Criminal Justice Concepts and Issues

An Anthology

Fourth Edition

Chris W. Eskridge
University of Nebraska

Roxbury Publishing Company
Los Angeles, California

Library of Congress Cataloging-in-Publication Data

Criminal justice: concepts and issues / [compiled by] Chris W. Eskridge—4th ed.
p. cm.
Includes bibliographical references and index.
ISBN 1-891487-85-X
1. Criminal justice, Administration of—United States. 2. Crime—United States. 3. Criminal law—United States. I. Eskridge, Chris W. II. Title.

HV9950.C744 2004
364.973—dc21 2001041938

Publisher: Claude Teweles
Managing Editor: Dawn VanDercreek
Production Editor: Sacha A. Howells
Production Assistants: Scott Oney and Josh Levine
Typography: SDS Design, info@sds-design.com
Cover Design: Marnie Kenney

Printed on acid-free paper in the United States of America. This book meets the standards for recycling of the Environmental Protection Agency.

ISBN 1-891487-85-X

ROXBURY PUBLISHING COMPANY
P. O. Box 491044
Los Angeles, California 90049-9044
Voice: (310) 473-3312 • Fax: (310) 473-4490
Email: roxbury@roxbury.net
Website: www.roxbury.net

Dedication

This book is dedicated to my students past, present, and future. It is hoped that the ideas and concepts presented in this volume will give pause for reflection and serve to stimulate critical thinking.

Dedication

This book is dedicated to my students past, present, and future. It is hoped that the ideas and concepts presented in this volume will give pause for reflection and serve to stimulate critical thinking.

Acknowledgments

Many people helped make the Fourth Edition of *Criminal Justice: Concepts and Issues* become a reality. I would like to offer thanks to those who reviewed the First, Second, and Third Editions of this anthology and made numerous helpful suggestions. I am especially grateful to Amy Aarsen and Katie Beckner who helped review, collect, and photocopy articles for the First Edition, and to Jenifer Green-Futchman and Jan Marie Lambert who helped in a similar vein with the Second and Third Editions respectively. A special thanks to Janis Searcy and Jessica Sabala who helped in various ways with this Fourth Edition.

I extend a special thanks to the production staff at Roxbury Publishing Company, particularly Sacha Howells, for seeing this project through to the finish. Finally, I must thank Claude Teweles. Without his vision, his help, his organization, his encouragement, and his attention to detail, this work would never have seen the light of day. ✦

Table of Contents

---

* Indicates chapters new to this edition

UNIT II: AMERICAN LAW ENFORCEMENT

---

* Indicates chapters new to this edition

UNIT III: AMERICAN COURTS

* Indicates chapters new to this edition

UNIT IV: AMERICAN CORRECTIONS

---

* Indicates chapters new to this edition

UNIT V: AMERICAN JUVENILE JUSTICE

* Indicates chapters new to this edition

---

* Indicates chapters new to this edition

APPENDICES

* Indicates chapters new to this edition

[illegible] Council [illegible]

[illegible]

[illegible] 2000 Presidential Address

[illegible]

[illegible]

APPENDIX [illegible]

A. [illegible] Organizations [illegible]

B. [illegible]

[illegible] of CSWE Regions [illegible]

Unit I

Crime and Justice in America

Unfortunately, crime is a relatively common aspect of life in America. We fear crime, and most of us will take whatever action we can to avoid becoming a victim of it. Criminal acts range in seriousness from the premeditated shooting of a police officer to jaywalking across a quiet city street. Some crimes are of such a dire nature that they demand our attention, and significant efforts are made to determine all we can about them.

What is crime? Consider the following excerpt from a report prepared by the Bureau of Justice Statistics (1988, 2–3):

> What is crime? Crimes are defined by law. In this report we define crime as all behaviors and acts for which a society provides formally sanctioned punishment. In the United States what is criminal is specified in the written law, primarily state statutes. What is included in the definition of crime varies among Federal, state, and local jurisdictions.
>
> Criminologists devote a great deal of attention to defining crime in both general and specific terms. This definitional process is the first step toward the goal of obtaining accurate crime statistics.
>
> To provide additional perspectives on crime it is sometimes viewed in ways other than in the standard legal definitions. Such alternatives define crime in terms of the type of victim (child abuse), the type of offender (white-collar crime), the object of the crime (property crime), or the method of criminal activity (organized crime). Such definitions usually cover one or more of the standard legal definitions. For example, organized crime may include fraud, extortion, assault or homicide.
>
> What is considered criminal by society changes over time. Some types of events such as murder, robbery, and burglary have been defined as crimes for centuries. Such crimes are part of the common law definition of crime. Other types of conduct traditionally have not been viewed as crimes. As social values and mores change, society has codified some conduct as criminal while decriminalizing other conduct. The recent movement toward increased "criminalization" of drunk driving is an example of such a change.
>
> New technology also results in new types of conduct not anticipated by the law. Changes in the law may be needed to define and sanction these types of conduct. For example, the introduction of computers has added to the criminal codes in many states so that acts such as the destruction of programs or data could be defined as crimes.
>
> What are some other common crimes in the United States?
>
> *Drug abuse violations.* Offenses relating to growing, manufacturing, making, possessing, using, selling, or distributing narcotic and dangerous non-narcotic drugs. A distinction is made between possession and sale/manufacturing.

Sex offenses. In current statistical usage, the name of a broad category of varying content, usually consisting of all offenses having a sexual element except for forcible rape and commercial sex offenses, which are defined separately.

Fraud offenses. The crime type comprising offenses sharing the elements of practice of deceit or intentional misrepresentation of fact, with the intent of unlawfully depriving a person of his or her property or legal rights.

Drunkenness. Public intoxication, except "driving under the influence."

Disturbing the peace. Unlawful interruption of the peace, quiet, or order of a community, including offenses called "disorderly conduct," "vagrancy," "loitering," "unlawful assembly," and "riot."

Driving under the influence. Driving or operating any vehicle or common carrier while drunk or under the influence of liquor or drugs.

Liquor law offenses. State or local liquor law violations, except drunkenness and driving under the influence. Federal violations are excluded.

Gambling. Unlawful staking or wagering of money or other things of value on a game of chance or on an uncertain event.

Kidnapping. Transportation or confinement of a person without authority of law and without his or her consent, or without the consent of his or her guardian, if a minor.

Vandalism. Destroying or damaging, or attempting to destroy or damage, the property of another without his or her consent, or public property, except by burning, which is arson.

Public order offenses. Violations of the peace or order of the community or threats to the public health through unacceptable public conduct, interference with government authority, or violation of civil rights or liberties. Weapons offenses, bribery, escape, and tax law violations, for example, are included in this category.

How do violent crimes differ from property crimes? The outcome of a criminal event determines if it is a property crime or a violent crime. Violent crime refers to events such as homicide, rape, and assault that may result in injury to a person. Robbery is also considered a violent crime because it involves the use or threat of force against a person.

Property crimes are unlawful acts with the intent of gaining property but which do not involve the use or threat of force against an individual. Larceny and motor vehicle theft are examples of property crime.

In the National Crime Survey a distinction is also made between crimes against persons (violent crimes and personal larceny) and crimes against households (property crimes, including household larceny).

How do felonies differ from misdemeanors? Criminal offenses are also classified according to how they are handled by the criminal justice system. More jurisdictions recognize two classes of offenses: felonies and misdemeanors.

Felonies are not distinguished from misdemeanors in the same way in all jurisdictions, but most states define felonies as offenses punishable by a year or more in a state prison. The most serious crimes are never "misdemeanors" and the most minor offenses are never "felonies."

Crime Rates

Each year the Federal Bureau of Investigation (FBI) publishes a document known as the Uniform Crime Report (UCR) that provides information regarding the amount and type of crimes known to the police. Nearly every law enforcement agency in the United States submits data to the FBI for this report (go to *http://www.fbi.gov/ucr/01cius.htm* for a synopsis of the most current report).

This report focuses primarily on what are called Type I or index crimes: murder, non-negligent manslaughter, forcible rape, robbery, aggravated assault, burglary, larceny, arson, and motor vehicle theft. The UCR includes crime information obtained from previous years, which allows for a multi-year analysis of crime trends.

Violent Crime

While recent trends suggest some upward movement, the UCR figures over the past decade have revealed a drop in the homicide rate in the U.S. Still, the chance of being murdered in one's lifetime in America is now about 1:150, the odds differing depending upon one's gender, race, and socioeconomic status. White females, for example, have only 1 chance in 600 of being murdered. On the other hand, the odds may be as high as 1:35 for young black males.

Despite the fact that our homicide rate has dropped somewhat over the past decade, it remains one of the highest of any Western industrialized nation. Why are we so violent in this country? The ready availability and the lethal nature of firearms, particularly handguns, is considered by many experts to be one of the chief factors. Firearms are used in more than 60 percent of all homicides, but social scientists have pointed to other factors that might also be at work, including the following:

- Drug use continues to spur deadly competition among rival drug suppliers.
- The ready availability and social acceptability of alcohol. More than half of the inmates in prison on a violent crime charge committed that offense while under the influence of alcohol.
- Juvenile gang activity continues to promote the subculture of violence, particularly within the inner cities.
- The general disintegration of the family and the community as value-stamping mechanisms may be leaving many young people with a limited sense of traditional moral direction; consequently, they may be more likely to engage in instinctual violence.
- Though we decry its use in our own homes and neighborhoods, American cultural values glorify violence in a number of arenas (i.e., sporting events, television, cartoons, movies). As a result of this mixed message, there seems to be some spillover into our communities.
- Decades of high unemployment in our inner cities have resulted in strong feelings of relative deprivation among many inner-city residents. This has become a source of great resentment that is often vented in acts of violence.
- The oppositional culture of the streets has its own code of behavior that subverts hope and civility and romanticizes violence.
- The number of children growing up in violent-prone families who, as they leave their homes and families, are more prone to inflict violence on their own spouses, children, and others.
- Media violence may contribute to a sense of callousness toward real-world violence.
- A general overexposure to violence as both recipients and observers has made us calloused, and more prone to both accept and engage in such acts.
- A sense of frustration and futility harbored by residents of the inner cities regarding what they see as a double standard of justice seems to have resulted in a measure of violent vigilantism, intensifying the cycle of violence.

Whatever the explanations may be, the fact remains that we are a violent nation when compared with the other countries of the world. Perhaps due to that fact, crime remains one of the most potent political issues of our day.

National Crime Victimization Survey

There are numerous problems with UCR data and they should be viewed with some caution. Reported crime rates have been found to be a function of many factors, including the education level of police officers, fiscal resources of local police departments, police department policies, the social class of the victims, and whether or not the victims had insurance. In addition, it is widely understood and accepted that the police do not file official reports on all crimes of which they are aware. In other words, there are more crimes actually committed than reported.

As a result of these concerns, researchers also employ other measures in an attempt to determine how much crime is actually committed. Their efforts have resulted in the development of the annual National Crime Victimization

Survey (NCVS). This survey is a joint undertaking of the Department of Justice and the Bureau of Census. Approximately 86,800 households containing roughly 159,420 people age 12 and over are now surveyed twice each year. They are asked if they have been victims of a crime during the six-month period prior to the interview.

The NCVS data indicates that there were 24 million victimizations in the year 2001. There were approximately 5.7 million violent crimes (rape, robbery, assault), and 18.3 million property crimes. Interestingly, just over one-third of the property crimes and just under one-half of the violent crimes were reported to the police. The data further revealed that the chance of personal victimization depends on a number of factors, including age, gender, race, family income, and type of residence. The highest rates of violent crime victimization are possessed by poor (annual income less than $7,500), young (age 16–19), single, black or Hispanic males who live in urban areas. By the same token, based on previous NCVS data, it does appear that at least 95 percent of us will be the victim of a serious crime in our lifetimes.

Illegal Drug Use

While the Uniform Crime Report contains data dealing with drug abuse arrests, actual drug-use estimates are not a part of that report. Drug-use estimates are not a part of the NCVS evaluation either. Efforts have been undertaken by other agencies and organizations to determine the extent of illegal drug use in the United States. Perhaps the most complete research efforts to address this issue on a national basis are supported by the Substance Abuse and Mental Health Services Administration, an agency within the U.S. Department of Health and Human Services.[1]

In 2001, this agency surveyed more than 70,000 people aged 12 and over and published a report entitled *The National Household Survey on Drug Abuse* (NHSDA). The 2001 survey revealed that roughly 14 million persons use illicit drugs at least once a month. The good news is that this is significantly lower than the 1979 estimate of 25 million. In fact, the NHSDA surveys have documented an apparent drop in the use of almost every kind of drug over the past decade, including alcohol and tobacco.

While there has been some progress in slowing the flow of illegal drug use in America, current research findings as well as street-level ethnographic observations are sending out very clear signals of possible future increases in general illicit drug use. At this juncture, methamphetamines seem poised to become the new "hot" drug of choice as we begin the new millennium, though marijuana will clearly continue to be the most commonly used illicit drug. Police reports suggest that the use of so-called "club drugs" such as ecstasy, GHB, ketamine, rohypnol, and the synthetic opioid OxyContin may be increasing.

As noted, marijuana remains the most frequently used illicit drug in America. The 2001 survey estimated that more than 10.5 million persons use marijuana monthly. Monthly marijuana use among the 18–25 age group is now nearly 36 percent. There were an estimated 1.2 million monthly cocaine users in 2001. The 2001 NHSDA report estimated that there were approximately 1 million persons who used hallucinogens monthly, and 130,000 persons who used heroin monthly. While these numbers may appear high, the Arrestee Drug Abuse Monitoring Program (ADAM) tends to corroborate the figures. The ADAM project (a research effort being undertaken in 34 cities) has found that in aggregate, some 65 percent of adult male arrestees test positive for illicit drug use.

While drug use is clearly lower today than it was a decade ago, there are still 14 million regular drug users, roughly 6 percent of the 12-and-over population, and there is no indication that that figure will get any smaller, despite rigorous law enforcement efforts and the many state and community anti-drug campaigns. There are warning signs, in fact, that the numbers may now start to increase, as noted above. Even more disconcerting is the fact that 6 percent is clearly an underreported figure. The NHSDA focuses on households and thus misses many of the homeless, people who are institutionalized, military personnel on active duty, and individuals in drug and alcohol clinics. Another significant problem with the survey is that in some cities, as many as 25 percent of those contacted refused and/or failed to participate. Given these gaps, the reported 14 million monthly users should be considered a minimum estimate. It must be emphasized that drug use was not always a criminal offense in America. The criminalization of drugs in this country has a long and interesting history. Today, of course, it is illegal to manufacture, deliver, or possess controlled substances. While the statutes differ from state to state, most states have patterned their laws after the 1970 Federal Comprehensive Drug Abuse Prevention and Control Act.

In the past few years, most states and the federal government have increased the severity of penalties for drug violations. However, despite the war on drugs, drug use continues at a very high rate. Overall, the world's drug trade in the year 2001 was estimated to be a $500+ billion industry, and there was no evidence of weakening demand. To the contrary, from all available evidence, it appears that the drug problem will be with us well into the century.

White-Collar/Corporate Crime

Another category of criminal behavior that is not represented in either the Uniform Crime Reports or the National Crime Victimization Survey is white-collar crime. White-collar crime is difficult to define, as it encompasses a variety of criminal activities. Price fixing, bid rigging, health-care fraud, embezzlement, stock manipulation, computer fraud, creative accounting, "cooked books," and kickback schemes are all examples of white-collar crimes.

White-collar crime involves manipulation and fraud in the area of business and government; it constitutes a violation of the social relationship of trust (Shapiro 1990). The cost of white-collar crime is far greater than that of traditional street crime, and yet street crime receives much greater attention from law enforcement officials. Due to the public outcry against the activities in the 1980s of such individuals as Charles Keating, Ivan Boesky, and Mike Milken, and the Enron and WorldCom debacles in the first few years of the twenty-first century, many thought that white-collar crime would receive increased law enforcement attention. President Bush even created a blue-ribbon commission to examine corporate corruption, but such interest has proved to be more show than substance, and white-collar crime continues to receive very little substantive systemic attention from the justice community.

Organized Crime

The results of many crime syndicate enterprises appear within the pages and tabular columns of the UCR and NCVS reports, but many also escape notice. As with white-collar crime, it is difficult to develop a firm definition of organized crime, for it covers a vast array of activities and ventures. Racketeering, extortion, loansharking, prostitution, gambling/numbers operations, smuggling (goods as well as people), fixing sporting events, black market/fencing, drug trafficking, illegal arms trading, and illegal toxic waste disposal are all examples of typical syndicate operations today.

Beginning in the late 1980s, the FBI undertook a high-profile campaign to "knock out" the so-called American Mafia or La Cosa Nostra, and has been somewhat successful. The old, traditional New York City–based crime families, whose organizational roots date back to Prohibition, do seem to be weakened at present. By the late 1990s, with the incarceration of John Gotti and Vinny "The Chin" Gigante, the fabled organized crime "Commission" was no longer functioning. Poised to fill the void, however, are, among others, the increasingly aggressive Russian mobs that are spilling into America, the Mexican and Colombian drug cartels, the Japanese Yakuza, and the Triads of China. Officials from both the Department of Justice and the Central Intelligence Agency have identified these criminal organizations as among the greatest external threats to the future of this country.

Domestic Terrorism

With the bombings of the World Trade Center complex in February of 1993 and the Alfred P. Murrah Federal Building in Oklahoma City in April of 1995, America was forcibly introduced, firsthand, to the world of terrorism. Up to that time, America had been relatively free from domestic terrorist acts of such magnitude. The matter came forcibly into focus with the episodes of September 11, 2001. Such an event of mass destruction and loss of life had not occurred on American soil since the Japanese attack on Pearl Harbor in December, 1941. It now appears that the proverbial Pandora's box has been opened, and the question today is not one of if, but of when the next attack will occur.

The United States has experienced many other terrorist-type episodes in the past, though the incidents may not have been classified as terrorism per se. One need merely leaf through the violence-strewn pages of American history to learn of the acts of terror perpetrated over the years by such groups as the Molly Maguires, the Ku Klux Klan, corporate America in its battles with organized labor, and more recently, anti-abortion activists. Terrorism has been a fact of life on the American streets and in the American culture for many years, from the Civil War–era draft riots, to the Haymarket Square bombing in 1886, to the World War I Bonus Riots in the early 1930s, to the racially based riots of the 1960s, to the Los Angeles riots of 1992. Four American presidents have been assassinated, and serious attempts on the lives of at least six other have been documented. Various immigrant groups such as the Chinese, Hispanics, Irish, and Italians have, in turn, been subjected to terroristic treatment over the course of the last century and longer.

The FBI includes hate crime data in the annual UCR. Generally, a quarter of those episodes are reported to have occurred in California. The greatest domestic terrorist threat today seems to be from right-wing radical groups. The Southern Poverty Law Center tracks such organizations, and reports that presently there are approximately 475 active hate groups and 450 active anti-government militias in the United States. In addition, there are approximately 600 entities that can be classified as religious cult groups.

While all of these entities certainly cannot be considered terrorist groups, many do have the potential for violence. Weapons have been stockpiled, and secured compounds and training grounds have been built by many of these organizations. The passage of the Brady Bill and the government's overreaction at Ruby Ridge and Waco served to intensify the resolve of the nationwide right-wing movement, and served to increase the size of the membership of many of these organizations. The aftermath of the Oklahoma City bombing, when images of mangled bodies of children were publicized served to somewhat "cool" this movement. Interestingly, the September 11 episode has seemed to further dilute recruiting efforts of these organizations.

There are a number of single-issue organizations that occasionally engage in domestic terrorist activities. For example, anti-abortion activists, who have a particularly strong presence in the South, have sporadically bombed abortion clinics and generally terrorized those who work there. A number of animal rights and environmental groups such as the Animal Liberation Front and Earth First! have engaged in selective acts of violence, and show no indication of backing off. Occasional loners, such as Ted Kacyznski (aka the Uni-bomber), and the still unknown individual who mailed a number of anthrax-laced letters in late 2001 surface from time to time, but pose no serious threat to national security or stability. Even at the height of their power, domestic radical organizations have not engaged in sustained campaigns of mass destruction, but instead have focused on propaganda efforts, paramilitary training, and relatively nonviolent harassment tactics.

Although the September 11 bombings surface as a notable exception, international entities have not been able to establish significant patterns of terrorist activity in America, nor have they been successful in their propaganda activities thus far. America will not be immune forever, however, and the potential for terroristic violence is ever present. Modern American law enforcement efforts have tended to focus on small but very vocal and volatile splinter domestic groups. In the aftermath of September 11, more and more law enforcement attention is being given to international terrorist organizations, with the newly created Office of Homeland Security attempting to coordinate activities. Questions and concerns about privacy, civil rights, and the extent of government intervention and regulation have also been raised, issues that have not truly been on the political agenda since the 1950s and '60s.

The Politics of Crime

Despite the fact that there has been a marginal decline in overall crime victimization rates in the last decade, the fear of crime has emerged as one of the most pressing issues of the day in this post–Cold War era. The public is legitimately frightened and frustrated by the crime problem, and the images of violent crime portrayed by the media only aggravate the situation. Citizens are further disillusioned by irresponsible politicians who play to those fears to win reelection rather than truly addressing fundamental community problems. The prevailing response among political leaders of both parties today is the simplistic and immensely popular message of "get tough." Fear, they believe, is what prevents people from doing wrong. This model proposes that crime prevention is achieved by adopting mandatory sentencing laws, building more prisons, hiring more police, and administering the death penalty more frequently. In point of fact, these responses have not proven effective and may even contribute to the crime problem, but this aggressive posture remains quite popular.

It is rather ironic that crime has emerged as the preeminent social issue of the day at a time when overall crime rates have actually fallen. What is disconcerting is that demographics reveal that a real crime wave is clearly on the horizon. There is a definitive relationship between age and crime. The age-crime curve suggests that youths 14 to 17 years old are particularly crime-prone. A bubble is working its way through the demographic pipeline of America, and there will be an increasing number of youths in that age category, peaking in the year 2005. These data clearly suggest that the real crime problem has only just begun. The problem will become all the more accentuated due to the fact that current crime-control policies show almost no ability to mitigate this threat, and in fact may actually be contributing to its intensity.

* * *

Concern with criminal activity in our society runs from the suites to the streets. While overall crime rates seem to have stabilized for now, the recent reported upturn in violent crime is a cause of concern. As a result, crime continues to be one of the most significant social-political issues of the day.

Note

1. The 2001 survey is the nineteenth in a series originally undertaken in 1971 by the National Commission on Marihuana and Drug Abuse. Responsibility for the survey transferred in 1992 from the National Institute of Drug Abuse to the Substance Abuse and Mental Health Service Administration, an agency within the U.S. Department of Health and Human Services.

References and Further Reading Materials

Abadinsky, Howard. 2000. *Organized Crime.* Belmont, CA: Wadsworth.

——. 2001. *Drug Abuse.* Belmont, CA: Wadsworth.

Braithwaite, John. 2002. *Restorative Justice and Responsive Regulations.* New York: Oxford University Press.

Bureau of Justice Statistics. 1988. *Report to the Nation on Crime and Justice.* Washington, DC: United States Department of Justice.

Bureau of Justice Statistics. 2002. *Criminal Victimization 2001.* Washington, D.C.: U.S. Department of Justice (see also http://www.ojp.usdog.gov/bjs).

Buzawa, Eve S. and Carl G. Buzawa. 2002. *Domestic Violence.* Thousand Oaks, CA: Sage.

Cullen, Francis and Robert Agnew. 1999. *Criminological Theory: Past to Present.* Los Angeles, CA: Roxbury.

Federal Bureau of Investigation. 2002. *Crime in the United States: 2001.* Washington, D.C.: U.S. Department of Justice (see also http://www.fbi.gov).

Inciardi, James A. 2002. *Criminal Justice.* Fort Worth, TX: Harcourt.

National Institute of Justice. 2002. *Arrestee Drug Abuse Monitoring Program, 2001.* Washington, D.C., U.S. Department of Justice (see also http://www.adam-nij.net).

Office of National Drug Control Policy. 2001. *Pulse Check: Trends in Drug Abuse.* Washington, D.C.:Executive Office of the President.

Rosoff, Stephen, Henry Pontell, and Robert Tillman. 1998. *Profit Without Honor: White-Collar Crime and the Looting of America.* Upper Saddle River, NJ: Prentice-Hall.

Shapiro, Susan P. 1990. "Collaring the Crime, Not the Criminal: Reconsidering the Concept of White-Collar Crime," *American Sociological Review,* June 1990, pp. 346–365.

Shover, Neal and John Paul Wright. 2001. *Crimes of Privilege: Readings in White-Collar Crime.* New York: Oxford University Press.

Siegel, Larry. 2002. *Criminology.* Belmont, CA: Wadsworth.

Substance Abuse and Mental Health Services Administration. 2002. *Summary of Findings from the 2001 National Household Survey on Drug Abuse.* Rockville, MD: Office of Applied Studies, U.S. Department of Health and Human Services (see also http://www.samhas.gov/oas/nhsda.htm).

Walker, Samuel, Cassia Spohn, and Miriam DeLone. 2000. *The Color of Justice.* Belmont, CA: Wadsworth.

White, Jonathan R. 2002. *Terrorism.* Belmont, CA: Wadsworth.

Wilson, James Q. and Joan Petersilia (eds). 2002. *Crime: Public Policies For Crime Control.* Oakland, CA: Institute For Contemporary Studies. ✦

Chapter 1

Justice and the American Justice Network[1]

Chris W. Eskridge

The author explores the general concept of justice and examines the historic response of governments to crime. The general administration of justice process in America is examined, and a basic discussion of prosecution, adjudication, sentencing, corrections, and the juvenile justice system is presented.

Justice?

What is justice? Can we be truly just? What is the cost of justice? Do we want all members of society to come under the umbrella of justice?

These and similar questions have fascinated politicians, patriots, philosophers, and the general public for centuries. There is no universal definition of justice. It is an over-arching concept that spans an infinite number of perspectives and views, each as valid as the other, even though they are often mutually exclusive and at times incompatible.

To dispense absolute justice requires the presence of four elements:

1. The absolute ability to identify law violators.
2. The absolute ability to apprehend law violators.
3. The absolute ability to punish law violators.
4. The absolute ability to identify the intent of law violators.

While not a practical proposal, if adequate resources were devoted to law enforcement efforts, arguably all law violators could be identified and apprehended. If draconian prosecutorial methods were utilized, all law violators could then be punished. But what is missing in this scenario is the accurate identification of intent. At present, we lack the absolute ability to identify intent. Thus, even with adequate resources, it is impossible to distribute absolute justice.

When societies attempt to administer justice, mistakes are inevitable. Types of mistakes include the following:

- The innocent are punished.
- The guilty escape punishment.
- The guilty are punished more severely than necessary.
- The guilty are punished less severely than necessary.

We read in Plato's *Republic* of Socrates considering whether justice is "nothing else than the interest of the stronger." If that is the case, then the poor would be more likely to be on the receiving end of the first and third mistakes listed above. Former U.S. Senator Philip Hart once noted that the justice system has two transmission belts, one for the rich and one for the poor, and the low-income transmission belt leads to prison in shorter order. The President's Crime Commission Report of 1967 came to the same conclusion, noting that "the offender at the end of the road in prison is likely to be a member of the lowest social and economic groups in the country." Cressey made a similar observation with respect to racial disparity:

> Numerous studies have shown that African Americans are more likely to be arrested, indicted, convicted, and committed to an institution than are whites who commit the same offenses, and many other studies have shown that blacks have a poorer chance than whites to receive probation, a suspended sentence, parole, commutation of a death sentence, or pardon. (Sutherland and Cressey 1974, 133)

Justice should be the equitable access and applicability of rights, privileges, and opportunities, but in practice this is not always the case. That fact has caused a significant degree of contention in this country. Consequently, the enforcement of law and the administration of justice have become much more difficult tasks in the United States than they were some years ago.

Systems of justice, in whatever societies or environments they develop, serve as mechanisms to enforce behavior standards deemed necessary to protect individuals and the general well-being of the community. Justice systems tend to possess a two-fold role, namely, the prevention of certain activities and the apprehension and formal processing of individuals who have committed illegal acts. What distinguishes the justice system of one country from that of another is the form of the process and the extent of the protections offered in that process.

A consensus has yet to be reached in this country as to the scope of the personal protection to be offered. What types of protection, freedoms, and rights should be given to what groups of people and how extensive should they be? When does the exercise of these protections and freedoms begin to flaunt the law? When does governmental control becomes excessive intervention? How much liberty is to be afforded to members of society and how much order should the state seek to maintain? Politicians, patriots, and philosophers have all grappled with these concepts for centuries.

The Constitution of the United States, and more particularly the Bill of Rights, is a product of the collective reasoning of a group of individuals who debated these very issues more than 200 years ago. The document they produced extended personal liberties and restricted governmental intervention like no legal document ever had before. The Constitution grants American citizens certain rights and directs that these rights cannot be withdrawn without due process of law.

There have been, however, rather intense disagreements over the years as to the proper definition of due process of law. In general, some advocate the need to limit the scope of due process protections and to expand the power of the State. Others clamor for an expansion of due process rights and the need to place powerful restrictions on the State's ability to interfere in citizens' lives. These two perspectives are known as the crime control model and due process model, respectively (Packer 1968).

The Due Process Model

Under the due process model, the primary concerns are the protection of individuals, individual freedom, and general maintenance of liberty. People are considered basically good. Individuals are presumed innocent until proven guilty. Concern is with rehabilitating and reintegrating offenders back into society, and more particularly in assisting law violators to make a deliberate conversion to a more responsible lifestyle. The government intervenes and actively encourages, aids, and assists. Social welfare programs, low-interest inner-city business loans, massive aid to cities, racial-preference programs, income redistribution policies, Project Head Start, Job Corps, and student loan programs would all indicate a due process philosophy.

Under the due process model, law enforcement officials conduct investigations according to strict guidelines. The courts take an active role in monitoring the operations of the police and the justice system in general. Every community has its own independent police department that brings a measure of local sensitivity and general humanitarian concern to law enforcement. The justice process is deliberate, formalized, thorough, and individualized. The due process model emphasizes treatment and not punishment of offenders. Treatment entails establishment of community-based alternatives to incarceration, such as pretrial release and pretrial diversion programs, neighborhood justice centers, probation, restitution, community service sentencing, parole, work release, halfway houses, and so on. Concern is with the normative, relative concept of fairness—doing the "right" thing. Police officers adopt a community-policing social service perspective, while probation and parole officers adhere to the advocacy model. Interest is in the development of long-term solutions at the cost of aggravating some nagging contingencies of the moment. There will be guilty persons who will escape punishment, and some guilty persons will be punished less severely than they should be. But on the other hand, there will be fewer innocent persons punished, and the number of guilty persons punished more severely than they deserve will also diminish.

The Crime Control Model

Under the crime control model, the primary concern is the immediate protection of society, in generally maintaining order. People are considered basically evil. Individuals are presumed guilty until proven innocent, and concern is with forcing conformity through an external deterrence system. Deterrence serves as the philosophic underpinnings of the entire model. The government rules through fear and intimidation, and the courts generally defer to the wishes of the law enforcement community. Law enforcement officials have large grants of discretionary powers and few if any restrictions placed upon their ability to collect evidence. They adhere to an aggressive, authoritarian enforcement philosophy. There are large numbers of law enforcement officers, and all law enforcement agencies are centrally organized as a national police force in a tight, closed bureaucratic structure. The justice process is quick and generally informal.

Once guilt has been determined, punishment is meted out with swiftness, certainty, and severity. The crime control model promotes punishment, rather than treatment. There is frequent use of the death penalty, as well as frequent mandatory commitment of individuals to large, dehumanizing prisons, authorization of electronic surveillance, elimination of bail, and adherence to a preventive detention perspective. There is no place under this model for diversion programs, rehabilitation programs, probation, or parole. Interest is in developing solutions to immediate problems. There will be some innocent persons punished, and some guilty persons will be punished more severely than they should be. But on the other hand, fewer guilty persons will escape punishment, and the number of guilty persons punished less severely than they deserve will diminish.

Regardless of which model is chosen, the administration of social justice involves a definite cost. America has tended to lean towards the due process model and has long prided itself in offering a substantial measure of legal protection to the accused. At the philosophic core of the American system is the concept that individuals may be punished by the state only if an impartial and deliberate process proves they have violated a law. To facilitate that process, and in an attempt to yield some sense of equity in our society, a network of institutions and procedures has evolved in America. Some aspects of it were inherited and adapted from the British, while others have been uniquely American developments.

The following excerpt, taken from the Bureau of Justice Statistics publication, *Report to the Nation on Crime and Justice* (1988, 56–59), provides an overview of the operation of the justice system in America:

> The response to crime is a complex process that involves citizens as well as many agencies, levels, and branches of government. The private sector initiates the response to crime.
>
> This first response may come from any part of the private sector: individuals, families, neighborhoods, associations, business, industry, agriculture, educational institutions, the news media, or any other private service to the public.
>
> It involves crime prevention as well as participation in the criminal justice process once a crime has been committed. Private crime prevention is more than providing private security or burglar alarms or participating in neighborhood watch. It also includes a commitment to stop criminal behavior by not engaging in it or condoning it when it is committed by others.
>
> Citizens take part directly in the criminal justice process by reporting crime to the police, by being reliable participants (for example, witnesses, jurors) in a criminal proceeding, and by accepting the disposition of the system as just or reasonable. As voters and taxpayers, citizens also participate in criminal justice through the policymaking process that affects how the criminal justice process operates, the resources available to it, and its goals and objectives. At every stage of the process, from the original formulation of objectives to the decision about where to locate jails and

prisons and to the reintegration of inmates into society, the private sector has a role to play. Without such involvement, the criminal justice process cannot serve the citizens it is intended to protect.

The Government Responds to Crime Through the Criminal Justice System

We apprehend, try, and punish offenders by means of a loose confederation of agencies at all levels of government. Our American system of justice has evolved from the English common law into a complex series of procedures and decisions. There is no single criminal justice system in this country. We have many systems that are similar, but individually unique.

Criminal cases may be handled differently in different jurisdictions, but court decisions based on the due process guarantees of the U.S. Constitution require that specific steps be taken in the administration of criminal justice.

The description of the criminal and juvenile justice systems that follows portrays the most common sequence of events in the response to serious criminal behavior.

Entry into the System

The justice system does not respond to most crime because so much crime is not discovered or reported to the police. Law enforcement agencies learn about crime from the reports of citizens, from discovery by a police officer in the field, or from investigative and intelligence work.

Once a law enforcement agency has established that a crime has been committed, a suspect must be identified and apprehended for the case to proceed through the system. Sometimes a suspect is apprehended at the scene; however, identification of a suspect sometimes requires an extensive investigation. Often, no one is identified or apprehended.

Prosecution and Pretrial Services

After an arrest, law enforcement agencies present information about the case and about the accused to the prosecutor, who will decide if formal charges will be filed with the court. If no charges are filed, the accused must be released. The prosecutor can also drop charges after making efforts to prosecute (*nolle prosequi*).

A suspect charged with a crime must be taken before a judge or magistrate without unnecessary delay. At the initial appearance, the judge or magistrate informs the accused of the charges and decides whether there is probable cause to detain the accused person. Often, the defense counsel is also assigned at the initial appearance. If the offense is not very serious, the determination of guilt and assessment of a penalty may also occur at this stage.

In some jurisdictions, a pretrial-release decision is made at the initial appearance, but this decision may occur at other hearings or may be changed at another time during the process. Pretrial release and bail were traditionally intended to ensure appearance at trial. However, many jurisdictions permit pretrial detention of defendants accused of serious offenses and deemed to be dangerous to prevent them from committing crimes in the pretrial period. The court may decide to release the accused on his/her own recognizance, into the custody of a third party, on the promise of satisfying certain conditions, or after the posting of a financial bond.

In many jurisdictions, the initial appearance may be followed by a preliminary hearing. The main function of this hearing is to discover if there is probable cause to believe that the accused committed a known crime within the jurisdiction of the court. If the judge does not find probable cause, the case is dismissed; however, if the judge or magistrate finds probable cause for such a belief, or the accused waives his or her right to a preliminary hearing, the case may be bound over to a grand jury.

A *grand jury* hears evidence against the accused presented by the prosecutor and decides if there is sufficient evidence to cause the accused to be brought to trial. If the grand jury finds sufficient evidence, it submits the court an *indictment* (a written statement of the essential facts of the offense charged against the accused). Where the grand jury system is used, the grand jury may also investigate criminal activity generally and issue indictments called grand jury originals that initiate criminal cases.

Misdemeanor cases and some felony cases proceed by the issuance of an *information* (a formal, written accusation submitted to the court by a prosecutor). *In some jurisdictions*, the indictments *may be* required in felony cases. However, the accused may choose to waive a grand jury indictment and, instead, accept service of an information for the crime.

Adjudication

Once an indictment or information has been filed with the trial court, the accused is scheduled for arraignment. At the arraignment, the accused is informed of the charges, advised of the rights of criminal defendants, and asked to enter a plea to the charges. Sometimes, a plea of guilty is the result of negotiations between the prosecutor and the defendant, with the defendant entering a guilty plea in expectation of reduced charges or a lenient sentence.

If the accused pleads guilty or pleads *nolo contendere* (accepts penalty without admitting guilt), the judge may accept or reject the plea. If the plea is accepted, no trial is held and the offender is sentenced at this proceeding or at a later date. The plea may be rejected if, for example, the judge believes that the accused may have been coerced. If this occurs, the case may proceed to trial.

If the accused pleads not guilty or not guilty by reason of insanity, a date is set for the trial. A person accused of a serious crime is guaranteed a trial by jury. However, the accused may ask for a bench trial where the judge, rather than a jury, serves as the finder of fact. In both instances the prosecution and defense present evidence by questioning witnesses while the judge decides on issues of law. The trial results in acquittal or conviction on the original charges or on lesser included offenses.

After the trial a defendant may request appellate review of the conviction or sentence. In many criminal cases, appeals of a conviction are a matter of right; all states with the death penalty provide for automatic appeal of cases involving a death sentence. However, under some circumstances and in some jurisdictions, appeals may be subject to the discretion of the appellate court and may be granted only on acceptance of a defendant's petition for a *writ of certiorari*. Prisoners may also appeal their sentences through civil rights petitions and *writs of habeas corpus* where they claim unlawful detention.

Sentencing and Sanctions

After a guilty verdict or guilty plea, sentence is imposed. In most cases the judge decides on the sentence, but in some states, the sentence is decided by the jury, particularly for capital offenses such as murder.

In arriving at an appropriate sentence, a sentencing hearing may be held at which evidence of aggravating or mitigating circumstances will be considered. In assessing the circumstances surrounding a convicted person's criminal behavior, courts often rely on presentence investigations by probation agencies or other designated authorities. Courts may also consider victim impact statements.

The sentencing choices that may be available to judges and juries include one or more of the following:

- the death penalty.
- incarceration in a prison, jail, or other confinement facility.
- probation—allowing the convicted person to remain at liberty but subject to certain conditions and restrictions.
- fines—primarily applied as penalties in minor offenses.
- restitution—which requires the offender to provide financial compensation to the victim.

In many states, state law mandates that persons convicted of certain types of offenses serve a prison term. Most states permit the judge to set the sentence length within certain limits, but some states have determinate sentencing laws that stipulate a specific sentence length, which must be served and cannot be altered by a parole board.

Corrections

Offenders sentenced to incarceration usually serve time in a local jail or a state prison. Offenders sentenced to less than one year generally go to jail; those sentenced to more than one year go to prison. Persons admitted to a state prison system may be held in prisons with varying levels of custody or in a community correctional facility.

A prisoner may become eligible for parole after serving a specific part of his or her sentence. Parole is the conditional release of a prisoner before the prisoner's full sentence has been served. The decision to grant parole is made by an authority such as a parole board, which has power to grant or revoke parole or to discharge a parolee altogether. The way parole decisions are made varies widely among jurisdictions.

Offenders may also be required to serve out their full sentences prior to release (expiration of term). Those sentenced under determinate sentencing laws can be released only after they have served their full sentence (mandatory release) less any "goodtime" received while in prison. Inmates get such credits against their sentence automatically or by earning it through participation in programs.

If an offender has an outstanding charge or sentence in another state, a detainer is used to ensure that when released from prison he or she will be transferred to the other state.

If released by a parole board decision or by mandatory release, the releasee will be under the supervision of a parole officer in the community for the balance of his or her unexpired sentence. This supervision is governed by specific conditions of release, and the releasee may be returned to prison for violations of such conditions.

The Juvenile Justice System

The processing of juvenile offenders is not entirely dissimilar to adult criminal processing, but there are crucial differences in the procedures. Many juveniles are referred to juvenile courts by law enforcement officers, but many others are referred by school officials, social services agencies, neighbors, and even parents, for behavior or conditions that are determined to require intervention by the formal system for social control.

When juveniles are referred to the juvenile courts, their *intake* departments, or prosecuting attorneys, determine whether sufficient grounds exist to warrant filing a petition that requests an *adjudicatory hearing* or a request to transfer jurisdiction to criminal court. In some states and at the Federal level prosecutors under certain circumstances may file criminal charges against juveniles directly in criminal courts.

The court with jurisdiction over juvenile matters may reject the petition or the juveniles may be diverted to other agencies or programs in lieu of further court processing. Examples of diversion programs include individual or group counseling or referral to educational and recreational programs.

If a petition for an adjudicatory hearing is accepted, the juvenile may be brought before a court quite unlike the court with jurisdiction over adult offenders. In disposing of cases juvenile courts usually have far more discretion than adult courts. In addition to such options as probation, commitment to correctional institutions, restitution, or fines, state laws grant juvenile courts the power to order removal of children from their homes to foster homes or treatment facilities. Juvenile courts also may order participation in special programs aimed at shoplifting prevention, drug counseling, or driver education. They also may order referral to criminal court for trial as adults.

Despite the considerable discretion associated with juvenile court proceedings, juveniles are afforded many of the due-process safeguards associated with adult criminal trials. Sixteen states permit the use of juries in juvenile courts; however, in light of the U.S. Supreme Court's holding that juries are not essential to juvenile hearings, most states do not make provisions for juries in juvenile courts.

The Response to Crime Is Founded in the Intergovernmental Structure of the United States

Under our form of government, each state and the Federal Government has its own criminal justice system. All systems must respect the rights of individuals set forth in court interpretation of the U.S. Constitution and defined in case law.

State constitutions and laws define the criminal justice system within each state and delegate the authority and responsibility for criminal justice to various jurisdictions, officials, and institutions. State laws also define criminal behavior and groups of children or acts under jurisdiction of the juvenile courts.

Municipalities and counties further define their criminal justice systems through local ordinances that proscribe additional illegal behavior and establish the local agencies responsible for criminal justice processing that were not established by the state.

Congress also has established a criminal justice system at the Federal level to respond to

Federal crimes such as bank robbery, kidnapping, and transporting stolen goods across state lines.

The Response to Crime Is Mainly a State and Local Function

Very few crimes are under exclusive Federal jurisdiction. The responsibility to respond to most crime rests with the state and local governments. Police protection is primarily a function of cities and towns. Corrections is primarily a function of state governments. More than three-fifths of all justice personnel are employed at the local level.

In general terms, the justice system consists of four components: the legislature, the police, the courts, and corrections. While each has distinct tasks, these four divisions are by no means independent of each other. The legislature creates the laws that the police enforce. The courts deal with individuals whom the police arrest. The correctional system handles those sentenced by the courts. Success in reforming convicts can be determined to some degree by whether or not the "ex-con" returns to the system as an offender. Correctional and police practices are subject to court scrutiny, as are the laws enacted by legislative bodies, which hold the purse strings for the entire system.

It has been argued by some that well-meaning reformers frequently fail to grasp the interconnected nature of these four divisions and consequently fail to understand the impact their recommendations will have upon the system as a whole. Proposals for reform also frequently face serious challenges from those within and outside of the system who have a vested interest in maintaining the status quo. As a result, it has been noted that while the justice system is often publicly reviled and attacked, ultimately it is left fundamentally unchanged (Neely 1982, 28).

Today, the police, the courts, and the correctional components are all being inundated by an unprecedented number of cases. The justice system is being overtaxed as it tries to respond to problems of a nature and magnitude that are beyond its collective capabilities. Just how much more it can handle has become one of the greatest concerns of our times.

Note

1. This section draws from the President's Commission of Law Enforcement and Administration of Justice, *The Challenge of Crime in a Free Society.* Washington, DC: U.S. Government Printing Office, 1967, pp. 7–12.

References and Further Reading Materials

Allen, Harry and Clifford Simonsen. 2001. *Corrections in America.* New York: Prentice Hall.

Bureau of Justice Statistics. 1988. *Report to the Nation on Crime and Justice.* Washington, DC: United States Department of Justice.

Cullen, Francis and Robert Agnew. 2003. *Criminological Theory: Past to Present.* Los Angeles: Roxbury.

Doerner, William and Steven Lab. 2002. *Victimology.* Cincinnati, OH: Anderson.

Gaines, Larry, Victor Kappeler, and Joseph Vaughn. 2002. *Policing in America.* Cincinnati, OH: Anderson.

Inciardi, James. 2002. *Criminal Justice.* Fort Worth, TX: Harcourt.

Neely, Richard. 1982. "Why Governments Don't Do What They Could to Reduce Violent Crime: The Politics of Crime," *The Atlantic Monthly,* August, pp. 27–31.

Neubauer, David. 2002. *America's Courts and the Criminal Justice System.* Belmont, CA: Wadsworth.

Packer, Herbert. 1968. *The Limits of Criminal Sanction.* Stanford, CA: Stanford University Press.

President's Crime Commission. 1967. *The Challenge of Crime in a Free Society.* Washington, DC: U.S. Government Printing Office.

Senna, Joseph and Larry Siegel. 2002. *Introduction to Criminal Justice.* Belmont, CA: Wadsworth.

Sutherland, Edwin and Donald Cressey. 1974. *Criminology,* p. 133. New York: Lippincott.

Walker, Samuel. 2001. *Sense and Nonsense About Crime and Drugs.* Belmont, CA: Wadsworth.

Walker, Samuel, Cassie Spohn, and Miriam DeLone. 2003. *The Color of Justice: Race, Ethnicity, and Crime in America.* Belmont, CA: Wadsworth.

Chapter 2

Explaining the American and Canadian Crime 'Drop' in the 1990's[1]

Marc Ouimet

Statistical analysis is an invaluable tool in studying the nature of crime, but linking changes in crime rates to a specific crime-fighting approach can lead to faulty assumptions between cause and effect.

Despite significant differences in their approaches to crime control, both the United States and Canada experienced declines in crime rates during the 1990s after decades of continuous increases. In the United States, the decline was often attributed to get-tough measures like increased incarceration, aggressive policing tactics, and more police officers. Canada, however, experienced the same decline in the same period without a significant change in its approach to incarceration and policing. Ouimet suggests that factors affecting both countries—economic prosperity, demographic shifts, education levels, and even a change in society's "moral conditioning"—may be more likely to explain declining crime rates.

Crime in Canada, as recorded by official statistics, increased annually during the 1960's and 1970's. This led to scepticism among many scholars regarding the validity of the crime figures. According to Hagan (1991), the growth in crime during that period can be explained partly by better recording practices and by a greater police enforcement of minor statutes. Despite distortions caused by these changes, Hagan concludes that there has been a real increase during that period in crime and violence, as well as in rates of alcohol and drug abuse. In the 1980's, official statistics for some types of offences show periods of stability and even slight decline, but trends for violence continued to grow sharply. The 1990's show a strikingly different picture. Since 1992, most categories of crimes have declined significantly in Canada.

In *The Crime Drop in America* (Blumstein and Wallman 2000), experts examine the unprecedented fall of crime in the USA throughout the 1990's which can be observed both in official crime statistics and the national crime survey (Rennison 2000). It is interesting to note that no one had foreseen the amplitude of the crime drop before it happened. Our collective inability to foresee future crime trends, even with the use of sophisticated time-series analytical models, demonstrates that criminological macro-theories have yet to be developed. The reality of the decline of crime has only been acknowledged in recent years and is now attracting research. Chaiken (2000:1) concludes, after reviewing a Statistics Canada publication, that 'the longer pattern in Canada is essentially flat'. This is troublesome because all data indicate that a drop in crime also occurred in Canada. Although Chaiken (2000) does not acknowledge that fact, drops in crime during the 90's have also been observed elsewhere. In Germany, the total offence rate dropped by 7.8% between 1993 and 1999 (PKS Berichtsjahr 2001). In England, the total number of crimes recorded by the British Crime Survey dropped by 15.6% between 1993 and 1999 (Povey 2001).

In this paper, long term crime trends in Canada and the United States are examined in order to establish the concordance between the two countries. Then, a detailed analysis of the evolution of crime between 1993 and 1999 is presented. Finally, factors that may help explain recent trends are examined

Our Two Nations

Canada is the country that most resembles the U.S. First, more than 90% of the 30 million Canadians live within 100 miles from the U.S. border. Second our history of colonisation is generally comparable, although Canada has retained a more continental influence than the U.S. (Lipset 1990). Third, both countries have historically been lands of immigration from around the world. Perhaps more important today is the fact that our popular cultural world is mostly undifferentiated, whether in movies, sports or television (Quebec being the exception). With the trend towards globalization and particularly the NAFTA agreement, exchanges between our countries have increased rapidly in the last decade. Canada is by far the largest trading partner of the U.S. (and vice versa) in both imports and exports, with a total trade figure of $434 billion in 1999 as compared to $284b with Japan, $251b with the U.K. and $238b for Mexico.[2] Our commercial exchanges amount to more than one billion U.S. dollars a day. There are, however, major differences between Canada and the United States. Canada is a more egalitarian society. This is most visible in easy access to education and in universal access to health care services. There are also less visible differences, such as differences in personal values. According to Lipset (1990), Canadians are more tolerant toward others and more open to different races, religions or sexual orientations.

In terms of crime incidence, there are similarities and differences between Canada and the United States. Mayhew and van Dijk (1997), who conducted an international crime victimization survey, found that in 1995 the overall national victimization risk was 24.2% for Americans and 25.2% for Canadians. The prevalence of most types of crimes is comparable even for crimes such as robbery (1.3% for Americans vs. 1.2% for Canadians). Two factors stand out in an analysis of the crime problem: the greater lethality of interpersonal conflicts in the U.S. because of easy access to firearms, and the disproportionate crime problem in large U.S. cities (Ouimet 1999).

In terms of crime control, Canada and the U.S. are very different. In the U.S., there are more police officers *per capita,* courts are more likely to sentence offenders to jail or prison, average terms of imprisonment are longer in the U.S., and possibilities for parole are more likely in Canada. All these factors, in association with high rates of violence, contribute to the fact that the incarceration rate in the U.S. is more than four times greater than in Canada.

In order to compare the general evolution of crime trends in both countries, long-term trends in the homicide rate were examined. This offence was chosen because data are available for long-term periods, it is an accurately measured variable, it shows few differences in definitions over time or space and is correlated with the incidence of less serious forms of crime. Figure 1 displays the Canadian and American homicide rate from 1901 to 1999.[3]

Although the homicide rate is three to four times higher in the U.S. than in Canada, trends are comparable. Figure 2.1 shows that in both countries, homicide rates increased in the three first decades of the century, culminating in the early thirties, a period of economic depression. Rates dropped considerably from the mid-thirties to the fifties, despite a small post-war jump. In both countries, the homicide rate increased dramatically between the early sixties and the late seventies before reaching a plateau in the early nineties, after which it decreased again. Homicide rates for both countries in 1999 are comparable to rates during the mid-sixties. The concordance in the general trends of both countries' homicide rates is remarkable. As one can imagine, the ratio between both curves is flat from 1962 to 1999 (it averages 3.6).[4] Such a result also rejects the hypothesis of a convergence between the U.S. and Canada that was proposed by Lenton (1989) and correctly rejected by Hagan (1991). The long-term parallelism be-

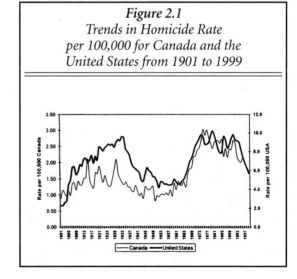

Figure 2.1
Trends in Homicide Rate per 100,000 for Canada and the United States from 1901 to 1999

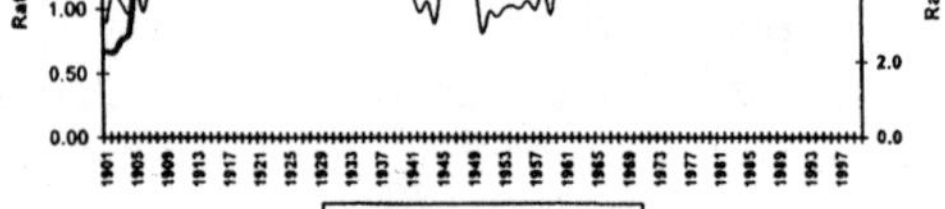

tween homicide trends in both countries can be interpreted as an indication that the forces behind these trends are very general and diffused across North America.

Explanations for the U.S. Drop in Crime

Many factors may have contributed to the last decade's decline in crime rates. In a recent book, editors Alfred Blumstein and Joel Wallman (2000) asked contributors to discuss the changes in specific areas that might have played a role in the downward trend of violence. In chapter two, Blumstein shows that the homicide peak of the early nineties is mostly attributable to an epidemic of young urban black handgun homicides. Yet, the homicide rate for whites, older people or non-urban people has also gone down in the 90's. There are three major explanations for the drop in crime that are examined in the book: demographic trends, incarceration policies, and police practices.

The demographic approach is to look at downward trends in crime as a consequence of the diminishing number of people in the crime-prone age category, namely teenagers and young adults. Steffensmeier and Harer (1999) argue that changes in age composition made only a small contribution to the downward trend of crime in the years of the Clinton administration. There is scepticism about the demographic explanation because the impact of changes in the population structure on crime should, for many observers, have taken place earlier. The number of teenagers and young adults peaked around 1980 and dropped during the 80's. The explanation for the lag between the two phenomena may well be the presence of a cohort effect. The cohort effect would specify that people born during the early 60's showed higher levels of crime involvement than any cohort before or after, and were criminally active for longer periods than other cohorts (in large part explainable by difficulties of integrating the job market during the 80's). Therefore, the impact of the diminishing number of youths has been delayed, and this explains the temporary lag between the two phenomena.

The role of increases in the incarceration rate on the crime rate was carefully examined by Spelman (2000). He estimates the relationship between incarceration and crime and comes up with an elasticity measure of –0.4, which means that an increase in incarceration of one percent will be followed by a drop in crime of 0.4%, or 4/1000. For Spelman, about one quarter of the drop in crime during the 90's can be explained by increases in incarceration. Not all scholars share the view that the use of incarceration is related to trends in the crime rate. An analysis provided by the Justice Policy Institute (2000) shows that the State of Texas increased its prison population throughout the 90's to reach an incarceration rate of 1,035 per 100,000 residents in 1999, second only to Louisiana, while its drop in crime for the 1995–1998 period was 5%, far behind the drop of 23% in California or 21% in New York.

Our own calculations of the correlation between the 1990–1998 percentage change in homicide rates and incarceration rates for 48 states (DC, Hawaii, and Alaska not included) stands at 0,085 and is not statistically different from zero (correlations for other index crimes are all positive but not non-significant at a 0,05 level). In other words, trends in states' incarceration levels are not associated to trends in crime levels. As explained elsewhere (Ouimet and Tremblay 1996), the error around the correlation between the 1993 murder rate and the incarceration rate (correlation of 0,768 in 1993) is strongly and positively related to the percent change in the incarceration level between 1993 and 1998, suggesting that American states are adjusting their incarceration levels to the states' norm given their crime rate.[5] For example, the stale of Delaware had an incarceration rate in 1993 of 394 (which was more than the rate of 226 which it should have had in light of its murder rate) "only" increased its incarceration by 8.8% between 1993 and 1998. At the other extreme, West Virginia, with an incarceration level of 98 in 1993 (much lower than expected) has managed to almost double its incarceration rate to 192 in 1998. Ouimet and Tremblay (1996) offer a political model for explaining these variations in incarceration rate.

Another explanation for the drop in crime concerns policing. Eck and Maguire (2000) examined the possible impact of changes in policing on the drop in crime, but are generally quite critical of the claims that have been made by police officials about their role in the general downward trend in crime. The main problem with the policing explanation is that innovative police practices such as gun patrols (stop and frisk) or CompStat type systems had been implemented after the crime rate had already been declining. Moreover, the rate of crime dropped even in cities that had not experienced major changes in policing. In sum, we know too little about the specific impact of different police strategies such as problem-oriented policing, community policing, or zero-tolerance policing to allow us to evaluate the causal relationship between policing and crime trends.

Other explanations have been advanced to explain the drop in crime. While Rosenfeld (2000) acknowledges the impact of demographic and incarceration factors, he argues that other variables have to be considered to explain the downward trend in homicide, one of which might be the "civilizing process" described by Elias (1939). Elias shows how people gradually become more sensitive to violence and are therefore gradually expressing greater intolerance towards such behaviors. Holloway (1999) advances an explanation developed by Levitt and Donohue that can account for diminishing crime rates in most places in the U.S., during the 90's (whether policing practices have changed or not, whether state imprisonment rates changed much or a little, etc.). They argue that increases in abortion during the late 70's and 80's resulted in the reduction of the numbers of unwanted children that would have grown to become delinquents. What the authors do not tell us is that the number of single-parent families also increased during the late 70's and 80's, and this should have contributed to a growth in juvenile delinquents during the 90's. Another explanation was proposed by Felson (1998), who concludes that the decline in the use of paper money bills has contributed to a general reduction in theft, robbery, and even homicide. It is not clear, however, why this trend would have had any impact on the rates of crimes such as car theft or burglary.

The contributing authors in *The Crime Drop in America* focus on serious violence, namely homicide and robbery. Sexual assault and aggravated assault are not examined because it is believed that UCR statistics are not reliable for these behaviours. Little mention is made of the fact that very common crimes such as burglary and car theft are also declining. The result of this selection by the authors is to look for specific factors, rather than those that may explain the many varieties of trends in crime. For example, if one concentrates on homicide, the question of guns becomes central, but guns play little role in explaining rates of burglary or car theft. Second, no effort is made to sort out comparatively the different possible causes of the decline.

Examining the Crime Trends for Canadian Regions and the U.S.

The year 1991 can be considered as the peak in the upward trend for many types of crimes in both Canada and the U.S. In the eight years that followed, the volume of several types of crime decreased annually. To study the Canadian context, five regions were constructed out of ten provinces: Prince Edward Island, New Brunswick, Nova Scotia and Newfoundland were grouped into the "Atlantic region", while Alberta, Saskatchewan and Manitoba were grouped in the "Prairies region". This has been done to provide an easier analysis of the trends in crime and because penitentiary data are only available on the basis of those regions.[6]

To study crime, we selected a few well-defined offences that are often used in trend analysis and represent the principal crimes that result in the incarceration of the offender. Canadian data were coded from Statistics Canada's CANSIM data sets, while American data were extracted from the Bureau of Justice Statistics website. In terms of definitions for homicide, robbery, burglary, and motor vehicle theft, the rates can be compared directly between both countries because the statutory definitions of these offences are fairly similar. The rates for sexual assault and assault should not be compared across countries since the American rape and aggravated assault concepts are more limited than in Canada (there is no way to isolate aggravated assault and aggravated sexual assault in Canadian statistics). Table 2.1 presents the crime data for Canada and the United States in 1991 and 1999.

Table 2.1 shows that there has been an important reduction in crime rates for most categories of crime in most regions of Canada. The drop varies from 23% (assault and robbery) to 43% for homicide. The homicide rate has declined in all regions; the reduction ranges from 35% to 58%. With the exception of motor vehicle theft, the frequency of all crimes decreased in all regions except robbery in the Prairies (no change). The only crime without a declining rate is motor vehicle theft, which nevertheless declines on a per 100,000 registered motor vehicles basis. Table 2.1 also reports crime figures for the U.S. in the years 1991 and 1999. It is difficult to determine in which country crime has decreased the most. In fact, our interpretation of the data is that crime has decreased at the same rate in both countries.

The data show that the drop in crime occurred in Canada as well as in the United States, and that the trends are comparable for most types of crime. This would indicate that the causes of the decline cannot be found in very specific factors that may have played a role in some jurisdictions. In this sense, searching for causes of the decline in specific forms of crime—such as the drop in youth firearm-related homicides—is misleading.

Explaining the Decline of Crime Rates in Canada

A number of factors may have played a role in the explanation of the recent trend in crime in Canada. We grouped them in two dimensions: endogenous or exogenous. Endogenous factors are those that are part of the criminal justice system and over which agencies have some control.

Table 2.1
Rate per 100,000 Population for Selected Offences for Canadian Regions and the U.S. in 1991 and 1999

	Atlantic	Quebec	Ontario	Prairies	British Columbia	Canada	U.S.
1991:							
Homicide	2,19	2,63	2,46	3,21	3,95	2,79	9,77
Sexual assault	176	57	105	151	154	113	42
Assault	949	583	971	1,139	1,296	938	272
Robbery	31	188	99	107	151	123	432
Burglary	1,106	1,876	1,289	1,748	2,143	1,603	1,248
Motor vehicle theft	201	697	379	524	759	514	660
Population	2,330,800	6,845,700	9,914,200	4,609,500	3,218,500	26,918,700	252,932,796
1999:							
Homicide	0,93	1,70	1,32	1,73	2,34	1,59	5,70
Sexual assault	99	47	72	107	97	77	33
Assault	765	447	661	1,005	1,005	721	150
Robbery	28	113	76	107	140	95	336
Burglary	826	1,158	810	1,208	1,447	1,047	770
Motor vehicle theft	223	587	439	643	731	531	421
Population	2,368,374	7,333,283	11,411,547	5,078,177	4,009,922	30,201,303	272,691,000
Difference 91–99							
Homicide	–58%	–35%	–46%	–46%	–41%	–43%	–42%
Sexual assault	–44%	–18%	–31%	–30%	–37%	–31%	–23%
Assault	–19%	–23%	–32%	–12%	–22%	–23%	–45%
Robbery	–9%	–40%	–23%	0%	–7%	–23%	–22%
Burglary	–25%	–38%	–37%	–31%	–32%	–35%	–38%
Motor vehicle theft	11%	–16%	16%	23%	–4%	3%	–36%
Population	2%	7%	15%	10%	25%	12%	8%

Exogenous factors are those which exist outside the scope of the criminal justice system.

Endogenous Factors

In Canada during the 1990's, there has been no sign of toughening in various sectors of the criminal justice system. In fact, given the difficult economic situation of the different governments during this period, federal and provincial governments were disinclined to develop initiatives that would increase government spending. Debt reduction was the main objective for most governments. Statistics Canada provides data to substantiate this claim: spending related to justice in Canada for 1992–93 and for 1996–97 were as follows: $5,717 vs. $5,856 millions for police, $867 vs. $857 millions for criminal courts, and $1,880 vs. $1,969 millions for adult correctional services. In fact, the growth in the budget of justice-related organizations was below the level of inflation. Table 2.2 presents information relating to policing and correctional sectors for both the U.S. and Canada in 1991 and 1999. For comparative purposes, the incarceration rate is based on the number of adults incarcerated in relation to the total population, not on the officially published adult incarceration rate per 100,000 adults, which stands at 140 in 1999 (Thomas 2000).[7]

Table 2.2 shows that in Canada both the number of police officers per 1,000 and the incarceration rate fell, respectively, by 11% and 3%. In the U.S. increases have been observed in both the number of police officers per 100,000 (+11%) and in the incarceration rate (+42%). The picture that emerges from both countries is therefore dramatically different. The fact that neither police nor correctional indicators show an increase in Canada during the nineties does not mean that no important changes have occurred within these sectors. For example, police organizations improved different aspects of their work throughout the nineties, including a greater use of computers and databases and the creation of specialized units or task forces. This was also true in the U.S. On the correctional side, agencies responded to increases in the number of people sent to prison in the early nineties by allowing early release for non-violent offenders. In Quebec, for example, since the early 90's, non-violent offenders have been expected to be put under community correctional supervision after serving one-sixth of their sentence (Corbo 2001).[8] Even courts help relieve the pressure by employing a new alternative form of imprisonment called a conditional sentence, which is a prison sentence that is served in the community.[9] Although not necessarily well understood or popular within the general population, these measures made it possible, in the early 1990's, to increase the number of people sentenced by courts and the number or people sent to prison without significantly increasing the average size of the incarcerated population. Another aspect relating to endogenous factors is the question or drug crimes. In Canada, there has simply not been a "war on drugs". On the other hand, this "war" has greatly contributed

Table 2.2
Endogenous and Exogenous Indicators in U.S. and Canada for 1991 and 1999

	United States			Canada		
	1991	1999	% change	1991	1999	% change
Population in millions	252.9	272.8	8%	27.9	30.5	9%
Rate of police officers per 1000 (numbers in parentheses)	2.1 (53,1706)	2.3 (63,5600)	11% (20%)	2.0 (56,768)	1.8 (55,300)	−11% (−3%)
Incarceration rate per 100,000 (numbers in parentheses)	481 (1,219,014)	682 (1,860,520)	42% (53%)	110 (30,634)	106 (32,411)	−3% (6%)
Global unemplyoment rate	6.7%	4.3%	−36%	10.4%	7.6%	−27%
Proportion of the population aged 20 to 34 (1990 and 1999)	25.1%	20.5%	−18%	26.2%	21.4%	−18%

to the incarceration trends in the U.S. in the 1980's and 1990's (Blumstein and Beck 1999).

Exogenous Factors

There are two major social forces that may have played a role in explaining the declining rate of crime in Canada during the 1990's: demography and economic prosperity. The "baby boom" has had a more important impact in Canada than in any other industrialized country (Foote 2000). The after-war boom continued into the early sixties, at which point the number of births dropped until the early seventies and has remained low since. Nineteen sixty two is the single year in which the greatest percentage of Canadians were born (Foote 2000). The large cohort born around 1960 became young adults at the turn of the eighties, when the recession arrived. During the 1980's, there were hiring freezes, shutdowns, and high unemployment rates. In 1992, the large cohort born around 1962 reached 30 years of age and, in 1999, people in this category were approaching 40. The traditional age-crime curve tends to point to 18 years of age as the most violence-prone age, while the average serious offender is older (Farrington 1986). Murderers, bank robbers and rapists are closer to 30 than to 20.

Therefore, if one concedes that serious crime is not only a teenager or very young adult problem (which is obvious for sexual assault and domestic violence), the downward trend in crime observed in Canada might very well be explained by a progressive decrease in high crime groups, such as the 18–24, 25–29, and 30–34 age groups. Hence, the crime trends in Canada are compatible with the demographic explanation; property crimes (highly associated with teenagers and young adults) levelled off during the 80's, while violent crimes (mostly committed by youths but also middle aged adults) decreased in the 90's. Data presented in Table 2.2 show that the number of people aged between 20 and 34 dropped by 18% in the U.S. and Canada between 1990 and 1999.

The other exogenous factor involves the economy. Canada had very high unemployment figures throughout the 1980's. The situation improved in the early 1990's and continued to improve thereafter. Table 2.2 shows that the total unemployment rate dropped by 36% in the U.S. and by 27% in Canada between 1991 and 1999. Employment is now more easily available for young adults, especially in the world of service oriented part-time jobs. More stable and rewarding jobs and opportunities have grown during the 1990's as a result of the massive retirement wave that took place amongst early baby-boomers. The economic situation for young adults has therefore improved greatly during the 1990's, explaining at least a part of the drop (Freeman 2000).

Besides demographic and economic changes, other factors may play a role in explaining decreasing crime trends in Canada and in the United States. One of those factors might be a growing proportion of young adults pursuing higher education. According to Statistics Canada (2000): "In 1990, 20% of people aged 25 to 29 in Canada had less than high school education. By 1998, that percentage had dropped to 13%. Also, between 1990 and 1998, the percentage of individuals in this age group who had university degrees rose from 17% to 26%." Another factor explaining the decline in the crime rate might be a decrease in public consumption of alcohol, presumably because of more stringent enforcement of DWI laws. In fact, the per-capita sale of spirits and beer in Canada has decreased slightly during the 90's (Statistics Canada 1999), but public consumption in restaurants and bars might have dropped even more rapidly. These two hypotheses, as well as others, have to be examined more closely in further research.

Conclusion

According to LaFree (1998; 1999), "The United States in the 1990's has experienced the greatest sustained decline in violent crimes since World War II". This decline applies to most types of street crimes. Crime trends in Canada are very similar to those observed in the U.S. The quest for a general explanation should therefore focus on changes that have affected both countries, in all regions and for most forms of crime. If changes in the use of incarceration is to be invoked as an explanation, it would have to be shown why it worked in the

U.S. but not in Canada. In terms of policing, contrary to the U.S., Canada has not increased the *pro rata* number of police officers. Nevertheless, advances in technology have characterized many police organisations during the 90's as well as changes in police operations. While police organisations are doubtlessly more efficient in 1999 than in 1991, we do not know what changes, if any, have had an impact on crime (Eck and Maguire 2000). In Canada, there has been no movement toward more aggressive policing, as was observed in many U.S. cities. As we have seen, the areas that are the most promising for explaining the crime drop in both countries have to do with demography and economic prosperity. It is also possible that the two nations, as well as others, may have gone through a period of important changes in collective values.

Collective values are the factors that are the most difficult to grasp for researchers. Nevertheless, they may play an important role in explaining recent crime trends. The work of Elias (1939), who studied the evolution of good manners across centuries, provides an understanding of how violent behaviour was progressively identified as "bad behaviour". In the early Middle Ages, knights took pleasure in torturing and killing peasants. As society evolved, this behaviour was no longer accepted. The process proposed by Elias seems quite straightforward: changes in social structures are accompanied by changes in people's sensibilities. Identifying what in our society changed during the 80's and 90's to cause our values regarding crime and violence to evolve so drastically would allow us to explain how and why crime rates decline.

Homicide rates were high in the first three decades of the 20th century. It might very well be that industrialization, massive immigration, and poverty were factors that disrupted family structure and the social fabric. At mid-century, a new ethos emerged in our society, with strong families, disciplinary schools, and religious fervour. Self-restraint was tantamount to good manners. The cultural revolution of the 60's and 70's, with liberalization and self-expression becoming the dominant ethos—or pathos—has profoundly changed our society (Wilson and Herrnstein 1985; Freeman 2000). Crime rates, but also the rates of automobile accidents and suicides, increased rapidly. The late 1980's and 1990's, however, can be characterized by the progressive integration of a new ethos of moderation in drinking, drug use, sexual activity, and even tobacco use. Many behaviours that were seen as acceptable or were not the object of public outrage only twenty years ago are now gradually integrated into our moral conditioning.

Notes

1. This research was supported by a grant from SSHRC. I would like to thank anonymous reviewers as well us the editor of the CJC for their comments on a earlier version of this paper.
2. For detailed statistics, see *www.canadianembassy.org*.
3. For Canada, data for 1901–1961 was obtained from Buckley (1963) and Leach (1983), while data for the 1962–1999 period come from Statistic Canada's CANSIM series. For the U.S., data for 1900–1959 come from Archer and Gartner (1984), from the Sourcebook of Criminal Justice Statistics for the period 1960–1992 and from the BJS website for the years 1993 to 1999.
4. In order to test the presence of a trend in the ratio, a regression was performed with T as the independent variable and the US-Canada ratio as the dependent variable for the 38 years since 1962. The equation is Y (ratio) = 3,669 – 0,0035 (Year), has a R square value of 1.2% and is not significant at the 0,5 level.
5. The unstandardized error term of the equation [Y(1993 incarceration rate) = a + b (1993 homicide rate)] shows a correlation of 0,408 with the 1993–1998 percent change in incarceration rate.
6. Canada's three territories, Yukon, the Northwest Territories and Nunavut were not included in the analysis because of their very small populations and specific crime problems.
7. Data on unemployment demography comes from *www.fedstats.org* and *www.statscan.ca*.
8. Passed in 1991, Bill 147 in Québec allows the prison warden to transfer to community correctional supervision an inmate who has served 1/6 of his/her sentence. According to Corbo (2001), wardens received internal messages from their organization asking them to try to release 83% of their inmates serving a sentence of less than six months.
9. This new disposition was created by the Sentencing Reform Bill (C-41) that was proclaimed in 1996.

References

Archer, Dane and Rosemary Gartner. 1984. Violence and Crime in International Perspective. New Haven, CT: Yale University Press.

Blumstein, Alfred and Allen Beck. 1999. Population Growth in U.S. Prisons 1980–1996. In Michael Tonry and Joan Petersilia (eds.), Prisons. New York: U.S. Department of Justice.

Blumstein, Alfred and Joel Wallman. 2000. The Crime Drop in America. New York: Cambridge University Press.

Buckley, K.A.H. 1963. Historical Statistics of Canada. Toronto: MacMillan.

Chaiken, Jan M. 2000. Crunching numbers: Crime and incarceration at the end of the millennium. National Institute of Justice Journal. January 10–17.

Corbo, Claude. 2001. Pour rendre plus sécuritaire un risque nécessaire. Rapport, Québec: Ministère de la sécurité publique du Québec.

Eck, John and Edward Maguire. 2000. Have changes in policing reduced violent crime? An assessment of the evidence. In Alfred Blumstein and Joel Wallman (eds.), The Crime Drop in America. New York: Cambridge.

Elias, Norbert. 1939. The Civilizing Process. New York: Blackwell (1994 edition).

Farrington, David. 1986. Age and crime. In Michael Tonry and Norval Morris (eds.), Crime and Justice, volume 7. Chicago: University of Chicago Press.

Felson, Marcus. 1998. Crime in Every Day Life. Second edition. Thousand Oaks, California: Pine Forge Press.

Foote, David. 2000. Boom, Bust and Echo. Second edition. Toronto: MacFarlane, Walter & Ross.

Freeman, Richard B. 2000. Does the booming economy help explain the drop in crime? In U.S. Department of Justice, Perspectives on Crime and Justice: 1999–2000 Lectures Series. Rockville, MD: Department of Justice.

Hagan, John. 1991. Disreputable Pleasures: Crime and Deviance in Canada. Third edition, Toronto: McGraw-Hill.

Holloway, Marguerite. 1999. The aborted crime wave. Scientific American, December 1999.

Justice Policy Institute. 2000. Texas Tough?: An Analysis of Incarceration and Crime Trends in the Lone Star State. Washington, DC: Center on Juvenile and Criminal Justice.

LaFree, Gary. 1998. Social institutions and the crime "bust" of the 1990s. Journal of Criminal Law and Criminology 88 (1): 325–1368.

——. 1999. Declining violent crime rates in the 1990s: Predicting crime booms and busts. Annual Review or Sociology 25: 145–168.

Leach, F.H. 1983. Statistiques historiques du Canada, Deuxième édition. Ottawa: Statistics Canada.

Lenton, Rhonda. 1989. Homicide in Canada and the USA: A critique of the Hagan thesis. Canadian Journal of Sociology 14: 163–178.

Lipset, Seymour M. 1990. Continental Divide: The Values and Institutions in the United States and Canada. New York: Routledge.

Mayhew, Pat and Jan J.M. van Dijk. 1997. Criminal Victimization in Eleven Industrialized Countries. Key findings from the 1996 International Crime Victims Survey. The Hague: Ministry of Justice, WODC.

Ouimet, Marc. 1999. Crime in Canada and the United States: A comparative analysis. Canadian Review of Sociology and Anthropology 36 (3): 389–408.

Ouimet, Marc and Pierre Tremblay. 1996. A normative theory of the relationship between crime rates and imprisonment rates. Journal of Research on Crime and Delinquency 33 (1): 109–125.

PKS Berichtsjahr. 2001. Police Crime Statistics—2000. Wiesbaden: Federal Republic of Germany.

Povey, David. 2001. Recorded crime, England and Wales—12 months to March 2001. Research Development Statistics. London. UK: Home Office.

Rennison, Callie Marie. 2000. Criminal victimization 1999. National Crime Victimization Survey. Bureau of Justice Statistics.

Rosenfeld, Richard. 2000. Patterns in adult homicides: 1980–1995. In Alfred Blumstein and Joel Wallman (eds.), The Crime Drop in America. New York: Cambridge.

Spelman, William. 2000. The limited importance of prison expansion. In Alfred Blumstein and Joel Wallman (eds.), The Crime Drop in America. New York: Cambridge.

Statistics Canada. 1999. The control and sale of alcoholic beverages in Canada. Ottowa: Statistics Canada. Ref: 63-202-XIB.

——. 2000. Education indicators in Canada. Ottowa: Statistics Canada. Ref: 81-582-XIE.

Steffensmeier, Darrell and Miles D. Harer. 1999. Making sense of recent U.S. crime trends, 1980 to 1996/1998: Age composition effects and other explanations. Journal of Research on Crime and Delinquency 36 (3): 235–274.

Thomas, Jennifer. 2000. Adult Correctional Services in Canada, 98–99. Juristat, 20 (3). Ottawa: Canadian Center for Justice Statistics. Statistics Canada.

Wilson, James. Q. and Richard J. Herrnstein. 1985. Crime and Human Nature. New York: Simon and Schuster.

Chapter 3

Armed Americans

The Impact of Firearm Availability on National Homicide Rates

Anthony W. Hoskin

The effect of gun access on homicide rates has long been politically controversial in the United States, generating arguments across the spectrum: some claim guns have no effect, others that they increase deadly violence, and still others that they actually reduce *the likelihood of homicide. But while many studies have tracked homicide rates as they correlate to gun ownership in the U.S. over time, few have closely examined the relationship between homicide and gun access across nations.*

Anthony Hoskin's study subjected thirty-six countries to a rigorous study that brought to light many of the difficulties in comparing statistics across nations and came up with a surprising conclusion—while countries with greater numbers of privately owned firearms are likely to have high incidences of lethal violence, it is far from a simple cause-and-effect relationship. Other factors which contribute to violence, and which happen to be part of the American makeup, combine to make the United States uniquely prone to homicide.

The United States has the questionable distinction of being a world leader in homicide. In their recent book *Crime Is Not the Problem,* Franklin Zimring and Gordon Hawkins (1997) used multinational victim surveys, official crime statistics, and health statistics to show that America's level of crime is not much different from that of other industrialized nations, but its level of lethal violence is much higher. Although the U.S. murder rate has declined in recent years to 5.4 deaths per 100,000 persons (Federal Bureau of Investigation 2000), it remains almost four times higher than that of the average industrialized nation and three times that of our neighbor Canada (World Health Organization 1998).[1]

Lethal violence is often thought to be associated with poverty, but the homicide rates in most poor countries are lower than in the United States. In fact, of the 25 developing nations that provided WHO (1996) with data, only a few countries of the former Soviet Union and only a few of the Latin American countries report homicide levels exceeding those in the United States. Yet one might expect pervasive violence in these regions, which currently are experiencing economic deprivation and rapid social change. Why does America experience so much violence? Public opinion on this question ranges from the effects of media violence to the breakdown of the family, from illicit drugs to a soft response by the criminal justice system. The large disparities between the wealthy and the poor have inspired criminologists to look to inequality as the principal national-level explanation of variation in homicide rates (Avison and Loring 1986; Braithwaite and Braithwaite 1980; Krohn 1976; Messner 1980, 1982; Unnithan and Whitt 1992; Unnithan et al. 1994).

Criminologists from other countries argue that the widespread access to firearms is *the* explanation for America's gun violence problem. They contend that any other explanation avoids the obvious:

> When discussing American lethal violence with any foreign criminologist, guns are always the first factor to be mentioned as an explanation of the distinctively high rates of death in the United States. What sets the foreign criminologists' comments apart from our American colleagues is not the unanimity with which they focus on guns, however, because this topic is inevitably mentioned by American criminologists as well. But our foreign colleagues are frequently unwilling to discuss any other feature of American society or government *except* gun ownership and use. (Zimring and Hawkins 1997:106; author's emphasis.)

There are at least two reasons to think that America's level of lethal violence may be high because of the widespread availability of firearms. First, gun possession in the United States, particularly handgun possession, exceeds that of every other country for which data are available. Second, the United States surpasses other countries by a much greater margin in gun homicides than in nongun homicides. According to data presented by Killias (1993), nearly one-half (48%) of American respondents report having at least one gun of any type in their home. The average for other high-income nations is only 16 percent. The difference is even more striking when the comparison is limited to the possession of handguns, the type of firearm most frequently used in homicides (at least in the United States). More than one in four (28.4%) American households report having at least one handgun in the home. This is more than four times the handgun possession rate of the other high-income countries, averaged together; handguns are present in only 6.8 percent of those households (Killias 1993).

Americans not only have widespread access to handguns, but also are killed by firearms at much higher rates than non-Americans. The nongun homicide rate in the United States is 2.5 times higher than the average for other countries; the U.S. gun homicide rate is 7.6 times higher than the combined rates of other nations (Killias 1993). The ratio of American gun homicides to gun homicides in other countries, when compared with the American/non-American ratio of nongun homicides, implies that some factor makes American gun homicide rates higher than one would expect on the basis of the pattern of nongun homicides. The widespread ownership of firearms accompanied by pervasive lethal violence is a co-occurrence that requires an explanation.

Theory

Researchers have offered several views on the role of firearms in interpersonal violence (Berkowitz and LePage 1967; Kleck 1991; Wolfgang 1958; Zimring 1968). Hypotheses typically have not been derived from general theories, but Kleck (1991:154–55) provides a general way of thinking about guns by conceptualizing them in terms of power. Personal power can be viewed as one's ability to impose some condition on others, despite their resistance, which ultimately rests on the capacity to use physical force and violence. Individual power is usually conceptualized as a static property that derives from a person's enduring characteristics and from his or her location in the social structure, but power also can come from situational resources such as the possession of a firearm. Guns, like other weapons, are tools designed to give humans the capacity to inflict a degree of physical harm that is more difficult to achieve when using nothing more than one's body. Although firearms can be used for destructive purposes, their power also can defend people from aggression by others.

Specific views of the link between guns and violent crime can be divided into three general types. The first claims that access to guns plays no role in the production of violence. According to the second view, greater availability of guns leads to more violence. By contrast, the third view proposes that the presence of guns acts to reduce violence.

In an early statement on how guns might affect violent outcomes, Wolfgang (1958:83) stated the following conclusions from his study of homicide: "[F]ew homicides due to shooting could be avoided merely if a firearm were not immediately present, and ... the offender would select some other weapon to achieve the same destructive goal." Wolfgang asserted that the extent of the harm inflicted on a victim is the result of the aggressor's specific intentions: the greater the degree of harm intended, the more lethal the weapon that would be chosen. The presence of a firearm in a violent incident reveals that the assailant's motivation is intensely violent; it does not reflect the fact that a gun happened to be close at hand. Wolfgang portrayed an aggressor as one who (1) plans the amount of damage to be done beforehand; (2) chooses the weapon that is appropriate for the desired injury; and (3) executes the attack as planned. Wolfgang's claim is captured nicely in the adage "Guns don't kill people; people kill people."

In contrast to Wolfgang, Zimring (1968, 1972) argued that there is a "weapon instrumentality" effect: the presence of a gun increases the likelihood of injury and homicide independent of the aggressor's motivation. According to Zimring, the outcome of a violent incident is largely a function of the deadliness of the aggressor's weapon. Assailants are not likely to plan, in any precise way, the extent of the injury that they inflict on victims. The motivation to attack someone is usually fleeting and indeterminate, and whether an attack only causes injury or results in death depends on the killing power of the weapon. With the same expenditure of effort, a gun will wound someone more severely than another weapon and is more likely to kill the victim.

According to Zimring and Hawkins (1997), gun use not only increases the mechanical killing power of an attack but also gives the capacity to kill at long distances. The only practical limit to the range of a gun is the shooter's marksmanship. No other commonly used weapon can inflict lethal injury at long distances. Moreover, aggressors with firearms have the capacity to attack multiple victims at the same time. Unlike knives or blunt instruments, most guns can inflict several injuries on different victims in a matter of seconds.

Guns also may produce violence by emboldening and empowering an aggressor. A firearm may give a person the power and the courage to commit an act of violence that he or she would not otherwise commit, a phenomenon that Kleck (1991:156) calls "facilitation." An unarmed person may elect not to show aggression against a stronger victim for fear of failure, but possession of a gun may lead someone to attack an otherwise stronger individual on the expectation that success is likely (Kleck 1991:156; Tedeschi and Felson 1994:201–02).

Related to the concept of facilitation is the idea that guns enable offenders to inflict injuries without the need for direct contact with the victim. Wolfgang (1958:737) suggested, in contrast to his position that access to guns does not affect violence, that squeamish offenders who are averse to killing someone with a knife or a blunt instrument might be able to kill someone at a distance with a gun.

Most accounts explaining how firearm possession leads to violence focus on the physical impact of the gun. Another approach is to focus on a firearm's symbolic aspects. It may be that the presence of a firearm serves as an aggressive stimulus. According to Berkowitz and LePage (1967), anger and frustration can lead people to violence; the sight of a weapon can evoke aggression in angry people because of the learned association between weapons and aggressive behavior. Berkowitz (1983) also argues that the presence of a gun may stir up negative thoughts that are accompanied by unpleasant emotions, thereby intensifying any existing negative emotion. Turner and his associates (1977:375–76) qualified Berkowitz's proposition by pointing out that the presence of a gun stimulates aggression only in people who associate weapons with the positive consequences of aggressive behavior; those who associate weapons with negative consequences of aggression are likely to be inhibited by the sight of a weapon.

In contrast to those who contend that firearm availability raises levels of violence, some scholars propose that private gun ownership and defensive gun use deter violent crime (Cook 1991:58–61; Kleck 1991:130–45). In their view, a criminal may be deterred from committing a crime that involves direct contact with a victim if the criminal anticipates armed resistance by the victim. An offender who confronts an armed victim is exposed to a higher risk of injury, which makes the prospect of victimization less attractive. In most instances, offenders will not know whether a potential victim has a gun, and must make a decision about committing a crime based on the expectation of gun possession. Offenders are aware that potential victims who are at home or who are working in the kinds of business establishments where proprietors keep guns (e.g., small shops, convenience stores, and gas stations) are much more likely than other potential victims to have access to firearms; such knowledge should decrease the likelihood of an attempt to victimize these individuals.

Kleck (1991:161–62) proposed that the use of a gun in committing a face-to-face crime reduces the chance of an actual attack by restraining the actions of both the perpetrator and the victim. In direct-contact crimes, criminals usually do not want to murder their victims; they want something from victims but do not want to kill them to get it. Criminals are motivated to use firearms because a weapon's deadliness is likely to intimidate the victim. On the other hand, the possession of a firearm gives the aggressor such deadly power that any use of it may inflict much more injury than desired. Thus one would expect that offenders will frequently threaten victims with a gun but will rarely use them.

The use of guns to threaten victims may serve as a substitute for an actual attack and thereby may reduce the incidence of attack, injury, and death to the victim (Kleck 1991:161–62). The possession of a firearm gives the power not only to injure or kill, but also to accomplish other ends: to force compliance, to frighten and humiliate, and to appear fearless and powerful. Without a gun, through threat alone, an aggressor may lack the intimidation power to attain some goal, and an actual attack may become necessary. Threatening someone with an object as deadly as a gun also may do more than eliminate the need to actually attack the victim: it may give an opponent a legitimate excuse to not fight back. An audience is likely to consider the decision to submit to an armed antagonist as prudent, not cowardly (Kleck 1991:161–62).

To summarize, scholars have made a number of competing claims about the effect of firearms possession on interpersonal violence. The simplest claim is that guns do not have an independent effect on violent crime; the use of a gun in a criminal act merely reflects the offender's intentions. In contrast, several claims have been made expressing how access to guns produces violence: (1) guns, because of their capacity to inflict serious physical harm with little effort, increase the degree of injury suffered by victims; (2) guns give weak aggressors the courage to attack stronger targets; and (3) guns are a cue to angry and frustrated people to act aggressively. Finally, gun possession has been portrayed as a practice that prevents violence: criminals are deterred from victimizing someone who is thought to possess a firearm. When the criminal possesses the gun, violence is avoided: the behavior of both the victim and the offender is likely to be very restrained. Also, by threatening someone with a gun, the criminal may gain the victim's compliance without the need to resort to an attack.

Macro-Level Research

Almost all macro-level research examining the relationship between gun availability and crime rates has been based on American data. Overall these studies have found that measures of firearm availability are related positively to rates of overall homicide (Brearley 1932; Brill 1977; Fisher 1976; Kleck 1979; Lester 1988; Maggadino and Medoff 1984; McDowall 1991; Newton and Zimring 1969; Philips, Votey, and Howell 1976; Seitz 1972; South 1984), robbery-related murder (Cook 1979, 1987), and burglary (Cook 1983). On the other hand, studies using more direct measures of firearm availability and those which have employed nonrecursive models have been less likely to report significant effects (Kleck 1979, 1984, 1991; Kleck and Patterson 1993; McDowall 1986, 1991).

Few macro-level studies have examined the role of access to guns in violent crime in other nations, and only a few have examined differences across nations. As a result, there is little systematic evidence on whether the United States leads the Western world in homicide because of high levels of private gun ownership. International comparisons of access to guns and levels of homicide are often limited to showing that the United States is much higher on these variables than some other country (e.g., Clark and Mayhew 1988; Newton and Zimring 1969).

A few studies have examined the relationship between gun availability across a sample of nations; most of these have reported a positive association (Curtis 1974; Etzioni and Remp 1973; Killias 1990, 1993; Kleck 1997; Lester 1974, 1991, 1996). These studies, however, suffer from a number of methodological limitations.

First, the sample sizes have been very small, usually fewer than 20 cases. Findings derived from a small number of cases are highly sensitive to sample composition. Second, the studies generally have limited their analysis to zero-order correlations and may have produced biased estimates by failing to control for confounding factors. Third, most of these studies use only single-year estimates of homicide. The infrequency of homicides increases the potential for measurement error, and it is standard practice in cross-national homicide research to reduce measurement error by averaging rates over several years. Fourth, this problem also exists in studies that use single-year estimates of gun availability based on rare events such as suicides, homicides, or fatal accidents involving the use of firearms.

Fifth, international comparisons often fail to match the time periods for the measures of homicide and of firearm availability. A statistically significant cross-sectional relationship between these two variables would probably be underestimated if they were measured at times several years apart. Sixth, the studies often fail to validate their indirect measures of access to firearms. In the absence of validating evidence, less confidence can be placed in proxy measures. Finally, all of the international studies have failed to investigate the possibility that gun availability may be associated with homicide because high homicide rates tend to increase firearm ownership for the purpose of self-defense: The association may not be due to the effect of firearm access on homicide rates.

In the present study I conduct a cross-national analysis of homicide that improves on macro-level research in the following ways: (1) I examine directly why the United States has such a high level of lethal violence in comparison with other countries; (2) I use a sample that is large enough to allow for multivariate analysis, in which confounding factors can be controlled; (3) I reduce measurement error in homicide rates by using multiple-year averages matched on time period with independent variables; (4) I validate an indirect measure of firearm availability; and (5) I use a recursive model of homicide and firearm availability that allows me to estimate the effect of firearm availability on homicide, net of homicide's effect on firearm availability.

Conceptualization and Measurement of Firearm Availability

Philip Cook (1991:37–42) has discussed three ways in which firearm availability has been conceptualized in the literature. First, in terms of gun ownership: gun owners obviously have more ready access to guns than do other people. Second, availability can refer to the cost and difficulty of acquiring a gun. Costs include not only the purchase price but also the obstacles presented by federal and state laws that regulate firearms commerce. Third, because many personal crimes occur in public places, carrying a gun outside one's home is another important conceptualization.

Zimring's (1968) proposition about the relationship between guns and homicide implies a particular conceptualization of firearm availability. As described above, Zimring argues that in many incidents of assault, aggressors are temporarily motivated to inflict an unspecified amount of physical harm on a target individual. The amount of injury actually suffered by the victim depends largely on the type of weapon that is readily available for use. If a loaded gun can be obtained before the desire to hurt the victim passes, the aggressor is likely to use it, and the killing power of the gun increases the risk that the victim will die from his or her injuries.

Zimring's argument portrays the typical assailant as a person who is irrational, impulsive, and highly responsive to immediate circumstances. Thus the concept of firearm availability that flows from the "instrumentality" thesis is that a gun is available for use if the time required to obtain a loaded, functioning gun is no longer than the time in which an aggressor is motivated to harm a target. In the theoretical maximum for firearm availability, the time it takes to obtain a loaded, functioning gun *never* exceeds the length of time in which an assailant is motivated to attack a victim. Conversely, in the theoretical minimum of availability, the time it takes to secure a gun *always* exceeds the time in which an offender is motivated to attack.

An ideal aggregate-level measure of this conceptualization of firearm availability would be the number of instances in a given period in which the length of time required for obtaining a loaded, functioning gun did not exceed the length of time when an individual was motivated to harm a victim as a proportion of the total number of instances in which individuals in a population were motivated to harm a victim. Because international data for this variable are not available, a substitute measure must be used.

Household gun possession is one conceptualization of availability which overlaps extensively with the conceptualization described above. Unless an aggressor is some distance from home, he or she can quickly obtain a gun that is kept at home, in a period shorter than the period in which one is motivated to attack a victim. Even a firearm kept unloaded under lock and key can ordinarily be obtained and loaded very quickly.[2]

Although no available data allow a direct operationalization of firearm availability as defined above, available cross-national data permit a straightforward operationalization of household gun possession. The International Crime Survey (del Frate, Zvekic, and van Dijk 1993) collected data on gun possession for households from 20 countries. Surveys were conducted by telephone in seven countries in 1989 and in five countries in 1992; surveys in eight countries were conducted in both years. Respondents were asked two questions about household gun possession. The first was asked of everyone: "Do you keep any firearms in your household?" If respondents answered "yes," they were asked a second question: "Is it a handgun, a rifle, or a shotgun?" (In the 1989 survey, rifles and shotguns were combined into one response category.)

From the data collected from this survey, Killias (1993) calculated the prevalence rates of household gun possession and household handgun possession for 18 developed countries. He used this measure to show a strong positive correlation between firearm availability and gun homicide rates, but the small number of cases made it impossible to conduct a multivariate analysis in which relevant factors could be controlled statistically. Although 18 cases are also insufficient for the present study, this measure can serve as the standard for assessing the validity of the availability measure to be used.

One indirect measure of firearm availability which is available for a much larger and more diverse sample of countries, is the percentage of all suicides committed with guns. Data for this measure were collected by Krug, Powell, and Dahlberg (1996) at the Centers for Disease Control (CDC). They obtained suicide mortality data for 36 highly and moderately developed nations for the most recent year available between 1990 and 1995.[3] Research has shown that the "percent gun suicide" measure is a valid proxy for firearm availability (Cook 1979; Killias 1993; Kleck 1991:194–95; Lester 1996).

To assess the validity of the gun suicide measure as a measure of gun availability, I correlated it with the International Crime Survey measure of household gun possession for 17 developed countries. The gun suicide measure is calculated from the CDC data, described above.

Calculations reveal that the Pearson correlation coefficient between the natural log of the percentage of suicides committed with guns and the percentage of households with any type of gun is .90 ($p < .001$) across 17 countries. This finding is very similar to the .91 correlation reported by Killias (1993), based on a sample of 16 European countries. These findings indicate that the gun suicide measure is related very closely to the survey-based measure of overall household firearm possession. The correlation between gun suicides and the survey measure of household handgun possession is lower: .62 ($p < .01$). It appears that the gun suicide measure taps household possession of any type of gun more strongly than household handgun possession. Consequently, firearm availability, as measured here, appears to be a proxy for household possession of firearms of any type.

Data on Homicides and Control Variables

Whereas a great deal of homicide research is based on arrest data or offenses known to police, numerous cross-national homicide studies are based on mortality data obtained from the *World Health Statistics Annual*, published by the World Health Organization (WHO). National-level homicide rates based on mortality data are valid and reliable measures, at least for assessing the relationship between national characteristics and crime (Bennett and Lynch 1990; Vidgerhous 1978).

I calculated homicide rates in the following way: (1) I found the numerator by summing the number of total homicides for each year in the 1990–1994 period and dividing by the number of years for which data were available; (2) the

1990 mid-year total population, taken from the *Demographic Yearbook* (United Nations, various years), served as the denominator; and (3) I multiplied the fraction by 100,000 to give the average number of homicides per 100,000 population. Analysis of the 1990–1994 average homicide rate indicated that conversion to natural log forms produced a distribution approximating normality. Descriptive statistics for the homicide measures are presented in Table 3.1. The large standard deviation relative to the measure's mean indicates substantial cross-national variation.

Findings from cross-national research indicate that a number of social factors affect homicide levels, and that these variables should be included as controls in the present analysis. One of the most reliable cross-national findings is that homicide varies directly with economic inequality (Avison and Loring 1986; Braithwaite and Braithwaite 1980; Krohn 1976; LaFree and Kick 1986; Messner 1980, 1982, 1989; Messner and Rosenfeld 1997; Neapolitan 1994, 1998; Unnithan et al. 1994; Unnithan and Whitt 1992). The Gini coefficient of household income distribution is a commonly used measure of economic inequality; I obtained circa-1990 data for this variable from the World Bank's (1998) *World Development Report*. Data for this variable and for all other controls were obtained for the year closest to 1990 for which data were available; I gave preference to data from 1990–1994.

According to a number of studies, homicide levels tend to be low in nations with higher levels of socioeconomic development (Krohn 1978; Krohn and Wellford 1977; Messner and Rosenfeld 1997; Neapolitan 1994), and rates of gun ownership are higher among wealthy individuals (Kleck 1991). Socioeconomic development is commonly operationalized as per capita GNP; I took data for this measure from the World Bank (1994).

At least three cross-national studies have reported a positive relationship between the youthfulness of the population and levels of homicide (Conklin and Simpson 1985; Hansmann and Quigley 1982; Messner 1989). The percentage of the population that is male as well as young should be related to homicide, and males are much more likely than females to own firearms (Kleck 1991). In the present analysis, the age-sex structure is measured as the percentage of the total population that is male between ages 15 and 34. In addition, at least one study reported a positive association between population density and homicide (Conklin and Simpson 1985). Urban populations also show lower levels of gun ownership (Kleck 1991). The appropriate data for the age-sex structure variable and for the number of persons per square mile were available in the *Demographic Yearbook* (United Nations, various years).

Two studies of welfare spending have reported a negative effect on homicide rates (Fiala and LaFree 1988; Messner and Rosenfeld 1997).

Table 3.1
Descriptive Statistics

Variable	Minimum	Maximum	Mean	SD
Percent Suicides With Guns, Unlogged	.21	60.95	14.65	13.60
Percent Suicides With Guns, Logged	−1.56	4.11	2.05	1.42
1990–94 Homicide Rate, Unlogged	.42	28.21	3.70	5.92
1990–94 Homicide Rate, Logged	−.71	3.03	.73	.91
Persons Per Square Mile, Unlogged	2.06	5,400.00	390.61	961.42
Persons Per Square Mile, Logged	.72	8.59	4.67	1.72
Percent Male Ages 15 to 34, Unlogged	11.00	25.70	15.91	2.38
Percent Male Ages 15 to 34, Logged	2.40	3.30	2.76	.14
Ethnic Heterogeneity Index	.00	.71	.26	.19
East Asia Dummy	.00	1.00	.14	.35
Welfare State Index	−5.52	4.72	.00	2.57
Economic Discrimination Index	.00	4.00	1.58	1.39
Nonlethal Violence Rate, Unlogged	17.90	707.10	204.82	168.47
Nonlethal Violence Rate, Logged	2.88	6.56	4.99	.84

NOTE: *N* = 36 nations

Messner and Rosenfeld found that a measure of the services available to citizens which reduce their reliance on the market for sustenance and support, called the "decommodification index," was related positively to national homicide rates. This index is a composite of a number of measures of the levels of social spending by the central government.

Three studies (Messner 1989; Messner and Rosenfeld 1997; Neapolitan 1994) report that homicide is related directly to economic discrimination. Messner and Rosenfeld's measure is "an ordinal rating scale based on expert judgments about the extent to which groups experience objective economic disadvantages that are attributable to deliberate discrimination. A nation's score represents the most extreme level of economic discrimination experienced by any minority group of that nation" (p. 1403). Data on the decommodifaction index and on economic discrimination were provided by the authors.

At least three studies report that homicide varies directly with ethnic heterogeneity (Avison and Loring 1986; Braithwaite and Braithwaite 1980; McDonald 1976). Data on ethnic group distributions are available in *The World Almanac and Book of Facts, 1999* (Famighetti 1998). I created an ethnic heterogeneity index using Blau's (1977:78) formula: heterogeneity score = $1 - \Sigma p_i^2$, where p_i is the ethnic group's size as a proportion of the total population. This measure takes into account both the relative size of the group and the number of groups in a population; a score of 1 reflects the theoretically maximum degree of heterogeneity.

WHO homicide data (World Health Organization, various years) reveal that rates are uniformly low in east Asia. Firearm ownership is also known to be rare in this region; consequently I constructed a dummy variable in which east Asian countries were scored 1 and all others were scored 0.

Research on firearms also suggests an additional control variable. Kleck (1991:185–86) points out that aggregate-level research on lethal violence and gun ownership is commonly limited by the failure to control for the "average lethality of the criminal population." It may be that an association between gun availability and homicide is produced by the criminal population's willingness to inflict lethal injury, as manifested by killing others and by carrying lethal weapons. To control for this possibility, I include the rate of nonlethal serious violent crime in the model as a proxy measure of criminal lethality, on the assumption that a willingness to inflict serious nonlethal harm is related closely to the willingness to kill. I computed this measure from data obtained from *International Crime Statistics* (INTERPOL, various years). To assess the validity of the measure, I calculated Pearson and Spearman correlation coefficients between the nonlethal violent crime rate and the percentage of International Crime Survey (del Frate et al. 1993) respondents who reported having been threatened or assaulted at least once in the past year. Both coefficients are .63, statistically significant at the .01 level (two-tailed test). Although at least one study (Kalish 1988) concluded that national differences in legal codes and data collection can reduce the reliability and validity of Interpol's data, the strong correlation between the nonlethal violent crime rate and the survey-based measure of violence suggests that the former is a valid measure of nonlethal violence.

Cross-national research is plagued by missing data. This problem is particularly serious in view of the fact that samples are small; even a few missing cases can severely reduce the sample of cases with nonmissing values. The data set to be used in the cross-sectional analysis contains only a small percentage of missing cases on several control variables (not on the firearm availability measure). I used mean substitution, which yielded a sample of 36 cases with no missing values.

I examined all of the variables to be included in the multivariate analysis to see whether they were distributed normally. I examined normality statistics for both the original variables and their natural log counterparts. The following variables more closely approximated a normal distribution: the natural log of homicides per 100,000 total population; the natural log of the percentage of suicides committed with guns;

the natural log of the number of persons per square mile; the natural log of the Gini coefficient of income distribution; per capita GNP; the percentage of the total population living in urban areas; the natural log of the percentage of the total population that is male between ages 15 and 34; the index of maximum economic discrimination; the decommodification index; the index of ethnic heterogeneity; and the natural log of the nonlethal violent crime rate.

Methods

Two-stage least squares regression is one estimation technique that enables an analyst to model the reciprocal relationship between two variables. The following description is taken from Gujarati (1988:603–08); the method involves two successive applications of ordinary least squares (OLS) regression.

In the first stage, one eliminates the likely correlation, in the homicide model, between firearm availability and homicide's error term by regressing firearm availability first on all the predetermined variables in the whole system: That is, all the exogenous variables in both the homicide and the firearm availability equations. Following OLS theory, the values of firearm availability predicted by the exogenous variables will not be correlated asymptotically with the error term. Predicted firearm availability, although it "resembles" the observed firearm availability variable (in the sense of being highly correlated), will be uncorrelated with the error term in the homicide equation. Such a proxy is also known as an *instrumental variable.*

In the second stage of two-stage least squares regression, firearm availability in the original homicide equation is replaced with the predicted firearm availability variable, and OLS then is applied to the transformed equation. The estimators thus are consistent: That is, they converge to their true values as the sample size increases indefinitely.

Results

Descriptive statistics are presented in Table 3.1. Variables that have been logged are also shown in their unlogged form. The proportion of suicides committed with guns ranges from .21 percent (in South Korea) to 60.95 percent (in the United States). National homicide rates vary widely as well, from .42 per 100,000 (in Austria) to 28.21 per 100,000 (in Estonia). Among control variables, the number of persons per square mile varies a great deal: from 2.06 (in Australia) to 5,400 (in Hong Kong). The percentage of a national population that is male and age 15–34 ranges from 11.00 (in Estonia) to 25.70 (in Kuwait). The ethnic heterogeneity index ranges from zero in South Korea to .71 in Canada. (Recall that the upper limit is 1.00.) Fourteen percent of the countries in the sample are east Asian: Hong Kong, Japan, Singapore, South Korea, and Taiwan. As for the welfare state index, the sample ranges widely from –5.52 (in Brazil) to 4.72 (in Sweden). Ten nations scored zero on the economic discrimination index; Israel and Brazil scored the maximum possible (4.00). The number of nonlethal violent crimes per 100,000 total population ranged from 17.90 in Japan to 707.10 in the United States.

Preliminary analysis revealed very high correlations between three variables: the Gini coefficient, per capita GNP, and the decommodification index. Principal-components analysis indicated that these variables largely reflected a single underlying factor: This one factor explained 73.6 percent of the variance in the three values, and only this factor had a eigenvalue greater than 1 (2.21). The values for the Gini coefficient (ln), which were all negative, were changed to positive so that the measure would have a positive loading on the factor, as did the other two variables. I converted the values of the three variables to *z*-scores and summed them to create a composite index. I decided to conceptualize this as a "welfare state index" because per capita GNPs in welfare states are comparatively high, levels of income inequality are comparatively low, [and] levels of spending on social welfare and programs are comparatively high. The latter is particularly important in the decision to label the measure as a welfare state index because the decommodification index had the highest factor loading (.90); this indicates that the factor taps

Table 3.2
Bivariate Correlations

Variables	1	2	3	4	5	6	7	8	9
1. % Gun Suicides	1.00								
2. Homicide Rate (ln)	.37*	1.00							
3. Persons/Mile^2 (ln)	–.66*	–.20	1.00						
4. % Male 15–34 (ln)	–.29*	–.06	.09	1.00					
5. Ethnic Heterogeneity	.34*	.55*	–.14	–.04	1.00				
6. East Asia Dummy	–.74*	–.24	.52*	.24	–.26	1.00			
7. Welfare State Index	.12	–.52*	–.05	–.39*	–.19	–.12	1.00		
8. Econ. Discrimination	.27	.30*	–.16	.04	.44*	–.09	–.34*	1.00	
9. Nonlethal Violence	.17	.11	–.08	–.09	.19	–.17	.10	–.06	1.00

NOTE: N = 36 nations; *p < .10, two-tailed test

heavily the extent of the state's protection of citizens from the vicissitudes of the market. With the newly created variable, statistics indicate no multicollinearity problem among the independent variables; the highest variance inflation factor score is 1.7 for the economic discrimination index.

The limited size of the sample requires minimization of the number of exogenous and endogenous variables to be included in the multivariate analysis. I decided to include in multivariate models only those variables which had zero-order correlations with the dependent variable at the .10 significance level (two-tailed test). As Table 3.2 shows, five variables meet this criterion with respect to firearm availability: homicide rate, persons per square mile, percent males age 15–34, the ethnic heterogeneity index, and the east Asia dummy. Four variables were correlated with homicide at the .10 level of significance: the percentage of suicides committed with guns, the ethnic heterogeneity index, the welfare state index, and the index of economic discrimination.

The two models are estimated in the present analysis:

Gun availability function: $Y_{1i} = B_{10} + B_{11}Y_{2i} + \gamma_{11}X_{1i} + \gamma_{12}X_{2i} + \gamma_{13}X_{3i} + \gamma_{14}X_{4i} + u_{1i}$

Homicide function: $Y_{2i} = B_{20} + B_{21}Y_{1i} + \gamma_{21}X_{3i} + \gamma_{22}X_{5i} + \gamma_{23}X_{6i} + u_{2i}$, *where*

Y_1 = percentage of suicides committed with guns (ln),

Y_2 = total homicide rate (ln),

X_1 = number of persons/mile^2 (ln),

X_2 = percentage of population male ages 15 to 34,

X_3 = ethnic heterogeneity index,

X_4 = east Asia dummy,

X_5 = welfare state index, and

X_6 = economic discrimination index.

In these two models, firearm availability and homicide are functions of each other, in addition to other factors.

The first step in two-stage least squares regression is to estimate two models. The measures of firearm availability and homicide are each regressed on all exogenous variables in the two equations written above: the numbers of person per square mile (ln), percent male ages 15–34(ln), the ethnic heterogeneity index, the east Asia dummy, the welfare state index, and the economic discrimination index. Table 3.3 presents least squares regression coefficients for the two models. The measure of firearm availability is related significantly (at the .01 level) to the number of persons per square mile (ln) and to the east Asia dummy. The R^2 statistic is .71, indicating that predicted firearm availability is correlated very closely to observed firearm availability. In the homicide model, homicide rates are related significantly to the percentage of the population male and ages 15 to 34, the ethnic heterogeneity index, and the welfare state index. The R^2 statistic is .57, an indication that predicted homicide is associated closely with observed homicide.

In the second step in two-stage least squares regression, we estimate the models written above, substitute the predicted homicide variable for observed homicide in the firearm avail-

Table 3.3
First-Stage Least Squares Regression Coefficients (Standardized Coefficients in Parentheses)

Exogenous Variables	Firearm Availability	Homicide
Number of Persons/Mile^2(ln)	–.30**	–.07
	(–.37)	(–.12)
% Male Ages 15–34(ln)	–1.07	–1.64*
	(–.10)	(–.25)
East Asia Dummy	–1.91**	–.20
	(–.47)	(–.08)
Ethnic Heterogeneity Index	.85	2.20**
	(.11)	(.46)
Welfare State Index	.04	–.21**
	(.08)	(–.59)
Economic Discrimination	.16	–.10
	(.15)	(–.14)
Constant	6.21*	5.16*
F-Statistic	11.66**	6.52**
R^2	.71	.57

NOTE: *N* = 36 Nations; **p* < .05; ***p* < .01 (one-tailed test)

ability model, and substitute the predicted firearm availability measure for observed firearm availability in the homicide model. Predicted homicide and predicted firearm availability serve as instrumental variables in their respective models; although they closely "resemble" their observed counterparts (in the sense of being highly correlated), each is asymptotically uncorrelated with the disturbance term in its own model.

Table 3.4 lists the second-stage least squares regression coefficients. The second column indicates that the measure of firearm availability is related significantly and negatively to the population density measure and to the east Asia dummy. Standardized coefficients indicate that these two variables have substantial effects on firearm availability. By contrast, firearm availability is unrelated to the age-sex structure, the ethnic heterogeneity index, and, most important for the present analysis, the predicted homicide rate. As indicated by the R^2 statistic, the model explains almost 70 percent of the cross-national variation in firearm possession.

In the second equation, higher homicide rates are associated at the .01 significance level

Table 3.4
Second-Stage Least Squares Regression Coefficients (Standardized Coefficients in Parentheses)

Independent Variables	Firearm Availability	Homicide
Number of Persons/Mile^2(ln)	–.33**	—
	(–.40)	
% Male Ages 15–34(ln)	–1.46	—
	(–.14)	
East Asia Dummy	–1.88**	—
	(–.46)	
Ethnic Heterogeneity Index	1.65	1.99**
	(.22)	(.41)
Welfare State Index	—	–.19**
		(–.53)
Economic Discrimination	—	–.10
		(–.14)
Predicted Homicide	–.17	—
	(.08)	
Predicted Firearm Availability	—	.20*
		(.26)
Constant	7.58**	–.04
F-Statistic	13.62**	9.00**
R^2	.69	.54

NOTE: *N* = 36 Nations; * *p* < .05; ** *p* < .01 (one-tailed test)

with nations registering high ethnic heterogeneity and a low welfare state index. The standardized coefficients for both variables are large. In contrast, the index of economic discrimination is unrelated to homicide rates. As for the independent variable of interest—firearm availability—the relationship is positive and significant at the .05 level. The standardized coefficient is .26; although it is only half the size of the welfare state coefficient, the relationship is moderately strong. The model explains 54 percent of the international variation in homicide, as indicated by the R^2 statistic.

Analyses of small samples can be affected greatly by outliers and sample composition. The United States is unique in possessing a very high level of both gun ownership and homicide. It may be that removing a case such as the United States from the sample would eliminate any correlation observed between firearm availability and homicide rates. To check for such a possibility (for other nations as well as the United States), I omitted each of the 36 nations in the full sample one at a time, and generated two-stage least squares regression coefficients for each of the 36 possible subsamples. Although the signs of all 36 firearm availability coefficients were positive and the values were approximately .2, *p*-values in four cases—Argentina, Brazil, Finland, and Kuwait—fell between .05 and .06 (one-tailed test). The former three are high gun ownership/high homicide countries; the latter is marked by low gun ownership and a low homicide rate. In spite of these exceptions, the overall results point to stability across various sample compositions. I made the same check for the firearm availability model to see whether higher homicide rates led to higher levels of firearm availability, at least in certain subsamples. In all 36 estimated models, the homicide coefficient was negative. The finding that levels of firearm availability are not affected by homicide rates is insensitive to the cases included in the analyzed sample.

Summary and Discussion

The primary purpose of the present analysis has been to test cross-nationally the hypothesis that greater access to firearms produces higher levels of lethal violence. The results are clear and stable: lethal violence is likely to be high in countries with greater supplies of privately owned guns. In addition, homicide rates are likely to be high in nations with ethnically heterogeneous populations and conservative welfare states. I found this to be the case after controlling for confounding factors and across various sample compositions. The case of the United States is consistent with the estimated model: it is an ethnically heterogeneous country that spends relatively little on social programs, and it leads the world in private firearm possession.

The findings reported here are consistent with Zimring's (1968) hypothesis that greater gun availability increases the likelihood that a gun will be used in an attack, which in turn increases the risk that the victim will die of his or her injuries. The findings do not support Wolfgang's (1958) position that homicides are unrelated to the availability of firearms. If access to a gun does not affect whether a homicide occurs, one would not expect to find a significant partial correlation between firearm availability and national homicide rates. Moreover, Kleck's (1991) contention that widespread gun ownership deters homicide is not supported in the present analysis. The methods used here do not permit us to rule out the possibility that firearm availability exerts a positive effect on homicide via weapon instrumentality *and* a negative effect on homicide via deterrence; the results, however, indicate that any deterrent effect must be much weaker than the positive effect of availability, because the observed correlation is positive and quite large.

Results do not support the hypothesis that high levels of lethal violence cause people to purchase firearms in order to protect themselves. Homicide rates had no effect on the measure of firearm availability; this was true for 37 different samples.

The present study has moved beyond prior cross-national research in a number of ways. First, the error associated with measuring homicide has been reduced by computing homicide rates that are averaged over multiple years. Second, larger samples that include developing nations have been analyzed. Third, relevant control variables have been included in models estimating the relationship between firearm availability and homicide. Fourth, the validity of the proxy measures of firearm availability used in the present study has been established. Fifth, the effect of firearm availability on homicide, net of homicide's effect on firearm availability, has been assessed. Finally, I made careful checks to rule out the possibility that findings were due to peculiarities of the selected sample.

Although this study has produced evidence that greater access to guns increases levels of lethal violence, the findings should be interpreted cautiously. The analysis is based on a relatively small number of cases. The estimation techniques used in this study assume a large sample, and we could place greater confidence in these results if the number of cases were considerably larger. In addition, the analyses reported here are based on proxy measures of firearm availability; although they are correlated highly with a survey-based measure of household gun possession, a direct measure of firearm availability would be preferable. I have already described the limitations associated with the measurement of violent cultures.

The limitations in the present study suggest possible avenues for future research. Direct measures of firearm availability are needed for more countries than currently are represented in available data. The International Crime Survey has gathered data on 18 developed nations and has conducted surveys in certain areas in 12 developing nations (del Frate et al. 1993). Data for a larger number of countries would make multivariate analyses possible; data for multiple years would allow us to estimate longitudinal models. Prior research and the present study have shown that the percentage of suicides committed with guns is a valid indirect measure of firearm availability, and access to gun suicide data for multiple years for a larger sample of countries would make possible an improvement in cross-national research.

Although a number of studies have examined the relationship between national-level rates of gun ownership and violent crime over time for the United States, little research has investigated this relationship for other countries. It would be interesting to see whether changes in firearm availability affect changes in violent crime in other nations.

Future research also might examine the cross-national relationship between firearm availability and other forms of violence. Few studies have examined whether nations with widespread access to guns show higher rates of robbery, suicide, or fatal firearm accidents. Cross-national research has done little to identify the national-level determinants of private gun ownership. What forces cause citizens in countries such as the United States to arm themselves?

Knowledge of the relationship between firearm availability and criminal violence is still relatively undeveloped. Although a number of excellent studies have been conducted, the evidence is still mixed and unconvincing. It is surprising that research on the link between gun availability and violence has not been pursued further, given the particular importance of this issue for American criminal justice policy. Thousands of human lives are taken by guns each year, and the endless political debates reveal many citizens' intense feelings about the proper place of firearms in American society. Yet analysts have not yet produced the kind of research that gives policy makers unambiguous guidance. Along with research that investigates the nontechnological sources of interpersonal violence, the need for further research on the relationship between guns and violent crime is clear.

Notes

1. I calculated the rates presented here from the raw data published by the World Health Organization. WHO (1996:xviii) defines homicides as "deaths by injury purposely inflicted by others." The comparison group consists of Australia, Austria, Belgium, Canada, Denmark, Finland, France, Germany, Hong Kong, Ireland, Israel, Italy, Japan, the Netherlands, New Zealand, Norway, Singapore, Spain, Sweden, and Switzerland.
2. In at least one area, household gun possession may not overlap with the conceptualization of firearm availability discussed above: a small percentage of people keep guns on their persons or in their automobiles (Kleck 1997:206). Such locations would place a gun in the "available" category. It may be, however, that many of these people keep these guns in their dwellings when they are at home, thus reducing the lack of overlap in these two conceptualizations of availability.
3. Data are available for the following 36 nations: Argentina, Australia, Austria, Belgium, Brazil, Canada, Denmark, Eng-

land, Estonia, Finland, France, Germany, Greece, Hong Kong, Hungary, Ireland, Israel, Italy, Japan, Kuwait, Mauritius, Mexico, the Netherlands, New Zealand, Northern Ireland, Norway, Portugal, Scotland, Singapore, Slovenia, South Korea, Spain, Sweden, Switzerland, Taiwan, and the United States. Gary Kleck, who obtained these data from Krug and colleagues, shared a copy with me.

References

Avison, W.R. and P.L. Loring. 1986. "Population Diversity and Cross-National Homicide: The Effects of Inequality and Heterogeneity." *Criminology* 24:733–49.

Bennett, R.R. and J.P. Lynch. 1990. "Does a Difference Make a Difference: Comparing Cross-National Crime Indicators." *Criminology* 28:153–81.

Berkowitz, L. 1983. "Aversively Stimulated Aggression: Some Parallels and Differences in Research with Animals and Humans." *American Psychologist* 38:1134–44.

Berkowitz, L. and A. LePage. 1967. "Weapons as Aggression-Eliciting Stimuli." *Journal of Personality and Social Psychology* 7:202–07.

Blau, P. 1977. *Inequality and Heterogeneity.* New York: Free Press.

Braithwaite, J. and V. Braithwaite. 1980. "The Effect of Income Inequality and Social Democracy on Homicide." *British Journal of Criminology* 20:45–53.

Brearley, H.C. 1932. *Homicide in the United States.* Chapel Hill, NC: University of North Carolina Press.

Brill, S. 1977. *Firearm Abuse: A Research and Policy Report.* Washington, DC: Police Foundation.

Clark, R.V.G. and P. Mayhew. 1988. "The British Gas Suicide Story and Its Criminological Implications." *Crime and Justice* 10:79–116.

Conklin, G.H. and M.E. Simpson. 1985. "A Demographic Approach to the Cross-National Study of Homicide." *Comparative Social Research* 8:171–85.

Cook, P. 1979. "The Effect of Gun Availability on Robbery and Robbery Murder: A Cross Section Study of Fifty Cities." Pp. 743–81 in *Policy Studies Review Annual,* vol. 3, edited by R.H. Haveman and B.B. Zellner. Beverly Hills, CA: Sage.

——. 1983. "Does Gun Ownership Deter Burglary?" Unpublished manuscript. Durham, NC: Duke University, Institute of Policy Sciences.

——. 1987. "Robbery Violence." *Journal of Criminal Law and Criminology* 78:357–76.

——. 1991. "The Technology of Personal Violence." Pp. 1–71 in *Crime and Justice,* edited by M. Tonry. Chicago, IL: The University of Chicago Press.

Curtis, L.A. 1974. *Criminal Violence: National Patterns and Behavior.* Lexington, MA: Lexington.

del Frate, A.A., U. Zvekic, and J.J.M. van Dijk, eds. 1993. *Understanding Crime: Experiences of Crime and Crime Control.* Rome: UNICRI.

Etzioni, A. and R. Remp. 1973. *Technological Shortcuts to Social Change.* New York: Praeger.

Famighetti, R., ed. 1998. *The World Almanac and Book of Facts, 1999.* Mahwah, NJ: World Almanac Books.

Federal Bureau of Investigation. 2000. *Crime in the United States.* Washington, DC: U.S. Government Printing Office.

Fiala, R. and G. LaFree. 1988. "Cross-National Determinants of Child Homicide." *American Sociological Review* 53:432–45.

Fisher, J.C. 1976. "Homicide in Detroit: The Role of Firearms." *Criminology* 14:387–400.

Gujarati, D. 1988. Basic Econometrics. New York: McGraw-Hill.

Hansmann, H.B. and J.M. Quigley. 1982. "Population Heterogeneity and the Sociogenesis of Homicide." *Social Forces 61:206–24.*

INTERPOL. (various years). *International Crime Statistics.* Paris: INTERPOL.

Kalish, C. 1988. *International Crime Rates.* Washington, DC: Bureau of Justice Statistics.

Killias, M. 1990. "Gun Ownership and Violent Crime: The Swiss Experience in International Perspective." *Security Journal* 1:169–74.

——. 1993. "Gun Ownership, Suicide and Homicide: An International Perspective." Pp. 289–302 in *Understanding Crime: Experiences of Crime and Crime Control,* edited by A.A. del Frate, U. Zvekic, and J.J.M. van Dijk. Rome: UNICRI.

Kleck, G. 1979. "Capital Punishment, Gun Ownership, and Homicide." *American Journal of Sociology* 84:882–910.

——. 1984. "The Relationship between Gun Ownership Levels and Rates of Violence in the United States." Pp. 99–135 in *Firearms and Violence: Issues of Public Policy,* edited by D.B. Kates, Jr. Cambridge, MA: Ballinger.

——. 1991. *Point Blank: Guns and Violence in America.* New York: Walter de Gruyter, Inc.

——. 1997. *Targeting Guns: Firearms and Their Control.* New York: Aldine de Gruyter.

Kleck, G. and G. Patterson. 1993. "The Impact of Gun Control and Gun Ownership Levels on Violence Rates." *Journal of Quantitative Criminology* 9:249–87.

Krohn, M. 1976. "Inequality, Unemployment, and Crime: A Cross-National Examination." *Sociological Quarterly* 17:303–13.

——. 1978. "A Durkheimian Analysis of International Crime Rates." *Social Forces* 57:654–70.

Krohn, M. and C.F. Wellford. 1977. "A Static and Dynamic Analysis of Crime and the Primary Dimensions of Nations." *International Journal of Criminology and Penology* 5:1–16.

Krug, E.G., K.E. Powell, and L.L. Dahlberg. 1996. "Firearm-Related Deaths in the United States and 35 Other High- and Upper-Middle-Income Countries." Unpublished paper. Atlanta, GA: Centers for Disease Control and Prevention.

LaFree, G.D. and E.L. Kick. 1986. "Cross-National Effects of Developmental, Distributional, and Demographic Variables on Crime: A Review and Analysis." *International Annals of Criminology* 24:213–35.

Lester, D. 1974. "A Cross-National Study of Suicide and Homicide." *Behavior Science Research* 9:307–18.

——. 1988. "Gun Control, Gun Ownership, and Suicide Prevention." *Suicide and Life Threatening Behavior* 18:176–80.

——. 1991. "Crime as Opportunity: A Test of the Hypothesis with European Homicide Rates." *British Journal of Criminology* 31:186–88.

——. 1996. "Gun Ownership and Rates of Homicide and Suicide." *European Journal of Psychiatry* 10:83–85.

Maggadino, J.P. and M.H. Medoff. 1984. "An Empirical Analysis of Federal and State Firearm Control Laws." Pp. 225–58 in *Firearms and Violence: Issues of Public Policy,* edited by D.B. Kates, Jr. Cambridge, MA: Ballinger.

McDonald, L. 1976. *The Sociology of Law and Order.* Boulder, CO: Westview Press.

McDowall, D. 1986. "Gun Availability and Robbery Rates: A Panel Study of Large U.S. Cities, 1974–1978." *Law and Policy* 8:135–48.

——. 1991. "Firearm Availability and Homicide in Detroit, 1951–1986." *Social Forces* 69:1085–1101.

Messner, S.F. 1980. "Income Inequality and Murder Rates: Some Cross-National Findings." *Comparative Social Research* 3:185–98.

——. 1982. "Social Development, Social Equality, and Homicide: A Cross-National Test of a Durkheimian Theory." *Social Forces* 61:225–40.

——. 1989. "Economic Discrimination and Societal Homicide Rates: Further Evidence on the Cost of Inequality." *American Sociological Review* 54:597–611.

Messner, S. and R. Rosenfeld. 1997. "Political Restraint of the Market and Levels of Criminal Homicide: A Cross-National Application of Institutional-Anomie Theory." *Social Forces* 75:1393–1416.

Neapolitan, J.L. 1994. "Cross-National Variation in Crime Rates: The Case of Latin America." *International Criminal Justice Review* 4:4–22.

——. 1998. "Cross-National Variation in Homicides: Is Race a Factor?" *Criminology* 36:139–55.

Newton, G.D., Jr. and F.E. Zimring. 1969. *Firearms and Violence in American Life.* Washington, DC: U.S. Government Printing Office.

Philips, L., H.L. Votey, and J. Howell. 1976. "Handguns and Homicide." *Journal of Legal Studies* 5:463–78.

Seitz, S.T. 1972. "Firearms, Homicides, and Gun Control Effectiveness." *Law and Society Review* 6:595–614.

South, S.J. 1984. "Unemployment and Social Problems in the Post-war United States." *Social Indicators Research* 15:391–416.

Tedeschi, J. and R. Felson. 1994. *Violence, Aggression, and Coercive Actions.* Washington, DC: American Psychological Association.

Turner, C.W., L.S. Simons, L. Berkowitz, and A. Frodi. 1977. "The Stimulating and Inhibiting Effects of Weapons on Aggressive Behavior." *Aggressive Behavior* 3:355–78.

Unnithan, N.P., L. Huff-Corzine, J. Corzine, and H.P. Whitt. 1994. *The Currents of Lethal Violence: An Integrated Model of Suicide and Homicide.* Albany, NY: State University of New York Press.

Unnithan, N.P. and H.P. Whitt. 1992. "Inequality, Economic Development and Lethal Violence: A Cross-National Analysis of Suicide and Homicide." *International Journal of Comparative Sociology* 33:182–95.

United Nations. (various years). *Demographic Yearbook.* United Nations Publishing Service.

Vidgerhous, G. 1978. "Methodological Problems Confronting Cross-Cultural Criminological Research Using Official Data." *Human Relations* 3:229–47.

Wolfgang, M. 1958. *Patterns in Criminal Homicide.* Philadelphia, PA: University of Pennsylvania Press.

World Bank. 1994. *World Development Report.* New York: Oxford University Press.

——. 1998. World Development Report. New York: Oxford University Press.

World Health Organization (WHO). (various years). *World Health Statistics Annual.* Geneva: WHO.

Zimring, F.E. 1968. "Is Gun Control Likely to Reduce Violent Killings?" *University of Chicago Law Review* 35:721–37.

——. 1972. "The Medium is the Message: Firearm Caliber as a Determinant of Death from Assault." *Journal of Legal Studies* 1:97–123.

Zimring, F.E. and G. Hawkins. 1997. *Crime Is Not the Problem: Lethal Violence in America.* New York: Oxford University Press.

Chapter 4

Black and White Differences in the Perception of Justice

Deane C. Wiley

A *number of studies have examined the racial divide between African Americans and whites in the criminal justice system: disparate incarceration rates, harsher sentences, and more guilty verdicts contribute to a system that many say is biased. Here, Deane Wiley turns away from statistics and instead focuses on perception—what blacks and whites* believe *about justice in the United States.*

Efforts to understand the legal system and its impact on African Americans have provided mixed results. Research has indicated that African Americans are likely to be judged more harshly by jurors (Feild, 1979; Ugwuegbu, 1979), are likely to receive more severe sentences (Chambliss, 1994, 1995; Hudson, 1989; Tonry, 1994) and are represented in the legal system in disproportionate numbers (McCaghy, Giordano, & Henson, 1977; Petersen, Schwirian, & Bleda, 1978). The magnitude of the issue is heightened by the numbers of African Americans in the system. For instance, in 1996 the incarceration rate for Whites was 289 per 100,000 people while for African Americans it was 1,860 per 100,000 (Kennedy, 1997). The chance of an African American male going to jail is one in four, while the chance of a White male going to jail is only one in twenty-three (U.S. Department of Justice, 1997). The reasons why these disparities exist is still unclear. Some researchers indicate that the disparities may be a result of social class biases (Hagan, Gillis, & Simpson, 1985). Others indicate that the problem can be blamed on racial discrimination (Baer & Chambliss, 1997; Maden, 1993; Morris, 1988; Petersilia, 1985).

Pfeifer (1991) suggests that the legal system may be biased against African Americans in the early stages of contact. Since the police are often responsible for determining who is involved in the legal system, they may provide the key to reported inequities. However, Delisi and Regoli (1999) found no evidence to support this type of bias. They performed a secondary analysis of the extant criminological literature and concluded that the justice system was not systematically discriminatory against African Americans. Other studies report no bias with regard to sentencing lengths (Zatz & Hagan, 1985) or in the shooting behavior of the police (Inn, Wheeler, & Sparling, 1977). However, most studies conclude that many officers engage in some type of bias toward African Americans (Alibhai, 1988; Baer & Chambliss, 1997; Fisher & Doyle-Martin, 1981; Hawkins, 1985; Hawkins & Hardy, 1989; Hill, 1982; Hudson, 1989; McCaghy *et al.*, 1977; Mercer, 1984; Petersen *et al.*, 1978; Smith, Visher, & Davidson, 1984; Tonry, 1994).

Although some studies have found that African Americans have a more negative view of the police (Berman, 1974, 1976; Woodbury , 1973), these studies primarily focused on individuals who had direct contact with the police. Some of the information was obtained from respondents after the police had taken them into custody, while others judged the police after calling for assistance. The results indicate that African Americans do not view the police as positively as Whites.

The purpose of this research is to add to the literature of inquiries about perceptions of justice. The present study examines the perceptions of individuals subsequent to their *observing* the interactions of citizens with the police. Although this area of research has received little attention, it may be useful in contributing to a better understanding of the distrust of the African American community for the justice system.

Method

Three hundred and eighteen research participants were recruited from the campus of a Midwestern community college. One hundred and twenty-four of the participants were African Americans, with 45 males and 79 females. One hundred and eighty-eight Whites participated in the study, with 66 males and 122 females.

The research participants were informed they were participating in a study to improve the public image of the police. They then viewed one of four different video taped scenarios in classes that ranged in size from 20 to 35 students in the Social Science Department of the college. The videotapes were produced with the assistance of a professional production company. The stimuli were approximately 4 minutes long and depicted an encounter between a uniformed law enforcement official and an ordinary citizen. The interaction involved a routine traffic stop in which the officer runs a set of routine checks. The actors in the videotape were pretested to ensure that they were perceived to be similar in attractiveness, size, aggressiveness, friendliness, courtesy, and so on. The scenes are identical except that the race of the actors was varied: (1) African American officer and African American citizen; (2) African American officer and White citizen; (3) White officer and African American citizen; (4) White officer and White citizen. Because the data were collected in group (i.e., class) settings, individual participants could not be randomly assigned to conditions. However, random assignment was used to determine which scene each group would view. An African American male and a White male collected all the data. After viewing the videotaped scenario, the research participants were asked to rate the scene. A 20-item questionnaire, adapted from Tyler (1987, 1989), was used to measure the research participants' perceptions of the interactions. Finally, a demographic sheet with a manipulation check was administered.

Results

An exploratory factor analysis with varimax rotation was performed on all the research participants' responses to determine which dimensions were measured by the survey. Four factors with eigenvalues greater than or equal to 1.00 accounted for 55.3% of the total measurement variance. Each factor was composed of items with loadings greater than .51 on only that item. Table 4.1 presents the results of the factor analysis.

The first factor appeared to be composed of items related to the appropriate behavior of the officer and was identified as a professional integrity factor. Reliability estimates of this factor produced an alpha of 0.88. The items in this factor were averaged and treated as a scale in subsequent analyses.

Factor 2 was composed of items mainly related to neutrality and impartiality. The factor was labeled lack of prejudice. However, it produced an initial reliability estimate of only 0.51. After one item, 'Overall I believe the motorist acted appropriately,' was removed, the alpha increased to 0.77. The remaining items were averaged and treated as a scale for subsequent analyses.

Factors 3 and 4 only produced alphas of 0.52 and 0.44, respectively. The removal of any single item did not improve the alpha and the factor appeared unreliable. They were not used for subsequent analysis. Table 4.2 summarizes the empirically derived dependent variables.

Separate 2 (race of research participant) × 2 (race of motorist) × 2 (race of officer) ANOVAs were performed using professional integrity and lack of prejudice to determine whether race affected the judgments made on these two scales. Main effects were found for race of the participant on the professional integrity scale $F(1, 304) = 4.44, p = .036$ and the lack of prejudice scale $F(1, 304) = 27.48, p < .001$. Table 4.3 reports the means for the scales broken down by race of the participants. The means indicate that African Americans judged the officer to be acting with less professional integrity and with more prejudice than the White research participants.

Lack of prejudice produced a significant main effect for race of officer; $F(1,304) = 6.12, p = .014$. The means for this scale indicate that the African American officer ($M = 4.12$) was reported to be more impartial than the White officer ($M = 3.93$). No other main effects were obtained for lack of prejudice.

There was a significant interaction between race of the research participant and race of the

Table 4.1
Results of the Exploratory Factor Analysis

Factor name	Explained variance	Constituent items	Loading
Professional integrity	31.9	I believe officer showed respect for the rights of the motorist	.81
		I believe the officer was rude to the motorist	.76
		I believe the officer acted improperly	.75
		I believe the motorist was treated fairly by the officer	.74
		I believe the officer was impolite	.74
		I believe the officer used proper procedures in handling the situation	.70
		Overall I believe the officer acted appropriately	.69
		I believe the motorist was allowed to present his side of the story	.54
Lack of Prejudice	10.4	I believe the officer's actions were influenced by the race of the motorist	.72
		I believe the officer's actions were influenced by the type of car driven	.70
		I believe the officer lied to the motorist about the reason for the stop	.63
		Overall I believe the motorist acted appropriately	–.57
		I believe the officer's actions were influenced by the sex of the motorist	.56
		I believe the officer was biased against the motorist	.51
Factor 3	7.8	I believe this officer's behavior was typical of the way the police behave	.71
		If need be, rude behavior could be reported and an apology received	.64
		I believe that all people are treated in a similar manner by the police	.59
		In general I believe the police do a good job	.52
Factor 4	5.1	I believe the officer's actions were influenced by the actions of the motorist	.83
		I believe the officer had a great deal of influence over the decision	.69
Total	55.3		

All factors have eigenvalues equal to or greater than 1.00.
To be considered part of a factor, a variable must load .51 or above on only that factor.
Participants indicated the degree to which they agree or disagree.

motorist on the lack of prejudice scale $F(1,304) = 13.47$, $p < .001$. Simple effects analysis revealed that only when the officer was White did race of the research participant reach significance, $F(1,304) = 37.65$, $p < .001$. The means indicate that the African American research

Table 4.2
Empirically Derived Dependent Variables

Variable name	Constituent items
Professional integrity	I believe officer showed respect for the rights of the motorist I believe the officer was rude to the motorist I believe the officer acted improperly I believe the motorist was treated fairly by the officer I believe the officer was impolite I believe the officer used proper procedures in handling the situation Overall I believe the officer acted appropriately I believe the motorist was allowed to present his side of the story
Lack of prejudice	I believe the officer's actions were influenced by the race of the motorist I believe the officer's actions were influenced by the type of car driven I believe the officer lied to the motorist about the reason for the stop I believe the officer's actions were influenced by the sex of the motorist I believe the officer was biased against the motorist

Table 4.3
Means for Race of the Participant

Variable name	African American	White
	M	*M*
Professional integrity[a]	3.76	3.96
Lack of prejudice[b]	3.81	4.23

[a]Significant at the .05 level.
[b]Significant at the .01 level

participants (M=3.58) were less likely to feel that the officer was impartial than the White research participants ($M = 4.29$).

Race of the officer by race of the motorist produced a significant interaction effect for professional integrity, $F(1,304) = 8.61$, $p = .004$). An analysis of the simple effects indicated that when the race of the officer was African American the race of the motorist reached significance, $F(1,304) = 7.51$, $p = .007$. As seen in Table 4.4, the officer was judged to have less integrity when dealing with the African American motorist than with the White motorist. Similarly, when the motorist was African American, the race of the officer reached significance $F(1,304) = 5.03$, $p = .026$. For the participants in the African American motorist condition, the officer had less integrity when he was African American than when he was White. No other significant interactions were obtained for the empirically derived scales.

Discussion

This study was a modest inquiry into understanding the possible basis for negative feelings of African Americans for the police. The major findings of this study are consistent with previous research, indicating that race plays a role in the perception of the police. After viewing videotaped interactions of motorists and police, African Americans did not view the police as positively as Whites. African Americans perceived the officer to possess less integrity. In addition, an interaction between the race of the motorist and the race of the officer indicated that when the officer was African American, he was seen as having less integrity when the motorist was also African American. This may have implications for programs that attempt to address concerns of the African American community by hiring more minority officers. Simply having African Americans serve on the police force may not increase positive feelings for the police. However, this is not a simple issue.

Overall, African American participants felt the officer was more prejudiced than the White participants did. However, a main effect was obtained for the race of the officer, indicating that the African American officer was seen as less prejudiced than the White officer. Furthermore, when the officer was White, the African Ameri-

Table 4.4
Means and Standard Deviations of Race of the Motorist by Race of the Officer for Professional Integrity

Condition	*M*	SD	*N*
Black motorist			
Black officer	3.71[a,b]	.91	71
White officer	3.99[b]	.77	89
White motorist			
Black officer	4.03[a]	.67	87
White officer	3.80	.91	71

[a]Significantly different at the .01 level.
[b]Significantly different at the .05 level.

can participants felt the officer was more prejudiced than the White participants.

The results suggest the race of the participants influenced how they perceived the interaction between the motorist and the officer. Although it might be assumed that African American participants would be less satisfied with the interaction when the motorist was also African American, regardless of the race of the officer, this was not the case. There was no interaction between race of the participant and race of the motorist. Nonetheless, the race of the officer played a significant role in the perceptions of the participants.

It might be expected that under conditions where the officer was African American, the White officer would be judged the most severe. However, the interaction effect indicated that the encounter was perceived as less satisfying and less fair when the officer and the motorist were African American. This may be partially explained by empathy that respondents felt for the motorist. The empathy may have led the participants to expect better treatment by one of their own, for one of their own.

Overall, the results of this study are consistent with other studies that have found African Americans and Whites view justice issues very differently from one another. African Americans judged the officers as less partial and more prejudiced. Negative feelings such as these may create a self-fulfilling prophecy that results in African Americans being arrested by police officers more frequently than Whites. Confrontations with police officers are highly charged situations and preexisting negative attitudes may serve to exacerbate an already tense situation. Specific research should be conducted to address this hypothesis. In addition, negative feelings, whether they come from past experiences or other factors, could implicate perceptions of justice at all levels of the legal system.

References

Alibhai Y. 1988. Criminal injustice: how the legal system treats Blacks. *New Statesman and Society* 5: 34–36.

Baer J., Chambliss W. 1997. Generating fear: The politics of crime reporting. *Crime, Law, and Social Change* 27: 87–107.

Berman J. 1974. Black-White differences among parolees in their perceptions of the justice system. *Personality and Social Psychology Bulletin* 1: 324–326.

Berman J. 1976. Parolees' perception of the justice system: Black-White differences. *Criminology: An Interdisciplinary Journal* 13(4): 507–520.

Chambliss W. 1994. Policing the ghetto underclass: The politics of law and law enforcement. *Social Problems* 41: 177–194.

Chambliss W. 1995. Another lost war: The cost and consequences of drug prohibition. *Social Justice* 22: 101–124.

Delisi M., Regoli B. 1999. Race, conventional crime, and criminal justice: The declining importance of skin color. *Journal of Criminal Justice* 27: 549–557.

Feild H. 1979. Rape trials and jurors' decisions: A psycholegal analysis of the effects of victim, defendant, and case characteristics. *Law and Human Behavior* 3: 261–284.

Fisher G.A., Doyle-Martin S.M. 1981. The effects of ethnic prejudice on police referrals to the juvenile court. *California Sociologist* 4(2): 189–205.

Hagan J., Gillis A., Simpson J. 1985. The class structure of gender and delinquency. *American Journal of Sociology* 90: 1151–1178.

Hawkins D.F. 1985. Trends in Black-White imprisonment: Changing conceptions of race or changing patterns of social control? *Crime and Social Justice* 24: 187–209.

Hawkins D.F., Hardy K.A. 1989. Black-White imprisonment rates: A state by state analysis. *Social Justice* 16(4): 75–94.

Hill G.D. 1982. Other things are not equal: Redirecting equity research on deviance processing. *Research in Social Problems and Public Policy* 2: 149–173.

Hudson B. 1989. Discrimination and disparity: The influence of race on sentencing. *New Community* 16: 23–34.

Inn A., Wheeler A.C., Sparling C.L. 1977. The effects of suspect race and situation hazard on police officer shooting behavior. *Journal of Applied Social Psychology* 7(1): 27–37.

Kennedy R. 1997. *Race, Crime, and the Law.* Pantheon: New York.

Maden T. 1993. Crime culture and ethnicity. *International Journal of Psychiatry* 5: 281–289.

McCaghy C.H., Giordano P.C., Henson T.K. 1977. Auto theft: Offender and offense characteristics. *Criminology: An Interdisciplinary Journal* 15: 367–385.

Mercer K. 1984. Black communities' experience of psychiatric services. *International Journal of Social Psychiatry* 30(1–2): 22–27.

Morris N. 1988. Race and crime: What evidence is there that race influences results in the criminal justice system? *Judicature* 72: 111–113.

Petersen D.M., Schwirian K.P., Bleda S.E. 1978. The drug arrest: Empirical observations on the age, sex and race of drug law offenders in a midwestern city. *Drug Forum* 6: 371–386.

Petersilia J. 1985. Racial disparities in the criminal justice system: A summary. *Crime and Delinquency* 31: 15–34.

Pfeifer J.E. 1991. Reviewing the empirical evidence on jury racism: Findings of discrimination or discriminatory findings? *Nebraska Law Review* 69: 230–250.

Smith D.A., Visher C.A., Davidson L.A. 1984. Equity and discretionary justice: The influence of on public arrest decisions. *The Journal of Criminal Law and Criminology* 75: 234–249.

Tonry M. 1994. Racial politics, racial disparities, and the war on crime. *Crime and Delinquency* 40: 475–494.

Tyler T.R. 1987. Conditions leading to value expressive effects in judgements of procedural justice: A test of four models. *Journal of Personality and Social Psychology* 52: 333–344.

——. 1989. The psychology of procedural justice: A test of the group-value model. *Journal of Personality and Social Psychology* 57(5): 830–838.

Ugwuegbu D. 1979. Racial and evidential factors on juror attribution of legal responsibility. *Journal of Experimental Social Psychology* 15: 133–146.

U.S. Department of Justice. 1997. *Lifetime Likelihood of Going to State or Federal Prison.* U.S. Government Printing Office: Washington, DC.

Woodbury R. 1973. Delinquents' attitudes toward the juvenile justice system. *Psychological Reports* 32(3): 1119–1124.

Zatz M.S., Hagan J. 1985. Crime, time and punishment: An exploration of selection bias in sentencing research. *journal of Qualitative Criminology* 1: 103–126.

Chapter 5

Genetic Factors and Criminal Behavior

Jasmine A. Tehrani
Sarnoff A. Mednick

Criminal behavior results from a complex interplay of social and genetic factors. Until recently, the majority of criminological research focused solely on social contributors, either minimizing or negating the importance of genetics on criminal behavior. In the past fifteen years, however, a large body of evidence has emerged suggesting that the etiology of criminal behavior may be better understood when genetic factors are taken into account.

What causes an individual to become a criminal? How does an individual who is raised in a stable adoptive home grow up to become Jeremy Strohmeyer, the young man convicted of raping and murdering an eight-year-old girl in a Nevada casino? The response to this question varies according to several factors, including the political climate and the theoretical orientation of the respondent. Social factors have received the majority of the attention; environmental variables such as socioeconomic status, for example, are most commonly studied in relation to criminal behavior. But social variables may not be sufficient to account for the wide range of variance observed in criminal behavior. For example, based on all accounts, Jeremy Strohmeyer was adopted into a loving and supportive environment. An investigation into Strohmeyer's biological background, however, revealed a history of schizophrenia and criminality in his biological parents. Perhaps other factors, alone or in concert with previously identified environmental variables, may better explain why some individuals travel down a criminal path.

Brennan (1999), in a recent issue of *Federal Probation*, addresses the gap found in current sociological and criminological literature in relation to acknowledging the influence of "non-social" factors.

Genetic factors, an important source of influence implicated in a variety of mental disorders such as schizophrenia, depression, and anxiety disorders, may play a role in predisposing certain individuals to criminal behavior. A genetic background positive for criminal behavior or mental illness, however, does not mean that the individual will develop the disorder later in life. In fact, most individuals who have a criminal biological parent do not become criminal. What we are stating is that certain individuals, due to genetic and/or environmental markers, may have an elevated risk of becoming criminal. Put another way, offspring of criminal biological parents may have a greater chance of engaging in criminal behavior than offspring of non-criminal biological parents.

The mention of genetic factors in relation to crime is sometimes met with resistance, a reaction which may be partially attributed to earlier efforts to identify observable physical characteristics associated with criminality. For example, in 1876, Cesare Lombroso proposed that criminals tended to have atavistic features, consisting of protruding jaws, receding foreheads and chins and asymmetrical facial features. Such theories have since been discounted. Genetic and biological research efforts today have largely moved away from this type of research. Nevertheless, there are still myths surrounding the role of genetics in relation to crime. To this end, several myths will be discussed, followed by evidence which links non-social or genetic factors to criminal behavior. These are by no means all of the myths, but may be the most commonly held inaccuracies regarding this type of research.

Myths

1. Identifying the Role of Genetics in Criminal Behavior Implies That There Is a 'Crime Gene'

It is difficult to imagine that a single gene encodes for criminal activity; a more plausible scenario is that multiple genes interact to create an increased risk for criminal behavior. Moreover, genetic factors are likely to be associated with other behavioral characteristics that are correlated with criminal behavior, such as impulsivity and sensation-seeking behaviors.

2. Attributing Crime to Genetic Factors is Deterministic

Genes alone do not cause individuals to become criminal. Moreover, a genetic predisposition towards a certain behavior does not mean that an individual is destined to become a criminal. The notion that humans are programmed for certain behaviors fails to acknowledge important environmental factors which are likely to mediate the relationship between genetics and crime. For example, the expression of a genetic liability towards a certain behavior may be minimized or neutralized by positive family rearing conditions. Negative family rearing conditions might trigger a genetic vulnerability. Such an occurrence suggests that genes and the environment interact to either elevate or reduce the risk for certain negative outcomes.

Genetic Epidemiological Studies

Family, twin, and adoption studies, three epidemiological designs which are employed to examine environmental and genetic sources of influence, suggest that criminal behavior may be genetically mediated. These three epidemiological designs, however, provide varying opportunities to test for genetic effects. The limitation of family studies, for example, is that genetics and environmental sources of influence cannot be separated. Therefore, given the limited utility of family studies to separate issues of nature versus nurture, this section will focus on two other epidemiological research designs which are better equipped to test for genetic effects.

Twin Studies

Twin studies compare the rate of criminal behavior of twins who are genetically identical or monozygotic twins (MZ) with the rate of criminal behavior of dizygotic twins (DZ) in order to assess the role of genetic and environmental influences. To the extent that the similarity observed in MZ twins is greater than that in DZ twins, genetic influences may be implicated.

To date, over 10 twin studies, carried out in different countries, have tested for a genetic effect in crime. Taken together, these studies support the interpretation that criminal behavior may be a genetically mediated outcome. Specifically, a greater concordance rate for criminal behavior is observed for MZ twins than for DZ twins. Some researchers believe that the twin methodology may be flawed in that MZ twins, in addition to sharing more genetic information than DZ twins, are also more likely to be treated more similarly than DZ twins. Studies comparing the concordance rates in MZ twins reared apart can avoid this problem, but it is difficult to obtain such subjects. Christiansen (1977) has noted that several of the earlier twin studies had cases in which a set of monozygotic twins were raised in separate environments; these preliminary data suggest that studying MZ twins reared apart may be an important behavioral genetics tool to investigate the etiology of criminal behavior. To our knowledge, only one modern twin study has employed this type of research design to test whether criminal behavior may be genetically mediated.

Grove et al. (1990) investigated the concordance of antisocial behavior among a sample of 32 sets of monozygotic twins reared apart (MZA) who were adopted by non-relatives shortly after birth. Grove found substantial overlap between the genetic influences for both childhood conduct disorders (correlation of 0.41) and adult antisocial behaviors (correlation of 0.28). Although these findings are based on a small number of subjects, the Grove findings are congruent with the findings from other twin studies and extend the twin literature by evaluating MZ twins raised in separate environments.

Adoption Studies

Adoption studies provide a natural experiment to test the existence and strength of inherited predispositions. Adoptees are separated at birth from their biological parents. Thus, similarities between the adoptee and biological parents can be regarded as estimates of genetic influences, while similarities between the adoptee and the adoptive parents may be thought of as estimates of environmental influences. Adoption studies have been carried out in three different countries: the United States, Sweden and Denmark.

Iowa. The first adoption study to explore the genetic transmission of criminal behavior was carried out in Iowa by Crowe (1974). The sample consisted of 52 adoptees (including 27 males) born between 1925 and 1956 to a group of 41 incarcerated female offenders. A group of control adoptees were matched for age, sex, race and approximate age at the time of adoption. Seven of the 52 adoptees sustained a criminal conviction as an adult whereas only one of the control adoptees had a conviction. Since these adoptees were separated from their incarcerated mothers at birth, this tends to implicate a heritable component to antisocial behavior. A separate series of adoption studies carried out in Iowa by Cadoret and colleagues have supported Crowe's original findings. These independent replications lend support to the notion that criminal behavior may have important genetic influences.

Sweden. Bohman et al. (1978) examined the criminality and alcoholism rates among 2,324 Swedish adoptees and their biological and adoptive parents, as determined by a check with national criminal and alcohol registries. The authors noted that a biological background positive for criminality contributed to an increased risk of criminality in the adopted-away children.

Denmark. Mednick, Gabrielli, and Hutchings (1984) carried out a study of the genetic influence on criminal behavior using an extensive data set consisting of 14,427 Danish adoptees (ranging in age from 29 to 52 years) and both sets of biological and adoptive parents. They found that adopted-away sons had an elevated risk of having a court conviction if their biological parent, rather than their adoptive parent, had one or more court convictions. If neither the biological nor adoptive parents were convicted, 13.5 percent of the sons were convicted. If the adoptive parents were convicted and the biological parents were not, this figure only increased to 14.7 percent. When examining sons whose biological parents were convicted and adoptive parents remained law-abiding, however, 20 percent of the adoptees had one or more criminal convictions. Moreover, as the number of biological parental convictions increased, the rate of adoptees with court convictions increased.

The finding that recidivism may be a genetically transmitted trait led us to investigate whether genetics play a role in persistent forms of criminal offending. Based on age of onset and duration of offending, Moffitt (1993) suggests the existence of two qualitatively different types of offenders; (1) individuals whose criminality is confined to adolescence, or adolescent-limited offenders, and (2)individuals whose criminality occurs during the adolescent period and extends into adulthood, or life-course persistent offenders. Genetic factors may play some role in explaining differences between the two groups. Moffitt suggests that life-course persistent antisocial behavior may have an underlying biological basis, whereas adolescent-limited antisocial behavior may be better explained by situational environmental factors. We tested this theory within the context of an adoption design. The results suggest that the biological parents with a criminal conviction were more likely to have an adopted-away son who evidenced life-course persistent offending than adolescent-limited offending (Tehrani and Mednick, in preparation). These data support the contention that genetics may play a role in persistent forms of offending.

These data, obtained from three different countries and in different laboratories, lend support to the notion that criminal behavior appears to have a strong genetic component. But what about serious forms of criminal behavior, such as violent offending? Our research group has investigated whether violent offending may be heritable.

Is There a Genetic Liability to Violence?

Twin and adoption studies have been employed to address this question, yielding mixed results. Cloninger and Gottesman (1987), for example, reanalyzed the twin data collected by

Christiansen (1977) and grouped subjects as either violent offenders or property offenders. Heritability for property offenses was found to be 0.78 while heritability for violent offenses was .50. Although the genetic effect for property offenses was greater than for violent offenses, the data suggest that violent offenses may also have a heritable underlying component. Two independent adoption studies, however, have failed to provide support for the hypothesis that violence is a heritable trait (Bohman et al., 1982; Mednick et al., 1984). The largest adoption study to date was carried out in Denmark by our research group (n=14,427). As stated earlier, Mednick, Gabrielli and Hutchings (1984) reported a significant relationship between the number of criminal convictions in the biological parent and the number of convictions in the adoptees. Subsequent statistical analyses revealed that this relationship held significantly for property offenses, but not significantly for violent offenses.

A study in Oregon provided an important clue that mental illness, particularly severe mental illness, may be genetically related to violence. In a classic study, Heston (1966) followed up a sample of 47 offspring born to schizophrenic mothers and compared them to a group of matched controls. These offspring were separated from their mothers shortly after birth and placed in foster care or orphanages. Heston was primarily interested in determining if adopted-away offspring of schizophrenic mothers were at increased risk of becoming schizophrenic themselves. The findings supported the original hypothesis, as 5 of the 47 offspring became schizophrenic. An interesting finding is that an even greater number of the adopted-away offspring of schizophrenic biological mothers actually had been incarcerated for violent offenses. Eleven (23.4 percent) of the adoptees had been incarcerated for violent offenses. Since these offspring were not raised by their schizophrenic mothers, this suggested the possibility that at least certain forms of mental illness and criminal violence may share a common genetic basis.

With the Heston study in mind, Moffit (1987) investigated the role of parental mental illness in the emergence of violent offending among the Danish adopted-away sons. When only the criminal behavior of the biological parents is considered, she found no increase in violent offending in the adoptees. A significant increase in the rate of violent offending is noted only among offspring whose biological parents were severely criminal (typically the biological father) and had been hospitalized one or more times for a psychiatric condition (typically the biological mother).

These findings suggest that a biological background positive for mental disorders may be associated with an increased risk of violent offending in the children. Other disorders in the biological parents may also in crease the risk of violent offending in the adopted-away offspring. One such disorder which may elevate the risk of violent offending in children is the presence of alcoholism in the biological parents.

The Genetic Link Between Violence and Alcoholism

Recent molecular genetics studies report that a gene related to the serotonin system may be associated with increased risk for the co-occurrence of violence and alcoholism. These efforts have been fueled by the robust finding that alcoholism and violence, in humans and non-human primates, may be related to serotonergic dysregulation (Virkkunen et al., 1989; Higley et al., 1992). In a reanalysis of data from the Swedish Adoption Study, Carey (1993) noted that paternal violence is linked to alcoholism in adopted-away males. We are currently investigating the possible genetic link between violence and alcoholism (Tehrani and Mednick, in preparation). Within the context of the Danish Adoption Cohort, we found that alcoholic biological parents were twice as likely to have a violent adopted-away son than non-alcoholic parents. In contrast, the risk for property offenses in adopted-away sons of biological parents with alcohol problems was not significantly elevated. The significant genetic effect was specific to violent offenders.

Moreover, violent offending (but not property offending) among the biological parents was related to severe alcohol-related problems in the adopted-away males. These findings from our adoption cohort are in agreement with data from the Swedish adoption study, and support the overall interpretations from recent molecular genetic studies.

Conclusions

Genetic factors represent one source of influence on criminal behavior. Until recently, their role had been ignored or discounted. The data that are emerging from research labs around the world indicate that excluding genetic factors from consideration may limit opportunities to advance the understanding of why some individuals become criminal. Apart from satisfying our scientific curiosity, this type of genetic research could potentially contribute to prevention efforts. Investigations into the etiological correlates of criminal behavior may lead to promising new directions for treatment and intervention. These etiological factors, either social or genetic, may help to identify individuals who are at elevated risk of certain negative outcomes. If, for example, we identify individuals who are at increased genetic risk for criminal offending, environmental buffers such as educational programs may be implemented to help reduce the risk that this genetic predisposition will be expressed. Put another way, the genetic vulnerability may be counterbalanced by positive environmental conditions. Two adoption studies have already noted this. For example, in the Danish and Swedish adoption studies, adopted-away children of criminal biological parents who were raised in higher socioeconomic adoptive homes evidenced a significantly reduced rate of criminal convictions, as compared to adoptees raised in low or middle class adoptive homes. Such an observation suggests that crime prevention efforts may be most effective when all risk factors, social and genetic, are evaluated.

References

Bohman, M. (1978). Some genetic aspects of alcoholism and criminality. *Archives of General Psychiatry* 35; 269–276.

Brennan, P.A. (1999). Biosocial risk factors and juvenile violence. *Federal Probation.*

Cadoret, R.J., Cain, C.A., Crowe, R.R. (1983). Evidence for gene-environment interaction in the development of adolescent antisocial behavior. *Behavior Genetics* 13:301–310.

Carey, G. (1993). Multivariate genetic relationships among drug abuse, alcohol abuse and antisocial personality. *Psychiatric Genetics* 3, 141.

Christiansen, K.O. (1977). A preliminary study of criminality among twins. In Mednick, S.A. and Christiansen, K.O. (Eds), *Biological Bases of Criminal Behavior.* New York: Gardener Press, pp. 89–108.

Cloninger, C.R., and Gottesman, I.I. (1987). Genetic and environmental factors in antisocial behavior disorders. In Mednick, S.A., Moffit, T.E., and Stack, S.A. (Eds). *The Causes of Crime: New Biological Approaches,* New York: Cambridge University Press.

Crowe, R.R. (1975). An adoption study of antisocial behavior. *Archives of General Psychiatry* 31: 785–791.

Grove, W.M., Eckert, E.D., Heston, L., Bouchard, T.J., Segal, N., Lykken, D.Y. (1990). Heritability of substance abuse and antisocial behavior: A study of monozygotic twins reared apart. *Biological Psychiatry* 27: 1293–1304.

Heston, L.L. (1966). Psychiatric disorders in foster-home reared children of schizophrenics. *British Journal of Psychiatry* 112: 819–825.

Higley, J.D., Suomi, S.J., Linnoila, M. (1992). A longitudinal assessment of CSF monoamine metabolite and plasma cortisol concentrations in young rhesus monkeys. *Biological Psychiatry* 32: 127–145.

Mednick S.A., Gabrielli, W.F., Hutchins B. (1984). Genetic influences in criminal convictions: Evidence from an adoption cohort. *Science* 224: 891–894.

Moffit, T.E. (1987). Parental mental disorder and offspring criminal behavior: An adoption study. *Psychiatry: Interpersonal and Biological Processes* 50, 346–360.

Virkkunen, M., DeJong, J., Bartko, F., Goodwin, F., Linnoila, M. (1989). Relationship of psycho-biological variables to recidivism in violent offenders and impulsive fire setters. *Archives of General Psychiatry,* 600–604.

Jasmine A. Tehrani and Sarnoff A. Mednick, "Genetic Factors and Criminal Behavior." Reprinted from *Federal Probation,* December 2000, 64 (2): 24–27. Published by The Administrative Offices of the United States Courts. ✦

Chapter 6
Estimating Wrongful Convictions

Tony G. Poveda

While individual cases of the innocent going to prison make big headlines, criminologists have long neglected to study the extent of wrongful conviction—an important measure of just how flawed the justice system may be. Poveda examines an array of methods for estimating the incidence of wrongful convictions before adopting two. By studying both official statistics of overturned convictions and inmates' claims of mistaken incarceration, the author attempts to enumerate what he calls the "dark figure" of wrongful convictions.

The extent of wrongful convictions has been a topic of much speculation and remains a "dark figure" in the study of criminal justice. One of the few attempts to estimate the prevalence of wrongful convictions was a 1986 study by C. Ronald Huff and associates. In that research a variety of justice system officials (mostly in Ohio) were surveyed for their perceptions of this type of miscarriage of justice in felony cases (Huff, Rattner, and Sagarin 1986, 1996).[1] More recently, a statistical study of errors in capital cases conducted by James Liebman and colleagues has highlighted the extent of reversible error in capital cases, some of which involve the erroneous conviction of the innocent (Liebman, Fagan, and West 2000).[2] Research on the scope of the wrongful-conviction problem is still in its infancy; it is plagued by methodological problems and by the absence of any central entity for tracking official errors in the justice system.

A 1998 scholarly exchange between Richard Leo, Richard Ofshe, and Paul Cassell underscores the difficulty of quantifying the wrongful-conviction problem but also highlights its importance for public policy[3] (Cassell 1998; Leo and Ofshe 1998a, 1998b).[4] The present article is a preliminary effort at exploring several methodologies for estimating wrongful convictions. I emphasize two approaches to the problem: the use of official records on court-ordered discharges from imprisonment, and data from inmates' self-reports.

Defining Wrongful Convictions

Wrongful convictions can be understood along a continuum of justice-system errors ranging from persons who are falsely accused (arrested, prosecuted, and tried), to those who are wrongly convicted and imprisoned, to death row inmates who are erroneously executed. In this article I focus on errors that result in the conviction and imprisonment of innocent persons. These are wrong-person errors, as distinct from procedural errors in the conviction of a defendant. Although this distinction is sometimes difficult to maintain in practice, wrong-person convictions are cases in which individuals are exonerated because they are factually (not merely legally) innocent of the crime for which they were convicted—and are not released solely on the grounds that their due process rights were violated (e.g., by illegal search, Miranda warning not given, trial-court error). This definition is in the tradition of Edwin Borchard's ([1932] 1970) classic study of wrongful convictions, the landmark work of Hugo Bedau and Michael Radelet (1987; Radelet, Bedau, and Putnam 1992) on erroneous convictions in capital cases, and the research of Huff and associates (1986, 1996) on convicted innocents.

On a conceptual level, wrongful convictions denote a distinct type of justice-system error: when a wrong person has been convicted and incarcerated. Operationally, however, it is difficult to determine when someone is factually innocent. The fact that an offender's conviction is overturned on appeal and that the offender is acquitted in a subsequent trial does not in itself establish innocence. It simply means that the state was not able to establish guilt beyond a reasonable doubt. Clearly, "not guilty" and "innocent" are not synonymous. For example, according to New York State's Court of Claims Act (Article II, Sec.8-b), if innocent persons wish to seek compensatory damages for unjust conviction and imprisonment, they must "demonstrate by clear and convincing evidence" that they did not commit the crime for which they were convicted and incarcerated (New York State Court of Claims 1998). More is required than merely showing that the conviction was vacated or that the indictment against them was dismissed.

The problem is illustrated further by the April 2000 verdict in the Sam Sheppard civil trial. The Sheppard jury had to determine "by the greater weight of the evidence" whether Sheppard was innocent and therefore wrongfully imprisoned by the State of Ohio for the 1954 murder of his wife. The civil jury ruled that Sheppard's family[5] had not met the burden of proof for innocence, even though a 1966 jury, in Sheppard's second criminal trial, had found him not guilty (Ewinger and Hagan 2000; Hagan and Ewinger 2000).

Thus, the operational definition of wrongful conviction for research is problematic. What constitutes evidence and criteria for innocence? How compelling should that evidence be? The tradition of studying wrongful convictions, beginning with Borchard in 1932, has erred on the side of a restrictive definition of wrongful conviction: evidence is required showing that someone else committed the offense or that the convicted person was uninvolved in the crime (Gross 1998:129; Radelet and Bedau 1998:106).[6] Bedau and Radelet (1987:47) maintained that "there is no quantity or quality of evidence that could be produced that would definitively prove innocence." At best, they argued, a "majority of neutral observers, given the evidence at our disposal, would judge the defendant in question to be innocent."[7] Huff and his colleagues similarly included only cases in which there was evidence of innocence "beyond a reasonable doubt" (Huff et al. 1986:519) or when convicted persons had been "clearly exonerated" (Huff et al. 1996:10).

An additional issue is whether such wrong-person errors must be acknowledged by officials in the criminal justice system, particularly by the courts. Surely the more restrictive definition would consider only officially acknowledged errors. This criterion is followed in Huff's database of felony cases (Huff et al. 1986:519). Bedau and Radelet also relied on official judgment of error (e.g., appellate court decisions, executive pardons, indemnity claims) in 90 percent of their 416 capital cases. In the other 10 percent, however, their decision to include the case was based on unofficial judgments. These latter cases included research by scholars or journalists who had reexamined evidence in a particular case (and often had discovered new evidence), and had concluded that the defendant was not guilty, even though no court had determined this (Radelet et al. 1992:17–18). Insofar as we allow unofficial judgments of error, we are shifting toward a more expansive definition of wrongful conviction.

Alternative Methodologies

A critical methodological problem in the study of wrongful convictions is how to determine the extent of such convictions and imprisonment in the criminal justice system. The dominant approach in the literature has been to catalogue individual cases of wrongful conviction. This approach has been pursued by legal scholars, journalists, sociologists, and other researchers (Borchard [1932] 1970; Connors et al. 1996; Dieter 1997; Huff et al. 1996; Radelet et al. 1992; Radin 1964; Rosenbaum 1990–1991; U.S. House 1994; Yant 1991); none claim to have identified all such cases. Indeed, many of these researchers point to the role of luck and chance in the discovery of wrongful-conviction cases (U.S. House 1994:12). Bedau and Radelet (1987:29) emphasized "how accidental and unsystematic the discovery of relevant cases actually is." Gross (1998:150) concluded that "most miscarriages of justice in capital cases never come to light"; when they do so, it is typically because of heightened judicial attention to the case, because the real criminal confesses, or simply because of luck.

The fundamental flaw of the case study approach is that there is no way to determine how many cases go undiscovered—the "dark figure" of wrongful convictions—and whether these cases differ systematically from those which are identified. The documenting of individual cases has helped to sensitize the public and policy makers to the existence of erroneous convictions, but it falls short as a method for determining the prevalence of such convictions.

Another approach, taken especially since the late 1970s, has been to employ laboratory or experimental methods in studying mistaken eyewitness identification, a significant factor in many wrongful convictions (Cutler and Penrod 1995; Loftus 1993, 1996; Wells 1993). This research has attempted to discover error rates of eyewitness identification under different experimental conditions, with emphasis on police identification procedures in lineups, event factors, and postevent information. Factors such as whether the culprit is present or absent in the lineup, police instructions given to the witness, the trauma of the crime, the use of a deadly weapon, and information obtained by the witness after the crime are all relevant to shaping the memory of an event and to eyewitnesses' accuracy (Devine 1995; Loftus and Ketcham 1991; Wells 1993).

One problem with this line of research is that it is often based on simulated events (staged crimes and lineups) rather than on actual crimes; thus it raises questions of generalizability from experimental to forensic ("real") contexts (Yuille 1993). Moreover, the purpose of eyewitness identification experiments is to isolate the role of particular factors in producing error, not to estimate the overall accuracy of eyewitness identifications in actual cases (Cutler and Penrod 1995). Thus, again, this methodology is limited in providing an empirical basis for estimating the prevalence of wrongful convictions. In 1999, however, when the Innocence Project examined the 62 DNA exonerations to date in the United States, it found that mistaken eyewitness testimony was a factor in 84 percent of those wrongful convictions (Scheck, Neufeld, and Dwyer 2000:246).

Another possible line of inquiry is the use of field research to determine the extent of error produced by a particular investigative practice. Leo and Ofshe's research on police interrogations reflects this approach (Leo 1996). Their fieldwork in a limited number of police departments has led to observations on how standard police interrogation practices can cause suspects to make false confessions (Leo and Ofshe 1998a; Ofshe and Leo 1997). These authors, however, make no claim that their methodology can be used to identify the universe of false confessions. On the contrary, they maintain that the "methodological problems inherent in arriving at a sound estimate [of the frequency of false confessions] are formidable and unsolved, and we have concluded that no well-founded estimate has yet been published" (Leo and Ofshe 1998b:560). Thus they are quite skeptical about the possibility of quantification, given the absence of official records on the number of police interrogations and the frequency of false confessions resulting from those interrogations.

Finally, another approach to discovering errors in the criminal criminal justice system is the use of appellate court decisions in which convictions or sentences have been overturned. This methodology has been adopted by Liebman and associates in their research on errors in capital cases. Liebman relied on published judicial decisions at three levels of the capital review process: state direct appeal, state postconviction appeal, and federal habeas corpus review. This is a monumental task, as noted by Liebman, Fagan, and West (2000:24): it requires a "painstaking search" for cases relying on various sources of information. To complicate this task, there is no central repository for these judicial decisions.

Liebman's study of capital errors between 1973 and 1995 began in 1991 and continues today. Although appellate courts (at the three review levels) found reversible error in 68 percent of capital cases during the study period, Liebman's findings on the outcomes of these reversals are limited to the 301 cases in the state postconviction appeals. Upon retrial, 247 of the plaintiffs in the state postconviction cases were sentenced to less than death, 22 (7%) were found not guilty, and 54 were resentenced to death (Liebman et al. 2000:132). As Liebman et al. (2000:27) pointed out, state postconviction decisions, unlike state direct appeal and federal habeas corpus reviews, often are not published and therefore are difficult to locate. At the present, the list of such cases is incomplete. The Liebman study has provided substantial evidence demonstrating a high rate of error in capital judgments. So far, however (except for the state postconviction results), it has provided only limited information on the outcome of these reversals, notably in regard to the prevalence of wrongful convictions.

As noted, criminal justice agencies do not keep statistics on errors made by officials at various stages of the justice process, including the number of persons wrongfully convicted and imprisoned. In the remainder of this paper, I consider two different approaches to this quantification problem. One approach employs official agency records or statistics as a basis for constructing a measure of wrongful convictions and imprisonment; the other relies on inmates' self-reports of their own criminal activity, including denial of committing the offense for which they were incarcerated. The development of multiple methods for estimating wrongful convictions has certain advantages. Insofar as each method has its own limitations, the use of multiple and independent measures to estimate the prevalence of wrongful convictions will increase our confidence in the findings of each approach, if we assume a consistency in results (Webb et al. 1966:3–5).

Use of Official Statistics on Court-Ordered Discharges

This approach develops an estimate of wrongful convictions based on actions taken by justice officials, namely court-ordered discharge of inmates from imprisonment. "Court-ordered discharge," however, is a broader category than "wrongful conviction": it encompasses not only substantive errors (wrong-person convictions) but also procedural errors in the conviction and sentencing of the offender. Ultimately it is necessary to distinguish these two types of errors if our use of these official data is to have merit.

Data from the New York State Department of Correctional Services

A series of research reports and the availability of data from the New York State (NYS) Department of Correctional Services (DOCS) make New York a convenient jurisdiction for examining the value of court-ordered discharges.[8] Every year the DOCS publishes reports on inmates under its jurisdiction, but its annual report, *Characteristics of Inmates Discharged,* is most relevant to this study. The DOCS recognizes 10 categories of inmate release, including parole, maximum expiration of sentence, escape, death, court-ordered discharges, and others.

A court-ordered discharge is defined by the DOCS as a case "where the individual is discharged from custody while further court proceedings take place (i.e., an appeal, new trial), or is discharged as a result of court proceedings in which the individual is found guilty of a lesser charge for which he may already have served the length of time legally required, or discharged because the original charge was dismissed" (DOCS 1997a:3). Over the 22-year period from 1976 through 1997, the DOCS has averaged 155 court-ordered discharges per year. There were 199 such discharges in 1995, the year that we examine here. Because of the relatively small number of inmates discharged under court order in any single year, the DOCS annual reports do not provide cross-tabulated data on inmate characteristics for those who are released in this manner. (Such data are available only for parole release.) The DOCS Office of Program Planning, Evaluation, and Research, however, provided me with more highly detailed information on the characteristics of court-ordered discharges for 1995.

Measures of Wrongful Conviction

Unfortunately, the data mentioned above need further elaboration and interpretation before we can make any inferences about the extent of wrongful convictions. As stated earlier, official data on court-ordered discharges do not distinguish between substantive and procedural errors, and we are concerned with the former (wrong-person convictions and imprisonment). Nothing in the official data makes this distinction, except a 1989 DOCS report on vacated murder sentences in New York. That study, conducted by the New York State Department of Correctional Services, identified 33 offenders who had been convicted of murder and released from DOCS custody between 1980 and 1987 for new trials. Those cases "represent current instances where appellate courts found error so substantial as to warrant the vacation of the conviction for murder" (DOCS 1989:1).

In the DOCS follow-up analysis on those 33 cases, it was found that on retrial the great majority (26, or 78.8%) were reconvicted of a lesser offense (17 for first-degree manslaughter). The remaining seven (21.2%) were acquitted after a new trial or after local prosecutors dismissed the original indictment.[9] If we regard these seven cases as wrong-person convictions, using acquittal after a new trial or dismissal of indictment (following a court-ordered discharge) as measures of wrongful conviction, this internal DOCS study offers some empirical basis for estimating the proportion of court-ordered discharges that represents substantive error (21.2%), at least in regard to murder convictions and commitments.

Samuel Gross (1996, 1998) argues persuasively that homicide cases in general, and capital cases in particular, are handled differently by officials in the criminal justice system, and for a variety of reasons are more likely to involve erroneous convictions. Therefore, in line with Gross's thesis (and the limits of DOCS data), we must limit our objective here to estimating the prevalence of wrongful murder convictions rather than wrongful felony convictions.

Findings

An examination of 1995 DOCS data on court-ordered discharges reveals that of the 199 inmates released from custody by the courts, 24 (12.1%) had been convicted of murder (DOCS 1997a).[10] If we assume that only 21.2 percent[11] of these court-ordered discharges represent substantive errors, then only five discharges represent wrongful murder convictions. However, the relevant population base for calculating prevalence of wrongful convictions is the number of murder commitments to the Department of Correctional Services. A study conducted by the New York State Defenders Association (NYSDA)[12] found that the median time from conviction to reversal (acquittal/dismissal) in wrongful homicide convictions in New York is approximately three years (NYSDA 1989; Rosenbaum 1990–1991).[13] Accordingly, murder inmates released by court-ordered discharge in 1995 were probably committed to the Department of Correctional Services in 1992, when 357 murder commitments were made to the DOCS (DOCS 1997b:10). If five of these were wrongful convictions, this translates to an error rate of 1.4 percent in murder convictions/commitments.[14]

The NYSDA study, described above, also attempted to catalogue wrongful homicide convictions in New York State from 1965 to 1988. As part of its Wrongful Conviction Study Project, the study identified 59 wrongful homicide convictions during this period, 45 of which involved murder convictions (Rosenbaum 1990–1991:807–08). The NYSDA's definition of wrongful homicide conviction, however, was broader than that employed in the present study. It included not only cases in which the defendant, whose conviction had been overturned, was acquitted on retrial or the charges were dismissed, but also cases in which the defendant was reconvicted of a nonhomicide crime. If the NYSDA study cases are limited to murder sentences reversed between 1980 and 1987 and to cases in which the defendant was subsequently acquitted on retrial or the indictment was dismissed (and omits cases in which the defendant was reconvicted of a lesser offense),[15] we were left with 23 wrongful murder convictions in New York State between 1980 and 1987. During the period 1977 to 1984,[16] 2,276 murder commitments were made to the Department of Correctional Services (Chapman and Zausner 1985); this translates to a 1.0 percent error rate in murder convictions/commitments.

The estimated prevalence of wrongful murder convictions reached by using the NYSDA study (1.0%) is comparable to the estimate of 1.4 percent calculated from DOCS data on court-ordered discharges. This is the case even though very different methodologies, each with its own assumptions and limitations, are used in each approach. Both, however, are based on officially acknowledged errors in which the convicted murder defendant has been released from custody and subsequently is acquitted on retrial, or in which the original indictment is dismissed.

Use of Inmates' Self-Reports

The use of inmates' self-reports is another methodological approach to estimating the prevalence of wrongful convictions. Unlike court-ordered discharges, which rely on the reliability and validity of agency records, inmates' self-reports depend on the reliability and validity of inmates' accounts of their own criminality. The use of these self-reports provides another approach, with a different set of assumptions and limitations, to the quantification problem.

The RAND Inmate Survey

In late 1978 and early 1979, the RAND Corporation of Santa Monica, California conducted surveys of convicted male offenders (in 14 jails and 12 prisons) in California, Michigan, and Texas (Peterson et al. 1982). The surveys were administered in small groups (10 to 30 inmates) by temporary RAND employees who were hired because of their experience in working with incarcerated inmates; prison officials did not participate in these sessions. The sample was representative of adult male inmates admitted to prisons and jails in the above jurisdictions at the time of the survey. Participation was voluntary and required informed consent.[17] Altogether self-report data were obtained from 1,380 prison inmates and 810 jail inmates.

The questionnaire, which took about 50 minutes to complete, asked for detailed information about crimes the inmates had committed in a one- to two-year period preceding their incarceration, including questions about arrests and convictions. The survey also questioned inmates about their current conviction offense, demographic characteristics, and other personal details. In addition, official criminal records were collected on 85 percent of the prison inmates who responded to the questionnaire (Peterson et al. 1982).

Measure of Wrongful Conviction

Although the purpose of the RAND Inmate Survey was to collect data on criminal careers and to develop policy implications from those data, two questionnaire items in the "1978 Jail/Prison Survey Booklet" (Chaiken and Chaiken 1982:App. E) are relevant to our research. These questions (Numbers 6 and 7 on p. 39 of the booklet) pertain to the inmate's current offense: "What charge(s) were you *convicted* of that you are serving time for *now*? (Check *all* that apply)," and "For these convictions, what crimes, if any, do you think you really did? (Check all that apply)." Each of these questions is followed by a list of 15 different offenses, plus an "other" category. In addition, the last response choice for the second question is "Did *no* crime." Inmates' denials of the conviction offense (i.e., self-reports that they "did *no* crime") provide another basis for measuring wrongful conviction. Clearly, inmates who claim that they are innocent of the offense for which they have been incarcerated meet the operational definition of wrongful conviction.

Certainly, inmates' self-reports raise serious questions of reliability and validity that must be addressed before we can take them at face value. Built into the RAND research design were several ways of checking on the internal consistency (reliability) as well as the validity of responses. These included asking respondents for essentially the same information in different parts of the questionnaire, retesting some of the respondents a week later, and comparing inmates' responses with official records. Overall, "83 percent of respondents tracked the questionnaire with a high degree of accuracy and completeness, and were very consistent in their answers" (Chaiken and Chaiken 1982:224–25).

When researchers compared questionnaire data with the prison inmates' official records,[18] they found a close correspondence. In fact, in California and Texas, respondents reported 6 percent more convictions than the records show; in Michigan, convictions were underreported by 6 percent (Marquis and Ebener 1981:34). Inmates were reluctant, however, to provide information on sex offenses, including rape; these are more likely than other offenses to be understated in self-reports (Peterson et al. 1982:21). There was also evidence that some errors in inmate-reported crimes were due to confusion about offense categories; thus the problem was one of misclassification rather than omission. For example, "robbery" and "theft" were sometimes confused (Marquis and Ebener 1981:38).

In assessing the quality of prisoners' self-reports, RAND researchers began with the conventional wisdom that respondents are likely to conceal undesirable information about themselves. After reviewing the methods literature as well as results from the RAND Inmate Survey, however, they concluded just the opposite: "We found evidence that respondents usually reveal more arrests and convictions in questionnaires or interviews than can be found in official records" (Marquis and Ebener 1981:2). Moreover, the RAND evaluation of inmates' self-reports specifically examined the quality of reports on questionnaire items pertaining to the current offense. The investigators concluded that "on a general level, the data are close to unbiased" (Marquis and Ebener 1981:32). Although the RAND researchers observed item-by-item variation, they found in general that reliability was "moderately high" (Marquis and Ebener 1981:32). Overall the RAND findings refute the widely held belief that inmates are likely to underreport their criminal activity: "In general, the prisoner respondents do not appear to be systematically denying their conviction offenses in the questionnaire" (Marquis and Ebener 1981:47).

Method

The RAND Inmate Survey (National Archive of Criminal Justice Data 2000; Peterson et al. 1982) is available to the public at the National Archive of Criminal Justice Data website.[19] Because I was interested in only a few of the variables contained in the survey, I extracted those variables from the RAND data set to create a smaller data set for analysis. Any cases with missing data were eliminated. The specific variables in the newer, smaller data set included current conviction offense, crimes actually committed, state, and type of institution. In addition, because in the present study I am interested in wrongful convictions and imprisonment at the felony level, I examined only data on prison inmates: 1,282 cases in Michigan, California, and Texas.

Findings

The basic finding is that 197 of the 1,282 prison inmates questioned in the RAND Survey, or 15.4 percent, claimed that they did *not* commit the crime for which they had been convicted and imprisoned (see Table 6.1). Those inmates also denied committing any of the other 15 crimes included on the "current conviction offense" checklist, including "other." This finding did not vary widely by state: 14.1 percent of Michigan prisoners denied having committed

Table 6.1
Current Conviction Crime by Self-Reported Denial

Current Conviction Offense	Did Not Commit *n*	Did Not Commit %
Rape	23	37.7
Sex Offense (Not Rape)	14	26.9
Murder	18	17.5
Weapons	20	13.4
Assault	22	12.8
Robbery	44	11.5
Forgery	8	9.9
Burglary	33	9.0
Drug Sale	7	8.1
Drug Possession	6	5.2
All Offenses	197	15.4

Source: National Archive of Criminal Justice Data (2000). NOTE: N = 1,272 (missing values in 10 of the 1,282 cases)

any crime, as did 14.6 percent in California and 16.7 percent in Texas.

Denials varied more widely, however, by current conviction offense. Rapists and other sex offenders denied their conviction offense at the highest rates by far: 37.7 and 26.9 percent respectively. Those convicted of murder, weapons violations, assault, and robbery fell into the middle range: 17.5, 13.4, 12.8, and 11.5 percent respectively denied their offense. Drug and nonviolent property offenders were least likely to deny their conviction offense.

It is possible that in this rather lengthy, complex questionnaire the inmate respondents misunderstood the two key questions that are of concern to us. Specifically, in marking "Did *no* crime," they may not have understood their response. As a check on respondents' confusion, I examined whether inmates who reported that they "did no crime" (in response to question 7 in the booklet) also indicated, nonetheless, that they really had committed another crime. Such a response, of course, would be contradictory to the question "What crimes, if any, did you really commit?" This did not seem to be a problem, however: only 19 (1.5%) of the inmate respondents indicated that they had committed no crime and yet checked one of the other crime categories on the list.

Overall, inmates' reports of their conviction crime corresponded to crime they actually committed. For example, 103 inmate respondents reported that they had been convicted of murder, and 70 of those respondents admitted that they had committed murder. Many of the remaining 33 respondents admitted to crimes less than murder (e.g., manslaughter, robbery) and therefore questioned the state's classification of the crime they had committed, but only 18 claimed that they had committed no crime at all. Similarly, 382 inmate respondents reported a conviction of robbery, and 287 admitted that they had committed that crime. Only 44 of the remaining 95 respondents convicted of robbery claimed that they had committed no crime. This pattern holds for the great majority of crimes; the exceptions are rape and other sex offenses, for which the rate of denial was much higher. In the case of rape, 61 inmate respondents reported a conviction of rape, only 17 conceded that they had committed that crime, and 23 claimed to have committed no crime at all.

Discussion and Conclusions

The prevalence of wrongful convictions as measured by inmates' self-reports is significantly greater than the estimate derived from using official data based on court-ordered discharges (15% versus 1%).[20] This finding perhaps is not surprising, but it does not support the idea that alternative methodologies might produce similar results.

Although the RAND assessment of prisoners' self-reports challenged the conventional wisdom that inmates in general deny their criminal activities, some prisoners nonetheless have a variety of self-serving motives for underreporting their crimes. Even though they have been convicted and imprisoned, some inmates still may have forthcoming appeals, and therefore, in spite of the anonymity or confidentiality of a survey, a personal stake in minimizing their involvement in the conviction crime. It is also possible, as Loftus (1996) argued so persuasively with eyewitness testimony, that postevent information may reshape inmates' memories of their criminal conduct, including their current conviction offenses.[21] Perhaps defense arguments and accounts of the crime presented at trial or on appeal, by minimizing or denying defendants' involvement, may subtly influence memories of the actual crime.[22]

It may also be that inmates' perceptions of their criminal conduct are at variance with the legal definition. For example, Koss, Gidycz, and Wisniewski (1987), who researched the prevalence of rape on college campuses, observed that male offenders tended not to recognize their conduct as rape; yet they admitted to having sex with a female against her will.[23] This disparity in definitions of rape (legal versus offender's definition) perhaps accounts for much of the underreporting of rape (and other sex offenses) in the RAND Inmate Survey. Another possibility, as noted by the RAND researchers, is that inmates misclassify their offense, perhaps confusing robbery with theft or murder with manslaughter. It is more difficult, however, to understand the complete denial of an inmate's conviction offense, short of lying or wrongful conviction.

An earlier RAND survey of 624 California male prisoners also concluded that "inmates did not deny committing crimes" (Peterson, Braiker, and Polich 1981:xxi), but found that 81 (13%) of those inmates denied committing any of the 11 crimes on the survey list. Peterson and his colleagues (1981:20) maintained that about half of the 81 had committed a crime not on their list; about 6 percent denied committing any crime, including the crime for which they had been imprisoned. Although this figure is less than the approximately 15 percent denial rate found in the 1978 RAND Inmate Survey, it is larger than the 1 percent estimate of wrongful convictions based on court-ordered discharges.

The two approaches employed in this study to estimate the prevalence of wrongful convictions not only resulted in different outcomes, but also are based on different methodologies. One draws on officially acknowledged error (court-ordered discharges); the other, on the uncorroborated claims of prisoners (inmates' self-reports), and thus on a more expansive definition of wrongful conviction. Because court-ordered discharges are the result of inmates who pursue their claims of justice-system error (whether substantive or procedural), it is not surprising that the outcome of that process will yield a smaller estimate, given the attrition of cases. Moreover, future research on court-ordered discharges must continue to distinguish between persons released for procedural and for substantive reasons, and must reexamine the proportion of cases involving wrong-person convictions.[24] Although the extent of wrongful convictions remains a "dark figure," the divergent findings of the two approaches used here may delineate the parameters of the problem: prevalence ranges from 1 to 15 percent, depending on assumptions and operational definitions.

Future research also must take into account variation in wrongful convictions over time. Drawing on Packer's (1968) distinction between "crime control" and "due process," Huff and his colleagues (1996:143–44) note a possible link between wrongful convictions and a crime-control model of the criminal justice process. This suggests that in historical periods which emphasize crime control over due process (as in "get tough" crime policies), errors of justice are also more likely, including wrongful convictions. Until now, the absence of a methodology for measuring justice-system error has made this proposition untestable.

Estimating the prevalence of wrongful convictions is not merely a matter of academic interest. Knowing the magnitude and scope of the problem has important public policy implications. Although we may never know exactly how many innocent persons have been convicted and imprisoned, the extent of this problem indicates how well (or how poorly) our criminal justice system is sorting the guilty from the not guilty; certainly this is a major goal of the system. The extent of error provides a quality control mechanism and alerts us to systemic flaws, whether they pertain to mistaken eyewitness identification, police interrogation practices, ineffective counsel, or the use of jailhouse informers.

In a 1999 report by the Institute of Medicine of the National Academy of Sciences (NAS), it was estimated that medical mistakes annually kill from 44,000 to 98,000 hospital patients (Corrigan, Kohn, and Donaldson 1999). The report emphasized the systemic basis for most errors in the health care system, rather than individual recklessness, and identified some of the organizational measures that can be taken to prevent death and injury from medical mistakes (NAS 1999). Although officials and providers in the health care system have been slow[25] to recognize the extent of medical mistakes and their implications for public safety, this report represents a reversal.

Officials in the criminal justice system can learn from the experience of other institutions by publicly acknowledging justicesystem errors, conducting inquiries when they occur, and beginning to quantify the extent of the problem.[26] Only then can the problem of wrongful convictions be addressed in terms of systemic flaws, not merely as individual wrongdoing nor as honest mistakes that are quickly forgotten.

Author's Note

An earlier version of this article was presented at the annual meetings of the American Society of Criminology, held in San Francisco on November 16, 2000. I am indebted to Paul H. Korotkin, assistant director, and to William Chapman of the DOCS office for Program Planning, Evaluation and Research for providing me with data on court-ordered discharges from imprisonment in New York State. I am also grateful to my colleague, Dr. Tie-ting Su, for writing a computer program to transform the data from the RAND Inmate Survey into a more manageable data set and for producing the resulting cross-tabulated tables.

Notes

1. The great majority of respondents (71.8%) in the Huff study estimated that fewer than 1 percent of felony convictions involved innocent persons (Huff et al. 1986:523).
2. In the Liebman study of capital cases, 7 percent of persons whose death sentences were overturned were found not guilty upon retrial, or charges against them were dismissed (Liebman et al. 2000:132).
3. This is most evident in the movement for a moratorium on the death penalty. The release of 95 innocent death row inmates nationwide since 1973 (as of May 7, 2001) has raised serious doubts about the administration of capital punishment in the United States (Death Penalty Information Center (DPIC) 2001; Dieter 1997). On January 31, 2000 Illinois became the first death-penalty state to issue such a moratorium. In that state, for each death row inmate executed over the last 20 years, another has been released because of innocence (Johnson 2000).
4. The exchange between Leo/Ofshe and Cassell centered on the role of police-induced false confessions in producing wrongful convictions, the magnitude of the problem, and the relevance of the Miranda warning to this issue. Cassell (1998) maintained that the false-confession problem is minor compared with the problem of lost confessions from guilty persons (and therefore lost convictions); this problem, he argued, is due to restrictions on police interrogation. Leo and Ofshe (1998b) challenged Cassell's attempt to quantify the false-confession problem and rejected his claim that quantification is even necessary for public policy decisions. In addition, they reaffirmed the importance of Miranda and the need to develop other procedural safeguards to minimize false confessions and other sources of wrongful convictions.
5. Dr. Sam Sheppard died of liver failure in 1970 at age 46 ("History of Sheppard Case" 2000).
6. Radelet and Bedau (1998:106–07) also note that the concept of innocence can be broadened in a variety of ways including the counting of accidental killings, self-defense, and killings by a mentally ill offender.
7. "The most one can hope to obtain is a consensus of investigators after the case reaches its final disposition. Consensus can be measured in degrees, and the cases that we have included in our catalogue are those in which we believe a majority of neutral observers ... would judge the defendant in question to be innocent" (Bedau and Radelet 1987:47).
8. The DOCS disseminates official statistics through its Office of Program Planning, Evaluation, and Research.
9. Five of the seven cases involved acquittals; the other two, dismissals. It is possible that the indictment dismissals were made on procedural grounds, but it is more likely that the conviction reversal in appellate court undermined the evidentiary basis for pursuing the case (e.g., recanted witness testimony, discovery of police report exonerating defendant).
10. Data on the specific characteristics, including the commitment crime, of 1995 court-ordered discharges were provided by Paul Korotkin, assistant director of program planning, evaluation, and research of the DOCS.
11. The 21.2 percent figure is based on the findings of the 1989 DOCS study on vacated murder sentences.
12. The New York State Defenders Association is a nonprofit organization of public defenders and legal aid attorneys who provide services to criminal defense lawyers throughout the state.
13. On the basis of the wrongful conviction cases cited in the NYSDA study, the median time between conviction and inmate's release was 38.5 months. The DOCS (1989:3) study placed the median at 29 months (from prison reception to reversal). Even if we allow for some variation in the reversal period (from one to four years), the average number of annual murder commitments in NYS between 1991 and 1994 was 370, only a slight departure from the 1992 figure of 357 that I used.
14. If we use the 7.3 percent figure (instead of the 21.2 percent from the DOCS study), derived from the Liebman study of state postconviction reversals, as the basis for estimating the proportion of errors involving wrong-person convictions in vacated murder cases, the error rate for murder convictions/commitments is only .5 percent. The Liebman study, however, is based on an incomplete sample of capital cases reviewed in state postconviction appeals (1973–1995) in 26 states (Liebman et al. 2000:53), not including New York (which did not restore the death penalty until September 1995). The 21.2 percent figure is based on New York vacated murder cases during the 1980–1987 period.
15. These parameters then correspond to those of the 1989 DOCS study.
16. This allows for a three-year lag period from conviction to reversal.
17. The response rate for jail inmates was 70 percent; for prison inmates in California and Michigan, 50 percent; for prison inmates in Texas, 82 percent (Peterson et al. 1982:viii). The RAND researchers attempted to correct the problem of nonrespondents with a replacement procedure. Moreover, although the survey was confidential, it was not anonymous. The questionnaires were coded to make future identification of respondents possible for subsequent research (Peterson et al. 1982:x).
18. This portion of the assessment of the quality of responses was limited to prisoner respondents because official records were available only for prisoners, not for jail inmates. RAND researchers used official records to check the correspondence between prisoners' self-reports and official arrests and convictions.
19. The NACJD is sponsored by the Bureau of Justice Statistics (U.S. Dept. of Justice), operated by the Inter-University Consortium for Political and Social Research, and headquartered at the University of Michigan.
20. Technically, the comparison here should be between 17.5 percent (the proportion of convicted murderers denying the charges in the RAND survey) and the 1.4 percent error rate for murder convictions/commitments based on court-ordered discharges.
21. This is evident in the growing number of cases where postconviction DNA testing provides incriminating evidence rather than exonerating the inmate. A case in point is that of Texas death row inmate Ricky McGinn. In June 2000 Governor George Bush gave McGinn a 30-day reprieve to allow time for DNA testing before his execution. All of the DNA results subsequently showed a match between McGinn and evidence recovered from the victim. Even so, McGinn maintained his innocence ("Texas Man" 2000). This also occurred in the Scott William Davi case in South Dakota: Davi's DNA results provided a match confirming the rape and murder of his ex-wife. Davi, too, maintained his innocence. The results of DNA testing at two major forensic laboratories (Forensic Science Associates and Cellmark) have confirmed prisoners' guilt in 60 percent of the cases (Cohen 2000:A1).

22. Pennington and Hastie (1993) have written about the "story model" of juror's decision making, arguing that prosecutors and defense attorneys construct stories of the crime to make it more understandable to the jury. The story then is a way to organize the facts of the case in a manner consistent with the prosecution or the defense version of events. These "stories" might later influence the defendants' recollections of their crimes.
23. In particular, respondents disagree about what constitutes coercive or consensual sexual relations.
24. The 21.2 percent estimate used in this study is based on one study, the 1989 DOCS research on vacated murder convictions, which needs to be explored more fully.
25. Action has been slow in relation to some other sectors of the economy in which public safety issues are well established, such as the airline and automobile industries and workplace safety in general. Medical malpractice suits, of course, have contributed to the health care system's reluctance to publicly acknowledge medical mistakes.
26. In May 2000, New York Governor George Pataki proposed legislation to create a DNA Review Committee. This committee would have the authority to review cases in which DNA has exonerated offenders, and to recommend legal or procedural changes to prevent future recurrences ("Gov. Pataki" 2000).

References

Bedau, H.A. and M. Radelet. 1987. "Miscarriages of Justice in Potentially Capital Cases." *Stanford Law Review* 40:21–179.

Borchard, E.M. [1932] 1970. *Convicting the Innocent: Errors of Criminal Justice.* New York: Da Capo.

Cassell, P. 1998. "Protecting the Innocent From False Confessions and Lost Confessions—And from Miranda." *Journal of Criminal Law and Criminology* 88:497–556.

Chaiken, J.M. and M.R. Chaiken. 1982. *Varieties of Criminal Behavior.* Santa Monica, CA: RAND.

Chapman, W.R. and S.A. Zausner. 1985. *Characteristics of Inmates Under Custody: A Ten-Year Trend Study.* Albany, NY: Department of Correctional Services.

Cohen, L.P. 2000. "Someone Who's Guilty Would Never Want DNA Testing, Right?" *Wall Street Journal,* July 12, pp. A1, A12.

Connors, E., T. Lundregan, N. Miller, and T. McEwen. 1996. *Convicted by Juries, Exonerated by Science: Case Studies in the Use of DNA Evidence to Establish Innocence After Trial.* Washington, DC: U.S. Department of Justice.

Corrigan, J., L. Kohn, and M. Donaldson, eds. 1999. *To Err Is Human: Building a Safer Health System.* Washington, DC: Institute of Medicine, National Academy of Sciences.

Cutler, B.L. and S.D. Penrod. 1995. *Mistaken Identification: The Eyewitness, Psychology, and the Law.* New York: Cambridge University Press.

Death Penalty Information Center (DPIC). 2001. "Innocence: Freed from Death Row." Death Penalty Information Center Website. Retrieved May 7, 2001 (http://www.deathpenaltyinfo.org).

Department of Correctional Services (DOCS). 1989. *Murder Commitments With Subsequent Sentence Vacations.* Albany, NY: Division of Program Planning, Research, and Evaluation.

——.1997a. *Characteristics of Inmates Discharged, 1995.* Albany, NY: Division of Program Planning, Research, and Evaluation.

——.1997b. *Characteristics of New Commitments, 1995.* Albany, NY: Division of Program Planning, Research, and Evaluation.

Devine, P.G. 1995. "Getting Hooked on Research in Social Psychology: Examples From Eyewitness Identification and Prejudice." Pp. 161–84 in *The Social Psychologists,* edited by G. Brannigan and M. Merrens. New York: McGraw-Hill.

Dieter, R.C. 1997. "Innocence and the Death Penalty: The Increasing Danger of Executing the Innocent." Death Penalty Information Center Website. Retrieved April 13, 2000 (http://www.deathpenaltyinfo.org).

Ewinger, J. and J.F. Hagan. 2000. "Jurors Issue Rapid Verdict." *Cleveland Plain Dealer,* April 13. Retrieved April 13, 2000 (http://www.cleveland.com/news).

"Governor Pataki to Establish DNA Review Committee." 2000. Press release, May 8. Retrieved Aug. 10, 2000 (http://www.state.ny.us/governor/press/year00/may8_00.htm).

Gross, S.R. 1996. "The Risks of Death: Why Erroneous Convictions Are Common in Capital Cases." *Buffalo Law Review* 44:1–21. Retrieved Dec. 22, 1998 (http://web.lexis-nexis.com/universe).

——.1998. "Lost Lives: Miscarriages of Justice in Capital Cases." *Law and Contemporary Problems* 61:125–52.

Hagan, J.F. and J. Ewinger. 2000. "Third Trial Fails to Overcome Burden of Proving Sheppard Was Innocent." *Cleveland Plain Dealer,* April 13. Retrieved April 13, 2000 (http://www.cleveland.com/news).

"History of the Sheppard Case." 2000. *Cleveland Plain Dealer,* Feb. 3. Retrieved April 13, 2000 (http://www.cleveland. . .indepth/sam/stories).

Huff, C.R., A. Rattner, and E. Sagarin. 1986. "Guilty Until Proved Innocent: Wrongful Conviction and Public Policy." *Crime and Delinquency* 32:518–44.

——.1996. *Convicted but Innocent: Wrongful Conviction and Public Policy.* Thousand Oaks, CA: Sage.

Johnson, D. 2000. "Illinois, Citing Verdict Errors, Bars Executions." *New York Times,* February 1, pp. A1, A16.

Koss, M.P., C.A. Gidycz, and N. Wisniewski. 1987. "The Scope of Rape: Incidence and Prevalence of Sexual Aggression and Victimization in a National Sample of Higher Education Students." *Journal of Consulting and Clinical Psychology* 55:162–70.

Leo, R.A. 1996. "Inside the Interrogation Room." *Journal of Criminal Law and Criminology* 86:266–303.

Leo, R.A. and R.J. Ofshe. 1998a. "The Consequences of False Confessions: Deprivations of Liberty and Miscarriages of Justice in the Age of Psychological Interrogation." *Journal of Criminal Law and Criminology* 88:429–96.

——.1998b. "Using the Innocent to Scapegoat Miranda." *Journal of Criminal Law and Criminology* 88:557–78.

Liebman, J.S., J. Fagan, and V. West. 2000. "A Broken System: Error Rates in Capital Cases, 1973–1995." The Justice Project Website. Retrieved June 30, 2000 (http://207.153.244.129/liebman1.pdf).

Loftus, E.F. 1993. "Psychologists in the Eyewitness World." *American Psychologist* 48:550–52.

——.1996. *Eyewitness Testimony.* Cambridge, MA: Harvard University Press.

Loftus, E.F. and K. Ketcham. 1991. *Witness for the Defense: The Accused, the Witness, and the Expert Who Puts Memory on Trial.* New York: St. Martin's.

Marquis, K.H. and P.A. Ebener. 1981. *Quality of Prisoner Self-Reports: Arrest and Conviction Response Errors.* Santa Monica, CA: RAND.

National Academy of Sciences (NAS), Institute of Medicine. 1999. "Preventing Death and Injury From Medical Errors Requires Dramatic, System-Wide Changes." *National Academies News,* November 29. Retrieved December 30, 1999 (http://www4.nationalacademies.org/news).

National Archive of Criminal Justice Data. 2000. "Survey of Jail and Prison Inmates, 1978: California, Michigan, and Texas." ICPSR Study 8169. Ann Arbor, MI: ICPSR. Retrieved May 2000 (http://www.icpsr.umich.edu/NACJD).

New York State Court of Claims. 1998. "Court of Claims Act." Retrieved June 10, 1998 (http://www.nyscourtofclaims.state.ny.us).

New York State Defenders Association (NYSDA). 1989. *Convicting the Innocent: Wrongful New York State Homicide Convictions, 1965–1988.* A Preliminary Report. Albany, NY: Public Defense Backup Center.

Ofshe, R.J. and R.A. Leo. 1997. "The Decision to Confess Falsely: Rational Choice and Irrational Action." *Denver University Law Review* 74:979–1122.

Packer, H. 1968. *The Limits of the Criminal Sanction.* Stanford, CA: Stanford University Press.

Pennington, N. and R. Hastie. 1993. "The Story Model for Juror Decision Making." Pp. 192–221 in *Inside the Juror: The Psychology of Juror Decision Making,* edited by R. Hastie. Cambridge, UK: Cambridge University Press.

Peterson, M.A., H.B. Braiker, and S.M. Polich. 1981. *Who Commits Crimes: A Survey of Prison Inmates.* Cambridge, MA: Oelgeschlager, Gunn, and Hain.

Peterson, M., J. Chaiken, P. Ebener, and P. Honig. 1982. *Survey of Prison and Jail Inmates: Background and Method.* Santa Monica, CA: RAND.

Radelet, M.L. and H.A. Bedau. 1998. "The Execution of the Innocent." *Law and Contemporary Problems* 61:105–24.

Radelet, M.L., H.A. Bedau, and C.E. Putnam. 1992. *In Spite of Innocence: Erroneous Convictions in Capital Cases.* Boston, MA: Northeastern University Press.

Radin, E.D. 1964. *The Innocents.* New York: Morrow.

Rosenbaum, M.I. 1990–1991. "Inevitable Error: Wrongful New York State Homicide Convictions." *Review of Law and Social Change* 18:807–30.

Scheck, B., P. Neufeld, and J. Dwyer. 2000. *Actual Innocence.* New York: Doubleday.

"Texas Man Gets New Execution Date." 2000. *New York Times,* August 15. Retrieved August 15, 2000 (http://www.nytimes.com).

U.S. House of Representatives. 1994. *Innocence and the Death Penalty: Assessing the Danger of Mistaken Executions.* Staff Report by Subcommittee on Civil and Constitutional Rights of the Committee on the Judiciary. 103rd Congress, 2nd Session. Washington, DC: U.S. Government Printing Office.

Webb, E.J., D.T. Campbell, R.D. Schwartz, and L. Sechrest. 1966. *Unobtrusive Measures: Nonreactive Research in the Social Sciences.* Chicago, IL: Rand McNally.

Wells, G.L. 1993. "What Do We Know About Eyewitness Identification?" *American Psychologist* 48:553–71.

Yant, M. 1991. *Presumed Guilty: When Innocent People Are Wrongly Convicted.* Buffalo, NY: Prometheus.

Yuille, J.C. 1993. "We Must Study Forensic Eyewitnesses to Know About Them." *American Psychologist* 48:572–73.

Chapter 7

The United States Supreme Court and the Fourth Amendment

Evolution from Warren to Post-Warren Perspectives

Jack E. Call

Throughout the 1960s, the Warren Court adjudicated a series of landmark cases that established the limits placed on police by the Fourth Amendment, which prohibits unreasonable searches and seizures and requires probable cause before the issue of a warrant. This "due process revolution" restrained police and defended the rights of suspects.

But the Warren Court didn't always have opportunity to clarify, elaborate, and delineate the boundaries of its controversial decisions. In the early 1970s, Warren Burger replaced Earl Warren as Chief Justice, and three new justices were appointed to the Court. Since 1974, the "post-Warren Court" has decided more than 140 cases involving Fourth Amendment issues. While only one Warren Court decision was actually overturned, in a series of decisions, the post-Warren Court has diminished standards for probable cause, condoned "pretext searches," and increased police authority.

The last 25 years constitute a distinct period in the United States Supreme Court's treatment of Fourth Amendment cases. The year 1975 is not itself a bold line of demarcation in the development of Fourth Amendment law, but in the mid-1970s the Court was clearly undergoing a shift in philosophy in this area that has resulted in a body of Fourth Amendment law that is very different from the Fourth Amendment law developed by the Warren Court in the 1960s.

The 1960s constituted one of the most remarkable periods in the history of the Supreme Court. The changes in constitutional law brought about by the Warren Court in that decade were so dramatic that they are sometimes referred to collectively as the due process revolution (Hall, 1992). It was a "due process" revolution because the due process clause of the Fourteenth Amendment was interpreted by the Court to require most of the rights in the Bill of Rights, which had previously applied only to the federal government, to be followed by state and local governments as well. It was a "revolution" because the changes brought about a redistribution of judicial power that gave federal courts the final authority to give meaning to those ambiguous rights contained in the Bill of Rights.

The due process revolution cut a wide path, extending to a broad range of rights. Two aspects of this sea change in the legal landscape are important to our discussion. The first is that the Warren Court not only made applicable to the states a broad range of rights that had previously applied only to the federal government but also interpreted those rights in a way that was very supportive of the individuals asserting them. The second important point is that, because of the broad range of rights that the Warren Court addressed and the relatively short duration of the due process revolution, the Court often made dramatic new expansions of a right without an opportunity to elaborate, in later cases, on the full scope or reach of these new pronouncements. In no area of constitutional law was this more true than in the Warren Court's treatment of Fourth Amendment issues.

This article begins by examining the important Fourth Amendment decisions of the Warren Court. The next sections examine the most important Fourth Amendment cases that were decided by the Supreme Court in the last 25 years (the post-Warren Court). The article concludes with some generalizations about the post-Warren Court's treatment of the Fourth Amendment.

The Warren Court and the Fourth Amendment

Perhaps the most important Warren Court decision interpreting the Fourth Amendment was *Mapp v. Ohio* (1961). In 1949, the Court held that the Fourth Amendment was applicable to the states through the due process clause in the Fourteenth Amendment, but it also held that the states did not have to exclude evidence obtained in violation of that amendment (*Wolf v. Colorado,* 1949). In *Mapp,* the Court changed its mind on this latter point and held that states must apply the exclusionary rule to evidence obtained unconstitutionally.

Mapp was undoubtedly one of the most controversial Warren Court decisions dealing with the rights of the criminally accused. It was perhaps the first decision that indicated the Warren Court's willingness to use the due process clause to dramatically alter the balance of power between state and federal courts on matters of criminal procedure. Along with *Gideon v. Wainwright* (1963) and *Miranda v. Arizona* (1966), *Mapp* became a focal point for the states' resentment of the intrusion of the federal courts into criminal matters, an area that the states believed had been left to their control under the Constitution without interference from the federal government.

The Warren Court decided other important Fourth Amendment cases as well. In *Aguilar v. Texas* (1964), the Court dealt with the establishment of probable cause to search or arrest based on information received from informants, especially anonymous informants. The Court established a two-pronged test to be used in these cases, holding that a judicial officer issuing a warrant based on information from an informant must satisfy himself or herself that the informant is reliable and that the basis of the informant's information is also reliable.

In *Katz v. U.S.* (1967), the Court considered the difficult but very important issue of what constitutes a search. In many cases, the police (without a warrant) seize evidence that is in plain sight, but the issue is whether the police, in getting to the evidence, conducted a search. If they did not, then the Fourth Amendment rules concerning warrants and probable cause do not apply. Prior to its decision in *Katz,* the Court had taken a property approach to this question, concluding that the police do not search unless they do something to intrude physically into a place that is protected by the Fourth Amendment. In *Katz,* the police had attached an eavesdropping device to the outside of a glass phone booth; therefore, they had not physically intruded into the phone booth. The Court abandoned the property approach and ruled that the police engage in a search whenever their actions intrude upon a reasonable expectation of privacy.

In *Chimel v. California* (1969), the Court dealt with another very significant issue–the scope of a search conducted incident to an arrest. This issue is of great practical significance because of the frequency with which such searches occur. Prior to its decision in *Chimel,* the Court had permitted a warrantless search of the entire premises where an arrest occurred. In *Chimel,* the Court continued to adhere to the notion that a warrantless search incident to an arrest is permissible for the protection of the arresting officer and in order to prevent the destruction of evidence that the arrestee might be able to access just before, during, or after the arrest. However, the Court held that in order to protect these interests adequately an arresting officer need only search the person arrested and the area within the person's immediate control.

The Court also made it clear in another case that such a search is invalid unless the arrest is lawful and that the lawfulness of the arrest must be assessed on the basis of the information that was available to the arresting officer *before* the officer conducted the search incident to that arrest (*Sibron v. New York,* 1968). In other words, the arresting officer may not use any information turned up during the search incident to the arrest as a justification for the arrest itself.

In the final Warren Court pro-defense case of significance under the Fourth Amendment, the Court dealt with the issue of whether a warrant based on probable cause was required for a housing inspector to make an ordinary search of premises for code compliance. In *Camara v. Municipal Court* (1967), the Court held that a warrant was required for such an inspection.

However, it also ruled that a warrant to make the inspection does not require probable cause to think that violations will be discovered at the place inspected, so long as the agency has promulgated reasonable regulations for determining when the inspections will be made. In coming to this conclusion, the Court balanced the need for the inspections without probable cause against the degree of intrusion that the inspections entail.

There were two very important Warren Court Fourth Amendment cases that were decided favorably to the police. In the first case, *Terry v. Ohio* (1968), Terry had been stopped by a police officer who had observed Terry engaging in suspicious behavior. The officer clearly lacked probable cause to arrest or search Terry. Terry argued that, under the Fourth Amendment, the only time a police officer can detain someone (a "seizure" in Fourth Amendment language) is when that person has been arrested, an action requiring probable cause to think that the person has committed a crime. The Warren Court rejected this argument, holding that there is another kind of permissible seizure under the Fourth Amendment. This seizure, which is now commonly referred to as a "Terry stop," is a brief detention of someone who an officer has reasonable suspicion to think has committed, is committing, or is about to commit a crime. Thus, *Terry* expanded the authority of the police to detain people against their will.

In the second Warren Court case decided in favor of the police, *Warden v. Hayden* (1967), the Court recognized explicitly for the first time a hot pursuit exception to the warrant requirement. The Court held that the police could enter, without a warrant, the house of an armed robbery suspect who had just been followed to that house immediately after the commission of the robbery. The Court indicated that, for their own protection, the officers pursuing Hayden could enter the home immediately to ensure that Hayden was the only person there who posed a threat to the officers. The Court also overturned a rule that prohibited police from seizing evidence other than contraband or fruits or instrumentalities of a crime while conducting a search and held that "mere evidence" of a crime could be seized as well.

The Post-Warren Court Record

Since 1974, the Supreme Court has decided more than 140 cases involving issues arising under the Fourth Amendment. Obviously, it is beyond the scope of this article to discuss all of these post-Warren Court decisions. Consequently, this article focuses on those decisions that have had the most significant impact on the development of Fourth Amendment jurisprudence. The decisions discussed have explored territory that was previously uncharted, have steered the law significantly in a direction different from that of the Warren Court, or have held in favor of the criminal defendant in a significant way that stands out from the general trend reflected in post-Warren Court decisions.

For purposes of analysis in this article, the period 1970–1974 will not be considered a part of either the Warren Court era or the present post-Warren Court era. Warren Burger replaced Earl Warren as Chief Justice in June 1969. In the next two and one half years, Justices Blackmun, Powell, and Rehnquist replaced Justices Fortas, Black, and Harlan. The period 1970–1974 can be viewed as a transition period, during which the Court, after undergoing such a large change of personnel in such a short period of time, was developing a new identity. The Court during this period will be referred to as the Transition Court.

What Is a Search?

In *Katz,* the Warren Court abandoned a property approach in favor of a privacy approach to determining whether the police have engaged in a search. Given the technological advances of the twentieth century that made it possible for the police to obtain information about individuals without physical intrusion into a constitutionally protected place, the shift to a privacy approach expanded the reach of the Fourth Amendment and thereby extended greater protections to individuals. However, in applying this new privacy approach, the post-Warren Court has been quite generous to the police.

In *Oliver v. U.S.* (1984), for example, the police had gone onto Oliver's land without a warrant, looking for marijuana that was reportedly growing on the property. Even though the land was fenced, locked, and marked with "no trespassing" signs, the Court concluded that the police had not intruded upon a reasonable expectation of privacy. The "open fields" that the police explored "do not provide the setting for those intimate activities that the [Fourth] Amendment is intended to shelter from government interference or surveillance" (*Oliver v. U.S.*, p. 179).

The post-Warren Court has shown its continuing commitment to the open fields doctrine by ruling that photographs taken from airplanes at an altitude of 1,000 feet (*California v. Ciraolo,* 1986), and at a higher altitude using highly sophisticated equipment (*Dow Chemical Co. v. U.S.*, 1986), and observations with binoculars from a helicopter at 400 feet (*Florida v. Riley,* 1989) are not searches. The post-Warren Court did indicate in *U.S. v. Dunn* (1987) that observations made by the police on land of things within the curtilage of the home (the area immediately surrounding the home) is a search, but then it held that a barn some 60 yards from the home was not within the curtilage.

The post-Warren Court also found no intrusion upon a reasonable expectation of privacy by the police in obtaining bank records containing important financial information (*U.S. v. Miller,* 1976) or in obtaining a list of phone numbers called from a particular phone (*Smith v. Maryland,* 1979). The Court concluded that, when an individual chooses to utilize the services of a bank or a phone company, that person assumes the risk that the information revealed to these organizations might be shared with third parties.

The post-Warren Court also found no reasonable expectation of privacy retained in garbage that had been placed on the street for collection (*California v. Greenwood,* 1988). The majority of the Court was unpersuaded by the observation of Justice Marshall in his dissenting opinion that the media had expressed outrage at the actions of one of its members who had rummaged through the garbage of Henry Kissinger to discover private information about him.

The post-Warren Court also held that the installation of an electronic "beeper" in the wheel well of a person's car (while it was in a public place) (*U.S. v. Knotts,* 1983) or in a package that had not yet been delivered to a person (*U.S. v. Karo,* 1984) is not a search. The use of such devices constitutes a search only when the device reveals information that the police could have obtained only by intruding upon a reasonable expectation of privacy (such as by making the police aware that a package in which a beeper is contained has been opened, when that package is in a home).

In a very recent case, *Bond v. U.S.* (2000), the post-Warren Court demonstrated that even its restrictive view of what constitutes a reasonable expectation of privacy imposes some limits on what police behavior will be viewed as a search. In a 7–2 decision, the Court held that the police conducted a search when they felt the contours of objects contained in a piece of "soft shell" luggage by manipulating the outer covering of a suitcase that had been placed in the luggage rack above the passenger seats in a bus. The Court accepted the government's contention that bus passengers know that their luggage will be handled by bus company employees and even other passengers. Nevertheless, the Court concluded that passengers do not expect that "other passengers or bus employees will, as a matter of course, feel the bag in an exploratory manner" (*Bond v. U.S.*, p. 1465).

Determining Probable Cause and Reasonable Suspicion

In *Aguilar v. Texas,* the Warren Court held that, when probable cause to search or arrest is being determined on the basis of information received from an informant, the person making the determination must have a reasonable basis for concluding that the informant is reliable and that the informant's information was obtained in a reliable manner (this is often referred to as the "basis of knowledge" prong). This decision made clear the Warren Court's desire to bring a certain degree of rigor to the probable cause determination (a desire that presumably extended as well to the reasonable suspicion determination established three years later in *Terry v. Ohio*).

In 1983, the post-Warren Court revisited this issue in *Illinois v. Gates.* In a 5-4 decision, the Court concluded that the two-pronged *Aguilar* approach had created legal technicalities that were causing lower courts to overturn too many probable cause determinations made by the police or magistrates on the basis of hearsay information. Consequently, the Court abandoned the *Aguilar* requirements in favor of a "totality of the circumstances" approach. Under this approach, the probable cause decision-maker need only make a commonsense determination of probable cause based on all of the available information. An informant's reliability and the basis of his or her knowledge are still relevant, but "a deficiency in one may be compensated for, in determining the overall reliability of a tip, by a strong showing as to the other" (*Illinois v. Gates,* p. 233).

In *Gates* the Court also made clear its feeling that lower courts should extend great deference to the probable cause determinations made by magistrates in issuing warrants. The next year, the post-Warren Court's confidence in magistrates came to full fruition in *U.S. v. Leon* (1984). In *Leon,* the Court held that evidence obtained by the police in executing a search warrant that should not have been issued because of a lack of probable cause was nevertheless admissible at trial to prove the defendant's guilt. In creating this limited good faith exception to the exclusionary rule, the Court demonstrated not only its confidence in the probable cause determinations of magistrates but also its lack of enthusiasm for the exclusionary rule.

In applying the exclusionary rule to the states in *Mapp v. Ohio,* the Warren Court had indicated that the exclusionary rule was designed not only to control the behavior of the police but also to preserve "judicial integrity." Speaking for the Court, Justice Clark observed in *Mapp* that "nothing can destroy a government more quickly than its failure to observe its own law" (*Mapp v . Ohio,* p. 659). In *Leon,* the post-Warren Court appears to have abandoned preservation of judicial integrity as a purpose of the exclusionary rule. This is the logical conclusion to be drawn from the Court's ruling that use of the exclusionary rule is unnecessary to control the decisions of magistrates, as opposed to actions of the police. Where evidence is obtained after an erroneous probable cause determination by a magistrate and is admitted as evidence at trial, the judicial system is failing to observe its own law.

In a case involving the basis for a reasonable suspicion determination in a Terry stop situation, the post-Warren Court again displayed a lax approach to the standard. In *Alabama v. White* (1990), the Court indicated that "reasonable suspicion is a less demanding standard than probable cause not only in the sense that reasonable suspicion can be established with information that is different in quantity or content than that required to establish probable cause, but also in the sense that reasonable suspicion can arise from information that is less reliable than that required to show probable cause" (*Alabama v. White,* p. 330).

In *Gates* and *White,* the post-Warren Court diminished the probable cause and reasonable suspicion standards not only through its rhetoric but also in its application of those standards to the facts in each case. In *Gates,* the police had received an anonymous letter indicating that Lance and Sue Gates were drug dealers. The letter described their usual procedure for picking up a load of drugs. Sue would drive to West Palm Beach, register in a hotel, and pick up the drugs. Lance would fly down a couple of days later to pick up the car and drive it back while Sue flew home. The letter specified the date of the next trip. The police verified that an L. Gates flew to Florida on the date specified and met a woman registered as Susan Gates, and observed them both in a car headed in the direction of Chicago. The Court concluded that the verification of most of the information contained in the letter gave the police sufficient confidence that the rest of the information in the letter was reliable and therefore gave them probable cause to search the Gates' car and home. However, as Justice Stevens pointed out in his dissent, all of the information verified was innocent behavior, and one piece of information (that Sue would fly back to Chicago) was inaccurate.

In *White,* an anonymous tip indicated that Ms. White possessed cocaine in an attaché case. The informant said that White would get into a particular car (with a broken taillight) parked in the parking lot of a particular apartment complex at a specified time and would drive that car to Dobey's Motel with the cocaine in the car. The police observed a woman (without an attaché case) get into the car described in the tip at the time predicted and drive in the direction of Dobey's Motel. The Court held that the verification of this information gave the police reasonable suspicion to stop White. Although the Court emphasized that the information that the police verified was predictive in nature, as in *Gates* the information verified was all innocent, and, unlike in *Gates,* this information was the kind that many people who knew Ms. White could easily have known. For example, it may have been that Ms. White worked at Dobey's Motel, or somewhere nearby, and went to work every day by the described route at the time predicted by the informant.

As with the issue of what constitutes a search, the post-Warren Court has again decided a very recent case demonstrating at least some willingness to draw some lines for the police. In *Florida v. J.L.* (2000), the police received an anonymous report that a young, black male in a plaid shirt on a specified street corner was carrying an illegal gun. When the police went to the street corner specified, they observed three young, black males standing together, one of whom was wearing a plaid shirt. A unanimous Court ruled that this information did not provide the police reasonable suspicion to stop and frisk the young man. The Court compared the facts in this case with those in *White,* noted that the Court had characterized *White* as a close case, and indicated that the police had less suspicion in this case than in *White.*

Searches Incident to Arrest and Pretext Arrests

The language of the Fourth Amendment prohibits unreasonable searches and seizures (the "reasonableness clause") and requires that warrants be issued only when probable cause exists (the "warrant clause"). The amendment does not specify when the police need a warrant before making a search or seizure. Historically, the Supreme Court has adhered to the principle that a warrant requirement is implicit in the Fourth Amendment, stressing the amendment's emphasis on the warrant clause.[1] The next several sections deal with the post-Warren Court's treatment of a number of the exceptions to the warrant requirement.

In *Chimel v. California,* the Warren Court held that a warrantless search incident to an arrest may extend no further than a search of the person arrested and the area within his immediate control (where he could reach a weapon or evidence). *Chimel* overturned a 1950 case (*U.S. v. Rabinowitz*) that had permitted the police to search the entire office where the defendant had been arrested and had led to a common police practice of searching, without a warrant, the entire premises where an arrest took place. In *Chimel* itself, for example, the police had searched a three-bedroom house without a warrant after arresting Chimel in the house.

When the post-Warren Court applied this new "arm span" rule to automobiles, it adopted an approach that seems inconsistent with the spirit and intent of *Chimel.* The Court held that, when the police conduct a search incident to an arrest that occurs in an automobile, the police may search the entire passenger compartment of the vehicle (*New York v. Belton,* 1981). The Court indicated that to adhere to a strict "arm span" approach where cars are involved would require the police to make too many difficult judgments as to which portions of the car are within the immediate control of the person arrested. Thus, there is a need to provide the police a "bright line rule" to follow.

Of course, this rule gives the police broad authority to search a vehicle when a person in the vehicle is arrested. The search incident to arrest requires no reason to think that the person arrested is armed or has evidence of a crime within his reach (*U.S. v. Robinson,* 1973)—only the existence of a custodial arrest. Because the search is for weapons or evidence of *any crime* (including possession of drugs), it can be very extensive in its scope (although, of course, it may not include the trunk or the engine compartment). What is more, in spite of the fact that the purpose for the "search incident to arrest" exception to the warrant requirement is to protect the arresting officer and to protect against the destruction of evidence, in the *Belton* case itself the Court permitted a warrantless search of the passenger compartment, even though at the time of the search Belton was outside the car and in handcuffs (and seemingly incapable of obtaining a weapon or evidence from the vehicle). Thus, the post-Warren Court has been quite generous to the police not only as to the scope of the search that may be conducted incident to an arrest at a car but also as to the circumstances under which it has permitted the search to be conducted.

In part because of this broad authority to search a vehicle incident to arrest, questions arose as to the authority of the police to time an arrest (or a Terry stop) so that it occurs at a car (often referred to as a "pretext arrest"), thus providing the police an opportunity to search the vehicle (or at least to look inside it). In *Whren v. U.S.* (1996), the post-Warren Court concluded (unanimously) that the subjective motivations of an officer in stopping or arresting someone are simply irrelevant, thereby condoning pretext arrests.[2] The only constitutional issue in such cases, the Court found, is whether there is a lawful, objective basis for the stop or arrest.

The defendant in *Whren* argued that a stop or arrest should be found to be pretextual if it deviates from normal police action. He contended that, without such a rule, the frequency with which traffic laws are technically violated is so great that the police can eventually stop anyone if they follow the person long enough. Without taking issue with the validity of this point, Justice Scalia responded that "we are aware of no principle that would allow us to decide at what point a code of law becomes so expansive and so commonly violated that infraction itself can no longer be the ordinary measure of the lawfulness of enforcement. And even if we could identify such exorbitant codes, we do not know by what standard (or what right) we would decide, as petitioners would have us do, which particular provisions are sufficiently important to merit enforcement" (*Whren v. U.S.*, 1996, pp. 818–819).

The post-Warren Court did recently hold that the police may not search a person incident to issuance of a citation (*Knowles v. Iowa*, 1998). The Court indicated that the concerns that justify warrantless searches when custodial arrests are made—removal of weapons and securing of evidence—are absent in cases where an officer issues a citation. However, the Court has never ruled on the issue of whether the Fourth Amendment permits custodial arrests for minor offenses. Justice Stewart suggested such a limitation in his concurring opinion in *U.S. v. Robinson*. It appears that this is the only practical way to establish meaningful limits on the ability of the police to stop persons into whose cars they want to look. Even this limitation would only prevent the police from *searching* a car that had been stopped for a minor offense (because making a custodial arrest for the offense would then be unconstitutional). The police would still not be prevented from making the stop for the purpose of looking into the car from outside it.

There is one other case (in addition to *Knowles*) in which the post-Warren Court has imposed a notable restriction on the ability of the police to conduct warrantless searches incident to arrest. In *Maryland v. Buie* (1990), the Court ruled on the authority of the police to make a protective sweep of a house in which they have made an arrest to ensure that there are no other persons in the house who might pose a danger to them. The Court held that the police may "look in closets and other spaces immediately adjoining the place of arrest from which an attack could be immediately launched" (*Maryland v. Buie*, p. 334) for persons who might be a threat to them. However, the police may not sweep beyond those areas "immediately adjoining the place of arrest" unless they have reasonable suspicion to think that they will find someone there.

Ironically, this may be one instance where the post-Warren Court has actually been more protective of the individual than prudence demands. A protective sweep is a very unintrusive procedure. Because it is limited to a quick inspection of places where a person can hide, it should be possible to complete the sweep in a matter of minutes, even in a large house. On the other hand, the danger to the police in such a situation is substantial. The police will often be unaware that there are other people in the home. Furthermore, it will not be unusual for friends or relatives of a person being arrested, who were not involved in the crime that is the basis for the arrest, to attempt to thwart the efforts of the police. Given the uncertainty of such a threat and the minimal intrusion involved in a protective sweep, the police should be permitted to sweep an entire home in which they have made an arrest, regardless of the likelihood that anyone will be found.

Buie demonstrates an important feature of the post-Warren Court Fourth Amendment jurisprudence. While the Court has been very deferential to the police, it also has been very protective of the privacy of the home. For example, in *U.S. v. Watson* (1976), the post-Warren Court held that the police do not need an arrest warrant to arrest a person in public, even if they have plenty of time to obtain one. However, the Court created an exception to this rule in *Payton v. New York* (1980) when it held that, in the absence of consent or of some emergency, the police need an arrest warrant to enter a home to make the arrest.

The post-Warren Court's protective concern for the home is also evident in two "knock and announce" cases decided in the mid-1990s. For years it had been assumed that the Fourth Amendment requires that the police knock and announce their purpose before entering a home to execute a search or arrest warrant, but the Court had never said so definitively. In *Wilson v. Arkansas* (1995), the Court unanimously affirmed this rule, although it indicated that no-knock entries are justified when the police have reason to believe that knocking and announcing will result in the destruction of evidence, the escape of a suspect, or the infliction of harm on the officers. Two years later, in *Richards v. Wisconsin* (1997), the Court held that the police only need reasonable suspicion (rather than probable cause) to believe that one of these exigencies is present, but in the same case the Court held that this finding of reasonable suspicion must be individualized in each case. In so holding, the Court rejected the rule approved by the Wisconsin Supreme Court that permitted the police to make no-knock entries in all felony drug cases.

Motor Vehicle Searches

In 1925, the Supreme Court permitted a warrantless search of a car (*Carroll v. U.S.*). Because the driver of the car in *Carroll* had not been arrested, it was thought for some time that this case represented a special exigent circumstances case. The Court has long recognized that warrants are unnecessary when some emergency justifies dispensing with a warrant. The most common emergency is the likelihood of destruction of evidence if the police wait to obtain a warrant before searching. Thus, in *Carroll,* if the police had obtained a warrant before searching, Carroll would probably have driven the car away while the police were getting their warrant.

In *Chambers v. Maroney* (1970), the Transition Court made it clear that *Carroll* had not simply created a special exigent circumstance. In *Chambers,* the police had seized the defendant's car and had it in their custody at the police station (with the defendant also in custody) when they searched the car without a warrant. Thus, any exigency had been eliminated, and there was no reason why delaying the search until a warrant had been obtained would have caused the police any harm. Nevertheless, the Court upheld the warrantless search, indicating that, once the car was in the possession of the police, there was little difference between searching the car without a warrant and immobilizing it until a warrant could be obtained.

The next year, the Transition Court disallowed a warrantless automobile search in *Coolidge v. New Hampshire* (1971). In that case, the police had searched Coolidge's car with a search warrant that the Court ruled had been improperly issued because it had not been issued by a neutral and detached magistrate. Thus, the prosecution needed to justify the search of the car under one of the exceptions to the warrant requirement. However, the Court declined to apply the motor vehicle exception because the police had probable cause to search the vehicle for days prior to the search.

Coolidge seemed to suggest that, if the police have a clear opportunity to obtain a warrant before searching a motor vehicle, they need the warrant. It was difficult to know whether this was really what the Court meant to say, because it decided so many other issues in *Coolidge,* there were so many separate opinions written by concurring Justices, and the "clear opportunity" holding seemed counter to motor vehicle exception cases decided before and after *Coolidge.*

In *Pennsylvania v. Labron* (1996), the post-Warren Court seems to have virtually overturned *Coolidge,* in effect, by upholding two warrantless searches of vehicles in situations where the police had time to obtain warrants before searching. In so holding, the Court indicated that "if a car is readily mobile and probable cause exists to believe it contains contraband, the Fourth Amendment . . . permits police to search the vehicle without more"[3] (*Pennsylvania v. Labron,* p. 940). Thus, if the police have probable cause to think that contraband or evidence is in a motor vehicle, they will nearly always be able to search the vehicle without a warrant.

The post-Warren Court has also broadened the motor vehicle exception by holding that, while conducting such a search, the police may look in closed containers found in the vehicle (*U.S. v. Ross,* 1982). This rule applies even if the police have an opportunity to search the container when it is not in the vehicle but wait instead until it is placed in a vehicle (*California v. Acevedo,* 1991). The rule also applies to containers that belong to passengers in the vehicle and not to the driver, even though the driver is the suspect and the person whose circumstances have provided probable cause to search the vehicle (*Wyoming v. Houghton,* 1999).

As these cases demonstrate, the post-Warren Court's approach to motor vehicles is much different from its approach to homes. While the Court (as discussed earlier) has demonstrated considerable sensitivity to the special privacy concerns associated with the home, it has recognized very little privacy associated with motor vehicles. This can be seen in the cases just discussed and in the *Belton* case that was discussed earlier in the section on searches incident to arrest. It is also evident in *Michigan v. Long* (1983). In that case, the Court held that, if the police lawfully make a Terry stop of someone in a motor vehicle (or someone who was just in a motor vehicle) and have reasonable suspicion to think that that person is armed, they may "frisk" the entire passenger compartment of the vehicle. The scope of this search differs from a Belton search (a search of the passenger compartment of a vehicle for weapons or evidence of a crime, incident to an arrest of an occupant of the vehicle) only in that in the Long search the police may look inside the vehicle only in places where they could reasonably expect to find a weapon. Given the fact that a pocket knife is a weapon, this limitation does not do much to distinguish the Belton and Long motor vehicle searches.

The Stop and Frisk Exception

In *Terry v. Ohio,* the Warren Court recognized a new exception to the warrant requirement—the stop-and-frisk exception. The Court held that, if the police have reasonable suspicion to think that criminal activity is afoot, they may briefly detain the persons reasonably thought to be involved in the activity. If they have reasonable suspicion to think that the person detained is armed and dangerous, they may frisk the person (limited to a patdown of the outer clothing). The post-Warren Court has elaborated on this exception in at least three ways that have been helpful to law enforcement: in its application of the reasonable suspicion standard, in its definition of what is a stop, and in its treatment of how long a stop may last.

The post-Warren Court has not provided the police a good definition of reasonable suspicion. This is not surprising, given the difficulty of the task and given that neither the post-Warren Court nor previous Courts have provided a good definition of probable cause either. Without a good definition, cases applying the standard become of critical importance as a source of guidance. The post-Warren Court has been willing to find an absence of reasonable suspicion on occasion. The Court found that there was no reasonable suspicion to stop a person whom the police had seen walking away from another person in an alley in a high crime neighborhood (*Brown v. Texas,* 1979). It also found no basis for stopping a person who had gotten off a plane from a drug source city at a time when law enforcement activity in the airport was minimal, who had no luggage other than a shoulder bag, who appeared to be trying to conceal that he was traveling with someone else, and who often looked back at that person (*Reid v. Georgia,* 1980).

However, the post-Warren Court has also found the existence of reasonable suspicion under circumstances where the level of suspicion was quite low. For instance, it permitted a Terry stop in an airport of a pale, casually dressed, young man arriving from a drug source city, carrying heavy luggage, who appeared to be nervous, had paid for his ticket with cash, and had written only his name and destination on the baggage identification tag (*Florida v. Royer,* 1983). It also found reasonable suspicion in another airport stop where the person stopped had purchased two round-trip tickets from Honolulu to Miami with $2,100 in cash, intended to be in Miami less than 48 hours, and gave the airlines a name that was different from the name under which his phone number was listed (*U.S. v. Sokolow,* 1989).

In the most recent, and perhaps most questionable, reasonable suspicion case, the Court found reasonable suspicion to stop a person who was in a high crime area and had run from the police (the Court referred to it as "headlong flight") when he saw them coming toward him (*Illinois v. Wardlow,* 2000). Although the Court had previously suggested that presence in a high crime area was a factor that could be considered in determining whether reasonable suspicion (and presumably, then, probable cause as well) exists, it had never upheld a case in which that had been a factor. Although on a purely logical basis this approach may have some appeal, the problem is that it means that people who live in high crime neighborhoods are more subject to being stopped by the police than people who do not live in such neighborhoods. We must add to this concern, if we will be honest, a racial element, because we know that African-Americans (and many other ethnic minority groups as well) are more likely to live in high crime areas than white people.

The post-Warren Court has also defined a Terry stop in a questionable manner. The Court has held that a person is not stopped simply because the police have made it clear to the person that they expect him to remain where he is. In *California v. Hodari D.* (1991), the Court held that a person has not been stopped unless he or she submits to a show of authority by the police or has been physically restrained by the police. Thus, even though the police may lack reasonable suspicion to stop someone, if that person discards evidence or does something incriminating after the police have *attempted* to stop the person but before the person submits to police authority or is physically restrained, the evidence can be used by the government.

A Terry stop is a kind of seizure, as that term is used in the Fourth Amendment. Until 1991, the Court had defined seizure as a situation created by the police in which a reasonable person would not feel free to leave (*U.S. v. Mendenhall,* 1980). In *Florida v. Bostick* (1991), the Court clarified the definition somewhat by indicating that, in order to have a stop, it must be the *actions* of the police that make a person feel not free to leave. It refined the seizure definition so that it is now defined according to whether a reasonable person would feel "free to decline the officers' requests or otherwise terminate the encounter." Although the Court sent the case back to the lower court for reconsideration in light of the Court's clarification of the seizure definition, the Court also made it clear that Bostick was not necessarily stopped by the police just because he did not feel free to leave the bus that the police had boarded. The bus was making a brief layover, and Bostick may well have not felt free to leave the bus because he was afraid of missing the continuation of his bus's trip.

What this slightly (but significantly) new approach to defining a seizure overlooks is that, when the police selected layover buses to board, they knew full well that the passengers continuing on would be reluctant to get off the bus to avoid the police. They also knew that being reluctant or unable to get off the bus would subject a passenger to more pressure from the police, who were using this occasion to ask passengers for consent to search their carry-on luggage. Thus, the situation picked by the police in which to use this tactic should be considered part of their behavior.

A third troublesome stop issue addressed by the post-Warren Court concerns the question of how long a stop may last. At some point, if a person stopped is not allowed to leave, the stop becomes an arrest. Crossing this line between a stop and an arrest is significant for at least two reasons. First, an arrest requires probable cause. Thus, if the stop becomes an arrest and the police still have only reasonable suspicion to justify the detention, any evidence obtained thereafter from the suspect will be inadmissible (*Florida v. Royer,* 1983). Second, the Court has indicated that Miranda warnings must be given to a suspect who is in custody (*Miranda v. Arizona,* 1966). A person is in custody if he or she has been arrested, but not if he or she has merely been stopped (*Berkemer v. McCarty,* 1984).

Initially, the post-Warren Court took a rather firm approach to this issue. In *Florida v. Royer* (1983), the Court indicated that a Terry stop could last "no longer than is necessary to effectuate the purpose of the stop" and held that the 15-minute detention of Royer in a large airport storage closet was too long to constitute a valid Terry stop. That same year, the Court held that a Terry stop had become an arrest because the suspect had been detained 90 minutes (*U.S. v. Place,* 1983).

Just two years later, the Court changed its approach significantly. In *U.S. v. Sharpe* (1985), the Court declined to impose any kind of strict time limit on how long a stop may last. Instead, the Court indicated that how long the police may detain someone short of arrest varies with the circumstances of each case. The detention appropriately remains a stop so long as the police have used due diligence to confirm or dispel their suspicions. This should be a much easier standard for the police to satisfy than the no-longer-than-necessary standard established (temporarily) by *Royer.*

Although the post-Warren Court adopted very favorable positions for law enforcement in the three areas just discussed, there are two important cases relating to stop-and-frisks where the post-Warren Court came down on the side of protecting individuals. In *Ybarra v. Illinois* (1979), the Court held that the police could not frisk the patrons of a tavern that the police were about to search with a warrant. The Court indicated that the arguable need for the searching officers to ensure their safety by determining whether any of the patrons in the dimly lit bar were armed was insufficient to justify dispensing with individualized suspicion as to whether any of the patrons were armed.

In *Chicago v. Morales* (1999), the Court dealt with Chicago's attempt to gain some control on drug dealing through an anti-loitering statute. The statute in question provided that "whenever a police officer observes a person whom he reasonably believes to be a criminal street gang member loitering in any public place with one or more other persons, he shall order all such persons to disperse and remove themselves from the area. Any person who does not promptly obey such an order is in violation of this section." The statute defined loitering as "remain[ing] in any one place with no apparent purpose" (*Chicago v. Morales,* p. 47).

The Court had struck down previous loitering statutes because they were so vague that they violated due process of law (*Kolender v. Lawson,* 1983; *Papachristou v. City of Jacksonville,* 1972). The government tried to distinguish those cases on the basis that the Chicago ordinance only permitted the arrest of persons who refused to follow the dispersal order and did not permit the arrest of every person deemed by the police to be loitering. The Court found that this ordinance still gave the police too much discretion to decide who, among those persons who refused to disperse, had "no apparent reason" for refusing.

Consent Searches

A very common warrantless search is the consent search. Consent searches are valid so long as the consent was given voluntarily. The Transition Court held that the consent can be voluntary even if the person giving the consent is unaware that he or she has a right not to consent (*Schneckloth v. Bustamonte,* 1973).

An issue of great significance concerning consent searches is the question of when a third party (someone other than the suspect) may consent to a search of premises in which the suspect has a privacy interest. The Transition Court took the approach that a person who has "common authority" over premises possesses the power to consent to a search of the premises (*U.S. v. Matlock,* 1974). This approach is quite reasonable. It is grounded on the notion that a person who mutually uses property with another person necessarily gives up much of his or her privacy in those premises and knows that the other person may invite others onto the premises as well.

In *Illinois v. Rodriquez* (1990), the Court took this reasoning one step further. In that case, the police acted with the consent of a Gail Fischer, who reasonably appeared to them to have common authority over the premises searched but in actuality no longer exercised control over them. Ms. Fischer had referred to the searched premises as "our" apartment and indicated that she had clothes and furniture there. She failed to tell the police, however, that she had moved out of the apartment nearly a month previously and never went back to the apartment except when the defendant was there.

The Court upheld the search on the basis that it reasonably appeared to the police that Ms. Fischer had common authority over the apartment. By shifting the analysis from common authority to apparent authority, the Court abandoned the "assumption of risk" reasoning that undergirded its decision in *Matlock.* One can assume the risk that a person with whom premises are shared will bring others there, but it is disingenuous to reason that, when a person shares premises with another, he or she assumes the risk that, if the sharing is discontinued, the person who used to have access to the premises will mislead others into thinking that he or she still does.

More troubling, though, is the effect of the apparent authority approach on police thinking. When common authority was the key, the police were well advised to inquire into the nature of the consenting party's status with respect to the premises to be searched, because if their judgment about common authority was wrong they could not use any evidence they discovered. Now that apparent authority is the key, however, the thinking is almost the opposite. Once the police know enough about the consenting party's status to permit them to conclude reasonably that he or she has common authority over the premises to be searched, they are well advised to make no further inquiries; if they do, they may discover something that will make it clear that they cannot act on this consent.

Regulatory Searches and Seizures

A relatively recent exception to the warrant requirement recognized by the Supreme Court is for regulatory searches and seizures. This is perhaps the most controversial exception discussed in this article. An initial difficulty is defining what constitutes a regulatory search or seizure. The exception has been applied to a wide variety of governmental conduct that involves enforcement of government regulations but does not involve what might be characterized as "police work" or traditional law enforcement. Whitebread and Slobogin have suggested that regulatory searches and seizures "share two features: (1) their predominant objective is to procure evidence for 'administrative' purposes that at most can result in a misdemeanor conviction (although sometimes evidence of serious crime is discovered in plain view during such searches); and (2) they are usually conducted by officials other than the police" (Whitebread & Slobogin, 2000, p. 291). In more recent cases, the Court has sometimes stressed that these cases involve "special needs" of the government that extend "beyond the normal need for law enforcement," although the Court has not been clear as to what it means by "special needs" (*New Jersey v. T.L.O.,* 1985, p. 351).

Unfortunately, the Court has not developed a consistent rationale that permits one to make a coherent whole of these cases, and not all cases that fall within this exception to the warrant requirement satisfy all of the criteria just mentioned. For example, many authors of criminal procedure textbooks include border searches within the exception, but often the border search is for drugs. If the search turns up drugs, the ensuing prosecution is not likely to be for a misdemeanor. What is more, the "predominant objective" of such searches is often *not* to obtain evidence for administrative purposes. In addition, many of the opinions in these cases make no mention of "special needs beyond the normal need for law enforcement."

A second difficulty is trying to make meaningful generalizations about the exception. The exception did not really exist until 1967, when the Warren Court decided *Camara v. Municipal Court.* In that case, the Court held that the Fourth Amendment applies to housing inspections, that a housing inspector needs a search warrant to make a non-emergency inspection of a house, and that such an administrative search warrant may be issued without probable cause to think that any particular violations will be found in the place inspected. In coming to these conclusions, the Court determined that administrative searches need only be reasonable in order to be constitutional. Most importantly, the Court indicated that, in making this reasonableness determination, a balancing approach is to be utilized. The importance of and need for the governmental action is to be weighed or balanced against the degree of intrusiveness that the action entails.

It is the application of this balancing approach that makes generalization about this warrant exception so difficult. In effect it makes every type of administrative inspection, search, or seizure a warrant exception of its own. With each type of governmental action, it must be determined whether a warrant is required and what level of suspicion (probable cause, reasonable suspicion, or something else), if any, is necessary before the action can be taken.

Although the Warren Court created this exception to the warrant requirement, its present scope is almost wholly a product of the post-Warren Court. In the chapter on regulatory searches and seizures in Whitebread and Slobogin's thorough treatment of criminal procedure (2000), 3 cases from the Transition Court are cited; 27 cases from the post-Warren Court are cited. Our discussion will be limited to five types of administrative actions (involving 8 of the 27 cases) that were selected as illustrative of the type of analysis employed by the Court and the degree of intrusiveness that the Court has condoned.

The first type of administrative action dealt with a Terry stop at the border of the United States (*U.S. v. Montoya de Hernandez,* 1985). The Court has indicated that persons and effects entering the United States at the borders may be searched thoroughly without either a warrant or suspicion. In *Montoya de Hernandez,* customs officials had reasonable suspicion to think that the defendant, who had just arrived in this country from Colombia, was a balloon swallower—a person who was attempting to smuggle drugs that had been placed in balloons and then swallowed just before departing for this country. When the defendant refused to submit to an X-ray examination that could have confirmed or dispelled the suspicions of the customs officials, she was detained for 16 hours awaiting "the call of nature." After growing impatient with the failure of the call to arrive, customs officials obtained a warrant that permitted them to "search" the defendant's alimentary canal. That search discovered 88 balloons of cocaine.

The post-Warren Court upheld this lengthy detention. Although the Court stressed that the defendant could have shortened the detention by agreeing to the X-ray examination, it seems highly unlikely that the Court would have condoned such a long detention had it not occurred at the border.

In the next type of administrative action, customs officials boarded a ship in United States territorial waters, ostensibly for the purpose of checking to see whether the vessel was carrying all of the documents that vessels in U.S. waters are required to carry by federal law (*U.S. v. Villamonte-Marquez,* 1983). Because customs officials brought along an ordinary police officer, it appeared that there was other business on their agenda as well. However, these officials had no particular reason to suspect the vessel of criminal activity. In the course of their search, they discovered marijuana on the vessel. The Court held that this warrantless, suspicionless boarding was constitutional because the government need (to ensure compliance with the complicated document requirements, which serve a variety of important public purposes) was great and the intrusion (a common and brief detention lasting no longer than necessary to inspect the documents) was small.

It is interesting to note that in its reasoning in support of this holding the Court stressed the difficulty of enforcing the documentation requirements for all vessels transiting the unconfined coastal waters of the United States, "particularly in waters where the need to deter or apprehend drug smugglers is great." Of course, this latter concern is not a "special need . . . beyond the normal need for law enforcement."

The third type of administrative action involved a search of a person on probation (*Griffin v. Wisconsin*, 1987). Griffin's probation officer searched his home without a warrant, looking for a weapon (which would have been a violation of his probation) based on a tip from an unidentified police officer that Griffin "had or might have guns" in his home. The Court indicated that this kind of search could be conducted without a warrant and on the basis of suspicion that is less than probable cause (although the Court was unclear as to just what the acceptable standard is). The Court again saw a special need—to respond quickly to possible violations of probation that would suggest a danger to the public from persons who have been convicted of a crime but permitted to serve a sentence short of incarceration. The intrusion was viewed as minimal, given the probationer's status as a convicted criminal who was permitted to be free as a result of the "grace" of the state.

The fourth type of administrative action was a search of a student by a public high school vice principal (*New Jersey v. T.L.O.*, 1985). The vice principal received a report from one of his teachers that T.L.O. had been discovered by the teacher smoking in a school rest room, a violation of school rules. The vice principal searched T.L.O.'s purse without a warrant and discovered evidence implicating the student in marijuana-dealing. The Court held that, although the vice principal's actions were subject to scrutiny under the Fourth Amendment, he needed neither a warrant nor probable cause to search T.L.O.'s purse. So long as the vice principal had "reasonable grounds" for concluding that evidence of a violation of law or school rules was contained in T.L.O.'s purse, the warrantless search of the purse was constitutional.

Again the Court balanced the government need against the intrusion. The Court viewed an efficient disciplinary system as essential to the special need of schools to maintain a proper educational environment. In this situation, the intrusiveness issue was examined a bit differently. So long as the intrusion is reasonable, in light of the student's age and sex and the nature of the infraction that was suspected, a student's interest in not being subjected to the intrusion is outweighed by the important government interest.

The last type of administrative action concerned drug testing of employees or students by government officials (*Chandler v. Miller*, 1997; *National Treasury Employees Union v. Von Raab*, 1989; *Skinner v. Railway Labor Executives' Association*, 1989; *Vernonia School District 47J v. Acton*, 1995). In three of these cases, the post-Warren Court upheld warrantless, suspicionless drug testing. In Skinner, the Court upheld the Federal Railroad Administration's testing of employees who had been involved in an accident or who were suspected of violating safety rules. The compelling government interest in avoiding future accidents outweighed the privacy interests of railroad employees, which were diminished by the fact that they could expect to be examined for their fitness to perform tasks that were directly related to the safety of passengers.

In *Von Raab*, the Court upheld U.S. Customs Service testing of employees who had applied for or were being promoted to positions that required the carrying of a gun, that were involved in drug enforcement, or that required access to classified material. The important government interest was in preventing impaired employees from using guns and ensuring that the drug enforcement program was not undermined by employees whose own drug use would make them unsympathetic to vigorous enforcement. On the other side of the ledger, employees working in these areas should expect that their fitness would be examined.

In *Acton*, the Court upheld testing of student athletes. School officials had been able to demonstrate that their schools were experiencing drug problems that negatively impacted the achievement of their educational goals and that student athletes were leaders in the local drug culture. The intrusion involved was viewed as minimal because the persons being tested were minors who were already subject to considerable control by school officials. In addition, the urine samples that were tested were obtained in locker rooms, where privacy expectations are greatly diminished.

Only in *Chandler* has the post-Warren Court struck down a drug testing program. In that case, the State of Georgia required all candidates for public office to pass a drug test in order to qualify for the office. The Court found this requirement unconstitutional because the state had not demonstrated a "concrete need" for it. The state conceded that there was no evidence of public officials in the state being impaired by drug usage.

These regulatory search and seizure cases demonstrate that if government officials can show a "special need . . . beyond the normal need for law enforcement" they stand a good chance of convincing the Court that warrant and probable cause requirements can be relaxed or even dispensed with altogether. It is also apparent that, although the special need is supposed to be separate from a law enforcement need, there will often be law enforcement implications to the regulatory search or seizure.

These cases (and others decided by the post-Warren Court that were not discussed here) also demonstrate that this exception to the warrant requirement has expanded in scope dramatically in the last 25 years. If the expansion continues, it could become so broad as to virtually swallow up the warrant requirement, replacing it, in effect, with a reasonableness standard. As alluded to in footnote 1, one way of interpreting the Fourth Amendment is to conclude that it simply requires reasonableness in the way searches and seizures are conducted (and does not establish a warrant requirement). However, if the Court decides to replace the present warrant requirement with a reasonableness standard, this change should occur directly and with full consideration of the implications of the change. The incremental expansion of the regulatory search exception to the warrant requirement has not included this kind of open and forthright discussion.

Conclusion

The cases discussed in this article demonstrate several important characteristics of the post-Warren Court's approach to the Fourth Amendment. First and foremost is the obvious conclusion that the post-Warren Court has been very pro-police in its approach. It has taken a rather narrow view of interpreting when police action intrudes upon a reasonable expectation of privacy. It has given the police considerable leeway in making probable cause and reasonable suspicion determinations. It has declined to explore an officer's motivations for a particular course of action so long as there is an objective basis for the officer's actions. It has removed virtually any requirement that the police seek judicial authorization to search a motor vehicle. It has removed any incentive for the police to inquire carefully about the status of a person who appears to have the authority to consent to a search of shared premises. And it has encouraged law enforcement and other government officials to look for special governmental needs that will justify dispensing with normal Fourth Amendment requirements.

A second trait of the post-Warren Court's Fourth Amendment decisions is that the Court has developed a body of conservative Fourth Amendment case law without overturning any of the controversial decisions of the Warren Court. The history of the Supreme Court's treatment of criminal procedure issues generally can be divided into four stages. The first stage, the period prior to 1960, can be referred to as the state law period. During this period, criminal procedure was largely a matter of state law. The protections extended to individuals in criminal matters by the Fourth, Fifth, Sixth, and Eighth Amendments applied only to the federal government and, therefore, only to federal criminal prosecutions. Because the overwhelming majority of criminal cases are prosecuted in state courts, the law of criminal procedure for most persons accused of criminal acts was to be found in state law.

The second stage is the decade of the 1960s. As we have seen, this period is sometimes referred to as the due process revolution. It witnessed the extension of most of the criminal rights contained in the Bill of Rights to the states through the incorporation of those rights into the due process clause of the Fourteenth Amendment. It was also characterized by the Court's interpretation of these rights in a way that was usually favorable to the accused.

The third stage is the transition period of 1970–1974. During this period, the personnel on the Court changed substantially. The new Justices, as a group, were more conservative than the Justices whom they replaced. Some criminal procedure cases during this period were decided in a way that would have been expected from the Warren Court. In other cases, the Court began to display a willingness to take a more pro-government stance.

The last (and current) stage can be called the retrenchment period. The tentative tilt to the right of the transition period became a consistent position. The Court has regularly (although certainly not always) decided criminal procedure issues in favor of the government. But, in doing so, it has not directly overturned the controversial decisions of the Warren Court (except *Aguilar v. Texas*). It has "retrenched" by limiting the reach and scope of those decisions in applying them to a variety of situations that the Warren Court did not have the opportunity to address. It is fair to say that these decisions are not faithful to the spirit and intent of the Warren Court decisions, but for the most part the movement away from the landmark decisions of the due process revolution has been incremental, in small steps, rather than through blockbuster decisions.

These periods are more apparent when all of the criminal procedure cases of the Supreme Court are examined, but the Fourth Amendment cases discussed in this article fit nicely into these periods.

A third characteristic of the post-Warren Court search and seizure cases is that they have often made seemingly minor changes or adjustments to Fourth Amendment jurisprudence, but those changes have sent a clear message that the restraints on the police are being relaxed and have given lower courts greater freedom to uphold police actions. For example, the shift from the two-pronged *Aguilar* approach to the totality-of-the-circumstances *Gates* approach was not a huge change in standards, but in making the change the Court stressed its concern about legal technicalities being applied by lower courts. In addition, totality-of-the-circumstances tests always turn in individual cases on the particular facts of those cases. This makes it quite easy for a lower court to distinguish a prior decision of an appellate court that had found against the police by indicating that the facts in the present case are different from the facts in the previous case in some significant way.

Another example is the Court's shift from the no-longer-than-necessary restriction on the length of Terry stops established in *Royer* to the due diligence approach of *Sharpe.* Again, this shift does not represent a great change in theory, but in practice it will be much easier for a court to explain why the actions of the police were diligent than it would be for the court to explain why an alternative action suggested by the defense that would have shortened the stop should not have been taken by the police.

The last trait of the post-Warren Court search and seizure cases is that they have been consistent in their overall posture. There are no areas of Fourth Amendment jurisprudence where a liberal surge of activity appears to be on the verge of breaking through. We have noted some very recent cases where the Court has imposed some limits on the police (*Bond v. U.S.; Chicago v. Morales; Florida v. J.L.; Knowles v. Iowa*). However, these were all instances where the authority of the police had been pushed to the extreme. Had the police won in these cases, many people would have been asking whether there were any constitutional limits left on what the police can do.

Nor does it appear that this pattern is likely to change any time soon. On Fourth Amendment issues, there is presently a relatively consistent conservative bloc of six Justices (Rehnquist, O'Connor, Scalia, Kennedy, Souter, and Thomas). Occasionally O'Connor, Kennedy, or Souter will shift to the liberal side on a particular issue, but it is rare for more than one of them to shift on the same issue. Of these six, only Chief Justice Rehnquist is over the age of 70. As it is common for Justices to remain on the Court well into their 70s and even 80s, it is unlikely that more than one of these six conservative Justices will leave the Court in the near future.

Even this possible loss to the conservative bloc is counterbalanced by the fact that one of the members of the more liberal or moderate bloc, Justice Stevens, is four years older than Chief Justice Rehnquist. Thus, if a Republican is elected President in 2000, it is conceivable that the Court could become even more conservative on Fourth Amendment matters before it becomes more moderate.

The last 25 years has witnessed a Supreme Court that views the law enforcement task as an important and difficult one. It does not view the Fourth Amendment as intended to embody rules that significantly impair the police in their efforts to ferret out and solve crimes. Prediction is always a risky business, but there is good reason to think that the trends of the post-Warren Court discussed in this article will continue for quite some time to come.

Notes

1. Over the years, there have been Justices who have disagreed with the conclusion that the Fourth Amendment creates a warrant requirement. These Justices have adhered to the principle that the Fourth Amendment only requires that searches be reasonable and that the presence or absence of a warrant is simply a factor to be considered in making the reasonableness determination. At least one set of commentators (Whitebread & Slobogin, 2000) believe that this reasonableness approach to the Fourth Amendment has "gained the ascendancy . . . in practice, if not in theory" (p. 138).

2. In a previous case (*Scott v. U.S.*, 1978), the post-Warren Court had permitted pretext searches. In a pretext search, the police search for Object A, for which they possess probable cause, hoping to find Object B, for which they do not possess probable cause.

3. It is possible to argue that *Coolidge* retains some limited vitality because the automobiles searched in *Labron* were on public property, whereas Coolidge's automobile was in his driveway. Thus, one could argue that the police need a warrant to search a motor vehicle when they have a clear opportunity to obtain the warrant *and* the vehicle is on private property (Whitebread & Slobogin, 2000, p. 199).

References

Aguilar v. Texas, 378 U.S. 108 (1964).
Alabama v. White, 496 U.S. 325 (1990).
Berkemer v. McCarty, 468 U.S. 420 (1984).
Bond v. U.S., 120 S.Ct. 1462 (2000).
Brown v. Texas, 443 U.S. 47 (1979).
California v. Acevedo, 500 U.S. 565 (1991).
California v. Ciraolo, 476 U.S. 227 (1986).
California v. Greenwood, 486 U.S. 35 (1988).
California v. Hodari D., 499 U.S. 621 (1991).
Camara v. Municipal Court, 387 U.S. 523 (1967).
Carroll v. U.S., 267 U.S. 132 (1925).
Chambers v. Maroney, 399 U.S. 42 (1970).
Chandler v. Miller, 520 U.S. 305 (1997).
Chicago v. Morales, 527 U.S. 41 (1999).
Chimel v. California, 395 U.S. 752 (1969).
Coolidge v. New Hampshire, 403 U.S. 443 (1971).
Dow Chemical Co. v. U.S., 476 U.S. 227 (1986).
Florida v. Bostick, 501 U.S. 429 (1991).
Florida v. J.L., 529 U.S. (2000).
Florida v. Riley, 488 U.S. 445 (1989).
Florida v. Royer, 460 U.S. 491 (1983).
Gideon v. Wainwright, 372 U.S. 335 (1963).
Griffin v. Wisconsin, 483 U.S. 868 (1987).
Hall, K. (1992). *The Oxford companion to the Supreme Court of the United States.* New York, NY: Oxford University Press.
Illinois v. Gates, 462 U.S. 213 (1983).
Illinois v. Rodriguez, 497 U.S. 177 (1990).
Illinois v. Wardlow, 528 U.S. (2000).
Katz v. U.S., 389 U.S. 347 (1967).
Knowles v. Iowa, 525 U.S. 113 (1998).
Kolender v. Lawson, 461 U.S. 352 (1983).
Mapp v. Ohio, 367 U.S. 643 (1961).
Maryland v. Buie, 494 U.S. 325 (1990).
Michigan v. Long, 463 U.S. 1032 (1983).
Miranda v. Arizona, 384 U.S. 436 (1966).
National Treasury Employees Union v. Von Raab, 489 U.S. 656 (1989).
New Jersey v. T.L.O., 469 U.S. 325 (1985).
New York v. Belton, 453 U.S. 454 (1981).
Oliver v. U.S., 466 U.S. 170 (1984).
Papachristou v. City of Jacksonville, 405 U.S. 156 (1972).
Payton v. New York, 445 U.S. 573 (1980).
Pennsylvania v. Labron, 518 U.S. 938 (1996).
Reid v. Georgia, 448 U.S. 438 (1980).
Richards v. Wisconsin, 520 U.S. 385 (1997).
Schneckloth v. Bustamonte, 412 U.S. 218 (1973).
Scott v. U.S., 436 U.S. 128 (1978).
Sibron v. New York, 392 U.S. 40 (1968).
Skinner v. Railway Labor Executives' Association, 489 U.S. 602 (1989).
Smith v. Maryland, 442 U.S. 735 (1979).
Terry v. Ohio, 392 U.S. 1 (1968).
U.S. v. Dunn, 480 U.S. 294 (1987).
U.S. v. Karo, 468 U.S. 705 (1984).
U.S. v. Knotts, 460 U.S. 276 (1983).
U.S. v. Leon, 468 U.S. 397 (1984).
U.S. v. Matlock, 415 U.S. 164 (1974).
U.S. v. Mendenhall, 446 U.S. 544 (1980).
U.S. v. Miller, 425 U.S. 435 (1976).
U.S. v. Montoya de Hernandez, 473 U.S. 531 (1985).
U.S. v. Place, 462 U.S. 696 (1983).
U.S. v. Rabinowitz, 339 U.S. 56 (1950).
U.S. v. Robinson, 414 U.S. 218 (1973).
U.S. v. Ross, 456 U.S. 798 (1982).
U.S. v. Sharpe, 470 U.S. 675 (1985).
U.S. v. Sokolow, 490 U.S. 1 (1989).

U.S. v. Villamonte-Marquez, 462 U.S. 579 (1983).

U.S. v. Watson, 423 U.S. 411 (1976).

Vernonia School District 47J v. Acton, 515 U.S. 646 (1995).

Warden v. Hayden, 387 U.S. 294 (1967).

Whitebread, C., & Slobogin, C. (2000). *Criminal procedure: An analysis of cases and concepts.* New York, NY: Foundation Press.

Whren v. U.S., 517 U.S. 806 (1996).

Wilson v. Arkansas, 514 U.S. 927 (1995).

Wolf v. Colorado, 338 U.S. 25 (1949).

Wyoming v. Houghton, 526 U.S. 295 (1999).

Ybarra v. Illinois, 444 U.S. 85 (1979).

Unit I

Discussion Questions

1. What is justice? What elements must be in place for a society to dispense absolute justice?

2. We read in Plato's *Republic* of Socrates considering whether justice is "nothing else than the interest of the stronger." Do you support this position? Why or why not?

3. Why does the crime rate appear to be dropping? Do you agree with the explanations outlined by Ouimet? Why or why not? What other factors might be contributing to the apparent reduction in crime?

4. Hoskins presents data suggesting that an armed America is a less safe America. Data aside, do you agree with his findings?

5. Would you support or oppose handgun control legislation? Why or why not?

6. Why do young people carry guns? Do you carry a handgun? Why or why not? Should programs be implemented to get guns out of the hands of young people? If so, describe how such a program would work.

7. Wiley's research clearly indicates that blacks and whites view the justice system very differently. What are those differences and what accounts for them? How do your perspectives regarding the "color of justice" compare to those of Wiley's respondents?

8. Do you feel that science has confirmed genetic links to crime and violence? Support your position by referring to scientific evaluations that have examined this issue.

9. Review the biological, sociological, and psychological causes of violence. Which theory seems to be the most powerful explanation to you? Why?

10. Describe the frustration you would feel were you to be wrongfully charged with and convicted of a felony. What course of action would you undertake to remedy the error? What obstacles would you likely face?

11. Call notes that the Supreme Court has moved to a propolice position on Fourth Amendment issues and has developed a rather conservative body of Fourth Amendment case law. Do you agree with the Court's position? Why or why not?

12. What specific Fourth Amendment Supreme Court case rulings do you agree and disagree with? How would you have ruled differently?

13. What new programs would you propose as possible crime prevention programs for the twenty-first century?

14. Design a research evaluation effort to determine whether the new crime prevention programs you propose would really prevent or reduce crime. ✦

Unit II

American Law Enforcement

Some of the latest estimates indicate that there are roughly 830,000 sworn law enforcement personnel and 300,000 civilians working in some 18,000 law enforcement agencies in this country. Recent federal incentives urging local agencies to expand their community policing efforts will push the numbers upward in coming years.

City police forces are perhaps the most visible law enforcement agencies. New York City boasts the largest city police force in the United States with nearly 40,000 officers. Sheriffs' departments function at the county level, with highway patrols and state bureaus of investigation serving state law enforcement needs. There are also approximately seventy federal agencies with law enforcement functions, the most visible of which are perhaps the Bureau of Alcohol, Tobacco and Firearms, the U.S. Secret Service, the Federal Bureau of Investigation, and the Drug Enforcement Administration. Law enforcement expenditures are now approaching $50 billion per year.

Public law enforcement is being increasingly augmented by a growing private sector. Private security currently employs more than twice as many officers and spends nearly twice as much money as does public law enforcement. This trend will surely continue well into the twenty-first century.

A Brief History

Law enforcement has not always been such a major industry in this country. Consider the following excerpt taken from a report prepared by the Bureau of Justice Statistics (1988, 63–65):

> Law enforcement evolved throughout U.S. history. In colonial times law was enforced by constables and a night watch made up of citizens who took turns watching for fires and unruly persons. By the beginning of the nineteenth century, most citizens who could afford it paid for someone else to take their watch.
>
> The first publicly supported, centralized, consolidated police organization in the United States was established in New York in 1844. It was modeled after the London Metropolitan Police created in 1829 by Sir Robert Peel. Other major American cities adopted the same system soon after. Today, more than 90% of all municipalities with a population of 2,500 or more have their own police forces.
>
> Rural policing in the United States developed from the functions of sheriffs. The office of sheriff, a direct import from seventeenth-century England, was used primarily in the rural colonies of the South. As elected county officials, sheriffs had detention and political functions along with law enforcement responsibilities.
>
> Originally responsible for large, sparsely populated areas, many sheriffs were faced with big-city law enforcement problems because of urban growth after World War II. In some

counties the sheriff's office has retained its detention functions, but law enforcement functions are handled by county police departments. In other counties the sheriff's office resembles many big-city police departments. There are more than 3,000 sheriff's departments in the United States today.

Traditionally, the police function has been dominated by local governments.

- In 1986 there were 11,743 municipal, 79 county, and 1,819 township general purpose police agencies in the United States. Together, they employ 533,247 full-time equivalent employees.

- Other state and local law enforcement groups include state agencies such as the 51 state police and highway patrols and some 965 special police agencies including park rangers, harbor police, transit police, and campus security forces. Along with their independent responsibilities, these agencies often support local law enforcement on technical matters such as forensics and identification.

- The Federal Government employs 8% of all law enforcement personnel. Among the more than 50 Federal law enforcement agencies are the Federal Bureau of Investigation (FBI), the Drug Enforcement Administration (DEA), the Bureau of Alcohol, Tobacco, and Firearms (ATF), the Secret Service, and the Postal Inspection Service.

Urbanization and social change have had great impact on policing.

- The dramatic shift in population to urban areas since World War II has had great impact on the demand for police service. The percentage of police officers employed in urban areas rose from 68% in 1977 to 82% in 1982.

- During the recent period of increasing concern about employment discrimination against women and minorities, mostly white, male police departments have added women and minorities to their ranks. The proportion of sworn officers who were women went from 2% in 1971 to almost 7% in 1985. The proportion of police officers and detectives who were black went from 9% in 1983 to 12% in 1985.

Professionalism and advanced technology have also transformed policing in the past half century.

- In 1982, 79% of police officers in a sample survey conducted by the FBI reported that they had done some college work. 23% of the respondents had received baccalaureate degrees (LeDoux and Tully 1982). Basic and in-service training is now regarded as indispensable. More than 670 training academies now exist in the United States (O'Leary and Titus 1986).

- In 1964 only one major police department was using automated data processing (Colton 1972). More recent surveys suggest that virtually all jurisdictions of 50,000 or more population were using computers by 1981 (PERF 1982).

- In 1922 less than 1,000 patrol cars were in use in the entire country (Locke 1982). At that time, only one city had radio-equipped cars. Today, the patrol car has almost replaced the "beat cop" and police communications enable the patrol officer to have access to citizen calls for service as well as data banks on a variety of critical information, including outstanding warrants and stolen property.

There is no standard level of police protection. Police employment in the United States ranges from 0 to 55 police per 1,000 residents; however, three-quarters of all counties have between 1 and 3 officers per 1,000 residents. The number of officers per 100 square miles ranges from 0 in some places in Alaska, where State police and Federal authorities enforce the law, to 8,667 in the boroughs of New York City. Yet, some counties that greatly differ in population and land area have similar levels of police protection. For example, San Diego county, with a population of more than 1.8 million in 1980, and Knox County, Tennessee (containing the city of Knoxville), with a population of over 300,000 both have about 2 officers per 1,000 residents.

No single factor determines the police strength of a given area. Decisions on the size of a police force may be determined by a variety of factors, including the budgetary constraints of a city or county.

- Many people believe that increased police employment will result in higher levels of protection and will lead to reductions in crime. Yet, researchers disagree about whether there is a relationship between either the number of police officers on duty and the rate at which crime occurs or between crime rates and budget allocations for law enforcement. Some contend that if a relationship is to be found between crime rates and police, it may be associated more with the tactics of law enforcement officers than with their numbers (Loftin and McDowell 1982).

- The rate of law enforcement officers per capita shows little relationship to county population. The analysis of per capita police rates per county shows that the size of the law enforcement contingent is influenced more by such special factors as the presence of universities and large numbers of commuters or tourists than by the size of the resident population.

- The area of a county also shows little or no relationship to either police employment levels or the number of police per square mile. Some studies have shown that the strength of the police force is lessened as the enforcement area in square miles goes up (Kakalik and Widhorn 1971, 90).

- One factor that appears to contribute to police strength is density. As the number of residents per square mile increases, there is likely to be an increase in the number of police per capita.

Role and Function

There has been a wide-ranging debate as to the proper role of law enforcement in this country. The debate is often blurred due to misconceptions held by the public and many elected officials regarding the reality of police work. Perhaps the greatest barrier in understanding American police, as Walker (1992, 61–62) has indicated, is their mythical, entertainment industry–enhanced image as *proactive* crimefighters. Contrary to the Hollywood image, time-and-motion studies clearly indicate that the bulk of police work consists of *reactive* social service activity.

While the debate continues, at present the law enforcement community appears to have five primary functions:

1. *Major emergency arm of the community.* The police are charged with the responsibility of using force to maintain law and order.

2. *Gatekeepers.* The police are charged with the power to decide whether or not to arrest possible offenders. They must determine if a law has been violated, whether an arrest should be made, and who should be arrested. The police in America are expected to use some measure of personal judgment in making these decisions. We have adopted a selective enforcement model in this country and do not require the police to systematically bring all law violators into the system for formal processing.

3. *Awareness agents.* The police are expected to be suspicious and keenly aware of the world around them, so as to detect those who violate the laws. There is a good deal of controversy today over how aware we wish the police to be, and what type of crimes are the most important to detect. Some would argue, for example, that there is a need for a greater awareness of white-collar crimes.

4. *Mediators.* The police are the mediators between the community and the legal system. They are the first line of contact between the public and the government. This has become an increasingly difficult role to fulfill as we have become an increasingly diverse nation in terms of racial heritage, culture, and language. These differences often inhibit communication with police personnel.

5. *Moral censors.* The police serve as "moral censors" in that they are asked to enforce a number of morality-based laws (i.e., laws against gambling, drug use, prostitution, pornography, under-age alcohol consumption, etc.).

This fifth function bears further elaboration, for it is a most troublesome and frustrating task. Justice officials, and law enforcement officers in particular, are expected to enforce a number of unpopular laws. The fact that the police enforce these moral laws serves to maintain a token image of societal morality. Many have noted that the enforcement of such laws serves a very important social/psychological function for society at large, for enforcement publicly verifies to "the people" that we are a moral society. Critics note that it is little more than a carefully constructed facade, and point to the high demand for illegal goods and services among "the people." Indeed, many individuals do consume these commodities, and are quite willing to pay the police and other government officials not to enforce such laws. The result is a serious corruption problem. Numerous studies have been undertaken in an attempt to understand the nature and extent of law enforcement corruption.

A related issue is the improper use of force by the police. Perhaps no other law enforcement issue evokes so much public outcry and criticism. The 1991 videotaped clubbing of Rodney King by Los Angeles police and the 1997 beating of Haitian immigrant Abner Louima by New York City police vividly brought the issue of police brutality to the public's attention. Just how many citizens are harmed by the police each year is the subject of considerable debate. A 1997 study undertaken by the Bureau of Justice Statistics concluded that there are roughly 500,000 situations each year when the police threaten to and/or actually do use force against citizens (Greenfeld et al. 1997). Utilizing studies undertaken by Matulia (1985) and Fyfe (1988), it is estimated that the police may kill as many as 1,000 persons a year. Others suggest the number is between 300 and 600 a year, with 1,500 persons beaten.

By the same token, it should not be overlooked that law enforcement officers are also often assaulted and killed on duty. While the numbers have varied in recent years, current data indicate that approximately 40–60 officers are murdered while in the line of duty each year. Heavily armed drug dealers and the recent increase in activity of urban gangs will likely result in a higher casualty rate among police officers in the future. It is likely that the number of citizens beaten and killed by police will also increase.

The law enforcement community has extended considerable effort in responding to so-called traditional street crimes. The challenge in the future is to also respond to the seemingly growing amount of transnational organized crime, corporate crime, white-collar crime, terrorism, and computer crime. Local police agencies typically have neither the expertise nor the financial resources to contend with these so-called nontraditional crimes. Consequently, enforcement in these areas has generally shifted into the federal realm.

Administrative Issues

In the past decade, several administrative issues have emerged.

Hiring Practices

Many police departments are lagging in hiring and promoting minorities and females. At present, a number of departments are under court order to rectify the situation.

Education

Few police departments have established a formal higher educational standard, despite encouragement to do so by the 1967 Presidential Crime Commission Report. While the results are somewhat mixed, it appears that officers with a higher education are able to perform their duties more effectively. As more educated officers reach the higher echelons of police administration, it is likely that many departments will establish higher educational standards for entry and promotion. A number of large departments across the country have already done so. However, it may yet take some time for small, rural departments to move in this direction.

Crime Prevention

The law enforcement community does a poor job in preventing crime. Marvell and Moody (1996, 610) note that crime prevention is not the primary focus of most police work, that to truly deter street crime there would need to be an unrealistically large increase in the number of line-level officers, and that most police strategies and activites inadequately address crime-prevention needs. As a result, progressive law enforcement agencies are moving away from traditional policing modes to community/problem-solving policing in an attempt to locate and remedy situations that foster crime.

Community Policing

Over the course of the past 30 years, there has been growing interest in the concept of community policing. "Community policing" is a catch-all phrase. It denotes a general effort on the part of the police to obtain the trust and respect of the citizens in the communities in which they serve. It also suggests a need for the police to take on a crime-prevention role, and to help develop and maintain a sense of cohesion within the community, instead of merely reacting to crime once it has occurred. Among other considerations, community policing suggests the need to set up precinct offices in neighborhoods to institute victim-witness assistance programs, to support neighborhood watch and home security programs, to increase the use of foot and bicycle patrols . . . in short, to increase the positive interaction between citizens and the law enforcement community.

Cutting-Edge Technology

Increasingly, the police are utilizing modern technology to help them respond to crime. Computers have found their way into nearly every law enforcement department, where they are used as management tools to design work schedules, to assess crime patterns and trends, to exchange information between departments, and to develop probability and solvability models. The communications industry has seen tremendous advancements in the past 30 years, and the police have stayed abreast of those changes.

Many departments have moved into the area of electronic surveillance. One mode of surveillance, known as the "photocop" program, is catching on across the country. Officers utilize a roadside device which detects speeders and automatically takes a picture of them and their license plates. Citations are then sent to the cars' registered owners. Recent advancements in forensic science technology have given the police a greater ability to find valuable clues from bomb fragments, paint chips, body organs, bones, gas residue, and clothing fibers. The giant strides achieved in DNA technology are revolutionizing violent crime investigations and prosecutions. Most progressive departments now have automated fingerprinting capabilities.

* * *

Perhaps the most difficult of all government service positions, police work demands a high degree of patience, tolerance, wisdom, and endurance. Much has been written regarding police stress and cynicism. Police work has been called the most psychologically demanding job in the world. It is no wonder that law enforcement officers suffer from high rates of alcoholism, health problems (particularly heart disease and cancer), suicide, marital difficulties, and divorce, and that law enforcement agencies have such a high rate of turnover. Given the environment in which the police must function, as well as the enormous pressures placed upon officers and agencies, it is a tribute to the law enforcement profession that it functions as well as it does.

References and Further Reading Materials

Bureau of Justice Statistics. 1988. *Report to the Nation on Crime.* Washington, DC: United States Department of Justice.

Delattre, Edwin J. 2002. *Character and Cops: Ethics in Policing.* Washington, DC: AEI Press.

Fyfe, James. 1988. "Police Use of Deadly Force: Research and Reform," Justice Quarterly, June 1988, pp. 165–205.

Glensor, Ronald W., Mark Correia, and Kenneth Peak. 2000. *Policing Communities.* Los Angeles, CA: Roxbury.

Greenfeld, Lawrence, Patrick Langan, and Steven Smith. 1997. *Police Use of Force.* Washington, DC: Bureau of Justice Statistics.

Kakalik, James S. and Sorrell Widhorn. 1971. *Aids to Decisionmaking in Police Patrol. A Report Prepared for the United States Department of Housing and Urban Development.* Santa Monica, CA: The RAND Corporation.

LeDoux, J.C. and Tully, E.J. 1982. *A Study of Factors Influencing the Continuing Education of Police Officers.* Washington, DC: Federal Bureau of Investigation.

Locke, Herbert G. 1982. "The Evolution of Contemporary Police Service," in Bernard L. Garmine (ed.), *Local Government Management.* Washington, DC: International City Management Association.

Loftin, Cohn and David McDowell. 1982. "The Police, Crime, and Economic Theory: An Assessment," *American Sociological Review,* Vol. 47(3), pp. 393–401.

Marvell, Thomas and Carlisle Moody. 1996. "Specification Problems, Police Levels and Crime Rates," *Criminology,* November 1996, pp. 609–646.

Matulia, K. R. 1985. *A Balance of Forces.* Gaithersburg, MD: International Association of Chiefs of Police.

O'Leary and Titus. 1986. *Monographs, Vol. I and II.: National Association of State Directors of Law Enforcement Training.* Columbia, SC: South Carolina Criminal Justice Authority.

PERF. 1978. *Survey of Police Operational and Administrative Practices: 1978.* Washington, DC: Police Executive Research Forum.

Roberg, Roy and Jack Kuykendall. 1997. *Police Management.* Los Angeles, CA: Roxbury.

Roberg, Roy, John Crank, and Jack Kuykendall. 2000. *Police & Society.* Los Angeles, CA: Roxbury.

Thurman, Quint and Edmund McGarrell. 1997. *Community Policing in a Rural Setting.* Cincinnati, OH: Anderson.

Trojanowicz, Robert, Victor Kappeler, Larry Gaines, and Bonnie Bucqueroux. 1998. *Community Policing: A Contemporary Perspective.* Cincinnati, OH: Anderson.

Walker, Sam. 1992. *The Police in America.* New York, NY: McGraw-Hill.

Walker, Sam and Charles Katz. 2002. *The Police in America.* New York, NY: McGraw-Hill. ✦

Chapter 8
Police Crackdowns

Lawrence W. Sherman

B*y constantly changing crackdown targets, police may be able to reduce crime through an accumulation of residual deterrence at several locations. This approach is more effective, the author argues, than utilizing deterrence efforts at a single location. Sherman examines the reasoning behind this hypothesis and explains how this technique may be used and evaluated more effectively. He also explores ways in which law enforcement agencies can adopt more of a social service role and manage personnel problems on the one hand, yet retain some degree of crime control deterrence capacity on the other. Different tactical methods used in crackdowns are also explored, and three methods of measuring residual deterrence are presented.*

Can you increase the deterrent effect of policing without increasing the police budget? Few people would say so. But it may well be possible.

The key to success may be *rotating*, rather than *permanent*, patrol priorities and plans. By frequent changes in targets, but with major enforcement efforts—crackdowns—during a brief time period, police may get a "free bonus" of deterrence each time they replace one target with another. By the time potential criminals figure out that police have switched targets, a police department may be ready to switch back again.

Crackdowns constitute one of the most widespread developments in American policing in the 1980s. Drunk driving, domestic violence, public drug markets, streetwalking prostitutes, illegal parking, and even unsafe bicycle riding have all been targets for publicly announced police crackdowns. What all these problems have in common is that they occur in such volume that police usually ignore most individual transgressions. What the crackdowns have in common is a sharp increase in law enforcement resources applied to the previously under-enforced laws, with a clear goal of deterring the misconduct.

Crackdowns can be defined as increases in either the certainty or severity of official police reaction to a specific type of crime or all crime in a specific area. More precisely, police crackdowns constitute a sudden, usually proactive change in activity. The activity is intended to drastically increase either the communicated threat or actual certainty of apprehension. Crackdowns are aimed at specific types of offenses or at all offenses in certain specific areas.

Crackdowns must be distinguished from formal police personnel allocation decisions. The distribution of officers around a city is normally unequal per square mile, since it is guided by such factors as the relative density of population, number of calls for service, and amount of reported crime in each area. Simply adjusting the allocation as those factors change is not a crackdown but a finetuning of permanent triage priorities.

Crackdowns focus on specific target problems,[1] and these provide the sole justification for reallocating police resources outside the usual formula.

The notion that crackdowns might have lingering, or "residual," deterrent effects even after the crackdown is over had led to an analysis of some cities' experience with crackdowns and a review of 18 case studies of police crackdowns (see box). The evidence from the case studies supports the notion of residual deterrence—that is, some crime reduction persists after a crackdown is over. Moreover, there is some decay of initial crackdown impact even if police resources remain in the targeted area.

By constantly changing crackdown targets, police may reduce crime more through the accumulation of residual deterrence at several locations than through initial deterrence at a single location. And by limiting the time period devoted to each target, police might also avoid wasting scarce resources trying to sustain initial deterrent effects in the face of inevitable decay.

This article examines the basic reasoning for this hypothesis. Its purpose is not to advocate crackdowns but rather to consider how they might be employed and evaluated more effectively.

Managing the Scarcity Problem

A basic theory of criminal justice is that crime can be deterred through certain punishment. But in modern America there is too much crime and too little law enforcement to make punishment very certain. The chances of being arrested for any given crime are very low because offenders have ample opportunity to choose a time and place that existing police resources cannot cover.

Despite continuing debate about the crime problem, few communities have raised budgets to make police more effective in arresting offenders. After 1978, in fact, the total number of police in big cities began to decline while reports of both serious and minor crimes increased substantially.[2]

Examples of Police Crackdowns

Police crackdowns can target specific neighborhoods or specific offenses, and their duration can range from a few weeks to several years. The following, selected from the 18 case studies reviewed for this article, illustrate this range. Initial and residual deterrent effects varied, sometimes based on factors outside the scope of the crackdowns themselves.

Drug crackdown, Washington, D.C. A massive police presence—60 police officers per day and a parked police trailer—in the Hanover Place neighborhood open-air drug market provided an effective initial deterrent.

Lynn, Massachusetts, open-air heroin market. A 4-year crackdown using four to six police officers led to 140 drug arrests in the first 10 months and increased demand for drug treatment.

Operation Clean Sweep, Washington, D.C. The city allocated 100 to 200 officers—many on overtime—to 59 drug markets, making 60 arrests a day. Tactics included roadblocks, observation of open-air markets, "reverse buy" sell-and-bust by undercover officers, and seizure of cars.

Repeat Call Address Policing (RECAP) Experiment, Minneapolis. A special unit of five police officers attempted to reduce calls for service from 125 residential addresses, increasing their presence with landlords and tenants. This short-term targeting of resources led to a 15-percent drop in calls from these addresses, compared to 125 control addresses.

Nashville, Tennessee, patrol experiment. A sharp increase in moving patrol at speeds under 20 miles per hour in four high-crime neighborhoods netted a measurable decrease in Part I Index Crime during two short crackdowns (11 days and 15 days).

Disorder crackdown, Washington, D.C. Massive publicity accompanied a crackdown on illegal parking and disorder that was attracting street crime to the Georgetown area of the city. Police raised their weekend manpower 30 percent and installed a trailer at a key intersection to book arrestees.

New York City subway crackdown. This massive crackdown involved increasing the number of police officers from 1,200 to 3,100, virtually guaranteeing an officer for every train and every station. Crime fell during the first 2 years of the crackdown but rose again during the following 6 years.

Cheshire, England, drunk driving crackdown. During two short-term crackdowns, one accompanied by continuing publicity, police increased breathalyzer tests up to sixfold between 10 p.m. and 2 a.m. Significant deterrent effects continued up to 6 months after the crackdowns ceased.

London prostitution crackdown. Stepped up arrest of prostitutes, pimps, and brothel keepers—combined with cautions of their customers—succeeded in reducing "curb-crawling," with no displacement.

New Zealand drunk driving crackdowns. Deterrent effects of two short-term crackdowns were felt even before they began, because of intensive publicity about the impending crackdowns and stepped-up administration of breathalyzer tests.

Given this situation of scarce resources, policymakers have two choices. They can constantly shift priorities as this article suggests but as rarely happens in practice. Or they can adopt the more common method of simply setting permanent triage priorities whereby some kinds of offenses are ignored or given very little attention so that resources can be concentrated on more serious problems.

In some cities, for example, police will not investigate burglaries unless the loss exceeds $5,000. In other cities, marijuana smoking and public drinking have been virtually decriminalized by police limitations. And until quite recently, police, prosecutors, and judges rarely took any action against minor domestic violence. These practical compromises were all seen as necessary ways to have enough law enforcement personnel and prison space for armed robbers, narcotics pushers, rapists, and murderers.[3]

One consequence of this triage approach is endless wrangling over what the priorities should be. Thus an early 1986 *New York Times* editorial took New York's police commissioner to task for failing to enforce bicycle traffic laws after three deaths and many injuries to pedestrians. The commissioner's public response was that he could not spare the personnel from dealing with the "crack" epidemic. Nonetheless, by July of that year New York police had launched an unannounced crackdown on cyclists, issuing 3,633 summonses in 2 weeks and prompting Buffalo, New York, police to follow suit.[4]

These sporadic pressures on policy are nothing new. Like the exhausted parent, police fail to crack down out of sheer poverty of resources rather than poverty of desire. But when political pressures or the news media focus attention on some law that has been little enforced, police resources may be temporarily diverted from normal priorities to deal with that long-ignored problem.

The effect is almost a change in the interpretation of the criminal law, a virtual admission that the offense had previously received too low a priority. The crackdown communicates to the lawbreaking public a statement that, in effect, the law is back on the books. Indeed, when Milwaukee police cracked down on misdemeanor domestic violence in May 1986 by adopting a new arrest policy, street officers often explained to the arrestees that the arrest was the result of a new law.

Characteristics of Crackdowns

Police crackdowns have three possible tactical elements: presence, sanctions, and media threats.

- *Presence* is simply an increased ratio of police officers per potential offender, either in places or in situations. Increased presence can be accomplished either through uniformed presence (which communicates a visible threat to potential offenders) or through plainclothes surveillance (which may make potential offenders less certain about the risk of apprehension).
- *Sanctions* denote any coercive police imposition on offenders or potential offenders: stopping cars or pedestrians for identification checks, issuing warnings, mounting roadblock checkpoints, conducting breathalyzer tests, making arrests, and so on.
- *Media threats* are announced intentions to increase the certainty of sanctions. They are reported in newspapers, public service announcements on television and radio, or even through billboard campaigns.

In practice, these tactical elements are combined in different ways. The interaction between presence and sanctions, for example, is ironically perverse: Greater presence can produce more sanctions, but sanctions can reduce presence by taking police away to process arrests. In a 1985 parking violation crackdown in the Georgetown district of Washington D.C.[5] police avoided this dilemma by installing a booking center in a trailer parked on the street on weekend nights, saving the police a 2-mile drive to the station for each arrest. Conversely, visible presence can reduce the number of sanctions imposed as would-be violators change their behavior in the face of almost certain arrest.

Area crackdowns tend to emphasize presence, while offense-specific crackdowns emphasize sanctions. Whether a media campaign is added to the other elements of a crackdown may depend on public interest in the problem as well as business interest in providing such advertising services free of charge.

A *backoff* is the usual sequel to a crackdown. For reasons of necessity (which may be a virtue), crackdowns rarely last forever. On rare occasions, some crackdown may become part of the permanent triage, realigning the previous priority system. But most will eventually terminate in a backoff, which can be defined as a reduction in the visible threat or actual certainty of apprehension created by the crackdown. Backoffs can occur suddenly or gradually. They can result from explicit police management decisions or uncorrected informal action of enforcement personnel, and they can take place through reduced presence or by reduced sanctioning.

Changing Policies or Increasing Police Presence

Police crackdowns take two frequently overlapping forms. One is a policy change about how to handle specific offenses, such as arresting wife beaters rather than counseling them, or towing illegally parked cars rather than just ticketing them. The other is an increase in police presence in specific geographical areas, constituting a temporary state of full enforcement of every law on the books for those particular areas. Both kinds of crackdowns attempt to communicate a more powerful threat of apprehension and punishment than "normal" policing.

Both kinds of crackdowns are highly controversial, although the geographically focused approach is probably more vulnerable to charges that police violate civil liberties. Most of the controversy centers on the effectiveness of crackdowns: Are they worth the cost in tax dollars and public inconvenience? Vocal constituencies may strongly support crackdowns, but critics often argue that police crackdowns are undertaken for political purposes or as an excuse for police to earn overtime pay. Police themselves at times have raised doubts about the crime reduction effects of crackdowns.

Similarly, academic observers have been skeptical about the effects of police crackdowns. The leading student of drunk driving enforcement has argued that such crackdowns fail to create lasting deterrence,[6] while a leading police scholar has suggested that massive, sudden increases in police patrol can deter street crimes temporarily but not over the long run.[7]

Distinguishing Among Different Deterrent Effects

All these debates fail to make important distinctions among the different kinds of deterrent effects crackdowns can produce. They fail to separate any initial deterrence in the immediate wake of a crackdown from the possible residual deterrence after the crackdown has been withdrawn. They also fail to take account of the varying speed with which any initial deterrence decays during or after the crackdown.

There is evidence that some crackdowns do initially deter or at least displace some kinds of offenses. However, it is hard to sustain many crackdowns over a long period, either because police eventually start backing off or because potential offenders gradually realize that their chances of being caught are not as great as they had thought. None of the successful short-term crackdowns reviewed in our study appeared to suffer deterrence decay, suggesting that the decay problem may be limited to longer crackdowns. Yet even in longer term crackdowns, deterrence may take as long as 2 years to diminish, under the right conditions.

The slow decay constitutes a bonus residue of deterrence from the crackdown period. This residue fits the growing body of theory and evidence about how people make decisions under conditions of uncertainty, since intermittent, unpredictable crackdowns make risks of apprehension far more uncertain than could any system of fixed police priority—including long-term crackdowns. But systematic empirical evidence for the residual deterrence hypothesis is still quite meager.

One NIJ experiment testing the residual deterrence hypothesis has just been completed by the Minneapolis Police Department and the Crime Control Institute.[8] This "hot spots" patrol experiment randomly assigned 55 high-crime areas to receive up to 3 hours of extra, unpredictable time of patrol car presence each day, and 55 other high-crime areas to receive normal patrol. The experiment is now being evaluated in terms of crime reports, calls for service, and more than 6,000 hours of systematic observation of the level of disorder.

Crackdown Effects

The effects of crackdowns revolve around five key questions:

- Was there any initial deterrent effect?
- Was there any increase in crime?
- Was there apparent local displacement?
- Did the initial deterrence decay?
- Was there any residual deterrence after the backoff?

Any crime reduction is arguably a general deterrent effect, even though it fails to distinguish between the reduction in the general crime rate and reduction in the criminal activity of individual active offenders.[9]

Interpreting any crime reduction as deterrence is problematic in other ways. A reduction could have been caused by incapacitation of a few active offenders early on in the crackdown. Or it could have been caused by changing transportation patterns, declining area population, or other factors.[10] But over short periods, with large enough numbers of offenses, it seems reasonable for police to interpret a crime reduction as a deterrent effect.

The more important point is the distinction between initial and residual deterrence. If a crime reduction is achieved while the crackdown tactic—presence, sanctions, or publicity—is still in operation, then it is plausibly an initial deterrence effect. But if the crime reduction is sustained after the tactic is terminated or reduced, then it is plausibly a residual deterrent effect. The perceived risk of apprehension that "hangs over" could influence decisions not to commit offenses after the risk (or the communicated threat) is actually reduced, at least until other evidence indicates that the risk has returned to its prior level. Decay, or a gradual decline from initial changes, is therefore a central concept for crackdowns in at least three ways.

Crackdown decay. Since a crackdown requires greater police effort, the tendency to regress to the former level of effort may cause the implementation of the crackdown itself to decay. Fewer arrests are made, fewer people are stopped, more officers are diverted to other duties—all of which could be planned by police commanders or just carried out by the lower ranks.

Operation Pressure Point

In early 1984, a newly appointed New York City police commissioner launched "Operation Pressure Point," a 2-year crackdown on the Lower East Side drug markets. Prior to the crackdown, the area had offered many blatant drug bazaars, with customers attracted from all over the New York area. Heroin buyers could be seen standing in long lines stretching around street corners.

The crackdown, at a cost of $12 million per year, used more than 150 uniformed officers, most of them rookies. The crackdown began with a high volume of drug arrests—65 per day for the first 6 weeks, then dropping to 20 per day. This rate continued until at least August 1986, by which time the police had made 21,000 drug-related arrests in the target area.

Tactics included observation-of-sale arrests, undercover buys, raids on dealing locations, arrests for unrelated misdemeanors and violations, tips from informers, and a "hotline" phone number.

The initial deterrent effect was a 47 percent reduction in robberies in 1984 compared to 1983, and a 62 percent reduction (from 34 to 13) in homicides during the same period. This initial effect was maintained until at least the first 8 months of 1986, with a 40 percent reduction in robbery and a 9 percent reduction in homicide compared to the first 8 months of 1983. While no displacement to the immediate vicinity was found, other parts of Manhattan experienced a growth in drug markets.

Initial deterrence decay. With or without a decay of police effort, an initial crime reduction might decay as potential offenders learn through trial and error that they have overestimated the certainty of getting caught.

Residual deterrence decay. The same learning process can take place gradually after the effort is actually reduced, with the residual deterrence slowly declining as word-of-mouth communication and personal experience show that it is once again "safe" to break the law.

Conclusions

The data gathered at the 18 sites suggest that crackdowns cause an initial shock to potential offenders. We cannot know how many of the cases where deterrence decayed might have shown residual deterrence if the crackdowns had been stopped sooner. But we can speculate that the rebounding crime rates might have looked much the same without continued expenditure of police resources. Aiming for residual deterrence could make wider use of crackdowns far more feasible than trying to achieve sustained deterrence over time.

Notes

1. Eck, John, and William Spelman. *Problem Solving: Problem-Oriented Policing in Newport News.* Washington, D.C.: Police Executive Research Forum, 1987.
2. U.S. Department of Justice, Bureau of Justice Statistics. *Police Employment and Expenditure Trends.* Washington, D.C.: U.S. Government Printing Office, 1986.
3. Federal Bureau of Investigation. *Crime in America: The Uniform Crime Reports* (annual), Washington, D.C.: Federal Bureau of Investigation, 1978–88.
4. Connelly, Mary, Carlyle C. Douglas, and Laura Mansnerus. "Cracking Down on City Cyclists." *New York Times* (August 24, 1986, eastern e.).
5. Sherman, Lawrence W., Anne Roschelle, Patrick R. Gartin, Deborah Linnell, and Clare Coleman. "Cracking Down and Backing Off: Residual Deterrence." Report submitted to the National Institute of Justice, Washington, D.C., by the Center for Crime Control, University of Maryland, 1986.
6. Ross, H. Laurence. *Deterring the Drinking Driver: Legal Policy and Social Control.* Lexington, Massachusetts: D.C. Heath, 1981.
7. Wilson, James Q. *Thinking About Crime* 2d ed. New York: Basic Books, 1983, p. 64.
8. Sherman, Lawrence W., and David Weisburd. "Policing the Hot Spots of Crime: An Experimental Research Design." Unpublished manuscript, Crime Control Institute, 1988.
9. Blumstein, Alfred, Jacqueline Cohen, Jeffrey Roth, and Christy Visher, eds. *Criminal Careers and "Career Criminals,"* 2 vols. Washington, D.C.: National Academy Press, 1986.
10. Cook, Thomas, and Donald T. Campbell. *Quasi-Experimentation: Design and Analysis Issues for Field Settings.* Chicago: Rand-McNally.

Lawrence W. Sherman, "Police Crackdowns." Washington, D.C.: National Institute of Justice Research in Action, March/April 1990, pp. 2–6. ✦

Chapter 9

Community Policing

Is It Changing the Basic Functions of Policing? Findings from a Longitudinal Study of 200+ Municipal Police Agencies

Jihong Zhao
Nicholas P. Lovrich
T. Hank Robinson

In the 1990s, community-oriented policing (COP) emerged as a significant innovation, prompted by federal legislation and public dissatisfaction with policing's prevailing professional model. Among COP's key tenets was a shift in policing's core function, from the crime control of the professional model to order maintenance. But despite widespread lip service, have police agencies truly shifted their fundamental approach, or have they merely adopted the rhetoric and symbols of innovation?

The authors conducted longitudinal surveys of more than 200 municipal police departments to explore which theory of organizational change best explains the widespread institutionalization of community policing: contingency theory, *which suggests that as the external environment changes, an organization changes its priorities and goals to respond, or* institutional theory, *which posits that an organization will adopt new programs and symbols to foster public support, but without true changes in functional priorities.*

Introduction

The term "organizational change" is commonly cited as a central element of community-oriented policing (COP) and reflects the belief that deep reform occurs in those American police agencies adopting this approach. At the federal level of government, community policing has enjoyed unprecedented bipartisan endorsement and sustained financial support from the Clinton administration and Congress as the 1994 Violent Crime Control and Law Enforcement Act (United States Congress, 1994) and its derivative statutes and programs evidence.[1]

A careful review of the police management literature, however, reveals little systematic conceptualization of a crucial question underlying COP: *At what level do police organizations do change?* The present widespread implementation of COP programs is often cited as prima facie evidence of the depth of change occurring in contemporary policing. Relevant research in management science, though, suggests strongly that investigations of organizational change must focus beyond program implementation and analyze the way operations are directed and maintained as core functional outcomes (e.g., Donaldson, 1995; Huber, Sutcliffe, Miller, & Glick, 1993; Van de Ven & Poole, 1995; Yin, 1979).

Scholars studying contemporary policing in the U.S. are divided on the possible reasons for the popularity of community policing. The more optimistic ones argue COP represents a genuine constructive revolution in policing practices because the changing societal environment that features a declining trust in government, efforts to "reinvent" government, efforts to stimulate civic engagement—forces police agencies to respond to new social and/or political demands in a thoughtful and enlightened way (e.g., Capowich & Roehl, 1994; Cordner, 1998; Kelling, 1988; Trojanowicz & Bucqueroux, 1990). The fundamental and enduring nature of police work—entailing the use of coercive force and repeated contact with offenders and social deviants in often dangerous settings—prompts pessimists to argue such change is almost impossible (e.g., Bittner, 1972; Buerger, 1994; Lyons, 1999; Manning, 1995). These researchers conclude [that police agencies are] adopting . . . COP to appear responsive to change, not to alter their work in adjustment to their environment (e.g., Klockars, 1988). At the moment, the voices of the optimistic perspective are the more prominent: the pessimistic perspective is present but less often noticed.

This study represented a continued effort to investigate the reasons for organizational change in the process of policing and built on a cross-sectional study conducted by Zhao and Thurman (1997). In this study, two competing theories of organizational change were tested: (1) *contingency theory* reflecting the salience of exogenous stimulants to change, and (2) *institutional theory* reflecting the broad influence of political and socioeconomic factors. This article focuses on the core functions of American police organizations and investigates the extent and nature of change of priorities among those functions over a period of three years within which community policing gained its greatest momentum across the country. This study attempted to shed light on the following two important research questions: *Did the priorities among core police functions change over time as suggested in the COP literature?* and *Was any observed reprioritization of core police functions due to discernible aspects of a police department's external environment?* A longitudinal panel study of over two hundred police agencies in forty-seven states was used for the analysis presented here.

Theoretical Considerations

Goal-Directed Activity as the Foundational Elements of Organizational Phenomena

There are many ways of defining the term organization, but virtually all the definitions operative in management science or the sociology of organization share one common element—namely, organizations are created to achieve a specific goal or a set of interrelated goals. In his classic work, Philip Selznick (1948, p. 25) defined organization as "the arrangement of personnel for facilitating the accomplishment of some agreed purpose through the allocation of functions and responsibilities." Similarly, the noted sociologist Talcott Parsons (1956, p. 63) viewed organization as featuring the "primacy of orientation to the attainment of a specific goal" (also see Donaldson, 1995; Lawrence & Lorsch, 1969). Organizations are created to achieve goals. Goals justify the very existence of the organization and set the boundaries of acceptable activity and structure the principal tasks of the staff and line functionaries (Thompson, 1967).

The Noble Laureate Herbert Simon closely examined organizational goal phenomena, and in his article "On the Concept of Organizational Goal" (1964, p. 1), argued that the construct organizational goal is "seldom unitary, but generally consists of a whole set of constraints the action must satisfy." Organizations are expected to undertake a number of functions in support of their goals. In this regard, Simon observed that while none of the goal-derived core functions can be completely ignored, limited resources force all organizations to prioritize their functions according to a rational process of assessment of internal and external operating conditions and long-term maintenance considerations (Lawrence & Lorsch, 1969).

Scholars of policing tend to agree that three distinct primary functions have been associated with American policing throughout its history—namely, *crime control, order maintenance,* and *service provision* (Trojanowicz & Bucqueroux, 1990; Walker, 1977). In his empirical study of police functions, for example, James Q. Wilson (1968) argued that police activities can be grouped into three general functions—crime control, order maintenance, and service. Kelling and Moore (1988) analyzed historical change in American policing and concluded that the priorities accorded these three core functions have varied among American police agencies over the course of the past one hundred years. For example, the bureaucratic or professional model of policing that came into prominence during the decades preceding the advent of community policing delineated crime control as the organization's primary core mission with a lesser emphasis on order maintenance and service provision (Kelling & Moore, 1988).

If reprioritizing police core functions connotes substantive organizational change within policing over the course of national history, then community policing presents another "paradigm shift" in policing only to the extent that it can be shown that the priorities of core police functions have shifted away from the professional model (Goldstein, 1990; Trojanowicz & Bucqueroux, 1990). Eck and Rosenbaum (1994, pp. 7–8) observed that "community policing rearranges priorities among functions and adds new ones. Nonemergency services take on greater importance." Similarly, Moore (1994) pointed out that a COP-directed rearrangement of police functions places greater emphasis on order maintenance and other nonemergency services. Typical COP programs such as foot patrol, storefronts and mini-stations, geographical assignment, and citizen-engaged neighborhood crime prevention activities are specifically directed toward the order maintenance and service provision functions (Weisel & Eck, 1994). Despite more than a decade of COP implementation across the nation, however, scholars and practitioners alike disagree about the extent to which it has prompted substantive organizational change. The next two sections introduce two theoretical perspectives regarding organizational change in policing that are useful in clarifying the ongoing disagreement about the extent of "real" change taking place in U.S. policing practices at the turn of the century.

Contingency Perspective of Change

Both contingency and institutional perspectives on organizational change have their intellectual roots in general systems theory originally developed in the biological sciences in the 1920s and adopted to the social systems in the 1950s (Bertalanffy, 1956); they differ mainly in the range of exogenous factors assumed to be at work (Donaldson, 1995). Contingency theory, for example, places an emphasis on the external task environment within which an organization operates (e.g. Hage & Aiken, 1970; Van de Ven & Drazin, 1985; Woodward, 1958), whereas the institutional perspective accords primary significance to the broad cultural and political environment within which an organization arises (DiMaggio, 1983; Meyer & Rowan, 1977; Selznick, 1948).

According to the contingency perspective, the driving force of organizational change is the external environment, particularly the task environment with which an organization is confronted. For example, in their study of twenty industrial firms in the United Kingdom, Burns and Stalker (1961) developed their well known and widely used categories of *mechanistic* vs. *organic* organizations and their environments.[2] Other contingency theorists have explored patterns in the incidence of innovation and use of technology (Dewar & Hage, 1978; Mobrman & Mobrman, 1990; Woodward, 1958), and the relationship between organizational size and environment (Blau & Schoenherr, 1971; Kimberly, 1976).

The contingency perspective features two cardinal assumptions regarding organizational change. First, individual organizations must adapt themselves to their external environment when their goal or goals are affected by change in their operating conditions. The external environment is conceptualized as posing demands to which organizations must respond (Hage & Aiken, 1970). In addition, organizational environments are perceived as being dynamic, leading to the second cardinal assumption that there must be a "fit" between an organization and its environment. A good fit between the two means higher levels of performance and efficiency (Van de Ven & Drazin, 1985). Donaldson (1995, p. 32) argues that in order to find an optimal fit, organizations have to be able to alter both their goals and operations over the course of time. For example, the characteristics of the task environment—e.g., stable vs. turbulent—may affect organizational arrangements. The theoretical framework for organizational change can be conceptualized as a cyclical process in which:

1. An initial fit exists between an organization and its environment;
2. Environmental change results in a disjuncture between structure and strategies and operating conditions;
3. Organization performance worsens, occasioning organized change in response;
4. If performance improves, a new structural and strategic equilibrium is institutionalized by the organizational decision-makers.

The contingency perspective would seem to apply to the analysis of organizational change in policing quite well. The traditional strategies of crime control developed under the professional model became increasingly ineffective in the late 1960s and 1970s (Greenwood, Chaiken & Petersilia, 1977; Kelling, Pate, Dieckman & Brown, 1974), suggesting a poor fit between the societal environment and the prevailing structural and strategic organization of policing (Brown & Wycoff, 1987; Kessler, 1993; Wycoff & Skogan, 1994). In order to be more effective, police agencies would have to change. For example, as early as thirty years ago, Angell (1971) and Germann (1969) argued that there was a need for American police agencies to change in order to adapt themselves to a changing environment (e.g., President's Commission on Law Enforcement and Administration of Justice, 1967). Similarly, examining what the proper role of American police should be in a democratic society, Goldstein (1977) argued that the bureaucratic model of policing was essentially contradictory to some of the basic values celebrated in American society.

Later, the publication of Wilson and Kelling's (1982) "Broken Windows" thesis helped to further support the claim that order maintenance should supplant crime control as the top priority of police work. They argued that because social disorder provides a promising climate in which criminal incidents can flourish, local police agencies should develop new strategies to resolve problems underlying crime rather than just responding to the actual incidence of crime (Goldstein, 1990).

The proponents of community policing tend to emphasize three primary positions concerning organizational change in American policing. The first proposition is that police agencies should respond to an environment that has changed dramatically with respect to its expectation about government in general, and police services in particular. Since empirical research findings and theoretical developments in the policing literature all questioned the continued utility of the professional model of policing, it follows that police organizations need to adapt themselves to the new demands and find a better fit with their environment (Kelling & Moore, 1988; Trojanowicz & Bucqueroux, 1990).

The second proposition is that organizational change in policing should lead to a corresponding reprioritization of police functions (Eck & Rosenbaum, 1994). A primary argument for this reprioritization is that police need to address real social disorder and social inequality underlying crime incidents (e.g., Capowich & Roehl, 1994; Eck & Spelman, 1987). The third proposition concerns the systematic linkage between a police agency's operational activities and its manifest organizational priorities. For example, Wasserman and Moore (1988) argued that the formal adoption of COP should lead to manifest activities directed toward social order and service provision, suggesting that the more COP programs a police agency has implemented (such as foot patrols, storefronts, school resource officers, geographic assignment), the more likely it will have reprioritized its core functions of crime fighting, promoting social order, and providing services.

The Institutional Perspective of Change

In broad terms, the institutional perspective posits that organizations are deeply embedded in a social and cultural context. Organizational goals and structural arrangements are influenced significantly by the distinctive cultural and political elements at play when an organization comes into being (Meyer & Rowan, 1977; Meyer & Scott, 1983). As a consequence, a rational analysis of the character of the immediate environment cannot solely explain organizational change phenomena and associated behavior (Scott, 1995). A crucial component of the theory is the concept of legitimacy; in the institutional perspective, the term legitimacy refers to "the degree of cultural support for an organization—the extent to which the array of established cultural accounts provide explanations for its existence, functioning, and jurisdiction" (Meyer & Scott, 1983, p. 201). According to institutional perspective theorists, legitimacy is not automatically given in a rationalized organizational setting and formal organizations have to work hard to gain it (Meyer & Rowan, 1977).

The response to a broader social context, as opposed to sensitivity to specific environment problems, makes the relationship between organizational goals and adaptive activities loosely coupled at best (Meyer, Boli & Thomas, 1995). Meyer and Scott (1983, p. 211) argue that "institutionalized organizations like local government are likely to . . . buffer themselves from work activities, through ritualization or decoupling of structure and activities." Simply stated, organizational change can reflect the purposeful organizational effort to both generate public support and build "legitimacy" by making the organization simultaneously look good to outsiders and appear stable to insiders. This means that organizational change can take the shape of a process of creating new programs and increasing the use of new symbols, and rituals, while at the same time the core mission of an organization and functional priorities remain substantially intact (Meyer & Rowan, 1977).

Some students of policing have argued that little or no substantive change in the nature of policing should be expected beyond the buffering strategy outlined in Meyer and Rowan's (1977) work. In his classic work, *Functions of Police in Modern Society,* Bittner (1972) pointed out that the authorized use of coercive force distinguishes police from any other public entity. Moreover, Bittner (1967) argues that a direct consequence associated with the exclusive legitimate right to use coercive force is that crime control becomes the top priority concern of police agencies.

Applying Bittner's theoretical framework to the analysis of COP, Klockars (1988, p. 41) has noted the following:

> the modern movement toward what is currently called "community policing" is best understood as the latest in a fairly long tradition of *circumlocutions* whose purpose is to conceal, mystify, and legitimate police distribution of nonnegotiable coercive force [emphasis added].

Klockars joins Bittner in arguing that the very nature of police work makes it impossible to change the priorities among the core crime control, order maintenance, and service provision functions in the way COP presents. Similarly, Manning (1988) views the COP movement as little more than "old wine in new bottles," a concept developed more to influence and manipulate public opinion than to reprioritize police functions (also see Manning, 1995). Viewed from the Bittner, Klockars, and Manning perspective, the primary purpose of COP programs is to make police agencies look good in front of their local constituents. Out of the limelight, however, agencies tend to police pretty much the same as they always have. Buerger (1994) added to this critique of COP by noting that community policing really entails little community empowerment, but rather emphasized community cooperation. In most COP programs, the community is expected to be the "ears and eyes" of the police providing information about crime and criminals. It is urged to rally to the support of the local police force on important occasions.

From the perspective of institutional theorists, the key to understanding police organizations is to comprehend the crime control, tradition-driven institution that defines the nature of police work. Institutional theory suggests that organizational change need not reprioritize core functions; it can, instead, initiate activities in highly visible environmental settings to enhance the external legitimacy of the organization and consciously buffer preexisting priorities.[3] The core mission of crime control and such adaptive operational activities can be loosely coupled in the police agency setting. Such new programs need not reflect a reprioritization if core police functions.

Methods

The data used in this analysis were derived from a longitudinal survey of police chiefs conducted by the Division of Governmental Studies and Services (DGSS) at Washington State University in 1993 and 1996. DGSS has conducted mail-out/mail-back surveys to the same set of 281 municipal police departments located in forty-seven states in three-year intervals since 1978. The cities in the sample were selected from among those municipalities initially included in a representative national survey of chiefs of police in cities with a population of over 25,000 conducted by the International City Management Association in 1969. After three waves of mailings sent in 1996, 245 (87.2 percent) out of 281 police departments completed and returned a survey questionnaire. In 1993, the survey responses of 215 departments were included in the final analysis. The consistently high return rate registered in 1993 and in 1996 yielded a sample of 201 police agencies that returned their survey instruments in both the 1993 and 1996 surveys. This panel data set represented 71.5 percent of the total original sample of 281 agencies. An additional source of information used beyond the survey for the same respondents were 1992 and 1995 Uniform Crime Reports (UCR) data for the four index crimes against persons.

Measurements and Variables of Interest

The dependent variables in the analysis reflect the level of priority assigned to core area police functions, as measured through responses to Wilson's (1968) list of sixteen police activities reflecting the crime control, order maintenance, and service provision functions. A four-point scale varying from very low priority to high priority was used in the police chief survey to gather priority ratings on each of the sixteen items. A factor analysis based on the 1993 survey data identified five distinctive factors (or clusters), representing identifiable police functions—CRM1 (violent crime), CRM2 (gang and drug offenses), CRM3 (property crime), ORDER (order maintenance), and SERVICE (service activities); a detailed discussion of the five factors was presented in Zhao and Thurman (1997). In this analysis, the police functions were constructed on the same scales for the 1996 data.

Three independent variables were used to test for the effects of a number of environmental and organizational conditions on the prioritization of police functions among these municipal police agencies. The first variable of interest was change in rate of serious crime reported to the police. It is reasonable to speculate that an increase in this type of crime rate in any community constitutes a direct challenge for the local police agency in the external environment.[4] The first hypothesis is:

> *Hypothesis 1:* An increase in serious violent crime will be associated with a shift in priority concerns.

The second independent variable of interest was the extent of adoption of COP programs. In both the 1993 and 1996 surveys, police departments were asked to identify which COP elements they implemented based on a list of nineteen specific archetypical COP programs derived from the community policing literature discussed earlier (see Appendix 9.2 for a list of the programs.)[5] A fundamental objective of community policing is to increase the importance of the order maintenance and service functions in public safety provision. This shift of police functions is justified by the "broken windows" theory, which asserts that order maintenance and service functions are as important as the crime control function in achieving the public safety goals of American policing. Given this line of reasoning, it seems reasonable to assume that municipal police agencies that adopted more innovative programs in this three-year period were more likely to alter the traditional ordering of police functions away from crime control than those that either remained the same or decreased the number of COP programs maintained. The second hypothesis is:

> *Hypothesis 2:* An increase in the number of community policing programs will be associated with a shift in priorities away from crime control and toward order maintenance and service provision.

The third independent variable of interest concerned a key organization resource that enables an agency to implement community policing—namely, the extent of increase in the number of commissioned officers. Community policing is a labor-intensive change in policing: under COP philosophy, police officers engage in more frequent individual interactions with local residents and initiate problem-solving activities. Since its inception in 1994, the OCOPS has been mandated with the task of promoting organizational change in U.S. policing by adding 100,000 community policing officers to local police agencies and funding a variety of community-focused projects and program evaluations. In the survey, over 74 percent of the participating police agencies reported receiving some form of funding from the COPS Office in the period 1993 to 1996. It seems reasonable to presume that an agency reporting an increase in community policing officers should also be likely to report some degree of reprioritization of police functions toward the order maintenance and service provision functions. The third hypothesis is:

> *Hypothesis 3:* The greater the increase in the number of commissioned officers between 1993 and 1996, the greater the extent of reprioritization of police functions away from crime control and toward order maintenance and service provision.

The first control variable was city size. Meagher (1985) found significant variation in police activities by city size in a national study of police functions in a survey involving 249 municipal departments of various sizes. For example, officers in smaller agencies spent significantly more time providing services than did their counterparts in larger agencies. Relatedly, officers in large departments tend to spend more time on the crime control function than their counterparts in smaller agencies (also see Crank & Wells, 1991; Flanagan, 1985; Weisheit, Wells & Falcone, 1994).[6] The fourth hypothesis is:

> *Hypothesis 4:* Police agencies in small cities will rate order maintenance and service functions as higher priorities than their counterparts in large cities.

The second variable was geographic region. Research using national data suggested that police operations and management practices vary predictably by geographic regions (Steel & Lovrich, 1986; Warner, Steel & Lovrich, 1989). Recently, based on the analysis of separate national data sets, Maguire (1997) and Zhao (1996) reported that police innovations tended to vary by geographic regions, and police agencies located in the West were more likely to initiate innovative programs than agencies in other regions. The fifth hypothesis is:

> *Hypothesis 5:* Police agencies located in the West will be more likely to report a shift of priorities away from crime control over the 1993 to 1996 time period than agencies located elsewhere in the country.

Findings

In this section, the mean ratings of three functions in the municipal police departments are discussed, followed by the multivariate analysis of the relationship between the priorities of police functions and three independent variables and two control variables. The comparison of mean ratings between the 1993 and 1996 surveys is shown in Table 9.1.

At the aggregate level, the mean ratings of five police functions in 1996 are quite similar to those of 1993. The three crime control functions (against persons, drugs and gangs, and property crime) are given the top priority in the police agencies surveyed. Similarly, the service function received the lowest priority. The alpha levels of the five scales as measures of functions are very consistent over time, as shown in Ap-

Table 9.1
Descriptive Analysis: Dependent and Independent Variables

	Mean ratings (S.D.)		Change from 93 mean rating (percent)	
Dependent variables: police functions 1996 (scale)[a]	**96**	**93**	**Above**	**Below**
Crime control: against persons (CRM1), *n* = 238	3.79 (0.36)	3.77 (0.36)	28.9	21.6
Crime control: drugs and gangs (CRM2), *n* = 238	3.61 (0.57)	3.54 (0.53)	41.7	15.1
Crime control: against property (CRM3), *n* = 238	2.95 (0.47)	2.83 (0.53)	46.2	32.5
Order maintenance (ORDER), *n* = 238	2.87 (0.55)	2.78 (0.53)	45.6	33.4
Service (SERCVICE), *n* = 227	2.47 (0.51)	2.37 (0.59)	48.6	34.5

[a] The mean ratings: 1 = very low priority, 2 = low priority, 3 = moderate priority, and 4 = high priority. The items and alpha level for each individual scale are set forth in Appendix A: Part A. For a detailed discussion on the construction of the five-factor analysis-derived scales, see Zhao and Thurman (1997).

pendix 9.1: Part A. This indicates the five police functions reflect the conceptual understanding of police activities measured by the sixteen items. Further, the mean aggregate ratings of police functions show that, *overall, there has been very little change in prioritizing police functions during this three-year period.*

Importantly, the use of panel data enables us to examine in greater detail the change in the ratings recorded by each individual municipal police department in the survey sample. Interestingly, there is a noticeable variation in mean ratings recorded in the two surveys. While 28.9 percent of the agencies accorded the crime control function (against person) a higher priority in 1996 than in 1993, 21.6 percent of the agencies rated crime control a lower priority than they did three years previously. Given these substantial changes in prioritizing core functions, the question is this: Did these changes in prioritizing core police functions reflect the external environment and internal measures available during the 1993 and 1996 period as contingency theory would predict?

The frequency distributions of three independent and two control variables are reported in Table 9.2. Overall, the 1996 crime rate in the reporting cities, was considerably lower than in 1993 (See Appendix 9.1: Part B). All four types of crimes showed a mean decrease. This is consistent with the overall national pattern of crime trends that leveled off in the early 1990s, and then went down later in the decade. There has been some increase in the number of community policing programs reported by the departments surveyed between 1993 and 1996, suggesting that community policing continues to gain standing in U.S. police agencies (for a list if the programs, see Appendix 9.2). At the same time, the sizable standard deviation (3.45) for this mean measure indicates that noticeable shifting between the initiation and termination of COP programs was taking place in this time period. On average, there was a 6.04 percent increase in the number of commissioned officers in the municipal police agencies surveyed; this seems consistent with the observation that over 74 percent of the responding agencies reported having received federal funding for doing community policing. The city size distribution shows a significant variation of city population in the sample. The smallest city in the sample had about 21,000 residents and the largest more than 1.5 million. Similarly, police agencies included in the sample were from all four geographic regions in the U.S.

A multivariate analysis was performed to determine the extent to which the five measures of "contingencies" account for the reprioritization among core police functions over the period of 1993 to 1996. Table 9.3 sets forth the results for the five indicators of crime control prioritization. The R^2 of the three models estimating the influence of independent variables on the mean priority ratings of police functions are very low. This finding strongly suggests that American police organizations share a high degree of consensus on the top priority to be accorded the crime control function. This priority remains in force regardless of the environmental and

Table 9.2
Independent Variables

	Mean (S.D.)
Change in crime rates (*z* score)[a], *n* = 219	0.001 (2.52)
Change in COP program[b], *n* = 190	1.02 (3.45)
Change in percent of officers, *n* = 197	6.04 (0.01)
City population, *n* = 238	190.115 (300.226)
Region (percent), *n* = 238	
West	27.6
North Central	30.4
South	29.0
Northeast	13.0

[a] For the average crime rates in the cities surveyed, see Appendix 9.1: Part B.
[b] For the list of nineteen COP programs, please see Appendix 9.2.

Table 9.3
Multiple Regression Analysis on the Effect of Independent Variables on the Crime Control Functions

Dependent variables	CRM1 (against persons)	CRM2 (drug and gangs)	CRM3 (against property)
Independent variables			
Change in crime rates (1995–1992)	.001	–.001	–.001
Percent of change in officers	–.29	.59	.25
Change in COP programs (1996–1993)	.001	–.002	.001
Control variables			
City population	.00	.00	–.00
North Central region	–.01	–.16	–.05
South region	–.002	–.01	–.14
Northeast region	.01	–.40	–.001
Constant	3.81*	3.69*	2.94*
R	.11	.27	.22
R^2	.01	.07	.05
n = 180			

Note: West region is the omitted contrast group.
* Significant at .001 level.

agency contextual conditions facing a department in the 1993–1996 period. None of the hypotheses regarding the effects of the independent variables was supported by the 1993 and 1996 panel survey data. The managerial changes in priority ratings documented between 1993 and 1996 represent random fluctuation among these police agencies: they do not support the expectations of contingency theory. Table 9.4 sets forth the analysis of priority ratings for order maintenance and service functions.

Once again, the influence of the several contingency theory–derived explanatory variables is insignificant, resembling closely the findings displayed in Table 9.3. Noteworthy, however, are the two multiple regression coefficients that are statistically significant (all other factors held constant) in the two statistical models, and the signs indicating an effect in the hypothesized direction. A change in the direction of more substantive implementation of COP programs is associated with increased assignment of priority to the order maintenance function. In addition, the priority ratings for the service function decline as the crime rate increases among these 200+ municipal police agencies. It should be noted, of course, that while the coefficients are significant, the statistical models producing these findings account for only 8 percent of the variance in the order maintenance and service provision functions, respectively.

Discussion and Conclusion

In their 1997 study based in 1993 survey results from 281 agencies, Zhao and Thurman reported that the priorities of American police strongly reflected the professional crime fighting model. Further, they reported that the priority ratings of the five-factor analysis generated functions were unrelated to variation in three environmental variables—crime rate, city size, and geographic region. This study examined the relationship between the priorities accorded core police functions and organizational environmental conditions with a particular focus on change away from crime control as a predominant priority in policing during a period of three years during which community policing became a broadly diffused innovation across the country. The primary findings of this research clearly indicate that the core functional priorities of American policing largely remain closely modeled after the professional model; these priorities were not affected significantly by the changes such as the addition of officers, the provision of funds for COP training or the adoption of COP programs between 1993 and 1996.

From a theoretical point of view, the finding suggest that contingency theory does a poor job of explaining organizational change in American policing. In contrast, the findings reported here suggest the utility of the institutional per-

Table 9.4
Multiple Regression Analysis on the Effect of Independent Variables on the Order Maintenance and the Service Functions

Dependent variables	Order maintenance	Service
Independent variables		
Change in crime rates (1995–1992)	.001	–.004*
Percent of change in commissioned officers	.25	.01
Change in number of COP programs (1996–1993)	.03*	.02
Control variables		
City population	.00	–.00
North Central region	.002	.01
South region	–.11	–.12
Northeast region	–.15	.13
Constant	2.83*	2.49*
R	.29	.28
R^2	.08	.08
$n = 180$		

Note: West region is the omitted contrast group.
* Significant at .001 level.

spective in the investigation of organizational change in municipal police agencies. Twenty-five years ago, Bittner argued that police functions were largely independent from the influence of environment given crime control's prominent priority in policing. The findings could be interpreted as supporting his argument, this time based on a longitudinal analysis.

Recent research reported by other scholars also suggested that some developments in contemporary policing could not be explained by the environmental factors widely believed to favor the adoption of a COP operating philosophy in policing. The rapid increase in the number of SWAT teams in American police agencies is a good example. The purpose of SWAT is straightforward—highly trained teams can be swiftly deployed with an impressive use of force in circumstances calling for a quasi-military police response. In their study of SWAT units in the population of police agencies serving jurisdictions between 25,000 and 50,000 citizens, Kraska and Cubellis (1997) found a rapid expansion of these units between 1985 and 1995 (an increase of 157 percent). More and more police agencies serving small jurisdictions have established SWAT teams for hostage situations, acts of terrorism, civil disturbances, and high-risk searches and arrests: activities that occur only rarely in small cities. The presence or absence of SWAT teams in these smaller cities is independent of local crime rates, again suggesting the inapplicability of contingency theory and the likely insight to be derived from an institutional theory perspective.

Similarly, in a qualitative, multiyear study on community policing in Seattle, Washington, William Lyons (1999, p. 13) found that implementation of community policing did not correspond to a systematic change in the operational efforts of the Seattle Police Department. Lyons concluded that "this meant that even in a National Institute of Justice Model of community policing (Seattle) there was nearly no change in police organization, patrol orientation, community-based crime prevention, or accountability six years after the first police-community partnership was established."

James Thompson (1967), in his classic work *Organizations in Action,* argued that organizations tend to develop buffers to protect their core mission processes and activities in times of uncertainty. Innovations proliferate along the boundaries of the organizational and environmental nexus in periods of crisis, while the core mission of the organization remains sealed off from the influence of an unstable environment. In both the 1993 and the 1996 surveys, police departments were asked to evaluate the extent of implementation of community policing in their agencies over the course of the previous three years. Over 70 percent of the survey respondents indicated that the implementation of COP had proceeded well, but this reported progress toward COP operations did not translate into the reprioritization of core police functions. Similarly, in their pioneering study on applying institutional theory to police research, Crank and Langworthy (1992, p. 341) forcefully argued, "As a result of this environmental context, police practices and organizational structures cannot be understood either simply in terms of production economies or solely from the perspective of technical efficiency and effectiveness."

The longitudinal data explored in this analysis covered too little time to permit a definitive judgment on the extent to which COP would ultimately cause a paradigm shift in American policing. Given the fact that it took police agencies about thirty years (1900s to 1930s) to complete the transition from the political model of policing to the predominant professional model, much more time must pass before community policing's impact can be assessed. Future research of the type reported here will need to be periodically undertaken and reported to determine whether a long-term pursuit of COP leads to a genuine reprioritization of core functions reflecting a new paradigm in American policing.

Acknowledgments

We thank Jeremy Miller for his contribution in the data collection process which made this paper possible.

Notes

1. As a direct result of this legislation, the federal government has now become the principal sponsor in the nationwide implementation of COP (National Institute of Justice, 1997). The Crime Act contains provisions to fund local governments for hiring and redeployment of 100,000 police officers who must be engaged in bonafide community policing activities. Similarly, the Office of Community Oriented Policing Services (the "OCOPS") was established at the federal level to coordinate and supervise the implementation of COP activities. In 1995, over thirty regional community policing institutes were created across the nation to provide COP train-

Appendix 9.1

Part A: Scales in 1996 and 1993 Surveys

	Alpha for the 1996 scales	Alpha for the 1993 scales
1. Crime control: against persons	.74	.71
Robbery		
Rape		
Stranger assault		
2. Crime control: drug and gangs[a]		
Drug dealing in the streets		
Gangs		
3. Crime control: against property	.62	.67
Burglary		
Vandalism		
Property damage		
4. Order maintenance	.63	.64
Neighborhood trouble		
Family trouble		
Vagrancy		
5. Service	.53	.71
Fire, power out, tree down		
Emergency services—accidents, ambulance calls		
Lost and found person or property		
Stray animals		
Drunkenness		

Part B: Four Types of Crime Rates in the Cities Surveyed (per 100,000 residents)[b]

	1995	1992
Murder rate	9.97	11.52
Rape rate	50.75	54.77
Robbery rate	332.95	390.99
Assault	529.35	633.47

[a] The correlation between the two items is .38 for 1996.

[b] Data are collected from FBI's *Uniform Crime Report* for 1995 and 1992, respectively.

Appendix 9.2
List of COP programs and strategies

Externally focused change/reorientation of police operations and crime prevention
1. Department sponsorship of community newsletter
2. Additional officers on foot, bicycle, or horse patrol
3. Use of storefronts for crime prevention
4. Use of task unit for solving special problems in a targeted area
5. Victim contact program
6. Crime prevention education of the general public
7. Fixed assignment of officers to neighborhoods or schools for extended periods
8. Permanent reassignment of some sworn personnel from traditional patrol to crime prevention
9. Use of citizen survey to keep informed about local problems
10. Neighborhood watch
11. Business watch
12. Increased hiring of civilians for non–law enforcement tasks
13. Community service officers (uniformed citizens who perform support and community liaison activities)
14. Unpaid civilian volunteers who perform support and community liaison activities

Internally or managerial focused change

15. Reassessment of rank and assignments
16. Reassigning some management positions from sworn to civilian personnel
17. Adding the position of "Master Police Officer" to increase rewards for line officers
18. Quality circles (problem solving among small groups of line personnel)

ing for local police agencies either wishing to adopt COP or desiring to deepen their knowledge of COP programs and practices already in use in other jurisdictions (OCOPS, 1997).

2. A key to understanding these two types of organizations is knowing that organization configuration (e.g., structure, supervision, and division of labor) is contingent upon an effective matching up with the organizational environment. In this regard, Lawrence and Lorsch's (1969) classical study concerning the impact of the external environment on three types of industries—pharmaceutical, chemical, and container firms—certainly constitutes an influential work. Their findings confirmed that organizational differentiation and integration are determined to some important degree by the specific environment that surrounds an organization.
3. Crank and Langworthy (1993) are the scholars who first applied institutional theory in the study of American police and analyzed the institutionalized environment of police agencies (also see Crank, 1994).
4. Similar to the 1993 study, the four Part I crimes against persons that are published in the UCR are included in the index (murder, rape, robbery, and assault). Furthermore, the index was constructed using *z* scores of these crimes because the frequencies of murder and rape were significantly lower than those of the other two crimes. The change in crime rates is measured as the change in *z* scores between 1992 and 1995 UCR index.
5. Use of innovative programs to measure the extent of change is common in organizational change literature (Damanpour, 1991; Kimberly, 1976). Further, based on the literature, two categories of COP programs are included—the externally focused and internally focused programs—to capture a broad spectrum of innovations in policing.
6. For more discussion on the variables city size and region, see Zhao and Thurman (1997).

References

Angell, J. E. (1971). Toward an alternative to the classic police organizational arrangements: A democratic model. *Criminology, 8,* 185–206.

Bertalanffy, L. (1956). General system theory. In: L. Bertalanffy (ed.), *General systems: Yearbook of the society for the advancement of general system theory* (vol. 1, pp. 1–10). Ann Arbor, MI: Mental Health Research Institute.

Bittner, E. (1967). Police on skid row: A study of peace keeping. *American Sociological Review, 32,* 699–715.

——. (1972). *The functions of the police in modern society* (2nd ed.). Washington, DC: National Institute of Mental Health.

Blau, P. & Schoenherr, R. (1971). *The structure of organizations.* New York: Basic Books.

Brown, L., & Wycoff, M. A. (1987). Policing Houston: Reducing fear and improving service. *Crime and Delinquency, 33,* 71–89.

Buerger, M. (1994). The limits of community. In: D. Rosenbaum (Ed.), *The challenge of community policing: Testing the promises* (pp. 270–273). Thousand Oaks, CA: Sage Publications.

Burns, T., & Stalker, G. (1963). *The management of innovation.* London: Tavistock.

Capowich, G., & Roehl, J. (1994). Problem-oriented policing: Actions and effectiveness in San Diego. In: D. Rosenbaum (Ed.), *The challenge of community policing: Testing the promises* (pp. 127–146). Thousand Oaks, CA: Sage Publications.

Cordner, G. (1988). Community policing: Elements and effects. In: G. Alpert & A. Piquero (eds.), *Community policing: Contemporary readings* (pp. 45–62). Prospect Heights, IL: Waveland Press.

Crank, J. (1994). Watchman and community: Myth and institutionalization in policing. *Law and Society Review, 28,* 338–363.

Crank, J., & Langworthy, R. (1992). An institutional perspective of policing. *Journal of Criminal Law and Criminology, 83,* 338–363.

Crank, J., & Wells, E. (1991). The effects of size and urbanism on structure among Illinois police departments. *Justice Quarterly, 8,* 169–185.

Damanpour, F. (1991). Organizational innovation: A meta-analysis of effects of determinants and moderators. *Academy of Management Journal, 34,* 555–590.

Dewar, R., & Hage, J. (1978). Size, technology, complexity, and structural differentiation: Toward a theoretical synthesis. *Administrative Science Quarterly, 23,* 111–136.

DiMaggio, P. (1983). State expansion and organizational fields. In: R. Hall & R. E. Quinn (Eds.), *Organizational theory and public policy* (pp. 147–161). Beverly Hills, CA: Sage Publications.

Donaldson, L. (1995). *American anti-management theories of organization: A critique of paradigm proliferation.* New York: Cambridge University Press.

Eck, J., & Rosenbaum, D. (1994). The new police order: Effectiveness, equality, and efficiency in community policing. In: D. Rosenbaum (Ed.), *The challenge of community policing: Testing the promises* (pp. 3–146). Thousand Oaks, CA: Sage Publications.

Eck, J., & Spelman, W. (1987). *Solving problems: Problem-oriented policing in Newport News.* Washington, DC: Police Executive Research Forum.

Flanagan, T. (1985). Consumer perspectives on police operational strategy. *Journal of Police Science and Administration, 13,* 10–21.

Germann, L. (1969). Community policing: An assessment. *Journal of Criminal Law and Criminology, and Police Science, 60,* 89–96.

Goldstein, H. (1977). *Policing a free society.* Cambridge, MA: Ballinger.

——. (1990). *Problem oriented policing.* New York: McGraw-Hill.

Greenwood, P., Chaiken, J., & Petersilia, J. (1977). The criminal investigation process. Lexington, MA: D.C. Heath.

Hage, J., & Aiken, M. (1970). *Social change in complex organizations.* New York: Random House.

Huber, G., Sutcliffe, K., Miller, C., & Glick, W. (1993). Understanding and predicting organizational change. In: G. Huber & W. Glick (Eds.), *Organizational change and redesign: Ideas and insights for improving performance* (pp. 215–254). New York: Oxford University Press.

Kelling, G. (1988). Police and community: The quiet revolution. *Perspectives on policing* (no. 1). Washington, DC: National Institute of Justice and Harvard University.

Kelling, G., & Moore, M. (1988). From political reform to community: The evolving strategy of police. In: J. Greene & S. Mastrofski (Eds.), *Community policing: Rhetoric or reality?* (pp. 3–25). New York: Praeger.

Kelling, G., Pate, A., Dieckman, D., & Brown, C. (1974). *The Kansas City preventive patrol experiment: A summary report.* Washington, DC: Police Foundation.

Kessler, D. (1993). Integrating calls for service with community- and problem-oriented policing: A case study. *Crime and Delinquency, 39,* 485–508.

Kimberly, J. (1976). Organizational size and the structuralist perspective: A review, critique, and proposal. *Administrative Science Quarterly, 21,* 571–579.

Klockars, C. (1988). The rhetoric of community policing. In: J. Greene & S. Mastrofski (Eds.), *Community policing: Rhetoric or reality?* (pp. 239–258). New York: Praeger.

Kraska, P., & Cubellis, L. (1997). Militarizing Mayberry and beyond: Making sense of American paramilitary policing. *Justice Quarterly, 14,* 607–629.

Lawrence, P., & Lorsch, J. (1969). *Organization and environment.* Homewood, IL: Richard D. Irwin.

Lyons, W. (1999). *The politics of community policing: Rearranging the power to punish.* Ann Arbor, MI: University of Michigan Press.

Maguire, E. (1997). Structural change in large municipal police organizations in the community policing era. *Justice Quarterly, 14,* 547–576.

Manning, P. (1988). Community policing as a drama of control. In: J. Greene & S. Mastrofski (Eds.), *Community policing: Rhetoric or reality?* (pp. 27–45). New York: Praeger.

——. (1995). TQM and the future of policing. *Police Forum,* vol. 5 (no. 2). Richmond, KY: Academy of Criminal Justice Sciences.

Meagher, S. (1985). Police patrol styles: How pervasive is community variation? *Journal of Police Science and Administration, 13,* 36–45.

Meyer, J., Boli, J., & Thomas, G. (1995). Ontology and rationalization in the western cultural account. In: R. Meyer, J. Meyer, et al. (Eds.), *Institutional environments and organizations: Structure complexity and individualism.* Thousand Oaks, CA: Sage Publications.

Meyer, J., & Rowan, B. (1977). Institutionalized organizations: Formal structure as myth and ceremony. *American Journal of Sociology, 83,* 340–363.

Meyer, J., & Scott, R. (1983). Centralization and the legitimacy problems of local government. In: J. Meyer & W. Scott (Eds.), *Organizational environments: Ritual and rationality* (pp. 199–215). Beverly Hills, CA: Sage Publications.

Mobrman, S. & Mobrman, A. (1990). The environment as an agent of change. In: A. Mobrman and Associates (Eds.), *Large-scale organizational change* (pp. 35–47). San Francisco: Jossey-Bass.

Moore, M. (1994). Research synthesis and policy implications. In: D. Rosenbaum (Ed.), *The challenge of community policing: Testing the promises* (pp. 285–289). Thousand Oaks, CA: Sage Publications.

National Institute of Justice. (1997). *Criminal justice research under the crime act—1995 to 1996.* Washington, DC: U.S. Department of Justice.

Office of Community Oriented Policing Services. (1997, February/March). *Community cops.* Washington, DC: U.S. Department of Justice.

Parsons, T. (1956). Suggestions for a sociological approach to the theory of organizations. *Administrative Science Quarterly, 1,* 63–85.

President's Commission on Law Enforcement and Administration of Justice. (1967). *The challenge of crime in a free society.* Washington, DC: U.S. Government Printing Office.

Scott, R. (1995). *Institutions and organizations.* Thousand Oaks, CA: Sage Publications.

Selznick, P. (1948). Foundations of the theory of organization. *American Sociological Review, 13,* 25–35.

Simon, H. (1964). On the concept of organizational goal. *Administrative Science Quarterly, 9,* 1–22.

Steel, B., & Lovrich, N. (1986). Fiscal stress, competing values, and municipal governance: What fate befell affirmative action in municipal police departments? *Journal of Urban Affairs, 15,* 15–30.

Thompson, J. (1967). *Organizations in action.* New York: McGraw-Hill.

Trojanowicz, R., & Bucqueroux, B. (1990). *Community policing: A contemporary perspective.* Cincinnati: Anderson Publishing.

United States Congress. (1994). *Congressional record: Proceedings and debates of the 103rd Congress, second session, 140* (120), H8772–H8878.

Van de Ven, A., & Drazin, R. (1985). The concept of fit in contingency theory. *Research in Organizational Behavior, 7* 333–365.

Van de Ven, A., & Poole, M. (1995). Explaining development and change in organizations. *Academy of Management Review, 20,* 510–540.

Walker, S. (1977). *A critical history of police reform.* Lexington, MA: D.C. Heath.

Warner, R., Steel, B., & Lovrich, N. (1989). Conditions associated with the advent of representative bureaucracy: The case of women in policing. *Social Science Quarterly, 70,* 562–578.

Wasserman, R., & Moore, M. (1988). Values in policing. *Perspectives on policing (no. 8).* Washington, DC: National Institute of Justice.

Weisel, D., & Eck, J. (1994). Toward a practical approach to organizational change: community policing initiatives in six cities. In: D. Rosenbaum (Ed.), *The challenge of community policing: Testing the promises* (pp. 53–72). Thousand Oaks, CA: Sage Publications.

Weisheit, R., Wells, E., & Falcone, D. (1994). Community policing in small town and rural America. *Crime and Delinquency, 40,* 549–567.

Wilson, J. Q. (1968). *Varieties of police behavior.* Cambridge, MA: Harvard University Press.

Wilson, J. Q., & Kelling, G. (1982). The police and neighborhood safety: Broken windows. *Atlantic Monthly, 249,* 29–38.

Woodward, J. (1958). *Management and technology.* London: Her Majesty's Stationery Office.

Wycoff, M. A., & Skogan, W. (1994). The effect of a community policing management style on officers' attitudes. *Crime and Delinquency, 40,* 371–383.

Yin, R. (1979). *Changing in urban bureaucracies: How new practices become routinized.* Lexington, MA: Lexington Books.

Zhao, J. (1996). *Why police organizations change: A study of community policing.* Washington, DC: Police Executive Research Forum.

Zhao, J., & Thurman, Q. (1997). Community policing: Where are we now? *Crime and Delinquency, 43,* 345–357.

Jihong Zhao, Nicholas P. Lovrich, and T. Hank Robinson, "Community Policing: Is It Changing the Basic Functions of Policing? Findings from a Longitudinal Study of 200+ Municipal Police Agencies." Reprinted from *Journal of Criminal Justice* 29 (5): 365–377.

Chapter 10

Police Culture, Individualism, and Community Policing

Evidence from Two Police Departments

Eugene A. Paoline, III
Stephanie M. Myers
Robert E. Worden

Police culture has long been seen as a uniform response to the dangers of police work and the ambiguity of the police role. Conventional wisdom supposes an authoritarian, aggressive police culture that engenders fierce loyalty to the group, a culture prone to abuses of authority and tension between police and society at large. But even research done in the 1970s belied the idea of this monolithic police culture, and changes in the last twenty-five years, including the rise of community policing and increased diversity in officers' gender, race, and education levels, suggest even further fragmentation.

Based on Project on Policing Neighborhoods data for two cities, the authors examined police officers' outlooks on seven issues, including order maintenance, aggressiveness, and distrust of citizens, to determine how officers saw the police role. Then the effects of officer characteristics on those outlooks were analyzed, yielding surprising results.

Introduction

Police officers' occupational attitudes and values are shaped by a working environment characterized by uncertainty, danger, and coercive authority. Officers' adaptations to this environment form the basis for the police culture—a set of outlooks widely shared among officers.[1] This is part of the conventional wisdom about police; it can be found in textbooks (e.g., Crank 1998; Peak and Glensor 1999:146–49) and heard at conferences. This culture idealizes a hard-nosed, aggressive approach to policing which accords priority to law enforcement and crime fighting, and which gives rise to abuses of authority and tension with the community. The police culture impedes efforts to detect and investigate corruption and other misconduct. Furthermore, contemporary reform efforts, especially including the implementation of community policing, confront resistance by police officers that is rooted in the culture (Lurigio and Skogan 1994; Skogan and Hartnett 1997:ch. 4; Sparrow, Moore, and Kennedy 1990).

Yet we also know that police officers' attitudes vary along a number of important dimensions. Studies based on field research conducted in the 1970s show that police officers differed, even then, in their conceptions of the police role and in their attitudes toward legal restrictions, legal institutions, discretionary enforcement, police supervision, and the citizenry (see R. Worden 1995). With changes in the composition of police forces and in departmental philosophies over the past two decades, one now might expect to find still greater variation in officers' attitudes, inasmuch as police officers are more diverse and their working environment is evolving with the implementation of community policing. Thus the conventional wisdom about the police culture must be refined.

Our primary thesis is that widely accepted portrayals of the police culture overstate the range of the outlooks that constitute the police culture: with respect to several of the outlooks that are normally ascribed to the culture, officers vary more widely than the conventional wisdom would lead us to expect. Thus we raise a question not about the existence of a police culture, but rather about the content and scope of that culture. We also posit that changes in policing—diversity in social backgrounds and the adoption of community policing—could be expected to have further attenuated the pull of cultural forces. On that basis we hypothesize that officers' characteristics—their sex, race, and education, and their exposure to community policing—are related to their occupational attitudes. These propositions are compatible with some recent research (Haarr 1997; Herbert 1998; Jermier et al. 1991; Manning 1994), which challenges the (implicit or explicit) view that police culture is monolithic.

In an effort to bring systematic empirical evidence to these propositions, we analyze data collected in two police departments for the Project on Policing Neighborhoods (POPN). Patrol officers in the Indianapolis Police Department (IPD) and the St. Petersburg Police Department (SPPD) were surveyed for POPN respectively in 1996 and 1997; both of these departments had begun to implement community policing.

First, we identify a number of occupational outlooks that echo themes of the police culture: officers' conceptions of the scope of the police role, beliefs about how that role should be performed, and attitudes toward citizens. We discuss recent changes in policing, explain how those changes might alter the working environment with which officers must cope, and examine the implications for officers' outlooks and police culture. From a consideration of those changes we derive some hypotheses about the relationships between officers' outlooks and their sex, race, education, length of service, training, and assignment. We then present findings on these questions based on our analysis of POPN data: the distributions of officers along these attitudinal dimensions, and the extent to which these outlooks are shaped by officers' backgrounds and characteristics. We find that the distributions of officers' outlooks do not conform to the conventional wisdom about police culture; we also find, unexpectedly, that race, sex, and other characteristics do not account for much of the variation in outlooks. We then discuss the implications for future research and practice.

Culture, Individualism, and Change in Policing

Police Culture: Conventional Wisdom

Accounts of the police culture that form the basis for conventional wisdom have focused on the mechanisms used by officers to cope with their occupational and organizational environments (Bittner 1974; Brown 1988; Drummond 1976; Farkas and Manning 1997; Fielding 1988; Kappeler, Sluder, and Alpers 1994; Manning 1995; McNamara 1967; Muir 1977; Reiner 1985; Reuss-Ianni 1983; Skolnick 1966; Sparrow et al. 1990; Tauber 1970; Van Maanen 1974; Westley 1970). The occupational environment includes physical danger intrinsic to police work and the unique coercive authority wielded by officers. The organizational environment includes unpredictable and punitive supervisory oversight, and the ambiguity of the police role. The police culture is thought to consist of widely shared attitudes, values, and norms that manage the strains which originate in these work environments (see Crank 1998). We briefly summarize this view here.

Officers cope with the danger and uncertainty of their occupational environment by *being suspicious* and *maintaining the edge.* Personal safety is an overriding concern; officers learn to "read" people and situations in terms of the potential danger that they pose (Van Maanen 1974:118). Officers "maintain the edge" with an authoritative, take-charge approach to policing as they create, display, and maintain their authority to be "one up" on citizens (Manning 1995; Sykes and Brent 1980).

Officers cope with the organizational environment by taking a *lay-low* or *cover-your-ass* attitude and adopting a *crimefighter* or *law-enforcement* orientation. They discover that when they are recognized, it is usually for something they have done wrong (procedurally) rather than for something they have done well (substantively), and they learn that hard work entails the risk of exposure and sanction. They also learn, however, that they can resolve the ambiguity of their role in society by identifying with the role that management has normally recognized as the official mandate of the police (Walker 1977), and in which they can find honor. Police training, the creation of specialized divisions, the focus on crime statistics, and performance evaluation and promotion traditionally have reinforced the law-enforcement orientation (Bittner 1974:21–22). Thus the police culture stresses law enforcement or "real" police work over order-maintenance or service roles, and the inner-directed, aggressive street cop is the cultural ideal. Because aggressive law enforcement entails bureaucratic risks, officers adopt a selective approach to law enforcement, focusing on more serious criminal incidents (i.e., felonies). They are careful to justify their actions post hoc or to conceal their mistakes and indiscretions.

The problems that officers confront in their working environment, as well as the coping mechanisms prescribed by the police culture, produce the defining characteristics of the police culture: *social isolation* and *group loyalty.* The dangerousness of their occupational environment prompts officers to distance themselves from the rest of society (Tauber 1970). The unique elements of their coercive authority separate them further from the public (Skolnick 1966). Some analysts hold that the professionalization of the police (i.e., taking the politics out of policing, focusing on scientific crimefighting, and using motorized patrol, along with anticorruption measures) has been a catalyst for this isolation and strengthening of the police culture (Brown 1988; Sparrow et al. 1990). In this context, officers develop a "we versus they" attitude toward the citizenry (Sparrow et al. 1990) and strong norms of group loyalty. New recruits are tested before being accepted as one of the group, and officers are expected to provide mutual support in the face of a hostile citizenry and a punitive bureaucracy.

Autonomy and Individualism in Policing

As Brown explains, "[L]oyalty and individualism are the opposite sides of the coin: the police culture demands loyalty but grants autonomy" (1988:85; also see Manning 1995:474). This individualism, according to Brown and others (Broderick 1977; Muir 1977; White 1972), manifests itself in attitudes that diverge from those ascribed to the culture, including beliefs about the scope and the proper performance of the police role and tactics, as well as attitudes toward the public. This research, which has generated typologies of police officers, contrasts with conventional views of the police culture, particularly with respect to the predominance of a role orientation defined by law enforcement, the idealization of an aggressive approach to policing, and an "us versus them" attitude toward citizens. While research on the police culture has emphasized what appeared to be the central tendencies in the occupational group, the typologies highlight the variance.

In forming a fourfold typology of officers, Brown (1988) found differences in officers' *aggressiveness* and *selectivity.* Aggressiveness is "a matter of taking the initiative on the street to control crime and the preoccupation with order that legitimizes the use of illegal tactics" (p. 223). The priority that officers place on the law-enforcement function, and on enforcement activities such as running license checks and conducting field interrogations, is one respect in which they exhibit attitudinal differences. Selectivity distinguishes among patrol officers "who believe that all laws should be enforced insofar as possible, and those who consciously assign felonies a higher priority" (Brown 1988:223); thus the importance of enforcing against even minor infractions is another respect in which officers' attitudes differ. Brown distinguishes four types of officers in terms of these two characteristics, and his typology demonstrates that many officers do not fit the traditional cultural mold. His "old-style crimefighter," who is both highly aggressive and selective, epitomizes the officer described in the literature on the police culture. The contrasting attitudes of the other types, however, reflect the individualism that prevailed among police even in the 1970s, when Brown conducted his field research. Brown's "service-style" officer, for example, accords higher priority to order maintenance and service than to law enforcement; the "professional-style officer" is quite receptive to performing the order-maintenance and service functions in addition to law enforcement.

William Ker Muir (1977) also formed a fourfold typology of police officers, based on their views of human nature and their moral outlook on coercive authority. The cynicism that characterizes Muir's "enforcer," and the ease with which the "enforcer" reconciles coercive authority with a code of morality, typify themes of the police culture. But two other types that Muir describes—the "professional" and the "reciprocator"—hold more benign views of human nature; these views not only temper their use of authority but also would appear to make them quite receptive to working cooperatively with citizens. Such officers regard people as fundamentally alike, rather than as either good or evil; thus one might expect that they maintain a functional suspiciousness without subscribing to a "we versus they" outlook.

This research suggests that officers cope in different ways with the strains created by their working environment. The coping mechanisms that are part of what we know as the police culture may have predominated at one time; some of these—such as strong group loyalty—still may be predominant today. Apparently, however, some officers manage the strains of their work without adopting all of the outlooks that we normally ascribe to the police culture. Furthermore, changes over the past two decades in the working environment, and in the backgrounds of officers (see Britz 1997; Haarr 1997; Walker 1985) who must cope with the environment, may have further attenuated the centripetal pull of cultural forces.

Changes in Policing

Over the past 25 years, policing has changed (and continues to change) in at least two major respects: the promulgation of a community-policing philosophy and the increasing diversity of police personnel. The adoption of and experimentation with community policing (and, before it, team policing) may have altered both the occupational and (especially) the organizational environments of policing, and within those environments the strains that officers must manage. Changes in the philosophy and practice of policing, then, might shift the distribution of occupational attitudes among officers, especially as new officers enter police work and older officers, whose outlooks were formed in an earlier era, retire. Increasing diversity in officers' race, sex, and education might be expected to alter patterns of interaction and socialization (Haarr 1997; Manning 1994) and to diminish the strength of officers' attachment to the occupation and the peer group.

Community Policing. Insofar as community policing changes the role of the police and the relationship between police and citizens, it might be expected to alter elements of both the occupational and the organizational environments of police. Community policing could be expected to affect the occupational environment in two ways. First, by providing for stable assignments to geographic areas and facilitating officers' familiarity with the people and places in those areas, and by providing for more frequent contacts with law-abiding and cooperative citizens, it might mitigate to some degree the perceived threats in officers' environments.[2] Second, as a result of extending officers' capacity to handle incidents and deal with problems using less conventional tactics that do not depend on their authority to invoke the criminal law, officers' coercive authority might become a somewhat less salient element of their occupational identity. Community policing might be expected especially to affect the organizational environment by expanding the range of functions that properly fall within the scope of the police role, and perhaps even by reordering the priorities attached to them. This process might result in greater attention to and recognition of officers' efforts to reduce disorders, solve neighborhood problems, and build rapport with citizens. With these changes, officers might be less likely to adopt a "we versus they" outlook toward citizens and less likely to define their role in narrow terms that emphasize law enforcement. Instead we might expect that officers will be more likely to internalize a community-policing "philosophy."

Community-policing training is a potentially important part of the transition to community policing (Skogan and Hartnett 1997; cf. Buerger 1998). Training that provides a rationale for an expanded police role, for problem solving, and for citizen involvement might legitimate these features of community policing for new officers and perhaps to change the outlooks of more experienced and traditional officers. Officers with (more) training in community policing might be more likely to have heard and understood the messages, and thus to hold broader conceptions of the role and more positive attitudes toward citizens. Moreover, training that enhances officers' capacity to perform community-policing functions—analyzing problems, working with community groups, developing and implementing responses that do not rely on the criminal law—could shape officers' outlooks on the police role and their attitudes toward the public.

Specialized community-policing assignments might provide positive experiences in problem solving and working with citizens that reinforce the messages of training. Such experiences provide immediate and concrete evidence that community policing is practicable and effective. The effects of such assignments possibly could extend beyond those who hold them—that is, officers assigned to traditional patrol duties could observe the work of community policing specialists and could learn, through such vicarious experience, about the virtues of community policing—but we would expect the effect to be strongest for those with direct experiences. In departments in which nonspecialists have occasion to experiment with community policing, we might expect to find smaller differences between specialists and other officers.

One might expect that officers who are socialized in this altered working environment would develop occupational attitudes which are more compatible with community policing and which diverge from cultural tenets. In this regard, the community era of policing might parallel the due process revolution:

> The hostility to standards of due process identified by Skolnick in his 1960's research may have declined by 1990. One important factor accounting for this change is the steady turnover of police personnel. Most police officers working today, and virtually all patrol officers, were hired after the Miranda decisions. The legal standards that prevailed at the start of their careers were very different from those prevailing when the officers studied by Skolnick began their careers. As a result, they were socialized into a different legal context than were older officers. (Walker 1992:336)

If the most recent cohorts of police officers are more likely than their predecessors to embrace community-policing outlooks, we would expect officers' outlooks to be related to their length of service.[3] Skogan and Hartnett (1997), however, report the opposite: in Chicago, older officers held more favorable attitudes toward community policing. In addition, Crank (1997) argues that successful community-policing reform depends on integrating "seasoned officers," who are "carriers" of police culture, into the strategic change.

Diversity. Police departments now include proportionally more women, more members of racial minorities, and more college-educated officers than in the past. Walker (1992:313–14) reports that in the mid-1960s, only 3.6 percent of all sworn officers were black; in 1972, only 2 percent of sworn officers in cities with populations of 50,000 or more were women. By 1993, on the basis of his analysis of Law Enforcement Management and Administrative Statistics (LEMAS) data collected in that year, Reaves (1996) estimates that of all the full-time sworn officers in local police departments of all sizes, 19 percent were members of minorities and 8.8 percent were women. Furthermore, officers' educational backgrounds have become more diverse: Carter, Sapp, and Stephens (1989:38) report that by 1988, 65.2 percent of officers had at least one year of college education, while 22.6 percent had earned at least a baccalaureate degree.

These changes in the composition of police personnel may contribute to a further fragmentation of the police culture and an even greater heterogeneity in their occupational outlooks. The demographic diversity of police has altered the patterns of interactions among officers because minorities and women have not been accepted readily into the traditional culture. Furthermore, because not all officers come from the same social background, and because they have career alternatives to policing, officers' attachments to the occupation and the peer group may be weaker than in the past (see Haarr 1997; Reuss-Ianni 1983). Acculturating forces therefore may be less powerful now than they once were; as a result, preservice socialization and outlooks would affect the development of officers' occupational outlooks more strongly. As police forces have become more diverse, then, one might expect to find greater variation in officers' adaptations to their working environment and greater covariation between their outlooks and their backgrounds.

Women in American society traditionally have been socialized to be caregivers; women tend to be more aware of, and more concerned with, people's needs (Gilligan 1982). Furthermore, women historically have been excluded from the police profession and the traditional police culture. Consequently one might expect that women would be less likely to internalize—or even more likely to challenge—cultural tenets (A. Worden 1993:207). Therefore, one might expect women's conception of the police role to be more expansive; also, insofar as women are less rule-oriented, they might be more selective in their enforcement. They might also be more likely than men to hold positive views of citizens, if they are less confrontational and encounter less resistance from citizens (A. Worden 1993:211). These expectations seldom have been subjected to empirical scrutiny. When they have been tested, they have not been confirmed (see Morash and Haarr 1995; A. Worden 1993), perhaps because women who are attracted to (and survive in) police work are unrepresentative of women generally, but also perhaps because of the powerful effects of the work environment. With changes in the work environment, we might find more support for these expectations in the 1990s and beyond (but cf. Skogan and Hartnett 1997).

Similarly, minority officers have not been accepted into the police culture as readily as whites. Thus we might expect that minority officers would be less likely to embrace—and perhaps more likely to reject—cultural values. Minority officers might have more insight and empathy regarding the perspective of minority communities, which place less trust in police authority (see, e.g., Durand 1976; Flanagan 1985; Shuman and Gruenberg 1972), and regarding minority communities' need for police services. Minority officers also might be more aware of, and sensitive to, the potentially detrimental consequences of aggressive policing and selective enforcement. In addition, they might appreciate more fully the beneficial forms that police service can take, to include order-maintenance and noncrime services. Finally, one might expect that minority officers would be less susceptible to stereotypes promulgated by the police culture and less estranged from the minority communities (see Buzawa 1981); thus they may be more likely than their white counterparts to see citizens as willing to cooperate. Skogan and Hartnett (1997) found some support for these expectations in their evaluation of community policing in Chicago.

One might expect college-educated officers to have a weaker attachment to the police culture, and thus to be more independent from that culture, inasmuch as their occupational options extend beyond their police careers (Reuss-Ianni 1983). Educational experiences might result in a greater appreciation of the multiple functions that police perform in modern society, of limitations on police authority, and of the social, economic, and psychological forces that shape the problems and behavior of the people with whom they have contact. Therefore one might expect that college-educated officers would subscribe to broader role orientations than their less-educated colleagues, that they would have more positive attitudes toward citizens, and that they would be less aggressive. College-educated officers also might expect to be more autonomous in exercising discretion, and to accept bureaucratic constraints with less equanimity, than would less highly educated officers, thus we might expect them to be more favorably disposed toward selective enforcement. These expectations are based, to some extent, on the premise of a liberal arts education; insofar as college curricula approximate such an education to varying degrees, the effect of a college education as such might be fairly weak. Indeed, empirical tests of such propositions have produced at best mixed support and, on balance, only modest confirmation (see Brooks, Piquero, and Cronin 1993; R. Worden 1990).

Previous research clearly shows that even during the reform era, police culture was much less than monolithic with respect to several outlooks, although the degree of dispersion cannot be estimated. With changes in the composition of police and in the working environment of police during the community era, we might expect to find still greater variation in occupational outlooks and less reliance on the culturally prescribed coping mechanisms. Although we would not dispute the existence of a police culture, we raise empirical questions about the content of the culture. Are each of the outlooks normally considered part of the police culture actually held by most officers? What are the social and organizational lines of attitudinal cleavage among officers? We cannot examine changes in the distribution of occupational outlooks over time, but we can compare the distributions that we observe with those which one would expect on the basis of conventional wisdom. We also can look for evidence that these outlooks are affected by characteristics which reflect changes in policing: social background (sex, race, and education) and exposure to community policing (training, assignment, and length of service).

Evidence from Indianapolis and St. Petersburg

The Project on Policing Neighborhoods (POPN) surveyed officers in two agencies, the Indianapolis Police Department (IPD) and the St. Petersburg Police Department (SPPD). Comparisons of minority and female representation using 1993 LEMAS data (Reaves and Smith 1995) show that IPD and SPPD were very near the national average for minority representation (with 19.1% and 18.3% respectively), and somewhat above the national average for female representation (with 15.1% and 12.6% respectively). Both departments had begun to implement community policing—IPD in 1992 and SPPD in 1990—although they practiced somewhat different conceptions of community policing (see Mastrofski, Worden, and Snipes 1995). IPD's top management espoused a form of community policing which resembles the "broken windows" model, and which was interpreted to street-level officers as directed, aggressive patrol. Community policing in St. Petersburg took a less aggressive approach: it emphasized community engagement (i.e., building positive relations between police and the citizenry) and a problem-oriented approach based on the (SARA) model (see Eck and Spelman 1987).[4] Hence we conduct separate analyses for each department, in the event that these differences affect attitudinal patterns.

POPN sought to survey all officers with patrol responsibilities. In Indianapolis, the survey was conducted during the summer of 1996; of the 426 patrol officers assigned to one of IPD's four patrol districts during the study period, 398 were interviewed, for a completion rate of 93 percent.[5] In St. Petersburg, the survey was conducted during the summer of 1997; 240 of the 246 patrol officers were interviewed, for a completion rate of 98 percent. At both sites, each officer was interviewed by a trained interviewer in a private room during the regular work shift. Interviewers followed a structured instrument designed to obtain information on officers' personal characteristics, training and education, work experience, perceptions of their beats, and attitudes toward the police role. Participation was voluntary, and each respondent was promised confidentiality.[6]

To better understand the distributions of officers' outlooks and their associations with officers' characteristics, we first briefly consider the work environments of IPD and SPPD as officers experienced them subjectively. We then examine the central tendencies and dispersion of officers' outlooks on the police role and on citizens, and we analyze patterns of association between officers' outlooks and their characteristics.

The Work Environments

The POPN survey data contain some clues about officers' familiarity with their beats, their self-assessed knowledge of approaches to their work that do not rely on the use of the criminal law, their perceptions of the use of rewards and sanctions by management, and their perceptions of management's priorities and the implementation of problem solving.[7] We have no baseline data with which to compare officers' responses, however; thus we cannot assess the degree to which officers' perceptions of their work environments have changed over time. Overall the survey data suggest that both of these departments, at the time of POPN data collection, were in a period of transition to community policing.

Many of the officers in IPD had regular beat assignments and had worked fairly regularly in their beats. This situation presumably allowed them to develop a knowledge of their beats that might make the working environment somewhat less threatening. A smaller but substantial fraction of SPPD officers had worked in their beats with comparable regularity. Furthermore, the majority of officers in both departments felt at least moderately knowledgeable about the use of mediation and civil remedies (on which modest levels of training had been provided). They felt more knowledgeable, however, about search and seizure, which of course is related to their authority to enforce the criminal law. Officers' authority to invoke the criminal law might be a less salient feature of their professional identity insofar as they feel knowledgeable about handling incidents and resolving problems through other means. These data do not permit a direct examination of officers' perceptions of the occupational environment, but they offer some reason to believe that modest changes might have taken place, insofar as the adoption of community policing can alter an occupational environment that is marked by danger and coercive authority.

Moreover, the organizational environments in these departments appear to differ somewhat from those described in accounts of the police culture. One-third (in SPPD) to one-half (in IPD) of the officers believed it was at least "somewhat" likely that officers who perform well would be recognized by management; and three-fourths or more of the officers believed that minor rule violations would be treated fairly by management. Officers also perceived that management priorities included community engagement and problem solving in addition to more traditional enforcement functions, although their perceptions also reflected some uncertainty about the relative priorities.[8] Furthermore, most officers (particularly in SPPD) believed that the implementation of problem solving in their department was not supported by clear direction and needed resources.

Overall, the organizational environments that officers perceived did not closely resemble the overridingly and unpredictably punitive environment that appears in the literature on the police culture. Nor did these environments focus, albeit only implicitly, on crime control and law enforcement. Officers, however, saw a need for further efforts to clarify roles and provide needed resources (especially time and information). Therefore we might expect that in these departments, the traditional police culture would not be so influential in shaping officers' adaptations to their working environment.

Outlooks

We examine seven outlooks: orientation to law enforcement, orientation to order maintenance, orientation to community policing, aggressiveness, selectivity, distrust of citizens, and perceptions of citizens' cooperation. Most of these outlooks revolve around officers' conceptions of the police role. The law-enforcement orientation reflects the priority that officers attach to the law-enforcement function. The order-maintenance orientation reflects the degree to which officers include in their role conception a responsibility for handling routine order-maintenance situations. The community-policing orientation reflects the degree to which officers' role conceptions encompass a responsibility for handling problematic conditions (e.g., nuisance businesses, graffiti, abandoned cars). Aggressiveness, following Brown (1988), concerns the extent to which officers endorse a proactive style of patrol involving frequent stops and field interrogations. Selectivity, also following Brown, concerns the degree to which officers endorse non-enforcement against minor offenses. Officers' attitudes toward citizens, and presumably the degree to which officers view citizens as "them" (versus the police as "we"), are reflected in two outlooks: officers' distrust of citizens, and officers' perceptions of citizens' cooperation. Overall the outlooks of officers in Indianapolis and St. Petersburg do not conform to the pattern that we would expect on the basis of conventional wisdom about the police culture. In their responses we find greater receptivity to community policing than the conventional wisdom would predict.

Our measures of four of these outlooks are each based on a single survey item; the other three measures are additive indices.[9] Table 10.1

Table 10.1
Frequency Distributions for Outlooks: Single-Item Measures (Percentages)

Single-Item Survey Questions	Disagree Strongly	Disagree Somewhat	Agree Somewhat	Agree Strongly
Enforcing the law is by far a patrol officer's most important responsibility (law enforcement)				
IPD	4.5	12.6	55.9	27.0
SPPD	2.1	10.1	48.1	39.7
A good patrol officer is one who patrols aggressively by stopping cars, checking out people, running license checks, and so forth (aggressive patrol)				
IPD	6.5	24.4	44.7	24.4
SPPD	5.9	19.8	47.3	27.0
Police officers have reason to be distrustful of most citizens (citizen distrust)				
IPD	27.1	43.7	25.4	3.8
SPPD	29.7	44.9	25.0	.4
	Never	Rarely	Sometimes	Often
How frequently would you say there are good reasons for not arresting someone who has committed a minor criminal offense? (selective enforcement)				
IPD	.8	10.7	71.4	17.1
SPPD	1.7	18.6	63.7	16.0

displays the response categories (and associated numerical values) and the distributions in each department on the single-item measures: law enforcement, aggressiveness, citizen distrust, and selectivity. Table 10.2 displays the same information about the additive indices: order maintenance, community policing, and citizen cooperation.

More than 80 percent of the officers believe that law enforcement is their most important responsibility (see Table 10.1), but more than half express some qualifications that law enforcement is *by far* their most important responsibility. We might surmise that those with reservations differ from other officers in *how much* more important a responsibility they believe law enforcement to be.[10] Thus, although we find nearly uniform agreement that law enforcement is an important function, we also find variation in the intensity of opinion, which probably reflects differences in priorities.

Officers' role definitions include the performance of traditional order-maintenance tasks—handling family disputes, neighbor disputes, and public nuisances—although we find notable variation among officers (see Table 10.2). We might expect that officers who have internalized cultural values would tend to say that police should never handle such incidents, or should do so only sometimes. Yet 70 percent to 80 percent of the respondents in each department said that police should handle neighbor disputes and family disputes always or much of the time. Half (in IPD) to two-thirds (in SPPD) said that police should handle public nuisances always or much of the time.

Officers vary widely in the extent to which their role conceptions include a responsibility for addressing conditions that give rise to or sig-

Table 10.2
Frequency Distributions for Outlooks: Additive Indices (Percentages)

Scale Survey Questions	3	4	5	6	7	8	9	10	11	12
Order Maintenance[a]										
1. Patrol officers should be expected to do something about public nuisances										
2. Patrol officers should be expected to do something about neighbor disputes										
3. Patrol officers should be expected to do something about family disputes										
IPD	—	—	1.3	9.6	11.3	18.9	16.1	17.6	13.1	12.1
SPPD	—	—	1.3	12.0	14.5	9.8	17.9	15.9	10.7	17.9
Community Policing[a]										
4. Patrol officers should be expected to do something about litter and trash										
5. Patrol officers should be expected to do something about parents who don't control their kids										
6. Patrol officers should be expected to do something about nuisance businesses that cause lots of problems for neighbors										
IPD	1.0	3.8	12.8	24.6	22.9	18.3	9.8	4.0	1.3	1.5
SPPD	2.6	6.4	15.3	17.9	17.0	13.2	11.9	8.5	3.8	3.4
Citizen Cooperation[b]										
8. How many of the citizens in [beat#] would call the police if they saw something suspicious?										
9. How many of the citizens in [beat #] would provide information about a crime if they knew something and were asked about it by police?										
10. How many of the citizens in [beat #] are willing to work with the police to try to solve neighborhood problems?										
IPD	—	—	—	4.8	13.4	17.4	21.5	16.6	15.0	11.3
SPPD	—	.4	.4	5.6	8.2	9.9	14.2	17.7	17.2	26.4

a 1 = never; 2 = sometimes; 3 = much of the time; 4 = always
b 1 = none; 2 = few; 3 = some; 4 = most

nify disorder: litter and trash, parents who fail to control their children, and businesses that cause many problems for their neighbors. We would expect that officers who subscribe to a traditionally narrow role orientation would tend to say that police should never handle such situations, or should do so only sometimes. By contrast, officers who have embraced a community-policing philosophy would say that police should do something about these conditions at least much of the time. Officers in IPD and SPPD, as a group, are more reluctant to attend to these matters of disorder than to more traditional order-maintenance matters (see Table 10.2). They are more receptive to handling nuisance businesses than to doing something about either litter and trash or irresponsible parents: about three-fifths of the respondents said that police should do something about nuisance businesses always or much of the time, and another one-third said that police should do something sometimes. About half of the respondents in both departments, however, said that police only sometimes should do something about the latter two conditions.

The officers expressed generally favorable attitudes toward aggressive patrol and selectivity in enforcement (see Table 10.1), but not as intensely as would the traditional police culture. If the cultural ideal is the "inner-directed, aggressive street cop" (Brown 1988:84), then one would expect most officers to agree strongly with the survey item about aggressive patrol. Yet only one-quarter of the officers agreed strongly, and about half agreed somewhat; one-quarter or (in IPD) more disagreed with the statement.[11] In addition, we might expect that officers socialized into the traditional occupational culture, with its emphasis on experientially based knowledge of how to work the street, would have favorable attitudes toward selective enforcement; thus respondents would say that police "often" have good reasons not to arrest someone who has committed a minor offense. Only about one-sixth of the officers responded in that way, however, while 65 to 70 percent said "sometimes." A fairly small fraction of the respondents appear to be nonselective, espousing a strict adherence to the law regardless of the seriousness of the offense.

A substantial majority of IPD and SPPD officers are not distrustful of the citizenry. Officers who subscribe to the conventional cultural view of the citizenry would agree, perhaps strongly, with the item about distrust of citizens. Only one-quarter of the respondents, however, agreed with the statement; about the same proportion disagreed strongly (see Table 10.1). In addition, officers' perceptions of citizens' cooperation are positive, on balance (especially in St. Petersburg); we did not find much evidence of the "we versus they" mentality that is ascribed to the police culture (see Table 10.2).[12]

We do not claim that we measured all the elements of the traditional police culture, but in those which we measured we found substantial variation among officers and considerable divergence from cultural views. The boundaries of police culture do not now—if they ever did—extend as far as these outlooks. Furthermore, in these very important respects, the police culture appears to represent less of a barrier to community policing in these departments than conventional wisdom implies.

Officers' Characteristics and Associations with Outlooks

We examine the effects of six characteristics of officers: sex, race, education, length of service, in training community policing, and assignment. For our analysis, both sex and race are treated as dummy variables. Women account for 16.6 percent of the respondents in IPD and 12.5 percent in SPPD. Nonwhite officers (almost 90% of whom were African-American) are 21.4 percent of the respondents in IPD and 22.5 percent of those in SPPD.

We assume that a bachelor's degree signifies the completion of a curriculum which might be expected to prompt the development of outlooks described above. Accordingly we use a dummy variable to indicate whether respondents have a bachelor's degree: 35.6 percent in IPD hold a bachelor's degree, as do 26.4 percent in SPPD. We use a second dummy variable to distinguish officers with some college education (but not a bachelor's degree) from other officers: 44.4 percent in IPD and 59.0 percent in SPPD have some college experience.

Officers varied widely in length of service, with a median of eight to nine years. Twenty-nine percent of the respondents in IPD had begun working there in or after 1992, when community policing was adopted by IPD; 44 percent of the respondents in SPPD had begun working there in or after 1990, when community policing initially was implemented in that department.

Training in community policing includes training on each of several topics: (1) the concepts and principles of community policing, (2) code enforcement and the use of civil regulations, (3) using crime data to analyze neighborhood problems, (4) organizing community groups, and (5) mediation.[13] The first of these topics—concepts and principles of community policing—corresponds to the kind of training that Buerger (1998) characterizes as "an exercise in presenting the justification for adopting a new philosophy" (p. 52) which is "decoupled from the actual work process" (p. 50). The other topics, especially 2, 3, and 4, concern skills that officers would have occasion to use in performing community policing; such "skills training components," according to Buerger (1998:52), are less common.

Such was the case in IPD and SPPD. The median in both departments was reported to be one to two days of training in concepts and principles of community policing. During the preceding three years, the median respondent in IPD had received less than one day of training on code enforcement, less than one day on using crime data to analyze problems, no training on organizing community groups, and less than one day on mediation. In SPPD, the median respondent had received no training on any of these four topics during the preceding three years. Overall, most officers in each department had received some training in the concepts and principles of community policing, and some officers had received some training in community-policing skills.

Finally, we use a dummy variable to indicate whether respondents were community-policing specialists. There were 24 such specialists in IPD and 61 in SPPD. The others were "run" or 911 officers and other types of specialists, such as accident investigators (in IPD).

We examine the associations between officers' outlooks and their characteristics by inspecting the simple bivariate relationships through cross-tabulations and correlation coefficients, and by statistically isolating, through regression analysis, the variation in outlooks for which each characteristic accounts independently.[14] The respondents constitute virtually the entire population of patrol officers with patrol responsibilities in each department. Thus our interpretation of results attends mostly to substantive significance, and addresses statistical significance only as a rough guide to the strength of associations.

The results of these analyses are consistent. The associations are generally quite weak: few product-moment coefficients exceed .2 in magnitude, and few gamma coefficients exceed .4; regression analyses (see Table 10.3) show that the characteristics, as a set, account for only small fractions of the variance in individual outlooks. Some of the larger associations have the (positive or negative) sign we expected, but the sign of others contradict our expectations. Some of the larger associations hold in one department but not in both. Overall it appears that the variation in officers' outlooks is patterned only to a limited extent by officers' characteristics.

Officers' sex bears hardly any of the expected associations with their outlooks. Women tend, as expected, to be less favorable toward aggressive patrol, and women in SPPD, but not in IPD, tend to attach somewhat lower priority to law enforcement than do men,[15] but the associations in each department are very weak. Moreover, women in IPD (but not in SPPD) are somewhat *less* likely than the men to assume responsibility for order-maintenance incidents or for the problematic conditions to which community policing directs attention. A very speculative interpretation is that IPD policewomen adopt more restrictive role conceptions lest they confirm prevailing female stereotypes. Yet because we lack data on the workplace climate for women in either department, we cannot assess

Table 10.3
Relationships Between Officers' Outlooks and Characteristics: Ordered Logit Regression Coefficients Frequency Distribution for Outlooks: Additive Indices

	Law Enforcement	Order Maintenance	Community Policing	Aggressive Patrol	Selective Enforcement	Citizen Cooperation	Citizen Distrust
Female							
IPD	–.006	–.716**	–.367	–.186	–.247	.167	.200
	(.286)	(.252)	(.255)	(.253)	(.334)	(.258)	(.247)
SPPD	–.251	.128	–.054	–.147	–.242	–.093	.015
	(.421)	(.397)	(.343)	(.414)	(.531)	(.470)	(.377)
Non White							
IPD	.281	.514**	.784**	–1.219**	–.828**	–.268	–.049
	(.262)	(.231)	(.224)	(.243)	(.309)	(.253)	(.244)
SPPD	.296	.351	.292	–.428	.862**	.045	–.470
	(.332)	(.295)	(.290)	(.302)	(.330)	(.294)	(.323)
Some College							
IPD	–.618**	–.445*	–.464*	–.292	.224	–.013	.612**
	(.278)	(.261)	(.266)	(.278)	(.329)	(.260)	(.263)
SPPD	.217	.237	.352	–.428	.790**	–.825**	–.152
	(.360)	(.336)	(.339)	(.359)	(.401)	(.339)	(.363)
Baccalaureate & Higher							
IPD	–.861**	–.522*	–.487*	–.444	.727**	–.202	.575**
	(.304)	(.276)	(.286)	(.291)	(.334)	(.276)	(.286)
SPPD	.310	.097	.329	–.502	.636	–.369	–.154
	(.432)	(.374)	(.382)	(.405)	(.454)	(.391)	(.434)
Length of Service							
IPD	–.018	.008	.020	–.064**	.043**	.076**	–.010
	(.014)	(.014)	(.014)	(.015)	(.018)	(.014)	(.014)
SPPD	–.007	.038**	.044**	–.068**	.059**	.061**	–.017
	(.021)	(.019)	(.020)	(.021)	(.024)	(.021)	(.021)
Community Policing Assignment							
IPD	–1.064**	–.148	–.494	.229	.175	–.082	–.071
	(.556)	(.465)	(.386)	(.405)	(.488)	(.427)	(.506)
SPPD	–.553	.635**	1.535**	.214	–.271	.202	–1.061**
	(.354)	(.302)	(.330)	(.322)	(.377)	(.325)	(.122)
Community Policing Concepts & Principles							
IPD	.173	.120	.112	.137	–.085	–.145	–.028
	(.118)	(.103)	(.109)	(.109)	(.131)	(.105)	(.113)
SPPD	.119	.046	–.055	.100	–.101	.091	.150
	(.125)	(.110)	(.107)	(.118)	(.123)	(.120)	(.115)
Code Enforcement & Civil Regulations							
IPD	.185*	–.010	.048	.051	–.091	–.078	–.133
	(.107)	(.092)	(.092)	(.010)	(.115)	(.099)	(.093)
SPPD	.335*	.276*	.215	.188	–.005	.064	–.184
	(.190)	(.169)	(.155)	(.170)	(.188)	(.190)	(.170)
Analyzing Neighborhood Problems							
IPD	–.188	–.011	.228*	.009	.018	.052	–.048
	(.130)	(.117)	(.130)	(.115)	(.150)	(.123)	(.115)
SPPD	–.362**	.002	.062	–.178	.128	–.110	–.126
	(.176)	(.140)	(.154)	(.202)	(.157)	(.150)	(.169)
Organizing Community Groups							
IPD	–.084	.167	–.082	–.316**	–.013	.212	–.103
	(.150)	(.135)	(.133)	(.133)	(.168)	(.157)	(.149)
SPPD	–.189	–.258	–.141	–.403*	.082	.074	.433*
	(.231)	(.217)	(.192)	(.212)	(.277)	(.212)	(.235)
Mediation							
IPD	.089	.079	.160	.351**	.066	.210**	.116
	(.126)	(.102)	(.100)	(.115)	(.131)	(.105)	(.119)
SPPD	.101	–.050	.024	.041	–.071	.001	–.074
	(.190)	(.169)	(.158)	(.178)	(.203)	(.176)	(.171)
N							
IPD	389	390	391	390	384	366	391
SPPD	233	231	232	233	233	228	232

Note: Standard errors of coefficient estimates shown in parentheses.
* p < .10; ** p < .05

such an interpretation. The most striking feature of the results for officers' sex is the degree of similiarity between the men's and the women's outlooks.

The outlooks of minority officers differ from those of white officers in several of the expected ways. Nonwhite officers in both departments have somewhat more positive orientations toward order maintenance and community policing than do white officers. The differences are not large, however, (and they achieve statistical significance only in IPD). Nonwhite officers also have less favorable attitudes toward aggressive patrol, and the difference among IPD officers is of notable magnitude. Even so, nonwhite officers in both departments place somewhat higher priority on law enforcement. Officers' race is also associated modestly with selectivity in both departments, but the nature of the association is not the same across departments: minority officers in IPD are less positive about selective enforcement, while those in SPPD are more positive. Nonwhite officers in SPPD are somewhat less distrustful of citizens, but among IPD officers we found no association between officers' race and distrust of citizens. Nonwhite officers in IPD are somewhat less positive about citizens' cooperation, although this could be a function of their beat assignments.[16] Thus we find mixed support in these departments, for our expectations that nonwhite officers might reject traditional cultural ideals.

Most of the differences in outlooks that are associated with educational background exist between officers with no college and those with at least some college, including a college degree; few differences can be detected between those with some college and those with a bachelor's degree. Some of the differences are in the expected direction; others are not. College-educated officers in IPD, as expected, place lower priority on law enforcement. Contrary to our expectations, however, college-educated officers in IPD have *less* favorable attitudes toward order maintenance and toward community policing, although the differences are small. In SPPD, by contrast, the outlooks of college-educated officers are not much different from those of other officers, and the small differences conform to our expectations: college-educated officers are (somewhat) *more* positive toward order maintenance and community policing.[17] College-educated officers in both departments, as expected, are less positive toward aggressive patrol and more positive toward selective enforcement, but the differences are small. Finally, college-educated officers in IPD are *more* distrustful of the citizenry, whereas education and distrust are unrelated in SPPD. Also, in SPPD but not in IPD, officers with only some college experience hold more negative perceptions of citizens' cooperation.

Officers' length of service is related to several outlooks, although most of the relationships are small in magnitude. More experienced officers tend to have less favorable attitudes toward aggressive patrol and more favorable attitudes toward selective enforcement, although the difference is very modest. More experienced officers have more positive perceptions of citizens' cooperation, although this could be an artifact of their beat assignments: more experienced officers, with more seniority, may be assigned to beats whose residents are more likely to cooperate with police, or whose social class leads officers to believe that they are. This interpretation can be corroborated somewhat by the null relationship between experience and citizen distrust; more experienced officers are neither more nor less distrustful of citizens. Finally, more experienced officers in SPPD (but not in IPD) are more favorable toward order maintenance and community policing; these differences are substantively small (albeit statistically significant). Length of service bears no appreciable relationship to officers' orientations toward law enforcement.

Training on any of the topics examined here bears only a modest association to officers' attitudes. In particular, training in concepts and principles of community policing has no apparent effect on officers' outlooks. The coefficients are uniformly small, indicating only negligible differences in the attitudes of officers with varying amounts of exposure to concepts and principles, as predicted by Buerger (1998). Training in community-policing skills bears inconsistent and sometimes unexpected relationships to attitudes, but overall the associations are weak. This finding may be due to the "dosage" of the training: very few officers had received more than a small amount of training, if any, on these topics. It may be that more extensive training, particularly if reinforced with direct experience in the application of the skills, would have demonstrable effects, but we can only speculate on this possibility.

Officers with assignments as community-policing specialists differ from other officers in some expected ways. Community-policing officers in SPPD are substantially more receptive to handling order-maintenance situations and problematic conditions than are other (911) officers. SPPD's community-policing officers also are less distrustful of citizens. In IPD, community-policing officers place somewhat less priority on the law-enforcement function, but they are *less* receptive to handling problematic conditions. These differences almost certainly reflect several influences: the self-selection of officers into community-policing assignments; the selection of officers, by the departments, for community-policing assignments; and the experiential effects of community-policing assignments. Moreover, these influences are probably not the same in the two departments, inasmuch as the nature of the community-policing specialist assignments differed. Therefore it is surprising that other differences—for example, in aggressiveness—were not manifested in officers' outlooks.

Overall, then, we find that while there is substantial variation in officers' occupational attitudes, this variation is not patterned strongly by their characteristics. We detect only modest differences associated with officers' race, and even smaller differences, if any, associated with their sex and education. We detect some differences among community-policing specialists, some modest differences associated with officers' length of service, and weak or no differences associated with training in community-policing topics. We do not find many large or consistent differences in these relationships across the departments.[18] Thus we might infer that the environments of these departments—both of which are moderately large, urban departments in the early stages of the transition to community policing, albeit different models of community policing—are similar in important respects. We might speculate further that these work environments are similar to those of many other departments, and thus that the patterns we find here hold elsewhere.

Discussion and Conclusions

We looked for manifestations of the traditional police culture in elements of officers' role conceptions and in their attitudes toward citizens. Among officers in both Indianapolis and St. Petersburg we found a substantial amount of variation in these important occupational outlooks. Some of the differences that we detected here almost certainly predate the dawning of the community era. Field research conducted in the 1970s shows that officers, despite their social homogeneity, did not all adapt to and cope with the strains of the police occupation in the same ways. They held varying conceptions of the police role; they differed in their outlooks on human nature in general and on citizens in particular. We might expect that the changes in policing since the 1970s would accentuate the differences among officers, and perhaps would shift the distributions of opinion. The implementation of community policing could be expected to alter the working environment of police. The increasing diversity of police officers could be expected to weaken cultural forces and to bring to policing an even greater variation in preservice outlooks. Though our data do not permit us to examine change over time, they show that officers vary along these attitudinal dimensions.

Not surprisingly, most officers believe that law enforcement is an important responsibility and that a good officer patrols aggressively. It is somewhat surprising, however, and perhaps a contradiction of the conventional wisdom about police culture, that many officers do not consider law enforcement their most important responsibility *by far*, and that many officers express at least some reservations about aggressive patrol. Furthermore, most officers accept a responsibility for handling incidents of disorder, and a substantial number extend their role to handling problematic conditions for which police executives only recently have assumed responsibility as part of problem solving. Many officers also express favorable views about the likelihood of cooperation from citizens. The implementation of community policing can build on all of these attitudes, even without the attitude change for which managers hope (in vain, according to Buerger 1998) when they conduct training in community policing. These findings also are at odds with popular views of police culture. They do not imply that the police culture does not exist; they suggest instead that the police culture does not encompass all of the attitudes and values that conventional wisdom specifies.

Though in these departments we find divergence from traditional depictions of police culture, we do not find that these differences are patterned by officers' characteristics: sex, race, education, length of service, training, and assignment. Although the cultural mold is not intact in these (and probably many other) departments, our analyses suggest that it is not broken cleanly along the lines of these social and occupational differences. In view of some recent findings on the cultural implications of diversity in race and sex, this result is particularly surprising and noteworthy. It appears, on the basis of the findings reported here, that just as white men with working-class backgrounds formed varying occupational outlooks in managing the strains of police work, so do women, members of minorities, and college-educated officers.[19] Further research may reveal patterns that we were unable to detect, but these present findings suggest that further research should look beyond race and sex in seeking to account for cultural fragmentation. In any case, it seems that the fractures in the police culture may afford better prospects for the successful implementation of community policing than conventional wisdom implies. Culture apparently is not determined by the nature of the work; it may be more malleable, and subject to organizational influences (see Wilson 1968).

The further implementation of community policing may rest more firmly on efforts to facilitate the practice of community policing than on efforts to win officers' hearts and minds more directly. The role conceptions and outlooks on citizens held by many officers are not incompatible with community policing. Their working environment, however, including supervision, performance appraisal, training in necessary skills, and information systems, must not impede but support the practice of community policing. If officers express negative views of community policing as such, those views will often be due to failures to change the working environment. Concerted efforts to enable officers to engage in community policing, rather than concerted efforts to change their attitudes, may hold more promise for successful reform (also see Crank 1997).

Future research should continue to attend to variation among officers; even some research on police culture has begun to do this (Haarr 1997; Herbert 1998; Manning 1994). Much remains to be done, however. For example, the observation that officers vary in the relative importance they attach to different "normative orders" (Herbert 1998) begs certain questions. Of what values, attitudes, and beliefs do these normative orders consist? How can these outlooks be measured validly and reliably? Unfortunately, no consensus exists on either conceptual definitions of attitudinal constructs or optimal measurement strategies (Worden 1995); thus research findings will not be readily cumulative.

Even so, analyses that examine patterns of attitudinal similarities and differences among officers, the bases (or at least the correlates) of the differences, and changes over time will nevertheless expand and deepen our understanding of officers' outlooks. Analyses exploring the attitudes of officers in presumably different work environments—departments of different size, or serving constituencies with different needs and demands—will reveal how extensively the differences in such environments are associated with differences in adaptations and outlooks. Furthermore, research on the connections between outlooks and behavior, and particularly forms of behavior on which contemporary reform depends, will hinge on the specification of attitudinal constructs. Analyses of police behavior, which may not be governed by officers' outlooks or even consistent with such outlooks (see R. Worden 1989), could reveal patterns of variation that call for still more sophisticated analytical frameworks for understanding police culture.

Authors' Note

This manuscript is based on data from the Project on Policing Neighborhoods, directed by Stephen D. Mastrofski, Roger B. Parks, Albert J. Reiss, Jr., and Robert E. Worden. The project was supported by Grant No. 95-IJ-CX-0071 by the National Institute of Justice, Office of Justice Programs, U.S. Department of Justice. Points of view in this document are those of the authors and do not necessarily represent the official position or policies of the U.S. Department of Justice.

Notes

1. We use the term *outlook* to refer to beliefs, attitudes, values, opinions and other kinds of "subjective outlooks" among which social psychologists sometimes distinguish. For a succinct discussion of the differences among these constructs, see Meddin (1975); also see Rokeach (1972).
2. Officers' perceptions of danger are disproportionate to the objective risk (Cullen et al. 1983) because of the unpredictability and potential severity of the threats; in some respects

it is functional for officers to err by overestimating the risks (see Muir 1977). Yet greater knowledge of the people and places with which officers have contact could reduce (but obviously never eliminate) both the actual and the perceived risk.

3. Attitudes may be related to length of service for other reasons, of course. Experience may tend to temper officers' enthusiasm for law enforcement; older and more experienced officers, for example, may come to doubt that aggressive patrol is worth the associated physical and bureaucratic risks, especially inasmuch as they may have more to lose. Veteran officers also may find more value in selective enforcement than do younger officers, insofar as they feel more knowledgeable and more comfortable using their discretion.
4. Both departments assigned selected officers as community policing specialists. For the most part, these officers were relieved of the responsibility for handling calls for service, while other patrol officers ("run" officers in IPD and 911 officers in SPPD) bore the call load. In SPPD, one community policing officer (CPO) was assigned to each of the 48 beats (called community policing areas, or CPAs); CPOs were expected to set their own hours in order to engage in problem solving. Additional CPOs were assigned to public housing projects and to the downtown area. The organization and operation of community policing specialists in each of IPD's four districts was subject to the discretion of the district commanders; community policing officers worked mainly as part of a district squad on the "day tact" shift (9 a.m. to 5 p.m.). Other ("run") officers had fairly stable assignments to shifts and beats, and were (loosely) expected to undertake problem-solving projects.
5. Of the 28 nonrespondents, interviewers were unable to contact 10 (three of those were reserve officers who did not work often), and 18 refused to participate.
6. We believe that the response rate was high at least partly because officers were invited to participate during their work shifts and not on personal time, and because the survey was part of a larger study that included systematic social observation of more than 300 patrol shifts in each department. The latter fact may have legitimated the survey as a serious, credible effort to learn about officers' work. The response rate may also reflect a more general climate of receptivity to research in these departments.
7. Space limitations preclude a detailed discussion of these findings. For a fuller consideration of the work environments in IPD and SPPD, see Paoline, Myers, and Worden (1999).
8. In this respect, IPD and SPPD may represent many departments that are making the transition to community policing; see Zhao and Thurman (1997).
9. Each of the indices correlates with the corresponding factor scale at or above .95. We use the additive indices in our analyses because they are more readily interpretable than the factor scales, and statistically indistinguishable from those scales.

   We began with a factor model that represented these survey items as a function of three factors: role conception, selectivity, and attitude toward citizens. Preliminary factor analyses, however, revealed a more complicated dimensional structure, which prompted us to revise the factor model. The results of confirmatory factor analysis accord with our expectation that the items constituting each of the indices in fact tap a single underlying dimension. Among IPD respondents, however, a factor analysis of the six items that make up the order-maintenance and community-policing indices yields two factors; among SPPD respondents, a factor analysis of these six items yields a single factor. Although we distinguish between these outlooks for our analyses, our measures display similar patterns of association with other variables; for some analytic purposes, these indices could be combined with little or no distortion.

   The reliabilities of the scales are acceptable: the alpha coefficients are .72, .63, and .74 respectively for the order-maintenance, community-policing, and citizen-cooperation scales.

   With only two exceptions, the measures of the seven outlooks are not intercorrelated even moderately. One exception is the (expected) association between officers' orientation to law enforcement and their aggressiveness, which are correlated at moderate levels (.23 in IPD and .42 in SPPD). The other exception is the (expected) association between officers' orientations to order maintenance and community policing: the correlation coefficients are .41 in IPD and .60 in SPPD. Otherwise, however, the correlations are fairly weak.
10. All but a very few of the officers also agreed (strongly or somewhat) with the statement "Assisting citizens is just as important as enforcing the law." Officers apparently are ambivalent about the priority attached to law enforcement.
11. We are somewhat surprised by the congruence between the distributions of responses in the two departments, given that IPD's management had endorsed aggressive policing as part of its model of community policing.
12. Much of POPN's data collection focused on 12 beats in each city. Officers who were not currently assigned to one of the 12 study beats were asked about one of those beats, provided that they had been assigned to such a beat at least one-fourth of the time in the preceding six months. Otherwise they were asked about the beat to which they were currently assigned.
13. Respondents were asked to indicate the amount of training they had received on each of several topics in the preceding three years, with response categories (and numerical values) that included none (= 1), less than one day (= 2), one to two days (= 3), three to five days (= 4), and more than five days (= 5).
14. Because the attitude measures were ordinal, we estimated several measures of association, including Pearson's *r*, Kendall's tau-*c*, and gamma, and we estimated the parameters of the regression models using ordered logistic regression.
15. Equivalent proportions of men and of women in SPPD strongly agree that "enforcing the law is by far a patrol officer's most important responsibility." Women, however, are less likely to agree somewhat, and correspondingly more likely to disagree.
16. Some previous research (Haarr 1997; A. Worden 1993) suggests that officers' sex and race may interact in shaping their attitudes: That is, the attitudinal differences between men and women may not be equivalent for whites and for nonwhites. We estimated the interaction effects of race and sex, and we found a discernible pattern of substantial interactions only among SPPD officers. Nonwhite women in SPPD held less favorable attitudes toward law enforcement, and more positive attitudes toward order-maintenance and community-policing functions, than one would expect on the basis of the main effects of race and sex alone. They also held more favorable attitudes toward citizen cooperation. Nonwhite women in SPPD, however, were more distrustful of the citizenry; this was the only interaction that reached statistical significance. It would appear, in view of these results, that race-by-sex interactions are contingent on organizational context. Future research should explore these relationships further.
17. The difference between the two departments in regard to education and orientations toward order maintenance and community policing might be explained by differences in their organizational environments. If (as one might suppose) college-educated officers are more highly motivated for advancement in the organization, their role conceptions may depend, to some extent, on the role performance for which they anticipate organizational rewards. If officers are skeptical that the performance of order maintenance and community policing functions will help them to advance, they may be disinclined to incorporate these functions into their conceptions of their role. This interpretation is very speculative; in support, we can only note that SPPD was im-

plementing a new performance appraisal system to encompass officers' performance of community- and problem-oriented policing. In neither department, however, did most officers believe that the department had done better than a "fair" job of rewarding officers who did well in problem solving.

18. In the text above, and with reference to Table 10.3, we noted differences of notable magnitude.

19. Other researchers (e.g., Jurik and Halemba 1984; Morash and Haarr 1995; A. Worden 1993; R. Worden 1990; Zhao, Thurman, and He 1999), finding that background characteristics bear only weak relationships to occupational attitudes, have inferred that the effects of preservice differences in background are overwhelmed by the effects of the work and role requirements. Yet work and role requirements, on the face of it, do not suffice to explain variation in occupational attitudes: role orientations, attitudes toward citizens, or even (we might speculate) the subjective perceptions of job dimensions that are related to job satisfaction.

References

Bittner, E. 1974. "Florence Nightingale in Pursuit of Willie Sutton: A Theory of the Police." Pp. 17–44 in *The Potential for Reform of Criminal Justice,* edited by H. Jacob. Beverly Hills, CA: Sage.

Britz, M.T. 1997. "The Police Subculture and Occupational Socialization: Exploring Individual and Demographic Characteristics." *American Journal of Criminal Justice* 21(2):127–46.

Broderick, J.J. 1977. *Police in a Time of Change.* Morristown, NJ: General Learning Press.

Brooks, L.W., A. Piquero, and J. Cronin. 1993. "Police Officer Attitudes Concerning Their Communities and Their Roles: A Comparison of Two Suburban Police Departments." *American Journal of Police* 12(3):115–39.

Brown, M.K. 1988. *Working the Street: Police Discretion and the Dilemmas of Reform.* New York, NY: Russell Sage Foundation.

Buerger, M.E. 1998. "Police Training as Pentecost: Using Tools Singularly Ill-Suited to the Purpose of Reform." *Police Quarterly* 1(1):27–63.

Buzawa, E.S. 1981. "The Role of Race in Predicting Job Attitudes of Patrol Officers." *Journal of Criminal Justice* 9:63–77.

Carter, D.L., A.D. Sapp, and D.W. Stephens. 1989. *The State of Police Education: Policy Direction for the 21st Century.* Washington, D.C.: Police Executive Research Forum.

Crank, J.P. 1997. "Celebrating Agency Culture: Engaging a Traditional Cop's Heart in Organizational Change." Pp.49–57 in *Community Policing in a Rural Setting,* edited by Q.C. Thurman and E.F. McGarrell. Cincinnati, OH: Anderson.

——. 1998. *Understanding Police Culture.* Cincinnati, OH: Anderson.

Cullen, F.T., B.G. Link, L.F. Travis III, and T. Lemming. 1983. "Paradoxes in Policing: A Note on Perceptions of Danger." *Journal of Police Science and Administration* 11(4):457–62.

Drummond, D.S. 1976. *Police Culture.* Beverly Hills, CA: Sage Publications.

Durand, R. 1976. "Some Dynamics of Urban Service Evaluations Among Blacks and Whites." *Social Science Quarterly* 56(1):698–706.

Eck, J.E. and W. Spelman. 1987. *Problem Solving: Problem-Oriented Policing in Newport News.* Washington, DC: Police Executive Research Forum.

Farkas, M.A. and P.K. Manning. 1997. "The Occupational Culture of Corrections and Police Officers." *Journal of Crime and Justice* 20(2):51–68.

Fielding, N.G. 1988. *Joining Forces: Police Training, Socialization, and Occupation Competence.* London: Routledge.

Flanagan, T.J. 1985. "Consumer Perspectives on Police Operational Strategy." *Journal of Police Science and Administration* 13:10–21.

Gilligan, C. 1982. *In a Different Voice: Psychological Theory and Women's Development.* Cambridge, MA: Harvard University Press.

Haarr, R.N. 1997. "Patterns of Interaction in a Police Patrol Bureau: Race and Gender Barriers to Integration." *Justice Quarterly* 14(1):53–85.

Herbert, S. 1998. "Police Subculture Reconsidered." *Criminology* 36(2):343–69.

Jurik, N.C. and G.J. Halemba. 1984. "Gender, Working Conditions, and the Job Satisfaction of Women in a Non-Traditional Occupation: Female Correctional Officers in Men's Prisons." *Sociological Quarterly* 25:551–66.

Kappeler, V.E., R.D. Sluder, and G.P. Alpert. 1994. *Forces of Deviance: Understanding the Dark Side of Policing.* Prospect Heights, IL: Waveland Press, Inc.

Lurigio, A.J. and W.G. Skogan. 1994. "Winning the Hearts and Minds of Police Officers: An Assessment of Staff Perceptions of Community Policing in Chicago." *Crime & Delinquency* 40(3):315–30.

Manning, P.K. 1994. "Dynamics and Tensions in Police Occupational Culture." Unpublished manuscript, Michigan State University.

——. 1995. "The Police Occupational Culture in Anglo-American Societies." Pp. 472–75 in *The Encyclopedia of Police Science,* edited by W. Bailey. New York, NY: Garland Publishing Co.

Mastrofski, S.D., R.E. Worden, and J.B. Snipes. 1995. "Law Enforcement in a Time of Community Policing." *Criminology* 33(4):539–63.

McNamara, J.H. 1967. "Uncertainties in Police Work: The Relevance of Police Recruits' Background and Training." Pp. 163–252 in *The Police: Six Sociological Essays,* edited by D. Bordua. New York, NY: John Wiley & Sons.

Meddin, J. 1975. "Attitudes, Values, and Related Concepts: A System of Classification." *Social Science Quarterly* 55:889–900.

Morash, M. and R.N. Haarr. 1995. "Gender, Workplace Problems, and Stress in Policing." *Justice Quarterly* 12:113–40.

Muir, W.K., Jr. 1977. *Police: Streetcorner Politicians.* Chicago, IL: University of Chicago Press.

Paoline, E.A. III, S.M. Myers, and R.E. Worden. 1999. *Police Culture, Individualism, and Community Policing: Evidence from Two Police Departments.* Report to the National Institute of Justice (Grant 95-IJ-CX-0071). Albany, NY: Hindelang Criminal Justice Research Center, University at Albany.

Peak, K.J. and R.W. Glensor. 1999. *Community Policing & Problem Solving.* Upper Saddle River, NJ: Prentice Hall.

Reaves, B.A. 1996. *Local Police Departments.* Washington, D.C.: U.S. Department of Justice.

—— and P.Z. Smith. 1995. *Law Enforcement Management and Administrative Statistics, 1993: Data for Individual State and Local Agencies with 100 or More Officers.* Washington, D.C.: U.S. Department of Justice.

Reiner, R. 1985. *The Politics of the Police.* New York, NY: St. Martin's Press.

Reuss-Ianni, E. 1983. *Two Cultures of Policing.* New Brunswick, NJ: Transaction.

Rokeach, M. 1972. *Beliefs, Attitudes, and Values: A Theory of Organization and Change.* San Francisco, CA: Jossey-Bass.

Schuman, H. and B. Gruenberg. 1972. "Dissatisfaction with City Services: Is Race an Important Factor?" Pp. 369–92 in *People and Politics in Urban Society, Urban Affairs Annual Reviews,* vol. 6, edited by H. Hahn. Beverly Hills, CA: Sage.

Skogan, W.G. and S.M. Hartnett. 1997. *Community Policing, Chicago Style.* New York, NY: Oxford University Press.

Skolnick, J.H. 1966. *Justice Without Trial: Law Enforcement in Democratic Society.* New York, NY: John Wiley.

Sparrow, M.K., M.H. Moore, and D.M. Kennedy. 1990. *Beyond 911: A New Era for Policing.* New York, NY: Basic Books.

Sykes, R.E. and E.E. Brent. 1980. "The Regulation of Interaction by Police: A Systems View of Taking Charge." *Criminology* 18:182–97.

Tauber, R.K. 1970. "Danger and the Police." Pp. 95–104 in *The Sociology of Punishment and Correction,* edited by N. Johnston, L. Savitz, and M.E. Wolfgang. New York, NY: John Wiley & Sons.

Van Maanen, J. 1974. "Working the Street: A Developmental View of Police Behavior." Pp. 83–130 in *The Potential for Reform of Criminal Justice,* edited by H. Jacob. Beverly Hills, CA: Sage.

Walker, S. 1977. *A Critical History of Police Reform: The Emergence of Professionalism.* Lexington, MA: Lexington Books.

——. 1985. "Racial Minority and Female Employment in Policing: The Implications of 'Glacial' Change." *Crime & Delinquency* 31(4):555–72.

——. 1992. *The Police in America.* New York, NY: McGraw-Hill.

White, S.O. 1972. "A Perspective on Police Professionalization." *Law and Society Review* 7(Fall):61–85.

Westley, W.A. 1970. *Violence and the Police: A Sociological Study of Law, Custom, and Morality.* Cambridge, MA: MIT Press.

Wilson, J.Q. 1968. *Varieties of Police Behavior: The Management of Law and Order in Eight Communities.* Cambridge, MA: Harvard University Press.

Worden, A.P. 1993. "The Attitudes of Women and Men in Policing: Testing Conventional and Contemporary Wisdom." *Criminology* 31(2):203–37.

Worden, R.E. 1989. "Situational and Attitudinal Explanations of Police Behavior: A Theoretical Reappraisal and Empirical Assessment." *Law & Society Review* 23 (4):667–711.

——. 1990. "A Badge and A Baccalaureate: Policies, Hypotheses, and Further Evidence." *Justice Quarterly* 7(3):565–92.

——. 1995. "Police Officers' Belief Systems: A Framework for Analysis." *American Journal of Police* 14:49–81.

Zhao, J. and Q.C. Thurman. 1997. "Community Policing: Where Are We Now?" *Crime & Delinquency* 43(3):345–57.

—— and N. He. 1999. "Sources of Job Satisfaction Among Police Officers: A Test of Demographic and Work Environment Models." *Justice Quarterly* 16(1):153–73.

Eugene A. Paoline, III, Stephanie M. Myers, and Robert E. Worden, "Police Culture, Individualism, and Community Policing: Evidence from Two Police Departments." Reprinted from *Justice Quarterly* 17 (3): 575–605.

Chapter 11

Patrol Officers and Problem Solving

An Application of Expectancy Theory

Christina DeJong
Stephen D. Mastrofski
Roger B. Parks

A *key element of community policing is problem solving, or problem-oriented policing (POP)—a "scientific" approach that aims to address the underlying causes of crime with data collection, interagency cooperation, and long-term approaches rather than short-term, reactive ones.*

While the idea of problem-oriented policing has clearly been embraced by police agencies, there is still considerable variation between individual officers' likelihood to use POP. The authors suggest that this variation can be explained by expectancy theory, which proposes that officers will be motivated to adopt problem-solving techniques if they have the opportunity and ability to do so, if they are likely to be recognized for doing so, and if the rewards for such approaches outweigh the costs. Using data from two police agencies with different bureaucratic styles of promoting problem solving, the authors compare officers' perceptions of how their superiors view POP with their actual time spent on POP techniques.

Criminal justice organizations are among the most popular targets of reform among contemporary America's public institutions. In particular, police have been the object of intensive reorganization and rehabilitation for the last decade, especially since 1994. In that year the president signed a bill passed by Congress to use federal support for hiring 100,000 more police as a means of promoting community policing.

"Community policing" is in part a reaction to a previous reform trend, which produced increasing bureaucratization in American police forces (Fogelson 1977; Reiss 1992; Walker 1977). Reformers seek, among other things, to replace the ideal of the "snappy bureaucrat" (Bittner 1970) with the "true professional." Such a person does not rely on rules and standard operating procedures to deal with crime, but rather harnesses creativity and flexibility to the rigors of the scientific method. Meanwhile, to solve problems, the professional extends the scope of routine activities to working "partners" outside the police organization (Goldstein 1990; Mastrofski and Uchida 1993; Sherman et al. 1997:8–30). In this model, the police officer serves as a "clinician" who engages in "problem solving" with the clientele he or she serves (Mastrofski 1998).

Problem solving contains the following key elements, as outlined by the person who introduced the idea to police (Goldstein 1990:ch. 4): identifying problems that are substantive concerns of the community; looking for patterns in events that allow police to establish the nature and causes of these problems; taking a proactive, long-term, preventive approach to solving the problem rather than a reactive, short-term approach; systematically gathering and analyzing data on the problem and on current efforts to deal with it; searching for a solution with the best prospects for reducing the problem (one that often may involve activities of other organizations and groups of citizens); and systematic evaluation of the solution implemented to determine what worked, what did not, and how future efforts might be improved.

Problem solving is a rational, empirical approach to police intervention, which calls for a great deal of thinking, observing, analysis, and collaboration throughout. In practice, it seems radically different from the traditional way to mobilize the police, which is based on following a routine in responding to separate calls for service. (Such calls are treated as independent and unrelated events.) Reactive or "911" policing focuses on doing only what is necessary to establish order in the short term; it values the speed and brevity of the response rather than thoroughness and long-term effectiveness; it relies on a narrow range of traditional law enforcement responses; and it views the police as agents who work independent of other government organizations and private collectivities whose actions might have some bearing on the problem (Eck and Spelman 1987; Wilson and Kelling 1989).

Problem-oriented policing has become a hallmark of many community policing efforts in departments around the nation, and large numbers of local police agencies report that they participate. As early as 1993, a large percentage of local police agencies (in a national survey of 1,606 departments) reported that their patrol officers were engaged in the following aspects of problem solving:

> Working with citizens to identify and resolve area problems (86 percent); Assisting in organizing the community (70 percent);
>
> Conducting crime analysis for the area of assignment (53 percent);
>
> Meeting regularly with community groups (77 percent);
>
> Working with other city agencies to solve neighborhood problems (78 percent) (Maguire and Mastrofski 1999:50).

High percentages of agencies receiving federal funding from the Office of Community Oriented Policing Services (COPS) reported that they were working with community groups and other government agencies to identify and solve problems, and were using computers to analyze data on problems (Maguire and Mastrofski 1999:54). Fully 44 percent of the 6,566 grantees completing initial progress reports for the period 1994–1997 stated that they were engaged in problem-oriented policing targeted at specific recurring problems through systematic analysis of the problems, implementation of strategy, and systematic assessment of results (Maguire and Mastrofski 1999:57).

The idea of problem-oriented policing has clearly taken hold in America's local police agencies, but these surveys do not indicate how far this approach has moved beyond program creation and occasional practice. To what extent has problem-oriented policing become part of the organization's routine practice? Because local police departments commit the largest share of sworn resources to patrol, and because patrol is the operational unit that most agencies target first for community policing reform, an examination of routine street-level patrol practices will help us understand more clearly the "dosage" of problem-oriented policing. The dosage question requires a detailed analysis of individual officers' behavior because patrol officers exercise high levels of discretion in what they do and how they do it. A department may have launched a vigorous problem-solving program, which nonetheless founders on the rocks of officers' discretion and contingencies that arise throughout the officer's workday.

If problem-solving effort is similar to other aspects of police behavior that have been studied closely (e.g., arrest or use of force), we can expect significant variation in the amount of problem solving by officers. What accounts for variation in officers' problem-solving efforts? Answering this question requires a model of police behavior. Most of the extant models are tied closely to officers as legal actors: whether they invoke the law, and how much they invoke (Black 1980) or the extent to which police behavior conforms to law (Skolnick 1994; Skolnick and Fyfe 1993). Neither of these approaches is very useful here because the purpose of problem solving is to find ways to go beyond the usual forms of legal intervention (e.g., making arrests, using force, investigating incidents, and filing crime reports), and indeed to do things that do not resemble what the police traditionally have regarded as their legal domain. Problem-oriented policing calls for creativity and flexibility in areas in which the law says very little about constraining police: for example, organizing neighborhood groups to work on neighborhood disorders, cleaning up trash-filled neighborhoods, and working to motivate disadvantaged and troubled youths to choose socially productive ways to spend their time.

In this article we employ a theoretical framework that treats problem-oriented policing as a particular kind of "work" and police officers as workers in an organization that (at least ostensibly) values such work. We draw on expectancy motivation theory to frame our analysis of field observations made in two agencies that implement problem-oriented policing.

Our research questions are relevant to crime policy in two ways. First, the answers will help us understand how the state's agents, charged with spearheading a new method of crime prevention and control, actually behave. That is, our inquiry will illuminate a relatively new process of crime prevention and control. Second, answers to these questions are essential in assessing the prospects of problem-oriented policing for preventing and controlling crime. Reformers around the nation have invested much hope in this rational, empirical approach. They believe it will fortify the police capacity to reduce crime (Sherman et al. 1997). A federally funded, systematic review of studies of crime prevention concluded that problem-oriented policing is a "promising" strategy, even while noting that the available evidence may be highly skewed by a selective reporting process in which failures are excluded (Sherman et al. 1997:8–30).

Whether researchers can demonstrate a crime prevention effect for problem-oriented policing is an important question. To answer this, we ask equally important questions: To what extent has the treatment been implemented? What promotes or impedes its implementation? As stated above, we address these with data from systematic field observation of patrol officers in two agencies that are implementing problem-oriented policing. Although such a sample obviously has little generalizability, it offers the first in-depth analysis of routine problem solving by police officers.

A Framework for Explaining Variation in Problem-Solving Effort

Police effort in problem solving can be measured and counted. Effort can be measured through counts of projects, activities, or people served. All are input or activity measures that tell us something about the extent of officers' problem solving. The most reliable input measure for our purposes, however, is one that tracks resources used for problem solving most directly and most precisely. Because personnel time accounts for most of the police budget, tracking time allocated to problem solving is a logical way to measure effort. Accounting for time expended on a given task tells us nothing about how effectively or how efficiently that time was spent, but it indicates the resources committed to program implementation. Such a measure is particularly relevant for understanding problem-oriented policing today, when so many agencies are struggling merely to convince their officers to try it. Although it is not a direct measure of productivity (problems solved, citizens helped, crimes prevented), it is a useful measure of workers' behavior that is linked closely to program dosage.

Organizational and industrial psychology has developed a large literature that attempts to account for variation in workers' effort and output. A framework known as expectancy motivation theory is particularly suited to our topic and to the available data. It attempts to explain workers' performance by taking into account their expectations about obtaining desired outcomes when they perform at higher levels (Campbell and Pritchard 1976; Mitchell 1974). According to expectancy theory, several factors influence workers' perception of the value of increased performance:

> Effort-performance expectancy: Workers must perceive that the desired performance is within their means—that they have the capability and opportunity to perform.
>
> Instrumentality of performance: Workers must know clearly what behaviors are expected of them—those actions which are viewed as instrumental to achieving rewards from the organization.
>
> Performance-reward expectancy: Workers need to know how the organization calibrates rewards for performance. What level of reward results from what level of performance?
>
> Reward-cost balance: Workers must place a sufficiently high value on the rewards available to be motivated to try to receive them.

All of these factors must be sufficiently high if a worker is to perform as the organization desires.

Expectancy theory has been tested in a variety of settings (the military, nursing, educational institutions, and private corporations) involving diverse performance indicators (occupational choice, sorority choice, job satisfaction and departure, and a wide range of on-the-job behaviors) (Mitchell 1982a, 1982b). The model's explanatory power varies with the type of organization and with workers' performance. Police organizations would offer an especially challenging test of the theory because police apparently operate in an organizational environment and an occupational culture that undercut the capacity of management initiatives to change workers' habits (Guyot 1991; Reuss-Ianni 1983; Rubinstein 1973; Van Maanen 1974). This literature strongly suggests that in a comprehensive test of expectancy theory, measures of reward-cost balance will include indicators of officers' beliefs about alternatives to problem-oriented policing in how to spend their time, and how their coworkers feel about problem-oriented policing and alternative approaches.

The model is highly relevant to the implementation of community and problem-oriented policing because many of the prescriptions for the transformation of policing actually depend on the efficacy of expectancy motivation theory. That is, effective implementation of problem-oriented policing is associated with giving officers the opportunity to perform it (e.g., sufficient time freed from responding to calls for service), sufficient capability (e.g., education and training), clear performance expectations (e.g., worker performance evaluations and career rewards), and getting officers to internalize the values or "philosophy" of community policing (Sparrow, Moore, and Kennedy 1990; Trojanowicz and Carter 1988).

Expectancy motivation theory has been used to account for variation in officers' DUI arrest rates in 19 Pennsylvania police departments (Mastrofski, Ritti, and Snipes 1994). Researchers were unable to estimate the complete expectancy model, and thus had to rely on proxy variables in some cases. After removing organizational effects, they found that available expectancy factors or their proxies explained more than one-fourth of the variation in officers' annual drunk-driving arrest tallies. Capability (experience and training) and opportunity (work shift and nonsupervisory responsibilities) were the most powerful predictors of officers' productivity. The reward-cost balance variables were less powerful: officers' personal feelings about the seriousness of drunk driving had no effect, and personal commitment to a legalistic style was a significant but not powerful intrinsic reinforcement for making arrests. Instrumentality variables showed weak effects, mostly opposite to what expectancy theory predicted: arrest productivity was lowest among the officers most inclined to perceive that the department provided incentives for drunk driving arrests. A few officers (8 percent, who made 44 percent of the arrests) accounted for much of the DUI productivity in the sample. These "rate-busters," like those identified by Whyte and colleagues (1955) in factories, were alienated both from their peers and from management. Although highly productive, they viewed the department as disinclined to reward this performance. Their performance was *decoupled* from their agencies' extrinsic reward system.

Mavericks accounted for most of their agency's DUI arrest productivity, flouting the department's incentive system. Does the same hold for problem-oriented policing, or are officers susceptible to the organizational interventions that are found in the contemporary reformer's tool kit? These include recruitment and selection (education), skill development (training), ensuring opportunity (in terms of time and place), and developing incentives by establishing goals and performance criteria, structuring job assignments, and linking rewards to performance. Or is the dosage of community policing more susceptible to the officers' belief system: Does it require that police organizations infuse their officers with a reformer's philosophical commitment to the goals and methods of problem solving? Must all expectancy factors be present to produce a substantial behavioral effect—as the theory posits—or are the effects of expectancy factors additive? We address these questions by analyzing the behavior of rank-and-file patrol officers in two municipal police agencies.

Problem-Oriented Policing at the Research Sites

Both the Indianapolis and the St. Petersburg police departments included problem-oriented policing as an important element in their public accounts of their community policing efforts. Some of Indianapolis's problem-solving projects were featured in a 1995 article in the *Law Enforcement News.* St. Petersburg's approach under Darrel Stephens's leadership since 1992 had achieved frequent national publicity as an attempt to reorient the entire department around problem solving. The two departments, however, differed as to the nature and extent of their problem solving.

Problem solving in Indianapolis was left largely to each of the four district commanders. These commanders established the problem-solving "themes" of their commands and structured officer efforts. One district emphasized bike patrol as a way to catch offenders more effectively and to establish better rapport with the public. Another focused on drug dealing, illegal firearms, and quality-of-life offenses, relying heavily on aggressive traffic enforcement and order maintenance. (Much of this was performed by a specially designated squad.) Another district also used aggressive order maintenance, employing crime and calls-for-service data to target hot spots and track the progress of interventions. These methods were supplemented with an array of community outreach endeavors such as foot patrol, crime watch, prayer vigils, school programs, and a citizen advisory task force. Finally, one district concentrated on drug problems by using code enforcement to condemn properties used for illicit dealing. A civilian employee worked closely with sworn officers to identify such properties and mobilize the city's code enforcement.

Although the themes and approaches varied somewhat, the four districts exhibited several common features. First, the district commanders tended to compartmentalize problem solving as the responsibility of specialist units. General patrol officers were encouraged to cooperate with these units, but the specialists took the lead in these endeavors; patrol generalists typically carried out problem-solving tasks assigned to them. Second, because problem solving tended to be a unit-level responsibility, direction in identifying problems and searching for solutions tended to come from specialists in problem solving, from management, and from unit supervisors, not from rank-and-file officers. Third, the department focused the search for problems on a relatively narrow range of issues, and similarly constrained the search for solutions. Illegal drugs, guns, and gang activity were the main focus; the search for problem-solving strategies tended to focus on street enforcement, aggressive interventions in public places, and code enforcement to shut down properties used for illicit purposes.

St. Petersburg decentralized problem solving to the individual officer level, structuring the entire process around teams of patrol generalists (911 officers) and community policing officer (CPO) specialists assigned to small geographic areas of approximately 5,000 residents. In contrast to Indianapolis, where district commanders played a central role in setting problem-solving priorities and selecting methods, district commanders and lower-level supervisors played only a small, supporting role in overseeing the problem-solving process. Each of St. Petersburg's 48 community policing areas (CPAs) contained a team of one CPO and several 911 officers who were assigned throughout the day. The CPO, under a team sergeant's supervision, was to identify problems in the assigned CPA, and plan and coordinate problem solving by the team. CPOs were given complete flexibility in scheduling their work: they were required only to log 40 hours per week and to log no more than 10 hours in a given day.[1] Sergeants also were given some flexibility in work schedules, although less than CPOs.

Officers were to identify problems using crime and calls-for-service data (made available to them through computer software accessed at headquarters) and by working closely with community groups active in the CPAs and with other organizations that could help with the problem. Officers were to document problem-solving projects on a computerized registry and to log time spent on problem solving on a computerized activity log.

Illicit drugs were reported as the most frequently targeted problem, but these accounted for less than half of the projects initiated. Disputes and disorders, theft, burglary, robbery, traffic, and numerous miscellaneous problems accounted for most of the projects. As in Indianapolis, traditional enforcement methods or increasing surveillance or visibility were the most frequent tactics selected. These were not instituted districtwide, however, but were tailored to the specific CPA's problem. Although used less frequently, nonenforcement strategies were employed in many projects such as coordinating enforcement with other agencies' interventions and working with citizen groups.

St. Petersburg's managers hoped that this geographically decentralized team approach would provide for maximum flexibility through a "bubble-up" process that made each CPO the key project initiator and link to community groups. Managers hoped that the CPO's efforts would infuse all of the officers assigned to each CPA with a problem-solving orientation and would give each officer a relevant role when specific projects called for it. Upper-level supervisors were expected to monitor progress and provide general guidance and support. Systematic reviews of ongoing projects were conducted through district- and department-wide staff meetings held every few weeks.

Thus we observed significant differences between the problem-solving approaches used by Indianapolis and by St. Petersburg. Indianapolis committed a much smaller proportion of its district officers to community policing specialist assignments (5 percent versus 17 percent in St. Petersburg). That city concentrated specialists in a single district unit, while St. Petersburg attempted to integrate its CPOs into teams working with generalists. In Indianapolis the district commanders played a central role in deciding problem-solving priorities and strategies, while their St. Petersburg counterparts supported problem-solving efforts initiated by the rank and file. Finally, Indianapolis focused its problem-solving efforts on a much narrower range of problems and strategies than did St. Petersburg.

Propositions

First, we wish to account for variation in the amount of time spent on problem solving. How well does our expectancy motivation model account for variations in problem solving in these departments? An available alternative to this model is offered by James Q. Wilson (1968), who argued that as police departments' leadership and policies differ, so too do their practices. He tested this point by comparing the arrest practices in agencies whose leaders and structures promoted a watchman, legalistic, or service style. Although the leadership in both of our agencies pursued the service style, their approaches to promoting and structuring problem solving were sufficiently different to offer a credible test of Wilson's thesis applied to problem solving. If the differences in leadership matter, we should find distinct differences in the inclinations of Indianapolis and St. Petersburg officers to engage in problem solving. Because of St. Petersburg's efforts to institutionalize problem solving at the rank-and-file level, we expect that St. Petersburg officers would be more inclined to engage in it. The greater the variation in problem-solving time explained by the officer's department, the stronger the agency-level effects articulated by Wilson. Insofar as organization-level effects are weak, we must look to the effects of expectancy motivation theory at lower levels of analysis.

Second, we wish to know which of the motivation expectancy factors will influence most strongly the amount of time spent on problem solving. Research on drunk-driving arrests shows that effort-performance expectancy variables (opportunity and ability) exert the greatest influence on officers' behavior. Although we might well expect ability and opportunity to affect the problem-solving effort, we anticipate that this task is so different from a DUI arrest decision that it will produce a distinctively different pattern in the weighting of effects among the model's elements. Drunk-driving arrests require a specific kind of opportunity (working on public roads at times when drunk driving is frequent) and specific skills (for detecting the offense, generating evidence, and presenting it effectively in court). The DUI arrest decision is supported by well-developed legal doctrine and technology for detection and evidence generation.

Problem solving is less demanding in these ways: it can be performed over a much broader range of times, events, and places, and the technologies that support it are far more diffuse. Indeed, as a set of specific tasks, it is simply less highly developed than DUI enforcement. Therefore, the training for problem solving is more diffuse and, we expect, less relevant to the willingness to engage in it.

The most important consideration in this task environment is how the organization structures incentives. We offer a hypothesis contrary to some reformers' claim that the successful implementation of community policing requires officers to adopt it as their personal philosophy. On the basis of prior research, we hypothesize that internalized values relevant to adopting problem-oriented policing are largely irrelevant to the actual practice (Buerger 1998). Rather, officers' use of problem solving depends on the external structures that departments provide for doing this kind of work.

Data

Data collection focused on officers assigned to 12 beats in each city. We matched the sampled beats as closely as possible, according to residents' level of socioeconomic distress. We measured socioeconomic distress as the sum of the percentages of families with children headed by a single female, the adult population unemployed, and the population below 50 percent of poverty level.[2] This index is similar to that used by Sampson, Raudenbush, and Earls (1997). The sample excluded beats in the lowest quartile of socioeconomic distress so that observations would concentrate in areas where police-citizen interactions were most frequent. Field observers were graduate students and honors undergraduates who had received a semester-long training course in systematic observation of the police, as well as on-site orientation rides.

Systematic observations were conducted in summer months according to procedures originally set forth by Reiss (1971) and detailed elsewhere (Mastrofski et al. 1998). Field researchers accompanied patrol officers assigned to the selected beats throughout a matched sample of work shifts. They took brief field notes and then spent the following day at the research office, transcribing their notes into detailed accounts and coding them according to a protocol. Observation sessions oversampled the busier days and times of the week. Both general patrol officers and community policing officers were observed in rough proportion to their representation in the personnel allocation to the study beats. The observers conducted a total of about 240 hours of observation with officers assigned to each of the selected beats.

Observers maintained a record documenting how officers spent their work time. This was divided into two general event categories: time spent engaged with the public on police business (encounters) and all other time (activities). Characteristics of each event were coded for when the event occurred, its location in the city, which actors participated, and what they did.

For the analysis reported here, the observation session serves as the unit of analysis. Researchers conducted 361 observation sessions in Indianapolis and 369 in St. Petersburg. The sessions averaged nearly eight hours at each site, but the length varied somewhat. Sometimes sessions ended before the scheduled time because officers left to attend training, attend an extended court proceeding, take the rest of the day off, or perform a special assignment unrelated to service to the assigned beat. Community policing officers in St. Petersburg were given flexibility to determine the days and hours they worked, so the beginning and end times of their observation sessions varied considerably.[3]

Sometimes officers worked longer than regularly scheduled because of an emergency, to finish an activity begun during the regularly scheduled shift, or to perform some specially arranged overtime activity. If a regularly scheduled observation session ended with more than two hours remaining, the field researcher began a new session with the officer who replaced the originally assigned officer.[4] Time spent on problem solving was aggregated for the entire observation session. Characteristics of the assigned beat and the observed officer were linked to the observation session.

Data on the officer's background and attitudes were drawn from in-person interviews with patrol officers at a time when they were not under field observation. Researchers who did not conduct field observations held the interviews in a private room. These interviews took approximately 25 minutes and covered the officers' views and experiences on the beats they served, the work of police, the department, and community policing. We merged interview data with observation data for this analysis, and lost only 5 percent of the cases because of officers who refused to be interviewed or were otherwise unavailable.

Variables

Variable definitions are described below and summarized in Table 11.1.[5] The distributions of all variables are presented in Table 11.2.

Dependent Variable: Problem-Solving Time

Problem-solving activity, unlike many of the police behaviors studied by scholars, is not always easy to recognize. Arrests, use of force, report writing, and rendering assistance are all identified readily by what officers do and say. Problem solving, however, often involves the officer's own observations and analysis. These cognitive processes are not necessarily verbalized nor otherwise manifested such that the researcher can distinguish them from other types of activity. For example, an officer might decide to conduct preventive patrol of a public park to look for drug dealing. The officer may do this as part of a long-term project to rid the park of drug dealers; alternatively, it may be a spur-of-the-moment choice unconnected to any of the rational planning and analysis that are the core of problem solving as conceived by community policing reformers (Eck and Spelman 1987; Goldstein 1990).

We attempted to overcome this challenge by training observers to get officers to talk about their actions (Mastrofski and Parks 1990). Observers did this routinely after officers had engaged in some focused activity, such as responding to a call for service. When the activity did not involve face-to-face interaction between the police and others, officers were encouraged to talk about it simultaneously (e.g., driving around the park looking for drug dealers). Field researchers did not ask directly, "Are you engaging in problem-solving now?" because of the reactivity such a question might stimulate. They were asked, however, to draw on all the information available to them for each event they observed, and to make a judgment about each of the following:

> Was this activity part of a long-term plan or project to deal with a problem?[6]
>
> Did the police try to determine the nature, extent, or causes of the problem?[7]
>
> Were the police trying to prevent the occurrence or recurrence of a problem?[8]
>
> Did the activity involve communicating with representatives of citizen organizations or representatives of other service-providing organizations?

If any of the above conditions were met, we considered the entire event to be oriented to problem solving. The duration of the event was calculated by the difference between the start and the end time of the event. We calculated the total amount of time spent on problem solving by summing the number of minutes spent on such events during an observation period.

Our measure has obvious limitations. Officers may have failed to signal that a given event was part of a problem-solving effort when in fact that was the case. This certainly occurred; even so, our measure appears to be preferable to the standard alternative, which would use officers' self-reports of their problem-solving activities. Officers in St. Petersburg were required to document their problem-solving activities and time spent on problem solving. Officers and supervisors, however, generally believed that these records were unreliable, primarily because the officers knew that they were rarely used by any of their supervisors or managers. A review of the activity logs revealed that even community policing specialists rarely logged more than a few minutes per shift on problem-solving activities. Some reports contained obvious errors: for example, more time was logged for problem solving than was available in the entire work period.

Our data have several advantages over self-report data supplied by the department. In particular, the observers did not emphasize problem solving in their note taking. Indeed, this was a very small part of the coding protocol. Also, the field researchers' *only* job was to note and record events, and they received training, detailed instructions, and supervision in doing so. Certainly this approach increased the reliability of observations if one wishes to go beyond defining problem solving as "whatever the officer says it is."[9]

Table 11.1
Description of Independent Variables

Variable	Direction of Expected Effect	Definition
Site (St. Petersburg)	+	St. Petersburg = 1; Indianapolis = 0
Opportunity		
Self-directed time	+	Time free of assignments from dispatch or supervisors
Day shift	+	Officer works morning and early afternoon
Afternoon shift	+	Officer works afternoon to early evening
Socioeconomic distress of beat	+	Percentage unemployed plus percentage below 50% poverty plus percentage female-headed households
District staffing level	+	Number of officers on duty per 1,000 residents in each beat
Ability		
College education	+	Officer has bachelor's degree or higher
Amount of community policing training	+	Officer has completed a number of training courses in community policing techniques
Years of police experience	+/–	Years of experience in any police department
Instrumentality of Performance		
CPO assignment	+	Officer is officially assigned to CP duties
Department rewards problem solving	+	Department rewards officers for good problem solving
Supervisor wants reduced repeat calls for service	+	Supervisor wants to reduce repeat calls for service
District mgr. wants reduced repeat calls for service	+	District manager wants to reduce repeat calls for service
Reward-Cost Balance		
Good officer asks about problems	+	A good officer asks residents about neighborhood problems
Officer supports handling disorder problems	+	Nuisance problem include family and neighbor disputes, noise, and trash
Enforcing the law is most important	+	Enforcing the law is an officer's most important responsibility
Ambitious for promotion	+	Would you say that, for you personally, getting promoted is very important, somewhat important, somewhat unimportant, or very important?
Peers distrust citizens	–	How may officers in your unit would say that police officers have reason to be distrustful of most citizens?
Peers believe law enforcement is most important	–	How many officers in your unit would say that enforcing the law is by far a patrol officer's most important responsibility?

Table 11.2
Descriptive Statistics for Sample

Variable	Range	Mean	SD
Dependent Variable			
Time spent problem solving (in minutes)	0–451	40.69	62.89
Site (St. Petersburg)	0–1	.52	.50
Opportunity			
Self-directed time (in minutes)	2–700	358.06	100.90
Day shift	0–1	.33	.47
Afternoon shift	0–1	.33	.47
Socioeconomic distress of beat	20.83–79.83	44.14	18.03
District staffing level	.43–4.59	2.17	.64
Ability			
College education	0–1	.35	.48
Amount of CP training	7–32	14.82	4.95
Years of police experience	1–32	9.57	6.62
Instrumentality of Performance			
CPO assignment	0–1	.18	.39
Department rewards problem solving	1–4	1.91	.79
Supervisor wants reduced repeat calls for service	1–3	2.25	.70
District mgr wants reduced repeat calls for service	1–3	2.09	.72
Reward-Cost Balance			
Good officer asks about problems	1–4	3.63	.58
Officer supports handling disorder problems	2–18	10.27	3.49
Enforcing the law is most important	1–4	3.11	.78
Ambitious for promotion	1–4	2.45	1.04
Peers distrust citizens	1–4	2.52	.82
Peers believe law enforcement is most important	1–4	3.36	.68

The average amount of problem-solving time per observation session was 41 minutes. Table 11.3 shows the considerable variation across shifts: nearly one-third include no problem-solving activity, but 37 percent show at least 30 minutes. Although problem solving did not dominate most work shifts, it accounted for an observable part of the officer's workday in a substantial portion of cases.

This variation is somewhat deceptive, however, because it is partially an artifact of our method of sampling officers' work time. The total length of each observation session sets the outer limit of time an officer might spend on problem solving. Because the length of observation sessions is variable, we must remove variation that is an artifact of the mechanics of field observation. We did this by regressing problem-solving time on the total observed time for each observation session, using the Studentized residual as the dependent variable.[10] The residual is what is left of problem-solving time after the effects of total observed time are taken into account. This residual is expressed in units of standard deviation of the observed value from the value predicted by the total observed time variable. For example, a value of –4.5 for an observation session indicates that the observed value of problem-solving time was much smaller than the value predicted by observed time alone. The length of the observation session accounted for 3.5 percent of the variance in problem-solving time. Hereafter, references to problem-solving time pertain to the residualized variable unless indicated otherwise.

Independent Variables: Organization Factors

Site. We use the identity of the site as a dummy variable to take into account any organizational differences between the sites. Specifically, this variable represents the somewhat different orientation to problem solving held by the leadership of the two agencies. Officers in St. Petersburg are expected on average to expend more time on problem solving than Indianapolis officers.

Independent Variables: Expectancy Motivation Factors

Opportunity. The opportunity to conduct problem solving was measured in several ways. An aspect of opportunity is the amount of time during the shift when the officer is free from

Table 11.3
Distribution of Time Spent on Problem Solving (N = 614)

Problem-Solving: Time in Minutes	Frequency	Percentage
0	192	31.3
1–10	95	15.5
11–30	93	15.1
31–60	88	14.3
61–90	54	8.8
91–120	33	5.4
121–150	17	2.8
151–180	17	2.8
over 180 minutes	25	4.1
Total	614	100.0

specific assignments from the dispatcher or superiors. Presumably the more of this self-directed time is available, the greater the opportunity to engage in problem solving. Officers working day and afternoon shifts typically have more frequent opportunities to engage citizens because most citizens are awake at these times. On the midnight shift, in contrast, large numbers of the public are asleep and otherwise inaccessible.

The social and economic character of the assigned area may be expected to reflect the number and severity of problems presenting themselves to police. More distressed areas typically make more demands on police agencies in terms of calls for service; presumably they present more, and more pressing, opportunities for problem-solving interventions. As stated earlier, we measure the socioeconomic distress of a beat by summing the percentage of unemployed residents in the work force, the percentage of residents living below 50 percent of the poverty level, and the percentage of households headed by a single female.

Opportunity is also reflected in the availability of police resources at any given time. The more resources available, the greater the opportunity for any given officer to engage in problem solving. We operationalize resource availability as the number of sworn officers on duty per thousand residents in the district in which the assigned beat is located. This measure is taken from department assignment records; it reflects the average number on duty during the period of standard shift, because there is some fluctuation due to overlapping shifts and officers working less than full shifts. The district is the appropriate level at which to estimate officers' availability because, in both departments, cross-beat dispatching is common within districts but rare across districts (Klinger 1997).

Ability. Ability to conduct problem solving was measured in three ways. First, we considered officers who possessed a baccalaureate college degree to have more of the skills necessary for problem solving. A college degree is presumed to strengthen an officer's theoretical and conceptual abilities, as well as empirical research and planning skills.

Second, training in topics directly relevant to community and problem-oriented policing is designed specifically to increase officers' effectiveness in problem solving. We calculated a scale of community policing by summing the amount of training each officer received in public speaking, using computers, community policing philosophy, code enforcement, mediation, crime analysis, and organizing community groups.[11]

Third, an officer's experience on the job is relevant to ability to solve problems. One might presuppose that such experience would increase the officer's knowledge of the community and the kinds of problems that occur repeatedly. Yet if one assumes a *zeitgeist* effect in terms of policing skills developed, more experienced officers (whose early work habits were formed under a different reform ideology) should be more inflexible: such officers would find it more difficult to adopt problem-solving methods than less experienced officers with fewer years on the force. We cannot say in advance which of these effects would dominate; it is possible that they cancel each other.

Instrumentality of Performance. Instrumentality variables reflect what the organization has communicated to officers about what constitutes job performance: what is expected of them. Will the department reward the officer for engaging in problem solving? Four variables show various aspects of instrumentality. First, having a specific community policing job assignment means that the department has given the officer a narrower set of tasks in which to specialize than the general patrol officer. A second measure indicates the officers' views on how well the organization rewards them for a successful problem-solving job.[12] Third, an attitudinal measure indicates the extent to which officers perceive that their supervisor gives priority to a highly valued problem-solving objective: reducing the number of repeat calls for service to the same address.[13] A fourth similarly constructed measure indicates officers' perceptions of their district manager's priorities for the same goal. As instrumentality scores for problem solving increase, so should the amount of time officers devote to problem solving.

Reward-Cost Balance. Even if a police worker perceives that he or she has the opportunity and ability to solve problems and that the organization desires and rewards this work, other influences may affect the worker's calculus of the net benefit in doing this work. Problem solving may be more or less intrinsically rewarding; it may or may not comport with the officer's view of what police should do; other tasks may take higher priority; and the officer's peers may value problem solving to a greater or lesser degree. Finally, officers may vary in the degree to which they value rewards that the organization can bestow on them.

Six variables tap various features that help us map how the officer may balance the rewards and costs of problem solving. In one questionnaire item, officers were asked whether they agreed that "[a] good patrol officer will try to find out what residents think the neighborhood problems are." The stronger the officer's agreement with this statement, the greater the value the officer places on obtaining community input, a key aspect of problem solving. Second, the public most often wants police to attend to minor disputes and quality-of-life matters. Officers who believe that these problems deserve police attention are more likely to engage in problem solving. We created an additive scale of the officer's belief that police should attend to these matters. The scale was composed of officers' views on how often they should be expected to do something about public nuisances, neighbor disputes, family disputes, litter and trash, parents who do not control their children, and nuisance businesses that cause many problems for neighbors. Possible responses were (0) never, (1) sometimes, (2) much of the time, and (3) always).[14]

On the other hand, officers who are oriented toward law enforcement as a goal should place a lower value on problem solving because the problem-solving literature emphasizes seeking the most effective solution from a broad range of options, including many that are not enforcement oriented; enforcement orientation is a fourth variable. Fifth, officers who desire promotion are more sensitive to the department's priorities. Where departments promote problem solving, these ambitious officers should engage in more of this activity than their less ambitious colleagues, other things being equal.

Regardless of how officers may feel personally, they also may be affected by their peer environment. In two questions we asked respondents to indicate how many of the officers in their work unit would say that police officers have reason to be distrustful of most citizens (the sixth variable), and that enforcing the law is by far a patrol officer's most important priority: (1) none, (2) a few, (3) about half, or (4) all or most. Higher responses indicate a more cohesive peer culture regarding each of these items. Where more peers distrust citizens, there is less informal peer support for working closely with the public in problem solving. Where more peers support law enforcement as the dominant priority, there is less support for the wide-ranging search for solutions associated with problem solving.

Performance-Reward Expectancy. As in previous applications of expectancy theory to policing (Mastrofski et al. 1994), our test is incomplete because data on performance-reward expectancy variables (how the organization calibrates rewards for performance) are unavailable. Therefore it is more appropriate to use the expectancy-motivation framework to interpret the results of the data available to us.

Analysis

We used ordinary least squares (OLS) to regress problem-solving time on the independent variables.[15] The variables are grouped in the table according to the factor they represent. Thus all models include variables measuring opportunity, skill, instrumentality (the perception of external incentives provided formally by the department), and reward-cost balance (a crude way of approximating officers' own values and informal peer norms that may either reinforce or contradict instrumental influences). Results from the OLS analysis are presented in Table 11.4.

The betas of the final model afford an opportunity to determine whether the effects of individual variables were in the expected directions, and to compare the magnitude of effects. Among opportunity variables, only self-directed time and district staffing level demonstrated significant effects. Self-directed time showed an effect opposite in direction to that hypothesized, probably because of the effects of correlation with total observed time. (The effects of total observed time are accounted for by using the residuals of its effects for the dependent variable.) The bivariate relationship between self-directed time and unresidualized problem-solving time was positive. Thus we do not make any inferences about the size and direction of this regression coefficient, but merely use it to account for any variance not already removed by the length-of-observation variable. Higher levels of district staffing were associated with more time spent on problem solving. Variables designed to capture temporal and spatial variation in opportunity for problem solving showed no significant effects.

Of the three variables representing ability to engage in problem solving, only amount of experience showed a significant effect. Officers with less than 10 years of experience were more

Table 11.4

Ordinary Least Squares Regression of Problem-Solving Time on Organization and Expectancy Variables (N = 614)

Variable Name	Coefficient	Beta	Sig.
Constant	–.791		
Site			
St. Petersburg	.045	.022	.659
Opportunity			
Self-directed time	–.001	–.096	.021
Day shift	.177	.080	.129
Afternoon shift	–.036	–.016	.732
Socioeconomic distress of beat	–.001	–.010	.802
District staffing level	.143	.088	.037
Ability			
College education	–.063	–.029	.484
Amount of CP training	.011	.054	.228
Less than 10 years of police experience	.367	.173	.000
Instrumentality of Performance			
CPO assignment	.666	.248	.000
PD rewards for good problem solving job	–.178	–.136	.001
Supervisor wants reduced repeat calls for service	.154	.104	.014
District manager wants reduced repeat calls for service	.014	.009	.830
Reward-Cost Balance			
Officer supports handling disorder problems	.000	.001	.974
Enforcing the law is most important	–.114	–.084	.064
Good officer asks residents about neighborhood problems	–.001	–.005	.909
Ambitious for promotion	.073	.073	.088
Peers believe enforcing law is most important	.128	.083	.059
Peers distrust citizens	.024	.019	.630
R^2 = .164			

inclined to spend time in problem solving; this finding suggests the challenges of changing work habits as they grow stronger over time.[16] Neither college education nor amount of community policing training showed a significant effect.

Three of the four instrumentality variables showed significant effects. By far, the strongest was the nature of the officer's work assignment (community policing officer versus patrol generalist). Surprisingly, officers who perceived that the department rewards officers for doing a good job in problem solving did *less* problem solving. We speculate that this response may reflect different standards: officers who do more problem solving may expect the department to offer more rewards for problem solving than do officers who do less. Conversely, low performers may view the department as providing more rewards for problem solving than justified. Officers who perceive that their supervisors give a higher priority to reducing repeat calls for service to the same address spend more time in problem solving, but their perceptions of the district manager's priorities have no effect. This finding is consistent with the ethnographic studies showing that the first-line supervisor has by far the greatest influence on the day-to-day performance of the rank and file (Muir 1977; Rubinstein 1973; Van Maanen 1983).

None of the reward-cost balance variables achieved a statistically significant effect, although two came close: officers' belief and their perception that peers believe enforcing the law is important. Officers who believe that law enforcement is most important tend to do less problem solving (as expected). Surprisingly, however, officers who believe that more of their peers support law enforcement as the top priority also engage in more problem solving. It may be that this variable too reflects a different evaluative standard for officers who engage in more problem solving. They may have heightened sensitivity to their deviation from the traditional reactive work model, and therefore may give more attention to their peers' enforcement efforts. Alternatively, this finding may reflect the tendency of officers in these departments to view enforcement strategies as the preferred approach in solving problems.

Given the skewed nature of the dependent variable, it is possible that a few observation sessions containing exceptionally large amounts of problem-solving time account for the effects noted. We performed a number of additional regressions excluding outliers, and found that the results were not affected substantially.

The relatively strong effect of the officer's duty assignment (CPO versus general patrol) raises the possibility that the motivation expectancy model may operate very differently for the two groups. Simply put, problem-solving work should be much more relevant to those whose job assignment and work expectations are focused specifically on this task. Hence we would expect the remainder of the variables in the model to be far more powerful in accounting for problem-solving effort among CPOs than among general patrol officers.

To test this possibility, we split the sample into these two groups: 500 observation sessions with general patrol officers and 114 sessions with CPOs. Table 11.5 shows that our expectation was correct. The model has over four times as much explanatory power for CPOs as for general patrol officers. Each model shows different significant effects: the factors that affect problem-solving time for beat officers are not those that affect problem-solving time for CPOs.

The last column in Table 11.5 shows the *t*-value for the comparison of coefficients between the two samples (see Paternoster et al. 1998). Five variables show a statistically significant difference. Two of these are in a direction readily expected. First, the desire for promotion significantly increases problem-solving time for CPOs but has an inconsequential effect for general patrol officers. Second, CPOs are differentiated from general patrol officers in that only the former are influenced by their perception of the district manager's priority to reduce repeat calls for service. In both departments, the problem-solving effort was viewed much more as a special management initiative than as a routine operation. Not surprisingly, CPOs are far more

Table 11.5
Ordinary Least Squares Regression of Problem-Solving Time on Organizational and Expectancy Variables, Comparing Community Policing Officers with Beat Officers

	Beat (911) Officers (*N* = 500)		Community Policing Officers (*N* = 114)		
Variable Name	**Coeff.**	**(SE)**	**Coeff.**	**(SE)**	$t_{(b1-b2)}$[a]
Constant	.15	(.45)	–1.44	(2.96)	
Site (St. Petersburg)	–.01	(.10)	–.78	(.60)	1.29
Opportunity					
Self-directed time	–.01	(.00)**	–.00	(.00)	–1.89
Day shift	.22	(.11)	.09	(.49)	.25
Afternoon shift	–.06	(.09)	–.09	(.50)	.05
Socioeconomic distress of beat	.00	(.00)	–.00	(.01)	.54
District staffing level	.04	(.07)	.40	(.21)	–1.65
Ability					
College education	–.03	(.08)	–1.15	(.49)*	2.26
Amount of CP training	–.00	(.01)	.05	(.04)	–1.18
Less than 10 years of police experience	.33	(.10)**	.30	(.41)	.06
Instrumentality of Performance					
PD rewards for good problem-solving job	–.12	(.05)*	–.29	(.23)	.75
Supervisor wants reduced repeat calls for service	.15	(.06)*	.34	(.38)	–.51
District manager wants reduced repeat calls for service	–.08	(.06)	.95	(.28)**	–3.57
Reward-Cost Balance					
Officer supports handling disorder problems	–.02	(.01)	.06	(.04)	–1.68
Enforcing the law is most important	–.04	(.06)	–.21	(.22)	.74
Good officer asks residents about neighborhood problems	.01	(.07)	–1.46	(.64)	2.31
Ambitious for promotion	.03	(.04)	.63	(.20)**	–3.02
Peers believe enforcing law is most important	–.04	(.06)	.96	(.30)**	–3.33
Peers distrust citizens	.00	(.05)	–.21	(.25)	.83
R^2	.08		.38		

[a] *T*-test for the difference in coefficients between patrol and community police officers.
*$p < .05$; **$p < .01$

sensitive to their district manager's perspective on problem solving.

The rationale is less obvious for the differential effects of a third variable, perceived peer attitudes about enforcement as the top priority. CPOs who perceived their peers as strongly oriented to enforcement also spent more time in problem solving. This may well reflect the application of different standards, whereby respondents rated their peers according to their own expectations rather than by some objective standard.

Most puzzling is a fourth variable, the differential effect of a college degree. It has virtually no effect for general patrol officers, but it seems to suppress problem solving among CPOs. We can only speculate about the cause. Problem solving may attract a different kind of college-educated officer to the specialist position than is found among the general patrol officers. Alternatively, the problem-solving aspects of the work may come to be viewed as undesirable or ineffective for college-educated officers who do a great deal of problem solving. Finally, attitude about whether an officer should ask residents about neighborhood problems differs significantly across models. Although this variable was not significant in either model, it approaches significance for 911 officers. Indianapolis and St. Petersburg differed in the nature and extent of problem solving. To determine whether expectancy motivation theory provides a stronger explanation for one site than for the other, we estimated separate regression equations for Indianapolis (298 rides) and St. Petersburg (316 rides). Table 11.6 contains OLS coefficients and *t*-tests for differences in coefficients.

Opportunity variables seem more important in Indianapolis than in St. Petersburg. In Indianapolis, district staffing levels exert a positive influence on problem-solving time, while in St.

Petersburg, no opportunity variables are related significantly to the dependent variable. One possible explanation for this finding is that CPOs in St. Petersburg "created" their opportunities to engage in problem solving by writing their own schedules. Typically they were not constrained by predefined shifts, and much of their time on duty was self-directed. Ability variables are not significant in either jurisdiction.

Community policing assignment is related strongly to problem-solving activity in St. Petersburg (beta = .266) but not in Indianapolis: officers assigned to a community policing detail in St. Petersburg engaged in more problem solving than beat officers in that city. This relationship does not hold for officers in Indianapolis, however. In St. Petersburg, community policing officers were given more autonomy to identify neighborhood problems and produce solutions. In Indianapolis, problems were identified by upper management, who created specific solutions. Perhaps the freedom to identify and solve problems led CPOs in St. Petersburg to do more of this. In addition, officers in Indianapolis (where supervisors define solutions to neighborhood problems) are significantly more likely to engage in problem solving if they believe that their supervisor wants to reduce repeat calls for service. This finding is not significant in St. Petersburg.

Perception of departmental rewards for problem solving is the only variable significant in both Indianapolis and St. Petersburg. As above, officers who feel that their department supports problem solving tend to do less of it. Finally, ambition for promotion is stronger (and significant) in St. Petersburg, where the structural reinforcements promoting problem solving are stronger and more diffuse than in Indianapolis.

Finally, expectancy motivation theory posits that all measures must be at a high level if workers are to perform as the organization desires. Our final task is to examine whether officers who are "high" on any one of these factors do so,

Table 11.6
Ordinary Least Squares Regression of Problem-Solving Time on Organizational and Expectancy Variables, Comparing Indianapolis with St. Petersburg

	Indianapolis (N = 298)		St. Petersburg (N = 316)		
Variable Name	Coeff.	(SE)	Coeff.	(SE)	$t_{(b1-b2)}$[a]
Constant	−.73	(.59)	−1.16	(.88)	
Opportunity					
Self-directed time	−.00	(.00)**	−.00	(.00)	−1.34
Day shift	.25	(.13)	−.07	(.24)	1.17
Afternoon shift	−.04	(.12)	−.17	(.20)	.53
Socioeconomic distress of beat	.00	(.00)	−.00	(.00)	.05
District staffing level	.38	(.13)**	.12	(.10)	1.64
Ability					
College education	−.02	(.10)	−.23	(.18)	1.06
Amount of CP training	.01	(.01)	.03	(.02)	−1.12
Less than 10 years of police experience	−.22	(.13)	.32	(.19)	−2.40
Instrumentality of Performance					
CPO Assignment	.28	(.18)	.73	(.21)**	−1.63
PD rewards for good problem-solving job	−.13	(.06)*	−.22	(.10)*	.77
Supervisor wants reduced repeat calls for service	.15	(.08)*	.11	(.11)	.30
District manager wants reduced repeat calls for service	−.02	(.08)	.06	(.11)	−.51
Reward-Cost Balance					
Officers support handling disorder problems	−.02	(.02)	.02	(.02)	−1.61
Enforcing the law is most important	−.06	(.08)	−.16	(.10)	.77
Good officer asks residents about neighborhood problems	.07	(.10)	−.08	(.13)	.96
Ambitious for promotion	.01	(.06)	.17	(.07)*	−1.74
Peers believe enforcing law is most important	.06	(.08)	.18	(.11)	−.90
Peers distrust citizens	.03	(.06)	.03	(.09)	−.07
R^2	.14		.20		

[a] *T*-test for the difference in coefficients between Indianapolis and St. Petersburg.
*$p < .05$; **$p < .01$

or whether all four factors must be present at a high level to generate significant amounts of problem solving. In other words, do opportunity, ability, instrumentality, and reward-cost balance interact to affect the amount of time officers spend in problem solving? To test this question, we created scales measuring each of the four aspects of expectancy-motivation theory. Because the variables contain different numbers of categories, we created scales by multiplying each variable by its unstandardized regression coefficient (see Table 11.4) and summing those values.[17] We derived OLS regression estimates first using these four scales alone (with research site included as a control variable) and then including the interaction of all four in a second model. The results of this analysis are displayed in Table 11.7.

The first columns in Table 11.7 indicate that the explanatory power of this model is similar to that of the model presented in Table 11.4. As in Table 11.4, 16.4 percent of the variation in problem-solving time is explained by the four expectancy motivation factors. As in the earlier regression model, research site does not affect time spent on problem solving. All four components of expectancy motivation, however, are related significantly to problem-solving time: officers with high levels of opportunity, ability, instrumentality, and reward-cost balance engage more often in problem-solving behaviors. This model also indicates that instrumentality of performance plays the most important role in problem solving (beta = .314).

The value of r^2 increases slightly when the interaction of all four factors is entered into the model ($r^2 = .168$), although the interaction itself is not related significantly to the dependent variable. Thus, although the individual components of expectancy motivation theory are important in explaining the amount of time spent on problem solving, a high level of all four components is not necessary for desired performance.

Conclusions

We have examined how fully patrol officers in two agencies committed their work time to problem-solving activities. As expected, problem solving has taken hold only modestly in these agencies. On many work shifts, officers spent little or no time on problem solving, but in a substantial portion of shifts, officers committed at least one-half hour to these tasks. Although the two departments differed as to their officers' tendency to spend time problem solving, the explanatory power of the department's identity was only a small fraction of the power of the motivation-expectancy factors. This finding determines the upper limits of top agency leaders' effects on the level of problem-solving effort; at least in this comparison, the effects were of little consequence.

Rather, the analysis shows that a model focused on police workers' motivation expectancy is considerably more powerful. Of all motivation expectancy considerations, instrumental-

Table 11.7
Test for Interactions Between Expectancy-Motivation Variables

Variable	Expectancy-Motivation Factors Alone: Coeff.	Beta	Expectancy-Motivation Factors with Interaction: Coeff.	Beta
Constant	–.79		–.80	
St. Petersburg	.05	.02	.04	.02
Opportunity	1.00**	.14	1.20**	.17
Ability	1.00**	.19	1.01**	.19
Instrumentality	1.00**	.31	.95**	.30
Reward-Cost Balance	1.01**	.11	1.07**	.11
Interaction (Opp x Ability x Instrum x Rcbal)			–7.63	–.07
R^2	.16		.17	

**$p < .01$

ity variables dominated. Especially powerful were the effects of giving an officer a specialized community policing job assignment. Opportunity and ability variables possessed modest explanatory power. Variables reflecting the officer's personal view of what police work should be, and the view of his or her peers, accounted for the smallest amount of the model's explanatory power.

Differences in regression coefficients between the two research sites suggest that the method of implementing community policing has a significant effect on officers' amount of problem solving. In St. Petersburg, where police officers were relatively autonomous and defined neighborhood problems themselves, community policing officers were more active problem solvers than CPOs in Indianapolis. In contrast, community policing officers in Indianapolis were just as likely as beat officers to engage in problem solving; in that city, problems were defined by upper management and CPOs were not freed from responding to calls for service. Also in Indianapolis, officers seem to be aware of the priorities placed on problem solving by upper management: they spent more time in problem solving if they thought it was a management priority. In addition, officers with more time to conduct problem-solving activities did so.

Many departments around the nation structure their problem-solving efforts similarly to the departments we studied. They create some special job assignments that focus officers' duties on problem solving, but use the great majority of the patrol force to conduct "reactive" policing tasks, and support the problem-solving specialists ad hoc, catch-as-catch-can.

Under these arrangements, it appears that the single most powerful thing a department can do to increase its problem-solving dosage is to assign more officers to these specialist jobs. In these circumstances, and even though top management may exhort *all* officers to embrace the community policing, problem-solving "philosophy," differences in officers' belief systems (and their perception of their peers' belief systems) are of practically no consequence. Perhaps some leaders may possess sufficient charisma to inspire widespread shifts in officers' views of what constitutes important goals and methods of policing. Perhaps departments that decline to create problem-solving specialists may successfully imbue a larger proportion of their patrol force with the opportunity and inclination to engage in problem solving. Testing these possibilities would require replication of this study in other departments with strikingly different structures and leaders, but we do not know whether such departments even exist.

We must be careful not to overplay the importance of our results. The motivation-expectancy model (with the organizational component as well) accounted for only 15 percent of the variance in problem-solving time. Although statistically significant, this explanatory power is quite modest even by social science standards. This finding certainly reflects the openness of the police organization and its workers to fluctuations in the demands placed upon it by its environment (Reiss 1992; Reiss and Bordua 1967).

Despite contemporary reformers' efforts to produce police who do more to change their work environment by solving problems proactively, the police remain one of society's principal means of responding to stochastically distributed social problems. The uncertainty of what each patrol officer will face as he or she leaves roll call creates tremendous challenges for increasing the planned, thoughtful, empirical, programmatic problem-solving approach. Police agencies have yet to create mechanisms that buffer their patrol forces from the uncertainties and fluctuations of their calls-for-service workload. Indeed, patrol forces serve as the buffer for other specialized units in the agency so that *they* can be removed from the need to respond to moment-by-moment fluctuations in work demands. More sophisticated measures and models incorporating these externally imposed work demands may well increase our capacity to account for variations in problem-solving time.

Authors' Note

This research is based on data from the Project on Policing Neighborhoods, directed by Stephen D. Mastrofski, Roger B. Parks, Albert J. Reiss Jr., and Robert E. Worden. The project was supported by Grant 95-IJ-CX-0071 by the National Institute of Justice, Office of Justice Programs, U.S. Department of Justice. Points of view in this document are those of the authors and do not necessarily represent the official position or policies of the U.S. Department of Justice.

Notes

1. Despite this requirement, several CPOs in St. Petersburg logged up to 13-hour days.
2. The reliability coefficient for the socioeconomic distress scale is .85.
3. In St. Petersburg, community policing officers were given great flexibility in deciding when they worked, as long as they logged 40 hours per week. They were allowed to select which days they worked and the hours they worked on any given day, without prior approval by a supervisor. Observations of these officers were scheduled without regard to day and shift, because day and shift were irrelevant to their own scheduling.
4. We made this change because the project was designed to sample the policing by officers assigned to the 12 selected neighborhoods, not the policing by a given set of officers. In some cases the department did not replace the officer with a full-time replacement, but instead assigned someone who had another beat assignment as well. In these cases, field researchers were transferred to officers who the sergeant expected would spend the most time working in the selected study beat.
5. The statistics are based on a listwise deletion for missing values. Virtually all of the missing values came from data taken from the officer surveys. A few observed officers were not interviewed (some refused) or declined to answer certain questions. Of the 728 observation sessions, 614 contained no missing values.
6. A long-term plan was defined as a plan developed before this observation session.
7. This investigation had to go beyond a mere attempt to identify suspects or wrongdoers.
8. An affirmative answer required some indication that the officer was trying to do more than deal only with the presenting situation. The police action had to be clearly oriented to the future (beyond the end of the work shift).
9. To assess reliability of our problem-solving measure, we conducted random comparisons of the observer narratives and the quantified, coded data. We randomly selected 100 encounters and compared the observer's written description with the coded data analyzed here.
10. We were unable to analyze problem-solving time directly because of collinearity between total ride length and amount of self-directed time. In addition, we could not use the proportion of time spent on problem solving because of differences in ride lengths, as discussed above.
11. Response options for each type of training were (1) none, (2) less than one day, (3) one or two days, (4) three to five days, and (5) more than five days. The reliability coefficient for the summary scale was .80.
12. Responses to the following item were coded as indicated: "How well has the [X] department done in rewarding officers who do a good job with problem solving?" (1) Poor, (2) fair, (3) good, (4) excellent.
13. Officers who rated this goal among the two most important of their supervisor's goals were assigned a value of 3; those who rated this goal among the two least important of their supervisor's goals were assigned a value of 1; all others received a value of 2, somewhere between the most and the least important goals held by their supervisor.
14. The reliability coefficient for this measure was .72 for all Indianapolis officers interviewed and .82 for all St. Petersburg officers interviewed.
15. The data are hierarchical. Many officers were observed more than once, but the average number of rides per officer was quite low (2.3). Of the 319 officers observed, 45 percent were observed only once, and 26 percent were observed twice. Only 9 percent of the sample were observed five or more times, well below the rule-of- thumb minimum of 10 needed to produce stable hierarchical regression coefficients. Thus, although a nonhierarchical OLS underestimates the standard error of regression coefficients for officer-level variables in this sample, this bias is relatively small in view of the great majority of officers observed only once or twice.
16. In exploratory bivariate analysis (not presented), the relationship between years of experience and time spent in problem solving was delineated clearly at 10 years of experience as an officer. Thus, rather than using the continuous variable "years of experience," we created a dummy variable indicating "less than 10 years experience" or "10 years or more."
17. For example, ability is measured with the following formula: $(-.029 \times \text{college}) + (.054 \times \text{CP training}) + (.173 \times \text{experience})$. This technique results in a model in which the regression coefficients are equal to 1, and the standardized coefficients can be compared directly (Coleman 1976).

References

Buerger, M.E. 1998. "Police Training as Pentecost: Using Tools Singularly Ill-Suited to the Purpose of Reform." *Police Quarterly* 1:27–64.

Bittner, E. 1970. *The Functions of the Police in Modern Society: A Review of Background Factors, Current Practices, and Possible Role Models.* Chevy Chase, MD: Center for Studies of Crime and Delinquency.

Black, D.J. 1980. *The Manners and Customs of the Police.* New York: Academic Press.

Campbell, J.P. and R.D. Pritchard. 1976. "Motivation Theory in Industrial and Organizational Psychology." Pp. 63–130 in *Handbook of Industrial and Organizational Psychology,* edited by M.D. Dunnette. Chicago, IL: Rand McNally.

Coleman, J.S. 1976. "Regression Analysis for the Comparison of School and Home Effects." *Social Science Research* 5:1–20.

Eck, J.E. and W. Spelman. 1987. "Who Ya Gonna Call? The Police as Problem-Busters." *Crime and Delinquency* 33:31–52.

Fogelson, R.M. 1977. *Big-City Police.* Cambridge, MA: Harvard University Press.

Goldstein, H. 1990. *Problem-Oriented Policing.* Philadelphia, PA: Temple University Press.

Guyot, D. 1991. *Policing as Though People Matter.* Philadelphia, PA: Temple University Press.

Klinger, D.A. 1997. "Negotiating Order in Patrol Work: An Ecological Theory of Police Response to Deviance." *Criminology* 35(2):277–306.

Maguire, E. and S.D. Mastrofski. 1999. "Patterns of Community Policing in the United States." *Police Quarterly.*

Mastrofski, S.D. 1998. "Community Policing and Police Organization Structure." Pp. 161–89 in *How to Recognize Good Policing: Problems and Issues,* edited by J. Brodeur. Thousand Oaks, CA: Sage.

Mastrofski, S.D. and R.B. Parks. 1990. "Improving Observational Studies of the Police." *Criminology* 29:475–96.

Mastrofski, S.D., R.B. Parks, A.J. Reiss, Jr., R.E. Worden, C. DeJong, J.B. Snipes, and W. Terrill. 1998. *Systematic Observation of Public Police: Applying Field Research Methods to Policy Issues.* Washington, DC: National Institute of Justice.

Mastrofski, S.D., R.R. Ritti, and J.B. Snipes. 1994. "Expectancy Theory and Police Productivity in DUI Enforcement." *Law and Society Review* 28:113–48.

Mastrofski, S.D. and C.D. Uchida. 1993. "Transforming the Police." *Journal of Research in Crime and Delinquency* 30:330–58.

Mitchell, T.R. 1974. "Expectancy Models of Job Satisfaction, Occupational Preference and Effort: A Theoretical, Methodological, and Empirical Appraisal." *Psychological Bulletin* 81:1053–77.

——. 1982a. "Expectancy-Value Models in Organizational Psychology." Pp. 293–312 in *Expectations and Actions: Expectancy-Value Models in Psychology,* edited by N.T. Feather. Hillsdale, NJ: Erlbaum.

——. 1982b. "Motivation: New Directions for Research, Theory, and Practice." *Academy of Management Review* 7:80–88.

Muir, W.K. 1977. *Police: Streetcorner Politicians*. Chicago, IL: University of Chicago Press.

Paternoster, R., R. Brame, P. Mazerolle, and A. Piquero. 1998. "Using the Correct Statistical Test for the Equality of Regression Coefficients." *Criminology* 36:859–66.

Reiss, A.J. 1971. "Systematic Observation of Natural Social Phenomena." Pp. 3–33 in *Sociological Methodogy* 1971, edited by H.L. Costner. San Francisco, CA: Jossey-Bass.

——. 1992. "Police Organization in the Twentieth Century." Pp. 51–97 in *Modern Policing*, edited by M. Tonry and N. Morris. Chicago, IL: University of Chicago Press.

Reiss, A.J. and D. Bordua. 1967. "Environment and Organization: A Perspective on the Police." Pp. 25–55 in *The Police: Six Sociological Essays*, edited by D. Bordua. New York: Wiley.

Reuss-Ianni, E. 1983. *The Two Cultures of Policing*. New Brunswick, NJ: Transaction Books.

Rubinstein, J. 1973. *City Police*. New York: Farrar, Straus & Giroux.

Sampson, R.J., S.W. Raudenbush, and F. Earls. 1997. "Neighborhoods and Violent Crime: A Multilevel Study of Collective Efficacy." *Science* 277:918–24.

Sherman, L.W., D. Gottfredson, D. MacKenzie, J. Eck, P. Reuter, and S. Bushway. 1997. *Preventing Crime: What Works, What Doesn't, What's Promising*. Washington, DC: U.S. Government Printing Office.

Skolnick, J.H. 1994. *Justice Without Trial: Law Enforcement in Democratic Society*. New York: MacMillian.

Skolnick, J.H. and J.J. Fyfe. 1993. *Above the Law: Police and the Excessive Use of Force*. New York: Free Press.

Sparrow, M.K., M.H. Moore, and D.M. Kennedy. 1990. *Beyond 911: A New Era for Policing*. New York: Basic Books.

Trojanowicz, R. and D. Carter. 1988. *The Philosophy and Role of Community Policing*. East Lansing, MI: National Neighborhood Foot Patrol Center, Michigan State University.

Van Maanen, J. 1974. "Working the Street: A Developmental View of Police Behavior." Pp. 83–130 in *The Potential for Reform of Criminal Justice*, edited by H. Jacob. Beverly Hills, CA: Sage.

——.1983. "The Boss: First-Line Supervision in an American Police Agency." Pp. 275–317 in *Control in the Police Organization*, edited by M. Punch. Cambridge, MA: MIT Press.

Walker, S. 1977. *A Critical History of Police Reform: The Emergence of Professionalism*. Lexington, MA: Lexington Books.

Whyte, W.F., M. Dalton, D. Roy, L. Sayles, O. Collins, F. Miller, G. Strauss, F. Fuerstenberg, and A. Bavelas. 1955. *Money and Motivation: An Analysis of Incentives in Industry*. New York: Harper & Bros.

Wilson, J.Q. 1968. *Varieties of Police Behavior: The Management of Law and Order in Eight Communities*. Cambridge, MA: Harvard University Press.

Wilson, J.Q. and G.W. Kelling. 1982. "The Police and Neighborhood Safety: Broken Windows." *Atlantic Monthly* (March), pp. 29–38.

——. 1989. "Making Neighborhoods Safe." *Atlantic Monthly* (February), pp. 46–52.

Chapter 12

Citizen Complaints and Problem Officers

Examining Officer Behavior

William Terrill
John McCluskey

Although a number of studies have examined citizens complaints against the police—studying the complaint process, comparing the characteristics of problem and nonproblem officers—all have equated complaints with officer misconduct. Here, Terrill and McCluskey examine the actual relationship between citizen complaints and officer behavior, comparing observational data of low-complaint and "problem" officers to see whether their behavior in the field justifies the label.

Do citizen complaints tell us nothing? Do they truly reflect an officer's propensity for misconduct? Or do they actually signify higher productivity, as officers who intervene more frequently are increasingly likely to receive complaints?

Introduction

The police, as a public institution, relies on a grant of legitimacy rooted in public trust and confidence. Citizen complaints of police misconduct represent a weakening of that foundation. Complaints that become news events can erode confidence among an even wider audience. Incidents such as the Abner Louima brutality case in New York grab headlines and reverberate throughout the popular, academic, and policy-making environments.

Systematic research on police misconduct suggests most citizen complaints are generated by a handful of officers. In 1991, the Christopher Commission released its review of the Los Angeles Police Department in the aftermath of the Rodney King riots (Independent Commission on the Los Angeles Police Department, 1991). From its investigation, the Commission reported that a small group of officers were responsible for a disproportionate number of citizen complaints. Forty-four such officers who had six or more allegations of excessive force or improper tactics were identified and subsequently labeled "problem officers." It stands to reason that officers who repeatedly receive citizen complaints will be looked upon with suspicion, reflecting the adage—"where there's smoke there's often fire." Police departments throughout the country have exerted much effort in recent years to identifying potential problem officers through the use of citizen complaint data. Several departments (e.g., Chicago and Detroit) have even experimented with computerized early warning systems to identify officers with a high number of citizen complaints (Kappeler, Sluder, & Alpert, 1994).[1]

Using data collected as part of an observational study of the police in St. Petersburg, FL, this article examines the relationship between citizen complaints and officer behavior in day-to-day encounters with the public. More specifically, do officers identified as problem officers (via their citizen complaint history) engage in physical force and discourteous behavior, stop suspected criminals, and engage in less inhibiting behaviors more often than those identified as nonproblem officers? Previous studies concerning citizen complaints have most often concentrated on the complaint process (Dugan & Breda, 1991; Wagner & Decker, 1997). Others have examined officer characteristics such as race, gender, and attitudes, in an attempt to identify patterns or differences between "problem officers" and their nonproblem counterparts, or rates of sustained complaints (Hudson, 1970; Lersch & Mieczkowski, 1996). What is lacking in this debate is an empirical examination of the relationship between citizen complaints and actual officer behavior. Equating complaints with behavior requires a leap of faith that is premature at this juncture.

Politicians, police administrators, and the public, whether fairly or unfairly, look upon those with extensive complaint histories as *potential* problem officers. Officers who are consistently identified as alleged violators merit attention, whether guilty of wrongdoing or not, whether being productive or not. Simply, it is these officers who pose the greatest risk to police departments in terms of public perception and financial liability. On the other hand, one has to question the validity of the "where there's smoke there's often fire" approach since there is little supporting evidence. The problem lies in the fact that it is difficult to uncover if there really is any fire beneath all that smoke, since most allegations of police misbehavior are rarely confirmed (Lersch & Mieczkowski, 1996).

This article provides the unique opportunity to combine citizen complaint data with actual observations. It examines the behavior of identified problem officers, as well as those who are not labeled as such. If there is fire under the smoke, one would expect differences in behavior between these two groups of officers. Do citizen complaint data truly identify problem officers who behave differently than their colleagues? What is it about these "potential problem officers," from a behavioral standpoint, that results in a high rate of repeat complaints from the public? Do these officers differ in how they discharge their duties?

Perspectives on Citizen Complaints and Problem Officers

The police-citizen encounter represents a special case of humans engaging in social interaction. The potential for conflict between actors is naturally heightened when individual actors battle for a differential outcome. This is not to say that overt conflict arises whenever this is the case. Most social interaction occurs without conflict. As Goffman (1959) argues, in most social interactions, a working consensus develops because "participants are sufficiently attuned to one another so that open contradictions will not occur" (p. 9). Generally, this type of peaceful scenario plays out even in the case of highly adversarial situations such as police-citizen interactions (Bayley & Garofalo, 1989). Most police-citizen encounters occur without conflict because of the "willingness of the actors to agree on the definition of the situation and to permit each actor to play out the role he has chosen for himself" (Hudson, 1970, p 180).

Nonetheless, as a result of the often adversarial nature of the police-citizen relationship, situations rise in which avoidance of conflict is not an option. Not every citizen willingly accepts an officer's definition of a situation; instead, he or she may choose to rebel against or challenge the authority of the police officer. Van Maanen (1978) noted that this type of citizen, termed the "asshole" by police, was likely to receive street justice in the form of a "thumping." Though Van Maanen's fieldwork took place three decades ago, police continue to confront citizens they label as "assholes" who challenge their authority (Mastrofski, Reisig, & McCluskey, 1999). Use of force against such suspects is, however, now receiving more careful scrutiny due to the aforementioned legal and financial implications. More precisely, "thumping" an "asshole" has garnered an increasing amount of both departmental and public attention (Skolnick & Fyfe, 1993).

When force is applied in conflict situations, the process or management of conflict becomes the focal concern (Mastrofski, 1999). It is one thing for an officer to use force, but another if such force is not delivered properly or legally (Klockars, 1995; Terrill, 2001; Toch, 1995). Legitimacy of the police institution is threatened when officers are unable or unwilling to resolve conflict situations in an appropriate manner (Kerstetter, 1995; Tyler, 1990). As a result, various mechanisms exist to restore legitimacy. For example, a citizen may bring a lawsuit against an officer or the police department alleging wrongdoing, letting the courts settle the issue, but this is expensive, time consuming, and realistically available only in cases where severe physical or monetary damage has resulted.

Another option is to file a complaint with the police department itself. Complaints indicate that citizens perceive something as "wrong," and they have a grievance requiring redress. This could be some noxious officer behavior (e.g., a racial epithet aimed at the complainant), it could be that the officer was perceived as rude or condescending, or it could be that the officer was alleged to have used excessive force. Regardless of the underlying source, a citizen complaint represents citizen frustration arising from an incident involving the named officer. Thus, if we know how many complaints officers have, *what exactly do we know?*

At least three different perspectives on the meaning of citizen complaints are possible. First, it may be that citizen complaints tell us little to nothing because they are unreliable or invalid indicators of officer behavior. Two arguments can be made in this respect. First, a citizen complaint is just that—a "citizen" complaint. It is the citizen's view or perception that the officer acted illegally or improperly, which is unlikely to be informed by rules and procedures promulgated by police departments for establishing uniform operating standards.[2] Second, a complaint is solely an allegation of wrongdoing and may have less to do with improper police behavior and more to do with the fact the citizen was the subject of an officer behavior (e.g., arrest, search) that the citizen simply does not like, thereby prompting a grudge on his or her behalf. These two points undermine the reliability of a noninvestigated complaint as a performance measure. One can presume that complaints that are subsequently sustained hold merit, but due to stringent evidentiary requirements, the ratio of sustained complaints to the total number of complaints is often extremely low in general, and even more so concerning serious complaints such as excessive force.

Second, it may be that complaints help to identity potential problem officers. Toch (1995) notes that complaints are subject to interpretation, but they may be a rough indicator of an officer's "propensity" for malpractice. Thus, officers with a high complaint rate, in particular, should be identifiable through variation in some behaviors when compared to nonproblem counterparts (Toch, 1995). To the extent that citizen complaints represent these behavioral propensities, they should be predictors of police behavior in encounters with citizens.[3]

Third, citizen complaints may actually be an indicator of officer productivity. It has been argued (Lersch & Mieczkowski, 1996; Wagner & Decker, 1997) that officers who receive repeated complaints may not actually be so-called problem officers, but rather productive officers. The surest way not to receive a complaint is to do little or no police work; or, to avoid probing or dealing with situations where conflict is likely (e.g., chasing drug dealers) (Muir, 1977; Willing, 1999). It is difficult to support or deny the merits of these arguments since all are rooted in plausible assumptions. Each perspective calls into question the inherent "meaning" of a complaint or what complaints actually represent.

These varying perspectives, and the fact police departments are increasingly relying on citizen complaints as a performance measure, illustrate the need to unpack the underlying meaning of citizen complaints.[4] This article examines whether a group of officers with identified complaint problems behaves differently in field contacts with citizens when compared with nonproblem counterparts. In particular, three domains of officer behavior are examined.

Physical Force and Discourtesy

The most serious complaints logged against an officer are those of excessive force and discourtesy. Excessive force complaints have long been a hot button topic, and departments engaged in community policing are increasingly sensitive to the issue of police discourtesy. Unfortunately, such complaints are also some of the most difficult to substantiate, and internal affairs investigations traditionally result in a finding of unfounded or not sustained.[5] Given the importance placed on these behaviors, do officers who received a high number of force and discourtesy complaints engage in such behaviors at a rate higher than their counterparts with few to no complaints?

Agitators

In addition to analyzing use of force and discourteous behaviors, various officer behaviors that may increase the likelihood of a complaint are examined. Officers with a high number of complaints may not necessarily engage in improper behavior, but they may be more apt to use tactics that tend to anger or frustrate the citizen. For instance, officers who receive complaints for force or discourtesy may have a tendency to order or threaten citizens more often, rather than negotiating or attempting to persuade. They may also be inclined to rely more heavily on interrogation and search tactics to gather information. Similarly, officers that are more proactive may prompt more complaints since they are placing the responsibility upon themselves to intervene in the lives of citizens, unlike a dispatched call for service. Previous studies of complaint data have shown that a disproportionate number of complaints stem from officer-initiated stops (Hudson, 1970; Lersch & Mieczkowski, 1996). This finding lends credence to those who argue that complaints correspond with productivity.

There is reason to question the productivity argument since the data from previous studies have often been taken only from the number of citizen complaints filed, which is akin to the problem of sampling on the dependent variable. For instance, two officers may each have ten complaints, with officer one having four complaints from officer-initiated stops while the other has two. Advocates of the productivity argument may argue that officer number one is being more productive by getting involved in more problem situations, which increases his or her chance of a complaint. The unknown is: How many of each officer's self-initiated stops lead to a complaint? By relying on complaint data as the source for a rate of proactivity there is no way to determine this. With observational data, a rate of officer proactivity can be ascertained more adequately. For example, by looking at observed proactivity for these two hypothetical officers, one may find that each made twenty proactive stops. If this were the case, they would have equivalent levels of productivity, yet, officer one is receiving twice the number of complaints. The argument could be made that it is not officer productivity that leads to an increased number of complaints, but is something about how he or she is handling proactive stops.

Inhibitors

While officers may use tactics that tend to agitate citizens, it is also plausible that some officers engage in inhibiting behaviors more readily. These behaviors are characterized as those that can soothe or tone down the encounter. For instance, offering comfort or reassurance may positively affect citizens who officers encounter, even when such an encounter is inherently negative. An officer placing a citizen under arrest may explain the subsequent booking process and reassure the suspect that the procedure will be carried out as expediently as possible. Similarly, satisfying citizen requests can possibly affect citizen satisfaction and reduce the probability of a citizen complaint. For example, a suspect being taken into custody may request a shirt or shoes to wear. Failure to fulfill such a request may set the tone for the rest of the encounter and eventually lead to a complaint. The force used in taking the suspect into custody may be completely appropriate, but a decision to further degrade the citizen by sending him or her to lockup without shoes may prompt a complaint stating the officer used force improperly.

In summary, three questions are posed—do officers with a high number of physical force/discourtesy complaints:

- use physical force or display discourtesy at a *higher* rate than those with a low number of complaints?
- command and threaten, interrogate, search, or initiate activity at a *higher* rate than those with a low number of complaints?
- offer comfort/reassurance or satisfy citizen requests at a *lower* rate than those with a low number of complaints?

Examining physical force and discourtesy provides a picture of the degree to which these behaviors occur on the street and how well citizen complaint data corresponds with such behavior. Analyzing various tactics that could "agitate" citizens may provide clearer insight on what might provoke a citizen to file a complaint against an officer. If problem officers have a propensity for misbehavior, they are expected to have engaged in more agitating behaviors than their nonproblem counterparts. Inhibitors represent a third set of behaviors that may distinguish high-complaint officers from their colleagues. It is hypothesized that inhibiting behaviors are most likely to leave a citizen "satisfied" with the police-citizen encounter, thereby reducing the likelihood of a complaint. Officers who are nonproblem officers should engage in these behaviors at a higher rate than their problem counterparts. Looking at possible agitating and inhibiting behaviors allows for a more comprehensive understanding of why some officers may be more complaint prone.

Data/Method

Data were collected during the summer of 1997 in St. Petersburg, FL as part of the Project on Policing Neighborhoods (POPN).[6] For the purpose of this article, two data elements from POPN were utilized: citizen complaint records and observation sessions. In reference to citizen complaints, POPN researchers were able to collect data on each officer dating back five years with the help of senior police officials and members of the internal affairs division. Contained in the complaint data is the type of case, including such categories as incompetence, inefficiency, conduct unbecoming, discourtesy, harassment, unnecessary force, as well as numerous minor violations.

Using these data, high-complaint officers were first identified. Complaints were restricted to those involving force and verbal harassment (arguably noxious and antisocial behaviors). An alternative approach would have been to use all citizen complaints to identify problem officers. Prior evidence suggests that officers engaged most often in forceful behavior are also most likely to receive citizen complaints for all types of behavior. For instance, as stated by Adams (1995), referring to identified problem officers in the Christopher Commission report on the Los Angeles police department, "[i]t is interesting to note that these officers received a large number of citizen complaints that did not necessarily involve use of force issues, suggesting the possibility that officers who are physically aggressive are associated with a wide variety of problems" (p. 65). Despite support for such an approach, it was decided to take a more conservative approach and restrict the identification of problem officers to only those involving physical force and discourtesy complaints.[7] Table 12.1 shows that ninety-four officers were responsible for 181 citizen complaints.

Table 12.1
Total Number of Complaints—Force and Discourtesy

Number of complaints	Number of officers
0	30
1	23
2	15
3	10
4	5
5	3
6	3
7	1
8	2
9	1
13	1
N = 181	*N* = 94
Mean = 1.93	
S.D. = 2.35	

Prior analysis of complaint data has generally grouped officers into two categories: problem officers and nonproblem officers. To do so, an arbitrary cutoff point is made to place officers into one of these two groups (e.g., the 1991 Independent Commission on the Los Angeles Police Department report identified those officers with five or more complaints). A similar approach was applied here, but only after first standardizing the number of complaints received based on time in service (up to the five-year limit complaint data were available). To just count the number of complaints per officer and then place each officer into one of the two categories fails to account for how long each officer has actually been on the job, and, hence, the rate at which he or she receives complaints. An officer with three complaints and one year on the department is quite different than an officer with the same number of complaints who has been working for five years. Therefore, officers with a rate of one or more complaints per year were placed in the problem officer category while those with less than .21 per year were designated to the nonproblem officer category.[8] While it is more customary to just split officers at a designated cutoff point and place them into problem and nonproblem groups, it was decided that the most powerful comparisons could be drawn by eliminating those officers with rates between 0.21 and one complaint per year.[9] Table 12.2 shows the rate of complaints per year for the ninety-four officers, which range from 0 to 2.6.

Table 12.2
Rate of Complaints Per Year—Force and Discourtesy

Rate of complaints	Number of officers
0.00	30
0.20	16
0.25	2
0.33	1
0.40	9
0.50	3
0.60	8
0.67	2
0.80	5
1.00	6
1.20	3
1.40	1
1.50	1
1.60	2
1.80	1
2.00	2
2.50	1
2.60	1
	N = 94

Mean = 0.488
S.D. = 0.582

One threshold concern regarding the complaint data was whether the St. Petersburg Police Department was typical of other city police agencies. Data collected by Pate and Fridell (1994) concerning the number of excessive force complaints across a number of departments were examined to determine whether St. Petersburg had a similar excessive force complaint rate when compared with other agencies. These data, when filtered to include only municipal agencies serving more than 50,000 people (arguably the group most similar to St. Petersburg), were used to make a department level comparison. The complaint rate generated by dividing excessive force complaints by the number of total sworn officers is 0.06 for St. Petersburg during 1996. This rate puts them squarely in the middle third of municipal departments reporting data to Pate and Fridell. Thus, it can be argued that, at the organizational level, the department under study does not vary significantly from other agencies in terms of excessive force complaints generated per sworn officer. This provides some confidence, in terms of the generation of complaints within the St. Petersburg Police Department, that this department is typical of similar municipal agencies.

The core element of POPN involved observing patrol officers in their natural setting.[10] Hence, the second core data element used here is taken from the observational database generated as part of POPN. Prior to beginning fieldwork, a team of observers (field researchers) underwent an intensive four-month training program on how to conduct Systematic Social Observation (SSO) of police (Mastrofski et al., 1998). Observers were a combination of undergraduate and graduate students from Michigan State University and the State University of New York at Albany who took a semester-long class specifically on SSO protocol. Observers were criminal justice majors, none of which were former law enforcement officers. During the classroom portion (a total of forty-five hours) of the training phase, each student was trained on the specifics of SSO (see Mastrofski et al., 1998 for a detailed description). Observers also pretested the protocol in the field while conducting five training rides with a local department willing to permit observation. In addition to the training received at the home universities, observers conducted a training ride once arriving on site to acclimate them to the city, beat boundaries, and the organizational structure of the department.[11]

Field researchers accompanied patrol officers throughout a sample of work shifts in selected beats throughout the city.[12] Beat selection was biased toward beats where POPN researchers expected to observe higher levels of police activity than the average in the city (i.e. areas that had higher levels of social and economic distress than characteristic of the entire city).[13] Officers observed within these neighborhoods serve as the unit of analysis.

While on patrol, observers took brief field notes indicating when various activities and encounters with the public occurred, who was involved, and what happened.[14] According to POPN protocol, an *encounter* involved a face-

Table 12.3
Observed Physical Force and Discourtesy (Police/Suspect Encounters) (N = 1487)

Number of forceful acts	Number of officers	Number of discourteous acts	Number of officers	Number of forceful/discourteous acts	Number of officers
0	16	0	43	0	11
1	17	1	16	1	13
2	10	2	19	2	10
3	11	3	7	3	12
4	9	4	5	4	10
5	5	5	1	5	3
6	6	6	2	6	4
7	5	7	0	7	5
8	4	8	0	8	2
9	1	9	0	9	5
10	4	10	0	10	6
11+	6	11+	1	11+	13
N = 369		*N* = 125		*N* = 494	
Mean = 3.93		Mean = 1.33		Mean = 5.25	

to-face communication between officers and citizens that took over one minute, involved more than three verbal exchanges between officer and citizen, or involved significant physical contact between the officer and citizen. The day following the ride, observers transcribed their field notes into detailed narrative accounts and coded them according to a structured protocol. One hundred and twenty-six officers were observed in St. Petersburg, covering 360 shifts and consisting of approximately 3300 encounters.[15]

To compile the behaviors of interest (e.g., force, discourtesy) from the observational data, the total number of encounters observed was pared down to only those involving suspect/disputants (*N*= 1487), since it is in these encounters that one would expect such behaviors to be most prevalent (as opposed to encounters involving witnesses or victims). Tables 12.3–12.5 present the number of times each behavior (e.g., force, discourtesy) was observed during these encounters.

For analyses purposes, as discussed in the Results, a rate was then given to each officer (per number of suspects observed) according to the selected behaviors of interest. These data were then matched with the complaint data. Finally, since interest lies in comparing the differences between two groups—problem officers with nonproblem officers (the rate at which each group displays the behaviors of interest noted), a two-sample *t* test of differences was used.

Table 12.4
Observed Agitators (Police/Suspect Encounters) (N = 1487)

Number of command/threats	Number of officers	Number of suspect searches	Number of officers
0	2	0	35
1	3	1	21
2	5	2	19
3	7	3	8
4	7	4	5
5	3	5	2
6	9	6	0
7	2	7	1
8	4	8	0
9	8	9	2
10	4	10	0
11+	40	11+	1
N = 1089		*N* = 150	
Mean = 11.58		Mean = 1.59	
S.D. = 10.24		S.D. = 2.11	

Number of suspect interrogations	Number of officers	Number of proactive encounters	Number of officers
0	0	0	4
1	1	1	13
2	5	2	5
3	7	3	10
4	5	4	13
5	11	5	14
6	8	6	4
7	7	7	1
8	8	8	5
9	5	9	2
10	5	10	2
11+	33	11+	21
N = 925		*N* = 633	
Mean = 9.84		mean = 6.73	
SD. = 6.79		S.D. = 6.17	

Table 12.5
Observed Inhibitors (Police/Suspect Encounters) (N = 1487)

Number of suspects offered comfort/reassurance	Number of officers	Number of suspect requests satisfied	Number of officers
0	37	0	22
1	28	1	19
2	10	2	12
3	7	3	12
4	7	4	12
5	2	5	7
6	0	6	3
7	0	7	1
8	2	8	2
9	0	9	0
10	0	10	0
11+	1	11+	4
N = 134		*N* = 266	
Mean = 1.42		Mean = 2.82	
S.D. = 7.94		S.D.=3.39	

Results

Physical Force/Discourtesy

The initial set of comparisons involved physical force and discourtesy. Physical force involved any physical act a citizen was subjected to by an officer. This included restraint techniques (e.g., firm grip, grasp, wristlock), striking with the body (e.g., punch, kick, takedown maneuvers), or striking with an external weapon (e.g., baton, flashlight, mace). Given the subjective nature of trying to determine excessive force, there was no attempt to make any assertions that the observed force behavior was excessive.[16] The focus was to determine the extent to which, if at all, potential problem officers use force at a greater rate. If they engage in forceful tactics at a significantly higher rate, then one could infer a potential increased probability of having a citizen complaint logged against them. Police discourtesy was defined as calling the citizen names, making derogatory statements about the citizen or the citizen's family, belittling remarks, slurs, cursing, shouting, or ignoring the citizen (except in an emergency), making obscene gestures toward the citizen, or spitting (Mastrofski et al., 1999).

A combined measure of physical force and discourtesy (rate per suspect) was used to first test for a difference between the two groups.[17] As Table 12.6 shows, there was no statistically significant difference between problem officers and nonproblem officers when comparing the rate in which they engage in physical force and discourtesy. In fact, their average rate of using one of these forms of behavior is almost identical, 0.28 for nonproblem officers and 0.29 for problem officers.

In addition to combining physical force and discourteous behavior together, each was also examined separately. Police "forcefulness" was analyzed in two different ways in an attempt to adequately measure this behavior. First, the rate of suspect encounters where officers used force at least once (prevalence) was compared. Second, the number of forceful tactics used in each encounter where force was used at least once (incidence) was examined. This second measure was used since force complaints are for "unnecessary" force, and it was conceived that officers with a high complaint rate may use force on the same number of suspects as low-complaint officers, but may use force more times during a given encounter, arguably a more accurate measure to capture the "excessive" aspect of police force.[18]

When looking at the difference between groups using rate of force per number of suspects (prevalence measure) as the dependent measure, there was not a statistically significant difference between groups (0.15 compared to 0.23, $P = .055$). Using rate of number of forceful tactics per suspect (incidence measure) as the dependent measure, high-complaint officers did apply force at a significantly greater rate than their low-complaint counterparts. On average, low-complaint officers used force at a rate of 0.21 compared to 0.31 for high-complaint officers ($P = .049$). It appears that while high-complaint officers do use a significantly greater number of forceful tactics against suspects, they do not apply force against a greater number of suspects. In looking at the P values for these two comparisons, only .006 separate the two ($P = .049$ vs. $P = .055$). In essence, regardless of the measure used, in only about five in one hundred cases would this finding be had by chance, thereby offering a fairly strong assurance (95 percent) that the difference between the prob-

Table 12.6
Comparisons of Means—Force and Discourtesy

Observed behavior	Officer Grouping	Mean	Standard Deviation
Rate of physical force and discourtesy used on suspects (P =.431)	Low complaints	0.279	0.192
	High complaints	0.288	0.146
Rate of physical force used on suspects (P = .055)	Low complaints	0.149	0.114
	High complaints	0.225	0.179
Rate of frequency of physical force used on suspects (P = .049)	Low complaints	0.209	0.180
	High complaints	0.309	0.290
Rate of discourteous behavior used on suspects (P = .356)	Low complaints	0.070	0.130
	High complaints	0.082	0.071
Rate of frequency of discourteous behavior used on suspects (P = .498)	Low complaints	0.090	0.227
	High complaints	0.090	0.079

lem and nonproblem groups, in terms of physical force, is, in fact, real. Following conventional protocol calls for an outright rejection of the prevalence measure. From a substantive standpoint, however, it is difficult to reject one measure that six in one hundred times would be had by chance, yet accept the other that five in one hundred times would be had by chance.

The final two comparisons found in Table 12.6 involve officer discourtesy. Regardless of whether rate of suspects (0.07 vs. 0.08) or rate of frequency (0.09 vs. 0.09) was used, no statistically significant difference between the two groups in terms of discourteous behavior emerged. This is not surprising given such similar average rates. High-complaint officers are no more likely to be discourteous than low-complaint officers.

Agitators

The first agitating behaviors analyzed were commands and threats. Commands involved "strong directive language" where an officer made it clear that he or she was not asking or requesting compliance, but rather ordering it (e.g., "drop the knife, don't move"). Threats were explicit statements made to the citizen, which signified a consequence if the command was not carried out (e.g., "don't move or I'll mace you").

As shown in Table 12.7, while high-complaint officers did rely on commands and threats at a rate greater than low-complaint officers (0.48 vs. 0.42, respectively), the difference between the two did not reach statistical significance. Again, like physical force and discourtesy, a measure of the number of times officers used commands and threats within individual encounters was also tested. In this instance, there was no statistically significant difference between the groups (0.82 vs. 0.73).

The second agitating behavior analyzed was searching.[19] Searches were classified as any time an officer searched a suspect's person, his personal belongings, or premises. With respect to this behavior, no differences between the groups were uncovered. Low-complaint officers searched 8 percent of suspects encountered while high-complaint officers did so in 12 percent of suspect encounters.

Interrogation was defined as those instances when an officer questioned a suspect in order to gain information that would establish whether the suspect or his/her colleagues were involved in wrongdoing. Table 12.7 shows officers in the problem group used interrogation tactics at a significantly higher rate than their counterparts. On average, identified problem officers used some form of interrogation in 69 percent of suspect encounters, while nonproblem officers used it 58 percent of the time.

Proactivity was distinguished by whether an officer self-initiated a suspect encounter as opposed to being summoned to one via dispatch or a citizen on-scene. The strongest effect was found on proactivity. As seen in Table 12.7, officers in the high-complaint group, on average, initiated 51 percent of their suspect encounters. Conversely, nonproblem officers were only involved in 36 percent of self-initiated encounters. This finding seems to support earlier stud-

Table 12.7
Comparisons of Means—Agitating Behaviors

Observed behavior	Officer grouping	Mean	Standard deviation
Rate of commands and threats used on suspects ($P = .138$)	Low complaints	0.426	0.175
	High complaints	0.480	0.181
Rate of frequency of commands and threats used on suspects ($P = .224$)	Low complaints	0.731	0.438
	High complaints	0.823	0.415
Rate of searches used on suspects ($P = .125$)	Low complaints	0.081	0.089
	High complaints	0.128	0.163
Rate of interrogations used on suspects ($P = .023$)	Low complaints	0.576	0.200
	High complaints	0.688	0.197
Rate of proactive encounters with suspects ($P = .012$)	Low complaints	0.359	0.235
	High complaints	0.511	0.242

ies showing that officers involved in more self-initiated activity tend to be at greater risk of garnering complaints.

Inhibitors

In contrast to potential agitating behaviors, it was believed that officers may also engage in inhibiting behaviors. More specifically, it was hypothesized that officers who offer comfort or reassurance to citizens are likely to lessen the likelihood of a complaint. As shown in Table 12.8, however, no significant difference was uncovered between the two groups of officers in terms of comforting and reassuring suspects. The nonproblem group offered comfort or reassurance in 10 percent of suspect encounters while the problem group did so in 6 percent of suspect encounters.

Rate of fulfilling citizen requests was the second inhibiting behavior examined. A variety of citizen requests were combined to form this measure including: requests for physical help, requests for information, and requests that police advise or persuade another citizen. A suspect request was considered fulfilled if the officer fulfilled it outright or explained why the request could not be addressed at that time. As shown at the bottom of Table 12.8, there was no significant difference in the rate at which citizen requests were granted (0.89 for low-complaint officers compared to 0.77 for high-complaint officers).

Discussion

When comparing officers with relatively high complaint rates to those with relatively low complaint rates in terms of force and discourtesy at least one (and arguably two) significant difference was found. Those officers in the high rate or problem group were more likely to use physical force than their nonproblem colleagues. While this supports the view of complaints as predictors of propensity for using force, the remaining comparisons—rate of physical force and discourtesy behavior combined, rate of discourtesy behavior, and rate of frequency of discourtesy behavior, proved insignificant. At first glance, this appears to undermine the utility of complaints as indicators of officer propensity for using force.

Two *agitators* occurred at significantly higher rates among the problem officer group: proactive stopping and interrogation. These

Table 12.8
Comparisons of Means—Inhibiting Behaviors

Observed behavior	Officer grouping	Mean	Standard deviation
Rate of comfort given to suspects ($P = .101$)	Low complaints	0.101	0.118
	High complaints	0.062	0.082
Rate at which officers grant requests of suspects ($P = .114$)	Low complaints	0.890	0.233
	High complaints	0.766	0.382

represent a partial affirmation that productivity (a self-directed effort at stopping individuals and performing field interrogations) is related to complaints. Officers who had higher complaints were more active in terms of proactively confronting suspects and attempting to gather information in field interrogations.

These results do not provide bedrock support to the productivity hypothesis, nor do they indicate that police scholars or administrators are necessarily incorrect in asserting that complaints are a measure of officer propensity to use force in encounters with citizens. The inferences that can be drawn from this research serve only to temper the two perspectives. It appears here that, in some respects, both conceptions of the citizen complaint (as a productivity indicator and as an indicator of behavioral propensity) are partially supported.

It is likely that some officers are very productive and generate high rates of complaints because they actively engage the public. These officers might benefit from developing their ability to leave citizens as satisfied customers, Wiley and Hudik's (1974) research indicates that citizens would be more satisfied with encounters when they are made aware of the police's purpose. Stressing the treatment of citizens as coproducers rather than adversaries might transform the "productive officer" into a nonproblem officer.

Similarly, the fact that the "problem officer" group was significantly more likely to use force against a suspect than a nonproblem colleague cannot be dismissed lightly. This indicates that officers with high complaint rates are resorting to force more often. It is possible that the identified problem officers represent two distinct groups. The first could be those who are unable to master the use of persuasion and negotiation and too quickly resort to force (Muir, 1977). The second could be those who are "gung-ho" and produce complaints because they are overly productive and fail to adopt an appropriate exit strategy (e.g., explaining why they have engaged a suspect) to leave the citizen satisfied with their interaction. With respect to this it was proposed that police might exhibit *inhibiting* behaviors such as comforting citizens or satisfying citizen requests, which, though not statistically significant, were behaviors that the low-complaint group *did* exhibit at a higher rate than their high-complaint counterparts.

Overall, the St. Petersburg Police Department offers only a conservative test of Toch's (1995) theory. The department is not large ($N =$ 512 officers) and the cross-section of officers observed further restricted that number to ninety-four. If a larger number of officers were observed, it is likely that an even sharper contrast between high- and low-complaint officers would have emerged. It could also be argued that the use of a one complaint per year cut off is too low to distinguish problem officers from nonproblem officers. Furthermore, the low complaint rate that existed in general in the St Petersburg Police Department may indicate that the administration judiciously weeds out those officers who have high complaint levels or appear to be on a behavioral trajectory that will injure the department's standing in the community.

An alternative conception of citizen complaints would integrate them into the molding of a police officer. The ruminations in the previous paragraphs conceive of officers as static beings Those with low complaint levels are permanently "good" officers and those with high complaint levels are "bad" officers. That is an oversimplification of reality since humans have the capacity to learn from mistakes, and if the citizen complaint is conceived of as a "lesson learned," it is not surprising that so much similarity between the two groups was found. Officers with high complaint rates may have internalized the lesson of the complaint and approach their work from a new perspective. One could appeal to Muir's (1977) discourse on the career of Tom Hooker, who had much difficulty early in his career but eventually developed into a "professional" as an example of a "made" officer. The extent that others can adjust behavior to avoid future complaints is unknown, but it could explain, for example, why rates of officer discourtesy do not vary between the two groups.

This research began with the assumption that equating citizen complaints with officer behavior required a leap of faith that was premature given the lack of prior research. The findings presented here offer a first step in better understanding complaints relative to officer behavior. Future research should examine the individual level police-citizen encounter as a unit of analysis. It is possible that high-complaint officers act differently from their counterparts when confronted with various stimuli such as disrespectful citizens, evidence of citizen misbehavior, or citizen resistance. The present research was an aggregated snapshot of two groups of officers, which may mask variation among these individuals and their response patterns to citizen actions.

Acknowledgments

Data for this article was supported by Grant No. 95-IJ-CX-0071 from the National Institute of Justice. Opinions or points of view expressed in the article do not necessarily represent the official positions or policies of the National Institute of Justice or the U.S. Department of Justice. We would like to thank Professor Lorraine Green Mazerolle, Professor Roger Parks, Professor Candace McCoy, Chief Darrel Stephens, Chief Goliath Davis, and members of the internal affairs division for their help, cooperation, and insight at various points in the project.

Notes

1. A 1997 review article written for *Law Enforcement News* concerning developments in the policing field refers to this as one of the year's most notable trends (Rosen, 1997).
2. A suspect being handcuffed for having a warrant issued against him for unpaid traffic tickets may feel like the officer is being unduly harsh in his treatment, but department procedures may call for handcuffing all suspects being taken into custody regardless of the crime. Nonetheless, the citizen may file a complaint alleging excessive force.
3. Officers who have developed defective routines for handling "the family beef" might be likely to consistently adopt different tactics when compared to counterparts who have developed more effective methods of resolving conflicts (Muir, 1977).
4. In St. Petersburg, Darrel Stephens, former Chief and well-known advocate of community policing, along with current Chief Goliath Davis, has contributed considerable effort to bridge the gap between the police and community. The department has developed an international reputation as a leader in the implementation of community policing. Within this framework, citizen complaints have become an important performance measure for determining how well officers go about managing conflict.
5. In 1996, there were thirty-two cases alleging unnecessary force with zero sustained (St. Petersburg Police Department, Internal Affairs Annual Report, 1996).
6. This study was funded by the National Institute of Justice. The intent of POPN was to provide a comprehensive picture of everyday policing in the 1990s and was a follow-up to the Police Services Study (PSS) from the 1970s and the Black/Reiss observational study from the 1960s.
7. It is important to note the issue of *assignment hazard* with respect to citizen complaints, which may be defined as "the risk of getting complaints as a function of opportunity." In this regard, it is reasonable to assume that the probability of receiving a complaint is increased for officers working the street as opposed to those working in administrative positions. Unfortunately, data on officer assignments over the period of time (1992–1997) when complaints were generated was not available. The authors were restricted to those items recorded by internal affairs investigators and made available under the Florida State Sunshine Law on public records, which contained little more than basic types of information regarding the complaint (e.g., type of complaint and officer number, gender, race, length of service, etc.). Hence, a determination cannot be made as to the type of assignment for officers at the time of complaints. Nonetheless, it is important to note that assignment hazard is not an issue with respect to the observational component of the study. All officers (both those in the high complaint and low complaint group) during the observation period were part of the patrol division. POPN did not observe any special high-risk entry warrant teams, vice or narcotics units, or administrative personnel. Hence, all observed officers were exposed to the same degree of opportunity during the observation time period, at least with respect to being assigned to the same sort of duties—in this case, patrol duties. While this levels the playing field in that all officers are assigned the same type of duties, it still leaves open the question of whether some patrol officer assignments have an increased chance of "opportunity" for forceful or discourtesy behavior. It may be argued that an officer assigned a low crime beat as opposed to a high crime beat would have a decreased opportunity for such behavior because he or she rarely deals with suspected offenders. As a result, to account for this issue, behavior was standardized by the number of suspects encountered.
8. While no specific number of complaints officially designates an officer in St. Petersburg as a "problem officer" or "nonproblem officer" according to department policy (every case is analyzed on a case by case basis), officials stated that the rate of one or more complaints per year is the general standard used by supervisors to warrant additional attention.
9. Models were also generated using numerous grouping strategies (everyone with less than one complaint per year compared to everyone with more than one, as well as those with less than 0.33 complaints per year compared to those with greater than 0.79). Regardless of the grouping strategy applied, findings remained consistent with those presented in the Results.
10. Field observation allows for "a direct, detailed account of what happens on patrol by someone whose sole job is to provide a *disinterested* account. Such detail, thoroughness, and accuracy are not available through popular social science methods of surveys (of the police or public) and official records" (Mastrofski, Parks, Reiss, & Worden, 1995, p. 20; see also Mastrofski et al., 1998).
11. As part of the training program, observers were trained extensively in what to look for, how to note it in the field, and how to record it for data analysis. POPN Principal Investigators included Albert Reiss Jr., Stephen Mastrofski, Roger Parks, and Robert Worden, three of [whom] have extensive experience with designing and carrying out large-scale police observational studies. Reiss (1966) conducted one of the first large-scale police observational studies. In the 1977 Police Services Study (PSS), Parks was one of the three Principal Investigators and Mastrofski served as Site Director. In 1993, Mastrofski conducted a pilot study in Richmond aimed at perfecting the techniques used for POPN. For additional description on observer training and reliability issues, see Mastrofski et al., 1998.
12. A quota sample was used that: (1) covered all work shifts for each beat, (2) included the diversity of patrol units that worked the study beats and larger areas that covered those beats, and (3) included both slow and busy days of the week. The study did not seek a strictly representative sample of pa-

trol shifts because it needed a sufficient number of observations of certain patrol units and encounters with the public (more likely to occur during some shifts). Consequently, busy days (Thursday through Saturday) were oversampled, as were shifts and units where problem-oriented activity was more likely.

13. This bias was intentional. POPN directors wished to observe large numbers of encounters between police and citizens. The bias is consistent with neighborhood selection in the earlier Police Services Study (1977) and by Reiss (1966).
14. Field researchers accompanied their assigned officer during all activities and encounters with the public during the shift, except on those rare occasions when the officer instructed the researcher not to do so because of danger or because it would impede police business. Field researchers were instructed to minimize involvement in police work (except for minor assistance or emergencies) and to refrain from expressing views about police work in general or what was observed on the ride. The researcher's function was not to judge the officer, only to note what happened during the observation session and to note how the officer interpreted situations he or she encountered. Officer interpretation of the situation was conducted through a "debriefing" session where the observer would inquire as to the officers' thoughts and motivation for handling the encounter (see Mastrofski & Parks, 1990 for explicit protocol on this technique).
15. Although 126 total officers were observed, only officers observed on five or more suspect/disputant encounters (N = 94) were included in analyses in an attempt to prevent the rare occasion where an officer might be "out of character."
16. According to POPN protocol, observers were only asked to document use of force behaviors, not make a determination as to whether such behavior was excessive or unnecessary.
17. A one-tail t test is used to compare groups since one-way direction is hypothesized.
18. Additionally, given such similarity found in the combined measure of force and discourtesy used against suspects, both forms of behavior were broken down to ensure effects were not being masked in some manner by only looking at the rate of the combined behaviors on suspects.
19. Unlike the previous measures on officer behavior, which examines a rate for the number of suspect encounters the behavior was present at least once, as well as the number of times within individual cases, all of the remaining behavioral measures are based solely on the former. A count on the number of times officers engaged in these behaviors during individual encounters was not coded by observers, only whether they engaged in the behavior at least once.

References

Adams, K. (1995). Measuring the prevalence of police abuse of force. In: W. A. Geller, & H. Toch (Eds.), *And justice for all: Understanding and controlling police abuse of force* (pp. 61–97). Washington, DC: Police Executive Research Forum.

Bayley, D. H., & Garofalo, I. (1989). The management of violence by police patrol officers. *Criminology, 27,* 1–26.

Dugan, J. R., & Breda, D. R. (1991). Complaints about police officers: A comparison among types and agencies. *Journal of Criminal Justice, 19,* 165–171.

Goffman, E. (1959). *The presentation of self in everyday life.* New York, NY: Doubleday Anchor Books.

Hudson, J. (1970). Police-citizen encounters that lead to citizen complaints. *Social Problems, 18,* 179–193.

Independent Commission on the Los Angeles Police Department. (1991). *Report of the independent Commission on the Los Angeles police department.* Los Angeles, CA: International Creative Management.

Kappeler. V. E., Sluder, R. D., & Alpert, G. P. (1994). *Forces of deviance: Understanding the dark side of policing.* Prospect Heights, IL: Waveland Press.

Kerstetter, W. A. (1995). A 'Procedural Justice' perspective on police and citizen satisfaction with investigations of police use of force: Finding a common ground of fairness. In W. A. Geller & H. Toch (Eds.), *And justice for all: Understanding and controlling police abuse of force* (pp. 223–232). Washington, DC: Police Executive Research Forum.

Klockars, C. B. (1995). A theory of excessive force and its control. In W. A. Geller & H. Toch (Eds.), *And justice for all: Understanding and controlling police abuse of force* (pp. 11–29). Washington, DC: Police Executive Research Forum.

Lersch, K. M., & Mieczkowski, T. (1996). Who are the problem-prone officers? An analysis of citizen complaints. *American Journal of Police, 15,* 23–44.

Mastrofski, S. D. (1999). *Policing for people.* Washington, DC: Police Foundation.

Mastrofski, S. D., & Parks, R. B. (1990). Improving observational studies of police. *Criminology, 28,* 475–496.

Mastrofski, S. D., Parks, R. B., Reiss Jr., A. J., & Worden, R. E. (1995). Community policing at the street level: A study of the police and the community. Proposal submitted to the National Institute of Justice, Washington, DC.

Mastrofski, S. D., Parks, R. B., Reiss Jr., A. J, Worden, R. E., DeJong, C., Snipes, J. B., & Terrill, W. (1998). Systematic observation of public police: Applying field research methods to policy issues. National Institute of Justice Research Report, NCJ 172859.

Mastrofski, S. D., Reisig, M. D., & McCluskey, J. D. (1999). Unpublished manuscript. Police disrespect toward the public: An encounter-based analysis. East Lansing, MI: Michigan State University.

Muir Jr., W. K. (1977). *Police: Streetcorner politicians.* Chicago, IL: Chicago University Press.

Pate, A. M., & Fridell, L. A. (1994). *Police use of force: Official reports, citizen complaints, and legal consequences, 1991–1992 [Computer file].* Ann Arbor, MI: Inter-University Consortium for Political and Social Research (ICPSR).

Reiss Jr., A. J. (1966). Police observation report instructions. *Internal document of the Center for Research on Social Organization.* Ann Arbor, MI: University of Michigan.

Rosen, M. (1997). Policing moves along parallel tracks of introspection and outreach. *Law Enforcement News, 480.*

Skolnick, J. H., & Fyfe, J. J. (1993). *Above the law: Police and the excessive use of force.* New York, NY: Free Press.

St. Petersburg Police Department. (1996). Internal Affairs Annual Report.

Terrill, W. (2001). *Police coercion: Application of the force continuum.* New York, NY: LFB Scholarly Publishing.

Toch, H. (1995). A theory of excessive force and its control. In: W. A. Geller & H. Toch (Eds.), *And justice for all: Understanding and controlling police abuse of force* (pp. 99–112). Washington, DC: Police Executive Research Forum.

Tyler, T. R, (1990). *Why people obey the law.* New Haven, CT: Yale University Press.

Van Maanen, J. (1978). The 'asshole.' In P. K. Manning & J. Van Maanen (Eds.), *Policing: A view from the street.* Santa Monica, CA: Goodyear Publishing.

Wagner, A. E., & Decker, S. H. (1997). Evaluating citizen complaints against the police. In R. G. Dunham & G. P. Alpert (Eds.), *Critical issues in policing* (3rd ed.) (pp. 302–318). Prospect Heights, IL: Waveland Press.

Wiley, M. G., & Hudik, T. L. (1974). Police-citizen encounters: a field test of exchange theory. *Social Problems, 22,* 119–129.

Willing, R. (1999). Community policing passes the 'Fort Apache' test. *USA Today* (June 15, 15A).

William Terrill and John McCluskey, "Citizen Complaints and Problem Officers: Examining Officer Behavior." Reprinted from *Journal of Criminal Justice* 30 (2): 143–156.

Chapter 13

Police Use of Deadly Force

Research and Reform

James J. Fyfe

This is an excerpt of an article that looks at historical aspects of deadly force, including past problems and past solutions. Police use of deadly force first became a major public issue in the 1960s when many urban riots were precipitated by police killings of citizens. Since that time scholars have studied deadly force extensively, police practitioners have made significant reforms in their policies and practices regarding deadly force, and the United States Supreme Court has voided a centuries-old legal principle that authorized police (in about half the states) to use deadly force to apprehend unarmed, nonviolent, fleeing felony suspects. This essay reviews and interprets these developments.

Most social science writing opens with a testament to the seriousness of the problem under study and a lament about the absence of prior related research. Where police deadly force is concerned, however, documenting the seriousness of the subject matter is no challenge: the police are the only American public servants authorized routinely to make quick, unilateral, and irreversible decisions that are likely to result in the deaths of other Americans.[1]

When police officers fire their guns,[2] the immediate consequences of their decisions are realized at the rate of 750 feet per second and are beyond reversal by any level of official review. As most police recruits learn in the academy, the cop on the street—who, with the corrections officer, generally can boast of fewer academic and training credentials than any other criminal justice official—carries in his holster more power than has been granted the Chief Justice of the Supreme Court. When used injudiciously, this power has led to riot and additional death, civil and criminal litigation against police and their employers, and the ousters of police chiefs, elected officials, and entire city administrations. Even when used with great restraint, police deadly force has created polarization, suspicion, and distrust on the part of those who need the police most.

Because this is a review essay and reexamination of existing data rather than a report on new research, it provides only limited opportunity for breast beating about scholarly indifference: one cannot agree to write a review essay without a sizable body of literature to review. Still, *sizable* is a relative term; the existing research on the only unilateral life-or-death decision available to any American criminal justice official is the work of only a few individuals, and is dwarfed by the volume of studies on most other (and less critical) decision points in the criminal justice process. My dining-room table could accommodate easily the number of contemporary social scientists who have devoted any serious attention to police deadly force.

This is not to say that earlier researchers answered all the questions: 20 years ago, those who had studied deadly force could have been driven to dinner in the back seat of a compact car. Until the late 1960s, when two presidential commissions reported that police shootings were the immediate precipitants of many of that era's urban riots (National Commission on Civil Disorders 1968:17–53) and that officers generally received little guidance in use of deadly force (President's Commission 1967:188–89), the professional criminal justice community and most of the public paid little heed to how wisely or how well this power was exercised and controlled.[3] Criminology and criminal justice scholars apparently did not notice that police officers in most states were authorized by law and by their departments to kill people whom they suspected of bicycle theft;[4] with the slight exceptions noted below, they left us no clue as to how often or in what circumstances the police shot suspected bicycle thieves or anybody else. The practitioners who wrote books for police chiefs offered advice on training officers how to shoot, but generally ignored questions of when—and when not—to shoot.

Before that period, as far as I can determine, there existed only two empirical studies of police deadly force incidents. Gerald Robin (1963) analyzed all fatal shootings by Philadelphia police during the 11 years from 1950 through 1960, and also obtained some comparative statistics from several other cities. The American Civil Liberties Union (1966) found that police in an unnamed city had discharged their firearms more than 300 times in two years, and that more than one-third of these incidents were precipitated by vehicle chases involving juvenile suspects. In his *Police Administration*, almost certainly the most widely read police text of the time, O.W. Wilson (1963) said nothing about police deadly force or firearms except to suggest locations and safety precautions for shooting ranges and weapons storage cabinets (443–44). *Municipal Police Administration*, the International City Management Association's voluminous guide for police chiefs, said only the following before recommending specifications for weapons:

> A firearm allows the officer to protect himself and at the same time extend his usefulness into space as well as his skill and effectiveness of his weapon permit. How wisely this power is used depends upon the officer, his training, and established procedures and policy. The weapon only projects the long arm of the law as it is enforced by individuals. (Eastman 1961: 444)

In the years since Robin's work was published and, more significantly for public policy, since the Presidential Task Force on the Police (President's Commission 1967:189–90) examined and commented on police power to kill, a comparative boom has taken place in the literature of deadly force. Even so, because the police rarely have been asked to report to public officials about how they use this power, and because few scholars have persuaded the police to be more forthcoming, there is much that we do not know. Thus my excoriation of scholars' past failure to study deadly force is also an exhortation to future research. Deadly force is a serious subject that deserves greater scholarly interest than it has received.

The Emergence of a Problem

Although Robin's 1963 study was the first systematic look at the use of deadly force, it had little apparent effect on either scholars or officials.[5] The subject did draw attention a year later when the first of the major urban disorders of the 1960s, in Harlem and in Bedford-Stuyvesant, followed immediately upon the fatal shooting of a 15-year-old black boy who reportedly attacked an off-duty police lieutenant with a knife.[6] Soon it became apparent, as the National Advisory Commission on Civil Disorders (the "Kerner Commission") reported four years later, that this pattern would not remain unique to New York. In May 1966, a year after Los Angeles had suffered its Watts riot, the Commission reported that the accidental shooting death of a young black man led to renewed demonstrations and increased tensions in that city (1968:38). In 1967 the National Guard was called in to restore order at Jackson State College in Mississippi after police attempts to disperse a crowd resulted in the shootings of three blacks, one of whom was killed (1968:41). The 1967 Tampa riots were triggered by the fatal police shooting of a black youth who was fleeing from the scene of a burglary (1968:42). The Commission also wrote that "only the dramatic ghetto appearance of Mayor Ivan Allen, Jr., had averted a riot" in Atlanta in 1966 (1968:53).

Legal and Administrative Controls on Deadly Force

President Johnson's other major blue-ribbon panel, the President's Commission on Law Enforcement and Administration of Justice, looked carefully at police-community relations. In the report of its Task Force on the Police—which, in my view, remains the single most significant and most influential contribution to American police policy and practice to date—the Commission made clear its dismay at the virtual absence of administrative policies to guide police officers' decisions to use deadly force (President's Commission 1967:189–90). In a report to the Commission, Police Task Force chair Samuel Chapman cited the full text of one unnamed police department's policy on use of firearms as an illustration of the need for direction in this most critical matter of police discretion:

> Never take me out in anger; never put me back in disgrace. (Chapman 1967)

Chapman also saw to it that the final report of the Task Force included a model administrative policy on use of firearms (President's Commission 1967:188–89). This was not the first time he had championed this cause; in 1963 he and Thompson Crockett reported on a 1961 survey of 71 Michigan police departments serving populations of 10,000 or more. They found that

> 54 percent (27 of 50) of the agencies furnishing information had no written policies in effect to govern the use of firearms. These twenty-seven departments, which relied upon "oral policy," were asked to indicate the main points of oral instructions given to their officers regarding when to use firearms. Of the twenty-seven, only five departments mentioned such basic situations as self-defense and fleeing felons where firearms may be used. Thus, based on the reported practice in these Michigan cities, it would appear reasonable to regard with grave reservation the suitability of relying singularly upon "oral policy." (Chapman and Crockett 1963:42)[7]

> Further:
>
> "[W]hen to fire" is frequently trusted to the "judgment" or "discretion" of officers as individuals. . . . (1963:41)
>
> The consequence is that while officers know *how* to care for and use their firearms, many have little or no understanding of *when* the weapon may be employed. This paradox is similar to teaching an employee how to maintain and drive an automobile while neglecting to instruct him on the subject of motor vehicle regulations. It might be argued, as it often is in the case of firearms regulations, that the driver's "common sense," coupled with a warning not to crash into anybody unless absolutely necessary, would suffice to enable the driver to operate his vehicle at large on the highways. This argument conveniently ignores the fact that driving regulations, like firearms regulations, are not based entirely on "common sense" or personal safety. (Chapman and Crockett 1963:41; emphasis in original)

The Breadth of Law

In the absence of such policies, police shooting discretion generally was limited only by state criminal statutes or by case law defining justifiable homicide. These laws have several inadequacies. First, even the most restrictive state laws permit police to use their weapons in an extremely broad range of situations. Every state historically has permitted police officers to use deadly force to defend themselves or others against imminent death or serious physical harm, a provision that cannot be debated seriously. Indeed, except that generally they are obliged to attempt to retreat to safety before resorting to deadly force, American citizens enjoy the same justification for homicide (see, for example, New York Penal Law 1967). Because we ask the police to put their lives on the line in our behalf, it follows that they should enjoy this slight advantage over the rest of us.

Yet many states also have codified some variant of the common-law "fleeing felon" rule, which authorizes use of deadly force as a means of apprehending persons fleeing from suspected felonies. The Tennessee statute that eventually became the focus of *Tennessee v. Garner* (1985), illustrates the broadest category of such laws:

> *Resistance to Officer*—If after notice of the intention to arrest the [felony] defendant, he either flees or forcibly resists, the officer may use all the necessary means to effect the arrest. (Tennessee Code Annotated sec. 40-7-108:55)

The breadth of such "any *fleeing* felon" statutes perhaps was questioned first by Mikell, who queried the American Law Institute:

> May I ask what we are killing [the suspect] for when he steals an automobile and runs off with it? Are we killing him for stealing the automobile? . . . It cannot be . . . that we allow the officer to kill him because he stole the automobile, because the statute provides only three years in a penitentiary for that. Is it then . . . for fleeing that we kill him? Fleeing from arrest . . . is punishable by a light penalty, a penalty much less than that for stealing the automobile. If we are not killing him for stealing the automobile and not killing him for fleeing,

what are we killing him for? (American Law Institute 1931:186–87)[8]

Years later, apparently unaware that the fleeing felon laws of about one-half the states fit precisely the specifications he deplored, Chief Justice Burger mused:

> I wonder what would be the judicial response to a police order authorizing "shoot to kill" with respect to every fugitive. It is easy to predict our collective wrath and outrage. We, in common with all rational minds, would say that the police response must relate to the gravity and need; that a "shoot" order might conceivably be tolerable to prevent the escape of a convicted killer but surely not for car thieves, pickpockets, or a shoplifter. (*Bivens v. Six Unknown Agents* 1971, W. Burger, C.J., dissenting)

The History of Deadly Force Law

The history of the *any* fleeing felon laws that Chief Justice Burger regarded as outrageously hypothetical in 1971 (but which he voted subsequently to affirm in joining the *Garner* dissent) has been well documented in other places (Boutwell 1977; Fyfe 1981a; Rummel 1968; Sherman 1980), and need be traced here only briefly. It dates back to the English Middle Ages, when virtually all felons were punished by death after trials that paid little heed to current standards of due process or to the distinctions that have been drawn between factual and legal guilt. At that time, if the suspect had committed the felony, he almost certainly would be convicted; if convicted, he almost certainly would be executed. Thus, for all practical purposes, it made little difference whether the felon died during pretrial flight or at the hands of the executioner.

The manner in which felony suspects are pursued and apprehended also has changed in important ways over the centuries. When the fleeing felon rule originated, those who typically pursued felons were ordinary male citizens who were obliged by law to respond to the *hue and cry* and to join in pursuit. Because they were usually armed only with clubs or knives, discharging their duty to arrest compelled them to overpower physically people who knew that arrest was likely to result in execution. These circumstances also are a far cry from more modern applications of the fleeing felon rule. The officer involved in *Garner*, for example, fired his fatal shot from the relative safety of 30 feet at the back of an unarmed, 5'4", 100-pound juvenile burglary suspect who, if apprehended alive, would likely have been sentenced to probation.[9]

Debates about the merits of *any* fleeing felon laws came to an abrupt end in 1985, when the Supreme Court ruled in *Garner* that the Tennessee statute, when applied against unarmed, non-dangerous fleeing suspects, violated the Fourth Amendment's guarantees against unreasonable seizure.[10] In his opinion for the majority, Justice White wrote that deadly force was a constitutional means of effecting arrest only when a felony "suspect threatens the officer with a weapon or there is probable cause to believe that he has committed a crime involving the infliction or threatened infliction of serious physical harm" (*Tennessee v. Garner*, 471 U.S. at 4). This decision affects the laws not only of the 23 states that followed the broad *any* fleeing felon rule; because Garner was a suspect in a nighttime residential burglary, it also affects the laws of several other states that included this offense under the limited category of offenses justifying deadly force for purposes of apprehension.[11]

The Law as a Control on Professional Discretion

Although *Garner* moots some of the arguments about the great breadth of deadly force statutes, it does little to ameliorate a second and more general limitation of law in describing police shooting discretion: in no field of human endeavor does the criminal law alone define adequately the parameters of acceptable occupational behavior. In the course of their work, doctors, lawyers, psychologists, professors, soldiers, nursing home operators, truck drivers, government officials, and journalists can do many outrageous, unacceptable, and hurtful things without violating criminal law. In exchange for the monopolies on the activities performed by those in their crafts, the most highly developed of these professions keep their members' behavior in check by developing and enforcing codes of conduct that are both more specific and more restrictive than are criminal definitions. Who would submit to treatment by a surgeon whose choices in deciding how to deal with patients were limited only by the laws of homicide and assault?

Apply that logic to use of police firearms. Even post-*Garner*, no state law tells officers whether it is advisable to fire warning shots into the air on streets lined by high-rise buildings. The law provides no direction to officers who must decide quickly whether to shoot at people in moving vehicles and thereby risk turning them into speeding unguided missiles. The law related to police use of force, in short, is simply too vague to be regarded as a comprehensive set of operational guidelines.[12]

Resistance to Rule Making Regarding Deadly Force

Even so, many police administrators did not act on policy recommendations like Chapman's until their officers had become involved in shootings that (although noncriminal) generated community outcries and crises (Sherman 1983). Their sometimes vigorous resistance to change was rooted in many considerations. First, police authority to restrict shooting discretion more tightly than state law was uncertain. In 1971, for example, the Florida Attorney General issued a written opinion that administrative policies overriding the state's any fleeing felon law were legally impermissible (Florida Attorney General 1971:68–75); this narrow view of the separation of powers has been cast aside since in favor of more realistic interpretations of police chiefs' administrative prerogatives. In addition, apparently on the theory that jurors were unlikely to find police behavior unreasonable unless officers had violated their own departments' formal rules and policies, some police officials refrained from committing deadly force policies to paper. Time also has shown that this rather self-serving attempt to avoid accountability and liability was counterproductive: jurors don't need a piece of paper to tell them whether an individual officer acted reasonably, but typically they do find that a police department's failure to provide officers with such paper is inexcusable.[13] Finally, many police officers feared that restrictive deadly force policies would endanger the public and the police; by removing whatever deterrent value inhered in the fleeing felon rule, such policies would result in an increase in crime and a decrease in police ability to apprehend fleeing criminals. Indeed, even when research suggested that this was not the case (Fyfe 1979), many police chiefs continued to regard restrictive deadly force policies as invitations to public accusations that they were "weak on crime" or had "handcuffed the police."[14]

By now, however, the question of whether police should promulgate restrictive deadly force policies has been answered in the affirmative; at least among larger agencies, it is the rare department whose manual does not include such a policy.[15] Social science research has played some part in easing police resistance to formulation of deadly force policy, and in the Supreme Court's *Garner* decision as well. Thus it is time now to turn from discussions of law and policy to consideration of what that research has shown.

Conclusions

On balance, and even though the available data are skimpier than we would like, it appears that the frequency of police use of deadly force is influenced heavily by organizational philosophies, expectations, and policies; that levels of community violence are marginal predictors, useful chiefly when organizational variables may be held constant (as in studying a single police jurisdiction); and that variations in law play a role in determining frequency of deadly force only when administrators abdicate their responsibility to see that propriety is not limited only by statutory definitions of criminal assault and homicide.

For this last reason, *Tennessee v. Garner* probably is not as sweeping as many suspect. By the time this case was decided, virtually all major police departments had adopted their own administrative policies that were at least as restrictive as the *violent* felon rule propounded by the Supreme Court. In his decision for the majority, in fact, Justice White made repeated suggestions that the Court's holding was not a major intervention into police administrative prerogatives because most large police departments already were in compliance. Indeed, the fact that Memphis itself had abolished administratively the *any* fleeing felon rule five years before the case came to the Court (Memphis Police Department 1979) weakened seriously the city attorney's oral argument that the *any* fleeing felon rule was a valuable adjunct to the effectiveness of law enforcement. Thus it is likely that the major effects of *Garner* will be (and have been) felt in smaller police jurisdictions where, as Neilsen (1983) suggests, administrative rule making related to deadly force has been less frequent.

Still, although *Garner* itself will not revolutionize American law enforcement, the process leading up to it has altered dramatically the police community's view of the whole deadly force issue. As recently as 1980, for example, attendees at the annual IACP meeting voted "by a 4-to-1 margin reaffirming [the association's] support of laws and policies permitting police to shoot fleeing felony suspects." (*St. Louis Post Dispatch* 1980). In the same year, the International Union of Police Associations passed a resolution seeking to remove Patrick Murphy "as President of a private corporation known as the Police Foundation and to boycott any organization or foundation that supports the Police Foundation" because Murphy had criticized "police officers' use of weapons," "notoriously accused our nation's police officers as the immediate cause of the riots that took place in the 60s," indicated that four police officers who had been acquitted in a Miami beating death (a verdict which sparked Miami's Liberty City riot) had committed the beating of which they were accused, and had "further stated that a restrictive shooting policy not only reduces police shootings of civilians but does not result in any increased danger to police officers or a rise in crime" (International Union of Police Associations 1980).

By 1982, however, IACP had promulgated a model policy on police use of force that would permit shooting at fleeing felony suspects only when "freedom is reasonably believed to represent an *imminent* threat of grave bodily harm or death to the officer or other person(s)" (Matulia 1982:164; emphasis in original). In 1983 IACP joined in recommending that the Commission on Accreditation for Law Enforcement Agencies adopt its present strict *defense of life only* standard for deadly force policies (1983:1–2). In 1984 the Police Foundation's *amici curiae* brief against Tennessee and the Memphis Police Department in *Garner* was joined by "nine national and international associations of police and criminal justice professionals, the chiefs of police associations of two states, and thirty-one law enforcement chief executives" (Police Foundation 1984).[16] Equally significant, and contrary to past practice in cases of substantial constitutional issues involving the police, no *amicus* briefs were filed on the other side of the case. In 1985, when *Garner* was decided, IACP's executive director hailed it as a great step forward. This remarkable turnaround and disavowal of tradition and professional dogma was stimulated in large measure by research findings which suggested that the value of broad police shooting authority was overrated; rarely have researchers had such an effect on criminal justice policies and practices.[17]

Research regarding the people involved in incidents of deadly force by police generally shows that blacks and other minorities are overrepresented at both ends of police guns. Explanations for these disparities vary, but at least by my interpretation they typically involve embarrassing realities over which police have little control. Black citizens are overrepresented in the most violent and most criminogenic neighborhoods; individual black officers, who are still underrepresented in American policing generally, are far more likely than individual white officers to draw the most hazardous police duties in those same neighborhoods. Until these realities are altered, we can expect continuing minority disproportion in deadly force statistics no matter how stringently police officers' discretion is controlled.

This probability, I think, illustrates the central theme that may be drawn from all the research on deadly force reviewed in this essay. Police officers and the people at whom they shoot are simply actors in a much larger play. When police officers' roles in this play are defined carefully by their administrators and when the officers have been trained well to perform those roles, their individual characteristics mean little; the young cop, the old cop, the male cop, the female cop, the white cop, and the black cop all know what is expected of them, and they do it. When such clear expectations are not provided, officers improvise, and often we give their performances bad reviews. Yet because we put them on the stage in the first place, we also should criticize ourselves for failing to assure that they have been directed adequately.[18] When black children's roles are defined so clearly by the conditions in which so many are raised, we should expect that some will end their lives at the wrong end of police guns. We should not blame the police for that; we should blame ourselves for creating the stages on which so many black lives are played out.

Notes

1. Others with quasi-police functions (e.g., correctional officers and workers at mental institutions) typically bear a more limited version of this authority.
2. Although police also have used such lethal means of force as neckholds, other martial arts techniques, and even bombs, gunshots are far more frequent. Thus, for purposes of this essay, deadly force and shooting at human beings will be treated as synonyms.
3. By and large, writers in law reviews also appear to have left this subject alone until the mid-1960s (see the literature reviews in Geller and Karales 1981 and Sherman 1980).
4. Although we cannot assess easily the extent to which state deadly force laws may have been modified by court decisions, in 1985 19 states had codified the *any* fleeing felon rule; four others had no statute but apparently followed the rule. Through statute or case law, 22 others followed some variety of the *violent* fleeing felon rule; the laws of the remaining states are unclear (see Fyfe 1986; Winter 1986).
5. The exception is Rodney Stark, who made the following comment on Robin's (1963) finding that Akron police were 45 times more likely than Boston police to have killed citizens: "[S]uch enormous differences in rates suggest either that the police in some cities are supermen, or that those in other cities are killers" (1972:65).
6. The lieutenant had intervened in a street altercation between the group of which the boy was a part and a building superintendent who apparently had sprayed them with a garden hose (National Advisory Commission 1968:36).
7. In a contemporaneous study of 45 of the 51 American police departments in cities with populations over 250,000, it was found that three forces had no written deadly force policies whatever and that in many other cases, deadly force policy consisted only of vague advice to use caution and good judgment (Cincinnati Police Department 1964).
8. See also, *United States v. Clark* (1887): Suppose, for example, a person were arrested for petit larceny, which is a felony at the common law, might an officer under any circumstances be justified in killing him? I think not. The punishment is altogether too disproportionate to the offense.
9. Under Tennessee law, 15-year-olds must be treated as juveniles unless they are accused of violent offenses, among which the law does not include burglary (Tennessee Code Annotated: 27-234 [1977]).
10. Readers who have not followed *Garner* might be surprised to learn that the case was decided on Fourth Amendment grounds rather than on an intuitively appealing Eighth Amendment argument of denial of due process/punishment without trial (see, e.g., Sherman 1980). During the 11 years of litigation between young Garner's death and the Supreme Court's resolution of his father's action, this argument was raised and rejected by lower courts on the grounds that punishment was a judicial rather than a police function. If that was true, reasoned Garner's attorneys, their case was framed best in terms of the police function—arrest—and shootings to apprehend were cast as a form of seizure (see *Garner v. Memphis Police Department* [1979]).
11. The relevant Illinois law at the time of *Garner*, for example, included burglary under the "forcible felony" heading in which deadly force for apprehension was justified (Illinois Revised Statutes 1975). Also see Fyfe (1986) and Uviller (1986) for more detailed discussion of *Garner's* apparent effects on state law.
12. There also are many problems related to enforcement of criminal statutes governing police deadly force. Except perhaps in cases of money corruption, prosecutors typically are reluctant to charge the police, with whom they regularly work closely, grand jurors are reluctant to indict officers, and petit juries rarely convict (see Kobler 1975a, 1975b; United States Civil Rights Commission 1981:101–16).
13. After consulting and testifying in 100-odd civil cases emanating from police shootings, I see clearly that jurors are far more sympathetic to street police officers than to police chiefs. Jurors typically are very reluctant to place blame for bad shootings on officers who sit before them at defense tables day after day, in obvious agony over the tragedies to which they have been a party. Yet in their anxiety to right the wrongs done to victims of bad shootings, jurors are far less charitable toward abstract bureaucracies or toward police brass—who do not appear in court, or who testify briefly and leave—when plaintiffs' attorneys suggest that both police shooters and the persons shot have been victimized by police chiefs' failure to give officers direction in their most critical decisions.
14. In both Birmingham and Kansas City, Missouri, for example, police chiefs who promulgated restrictive shooting policies suffered severe criticism from segments of both their departments and the public (see, e.g., Sherman 1983).
15. Matulia's (1982:161) survey reported that as of 1980, 46 (86.8%) of 54 respondent police departments in cities with populations of more than 250,000 had administratively prohibited shooting at unarmed nonviolent fleeing felony suspects. An unpublished survey (Police Executive Research Forum 1982) of 75 police departments in jurisdictions with populations over 100,000 reported that 74 departments prohibited such shootings.
16. One of the joiners was the Academy of Criminal Justice Sciences. Two additional state police chiefs' associations agreed to join the brief too late to be included among signers.
17. This observation is tempered by the knowledge that increased governmental exposure to civil liability for failure to supervise police officers adequately has served also as a major stimulant to reform of deadly force policies and practices. Almost certainly, *Monell v. New York City Department of Social Services* (1978), in which the Supreme Court holds government entities liable when unreasonable policies and practices are proven to be the causes of constitutional violations suffered at the hands of individual agents, has had more effect on police operations than have any of the court's more celebrated rulings related to criminal procedure.
18. One area in which such direction apparently is needed involves police encounters with the mentally disturbed. During the 1970s, such events accounted for very small percentages of police shootings (1.6% in New York, Fyfe 1978:679; 0.6% in Chicago, Geller and Karales 1981:89). Since that time, however, I have received the impression that at least

among shootings that result in controversy and civil suits against police, far higher percentages result from police encounters with mentally disturbed people. Apparently the deinstitutionalization movement of the last decade has created a major new problem for police (see Murphy 1986).

References

American Civil Liberties Union (1966) *Police Power vs. Citizens' Rights.* New York: American Civil Liberties Union.

American Law Institute (1931) 9 *ALI Proceedings* 186–87 (Statement of Professor Mikell).

Baldwin, J. (1962) *Nobody Knows My Name.* New York: Dell.

Binder, A. and P. Scharf (1980) "The Violent Police-Citizen Encounter." *Annals of the American Academy of Political and Social Science* 452:111–21.

Binder, A., P. Scharf, and R. Galvin (1982) "Use of Deadly Force by Police Officers." Final Report Submitted to the National Institute of Justice, Grant 79-NI-AX-0134, December 1982.

Bivens v. Six Unknown Agents, 403 U.S. 388 (1971).

Blumberg, M. (1981) "Race and Police Shootings: An Analysis in Two Cities." In J. Fyfe (ed.), *Contemporary Issues in Law Enforcement.* Beverly Hills: Sage, pp. 152–166.

—— (1983) "The Use of Firearms by Police Officers: The Impact of Individuals, Communities and Race." Ph.D. dissertation, State University of New York at Albany. Ann Arbor: University Microfilms.

Boutwell, J.P. (1977) "Use of Deadly Force to Arrest a Fleeing Felon—A Constitutional Challenge." *FBI Law Enforcement Bulletin* 46:9–14.

Chapman, S.G. (1967) *Police Firearms Use Policy.* Report to the President's Commission on Law Enforcement and Administration of Justice. Washington, D.C.: United States Government Printing Office.

—— and T.S. Crockett (1963) "Gunsight Dilemma: Police Firearms Policy." *Police* 6:40–45.

Chicago Police Department (1980) General Order 80-20, December 23.

Cincinnati Police Department (1964) *Police Regulations Governing Use of Firearms Survey,* mimeo: April 22.

Clark, K.B. (1974) "Open Letter to Mayor Abraham D. Beame and Police Commissioner Michael J. Codd." Unpublished, New York, September 17, 1974.

Commission on Accreditation for Law Enforcement Agencies, Inc. (1983) *Standards for Law Enforcement Agencies.* Fairfax, VA: Commission on Accreditation for Law Enforcement Agencies, Inc.

Davis, A.J. (1980) Letter to Burton A. Rose of Peruto, Ryan and Vitullo, counsel for the Philadelphia Chapter of the Fraternal Order of Police, October 15.

Eastman, G.D. (1961) "Other Police Problems." In L. Holcomb R. (ed.), *Municipal Police Administration.* Fifth edition. Chicago: International City Management Association, pp. 422–454.

Florida Attorney General (1971) *Annual Report.* In Herman Goldstein (ed.), *Policing a Free Society.* Cambridge, MA: Ballinger, p. 127.

Friedrich, R.J. (1980) "Police Use of Force: Individuals, Situations, and Organizations." *Annual of the American Academy of Political and Social Science* 452:82–97.

Fyfe, J.J. (1978) "Shots Fired: An Analysis of New York City Police Firearms Discharge." Ph.D. dissertation, State University of New York at Albany. Ann Arbor: University Microfilms.

—— (1979) "Administrative Interventions on Police Shooting Discretion: An Empirical Examination." *Journal of Criminal Justice* 7:309–24.

—— (1980a) "Always Prepared: Police Off-Duty Guns." *Annals of the American Academy of Political and Social Science* 452:72–81.

—— (1980b) "Geographic Correlates of Police Shooting: A Microanalysis." *Journal of Research in Crime and Delinquency* 17:101–13.

—— (1981a) "Observation on Police Deadly Force." *Crime and Delinquency* 27:376–89.

—— (1981b) "Race and Extreme Police-Citizen Violence." In R.L. McNeely and C.E. Pope (eds.), *Race, Crime, and Criminal Justice.* Beverly Hills: Sage, pp. 89–108.

—— (1981c) "Toward a Typology of Police Shootings." In J.J. Fyfe (ed.), *Contemporary Issues in Law Enforcement.* Beverly Hills: Sage, pp. 136–151.

—— (1981d) "Who Shoots? A Look at Officer Race and Police Shooting." *Journal of Police Science and Administration* 9:367–82.

—— (1982) "Blind Justice: Police Shootings in Memphis." *Journal of Criminal Law and Criminology* 73:707–22.

—— (1986) "Enforcement Workshop: The Supreme Court's New Rules for Police Use of Deadly Force." *Criminal Law Bulletin* 22:62–68.

—— (1988) "Police Shooting Environment and License." In J.E. Scott & T. Hirschi (eds.), *Controversial Issues in Crime and Justice.* Beverly Hills: Sage, pp. 79–94.

Gain, C. (1971) "Discharge of Firearms Policy: Effecting Justice through Administrative Regulation: Unpublished statement, Oakland, CA, December 23.

Garner v. Memphis Police Department, 600 F.2d 52 (6th Cir. 1979).

Garner v. Memphis Police Department, Civil Action No. C-75-145, Memorandum Opinion and Order, slip op. (W.D. Tenn. July 8, 1981).

Garner v. Memphis Police Department, 710 F.2d 240 (6th Cir. 1983).

Geller, W.A. and K.J. Karales (1981) *Split-Second Decisions: Shootings of and by Chicago Police.* Chicago: Chicago Law Enforcement Study Group.

Goldkamp, J.S. (1976) "Minorities as Victims of Police Shootings: Interpretations of Racial Disproportionality and Police Use of Deadly Force." *Justice System Journal* 2:169–83.

Harding, R. and R. Fahey (1973) "Killings by Chicago Police, 1966–1970: An Empirical Study." *Southern California Law Review* 46:284–315.

Harring, S., T. Platt, R. Speiglman, and P. Takagi (1977) "The Management of Police Killings." *Crime and Social Justice* 8:34–43.

Hart, W.L. (1979) "Fatal Shootings by Police Officers." Unpublished report to the Detroit Board of Police Commissioners, October 22.

Heaphy, J.F. (ed.) (1978) *Police Practices: The General Administrative Survey.* Washington, D.C.: Police Foundation.

Horvath, F. and M. Donahue (1982) *Deadly Force: An Analysis of Shootings by Police in Michigan, 1976–1981.* East Lansing: Michigan State University.

Illinois Revised Statutes (1975) Chapter 38, Para. 2–8.

International Union of Police Associations (1980) *Resolution of July 15, 1980.* Washington, D.C.: mimeo.

Jenkins, B. and A. Faison (1974) *An Analysis of 248 Persons Killed by New York City Policemen.* New York: Metropolitan Applied Research Center.

Kania, R.R.E. and W.C. Mackey (1977) "Police Violence As a Function of Community Characteristics." *Criminology* 15:27–48.

Knoohuizen, R., R. Fahey, and D. Palmer (1972) *The Police and Their Use of Fatal Force in Chicago.* Chicago: Chicago Law Enforcement Study Group.

Kobler, A. (1975a) "Figures (and Perhaps Some Facts) on Police Killings of Civilians in the United States, 1965–1969." *Journal of Social Issues* 31:185–91.

—— (1975b) "Police Homicide in a Democracy." *Journal of Social Issues* 31:163–81.

Law Enforcement News (1981) "NYPD May Disarm Off-Duty." April 13:3.

Matulia, K.R. (1982) *A Balance of Forces.* Second edition. Gaithersburg, MD: International Association of Chiefs of Police.

—— (1985) *A Balance of Forces.* Second Edition. Gaithersburg, MD: International Association of Chiefs of Police.

McCleskey v. Georgia.—U.S.—, 95 L.Ed. 262, 107 S. Ct. 1756, 55 U.S.L.W. 4537 (1987).

Memphis Police Department (1979) *General Order 95-79, Deadly Force Policy,* July 16.

Meyer, M.W. (1980a) "Police Shootings of Minorities: The Case of Los Angeles." *The Annals* 452:98–110.

—— (1980b) *Report to the Los Angeles Board of Police Commissioners on Police Use of Deadly Force in Los Angeles: Officer-Involved Shootings,* Part IV. Los Angeles: Los Angeles Board of Police Commissioners.

Milton, C., J.W. Halleck, J. Lardner, and G.L. Abrecht (1977) *Police Use of Deadly Force.* Washington, D.C.: Police Foundation.

Monell v. New York City Department of Social Services, 436 U.S. 658 (1978).

Murphy, G. (1986) *With Special Care.* Washington, D.C.: Police Executive Research Forum.

National Advisory Commission on Civil Disorders (1968) *Report of the National Advisory Commission on Civil Disorders.* New York: Dutton.

National Center for Health Statistics (1967) *International Classification for Diseases, Adapted for Use in the United States* 8th Revision. Washington, D.C.: United States Government Printing Office.

National Commission on the Causes and Prevention of Violence (1969) *To Establish Justice, To Insure Domestic Tranquility.* Washington, D.C.: United States Government Printing Office.

New York State Penal Law (1967).

Nielsen, E. (1983) "Policy on the Police Use of Deadly Force: A Cross-National Analysis." *Journal of Police Science and Administration* 11:104–8.

Pennsylvania Statutes Annotated (1973).

Philadelphia Police Department (1980) *Directive 10,* April 2.

Police Executive Research Forum (1982) "Survey of Police Deadly Force Policies." Unpublished report, Washington, D.C.

—— and Police Foundation (1981) *Survey of Police Operational and Administrative Practices 1981.* Washington, D.C.: Police Executive Research Forum and Police Foundation, 1981.

Police Foundation, joined by Nine National and International Associations of Police and Criminal Justice Professionals, the Chiefs of Police Associations of two States, and Thirty-one Law Enforcement Chief Executives (1984) *Amici Curiae Brief in Tennessee v. Garner.* United States Supreme Court 83-1035, 83-1070. Washington, D.C.: August 6.

President's Commission on Law Enforcement and Administration of Justice (1967) *Task Force Report: The Police.* Washington, D.C.: United States Government Printing Office.

Rizzo v. Goode, 423 U.S. 362 (1976).

Robin, G. (1963) "Justifiable Homicide by Police." *Journal of Criminal Law, Criminology and Police Science* (May/June): 225–31.

Rummel, B. (1968) "The Right of Law Enforcement Officers to Use Deadly Force to Effect an Arrest." *New York Law Forum* 30:749.

Scharf, P. and A. Binder (1983) *The Badge and the Bullet.* New York: Praeger.

St. Louis Post-Dispatch (1980) "The Police Chiefs on Deadly Force." Editorial, September 21:16.

Sherman, L.W. (1980) "Execution without Trial: Police Homicide and the Constitution." *Vanderbilt Law Review* 33:71-110.

—— (1983) "Reducing Police Gun Use: Critical Events, Administrative Policy and Organizational Change." In Maurice Punch (ed.), *The Management and Control of Police Organizations.* Cambridge, MA: M.I.T. Press, pp. 98–125.

—— and R. Langworthy (1979) "Measuring Homicide by Police Officers." *Journal of Criminal Law and Criminology* 70:546–60.

Stark, R. (1972) *Police Riots.* Belmont, CA: Wadsworth.

Takagi, P. (1974) "A Garrison State in a 'Democratic' Society." *Crime and Social Justice.* 5:34–43.

Tennessee Code Annotated (1977).

Tennessee v. Garner, 471 U.S. 1, 105 S. Ct. 1694, 85 L. Ed. 1 (1985).

Uelman, G. (1973) "Varieties of Public Policy: A Study of Police Policy Regarding the Use of Deadly Force in Los Angeles County." *Loyola of Los Angeles Law Review* 6:1–65.

United States v. Clark, 31 F. 710 (6th Cir., 1887).

United States Bureau of the Census (1974) *The Social and Economic Status of the Black Population in the United States.* Washington, D.C.: United States Government Printing Office.

United States Civil Rights Commission (1979) *Police Practices and Civil Rights Hearing Held in Philadelphia, Pennsylvania Volume I, Testimony.* Washington, D.C.: United States Government Printing Office.

—— (1981) *Who is Guarding the Guardians?* Washington, D.C.: United States Government Printing Office.

Uviller, H.R. (1986) "Seizure by Gunshot: The Riddle of the Fleeing Felon." *New York University Review of Law and Social Change* XIV: 705–20.

Waegel, W.B. (1984) "The Use of Lethal Force by Police: The Effect of Statutory Change." *Crime and Delinquency* 30:121–40.

Wilson, O.W. (1963) *Police Administration.* Second edition. New York: McGraw-Hill.

Winter, S.L. (1986) "*Tennessee v. Garner* and the Democratic Practice of Judicial Review." *New York University Review of Law and Social Change* XIV: 679–704.

Yorke, Jeffrey (1988) "P.B. Police to Boost Firepower." *Washington Post* February 21:C-1,C6.

Chapter 14

Transnational Crime

Implications for Local Law Enforcement

Kip Schlegel

Economic globalization has given rise to globalized crime, particularly organized and white-collar crime. And with transnational crime on the rise, it has increasingly become a problem for local agencies. The challenges for local law enforcement agencies are largely those they already face in addressing white-collar crime—lack of resources and expertise in investigating technologically and organizationally complex practices, and a web of interagency jurisdictional conflicts with everyone from the FBI to the Postal Service—all of which are only compounded by the language, culture, and policy barriers between countries. Schlegel discusses the problems facing local law enforcement, and suggests some solutions.

We need not look outside the borders of the United States to understand the most significant issues facing local law enforcement as it attempts to deal with transnational crime. Although technological innovation, advances in rapid transit, and information systems have led to the globalization of crime, local law enforcement is confronted with much more basic and mundane problems that affect its ability to respond to these offenses. This is not to say that transnational crime does not pose unique and important problems for local law enforcement or that we should ignore the permutations of crime and social control that are products of different cultures, legal structures, and systems of enforcement found throughout the world. Rather, the contention here is that the most significant issues facing local law enforcement are not so much a function of geography as they are a function of the nature of the offenses themselves. The premise of this article is that much of transnational crime, or at least the most significant transnational crimes, are organized and economic crimes, and by the latter, I mean white-collar crimes. These kinds of offenses pose particular problems for local law enforcement, regardless of their geographic location. This article focuses on two such problems. First, the very nature of organized and white-collar crime taxes the capabilities of local law enforcement to investigate and prosecute these offenses. For the most part, local law enforcement is not well situated to respond effectively to offenses that are technologically or organizationally complex. Their mission is to respond rapidly and reactively to citizens in need, and they are strained as it is to meet this demand. Second, the nature of organized and white-collar crimes entails an interorganizational response from law enforcement. There are significant regulatory conflicts that are inherent in these interorganizational relationships and merit attention. For us to frame an adequate understanding and response to transnational crime at the local level, we must examine more closely the nature of these crimes and study the problems law enforcement faces in responding to these offenses within our own borders.

Although there is a wide array of transnational crimes—indeed, virtually any crime could become transnational merely by the offender hopping on board a plane, train, or automobile for another country—I limit the scope of this article to organized and white-collar offenses because they pose a systemic, rather than random, threat to the global community. For better or for worse, I wish to limit my contribution even further by focusing principally on white-collar offenses; however, I believe separating white-collar crimes from organized crime is more fiction than reality. The first part of this article will address the nature of these offenses and discuss the implications they pose for local law enforcement generally. The second part of this article will focus on the potential for regulatory conflict that arises with these kinds of offenses. This will frame the discussion of this regulatory conflict from an organizational-set perspective. I will conclude with a discussion of the implications for transnational crime and directions for future research on these areas.

The Nature of Organized and White-Collar Crime

Far too much ink has been spilled on the definitions of organized and white-collar crime (Geis, 1992; Helmkamp, Ball, & Townsend, 1996; Kelly, 1986; Schrager & Short, 1978). In fact, the limited systematic research on both areas inevitably bogs down in these definitional debates. It is neither possible nor necessary to resolve these issues here because the focus is primarily on larger conceptual issues. Nonetheless, it is important to be clear what is meant by organized and white-collar crime for the purposes of this analysis. *White-collar crime* is defined broadly here as illegal behavior governed by criminal statutes committed by individuals or organizations in the course of their legitimate economic activity. *Organized crime* is defined here as illegal behavior governed by criminal statutes committed by organized groups of individuals for the purposes of supplying illegal goods and services. As noted earlier, there is a distinction between organized crime and white-collar crime, but too much can be made of these differences. Using Dwight Smith's (1982) notion of a "spectrum of legitimacy," it may be argued that both forms of crime can be seen along a continuum of illegal behavior characterized by the degree of legitimacy of the acts and actors. White-collar offenses are largely offenses that feed off legitimate economic behavior, as in the sales of securities, manufacturing, banking operations, and political behavior. The actors occupy roles of power, trust, and privilege that are both personal and positional. Organized crime is largely illegitimate activity— that is, the manufacturing, production, distribution, or sales of illicit goods and services. The actors' status is primarily derived from their positions within the organization created for the expressed purposes of committing the illegal behavior.

The amount of white-collar and organized crime has also been hotly debated, and here again, no resolution is in sight. The National White-Collar Crime Center (Helmkamp et al., 1996) has estimated annual losses from white-collar crime to range from 260 billion to 1 trillion dollars. Of course, these losses are calculated in terms of the United States alone. Recent figures on the amount of harm generated from organized crime are of similar magnitude. Again, it is not necessary to come to terms with these figures. What is important is to note the size and scope of the problems and the grim reality that they are, in all probability, on the rise. More significant is the direction these forms of illegal behavior appear to be taking, because it is their permutations that pose significant problems for law enforcement. The old maxim holds true: If you want to understand white-collar crime, follow the money. Indeed, transnational crime has become the problem it is primarily because the social organization of money has itself become transnational. This shift is a product of both the nature of business activity as it seeks to maximize profits and the mechanisms or technology available to make it possible. Thus, if we follow the patterns of white-collar crime, we see the movement from manufacturing and small retail business activities that characterized the first half of the century, through the development of computers and information technology, and toward securities and commodities, banking, and insurance. Telemarketing, high-speed wire transfers, and global communication via the Internet have become the modus operandi of business at the millennium. At the same time, we have witnessed the creation of satellite occupations that service these new activities—from large brokerage firms, health maintenance organizations, law firms and the like. White-collar crimes are evident in these satellite occupations because of the trust that is inherent in their fiduciary roles as agents (Shapiro, 1990). White-collar and organized crime often intersect at this point, as organized criminals seek means to move and hide money and goods and thus turn to these specialized functions to carry this out.

It is within this context of legitimacy and change that we can begin to see the problems posed to law enforcement. For the sake of clarity, I discuss these offenses in terms of two central components: harm and complexity. Harm entails both the injury caused by the act, and the intent of the actor. White-collar crime poses particular problems with respect to injury because of the nature of the victimization that often occurs. Injury can be both direct and diffuse, and it can affect specific individual welfare interests, such as physical well-being and economic security, or it can affect generic societal interests, such as political democracy or fair markets. Crime is more easily understood and acted on when the injury is direct, and it affects specific individual welfare interests. Although many forms of white-collar crime are of this nature, much of white-collar crime finds itself on the other end of this continuum, where the injury is more diffuse and defined more readily with respect to societal welfare interests. Thus, a securities fraud that hypes either a product or a company in order to escalate its short-term value (what is referred to as "pump and dump") may be spread over a large number of victims, many of whom may not be people at all (that is, they may be organizational investors), with relatively minimal individual monetary loss. However, the harm is indeed significant from the standpoint of a societal interest in fair markets when the perception of a level playing field is blurred.

The second component of harm, the intent of the actor, is perhaps the most significant dilemma (at least as it pertains to white-collar crime) because it affects both the perception of victimization, which initiates the social control response, and the degree of culpability, which pushes that social control into the criminal remedy (Mann, 1992). As noted earlier, a key component to white-collar crime is that it thrives off the opportunity structures created by legitimate activity. Indeed, the most difficult forms of white-collar crime to enforce are those that mimic acceptable legal behavior. Most Americans could not explain what crimes Michael Milken engaged in during the 1980s that led him to be on the front pages of most major newspapers and magazines. In fact, the Securities and Exchange Commission (SEC) had difficulty itself trying to understand what it was exactly that Milken was doing and whether he was engaging in insider trading with an expressly criminal intent. More will be said later about the regulatory conflict that may arise with respect to the remedial jurisdiction of much of the illegal economic activity, but suffice it to say that the focus of law enforcement is the establishment of criminal intent, and this becomes difficult when either the activity approximates acceptable activity or the means to engage in the illegal activity are themselves legal as in, for example, the wiring of money to offshore accounts.

This component of intent is closely tied to another attribute of many white-collar offenses, or at least those offenses for which we ought to be concerned: offense complexity. The idea that white-collar offenses are particularly complex has been the subject of considerable academic debate. Michael Gottfredson and Travis Hirschi (1990) have argued, for example, that patterns of white-collar crime are not particularly different from other "common crimes"; they are largely spontaneous, relatively trivial, and lead to little monetary reward. Research by Weisburd, Wheeler, Waring, and Bode (1991) also suggests that many white-collar crimes prosecuted in federal district courts are relatively mundane and uncomplicated, committed by individuals who more closely fit the characteristics of the broad middle class of society. They note, however, that there is a hierarchy of white-collar offenses that is based, in part, on offense complexity. Two important caveats are needed here. First, the data drawn from this research include convicted offenders in a wide range of behaviors deemed by some, but not others, as white-collar crimes. Thus, the impoverished person who cashes someone else's welfare check and a young clerk who pilfers from her employer's cash register might find themselves labeled white-collar criminals. Second, the debate about whether offenses are or are not white-collar crimes aside, transnational crimes of all types are certainly more likely to involve more systemic and complicated forms of economic criminality.

Many factors make up offense complexity, but I will limit the discussion here to three issues: (a) organizational complexity, (b) technological complexity, and (c) spatial and temporal complexity. These issues are obviously connected, but each will be addressed briefly. As

Reiss and Tonry (1993) have noted, the tendency of much of the research on white-collar crime has been to focus primarily on individuals acting in their occupational roles, with minimal attention given to the role of organizations or, to put it more broadly, the organization of crime. Although all crime is socially organized in some fashion or another, most of the crimes we are concerned with here are embedded within both formal and informal organizations of varying complexity. Organizational complexity is a function of the number of component parts of the organization and of their position within the organization. It entails structure and function, including the formal and informal operating policies, task specializations, communication and decision-making systems, and organizational culture and norms (Vaughan, 1996). Much of the literature on organized crime has dealt with these kinds of issues, including the extent to which organized crime groups maintain formal structures and functions and the role that ethnicity plays in the organization's development and maintenance over time (Albanese, 1996; Cressey, 1969; Ianni, 1972; Reuter, 1983; Smith, 1975). Of course, organized crime need not be conceptualized in terms of bureaucratic structures. Indeed, increasing evidence suggests that many types of organized crimes are better depicted as taking place within networks of individuals and groups. These networks expand and contract according to the particular criminal opportunities that are available. Specialists may be required to pull off certain jobs, or resources and capital may be needed to bankroll a particular operation. Networks take on their own complexities and in many ways make it harder for law enforcement to develop any systematic response because of their fluid and dynamic nature. Networks form and disband, acting in many ways like a virus attacking the body. They mutate in response to the conditions in the environment and to the reactions of the host. Just when law enforcement might have a handle on the structure and activities of the network, the network alters its shape or changes its direction. There is no doubt that criminal organizations take a variety of forms, some more complicated than others, but clearly, the size of the organization and the ability and mechanisms to delineate specific actors and their functions are crucial ingredients to effective investigation and prosecution.

Organizational complexity may be embedded in the organization itself, or it may be a function of its specific core technology. Organizations involved in white-collar crime function for the specific purpose of completing particular tasks because those tasks are established (mostly) in the context of legal behavior. To understand the technology of white-collar crime, it is crucial to understand individuals' roles within the organization and the organization's role within markets or a network of organizations that make up particular institutional arrangements (Reiss & Tonry, 1993). A central issue for the investigation and prosecution of these crimes is to determine the degree of organizational criminality (as opposed to individual criminality), and this can be a particularly daunting task for law enforcement when the behavior takes place in the context of legitimate activity within complex market or industrial systems.

Technological complexity is perhaps the defining component of most serious forms of white-collar crime. Most white-collar offenses are crimes of deception—deception that attempts to convince others that the products are safe, that the activities are lucrative, or that leads to specific beneficial outcomes for the victims. The more complicated the activity, the greater the reliance on the part of the victim to trust the offender. As noted earlier, the complexity may be a function of the activity itself (for example, most of us would be unable to read blood assays that indicate the need for surgery, much less be able to perform that surgery or know that it was performed unnecessarily), or it may be a function of the procedures used to engage in the activity, such as the use of high-tech equipment, complicated financial laws, or money transfer technology. In either instance, the victim is typically at the mercy of the actor to interpret the event.

Finally, temporal and spatial complexities are key components to many forms of organized and white-collar crime. It is seldom the case that organizations that move illicit goods or provide illegal services are geographically centralized, and many forms of white-collar crime evolve out of special circumstances and conditions that blend over time to create the right opportunity structures. Furthermore, the more organizationally and technologically complicated the activity, the greater the temporal and spatial complexities. The greater the temporal component, the harder it is to establish cause and effect. The greater the spatial component, the harder it is to link offender to victims.

Organized and white-collar crimes have some unique features, and I have outlined two of these to demonstrate the points. These offenses have particular aspects of injury and intent that make the harm difficult to ascertain. Furthermore, relative to other forms of crime, they are far more complex in terms of organization, technology, and spatial and temporal distribution. How then do these particular features translate to local law enforcement? Before answering this question, it is useful to outline what we know about local law enforcement efforts to respond to these kinds of crimes.

Local Law Enforcement Response

From a research standpoint, we know precious little about the policing of organized crime and even less about the policing of white-collar crime. Most of our knowledge of the former comes from anecdotal accounts, which has tended to focus on issues relating to regulatory enforcement in areas such as the environment, health care, and markets. In 1987, the U.S. Department of Justice (DOJ) released figures indicating that 31% of the cases investigated by U.S. attorneys were classified as white-collar crimes, whereas 6% of state felony cases were for such offenses. Between 1980 and 1985, the number of federally convicted white-collar offenders increased by 18%. In spite of these numbers, virtually no systematic research exists on the subject of white-collar crime at the state and municipal levels of law enforcement. Researchers at the Police Executive Research Forum (Coe & Ellis, 1990) conducted an exploratory study of law enforcement agencies in all 50 states to try to determine state responses to white-collar crime. They found that white-collar crime investigations were increasing in scope. Twenty-three state law enforcement agencies had created separate units to investigate white-collar crimes, whereas another 9 states had plans to do so. Fourteen states planned to expand their operations. Of the 23 agencies, 14 were centralized in a single location in order to provide the technical support necessary to investigate specialized areas such as computer fraud analysis, auditing, and money laundering. Centralized records allowed investigators easy access to information on similar cases. States with decentralized units did so largely to limit travel time and expenses in covering large territories or because they are situated in major metropolitan areas with unique problems.

As noted earlier, the complex nature of white-collar crime requires a degree of specialized training or educational background, particularly in the fields of accounting, auditing, and business administration. All of the states with specialized units required their officers to have some specialized training, primarily provided by the Federal Law Enforcement Training Center, the FBI Academy, the Treasury Department, or the National White Collar Crime Center. Most of these courses, however, are only 1 week long, covering such areas as financial fraud investigations and computer fraud. Thirteen states require some or all of their investigators to be accountants, attorneys, or masters of business administration. Although the survey provides little additional information, the findings indicate that all states intended to increase their investigative efforts, particularly in the direction of money laundering and asset seizure and forfeiture. Clearly these units were moving in the direction of drug trafficking and distribution by large narcotics organizations. However, the units were also planning on expanding in the area of computer fraud detection, particularly in the area of electronic fund transfer systems.

This cursory research tells us two things. First, there is a dearth of information available on state and local responses to white-collar crime. Virtually no research exists on the type or amount of crimes enforced at these levels or on the issues relating to enforcement response. Second, this research, or perhaps more appropriately the lack of it, testifies to the huge obstacles that face local law enforcement in areas of criminal behavior that have become increasingly transnational in scope. The elements of harm noted above, that is to say injury and intent, affect law enforcement primarily by limiting both the reporting mechanisms and the development of evidence to support and maintain what are certain to be complex and time-consuming investigations. It is evident that local law enforcement can do little more than respond in piecemeal fashion to random complaints that are filtered their way. They are ill equipped to develop systematic and structured mechanisms whereby cases are prioritized, delegated, and managed. It is also clear that local law enforcement lacks the resources and personnel to respond to sophisticated cases that are organizationally or technologically complex. Instead, white-collar and organized crime cases are likely to be those whose harm is largely direct and individualized; smaller cases are contained within a succinct time frame and have a minimum number of victims. Large-scale white-collar and organized criminal cases not only require the resources, but more important, they also require a level of expertise to understand complex business and financial activities and transactions and to decipher the organizational structure and operations of the offense. Agents must also demonstrate proof of the crime beyond a reasonable doubt. This, in turn, requires a blending of specialized knowledge in the core technological activity and in the law. Yet, data indicate clearly that to the extent that local law enforcement has specialized units, the expertise of the officers is limited to a basic overview or foundational knowledge. Most expertise is developed in the field, and although this has its benefits, a major drawback is that it provides for a self-selection of cases that fit a particular profile the officer is accustomed to seeing. Susan Shapiro (1984) noted this problem in her study of the U.S. SEC enforcement program. Although investigators are highly trained in both securities and law (most are lawyers), they tend to specialize, even within the relatively specialized field of securities fraud. Thus, attorneys who are familiar with insider trading cases pursue such cases, whereas other crimes that are perhaps more harmful and sophisticated go undetected or fail to be investigated because the enforcement net is simply not cast for such behaviors.

These enforcement dilemmas lead to one primary and indisputable conclusion—local law enforcement cannot expect to handle these sophisticated cases on their own. They must turn to other agencies and other partnerships for help and support; in particular, they must turn to assistance at the federal level from regulators and criminal authorities. Yet, significant obstacles often arise from the nature of these interagency relationships, which limit effective responses to white-collar crime and organized crime. We might learn something of value by studying sources of interagency conflict that have arisen at the federal law enforcement level in efforts to respond to these crimes. Without examining these interorganizational relationships and the problems that are contained within them, many misfortunes are bound to repeat themselves as local law enforcement begins to grapple with transnational crime. To look at these issues, I draw from the notions of regulatory conflict and organizational theory and I use examples in securities enforcement to illustrate these problems.

The Nature of Regulatory Conflict

The study of regulatory conflict has largely focused on the impact that conflicting regulations have on those to whom the laws apply (Diver, 1980). For the most part, discussion has centered on the formation of laws, but the enforcement of those laws and the conflict arising from the enforcement process itself have received little attention. However, regulatory conflict is limited neither to the laws themselves nor to the impact that such discrepancies of the law may have on those to whom the laws apply. Conflict may also arise between the regulated and the regulators with regard to the goals of enforcement and the process by which those goals are carried out, as well as between the regulatory agencies themselves charged with enforcing the laws. It is this latter area that I address here.

Much of the literature on regulatory conflict pertaining to white-collar crimes focuses on the conflicting goals of enforcement, with the bulk of attention given to the problems that arise between compliance- and deterrence-oriented enforcement systems (Braithwaite, 1985; Reiss, 1984; Scholz, 1984). Although most of that literature deals with the relationship between the regulator and the regulated, there has been some spillover to the differences between agencies charged with regulating a given industry with respect to their goals. Differences in goals account for only one dimension in the complex set of relationships that ultimately explain regulatory conflict. Conflict may also arise as a result of other aspects of the organizational relationships between enforcement agencies, and organizational theory can provide us with some clues to the causes of this interagency conflict. Although there are myriad organizational theories to turn to, I have incorporated an organizational-set model here to guide the discussion of interagency conflict in the area of securities enforcement (Evans, 1966). Organizational-set models apply a systems approach to examine specifically the interactions of an organization (or class of organizations) with other organizations in its environment. This organization set may be partitioned into an input organization set and an output organization set, which supply and receive resources, goods, and services from a focal organization. This model is, of course, applicable to the relationship between regulators and an industry, or between regulators themselves.

Although there are many dimensions to organizational-set models, I will focus on only a few dimensions to illustrate potential sources of interagency conflict in the area of white-collar crime enforcement. First, attention is given to the size and diversity of the input and output sets and to the configuration of the network that comprises the organizational arrangements. Such components are likely to affect the degree of bargaining, amalgamation, domination, and co-optation found in organizational relationships. Second, at a more microlevel of analysis, organizational-set theory emphasizes the important linkages to the organizational system played by boundary personnel at both the input and output stages. Such factors as task specialization, status of the actors, and normative reference group orientation account for the nature and shape of organizational relationships.

Sources of Regulatory Conflict

As Evans (1966, p. 79) notes, much can be learned about organizational relationships by depicting their position within the organizational network. An input organization set is the network of organizations that provides resources to the focal organization. An output organization set is the complement of organizations that receives goods and services generated by the focal organization. The particular structure of input organization sets and output organization sets allows a focal organization the ability to assess the status and prognosis of its resources and thereby stabilize and protect its functions. It does this in part by clearly defining the nature of organizational dependency. Applying this systems approach to the traditional criminal justice system, we find that the functions of major components of the system are, relatively speaking, linear, clearly defined, and delegated. The input organizations are largely fixed temporally and functionally, and the dependency is, for the most part, predictable. Evans refers to this model as a chain network, in which members of a set are linked in a series with the focal organization that has only direct interaction with the first link in the chain, (e.g., victims and witnesses typically report to the police who conduct investigations and forward information to prosecutors) and in which the ability of one organization to carry out its activities depends on the effectiveness of the other in a cumulative fashion.

When it comes to white-collar crime enforcement, the structure of organizational relations is far more complex, both in terms of the size and the configuration of the organization sets (Schlegel, 1994). For example, a host of agencies may serve to detect, investigate, prosecute, and even punish illegal behavior in the securities industry—including state securities commissions, the National Association of Securities Dealers, the securities exchanges, the U.S. Attorneys Office, the FBI, the SEC, the Postal Service, and the Internal Revenue Service. Depicting the linkages between these agencies can be problematic, with the relationships at times approximating an all-channel network, in which all members of the set may interact with each other and each interacts with the focal organization, and at other times resembling a wheel network, in which the focal organization interacts with more than one organization of a particular type, but in which there are no mutual interactions between members of the set. More problematic, the functions of these different agencies may overlap in significant ways, and this commingling of functions becomes even [more] complex as the social control process advances. Not only can regulatory organizations perform similar kinds of activities but also their core technologies are similar, and from an organizational-set perspective, any single organization may serve as both input and output organizations for others within the regulatory structure. Thus, in the case of securities, the SEC may detect, investigate, and sanction insider trading, or it may detect and investigate it and forward the information to the exchange for enforcement action, or it may serve as the reporting party, further it to the exchange for investigation, and receive information back for sanctioning (or referral to the Department of Justice for criminal prosecution).

Regulatory conflict may be exacerbated in such organizational relationships by the fact that changes in the configurations of input and output sets affect the nature and frequency of interactions within the networks, leading to the development of dominance, fragmentation, or coalition formation. Furthermore, the structure of the organizational relationships will have reverberations in the internal structure and internal processes of the focal organization (Evans, 1966, p. 84). In the social organization of securities enforcement, the best example can be found in the relationship between the SEC and the DOJ. In the past, the SEC has typically served as an input organization for the DOJ in that many of the criminal cases investigated by the FBI and prosecuted by the U.S. Attorneys Office were referrals from the SEC that either met a threshold of harm or involved individuals or firms that were not amenable to compliance-oriented sanctions (e.g., con artists and fraudulent enterprises acting solely for the purposes of committing crime in the securities markets). Although it is not always the case, in such an arrangement, the SEC may run its course and then forward the matter for criminal action, having completed most of its investigation and litigation. Within the past decade, however, this arrangement has changed, bringing with it a certain amount of conflict between the two agencies. In recent years, securities and commodities frauds have become important program areas for both the FBI and the DOJ, demonstrated by the FBI's undercover operations in the commodities futures markets and by federal prosecutors' (particularly, the Southern District of New York) efforts to stem the tide of illegal activity on Wall Street. This change in targeting has substantially altered the organizational relationships between the two agencies in two substantial ways. First, greater competition can now be found between the two agencies as the DOJ has been taking on securities-related cases that may be simultaneously investigated and litigated by the SEC. Because Congress funds both the DOJ and the SEC in part on their ability to generate closed cases, these agencies are understandably wary of any action that might reduce their performance indicators. The natural course of such competition is to increase control of a case by closing ranks and reduce information sharing in instances in which such duplicity might be suspected.

This emphasis on securities cases has led to a second structural change by introducing the FBI as a more central actor in the enforcement process. Prior to this change, the central relationship in securities cases was between the SEC and the U.S. Attorneys Office. Basically, the SEC acted in an investigative capacity and passed that information on to the prosecutor. This relationship was compatible largely because the SEC is staffed by attorneys who are familiar with both securities fraud and legal procedure. As the role of the FBI in investigations has increased, the tasks and responsibilities of both the SEC and the U.S. Attorneys Office have changed correspondingly. The increase in securities cases brought to the attention of the DOJ has meant a greater reliance on the FBI to conduct the investigations necessary to take the case further. Yet, the FBI is often viewed as being ill equipped to handle such cases, largely due to the strained resources available for white-collar crime investigations. Similarly, although the FBI has agents who are skilled in securities cases, assistant U.S. attorneys have sometimes expressed concern over the general ability of agents to investigate sophisticated financial cases with complex audit trails. Prosecutors expressed the desire to have a closer working relationship with FBI investigators, with agents and prosecutors working in coordination during the investigation to obtain the best evidence for prosecution, but such cooperative arrangements have not been a traditional method of operation for either agency. These examples, I think, demonstrate the dynamic nature of agency relationships and the effect that these relationships can have on the core activities of the agencies themselves.

These concerns lead directly to a second area of organizational theory that may help to better understand regulatory conflict—the role of boundary personnel. As Evans (1966) notes, it is important to examine the "system linkages" that arise in the role relations of boundary personnel because "it is through the behavior of incumbents of various statuses at the boundary of the focal organization, such as top executives, lawyers, purchasing agents, marketing specialists, personnel officers, etc., that various environmental interactions are mediated" (p. 84).

Three aspects related to boundary personnel—task specialization, professional status, and normative orientation—allow us to better understand the potential conflict between enforcers. As highlighted earlier, one common concern raised by SEC officials with respect to the DOJ concerns the absence of specialization or expertise in securities-related matters. Securities activities are governed predominantly by five major acts of legislation with the 1933 and 1934 acts serving as the foundation for enforcement. These civil laws contain criminal sanctions as last resort measures. The laws cover a vast array of activities and behaviors, activities that change in response to market conditions and which, by necessity, lead businesses to push at the boundaries of acceptability in search of profit. Not only must regulators understand the form and scope of the laws themselves, but also and more important, they must understand the legitimate machinations of market activity from which the illegal activity derives. SEC regulators are, of course, trained in securities laws. With some exceptions, SEC staff are also trained broadly in securities-related matters, that is to say, most SEC lawyers handled an array of different cases—from insider trading to broker-dealer misappropriations to false filings. They are, thus, highly specialized.

Such is not the case with either the FBI or the U.S. Attorneys Office. Their agency mandates are much broader, ranging from terrorism to bank robbery to drug trafficking and possession. Given these larger mandates, the individuals who occupy boundary roles with respect to securities offenses also serve in numerous other boundary roles and must interact with multiple agencies and actors concerned with vastly different agendas.

Although it is often the case that the larger U.S. Attorneys Offices and regional field offices of the FBI maintain their own economic crimes units, this is not the case for most offices across the United States. In addition, there is not much sanctuary from the winds of Congress that on apparent whim, may shift national priority areas quickly or cut resources in dramatic fashion. The agency itself must be prepared to adjust to such uncertainties, and such preparation, of course, affects the activities and dedication of those occupying boundary roles.

Although there are some differences within offices that do maintain an economic crime unit, these units are susceptible to similar shifts within economic crime areas. The most notable economic crime of the 1980s and early 1990s was savings and loan fraud, and most economic crime units were tied up in lengthy and complicated investigations and prosecutions of those cases. Bank and thrift fraud is only one of a half dozen or so national economic crime priorities. Within those national priorities, regional differences may emerge, with telecommunications crimes being a more severe problem in one area, and political corruption or securities offenses in another. This juggling of activity places severe strains on an agency.

It is in the context of this shifting of tasks that we can better understand the relationships between boundary personnel. Securities and exchange staff often see U.S. attorneys as being reluctant to take on securities-related cases generally and being even more unwilling to tackle the more complex cases, a view shared by many prosecutors as well. A good case can take from 1 to 2 years from the first investigative tip to the end (compared to drug cases that can take a week to 10 days). Because of this, prosecutors look instead for the simple case with a quick outcome and measurable benefit—a "bullet between the eyes"—and these different perspectives on what is considered important create tension between the two offices.

Given the lack of expertise in the securities area and the competing demands from other areas, both the FBI and prosecutors depend on SEC personnel for assistance in understanding securities frauds. Yet, because of limited resources, competition, and learning curves, information sharing seldom takes place, and when it does, it is often done so grudgingly. Without proper training sessions with those who are most familiar with the securities industry generally and securities fraud in particular, it is virtually impossible for investigators and prosecutors to fully understand how schemes work or how regulations are circumvented.

A final characteristic of SEC enforcement staff reflects their professional status and normative orientation and distinguishes them from other boundary personnel in other agencies. Most of the enforcement division consists of lawyers who often discover, investigate, and ultimately litigate their own cases. This characteristic affects boundary relationships in several obvious ways. First, SEC personnel are likely to have a greater stake in the outcome of the case because they are responsible for all aspects of the case. Second, because they are the ones who will negotiate a settlement, their investigatory functions are more clearly delineated toward the outcome desired. By virtue of their occupation and specialization, they are cognizant not only of the activity itself (the illegal conduct) but also of the regulations and, perhaps more important, the legal procedure. One often-cited criticism of the FBI is that their expertise is limited to the techniques of criminal investigation, not to those of legal procedure.

The significance of these differences is clear from an organizational perspective that examines information flow and feedback mechanisms. Actors occupying these important boundary roles often speak at cross purposes. They gather different kinds of information through different means. They ask different questions and, perhaps more important, interact with violators in very different ways. When these factors are considered within the context of the organizational structure of social control noted above (especially considering the growth of parallel filings), the foundation for regulatory conflict becomes apparent.

In this brief discussion of securities enforcement, I have attempted to illustrate sources of apparent conflict in interagency relationships. Two organizational components were examined: (a) the structural arrangement that characterizes regulation and enforcement and (b) the role of boundary personnel and the factors that lead to the patterns of relationships found between agencies. What can we draw from this discussion that might inform us about the implications for local law enforcement with respect to white-collar crime generally and transnational crime specifically? First, it is important to emphasize that many, if not most, transnational crimes are white-collar offenses and include securities frauds, credit card schemes, bank frauds, technology crimes, and the like. As such, many of the offenses fall under the jurisdiction of one or more federal regulatory agencies that monitor the legitimate markets in which the illegal activity takes place. As local law enforcement agencies become more systematically involved in the investigation and prosecution of white-collar and organized offenses, they will be confronted with new organizational relationships that fundamentally alter their core activities. As these offenses cross national and international boundaries, the issues facing interagency relationships will be compounded dramatically. These units, which have typically been relatively self-contained (that is to say, they initiate, investigate, and prosecute cases largely on their own), will find that their input and output relationships change as they turn to and are turned to for assistance with more complex cases. As agencies attempt to define their goals and objectives, they must clearly define their domain in these new relationships. Yet, this will not be easy. The variety and complexity of white-collar crimes make it difficult to anticipate and plan systematic tasks and activities to formalize goals and criteria. Money laundering cases are considerably different from securities cases, which are considerably different from corruption cases. Because these agencies are understandably incapable of responding adequately to the myriad forms of fraud, they will be faced with greater reliance or dependency on other organizations that can perform specialized functions such as investigations or prosecutions. These organizations must be considered in the formation of goals and objectives, including jurisdiction, authority, and credit for cases. This requires that considerable attention be given to the development and maintenance of these boundary relationships. However, as activities and functions shift, the dependencies will shift and new sets of organizational relationships will be necessary, with perhaps different, conflicting, or competing goals and objectives, in turn requiring new sets of boundary personnel to maintain those relationships. Such personnel must have both an expertise in the area and an understanding of the functions and tasks of those who occupy the boundary relationships. As demonstrated with federal securities enforcement, these challenges are difficult enough when we consider them in the context of a specialized unit or agency acting as a focal organization in its own right. When we consider that these state and local white-collar and organized crime units are themselves contained within larger law enforcement organizations, whose mission, function, and activities are different from those of the units themselves, we begin to see the magnitude of the obstacles involved.

These obstacles become magnified manyfold when we introduce transnational crime, in which different systems of law, policing, and investigative authority are made all the more problematic by cultural and language barriers. Local law enforcement agencies have limited understanding of transnational crime, much less an understanding of the structure and management of law enforcement in the various countries across the seven continents. Under such circumstances, no local agency could possibly create an organizational structure that would adequately anticipate an effective response, and it would not be wise to attempt to do so. There are, however, some implications that arise from these discussions that we might consider.

Meaning for Local Law Enforcement

The central thesis of this article is that the most significant issues posed by transnational crime are inherent in the nature of the criminal activity and the structure of interagency relationships that arise to combat that activity. Transnational crimes are for the most part organized and white-collar crimes, and effective responses to the problems of complex white-collar and organized crime require a fundamental retooling of the law enforcement mission. Of course, it is important to note that most local law enforcement agencies do not, [n]or will they ever, have the capacity to respond to these forms of crimes, and so the issues and implications suggested here pertain only to the largest state and local law enforcement agencies covering major population areas. That being said, if serious attention is to be given to these offenses, local law enforcement agencies must concentrate on two central areas. First, local agencies must commit the resources to develop a critical mass of investigators and prosecutors with the knowledge and expertise necessary to mount long-term investigations of technologically and organizationally complex cases. Agencies must be willing to expand beyond the typical recruiting process to bring in accountants, attorneys, and computer technologists who can distinguish illegitimate from legitimate business practices and follow complex paper trails and audits. These individuals must have a knowledge that transcends criminal investigation and criminal procedure and that entails an understanding of organizations and the industrial, commercial, and technological systems and environments that foster criminal behavior. Agencies must also be willing to expend time and resources to investigate and prosecute long-term cases that are organizationally and technologically more complex and in which the determination of harm is more complicated.

Second, local law enforcement agencies must dedicate the time and resources necessary to develop an organizational structure that facilitates, rather than impedes, interorganizational relationships. Indeed, as much, if not more, attention and training should be given to the development of formalized cooperative working relationships with other agencies as given to learning about the criminal behavior itself. Simply put, we tend to view problems of crime as problems of resources and technology, and ignore the fact that much of the inertia in responding to the problems is generated from the intraorganizational and interorganizational relationships of the law enforcement agencies themselves. Efforts should be made to view other agencies as resources rather than as competitors, by establishing formalized channels of consistent communication. Unfortunately, to the extent that such communication is evident between agencies, it is often limited to the reactive solicitation of information with regard to a specific case, crime, organization, or individual. Furthermore, much of what may be called communication is of an informal nature—an officer in one department knows an agent in another office who might be able to shed some light on a particular problem. As Benson and Cullen (1998) have noted, these informal relationships are typically the norm and are often viewed as being more conducive to information sharing than are formal channels. Little attention is given to the development of formalized relationships that involve training, resources, and information sharing about the illegal activity; the environment that produces the opportunity structures for that activity; the mechanisms available for controlling that environment; or the functions, duties, activities, priorities, and problems of the agencies themselves. This is of particular importance to transnational crime because, in all likelihood, transnational criminal behavior will not be limited to one particular jurisdiction within the United States but will include a large number of law enforcement jurisdictions at both the local and federal levels.

One solution to these concerns is to develop multiagency task forces. These task forces can take a variety of forms, but they typically involve some formalized relationships between agencies with specific agreements that pertain to a specific case or type of crime. These task forces can provide a means to pool resources and information and develop a set of guidelines for the coordination of efforts between the agencies. However, these task forces are often viewed skeptically by agencies for several reasons. First, they can be seen as drains on already limited time and resources. Unless there is some direct benefit from their participation, many see task force participation as energy that could be spent more effectively on other matters. As Benson and Cullen (1998) note in their interviews with white-collar crime task forces, the key to these task forces is the steady flow of important and solvable cases that focus attention and provide a set of common problems to work on. Typically, however, task forces are often created only to demonstrate that some action is being taken to address some particular problem without a concerted effort to define the tasks of the group as a whole, the functions of the participating agencies, or even the general organizational mission. Given the demands on resources, it is not enough to simply get together on every third Tuesday to talk about a problem. Unless a set of common, shared problems is established, with clear delineation of responsibility and credit, the tendency is for individual agencies to approach the task force solely for the purposes of seeing what they can get from others, bartering with pieces of information in hopes of getting the better end of the trade. Task forces that move beyond public relations and enter into structured arrangements are far more likely to generate greater stakeholding and increase both formal and informal working relationships.

Areas of Future Research

To discuss areas of future research, I return to my original premise. Although transnational crime is and will be a growing problem for law enforcement at all levels of government, the core problems facing law enforcement that merit our attention are far more fundamental and certainly less titillating than the threat of globe-trotting criminals. How can we hope to understand the impact of transnational bank fraud, money laundering, weapons sales, and the like when we know so little about the nature of those kinds of crimes to begin with? How can we hope to understand the ramifications of international cooperation when we have only a limited understanding of law enforcement interagency cooperation and relationships within our own boundaries? We only need to examine the requests for proposals for research in the areas of crime and criminal justice in the past 10 years to see that white-collar and organized crime continue to be relegated to the periphery of public policy. When these topics occasionally get funded, they tend to focus on specific isolated events rather than the more relevant, but far more complicated, core problems. Instead of focusing on the structure of the most recent ethnic mob, we might want to explore the structure of illicit goods and services and the factors that create the opportunities for the organization of crime in particular markets, regions, and populations, of which ethnicity is one, but perhaps the least, relevant factor. Instead of examining the most recent health care conspiracy and the means by which sentences can be increased to deter it, we might instead examine the health care industry itself and the factors and conditions that facilitate and impede fraudulent behavior, including the relationship between the regulated and the regulators.

The same concerns hold true for issues of interagency relationships. The President's Crime Commission (1967) noted that "jurisdictional disputes have been persistent and troublesome features of local criminal justice and regulatory control systems" (p. 4), yet we often take the approach that turf battles come with the territory, and thus we treat them as mere background noise to a more interesting problem, such as drug enforcement or community policing. Much can be learned from research on organizational behavior, personnel management, and information technology that would be applicable to intraorganizational and interorganizational relationships in law enforcement.

Finally, we often proceed to solutions without fully understanding the nature of the problem. Nowhere is this more evident than in the area of white-collar crime, in which so many theories have been constructed and policies formulated on virtually nonexistent data. Greater attention should be given to epidemiology—to the study of the frequency, incidence, and prevalence of the problems. Although epidemiology began in the medical field as a means of studying communicable diseases, it soon expanded to mass diseases such as cancer, diabetes, and heart ailments. Scientists interested in broader issues of public health soon recognized that injuries are equally susceptible to an epidemiologic method, arguing that events such as train and airplane accidents conform to the same biological laws as do disease processes and that they demonstrate distribution patterns and clustering that may be systematically studied. If we conceive of these white-collar and organized crimes as forms of social or organizational pathology, we can turn our attention to their incidence and search for those things that serve as hosts for the pathos, as well as study the environment that brings the host and the pathos together. The point is that we must have a stronger understanding of the nature and incidence of the problems before we can adequately develop a theory of their origins and solutions, and we must recognize that in doing so, we will not find answers overnight. Hopefully, our new interest in transnational crime will not merely be transitory until something more exciting comes along but instead will offer the opportunity to grapple with both new and old problems and generate systematic attention from a wide range of disciplines and perspectives.

References

Albanese, J. (1996). *Organized crime in America* (3rd ed.). Cincinnati, OH: Anderson.

Benson, M. L., & Cullen, F. T. (1998). *Combatting corporate crime: Local prosecutors at work.* Boston: Northeastern University Press.

Braithwaite, J. (1985). *To punish or persuade: Enforcement of coal mine safety.* Albany: State University of New York Press.

Coe, C., & Ellis, C. (1990). *White-collar crime investigation by state law enforcement agencies.* Unpublished manuscript.

Cressey, D. (1969). *Theft of the nation.* New York: Harper and Row.

Diver, C. (1980). A theory of regulatory enforcement. *Public Policy,* 28, 25–99.

Evans, W. (1966). The organizational set. In J. Thompson (Ed.), *Approaches to organizational design* (pp. 173–191). Pittsburgh, PA: University of Pittsburgh Press.

Geis, G. (1992). White-collar crime: What is it? In K. Schlegel & D. Weisburd (Eds.), *White-collar crime reconsidered* (pp. 31–52). Boston: Northeastern University Press.

Gottfredson, M., & Hirschi, T. (1990). *A general theory of crime.* Stanford, CA: Stanford University Press.

Helmkarnp, J., Ball, R., & Townsend, K. (Eds.). (1996). *Proceedings of the academic workshop: White collar crime definitional dilemma.* Morgantown, WV: National White Collar Crime Center Training and Research Institute.

Ianni, F. A. J. (1972). *A family business.* New York: Russell Sage.

Kelly, R. J. (Ed.). (1986). *Organized crime.* Totowa, NJ: Rowman and Littlefield.

Mann, K. (1992). Procedure rules and information control: Gaining leverage over white-collar crime. In K. Schlegel & D. Weisburd (Eds.), *White-collar crime reconsidered* (pp. 332–351). Boston: Northeastern University Press.

President's Commission on Law Enforcement and Administration of Justice. (1967). *The challenge of crime in a free society.*

Reiss, A. J., Jr. (1984). Selecting strategies of social control over organizational life. In K. Hawkins & J. M. Thomas (Eds.), *Enforcing regulation* (pp.23–35). Boston: Kluwer-Nijhoff.

Reiss, A. J., Jr., & Tonry, M. (1993). Organizational crime. In A. J. Reiss, Jr. & M. Tonry (Eds.), *Beyond the law: Crime in complex organizations* (pp. 1–10). Chicago: University of Chicago Press.

Reuter, P. (1983). *Disorganized crime: The economics of the visible hand.* Cambridge, MA: MIT Press.

Schlegel, K. (1994). *Securities lawbreaking: The enforcement response* (Final Report to the National Institute of Justice). Unpublished report.

Scholz, J. T. (1984). Cooperation, deterrence and the ecology of regulatory enforcement. *Law and Society Review, 18,* 179.

Schrager, L. S., & Short, J. F., Jr. (1978). Toward a sociology of organizational crime. *Social Problems,* 25, 407–419.

Shapiro, S. (1984). *Wayward capitalists: Target of the Securities and Exchange Commission.* New Haven, CT: Yale University Press.

——. (1990). Collaring the crime, not the criminal: Liberating the concept of white-collar crime. *American Sociological Review, 55,* 346.

Smith, D. (1975). *The mafia mystique.* New York: Basic Books.

——. (1982). White-collar crime, organized crime, and the business community: Resolving a crisis in criminological theory. In P. Wickman & T. Daily (Eds.), *White-collar and economic crime* (pp. 108–132). Lexington, MA: Lexington Books.

U.S. Department of Justice. (1987). *Special report: White-collar crime.* Washington, DC: Author.

Vaughan, D. (1996). *The Challenger launch decision: Risky technology, culture, and deviance at NASA.* Chicago: University of Chicago Press.

Weisburd, D., Wheeler, S., Waring, E., & Bode, N. (1991). *Crimes of the middle classes.* New Haven, CT: Yale University Press.

Unit II

Discussion Questions

1. What are the elements of a police crackdown program? Describe proactive policing.
2. If you were a chief of police, would you institute a crackdown program? Why or why not?
3. What is community policing?
4. What impact has community policing had on American law enforcement and on American communities? How has it changed core policing activities?
5. What has been the impact of community policing on law enforcement from an organizational context?
6. Who should have the prime responsibility for bringing peace and tranquility to a neighborhood? What role does the law enforcement community have in achieving this end?
7. What responsibility rests with the law enforcement community regarding such social problems as racism, poverty, homelessness, and unemployment?
8. What type of education and training should law enforcement officers receive so that they can become more effective community/neighborhood problem solvers?
9. What are some typical activities in which a community-based foot patrol officer should engage?
10. Develop a research methodology that could be used to shed more light on the foot-patrol issue.
11. What has been the impact of the community policing movement on police culture? What other factors impact police culture?
12. What is expectancy motivation theory and how is it useful in explaining variations in police officers' problem-solving behavior?
13. In light of Terrill and McCluskey's findings, what is a "problem" officer? What should be done to respond to "problem" officers?
14. Some believe that court-ordered restrictions placed on the use of deadly force have "handcuffed" law enforcement officers. Do you agree or disagree?
15. How should law enforcement personnel be trained so that they might better respond to our changing society?
16. How can the law enforcement community positively respond to the challenges of transnational organized crime?
17. What can be done to enhance law enforcement agency cooperation at the federal, state, and local levels?
18. What law enforcement programs or policies should be implemented to achieve a significant community crime-prevention effect?
19. Design a research evaluation effort to determine whether the new law enforcement programs or policies you propose would positively impact the actual crime perpetration rate. ✦

Unit III

American Courts

The most important decisions of the justice process are made in the courtroom. This complex social milieu defies simple description, due in large part to the many varying interests that collide in court. Judges, prosecutors, defense attorneys, defendants, victims, jurors, probation personnel, court administrative personnel, law enforcement personnel, and media representatives all have their own agendas. Understanding the operations of the court becomes all the more complex when we realize that many of these courtroom players are elected officials or work for elected officials, which politicizes the process.

Traditionally, the courtroom is viewed as the stage for a legal joust between competing parties. In reality, however, adversarial relationships are generally discouraged and out-of-court settlements are the rule. At present, roughly 90 percent of all criminal convictions result from guilty pleas rather than trials.

Pluralism

Pluralism is the overriding feature of the American courts. Each state has its own independent court system. In addition, the federal government has a court system. There is at least one United States District Court seated in every state. Several states have more than one: there are four U.S. District Courts in the states of California, Texas, and New York, for example. A total of ninety-four district courts and 646 district court judgeships are spread out over the fifty states, the District of Columbia, and overseas U.S. territories.

The number of judges in each federal district court varies from one in Guam and the Mariana Islands to twenty-eight in the New York Southern District. All federal judges are appointed by the president and confirmed by the Senate. This appointment and confirmation process takes time and generally has political overtones. As a result, at any given moment there are a number of district court judgeship vacancies, a sizable number in recent years. This has had a negative impact on federal court operations. U.S. District Court judges serve for life and can only be removed by a congressional impeachment proceeding.

Every U.S. District Court has a number of U.S. magistrates assigned to handle cases in the district. Their role has expanded tremendously in recent years. There are 429 full-time U.S. magistrates (called magistrate judges), and seventy-nine part-time magistrates. U.S. magistrates are appointed by the district court and serve an eight-year term. Most U.S. District Courts also have a number of "senior" or retired judges who serve part and even full time. At present, there are more than 350 judges with senior status currently working in the U.S. District Courts nationwide.

U.S. District Courts are assigned to handle violations of federal law, appeals from state courts, and a variety of civil cases. Currently, the U.S. District Courts handle in excess of 275,000 civil cases and over 50,000 criminal cases a year. In addition, the U.S. District Courts are also responsible for bankruptcy issues, and handle more than 1.4 million such filings a year.

There are thirteen United States Courts of Appeals and 179 judges as of this writing. One Court of Appeals handles cases in the District of Columbia, another serves as the appellate court for the federal circuit, and the rest are organized on a regional basis. As with U.S. District Courts, the number of judges in each of the U.S. Courts of Appeals varies from six in the First Circuit to twenty-eight in the Ninth Circuit. Like district court judges, appellate court judges are also appointed by the president and confirmed by the Senate. Politics does have a bearing on the appointment process. Appellate court judges serve for life. The U.S. Appellate Courts handle difficult and complex appeals, but do not retry cases. They currently handle more than 50,000 cases a year.

The U.S. Supreme Court is the highest court in the country. There are nine justices on the Supreme Court. The Chief Justice at this writing is William H. Rhenquist. He, like his eight associates, was appointed by the president and confirmed by the Senate. All Supreme Court justices are appointed for life. To date, 110 men and two women have served on the U.S. Supreme Court.

The Supreme Court hears appeals coming up through the federal and state systems. Each year, the Supreme Court receives 7,000 to 8,000 requests to have cases heard, but certiorari is granted to (the court agrees to hear) just 200 to 300 cases. Four judges must agree to hear a case before certiorari is granted. Even then, a complete, signed opinion of the Court will be prepared in only seventy-five to 100 of the cases heard each year. The number of cases granted cert and, as a result, the number of signed opinions, has been steadily dropping in the past few years.

There are currently some 17,000 state and local courts which handle in excess of 120 million cases a year. The courts can be divided into these five categories:

1. *Minor trial courts.* Minor trial courts are the workhorses of the American criminal justice system, handling upwards of 90 percent of all criminal cases. They are often called county courts or municipal courts, and generally handle misdemeanor cases (including most traffic and parking violations), preliminary hearings, initial appearances/arraignments, and minor civil cases.

2. *Major trial courts.* Major trial courts are commonly called district, circuit, or superior courts. Their jurisdiction covers several counties. Major trial courts hear major civil cases, felony cases, and appeals from minor trial courts.

3. *Courts of appeals.* Courts of appeals hear cases on appeal from the trial courts in a given state. There are no juries present, no evidence is introduced, and no witnesses testify. A panel of judges listens to attorneys who present arguments regarding various points of law.

4. *Supreme courts.* These are the highest tribunals in the system. Their jurisdiction is limited to hearing appeals from lower state courts. Once again, no juries are present, no witnesses testify, and no evidence is introduced. Rather, points of law are argued by competing attorneys.

5. *Miscellaneous courts.* Every state has developed a court system to meet its specific needs. A wide array of judicial bodies exists, each unique to the state or community. Rulings in these courts are all subject to decisions of the State Supreme Court where they are located, and ultimately to the United States Supreme Court. Courts that fall into this category include such entities as small claims courts, juvenile courts, courts of industrial relations, tax courts, customs courts, and copyright courts.

Juries

Trial by jury is one of the most interesting features of the American justice system. Consider the following excerpt taken from a report prepared by the Bureau of Justice Statistics (1988, 86):

> Defendants are entitled to trial by a jury of their peers. All states require 12-member juries in capital cases; six states permit less than 12-member juries in felony trials.
>
> Names of prospective jurors are selected from lists intended to make jury pools representative of the community. In 16 states the voter registration list is the sole source of names for jury service. Maine; Las Vegas, Nevada; and 62 of Alabama's 67 counties use the driver's license list as the sole source of jury coverage. The use of merged voter and driver's license lists is either permitted or required by 25 states and the District of Columbia.
>
> Most states have statutory exemptions from jury service. The most common statutory exemptions are for undue hardship or public necessity, for personal bad health, or for persons serving as judicial officers. Many states also exempt specific occupations such as attorneys, doctors, dentists, clergy, elected officials, police officers, firemen, teachers, and sole proprietors of businesses. Twenty-seven states now have limited or no class exemptions from jury service.
>
> An estimated 15 percent of American adults have ever been called for jury duty. According to the Center for Jury Studies, the limited number of adults who have served as jurors results from such factors as:
>
> - the age limits on prospective jurors set by many states.
> - the use of voter registration lists that represent only a portion of eligible voters (67 percent at the 1980 presidential election).
> - replacement of names of jurors into the jury pool at too-frequent intervals.
> - the number of exemptions to service permitted by law or granted by the court.
>
> The maximum period of service required of a juror varies by state:
>
> - six states (Alabama, Florida, Louisiana, Mississippi, North Carolina, and South Carolina) have terms of service of one week.
> - fourteen states limit terms to two weeks.
> - eight states do not specify terms.
> - Vermont has the longest statutory limit with a two-year term.
>
> Innovations have eased the burden of being a juror:
>
> - twenty-seven states have at least one jurisdiction where a juror is called on for only one day to be available to sit in a single trial. The District of Columbia has this same system. Only if selected for a trial would a juror serve more than one day, until again randomly selected for jury service. It has been estimated that 11 percent of the U.S. population resides in one-day/one-trial jurisdictions.
> - courts in 50 states (including all courts in two states) use a juror call-in system. In these states jurors can dial a number to learn whether their attendance is needed on a particular day during their term of service.
>
> All states and the federal government pay trial jurors. . . . Thirty-eight states [also] pay for travel ranging from two cents per mile in New Jersey to 20 cents per mile in Hawaii. Some jurisdictions also require employers to pay the salaries of employees while serving on jury duty.

Prosecution

A key player in the courtroom is the prosecutor. Consider the following excerpt taken from the aforementioned Bureau of Justice Statistics Report (1988, 71–73):

> The prosecutor provides the link between the law enforcement and adjudicatory processes. The American prosecutor is unique in the world. First, the American prosecutor is a public prosecutor representing the people in matters of criminal law. Historically, European societies viewed crimes as wrongs against an individual whose claims could be pressed through private prosecution. Second, the American prosecutor is usually a local official, reflecting the development of autonomous local governments in the colonies. Finally, as an elected official, the local American prosecutor is responsible to the voters.

Prosecution is the function of representing the people in criminal cases. After the police arrest a suspect, the prosecutor coordinates the government's response to crime—from the initial screening, when the prosecutor decides whether or not to press charges, through trial. In some instances, it continues through sentencing with the presentation of sentencing recommendations.

Prosecutors have been accorded much discretion in carrying out their responsibilities. They make many of the decisions that determine whether a case will proceed through the criminal justice process.

Prosecution is predominantly a state and local function. Prosecuting officials include state, district, county, prosecuting and commonwealth attorneys; corporation counsels; circuit solicitors; attorneys general; and U.S. attorneys. Prosecution is carried out by more than 8,000 state, county, municipal, and township prosecution agencies (Bureau of Justice Statistics 1988). In all but five states, local prosecutors are elected officials. Many small jurisdictions engage a part-time prosecutor who also maintains a private law practice. In some areas police share the charging responsibility of local prosecutors. Prosecutors in urban jurisdictions often have offices staffed by many full-time assistants. Each state has an office of the attorney general, which has jurisdiction over all matters involving state law but generally, unless specifically requested, is not involved in local prosecution. Federal prosecution is the responsibility of 93 U.S. attorneys who are appointed by the President subject to confirmation by the Senate.

The decision to charge is generally a function of the prosecutor. Results of a 1981 survey of police and prosecution agencies in localities of over 100,000 indicate that police file initial charges in half the jurisdictions surveyed. This arrangement, sometimes referred to as the police court, is not commonly found in the larger, urban areas that account for most of the UCR Index crime. Usually, once an arrest is made and the case is referred to the prosecutor, most prosecutors screen cases to see if they merit prosecution. The prosecutor can refuse to prosecute, for example, because of insufficient evidence. The decision to charge is not usually reviewable by any other branch of government.

Some prosecutors accept almost all cases for prosecution; others screen out many cases. Some prosecutors have screening units designed to reject cases at the earliest possible point. Others tend to accept most arrests, more of which are dismissed by judges later in the adjudication process. Most prosecutor offices fall somewhere between these two extremes.

Arrest disposition patterns in 16 jurisdictions range from 0 to 45 percent of arrests rejected for prosecution. Jurisdictions with high rejection rates generally were found to have lower rates of dismissal at later stages of the criminal process. Conversely, jurisdictions that accepted most or all arrests usually had high dismissal rates.

Prosecutorial screen practices are of several distinct types. Several studies conclude that screening decisions consider:

- evidentiary factors.
- the views of the prosecutor on key criminal justice issues.
- the political and social environment in which the prosecutor functions.
- the resource constraints and organization of prosecutorial operations.

Jacoby's study confirmed the presence of at least three policies that affect the screening decision:

- Legal sufficiency—an arrest is accepted for prosecution if, on routine review of the arrest, the minimum legal elements of a case are present.
- System efficiency—arrests are disposed as quickly as possible by the fastest means possible, which are rejections, dismissals, and pleas.
- Trial sufficiency—the prosecutor accepts only those arrests for which, in his or her view, there is sufficient evidence to convict in court.
- Once charges are filed, a case may be terminated only by official action. The prosecutor can drop a case after making efforts to prosecute (*nolle prosequi*), or the court can dismiss the case on motion of the defense on grounds that the government has failed to establish that the defendant committed the crime charged. The prosecution also

may recommend dismissal, or the judge may take the initiative in dismissing a case. A dismissal is an official action of the court.

What are the most common reasons for rejection or dismissal? Many criminal cases are rejected or dismissed because of

- *insufficient evidence* that results from a failure to find sufficient physical evidence that links the defendant to the offense.
- *witness problems* that arise, for example, when a witness fails to appear, gives unclear or inconsistent statements, is reluctant to testify, is unsure of the identity of the offender or where a prior relationship may exist between the victim/witness and offender.
- *the interests of justice,* wherein the prosecutor decides not to prosecute certain types of offenses, particularly those that violate the letter but not the spirit of the law (for example, offenses involving insignificant amounts of property damage).
- *due process problems* that involve violations of the constitutional requirements for seizing evidence and for questioning the accused.
- *a plea on another case,* for example, when the accused is charged in several cases and the prosecutor agrees to drop one or more of the cases in exchange for a plea of guilty on another case.
- *pretrial diversion* that occurs when the prosecutor and the court agree to drop charges when the accused successfully meets the conditions for diversion, such as completion of a treatment program.
- *referral for other prosecution,* such as when there are other offenses, perhaps of a more serious nature, in a different jurisdiction, or deferral to federal prosecution.

Defense Counsel

Another unique feature of the American justice system is the constitutional right of individuals who are accused of a crime to the assistance of legal counsel. The following excerpt is from Robert L. Spangenberg et al. of Abt Associates, Inc., *BJS National Criminal Defense Systems Study,* October 1986, reprinted by the Bureau of Justice Statistics (1988, 74–75):

> The Sixth Amendment of the Constitution provides the accused the right to be assisted by counsel. The defense attorney's function is to protect the defendant's legal rights and to be the defendant's advocate in the adversary process. Defendants have the right to defend themselves, but most prefer to be represented by a specialist in the law. Relatively few members of the legal profession specialize in criminal law, but lawyers who normally handle other types of legal matters may take criminal cases.
>
> The right to the assistance of counsel is more than the right to hire a lawyer. Supreme Court decisions in *Gideon v. Wainwright* (1963) and *Argersinger v. Hamlin* (1972) established that the right to an attorney may not be frustrated by lack of means. For both felonies and misdemeanors for which jail or prison can be the penalty, the state must provide an attorney to any accused person who is indigent.
>
> The institutional response to this constitutional mandate is still evolving as states experiment with various ways to provide legal counsel for indigent defendants.
>
> A defendant is entitled to representation by counsel at every critical step in the criminal justice process. The Sixth Amendment provides the right to counsel in criminal prosecution but does not specify what steps or proceedings are included. Through the years the Supreme Court has held that a defendant has the right to counsel at such critical steps as police interrogation, police lineup, preliminary hearing, and appeal, as well as probation and parole revocation proceedings.
>
> Assigned counsel systems continue to dominate defender systems. About 60 percent of U.S. counties used assigned counsel in 1983 (down from 72 percent in 1973); 34 percent, public defenders; and 6 percent, contract attorneys.
>
> Each state adopts its own approach to providing counsel for indigents. Among the states
>
> - some provide counsel to all indigents charged with a misdemeanor; other states provide counsel only to those for whom a jail or prison term is possible.

- some assess the cost of an attorney against the defendant and collect for it in installments after the trial; others provide counsel completely free of charge.

These options are often used in combination.

Standards and procedures vary for determining indigency. Estimates of indigency rates from the National Indigent Defense Survey indicate that more than 40 percent of all defendants charged with felonies are classified as indigent even though the states use different levels of income to determine indigency. Indigency rates for defendants charged with a misdemeanor are much lower because the eligibility criteria for misdemeanors are more restrictive in many states.

Organization and funding of indigent defense programs also vary among the states. Indigent defense

- is completely funded in 18 states and the District of Columbia.
- is partially funded in 22 states.
- is funded by the county, sometimes assisted by municipalities, the federal government, and private grants in 11 states.

In 33 states indigent defense services are organized at the county level alone or in combination with a statewide system or with judicial districts; 13 states have statewide organizations only; four states rely on judicial districts.

Case assignments to attorneys representing indigents usually are made within 48 hours of arrest. Traditionally, in many jurisdictions attorneys who provide indigent defense services were not appointed until formal arraignment. The time between arrest and arraignment may exceed 30 days in some counties. A third of all counties surveyed in the last national survey of public defense services reported that counsel was appointed within one day of arrest. More than half of all sample counties (58 percent) reported appointment within 48 hours of arrest.

Early representation is most likely to occur in counties serviced by public defenders; 39 percent of all public defender counties reported that representation was provided within 24 hours; 33 percent of counties serviced by assigned counsel and 12 percent of counties served by contract systems reported similar representation.

Who defends indigents?

Public defender programs are public or private nonprofit organizations with full- or part-time salaried staff. Within the public defender classification, there are two categories—statewide and local. Under statewide systems, one person, designated by statutes of the state as the public defender, is charged with developing and maintaining a system of representation for each county in the state. Often a governing board shares responsibility for program operation. By contrast, most local public defenders operate autonomously and do not have a central administrator.

Local public defenders operate autonomously in 32 states and the District of Columbia, and 15 states have a state-administered system. Public defender systems are the dominant form in 43 of the 50 largest counties and, overall, serve 68 percent of the nation's population.

Assigned counsel systems involve the appointment by the courts of private attorneys as needed from a list of available attorneys. There are two main types of assigned counsel systems: *Ad hoc assigned counsel systems* in which individual private attorneys are appointed by individual judges and provide representation on a case-by-case basis. *Coordinated systems* have an administrator who oversees the appointment of counsel and develops a set of standards and guidelines for program administration; coordinated systems are sometimes indistinguishable from public defender programs.

Ad hoc systems represent about 75 percent of all assigned counsel programs. The others are part of a coordinated system of indigent defense. Though such counsel systems operate in almost two-thirds of the counties, they predominate in small counties with fewer than 50,000 residents.

Contract systems involve government contracting with individual attorneys, bar associations, or private law firms to provide services for a specified dollar amount. County agencies are usually responsible for the award of defender services contracts, and they are now frequently awarded to individual practitioners as opposed to law firms or other organized groups.

Contract systems are a relatively new way to provide defense services. They are found in small counties (less than 50,000) and very large ones. They vary considerably in organization, funding, and size. In about a fourth of the counties reporting them, they serve as an overflow for public defender offices and also represent codefendants in cases of conflict of interest.

Problems in the Courts

The courts have come under intense criticism in recent years for a variety of reasons, including political aspects of the judicial selection process, inadequate legal representation for defendants, difficulties with the evolving concept of the jury, inappropriate plea bargaining practices, and disparate sentencing. Plea bargaining is considered a particularly controversial aspect of the justice process. It has come to be seen by many as an unsavory practice that is only tolerated because of the huge backlog of cases.

Perhaps the most pressing problem facing the courts today is case overload, which is reaching crisis proportions, particularly in the federal courts. Case complexity and a sharp rise in civil litigation in the past decade have been the primary factors contributing to this problem. A number of reforms have been proposed and are currently being implemented, including the adoption at the federal level of a modified "English rule," where, within some bounds and restrictions, the losing side in a civil suit must pay the legal fees of the winner. It is hoped that this will reduce the number of nuisance or frivolous suits that jam the courtrooms. In a national survey of judges conducted in 1988, 39 percent indicated that they needed stress-management training to help them deal with job tensions caused by their heavy workload ("Too Many Continuances" 1988). The situation has deteriorated since then.

Another issue of concern that has been on the public agenda for some time is sentencing disparity. While justice demands similar sentences for similar crimes, the data clearly reveal that this has not been the case in the American courtroom. As a result, a number of jurisdictions (17 states and the federal government as of this writing) have moved toward determinate sentencing laws. Federal sentencing guidelines went into effect on November 1, 1987. The federal guidelines were immediately challenged in court, but were upheld by the U.S. Supreme Court. A number of states have also adopted various determinate/presumptive/prescriptive sentencing guideline models (Minnesota, Oregon, Pennsylvania, Washington). There is some evidence that such sentencing models achieve more uniform and socioeconomically neutral sentences. There have been a number of collateral impacts, however, and consequently the matter is subject to a significant measure of debate. Many practitioners and scholars are actively calling for the abolition of such models, particularly the federal guidelines (Tonry 1993).

International Courts

While this text is focused on the American system, there is a need to make mention of a tier of courts that are fast evolving into entities of some power—the so-called "world courts."

In the aftermath of World War II, the United Nations began to discuss the need to create a number of permanent international judicial tribunals. The idea of a "world court," and international law in general, was first developed by Hugo Grotius in 1625 in his book, *De Jure Belli ac Pacis.* He noted then, as we note to this day, that international law is custom, tradition, and common consent rather than hard and definitive substantive code. He further recognized that a world court would not possess the mechanisms necessary to enforce its rulings. Despite these limitations, and drawing upon the experience of the League of Nations–established Court of International Justice which sat from 1921 until 1939, the United Nations moved forward with its plans to create a world court, establishing the officially titled International Court of Justice in late 1945.

This court currently meets in The Hague, in the Netherlands. It is composed of fifteen judges elected to a nine-year term by the United Nations General Assembly. The judges act as independent magistrates and do not represent any particular government.

In some ways, the World Court has been more of a symbolic and ceremonial entity, used to sway public opinion and allow for international diplomatic positioning and posturing.

There is evidence, however, that the World Court is gaining in stature of late. The World Court, like other courts, is an evolving entity that, with the emergence of the European Union, may actually become a greater force in the world in the twenty-first century.

The real challenge is to establish, clarify, and articulate points of international law. At this point, the World Court defines international law as principles reflected in international conventions, international custom, general principles of law recognized by civilized nations, judicial decisions, and writings of the most highly qualified experts on international law.

In addition to the World Court, which deals primarily with criminal matters, there are two other international courts that also meet in the Netherlands: the Permanent Court of Arbitration, which deals with civil matters, and the International Criminal Tribunal, or the so-called War Crimes Tribunal.

* * *

The role of the courts, and particularly the federal courts, continues to expand in this country. We live in an era of judicial activism. The courts are no longer limiting themselves to handling individual criminal and civil cases; increasingly they are making public policy decisions as well. Some argue that the courts have extended their powers far beyond what the constitution set forth, while others believe that such activities are the natural product of an evolving nation. As the courts' influence continues to grow, in time they may well become the most powerful of the three branches of government.

References and Further Reading Materials

Abraham, Henry J. 1998. *The Judicial Process.* New York, NY: Oxford University Press.

Abraham, Henry J. and Barbara A. Perry. 1994. *Freedom and the Court.* New York, NY: Oxford University Press.

Argersinger v. Hamlin 407 U.S. 25 (1972).

Austin, James. 1998. "Sentencing Guidelines: A State Perspective," *National Institute of Justice Journal,* March 1998, pp. 25–26.

Boland, Barbara. 1983. *The Prosecution of Felony Arrests.* Washington, DC: U.S. Government Printing Office.

Bureau of Justice Statistics. 1988. *Justice Agencies in the United States, 1986.* Washington, DC: United States Department of Justice.

——. 1988. *Report to the Nation on Crime and Justice.* Washington, DC: United States Department of Justice.

Champion, Dean. 2001. *The American Dictionary of Criminal Justice: Key Terms and Major Court Cases.* Los Angeles, CA: Roxbury.

Gideon v. Wainwright 372 U.S. 335 (1963).

McGuire, Kevin T. 2001. *Understanding the U.S. Supreme Court: Cases and Controversies.* Boston, MA: McGraw-Hill.

Murphy, Walter, C. Herman Pritchett, and Lee Epstein. 2002. *Courts, Judges and Politics.* Boston, MA: McGraw-Hill.

Neubauer, David W. 2002. *America's Courts and the Criminal Justice System.* Belmont, CA: Wadsworth.

Samaha, Joel. 2002. *Criminal Procedure.* Belmont, CA: Wadsworth.

Schwartz, Bernard. 1993. *A History of the Supreme Court.* New York, NY: Oxford.

Spangenberg, Robert L. and Tessa Schwartz. 1994. "The Indigent Defense Crisis Is Chronic," *American Bar Association Journal on Criminal Justice,* Vol. 9, pp. 12–21.

Tonry, Michael. 1993. "The Failure of the U.S. Sentencing Commission's Guidelines," *Crime and Delinquency,* Vol. 39, pp. 131–149.

"Too Many Continuances #1 Factor in Court Delays, Survey Finds." 1988. *Criminal Justice Newsletter,* November 15, 1988, p. 7F. ✦

Chapter 15

The Origins and Development of Courts

Richard E. Messick

M*essick discusses the development of modern courts by examining their historical and cultural roots. Although political, social, and economic forces shaped different court systems over time and across cultures, an "element of universality" does appear in different societies' approaches to the fundamental role of a court: to resolve conflict in such a way that constrains the human desire for revenge.*

The oldest surviving courtroom drama in world literature closes with the presiding judge appealing to the parties to accept the court's decision and end their pursuit of revenge:

> Fair trial, fair judgment . . .
> Evidence which issued clear as day. . .
> . . . [Q]uench your anger; let not indignation rain
> Pestilence on our soil, corroding every seed
> Till the whole land is sterile desert. . .
> . . . [C]alm this black and swelling wrath.
>
> —Aeschylus, *The Eumenides*, 458 BCE

The plea succeeds, and the play concludes with the restoration of social peace and the promise of prosperity.

The drama's enduring appeal rests in large measure on the solution it offers to a problem all societies face. Without some kind of machinery to settle disputes, the only recourse open to those who seek justice is revenge. But the taking of revenge can spark an endless cycle of violence as first one side and then the other retaliates. The adjudication of a dispute by a court of law offers an alternative, one where facts are carefully assayed and self-defense and such other considerations as may excuse or explain the conduct are reviewed. In short, courts are a way to resolve disputes justly, and as the *Eumenides* shows, justice can form the basis of a lasting social order.

Aeschylus is not the only one to locate the origins of courts in society's need to contain the impulse for revenge.[1] The authors of the *Gongyang Commentary* to the *Spring and Autumn Annals*, a 4th century BCE (Before the Common Era) text on law in China, make a similar point in analyzing a son's responsibility when the state has unjustly executed his father. While they concede that when the execution was unjust a loyal son must revenge his father's death, if the execution was justified, they argue that the taking of revenge can lead to chaos, what they term "the way of the thrusting sword." Accordingly, they conclude that the legal system must provide a method for determining the truth or justice of state action.

Although the *Eumenides* suggests that courts emerge suddenly and fully formed to answer society's need to contain the impulse for revenge, in fact they develop gradually, reflecting a society's own development. When society is a small, close knit collection of kin, informal, low-cost methods of intervention suffice to resolve conflicts. But as the population grows and trade expands, group ties weaken. As these ties lessen, the means of intervention grow progressively more formal.

The rise of a court system parallels, and also signals, the rise of formal government. A decision of a court represents a collective response to a dispute. But these decisions are only enforceable when society has become sufficiently cohesive that it can act collectively in a firm and decisive manner. This is, of course, one way to mark the appearance of government itself, and the close connection between courts and government has not escaped notice. The *dharmasastra* attributed to Narada, a principal source of Hindu law, asserts that government is created to put an end to disputes among the citizenry, and almost two millennia later James Madison wrote that no political system deserved to be called a government unless it had a court system. Modern scholars suggest that while a certain degree of state power is a prerequisite to the establishment of courts, once created courts help consolidate and extend this power.[2]

Negotiation and Mediation

The simplest means for resolving disputes is mediation. An elder, community leader, or other figure the disputants respect, will try to help them find common ground but will have no power to impose a solution. A pure negotiator presents each side's position to the other while a mediator can suggest solutions of her own. In either case, the only requirement is that the solution be acceptable to both parties.

Simplicity and low cost explain why negotiation and mediation are found in every society. Unlike judges, mediators and negotiators do not have to sort out conflicting legal or factual claims. Nor do they have to prepare a written opinion showing how the settlement conforms to the law. Hence, unlike judges, they require no specialized training or expertise. Negotiation and mediation do not require enforcement machinery either. Compliance is assured because the settlement rests on both parties' consent.

Perhaps the first step in the evolution of more complex dispute resolution mechanisms occurs when social norms arise to complement mediation or negotiation. Since a mediated or negotiated settlement is most often one that splits the difference between the parties, they each have an incentive to overstate their claim. An individual suffering $50 in damages is more likely to be fully compensated if he claims his loss was $100. In the extreme case, a person may falsely claim a loss or injury in the expectation a compromise settlement will yield at least something. Chinese society very early developed a norm against such over-claiming. Confucian moralists taught that when a conflict arose, the person less assertive in pressing a claim or who sacrifices his interests to restore harmony acquired the greater moral status.

While a mediator is free to suggest any settlement the parties can agree upon, in virtually all societies norms appear that reflect a consensus on what is a reasonable settlement under the circumstances. Tacitus, the first century Roman historian, reports that among German tribes a murder could be compromised by the payment of a certain number of cattle or sheep to the victim's family, and the Celtic cultures of Wales and Ireland also had guidelines for compromising homicides. Ethnographic studies of more contemporary tribal societies describe similar practices. The Nuer of Sudan have rules that specify the compensation generally required to settle cases of murder, bodily injury, adultery, and other wrongs.[3] While such norms reflect moral judgments, they serve a practical end as well. By providing the mediator a point of reference in discussions with the two sides they reduce the cost of reaching a settlement.

But even when underpinned by supportive social norms, mediation and negotiation have their limitations. There is nothing to compel a party to a dispute to settle it. A bargaining impasse is always a possibility and with it the threat of private warfare. As an early code of the Anglo-Saxons put it, one accused of wrongdoing can either "buy off the spear or bear it."[4] Nor do even the most powerful social norms assure conflicts will always be settled. Deviants are present in all societies.

Imposing Settlements

A significant step in the development of a court system comes when a society moves beyond simply urging the parties to settle their dispute and begins to pressure one side or the other to agree to a resolution. The shift may be very subtle. In tribal societies mediators may suggest that a failure to accept a compromise carries the risk of offending supernatural forces. Public opinion may also be mobilized. In Zambia, if the village elders appointed to mediate a dispute conclude one party is unreasonably refusing to settle, the community will ostracize the individual.[5]

A more formal method for exerting public control over disputants is described in the *Eumenides*, and similar methods were employed in the ancient Near East, the Carolingian empire, and medieval France. The process was initiated by one who was the target of a self-help remedy. In the *Eumenides* this was the person sought by the forces of revenge. In ancient Babylon, it could be a debtor fearful a creditor was about to seize his property to satisfy the obligation. The initiating party would request a declaration that under the circumstances self-help was unjustified. If the tribunal hearing the case agreed, the target of the expected attack was entitled to society's protection. If it disagreed, the community would not interfere with the use of private force to secure redress.

Elements of a Court

The seeds of a modern court are visible in tribunals like these. Rather than urging or pressuring a party to accept a resolution, society is now imposing one. Nor is the solution it is imposing arbitrarily chosen. In the *Eumenides,* the tribunal exonerated the individual sought by the forces of revenge after concluding that his actions were what Greek society would have expected of any one who confronted similar circumstances. Besides grounding their judgments in accepted norms or customs, these tribunals often had means, however primitive, for sorting out conflicting factual assertions.

These three elements—(i) state-backed decisions that are (ii) reached after a fact-finding process and that are (iii) grounded in prevailing norms—are what distinguish courts from mediation and other non-state dispute resolution mechanisms.[6] Where a court differs from a tribunal like that described in the Eumenides is that enforcement is taken out of the hands of private individuals entirely. Had the tribunal there found the killing complained of was unjustified, it would have left it up to the forces of revenge to retaliate as they saw fit. By contrast, with a court responsibility for punishment always rests with the state.

When a formal court system appears is to some degree definitional. Some stress that decisions must be the product of reasoned argument.[7] Under this view, until the taking of testimony and the examination of documents replace ordeals, trials by combat, and other irrational means for determining facts, the institution is at best a prototypical court. Other definitions emphasize that for a court to exist, it must be presided over by a judge who is independent of the other branches of government.[8] If this is the criterion, courts do not appear in a number of industrialized countries until the mid-20th century, and many developing nations are still awaiting their appearance.

Reflecting early government's need to preserve social peace, the first disputes a nation's courts, or court-like institutions, hear almost always involve those that have the potential to spark private warfare. These generally arise from criminal acts—homicide, assault, theft, and so forth. In return for providing crime victims with an alternative to private revenge, governments

Litigation: A View from Ancient China

In 536 BCE, Tzu-ch'an, prime minister of the Chinese state of Cheng, had the law inscribed on a set of bronze tripod vessels. But many Chinese feared that once citizens could determine the law for themselves, litigation, followed by the collapse of public order, would surely ensue. In a letter to Prime Minister Tzu, an official of a neighboring state explains why:

> [W]hen the people know what the penalties are, they lose their fear of authority and acquire a contentiousness which causes them to make their appeal to the written words [of the penal laws], on the chance that this will bring them success [in court cases]. . . . As soon as the people know the grounds upon which to conduct disputation, they will reject the [unwritten] accepted ways of behavior (*li*) and make their appeal to the written word, arguing to the last over the tip of an awl or knife. Disorderly litigation will multiply and bribery will become current.[1]

Note

1. Bodde & Morris, LAW IN IMPERIAL CHINA 16 (1967).

typically demand that victims eschew the use of private force altogether. Revenge was outlawed in China in the 2nd century, and the first national legal code to appear in Europe after the fall of the Roman Empire, the *Liber Augustalis* of Norman Sicily, permitted self-help only to ward off an immediate attack.

In some societies, courts never expand much beyond hearing criminal cases. In China, at least initially, few disputes over contracts, property rights, and other non-criminal matters were brought to court. The Chinese aversion to litigation is legendary (see "Litigation: a view from ancient China") and is most often explained by Confucian principles stressing social harmony. Mediation, facilitated by norms such as that against over-claiming, provided a substitute for lawsuits, although recent archival research suggests that by the late Qing era this substitute was not as effective as once thought.[9]

Private and State Courts

While norms against resort to formal, state-run courts may not be as powerful elsewhere as they are in China, other substitutes for state-supervised litigation exist. In medieval Europe the Roman Catholic Church operated an elaborate network of courts, and many towns, merchant associations, and large landowners also ran tribunals that competed with state-run courts.[10] The "judges" were privately named, and court fees and fines paid to the tribunal's operator. A similar situation seems to have obtained in ancient India where townspeople and merchants and artisans also ran court-like institutions (*pûgas and srenî*).[11] Community pressure, the threat of ostracism or excommunication, and other informal enforcement mechanisms ensured that the litigants would appear and comply with the tribunals' decisions.

A More Efficient Remedy for Protecting Possession

For most of the 12th century England suffered from a crime wave brought on by a bitter civil war. Roving bands of marauders would descend upon an estate and forcibly eject its occupants. The bandits might stay for years, exploiting the serfs and livestock attached to the land.

While the dispossessed could appeal to the court of their feudal overlord, this remedy often provided little relief. If the occupiers were from outside the area, the court was without jurisdiction. Even if the court could hear the case, a defendant had many ways of delaying it. He could, for example, claim illness and take to bed, which automatically postponed the trial for a year. Nor did trial guarantee the land would be restored to its rightful possessor, for the matter was decided by combat.

Somewhere around 1166 the royal courts devised a new procedure to handle these cases. The Assize of Novel Disseisin provided for a trial by 12 jurors with the jury limited to deciding a single issue: Was the plaintiff unjustly forced off the land? If the answer was yes, the court ordered that possession be restored immediately. No adjournments were permitted, and if the defendant did not show, the agent in charge of the property was deemed to be appearing in his place. Nor was the dispossessor allowed to raise a claim of rightful ownership as a defense. Claims based on title had to be litigated in a separate proceeding.[1]

The new procedure proved extremely popular. Within 50 years people of modest means were bringing actions to recover possession of very small parcels.[2] The procedure cemented the hold of the central government over the citizenry and fostered social peace by reducing the use of private force.[3]

The Assize of Novel Disseisin marks the beginning of the civil action in England. For the first time plaintiffs could secure relief in a national court. It is the beginning too of the system of using juries to decide questions of fact. Finally, it represents a key step in the development of property law. With its advent, English law begins to split the idea of property into different bundles of rights. One bundle is denominated "ownership" and another "possession." The notion of divided interests in property stems from this innovation, and thus the example ultimately demonstrates how a procedural innovation—here a speedy remedy to restore possession—and substantive law—the law of property—are intertwined.

Notes

1. Simpson, A HISTORY OF THE LAND LAW 28–30 (2d ed. 1986).
2. Pollock & Maitland, THE HISTORY OF THE ENGLISH COMMON LAW 48 (2d ed. 1968) (1898).
3. Van Caenegem, THE BIRTH OF THE ENGLISH COMMON LAW 40–41 (2d ed. 1998).

Government-run courts in many countries began to absorb the dispute resolution business handled by private bodies. Part of this expansion is attributable to state building. The resolution of important disputes was a way governments could win the loyalty of their subjects and weaken ties to local lords.

State-run courts also offered litigants, or at least claimants, certain advantages. Unlike their private counterparts, courts can mobilize public force to compel a defendant to submit to their processes and be bound by their decisions.[12] In some instances they also can provide better service. The royal courts established after the Norman invasion of England are a well known example. Matters once heard by feudal or local courts were increasingly brought to the royal courts because of their streamlined procedures and more effective remedies. In cases arising from a violent seizure of land, a common problem in 13th century England, the royal courts provided a quick and easy method for restoring the land to the one entitled to it. (See "A More Efficient Remedy for Protecting Possession.")

But state-run courts could lose business to more efficient rivals, something that happened to the Qadis' courts during the Abbasid dynasty. On the assumption that no Muslim would lie under oath, fact-finding in these courts rested solely on the sworn testimony of the parties. But as the Muslim community expanded its contacts with the Byzantine and Persian empires, more and more contracts were reduced to writing, and when disputes about them arose, the value of referring to the contract itself to resolve conflicting testimony became clear. The Qadi courts eventually amended their procedures to accept written documents as proof of private transactions, but not before traders had turned to other tribunals to resolve their disputes.

Unlike the Qadis' courts, the expansion of trade in Europe in the 15th and 16th centuries brought state-run courts there much new business. During the Middle Ages, European merchants created their own courts to resolve disputes among themselves. Before contracting with a stranger, a merchant would investigate his background. If the potential trading partner had failed to comply with a decision of one of these courts, the merchant would refuse to contract with him. But as trade expanded, the number of background checks merchants had to conduct rose dramatically, and the growing expense this entailed has been advanced to explain why traders began turning to state-operated courts to enforce their contracts.[13]

In England, the common law courts absorbed the influx of commercial disputes, whereas on the continent special courts separate from those hearing ordinary civil matters were created to meet merchant needs. The difference again reflects competitive considerations. English common law courts were more powerful than their continental counterparts, and thus their judgments were more likely to be observed. English judges were also willing to incorporate into the law the substantive rules, particularly those concerning negotiable instruments, that traders had devised to facilitate commerce. Continental judges, on the other hand, were bound by legal doctrines that were often at odds with commercial law principles.[14]

Competition for "dispute resolution business" occurs not just between different kinds of courts. Other societal institutions enforce social norms and uphold order, and how well they perform these functions helps determine what is left for the courts to do. In Africa, religion, morality, and kinship systems all affect the scope of courts.[15] In the United States and South Asia "public interest" litigation can result in courts' ordering changes in the administration of government programs and even lead to their assuming responsibility for the operation of an entire department or ministry.[16] By contrast, such litigation is less common in many European states where institutions such as the ombudsman play a much more active role in overseeing government.[17] Some nations may consciously discourage the use of courts, as Japan did until recently by limiting the number of lawyers and judges and otherwise making litigation a time-consuming and costly exercise.[18]

Assuming New Functions

Although dispute resolution is what gives rise to courts, in some societies courts begin performing additional functions as well. Often these new functions represent nothing more than an ingenious bending of the litigation process to serve a new end. In medieval England parties wanting to enter into a land transaction would manufacture a lawsuit between themselves. The purchaser would bring a suit asserting that he owned the property and the seller would admit the claim. Entry of judgment provided written evidence of the transfer title and made it difficult for third parties to contest the transaction later.[19]

A far more significant function that courts began to assume is the making of law. A court opinion issued in one case can provide guidance to a judge handling a similar dispute later. Following earlier decisions economizes on judicial resources. Judges need not spend time devising new solutions to problems others have already solved. And because it makes the law more predictable, following precedent also discourages litigation altogether. If the parties to a lawsuit can predict how a court is likely to decide the case, the chances of settlement increase dramatically.[20]

While the law making power of courts is most closely identified with the English common law tradition, it is by no means unique to it. A Thai legal code dating from the middle of the 14th century directed judges to follow precedent, and under Islamic law opinions rendered by legal specialists in the course of litigation provide authority in later disputes. Even in those nations following the civil law tradition, court opinions serve as a source, albeit informally, of law.

Judicial Review

The most recent step in the evolution of courts has been their assumption of the responsibility for seeing that the other branches of government obey the law. Ensuring that rulers follow the law is a problem as old as government itself. Even when a ruler accepts the principle, there is, as the Islamic jurist Al-Jahiz observed in the 8th century, the challenge of devising an institution that can determine when government has violated the law and fix an appropriate sanction.[21]

The United States originated the practice of using courts to make this determination. In *Marbury v. Madison,* the Supreme Court held that it had the power to review whether legislative and executive actions conformed to the constitution. Political leaders criticized the Supreme Court for overstepping its bounds, and until the later part of the 19th century American courts used this power sparingly.[22] Despite some limited experiments, other nations were also reluctant to grant their courts wide-ranging powers to review the actions of other branches of government. Only after World War II, when many laid at least a part of the blame for the war on lawless government, did European states give their courts the power of judicial review. The practice spread to developing countries, and in the 1990s almost all of the former communist states adopted some form of judicial review.[23]

Borrowing and Colonization

As the experience with judicial review shows, courts do not develop solely in response to internal pressures. When Japan's rulers decided to modernize the economy in the latter half of the 19th century, they borrowed several features from European civil law systems.[24] Many Asian, African, and Latin American nations did not have the luxury of a choice, of course. The court systems of colonizing states were imposed on their own indigenous dispute resolution mechanisms, often with disastrous results. (See "The Unintended Consequences of Creating a Court.")

***

The development of modern courts is a difficult story to tell. No small set of variables explains the rise of courts or the reasons why they differ from one country to the next. Whereas an early generation of scholars posited a universal evolution of law and legal institutions,[25] it is now clear that social, economic, and political forces, both within and without, shape a nation's courts and its legal system. On the other hand, the striking similarities among specialized, state-run dispute resolution institutions across so many cultures separated by both time and space suggest that there is an element of universality to courts. As Aeschylus shows in the

The Unintended Consequences of Creating a Court

Shortly after the British took control of the Deccan Plateau in the early part of the 19th century, they introduced formal, state-run courts modeled after those in England. One of the reasons was to increase the flow of capital to small farmers. Without courts, only those who could avail themselves of "informal" means for enforcing debt contracts lent to farmers. In practice only a well-connected villager could bring sufficient pressure to bear on a defaulting borrower. The result was that agricultural lending was dominated by a series of local monopolists. The creation of a court system had the desired impact. New lenders entered the market, and competition drove interest rates down.

But, when drought hit several villages in the region in 1875 and lenders turned to the courts to foreclose on defaulting debtors, rioting broke out. Scores were killed or injured, and in several areas the courthouses were sacked and the documents evidencing the debts destroyed.

The commission formed to examine the cause of the riots concluded that courts had upset what was, under the circumstances, a desirable institutional arrangement. Local money-lenders had enjoyed what was in effect an exclusive right to lend to farmers. While the lender realized supra-competitive interest rates, these earnings provided him with a financial cushion that allowed him to carry debtors in bad times. The commission concluded that the lower rates brought about by the introduction of formal courts had robbed the lenders of this cushion and forced them to foreclose at the first sign of a downturn.

A formal economic analysis confirms the commission's view.[1] Its authors note that had the courts been able to recognize and enforce the kind of exclusive dealing contract that was implicit in the relationship between the money lender and the farmer, foreclosures and the ensuing riots might have been avoided. But when an institutional reform takes place in the world of "second best," here a situation in which not all contracts could be enforced, the reform can have unintended, and deleterious, consequences.

Note

1. Kranton & Swamy, *The Hazards of Piecemeal Reform: British Civil Courts and the Credit Market in Colonial India,* 58 J. DEV. ECON. 1 (1999).

Eumenides, they are a means of achieving an objective that is universal: the just resolution of conflict.

Notes

This article originated as a background report for the World Bank's *World Development Report 2002: Building Institutions for Markets.* The author gratefully acknowledges comments provided by Simeon Djankov, Roumeen Islam, William Mayville, Antonio Parra, Matthew Stephenson, Rebecca Kleinfeld, Luis López Guerra, and Rita McWilliams.

1. Pound, JURISPRUDENCE 387 (1959); Posner, *Revenge as Legal Prototype and Literary Genre,* in LAW AND LITERATURE: A MISUNDERSTOOD RELATIONSHIP 35 (1988).
2. Becker, COMPARATIVE JUDICIAL POLITICS: THE POLITICAL FUNCTIONING OF COURTS 371 (1970).
3. Evans-Pritchard, THE NUER: A DESCRIPTION OF THE MODES OF LIVELIHOOD AND POLITICAL INSTITUTIONS OF A NILOTIC PEOPLE 162 (1940).
4. Pound, AN INTRODUCTION TO THE PHILOSOPHY OF LAW 74 (1922).
5. Canter, *Dispute Settlement in Zambia,* in THE DISPUTING PROCESS—LAW IN TEN SOCIETIES 247, 260–61 (Nader & Todd eds., 1978).
6. Compare Becker, *supra* n. 2, at 13 (identifying seven characteristics of a court including independence and a belief by the judges that they should behave impartially).
7. Fuller, *The Forms and Limits of Adjudication,* in THE PRINCIPLES OF SOCIAL ORDER: SELECTED ESSAYS OF LON L. FULLER 86, 93 (Winston ed., 1981).
8. Shapiro, COURTS: A COMPARATIVE AND POLITICAL ANALYSIS 1 (1981).
9. Huang, CIVIL JUSTICE IN CHINA: REPRESENTATION AND PRACTICE IN THE QING 177–79 (1996).
10. Dawson, *A History of Lay Judges* 6–8 (2000) (1960).
11. Lingat, *The Classical Law of India* 246 (J. Duncan, M. Derrett ed. and trans., 1998) (1973) .
12. Landes & Posner, *Adjudication as a Private Good,* 8 J. LEGAL STUD. 235, 247 (1979).
13. Milgrom et. al., *The Role of Institutions in the Revival of Trade: The Law Merchants, Private Judges, and the Champagne Fairs,* 2 ECON. AND POL. 1 (1990).
14. Schlesinger et. al., COMPARATIVE LAW 303–04 (5th ed. 1988); Tallon, *Civil Law and Commercial Law* 136–142 (8 INTERNATIONAL ENCYCLOPEDIA OF COMPARATIVE LAW, 1983).
15. Wachuke, *Law and Negative Sanctions in African Societies,* in POLITICAL ANTHROPOLOGY: THE STATE OF THE ART 243 (Seaton and Claessen eds., 1979).
16. Ahmed, PUBLIC INTEREST LITIGATION: CONSTITUTIONAL ISSUES AND REMEDIES (1999).
17. See Gellhorn, OMBUDSMEN AND OTHERS: CITIZENS' PROTECTORS IN NINE COUNTRIES (1966); Galligan, ADMINISTRATIVE PROCEDURES AND THE SUPERVISION OF ADMINISTRATION IN HUNGARY, POLAND, BULGARIA, ESTONIA, AND ALBANIA 77–88 (Org. Econ. Coop. & Dev. SIGMA Paper No. 17, 1997).
18. Haley, *The Myth of the Reluctant Litigant,* 4 J. JAPANESE STUD. 359 (1978).
19. Simpson, A HISTORY OF THE LAND LAW 122–23 (2d ed. 1986).
20. Hay & Spier, Settlement of Litigation, in THE NEW PALGRAVE DICTIONARY OF ECONOMICS AND THE LAW 442 (Newman ed., 1998); Galanter, Justice in Many Rooms, 19 J. LEGAL PLURALISM 1, 3–10 (1981).

21. Lambton, STATE AND GOVERNMENT IN MEDIEVAL ISLAM 64 (1981).
22. Abraham, THE JUDICIAL PROCESS 311–334 (6th ed. 1993).
23. Schwartz, THE STRUGGLE FOR CONSTITUTIONAL JUSTICE IN POST-COMMUNIST EUROPE (2000).
24. Ishii, *Japanese Legislation in the Meiji Era 493–511* (Chambliss ed. & trans., 9 JAPANESE CULTURE IN THE MEIJI ERA: LEGISLATION, 1969).
25. Stein, LEGAL EVOLUTION: THE STORY OF AN IDEA (1980).

For Further Reading

A.N.E. Amissah, THE CONTRIBUTION OF THE COURTS TO GOVERNMENT: A WEST AFRICAN VIEW (1981).

Theodore L. Becker, COMPARATIVE JUDICIAL POLITICS: THE POLITICAL FUNCTIONING OF COURTS (1970).

Harold J. Berman, LAW AND REVOLUTION: THE FORMATION OF THE WESTERN LEGAL TRADITION (1983).

R.C. Van Caenegem, THE BIRTH OF THE ENGLISH COMMON LAW (2d ed. 1998).

N.J. Coulson, A HISTORY OF ISLAMIC LAW (1964).

Michael Dalby, *Revenge in Traditional China,* 25 AM. J. LEGAL HIST. 267 (1981).

Max Gluckman, POLITICS, LAW AND RITUAL IN TRIBAL SOCIETY (1965).

Robert Lingat, THE CLASSICAL LAW OF INDIA (J. Duncan M. Derrett ed. & trans., 1998).

Maurizio Lupoi, THE ORIGINS OF THE EUROPEAN LEGAL ORDER (Adrian Belton trans. 2000) (1994).

John Merryman et. al., THE CIVIL LAW TRADITION: EUROPE, LATIN AMERICA, AND EAST ASIA (1994).

David Pearl & Werner Menski, MUSLIM FAMILY LAW (3d ed. 1998).

Martin Shapiro, COURTS: A COMPARATIVE AND POLITICAL ANALYSIS (1981).

Hans Julius Wolf, *The Origin of Litigation Among the Greeks,* 4 TRADITIO 31 (1946).

Chapter 16

The Drug Court as a Sentencing Model

Gene Kassebaum
Duane K. Okamoto

In response to ballooning incarceration rates, due in part to increased drug convictions, criminal justice practitioners were forced to seek out new approaches to preventing nonviolent drug offenses. Punitive incarceration has little effect on addicted defendants, and probation is frequently ignored. Drug courts were conceived as an intermediate between the two extremes–immediate, short term confinement for drug violations accompanied by a spectrum of long-term treatment options, all presided over by a single judge familiar with each particular case. Here Kassebaum and Okamoto analyze data from the Hawaii Drug Court to discuss how the program functioned as a sentencing model, and whether it succeeded in promoting drug and alcohol abstinence in its clients.

Sentencing of criminal defendants in the United States in recent years is driven and constrained by the preeminence of the prison as our major idea for crime control. The massive increase in the incarcerated population in the United States is due in part to large increases in original court commitments of convicted drug offenders (Blumstein, 1993) and returns to custody by parole violators. Many of those paroles are revoked because of positive drug use test results (National Institute of Justice, 1994). Simple punitive sentences are not effective in changing the behavior of chemically dependent and socially marginalized defendants. Yet, if chronic drug users with histories of program nonattendance and missed court hearings are simply directed to report for treatment, the problem of attrition dissipates any effect. Often, nothing happens to dropout probationers; unless a new crime is committed, dropouts are listed as "whereabouts unknown," "absconded," or the like (National Institute of Justice, 1994, pp. 25–34). Assuming probation is revoked for a technical drug violation, the time gap between violation and revocation of probation reinforces the impression that there are no consequences for continued drug use. All this has led to a search for a sentencing option between prison and probation and has led to a serious interest in linking the sanctioning authority of the court with a supportive but demanding treatment program. That is the objective of the Hawaii Drug Court.

The Drug Court in Honolulu

The broad term *drug court* may designate any of a variety of court models, ranging from simply channeling felony drug cases into an enhanced prosecution and plea arrangement to an ambitious program of court-enforced treatment programs (see Bureau of Justice Assistance, November 1993). The expedited case processing drug court model is exemplified by New York City's N Part Courts (see New York City Criminal Justice Agency, Inc., August 1993). A second major type, the dedicated court managed treatment program, generally describes such programs as the Felony Drug Court of Dade County, Miami (see Goldkamp & Weiland, 1993), and the Hawaii Drug Court.[1]

The mission of the Hawaii Drug Court program is as follows:

> To channel nonviolent pretrial and post-conviction defendants, who would otherwise be incarcerated in Hawaii's correctional institutions, into a comprehensive and integrated system of judicial and treatment services. More specifically, the program's mission supports the aim of Hawaii's Judiciary by enhancing public safety and ensuring the equitable and expeditious resolution of cases. (Hawaii Drug Court Program Grant Application, Bureau of Justice Assistance, Correctional Options Program, FY 95)

The goals of the drug court program are as follows: (a) to reduce jail admissions and average length of stay for the target population, thus freeing existing incarceration resources for violent offenders; (b) to reduce recidivism of offenders with significant alcohol and other drug involvement; (c) to shorten the response time of the judicial system to violations by offenders; and (d) to reduce costs to the criminal justice system in handling alcohol and drug abusers. The program's goals will be achieved by establishing an integrated continuum of judicial supervision and rehabilitation services.[2]

The Hawaii Drug Court may be viewed as a sentencing model with the drug court judge and the contracted and in-court treatment organizations implementing the intervention model. This general concept addresses the problem of attrition in treatment programs and the limitation of standard court procedures for sentencing offenders whose major problem is chemical dependency. This concept of the drug court represents a simple but basic innovation in thinking about drug use abatement. The idea is that for many problem substance abusers, legal penalties are not effective because of chemical dependency, and treatment is often to no avail because addicts do not stay in treatment.

The sentencing model of the drug court puts a single judge, dedicated to the drug court, into direct and frequent contact with defendants under supervision of the court. The judge, who is not an officer in a probation division, monitors such defendants and sanctions program noncompliance by immediate, short-term jail confinement. These short-term jail confinements do not, unless a critical threshold is reached, permanently displace the client from the drug court program. The court's treatment program component motivates client participation by positive reinforcement and provides a continuum of services aimed at the self-sufficiency of the client and if possible reintegration of the client with a family or group that supports a drug-free lifestyle. The two aspects of the drug court sentencing model thus are as follows: (a) court monitoring and immediate, tangible punitive consequences for noncompliance with program requirements and (b) a strongly supportive group that provides a range of treatment options. These are, through the courtroom presence and biweekly contacts with the judge, tightly joined. The detection of noncompliance with court-ordered abstinence or treatment participation results in immediate and authoritative sanctions by the judge.

The implementation of this model requires that the model's integrity must be maintained despite operational demands of a busy court, the need for staff to learn and assume new roles in the judiciary, and the notorious resistance and evasiveness of drug-dependent and alcohol-dependent persons.

Data used in this article are mainly from three sources that were developed as part of an evaluation of the Hawaii Drug Court conducted in 1997. These sources are as follows:

1. *A database of accepted and rejected cases.* Hard copies of records of cases either accepted or rejected by the drug court were reviewed and entered into a database for the study period of January through June 1996. Prior criminal history on all reviewed defendants was obtained from the Offender Base Transaction System. These case summaries were coded and entered into the project database. Prior court appearances of all reviewed defendants were obtained from the Hawaii Judiciary Information System and entered into the database. Finally, data on confinement, progress through Phases I, II, and III, and other program dispositions including termination were extracted from the Hawaii Drug Court Master Index. This consolidated database is the source of tabulations presented in this article. Records of cases accepted and rejected for the drug court, and also between cases graduating, cases terminated, and cases retained in the program as of September 1997 were compared, subdivided by track and by risk level.

2. *Interviews with treatment providers.* Personal interviews were conducted with directors and, in some cases, other staff at treatment sites with which the drug court has purchase-of-service contracts.

3. *Interviews* with judges and administrators in the judiciary and in the executive branch who attend court sessions (hearings) and drug court graduations.

Our data collection was scheduled and completed to determine the extent to which the Hawaii Drug Court was recruiting from its designated target population, to determine if it had formed working connections with drug treatment groups in the community, to determine if it was providing both court monitoring and sanctions and a continuum of treatment services, and if it was having an impact on cell space use and transaction costs.[3] In this article, we discuss only the manner in which the drug court functions as a sentencing model and present some data on the immediate effect of program participation.

Program Entry

To be eligible for admission to the drug court, petitioners must meet the following criteria: (a) the petitioner must volunteer for the program; (b) the petitioner is facing charges, or is charged with, or is on probation for a Class B or Class C felony; (c) petitioner is a nonviolent offender, which is defined as a person who has not committed a serious and/or substantial bodily injury crime (assault in the second degree) within the previous 5 years and is not currently charged with committing such injury; (d) is in noncompliance with the terms and conditions of his or her probation and is in need of drug/alcohol treatment; and (e) the petitioner admits to an alcohol or drug problem.

Drug court petitioners enter from one of three tracks. Track 1 petitioners enter the drug court prior to charges being filed. Track 2 petitioners have been previously charged but have not yet gone to trial. Track 3 petitioners are on probation and may enter before or after a motion for revocation or modification of probation is filed. Upon acceptance into drug court, petitioners are referred to as clients of the drug court.

Program Phases

The Hawaii Drug Court program consists of three phases. Phase I is a 30-day program to orient and assess clients and to develop a case plan. During this phase, clients will participate in the Life Skills Training Course (LSTC). The course includes alcohol and other drug education, critical thinking and cognitive restructuring, and social skills training. Phase II is a 6- to 8-month alcohol and other drug treatment phase. The treatment may consist of an outpatient treatment (3 days a week, for a total of less than 9 hours per week) group, individual or combination therapy sessions, intensive outpatient treatment (which provides 24 contact hours per week), or an inpatient program (which is a 24-hour-per-day residential program). Phase III is a 3- to 4-month aftercare phase. Clients continue to receive supervision and participate in activities that reinforce positive lessons learned from Phase I and Phase II.

Program Requirements

Clients must cooperate with an assigned case manager and supervising officer at all times. They are expected to show respect to all staff and fellow clients and to strictly adhere to the policies and procedures of the Hawaii Drug Court. To advance from Phase I to Phase II, clients must have no positive urine tests or unexcused absences from the program for 14 consecutive days; clients must complete all the required forms and waivers, including the Addiction Severity Index and the individual master case plan; and clients must be employed or looking for employment or must be enrolled in or seeking an educational program. To advance from Phase II to Phase III, clients must have no positive urine tests or unexcused absences from the program for 60 consecutive days, clients must successfully complete drug or alcohol treatment and develop a continuing care plan with staff; and clients must be employed or enrolled in a vocational or educational program. To graduate, clients must have had no positive urine tests or unexcused absences from the program for 90 days prior to graduation, clients must be enrolled in a vocational/educational program or [have] obtained employment, and clients must have attained the goals as stated in the continuing care plan. Successful graduates will have all charges dismissed by the court. Six months after graduation, graduates will take a urine test. In the event of a positive test, graduates will be referred to services but will not be criminally charged.

The Drug Court Judge

In the drug court the judge is robed and elevated in standard courtroom fashion, flanked by the courtroom staff (clerk, bailiff, and stenographer), with a deputy prosecutor and public defender at small tables facing the bench. The behavior of the judge alternates between legal formality at decision points and informal when calling the long roster of defendants scheduled for that particular session (defendants appear every 2 weeks, sometimes weekly). Quickly as each is called, he or she steps in front of the bench, exchanges greetings with the judge, and then responds to the judge's brief and often routine questions, the first of which is usually "Are you clean and sober?" or a variation thereof. As the judge becomes more familiar with the client, he or she will expand the questions to inquire about the client's specific activities since they last met. Over time, the judge will demonstrate to the client an awareness of much of what is going on in the client's life by the type of questions he or she asks. The communication is on a colloquial level, with the judge using local words and pronunciation. When appropriate, the judge may use humor to make a comment about the defendant's problematic life. Sometimes there is a matter to be gone into in some detail and the questioning shifts to a more serious tone. On occasions, when a defendant passes a milestone the judge will offer praise, incentives such as movie tickets or ribbons, and initiate applause for the client. Defendants are praised by the judge for performance in line with program objectives. Continued sobriety is regularly recognized and commended.

But the judge promptly and sharply disposes of rule violators, the important lapses being missing a scheduled hearing, going AWOL from treatment, testing positive for drug use, and most serious, lying to direct questions about relapse. The judge immediately sends the defendant to custody.

The judge is thus activist, informal and formal. The judge imposes sanctions or grants clemency and positive recognition without delay. The judge is the clearly visible authority through which the program operates. The judge articulates the expectations of both the law and the treatment program in which the defendant is a client. The judge is a gateway not only to jail but also to a program that is widely seen as offering at least the possibility of escape from a marginalized and continually penalized existence. This dual capacity is the key element in the drug court as a sentencing model.

The central role of the judge is recognized in the elaborate ceremony that is held when a cohort of defendants has successfully completed the drug court's prescribed course. The first such graduation was held in the auditorium of a large and prestigious private school for children (K–12) of native Hawaiian extraction. The setting was particularly meaningful for the predominately Hawaiian clients in the drug court program. The chief justice of the supreme court of Hawaii and members of both houses in the state legislature were featured speakers. The master of ceremonies and the person who passed out certificates of completion, and who embraced each graduate, was the drug court judge. Subsequent graduations have been held in the supreme court, a restored Victorian legal setting across from Iolani Palace. The audience consisted of spouses, parents, partners, and children of graduates. There were all the features of a Hawaii-style academic graduation: flower leis, guitar playing, Hawaiian chanting, applause, and singing. The judge spoke; graduates shared their feelings about the drug court experience, usually giving their interaction with the judge a prominent place. For the senior author, it was the first occasion on which he saw a sitting felony court judge hug defendants.

Analysis

For purposes of assessing program performance, we selected cases reviewed for Hawaii Drug Court admittance from January through June 1996. This was to produce a sample that would have had between 14 and 20 months in which to traverse the program and have some postgraduation experience. A total of 103 cases were admitted to the Hawaii Drug Court during this period, and we were able to obtain sufficient information on 102 to make analysis useful. We were able to obtain information on all 120 of the eligible applicants who ultimately declined or were rejected for this same period.

Comparisons of Accepted Drug Court Clients and Rejected Applicants

After preliminary identification of appropriate (target) defendants for drug court, a review is conducted by deputy prosecutors and deputy public defenders in pretrial cases, and by Adult Probation for cases facing modification or revocation of probation. Surviving cases are then reviewed by program staff of the drug court, and lastly by the judge. The files of cases accepted, as well as cases rejected, contain terse but useful indications of factors taken into account. There was no indication that the drug court was endeavoring to take cases that were inappropriate. Most notes showed that the major cases avoided were those people who appeared not to recognize that he or she had a major problem with substance abuse. Other cases rejected were those of people who repeatedly had evaded programs and restraints on drug use.

A comparison of the 102 persons admitted to drug court and the 120 reviewed and rejected showed that the two groups did not differ on many characteristics, but on several they did. Prior arrests for property offenses did not differ between defendants accepted and those rejected by drug court, nor did the number of citations for contempt of court. Defendants admitted and those rejected frequently had extensive records of theft (usually petty theft and shoplifting) and contempt of court, indicating a pattern of disregard for the law but not typically a danger to the community. Prior arrests for drug offenses were nearly the same in the two groups. The average client reviewed had repeatedly been arrested for drug law violations. Defendants accepted less often had an arrest for an offense against persons (23.5% vs. 40% of those rejected), as shown in Table 16.1.

The most substantial difference between rejected and accepted cases is prior felony convictions. Persons rejected had significantly more felony convictions than persons admitted to the program (see Table 16.2).

The tables reveal that although the drug court avoids admitting defendants who have violent criminal records it does accept persons who have been convicted of one and sometimes more felonies. Also, its clients have repeatedly been arrested and have repeatedly failed to appear at court hearings. The population served by the drug court, by intention and in fact, is not a first-offender population with good prospects of dismissal or a deferred acceptance of guilty plea.

Table 16.1
Comparison of Prior Arrests for Offenses Against Persons Committed by Defendants Accepted and Rejected by Hawaii Drug Court (In Percentages)

Prior Arrests, Offenses Against Persons	Defendants Rejected	Defendants Accepted
None	76.5	60.0
One	10.8	17.5
Two or more	12.7	22.5

Role of the Treatment Providers in Assessment and Treatment

The Hawaii Drug Court contracts with four treatment providers to provide residential and outpatient treatment to clients. The four treatment providers also provide services to non–drug court referrals from the judiciary. They do not differentiate in the treatment of drug court and non–drug court referrals other than the need to schedule treatment around the drug court clients' frequent appearances in court. Funding for treatment is crucial and can have a major impact on the continuum of assessment and treatment. In some cases, treatment has served as a sanction to encourage positive behavior. More often, it is a necessary part of the client's recovery; without it, the client cannot

Table 16.2
Comparison of Prior Felony Convictions for Persons Accepted into or Rejected by Hawaii Drug Court (In Percentages)

Prior Felony Convictions	Defendants Accepted	Defendants Rejected or Declining
None	41.2	21.7
One	23.5	25.8
Two	14.7	14.2
Three	8.8	14.2
Four	5.9	12.5
Five or more	5.9	11.6
Total percentage	100	100
Number of cases	102	120

progress through the program. This in turn has a major impact on the number of clients served and the cost per client. The consumption of residential treatment funds at a higher than expected rate, and the funds' expected exhaustion by February 1998 slowed case flow, as shown in Table 16.3.

Table 16.3
Changes in Admissions and Enrollment in Residential Treatment

Intake	January Through June 1996	July Through December 1996	January Through June 1997
Cases admitted HDC	102	45	40
Cases in residential treatment	91	24	18
Residential treatment as % of admissions	89	53	45

It was initially planned that the Hawaii Drug Court program would take 10 to 13 months to complete. In fact it took longer. As of our assessment cut-off date of September 30, 1997, graduates ($n = 36$) entering during the study period (January through June 1996) took an average of 15 months to complete it. Those who terminated unsuccessfully ($n = 32$) lasted an average of 9.3 months. Clients in the program ($n = 35$) stayed an average of 16.6 months. When the last of the 103 entering in 1996 has graduated or terminated, the mean length of stay will be longer than 15 months.

Assessment of Program Outcomes

Assessing the initial effects of the Hawaii Drug Court is constrained by the impracticality of a randomly assigned control group in the start-up phase[4] and the lack of information after leaving the supervision of the drug court program. As of our assessment in December 1997, only 36 had graduated from the study cohort. By October 15, 1998, more than half (54%) had graduated, but terminations had risen to 40%

Table 16.4
Graduation, Termination and In Program for Original 103 Admissions to Hawaii Drug Court

Status	As of September 30, 1997	%	As of October 15, 1998	%
Graduated	36	35	56	54
Terminated	32	31	41	40
In program	35	34	6	6
Total	103	100	103	100

(see Table 16.4).

Four of the 6 defendants who were still in the program as of October 15, 1998, graduated in 1999; 3 in January and the fourth in September. The other 2 defendants were terminated in 1999; 1 in January and the other in February. In the analysis that follows, graduation and termination are as of the end of the study in September 1997.

Until a follow-up study of the original cohort is conducted, there is no basis for reliably estimating the long-term impact of drug court on crime or drug use. Program outcome in this article is mainly gauged by the success of the program in promoting alcohol and drug abstinence in clients while in the drug court.

First, the effect of the drug court varied with the risk level of the clients. There are approximately two sources of defendants for review. The first source is pretrial cases, which consisted of defendants not yet formally charged in court, termed Track I, or charged but not yet tried, referred to as Track II. Four defendants had a

Table 16.5
Persons Admitted With Prior Felony Convictions January Through June 1996 (In Percentages)

Source of Intake	No Prior Felony Conviction	One Prior Felony Conviction	Two Prior Felony Convictions	Three or More Prior Felony Convictions	Total Cases for 100%
Pretrial (precharge and predisposition)	62.3	13.1	16.4	8.2	61
Probation violation	9.8	39.0	34.1	17.1	41

Table 16.6
Source of Intake and Prior Convictions for Drug Offenses (In Percentages)

Source of Intake	No Prior Drug Conviction	One Prior Drug Conviction	Two or More Prior Drug Convictions	Total Cases for 100%
Pretrial defendant	75.4	11.5	13.1	61
Probation violation	43.9	43.9	12.2	41

charge in both Track I and Track II. There were a total of 61 pretrial defendants admitted to Hawaii Drug Court during the first 6 months. The second source of cases consisted of persons, referred to as Track III, brought in for probation violation. There were nine cases with a charge in both Track III and Track II, and they were treated as probation violations. There were 41 probation violation cases admitted to Hawaii Drug Court in the first 6 months.

Pretrial and probation violators differ in length and seriousness of prior criminal history. Probation violators, compared with pretrials, are more likely to have a more extensive felony conviction history. Almost two thirds (62.3%) of pretrial defendants had no prior felony conviction and only 4, or 9.8%, of probation violators had no prior felony conviction. Twice as many probation violators had two or more felony convictions compared with pretrials (see Table 16.5).

Fewer pretrials had a prior conviction for a drug offense. Seventy-five percent of pretrials had no prior drug conviction, whereas 44% of probation violators had none (see Table 16.6).

Probation violators were more likely to be terminated in drug court and less likely to graduate compared with pretrials. Only 24% of probation violators graduated, and 41.5% were terminated. For pretrials, these figures were reversed: 42.6% graduated, and 23% were terminated (see Table 16.7).

Conclusions

It may be that the differences in prior record, rather than the status of pretrial or probation, are the reason for the differences in success rates. Both prior felony convictions and prior drug convictions are indicators of a higher risk of termination.

There is an indication that pretrial cases do better even when controlling for prior record, but probation violators with better prior records do not do significantly better than probation violators with more serious records. Looking at the two together in a risk measure, risk predicts program outcome. Only 22% of the high-risk clients graduated and 47% were terminated, whereas 60% of the low-risk clients graduated and only 5% were terminated (see Table 16.8).

However, the number of cases is small when subdivided in this way, and this conclusion is tentative, to be checked later when more cases have gone through the drug court.

At any rate, although the odds of success are higher for pretrial cases it must be recognized that some probation violators, even those with prior felony convictions and prior drug offense convictions, have graduated. Ten probation violators did graduate, including seven who had two or more prior felony convictions. Seven of these 10 persons had prior drug convictions yet graduated. Although the odds were against them, even having both risk indicators did not

Table 16.7
Source of Intake and Program Outcome (In Percentages)

Source of Intake	Enrolled in Hawaii Drug Court	Terminated From the Drug Court Program	Graduated From the Drug Court Program	Total Cases for 100%
Pretrial	34.4	23.0	42.6	61
Probation violation	34.1	41.5	24.4	41

Table 16.8
Outcome by Risk Level for Clients

	High Risk		Moderate Risk		Lower Risk	
Program Outcome	n	%	n	%	n	%
In drug court program	11	31	10	38.5	14	35
Terminated from program	17	47	12	46.1	2	5
Graduated from program	8	22	4	15.4	24	60
Total	36		26		40	

Note: High risk means both prior drug offense and felony convictions; moderate risk means either prior felony or prior drug conviction; lower risk means neither a prior drug conviction nor a prior felony conviction.

prevent some defendants from graduation. To bar them from the drug court program would have closed off what proved in the end a successful completion of the program.

Termination from the drug court program may be taken as an indication of relapse or at-risk conduct. For the study cohort (January through June 1996), 30% of the clients admitted were terminated unsuccessfully. The drug court program, on that criterion, was successful in retaining or graduating 70% of clients admitted. The requirements of remaining in the program (including 14, 60, and 90 consecutive days of drug-free and alcohol-free status) and the level of monitoring to which these clients were subject, makes this an impressive contrast to the records of arrests and conviction for drug use (see Table 16.8) and contempt of court (see Table 16.9) that these clients amassed preceding admission to drug court.

A lesser level of relapse may also be estimated from numbers of clients subject to the short-term sanction of confinement. Overall, 52.9% of drug court clients had no confinement and 47.1% had one or more episodes of jail time. Table 16.10 displays the totals with and without confinement, and for those who were confined the mean number of times confined, the mean total days per client, and the percentage confined of graduates, terminated, and clients remaining in the program. Thus, 30 clients received some sanction of confinement without being terminated. These were 42% of the persons graduated or retained. Of those persons eventually terminated, 18, or 58%, were confined. Of those who graduated, 28% experienced some confinement as a program sanction, and they were confined on the average for shorter periods of time (mean of 14.3 days for graduates, 25.6 days for terminations). Of those remaining in the program, more than half were confined. Confinement is thus not itself decisive but it is correlated with not graduating (see Table 16.10).

The 6-month follow-up of HDC graduates includes a review of arrests and dispositions in the Offender Based Transaction System (OBTS). Except for two clients noted as being on the mainland, OBTS should be a reliable record of whether a person has been arrested, con-

Table 16.9
Program Outcome and Prior Citations for Contempt of Court

Program Outcome	**Measure**	**Value**
Still enrolled in drug court program	Mean	12.8
	Median	7
	Number of cases	35
Terminated from drug court program	Mean	10.9
	Median	7
	Number of cases	31
Graduated from drug court program	Mean	5.1
	Median	4
	Number of cases	36

Table 16.10
Confinement by Program Outcome

Program Outcome	Total Cases	No Confinement	Confinement	% Confined	Mean Number Confinement	Mean Number of Days
In program currently	35	15	20	57.0	1.35	24.3
Graduated from program	36	26	10	27.8	1.10	14.3
Terminated from program	31	13	18	58.0	1.72	25.56
Total	102	54	48		1.44	22.69

victed, or sentenced. Only four offenses are noted: two persons arrested for theft in the second degree, both of whom are noted to have had a relapse, and two persons arrested for driving under the influence of alcohol (DUI). Neither of the two graduates charged with theft were charged with drugs or alcohol. One of the graduates involved in the theft cases was sent to prison, and the other was dismissed. The two graduates charged with DUI were both employed. Both graduates charged with DUI received fines. In addition, there are two other graduates who the drug court staff mentioned as experiencing a relapse but have no indication of arrest on the OBTS.

Based on our analysis of the clients admitted during the first 6 months of the drug court program, we would conclude that the program has adhered to its mission statement and met its stated goals. Without a follow-up study of the graduated clients, it is premature to conclude that the Hawaii Drug Court is a proven success.

Another reason for caution is that the program enjoyed significantly higher funding during the evaluation period than is now available. Funding for purchase of service contracts with private organizations, especially for residential treatment, is a necessary element in the continuum of services called for in the drug court model. It would be inappropriate to generalize the experience of the first clients in the program to those subsequently admitted. There was an increase in the amount of time spent in the program, a decrease in residential treatment resources, and increased processing time. All of these factors can be attributed to the decrease in funding after July 1, 1997.

We are, however, optimistic about the future of the Hawaii Drug Court. The foundation for a successful program has been established in the first 18 months of the program. The working model of the program has been modified and improved during the first 18 months, and the first two judges developed a work style and set a high standard for future drug court judges. A dedicated and committed staff has been assembled and many of the administrative and management issues have been resolved. An awareness of the program has been developed within the judiciary, the legislature, and the general public, and the drug court enjoys a positive reputation.

Notes

1. A review of the now extensive literature on drug courts is beyond the scope of this article. The most direct federal predecessor is perhaps the Treatment Alternatives to Street Crime program, begun under the Law Enforcement Assistance Administration nearly 25 years ago. A useful overview of drug courts and what preceded them may be found in Inciardi, McBride, and Rivers (1996).
2. The Hawaii Drug Court program is administered within the Judiciary, Adult Probation Division, First Circuit Court, State of Hawaii. It was established through funding from a $500,000 federal grant from the Bureau of Justice Assistance Correctional Options Program, general funds from the State of Hawaii in the amount of $1,075,642, and $58,818 in funding from the Edward Byrne Memorial State and local Law Enforcement Assistance Program. First-year expenditures (1995 to 1996) were $38,751 (federal) and $418,568 (state). Second-year expenditures (1996 to 1997) were $457,984 (federal), $657,074 (state), and $58,818 (Edward Byrne Memorial). Total expenditures for the initial 18 months (December 1995 to June 1997) were $1,631,195. Since July 1, 1997, the Hawaii Drug Court has been solely supported by state funding and is receiving $796,301 annually to continue operations.
3. These questions are addressed in Okamato Consulting Group (1998).
4. Because determining true eligibility entails getting a decision from the deputy prosecutor, the drug court program and the drug court judge, as well as the concurrence of the public defender and the defendant, a randomly assigned control group would be expensive and disruptive. Given, however, the similarities in background between defendants accepted and rejected, a risk scale could be developed that would be used to create categories for both program participants and rejects, to partially adjust for differences in risk. That is, current referral for review eliminates defendants

with a history of felony violence and defendants without a confirmed dependency on alcohol and drugs.

References

Blumstein, A. (1993). Making rationality relevant: The American Society of Criminology 1992 presidential address. *Criminology, 31,* 1–16.

Bureau of Justice Assistance. (1993). *Program brief: Special drug courts* (NCJ 144531). Washington, DC: Bureau of Justice Assistance, Department of Justice.

Goldkamp, J. S., & Weiland, D. (1993). *Assessing the Impact of Dade County's Felonv Drug Court* (National Institute of Justice: Research in Brief). Washington, DC: Department of Justice.

Inciardi, J., McBride, D., & Rivers, J. (1996). *Drug control and the courts.* Thousand Oaks, CA: Sage.

National Institute of Justice. (1994). *Responding to probation and parole violations* [Bulletin]. Washington, DC: Department of Justice.

New York City Criminal Justice Agency, Inc. (1993). *New York City's Special Drug Courts: Recidivism Patterns and Processing Costs.* New York: New York City Criminal Justice Agency.

Okamoto Consulting Group. (1998, January). *Draft Report: Evaluation of the Hawaii Drug Court.* Submitted to the Judiciary, State of Hawaii.

Chapter 17

The Impact of Victim-Offender Mediation

Two Decades of Research

Mark S. Umbreit
Robert B. Coates
Betty Vos

While innovative programs can generate public interest and newspaper headlines, most are so new that real empirical evidence of success or failure is hard to come by. But as the oldest form of restorative justice, victim-offender mediation (VOM) has twenty years of research behind it. Here the authors examine the results of thirty-eight VOM studies to provide an overall picture of its performance in areas like client satisfaction, restitution, and recidivism rates.

Innovation is often used in criminal justice as a code word for reform. From a jail to a penitentiary (theoretically inspiring penance), to a reformatory, to a corrections center, to a halfway house, to a therapeutic community, to community corrections, to boot camps, to restorative justice, to whatever the next catchphrase might be, reform has too often meant changing the name without radically changing program content or underlying values. It has also often been the case that the latest justice innovation captures the imagination and zeal of a vocal following without the slightest scrutiny. Thus policies and supporting dollars outdistance the needed empirical research to determine impact and to help shape programming. Frequently, the result of enthusiasm without a critical eye is flash-in-the-pan programming, frustrated policy-makers, disheartened workers, and ill-treated victims and offenders.

As the oldest and most widely used expression of restorative justice throughout the world, with more than 1,300 programs in 18 countries (Umbreit, 2001), victim-offender mediation, too, has, at times, attracted more zeal than substance. Some see VOM as the solution for an entire juvenile court jurisdiction, or the means to handle efficiently all restitution cases, or to mollify victims while staff get on with what really needs to be done. Some have said, "This is what we have been waiting for. We will assign one probation officer to manage the 1 ,000 cases that we expect will involve restitution and that can be handled through the VOM process." Other justice system officials ask, "How do we fold VOM into what we already do without costing more or changing how we handle youth?"

Fortunately, many have tried to keep the expectations of VOM reasonable while assuring officials and policy-makers that it is not a single-program panacea. And there have been numerous efforts to empirically evaluate and assess the working of the programs in a variety of settings during the last 20 years or so. In fact, more studies have examined the impact of victim offender mediation than numerous other mainstream correctional interventions that our nation spends millions of dollars on each year.

While modest in proportion to many larger scale reforms, victim offender mediation is one of the more empirically grounded justice interventions to emerge. This overview of empirical studies designed to assess the growth, implementation, and impact of victim-offender mediation programs is based on a review of thirty-eight (38) evaluation reports. No doubt there are more. These studies have taken place in 14 states and the District of Columbia, four Canadian provinces as well as in England, Scotland, and New Zealand. Included are simple but informative post facto studies along with 12 that incorporate comparison groups. Five of the studies consist of in-depth secondary analysis, which often is a mark of a field of inquiry moving beyond immediate programmatic and policy questions to longer-range questions of causality. Most of the studies are quasi-experimental designs. Several studies offer more rigorous experimental designs with random assignment of subjects and higher-level statistical analysis.

While specific studies focus on particular sets of questions germane to local interest, overall, they address questions of consumer satisfaction with the program and the criminal justice system, victim-offender mediation as a means for determining and obtaining restitution, victim-offender mediation as diversion from further penetration into the system, and the relationship of victim-offender mediation to further delinquency or criminality.

The remainder of this article considers the consequences of victim-offender mediation over the past 20 years. Those consequences are divided into the following topics: 1) client satisfaction, 2) client perception of fairness, 3) restitution, 4) diversion, 5) recidivism, 6) costs, and 7) VOM and crimes of violence.

Some topics such as client satisfaction, client perception of fairness, and restitution are considered in most of the studies under review and we are only able to provide a sense for the overall findings while offering an illustrative flavor of a few specific studies. Other topics, such as recidivism and costs, are addressed by only a handful of studies and we will provide a bit more detailed information regarding these.

As one might expect, victim-offender mediation programs are called by many names and share an array of acronyms reflecting philosophical, regional, and cultural characteristics. Whether referred to as "victim-offender mediation," "victim-offender dialogue," "victim-offender conferencing," or "victim-offender meetings," nearly all of these programs provide an opportunity for crime victims and offenders to meet face-to-face to talk about the impact of the crime on their lives and to develop a plan for repairing the harm. Most programs work with juvenile offenders, a growing number with adult offenders, and some with both. The vast majority of victim-offender mediation programs are "dialogue driven" rather than "settlement driven" (Umbreit, 1997). To reduce confusion in the following discussion of a large number of studies, programs will simply be referred to as victim-offender mediation, or VOM.

Client Satisfaction

Victim-offender mediation proponents often speak of humanizing the justice system. Traditionally, victims have been left out of the justice process. Neither victim nor offender have had opportunities to tell their stories and to be heard. The state has somehow stood in for the victim, and the offender has seldom noticed how his or her actions have affected real, live people. Victims, too, have been left with stereotypes to fill their thoughts about offenders. Reformers believed VOM offered opportunities for both parties to come together in a controlled setting to share the pain of being victimized and to answer questions of why and how. Personalizing the consequences of crime, it was thought, would enhance satisfaction levels with the entire justice process.

The vast majority of studies reviewed reported in some way on satisfaction of victims and offenders with victim-offender mediation and its outcomes. Researchers found high levels of participant satisfaction across program sites, types of offenders, types of victims, and cultures.

Before exploring the nature of this satisfaction further, we should note that across these studies, from 40 to 60 percent of those offered the opportunity to participate in VOM refused, making it evident that participation is a highly self-selective process. Typically, these refusals came from victims who 1) believed the crime to be too trivial to merit the time required, 2) feared meeting the offender, or 3) wanted the offender to have a harsher punishment (Coates and Gehm, 1985; Umbreit, 1995). Gehm, in a study of 555 eligible cases, found 47 percent of the victims willing to participate (Gehm, 1990). In this study victims were more likely to participate if the offender was white, if the offense was a misdemeanor, and if the victim was representing an institution. The practical experience of VOM programs, however, is not consistent with this finding.

Offenders were sometimes advised by lawyers not to participate (Schneider, 1986). And some simply didn't want "to be bothered" (Coates and Gehm, 1985).

The voluntary nature of VOM is a self-selection factor overlaying these findings. The high levels of satisfaction may have something to do with the opportunity to choose. Perhaps those who are able to choose among justice options are more satisfied with their experiences.

Several studies noted victims' willingness to participate was driven by a desire to receive restitution, to hold the offender accountable, to learn more about the why of the crime and to share their pain with the offender, to avoid court processing, to help the offender change behavior, or to see that the offender was adequately punished. Offenders choosing to participate often wanted to "do the right thing" and "to get the whole experience behind them" (Coates and Gehm, 1985; Perry, Lajeunesse, and Woods, 1987; Umbreit, 1989; Roberts, 1995; Umbreit, 1995; Niemeyer and Shichor, 1996).

Expressions of satisfaction with VOM are consistently high for both victims and offenders across sites, cultures, and seriousness of offenses. Typically, eight or nine out of ten participants report being satisfied with the process and with the resulting agreement (Davis, 1980; Coates and Gehm, 1985; Perry, Lajeunesse, and Woods, 1987; Marshall, 1990; Umbreit, 1991, 1994, 1995; Umbreit and Coates, 1993;Wamer, 1992; Roberts, 1995; Carr, 1998; Roberts, 1998).

Participants in one British study (Umbreit and Roberts, 1996) yielded some of the lowest satisfaction scores among the studies reviewed. While 84 percent of those victims engaged in face-to-face mediation were satisfied with the mediation outcome, the bulk of the victims did not meet face to face with an offender. For those involved in indirect mediation, depending on shuttle mediation between parties without face-to-face meetings, 74 percent were satisfied with their experience. These findings were consistent with an earlier study based in Kettering, where a small sub-sample of participants were interviewed, indicating 62 percent of individual victims and 71 percent of corporate victims were satisfied (Dignan, 1990). About half of the offenders responding reported being satisfied. Participants involved in face-to-face mediation were more satisfied than those who worked with a go-between.

Victims often reported being satisfied with the opportunity to share their stories and their pain resulting from the crime event. A victim stated she had wanted to "let the kid know he hurt me personally, not just the money . . . I felt raped" (Umbreit, 1989). Some expressed satisfaction with their role in the process. One victim said: "we were both allowed to speak . . . he (mediator) didn't put words into anybody's mouth" (Umbreit, 1988).

Another female victim indicated, "I felt a little better that I've [a] stake in punishment" (Coates and Gehm, 1985). Another indicated that "it was important to find out what happened, to hear his story, and why he did it and how" (Umbreit and Coates, 1992). Numerous victims were consumed with the need for closure. A victim of violent crime indicated that prior to mediation, "I was consumed with hate and rage and was worried what I would do when he got out" (Platen, 1996).

Of course not all victims were so enamored of the process. A distinctly small but vocal minority of victims were not pleased with the program. A male victim complained: "It's like being hit by a car and having to get out and help the other driver when all you were doing was minding your own business" (Coates and Gehm, 1985). A Canadian stated: "The mediation process was not satisfactory, especially the outcome. I was not repaid for damages or given compensation one year later. The offender has not been adequately dealt with. I don't feel I was properly compensated" (Umbreit, 1995).

Offenders generally report surprise about having positive experiences. As one youth said, "He understood the mistake I made, and I really did appreciate him for it" (Umbreit, 1991). Some reported changes: " After meeting the victim I now realize that I hurt them a lot . . . to understand how the victim feels makes me different" (Umbreit and Coates, 1992). One Canadian offender stated his pleasure quite succinctly: "Without mediation I would have been convicted" (Umbreit, 1995).

The following comment reflects the feelings of a relatively small number of offenders who felt that victims at least occasionally abused the process: "We didn't take half the stuff she said we did; she either didn't have the stuff or someone else broke in too" (Coates and Gehm, 1995).

An offender in Albuquerque (Umbreit and Coates, 1992) also believed that the process allowed the victim too much power: "the guy was trying to cheat me . . . he was coming up with all these lists of items he claimed I took." Some offenders felt powerless to refute the accusations of victims.

Secondary analysis of satisfaction data from a U.S. study and a Canadian study yielded remarkably similar results (Bradshaw and Umbreit, 1998; Umbreit and Bradshaw, 1999). Using step-wise multiple regression procedures to determine those variables most associated with victim satisfaction, three variables emerged to explain over 40 percent of the variance. In each study, the key variables associated with victim satisfaction were: 1) the victim felt good about the mediator, 2) the victim perceived the resulting restitution agreement as fair, and 3) the victim, for whatever reason, had a strong initial desire to meet the offender. The last variable supports the notion that self-selection and choice are involved in longer-run satisfaction. These findings also underscore the important role of the mediator, and, of course, the actual outcome or agreement resulting from mediation.

These high levels of satisfaction with victim-offender mediation also translated into relatively high levels of satisfaction with the criminal justice system. Where comparison groups were studied, those victims and offenders going through mediation were far more satisfied with the criminal justice system than those going through traditional court prosecution (Davis, 1980; Umbreit and Coates, 1993; Umbreit, 1995). For example, a multi-site U.S. study of VOM in four states (Umbreit & Coates, 1993) found that victims of juvenile crime were significantly more likely to be satisfied (79 percent) with the manner in which the justice system dealt with their case than similar victims (57 percent) who went through the regular court process.

Fairness

Related to satisfaction is the question of fairness. Many of the studies reviewed asked participants about the fairness of the mediation process and of the resulting agreement (Davis, 1980; Coates and Gehm, 1985; Umbreit, 1988, 1989, 1991, 1995; Coates and Umbreit, 1992).

Not surprisingly, given the high levels of satisfaction, the vast majority of VOM participants (typically over 80 percent) across setting, cultures, and types of offenses reported believing that the process was fair to both sides and that the resulting agreement was fair. Again, these experiences led to feelings that the overall criminal justice system was fair. Where comparison groups were employed, people exposed were more likely to feel that they had been treated fairly than those going through the traditional court proceedings. In a study of burglary victims in Minneapolis, Umbreit found that 80 percent of those undergoing VOM experienced the criminal justice system as fair, compared with only 37 percent of burglary victims who did not participate in VOM (Umbreit, 1989).

As expected from the quantitative numbers on fairness, statements from victims and offenders about fairness reflected that assessment. Common comments included: "The mediator was not biased, she was not judgmental" (victim) and "he listened to everyone during the meeting" (offender). (Umbreit and Coates, 1992). A few, however, did not feel the same way. "He seemed more like an advocate for the kid, " and "she seemed kind of one-sided to the victim" (Umbreit and Coates, 1992) reflect perceived imbalance and unfairness in the mediation process. While the negative data that emerged was quite small in proportion to the overall positive findings, negative statements offered helpful insight into how the mediation process may have unintended consequences for the participants.

These overall positive experiences of satisfaction and fairness, however, have generated support for VOM as a criminal justice option. When asked, typically nine out of ten participants would recommend a VOM program to others (Coates and Gehm, 1985; Umbreit, 1991).

Restitution

Early on, restitution was regarded by program advocates as an important by-product of bringing offender and victim together in a face-to-face meeting. Restitution was considered somewhat secondary to the actual meeting where each party had the opportunity to talk about what happened. The current emphasis on humanistic "dialogue-driven" mediation (Umbreit, 1997) reflects this traditional emphasis on restitution being of secondary importance. Today, a few jurisdictions see VOM as a promising major vehicle for achieving restitution for the victim. These jurisdictions view the meeting as necessary to establish appropriate restitution amounts and garner the commitment of the offender to honor a contract. Victims frequently report that while restitution was the primary motivator for them to participate in VOM, what they appreciated most about the program was the opportunity to talk with the offender (Coates and Gehm, 1985; Umbreit and Coates, 1992).

In many settings, restitution is inextricably linked with victim-offender mediation. About half the studies under review looked at restitution as an outcome of mediation (Collins, 1984; Coates and Gehm, 1985; Perry, Lajeunesse and Woods, 1987; Umbreit, 1988; Galaway 1989; Umbreit, 1991; Umbreit and Coates, 1992; Warner, 1992; Roy, 1993). Of those cases that reached a meeting, typically 90 percent or more generated agreements. Restitution in one form or another (monetary, community service, or direct service to the victim) was part of the vast majority of these agreements. Looking across the studies, it appears that approximately 80–90 percent of the contracts are reported as completed. In some instances, the length of contract exceeded the length of study.

One study was able to compare restitution completion between those youth participating in VOM with a matched group who did not (Umbreit and Coates, 1993.) In that instance, 81 percent of participating youth completed their contracts contrasted with 57 percent of those not in the VOM program, a finding that was statistically significant. In another study comparing an Indiana county that integrated restitution into victim-offender mediation with a Michigan county that imposed restitution without mediation, no difference in completion rates were found (Roy, 1993). Each was just shy of 80 percent completion.

Diversion

Many VOM programs are nominally established to divert youthful offenders into less costly, time consuming, and (it is believed) less severe options. Although diversion is a goal lauded by many, others express concern about the unintended consequence of widening the net, that is, ushering in youth and adults to experience a sanction more severe than they would have if VOM did not exist. While much talk continues on this topic, there is a dearth of study devoted to it. Only a handful of the studies reviewed here address this question.

One of the broadest studies considering the diversion question was conducted over a three-year period in Kettering, Northamptonshire, England (Dignan, 1990). Offenders participating in the VOM program were matched with similar non-participating offenders from a neighboring jurisdiction. The author concludes that at least 60 percent of the offenders participating in the Kettering program were true diversions from court prosecution. Jurisdictional comparisons also led him to conclude that there was a 13 percent widening-the-net-effect, much less than local observers would have predicted.

An agency based in Glasgow, Scotland, where numbers were sufficiently large to allow random assignment of individuals between the VOM program and a comparison group going through the traditional process, found 43 percent of the latter group were not prosecuted (Warner, 1992). However, most of these pled guilty and were fined. This would suggest that VOM in this instance was a more severe sanction and indeed widened the net of government control.

In a very large three-county study of mediation in North Carolina, results on diversion were mixed (Clark, Valente, Jr., and Mace, 1992). In two counties, mediation had no impact on diverting offenders from court. However, in the third county the results were quite dramatic. The authors concluded: "The Henderson program's effect on trials was impressive; it may have reduced trials by as much as two-thirds."

Mediation impact on incarceration was explored in an Indiana-Ohio study by comparing consequences for 73 youth and adults going through VOM programs with those for a matched sample of individuals processed in the traditional manner (Coates and Gehm, 1985). VOM offenders spent less time incarcerated than did their counterparts. And when incarcerated, they did county jail time rather than state time. The length and place of incarceration also had substantial implications for costs.

Recidivism

While recidivism may be best regarded as an indicator of society's overall response to juvenile and adult offenders, it is a traditional measure used to evaluate the long-term impact of justice programs. Accordingly, a number of studies designed to assess VOM have incorporated measures of recidivism.

Some simply report rearrest or reconviction rates for offenders going through the VOM program understudy (Carr, 1998; Roberts, 1998). Since no comparison group or before/after outcomes are reported, these recidivism reports have local value, but offer very little meaning for readers unfamiliar with typical rates for that particular region.

One of the first studies to report recidivism on VOM was part of a much larger research project on restitution programs (Schneider, 1986).Youth randomly assigned to a Washington, D.C. VOM program were less likely to have subsequent offenses resulting in referral to a juvenile or adult court than youth in a comparison probation group. These youth were tracked for over 30 months. The results were 53 percent and 63 percent; the difference was statistically significant. A third group, those referred to mediation but refusing to participate, also did better than the probation group. This group's recidivism prevalence was 55 percent.

Marshall and Merry (1990) report recidivism on two programs handling adult offenders in Coventry and Wolverhampton, England. The results are tentative but encouraging. In both sites, the offenders were divided into the following groups: those who did not participate in mediation at all, those who were involved in discussions with staff even though their victims were unwilling to participate, those who were involved in indirect mediation, and those who met their victims face-to-face. Offender records were analyzed to determine criminal behavior for comparable periods before referral to program and after program intervention.

In Coventry, while there was no statistically significant differences between the "no work" or no participation group and the others, those who went through direct mediation and those who received individual attention even though their victims were unwilling to meet, did better, that is, either they committed fewer crimes or less serious offenses.

In Wolverhampton, the indirect mediation group fared best, with 74 percent improving their behavior compared to 55 percent direct mediation, 45 percent individuals receiving staff attention only, and 36 percent for those not involved in the program. The authors regard these findings as highly tentative and remain puzzled about why in one site indirect mediation fared so much better than direct while the reverse was found in the other.

The study based in Kettering, England (Dignan, 1990) compared recidivism data between the VOM offenders who went through face-to-face mediation with those who were exposed only to "shuttle mediation." The former group did somewhat better than the latter: 15.4 percent and 21.6 percent. As with satisfaction measures reported earlier, face-to-face mediation seems to generate better results both in the short run and in the longer run than the less personal indirect mediation.

In a study of youth participating in VOM programs in four states, youth in mediation had lower recidivism rates after a year than did a matched comparison group of youth who did not go through mediation (Umbreit and Coates, 1992). Overall, across sites, 18 percent of the program youth re-offended, compared to 27 percent for the comparison youth. Program youth also tended to reappear in court for less serious charges than did their comparison counterparts.

The Elkhart and Kalamazoo county study (Roy, 1993) found little difference in recidivism between youth going through the VOM program and the court-imposed restitution program. VOM youth recidivated at a slightly higher rate, 29 percent to 27 percent. The author noted that the VOM cohort included more felons than did the court-imposed restitution cohort.

A study of 125 youth in a Tennessee VOM program (Nugent and Paddock, 1995) reported that these youth were significantly less likely to re-offend than a randomly selected comparison group: 19.8 percent to 33.1 percent. The VOM youth who did re-offend did so with less serious charges than did their comparison counterparts.

A sizeable cohort of nearly 800 youth going through mediation in Cobb County, Georgia between 1993 and 1996 was followed along with a comparison group from an earlier time period (Stone, Helms, and Edgeworth, 1998). No significant difference in recidivism rates was found: 34.2 percent mediated to 36.7 percent non-mediated. Three-quarters of the mediated youth who returned to court did so because of violation of the conditions of mediation agreements.

In a recent article, Nugent, Umbreit, Wiinamaki and Paddock (2001) conducted a rigorous reanalysis of recidivism data reported in four previous studies involving a total sample of 1,298 juvenile offenders, 619 who participated in VOM and 679 who did not. Using logistic regression procedures, the authors determined that VOM youth recidivated at a statistically significant 32 percent lower rate than non-VOM youth, and when they did re-offend they did so for less serious offenses than the non-VOM youth.

All in all, recidivism findings across a fair number of sites and settings suggest that VOM is at least as viable an option for recidivism reduction as traditional approaches. And in a good number of instances, youth going through mediation programs are actually faring better.

Cost

Relative costs of correctional programs are difficult to assess. Several studies reviewed here addressed the issue of costs. Cost per unit case is obviously influenced by the number of cases handled and the amount of time devoted to each case. The results of a detailed cost analysis in a Scottish study were mixed (Warner, 1992). In some instances, mediation was less costly than other options and in others more. The author notes that given the "marginal scope" of these programs it remains difficult to evaluate how much they would cost on a scale large enough to affect overall program administration.

Evaluation of a large-scale VOM program in California led authors to conclude that cost per case was reduced dramatically as the program went from being a fledgling to being a viable option (Niemeyer and Schichor, 1996). Cost per case was $250.

An alternative way of considering the cost impact of VOM is to consider its effect on the broader system. Reduction of incarceration time served can yield considerable savings to a state or county (Coates and Gehm, 1985). Reduction of trials, such as in Henderson County, North Carolina, where trials were reduced by two-thirds, would have tremendous impact at the county level (Clarke, Valente Jr., and Mace, 1992). And researchers evaluating a VOM program in Cobb County, Georgia point out that while they did not do a cost analysis, time is money (Stone, Helms, and Edgeworth, 1998). The time required to process mediated cases was only a third of that needed for non-mediated cases.

The potential cost savings of VOM programs when they are truly employed as alternatives rather than as marginal showcase add-ons is significant. Yet a cautionary note must continue to be heard. Like any other program option, these programs can be swamped with cases to the point that quality is compromised. And in the quest for savings there is the temptation to expand the eligibility criteria to include those who would not otherwise penetrate the system or to take on serious cases that the particular program staff are ill equipped to manage. Staff and administrators must be prepared to ask, "Cost savings at what cost?"

VOM and Crimes of Violence

In 1990, a survey of victim-offender mediation programs in the juvenile justice system noted that most programs excluded violent offenders and sex offenders (Hughes and Schneider, 1990). Two-thirds of cases reported by VOM programs in a 1996–97 survey (Greenwood and Umbreit, 1998) involved offenders with misdemeanor offenses. Forty-five percent of reporting programs worked only with juveniles while nine percent handled adults only. The remainder worked with both. These figures support the notion that VOM is often used as a "front-end" diversionary option often working with "less serious" cases. In fact, the largest VOM programs in the United States, some receiving over 1,000 referrals a year, serve as a diversion of young offenders with little or no prior court involvement from formal processing in the juvenile court.

Many program staff contend that in order to work with burglary and moderately serious assault cases programs must accept the less serious cases. Others would argue that these so-called "less serious" cases still involve human loss and tragedy. And still others claim that making crime a human problem for offenders at these less serious levels will prevent more serious crimes from occurring. As indicated above when discussing recidivism, there is at least some modest empirical support for these contentions.

Without disparaging the work of VOM programs dealing in cases perceived and defined as "less serious," there are signs of at least a subtle shift in the utilization of VOM. In the above-mentioned 1996–97 survey, many program administrators indicated that programs "are being asked to mediate crimes of increasing severity and complexity." And "virtually all interviewees indicated that advanced training is necessary in working with cases of severe violence" (Greenwood and Umbreit, 1998).

Apart from the general pressure to take on more severe and complex cases, some individuals and programs specialize in working with the most violent kinds of crime. Studies involving murder, vehicular homicide, manslaughter, armed robbery, and sexual assault in such disparate locations as New York, Wisconsin, Alaska, Minnesota, Texas, Pennsylvania, Ohio, and British Columbia (Umbreit, 1989; Roberts, 1995; Flatten, 1996; Umbreit, Bradshaw, and Coates, 1999; Umbreit and Brown, 1999; Umbreit and Vos, 2000) are yielding important data for shaping mediation work with violent offenders and victims of violent crime.

These very intense, time-consuming mediation efforts have shown promising, positive results. Victims who seek and choose this kind of encounter and dialogue with an individual who brought unspeakable tragedy to their lives report feelings of relief, a greater sense of closure, and gratitude for not being forgotten and unheard. In several states, lists of victims seeking to meet with violent offenders far exceed the resources available to accommodate the victims' desires.

Conclusion

Victim-offender mediation has received considerable research attention—more than many other justice alternatives. With over 20 years of experience and research data, there is a solid basis for saying: 1) for those choosing to participate—be they victims or offenders—victim-offender mediation and dialogue engenders very high levels of satisfaction with the program and with the criminal justice system; 2) participants typically regard the process and resulting agreements as fair; 3) restitution comprises part of most agreements and over eight out of 10 agreements are usually completed; 4) VOM can be an effective tool for diverting juvenile offenders from further penetration into the system, yet it may also become a means for widening the net of social control; 5) VOM is as effective (if not more so) in reducing recidivism as traditional probation options; 6) where comparative costs have been considered, VOM offers considerable promise for reducing or containing costs; 7) there is growing interest in adopting mediation practices for working with victims and offenders involved in severely violent crime and preliminary research shows promising results, including the need for a far more lengthy and intensive process of preparing the parties.

For at least a significant minority of folks involved in the justice system, VOM is regarded as an effective means for holding offenders accountable for their actions. While there is a fairly extensive base of research on victim-offender mediation across many sites supporting this contention, far more work needs to be done. Most of the studies reported offer results that are at best suggestive because of the limitations of their research methodology. Far more rigorous studies, including random assignment, control groups and longitudinal designs, are required. Yet in the real world of field research in the criminal justice system, the 25-year experience of victim-offender mediation has become one of the more promising and empirically grounded reform movements to emerge during the last quarter of the twentieth century.

References

Bradshaw, W. and Umbreit, M. "Crime Victims Meet Juvenile Offenders: Contributing Factors to Victim Satisfaction with Mediated Dialogue," *Juvenile and Family Court Journal* Vol. 49 (Summer 1998), pp. 17–25.

Carr, C. (1998). *VORS Program Evaluation Report.*

Clarke, S., E. Valente, Jr., and R. Mace (1992). *Mediation of Interpersonal Disputes: An Evaluation of North Carolina's Programs.* Chapel Hill: Institute of Government, University of North Carolina.

Collins, J.P. (1984). *Final Evaluation Report on the Grande Prairie Community Reconciliation Project For Young Offenders.*

Coates, R. and J. Gehm (1985). *Victim Meets Offender: An Evaluation of Victim-Offender Reconciliation Programs.* Valparaiso, IN: PACT Institute of Justice; Coates, R. and J. Gehm (1989), "An Empirical Assessment" in M. Wright and B. Galaway (eds.), *Mediation and Criminal Justice.* London: Sage, pp. 251–263.

Davis, R. et. al. (1980). *Mediation and Arbitration as Alternative to Prosecution in Felony Arrest Cases, An Evaluation of the Brooklyn Dispute Resolution Center.* New York, NY: VERA Institute of Justice.

Dignan, J. (1990). *Repairing the Damage: An Evaluation of an Experimental Adult Reparation Scheme in Kettering, Northamptonshire.* Sheffield: Centre for Criminological Legal Research, Faculty of Law, University of Sheffield.

Fercello, C. and Umbreit, M. (1999) *Client satisfaction with victim offender conferences in Dakota County, Minnesota.* St. Paul, MN: Center for Restorative Justice & Mediation, University of Minnesota, School of Social Work.

Flaten, C. (1996). "Victim-Offender Mediation: Application with Serious Offences Committed by Juveniles." In B. Galaway and J. Hudson (eds.), *Restorative Justice: International Perspectives.* Monsey, NY: Criminal Justice Press, pp. 387–401.

Galaway, B. (1989). "Informal Justice: Mediation between Offenders and Victims." In P. Albrecht and O. Backes (eds.), *Crime Prevention and Intervention: Legal and Ethical Problems.* NY, NY: Walter de Gruyter, pp. 103–116.

Galaway, B. (1995). "Victim-Offender Mediation by New Zealand Probation Officers: The Possibilities and the Reality." *Mediation Quarterly* Vol. 12, pp. 249–262.

Gehm, J. (1990). "Mediated Victim-Offender Restitution Agreements: An Exploratory Analysis of Factors Related to Victim Participation." In B. Galaway and J. Judson (eds.), *Criminal Justice, Restitution, and Reconciliation.* Monsey, NY: Criminal Justice Press, pp. 177–182.

Hughes, S. and A. Schneider, (1990). *Victim-Offender Mediation in the Juvenile Justice System.* Washington, D.C.: Office of Juvenile Justice and Delinquency Prevention.

Marshall, T. (1990). "Results of Research from British Experiments in Restorative Justice." In B. Galaway and J. Hudson (eds.), *Criminal Justice, Restitution, and Reconciliation.* London: Sage, pp. 83–107.

Niemeyer, M. and D. Shichor (1996). "A Preliminary Study of a Large Victim/Offender Reconciliation Program," *Federal Probation,* Vol. 60 (September) pp. 30–34.

Nugent, W. and J. Paddock (1995). "The Effect of Victim-Offender Mediation on Severity of Reoffense," *Mediation Quarterly* Vol. 12, Summer, pp. 353–367.

Nugent, W., M. Umbreit, L. Wiinamaki, and J. Paddock (2001). "Participation in Victim-Offender Mediation and Severity of Subsequent Delinquent Behavior: Successful Replications?" *Journal of Research in Social Work Practice.*

Perry, L., Lajeunesse, T. and Woods, A. (1987). *Mediation Services: An Evaluation.* Manitoba Attorney General: Research, Planning and Evaluation.

Roberts, L. (1998). *Victim-Offender Mediation: An Evaluation of the Pima County Juvenile Court Center's Victim Offender Mediation Program (VOMP).* Available from Frasier Area Community Justice Initiatives in Langley, British Columbia.

Roberts, T. (1995). *Evaluation of the Victim-Offender Mediation Project, Langley, BC: Final Report.* Victoria, BC: Focus Consultants.

Roy, S. (1993) "Two Types of Juvenile Restitution Programs in Two Midwestern Counties: A Comparative Study," *Federal Probation,* Vol. 57, pp. 48–53.

Schneider, A. (1986). "Restitution and Recidivism Rates of Juvenile Offenders: Results from Four Experimental Studies," *Criminology,* Vol. 24, pp. 533–552.

Stone, S., W. Helms, and P. Edgeworth (1998). *Cobb County Juvenile Court Mediation Program Evaluation.*

Umbreit, M. S. (1988). "Mediation of Victim-Offender Conflict," *Journal of Dispute Resolution,* pp. 85–105.

Umbreit, M. (1989). "Crime Victims Seeking Fairness, Not Revenge: Toward Restorative Justice," *Federal Probation* (September 1989), pp. 52–57.

Umbreit, M. (1989). "Violent Offenders and Their Victims." In M. Wright and B. Galaway (eds.), *Mediation and Criminal Justice.* London: Sage, pp. 99–112.

Umbreit, M. (1991). "Minnesota Mediation Center Produces Positive Results," *Corrections Today* (August), pp. 194–197.

Umbreit, M. (1995). *Mediation of Criminal Conflict: An Assessment of Programs in Four Canadian Provinces.* St. Paul, MN: Center for Restorative Justice and Mediation, University of Minnesota, School of Social Work. Other publications related to this study include: Umbreit, M. (1996), "Restorative Justice Through Mediation: The Impact of Programs in Four Canadian Provinces," in B. Galaway and J. Hudson, (eds.) Restorative Justice: International Perspectives. Monsey, NY: Criminal Justice Press; Umbreit, M. (1999) "Victim-Offender Mediation in Canada: The Impact of an Emerging Social Work Intervention," International Social Work.

Umbreit, M. S. (2001). *The Handbook of Victim-Offender Mediation: An Essential Guide for Practice and Research.* San Francisco: Jossey-Bass.

Umbreit, M. and R. Coates, (1992). *Victim-Offender Mediation: An Analysis of Programs in Four States of the U.S.* St. Paul, MN: Center for Restorative Justice and Mediation, University of Minnesota, School of Social Work. Other publications related to this study include: Umbreit, M. & R. Coates, "The Impact of Mediating Victim-Offender Conflict: An Analysis of Programs in Three States," *Juvenile & Family Court Journal* (1992), pp. 1–8; Umbreit, M. & R. Coates, "Cross-Site Analysis of Victim-Offender Mediation in Four States," *Crime & Delinquency* Vol. 39 (Oct. 1993), pp 565–585; Umbreit, M. "Juvenile Offenders Meet Their Victims: The Impact of Mediation in Albuquerque, New Mexico," *Family and Conciliation Courts Review,* Vol. 31 (Jan. 1993), pp.90–100; Umbreit, M. *Victim Meets Offender.* Monsey, NY: Criminal Justice Press, 1994; Umbreit, M. "Crime Victims Confront Their Offenders: The Impact of a Minneapolis Mediation Program," *Research On Social Work Practice* Vol. 4 (Oct. 1994), pp. 436–447; Umbreit, M. "Restorative Justice through Mediation: The Impact of Offenders Facing Their Victims in Oakland," *Journal of Law and Social Work* Vol. 5 (Spring 1995), pp. 1–13; Umbreit, M. "Restorative Justice Through Victim-Offender Mediation: A Multi-Site Assessment," *Western Criminology Review* Vol. 1 (1998).

Umbreit, M. and A. Roberts (1996). *Mediation of Criminal Conflict in England: An Assessment of Services In Coventry And Leeds.* St. Paul, MN: Center for Restorative Justice and Mediation; and Roberts, A. and M. Umbreit (1996), "Victim-Offender Mediation: The English Experience," *MEDIATION UK,* Vol. 12, Summer.

Umbreit, M. and W. Bradshaw (1997). "Victim Experience of Meeting Adult vs. Juvenile Offenders: A Cross-National Comparison," *Federal Probation* Vol. 61 (December), pp. 33–39.

Umbreit, M. and J. Greenwood (1999). "National Survey of Victim Offender Mediation Programs in the US," *Mediation Quarterly* 16(3), pp. 235–251.

Umbreit, M., R. Coates, and A. Roberts (1998). "Impact of Victim-Offender Mediation in Canada, England and the United States," *The Crime Victims Report* (January/February) pp. 20–92.

Umbreit, M. and W. Bradshaw (1999). "Factors that Contribute to Victim Satisfaction with Mediated Offender Dialogue in Winnipeg: An Emerging Area of Social Work Practice," *Journal of Law and Social Work.*

Umbreit, M., W. Bradshaw, and R. Coates (2001). "Victims of Severe Violence Meet the Offender: Restorative Justice Through Dialogue." *International Journal of Victimology.*

Umbreit, M. and K. Brown (1999). "Victims of Severe Violence Meet the Offender in Ohio." *The Crime Victim Report,* Vol. 3 (3).

Umbreit, M. and Betty Vos (2000). "Homicide Survivors Meet the Offender Prior to Execution: Restorative Justice Through Dialogue." *Homicide Studies,* Vo1. 4 (1).

Warner, S. (1992). *Making Amends: Justice for Victims and Offenders.* Aldershot: Avebury.

Wiinamaki, K. (1997). Doctoral dissertation. School of Social Work, University of Tennessee.

Wynne, J. (1996). "Leeds Mediation and Reparation Service: Ten Years Experience of Victim-Offender Mediation." In B. Galaway and J. Hudson (eds.), *Restorative Justice: International Perspectives.* Monsey, NY: Criminal Justice Press, pp. 443–461.

Mark S. Umbreit, Robert B. Coates, and Betty Vos, "The Impact of Victim-Offender Mediation: Two Decades of Research." Reprinted from *Federal Probation,* September 2001, 65 (3): 29–35. Published by The Administrative Offices of the United States Courts. ✦

Chapter 18

Prosecutors Discover the Community

Brian Forst

While community prosecution has been touted as a reform along the lines of community policing or sentencing guidelines, Forst questions whether it is truly the paradigm shift the system needs. The successes of community policing programs, especially in the press, have led District Attorneys to adopt similar programs aimed at community outreach and involvement. But while community prosecution has led to well-received press conferences, Forst argues that the elected nature of the office actually steers DAs away from real reform. Beyond the rhetoric of "community outreach" and "cooperation," he suggests several areas where real reform could, and should, be implemented.

> The vice of our leading parties in this country is that they do not plant themselves on the deep and necessary grounds to which they are respectively entitled, but lash themselves to fury in the carrying of some local and momentary measure, nowise useful to the commonwealth.
>
> —Ralph Waldo Emerson
> *Essays, Second Series, Politics*

For all the well-deserved attention that has been given to revolutionary developments in policing, sentencing, and corrections during the last two decades of the 20th century, the prosecution scene has remained remarkably tranquil. Some view community prosecution programs as nothing less than a paradigm shift in prosecution,[1] but there are several reasons to question whether those programs really improve prosecution, much less offer the sort of breakthroughs that have occurred in other parts of the criminal justice system.

This article reviews the state of prosecution generally at the beginning of the 21st century and considers the prospects for reform, giving special attention to community prosecution programs and the potential for truly fundamental reform. One might reasonably conclude that the potential for a genuine revolution in prosecution is considerable, and that the opportunities for radical change in prosecution—change that could significantly advance the public's interests in justice and order—lie beyond the domain of contemporary community prosecution programs.

District attorneys from Boston and Brooklyn to Kansas City and Portland have launched programs of community outreach, assigning cases to assistant DAs by neighborhood rather than in the order they arrive, and encouraging the prosecutors to spend more time in the community. A common denominator is that the programs typically aim to redirect service outside the court, with more sensitivity to the cultures and special needs of those served.

Prosecutors who have announced these goals of service and sensitivity are putting a variety of programs in place to achieve them: working more closely with police officers and others who understand the unique characteristics of particular neighborhoods, sometimes assigning assistant district attorneys to work out of police precincts or storefronts, supporting community crime prevention programs, and converting from a production line approach that moves cases along impersonally to a system known as "vertical prosecution" that reduces the need for traumatized victims to repeat harrowing experiences to a sequence of strangers. A corollary activity has been to deal with crimes involving offenders who operate across communities by collaborating more closely with prosecutors in other jurisdictions.

A focus group commissioned by the Bureau of Justice Assistance developed this definition of community prosecution: "a long term, proactive strategy involving a partnership among the prosecutor's office, law enforcement, the community and public and private organizations whereby the authority of the prosecutor's office is used to solve problems and improve public safety and the quality of life in an identified community."[2]

Why the Sudden Interest?

These certainly seem like healthy, public-spirited developments but one can't help but wonder: Why now? Where does this sudden interest in the community by prosecutors come from?

The success of community policing programs surely plays an important role. District attorneys did not appear to notice the emergence of community policing in the 1980s, but when it matured into a full-fledged mass movement in the 1990s they started showing interest. The community policing movement is one of the reasons often cited for the 30 percent reduction in violent crime rates in the US since 1992.[3] Municipal police departments throughout the country have worked to build bridges to the community and improve public relations by moving officers from squad cars to foot and bicycle patrols, sending officers to schools to speak about drugs, and focusing more on prostitution, vandalism, and other crimes of disorder.

Anecdotal evidence in support of these activities is compelling, but whether they really reduce serious crime remains unclear. Wesley Skogan's exhaustive review of the experimental research in several cities has found these efforts to have done more to reduce fear and increase public satisfaction with police service than to reduce crime rates, at least in the short term.[4]

Community policing and community prosecution are rooted more fundamentally in two larger social movements of the 1980s and '90s: consumerism and communitarianism. The consumer movement itself has two distinct roots, one emphasizing excellence in service delivery, stimulated by the work of Tom Peters and Bob Waterman, the other emphasizing consumer rights, stimulated by the work of Ralph Nader. The combined effects of these influences on the attitudes, expectations, and behaviors of people acting both as public sector citizens and private sector consumers paved the way for criminal justice interest in the community.

The communitarian movement was stimulated largely by the work of Amitai Etzioni, especially his 1993 book, *The Spirit of Community.* Etzioni describes the movement broadly as "dedicated to the betterment of our moral, social, and political environment . . . Communitarians are dedicated to working with our fellow citizens to bring about the changes in values, habits, and public policies that will allow us to . . . safeguard and enhance our future." He goes on to outline the implications of this perspective for public safety: people working together more closely in crime watches, community policing and prosecution programs, sentencing nonviolent offenders to community service, and strengthening informal social control mechanisms.

By the late 1990s, federal funding became widely available to district attorneys to sweeten the community prosecution pot. Byrne Grant program funds, administered by the Bureau of Justice Assistance (BJA), provide support to prosecutors to establish and participate in community prosecution programs generally and community justice centers and multi-jurisdictional task forces in particular.

So now prosecutors are climbing aboard the community bandwagon. They're doing so in much the same way as did police chiefs: first a few brave souls, then others, aware of the political capital to be exploited. Most may be doing so with noble intentions. There is, in any case, merit in bringing prosecutors down from the ivory tower, to induce greater sensitivity to the lives of the people whose fates are often at the mercy of the prosecutor's decisions. Still, it may be no coincidence that such programs are unheard of in other countries, where prosecutors are appointed rather than elected. Ten years ago it was common to hear police officers complain about learning of their department's conversion to "community policing" on the evening news. Today, assistant district attorneys are telling similar stories.

Los Angeles County District Attorney Gil Garcetti is a recent convert to community prosecution. A picture of him walking through a crime-ridden apartment complex appeared prominently in local papers in Los Angeles in July 1999, his way of introducing a federally supported community prosecution initiative there. Garcetti is better known for his work supervising the prosecution of the O.J. Simpson case, which nearly cost him his job; he was narrowly re-elected in 1996 despite spending $2.4 million on his campaign, six times the level spent by his opponent.

Resistance to Reform

Photo opportunities and public proclamations tell one story; the historical record another. Prosecutors have in fact not been at the vanguard of either community consciousness or criminal justice reform. The end of the 20th century finds sea changes in every other sector of the criminal justice system. Policing is going through not only the community-oriented revolution, but also a transformation in privatization. As recently as 1965 there were more sworn police officers than private security personnel; 30 years later the number of private security personnel was about triple the number of sworn officers.[5]

We have seen equally remarkable changes in sentencing and corrections: the conversion from judicial discretion in sentencing to mandatory terms and legislatively imposed sentencing guideline systems, large-scale shifts from a dichotomous incarceration-or-probation world to one with a myriad of intermediate sanction options ranging from intensive supervision and electronically monitored home detention to more widespread use of community-based sanctions, and the expansion of privatization alternatives throughout the corrections sector.

Changes in prosecution have been fairly modest by comparison. The typical prosecutor's office has a more modern appearance than it did in the mid-20th century, with desktop computers supporting operations and access to vastly greater sources of information and forensic technologies than ever before. Women and minorities play larger roles as prosecutors than in earlier times, along with their gains in virtually every other profession. And now we have attempts at community outreach.

The fundamentals of prosecution, however, remain as they have for decades. The basic nature and goals of prosecution, the role of the citizen as victim or witness in a matter between the state and the defendant, the essential steps in processing cases through the courts, and systems of public accountability have all remained essentially unchanged since 1970.

Prosecutors are not more inherently resistant to change than others. They tend to be well-educated, they must understand fine points of the law, and they must be able to decipher intricate case details quickly and interpret complex human behaviors accurately. Prosecutors deal daily with unpredictability. Their work calls for intelligence and ingenuity, resourcefulness and hard work. They are sworn to serve the public. And they know that some innovations produce welcome political capital.

Still, as elected officials, district attorneys aim to avoid embarrassment. This is usually accomplished by keeping the bulk of the work of the office below the horizon, staying away from risky ventures and drastic departures from conventional modes of office management and from collaborations with researchers on the assessment of policies, procedures, or performance, assessments that could become tomorrow's negative headline.

A 1998 survey of more than 500 scientific evaluations of crime prevention programs, sponsored by the National Institute of Justice and conducted by Lawrence Sherman and his colleagues at the University of Maryland, found but a single evaluation of an innovative prosecution program, an experiment run by David Ford that tested three alternative domestic violence interventions in Indianapolis. Innovation was found mostly elsewhere—programs initiated by the police, social service agencies, schools, drug treatment specialists, housing, and correctional authorities.

The prosecutor's insulation derives in part from legal training. Prosecutors are trained in our adversarial system of law, not in principles of service delivery or systems of management. To the extent that they receive administrative training in law school, it is usually about the management of private law practice rather than the administration of a prosecutor's office.

A first rule of prosecution derives from the legal-adversarial culture: Don't divulge the particulars of your case to anyone who isn't in a position to help you win it. Prosecutors become accustomed to keeping their options open by revealing little about their objectives and about the information they have and don't have. They typically see little to gain and much to lose by divulging any information that is not required by law. Internal office policy manuals indicating the prosecutor's guidelines for screening cases and negotiating pleas are typically unavailable to the defense bar and the general public.

This culture stands in contrast to innovative efforts by other criminal justice agents, who sometimes find themselves attempting unsuccessfully to obtain needed support from the prosecutor. Sally Hillsman has reported finding prosecutors converting an innovative attempt at rehabilitation in New York into a vehicle for controlling offenders who would otherwise have had their cases dismissed following diversion and completion of job training. Sherman and his colleagues have similarly documented pretrial diversion programs that "tend to get co-opted by prosecutors for purposes other than the intended purpose of rehabilitating offenders."[6]

The prosecutor is insulated also by the virtual absence of a system of measured public accountability in most states. The success of prosecutors is assessed principally in terms of the public's perception of the prosecutor's ability to convict offenders. These perceptions are shaped primarily by a few prominent cases in the news and by occasional public pronouncements by a district attorney or attorney general asserting toughness against any and all who would dare to violate the law. Most prosecution offices are headed by elected district attorneys. Unlike police chiefs, who are appointed by and accountable to mayors, prosecutors do not report to a higher political authority in position to call for a more comprehensive system of accountability. Political opponents have not been able to distract the voters from their preoccupation with celebrity cases and their obliviousness to the importance of systematic measures of performance. And the media, capable of enlightening the public on the folly of weak accountability for the vast majority of felony cases, have opted to feed the public's appetite for information about exceptional cases.

Of course, most chief prosecutors are directly accountable to the voters. But they are politicians who have it in their best interest not to subject themselves to systems of accountability that opponents could use against them. Unlike the police chief, who may benefit from falling crime rates but must also suffer the inevitable upward swings in crime, the prosecutor is rarely called to task by the local press for a drop in the conviction rate. Conviction rates are not routinely reported to a national agency in the same way that crimes reported to the police and arrests made by the police are documented annually by the FBI. The National Judicial Reporting Program (NJRP) reports felony convictions and arrests for about 300 of the nation's 3,195 counties, but the data are aggregates rather than based on individually tracked felony cases.[7] Many of the convictions reported for a given year relate to arrests made in earlier years, which creates distortions especially when the aggregates change from one year to the next. NJRP gives no information about cases rejected or dropped by prosecutors.

Nor are the prosecutors in most jurisdictions required to provide systematic information about case outcomes to other criminal justice agencies that deal with and rely on the prosecutor, especially the police and victim-witness organizations. Some prosecutors do provide feedback, but it is usually voluntary and episodic.

Some prosecutors select cases and handle them in a way that gives more than the usual degree of political visibility, but this too tends to be opportunistic rather than systematic. Prosecutors in New York have established a tradition of pursuing high-profile cases aggressively, accepting pleas well beyond national norms in other cases, and eventually running for higher public office. A prosecutor's career path can be driven, for better or worse, by the outcome of a single case that attains local or national prominence.

No Bottom Line

The irony of community prosecution is that even the best of the programs lack systematic bottom-line public accountability. This is a problem that is endemic to the prosecutor's operations generally. Except for the rare case that makes the front-page news, the bulk of the prosecutor's work in most metropolitan jurisdictions is invisible to the communities about which prosecutors are expressing new-found interest. Prosecutors are occasionally overruled by judges, but those rulings are not routinely tallied to provide any systematic degree of public accountability. Opportunities for judicial oversight are limited more fundamentally by the fact that judges are unable to scrutinize the vast majority of cases that come to the prosecutor; for every felony case that a judge presides over in trial, the prosecutor in most jurisdictions rules on the handling of between 10 to 15 felony cases brought by the police.[8] And for every case that makes the evening news, the typical urban prosecutor determines the fate of more than 100 that do not.

District Attorney Gil Garcetti's conversion to community prosecution is instructive. Most of the same L.A. County voters who know scores of fascinating details about his handling of the Simpson case have no clue as to how effectively he has managed his office or how the office has performed in many thousands of other felony cases during his tenure, in comparison with earlier years, or with other big-city offices. A display of interest in crime in apartment complexes may provide splendid publicity spreads, but that is a poor substitute for a comprehensive system of accountability.

Does It Work?

As appealing as community prosecution seems, it is really not clear that the prevailing bundle of interventions that have become associated with the community prosecution movement are really the most effective ones for giving prosecutors their needed training on sensitivity toward community residents and problems. Should prosecutors be spending much time lecturing to school children? Assessments of police doing so under the Drug Abuse Resistance Education (DARE) programs have consistently found that those programs have done nothing to achieve the professed objectives of reduced drug use and delinquency.[9]

And precisely how should prosecutors be working more closely with police officers? It certainly makes sense for prosecutors to engage in ride-alongs with the police and set up operations in precincts and store fronts, to get to know both the neighborhoods and the police better. Yet there is no guarantee that those experiences will ensure that the prosecutors, thus enlightened, will exercise discretion more wisely from the case screening stage through final adjudication.

And how much time should prosecutors spend supporting community crime prevention programs? Surely crime prevention is a worthy goal, but it is not clear that prosecutors are better situated to engage effectively in those efforts than are the police.

Post-arrest options are another matter: focusing on dispute resolution, mediation, community service, restitution, and other community-based approaches to resolve minor crimes and problems at early stages before they blossom into serious felonies. These programs have yet to be subjected to rigorous experimental assessment, but they make sense theoretically: they fit the prosecution mandate more closely than many conventional crime prevention programs.

Converting from a production line approach to a vertical prosecution system may make sense in rape cases and cases involving victims who are very young or otherwise especially vulnerable. For a variety of less serious crimes, however, large municipal prosecution offices could be wasting resources and losing cases if they were to rely on systems of prosecution better suited to rural settings.

Multi-jurisdictional task forces may also be an effective way of sharing information to facilitate the solving of crimes and collection of strong evidence that secures convictions, but it may be much more effective in some settings and for certain types of cases than others. Task force successes appear to depend largely on the unique chemistries of the people involved.

The strongest evidence that interventions associated with community prosecution may reduce crime, especially cooperation between prosecutors and others in positions to prevent and solve crime, is from Boston. A constellation of projects are credited with reducing gun homicides in that city, especially among juveniles. The number of homicides dropped from about 100 annually in the late 1980s, before the projects were launched, to 35 by 1998 and not a single juvenile homicide in that year. The number of shootings also plummeted. Ralph Martin II, the District Attorney for Suffolk County (comprising Boston and immediately surrounding communities), played a pivotal leadership role in these projects.

A centerpiece of the Boston crime reduction efforts was the Safe Neighborhood Initiatives (SNI), which coordinated law enforcement activities, supported neighborhood revitalization efforts, and complemented conventional response activities with a focus on prevention. SNI prosecutors spoke at all the local schools and at various community organization meetings. They also participated in the Boston Youth Violence Strike Force (YVSF), which coordinated Martin's SNI with the Massachusetts Attorney General and local U.S. attorney, as well as with 45 full-time Boston Police Department officers, 15 officers from nearby police departments, and federal agents, together with probation, parole, and other correctional agents. A third element of collaboration was the Boston Gun Project, which included the close support of agents from the Bureau of Alcohol, Tobacco and Firearms.

In all three projects, coordination among prosecutors provided an array of creative options in determining which charges to file where. Cross-deputization of prosecutors provided opportunities to file cases that fell under multiple jurisdiction authority in Suffolk County juvenile court, adult court, or federal court. Coordination with law enforcement officials appears to have been equally important, to ensure that the elements needed to satisfy various charging requirements were met.

A broader set of prosecution strategies emerged from this coordination than had been traditionally applied. The Suffolk County D.A. aggressively filed charges against crimes of disorder—graffiti, truancy, noise, public drinking, and so on—to improve the quality of life, especially in areas of Boston that had suffered from chronic private abuse and public neglect. Federal, state, and local statutes were creatively applied to remove guns from the streets under laws against gun use, possession, and trafficking. The Massachusetts Commonwealth's criminal and civil forfeiture laws were exploited to take over drug dens and permit their renovation into suitable low-income housing. Civil sanctions were also more aggressively applied to target chronic public blemishes such as mechanics doing major vehicle repairs on the street and commercial establishments improperly disposing of waste.

A variety of interventions thus appears to have reduced crime in Boston, but this is by no means a clear victory for community prosecution. It may be a victory for aggressive programs to remove guns from juveniles and dangerous juveniles from the streets. It may be a victory for a unique way of targeting drugs. It may even be a victory for prosecutors who are effective at inducing support from others in positions to control crime. Several interventions were used, some having little to do with community prosecution, and we have no way of knowing which ones were the most effective; one or two may have even been counterproductive.

The key ingredient missing from the Boston experience was that the interventions were not individually tested by experimentation. Prosecutors in Boston and elsewhere are spending scarce resources on a loosely defined set of interventions having to do with "community outreach" and "cooperation" without the benefit of empirical evidence validating that some are really more effective than others, or indeed that any of those usually associated with community prosecution are useful for achieving the goals of prosecution.

The interventions are based on common sense and theory. Time and again, however, criminal justice interventions based on common sense and theory—from random police patrols and rapid police response to boot camps and DARE programs—have been found to be ineffective when subjected to properly designed and executed experimental research. In some cases, such as mandatory arrests of unemployed spouse assaulters and three-strikes-and-you're-out for old offenders, the intervention has been shown to be worse than neutral.[10] Over the years, a few courageous police chiefs—Clarence Kelley, Hubert Williams, and Darrel Stephens are three notable examples—have distinguished themselves and advanced their calling by allowing researchers to alter normal operations for the sake of learning from experiments what works, and there is no good reason why this should not happen in prosecution.

Why Change?

More than a few citizens are growing weary of political posturing when genuine accountability may be more welcome. A few have grown cynical enough to see that community prosecution offers a unique opportunity for elected public officials to spend more time shaking hands at the public's expense. Private sector marketing is, of course, even more extravagant, but there is an important difference: an office of prosecution is guaranteed survival regardless of what the citizen thinks of its performance. Private sector organizations have long used a variety of sources to obtain reliable feedback about the perceived effectiveness of service delivery. Police departments are turning increasingly to such assessment systems, in part because they have been losing market share, as noted earlier.

Prosecutors in the U.S. have little reason to worry about market share; they have a monopoly on prosecution. That is not the case in England and elsewhere, where private lawyers can prosecute a variety of criminal offenses. Signs of change are in the air here, however; civil courts already provide an alternative to criminal prosecution in the U.S. This provided a small moral victory to the families of the victims in the Simpson case. If our prosecutors don't move well beyond expressions of concern about the community, stronger private alternatives may emerge here as well.

The public has become deeply suspicious of officials who are less than honest about the essentials of their performance. If prosecutors really wish to serve the community, they will subject their new programs to objective assessment and more systematic reporting. They will make data available to the public on the number of arrests in each neighborhood by offense category and the disposition of those arrests at each stage of prosecution from the screening room until the case leaves the court. They will routinely communicate information about the status and outcome of each case to the police, victims, and witnesses. They will work more diligently to nurture, maintain, and monitor the cooperation of witnesses and victims.

Prospects for Reform

One prosecution event dwarfed all others in the late 1990s: independent prosecutor Kenneth Starr's impeachment investigation of the President. For all the media attention given to Starr's freewheeling exercise of discretion in building a case against Bill Clinton, remarkably little was paid to the power of prosecutors generally. The fact that Starr's target was no less than the President of the United States is, of course, what made that investigation so remarkable. Still, one might have expected a greater expression of concern about the broader implications of Starr's methods, that extraordinary means are available to prosecutors to damage personal reputations in the name of other ends.

This concern is not new. In 1940 former U.S. Attorney General and Supreme Court Justice Robert H. Jackson observed, "The prosecutor has more control over life, liberty, and reputation than any other person in America."[11] Jackson's remark had more resonance 60 years ago than today; a public that has grown intolerant of crime can be expected to accept extremes in the prosecutor's use of authority. But Starr's interests were not about street crime, and there is ample reason to suspect that for all the lip service paid to crime, most prosecutors appear to have other political interests that profoundly shape their operations.

While the operations of most other institutions are much more open to scrutiny today than when Justice Jackson made his observation about the prosecutor's power nearly 60 years ago, systematic accounting of the prosecutor's day-to-day operations remain absent from public view. Much of the work of the prosecutor remains very much subject to abuses of discretion, despite posturing to the contrary. Contemporary standards of accountability warrant the casting of a brighter light on the work of prosecutors, to move beyond rhetoric and strengthen legitimacy by making their operations more transparent and subject to systematic evaluation.

The potential for truly fundamental change in prosecution goes beyond even the critical matter of accountability. The prospects for such change do not necessarily lie beyond our grasp. Change that could significantly advance the public's interests in justice and order will probably require a shift from our current system, which treats the victim primarily as a resource for promoting the interest of the state, to one that recasts justice as a matter of balancing the right of the defendant to a fair and full hearing under the presumption of innocence with the fundamental right of the victim to be restored. Under current arrangements, victims are inadequately compensated for costs imposed by the criminal justice system: lost income, time spent with police and court officials, out-of-pocket costs for transportation, child care, and related costs.

Victims are not generally included in any meaningful way in case processing decisions following arrest. Most significantly, they are then rarely compensated for losses associated with the crime. Victims commonly end up feeling used, like mere items of evidence, deprived even of basic rights corresponding to those extended to offenders. Even when the offenders are convicted, victims rarely benefit in any tangible way from conventional sentences of incarceration and probation. Nor are intermediate sanctions typically of much help to victims: community service does little for the community and less for the victim; fines are rarely collected, and when they are, the proceeds typically do not go to the victim. In the exceptional case in which the judge orders restitution, the court rarely follows up to ensure that the terms of restitution are fully met. Victims are too often left with little incentive to cooperate in subsequent episodes.

Ironically, when victims are asked how they have been treated by various components of the criminal justice system, prosecutors fare less well than police, despite the fact that the chief prosecutor is usually an elected official and the police chief is not.[12] Community prosecution programs aim principally to connect the prosecutor more closely to the community, not primarily to restore the victim. These programs leave intact the fundamental principle that the prosecutor represents the state, not the victim, in all criminal matters.

Bruce Benson and others have suggested that a shift to a process resembling our tort system might effectively work to remedy these serious deficiencies. Genuine opportunities for victims to be restored could well increase their incentives to report crimes to the police, thus reducing recidivism rates and crime costs, stimulating general deterrent effects, and raising the perception of system legitimacy throughout society.[13]

As currently conceived, community prosecution programs do little either to make prosecutors more systematically accountable to citizens for their workaday, behind-the-scene performance in all felony cases or to promote a deep, transformational sense of justice. While these programs may offer superficial political advantages for prosecutors, and may even produce marginal gains in crime abatement, they represent no "paradigm shift." They may, in fact, divert the attention of prosecutors from reforms that could really serve members of the community most in need of relief from crime. Prosecutors might do well to consider, instead of or in addition to community prosecution, truly radical departure from current arrangements. Not just for political gains, but primarily for the sake of victims and the well-being of the community.

Notes

The author wishes to acknowledge helpful comments on earlier drafts from Kristen Bender, Tom Brady, David Ford, Phil Heymann, Gerard Rainville, and two anonymous referees.

1. Coles and Kelling offer this assessment: "Today, a new movement, 'community prosecution,' is capturing the attention of many prosecutors. In many senses, community prosecution represents the next stage in the dismantling of the old paradigm." Coles and Kelling, *Prevention Through Community Prosecution,* 136 THE PUBLIC INTEREST, 69, 73 (Summer 1999).
2. Stevens, *Defining Community Prosecution,* 28 THE PROSECUTOR 13 (March/April 1994).
3. President Bill Clinton has been a prominent advocate: "More community police on our streets and fewer guns in the hands of criminals have helped make our communities the safest they have been in a generation." Suro, *Figures Show 7% Decline in Crime for 1998,* The Washington Post (May 17, 1999), at A5.
4. Skogan, DISORDER AND DECLINE: CRIME AND THE SPIRAL OF DECAY IN AMERICAN NEIGHBORHOODS (New York: Free Press, 1990). Skogan has reported evidence of crime reduction effects of community policing in Chicago in more recent research. Skogan and Hartnett, COMMUNITY POLICING, CHICAGO STYLE (New York: Oxford University Press, 1990).
5. Forst and Manning, THE PRIVATIZATION OF POLICING: TWO VIEWS at 16 (Washington, DC: Georgetown University Press, 1999).
6. Hillsman, PRETRIAL DIVERSION OF YOUTHFUL ADULTS: A DECADE OF REFORM AND RESEARCH, 7 JUST SYS J. 361–87 (1982). Sherman, Gottfredson, MacKenzie, Eck, Reuter, and Bushway, PREVENTING CRIME: WHAT WORKS, WHAT DOESN'T, WHAT'S PROMISING, Chapter 6, at 14 (Washington, DC: National Institute of Justice, 1998).
7. Brown, Langan, and Levin, FELONY SENTENCES IN STATE COURTS, 1996, at 5 (Washington, DC: Bureau of Justice Statistics, 1999).
8. Forst, *Prosecution and Sentencing,* in Wilson and Petersilia, (eds.) CRIME 374. (San Francisco: ICS, 1995).
9. Sherman, et al., *supra n.* 6.
10. *Id.*
11. Jackson, *The Federal Prosecutor,* 24 JOURNAL OF THE AMERICAN JUDICATURE SOCIETY 18 (1940).
12. See Rosen's interview with Susan Herman, director of the National Center for Victims of Crime. Rosen, *LEN Interview with Susan Herman,* 25 LAW ENFORCEMENT NEWS 8,9 (November 30, 1999).
13. Benson, TO SERVE AND PROTECT: PRIVATIZATION AND COMMUNITY IN CRIMINAL JUSTICE (New York University Press, 1998).

Chapter 19

The Effects of Pretrial Publicity on Jurors

Norbert L. Kerr

M*any assert that pretrial publicity rarely prejudices the outcome of a trial. According to the growing research literature, however, not only can pretrial publicity bias jurors, but common remedies may not be effective in preventing or overcoming such bias.*

Perhaps nowhere do basic constitutional rights come into clearer conflict than on the issue of pretrial publicity. On the one hand, the First Amendment guarantees the press the freedom to investigate and report on matters of public concern, including the operation of the courts. On the other hand, the Sixth Amendment guarantees defendants the right to a public trial by an impartial jury. The conflict arises when the content of pretrial publicity may be prejudicial, threatening jurors' impartiality. Recent prominent cases such as those involving O.J. Simpson, Susan Smith, Manuel Noriega, Oliver North, and Rodney King have raised these issues and called them to the public's attention.

At the core are a number of behavioral questions: Under what, if any, conditions does pretrial publicity affect juror impartiality? What kinds of publicity create the greatest risk of bias? How well do existing safeguards and remedies for exposure to prejudicial pretrial publicity work? This article examines a number of the attempts by behavioral scientists to explore such questions.[1]

One could argue that bias due to pretrial publicity is not much of a problem. Relatively few crimes appear to receive more than cursory attention in the media. For example, Frasca has estimated that only about 7 percent of all felony arrests are covered by the press.[2] However, he also estimates that reporting in 70 percent of crimes that do receive press coverage contain some information that is prejudicial under American Bar Association guidelines (such as results of fingerprint tests).[3] Overall, according to Frasca, only about 5 percent of defendants must confront the potential problem of prejudicial pretrial publicity.

For the few cases that do receive extensive pretrial publicity, most of the parties involved think it has no significant effect on jury behavior. This was evident in the responses of judges, prosecutors, defense attorneys, and journalists interviewed as part of research on pretrial publicity.[4] Judges, who are responsible for using the available remedies to ensure an impartial jury, generally thought that these remedies (particularly voir dire) are quite effective.[5] Prosecutors, whose cases are usually bolstered by pretrial publicity, likewise tended to believe that such publicity does not pose an insuperable problem. Journalists, who are understandably zealous in defending First Amendment press freedoms, offered a variety of reasons why they believe pretrial publicity is not really a problem. Only defense attorneys, whose clients could be most directly and adversely affected by such publicity, said that pretrial publicity can and regularly does bias jury verdicts.

Why should anyone besides defense attorneys be concerned about this issue? Although proportionally few cases receive prejudicial pretrial coverage, the absolute number is not trivial (more than 12,000 per year in the United States).[6] Further, most of the judges and trial attorneys interviewed in the above study have or will handle one or more such cases. And the same public interest that makes these cases newsworthy prior to trial often results in close media attention throughout, making these cases important for counsel's reputation and for public opinion about the justice system. Most important, a growing research literature suggests not only that pretrial publicity can bias jury opinion, but that common remedies may not be very effective in preventing or overcoming such bias.

Publicity and Public Opinion

A number of investigators have surveyed public opinion following extensive pretrial publicity. The intent of most of this research has been to show that such publicity can affect public opinion about cases, particularly regarding the defendant's guilt or innocence. For example, Simon and Eimermann surveyed 130 registered voters concerning publicity surrounding a pending murder case.[7] During the two months that passed between the murder and the survey, 25 articles appeared in the local newspapers. Fifty-nine percent of those surveyed heard or read about the case and could supply details about the crime. Members of this exposed group were more likely to describe their current feelings about the case as pro-prosecution (65 percent versus 41 percent in the non-exposed group). They also were less likely to think that the defendants could receive a fair trial and to be willing to be tried by a jury in the same frame of mind as their own. Yet despite these differences, members of the exposed group were just as likely to believe they personally could hear the evidence with an open mind.

This and similar studies show that extensive prejudicial pretrial publicity can be associated with prejudgment of a defendant—a stronger belief that the defendant is guilty and stronger doubts about jurors' ability to impartially consider the evidence presented at trial.[8] However, even when pretrial publicity has been intense, most people feel they could be impartial jurors and that a fair trial could be obtained.

There have also been a number of surveys by litigants to bolster motions for change of venue.[9] They document that specific knowledge of a case and anti-defendant/pro-prosecution attitudes are more likely in local communities with high levels of pretrial publicity than in alternative more distant counties. However, few public opinion surveys presented by defense counsel have succeeded in winning a change in venue.[10]

What Is Prejudicial?

To identify aspects of pretrial publicity that produce the greatest degree of prejudgment, a number of investigators (primarily journalism researchers) have systematically varied the publicity's content.[11] Unsurprisingly, such research suggests that pretrial publicity that indicates culpability in the present crime (such as a confession) or a general predisposition to crime (such as an extensive record) can affect readers' impressions of guilt. Also, the more prejudicial information included in the pretrial publicity, the more likely the reader is to infer guilt.

For example, DeLuca gave one of seven news stories to 206 undergraduate journalism students who rated the suspect's likely degree of guilt. Reports of a confession significantly increased mean guilt ratings. Adding a report of a failed lie detector test significantly increased this mean rating. And the addition of a prior arrest record produced yet another significant increase in mean guilt ratings.[12]

Naturally, the most troublesome forms of pretrial publicity involve information that jurors may have seen or heard concerning the case they must try. Greene calls this "case-specific" pretrial publicity.[13] However, it is also possible that what she terms "general pretrial publicity," information that is prominently in the news but unrelated to the particular case being tried, may also affect jurors' verdicts.[14] For example, consider the case of Gary Dotson, who was convicted of the rape of Cathleen Webb in 1977. In 1985 Webb recanted her testimony, claiming she falsely lodged the original rape charge. According to Greene, such general publicity about the possibility of a false rape charge could affect juror behavior in a completely unrelated rape trial.

Research has demonstrated such general publicity effects.[15] In one study, three groups of mock jurors were compared: (a) a group that first read newspaper articles about a defendant mistakenly identified and convicted of rape (the miscarriage condition); (b) a group that read different articles describing how the testimony of an eyewitness led to the arrest and conviction of a mass murderer (the heinous crime condition); and (c) a control group that was exposed to no pretrial publicity. All mock jurors then considered a case of alleged armed robbery and murder. The prosecution's case depended primarily on eyewitness testimony. The acquittal rate in the miscarriage condition (57 percent) was significantly higher than either of the two others (control, 40 percent not guilty; heinous crime, 25 percent not guilty).[16] In a follow-up study, the investigators showed that the more similar the publicized case was to the case being tried, the stronger the effects of the general pretrial publicity.

Greene has argued that such effects are not isolated.[17] She has suggested, for example, that juror attitudes and behavior in unrelated cases can be and are affected by news or entertainment media depictions of courtroom procedures (such as the feature movie *The Verdict*),[18] of particular classes of witnesses (such as psychiatric testimony),[19] of law enforcement efficiency,[20] of insurance industry advertising,[21] and of violent pornography.[22]

Actual vs. Experimental Verdicts

Despite the generally sanguine attitudes expressed by journalists, prosecutors, and trial judges about the risks to fair trial created by prejudicial pretrial publicity, appellate courts have conceded that in certain cases the level and content of pretrial publicity has been so prejudicial that it has infringed on the defendant's due process rights.[23] Thus, case law recognizes the possibility that pretrial publicity may bias jurors and charges the trial court judge to deal with this possibility. The empirical question is whether such prejudice survives the remedies the court applies.

The most direct way to examine this question would be to associate the occurrence of pretrial publicity with actual jury verdicts—is the conviction rate higher in cases receiving prejudicial pretrial publicity? There have been a few isolated attempts to do this.[24]

The problem with such investigations is that they fail to examine a matched sample of cases without pretrial publicity. Without such data it is not possible to establish whether there is an association between the amount or type of pretrial publicity and the jury verdict. Apparently, no one has yet collected the appropriate data to answer this question. One reason is that it is very difficult to identify trials that are unequivocally comparable to those receiving extensive pretrial publicity. Cases that attract publicity may be systematically different in a variety of important ways (for example, they may involve more experienced counsel, counsel may prepare their cases more thoroughly, or judges may be more meticulous in their handling of the case).

The ideal comparison case, of course, is the same case and trial unchanged in any way except for the absence of pretrial publicity. That ideal is unachievable in examining actual jury trials, but it can be achieved in experimental studies. In laboratory trial simulations, an experimenter can ensure that the only difference between two sets of jurors is their exposure to pretrial publicity of known characteristics, and can then draw direct and confident inferences about the impact of such publicity on simulated or mock jurors' behavior.

The greater experimental control available in the laboratory is purchased at a cost—the laboratory simulation is necessarily artificial. But despite its artificiality, many behavioral scientists maintain that the findings of experimental simulations may help illuminate behavior in actual trial settings. This is not just a scientist's leap of faith. The utility of laboratory experimentation has been sufficiently well demonstrated that the public is quite used to paying attention to the fruits of such research. For instance, many diet soft drink consumers and smokers do not blissfully continue to use products containing saccharin or nicotine simply because they dismiss out of hand the highly artificial experimental research with laboratory animals that suggests the health risks of these substances. Instead, they grant that humans might want to limit or eliminate entirely from their diets substances that do produce cancer when fed in massive doses to laboratory rats.

Similarly, attorneys, judges, and legislators might want to carefully consider certain demonstrated risks to a fair trial of exposure to pretrial publicity, even when those risks are documented under highly artificial laboratory conditions. A number of studies have determined that the artificialities of the typical trial simulation study generally do not bias verdicts.[25] For all of these reasons, laboratory research on pretrial publicity and mock juror behavior (which constitutes the larger part of the pretrial publicity literature) is highly relevant.

From Publicity to Verdict

Does the well-documented effect of prejudicial pretrial publicity on public opinion reflect similar effects on juror judgment? A number of experiments have compared the verdicts of two groups of jurors for a single trial, one group having been first exposed to pretrial publicity, the other having not.[26] For example, Hoiberg and Stires examined two types of potentially prejudicial publicity—what might be called emotionally biasing publicity and factually biasing publicity.[27] The former refers to publicity that may shock or offend the public, and may arouse the public's passions surrounding a crime, but contains no inculpatory information about the defendant. Half of Hoiberg and Stires' mock jurors saw highly emotionally biasing publicity—an extremely lurid and graphic newspaper description of a rape-murder. The rest saw a news article that simply reported that "the girl had died as the result of a head injury."

Factually biasing publicity does contain specific inculpatory information about the defendant. Half of Hoiberg and Stires' mock jurors read a news article in which it was reported that the defendant had confessed to the crime. The rest read a report that indicated that questioning of the defendant had produced no clues or breakthroughs. Females (but not males) were significantly more certain of the defendant's guilt if exposed to either the emotionally or the factually biasing publicity.

This study, which used high school students as mock jurors, is an extreme example of a very unrealistic simulation of an actual trial. One might ask whether similar sensitivity to publicity would occur if the experiment provided a more accurate simulation of a real trial. Two experiments by Padawer-Singer and colleagues represent the most ambitious attempts to achieve realism in a jury simulation study of pretrial publicity.[28] They examined the combined effects of two types of prejudicial pretrial publicity—reports of a prior criminal record and of a withdrawn confession. The subjects were randomly selected from juror pools for two actual courts, the experiments were conducted in actual courtrooms, the stimulus trial was based on an actual murder trial, all standard trial elements were included, and deliberation was allowed to continue for several hours. The trial was presented in a three-hour audio tape recording based on an actual trial transcript.

The variation of exposure to pretrial publicity was achieved through two sets of simulated newspaper clippings. In the "neutral" set, only facts that were admissible in court were included. The "prejudicial" set also included a report of the criminal background of the defendant and another report that alleged that the defendant had retracted a confession. This publicity was factually biasing, yet care was taken to avoid any sensationalism in the news clippings.

In their first study, the authors reported that at the end of deliberation 78 percent of the jurors in the prejudiced condition favored conviction. In the neutral condition only 55 percent favored conviction. In a similar, second study, they found that 60 percent of prejudiced juries convicted the defendant while only 15 percent of neutral groups did so. Such results suggest that the biasing effects of pretrial publicity on mock juror verdicts is not restricted to highly artificial experimental conditions.

Although there is considerable evidence that prejudicial publicity can and does bias verdicts, there is far less direct evidence on why this bias occurs. A recent study by Otto, Penrod, and Dexter offers some suggestive evidence.[29] They found that several types of prejudicial publicity (such as negative character information and inadmissible evidence) affected jurors' initial, pretrial judgment of the defendant's likely guilt. This initial impression then seemed to exert both direct and indirect effects on jurors' final, post-trial verdicts. The latter, indirect effects resulted from pretrial publicity coloring jurors' assessment of evidence and their degree of sympathy for the defendant. Another type of prejudicial publicity (namely, prior record information) did not affect jurors' initial assessment of guilt, but seemed to affect their final verdicts. Thus, different types of pretrial publicity may affect verdicts through different routes.

Remedying the Effects

Trial court judges have a variety of remedies available to combat biasing effects of pretrial publicity. One rarely employed remedy is to impose a prior restraint or "gag" order on local media prohibiting publication or broadcast of potentially prejudicial material. Because this raises serious First Amendment questions, appellate courts have tended to discourage its use.[30] When publicity is localized, other remedies are changes of venue or of venire. If another venue can be found where the problematic publicity has been absent or muted, such remedies may be effective. Judges appear to be hesitant to employ such remedies for a number of reasons. For instance, they are expensive and they undermine a defendant's right to trial in the local community.[31] Thus, they are rarely used and there is practically no available research evidence on their effectiveness. However, there are four other remedies that are common and for which relevant behavioral research exists: granting a continuance, conducting extensive voir dire, instructing jurors to disregard pretrial publicity, and self-policing by the jury during deliberation.

Granting Continuances

A few very sensational cases manage to maintain more than a brief hold on the public's, and hence the media's, attention. For the majority of defendants, however, notoriety is a fleeting thing. Likewise, human memory is also fleeting. So, for those cases where publicity containing prejudicial content is limited in duration, one potentially effective remedy is for the trial judge to grant a continuance or to delay the trial starting date in the hope that potential jurors will have forgotten the publicity by the time the trial begins (and that there will not be a renewal of media interest).

A recently published experimental study focused on the effectiveness of this remedy.[32] It examined publicity that was both emotionally and factually biasing; the latter consisted of news reports detailing the defendant's previous two convictions for armed robbery and the discovery of incriminating physical evidence at his girlfriend's apartment. Neither piece of information was introduced into evidence during the trial. The emotionally biasing publicity identified the defendant as a suspect in a second offense—a fatal hit-and-run of a child involving the same vehicle used in the robbery. Care was taken to ensure none of the information conveyed in the emotionally biasing publicity bore in any way on the identity of the robber of the store (i.e., that it would also have factually biasing content). Mock jurors were exposed to both types of publicity, to only one, or to neither.

For approximately half of the jurors, this exposure occurred several days (12 on average) prior to the trial, simulating a brief continuance.[33] The remaining jurors were exposed to the pretrial publicity immediately prior to the trial. Juries exposed to the factual publicity were significantly more likely to convict the defendant than those not exposed, but only when there had been no delay between exposure and trial. When there had been a delay, factual publicity had no significant effect. Thus, the study offered some support for the effectiveness of a continuance as a means for ameliorating the influence of factually biasing pretrial publicity. Interestingly, though, the strong biasing effect of exposure to the emotionally biasing publicity was not attenuated at all by introducing such a delay. Thus, continuances (and perhaps other remedies) may be relatively more effective for one type of pretrial publicity than for another.

Jury Selection

From interviews and other surveys of attorneys and judges, it appears that voir dire and judicial admonitions are the most commonly used remedies for prejudicial pretrial publicity.[34] This reflects a widespread confidence that a careful and extensive voir dire is quite effective in identifying and eliminating jurors who might be tainted by exposure to pretrial publicity. In cases receiving limited publicity, this may well be true, since any juror who can remember seeing anything about the case can be excused. But in cases receiving extensive and intense publicity, such as O. J. Simpson's, it may be difficult to find jurors who have seen or heard nothing about the case (and one can question the qualifications for jury service of those who are so poorly informed).[35] Nevertheless, even for such cases it is commonly assumed that, with effort, a sufficient number of unexposed jurors can be found, that those exposed jurors who will assert their ability to disregard any publicity can and will do so, and that peremptory challenges may be used to remove those whose bias is not sufficiently demonstrable to warrant a challenge for cause.

As noted above, in high-publicity cases it is not uncommon for causal challenges to hinge upon the juror's own judgment of his or her impartiality. A juror who both remembers seeing publicity and doubts his or her ability to be impartial will routinely be excused for cause. A juror who remembers seeing publicity but assures the court that he or she could disregard it and attend exclusively to the trial evidence will not routinely be excused for cause.[36] Can such assertions of impartiality be accepted at face value? Sue, Smith, and Pedroza asked mock jurors who had been exposed to prejudicial factual publicity the generic impartiality question, "Can you, in view of the publicity you have seen, judge the defendant in a fair and unbiased manner?"[37] Those who answered "no" were indeed more likely to find the defendant guilty. But more important, those who answered "yes" were still much more likely to convict than jurors never exposed to the publicity (53 percent guilty versus 23 percent guilty, respectively).

Another recent study looked at the same questions.[38] Mock jurors who had been shown prejudicial factual or emotional publicity were asked in a simulated voir dire, "Can you put out of your mind any information you might have received from the newspapers or television and decide this case solely upon the evidence to be presented in court?" Mock jurors' responses to this question were unrelated to their subsequent verdicts. That is, those who doubted their ability to be impartial were no more or less likely to convict than those who had no such doubts. In both of these studies it is unclear whether the jurors were unaware of the biasing effect of the publicity or were simply not admitting a bias. What is clear is that jurors' simple assertions of impartiality were not sufficient to identify and eliminate bias due to exposure to pretrial publicity.[39]

Do peremptory challenges manage to catch and eliminate those jurors who fail to recognize or admit their own bias? A small but suggestive body of research has examined the effectiveness of attorney use of peremptory challenges in cases where pretrial publicity is not an issue.[40] There is little solid evidence that attorneys' peremptory challenges are reliably related to jurors' verdict preferences in such cases. However, perhaps pretrial publicity presents a less difficult task for counsel and the court. The immediate task is to detect specific knowledge about specific publicity rather than to detect a juror's general receptiveness to one side or the other's case. Furthermore, the voir dire is often much more extensive when there has been extensive publicity. Perhaps the greater scope of questioning and the greater number of peremptory challenges enhance the effectiveness of voir dire as a remedy for pretrial publicity.

In a study by Kramer et al., many of the mock jurors were videotaped as they responded to a series of generic voir dire questions for a high-publicity case (for example, "has . . . the publicity you've seen . . . caused you to form an opinion?").[41] In a followup study, these tapes were then mailed to a national sample of experienced prosecutors, defense attorneys, and trial judges.[42] Included was other information that would normally be available at the time of trial—summaries of the full range of publicity that jurors might have been exposed to, the background questionnaires collected by the jury commissioner, and the basic outlines of the prosecution and defense cases in the pending armed robbery trial. The attorneys and judges were asked to indicate which prospective jurors they would have excused had they been in their usual professional role in the armed robbery trial.

The judges' causal challenges and the defense attorneys' peremptory challenges were unrelated to jurors' verdicts. That is, those excused were no more or no less likely to convict than those who were acceptable to judges and defense attorneys. Prosecutors exercised fewer challenges (presumably since the publicity bolstered their case), but did somewhat better in identifying jurors sympathetic to their case. For example, the conviction rate among those retained by the prosecutors was significantly higher than those they peremptorily challenged (50.5 percent versus 16.7 percent, respectively). But the important question was, what was the net effect of all challenges? Were those who survived the scrutiny of experienced judges and attorneys just as bias-free as jurors never exposed to the publicity? The answer was no. Jurors exposed to prejudicial pretrial publicity who passed through the entire voir dire gauntlet were no more or less likely to convict than those who were excused (by anyone), but both groups were significantly more likely to convict than jurors unexposed to the publicity. Thus, the net effect of the voir dire process as simulated in this study was nil—the biasing effect of exposure to prejudicial pretrial publicity survived this voir dire process unscathed.

As noted above, though, there seems to be high confidence that voir dire is an effective way of recognizing and eliminating juror bias. This unfounded confidence was also documented in the study by Kerr et al.[43] Participating attorneys were asked to guess, based on the voir dire, which way each prospective juror was leaning—was he or she likely to vote guilty or not guilty? Overall, attorneys estimated that their predictions were correct 71.9 percent of the time. In fact, their predictions were correct only 45.4 percent of the time, about as well as one might do by flipping a coin.

Is it really surprising or disturbing that the existing evidence fails to bolster confidence in voir dire as a remedy for pretrial publicity? Jurors' awareness of and willingness to admit bias is clearly imperfect. Voir dire questioning is necessarily limited in content, length, and detail. Available challenges are limited. The need to seat a jury in a reasonable amount of time places constrains on even the judges' theoretically unlimited opportunities to challenge for cause. Those charged with making juror selection decisions receive little formal training for the task, and what little is provided is largely anecdotal or based on folklore or stereotypes. Further, even if there were reliable clues to juror bias, it is difficult to "learn on the job" largely because there is no effective feedback of how good one's decisions have been. Judges and attorneys never know how those they have challenged would have decided had they been seated as jurors. What is really surprising is not that voir dire accomplishes so little, but that it is expected to accomplish so much.

Judicial Instructions

A sizeable research literature calls into question the effectiveness of cautionary instructions from the bench as a means of eliminating the effect of legally inadmissible or prejudicial material.[44] For example, instructions to disregard such factors as inadmissible evidence[45] or a prior criminal record[46] seem to do little to reduce the impact of such extra-legal information. In fact, in a few studies instructions designed to reduce bias actually increased it.[47] Such findings are consistent with other recent social psychological research that indicates that telling someone not to think of something may well increase attention to it.[48]

As far as instructions to ignore pretrial publicity in particular are concerned, at least seven experiments have included specific judicial instructions prohibiting consideration of pretrial publicity, and none of them has observed any remedial effect.[49] For example, in the study by Kramer et al.,[50] half of the jurors were given the Wisconsin pattern jury instructions concerning pretrial publicity. For the other half, there was no mention of pretrial publicity, although there was the standard charge to disregard anything seen or heard when the court was not in session. Receiving the former instruction did not lessen the biasing effect of exposure to either the factually or emotionally biasing publicity.

The research evidence is very consistent. It suggests that reliance on standard judicial instructions as a remedy for exposure to pretrial publicity is unwarranted. If anything, such instructions seem to make matters worse. Judicial admonitions seem incapable of silencing pretrial publicity in jurors' minds.

Jury Deliberations

It has been suggested, both by legal scholars and behavioral scientists, that juries may effectively police themselves during deliberation.[51] If someone begins to discuss anything proscribed by the judge's instructions, other jurors may point this out and thereby help steer the deliberation back onto prescribed information. This line of argument suggests that whatever biasing effect pretrial publicity might have on individual juror judgment should be reduced through the process of jury deliberation. On the other hand, the usual effect of group discussion and decision making is to polarize opinion—that is, groups are usually more extreme in whatever direction individuals typically favor.[52] This suggests, for example, that if individual jurors tend to favor conviction, deliberating juries would be even more likely to convict. Indeed, this result has been observed.[53] This polarization phenomenon makes exactly the opposite prediction—namely, that biases at the individual juror level should be even larger among juries.

The existing research evidence seems most consistent with the latter prediction—if anything, jury deliberation seems to strengthen, not eliminate, bias. For example, in the Kramer et al. study the difference in juror conviction rates prior to deliberation between those exposed and not exposed to emotionally biasing publicity was only 5.9 percent; after deliberation this difference for non-hung juries was 43.3 percent. In this and other research,[54] rather than remedying exposure to publicity, deliberation tended to magnify its effect.

It is not entirely clear why this occurs. Kramer et al. videotaped their mock juries' deliberations to see whether and how exposure to pretrial publicity may have changed what jurors discussed.[55] Few juries exposed to publicity spent very much time discussing it directly. And the juries did seem to police themselves—mentions of publicity were nearly always followed by reminders that the jury should not consider such information. So the bias-enhancing effects of deliberation are probably more subtle and indirect. One possibility for which Kramer et al. found some support is that the usual and prescribed rule of giving the defendant the benefit of the doubt may be weakened among juries exposed to prejudicial pretrial publicity. This suggests that exposure to pretrial publicity not only can alter individual juror evaluations of trial evidence,[56] but may affect aspects of the jury deliberation process itself.

The use of lay petit juries as triers of fact has a long and important tradition in common law, and most observers agree that such juries generally do a very difficult job very well. However, whatever useful functions juries may serve, the available research suggests that jury deliberation should not be counted upon as a generally effective remedy for exposure to prejudicial pretrial publicity.

* * *

There are many confident voices among judges, lawyers, journalists, and jurors asserting that pretrial publicity rarely prejudices the outcome of a trial. Such assertions are based largely on personal experience, informal observation, and anecdote. However, systematic research tends to belie this rosy conclusion. This overview of the research literature suggests that intensive pretrial publicity can adversely affect public opinion and jury verdicts. Moreover, with but few exceptions, this research consistently calls into question the effectiveness of the most commonly relied upon remedies for such publicity. Of course, such research does not (indeed, cannot) prove that pretrial publicity will bias jury decision making in any particular trial. But it should alert the press, the courts, the bar, and the public not to turn a blind eye to the genuine risks of intensive pretrial publicity.

Notes

This article is based on Kerr, "Behavioral research on the effects of pretrial publicity," *From the Mind's Eye*, Vol. I, Issue 3 (1992).

1. Note in this summary of the literature that although much of the actual research was done with criminal cases, the principles of memory and judgment that underlie the reported effects should produce similar effects for civil cases.
2. Frasca, "Estimating the occurrence of trials prejudiced by press coverage," 72 *Judicature*, 162–169 (1988).
3. Tankard, Middleton, and Rimmer, "Compliance with American Bar Association fair trial-free press guidelines," 56 *Journalism Q.* 464 (1979).
4. See Carroll, Kerr, Alfini, Weaver, MacCoun, and Feldman, "Free press and fair trial: The role of behavioral research," 10

Law and Hum. Behav. 187–202 (1986) for a summary of these interviews.

5. Siebert, "Trial judges' opinions on prejudicial publicity," in Bush (ed.) *Free Press and Fair Trial: Some Dimensions of the Problem* (Athens, Ga.: University of Georgia Press, 1970); Weaver, "Prejudicial publicity: The judges' perspective." American Judicature Society Working Paper (1983).
6. *Supra* n. 2.
7. Simon and Eimermann, "The jury finds not guilty: Another look at media influence on the jury," 48 *Journalism Q.* 343–344 (1971).
8. See, e.g., Costantini and King, "The partial juror: Correlates and causes of prejudgment," 15 *Law & Soc'y Rev.* 9–40 (1980); Riley, "Pretrial Publicity: A field study," 50 *Journalism Q.* 17–23 (1973); Rollings and Blascovich, "The case of Patrica Hearst: Pretrial publicity and opinion," 27 *J. of Comm.* 58–65 (1977).
9. See Pollock, "The use of public opinion polls to obtain changes of venue and continuances in criminal trials," 51 *Crim. Jus. J.* 269–288 (1977) for a description of several unpublished surveys. Published surveys include Nietzel and Dillehay, "Psychologists as consultants for changes of venue: the use of public opinion surveys." Paper presented at the annual meeting of the Academy of Criminal Justice Sciences, Louisville, Kentucky, March, 1982; McConahay, Mullin and Frederick, "The uses of social sciences in trials with political and racial overtones: The trial of Joan Little," 41 *Law and Contemp. Probl.* 205–229 (1977).
10. There are a number of reasons, both legal and methodological, for this. See Pollock, *supra* n. 9, and Hans and Vidmar, "Jury selection," in Kerr and Bray (eds.), *The Psychology of the Courtroom* (New York: Academic Press, 1982). Still, there are ways of improving one's chances of success, see Vidmar and Judson, "The use of social sciences in a change of venue application," 59 *Canadian B. Rev.* 76–102 (1981) for an exemplary use of survey data with testimony to obtain a change of venue.
11. Hvistendahl, "The effect of placement of biasing information," 56 *Journalism Q.* 863–865 (1979); Sohn, "Determining guilt or innocence of accused from pretrial news stories," 53 *Journalism Q.* 100–105 (1976); Tans and Chaffee, "Pretrial publicity and juror prejudice," 43 *Journalism Q.* 647–654 (1966); Wilcox and McCombs, "Crime story elements and fair trial/free press." Unpublished paper, University of California (1967).
12. DeLuca, "Tipping the scales of justice: The effects of pretrial publicity." Unpublished master's thesis, Iowa State University (1979).
13. Greene, "Media effects on jurors," 14 *Law and Hum. Behav.* 439–450 (1990).
14. *Id.* at 441.
15. Greene and Loftus, "What's new in the news? The influence of well-publicized news events on pschological research and courtroom trials," 5 *Basic and Applied Soc. Psychology* 211–221 (1984).
16. Greene and Wade, "Of private talk and public print: General pre-trial publicity and juror decision-making," 2 *Applied Cognitive Psychology* 123–135 (1988).
17. *Supra* n. 13, and Riedel, "Effects of pretrial publicity on male and female jurors and judges in a mock rape trial," 73 *Psychological Reports* 819–832 (1993).
18. Shipp, "Message of 'The Verdict' is debated," *New York Times*, April 13, 1983, at A12.
19. Sharf, "Send in the clowns: The image of psychiatry during the Hinckley trial," 36 *J. of Comm.* 80–93(1986); Yoder, "The price we pay for insanity defense," *Chicago Sun-Times*, June 25, 1982, at 35.
20. Haney and Manzolati, "Television criminology: Network illustrations of criminal justice realities," in Aronson (ed.), *Readings About the Social Animal* (New York: Freeman, 1984).
21. Loftus, "Insurance advertising and jury awards," 65 *A.B.A.J.* 68–70 (1979).
22. Linz, Donnerstein and Penrod, "Effects of multiple exposures to filmed violence against women," 34 *J. of Comm.* 130–147 (1984); Zillman and Bryant, "Pornography, sexual callousness, and the trivialization of rape," 32 *J. of Comm.* 10–21 (1982).
23. See, e.g., Irwin v. Dowd, 366 U.S. 717 (1961); Rideau v. Louisiana, 373 U.S. 723 (1963); Sheppard v. Maxwell, 384 U.S. 333 (1966).
24. Hough, "Felonies, jury trials and news reports," in Bush (ed.), *Free Press and Fair Trial: Some Dimensions of the Problem* (Athens, Ga.: University of Georgia Press, 1970); Reuben, Confidential study cited "The Men at the Bar Meeting Debate, Gannet v. DePasquale" 68 *The Quill* 8 (1974).
25. Among the artificialities examined are the use of students as mock jurors [Simon and Mahan, "Quantifying burdens of proof: A view from the bench, the jury, and the classroom," *Law & Soc'y Rev.* 319–330 (1971); MacCoun and Kerr, "Asymmetric influence in mock jury deliberation: Jurors' bias for leniency," 54 *J. of Personality and Soc. Psychology* 21–33 (1988)]; the use of abbreviated stimulus trials [Kramer and Kerr, "Laboratory simulation and bias in the study of juror behavior: A methodological note," 13 *Law and Hum. Behav.* 89–100 (1989)]; the use of non-live trials [Miller, "Jurors' responses to videotaped trial materials," 1 *Personality and Soc. Psychology Bull.*, 561–569 (1975)]; the use of mock jurors instead of juries [Stasser, Kerr and Bray, "The social psychology of jury deliberations: Structure, process, and product," in Kerr and Bray (eds.), *The Psychology of the Courtroom* (New York: Academic Press, 1982)]; and mock jurors' knowledge that the case is not a real one [Kerr, Nerenz and Herrick, "Role playing and the study of jury behavior," 7 *Soc. Methods and Res.* 337–355 (1979)]. For a discussion of these issues, see Bray and Kerr, "Methodological issues in the study of the psychology of the courtroom," in Kerr and Bray (eds.), *The Psychology of the Courtroom*, id.
26. For a review, see *supra* n. 4.
27. Hoiberg and Stires, "The effect of several types of pretrial publicity on the guilt attributions of simulated juries," 3 *J. of Applied Soc. Psychology* 267–271 (1973).
28. Padawer-Singer and Barton, "Free press, fair trial," in Simon (ed.), *The Jury System: A Critical Analysis* (Beverly Hills, Calif.: Sage Publications, 1975); Padawer-Singer, Singer and Singer, "Voir dire by two lawyers: An essential safeguard," 57 *Judicature* 386–391 (1974), Padawer-Singer, Singer and Singer, "Legal and social-psychological research in the effects of pretrial publicity on juries, numerical makeup of juries, non-unanimous verdict requirements," 3 *Law and Psychology Rev.* 7–79 (1977).
29. Otto, Penrod and Dexter, "The biasing impact of pretrial publicity on juror judgments," 18 *Law and Hum. Behav.* 453–470 (1994).
30. See, for example, Press-Enter. Co. v. Superior Court, 464 U.S. 501-510 (1984); Richmond Newspapers, Inc. v. Virginia, 448 U.S. 555-581 (1980); Gannett v. DePasquale, 443 U.S. 368-380 (1979).
31. Siebert, *supra* n. 5.
32. Kramer, Kerr and Carroll, "Pretrial publicity, judicial remedies, and jury bias," 14 *Law and Hum. Behav.* 409–438 (1990).
33. Practical considerations (e.g., the difficulty of recontacting and scheduling participants after too long a delay; time constraints on the total length of the study) required this relatively short interval. Of course, actual continuances are typically much longer. (On the other hand, in actual cases, jurors may also be exposed to much longer or repeated instances of actual publicity).
34. See Seibert, *supra* n. 5.

35. Minow and Cate, "Who is an impartial juror in an age of mass media?," 40 *Am. U. L. Rev.* 631–664 (1991). There may also be some risk for a very high profile case like that of O.J. Simpson that jurors may actually want to serve on the jury (and share in the limelight) rather than, as is more typical, wanting to minimize or avoid the burden of jury duty.
36. For example, the U.S. Supreme Court has recently held that even when the majority of prospective jurors admit exposure to unfavorable publicity about a defendant, trial courts may rely upon jurors' professions of impartiality without inquiring into the content of the publicity to which they have been exposed. *Mu'min v. Virginia,* 111 S.Ct. 1899 (1991).
37. Sue, Smith and Pedroza, "Authoritarianism, pretrial publicity, and awareness of bias in simulated jurors," 37 *Psychological Rep.* 1299–1302 (1975).
38. Kerr, Kramer, Carroll, and Alfini, "On the effectiveness of voir dire in criminal cases with prejudicial pretrial publicity: An empirical study," 40 *Am. U. L. Rev.* 665–701 (1991).
39. Also see Moran and Cutler, 21 *J. of Applied Soc. Psychology* 345–367 (1991).
40. For a review, see Fulero and Penrod, "Attorney jury selection folklore: What do they think and how can psychology help?," 3 *Forensic Rep.* 233 (1990), or Hastie, "Is attorney-conducted voir dire an effective procedure for the selection of impartial juries?" 40 *Am. U. L. Rev.* 703–726 (1991).
41. See *supra* n. 32.
42. See *supra* n. 38.
43. See *supra* n. 38. Also see Dexter, Cutler and Moran, "A test of voir dire as a remedy for the prejudicial effects of pretrial publicity," 22 *J. of Applied Soc. Psychology* 819–832 (1992).
44. For reviews see Lind, "Psychology of courtroom procedure," in Kerr & Bray (eds.), *The Psychology of the Courtroom* (New York: Academic Press, 1982); or Hans and Vidmar, *Judging the Jury* (New York: Plenum, 1986).
45. Thompson, Fong, and Rosenhan, "Inadmissible evidence and juror verdicts," 40 *J. of Personality and Soc. Psychology* 453–463 (1981).
46. Hans and Doob, "Section 12 of the Canada Evidence Act and the deliberations of simulated juries," 18 *Crim. L. Q.* 235–253 (1976).
47. Wolf and Montgomery, "Effects of inadmissible evidence and level of judicial admonishment to disregard on the judgments of mock jurors," 7 *J. of Applied Soc. Psychology* 205–219 (1977); Tanford and Cox, "Decision processes in civil cases: The impact of impeachment evidence on liability and credibility judgments," 2 *Soc. Behav.* 1–l9 (1987); and Broeder, "The University of Chicago Jury Project," 38 *Neb. L. Rev.* 744–761 (1958).
48. Wegner, *White Bears and Other Unwanted Thoughts: Suppression, Obsession, and the Psychology of Mental Control* (New York: Viking, 1989).
49. See *supra* n. 29; *supra* n. 37; Padawer-Singer et al., *supra* n. 28, *supra* n. 32, Kline and Jess, "Prejudicial publicity: Its effects on law school mock juries," 43 *Journalism Q.* 113–116 (1966); Sue, Smith and Gilbert, "Biasing effects of pretrial publicity on judicial decisions," 2 *J. of Crim. Just.* 163–171 (1974); and Prager, "Timing of judicial instructions and pretrial publicity," 4 *Forensic Rep.* 451–453 (1991). Two other studies (viz. Simon, "Murder juries and the press," *Trans-Action* 64–65 (May–June 1966); and Keelin, "An experimental study of the effect of prejudicial pretrial publicity on jury verdicts," Unpublished master's thesis, Indiana University, 1979) suggest that such instructions are beneficial, but suffer from methodological flaws that invalidate their conclusions.
50. *Supra* n. 32.
51. Kaplan and Miller, "Reducing the effects of juror bias," 36 *J. of Personality and Soc. Psychology* 1443–1455 (1978).
52. See, e.g., Myers and Lamm, "The group polarization phenomenon," 83 *Psychological Bull.* 602–627 (1976).
53. See Stasser, et al., *supra* n. 25.
54. Also see Zanzola, "Effect of pretrial publicity on the verdicts of jurors and juries." Unpublished study, Department of Psychology, Northern Illinois University (1977).
55. *Supra* n. 32.
56. See *supra* n. 29.

Chapter 20

Expectations of Privacy?

Jurors' Views of Voir Dire Questions

Mary R. Rose

***D**uring the voir dire process of jury selection, attorneys are free to inquire into aspects of a juror's life that he or she may prefer to keep private, like religious practices, marital status, and criminal record. But when is a defendant's right to a fair trial outweighed by an individual juror's right to privacy? While some studies have addressed whether jurors feel that voir dire invades privacy, most have done so only in general terms, and without investigating the source of offense to jurors. Rose's study looks at what kinds of questions bother jurors, and specifically why—because they seem irrelevant, because they make jurors "uncomfortable," or because they are genuine invasions of privacy.*

Consider the following scenario:

You are summoned to appear in court although you have broken no law. When you arrive, you must sit and wait—sometimes for hours on end—not knowing when or if you will be seen. Should the court authorities call for you, your task is to provide whatever information they deem necessary for you to share. This might include simple facts about your identity, such as whether you are married or where you work. However, depending on the nature of the proceedings, you may also be asked to divulge information you do not routinely share with strangers, such as whether you have ever been victimized in a crime, have had to appear in court before, or know anyone who has broken the law or abuses alcohol or drugs. In some locations, you disclose this information in a room that is open not only to court personnel but to anyone wishing to attend. This might include members of the press. It is apparent that your answers determine whether you will be dismissed from this appearance; however, if you are dismissed, in most instances, you will not be told what about you or your answers was deemed inappropriate. On the other hand, if your responses are satisfactory, you may need to remain in the courtroom for several more days, or perhaps several more weeks. The court's compensation to you: Probably about $12 a day.

Someone unfamiliar with the American legal system might read the above description as a bizarre exercise of state power. Law-abiding citizens are corralled into court and subject to potential invasions of privacy; the procedure holds the possibility of unknowable and unreviewable arbitrariness in decision making; and compensation for the experience is, at best, minimal. Nonetheless, lacking nuance, this is essentially what the jury selection process in the United States entails.

Thankfully there has been increased attention to improving the experience of jury duty.[1] At the same time, there has been recognition that jurors have some rights.[2] Some commentators have specifically called for a recognition of a juror's right to privacy.[3] Outright conflicts over juror privacy do arise: In 1994 a prospective juror refused to answer several items on her juror questionnaire, maintaining that questions about her income, religion, television and reading habits, political affiliations, and health were "very private" and irrelevant. She was cited for contempt, which a federal magistrate judge later overturned, arguing that the trial court judge had not determined that the questions were, in fact, relevant. According to this ruling, judges should balance jurors' right to privacy against the needs of the parties and the rights of the public to have open voir dire.[4]

Balancing jurors' privacy interests when determining the scope of voir dire is a complex task for judges, in part because what "privacy" means is not well understood. *Brandborg* draws attention to a juror's potential focus on the relevance of questions. However, as the opening scenario suggested, a voir dire question could be highly pertinent—such as asking about jurors' experiences with crime—yet nevertheless perceived as an invasion of personal privacy. Thus, in thinking about juror privacy, judges may have to determine not only whether a question can be asked but how and under what circumstances.

Jurors' Views

Absent from discussions of juror privacy is a systematic account of the concerns of jurors. The literature is contradictory with respect to how often jury selection procedures invade or offend juror privacy, with some studies indicating that concerns about juror privacy are overstated.[5] On the other hand, there is evidence of potential problems, as jurors sometimes withhold information during voir dire,[6] suggesting that privacy interests may be asserted only surreptitiously. In addition, privacy has been called a "frequent complaint"[7] from jurors. The mix in estimates of jurors' sensitivity to privacy across various studies may reflect differences in the studies' sampling, question formats, or designs. In particular, most studies have asked about privacy in only general terms (for example, whether jurors feel negatively towards questions) or with a single question, making it difficult to obtain good estimates.

Prevalence aside, existing data also provide little sense of the source of offense to jurors. Possibly, as in *Brandborg,* jurors' negativity towards a question stems from its perceived lack of relevance, whereas jurors may tolerate even highly personal, uncomfortable questions if the questions seem probative and necessary to the proceedings. On the other hand, it could be that the greater offense comes when jurors must reveal sensitive information publicly, even if these revelations share a close connection to the case at hand. Knowing what types of questions are most problematic could provide guidance to courts in structuring voir dire.

In addition, the potential configuration of jurors' opinions could shed light on which remedies, if any, would be most useful to jurors and the courts. Questionnaires, in camera questioning, or in unusual cases, sealing transcripts of voir dire are potential accommodations for jurors wary of disclosing information that might embarrass them or that bears on highly private domains. In addition, the routine use of anonymous juries has been suggested as a mechanism to address both the privacy and safety concerns of jurors.[8] Nevertheless, these remedies are likely to be extreme or inappropriate when questioning is seen as irrelevant or unnecessary. Instead, greater judicial control over voir dire content, restricting the permissible basis for voir dire questions, or the reduction or wholesale elimination of the peremptory challenge are the purported solutions.

The aim of the present study is to provide empirical data about jurors' impressions of privacy during voir dire vis-a-vis the scope of questioning. The sample consists of people who were either selected for or excused from a series of felony criminal cases. Participants rated the extent to which their privacy was violated during jury selection, the types of questions that engendered dissatisfaction, why a question was bothersome, and how offended they felt.

Method

Cases

I interviewed 209 former jurors who had completed jury service in 13 criminal trials in a single North Carolina county. The trials involved four cases of homicide, one case of felonious assault (which included first-degree sex offenses), two cases of robbery with a dangerous weapon, two felony drug offenses, two accusations of breaking and entering/possession of stolen goods, and two cases of obtaining property by false pretenses. Trials were chosen because they were the most serious felony case commencing in a given week. I observed all the voir dires, which ranged in length from 1.5 hours to 1.5 days.

Typically the judge would introduce the case and the parties and ask jurors to state their name, marital status, employment, and whether they knew of any reason they could not be fair. Attorneys, beginning with the prosecutor, conducted the vast majority of the voir dire questioning. Selection followed a "sequential method,"[9] with six peremptory challenges per side (per defendant) and one additional for an alternate juror. For all trials, the parties conducted voir dire in open court and did not use questionnaires or anonymous juries. Only two trials received press coverage in the region's largest paper, one substantially so (a traffic accident that resulted in multiple deaths). In approximately half the trials, jurors were told to indicate whether a question bothered them. In one case, the judge said to speak to him; additionally, two prosecutors, who separately served in six cases, routinely told jurors the same.

Participant Profile

Across trials, 348 people underwent voir dire. Of these, 89 percent (n = 309) were deemed eligible for recruitment for a follow-up interview.[10] Completed and usable interviews were obtained from 207 former jurors (response rate = 67 percent). Despite additional recruitment efforts, people with unlisted phone numbers are under-represented (40 percent of all unlisted persons, compared with 80 percent of those listed, completed the interview). Across trials, participation rates ranged from a low of 39 percent to a high of 88 percent. Of the interviews, 105 (51 percent) were from excused jurors. Fifty-five percent of respondents were women and 72 percent were married. African Americans were 24 percent of respondents but 42 percent of nonrespondents. This under-representation is accounted for almost entirely by their being more likely to have unlisted phone numbers (51 percent, compared with only 24 percent of Whites) and thus being harder to recruit. Per 1990 U.S. Census data, the county is largely biracial, and only two participants in the study were Asian American. The sample is well educated (54 percent have a college degree or higher) with middle-class or higher household incomes (62 percent made $45,000 a year or more). For 54 percent, the target trial was their first experience with voir dire.

Privacy Questions

I assessed privacy violations through two separate measures, each of which inquired about three issues. First, jurors responded "yes" or "no" to the following questions: (1) "Did any of the questions, asked either of you or of anyone else, seem unrelated to or unnecessary for selecting jurors for that particular case?"; (2) "Were there any questions asked either of you or anyone else that made you feel uncomfortable in any way?"; (3) "Were there any questions asked of you or anyone else that seemed too private or too personal?" I asked jurors who responded "yes" to any of these three inquiries to give one or more examples of questions that fit the description. I also asked these people to explain why the exemplar question bothered them and how "offended" they felt by that question being asked during jury selection.[11]

In addition to these yes or no questions respondents rated on a 7-point scale (1) whether, taken as a whole, the questions seemed useful for deciding if people could be fair and impartial; (2) how comfortable the respondent felt during jury selection questioning; and (3) how much the lawyers seemed to care about protecting the personal privacy of the respondent and of others.[12] Lower scores on these scales correspond to less usefulness, comfort, and concern among lawyers about protecting privacy.

Results

Number and Types of 'Violations'

A larger proportion of respondents answered "yes" when asked if some of the voir dire questions seemed unrelated or unnecessary (43 percent) compared with those who said some questions made them uncomfortable (27 percent) or seemed "too private" (27 percent). Taken together, 53 percent of the sample said a question, asked either of them or another juror, appeared either unnecessary, made them uncomfortable, or seemed too private.

The mere fact of having been excused versus selected for a jury did not predict any of the proportions. However, I could not interview those selected for trial until after the trial ended. To the extent possible, I checked for effects associated with having been exposed to a trial by comparing responses of those selected for cases that completed versus a small subset (n = 4 cases) that did not.[13] Those who heard a full trial and deliberated were less likely to name a question as unnecessary (30 percent) than were those who did not (that is, those excused or "selected" people who did not hear the case; 49 percent). Providing examples of uncomfortable or "too private" questions was not associated with having heard the entire case. Privacy views did not differ by gender. African Americans were somewhat more likely to give examples of troublesome questions (61 percent) than were Whites (51 percent), but this difference was not statistically significant. In addition, those with listed versus unlisted phone numbers had comparable impressions.

Turning now to ratings made on the 7-point scales, results suggest that perceptions were positive, but not strongly so: ratings were typically just above the midpoint of the scales. Further, excused and selected jurors generally did not differ in these ratings, except that excused persons reported significantly lower comfort levels during questioning. As with the yes/no questions, gender, race, or having a listed phone did not predict these ratings.

Jurors gave significantly higher ratings to the questioning as useful (M = 5.36) and as comfortable (M = 5.38) than to lawyers' concern for protecting the privacy of the respondent (M = 4.69). In addition, the rating of lawyers' concern for privacy had more variability (SD = 1.97) than did the ratings of relevance (SD = 1.38) or comfort (SD = 1.73). Possibly, jurors' views of lawyers' concern are simply more variable and subjective. Alternatively, it is possible that this measure is more sensitive to the specific features of the trial (for example, the nature of the case) or the attorneys. To examine this possibility, I calculated the intraclass correlation, which reflects how much variability stems from differences in the ratings across trials. Approximately 10 percent of the variance in lawyers' concern for privacy protection was attributable to between-trial differences, whereas only about 6 percent of the comfort measure was. The usefulness of voir dire questions showed the least trial-to-trial variability, only about 2 percent.

Problematic Questions

Questions offered as examples of issues deemed unnecessary, uncomfortable, or "too private" appear in Table 20.1. A few caveats about the table are in order. First, not all questions listed were asked during every trial, especially those in the bottom third of the table. Second, in order to minimize idiosyncrasies in the results, Table 20.1 presents only questions mentioned by five or more respondents (that is, greater than 2.5 percent of the sample), and none that were specific to only one trial. As examples of omitted responses, four jurors from one drug case disliked being asked whether they knew people with drug or alcohol problems; however, no one reached from the other drug case mentioned this issue. Two jurors in another case disliked how much information a juror had to give about the medical condition of his ailing wife—described when the juror sought a hardship excuse, which was denied. In only one trial were jurors asked about reading habits, to which four people objected. Finally, two people in one case responded "all the questions by the defense attorney" when asked about unnecessary inquiries.

Uncomfortable or Too Private

Experiences with the courts or with crime predominate examples of unnerving inquiries. This broad category included questions about whether the juror has been charged with an offense, has been a victim of crime, or whether the jurors' family members have either been charged with something or been crime victims. In all, 52 people (25 percent of the sample) mentioned these issues as either uncomfortable, too private, or unnecessary—but the latter charge of irrelevance was infrequent.

Information about experiences with crime or the courts was usually elicited from jurors through direct questions such as: "Do you know anyone charged with a crime similar to the one at issue today?"; "Do you know anyone charged with any crime?"; "Have you or anyone you know ever been a victim of a violent crime?"; or, "Have you or your family been especially affected by guns or violence, or have you ever been the victim of a crime involving guns or violence?" In addition, more general questions elicited this information, for example "Have you ever been to court before, for any reason at all?"; or, "Have you ever had to hire an attorney?" Some type of question about experiences with crime or involvement in the courts appeared in every trial. In turn, at least one juror from every

Table 20.1
Questions Identified as Either Unnecessary, Uncomfortable, or Too Private (n = 110)

Questions pertaining to:	(Total N)	Not necessary	Uncomfortable	Too private	How offended (M)
Involvement with the courts or crime:					
Crime/court experiences in one's family	(24)	2[a]	12	13	4.35
Juror has been a crime victim	(17)	1	9	9	3.88
Juror has been charged with an offense	(15)	4	9	6	4.35
Non-specific crime/court questions[b]	(10)	0	7	5	4.30
Juror and family demographic:					
Parental status[c]	(24)	19	5	6	3.25
Spouse's type or place of employment	(18)	14	4	6	4.06
General location where juror resides[d]	(17)	11	4	6	3.11
Children's type or place of employment[e]	(15)	14	2	4	4.36
Jurors' type or place of employment[f]	(12)	8	3	6	3.63
Marital status	(11)	9	3	4	2.64
Interests and associations:[g]					
Religious affiliation	(10)	10	2	1	2.80
Voluntary organizations	(8)	6	2	2	3.78
Hobbies	(6)	6	0	0	2.83
Gun ownership	(5)	4	4	3	3.67

Notes: Numbers in parentheses refer to total number of participants mentioning this type of question. Unless otherwise indicated in footnotes below, questions appeared in all trials (n = 207). Offense ratings were made on a 7-point scale with lower values indicating feeling less offended.

a. Numbers across rows will not sum to total n listed in parentheses because participants could rate a question in multiple categories (e.g., as unnecessary and as uncomfortable).

b. Includes, e.g.: "Have you ever been to court before?" or "Have you ever hired an attorney?"

c. Includes, e.g.: "Do you have children?"; "What are their ages?"; or "How many children do you have?" One of these items appeared in all but one trial; in all, 170 people in this sample heard these questions.

d. Jurors were asked to indicate only the general area of the county in which they lived; however, this category includes a question about whether the juror lived close to the crime scene.

e. These items were asked in all but two trials; in all 155 jurors in this sample heard these questions.

f. Includes, e.g.: "What do you do for a living?"; "What did you do before your present job?"; or "Where do you work?"

g. These questions were not asked in every trial. The number of jurors exposed to these questions are as follows: n = 49 for religion; n = 87 for voluntary associations; n = 49 for hobbies; and n = 64 for gun ownership.

trial indicated concern about having this information divulged by themselves or others during jury selection.

Jurors provided multiple rationales for why these questions threatened privacy. First, the topics unearth painful life experiences. All of the following were mentioned during these trials: family members were currently incarcerated; jurors had been charged with DUI violations, drugs, larceny, or spousal abuse; jurors or family members had been victims of sexual assault or other violent crimes; also, jurors said they had been victims of domestic violence, had lost a son to an accidental shooting, or had a family member who committed a murder or suicide. Thus, in a public voir dire, jurors may have to describe—or watch others describe—information that might not be shared with close associates, let alone strangers. Referring to admitting his own DUI, one man said: "I didn't want to talk about it in front of a room filled with 100 or so people."

Second, jurors sometimes named questions that made them uncomfortable solely on behalf of another person. The actual target of the question may or may not have found it objectionable. To take a stark example, in a case involving a charge of a serious sexual offense, a female juror said she had been raped but had never reported it to the police. After the juror hedged about her abilities to be fair and impartial, the prosecutor launched into a blunt description of the alleged facts. Given these details, the juror burst into tears, said she could not be fair, and was quickly excused for cause. Not surprisingly, several jurors who witnessed this event later mentioned it as uncomfortable or too private. Nevertheless, in a subsequent interview with the juror, she referred to the event but added: "it was no one's fault in that room. It [my own experience] just came back and overwhelmed me.

That wasn't due to the process; that just happened. The process was fine."

When asked about privacy during voir dire, this juror did not mention the crime question as problematic but rather as effective given the nature of the case. She was, however, extremely unhappy about having revealed in front of the defendants the company for which she worked.

Finally, some jurors felt that inquiries about experiences with courts and crime invited questionable assumptions about one's abilities to be fair:

> I could see a criminal record, but even with a misdemeanor, if you've served your time, why you got to keep paying? The questions they asked had nothing to do with how a person would be as a juror. Your family isn't going to be on the jury, you are. If it's my [criminal] record, OK, but [a family member] could die in the gas chamber, and it's not you. They dig too much into the family, and that's why some don't want to be on the jury. They avoid it.

People who named problematic questions also rated how "offended" they were by their being asked. For court and crime items, offense was just above a "4," or the mid-point of a 7-point scale. Offensiveness means were lower for instances in which jurors had to relate their own experiences as victims of crime (M = 3.88) compared with admitting to having been charged personally with an offense (M = 4.35) or having to recount things that happened to family members (M = 4.35). Generic questions (for example, Have you ever been to court before?) also had a fairly high offensiveness rating (M = 4.30).

Juror and Family Demographics

Jurors cited two general domains of questions as being unrelated to or unnecessary for selecting a fair and impartial jury. The first concerns questions about their families and the jurors' own demographic information. In order of frequency, the questions cited were: parental status (for example, "Do you have any children?" "How many?" What are their ages?"); spouse's place or type of employment ("What does your spouse do for a living?" "Where does your spouse work?"); the general area of the county in which they reside (including having to say whether they live close to the crime scene); employment information about children; employment information about the juror; and marital status. An inquiry about the area of town in which jurors reside, jurors' employment, their marital status, and spouses' employment appeared in every trial. Questions about jurors' children appeared in 12 of the 13 cases, and 11 of the 13 cases asked specifically about children's employment. In all, 25 percent of jurors cited at least one question concerning family and juror demographics as either unnecessary, uncomfortable, or too private.

Jurors' rationales for providing these examples were of two types. First, some jurors cited safety concerns. On occasion this reflected a questionable ability to presume innocence. Referring to the defense table, at which four defendants and their lawyers sat, a man in the follow-up interview said: "You got eight of them staring at you, and four are criminals." More commonly, safety concerns stemmed from fear of retaliation from a convicted defendant or relative. For instance, some jurors would grant that the nature of their occupations is relevant but not the names of the entities for whom they or their families worked. From this perspective, more information identifying jurors or their families, especially their children, entails more vulnerability. Those who labeled these demographic issues as "uncomfortable" or "too private" tended to cite safety as a rationale.

More frequently, jurors felt that the questions about family members or employment invited stereotyping or broad assumptions about jurors' abilities to be fair and impartial. That is, the questions were not relevant. One woman, who had been divorced more than once, had to describe the occupations of her former spouses and commented: "I wasn't offended by the fact of having to give the information, but I was offended by the fact that they thought it mattered."

According to another prospective juror: "It's like they're looking at what's in your heart. I would rather base it [the selection decision] on the evidence."

Some jurors acknowledged that a spouse's or family member's experiences and occupations might bear upon one's own attitudes or reactions to the trial (for example, to a police officer testifying). However, a few jurors also felt that the remedy would be to ask not, "What does your grown son do for a living?" but instead, "Do any of your family members work in" and then to name specific fields (for example, law enforcement).

Interests and Associations

The other domain viewed as irrelevant or unnecessary concerned jurors' interests and associations, issues not necessarily raised in each trial. Ten people objected to having to state their religious affiliation (for example, "What church do you attend, if any?"). This relatively small number actually reflects a fairly high percentage (20 percent), as an inquiry about religious affiliation was posed in only four trials, with 49 people from this sample exposed to it.[14] Nine jurors (10 percent) mentioned an inquiry about organizations with which the juror strongly identifies or to which the juror gives money (asked in 7 trials, or to 87 people in this sample). Six (12 percent) said giving information about hobbies was unnecessary (asked in 3 trials to 49 people). Finally, five (8 percent) disliked having to say whether they owned guns (asked to 64 people in 3 trials, all of which involved a violent offense).

With the exception of the gun question, jurors typically explained that questions about their hobbies, religious affiliations, or organizational ties invited stereotyping and unfounded assumptions about them. Those uncomfortable with questions about gun ownership tended to be more concerned about safety, that is, they disliked that the defendant knew a gun could be found in their homes.

Violating Privacy

Inquiring about multiple dimensions of privacy, this study found that more than half of the participants (53 percent) could identify at least one question that seemed either unnecessary, made them uncomfortable, or seemed too private or personal. In short, for this sample, reports of some type of privacy violation were common. In addition, mean ratings on several privacy measures revealed only a modestly positive view of voir dire.

Given that this study took place in a single jurisdiction, one in which attorneys conducted open-court voir dire with no questionnaires, it could be argued that the high rate of violations is specific to this courthouse. Several facts argue against such a dismissive interpretation. First, few courts take the time to conduct one-on-one voir dire in the routine types of cases studied here;[15] thus the results may be pertinent to several jury selection systems in the U.S. in which jurors answer questions in front of other jurors and the public. Second, even though attorneys dominated questioning and conceivably might have been more intrusive than a judge, jurors in the present study tended to express comfort with attorneys. During the interview, I asked participants whether they would have preferred that the judge do more of the questioning during jury selection. A minority, 21 percent, said "yes"; 35 percent said "no"; and the remainder (44 percent) said they had no preference. Comfort with attorney-led questioning is supported by other studies.[16] Thus, aspects of attorney behaviors likely do not fully account for the results here, and this further argues against viewing these results as simple flukes of regional voir dire practices.

Most importantly, the types of questions jurors named as violations make the results noteworthy. The lines of inquiry cited most often as problematic did not typically mirror the issues for which Dianna Brandborg stood in contempt. Certainly, like Brandborg, some mentioned questions about hobbies or organizational affiliations as irrelevant. However, these questions were posed in only a few trials, and there is little evidence that these more infrequent inquiries account for jurors' views of relevance. The ratings for the usefulness of questions exhibited remarkably little trial-to-trial variability (about 2 percent), reflecting a fairly consistent view, on average, across cases. Instead, for multiple reasons—painful admissions, compassion for others, concerns about safety, and reaction to stereotyping—this sample expressed distaste for the more routine questions, those which required them to discuss experiences with crime and the courts, or to provide demographic information about themselves or their families. These jurors' privacy concerns went to the heart rather than to the fringes of the typical voir dire, and there is reason to believe that the types of privacy issues emanating from this courthouse will emerge in other courts as well.

Given this, and the fairly high rates of reported violations, should one conclude that privacy threats during voir dire are an epidemic in need of drastic remedy? As with a dismissive interpretation, an alarmist response likewise seems unwarranted, for other indicators are reassuring. First, far fewer people cited questions as uncomfortable (27 percent) or too private (27 percent) compared with instances in which jurors simply could not see the point of some inquiries (43 percent). Confusion about the need for some questions is perhaps to be expected when potential jurors undergo voir dire prior to hearing much information about the case. Indeed, the subset of selected jurors who sat for the entire trial were less likely to name questions as irrelevant than were those who did not hear the case (although note that 30 percent of the former group still did so).[17] Second, those who reported violations did not tend to report feeling greatly offended. Average ratings of offense typically fell near the midpoint of a 7-point scale. In short, this sample—although cognizant of privacy issues during voir dire—was not a particularly outraged group.

Implications for Reforms

The configuration of results allows for some reflection on various reforms aimed at improving jurors' sense of privacy protection. Note, for instance, that in all likelihood the issues mentioned as problematic in this study would still be asked in a voir dire system that adhered only to the parameters of the challenge for cause. This is because, as the jurors in this sample recognized, one's experiences with crime or the courts can be pertinent, even if they hold the potential for negative feelings. Thus, eliminating or drastically curtailing the peremptory challenge is not likely to alleviate privacy concerns fully. Cases involving traumatic or sensitive topics will still elicit discomfiting information from jurors.

Questionnaires can be advantageous for lessening jurors' worries about privacy,[18] allowing them to disclose sensitive information out of the public light. However, they cannot ameliorate all bases for concern, including safety fears and questions about who will have access to the written information. In addition, jurors may still feel that lawyers use answers to make unjustified assumptions about their ability to serve fairly—a long-standing complaint among former jurors.[19] Thus questionnaires are best viewed as only one portion of a strategy for addressing juror privacy concerns.

Another strong reform would involve the routine use of anonymous juries, which are designed to protect jurors' safety in criminal cases and to restrict media access to them in high profile cases. Note that this reform need not address this study's primary focus, that is, views of the proper scope of voir dire. Juries can be anonymous but still be subjected to an intensive voir dire. The degree to which jurors desire anonymity was not specifically explored here, although one person spontaneously mentioned her preference that juries be anonymous in cases involving a violent crime. It is notable that this study's high response rate, especially among those with listed numbers, did not suggest that jurors resented being contacted post-voir dire; in fact, very few expressed any discomfort with my having "found" them. Nonetheless, a more systematic examination of desire for anonymity would be useful in future investigations of juror privacy.

Some Simple Interventions

Given the complexity of more sweeping reforms, one should not ignore the potential benefits of simple attempts to demonstrate to jurors that privacy is a concern and a priority. First, to alleviate safety fears, specific information about jurors or their families (for example, the name of a company where the juror works) can be curtailed when more general information (for example, what the person does for a living) would suffice. Lawyers and judges would do well to remember that jurors can be particularly sensitive about questions regarding their children, especially where their children work or go to school. Most importantly, jurors can be reminded regularly that they can request to answer questions *in camera* or to speak with the judge and attorneys at the bench. In these trials, requests for jurors to "speak up" about privacy occurred in just about half the trials. Others have found one-on-one questioning of particular value.[20] All these sorts of efforts would communicate to jurors that the court and parties are aware of the challenge of providing sensitive information in a setting that otherwise restricts jurors' control over the proceedings.

That some jurors will respond negatively to a sense that they or others are being stereotyped is perhaps the most difficult dimension of privacy to confront. No doubt, some amount of stereotyping is unavoidable, as decision makers need to make best guesses about a juror's fitness for the case. Short of decisions based solely on a juror's race or gender, there are no legal barriers to prevent lawyers from acting on the basis of stereotypes and bald assumptions. When feasible, lawyers and judges concerned about this reaction might consider explaining the rationale for questions. In this way, jurors can understand that questions are not being asked without purpose (and lawyers themselves can consider precisely why they are seeking the information).

In one trial in this study, for instance, the prosecutor asked jurors if they had any children in college or if the jurors or their children worked while in college—odd inquiries when asked without explanation. The district attorney explained what about the case (the circumstances under which a witness was testifying) made the issue relevant. In that trial, only two jurors mentioned any questions as unrelated, uncomfortable, or too private. Although it is not possible to say that these favorable results are due to the prosecutor's explanation or to some other feature of the attorneys or the case, the example seems instructive. Short opening statements to the entire jury panel might also serve a similar purpose as providing specific rationales for inquiries.

Finally, with respect to stereotyping, counsel might also consider whether the informative value of a question outweighs its potential for misunderstanding or offense. In a murder trial in this sample, one juror said he disliked that jurors were asked to say whether they went to a local church or not (and if so, which one).

> I had a Jewish man who sat next to me and he said he went to a synagogue.I know there are troubles between Blacks and Jews in larger cities like New York. They didn't give me any real reason why they didn't select him, and it left in my mind that the defense attorney didn't want him on because [the juror] was Jewish and [the attorney] was defending a Black man.

I saw several other plausible explanations for why the defense attorney excused the juror just described (he had strong views against gun ownership and a remote connection to the prosecutor's spouse). Nevertheless, the raising of religion during voir dire—by the district attorney, who explained that the question pertained to jurors' "ties to the community"—allowed the above rival explanation to emerge in one juror's mind. Religion is a particularly sensitive topic; when posed in a voir dire, jurors in this sample consistently questioned its appropriateness.

***

The Supreme Court has not settled whether jurors have a "right" to privacy during voir dire, in part because at least one justice worried that acknowledging such a right would "unnecessarily complicate" the lives of trial judges.[21] This study examined juror privacy in detail and found that grappling with juror privacy is indeed a potentially complicated matter. Contending with juror privacy involves a balancing act between the multiple interests in voir dire: those of the parties, the public, and the jurors. These data further point to multiple privacy interests of the jurors: to limit public disclosures of highly sensitive information, to feel reassured that their own safety and that of their families is secure, and to feel that they have not been grossly stereotyped. Although some may entertain strong jury reforms, reassurances and explanations about voir dire inquiries, as well as proactive attention to the necessity of some questions, may work to increase jurors' sense of privacy protection without drastically compromising other important interests.

NOTES

The author gratefully acknowledges Shari Diamond, Nancy King, Neil Vidmar, and reviewers for this journal for their help in reading drafts of this work.

1. *See* generally, REPORT FROM THE COUNCIL ON COURT EXCELLENCE, JURIES FOR THE YEAR 2000 AND BEYOND: PROPOSALS TO IMPROVE THE JURY SYSTEMS IN WASHINGTON, D.C. (1998); Munsterman, Hannaford, and Whitehead (eds.), JURY TRIAL INNOVATIONS (1997). With respect to compliance with summonses, *see* Boatright. *Why citizens don't respond to jury summonses and what courts can do about it,* 82 JUDICATURE 156 (1999).
2. *See, e.g.,* Leipold. *Constitutionalizing jury selection in criminal cases: A critical evaluation.* 86 GEO. L J. 945 (1998); Underwood. *Ending Race Discrimination in Jury Selection: Whose Right Is It, Anyway?* 92 COLUM. L REV. 725 (1992).
3. *See, e.g.,* Glover. *The right to privacy of prospective jurors during voir dire,* 70 CAL. L. REV. 709 (1982); Weinstein. *Protecting a juror's right to privacy: Constitutional constraints and policy options,* 70 TEMP. L. REV. 1 (1997).
4. *Brandborg v. Lucas,* 891 F. Supp., 352 (E.D. Tex, 1995).
5. *See, e.g.,* Consolini. LEARNING BY DOING JUSTICE: JURY SERVICE AND POLITICAL ATTITUDES. Unpublished doctoral dissertation, University of California, Berkeley (1992) (finding that only 6.6 percent felt "very negative" about voir dire questioning; 23 percent felt "somewhat negative"); Diamond. *What jurors think: Expectations and reactions of citizens who serve as jurors,* in Litan, (ed.), VERDICT: ASSESSING THE CIVIL JURY SYSTEM 282, 289 (1993) (concluding that jurors have a "generally accepting attitude" toward questioning); Grisham and Lawless. *Jurors judge justice: A survey of criminal jurors,* 3 NEW MEX. L. REV. 353 (1973) (finding that only 6 percent thought voir dire questions were "too personal" but 11 percent saying questioning was "not personal enough"); Seltzer, Venuti and Lopes. *Juror Honesty During the Voir Dire,* 19 J. CRIM. JUST. 451, 455 (1991) (finding that only 8 percent said questioning was too personal).
6. Seltzer et al., *id* at 457.
7. Weinstein, *supra n.* 3 at 3, citing THE JURY PROJECT: REPORT TO THE CHIEF JUDGE OF THE STATE OF NEW YORK 49 (March 31, 1994); and Curriden. *The death of the peremptory challenge,* 80 ABAJ 62, 65 (which cites the results of an Atlanta Constitution poll that found that two-thirds of a sample of 100 jurors thought lawyers' questions were "personal and offensive").
8. King, *Nameless justice: The case for the routine use of anonymous juries in criminal trials,* 49 VANDERBILT L. REV. 123 (1996)
9. Bermant and Shapard, *The voir dire examination, juror challenges, and adversary advocacy,* in Sales (ed.), 2 PERSPECTIVES IN LAW AND PSYCHOLOGY: THE TRIAL PROCESS (1981). Through this method, the district attorney posed questions to a panel of 12 prospective jurors, exercised challenges, and then queried jurors replacing those excused. The defense did not begin questioning until the prosecutor had passed a panel of 12. After the defense exercised his or her challenges, the process repeated until both parties passed the panel.
10. To be eligible, the person must have been asked at least one question by an attorney (i.e., not immediately excused for cause), and must have been part of the same pool of jurors who were initially oriented for the case.
11. Respondents used a 1–7 scale in which "1" is "not at all offended" and "7" is "very offended."
12. The last inquiry was asked in two parts: privacy of self and then privacy of others; however, the items correlated almost perfectly, $r = .98$ and are discussed as a composite.
13. In two cases, juror comments tainted the panel (one made at the end of voir dire and another after opening statements); in two cases the defendant pled or had his charges dismissed after voir dire.
14. This question is distinct from one that asked whether jurors had religious or moral convictions that prohibited them from sitting in judgment, which was asked in all but one trial. Only one juror from one trial expressed discomfort over this, saying it "bordered on (asking about) religion."
15. Although *see:* Mize, *On better jury selection: Spotting UFO jurors before they enter the jury room,* COURT REVIEW 10 (Spring, 1999) (description of and argument for value of one-on-one questioning).
16. Jones, *Judge-versus attorney-conducted voir dire: An empirical investigation of juror candor,* 11 LAW AND HUM. BEHAV. 131, 142 (1987) (showing that even attempts by the judges to be less formal in order to put jurors at ease had no effect on perceptions).
17. Note that it is also possible that the trials that did not proceed to deliberations simply raised different issues during voir dire compared to those that did. A review of the topics covered in the trials did not show obvious substantive differences in the questions posed; however, there is no way to tell with certainty whether something specific to each case accounts for the differing perceptions of relevance.
18. JURIES FOR THE YEAR 2000 AND BEYOND, *supra n.* 1 at 34. Munsterman et. al., *supra n.* 1 at 62.
19. Broeder, *Voir dire examinations: An empirical study,* 38 SO. CAL. L. REV. 503, 517 (1965) (describing questions such as, "Can you (as a crane operator or as a school teacher or as a doctor's wife) be fair and impartial?" as "especially resented").
20. See Mize, *supra n.* 15.
21. *Press-Enterprise v. Superior Court of California,* 464 U.S. 501, 515 (1984, Blackmun, J. concurring).

Chapter 21

Victim Cooperation and the Prosecution of Domestic Violence in a Specialized Court

Myrna Dawson
Ronit Dinovitzer

Domestic violence cases can prove difficult to prosecute, as there are often no witnesses and victims can be uncooperative. As domestic violence became an increasing priority in the 1990s, mandatory policies resulted in huge arrest numbers, but still relatively low prosecution rates—just 10 percent in some communities. A special court in Toronto, Ontario was developed to provide extra victim support and increase domestic violence prosecutions by relying on evidence besides victim testimony.

Dawson and Dinovitzer's study examines the role of victim cooperation in the likelihood of prosecution, finding that even in a specialized court designed to operate without victim cooperation, prosecution was seven times more likely when victims did indeed cooperate. Given the importance of victim cooperation, they went on to analyze more than seventy characteristics, from demographics to the legal process, to single out elements that may make victims more likely to participate in the prosecution of their abusers.

The last several decades have been marked by careful scrutiny of criminal justice responses to domestic violence. Considerable research has examined both the role of police discretion in responding to domestic violence calls and the effect of arrest on recidivism rates (Fagan 1995; Sherman and Berk 1984; for review of arrest studies, see Fagan et al. 1995; Garner, Fagan, and Maxwell 1995). This attention to police practices, however, has not been paralleled by similar attention to the prosecution of domestic violence and to the role played by victims of domestic violence in the criminal justice process.

With the implementation of mandatory arrest policies in many jurisdictions, charges laid by police have flooded prosecutors' offices (Cahn 1992). The rate of prosecution for such cases is extremely low, however. It is estimated to be less than 10 percent in many communities (Fagan 1995; Ford 1991; Sherman 1992). Prosecutors often explain low rates of prosecution by emphasizing that victims of domestic violence tend to change their minds about pressing charges, often recanting their testimonies and/or becoming "noncooperative witnesses" (Ursel 1995; Vera Institute 1977). Because these cases rely heavily on the victim's testimony, some prosecutors argue that they have no choice but to withdraw the charges when the victim does not cooperate. In fact, at a 1996 meeting of the National Institute of Justice, there was strong consensus that "the most serious impediment to full prosecution of domestic cases is victims who refuse to cooperate from the start or who change their minds during the course of the case" (Davis, Smith, and Nickles 1997:5). Critics of this explanation, however, counter that victims are deterred from cooperating by prosecutors who ignore the realities of domestic violence; this situation contributes to an environment in which women[1] are revictimized by the criminal justice process (Field and Field 1973; Ford 1983; Gayford 1977; Hilton 1989; Lerman 1986).

Despite the commonly held assumption that prosecutors typically drop cases when victims do not (or cannot) cooperate (Ursel 1995; Vera Institute 1977), few empirical analyses have sought to determine whether this is the case. In this paper, we address the role of victim cooperation in the prosecution of domestic violence cases by examining case files from a specialized domestic violence court in Toronto, Canada. This court is designed to proceed with prosecutions more easily without the victim's cooperation. Our objective is to assess whether perceptions of a victim's willingness to cooperate are associated with the likelihood of prosecution, even when the efforts and procedures of a specialized court are designed to address this concern. In the second part of our analysis, we identify the characteristics of victims who are most likely to cooperate with the prosecution process in a specialized domestic violence court.[2]

Literature Review

Introduction

In understanding the role of victim cooperation in the prosecution of domestic violence, we can draw on past research concerning victim/witness cooperation and the prosecution process more generally. Considerable research has focused on case attrition at the prosecution stage of the criminal justice process. Most of these studies have dealt either with crimes in general (Albonetti 1986; Albonetti and Hepburn 1996; Forst, Lucianovic, and Cox 1977; Myers and Hagan 1979) or with sexual assault in particular (Frohman 1991; Kingsnorth, MacIntosh, and Wentworth 1999; Spears and Spohn 1997). They have highlighted some of the general factors associated with the likelihood of prosecution, including the role of victim/witness cooperation. Yet it is uncertain whether the findings from this research can be generalized to domestic violence because violence between intimates may have distinctive features. For instance, prosecutors apparently are less likely to pursue cases generally when there is a prior relationship between the victim and the accused (Davis and Smith 1981; Elliott 1989; Vera Institute 1977). Davis and Smith (1981) showed that the presence of such a relationship led to less serious case assessments in prosecutorial screening, even after controlling for victim injury and weapon use. In domestic violence cases, however, it may be that the likelihood of prosecution is affected by the intimate nature of the relationship, rather than by its mere existence (Stanko 1982). In other words, the nature of the victim's prior relationship with the accused may persuade a prosecutor that the victim may choose to resume this relationship and subsequently recant her testimony (Schmidt and Steury 1989), because intimate partner relationships often are characterized by frequent and intense interaction (Silverman and Kennedy 1993).

Researchers continue to speculate about the factors that predict whether a domestic violence case proceeds to prosecution. Some suggest that concerns about the victim's safety influence the decision to prosecute, out of fear that further criminal justice intervention will lead to escalation of the violence (Ellis 1984). Other researchers contend that prosecutors historically have perceived battering as inappropriate for criminal prosecution because it is viewed as a private family matter or a minor dispute that is difficult to prosecute due to a lack of victim cooperation (Cahn and Lerman 1991; McLeod 1983). Still others have explained the difficulty in prosecuting these cases as the result of a "self-fulfilling prophecy": prosecutors' beliefs that victims will not cooperate reinforce victims' negative views of the criminal justice system, thereby discouraging them from following through at the prosecutorial stage (Cahn 1992; Ellis 1984). Finally, the prosecution process has been described as a haphazard or random event over which the victim has little control (Ford 1983). As a result, it may not be possible to discern an underlying logic in the determinants of prosecution other than attributing it to "the luck of the draw" (Ford 1983:467). Therefore the unique factors presented by domestic violence require specific empirical study. Here we examine the complex fabric of assumptions underlying prosecutors' perceptions of victim cooperation and their effect on whether a case proceeds to prosecution.

Research on Victim Cooperation and the Prosecution Process

What Prosecutors Say: Descriptive Studies. A number of studies explore prosecutors' accounts of the role played by victim cooperation in the prosecution of domestic violence cases. In a survey of Alabama prosecutors, about half of the respondents stated that they failed to prosecute cases because the victim recanted or was a poor witness (Sigler, Crowley, and Johnson 1990:448, Table 1). Other studies have corroborated the finding that victim cooperation is pivotal (Sander 1988; Ursel 1995). Using data from the Manitoba Family Violence Court in Canada,

Ursel (1995) found that, according to prosecutors, almost 60 percent of all decisions not to prosecute were due to noncooperation by the victim. In these cases, a victim usually refused to testify, recanted or retracted her testimony, failed to attend court, or was not served a subpoena (p. 31, Table 3.3).

In contrast, in a study of domestic violence cases in Arizona from 1987 to 1988, factors other than victim cooperation, such as incomplete or vague police reports, were noted almost as often by prosecutors in their decision to drop the charges, and seemed to play an equally important role (Ferraro and Boychuk 1992:213). In a recent national mail survey of prosecutors in the United States, 80 percent of respondents indicated that they would continue to prosecute a domestic violence case even if the victim was uncooperative (Rebovich 1996:182).[3] Rebovich (1996) concluded:

> In the recent past, prosecutors were widely thought to be insensitive to the needs of domestic violence victims and negligent in the consistent prosecution of these cases.... [T]he survey results... demonstrate a growing commitment by district attorneys to vigorously prosecute domestic violence ... [and] a pronounced willingness to move forward in cases in which victims do not participate as witnesses. (p. 189)

Similarly, in the evaluation of the domestic violence program in the Quincy (Massachusetts) District Court, prosecutors reported that around 30 percent of the domestic violence cases were dismissed or *nolle prossed* because the victim requested that the case be dismissed, invoked her marital privilege, or refused to testify (Buzawa et al. 1999:Table 6.9).

Prosecutors' accounts provide valuable information on the relative importance of victim cooperation to the decision to prosecute, and there is no reason to assume that these accounts are inaccurate. Yet the picture they provide may be incomplete because social actors are embedded in their daily activities. They may be unable to articulate all of the implicit guidelines that inform their behavior (Bourdieu 1977). Accordingly, although self-report data reflect valuable information on prosecutors' own accounts explaining why charges are dropped, we need to supplement such data with models that can control for the more complex interplay of factors in the decision to prosecute.

What Prosecutors Do: Multivariate Analyses. Although researchers have made a number of empirical analyses of the prosecution of domestic violence cases, studies generally have focused on the rate at which cases are prosecuted and on the characteristics of these cases, rather than analyzing the factors that influence prosecutorial decisionmaking. For instance, in the report on the Quincy District Court mentioned above, the researchers report the distribution of cases that were dismissed or *nolle prossed*, state the reasons for the dismissals, and analyze the characteristics of the cases by initial disposition (Buzawa et al. 1999). Although this information is valuable, we must conduct multivariate analyses of the decision to prosecute in order to understand more clearly how multiple factors might influence prosecutorial decision making.

Multivariate analyses of victim cooperation in the prosecution process have been scarce. Schmidt and Steury (1989), however, made an informative examination of 400 misdemeanor domestic violence cases in Milwaukee from 1983 to 1984. Their multivariate analysis revealed that defendant-related factors were more important than victim-related variables in prosecutors' decisions to pursue charges. Schmidt and Steury found that the strongest predictors of prosecution were whether the defendant was present at the charging conference, whether he was intoxicated at the time of the incident, and whether he supported himself financially (p. 505). Therefore, these findings suggest that a great deal turns on the defendant himself (also see Rauma 1984). "There is much to suggest that the decision to prosecute is largely based on the defendant's past and current actions and choices" (Schmidt and Steury 1989:508), and is not a result of "victim-blaming" (p. 505). Schmidt and Steury's (1989) data, however, do not provide insight into the role of victim cooperation at the prosecution stage of the process. Although prosecutors' notations suggested that victims' wishes to drop the charges accounted for nearly half of the cases in which the prosecutor chose not to proceed (p. 495), a variable controlling for victim cooperation was not included in the multivariate analysis and therefore was not systematically evaluated. Thus, even though Schmidt and Steury's (1989) multivariate analysis suggests that the decision to prosecute is based largely on defendant characteristics, their descriptive data indicate that victim cooperation is a key factor.

In a more recent study based on a specialized domestic violence court in Milwaukee, the researchers address the effects of victim cooperation on prosecutors' charging decisions over two time periods (Davis, Smith, and Nickles 1997). In the first period, the district attorney's office prosecuted a case only if the victim attended the charging conference (p. 64). In the second period, the policy was changed such that the victim's attendance would no longer be required for the filing of cases; instead, cases would be charged according to the seriousness of the offense, their legal merit, and the defendant's criminal history.

In their multivariate analyses of the charging decision in the first time period, Davis, Smith, and Nickles (1997) found that attendance by the victim was the most important determinant of whether cases were charged; other significant predictors were type of offense, defendant's gender, prior convictions, and previous battery arrests for which the defendant was not charged (p. 79). In contrast, police assessments of the victim as intoxicated decreased the likelihood of prosecution. In their analyses of charging decisions in the second period, where the victim's attendance no longer was required, Davis, Smith, and Nickles (1997) still found that attendance by the victim was the most important predictor despite the change in policy, though none of the criminal history variables remained statistically significant predictors. Victim's attendance at the charging conference, then, was a central factor in prosecutorial decisionmaking, despite an explicit change in prosecutorial policy. Whether the arresting police officer found a victim to be cooperative, however, did not predict the likelihood of prosecution in either period.

The Decision to Cooperate

Researchers are beginning to establish why victims of domestic violence are reluctant to cooperate with the criminal justice system, and are starting to identify the characteristics of those victims who do cooperate. This literature suggests that the victim's decision to cooperate is constrained by concern for her physical, emotional, and financial well-being, and is conditioned by her experiences in the criminal justice system. Furthermore, these concerns are not limited to victims of domestic violence, but often are expressed by crime victims generally (see, e.g., Davis 1983; Norton 1983).

For victims of domestic violence, however, research suggests that one of the major obstacles to cooperating is intimidation by the accused or fear of reprisal if they cooperate (Cannavale 1976; Erez and Belknap 1998; Ford 1983; Singer 1988). Other factors are the criminal justice system's lack of responsiveness to the victims' needs and the "attitudes, comments, opinions or assumptions of criminal processing personnel who deal with battered women" (Erez and Belknap 1998:263; also see Byrne et al. 1999; Field and Field 1973; Ford 1983); a desire to continue the relationship or to reconcile with the accused (Walker 1979); the economic hardship for the victim and her family posed by prosecution (Chapman 1978; Erez and Belknap 1998); and the socialization of women to live with male violence (Shainess 1977; Walker 1979). In a recent study, three major obstacles to victims' participation in the court system were uncovered: victims were confused by the court process, found the criminal justice system to be frustrating, and were extremely fearful during the time period between the batterer's arrest and the resolution of the court case (Bennett, Goodman, and Dutton 1999).

These studies describe why domestic violence victims may not cooperate with the prosecution; others focus on the characteristics of victims who do cooperate. Although one multivariate study found no association between any victim or case characteristics and the likelihood that victims will cooperate in the prosecution process (Lerman 1986), another found that injury to the victim played a significant role in understanding a victim's willingness to cooperate: injured females were three times more likely than uninjured females to continue to cooperate at the prosecutorial stage (McLeod 1983). In the same study, the relationship between the victim and the offender was also significant: separated and divorced females were most cooperative, and also were the group for which prosecutors were most likely to file charges. Finally, in a multivariate analysis of victim cooperation, Goodman, Bennett, and Dutton (1999) found that victims were more likely to cooperate when they had social support, when they suffered severe violence, when they had children in common with the abuser, and when they reported higher levels of substance abuse. In short, their analyses revealed a number of victim-related characteristics that are important to understanding the likelihood of cooperation.

Research Setting

The data for this study were gathered from the files of a specialized domestic violence court in Toronto, Canada (hereafter called K-Court).[4] Prosecution files, that included police investigation reports, were supplemented by files kept by the Victim/Witness Assistance Program (VWAP), described in greater detail below. The K-Court was established to improve the criminal justice response to intimate partner violence and related crimes. In keeping with the cases that fall within K-Court's operational mandate, domestic violence is defined here as violence between intimate partners; it may take the form of assaults, sexual assaults, threats, and/or harassment. The term *intimate partners* includes legally married spouses, common-law partners, or dating couples, whether current or estranged, including persons in same-sex relationships.

In the data collection process we tracked all cases from the initial laying of a charge to final disposition. We also tracked cases in which all charges were withdrawn by the prosecutor; we documented the reasons for this case attrition on the basis of notations in the court files.[5] Case tracking was conducted from April 1, 1997 to March 31, 1998, a period roughly corresponding to the first year of the K-Court initiative. We tracked a total of 474 cases during that one-year period, reflecting all police-laid domestic assault and related charges brought to K-Court and completed during the evaluation period.[6] Although operation of K-Court actually began in mid-January 1997, we hoped that a delayed start in case tracking would give participants in the project an opportunity to become accustomed to their responsibilities, so that they would be more likely to follow the general principles and observe the operational goals when we began tracking. We acknowledge, however, that the case outcome data still may reflect the early stage of the project's evolution.[7]

We made regular visits to the court office to collect data from both prosecutor files and case files kept by the Victim/Witness Assistance Program. We gathered information on more than 70 variables pertaining to victim, offender, and offense characteristics as well as criminal justice variables and outcomes. In addition, we conducted interviews with victims who were prepared to participate in the evaluation. Unfortunately, because it proved extremely difficult and time-consuming to find participants, and to arrange and hold the interviews, only 60 such interviews were conducted; these represent less than 15 percent of the total sample. Although this low response rate prevents us from drawing conclusions from the qualitative data, we use victims' comments for illustration.

From Domestic Violence Prosecution in Ontario to K-Court

In Ontario, the Crown Policy Manual (hereafter called CPM), maintained by the Ministry of the Attorney General, provides prosecutors with guidance on how to conduct their prosecutions.[8] The CPM defines spouse/partner assault as "any physical or sexual assault or threat of physical or sexual assault on a woman or man by anyone with whom he or she has cohabited or had a long term relationship, whether or not they are legally married or living together at the time of assault or threat" (1993:SP-1, p. 1).[9]

The CPM not only provides a general framework for prosecutors in dealing with victims of domestic violence, but specifically addresses the "withdrawal of charges." When ought a prosecutor withdraw charges, and thus not proceed with a domestic violence prosecution? In Ontario, where the police generally lay the charge, they have been directed to lay charges in these cases, so long as reasonable and probable grounds exist. Police discretion beyond that point has been eliminated. The prosecutor, however, determines whether to proceed with the prosecution of the charge. Withdrawing charges of spouse/partner assault, though within the prosecutor's discretion, "is not appropriate unless exceptional circumstances exist." Before doing so, a prosecutor must consult with a more senior prosecutor (the Crown Attorney) or with a domestic violence coordinator (1993:SP-1, p. 4); furthermore, although it is the prosecutor's decision to withdraw charges (the victim does not control the prosecution), the victim also *must* acknowledge, in court, that she wants the charges withdrawn, and must state the reasons for wanting the prosecution terminated.

Stressing the importance of sound prosecutorial discretion in these cases (1993:3), the CPM provides a partial checklist of relevant factors to consider in helping prosecutors to determine whether to withdraw charges in a domestic violence case. This list includes the strength of the case, the history of violent behavior by the accused, evidence of harassment by the accused once charges have been laid, the extent of injuries suffered by the victim, the reasons that the victim states for not wanting the prosecution to proceed, and the results of an interview between the prosecutor and the victim, in which "Crown counsel discusses the public wrong aspect of domestic violence and tries to respond to any concerns the victim may have" (1993:SP-1, pp. 4–5).

Though the CPM is designed to provide guidelines to prosecutors across Ontario, K-Court was designed to provide for a more vigorous prosecution of domestic violence cases and to increase cooperation between prosecutors and participating police divisions. The initiative is premised on the belief that a commitment to these goals will improve the quality of investigations and will increase the number of successful outcomes.[10] Case screening decisions are made by a small group of prosecutors assigned to K-Court full-time.[11] This assignment ensures that cases are handled from start to finish by the same prosecutor who is assigned to the case early in the process, and offers the victim greater continuity. K-Court prosecutors also are expected to meet with all willing victims well before trial to discuss the facts of the case, to determine the victim's readiness to testify, to answer any questions on the part of the victim, and present a supportive, understanding position regardless of the victim's decision to cooperate with the prosecution. The overall objectives are to provide a sense of continuity to the prosecution process, to increase the quality of prosecutions, to increase the likelihood that a victim will cooperate with the prosecution, and to improve service to the victims.

Central to the K-Court initiative is the systematic collection of evidence by police so that the prosecution need not rely solely on victims' testimony. As a result, beginning in the year before the K-Court project and continuing through its first year of operation, the prosecutors worked with police at the three participating police divisions to develop new practices for collecting additional evidence. These include detailed descriptions of the crime scene, the seizing of items that may have been used as weapons, photographs (primarily of victims' injuries), transcripts of emergency 911 tapes, medical reports, and background information on the victim-offender relationship.[12]

A significant practice emphasized in this court is the procurement of videotaped statements from victims as soon as possible after the incident, provided that the victims agree to be videotaped. (Audiotaping is also considered an alternative.) The goal is to have a videotaped statement recorded immediately after the incident, or at least within 24 hours. The police are responsible for taping victims' testimony; generally these informal interviews are held at the police station. In extreme circumstances, the police may videotape victims' testimony outside the police station. In one case, for example, the police videotaped the victim's statement in her hospital room, where she was taken as a result of the violent incident and was expected to remain for several days. Prosecutors may use this videotape in lieu of victims' testimony in cases where victims cease to cooperate with the prosecution. Prosecutors are committed to pursuing the admission of this evidence more actively at trial; it is expected that this initiative could lead both to increased convictions at trial and to a greater number of guilty pleas on the strength of the available evidence, without requiring the victim to testify at trial.

A final component of the specialized domestic court is the Victim/Witness Assistance Program (VWAP).[13] Although this program is not dedicated exclusively to K-Court, the court generates a large proportion of the VWAP clients. Victim/witness workers attempt to contact the victims in all K-Court cases, by telephone or by letter, soon after the bail hearing or detention order.[14] This step can play an important role in preventing future violence, because victims are most open to information about how to reduce their vulnerability immediately or soon after the crime (Davis, Lurigio, and Skogan 1997; Friedman and Tucker 1997).

The role of the VWAP is to provide victims with information about the court process, referrals to community organizations and government agencies, personal escort and support at trial, and support during meetings with the prosecutor. More specifically, victim/witness workers notify their clients when court appearances are scheduled, solicit their input before a guilty plea by their abuser, and offer a tour of the court to make them more comfortable with the process. Where victims agree to meet with the representatives of this program, it is expected that victim/witness workers will provide them with enough support to prepare them and make them comfortable with testifying at trial. The main objective of the VWAP program, however, is to support the victim throughout the process, regardless of whether she chooses to testify.

Methods and Measurement

Variables and Measurement

The purpose of our analysis is twofold. First, we examine whether prosecutors' perceptions of a victim's willingness to cooperate increase the likelihood that a case will be prosecuted, while controlling for a number of legal and extralegal variables. The dependent variable was coded 1 if the case was prosecuted: that is, it proceeded to trial (regardless of whether the accused was found guilty or not guilty) or was resolved through the entry of a guilty plea. In a case that was not prosecuted, the prosecutor withdrew all the charges.

Because defendants may be charged with multiple offenses, we constructed a variable to summarize the dispositions for all the charges in each case in order to determine whether a case was prosecuted. When any of the charges in a case were resolved by trial or guilty plea, we considered the case to have been prosecuted (coded 1), even if the primary, or most serious, charge was withdrawn. This definition allows us to track cases even if the charges were reduced, and enables us to predict the likelihood that a defendant will be prosecuted on *any* charge related to domestic violence. The variable was coded 0 only if all the charges laid against an accused were withdrawn, and the case thus was not prosecuted.

The first part of our analysis focuses on the relationship between victim cooperation and the likelihood of prosecution. We determined whether a victim had cooperated after examining notes and assessments made in both the prosecutor's files and the files from the VWAP office. Evidence of the extent of victim cooperation includes notations in the files regarding whether a victim recanted or requested that charges be dropped, or whether prosecutors perceived the victim to be "hostile" or "on-side." The method undertaken in coding these variables does not rely on objective criteria for "cooperation," in that this determination inevitably involves some subjective assessment by each prosecutor. Such subjective assessment, however, is precisely what we wish to evaluate: whether prosecutors decide not to prosecute when they believe that the victim is not cooperating.

We model these data as three separate dummy variables indicating whether the victim cooperated fully (0,1) or was reluctant but cooperated (0,1).[15] "No victim cooperation" was the reference category. Hypothesizing that prosecutors may act differently depending on the extent or quality of a victim's cooperation, we defined "cooperative victims" as those who participated in the process from the point when the charge was laid through the completion of the case by trial or guilty plea. Victims who cooperated, but did so reluctantly, are those who indicated at some point during the process that they wanted the charges dropped or did not want to testify, but who subsequently participated in the prosecution until the case was resolved. Noncooperative victims are those who had no involvement after the charges were laid, or who were involved initially, but then ceased to cooperate altogether.

In the second part of our analysis, we seek to identify the demographic or situational factors associated with a victim's decision to cooperate. Here the dependent variable "victim cooperation" is dichotomized (cooperation = 1) because we are interested in whether victims cooperate, rather than in the quality of that cooperation.[16] The category of cooperative victims includes both those who cooperated fully and those who cooperated reluctantly. We include similar controls for legal and process variables as well as defendant characteristics in both analyses; these are discussed in greater detail below.

Legal Variables. Legal variables include seriousness of offense and strength of evidence. Indicators of offense seriousness are the degree of injury resulting from the incident (also see Rauma 1984; Schmidt and Steury 1989) and the use of a weapon to threaten or assault the victim during the incident. Degree of injury is entered as three separate dummy variables indicating whether the victim suffered "minor" injuries (0,1) such as cuts and/or bruises, or "serious" injuries (0,1) including sexual assaults or injuries requiring medical attention.[17] The reference category was comprised of those cases in which no injuries resulted. We also entered use of weapon as a dichotomy: cases involving threats or assaults with weapons were coded 1, and those involving no weapons were coded 0.

The procurement of additional evidence is a key component of K-Court, and may affect the importance of victim cooperation in this setting. Thus we introduce detailed measures of available evidence and the presence or absence of witnesses. First, we measure the strength of available evidence with seven dummy variables indicating the presence or absence of each type of evidence (presence is coded 1 for all variables): statements from victims, statements from others (witnesses or otherwise), photographs of victim injuries and/or the scene of the incident, videotaped victim statements, transcripts of the emergency 911 call, medical records, and other evidence (e.g., background evidence on the victim-offender relationship). Then we model the presence of witnesses as two separate dummy variables indicating whether the witnesses were adults (0,1) or children (0,1).[18] The reference category is "no witnesses present."

Process Variables. The frequency and/or occurrence of interactions between victims of domestic violence and criminal justice officials also may influence both the likelihood of prosecution and victim cooperation. A victim who is willing to meet with representatives of the court may be perceived as more cooperative. On the other hand, if a prosecutor or victim/witness assistance worker involves the victim in the process, she may feel more positive about the experience, and thus may be more willing to continue cooperating. One objective of the K-Court project is to work more effectively with victims; thus information on meetings between victims, prosecutors, and VWAP workers was recorded regularly. We included these variables as separate dichotomous variables (meetings = 1) in both logistic regression models to capture whether such meetings affected the likelihood of prosecution and (more important) whether a victim cooperated.

Defendant Characteristics. As noted earlier, researchers have identified a number of defendant characteristics that may affect whether a case proceeds to prosecution (Ellis 1984; Schmidt and Steury 1989; Stanko 1982). Three variables were available in this study for analysis, and we introduce them as controls: the defendant's relationship to the victim and the defendant's age and gender. Age is measured in years; gender is a dichotomous variable (male = 1).[19] Because the victim-defendant relationship is of particular interest in cases of domestic violence, we use more refined categories than did previous researchers to determine whether some types of intimate relationships are prosecuted more often than others and whether relationship type affects the victim's decision to cooperate. With legal spouse representing the reference category, we enter separate dummy variables for ex-legal spouse (0,1), common-law partner (0,1), ex-common-law partner (0,1), boyfriend/girlfriend (0,1), and ex-boyfriend/girlfriend (0,1).

Finally, research has shown that a defendant's criminal history is often related to the decision to prosecute (Rauma 1984; Schmidt and Steury 1989). We constructed dummy variables for prior domestic record (0,1),[20] other violent record (0,1), and nonviolent record (0,1). These dummy variables are mutually exclusive: for instance, where an individual was convicted of both domestic violence and assault, we classified the conviction as domestic violence. "No prior record" is the reference category.

The Sample

Table 21.1 provides an overview of sample characteristics and bivariate relationships among the independent and outcome variables. As expected, the great majority of victims were women: they accounted for 91 percent of our sample, while males made up 93 percent of the defendants. The average age of the victim was 33 years; the youngest was 15 and the oldest 75. The average age of the defendant was 35 years; the youngest defendant was 18 and the oldest 75. Overall, victims and defendants in our sample were slightly older than in other studies (see Schmidt and Steury 1989).

Almost half of the defendants had been involved previously with the criminal justice system, with charges for both violent and nonviolent offenses; 17 percent had prior domestic offenses. Many of the victims and defendants in our sample were or had been in common-law relationships (42%); close to one-quarter of the couples were estranged at the time of the incident. Forty-six percent of victims in our sample suffered minor injuries including bruises, cuts, and black eyes; weapons were used to threaten or assault a victim in about 16 percent of the cases. Witnesses were present in 42 percent of the cases; the majority of these were children of the victim and/or the offender.

Eighty-three percent of the cases proceeded to trial or were resolved through a plea agreement; the other 17 percent were withdrawn. The proportion of cases prosecuted in K-Court is higher than reported in other studies on the prosecution of domestic violence (Fagan 1995; Ford and Regoli 1993; Sherman 1992). This is not surprising, however, given that the K-Court is a specialized domestic violence court with a vigorous prosecution policy. Furthermore, as mentioned earlier, we considered a case as prosecuted even if a number of the charges in the case were withdrawn, as long as at least one of the

Table 21.1
Descriptive Characteristics of K-Court and Zero-Order Correlations (N=474)

Variable	Mean	Decision to Prosecute [a]	Victim Cooperation [b]	N
Victim Characteristics				
Mean age of victim (years)	33	–.02	.12*	474
Female victim	.91	.19***	.06	474
Offender Characteristics				
Mean age of offender (years)	35	–.05	.12*	474
Male offender	.93	.21***	.08	474
Prior domestic offenses	.17	.04	–.06	430
Prior violent offenses, nondomestic	.13	.04	.04	430
Prior nonviolent offenses	.18	–.04	–.09	430
Victim-Offender Relationship				
Legally married	.31	.05	–.02	462
Ex-legal spouse	.08	.06	.05	462
Common-law partner	.34	.02	–.03	462
Ex-common-law partner	.08	–.07	.10	462
Boyfriend/girlfriend	.10	–.12*	–.10	462
Ex-boyfriend/girlfriend	.07	.01	–.00	462
Estranged relationship	.23	–.01	.10	462
Incident Characteristics				
Minor injuries	.46	-.05	–.09	459
Serious injuries	.13	.04	–.00	459
Witnesses present, children	.14	.06	.05	402
Witnesses present, adults	.34	–.04	–.01	402
Weapons used	.16	–.02	–.03	474
Case Characteristics				
Decision to prosecute	.83	—	.28***	474
Victim cooperated	.40	.20***	—	370
Victim cooperated reluctantly	.15	.06	—	370
Victim met victims/witness workers	.50	.15**	.29***	390
Victim met with prosecution	.32	.09	.17**	390
Evidence, victim statement	.23	–.01	.08	390
Evidence, other witness statement	.16	.05	.10	390
Evidence, photographs (injuries/scene)	.32	–.00	.05	390
Evidence, victim's video testimony	.26	.13**	.20***	390
Evidence, emergency 911 tape	.27	–.02	.08	390
Evidence, medical reports	.08	.02	.09	390

a Zero-order correlations with dependent variable: decision to prosecute

b Zero-order correlations with dependent variable: victim cooperation

* $p < .05$; ** $p < .01$; *** $p < .001$

domestic violence charges was resolved by trial or guilty plea.

In 32 percent of all cases, the victim met at least once with the prosecutor; in half of all cases, she met with representatives of the victim/witness assistance program.[21] Victims who met with prosecutors and victim/witness assistance workers, however, did not necessarily cooperate with the prosecution; they may have attended these meetings to request withdrawal of the charges.

On the basis of the available data, approximately 55 percent of all victims cooperated with the prosecution.[22] This figure includes both the victims who cooperated from the beginning and continued to do so throughout and the victims who were initially reluctant but subsequently cooperated. In the remainder of the cases, the victims either were not involved with the process or asked to have the charges dropped and disengaged from the process.

The Decision to Prosecute

Findings

Table 21.2 reports the findings from five separate models predicting the likelihood of prosecution in cases of domestic violence. We employ logistic regression, a technique commonly used for dichotomous and highly skewed outcome variables, which allows us to predict the odds that an event will occur (Demaris 1992). For three of our independent variables (victim cooperation, evidence, and presence of witnesses), data were missing for over 10 percent of the cases; therefore our models include dummy variables for each of these variables, coded 0 if data are present and 1 if the data are missing (Cohen and Cohen 1975; Orme and Reis 1991). This strategy allows us to retain the maximum sample size, to increase statistical power, to reduce bias in estimation of regression parameters, and to test the extent to which data are missing randomly (Orme and Reis 1991). The missing-value dummies are shown in each of the two logistic regression tables; the extent of missing data is displayed in Table 21.1, for victim cooperation,[23] evidence, and presence of witnesses.[24]

The first model examines the relationship between the severity of the offense and the decision to prosecute, using controls for defendant and case characteristics. As shown in the first column of Table 21.2, male defendants are more likely to be prosecuted than female defendants.

Table 21.2

Logit Estimates of Effects of Legal and Background Variables and Victim Cooperation on Likelihood of Prosecution in Domestic Violence Cases

Variable	Model 1		Model 2		Model 3		Model 4		Model 5	
	Coefficient	Odds	Coefficient	Odds	Coefficient	Odds	Coefficient	Odds	Coefficient	Odds
Def. Characteristics										
Defendant age	−.02 (.01)	.98	−.03* (.01)	.97	−.03* (.01)	.97	−.04** (.01)	.96	−.04** (.01)	.96
Male	1.61*** (.39)	4.98	1.61*** (.40)	4.99	1.55*** (.42)	4.69	1.32** (.43)	3.74	1.34** (.44)	3.81
Case Characteristics										
Weapon used	.14 (.34)	1.15	.07 (.35)	1.08	.05 (.36)	1.05	.06 (.37)	1.06	.20 (.38)	1.22
Domestic prior record	.31 (.37)	1.36	.40 (.39)	1.49	.37 (.40)	1.45	.46 (.40)	1.59	.54 (.42)	1.72
Violent prior record	.25 (.42)	1.29	.50 (.44)	1.65	.45 (.45)	1.56	.53 (.46)	1.70	.46 (.47)	1.59
Nonviolent record	−.22 (.33)	.80	−.14 (.34)	.87	−.10 (.35)	.91	−.05 (.35)	.96	.07 (.36)	1.08
Injury	−.09 (.26)	.91	−.02 (.27)	.98	−.15 (.30)	.86	−.08 (.31)	.92	−.03 (.32)	.97
Relationship Type										
Ex–spouse			.19 (.60)	1.21	.16 (.61)	1.17	.22 (.61)	1.25	−.03 (.62)	.97
Common–law			−.41 (.34)	.66	−.35 (.36)	.71	−.37 (.36)	.69	−.42 (.37)	.66
Ex–common–law			−.99* (.47)	.37	−1.03* (.49)	.36	−.99* (.50)	.37	−1.36** (.52)	.26
Boyfriend/girlfriend			−1.28** (.43)	.28	−1.20** (.45)	.30	−1.20** (.46)	.30	−1.30** (.48)	.27
Ex–boyfriend/girlfriend			−.60 (.57)	.55	−.49 (.59)	.62	−.46 (.60)	.64	−.56 (.62)	.57
Legal Variables										
Victim statement					−.12 (.34)	.90	−.16 (.34)	.85	−.22 (.36)	.81
Witness statement					.60 (.44)	1.80	.55 (.46)	1.74	.49 (.46)	1.63
Photos					.12 (.33)	1.12	.01 (.34)	1.01	−.03 (.35)	.97
Video					.89* (.37)	2.44	.90* (.38)	2.47	.75* (.39)	2.11
Emergency tape					−.21 (.32)	.81	−.23 (.32)	.79	−.34 (.33)	.71
Medical evidence					.07 (.50)	1.08	−.10 (.51)	.90	−.11 (.53)	.89
Other evidence					.23 (.33)	1.26	.19 (.33)	1.20	−.01 (.34)	.99
Missing evidence					.18 (.44)	1.19	.13 (.45)	1.14	.18 (.46)	1.20
Child witness					.30 (.46)	1.35	.26 (.46)	1.29	.26 (.47)	1.29
Adult witness					−.34 (.32)	.71	−.29 (.32)	.75	−.38 (.33)	.69
Missing witness					.22 (.34)	1.36	.17 (.35)	1.22	.19 (.36)	1.27
Process Variables										
Victim met w/ VW AP							.77* (.37)	2.15	.53 (.39)	1.69
Victim met w/ Crown							.01 (.41)	1.01	−.01 (.43)	.98
Victim Cooperation										
Cooperated fully									2.01*** (.50)	7.48
Cooperated reluctantly									.81 (.57)	2.25
Missing cooperation									.22 (.32)	1.25
Constant	.80 (.55)		1.47 (.62)		1.42 (.71)		1.39 (.71)		1.21 (.73)	
−2 Log Likelihood	409.96		398.26		387.07		379.38		356.26	

NOTE: Numbers in parentheses are standard errors.
* $p < .05$; ** $p < .01$; *** $p < .001$

The second model introduces variables controlling for the relationship between the victim and the offender. The findings indicate that if the case involves a boyfriend/girlfriend relationship or an ex-common-law partner, the accused is less likely to be prosecuted for the offense than an accused who is legally married to the victim. Defendant's age is significant (older offenders are less likely to be prosecuted than younger offenders), and gender remains significant.

The third model introduces nine legal variables. The only legal variable with a significant effect on prosecution is the availability of videotaped statements, which increases the likelihood of prosecution. As in Model 2, involvement in an ex-common-law or boyfriend/girlfriend relationship decreases the likelihood of prosecution. Again, defendant's gender and age are significant in this model, with controls for victim-offender relationship and the presence of other types of evidence. Model 4 incorporates the process variables and shows that if a victim meets with representatives of the VWAP, the case is more likely to be prosecuted.

The final model, which incorporates the victim cooperation variables, demonstrates that when the victim cooperates, the odds of prosecution are more than seven times higher than if the victim does not cooperate. In other words, with controls for other relevant factors, victim cooperation is associated independently and positively with the likelihood of prosecution. All other previously significant variables still affect the likelihood of prosecution. Although our models cannot address the effects of other variables beyond the scope of our data (such as individual victims' perceptions of safety, or victims' hopes that offenders will receive counseling), our analysis demonstrates that neither offense seriousness nor defendant characteristics predict the likelihood of prosecution.

These findings are important not merely because they highlight the key role of victim cooperation in the likelihood that a case will proceed to prosecution, but rather because of the setting from which these data were collected: a specialized court, dedicated to prosecuting cases even without victim cooperation. Our findings suggest that, even in a setting where cases are mandated to proceed without victim cooperation through the use of other evidence, victim cooperation still plays the most significant role in determining whether a case is prosecuted.

Victim Cooperation

Our multivariate analysis confirms prior research suggesting that victim cooperation in cases of domestic violence is one of the key factors related to the likelihood of prosecution. Here we examine the correlates of victim cooperation during the prosecution process. Our goal is to determine what demographic, situational, or process variables are associated with victim cooperation in the prosecution of this offense. Our analysis is restricted to the 304 cases of domestic violence heard in K-Court for which we had information on victim cooperation.[25]

In the model predicting victim cooperation, our dependent variable is coded 1 if the victim cooperated with the prosecution, and 0 if the victim did not cooperate. Here we dichotomize the variable representing victim cooperation because we are interested in the determinants of any victim cooperation, rather than in the quality of that cooperation. Victim's age (measured in years) and victim's sex (female = 1) replace the variables for offender's age and offender's sex included in the first analysis. All other variables remain identical to those in the first analysis.

Findings

Table 21.3 shows that none of the demographic or situational characteristics are associated significantly with victim cooperation, once we control for the legal and process variables. Victim's age is significant in the first three models (older victims are more likely to cooperate), but becomes nonsignificant when process variables are introduced. Only one of the two criminal justice process variables, however, is related significantly to the likelihood that a victim of domestic violence will cooperate with the prosecution: the odds of cooperation are more than three times higher if the victim met with representatives of the victim/witness assistance program. Moreover, if the victim gave a videotaped

Table 21.3
Logit Estimates of Legal, Background, and Victim/Court Process Variables on Victim Cooperation

Variable	Model 1			Model 2			Model 3			Model 4		
	Coefficient		Odds	Coefficient		Odds	Coefficient		Odds	Coefficient		Odds
Victim Characteristics												
Victim age	.03*	(.01)	1.03	.03*	(.01)	1.03	.03*	(.01)	1.03	.02	(.01)	1.02
Female	.40	(.46)	1.50	.43	(.47)	1.54	.14	(.50)	1.15	−.18	(.53)	.84
Case Characteristics												
Weapon used	−.10	(.32)	.90	−.07	(.33)	.93	−.16	(.35)	.85	−.24	(.36)	.79
Domestic prior record	−.69*	(.35)	.50	−.77*	(.36)	.46	−.69	(.38)	.50	−.68	(.39)	.51
Violent prior record	.18	(.38)	1.20	.16	(.40)	1.18	.09	(.42)	1.09	.23	(.43)	1.25
Nonviolent record	−.48	(.32)	.62	−.46	(.33)	.63	−.47	(.34)	.62	−.43	(.35)	.65
Injury	−.33	(.25)	.72	−.24	(.26)	.79	−.48	(.29)	.62	−.38	(.30)	.68
Relationship Type												
Ex–spouse				.48	(.50)	1.61	.64	(.52)	1.90	.95	(.55)	2.59
Common–law				.12	(.31)	1.13	.11	(.33)	1.12	.22	(.35)	1.25
Ex–common–law				.78	(.52)	2.19	.59	(.56)	1.81	.84	(.58)	2.31
Boyfriend/girlfriend				−.22	(.42)	.80	−.13	(.44)	.88	.03	(.47)	1.03
Ex–boyfriend/girlfriend				.08	(.50)	1.08	.17	(.54)	1.19	.31	(.56)	1.37
Legal Variables												
Victim statement							.33	(.34)	1.40	.27	(.35)	1.31
Witness statement							.72	(.41)	2.05	.65	(.43)	1.91
Photos							.45	(.31)	1.57	.29	(.32)	1.34
Video							.99**	(.32)	2.69	.97**	(.34)	2.63
Emergency tape							.40	(.31)	1.49	.48	(.32)	1.61
Medical evidence							.67	(.49)	1.95	.37	(.50)	1.45
Other evidence							.49	(.31)	1.64	.38	(.32)	1.46
Missing evidence							.59	(.44)	1.79	.44	(.46)	1.55
Child witness							.06	(.41)	1.06	.10	(.42)	1.11
Adult witness							−.08	(.30)	.92	.05	(.32)	1.05
Missing witness							.23	(.42)	1.14	.26	(.33)	1.11
Process Variables												
Victim met w/ VW AP										1.16***	(.34)	3.20
Victim met w/ Crown										−.01	(.35)	.99
Constant	−.64	(.60)		−.85	(.66)		−1.35	(.75)		−1.71	(.79)	
−2 Log Likelihood	404.79			400.74			379.67			360.82		

NOTE: Numbers in parentheses are standard errors.
* $p < .05$; ** $p < .01$; *** $p < .001$

statement, the odds of subsequent cooperation are also significantly higher. In the full model, no other variable is associated significantly with victim cooperation.[26]

Discussion

In this [chapter] we first assessed the role of victim cooperation in the decision to prosecute domestic violence cases. Although it is commonly argued that lack of victim cooperation is the primary reason why prosecutors choose not to proceed in cases of domestic violence, this issue has received little systematic analysis (see Davis, Smith, and Nickles 1997). Using multivariate analysis to control for other factors relevant to the likelihood of prosecution in a specialized domestic violence court, we found that victim cooperation is a significant predictor of prosecution. In this sample, when victims cooperated, prosecutors were seven times more likely to pursue charges, even after we took into account the effects of defendant characteristics, the victim-defendant relationship, the type of evidence, and the presence of witnesses. This finding is especially interesting, given that our data are derived from a court designed to minimize the importance of victim cooperation in the prosecution of domestic violence cases.

Having found that victim cooperation remains a significant predictor of prosecution in our sample, in the second part of our analysis we sought to determine the factors associated with the victim's decision to cooperate with the prosecution. In contrast to past research, our findings demonstrated that neither demographic nor situational correlates of the incident were associated with victim cooperation. Rather, the two most important determinants were the availability of videotaped testimony and meetings between victims and victim/witness assistance workers.

One interpretation of these findings is based on common sense: victims who agreed to meet with victim/witness workers, or who were willing to have their testimony videotaped for evidence, are precisely those victims who were more likely to cooperate with the prosecution in the first place. In other words, cooperative victims tend to cooperate. From both research and policy perspectives, however, a fuller explanation is necessary. How might we explain the positive effects, on victim cooperation, of videotaped statements and meetings with victim/witness assistance workers?

Videotaped Testimony and Victim Cooperation

In exploring the correlates of victim cooperation, our analysis demonstrated that victims were more likely to cooperate when videotaped testimony from the victim was available to prosecutors as evidence. The significance of this variable in predicting cooperation may be explained by the complex relationship between prosecutors and victims of domestic violence. Some observers believe that victim noncooperation may be due to a "self-fulfilling prophecy" which begins with the actions and attitudes of prosecutors and other criminal justice officials (Buzawa and Buzawa 1996; Ellis 1984; Ford and Regoli 1993). From this perspective, victims' negative impressions and general distrust of the criminal justice system are reinforced by prosecutors' assumptions that the victim is not committed to cooperating; thereby victims are discouraged from following through at the prosecutorial stage. Many victims may be intimidated by the criminal justice system, and thus are uninformed about what they are expected to do (Cannavale 1976; Erez and Belknap 1998). Such victims, when faced with an ambivalent prosecutor, may conclude that the prosecutor is not committed to their case and consequently may disengage from the process. The following statements illustrate this point:

> I didn't find her [the prosecutor] very helpful. I provided names of witnesses and told her about the doctor's report, but she never followed up. (Case 98)

> I never got the information I wanted from him [the prosecutor]. I had to go to go elsewhere [victim/witness office] for information. In fact, I cornered him one day to ask him a question and he still didn't have time to speak with me. (Case 85)

In contrast, when the victim has already agreed to have her testimony videotaped, a prosecutor may be less inclined to question her commitment for two reasons. First, the prosecutor may perceive the victim's videotaped testimony as an indication of her commitment to the prosecution and to her role in the process. Second, and alternatively, the prosecutor may be less inclined to question the victim's commitment because the availability of videotaped testimony minimizes prosecutors' reliance on victim cooperation. In other words, should the victim recant, the videotape may stand in lieu of her testimony. The victim, as a result, is not perceived as the "weak link" in the process, and her treatment by the prosecutor may dispose her to cooperate throughout.[27]

Victim/Witness Assistance and Victim Cooperation

Our analysis also indicated that victims who met with victim/witness workers were more likely to cooperate with the prosecution. It may be that victims who do so gain the support they need to follow through with the prosecution of their abusive partners. Legal advocacy programs commonly have been used for victims of crime that occur in the private sphere, particularly against women and children (Sebba 1996; U.S. Department of Justice 1995). In cases of domestic violence, victims are often fearful and anxious about the criminal justice proceedings; support by victim advocates may help them negotiate the system more easily (Tomz and McGillis 1997). Advocacy programs have been instituted so that victims can understand their options and make informed decisions that will ensure their safety and/or improve their lives (Tomz and McGillis 1997; U.S. Department of Justice 1998). Moreover, battered women are often concerned about their safety and are uncertain about their future if their abusive partners are charged and/or convicted. Therefore, information about the criminal process, community service programs, and shelters is critical.

Tomz and McGillis (1997) argue that without the support of victim advocates, witnesses who are already inconvenienced, distressed by their involvement with the courts, or afraid that a court appearance will bring reprisals from the defendant will fail to testify. Meeting with victim/witness advocates, however, may encourage victims to continue cooperating with the prosecution. In turn, fewer cases may be dismissed for lack of "prosecutability" (Tomz and McGillis 1997). This interpretation is supported by the following statements from victims interviewed as part of the evaluation of K-Court:

> They [victim/witness workers] made me feel comfortable and were encouraging. If not for the victim/witness people, I wouldn't have gone through with it. I had a hard time understanding what was going on. They were patient and explained everything to me. The experience was not as bad as I thought it was going to be because of the support I got from them. (Case 146)

> I did not want to testify on the date of the trial. They convinced me that he [the abuser] needed help and would only get that help if I testified against him. (Case 99)

> The victim/witness people were very nice and accommodating . . . having a victim/witness worker there made it easier for me to face him . . . they made the process less intimidating. (Case 313)

> She [the victim/witness worker] was very helpful the day of the trial. She stayed with me through the whole thing and I found this calming. (Case 446)

Finally, it has been argued that women have been socialized to live with male violence (Shainess 1977; Walker 1979). Advocacy programs such as the victim/witness assistance program, however, may be able to inform victims that other options are available. As one woman commented on the message given to her by VWAP workers:

> The victim/witness people explained to me that I have rights and that I don't have to put up with being abused. I always thought that it was my fault . . . that I asked for it somehow. I have been beaten my whole life . . . I didn't know any better. (Case 166)

Although there has been little concrete research on the effects of victim/witness assistance programs or other types of crisis intervention programs (Young 1990), a recent study on the prosecution of child sexual abuse from 1983 to 1989 found that the introduction of the victim/witness assistance program doubled the success rate at trial for these cases (Dible and Teske 1993). Therefore, such programs not only may increase the likelihood of victim cooperation, but also may strengthen the prosecution as a whole.

Conclusion

In this analysis we examined a specialized domestic violence court in one city; it may not necessarily reflect dynamics in other jurisdictions. We believe, however, that our findings may have general implications beyond this particular context. These findings stress the importance of victim cooperation to prosecutorial decisionmaking; on a policy level, then, we must give special attention to the determinants and correlates of such cooperation. Two main issues emanate from the findings.

First, our data demonstrate the importance of victim/witness programs for victim cooperation. Therefore, continued evaluations of such programs are needed to further specify their relationship to victims' willingness to cooperate (Sebba 1996). If victim/witness assistance programs indeed make the criminal justice process less intimidating for victims, it may be desirable to increase funding to such advocacy agencies so that increased support is offered to victims of violence in general.

Second, if the availability of videotaped statements exerts a positive influence (as we have suggested) on the interaction between prosecutors and victims, continued and increased use of this procedure in courts would be beneficial. Where this practice has not been instituted, police and prosecutors should be trained in the uses and procedures for such evidence.

The response of criminal justice officials can make a difference to victims' willingness to cooperate; as Erez and Belknap (1998:264) demonstrate, helpful responses can encourage domestic violence victims to "sustain the frustration they face, or withstand the difficulties they have to overcome to reach a satisfactory solution." The responsiveness of criminal justice personnel to victims' needs is an important predictor of cooperation for victims of crime: victims who do not receive sufficient information, or who are not recognized as a party to the process, may disengage or cease to cooperate (Norton 1983; Sebba 1996; Shapland, Willmore, and Duff 1985).

Of course, we must not focus narrowly on the prosecutorial process. One victim's comment highlights the importance of interactions with other criminal justice personnel:

> The Crown and the victim/witness people can only be effective if the initial contact with police is a positive experience. Otherwise, we [the victims] are intimidated and scared off. The police are often the weak link in the chain. (Case 407)

To be effective, then, policies that seek to improve the criminal justice response to domestic violence must be informed by the victims' experience *throughout* the process. Such an approach will help us to address more effectively the issue of victim cooperation: in concentrating on the prosecutorial process, we have demonstrated the continued importance of such research.

With this focus on a specialized domestic violence court in Toronto, this [chapter] presents an important case study that should spur future research on domestic violence. Such research should continue to examine the determinants of both prosecutorial decisionmaking and victim cooperation, both in and out of specialized courts. As our case study demonstrates, how individual victims and prosecutors respond to criminal justice initiatives matters a great deal. This point ought not to be lost in criminal justice policymaking.

Authors' Note

We thank the three anonymous *Justice Quarterly* reviewers for their helpful comments, the Ministry of the Attorney General of Ontario for access to the data, and Rosemary Gartner, John Hagan, Ron Levi, and Mariana Valverde for their helpful comments and criticisms on previous drafts. This paper received first prize in the Gene Carte Student Paper Competition, sponsored by The American Society of Criminology, as well as the Sociology of Law Graduate Student Paper Award, given by the American Sociological Association. Authors are listed alphabetically.

Notes

1. We included gender as a variable in our analyses in order to compare victim cooperation in cases where women were victims and where men were victims. Most of the research, however, focuses on women as the primary victims of domestic violence, and the distribution of our sample supports this: women make up 91 percent of the victims. Thus, throughout, we use the female pronoun in referring to victims.
2. Some may suggest that, by using the term *victim cooperation*, we are implicitly blaming those victims who do not cooperate with the criminal justice process. We do not wish to imply that victims should always cooperate with prosecutions, nor do we suggest that victims should not be free to determine their degree of involvement in the prosecutorial process. Rather, our goal in this paper is to increase the understanding of the role that victims of domestic violence play in the prosecutorial process, and of the relationship between prosecutors and victims in responding to domestic violence.
3. These findings, however, were subject to significant regional variation: only 8 percent of prosecutors in the largest jurisdictions (population over 500,000) agreed that victim cooperation affected their decision to prosecute, compared with 36 percent of prosecutors in medium-sized jurisdictions (population between 250,000 and 500,000).
4. K-Court is part of the Provincial Court in Ontario. Although all criminal matters begin in Provincial Court, only certain offenses can be tried by a Provincial Court judge. Offenses under the Criminal Code can be classified either as summary conviction offenses (e.g., trespassing at night or vagrancy), indictable offenses (e.g., murder, forcible confinement, or aggravated assault), or hybrid offenses, for which the prosecution elects to proceed either summarily or by indictment (such as assault, uttering threats, or criminal harassment). The jurisdiction of the Provincial Court in criminal matters is limited to summary conviction offenses, hybrid offenses for which the prosecution elects to proceed summarily, or proceedings by way of indictment, in which the defendant elects, when permitted by the Code, to be tried in front of a Provincial Court judge. Finally, because no jury trials are held in Provincial Court, all trials in K-Court are heard by the judge alone.
5. We recognize that written reports and notes offer researchers a less accurate picture of the case than is available to the prosecutor at the time of his or her decision. Prosecutors, however, generally noted information clearly and consistently on the primary variables used in this analysis.
6. K-Court does not hear all charges related to domestic violence for the city of Toronto. There are 19 police divisions in Toronto; only three of these participated in the specialized court project. Thus, although the sample of 474 cases constitutes the whole population of cases brought to K-Court, it does not represent all charges of domestic violence laid in the city as a whole.
7. In the first year of operation, any innovative program—in this case a specialized domestic violence court—may perform optimally. In other words, people who staff the program are likely to be highly committed. Over time, however, it is possible that people become less committed, or high turnover means that staff members are less well trained or overwhelmed by workloads. Alternatively, staff members may not achieve the objectives of the new program until it has been running for some time. Regardless of the situation, the external validity of this analysis may be weakened somewhat because of the newness of the project.
8. Although the policies are not always mandatory—the CPM explicitly states that they are not designed to eliminate prosecutorial discretion or "flexible decision-making at the local level" (1993:3)—the Policy Manual provides a general framework for prosecutors in the Province of Ontario.
9. Stating clearly that spouse/partner assault "should be treated as seriously as any other serious criminal matter" (1993:SP-1, p. 1), much of the spouse/partner assault policy is geared toward assisting prosecutors in their relationship with the victim. Providing statistics on the likelihood of past victimization suffered by complainants, the Policy Manual states that "[t]hese prosecutions clearly require special sensitivity on the part of Crown counsel when dealing with them." (1993:SP-1, p. 2). Further, "Crown counsel are reminded that

the victims of spouse/partner assault are frequently ambivalent about the court process" (1993:SP-1, p. 3). In view of this frequent ambivalence, "[a]dditional care in listening to [victims'] concerns and explaining the process, though time consuming, is necessary to the conduct of the case" (1993:SP-1, p. 3). To allay victims' concerns it is suggested that prosecutors rely on studies showing that violence declines or terminates when the criminal process is instituted (1993:SP-1, p. 3). In addition, legal mechanisms for dealing with victims/witnesses who fail to appear at trial, and for victims/witnesses who are forgetful, adverse, or hostile at trial are provided (1993:SP-1, p. 6).

10. A "successful prosecution" refers to those cases in which charges were not withdrawn, even if the victim chose not to testify, and where convictions were secured through either a trial or a guilty plea. This is the language used by those involved in the K-Court initiative.
11. At any given time, four prosecutors were assigned to K-Court, though 13 different prosecutors were assigned during the year of the evaluation. The court itself is presided over by judges who are assigned to K-Court in rotation for one week each month for a period of three months. This approach is intended to keep the same judges involved in K-Court for the length of any one case, and thereby to keep the case wholly within K-Court. At the same time, rotation of judges out of K-Court during this time prevents identification of those judges as part of a court designed to successfully prosecute such cases, and allows judges to deal with cases other than domestic violence during that period.
12. Some of the practices were in place in some or all of the participating police divisions before the implementation of K-Court, but they were confirmed as priorities for this project.
13. This program is funded by the Attorney General of Ontario and is separate and independent of the prosecutors' office. Its mandate is to provide support to victims of crime.
14. The only exceptions are cases in which a guilty plea is entered at the bail hearing.
15. A victim's reluctance to continue cooperating with the criminal justice process was usually indicated in the victim/witness assistance files when it was noted that workers had to discuss the "ministry policy" with a client/victim. The ministry policy relates to the mandatory charging initiative in the Province of Ontario; when victims asked that charges be dropped, VWAP workers explained the mandatory charging policy to them and noted this action in the file.
16. To ensure that collapsing the variable in this way did not cause us to lose valuable information, we ran separate analyses using the trichotomous victim cooperation measure. The results demonstrated few differences in the factors that predicted full cooperation and reluctant cooperation. This point is discussed in greater detail in the section on results.
17. *Minor,* of course, is a relative term when used to describe injuries sustained during a violent incident. Furthermore, a focus on physical injuries disregards the emotional and verbal abuse which a victim may sustain, and which also may affect her willingness to cooperate.
18. The presence of children in the home or as witnesses to violent incidents may also be an important predictor of victim cooperation (Goodman, Bennett, and Dutton 1999) and of the prosecution's decision to proceed with a case. We gathered this information where possible, but it was not noted consistently in the files. Therefore the high proportion of missing data precluded inclusion of this variable in our models. Future researchers should strive to collect such information because the presence of children may be an important factor in predicting victims' actions in cases of domestic violence.
19. There were too few cases to permit separate analyses for male victims of domestic violence; thus we introduced gender as a control. We are not suggesting that male and female victims have similar experiences in the criminal justice system; rather, we wish to determine whether males were more likely than female victims to have their cases prosecuted or were more likely to cooperate.
20. Prior domestic record indicates that the offender had been convicted of a previous domestic violence offense involving either the same or a different victim.
21. As part of the VWAP's mandate to meet with all victims willing to do so, all K-Court victims were contacted by mail or telephone to arrange a meeting with program workers. Yet because some victims declined to meet, and because the VWAP could not find others, program workers met with only half the victims in this sample.
22. This variable was missing data in approximately 30 percent of cases. Below we describe the procedures used to deal with this missing data and discuss the implications.
23. The results of our analyses indicate a significant negative correlation between missing data on victim cooperation and the variable for meetings with victim witness assistance workers. That is, cases in which data were missing on cooperation were more likely to be those in which the victim did not meet with the victim/witness assistance workers (see Orme and Reis 1991). As shown in Table 21.2, the regression coefficient for missing data on the victim cooperation variable is nonsignificant; this indicates that after controlling for other variables, dependent variable means for subjects with missing data on the victim cooperation variable do not differ significantly from the dependent variable mean of the reference group (Orme and Reis 1991:78). This pattern suggests that the missing data are not missing in a systematic manner; as a result, our obtained sample should be representative of the population sampled (Orme and Reis 1991:84). As a further check, we conducted a sensitivity analysis, including only cases with complete data on victim cooperation. The results of the analysis on this subset of cases were substantively the same as those based on the larger sample; in particular, the effects of victim cooperation remained significant.
24. The missing-data dummies for evidence and witnesses were not correlated significantly with any other variables, and the regression coefficients were nonsignificant. This finding indicates that these data are missing randomly and do not cause bias in our sample.
25. We dropped from the analysis the cases for which data was missing on victim cooperation.
26. As noted previously, to ensure that collapsing the victim cooperation variable in this way did not cause us to lose valuable information, we ran a separate analysis that distinguished between victims who cooperated fully and victims who cooperated reluctantly. The two key predictors for both categories of victims, when examined separately, were the same as those identified in the analysis using the collapsed victim cooperation variable. That is, if videotaped testimony was available as evidence or if victims had met with victim/witness workers, they were more likely to cooperate with the prosecution. The one difference was that the availability of an emergency 911 tape predicted greater cooperation by reluctant victims, but not by victims who cooperated fully.
27. To verify this interpretation, one would need to hear from the prosecutors themselves. Although interviews were conducted with prosecutors involved in K-Court as part of the larger evaluation, this information was not recorded systematically and thus is not available for analysis.

References

Albonetti, C.A. 1986. "Criminality, Prosecutorial Screening, and Uncertainty: Toward a Theory of Discretionary Decision Making in Felony Case Processings." *Criminology* 24:623–44.

Albonetti, C.A. and J.R. Hepburn. 1996. "Prosecutorial Discretion to Defer Criminalization: The Effects of Defendant's Ascribed and Achieved Status Characteristics." *Journal of Quantitative Criminology* 12:63–81.

Bennett, L., L. Goodman, and M.A. Dutton. 1999. "Systemic Obstacles to the Criminal Prosecution of a Battering Partner: A Victim Perspective." *Journal of Interpersonal Violence* 14:761–72.

Bourdieu, P. 1977. *Outline of a Theory of Practice.* New York: Cambridge University Press.

Buzawa, E.S. and C.G. Buzawa. 1996. *Domestic Violence: The Criminal Justice Response.* Newbury Park, CA: Sage.

Buzawa, E., G.T. Hotaling, A. Klein, and J. Byrne. 1999. *Response to Domestic Violence in a Pro-Active Court Setting—Final Report.* Washington, DC: National Institute of Justice.

Byrne, C.A., D.G. Kilpatrick, S.S. Howley, and D. Beatty. 1999. "Female Victims of Partner Versus Nonpartner Violence: Experiences With the Criminal Justice System." *Criminal Justice and Behavior* 26:275–92.

Cahn, N.R. 1992. "Innovative Approaches to the Prosecution of Domestic Violence Crimes: An Overview." Pp. 161–80 in *Domestic Violence: The Changing Criminal Justice Response,* edited by E.S. Buzawa and C.G. Buzawa. Westport, CT: Auburn House.

Cahn, N.R. and L.G. Lerman. 1991. "Prosecuting Woman Abuse." Pp. 95–112 in *Woman Battering: Policy Responses,* edited by M. Steinman. Cincinnati, OH: Anderson.

Cannavale, F.J. 1976. *Witness Cooperation.* New York: Lexington Books.

Chapman, J.R. 1978. "The Economics of Women's Victimization." Pp. 251–68 in *The Victimization of Women,* edited by J.R. Chapman and M. Gates. Beverly Hills, CA: Sage.

Cohen, J. and P. Cohen. 1975. *Applied Multiple Regression/Correlation Analysis for the Behavioral Sciences.* Hillsdale, NJ: Erlbaum.

Davis, R.C., A.J. Lurigio, and W.G. Skogan. 1997. *Victims of Crime.* 2nd ed. Thousand Oaks, CA: Sage.

Davis, R.C. 1983. "Victim/Witness Noncooperation: A Second Look at a Persistent Phenomenon." *Journal of Criminal Justice* 11:287–99.

Davis, R.C. and B.E. Smith. 1981. "Crimes Between Acquaintances: The Response of Criminal Courts." *Victimology* 6:175–87.

Davis, R.C., B.E. Smith, and L. Nickles. 1997. "Prosecuting Domestic Violence Cases With Reluctant Victims: Assessing Two Novel Approaches in Milwaukee." Report to the National Institute of Justice.

Demaris, A. 1992. *Logit Modeling: Practical Applications.* London: Sage.

Dible, D.A. and R.H.C. Teske, Jr. 1993. "An Analysis of the Prosecutory Effects of a Child Sexual Abuse Victim-Witness Program." *Journal of Criminal Justice* 21:79–85.

Elliott, D.S. 1989. "Criminal Justice Procedures in Family Violence Crimes." Pp. 427–80 in *Family Violence, Crime and Justice,* vol. 11, edited by L. Ohlin and M. Tonry. Chicago, IL: University of Chicago Press.

Ellis, J.W. 1984. "Prosecutorial Discretion to Charge in Cases of Spousal Assault: A Dialogue." *Journal of Criminal Law and Criminology* 75:56–102.

Erez, E. and J. Belknap. 1998. "In Their Own Words: Battered Women's Assessments of the Criminal Processing System's Responses." *Violence and Victims* 13:251–68.

Fagan, J. 1995. *The Criminalization of Domestic Violence.* Washington, DC: National Institute of Justice.

Fagan, J., C. Maxwell, L. Macaluso, and C. Nahabedian. 1995. *Evaluation of the Domestic Violence Hearing Officer Pilot Program: Final Report.* Trenton, NJ: Administrative Office of the Courts.

Ferraro, K.J. and T. Boychuk. 1992. "The Court's Response to Interpersonal Violence: A Comparison of Intimate and Nonintimate Assault." Pp. 209–26 in *Domestic Violence: The Changing Criminal Justice Response,* edited by E.S. Buzawa and C.G. Buzawa. Westport, CT: Auburn House.

Field, M.H. and H.F. Field. 1973. "Marital Violence and the Criminal Process: Neither Justice nor Peace." *Social Service Review* 47:221–40.

Ford, D.A. 1983. "Wife Battery and Criminal Justice: A Study of Victim Decision-Making." *Family Relations* 32:463–75.

——. 1991. "Prosecution as a Victim Power Resource: A Note on Empowering Women in Violent Conjugal Relationships." *Law and Society Review* 25:313–34.

Ford, D.A. and M.J. Regoli. 1993. "The Criminal Prosecution of Wife Assaulters." Pp. 127–64 in *Legal Responses to Wife Assault,* edited by N.Z. Hilton. Newbury Park, CA: Sage.

Forst, B., J. Lucianovic, and S.J. Cox. 1977. *What Happens After Arrest?* Washington, DC: Institute for Law and Social Research.

Friedman, L.N. and S.B. Tucker. 1997. "Violence Prevention Through Victim Assistance: Helping People Escape the Web of Violence." Pp. 63–82 in *Victims of Crime,* edited by R.C. Davis, A.J. Lurigio, and W.G. Skogan. Thousand Oaks, CA: Sage.

Frohman, L. 1991. "Discrediting Victims' Allegations of Sexual Assault: Prosecutorial Accounts of Case Rejections." *Social Problems* 38:213–26.

Garner, J., J. Fagan, and C. Maxwell. 1995. "Published Findings From the Spouse Abuse Replication Program: A Critical Review." *Journal of Quantitative Criminology* 11:3–28.

Gayford, J.J. 1977. "The Plight of the Battered Wife." *International Journal of Environmental Studies* 10:283–86.

Goodman, L., L. Bennett, and M.A. Dutton. 1999. "Obstacles to Victims' Cooperation With the Criminal Prosecution of Their Abusers: The Role of Social Support." *Violence and Victims* 14:427–44.

Hilton, N.Z. 1989. "One in Ten: The Struggle and Disempowerment of the Battered Women's Movement." *Canadian Journal of Family Law* 7:315–35.

Kingsnorth, R.F., R. MacIntosh, and J. Wentworth. 1999. "Sexual Assault: The Role of Prior Relationship and Victim Characteristics in Case Processing." *Justice Quarterly* 16:275–302.

Lerman, L.G. 1986. "Prosecution of Wife Beaters: Institutional Obstacles and Innovations." Pp. 250–95 in *Violence in the Home: Interdisciplinary Perspectives,* edited by M. Lystad. New York: Brunner/Mazel.

McLeod, M. 1983. "Victim Noncooperation in the Prosecution of Domestic Assault." *Criminology* 21:395–416.

Myers, M.A. and J. Hagan. 1979. "Private and Public Trouble: Prosecutors and the Allocation of Court Resources." *Social Problems* 26:439–51.

Norton, L. 1983. "Witness Involvement in the Criminal Justice System and the Intention to Cooperate in Future Prosecutions." *Journal of Criminal Justice* 11:143–52.

Orme, J.G. and J. Reis. 1991. "Multiple Regression With Missing Data." *Journal of Social Service Research* 15:61–91.

Province of Ontario, Ministry of the Attorney General. 1993. *Crown Policy Manual.* Toronto: Ministry of the Attorney General.

Rauma, D. 1984. "Going for the Gold: Prosecutorial Decision Making in Cases of Wife Assault." *Social Science Research* 13:321–51.

Rebovich, D.J. 1996. "Prosecution Response to Domestic Violence." Pp. 176–91 in *Do Arrests and Restraining Orders Work?,* edited by E. Buzawa and G. Buzawa. Thousand Oaks, CA: Sage.

Sander, A. 1988. "Personal Violence and Public Order: The Prosecution of 'Domestic' Violence in England and Wales." *International Journal of the Sociology of Law* 16:359–82.

Schmidt, J. and E.H. Steury. 1989. "Prosecutorial Discretion in Filing Charges in Domestic Violence Cases." *Criminology* 27:487–510.

Sebba, L. 1996. *Third Parties: Victims and the Criminal Justice System.* Columbus, OH: Ohio State University Press.

Shainess, N. 1977. "Psychological Aspects of Wife Battering." Pp. 111–19 in *Battered Women: A Psychosociological Study of Domestic Violence,* edited by M. Roy. New York: Litton.

Shapland, J., J. Willmore, and P. Duff. 1985. *Victims in the Criminal Justice System.* Aldershot, UK: Gower.

Sherman, L. 1992. "The Influence of Criminology on Criminal Law: Evaluating for Misdemeanor Domestic Violence." *Journal of Criminal Law and Criminology* 85:901–45.

Sherman, L. and R.S. Berk. 1984. "The Specific Deterrent Effects of Arrest for Domestic Assault." *American Sociological Review* 49:261–72.

Sigler, R.T., J.M. Crowley, and I. Johnson. 1990. "Judicial and Prosecutorial Endorsement of Innovative Techniques in the Trial of Domestic Abuse Cases." *Journal of Criminal Justice* 18:443–53.

Silverman, R.A. and L. Kennedy. 1993. *Deadly Deeds: Murder in Canada.* Toronto: Nelson Canada.

Singer, S.I. 1988. "The Fear of Reprisal and the Failure of Victims to Report a Personal Crime." *Journal of Quantitative Criminology* 4:289–302.

Spears, J.W. and C.C. Spohn. 1997. "The Effect of Evidence Factors and Victim Characteristics on Prosecutors' Charging Decisions in Sexual Assault Cases." *Justice Quarterly 14:501–24.*

Stanko, E.A. 1982. "Would You Believe This Woman?" Pp. 63–82 in *Judge, Lawyer, Victim, Thief: Women, Gender and Criminal Justice,* edited by N.H. Rafter and E.A. Stanko. Boston, MA: Northeastern University Press.

Tomz, J.E. and D. McGillis. 1997. *Serving Crime Victims and Witnesses.* 2nd ed. Washington, DC: U.S. Department of Justice.

Ursel, J. 1995. "Winnipeg Family Violence Court Evaluation." Working Document WD1995-2e, Department of Justice, Ottawa, Canada.

U.S. Department of Justice. 1995. *Victim Assistance Programs: Whom They Service, What They Offer.* Washington, DC: U.S. Department of Justice.

——. 1998. *New Directions From the Field: Victims' Rights and Services for the 21st Century.* Washington, DC: U.S. Department of Justice.

Vera Institute of Justice. 1977. *Felony Arrests: Their Prosecution and Disposition in New York City's Courts.* New York: Vera Institute of Justice.

Walker, L. 1979. *The Battered Woman.* New York: Harper and Row.

Young, M.A. 1990. "Victim Assistance in the United States: The End of the Beginning." *International Review of Victimology* 1:181–90.

Unit III

Discussion Questions

1. Review the evolution of the court as an institution. Compare the development of the courts in the West to those in China and the Islamic world. What similarities and differences do you find?
2. What factors have affected the courts' evolution in England?
3. How do drug courts differ from traditional courts? How effective are drug courts in assisting offenders?
4. What types of offenders do you think should be diverted to drug courts and what types should be processed in the traditional court system?
5. What could drug courts do to improve their effectiveness?
6. Explain how victim-offender mediation programs work. Are they effective? Would you support the implementation of such a program in your community? Why or why not?
7. What are community prosecutor programs and why have they developed?
8. What are the weaknesses of the community prosecutor programs? What can be done to improve them? Would you support the use of community prosecution programs?
9. What effect does pretrial publicity have on jurors' decision making?
10. What can be done to minimize the negative effects of pretrial publicity on juror decision making?
11. There has recently been growing dissatisfaction with juries. Should the use of juries be restricted to certain types of cases, or perhaps even eliminated altogether? Why or why not?
12. What are some alternative options to the use of the traditional "jury of your peers" in a criminal trial; in a civil trial?
13. Why were jurors in the Rose study threatened by the questions asked during the voir dire process? How much privacy should jurors be able to maintain during the voir dire process, and how much does the court need to know?
14. How would you change the voir dire process and procedure to balance individual juror privacy against the need for public disclosure?
15. Why does victim cooperation in a domestic assault case result in such a high probability of prosecution?
16. Why are some victims less inclined to cooperate in domestic assault cases?

17. Should defendants continue to be allowed to plead guilty in exchange for reduced sentences and/or reduced charges? Why or why not?

18. Develop a new sentencing model, drawing upon the experience of jurisdictions that have various sentencing methodologies currently in place. ✦

Unit IV

American Corrections

Once an individual has been convicted of a criminal offense, the government has the right to administer a sanction. That sanction or criminal sentence may include a fine, community service, restitution, probation, commitment to a halfway house, mandatory drug or alcohol counseling, some period of incarceration followed by parole, or a combination of the above.

Unfortunately, not only are there problems in administration, but no uniform agreement exists regarding the goal of punishment itself. What exactly is the purpose of punishment? Are we seeking to deter, to rehabilitate, or to extract some measure of revenge? And how much punishment is enough? What is just punishment? What measure of punishment will have a long-range correcting effect? We have no firm answers to any of these questions as we administer our correctional programs.

The Prison Population

The total number of inmates in the United States grows by more than 1,000 persons every week, most of whom will cost roughly $21,000 per year to feed, house, and guard. As of this writing, there were approximately 1.5 million offenders in our 1,550 state and federal prisons. Included in this count are approximately 100,000 adult offenders housed in private prisons that operate in more than 30 states. All told, this yields an adult prison incarceration rate of approximately 472 per 100,000.

In addition to those incarcerated in prison facilities, approximately 630,000 individuals are detained in city and county jails. The overall adult incarceration rate (including prisons and jails) in the United States as of this writing was approximately 690 per 100,000. By comparison, the rate of incarceration among the nations of Western Europe is generally between 50 and 125 per 100,000.

For many years, the U.S. incarceration rate was roughly the same as Western Europe's, but beginning in the mid-1970s, we began a steady upward climb. Why the surge? Some researchers have speculated that prison populations mirror growth in the general population and concurrent increases in crime; however, others point out that the prison population has grown much faster than the general population. For example, from 1975 to 2000 the American population grew about 17 percent, but the prison population more than quadrupled. Nor does the growth in the prison population reflect crime rates. From 1981 to 2000, overall crime rates went down, while the prison population nearly tripled.

One of the chief reasons why prison populations have increased is that elected officials have bowed to public demand. The public seems to be convinced that imprisonment reduces crime, and has urged policy makers and judges to increase the severity of sentences, particularly with respect to drug law violations. The result has been more people being sent to prison, and being sent there for longer periods of time, than ever before. There is also evidence that some parole officials are returning parolees to prison at a higher rate than in the past, again due to public pressure. Thus, researchers argue that America's prison bulge is not the result of increased population or higher crime rates; rather, it is the result of decision making in the political arena.

Among other concerns, the current surge in prison commitments has resulted in very serious overcrowding problems. Nearly every state has prison facilities that are operating well over 100 percent of their designed capacity. Among other problems, this has led to increased emotional instability among inmates and a corresponding increase in the number of assaults and suicides. Many institutions report lower levels of morale among guards and a marked decrease in the number and quality of rehabilitation programs and work projects implemented. The population increase has also caused logistical nightmares for corrections staff with respect to the proper management of sanitary facilities, food distribution, bed space, legal needs, phone access, bedding, laundry, and so forth. Medical problems, particularly since the advent of the AIDS epidemic, further compound the difficulties of managing overcrowded prison facilities.

The impact of the increased use of incarceration is beginning to be felt within the confines of the justice system and the pocketbooks of American taxpayers. Not factoring in finance charges, it currently costs in excess of $33,000 for each new minimum-security prison bed constructed in the United States, $65,000 for each new medium-security bed, and over $85,000 for each new maximum-security bed. These costs vary by state. The cost of building a maximum-security bed in New York, for example, is in excess of $100,000, and with finance charges added is really closer to $300,000. In addition, as noted previously, it costs roughly $21,000 a year to house each inmate. Consequently, a 500-bed medium-security facility not only costs taxpayers more than $30 million to build, but will reduce the state treasury by at least $10 million per year in perpetuity. Prisons are massive revenue-absorbing institutions.

Alternatives to Incarceration

The high cost of incarceration has caused many states to turn more attention to a number of alternatives to incarceration. Most individuals sentenced to receive correctional supervision are placed on probation. As of this writing, there were approximately 3.9 million people on probation in America. Typically, probationers are allowed to move about in the community within certain court-mandated restrictions and rules. Alcohol use is becoming almost universally prohibited for probationers. To insure adherence, increasing numbers of probationers are required to participate in alcohol and drug screening by providing urine samples to authorities on a regular basis. In addition, probationers may be required to continue their schooling, pay fines and restitution, move into halfway houses, obtain psychological counseling, or participate in drug and alcohol treatment programs. The terms and conditions of probation are generally established for each individual by the court.

A probation officer is assigned to insure that the probationer abides by the rules. However, close supervision is quite difficult, as a probation officer may be responsible for as many as 100 or 200 probationers. If it is determined that a probationer has violated the terms and conditions of the probation sentence, that individual could have his or her probation revoked and be returned to jail or prison.

Probation and other similar forms of punishment, known collectively as intermediate sentences, are emerging as the new mode of punishment for the twenty-first century. Electronic monitoring of probationers is one approach that is catching on throughout the country, as are intensive probation supervision programs. Some intensive supervision programs assign as few as five clients to each probation officer.

Another form of correctional supervision is parole. As of this writing, there were over 750,000 offenders on parole in America. After completing a minimum period of time in prison, as outlined by state law, individuals are eligible to receive parole. The courts have made it quite clear that parole is a privilege, not a right; eligible individuals will not necessarily receive parole. Nearly all inmates, however, are eventually released from prison to parole. This decision is generally made by a parole board.

As with probation, an individual placed on parole is allowed to move about in the community, with certain rules and regulations governing his or her behavior. A parole officer is assigned to monitor parolee behavior. Typically, parolees have more restrictions and are more closely monitored than probationers. Still, close supervision of parolees is not practical. A typical parole officer will have as many as 50 clients. If it is determined that the parolee has violated the terms and conditions of parole, he or she could have parole revoked and be returned to prison. Electronic monitoring of parolees is becoming a common practice in most states, as are intensive parole supervision programs, which are similar to intensive probation supervision programs.

As of December 1981, there were slightly more than 2 million persons under some form of correctional supervision in America. Roughly two decades later, the figure has risen to nearly 7 million, with no indication of any change in this trend. Somewhat comically (were it not such a serious matter), a study undertaken in Washington state concluded that by the year 2056, every adult in that state would either be in prison or would be working for one (Associated Press 1993). An equally sobering statistic is the fact that many states now spend more money on prisons and jails than on higher education. While higher education used to be the largest item in most states' budgets, corrections will replace it as the largest budget item in the majority of the states in the coming years.

Overall, approximately 4 percent of all adult males in America are currently under some form of correctional supervision. Approximately 40 percent of young African-American males in America are now under some form of correctional supervision.

The Death Penalty

At present, 38 states have capital punishment statutes, but not all of those states have performed an execution since the moratorium was lifted by the Supreme Court in 1977. As of this writing, we have executed some 900 people in this country since 1977, 4,000 since 1930, and roughly 13,000 since 1630. Lethal injection has now emerged as the most common form of execution in the United States.

There are more than 3,750 inmates currently on death row, and the number is growing. About 300 new death sentences are handed down each year, which represents roughly 2 percent of the persons who are annually charged with murder. Approximately 40 percent of death sentences are eventually vacated or commuted. As implied, those sentenced to death row have access to a variety of appellate options, and can delay their execution for many years. The fact that the most common form of death for death row inmates is "natural causes" is exceedingly frustrating to many death penalty proponents, who have called for a reduction in the number of appellate options.

Numerous arguments have been made for and against the death penalty. At present, the pro–death penalty sentiment seems to be winning the public relations war. The polls consistently report that more than 80 percent of the public favor capital punishment, in contrast to polls conducted in the 1960s which showed a majority in opposition. Current support may even be more deep-seated than polls indicate. Durham, Elrod, and Kinkade (1996) found that 95 percent of those surveyed considered the death penalty appropriate for at least one of the situational vignettes they put forward. In other words, only 5 percent seem to have a principled objection to capital punishment per se as a form of punishment.

Other survey research on public support for capital punishment comes to different conclusions, which is typical of the issue. A number of studies have found that when people were offered another option, support for the death penalty dropped off dramatically. Only about a third of the respondents typically support the death penalty when given the option of sentencing the individual to life in prison without parole and requiring restitution to the victim's family.

Recently, a number of polls have reported that as many as 80 percent feel that the death penalty is too arbitrary in its administration. A few voices are just now beginning to venture into the public arena, noting that the system tends to execute a disproportionate number of poor minorities, and that innocent persons have been convicted and executed. There also seems to be a growing public awareness that changes in homicide rates are due to many factors, not just the presence or absence of a death penalty.

A series of relatively high-profile international criticisms of the American death penalty in the late 1990s may have begun to impact public debate. Specifically, Pope John Paul II and two entities of the United Nations have called upon the United States to consider abolishing capital punishment. In addition, in 1997 the American Bar Association, noting that "the death penalty is a maze of unfair practices with no internal consistency," called for a moratorium. The fact that over 100 persons have been released from death row as a result of DNA testing has also contributed to the public discussion. This will surely be a topic of heated debate well into the twenty-first century.

* * *

To many, the problems that now plague the correctional system seem almost unmanageable. In his assessment of the situation, written at the beginning of the 1990s, DiIulio (1991) saw little chance for escape from those problems in the then-foreseeable future. His assessment rings true all the more today, and for the contemporary foreseeable future. Despite the warnings and concerns that have been aired publicly, he and others predict that we will continue to see an increasing number of individuals brought into the justice system, more prisons will need to be built, and an ever-increasing number of persons will be placed on probation and parole supervision, among other correctional options. Corrections is now poised to emerge in the twenty-first century as the largest single expense in most state budgets.

References and Further Reading Materials

Abadinsky, Howard. 2003. *Probation and Parole: Theory and Practice.* Upper Saddle River, NJ: Prentice-Hall.

Allen, Harry E. and Clifford Simonsen. 2001. *Corrections in America: An Introduction.* Upper Saddle River, NJ: Prentice Hall.

Associated Press. 1993. "Prisons Packed, Costly." April 12, 1993.

Austin, James and John Irwin. 1993. *Does Imprisonment Reduce Crime?* San Francisco: National Council on Crime and Delinquency.

Blomberg, Thomas G. and Karol Lucken. 2000. *American Penology.* New York: Aldine de Gruyter.

Bohm, Robert M. 1999. *Deathquest.* Cincinnati, OH: Anderson.

Braithwaite, John. 2002. *Restorative Justice and Responsive Regulation.* New York: Oxford University Press.

Clear, Todd and George F. Cole. 2003. *American Corrections.* Belmont, CA: Wadsworth.

Durham, A.M., H.P. Elrod, and P.T. Kinkade. 1996. "Public support for the death penalty: Beyond Gallup." *Justice Quarterly* Vol. 13 No. 4, pp. 705–736.

Haworth, Karla. 1997. "U.S. Said to Spend More on Jails Than on College," *Chronicle of Higher Education,* March 7, p. A30.

Latessa, Edward J. and Harry E. Allen. 1999. *Corrections in the Community.* Cincinnati, OH: Anderson.

Latessa, Edward J., Alexander Holsinger, James W. Marquart, and Jonathan R. Sorensen. 2001. *Correctional Contexts.* Los Angeles: Roxbury.

Tonry, Michael (Ed.). 2001. *Penal Reform in Overcrowded Times.* New York: Oxford University Press.

Voorhis, Patricia, Michael Braswell, and David Lester. 2000. *Correctional Counseling and Rehabilitation.* Cincinnati, OH: Anderson. ✦

Chapter 22

The Future of Probation

Reintroducing the Spiritual Dimension into Correctional Practice

John T. Whitehead
Michael C. Braswell

At the beginning of the twenty-first century, probation has become the United States' most common correctional option; the number of probationers has almost quadrupled since 1980, and three times as many people are on probation as are in prison. Whitehead and Braswell look at how probation has developed in the last twenty-five years and suggest how it should change in future to address the growing needs of an overburdened criminal justice system. Their most intriguing suggestion actually returns to probation's roots: they assert that what is missing from modern probation is an element of spirituality that addresses emotional needs—through organized religion or otherwise—which they believe holds the most potential for reforming offenders.

The last 25 years have seen fundamental changes in probation. What once was a mix of social work and law enforcement, which varied from jurisdiction to jurisdiction, has seen a plethora of developments including electronic monitoring, intensive supervision, house arrest, restitution programs, victim-offender mediation, and even abolition. Probation officers have gone from social casework to urine testing, from brokerage activities to curfew monitoring, from acting as mentors to arresting for technical violations. Probation officers have changed their ideal role model from John Augustus, acting as avuncular advisor, to Dirty Harry Callahan, waiting for a violation to "make their day."

This [chapter] will review the changes in probation in the last 25 years in an effort to better understand where probation will go and should go in the next 25 years. Crystal balls are fictional. Therefore we make no claim to prognostication. However, we will try to examine as best we can the positive and negative consequences of possible probation models as legislators and correctional policy makers enter the twenty-first century.

The Numbers

As Table 22.1 indicates, like the rest of corrections in the last 25 years, probation has been in a growth mode. In 1980 there were just over 1 million adults on probation. By 1990 that number had increased to more than 2.5 million adults. By 1995 the number exceeded 3 million adults; it reached 3.4 million in 1998 and approximately 3.8 million in 1999. For purposes of comparison, in 1998 and 1999 about 1.2 million adults were in prison (Bonczar & Glaze, 1999; U.S. Department of Justice, Bureau of Justice Statistics [On-line]). Thus probation outstrips prison by a ratio of about 3 to 1, making it the most frequently used correctional option in the country. These numbers alone probably guarantee that probation will continue to be a correctional mainstay in the next 25 years. The

Table 22.1
Adults on Probation and Parole

	Probation	Parole
1980	1,118,097	220,438
1985	1,968,712	300,203
1990	2,670,234	531,407
1995	3,077,861	679,421
1996	3,164,996	679,733
1997	3,296,513	694,787
1998	3,417,613	704,964
1999	3,773,600	713,000
Percent change 1990–1998	28%	32.7%
Average annual percent change 1990–1998	3.1%	3.6%

Note: From *Probation and Parole in the United States, 1998*, by T. P. Bonczar and L. E. Glaze, 1999, Washington DC: U.S. Department of Justice; and from U.S. Department of Justice, Bureau of Justice Statistics [On-line]. Available: http//www.ojp.usdoj.gov/bjs

simple reality of bureaucratic inertia dictates that judges and legislators will continue to use probation as an all-purpose correctional intervention that serves various purposes, even some that conflict with one another.

As probation continues as one of the two basic correctional options—the other being prison—there are several directions that it can take. We will outline those directions, explore the positive and negative consequences of each, and conclude with a recommended direction for probation in the new millennium.

Several authors have outlined the possible directions that probation can take in shaping its mission. Duffee and O'Leary (1986), for example, argued that probation can follow one of four models, depending on the amount of emphasis given to either the offender or the community or both. The models they articulated were restraint (low emphasis on both offender and community), rehabilitation (high emphasis on the offender along with low emphasis on the community), reform (high emphasis on the community but low emphasis on the offender), and reintegration (high emphasis on both). To a considerable degree, this seminal article set the stage for any discussion of possible models of probation policy and practice.[1] What has changed, however, is an introduction of a new term—emphasis on the victim in addition to emphasis on the offender or the community—and the introduction of a different meaning of emphasis on the offender. Whereas Duffee and O'Leary defined emphasis on the offender as the rehabilitation model, we see emphasis on the spiritual dimension of human existence as a different type of emphasis on the offender and as something just as essential as any rehabilitative focus on personal problems.

Rehabilitation: From John Augustus to Sheriff Andy Taylor

One model of probation is the rehabilitation model (Duffee & O'Leary, 1986). Glaser (1969) called this the welfare model where the probation officer exhibits high concern for the offender and low concern for the community. Klockars (1972) would call it the therapeutic model.

In its basic form, this is the original model of probation, begun by John Augustus and living on in the 1960s television character of Sheriff Andy Taylor played by Andy Griffith. The focus is on the efforts of a concerned individual who takes a probationer under his or her wing and tries to do whatever he or she can to help. The contemporary terminology for this role is "mentor," recalling the way a dissertation chair would guide a graduate student through the dissertation process and even help the student to get all or parts of the dissertation published. Andy Griffith once portrayed this model in his efforts to assist a young man who had been accused of theft. Andy got him a job at Wally's filling station and stood by the youth even when some parts were stolen from the station. In the end, Andy's trust and assistance won out. Contemporary figures like General Colin Powell (Alliance for Youth [On-line]) have called on middle-class citizens, especially successful African-Americans, to mentor troubled youths.

Recent mentoring programs have attempted to foster prosocial involvement and bonds with adults and have tried to address alienation and lack of commitment to school. Unfortunately, most studies of mentors have shown no positive impact (Catalano, Loeber, & McKinney, 1999).

Psychologists and social workers have attempted to professionalize the helper role by transforming it into a counseling or social casework role (Garvin & Seabury, 1997; Landon & Feit, 1999). Here the probation officer would be a therapist rather than a simple mentor. The probation task would be to use reality therapy or rational emotive therapy or the therapy *du jour* to cure the probationer (new therapies come out periodically, much like new car models).

Some have argued that the officer could not be a therapist because of skill and time constraints. Instead, the officer could be a case manager (Dietrich, 1979) who would refer the offender to the appropriate professional services in the community (psychological counseling, social work, drug abuse programs, etc.). This is a task requiring considerable skill and effort. Referral is more than just giving a probationer the name of a program. Referral involves preparing the offender for the service and monitoring his or her attendance and participation in any referred program. Anyone familiar with probation and probationers knows that there can be many reasons for probationers not following up on referrals.

What is the future of rehabilitation in probation? Several scenarios are possible. Based on the research on the effectiveness of rehabilitation efforts (Gendreau, 1996; Lipsey, 1992; Lipsey, Wilson, & Cothern, 2000), probation might try to return to a rehabilitation model by implementing the latest findings on effective interventions. Effective interventions should be intensive and cognitive-behavioral, should be matched with the probationer's learning style and personality, should match offender and therapist, should be reinforced positively and fairly, and should utilize therapists who are appropriately trained and supervised (Gendreau, 1996). If these findings are implemented, recidivism reductions—but not the elimination of recidivism—can be expected.

Another possibility is the remedicalization of probation. Although prior medical models were tried and found wanting, more and more problems, such as generalized anxiety disorder, obsessive-compulsive disorder, hyperactivity, and depression, are being "pathologized" (Groopman, 2000)—treated as diseases with medications such as venlafaxine, paxil, prozac, and ritalin. Related to this are medical treatments for nicotine addiction; patches and gum help cigarette smokers to get off their addictions. If psychiatry and medicine continue to discover physiological or neurological bases of behavior amenable to pharmacological treatments, the next 25 years may see more and more opportunities to medicalize criminal behaviors (Raine, Brennan, Farrington, & Mednick, 1997).

On the other hand, there have been excesses in the use of drugs when other approaches could have done as well or could have done much better than the administration of a drug. A real danger with the medicalization of rehabilitation is the temptation to use a pill instead of taking the time and effort to address the underlying problem. It appears that health maintenance organizations (HMOs) foster the reliance on medications and the neglect of talk therapy because the former is much cheaper than the latter (Groopman, 2000). Still another danger with the medicalization of deviance is that often harmful side effects of the drugs come to light after initial positive results, outweighing any initial claims of effectiveness.

A positive aspect of any refocusing on rehabilitation would be the provision of options for probationers. Given the needs of probationers in terms of education, vocational training, counseling, and drug and alcohol problems, there is no question that probationers could benefit from programs in several or all of these areas. The recent emphasis on retribution has reduced some of the positive programs available to probation officers. Funding constraints have always been a problem. Duffee and Carlson (1996), for example, found that lengthy waiting periods existed for various drug treatment programs.

Several problems, however, face any rehabilitation emphasis in probation. One is the public and political clamor for punishment (Austin & Irwin, 2001). With certain crimes, particularly atrocious crimes inspiring horror, there is a certain demand for retribution. Even when psychiatric conditions, prior abuse, or other mitigating factors are well documented, the courts, the public, and politicians resist abandoning the rhetoric of responsibility and accountability. Governor of Arkansas Bill Clinton refused to stop the execution of a man who shot a police officer but then shot himself. The offender basically self-administered a lobotomy that left him with an IQ below 70. On the eve of his execution, he put away his dessert (a piece of pie) like he always did, planning to eat it the next morning even though he would be dead at 12:01 a.m. (Frady, 1993). Governor George W. Bush did not stop the execution of Karla Faye Tucker despite protests that she was a changed woman.

A second problem is public and political unwillingness to spend scarce tax dollars on the rehabilitation of criminals. Barry Feld's remarks about the failure of rehabilitation in juvenile justice apply equally well to its failure in the adult system: "Juvenile courts lack necessary resources because providing for child welfare is a societal responsibility, not simply a judicial one. Historically and currently, public officials deny juvenile courts resources because of pervasive public antipathy to their clients, those who are poor, disadvantaged and minority offenders" (Feld, 1999, p. 291). In other words, while individuals may follow the example of media Sheriff Andy Taylor and go out of their way to help individual offenders, cities, counties, states, and the nation do not want to commit the resources to corrections. Politicians, Republican and Democrat alike, are willing to build spartan prisons but are unwilling to commit the funding that would be necessary to provide what the rehabilitation researchers (Gendreau, 1996, for example) say is necessary for rehabilitation to work. Such politicians would rather grant tax breaks for the rich than fund Pell grants for the offender.

A major reason for reluctance to fund rehabilitation is a refusal to spend monies on the poor and on minorities. Public schools, for example, are far from uniform across the country. In many suburbs and upper-middle-class urban areas, public schools are well funded and the students achieve well above average. In abandoned inner cities and frost belt cities, the schools and their environs have been abandoned to those who are too poor to leave and the schools are problem-riddled. If taxpayers and governmental units do not want to fund public schools at adequate levels, it is no surprise that they are not willing to fund the rehabilitation programs that the research literature has found can be effective (Gendreau, 1996).

The Dirty Harry (Law Enforcement) Model of Probation

A second current model of probation is what might be called the Dirty Harry or law enforcement model: Shoot first and ask questions later. Klockars (1972) called probation officers using this model law enforcers, Glaser (1969) labeled this the punitive model, and Duffee and O'Leary (1986) dubbed it the reform model. In this model the goals are punishment, incapacitation, and deterrence. Here probation should be tough enough to hurt, should deter both the offender and would-be offenders, and should limit the opportunities for committing crime. Examples of this model include electronic monitoring, house arrest, and intensive supervision. The officer becomes a quasi-cop (a Dirty Harry, Wyatt Earp, or Andy Sipowicz) who is armed with urine cups, ankle devices, and curfew checks. One version is a variation of "hot spots" policing, where the probation officer goes to high-crime areas (hot spots) looking for probationers who might be violating their curfews or other probation conditions. The officer either warns them to go home or arrests them for violating their probation conditions (Kurlychek, Torbet, & Bozynski, 1999).

Still another version of this model is James Q. Wilson's suggestion that we give police officers the names and addresses of probationers who live in their beats. Then officers can check on these probationers to make sure that they are not carrying guns or violating other laws (Wilson, 1995). Grant monies have already been allocated to test such efforts to involve police officers in the supervision of probationers and parolees (Knoxville Public Safety Collaborative, 2000).

'Broken Windows' Probation

Perhaps the most well articulated version of this model is the "broken windows" probation model (Corbett, et al., 1999). As the name implies, Corbett and his colleagues have translated "broken windows" policing (see Wilson & Kelling, 1982, for the origin of this term) into the field of probation. The principles are to put public safety first, to supervise probationers in the neighborhood rather than in the office, to enforce conditions quickly and strongly, to develop partners in the community, to hold leaders accountable, and to apply business principles to probation. In this model, probation officers would be expected to do several things: collaborate with police in supervision efforts, react quickly to violations, participate in community crime prevention and betterment activities, and allocate resources to offenders who are at highest risk.

Although this broken windows model mentions treatment as one component, the focus is clearly on law enforcement. In fact, the authors picture the probation officer as carrying a laptop computer, palmcorder, cell phone, and flashlight—the tools of the modern patrol officer. Thus this model is quite congruent with the "new penology" as outlined by Feeley and Simon (1992). (See below for further discussion.)

There are several problems with this model. One is the well criticized problem of continuing the current losing war on crime and drugs. As several authorities have noted (Austin & Irwin, 2001), both the federal government and many of the states have been building more and more prisons in the ever escalating war on drugs and crime. One problem is money. We keep spending more and more but crime stays around, refusing to be knocked out. A related problem is that the color of justice in any modern Dodge City is predominantly black. African-Americans are the prime recipient of any form of probation as law enforcement. (For more discussion of race and justice, see Walker, Spohn, & DeLone, 2000.)

Still another problem is that recidivism, the traditional measure of failure for probation, gets turned on its head. Recidivism can be defined as success here because law enforcement–punitive efforts by officers result in greater detection of technical violations. These technical violations result in revocations of probation and prison commitments. Supporters argue that such revocations and commitments are positive because they take offenders who are at risk of committing new crimes off the street.

Concerning the broken windows model of probation specifically, its problems are similar to those of its parent, community policing. Specifically, this model of probation assumes that communities are able and willing to participate in the effort to make probation effective. And it assumes that probation officers can mobilize communities into all sorts of crime prevention and community betterment activities. These assumptions are often major leaps of faith. For example, a major study of community policing in eight cities found that the most difficult problem was "the inability of the police departments to organize and maintain active community involvement in their projects" (Grinc, 1994, p. 437). A subsequent community policing effort in Chicago "made some limited headway" in this area (Skogan & Hartnett, 1997, p. 158). This does not mean that such efforts are fruitless. It simply means that the task may be harder than the proponents of broken windows probation acknowledge.

New Penology Probation

At some point models such as broken windows probation can or do turn into what Feeley and Simon (1992) label "the new penology." Here expectations are lowered; no one expects probation to rehabilitate or even to deter offenders out of crime. Goals such as rehabilitation, deterrence, and punishment are not considered. Instead, the objective is simply "cost-effective ways of imposing long-term management on the dangerous" (Feeley & Simon, 1992, p. 456). The concern is efficiency—specifically, efficiency in keeping track of offenders in terms of following the conditions of probation. If offenders follow their conditions, success is terminating the probation order at the appropriate time. If the conditions are not followed, officers are held accountable for processing violations. Ironically, whereas violations and revocations used to be considered signs of failure, they now become indicators of success. They are performance measures of the bureaucracy at work managing caseloads of offenders. In Crank's terms, the ideal is the rationalization of the work process, and one key component is the "elaboration of record-keeping systems" (Crank, 1996, p. 270). So the ideal probation officer is a pencil pusher, updated to a laptop computer whiz.

Another term for this is the managerial model (Simon, 1993). In his study of parole, Simon has argued that California adopted this model after abandoning its clinical model. In the managerial model the focus has shifted from reintegration of parolees into the community to "isolating and containing this population" (Simon, 1993, p. 228). So the major activity of parole has become revocation because this fits in with the current correctional creed that "custody is the necessary and sufficient solution to criminal risk while at the same time meeting the managerial impetus to define and meet performance standards" (Simon, 1993, p. 229).

The Public Safety Model

Smith and Dickey (1999) advocate a "just punishment and public safety" model of probation. First, the sentencing court would specify the primary purpose of the sentence (just desert or public safety). The court would then order a sentence designed to advance the primary purpose for the particular offender being sentenced. Analogous to community policing officers, probation officers would utilize active rather than passive supervision. Active supervision means that officers would try to find and maintain informal methods of social control over their cases. Officers would seek the help of naturally occurring guardians; an example might be a neighbor who could act as a mentor for a juvenile delinquent. Because stable housing, a decent job, and a support network are important for offenders in avoiding crime, correctional agencies like probation would be involved in seeking and developing these resources. Probation might also have to consider radical departures from past practices. A task force in Wisconsin, for example, recently recommended abandoning felony probation and replacing it with Community Confinement and Control, which would combine confinement with some level of freedom and responsibility in the community (Smith & Dickey, 1999).

There are several questions that Smith and Dickey's proposal raises. One question is how it will be possible for judges to focus on only two goals, desert and public safety. One constant in the research on punishment attitudes is that judges, prosecutors, and the public have conflicting goals. Criminal justice actors and the public both want criminal sanctions to serve the ends of retribution, incapacitation, deterrence, and rehabilitation (Maguire & Pastore, 1999). Probation cannot possibly be limited to two goals.

A second problem is that the role of the probation officer suddenly becomes unlimited. Just as some call for community policing to solve all community problems, so also Smith and Dickey's suggestion that probation officers practice "active supervision" and "creative program development . . . to create jobs and job placement services" is ambitious at best and utopian at worst. Advocating the finding of naturally occurring guardians, for example, ignores the simple fact that if naturally occurring guardians were available the person would probably not be an offender. Creating jobs and job placement services is something that presidential candidates claim they can do. A probation officer is lucky to be able to place a half dozen offenders a year in jobs that he or she hears about in a myriad of ways.

Abolishing felony probation and creating "a new form of confinement" sounds creative and exciting until one realizes that the description of the creation—one "merging features of prisons with varying degrees of liberty and obligations of the offender in the community"—sounds amazingly similar to what old-fashioned, noncreative corrections personnel called halfway houses. It is fine to say that halfway houses are a viable option in corrections, but to suggest that they are the panacea for community corrections, given the record of recidivism in halfway houses (Hartmann, Friday, & Minor, 1994), is unrealistic.

Probation in a Set of Intermediate Sanctions

Still another conceptualization of probation is that probation can and should be part of a set of intermediate sanctions. Morris and Tonry (1990) argue that corrections should encompass a graduated set of sanctions ranging from the least severe—perhaps a simple fine—through regular supervision, intensive supervision (with or without electronic monitoring), house arrest, interrupted confinement (weekend jail plus probation supervision), to incarceration. They argue that in the past judges had inadequate choices: either incarceration or simple probation. Often incarceration was too harsh a choice and probation was too lenient an option. Providing more options would match the variety of supervision needs of offenders.

One problem with the vision of a set of intermediate sanctions is that the actual effectiveness of some of these sanctions has been less than hoped for. A study of intensive supervision found that 37 percent of the intensives were rearrested within one year and 65 percent committed a technical violation of the conditions of supervision (Petersilia & Turner, 1993). Although the argument can be made that intensive supervision was successfully catching these crimes and violations and sending the offenders to prison—24 percent were sent to prison—the hope had been that the recidivism statistics would be much lower than this.

Related to this is the fact that the public and politicians are not very tolerant of recidivism. Often one dramatic case of an offender on probation or parole committing a horrifying or spectacular crime is enough to start cries for abolishing parole, weekend furloughs, felony probation, or whatever program it was that had the offender at large in the community. Wisconsin's recent proposal for the abolition of felony probation is evidence of the lack of tolerance by the public and politicians for any variation of community corrections that has less than optimal recidivism levels.

Restorative and Community Justice

Still another model for probation is that of restorative and community justice. In this model, the focus is on the victim and the community as well as the offender. Restitution and victim–offender mediation are two ways of addressing the victim's perspective and needs, in contrast to the more traditional approach that often leaves the victim out of the process, relying instead on the defense attorney and prosecutor engaging in adversarial legal maneuvers in the symbolic, though artificial, community of the courtroom. Another tenet of restorative justice is competency development for the offender rather than traditional rehabilitation (Bazemore, 1999; Bazemore & Umbreit, 1995; Umbreit & Coates, 1999).

Some of the latest twists in this model put the real community back into the criminal justice process. In "sentencing circles," for example, community members take an active role in sentencing (Stuart, 1996). This particular example is drawn from Native American justice traditions, which involve the tribal community in the justice process. In a noncriminal context, the Quaker Community meets together and remains until problems and differences among its members are resolved and reconciliation begins to take place before it adjourns. (For more on the Quakers, see Trueblood, 1966.)

One problem with sentencing circles and similar approaches is that some academics and professionals may characterize such efforts as essentially nostalgic visions of a community that no longer exists. To use the Andy Griffith–Mayberry example once again, Sheriff Andy Taylor lived in a time and place where he could have lunch at the local café where everyone knew each other, get his hair cut at Floyd's barbershop, fill up his patrol car at Wally's gas station, and get a soda at the corner drug store before checking to make sure that Deputy Barney Fife hadn't accidentally shot himself or some innocent bystander with the single bullet that he was issued. If Sheriff Taylor were around today, the town of Mayberry might be a sprawling suburb of a major city with no local café, barbershop, or corner drug store. Sheriff Andy might instead pick up a hamburger at the drive-through of a national fast-food chain and eat it while talking to his stockbroker on his cell phone on his way to a fancy hair salon. After having his hair tinted, trimmed, and styled, he might find himself pulling into an Exxon/TacoBell/Dunkin Donuts Convenience Center to gas up his police cruiser from one of a dozen or more pumps. No familiar gas station attendant would rush out to assist him; rather, he would be greeted by a nameless, faceless recorded voice that would instruct him how to properly insert his credit card.

More importantly, many if not most of us no longer live in neighborhoods or old-fashioned communities. We live in subdivisions with an emphasis on property lines and privacy. Instead of interacting with our neighbors, we join chat groups in cyberspace, shop on the Internet, and surf our digital televisions to observe rather than participate in life. In the 1950s there were only three television networks and, as in the initial age of radio, many communities only had one or two families who owned television sets. As a result, watching a popular program often became a community affair, not to mention neighbors sipping lemonade in the evening on numerous front porches, or children playing together in front and back yards until night fell. Now, with videos, cable television, and video games, adults and children can watch whatever they want on their own television set in the privacy and isolation of their own room.

To expect and assume the existence of community in this context is at best difficult and at worst absurd. It reflects to some extent the nostalgia of middle-aged criminologists for the days, real or imagined, of their childhood. They may be able to buy new Lionel trains with digital sound systems but they play alone. At a time when voluntary associations like the PTA, Kiwanis, Rotary, and the Lions Club are experiencing dwindling memberships, some may say that it is unrealistic for advocates of community justice to expect atomized individuals to step forward to serve communities that do not exist. Sheriff Andy Taylor lived in a community where people interacted and knew and cared for one another. Today many of us live in suburban developments (or, worse, gated communities) where we do not even know our neighbors' names let alone care or demonstrate any concern for them. We build "privacy" fences around backyard decks and patios to keep our neighbors out rather than open front porches to invite them in.

Another problem is how to monitor the sentencing done by community members, sentencing circles, and so forth. Judicial sentencing has some built-in constraints. All judges are law school graduates and are familiar with both civil and penal law. They know (or should know) that there are legal limits that must be adhered to. Community judging boards are not law school graduates and do not know the law.

Still, with all the negatives, there is a part of us that still yearns for a "flesh and blood" community where we can participate and engage in responsible relationships with each other rather than engage in the noncommitted voyeurism of the Internet. The homeless don't live on the Internet, nor do the probationers. They live down the street and, in some cases, on the street. Yes, there are problems and challenges regarding how to monitor the sentencing and alternative sanctions enacted by community members in sentencing circles. And it is true that judicial sentencing has some built-in constraints such as the requirement for judges to be law school graduates familiar with both civil and penal law. Although community sentencing boards are not law school graduates and may not always know the law, and this can result in inappropriate actions, they can, like jurors, also discern the commonsense truth of a given situation and recommend a fair and compassionate course of action that transcends the adversarial nature of legal technicalities.

There are other problems with restorative justice. Offenders do not always complete their restitution payments, the model would require drastic changes in probation agency practices, and there may be race or class biases (Levrant, Cullen, Fulton, & Wozniak, 1999). Most critically, Levrant et al. question whether restorative justice can answer the question of "how to control crime. . . . In contrast, restorative justice provides few answers for how to deal with serious and persistent offenders. . . . The failure to control crime inevitably will lead to a new round of penal harm" (Levrant et al., 1999, pp. 22–23). Although we think these criticisms are overstated, they do indicate that the call for restorative justice is not without difficulty.

A Focus on Accountability: The Balanced Approach

The United States Department of Justice has been promoting research on the causes of delinquency and on intervention strategies. A key finding about the causes of delinquency is that there is no one cause of delinquency. Rather, there are a number of identified risk factors that place youths in jeopardy of becoming delinquent and there are protective factors such as bonding and clear behavioral standards that help to prevent delinquency (Kurlychek et al., 1999). Related research on interventions suggests that effective intervention programs are those that provide prosocial skills, concentrate on problem solving, use multiple modes of intervention, and are both structured and intensive. The suggestion for probation is to consider the research on causes and on effective interventions and to attempt to incorporate the research findings into local probation programs. Furthermore, the local departments need to conduct research on their programs to see what works best in reducing recidivism. A key aim is promoting a sense of accountability in juvenile offenders so that the offender will develop "a sufficient understanding of the harm caused by his or her delinquent behaviors and a sense of responsibility for the consequences of future actions. An offender should also leave more capable of being a law-abiding, productive member of society" (Kurlychek et al., 1999, p. 5).

The so-called balanced approach has elements of the rehabilitation model, the restorative justice model, and the law enforcement model. From the rehabilitation model the balanced approach borrows the concept that offenders have problems that can be addressed via appropriate services. From the restorative justice model the balanced approach borrows an emphasis on the victim and restitution. From the law enforcement model the balanced approach borrows the assumption that offenders are free, culpable actors who deserve to be held accountable for their behaviors.

The positive feature of the balanced approach is its eclectic nature; it borrows the best of the three mentioned models. Negatively, it shares the limitations of each approach from which it borrows. One additional negative feature of the balanced approach is that it does this borrowing without paying sufficient attention to the basic contradiction between the rehabilitation model and the law enforcement model. With its emphasis on determinism, the rehabilitation model is in direct conflict with the law enforcement model's emphasis on free will and accountability. If problems or defects cause one to become delinquent or criminal, then it is illogical to hold that the individual is responsible for his or her choice. The fact that the balanced approach blithely ignores this problem does not eliminate the problem.

Abolition and Privatization

Although they are not models of probation, any discussion of the future of probation would be incomplete without some mention of the two issues of abolition and privatization. Some are calling for the end of probation. For example, a recent governor's task force in Wisconsin recommended the termination of felony probation. In its place the task force recommended a residential type of corrections—Community Confinement and Control—that amounts to a halfway house (Smith & Dickey, 1999). Felony probation was deemed too lax. This residential type of corrections is seen as sufficiently punitive.

Probation will probably not be abolished. One practical reason for this is the sheer numbers of people who are on probation. As noted above, in 1998 there were almost 3.5 million persons on probation supervision (Bonczar & Glaze, 1999). Bureaucratic inertia suggests that governmental agencies will maintain programs that have such large numbers of clients. Also, the alarming recidivism data that Petersilia, Turner, Kahan, and Peterson (1995) claimed about felony probation in California—65 percent—have been proven misleading. A recent study of adult property offenders on felony probation, for example, found that instead the success rate was 67.7 percent, "in essence the antithesis of Petersilia's finding" (Benedict & Huff-Corzine, 1997, p. 248).

Another reason that probation will survive is that it is at least a token punishment. Politicians and citizens do not want to send a message that nothing will be done to certain criminals. Wisconsin, for example, only recommended abolishing felony probation and did not actually abolish it. Also, probation for misdemeanants would still continue. So the fact that probation sends at least a minimal message that crime will be punished is indication that it will survive.

Another possible development in probation is privatization. Florida, for example, has contracted out for mental health services (including anger management) and substance abuse services for community corrections clients (Lucken, 1997). Tennessee contracts out certain community corrections functions while retaining others as public operations.

Whether public or private, probation must still follow one of the models that are discussed above and below. In other words, privately operated probation would still have to choose to adopt a rehabilitation, law enforcement, restorative justice, or spiritual function approach to clients.

As is the case with prisons, an alleged advantage of privatized probation would be cost savings. Research on private prisons, however, suggests that claims of savings may not be supported in practice (Pratt & Maahs, 1999). Worse, abuses such as unconstitutional treatment of prisoners and riots have been very much a part of recent privatization efforts (Dyer, 2000). Thus, although some strongly advocate privatization efforts in corrections (see, for example, Harding, 1997), it appears that a completely convincing case has yet to be made.

Probation as a Spiritual Function

In today's secular society it may seem anachronistic to try to discuss the spiritual dimension of probation. How quickly we forget that the Quakers are very much a part of American correctional history (Rothman, 1971). The Quakers called prisons penitentiaries because of their desire to assist offenders in spiritual reformation. Bibles and enforced silence were provided to help offenders repent their sins and reform their lives. Many of us who are professors teach this in corrections courses, but, once we cover the Quakers in our first or second class, we blithely move on to supposedly more important issues.

What we are forgetting is that the Quakers had it right. They knew that the spiritual is the core of life. If you get the core right, the rest will follow. In many ways we have chosen to ignore the core, and the result is an emptiness at the center of our lives. Staples, for example, believes that the underlying reason for school violence is that many youths find contemporary society devoid of significance:

> The world in which our young live—indeed, in which we live—is essentially broken. We live fragmented lives in which work, for most people, provides little emotional, social, or spiritual sustenance beyond the necessary fulfillment of basic needs and in which leisure becomes, for [the] most part, distraction. . . . Until we find a way to address this issue, violence [drug addiction and other types of crime] will continue unabated because it is a response to the distortion of our fundamental yearning for meaning. (Staples, 2000, p. 31)

More generally, despite the presence of churches, our culture is not committed to the spirit but to material success via competition, culminating in the accouterments of a middle-class lifestyle: "a car, a house, education for the children, a secure retirement" (Messner & Rosenfeld, 1997). Thus Christmas in America is less the celebration of a spiritual leader's birth than the excuse for a shopping season that begins earlier and earlier each year and ends with the end of Christmas returns some time in January.

In addition to commentators like Staples describing the lack of meaning in contemporary culture, prisoners themselves attest to how such lack can contribute to their involvement in drugs and crime and how finding a sense of meaning can help them get out of a life of crime. One apparently successful businessman, for example, felt that despite his material success "deep down inside, nothing was ever enough" and he turned to cocaine to fill the void. Later, in prison, he turned to Christianity "in search of something that could fill the void inside" (p. 112), for "Who else could fill the God-shaped void but God Himself?" (Johnson & Toch, 2000, p. 112). An addict turned to Jesus in prison and found a "peace that surpasses all understanding . . . reaching inside and touching my heart and soul" (Johnson & Toch, 2000, p. 118). A robber realized "that my lack of purpose had caused me to drift and be unfocused" (Johnson & Toch, 2000, p. 124); in prison he learned to seek God and now he feels blessed. In California Jarvis Masters became a Buddhist on San Quentin's death row, where every night he folds his "blanket under me and meditate[s] on the floor of my cell" (Masters, 1997).

Not all offenders are this reflective. Not all are seeking greater significance and meaning in their lives. In their ethnographic studies of both burglars (1994) and robbers (1997), for example, Wright and Decker emphasize that many of the offenders whom they studied were wrapped up in the street culture with its "relentless pursuit of action, whether in the form of heavy drinking, drug use, or high-stakes gambling" (Wright & Decker, 1997, p. 39). They eschewed long-range planning for present enjoyment—"desperate partying"—in their immediate surroundings (Wright & Decker, 1997).

Offenders who are reflective and sense an emptiness in their lives are vivid testimony to the importance of the spiritual dimension of life. Offenders who are so absorbed in partying and street culture that there is no awareness of deeper meaning give indication why many criminal justice approaches—probation, prison, parole, for example—do not work. Offenders experience these interventions as mere externals that do nothing to change their superficial spirituality—if it can be called that—of desperate partying. If probation or prison do nothing to help offenders question whether street culture really fulfills their true needs, then they will continue to hustle to get the money that the street culture requires for drugs, alcohol, women, and fashionable clothes. If probation or other correctional options help offenders to ask questions about the meaning of life, then perhaps there is a chance for rehabilitation.

Definitions of Spiritual

What does the spiritual mean? Canda and Furman define the spiritual as "the person's search for a sense of meaning and morally fulfilling relationships between oneself, other people, the encompassing universe, and the ontological ground of existence, whether a person understands this in terms that are theistic, atheistic, nontheistic, or any combination of these" (Canda & Furman, 1999, p. 44). Canda and Furman go on to note that spiritual drives seek profound experiences, meaning or purpose, and "a sense of integration and wholeness within ourselves and in relation with the world (Canda & Furman, 1999, p. 49). Morgan defines spirituality as "a personal affirmation of transcendence" that is distinct from religion, which is "the institutional, ritual, and creedal expressions of this affirmation" (Morgan, 2000, p. 174).

In one sense we have turned over the spiritual dimension of our lives to psychology and psychiatry. Psychologists and psychiatrists are our contemporary priests and medicine men who help us to find meaning in our lives, to deal with loss such as the death of a spouse or child, and to face the ultimate human question of death. One possible reason for this is that organized religion may not be meeting the spiritual needs of many seekers. Another reason may be that some see therapists as better equipped to help them explore life's questions. And some of the major writers in psychology—Allport, Fromm, Frankl, and May—see spirituality as central to psychological functioning (Elkins, 1999). One guest on *The Oprah Winfrey Show,* Phillip C. McGraw, is called a life consultant. He is a PhD who gives advice on television and in his books (McGraw, 1999, 2000) on dealing with spouses, children, and jobs. So these professionals fill the role that priests and ministers have filled since the 1800s.

Just as individuals have turned to psychology and psychiatry for guidance, so also corrections has turned to these professions. Some time in the 1960s or 1970s state correctional systems like California put resources and hope into group counseling programs to rehabilitate prisoners (Irwin, 1980). One reason for this was that leadership was sympathetic to rehabilitation efforts. Another was the identification of a sizable problem of narcotic addiction in California (Simon, 1993). So the counselor in many ways replaced the chaplain as the purveyor of meaning in prison.

The question of who performs the function of trying to help offenders find meaning in their lives may not be as important as the issue of whether someone tries to fulfill that function. The empirical evidence is clear that many offenders use drugs or alcohol at the time of their offense and have drug or alcohol problems (Mumola & Bonczar, 1998). A simplistic response to this problem is the "war on drugs" (Walker, 1998). A problem with this response is that no war on drugs is going to help offenders find what they are looking for when they seek out drugs; if they are looking for meaning and a sense of purpose in their lives, some deeper satisfaction rather than a momentary high, then their search becomes a spiritual endeavor.

Some, of course, do not see a problem in drug use. Lenson, for example, argues that "the practice of getting high has existed from the dawn of time, and all efforts to eradicate it are based on an incomplete understanding of human nature" (Lenson, 1995, p. 190). Venturelli uses this fact to argue for including "diversity of consciousness as another right that citizens should have in our democracy" (Venturelli, 2000, p. 85). Somewhat differently, Pepinsky (2000) argues that the drug war is actually "a monumental exercise in enforcing obedience to patriarchal authority," because society is not so much concerned about drugs as it is about the use of approved drugs. Pepinsky contends, for example, that ritalin and cocaine are indistinguishable pharmacologically. One is socially approved while the other is condemned. Pepinsky sees the real question as encouraging discussion of how drugs make individuals feel and "whether they ought to be taking even what the doctor ordered" (Pepinsky, 2000, p. 167).

We refrain from this debate because we simply argue that many offenders and drug users may be coping with lack of meaning by turning to drugs. We see turning to drugs as evidence of a thirst for the spiritual. And there is a growing interest in religion and spirituality. In the mid-1990s best-selling books were exploring spiritual topics, major news magazines published articles about God, Gregorian chant CDs became best-sellers, and the television program *Touched by an Angel* achieved ratings success (Myers, 2000).

In addition to books and articles specifically addressing this topic (Myers, 2000), researchers and writers in a number of fields have begun to address the relevance of spirituality. This is true in counseling, social work practice, and even public administration. In health, for example, a number of investigators have uncovered positive benefits of religion or spirituality on blood pressure, frequency of hospitalization, depression, healthy lifestyles, well-being and satisfaction, the health of the immune system, and longevity (Koening, 1999; Mitka, 1998). There appear to be "wide-ranging effects that devout religious faith and practice may have on mental and physical health and on quality of life" (Koening, 1999, p. 296). In education some experts argue that mindfulness enhances memory, and the Waldorf schools emphasize meditation as one way to integrate the curriculum and spirituality (Iannone & Obenauf, 1999).

Ways to Address the Spiritual Dimension in Probation Practice

Obviously, the First Amendment prohibits the state from compelling prisoners to turn to religion in prison or on probation. Both prisons and probation, however, can attempt to address the spiritual needs of prisoners. Prisons traditionally have had both church services and chaplains as part and parcel of their institutional life. Likewise, volunteer organizations such as the Prison Fellowship Ministry founded by Charles Colson have played an important role in attempts to help prisoners (Prison Fellowship Ministry [On-line]). Church services and chaplains have not been a regular part of probation. There are ways, however, for probation agencies and officers to introduce a spiritual dimension into probation for those probationers who are interested.

A probation officer with whom one of the authors worked when he was a probation officer used group reporting instead of individual reporting. This probation officer then used these group reporting sessions as discussion groups. Probationers discussed their problems and their lives in these sessions. Videos could be used to get discussions going. Such group sessions could be occasions for probationers to discuss questions of purpose, meaning, and morality in their lives—spiritual questions. Reality therapist William Glasser noted that one client of his had never been asked what he intended to do with his life! When Glasser asked this simple question, it was like a draft of fresh air refreshing the client. It encouraged the young man to open up and to start thinking about what he intended to do with his life (Glasser, 1965). It is not a violation of the First Amendment for a probation officer to ask a probationer what he intends to do with his life. Thus, officers who ask such questions might be getting probationers to think about purpose, meaning, and morality in their lives—again fulfilling the definition of "spiritual" according to Canda and Furman (1999).

Still another way for officers to inject the spiritual dimension into their work with offenders is the simple but potentially profound example of their own lives. The example of guards, counselors, and probation officers can be spiritually instructive and inspiring for offenders. On the negative side, women prisoners in North Carolina once complained that the correctional officers came to work and plopped down in front of the television sets demanding to watch the shows that they preferred, forcing the offenders to switch channels from their favorite shows (Girshick, 1999). The message that this sends is loud and clear: My life is empty; I have nothing better to do than to mindlessly view meaningless television programs and annoying commercials for eight hours.

What if officers, prison or probation, instead sat down with offenders and talked to them about their lives? The three fundamental questions of human existence—Who am I? Where am I going? and Why?—have been discussed by philosophers, theologians, and social analysts throughout the ages (Fromm, 1941; May, Angel, & Ellenberger, 1958). What if officers came to work with enthusiasm and acted as if they themselves had a sense of purpose and meaning in their lives—that they really wanted to be there and to be of service and help to offenders? Someone like the late Mother Theresa or Sister Helen Prejean provides an example of someone who enjoys what they do, someone with a sense of purpose in their lives.

Perhaps the biggest problem with envisioning part of probation as spiritual is that this goes against the grain of much in American society. Part of corrections has operated in concert with our consumer culture. Part of the correctional mission has been to make offenders "successful" jobholders who will become compulsive spenders like the rest of us. Traditional anomie à la Merton and Cohen theory argues that most of us are pursuing the American Dream—a job, a spouse, two kids, and a house in the suburbs. Hirschi's control theory argues that offenders just lack social bonding. There is no questioning of the society that law-abiding youths are bonded to. So anomie theory would argue that we should teach offenders a job skill so that on weekends they can run to the mall and use their MasterCards to pursue the illusion of monetary bliss. And control theory would increase social bonds so that offenders can become active consumers of goods and the entertainment media: Buy now and pay later—a morally questionable, profit-driven philosophy that requires one's self-respect as the price of admission.

The spiritual dimension of life asks whether constant spending and media absorption breed happiness or whether there are deeper questions and goals in life. Prison ministry worker Bo Lozoff believes that the latter is true. He visits prisons and publishes a newsletter that blends the world's great religions into their common questions and answers—into their simple, universal truths.[2] He reminds prisoners that all of us—prisoner or free citizen—are serving time in our life's journey rather than simply pursuing the avaricious accumulation of wealth and profligate spending on industry- and mass media–created wants.

Lozoff and Braswell (1989) recommend a variety of ways for offenders to experience the spiritual journey including meditation, yoga, the path of service to others, and turning information into wisdom. More recently, Braswell, Fuller, and Lozoff (2000) have written a book on what they refer to as a peacemaking model for corrections. They suggest that, although personal transformation and institutional transformation may be pursued simultaneously, personal transformation takes priority. Persons who live their lives from the inside out can have a positive influence in oppressive institutional environments, whereas the most well intentioned system cannot overcome self-absorbed, morally bankrupt professionals. "The theme of care in community justice reminds us that we are all connected and whatever we do to the 'least of us,' whether prisoners, the homeless, or victims of abuse, we finally in the end do to ourselves and our children" (Braswell et al., 2000, p. 9).

In the field of professional social work, Canda and Furman (1999) incorporate the spiritual dimension in real-life social work job situations. In their national survey of social workers, surprising percentages of the workers polled indicated that they thought it appropriate to raise spiritual issues when a client is experiencing life events such as terminal illness, loss of a loved one, or a criminal justice event like arrest or sentencing. Specifically, 73 percent considered it appropriate with clients experiencing terminal illness and 40 percent considered this appropriate in criminal justice–related problems. More importantly, these authors argue that spirituality is the motivation for many to enter social work practice and that spirituality provides the deeper dimension of what social workers are trying to achieve. More specifically, the meaning of life is a spiritual question and social workers can only help their clients find meaning in their lives if they assist clients in reaching for the spiritual dimension.

Another perspective on the spiritual dimension of human life and of probation is that of Abraham Maslow (1968, 1971). Maslow distinguished between basic human needs such as hunger, affection, security, and self-esteem and metaneeds such as justice, goodness, beauty, order, unity, and so forth. Generally, prison and probation have focused on the basic needs or the goal of keeping offenders from committing new crimes. Metaneeds are considered to be beyond the scope of corrections or to be matters for humans to pursue on their own. Once again, our First Amendment tradition of freedom of religion and separation of church and state makes us understandably and properly wary of imposing any religious tradition on offenders. But Maslow's theory of personality suggests that limiting our concerns to the basic human needs is only part of the equation. To ignore the spiritual dimension of human existence is to turn our back on a primary aspect of the meaning of life.

The importance of Maslow's hierarchy of human needs is that it provides nonreligious affirmation that there are aspects of human existence that go beyond the basic demands of everyday existence. Maslow's is a nontraditional testimony that life is more than eating, sleeping, and getting by.

So one task of probation may be to help the segment of probationers who are open to asking and seeking answers to the perennial questions about human existence. Why am I here? What is the meaning of life? What is happiness? Should I just seek more and more money and spend more and more or are there other, more satisfying aspects of life? Will a bigger house, a fancier car, more expensive clothes, more CDs, more video games, and more hours surfing the Internet make me happy or is there something else? Do the choices that I make take into consideration the needs of others? Are the choices that I am making in my life moral or immoral? Am I just seeking distraction through greed or am I seeking "significance through engagement in the processes of reflection, creativity, compassion, and the gift of self to others" (Staples, 2000, p. 33)?

Perhaps the current "epidemic" of drug use should inspire us to ask deeper questions. Perhaps many see the emptiness of our consumer-, media-, Web-based culture and turn to drugs as a way of numbing themselves or filling the existential hole in their lives. If all we are teaching our kids is that money is everything, perhaps we are reaping the vapidity of our message and our example. Similarly, school violence can be seen as a response to the alienation in our schools, where consumerism has transformed education into just preparation for college or for a career (Staples, 2000).

A positive aspect of considering probation to have a spiritual dimension is that such an approach might be able to enrich lives. It is possible that a number of probationers are in need of encouragement regarding this dimension of their lives. Another positive aspect would be job enrichment for probation officers. Officers would be involved in the noble duty of helping offenders to find hope and meaning in their lives. We contend that officers want to do more in their jobs than simply administer urine tests for drugs, monitor curfews, and do paperwork; they want a sense of personal accomplishment (Whitehead, 1989). In short, we agree with Harris that many probation workers "entered the field with hopes of making a difference in the lives of people in conflict with the law" (Harris, 1998, p. 83).

One negative consequence of putting a spiritual dimension into probation is the danger of proselytizing. Officers belonging to a particular religious denomination may attempt to convert offenders rather than simply help offenders to discover their own spiritual journey. In one southern women's prison, for example, the prison chaplains viewed homosexuality as sinful. Rather than allow women to explore their sexual identities, chaplains tried to turn women away from their sinful ways so as to avoid eternal damnation (Maeve, 1999).

A related danger is violation of the First Amendment, which protects freedom of religion and mandates the separation of church and state. Officers could not be permitted to engage in any activities that would deny offenders religious freedom or violate the separation of church and state. The Supreme Court, for example, ruled unconstitutional even a nonsectarian prayer at a school graduation ceremony (*Lee v. Weisman,* 1992) and at football games (*Santa Fe Independent School District v. Doe,* 2000).

One further negative aspect is that attempting to inject the spiritual into probation is perhaps too ambitious a project. If probation cannot even accomplish the basic objective of keeping offenders crime-free, then how can it be expected to help offenders become better persons spiritually? On the other hand, perhaps we have it backwards. Perhaps one reason that probation has had such a bad track record with recidivism is that it makes no effort to help offenders in a search for meaning and purpose in their lives. As noted above, if the implicit view of probation is that offenders only need to become part of the American Dream and if that dream is questionable and uninspiring and ignores the deeper potential of human living, then it may be no surprise that probation does little to improve recidivism. If probationers are simply being encouraged to earn and spend, turning to crime is not all that different in terms of motive than more legal alternatives.

Another danger of trying to introduce the spiritual into probation is one of hypocrisy. An example of alleged religious hypocrisy is to be found in Angola State Penitentiary in Louisiana. According to Bergner's account in *God of the Rodeo* (1999), the warden promotes religion. When there was a danger of flooding, for example, the warden told the prisoners to bring just a blanket and their Bible as they evacuated the cell blocks for higher ground. Despite this emphasis on religion, Angola allows an inmate rodeo every year, which appears to be extremely dangerous and appears to detract from inmate dignity (Bergner, 1999). The lesson is that correctional officials or workers who preach spirituality and religion for offenders will not be very convincing spokespersons if their practices are inconsistent with spiritual consideration for inmates.

Another danger is that of conceiving of the spiritual as the only answer or as a panacea for crime. The spiritual is not the only answer and it is not an appropriate answer for everyone. Many offenders have very specific problems—lack of education, lack of employment, poor parenting, etc.—that directly contributed to their criminality. In a Marxist sense, it can be distracting to focus on religion or spirituality as the key when very real problems need addressing. As Maslow's hierarchy suggests, basic needs come first. A focus on spirituality cannot be an excuse to ignore the basic needs of offenders. But the spiritual dimension is something that always remains.

One reason that there is reluctance to say that probation in particular and corrections in general should have a spiritual dimension is a subtle viewpoint that religion is irrelevant in modern secular society. Some have taken the separation of church and state and extended it to maintain that religion has no voice in current affairs.[3] Religion is dismissed as being both irrelevant and fictitious. It is equated with superstition or witchcraft and not taken seriously. As Carter (1994) points out, however, if religion is allowed its legitimacy, then it can serve the useful role of critiquing society. At its best, religion serves as the conscience of both the individual and society in general. In addition, all religions espouse certain universal virtues such as compassion, personal responsibility, and reconciliation that are conducive to helping probationers find meaning in their lives and become law-abiding, prosocial citizens.

One final objection to injecting a spiritual dimension into probation is a postmodern or empiricist position that notions of transcendence and ultimate meaning are relics of religion or premodern philosophies that assert some sort of absolute truth about ontological reality that contemporary epistemologies fail to support. One solution is for the probation officer to refrain from judging the ontological reality of the probationer's belief in any ultimate meaning or absolute reality. Here the officer simply helps the offender to explore and affirm his or her own definition of meaning and reality without endorsing that definition as true apart from the subjective perspective of that offender. Or the officer can take the advice of Moules who cautions that postmodernism can go too far if it claims that all there is is human construction:

> [Such a view] leaves out the mystery, the sacred, and the greater-than-me ecology of this world. It leaves the earth—the humus—out of being human. What of the other things of the world, living and not living, and what of things beyond this world and unknown to us? . . . The earth is not here for us. We are obligated to serve and suffer it, to be in relationship with it, and to see ourselves of the earth in fleshy humus. What we do not know has its own integrity and organization, it's greater than our knowledge of it, and we do not get to make it up. (Moules, 2000, p. 234)

Conclusion

The pessimistic view is that the most likely future of probation is more of the same. Probation will stumble on with high caseloads, technological innovations, concern for surveillance and risk management, varying levels of recidivism, and technical violations for drug use and other problems. Band-aid solutions will persist. Sending the technical violators to prison offers the illusion that we are doing something about crime. Traditional jobs training programs offer the illusion that we are opening the American Dream to offenders. So traditional programming offers the hope that offenders can become more like many of us. They will work long hours at jobs that they might not like so that they can increase their spending power and then consume more and more goods, services, and entertainment.

But at least two meaningful alternatives exist. One is to pursue the model of restorative and community justice. The other is to attempt to reintroduce the spiritual dimension of life into probation. The restorative and community justice model would put emphasis on the victim, on enhancing offender competency, and on involving the community in the determination and implementation of justice. This model is already being attempted and has considerable promise for reinvigorating probation.

But perhaps the Quakers had it right. The spiritual dimension of life is critical. The path to the spiritual dimension does not lie in silence and the Bible for everyone. That can and will be the path for some. Others follow Buddha or Mohammed. Others follow New Age writers and still others find meaning in such areas as art, literature, movies, the theater, painting, and sculpture. No one has a monopoly on the spiritual context of life. If probation is ever to achieve the hopes of its founder John Augustus, it must somehow address the spiritual needs of offenders. Ignoring the spiritual dimension of life is ignoring its most important element.

As noted above, several dangers exist in any effort to add a spiritual dimension to probation. One is the danger of proselytizing. Some might see this as an effort to convert probationers to a particular religious denomination. Proselytizing must be avoided. Any effort at adding the spiritual dimension to probation must define the spiritual in broad terms and allow each offender to define it in his or her own manner. A second and related danger is the danger of violating the constitutional protection for freedom of religion and the constitutional provision for the separation of church and state. Any effort to put a spiritual dimension back into probation must continue to protect the offender's freedom of religion (including the freedom to be atheistic or areligious) and to do so within the constraints of the separation of church and state.

The constraints can be problematic at times. The alternative, however, is to administer probation as if the spiritual dimension of life is nonexistent or unimportant. We have been doing that for decades and the results have been far from ideal. Perhaps if we went back to our correctional roots and reintroduced the spiritual into probation—with appropriate safeguards against proselytizing and violating individual freedom of religious choice—the future of probation would become more promising.

Notes

1. For a contemporary delineation of sanctioning models and their implications for probation and corrections that differs from our probation models and does not include any reference to a spiritual function, see Harris (1998). For a discussion of the models of probation as control, case management, and offender reform, see Sluder, Sapp, and Langston (1994). For a classic discussion of the conflict between surveillance and service in parole, see Studt (1972). For a discussion of a managerial model versus a clinical model, see Simon (1993). For a discussion of control, bifurcated, case-manager, individualized, and rehabilitation models, see Whitehead (1984). For placing probation in the context of a graduated sanctions scheme, see Morris and Tonry (1990) and below.
2. For more information about Bo Lozoff and his prison ministry (the Prison-Ashram Project) and newsletter, his website is www.HumanKindness.org.
3. Supreme Court Chief Justice William Rehnquist echoed this sentiment in Santa Fe Independent School District v. Doe (2000). There he dissented to the ruling against student-led prayer at football games by saying that the majority opinion "bristles with hostility to all things religious in public life."

References

Alliance for Youth [On-line]. Available: http://www.americaspromise.org

Austin, J., & Irwin, J. (2001). *It's about time: America's imprisonment binge* (3rd ed.). Belmont, CA: Wadsworth Publishing Co.

Bazemore, G. (1999). The fork in the road to juvenile court reform. *Annals of the American Academy of Political and Social Science, 564,* 81–108.

Bazemore, G., & Umbreit, M. (1995). Rethinking the sanction function in juvenile court: Retributive or restorative responses to youth crime. *Crime and Delinquency, 41,* 296–316.

Benedict, W. R., & Huff-Corzine, L. (1997). Return to the scene of the punishment: Recidivism of male property offenders on felony probation. *Journal of Research in Crime and Delinquency, 34,* 237–252.

Bergner, D. (1999). *God of the rodeo: The quest for redemption in Louisiana's Angola prison.* New York, NY: Ballantine Books.

Bonczar, T. P., & Glaze, L. E. (1999). *Probation and parole in the United States, 1998.* Washington, DC: U.S. Department of Justice.

Braswell, M. C., Fuller, J., & Lozoff, B. (2000). *Corrections, peacemaking, and restorative justice.* Cincinnati, OH: Anderson Publishing Company.

Canda, E. R., & Furman, L. D. (1999). *Spiritual diversity in social work practice.* New York, NY: The Free Press.

Carter, S. L. (1994). *The culture of disbelief: How American law and politics trivialize religious devotion.* New York, NY: Anchor Books.

Catalano, R. F., Loeber, R., & McKinney, K. C. (1999). *School and community interventions to prevent serious and violent offending.* Washington, DC: U.S. Department of Justice.

Corbett, R. P., Beto, D. R., Coen, B., DiIulio, J. J., Faulkner, J. R., Fitzgerald, B. L., Gregg, I., Helber, N., Hinzman, G. R., Paparozzi, M., Perry, J., Pozzi, R., & Rhine, E. E. (1999). *"Broken windows" probation: The next step in fighting crime.* New York, NY: Manhattan Institute.

Crank, J. P. (1996). The construction of meaning during training for probation and parole. *Justice Quarterly, 13,* 263–290.

Dietrich, S. G. (1979). The probation officer as therapist. *Federal Probation, 43*(2), 14–19.

Duffee, D. E., & Carlson, B. E. (1996). Competing value premises for the provision of drug treatment to probationers. *Crime and Delinquency, 42,* 574–592.

Duffee, D., & O'Leary, V. (1986). Formulating correctional goals: The interaction of environment, belief, and organizational structure. In D. Duffee (Ed.), *Correctional management: Change and control in correctional organizations* (pp. 75–102). Prospect Heights, IL: Waveland Press.

Dyer, J. (2000). *The perpetual prisoner machine: How America profits from crime.* Boulder, CO: Westview Press.

Elkins, D. N. (1999, September). Spirituality: It's what's missing in mental health. *Psychology Today, 32,* 44–50.

Feeley, M. M., & Simon, J. (1992). The new penology: Notes on the emerging strategy of corrections and its implications. *Criminology, 30,* 449–474.

Feld, B. (1999). *Bad kids: Race and the transformation of the juvenile court.* New York, NY: Oxford University Press.

Frady, M. (1993, February 22). Death in Arkansas. *The New Yorker,* pp. 105–133.

Fromm, E. (1941). *Escape from freedom.* New York, NY: Holt, Rhinehart, & Winston.

Garvin, C. D., & Seabury, B. A. (1997). *Interpersonal practice in social work: Promoting competence and social justice.* Boston, MA: Allyn & Bacon.

Gendreau, P. (1996). The principles of effective intervention with offenders. In A. T. Harland (Ed.), *Choosing correctional options that work: Defining the demand and evaluating the supply* (pp. 117–130). Thousand Oaks, CA: Sage.

Girshick, L. B. (1999). *No safe haven: Stories of women in prison.* Boston, MA: Northeastern University Press.

Glaser, D. (1969). *The effectiveness of a prison and parole system.* Indianapolis, IN: Bobbs-Merrill.

Glasser, W. (1965). *Reality therapy.* New York, NY: Harper & Row.

Grinc, R. M. (1994). "Angels in marble": Problems in stimulating community involvement in community policing. *Crime and Delinquency, 40,* 437–468.

Groopman, J. (2000, April 10). The doubting disease. *The New Yorker,* pp. 52–57.

Harding, R. W. (1997). *Private prisons and public accountability.* New Brunswick, NJ: Transaction Publishers.

Harris, M. K. (1998). Exploring the implications of four sanctioning orientations for community corrections. *Federal Probation, 62*(2), 81–94.

Hartmann, D. J., Friday, P. C., & Minor, K. I. (1994). Residential probation: A seven year follow-up of halfway house discharges. *Journal of Criminal Justice, 22,* 503–515.

Iannone, R. V., & Obenauf, P. A. (1999). Toward spirituality in curriculum and teaching. *Education, 119,* 737–744.

Irwin, J. (1980). *Prisons in turmoil.* Boston, MA: Little, Brown, & Company.

Johnson, R., & Toch, H. (2000). *Crime and punishment: Inside views.* Los Angeles, CA: Roxbury Publishing Company.

Klockars, C. B. (1972). A theory of probation supervision. *Journal of Criminal Law, Criminology and Police Science, 63,* 550–557.

Knoxville Public Safety Collaborative. (2000). *Mission statement.* Unpublished document (State of Tennessee Board of Paroles and Knoxville Police Department).

Koening, H. G. (1999). *The healing power of faith: Science explores medicine's last great frontier.* New York, NY: Simon & Schuster.

Kurlychek, M., Torbet, P., & Bozynski, M. (1999). *Focus on accountability: Best practices for juvenile court and probation.* Washington, DC: U.S. Department of Justice.

Landon, P. S., & Feit, M. (1999). *Generalist social work practice.* Dubuque, IA: Eddie Bowers Publishing, Inc.

Lee v. Weisman, 505 U.S. 577 (1992).

Lenson, D. (1995). *On drugs.* Minneapolis, MN: University of Minnesota Press.

Levrant, S., Cullen, F. T., Fulton, B., & Wozniak, J. F. (1999). Reconsidering restorative justice: The corruption of benevolence revisited? *Crime and Delinquency, 45,* 3–27.

Lipsey, M. W. (1992). Juvenile delinquency treatment: A meta-analytic inquiry into the viability of effects. In T. Cook, H. Cooper, D. Corday, H. Hartman, L. Hedges, R. Light, T. Louis, & F. Mosteller (Eds.), *Meta-analysis for explanation: A casebook* (pp. 83–127). New York, NY: Russell Sage Foundation.

Lipsey, M. W., Wilson, D. B., & Cothern, L. (2000). *Effective intervention for serious juvenile offenders.* Washington, DC: U.S. Department of Justice.

Lozoff, B., & Braswell, M. (1989). *Inner corrections: Finding peace and peace making.* Cincinnati, OH: Anderson Publishing Company.

Lucken, K. (1997). Privatizing discretion: "Rehabilitating" treatment in community corrections. *Crime and Delinquency, 43,* 243–259.

Maeve, M. K. (1999). The social construction of love and sexuality in a women's prison. *Advances in Nursing Science, 21,* 46–65.

Maguire, K., & Pastore, A. L. (Eds.). (1999). *Sourcebook of criminal justice statistics 1998.* Washington, DC: U.S. Department of Justice.

Maslow, A. H. (1968). *Toward a psychology of being.* Princeton, NJ: Van Nostrand.

Maslow, A. H. (1971). *The farther reaches of human nature.* New York, NY: Viking Press.

Masters, J. J. (1997). *Finding freedom: Writings from death row.* Junction City, CA: Padma Publishing.

May, R., Angel, E., & Ellenberger, H. (1958). *Existence: A new dimension in psychiatry and psychology.* New York, NY: Simon & Schuster.

McGraw, P. C. (1999). *Life strategies: Doing what works, doing what matters.* New York, NY: Hyperion.

McGraw, P. C. (2000). *Relationship resource: A seven-step strategy for reconnecting with your partner.* New York, NY: Hyperion.

Messner, S. F., & Rosenfeld, R. (1997). *Crime and the American dream* (2nd ed.). Belmont, CA: Wadsworth Publishing Company.

Mitka, M. (1998, December 9). Getting religion seen as help in being well. *Journal of the American Medical Association, 280*(22), 1896–1897.

Morgan, O. J. (2000). Counseling and spirituality. In H. Hackney (Ed.), *Practice issues for the beginning counselor* (pp. 170–182). Boston, MA: Allyn & Bacon.

Morris, N., & Tonry, M. (1990). *Between prison and probation: Intermediate punishments in a rational sentencing system.* New York, NY: Oxford University Press.

Moules, N. J. (2000). Postmodernism and the sacred: Reclaiming connection in our greater-than-human worlds. *Journal of Marital and Family Therapy, 26,* 229–240.

Mumola, C. J., & Bonczar, T. P. (1998). *Substance abuse and treatment of adults on probation, 1995.* Washington, DC: U.S. Department of Justice.

Myers, D. G. (2000). *The American paradox: Spiritual hunger in an age of plenty.* New Haven, CT: Yale University Press.

Pepinsky, H. (2000, January). Educating for peace. *Annals of the American Academy of Political and Social Science, 567,* 157–169.

Petersilia, J. (1997). Probation in the United States. In M. Tonry (Ed.), *Crime and justice: A review of research* (Vol. 22, pp. 149–200). Chicago, IL: University of Chicago Press.

Petersilia, J., & Turner, S. (1993). *Evaluating intensive probation/parole: Results of a nationwide experiment. Research in brief.* Washington, DC: National Institute of Justice.

Petersilia, J., Turner, S., Kahan, J., & Peterson, J. (1985). *Granting felons probation: Public and alternatives.* Santa Monica, CA: The Rand Corporation.

Pratt, T. C., & Maahs, J. (1999). Are private prisons more cost-effective than public prisons: A meta-analysis of evaluation research studies. *Crime and Delinquency, 45,* 358–371.

Prison Fellowship Ministry [On-line]. Available: http://www.pfm.org

Raine, A., Brennan, P., Farrington, D. P., & Mednick, S. A. (Eds.). (1997). *Biosocial bases of violence.* New York, NY: Plenum Press.

Rothman, D. J. (1971). *The discovery of the asylum: Social order and disorder in the new republic.* Boston, MA: Little, Brown.

Santa Fe Independent School District v. Doe, 530 U.S. 290 (2000).

Simon, J. (1993). *Poor discipline: Parole and the social control of the underclass, 1980–1990.* Chicago, IL: University of Chicago Press.

Skogan, W. G., & Hartnett, S. M. (1997). *Community policing, Chicago style.* New York, NY: Oxford University Press.

Sluder, R. D., Sapp, A. D., & Langston, D. C. (1994). Guiding philosophies for probation in the 21st century. *Federal Probation, 58*(2), 3–10.

Smith, M. E., & Dickey, W. J. (1999). *Reforming sentencing and corrections for just punishment and public safety.* Washington, DC: U.S. Department of Justice.

Staples, J. S. (2000). Violence in schools: Rage against a broken world. *Annals of the American Academy of Political and Social Science, 567,* 30–41.

Stuart, B. (1996). Circle sentencing—turning swords into ploughshares. In B. Galaway & J. Hudson (Eds.), *Restorative justice: International perspectives* (pp. 193–206). Monsey, NY: Criminal Justice Press.

Studt, E. (1972). *Surveillance and service in parole: A report of the parole action study.* Washington, DC: National Institute of Corrections.

Trueblood, D. E. (1966). *The people called Quakers.* New York, NY: Harper & Row.

U.S. Department of Justice, Bureau of Justice Statistics [On-line]. Available: http://www.ojp.usdoj.gov/bjs

Umbreit, M. S., & Coates, R. B. (1999). Multicultural implications of restorative juvenile justice. *Federal Probation, 63*(2), 44–51.

Venturelli, P. J. (2000). Drugs in schools: Myths and realities. *Annals of the American Academy of Political and Social Science, 567,* 72–87.

Walker, S. (1998). *Sense and nonsense about crime and drugs: A policy guide* (4th ed.). Belmont, CA: West/Wadsworth Publishing Company.

Walker, S., Spohn, C., & DeLone, M. (2000). *The color of justice: Race, ethnicity, and crime in America* (2nd ed.). Belmont, CA: Wadsworth Publishing Company.

Whitehead, J. T. (1984). Probation mission reform: Implications for the forgotten actor—the probation officer. *Criminal Justice Review, 9,* 15–21.

Whitehead, J. T. (1989). *Burnout in probation and corrections.* New York, NY: Praeger Publishers.

Wilson, J. Q. (1995). Crime and public policy. In J. Q. Wilson & J. Petersilia (Eds.), *Crime* (pp. 489–507). San Francisco, CA: Institute for Contemporary Studies.

Wilson, J. Q., & Kelling, G. L. (1982, March). Broken windows: The police and neighborhood safety. *Atlantic Monthly,* pp. 29–38.

Wright, R. T., & Decker, S. H. (1994). *Burglars on the job: Streetlife and residential break-ins.* Boston, MA: Northeastern University Press.

Wright, R. T., & Decker, S. H. (1997). *Armed robbers in action: Stickups and street culture.* Boston, MA: Northeastern University Press.

Chapter 23

Intermediate Sanctions in Sentencing Guidelines

Michael Tonry

Intermediate sanctions have been developed in every state since 1980, and nearly half the states have, have had, or are developing sentencing guidelines. Looking back just three decades, both developments are dramatic; then, few states had programs that would today be considered intermediate sanctions, and not one had sentencing guidelines. From a twenty-first century perspective, neither intermediate sanctions nor guidelines can be considered novel. What is novel, however, is that policymakers in many states have begun to recognize that intermediate sanctions and guidelines, taken together, may assist each to achieve its primary purposes. A number of different approaches have emerged. This chapter describes and assesses these approaches and others under consideration, so that states attempting such coordinated approaches in the future can build on the experiences of their predecessors.

More States have adopted and are developing sentencing guidelines than ever before, and intermediate sanctions continue to proliferate. Both assertions may surprise people who are not actively involved in these developments. Programs in the States get much less media and scholarly attention than do Federal developments. Owing to the unpopularity of the Federal sentencing guidelines and the near absence of intermediate sanctions in the Federal courts, a person who knew only of Federal developments could be excused for believing that both are failed or passe innovations of the 1980s.

In the States, however, both guidelines and intermediate sanctions are thriving. Guidelines were in effect in more States in early 1997 than ever before, and both the number of intermediate sanctions programs and the number of people supervised in them grow every year.

A principal reason both are thriving is that in important respects they can accomplish the goals policymakers set for them. A second reason is that policymakers in many States are worried about the fiscal consequences for State budgets of recently enacted mandatory minimum sentence laws, "three-strikes" laws, and general increases in severity of sentences for violent offenders. Legislators in a number of States, notably North Carolina, Ohio, and Pennsylvania, have enacted laws that will increase use of prison sentences and lengthen terms for violent offenders, while reducing use of prison sentences for nonviolent offenders and diverting them into intermediate sanctions instead. In all of these States, funds have been authorized both to build more prisons and to pay for more community-based programs. Coordinating sentencing policies expressed in guidelines with operation of intermediate sanctions may be the way to make ambitious new punishment policies workable and affordable.

Sentencing Guidelines

Consider guidelines first. State guidelines received considerable national attention in the 1980s and much less since. Yet there are many more guidelines systems in operation in the 1990s than in the 1980s, and they are typically more effective. Guidelines come in two broad forms: presumptive and voluntary. Presumptive guidelines, as the words suggest, establish rebuttable presumptions about appropriate sentences in individual cases. Judges can impose some other sentence by "departing," but must then give reasons for the departure which are subject to appellate review if a party appeals. Voluntary guidelines create no presumptions. They are in effect suggestions that the judge may accept if he or she wishes to do so.

Although as many as 10 States adopted voluntary guidelines in the late 1970s and the 1980s, the few that were evaluated were shown to have few or no effects on sentencing patterns and most were abandoned or fell into desuetude. Delaware adopted voluntary guidelines in 1987 which remain in effect. Florida established voluntary guidelines in the early 1980s and later made them presumptive. More recently, Arkansas and Missouri adopted voluntary guidelines.

Only a few States initially adopted presumptive guidelines—Minnesota in 1980, Pennsylvania in 1981, and Washington in 1984—but they were adjudged reasonably effective at reducing disparities, diminishing scope for gender and racial bias, and improving coordination between sentencing policy and corrections resources. Newer presumptive schemes have since taken effect in Oregon, Kansas, North Carolina, and Ohio. Commissions early in 1997 were at work on guidelines in Maryland, Massachusetts, Michigan, Montana, Oklahoma, and South Carolina (and probably in other States of which I am unaware).

A principal criticism of guidelines systems is that they are too limited in scope. The successful Minnesota, Washington, and Oregon guidelines in the 1980s governed decisions of who was sent to prison, and for how long, but set no standards for imposition of jail sentences, intermediate sanctions, or standard probation. Since fewer than 25 percent of convicted felons in many States are sentenced to State prison, those early guidelines systems were far from comprehensive. Why, the argument goes, if guidelines can reduce disparities and make sentencing more predictable, should they not apply to all sentences?

Intermediate Sanctions

The story concerning intermediate sanctions is similar—more attention and excitement in the 1980s than today but more, and more sophisticated, activity today.

Corrections programs less restrictive than total confinement but more so than probation are not new. Halfway houses, curfews, and intensive probation programs existed in the 1950s and 1960s . . . conceptualized as rehabilitative programs. With the collapse of confidence in the ability of corrections programs to rehabilitate offenders, these programs lost credibility and support.

During the 1970s, community service, intensive probation, and restitution programs were established in many jurisdictions; they were conceptualized as alternatives to imprisonment. There was little evidence that alternatives reduced recidivism rates, and there was much evidence that they resulted in "net widening," used by judges as alternatives to standard probation rather than imprisonment. Alternatives too soon lost credibility and support.

In the 1980s, a series of new "intermediate sanctions" appeared and quickly spread. They included various forms of intensive probation, house arrest, electronic monitoring, boot camps, day-reporting centers, and day fines. Except for day fines, all these sanctions can be run as "front-end" or "back-end" programs. Entry into front-end programs is controlled by judges; corrections officials control entry into back-end programs, often in connection with early-release systems.

Intermediate sanctions were typically conceptualized as punishments located on a continuum between prison and probation and were supposed to be more intrusive and burdensome than standard probation. Proponents sometimes promised that the new punishments would cost less than jail or prison, reduce prison crowding, and cut recidivism rates. Although major evaluations of day-reporting centers and day fines had not been published by the end of 1996, evaluations of intensive probation, house arrest, electronic monitoring, and boot camps were available, and they did not confirm overenthusiastic proponents' predictions. Evaluated front-end programs typically experienced recidivism rates for new crimes neither higher nor lower than those of other sanctions for comparable offenders (but often much higher rates of technical violations and revocations), but because of extensive net widening and high rates of technical violations and revocations, they often cost more than confinement and worsened prison crowding. Back-end programs had similar recidivism-rate experiences but because corrections officials' control of entry prevented net widening, they were more effective at achieving cost savings and reducing prison-population pressures.

Because intermediate sanctions have multiple purposes, the evaluation findings do not deprive them of credibility and support. First, implementation evaluations show that intermediate sanctions can deliver much more intrusive and burdensome punishments than standard probation; that is why technical violation and revocation rates are high. From a retributive perspective, intermediate sanctions can be much more punitive than probation and can be scaled in severity to the seriousness of the crime. Second, national evaluations of intensive probation and boot camps suggest (but do not prove) that intermediate sanctions with strong treatment components can improve treatment effectiveness and thereby reduce recidivism rates. Third, experience with back-end programs shows that intermediate sanctions can save money and prison resources if ways can be found to eliminate or greatly diminish net widening.

Thus, intermediate sanctions can be used to save money and prison use, without significant sacrifices in public safety. The trick is to reduce net widening in front-end programs. In the American legal system, judges decide who is not sentenced to prison.

Since that power is unlikely to be taken away, some way needs to be devised to set enforceable standards for sentences other than . . . imprisonment. Sentencing guidelines may be the answer.

Combining Guidelines with Intermediate Sanctions

North Carolina and Ohio have adopted new guidelines systems incorporating standards for the use of intermediate sanctions. Pennsylvania in 1994 overhauled its 13-year-old guidelines to do the same thing. The Massachusetts sentencing commission in 1996 presented a proposal for a similar set of guidelines to the Massachusetts legislature. Commissions are at work on similar plans in several other States, and the pressures of rising prison populations and corrections budgets are likely to lead more States to similar efforts.

The early evidence from North Carolina suggests that guidelines incorporating intermediate sanctions can work. The North Carolina guidelines cover all felonies and misdemeanors and attempt to increase use of prison sentences for violent crimes. They also attempt to reduce prison use for nonviolent crimes by directing judges to sentence more offenders to intermediate sanctions. Both things happened in 1995, the guidelines' first full year of operation. Eighty-one percent of violent felons received prison sentences, up from 67 percent in 1993. Twenty-three percent of nonviolent felons were sent to prison, down from 42 percent in 1993. For all imprisoned felons, the mean predicted time to be served increased from 16 to 37 months.

Notwithstanding North Carolina's apparent success, it is small wonder that earlier guidelines dealt only with prison (and occasionally jail) sentences. A number of serious impediments prevented the development of guidelines with broader scope. First, judges in many States fiercely resisted the very idea of guidelines, and overcoming that resistance for prison guidelines was challenge enough. In some States, including New York, Maine, Connecticut, and South Carolina, judicial resistance could not be overcome and no guidelines were adopted.

Second, guidelines cannot realistically set standards for non-confinement sentences, nor can judges be expected to follow them, unless credible programs exist to which offenders can be sentenced. Until recently, few States had extensive community corrections programs, especially outside the big cities. A number of States have now begun to provide community corrections funding to counties that makes operation of well-managed intermediate sanctions feasible; many States as yet have not.

Third, non-confinement guidelines present more complex issues than do prison guidelines. For serious violent crimes, and for chronic offenders, the current crime and the past criminal record are in most cases the primary considerations relevant to sentencing. Guidelines grids that array crime categories along one axis and criminal history along the other can efficiently encapsulate the major criteria for those cases.

Sentencing for less serious crimes and offenders entails other considerations for many judges: might drug or sex-offender treatment be more effective than confinement, what are the likely collateral effects of imprisonment on the offender and his family, and are there special circumstances of the offense or the offender's characteristics that make one kind of sentence more appropriate than another? The two-axis grid by itself is not a very efficient way to address these and other offender-specific considerations.

Incorporation of intermediate sanctions into sentencing guidelines is in its earliest days. There are, nonetheless, a number of techniques that have been developed and ideas that have been examined. They are discussed briefly in this [chapter] and at length in the [complete report].[1]

Zones of Discretion

Most guidelines commissions that have tried to expand their guidelines' coverage to include non-confinement sentences have altered the traditional guidelines format to include more zones of discretion. The first guidelines in Minnesota, Pennsylvania, and Washington divided their grids into two zones. One contained confinement cells setting presumptive ranges for prison sentences, and the other contained non-confinement cells that gave the judge unfettered discretion to impose any other sentence, often including an option of jail sentences of up to one year. Minnesota's guidelines, for example, contained a bold black line that separated the confinement and non-confinement zones.

New North Carolina, revised Pennsylvania, and proposed Massachusetts guidelines, by contrast, have four or more zones. The details vary but they follow a common pattern. Sentences other than those authorized by the applicable zone are departures for which reasons must be given which are subject to review on appeal. One zone contains cells in which only prison sentences are presumed appropriate. A second might contain cells in which judges may choose between restrictive intermediate sanctions, such as residential drug treatment, house arrest with electronic monitoring, and a day-reporting center, and a prison sentence up to a designated length. A third might contain cells in which judges may choose among restrictive intermediate punishments. A fourth might authorize judges to choose between restrictive intermediate sanctions and a less restrictive penalty like community service or standard probation. A fifth might authorize sentencing choices only among less restrictive community penalties.

Punishment Units

A second approach that Oregon adopted and several other States considered is to express punishment in generic "punishment units" into which all sanctions can be converted. A hypothetical system might provide, for example, for the following conversion values:

- One year's confinement: 100 units
- One year's partial confinement: 50 units
- One year's house arrest: 50 units
- One year's standard probation: 20 units
- 25 days' community service: 50 units
- 30 days' intensive supervision: 5 units
- 90 days' income (day fines): 100 units
- 30 days' electronic monitoring: 5 units

That is by no means a complete list; such things as drug testing, treatment conditions, and restitution might or might not be added. The values could be divided or multiplied to obtain values for other periods (for example, 75 days' confinement equals 20 units).

If guidelines, for example, set "120 punishment units" as the presumptive sentence for a particular offender, a judge could impose any combination of sanctions that represented 120 units. One year's confinement (100 units) plus 60 subsequent days' intensive supervision (10 units) on electronic monitoring (10 units) would be appropriate. So would a 90-unit day fine (100 units) plus one year's standard probation (20 units). So would 25 days' community service (50 units) and six months' intensive supervision (30 units), followed by two years' standard probation (40 units).

In practice, the punishment unit approach has proven too complicated to be workable. Oregon's original guidelines had two zones of discretion and in every cell in the non-confinement zone specified the maximum number of punishment units for cases falling in that cell. However, detailed conversion rates were not established. All forms of confinement were given the same weight, and 16 hours' community service was made equivalent to 1 day's confinement. The commentary to the Oregon guidelines indicated that the provision of custody units was a foundation for later elaboration of conversion rates. The elaboration never happened. Pennsylvania likewise considered including the punishment unit concept in its revised 1994 guidelines but abandoned the idea as unworkable.

Exchange Rates

Another approach is simply to specify equivalent custodial and non-custodial penalties and to authorize judges to impose them in the alternative. Washington's commission did this in a modest way and later proposed a more extensive system, which the legislature did not adopt. Partial confinement and community service were initially authorized as substitutes for presumptive prison terms on the basis of 1 day's partial confinement or 3 days' community service for 1 day of confinement. The partial confinement/confinement exchange is probably workable (for short sentences; house arrest, assuming that to count as partial confinement, is seldom imposed for more than a few months), but the community service exchange rate is not.

Like the punishment unit proposals, so far the exchange-rate approaches have been unable to overcome the psychological and political pressures to make "equivalent" punishments as objectively burdensome as prison, which limits their use to the most minor offenses and offenders. Under Washington's 3-days'-community-service-equals-1-day's-confinement policy, that range would permit community service in place of 3 to 10 days' confinement if existing successful programs were used as models.

The difficulty is that community service programs, to be credible, must be enforced, and experience in this country and elsewhere instructs that they must be short. That is why the best-known American program in New York set 70 hours as a standard, and the national policies in England and Wales, Scotland, and the Netherlands set 240 hours as the upper limit. Those programs were designed to be used for offenders who otherwise would receive prison sentences of up to 6 months.

Exchange rates are limited in their potential uses for the same reason punishment units are. For so long as prevailing views require that imprisonment be considered the normal punishment and that substitutes for imprisonment be comparably burdensome and intrusive, exchange rates are unlikely to play a significant role in sentencing guidelines.

Categorical Exceptions

Categorical exception policies, focusing not on the sanction but on the offender, are permissive. They authorize, but do not direct, judges to disregard otherwise applicable sentencing ranges if offenders meet specified criteria. One example is Rule 5.K.1 in the Federal guidelines that empowers judges to depart from guidelines if the prosecution files a motion proposing such a departure because the defendant has provided "substantial assistance [to the government] in the investigation or prosecution of another person." Once the motion is made, the judge is free from guidelines presumptions about appropriate sentences.

The Federal categorical exception concerning substantial assistance, however, has no special relevance to intermediate sanctions. Only one State, Washington, has developed extensive categorical exception policies. Under the First-Time Offender Waiver, judges may disregard otherwise applicable guidelines in sentencing qualifying offenders and, guidelines commentary indicates, "The court is given broad discretion in setting the sentence." Available alternatives include up to 90 days [in] jail or 2 years [on] probation and financial penalties, compulsory treatment, and community service. To be eligible, the offense must be a first conviction for a nonviolent, nonsexual offense (some drug offenders are also ineligible). In 1993, 2,139 offenders (of 7,224 eligible) were sentenced under the first-time offender exception.

Washington's Special Sex Offender Sentencing Alternative authorizes judges to suspend prison sentences for most first-time sex offenders. To qualify, the offender must agree to two examinations by certified sex-offender treatment specialists and to preparation of a treatment plan. Offenders whose otherwise applicable presumptive sentence does not exceed 8 years are eligible. Following a decision that the offender is amenable to treatment, the judge may suspend the presumptive sentence and impose a community sentence that includes sex-offender treatment, up to 90 days in jail, community supervision, various financial obligations, and community service. In 1993, of 940 eligible offenders, 400 received special sex-offender departures.

No other State has attained as much experience with use of categorical exceptions to sentencing guidelines (Washington also has a "work ethic [boot] camp" program that permits substitution of 4 to 6 months' boot camp for 22 to 36 months in prison). The idea, however, has potentially broad application to guidelines systems.

Likely Future Developments

Past experience suggests that some of the devices used to date are likely to be useful tools in incorporating intermediate sanctions into guidelines, and that others are not. At least in America in the 1990s, punishment units and exchange rates appear to be at dead ends. The most ambitious efforts to implement either concept have had negligible scope.

Zones of discretion and categorical exceptions, however, do have roles to play. Use of zones of discretion has permitted policymakers to specify categories of offenses and offenders for which only particular kinds of sanctions are presumptively appropriate (only imprisonment, or only intermediate sanctions, or only less intrusive community penalties). Little guidance has as yet been provided to judges in choosing between imprisonment and other sanctions or among intermediate sanctions. Categorical exceptions are the most promising tools available for providing that guidance.

Future sentencing commissions will probably develop current ideas in new ways. None of the commissions that have adopted a zones-of-discretion approach, for example, has attempted to provide guidance to judges on how to choose among authorized intermediate sanctions or community penalties or between intermediate sanctions and authorized confinement or community sanctions. This could easily be done by setting policies that particular kinds of sanctions are appropriate for particular kinds of offenders: an obvious example would be a policy that residential drug treatment be presumed appropriate for a drug-dependent chronic property offender. Depending on how convinced the commission was about the wisdom of the policy, it could be made presumptive (and thus require a "departure" with reasons given for any other sentence) or only advisory.

Use of categorical exceptions likewise could be fine-tuned. The Federal and Washington State examples given above, for example, are permissive, entirely within the judge's discretion. A State might, however, want to make some categorical exceptions permissive and others presumptive. A first-time offender exception, like Washington's, might be permissive, while the Federal "substantial assistance" exception might be made presumptive.

More States will be facing the kinds of issues discussed in this [chapter]. Most States have in recent years enacted laws mandating greatly lengthened sentences for violent offenders and for some drug and repeat offenders. Under the incentive of Federal funds for prison construction, many States now require that violent offenders serve at least 85 percent of those longer sentences. Forecasts of enormous resulting increases in prison operating costs led the North Carolina legislature to adopt guidelines intended to carry out those policies for violent offenders but also to divert many nonviolent offenders from prison to less expensive intermediate sanctions. Many States will face the same financial choices, and some at least are likely to try to follow the path that North Carolina and Pennsylvania have charted.

Together the suggestions offered in this [chapter] for incorporating intermediate sanctions into sentencing guidelines may appear complicated, but that is a misimpression. Singly or together they constitute modest incremental steps toward creating comprehensive sentencing systems that incorporate confinement and non-confinement sanctions and attempt to achieve reasonable consistency in sentencing while allowing judges to take account of meaningful differences between cases.

Note

1. For the complete report, see Michael Tonry, *Intermediate Sanctions in Sentencing Guidelines.* Washington, DC: National Institute of Justice, May 1997, 101 pp. (NCJ 165043).

Michael Tonry, "Intermediate Sanctions in Sentencing Guidelines." Washington, D.C.: National Institute of Justice, May 1997, 101 pp. (NCJ 165043). ✦

Chapter 24

Prison-Based Programming

What It Can Do and Why It Is Needed

Daniel P. Mears
Sarah Lawrence
Amy L. Solomon
Michelle Waul

D*ue to declining funding and ideological support, prison-based programming has failed to keep up with growing prison populations in recent years. Yet inmates, who typically suffer from multiple behavioral, physical, mental, educational, and social adjustment problems, are badly in need of the services such programs provide. Only half of all inmates possess a high school degree, typically more than 70 percent of parolees are unemployed, some 80 percent of all inmates have histories of substance abuse, more than 15 percent suffer from serious mental disorders, and many suffer from serious multi-level health problems (i.e., HIV/AIDS, hepatitis C, tuberculosis). Even ignoring the moral component of assisting individuals, it can be argued that since the vast majority of inmates eventually return to society, society must provide a range of prison-based programs that aggressively seek to respond to inmate needs, or we will face serious consequences in the coming years.*

Figure 24.1
Sentenced Inmates Admitted and Released from State and Federal Prisons, 1977–1997

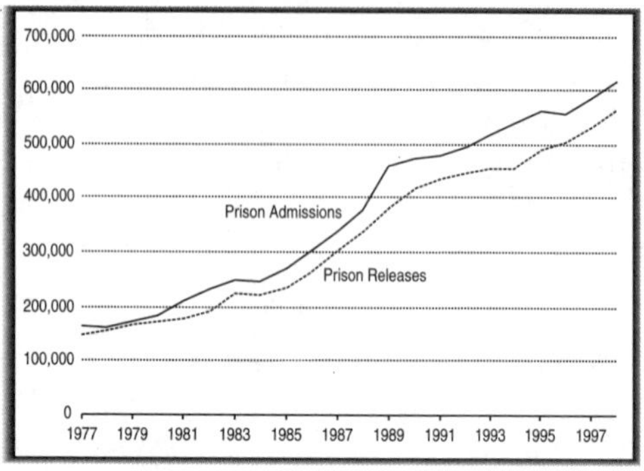

Source: Travis, Jeremy, Amy L. Solomon and Michelle Waul. 2001. *From prison to home: The dimensions and consequences of prisoner re-entry.* Washington, D.C.: The Urban Institute. Based on analysis by James P. Lynch and William J. Sabol of Bureau of Justice Statistics' *National Prisoner Statistics* data.

During the past two decades, the prison population grew more rapidly and now is larger than at any other juncture in U.S. history. This growth was fueled by two trends. The first consisted of a dramatic increase in admissions to state and federal prisons (see Figure 24.1). This growth far exceeded and, therefore, cannot be explained by increases in the general resident population. For example, between 1973 and 1999, the rate of incarceration rose from 110 to 476 per 100,000 residents.[1]

The second trend consisted of inmates serving longer sentences. Because of the increasing number of prison admissions, the lengthier sentences exerted an even greater impact on prison population growth.[2] The growth in the prison population was paralleled by similar growth in the number of inmates released into society. Indeed, despite tougher sentences, nearly every offender sentenced to prison eventually is released into society. The vast majority of these offenders are rearrested within three years of release, contributing to prison population growth and, in turn, to inmate re-entry.[3]

Such growth suggests that prison-based programming, including educational classes; mental health and drug treatment; vocational training and prison industries; and prerelease preparation; should be increasing. These programs have the potential to help maintain control of and improve safety in prisons, reduce the recidivism rate, and help inmates address a range of problems that can affect their ability to successfully transition into society.[4] Yet, programming has not kept pace with the number of offenders entering prison. In fact, the proportion of inmates receiving programming has steadily declined during the past decade.[5]

Figure 24.2
Inmates to Be Released During the Next 12 Months: Estimated Distribution of Expected Time Served Until Release, 1991 and 1997

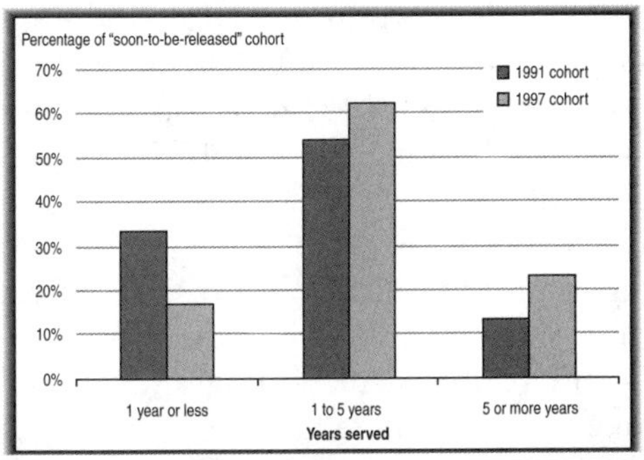

Source: Travis, Jeremy, Amy L. Solomon and Michelle Waul. 2001. *From prison to home: The dimensions and consequences of prisoner re-entry.* Washington, D.C.: The Urban Institute. Based on analysis by James P. Lynch and William J. Sabol of Bureau of Justice Statistics' *Survey of inmates of state correctional facilities,* 1991 and 1997 data.

Figure 24.3
Inmates to Be Released During the Next 12 Months: Percentage Participating in Prison Programs, 1991 and 1997

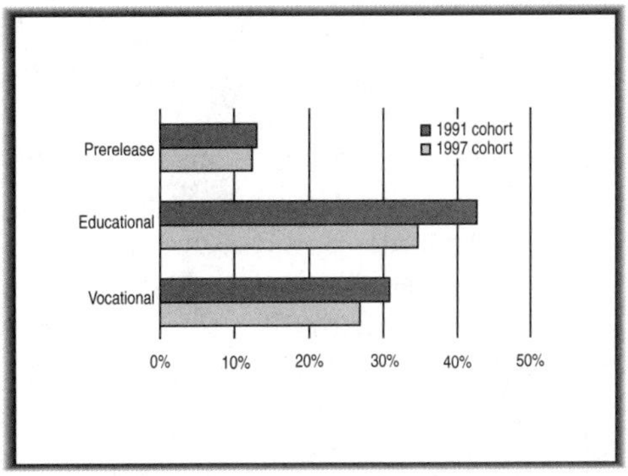

Source: Lynch, James P. and William J. Sabol. 2001. *Prisoner re-entry in perspective.* Washington, D.C.: The Urban Institute. Analysis of Bureau of Justice Statistics data: *Correctional populations in the United States: 1990–98* and *National corrections reporting program, 1990–98.*

Given a context in which prison control is a challenge and inmate re-entry looms large, correctional administrators and policy-makers should be eager to implement programming that has been proved to work.[6] But they would find that until recently, there has been little research directly addressing the question: What programs work best and for whom? Increasingly, however, research provides some guidance for how correctional policies might be structured to benefit both inmates and society.

The Need for Programming

Whether due to declines in funding or support, prison-based programming has not kept pace with the dramatic growth in incarcerated offenders. Consider the changes that occurred between 1991 and 1997, among the peak years of prison growth in the United States. In 1991, 43 percent of inmates received educational programming. By 1997, this figure dropped to 35 percent (see Figure 24.3). During this same period, rates of vocational programming participation dropped from 31 percent to 27 percent.

The decline of prerelease programming was negligible. In both 1991 and 1997, only about 10 percent of inmates released into society had participated in prerelease programs. This low percentage, coupled with the fact that the number of inmates released from prison grew rapidly during the 1990s, means there has been a corresponding growth in the number of inmates re-entering society without the training and skills necessary to successfully transition back to their families and communities.

Is there really a need for prison-based programming? The short answer is "Yes." The best available estimates indicate that most inmates suffer from multiple problems. For example, up to 11 percent of inmates have learning disabilities, compared with 3 percent of the general population.[7] Approximately half the inmates have high school diplomas or the equivalent. By contrast, more than three-quarters of the U.S. population has high school diplomas or the equivalent.[8]

Employment estimates among released offenders identify a significant challenge to successful inmate re-entry. A study of California offenders suggests, for example, that between 70 percent and 90 percent of parolees are unemployed.[9] Most of the parolees who obtained full-time employment earned 10 percent to 20 percent less than similarly situated individuals who had not been incarcerated.[10]

There are other problems as well. Nearly 80 percent of inmates have histories of substance abuse, and about 16 percent suffer from serious mental disorders. Yet, only one-third receive either substance abuse or mental health treatment while in prison.[11] It is estimated that only 10 percent of state inmates in 1997 received any type of formal substance abuse treatment, down from 25 percent in 1991.[12]

Physical health problems also are a major concern. Rates of infectious diseases such as HIV/AIDS, hepatitis C and tuberculosis are up to 10 times greater in prison than in the general population.[13] Additionally, the aging of the prison population means that there is an increasing need to address the diverse medical problems of older inmates.[14]

To compound matters, many inmates suffer from co-occurring disorders. They may, for example, have physical and mental health problems, including dual diagnoses, as well as educational and employment skills deficits. In these cases, the risks of recidivism, relapse into drug use, unemployment, etc., are compounded.[15]

The high number of offenders entering and leaving prisons—and the many problems they have—raise two critical issues. First, prisons increasingly will need effective strategies for managing inmates. Second, society will have to face any consequences associated with not addressing inmates' many problems and needs.

The Logic of Programming

Why have prison programs? The simple answer is that effective prison programs can potentially heighten the stability and order of prisons, reduce criminal behavior, and improve the lives of ex-offenders and their families, and the well-being of the communities to which they return.[16] The operative word is "potentially": Not all programs are effective and few, if any, are effective for all inmates. To know why, it helps to understand the underlying logic of prison-based programs.

Individuals enter prison with varying backgrounds. They have different work histories, health conditions, life skills, criminal records and differ as well in terms of age, sex and race/ethnicity. Although few programs systematically take into account these factors, they, nonetheless, can have profound impacts on the effectiveness of programs.

The range of prison-based programs offered to inmates includes academic instruction, vocational training, prison industries and employment services that can aid in obtaining post-release employment. Prisons also may offer a range of additional programs, including life skills training, such as how to obtain housing and balance a checkbook, mental health and drug abuse treatment, faith-based programs, and re-entry/transitional programming.

Participation in these programs typically is thought to contribute to enhancing the goal of public safety. However, some correctional administrators and researchers have advocated for a broader view of the benefits of prison-based programs. They point to other long-term goals that these programs may be able to achieve, such as helping ex-offenders become contributing, healthy members of society; promoting the health and functioning of the children and families of ex-offenders; and supporting the well-being of communities to which inmates are released. But how exactly might these goals be achieved through prison programming?

Generally, there are two paths. The first, the direct route, is through achieving specific post-release outcomes, such as reduced recidivism, drug abuse or addiction, increased employment and housing, improved physical and mental health, and healthier family relationships. The second, the indirect route, is through the provision of additional post-release programming, which, in turn, leads to similar outcomes.

Often, the combination of both prison-based and post-release programming can lead to long-lasting positive outcomes than either could provide alone. In both instances, research suggests that fulfillment of the different outcomes, including reduced recidivism and drug use, stable employment and housing, and healthy family relationships, can contribute to long-term goals such as public safety and ex-offender, family and community well-being. Although these outcomes and goals are frequently difficult to measure, they nonetheless can and often do set the parameters for justifying and, ultimately, assessing the merits of prison-based programs.[17]

How Programs Should Work

To date, few data sources precisely identify the number of inmates who can be served by prison programs (e.g., what is the supply of available programs?). Similarly, few data allow researchers to assess the duration, content or quality of prison-based programming.[18] In fact, most departments of correction provide little information about their programs beyond mission statements, desired impacts and, possibly, the number of participants.

The problem thus arises: How can these programs be adequately evaluated? The answer is that most cannot. Evaluations generally are meaningless unless they measure what a program is supposed to change both in the short term (while an inmate is in prison) and in the long term (while an inmate is back in society). Although some programs may reduce the criminal behavior of released inmates, this may not be their primary outcome, or it may be an outcome that can be achieved only after other outcomes have been achieved.

The risk lies in applying an inappropriate standard of evaluation and, thus, concluding, methodological issues aside, that a program does not "work."[19] When held to the sole criterion of reduced recidivism, many programs, in fact, may not be effective. Other measures, such as reduced drug use or increased employment, may be more appropriate for assessing their effectiveness. Even if recidivism is the primary focus, attainment of other outcomes may constitute necessary first steps.

Consider a popular, long-standing programming effort: prison industries.[20] The more common industries include textiles and apparel, office furniture, wood and metal products, computers, automotive services, medical products and the traditional license plate industry. Before evaluating any of these industries, a critical first step is to identify the underlying logic of having inmates participate. That is, what is participation supposed to do or achieve?

In most cases, prison officials justify inmate involvement in prison industries on the grounds that it can reduce future criminal activity.[21] But the focus on reduced crime substantially understates the range of outcomes and goals that prison industries may yield and that are frequently included to justify them.[22]

For example, while incarcerated, participants in prison industries may internalize a work ethic, develop specific work skills and establish work histories. These changes may indirectly facilitate other positive outcomes, including improved behavior and performance in other areas of programming (e.g., education, drug treatment) and in their day-to-day behavior.

One result of these in-prison changes may be reduced recidivism upon re-entry. But other post-release outcomes may result as well, including reduced drug use/abuse, stable employment and housing, and improved physical and mental health and family relationships. These outcomes might interact as well. For example, stable employment might result in reduced stress and improved family relations. In turn, this interaction might result in increased public safety and improvements to the well-being of ex-offenders, their families and communities.

Thus, a successful prison industry might successfully affect more than recidivism. Indeed, the ability of many programs to exert a strong and direct effect on recidivism may be relatively nominal, especially given the range of factors that can contribute to criminal behavior. In many cases, measures other than recidivism might represent more appropriate criteria of success.

For this reason, it is important to identify how exactly a given prison industry is intended to affect participating inmates. Since different industries may imply different orientations and goals, the logic of each must be clearly articulated and then empirically assessed.

The same holds true for prison programs in general. For example, education programs presumably have different shorter-term outcomes than drug treatment programs, and the pathways to longer-term outcomes, including recidivism, also presumably differ. It is this "black box"—the way in which a program is supposed to change participants over time—that needs to be illuminated if research is to provide fair and appropriate assessments of any type of prison programming. With greater understanding of this black box, correctional officers may be able to identify and overcome the many different challenges to effective program implementation.[23]

Prison Programming: What Works?

Despite decades of research on prison programming, relatively little provides solid guidance about specific programs that correctional administrators should implement. This literature suggests that, generally speaking, education and employment-oriented programs, as well as drug and mental health treatment programs, can be effective along a range of dimensions.[24] But for the most part, research is largely silent about which specific programs work and for whom. And it is generally silent as well about how specific types of programs should be implemented.[25]

The good news, however, is that recent research identifies general principles that underlie effective prison-based programming.[26] Some of these principles confirm what common sense might dictate. For example, programs typically are more effective when they address each inmate's particular needs. If an inmate has a solid educational background, it would make little sense to provide educational programming, especially if it was to the exclusion of addressing other needs (e.g., mental health or drug treatment).

The principles of effective programming include:[27]

- Matching offender needs with program offerings;
- Targeting offender needs that are changeable and that may contribute to crime, such as attitudes and anti-social activities;
- Providing programs that cover each individual's needs and are well-integrated with other prison programs to avoid potential redundancy or conflict across programs;
- Providing programming for at least several months;
- Ensuring incarceration is followed by integrated treatment and services;
- Relying on effective program design, implementation and monitoring; and
- Involving researchers and practitioners in collaborative program evaluation efforts.

Some programs may be effective even if they do not include all these principles. In general, however, programs that adhere to them yield more positive outcomes. Correctional and program administrators, thus, can use these principles to guide programming decisions and to determine whether existing programs should be modified.

The integration of different programming efforts (e.g., substance abuse, education and vocational training) can help reduce redundancy as well as conflicts that may arise from differences in how inmates are viewed or treated from one program to the next. In addition, for any program to have a significant impact, inmates typically must participate for at least three to six months. The basic rule of thumb is that the greater the exposure to programming, the greater the impact. However, much remains unknown about exactly how much programming is ideal or whether programming is more effective at the beginning, end or throughout an inmate's incarceration.

Finally, the effective integration of prison-based programming with re-entry programs and services represents a neglected but critical strategy for enhancing desired longer-term outcomes. As noted earlier, the transition to society can be traumatic. Numerous obstacles, such as barriers to employment and medical care, can affect post-release transition.[28] Difficulties in obtaining stable housing pose considerable challenges and undermine the ability of ex-offenders to effectively reintegrate into society.[29] Aftercare services can be critical to overcoming these obstacles and ensuring that the impacts of prison-based interventions are realized.[30]

Conclusion

Effective programming constitutes a potentially critical and cost-effective strategy for promoting public safety and other long-term goals, such as the well-being of ex-offenders, their families and the communities.[31] It does not have to preclude a "get tough" approach to sanctioning. Indeed, tougher sanctioning (e.g., lengthier sentences) can go hand-in-hand with prison programming.

But without an increasing emphasis on enhancing and improved programming in prisons, the potential benefits of investing in prisons may not be fully realized. To be sure, there appears to be a modest incapacitating effect of prisons (i.e., offenders in prison cannot commit crimes), one that presumably can be realized without investing in programming.[32] Similarly, retribution and justice, which represent important considerations for policy-makers, do not necessarily require the provision of prison-based programs.

However, to increase the likelihood that inmates returning to society will successfully transition into productive citizens, with positive impacts on their families and communities, prison-based programming may represent one of society's best hopes for breaking the cycle of offending. Indeed, incarceration without programming can potentially aggravate the many problems that inmates face upon release. The cycle of release and return, therefore, can ensue and society suffers the consequences.

Fortunately, correctional administrators can point to an emerging body of research showing significant public safety impacts due to prison-based programming. They also can draw on a set of general principles of effective programming to guide both the implementation of new programs and modification of existing ones. As they do, they should strive to define explicitly what these programs are supposed to do, assess their operations and impacts, address particular obstacles to effective implementation and weed out programs that simply do not work.

If this process is seriously and consistently undertaken by correctional and program administrators, the chances increase that they can garner support from legislators for effective prison-based programming. They can do so by showing that investing in specific types of programming can result in improved prison management and longer-term positive post-release outcomes. From this perspective, prison programming represents an investment that can benefit inmates, correctional administrators and, ultimately, society.

Notes

1. Blumstein, Alfred and Alan J. Beck. 1999. Population growth in U.S. prisons, 1980–1996. In *Prisons*, eds. Michael H. Tonry and Joan Petersilia, vol. 26 of *Criminal justice: A review of research*, 17–61. Chicago: University of Chicago Press.
2. Lynch, James P. and William J. Sabol. 2001. *Prisoner re-entry in perspective*. Washington, D.C.: The Urban Institute.
3. General Accounting Office. 2001. *Prisoner releases: Trends and information on reintegration programs*. Washington, D.C.: U.S. General Accounting Office.
4. Gaes, Gerald G., Timothy J. Flanagan, Lawrence L. Motiuk and Lynn Stewart. 1999. Adult correctional treatment. In *Prisons*, eds. Michael H. Tonry and Joan Petersilia, vol. 26 of *Criminal justice: A review of research*, 361–426. Chicago: University of Chicago Press.
5. Travis, Jeremy and Joan Petersilia. 2001. Re-entry reconsidered: A new look at an old question. *Crime and Delinquency*, 47(3):291–313.
6. General Accounting Office.
7. LoBuglio, Stefan. 2001. Time to reframe politics and practices in correctional education. In *Annual review of adult learning and literacy*, ed. National Center for the Study of Adult Learning and Literacy, 111–150. New York: Jossey-Bass Publishers.
8. LoBuglio.
9. California Department of Corrections. 1997. *Preventing parolee failure program: An evaluation*. Sacramento, Calif.: California Department of Corrections.
10. California Department of Corrections.
11. Beck, Alan J. 2000. State and federal prisoners returning to the community: Findings from the Bureau of Justice Statistics. Paper presented at the First Re-Entry Courts Initiative Cluster Meeting, 13 April in Washington, D.C.
12. Bureau of Justice Statistics. 2000. *Correctional populations in the United States, 1997*. Washington, D.C.: Bureau of Justice Statistics.
13. Hammett, Theodore M. 2000. Health-related issues in prisoner reentry to the community. Paper presented for the Re-Entry Roundtable, 12 and 13 Oct. in Washington, D.C.
14. Maruschak, Laura M. and Alan J. Beck. 2001. *Medical problems of inmates, 1997*. Washington, D.C.: Bureau of Justice Statistics.
15. Travis, Jeremy, Amy L. Solomon and Michelle Waul. 2001. *From prison to home: The dimensions and consequences of prisoner re-entry*. Washington, D.C.: The Urban Institute.
16. Travis and Petersilia.
17. Travis and Petersilia.
18. Lawrence, Sarah, Daniel P. Mears, Glenn Dubin and Jeremy Travis. 2001. *Prison programming: A preliminary investigation of knowledge, practice and opportunities*. Washington, D.C.: The Urban Institute.
19. Gaes et al.
20. Sexton, George E. 1995. *Work in American prisons: Joint ventures with the private sector*. Washington, D.C.: National Institute of Justice.
21. Austin, James and John Irwin. 2001. *It's about time: America's imprisonment binge*. Belmont, Calif.: Wadsworth.
22. Gaes et al.
23. Farabee, David, Michael Prendergast, Jerome Cartier, Henry Wexler, Kevin Knight and Douglas M. Anglin. 1999. Barriers

to implementing effective correctional drug treatment programs. *The Prison Journal,* 79(2):150–162.

24. Gaes et al.
25. Gaes et al.
26. Gerber, Jurg and Eric J. Fritsch. 1995. Adult academic and vocational correctional educational programs: A review of recent research. *Journal of Offender Rehabilitation,* 22(1 and 2):119–142.
27. Lawrence et al. Based on Cullen, Francis T. and Paul Gendreau. 2000. Assessing correctional rehabilitation: Policy, practice and prospects. In *Criminal justice 2000: Policies, processes and decisions of the criminal justice system,* ed. Julie Horney, 109–176. Washington, D.C.: U.S. Department of Justice.
28. Travis et al.
29. Bradley, Katherine H., R.B. Michael Oliver, Noel C. Richardson and Espeth M. Slayter. 2001. *No place like home: Housing and the ex-prisoner.* Boston: Community Resources for Justice.
30. Cullen and Gendreau.
31. Cullen and Gendreau.
32. Spelman, William. 2000. The limited importance of prison expansion. In *The crime drop in America,* eds. Alfred Blumstein and Joel Wallman, 97–129. New York: Cambridge University Press.

Chapter 25
Denial of Parole

An Inmate Perspective

Mary West-Smith
Mark R. Pogrebin
Eric D. Poole

Research on parole decision making has focused almost exclusively on parole board members and how they decide whether to grant or deny parole. Here, the authors consider the inmates' perspective, specifically the viewpoint of inmates whose parole has been denied. Based on letters written by inmates to the Colorado parole board, the nature of the problems inmates experience is explored.

Like many other discretionary decisions made about inmates (e.g., classification, housing, treatment, discipline, etc.), those involving parole are rather complex. Parole board members typically review an extensive array of information sources in arriving at their decisions, and empirical research has shown a wide variation in the decision-making process. The bulk of research on parole decision-making dates from the mid 1960s to the mid 1980s (e.g., Gottfredson & Ballard, 1966; Rogers & Hayner, 1968; Hoffman, 1972; Wilkins & Gottfredson, 1973; Scott, 1974; Carroll & Mondrick, 1976; Heinz et al., 1976; Talarico, 1976; Garber & Maslach, 1977; Sacks, 1977; Carroll et al., 1982; Conley & Zimmerman, 1982; Lombardi, 1984). Virtually all of this research focuses on the discretion exercised by parole board members and the factors that affect their decisions to grant or deny parole. Surprisingly, only one study, conducted over 20 years ago, has examined the inmate's perspective on the parole decision-making process (Cole & Logan, 1977). The present study seeks to advance the work on parole decision-making from the point of view of those inmates who have had their release on parole denied.

Inmates denied parole have often been dissatisfied with what they consider arbitrary and inequitable features of the parole hearing process. While those denied parole are naturally likely to disagree with that decision, much of the lack of acceptance for parole decisions may well relate to lack of understanding. Even inmates who have an opportunity to present their case through a personal interview are sent out of the room while discussions of the case take place (being recalled only to hear the ultimate decision and a summary of the reasons for it). This common practice protects the confidentiality of individual board members' actions; however, it precludes the inmate from hearing the discussions of the case, evaluations of strengths and weaknesses, or prognosis for success or failure. More importantly, this practice fails to provide guidance in terms of how to improve subsequent chances for successful parole consideration. A common criticism of parole hearings has been that they produce little information relevant to an inmate's parole readiness (Morris, 1974; Fogel, 1975; Cole & Logan, 1977); thus, it is unlikely that those denied parole understand the basis for the decision or attach a sense of justice to it.

Parole Boards

The 1973 Supreme Court decision in *Scarpa v. United States Board of Parole* established the foundation for parole as an "act of grace." Parole is legally considered a privilege rather than a right; therefore, the decision to grant or deny it is "almost unreviewable" (Hier, 1973, p. 435). In fact, when federal courts have been petitioned to intervene and challenge parole board actions, the decisions of parole boards have prevailed (see *Menechino v. Oswald*, 1970; *Tarlton v. Clark*, 1971). While subsequent Court rulings have established minimal due process rights in prison disciplinary proceedings (*Wolff v. McDonnell*, 1974) and in parole revocation hearings (*Morrissey v. Brewer*, 1972), the parole hearing itself is still exempt from due process rights. Yet in *Greenholtz v. Nebraska* (1979) and *Board of Pardons v. Allen* (1987), the Supreme Court held that, although there is no constitutional right to parole, state statutes may create a protected liberty interest where a state's parole system entitles inmates to parole if they meet certain conditions. Under such circumstances, the state has created a presumption that inmates who meet specific requirements will be granted parole. Although the existence of a parole system does not by itself give rise to an expectation of parole, states may create that expectation or presumption by the wording of their statutes. For example, in both *Greenholtz* and *Allen*, the Supreme Court emphasized that the statutory language—the use of the word "shall" rather than "may"—creates the presumption that parole will be granted if certain conditions are met. However, if the statute is general, giving broad discretion to the parole board, no liberty interest is created and due process is not required. In Colorado, as in most other states with parole systems, the decision to grant parole before the inmate's mandatory release date is vested entirely within the discretion of the parole board. The legislatively-set broad guidelines for parole decision-making allow maximum exercise of discretion with minimal oversight.

In Colorado, the structure of parole board hearings depends on the seriousness of the inmate's offense. A full board review is required for all cases involving a violent crime or for inmates with a history of violence. A quorum for a full board review is defined as four of the seven parole board members and a decision to grant parole requires four affirmative votes. However, two parole board members conduct the initial hearing and submit their recommendation to a full board review. Single board members hear nonviolent cases. The board member considers the inmate's parole application, interviews the inmate, makes the release decision, and decides the conditions of parole. The personal interview may be face-to-face or by telephone. If the decision is to grant parole, an additional board member's signature is required. Given the variety of backgrounds and experiences board members bring to the job, individual interpretation and application of the broad statutory guidelines can make parole decision-making appear idiosyncratic.

In their 1986 study of parole decision-making in Colorado, Pogrebin and his colleagues (1986) concluded from their observations that the "overriding factor in parole decisions was not the relative merits of the inmate's case, but the structure of the board itself" (p. 153). At the time of their study, at least two board members rather than the current single board member made the majority of decisions. One may speculate that with only one decision-maker the decision to grant or deny parole is now even more dependent on the individual board member's background and philosophy.

Normalization and Routinization

Sudnow's (1965) classic study of the processes of normalization and routinization in the public defender's office offers insights into the decision-making processes in parole board hearings. Like Sudnow's public defender, who works as an employee of the court system with the judge and prosecutor and whose interests include the smooth functioning of the court system, the parole board member in Colorado works with the prison administration, caseworkers, and other prison personnel. Public defenders must represent all defendants assigned to them and attempt to give the defendants the impression they are receiving individualized representation. However, public defenders often determine the plea bargain acceptable to the prosecutor and judge, based on the defendant's prior and current criminal activities, prior to the first meeting with the defendant (Sudnow, 1965).

The parole board theoretically offers individual consideration of the inmate's rehabilitation and the likelihood of future offending when deciding whether or not to release an inmate. However, the parole board, like the public defender, places a great deal of emphasis on the inmate's prior and current criminal record. The tremendous volume of cases handled by the public defender necessitates the establishment of "normal crime" categories, defined by type and location of crime and characteristics of the defendant and victim, which permit the public defender to quickly and easily determine an appropriate and acceptable sentence. Such normalization and routinization facilitate the rapid flow of cases and the smooth functioning of the court system. Similarly, a two-year study of 5,000 parole decisions in Colorado in the early 1980s demonstrated that the parole board heard far too many cases to allow for individualized judgments (Pogrebin et al., 1986, p. 149).

Observations of parole hearings illustrate the rapid flow of cases and collaboration with other prison personnel. Typically, the case manager, in a brief meeting with the parole board member, discusses the inmate, his prior criminal history, current offense, institutional behavior, compliance with treatment programs, progress and current attitude, and makes a release or deferral recommendation to the parole board member prior to the inmate interview. The inmate and family members, if present, are then brought into the hearing room. The parole board member asks the inmate to describe his prior and current crimes, his motivation for those crimes, and the circumstances that led to the current offense. Typical inmate responses are that he was "stupid," "drunk," or "not thinking right." Inquiries by the parole board about the programs the inmate has completed are not the norm; however, the inmate is often asked how he thinks the victim would view his release. The inmate typically tries to bring up the progress he has made by explaining how much he has learned while institutionalized and talks about the programs he completed and what he learned from them. A final statement by the inmate allows him to express remorse for the pain he has caused others and to vow he will not get into another situation where he will be tempted to commit crimes. Family members are then given time to make a statement, after which the inmate and family leave the hearing room. A brief discussion between the parole board member and the case manager is followed by the recommendation to grant or defer parole. A common reason given for a deferral is "not enough time served." If parole is granted, the parole board member sets the conditions for parole.

"Normal" cases are disposed of very quickly. The time from the case manager's initial presentation of the case to the start of the next case is typically ten to fifteen minutes. Atypical cases require a longer discussion with the case manager before and after the inmate interview. Atypical cases also can involve input from other prison personnel (e.g., a therapist), rather than just the case manager. Those inmates who do not fit the norm, either through their background or the nature of their crime, are given special attention. The parole board member does not need to question the inmate to discover if the case is atypical since the case manager will inform him if there is anything unusual about the inmate or his situation.

During the hearing, the board member asks first about the prior and current crimes and what the inmate thinks were the causal factors that led to the commission of the crimes. Based on his observations of public defenders, Sudnow (1965) concludes, "It is not the particular offenses for which he is charged that are crucial, but the constellation of prior offenses and the sequential pattern they take" (p. 264). Like the public defender who attempts to classify the case into a familiar type of crime by looking at the circumstances of prior and current offenses, the parole board member also considers the criminal offense history and concentrates on causal factors that led the inmate to commit the crimes. It is also important for the board member that the inmate recognize the patterns of his behavior, state the reasons why he committed his prior and current crimes, and accept responsibility for them. The inmate, in contrast, generally wants to describe what he has learned while incarcerated and talk about the classes and programs he has completed. The interview exchange thus reveals two divergent perceptions of what factors should be emphasized in the decision-making process. In Sudnow's (1965) description of a jury trial involving a public defender, "the onlooker comes away with the sense of having witnessed not a trial at all, but a set of motions, a perfunctorily carried off event" (p. 274). In a similar manner, the observer at a parole board hearing has the impression of having witnessed a scripted, staged performance.

As a result of their journey through the criminal justice system, individual inmates in a prison have been typed and classified by a series of criminal justice professionals. The compilation of prior decisions forms the parole board member's framework for his or her perception of the inmate. The parole board member, with the help of previous decision-makers and through normalization and routinization, "knows" what type of person the inmate is. As Heinz et al. (1976) point out, "a system premised on the individualization of justice unavoidably conflicts with a caseload that demands simple decision rules.... To process their caseloads, parole boards find it necessary to develop a routine, to look for one or two or a few factors that will decide their cases for them" (p. 18). With or without the aid of parole prediction tools to help in their decision, parole board members feel confident they understand the inmate and his situation; therefore, their decisions are more often based on personal intuition than structured guidelines.

Theoretical Framework

Based on a combination of both formal and informal sources of information they acquire while in prison, inmates believe that satisfactory institutional behavior and completion of required treatment and educational programs, when combined with adequate time served, will result in their release on parole. They also believe that passing their parole eligibility date denotes sufficient institutional time. Denial of parole, when the stated prerequisites for parole have been met, leads to inmate anger and frustration. As stories of parole denials spread throughout the DOC population, inmates are convinced that the parole board is abusing its discretion to continue confinement when it is no longer mandated.

Control of Institutional Behavior

The majority of inmates appearing before the parole board have a fairly good record of institutional behavior (Dawson, 1978). Inmates are led to believe that reduction in sentence length is possible through good behavior (Emshoff & Davidson, 1987). Adjustment to prison rules and regulations is not sufficient reason for release on parole; however, it comprises a minimum requirement for parole and poor adjustment is a reason to deny parole (Dawson, 1978). Preparation for a parole hearing would be a waste of both the prisoner's and the case manager's time and effort if the inmate's behavior were not adequate to justify release.

Research suggests that good behavior while incarcerated does not necessarily mean that an inmate will successfully adapt to the community and be law-abiding following a favorable early-release decision (Haesler, 1992; Metchik, 1992). In addition, Emshoff and Davidson (1987) note that good time credit is not an effective deterrent for disruptive behavior. Inmates who are most immature may be those most successful at adjusting to the abnormal environment of prison; inmates who resist conformity to rules may be those best suited for survival on the outside (Talarico, 1976). However, institutional control of inmate behavior is a crucial factor for the maintenance of order and security among large and diverse prison populations, and the use of good time credit has traditionally been viewed as an effective behavioral control mechanism (Dawson, 1978). Inmates are led to believe that good institutional behavior is an important criterion for release, but it is secondary to the background characteristics of the inmate. Rather than good behavior being a major consideration for release, as inmates are told, only misbehavior is taken into account and serves as a reason to deny parole.

Inmates are also told by their case managers and other prison personnel that they must complete certain programs to be paroled. Colorado's statutory parole guidelines list an inmate's progress in self-improvement and treatment programs as a component to be assessed in the release decision (Colorado Department of Public Safety, 1994). However, the completion of educational or treatment programs by the inmate is more often considered a factor in judging the inmate's institutional adjustment, i.e., his ability to conform to program rules and regimen. Requiring inmates to participate in prison programs may be more important for institutional control than for the rehabilitation of the inmate. Observations of federal parole hearings suggest that the inmate's institutional behavior and program participation are given little importance in release decisions (Heinz et al.,

1976). Noncompliance with required treatment programs or poor institutional behavior may be reasons to deny parole, but completion of treatment programs and good institutional behavior are not sufficient reasons to grant parole.

Release Decision Variables

Parole board members and inmates use contrasting sets of variables each group considers fundamental to the release decision. Inmates believe that completion of treatment requirements and good institutional behavior are primary criteria the parole board considers when making a release decision. Inmates also feel strongly that an adequate parole plan and demonstration that their families need their financial and emotional support should contribute to a decision to release on parole.

In contrast, the parole board first considers the inmate's current and prior offenses and incarcerations. Parole board members also determine if the inmate's time served is commensurate with what they perceive as adequate punishment. If it is not, the inmate's institutional behavior, progress in treatment, family circumstances and parole plan will not outweigh the perceived need for punishment. Inmates, believing they understand how the system works, become angry and frustrated when parole is denied after they have met all the stated conditions for release.

Unwritten norms and individualized discretion govern parole board decision-making; thus, the resulting decisions become predictable only in retrospect as patterns in granting or denying parole emerge over time. For example, one of the difficulties Pogrebin et al. (1986) encountered in their study of parole board hearings in Colorado was developing a written policy based on previous case decisions:

> This method requires that a parole board be convinced that there exists a hidden policy in its individual decisions. . . . [M]ost parole board members initially will deny that they use any parole policy as such . . . [and] will claim that each case is treated on its own merits. . . . [However] parole decisions begin to fit a pattern in which decisions are based on what has been decided previously in similar situations (p. 149).

Method

In October of 1997, Colorado-CURE (Citizens United for Rehabilitation of Errants), a Colorado non-profit prisoner advocacy group, solicited information through its quarterly newsletter from inmates (who were members of the organization) regarding parole board hearings that resulted in a "setback," i.e., parole deferral. Inmates were asked to send copies of their appeals and the response they received from the parole board to Colorado-CURE. One hundred and eighty inmates responded to the request for information with letters ranging in length from very brief one- or two-paragraph descriptions of parole board hearings to multiple page diatribes listing not only parole board issues, but complaints about prison conditions, prison staff, and the criminal justice system in general. Fifty-two letters were eliminated from the study because they did not directly address the individual inmate's own parole hearing. One hundred and twenty-eight inmate letters were analyzed; one hundred and twenty-five from male and three from female inmates. Some letters contained one specific complaint about the parole board, but most inmates listed at least two complaints. Several appeals also contained letters written to the parole board by family members on the inmate's behalf. Two hundred and eighty- five complaints were identified and classified into thirteen categories utilizing content analysis, which "translates frequency of occurrence of certain symbols into summary judgments and comparisons of content of the discourse" (Starosta, 1984, p. 185). Content analytical techniques provide the means to document, classify, and interpret the communication of meaning, allowing for inferential judgments from objective identification of the characteristics of messages (Holsti, 1969). In addition, parole board hearings, including the preliminary presentation by the case manager and the discussion after the inmate interview, were observed over a three-month period in 1998. These observations were made to provide a context for understanding the nature of the hearing process from the inmate's perspective and to document the substantive matter of parole deliberations.

The purpose of the present study is not to explore the method the parole board uses to reach its release decisions; rather, our interest is to examine the content of the written complaints of inmates in response to their being denied parole.

Findings

Table 25.1 presents the frequency of complaints regarding parole denial and the percentage of inmates having each complaint. Those complaints relating to parole hearings following a return to prison for a parole violation and those complaints regarding sex offender laws will not be addressed in the following discussion. Parole revocation hearings are governed by different administrative rules and are subject to more rigorous due process requirements and are thus beyond the scope of the current study. In addition, sex offender sentencing laws in Colorado have evolved through dramatic changes in legislation over the past several years and a great deal of confusion exists regarding which inmates are eligible for parole, when they are eligible, and what conditions can be imposed when inmates are paroled. Future analysis of sex offender laws is necessary to clarify this complex situation. We now turn to an examination of the remaining categories of inmate complaints concerning parole denial.

Inadequate Time Served

Forty-eight percent of the inmates reported "inadequate time served" as a reason given for parole deferment. Their attempt to understand the "time served" component in the board's decision is exemplified by the following accounts:

> . . . if you don't meet their [the parole board's] time criteria you are "not" eligible. Their time criteria is way more severe than statute. . . . [The risk assessment] also says, if you meet their time amounts and score 14 or less on the assessment you "shall" receive parole. This does not happen. The board is an entity with entirely too much power. . . .

* * *

> I don't understand how your P.E.D. [parole eligibility date] can come up and they can say you don't have enough time in.

* * *

> If the court wanted me to have more time, it could have aggravated my case with as much as eight years. Now the parole board is making itself a court!

* * *

> . . . I [was] set back again for six months with the reason being, not enough time spent in prison. I've done 5 calendar years, I'm two years past my P.E.D., this is my first and only felony of my life, I've never been to prison, it's a

Table 25.1
Frequency of Complaints and Percentage of Inmates Having Complaint

Nature of Complaint	Frequency of Complaints	Percentage of Inmates with Complaint
1. Inadequate time served, yet beyond P.E.D.	61	48%
2. Completed required programs	45	35%
3. Denied despite parole plan	35	27%
4. Board composition and behavior	27	21%
5. Longer setbacks after parole violation	26	20%
6. Family need for inmate support ignored	22	17%
7. Case manager not helpful	17	13%
8. New sex offender laws applied retroactively	16	12%
9. Required classes not available	11	9%
10. Few inmates paroled on same day	7	5%
11. Appeals not considered on individual basis	6	4%
12. Miscellaneous	12	9%
	N = 285	N = 128

> non-violent offense, it's not a crime of recidivism, I do not earn a livelihood from this crime or any criminal activity. So what is their problem?
>
> * * *
>
> [Enclosed] is a copy of my recent deferral for parole, citing the infamous "Not enough time served" excuse. This is the third time they've used this reason to set me back, lacking a viable one.

These responses of the inmates to the "inadequate time served" reason for parole deferral demonstrate that they believe the parole board uses a different set of criteria than the official ones for release decisions. Inmates do not understand that the "time served" justification for parole deferment relates directly to the perception by the parole board member of what is an acceptable punishment for their crime. They believe the parole board is looking for a reason to deny parole and uses "time served" when no other legitimate reason can be found.

Completed Required Programs

Thirty-five percent of the inmates complained that their parole was deferred despite completing all required treatment and educational programs. Related complaints, expressed by 9 percent of the inmates, were the lack of mandatory classes and the long waiting lists for required classes. The following excerpts from inmate letters reflect this complaint:

> When I first met with them [the parole board] I received a 10 month setback to complete the classes I was taking (at my own request). But [I] was told once I completed it and again met the board I was assured of a release. . . . Upon finishing these classes I met the board again [a year later]. . . . I noticed that none of my 7 certificates to date were in the file and only a partial section of the court file was in view. I tried to speak up that I was only the 5th or 6th person to complete the 64 week class and tell about the fact that I carry a 4.0 in work plus have never had a COPD conviction or a write-up. He silenced me and said that meant nothing. . . . I later was told I had been given another one year setback!!!
>
> * * *
>
> They gave me a six month setback because they want me to take another A.R.P. class. . . . [I]t was my first time down [first parole hearing], and I have taken A.R.P. already twice. . . . I have also taken . . . Independent Living Skills, Job Search, Alternatives to Violence, workshops and training in nonviolence, Advanced Training for Alternatives to Violence Project, mental health classes conducted by addiction recovery programs. I also chair the camp's A.A. meetings every week and just received my two year coin. I have also completed cognitive behavioral core curriculum. . . .
>
> * * *
>
> I'm one of the Colorado inmates that's been shipped to Minnesota. . . . I went before the parole board [in Colorado] . . . and they set me back a year, claiming that I needed to complete the mental health classes. . . . Then Colorado sends me to Minnesota where they don't even offer the mental classes that the board stated I needed to complete.

Inmates view completion of required programs as proof that they have made an effort to rehabilitate themselves and express frustration when the parole board does not recognize their efforts. The completion of classes was usually listed with other criteria the inmates viewed as important for their release on parole.

Parole Denied Despite Parole Plan

Deferral of parole even though a parole plan had been submitted was a complaint listed by 27 percent of inmates. It is interesting to note that this complaint never appeared as a solo concern, but was always linked to other issues. These inmates seem to believe that a strong parole plan alone will not be sufficient to gain release and that the parole plan must be combined with good institutional behavior and the completion of required classes. Even when all required criteria are met, parole was often deferred. The frustration of accomplishing all of the requirements yet still being deferred is expressed in the following excerpts:

> . . . I was denied for the third time by the D.O.C. parole board even though I have completed all recommended classes (Alcohol Ed. I and II,

> Relapse Prevention, Cognitive Skills and Basic Mental Health). I have a place to parole to [mother's house], a good job and a very strong support group consisting of family and friends. . . . To the present date I have served 75% of my 3-year sentence.
>
> * * *
>
> I had everything I needed to make parole, i.e. an approved plan, job, adequate time served. . . . [The parole board member] listed "release" on my paperwork, but "release denied" on my MRD (mandatory release date).
>
> * * *
>
> [After having problems with a previous address for the parole plan] . . . my parents and family . . . were assured . . . that all I needed to do is put together an alternative address. I managed to qualify for and arrange to lease a new low-income apartment at a new complex. . . . My family was helping with this. I also saw to it that I was preapproved at [a shelter in Denver], a parole office approved address, so that I could go there for a night or two if needed while I rented and had my own apartment approved by the parole office. My family expected me home, and I had hoped to be home and assisting them, too. I arranged employment from here, and looked forward to again being a supportive father and son. . . . I received a one-year setback! I was devastated, and my family is too. We are still trying to understand all of this. . . . I am . . . angry at seeing so many sources of support, employment, and other opportunities that I worked so hard at putting together now be lost.

Preparing an adequate parole plan requires effort on the part of both the inmate and the case manager. When a parole plan is coupled with completion of all required treatment and educational programs and good institutional behavior, the inmate is at a loss to understand how the parole board can deny parole. Inmates often expressed frustration that the plans they made for parole might not be available the next time they are eligible for parole. "Inadequate time served" is often the stated reason for parole deferment in these cases and does not indicate to the inmate changes he needs to make in order to be paroled in the future.

Parole Board Composition and Behavior

Twenty-one percent of the inmates complained about the composition of the parole board or about the attitude parole board members displayed toward the inmate and his or her family. Several inmates expressed concern that at the majority of hearings, only one parole board member is present and the outcome of an inmate's case might depend on the background of the parole board member hearing the case:

> The man [parole board member] usually comes alone, and he talks to the women worse than any verbal abuser I have ever heard. He says horrible things to them about how bad they are and usually reduces them to tears. Then he says they are "too emotionally unstable to be paroled!" If they stand up for themselves, they have "an attitude that he can't parole." If they refuse to react to his cruel proddings, they are "too cold and unfeeling." No way to win!! Why in the world do we have ex-policemen on the parole board?? Cops always want to throw away the key on all criminals, no matter what. Surely that could be argued . . . as conflict of interest!
>
> * * *
>
> As I was sitting in the parole hearing for me I was asked some pretty weird questions. Like while I was assaulting my victim was I having sex with my wife also. My answer was yes. Then this man [the parole board member] says, "Sounds like you had the best of both worlds, huh?" I was taken back by this comment and wonder why in the world this guy would think that this was the best of any world.
>
> * * *
>
> My hearing was more of an inquisition than a hearing for parole. All of the questions asked of me were asked with the intent to set me back and not the intent of finding reasons to parole me. It was my belief that when a person became parole eligible the purpose was to put them out, if possible. My hearing officer did nothing but look for reasons to set me back.

Inmates often expressed the view that the parole board members conducting their hearings did not want to listen to their stories. However, if parole board members have generally reached a decision prior to interviewing the inmate, as indicated by the routinization of the hearing process, it is logical that the board member would attempt to limit the inmate's presentation. In addition, if board members have already determined that parole will be deferred, one would expect the questions to focus on reasons to deny parole. One inmate stated, "I believe that the parole board member that held my hearing abused his discretion. I had the distinct feeling that he had already decided to set me back before I even stepped into the room."

Family's Need for Inmate's Support

Many inmates criticized the parole board for failing to take into account their families' financial, physical, and emotional needs. Seventeen percent of the inmates expressed this concern, and several included copies of letters written by family members asking the board to grant parole. The primary concerns were support for elderly parents and dependent young children:

> My mom has Lou Gehrig's disease. . . . [S]he can't walk and it has spread to her arms and shoulders. . . . [No] one will be there during the day to care for her. The disease is fast moving. . . . My mom is trying to get me home to care for her. . . . I am a non-violent first time offender. I have served 8 years on a 15. I have been before the parole board 5 times and denied each time. . . . (I got 6, 6, 9, 6, 12 month setbacks in that order). Why I'm being denied I'm unsure. I've asked the board and wasn't told much. I've completed all my programs, college, have a job out there, therapy all set up, and a good parole plan.

* * *

> I have everything going for me in the community. I have a full-time job. I have a 2-year-old son that needs me. I have a mother that is elderly and needs my help. This is all over an ounce of marijuana from [1994] and a walkaway from my own house. I have over 18 months in on an 18 month sentence.

* * *

> [My 85-year-old mother] has no one. Her doctor also wrote [to the chair of the parole board] as well as other family members, including my son. All begging for my release. She needs me!! I wish you could [see] . . . how hard I have worked since I have been in prison. . . . Being good and trying hard does not count for much in here. . . . This is my 5th year on an 8 year sentence.

The parole board does not consider a dependant family as a primary reason to release an inmate on parole; however, inmates regard their families' needs as very important and are upset that such highly personal and emotionally charged circumstances are given short shrift during their parole hearing. And if they believe they have met the conditions established for release, inmates do not understand why the parole board would not allow them to return home to help support a family.

Case Manager Not Helpful

Thirteen percent of the inmates expressed frustration with their case manager, with a few accusing the case manager of actually hurting their chances to make parole. Although the inmate was not present during the case manager's presentation to the board member, many inmates declared satisfaction with their case manager and felt that the board did not listen to the case manager's recommendation. Since the present study focuses on inmate complaints, the following excerpts document the nature of the dissatisfaction inmates expressed concerning their case managers:

> [The case manager] has a habit of ordering inmates to waive their parole hearings. Many inmates are angry and do not know where to turn because they feel it is their right to attend their parole hearings. . . . [He] forces most all of his caseload to waive their parole hearing. That is not right! . . . How and why is this man allowed to do this? I would not like my name mentioned because I fear the consequences I will pay. . . . [T]his man is my case manager and I have not seen the parole board yet.

* * *

> I have not had any writeups whatsoever and I have been taking some drug and alcohol classes since I have been back [parole revoked for a dirty U.A.]. I had a real strong parole plan that I thought that my case manager submitted but he never bothered to. I was planning on going to live with my father who I never asked for anything in my life and he was willing to help

> me with a good job and a good place to live. My father had also wrote to [the chair of the parole board] and asked if I could be paroled to him so he can help me change my life around.
>
> * * *
>
> [Some] case managers are not trained properly and do not know what they are doing. Paperwork is seldom done properly or on time. Others are downright mean and work against the very people they are to help. Our liberty depends on these people, and we have no one else to turn to when they turn against us.

Inmates realize they must at least have a favorable recommendation by the case manager if they are to have any chance for parole. Yet they generally view the case manager as a "marginal advocate," often going through the motions of representing their interests but not really supporting or believing in them. Case managers after all are employees of the Department of Corrections, and their primary loyalties are seen by inmates to attach to their employer and "the system."

Few Inmates Paroled the Same Day

Five percent of the inmates related in their letters that very few inmates were paroled on a given hearing day, leading them to suspect that the parole board typically denies release to the vast majority of inmates who come up for a hearing.

> I just received a letter . . . and she told me that 2 out of 24 made parole from [a Colorado women's facility]. . . . [Also] out of 27 guys on the ISP non-res program from [a community corrections facility] only 4 made parole!! . . . What is going on here?!! These guys [on ISP] are already on parole for all intents and purposes.
>
> * * *
>
> Went [before parole board] in June '97. 89 went. 2 made it (mandatory).
>
> * * *
>
> I realize they're not letting very many people go on parole or to community. It's not politically correct to parole anyone. Now that Walsenburg is opening, I'm sure they will parole even less people. I have talked to 14 people that seen the Board this week. 2 setbacks. . . .

Inmates circulate such stories and cite them as evidence that the parole board is only interested in keeping prisoners locked up. Many inmates express their belief that the parole board is trying to guarantee that all the prisons are filled to capacity.

Appeals Not Considered on an Individual Basis

Although Colorado-CURE asked inmates to send copies of their appeal and the response to the appeal, the majority of inmates mailed copies of their appeal before they received the response. Thus, it is not surprising that only four percent of the inmates discussed the apparent uniformity of appeal decisions. The standard form letter from the chair of the parole board, included by those who stated this complaint, reads as follows:

> I have reviewed your letter . . . , along with your file, and find the Board acted within its statutory discretion. Consequently, the decision of the Board stands.

Word of the appeals circulates among the general prison population and between prisons via letters to other inmates. Inmates suggest that the form letters are evidence that the parole board is not willing to review cases and reconsider decisions made by individual board members.

> I finally got their response. They are basically sending everyone the same form letter. I was told by someone else that it [is] what they were doing and sure enough that is what they are doing.
>
> * * *
>
> After receiving the denial of my appeal, I spoke with a fellow convict about his dilemma, which prompted him to show me a copy of his girlfriend's denial of her appeal. . . . It seems that [she] was given an unethical three (3) year setback, even though she has now completed 3/4 of her sentence. And she too received a carbon copy response from the [chair of the parole board's] office. It should be crystal clear that these files are not being reviewed as is stated in [the] responses, because if they had

been, these decisions would surely seem questionable at best.

Conclusion

The nature of the written complaints reflects the belief among many inmates that the parole board in Colorado is using criteria for release decisions that are hidden from inmates and their families. A parole board decision, made without public scrutiny by members who have no personal knowledge of the inmate, depends on the evaluation of the likelihood of recidivism by others in the criminal justice system. While guidelines and assessment tools have been developed to help with the decision-making process in Colorado, it is unclear the extent to which they are used. Release decisions by the parole board appear to be largely subjective and to follow latent norms that emerge over time. The emphasis on past and current crimes indicates that inmates—regardless of their institutional adjustment or progress in treatment, vocational, or educational programs—will continue to be denied parole until they have been sufficiently punished for their crimes. As one inmate lamented in his letter of complaint,

> When the inmate has an approved parole plan, a job waiting and high expectations for the future and then is set back a year . . . , he begins to die a slow death. They very often use the reason: Not enough time served to set people back. If I don't have enough time served, why am I seeing the parole board? Or they will say: *Needs Continued Correctional Treatment.* If I have maintained a perfect disciplinary record and conformed to the rules, what more correctional treatment do I need. . . . I had a parole plan and a job in May when I seen the Board. I was set back one year. I will see them in March. . . . I will have no job and nowhere to live. . . . The Colorado Dept. of Corrections does not rehabilitate inmates. That is solely up to the inmate. What they do is cause hate and bitterness and discontent.

Findings of this study indicate that the factors inmates believe affect release decisions are different from the factors the parole board considers and thus suggest why inmates fail to understand why their parole is deferred despite compliance with the prerequisites imposed upon them. As evidenced by the above examples, inmates are not only confused and angry when they believe parole should be granted, they begin to question whether or not it is worth the effort if they are only going to "kill their numbers" (i.e., serve the full sentence). The prison grapevine and the flow of information among the entire Department of Corrections inmate population allow such stories and theories to spread. Prison officials should be concerned that if inmates feel compliance with prison rules and regulations is pointless, they will be less likely to conform to the administration's requirements for institutional control. Currently, inmates who are turned down for parole see themselves as victims, unfairly denied what they perceive they have earned and deserve. Each parole eligible case that is deferred or set back becomes another story, duly embellished, that makes its rounds throughout the prison population, fueling suspicion, resentment, and fear of an unbridled discretionary system of power, control, and punishment.

Inmates denied parole are entitled to a subsequent hearing usually within one calendar year. But the uncertainty of never knowing precisely when one will be released can create considerable tension and frustration in prison. While discretionary release leaves them in limbo, it is the unpredictability of release decisions that is demoralizing. As we have found, this process has resulted in bitter complaints from inmates. Perhaps the late Justice Hugo Black of the U.S. Supreme Court best summarized the view of many inmates toward the parole board:

> In the course of my reading—by no means confined to law—I have reviewed many of the world's religions. The tenets of many faiths hold the deity to be a trinity. Seemingly, the parole boards by whatever names designated in the various states have in too many instances sought to enlarge this to include themselves as members. (Quoted in Mitford, 1973, p. 216)

References

Board of Pardons v. Allen, 482 U.S. 369 (1987).

Carroll, J.S., Wiener, R.L., Coates, D., Galegher, J., & Alirio, J.J. (1982). Evaluation, diagnosis, and prediction in parole decision making. *Law and Society Review, 17*, 199–228.

Carroll, L., & Mondrick, M.E. (1976). Racial bias in the decision to grant parole. *Law and Society Review, 11,* 93–107.

Cole, G.F., & Logan, C.H. (1977). Parole: The consumer's perspective. *Criminal Justice Review, 2,* 71–80.

Colorado Department of Public Safety. (1994). *Parole guidelines handbook.* Denver, CO: Division of Criminal Justice.

Conley, J.A., & Zimmerman, S.E. (1982). Decision making by a part-time parole board: An observational and empirical study. *Criminal Justice and Behavior, 9,* 396–431.

Dawson, R. (1978). The decision to grant or deny parole. In B. Atkins and M. Pogrebin (Eds.), *The invisible justice system: Discretion and the law* (pp. 360–389). Cincinnati: Anderson.

Emshoff, I.G., & Davidson, W.S. (1987). The effect of "good time" credit on inmate behavior: A quasi-experiment. *Criminal Justice and Behavior, 14,* 335–351.

Fogel, D. (1975). . . . *We are the living proof: The justice model for corrections.* Cincinnati: Anderson.

Garber, R.M., & Maslach, C. (1977). The parole hearing: Decision or justification? *Law and Human Behavior, 1,* 261–281.

Gottfredson, D.M., & Ballard, K.B. (1966). Differences in parole decisions associated with decision-makers. *Journal of Research in Crime and Delinquency, 3,* 112–119.

Greenholtz v. Nebraska Penal Inmates, 442 U.S. 1 (1979).

Haesler, W.T. (1992). The released prisoner and his difficulties to be accepted again as a "normal" citizen. *Euro-Criminology, 4,* 61–68.

Heinz, A.M., Heinz, J.P., Senderowitz, S.I., & Vance, M.A. (1976). Sentencing by parole board: An evaluation. *Journal of Criminal Law and Criminology, 67,* 1–31.

Hier, A.P. (1973). Curbing abuse in the decision to grant or deny parole. *Harvard Civil Rights—Civil Rights Law Review, 8,* 419–468.

Hoffman, P.B. (1972). Parole policy. *Journal of Research in Crime and Delinquency, 9,* 112–133.

Holsti, O.R. (1969). *Content analysis for the social sciences and humanities.* Reading, MA: Addison-Wesley.

Lombardi, J.H. (1984). The impact of correctional education on length of incarceration: Non-support for new paroling policy motivation. *Journal of Correctional Education, 35,* 54–57.

Menechino v. Oswald, 430 F.2d 402 (2nd Cir. 1970).

Metchik, E. (1992). Judicial views of parole decision processes: A social science perspective. *Journal of Offender Rehabilitation, 18,* 135–157.

Mitford, J. (1973). *Kind and unusual punishment: The prison business.* New York: Knopf.

Morris, N. (1974). *The future of imprisonment.* Chicago: University of Chicago Press.

Morrissey v. Brewer, 408 U.S. 471 (1972).

Pogrebin, M.R., Poole, E.D., & Regoli, R.M. (1986). Parole decision making in Colorado. *Journal of Criminal Justice, 14,* 147–155.

Rogers, J., & Hayner, N.S. (1968). Optimism and accuracy in perceptions of selected parole prediction items. *Social Forces, 46,* 388–400.

Sacks, H.R. (1977). Promises, performance, and principles: An empirical study of parole decision making in Connecticut. *Connecticut Law Review, 9,* 347–423.

Scarpa v. U.S. Board of Parole, 414 U.S. 934 (1973).

Scott, I.E. (1974). The use of discretion in determining the severity of punishment for incarcerated offenders. *Journal of Criminal Law and Criminology, 65,* 214–224.

Starosta, W.J. (1984). Qualitative content analysis: A Burkean perspective. In W. Gudykunst & Y.Y. Kim (Eds.), *Methods for intercultural communication research* (pp. 185–194). Beverly Hills, CA: Sage.

Sudnow, D. (1965). Normal crimes: Sociological features of the penal code in a public defender's office. *Social Problems, 12,* 255–276.

Talarico, S.M. (1976). The dilemma of parole decision making. In G.F. Cole (Ed.), *Criminal justice: Law and politics,* 2nd edition (pp. 447–456). North Scituate, MA: Duxbury.

Tarlton v. Clark, 441 F.2d 384 (5th Cir. 1971), *cert. denied,* 403 U.S. 934 (1971).

Wilkins, L.T., & Gottfredson, D.M. (1973). *Information selection and use in parole decision-making: Supplemental report V.* Davis, CA: National Council on Crime and Delinquency.

Wolff v. McDonnell, 418 U.S. 539 (1974).

Mary West-Smith, Mark R. Pogrebin, and Eric D. Poole, "Denial of Parole: An Inmate Perspective." Reprinted from *Federal Probation,* December 2000, 64 (2): 3–10. Published by The Administrative Offices of the United States Courts. ✦

Chapter 26

Community Supervision, Prosocial Activities, and Recidivism

Doris Layton MacKenzie
Robert Brame

Control theory maintains that when children are coerced into prosocial behavior, they form stronger attachments, conform to societal mores, and are less likely to fall into delinquency. The authors propose that the same coercion can be used to rehabilitate criminal offenders, that those who become involved in prosocial behaviors will be less likely to commit new crimes. Using data from four states, they analyze inmates' involvement in prosocial activities and recidivism rates to explore a possible correlation.

Theorists in the control tradition (Gottfredson and Hirschi 1990; Hirschi 1969; Nye 1958; Sampson and Laub 1993) have emphasized the importance of coercion in normal socialization processes. Although many control theorists focus on the importance of coercion and direct control during childhood, this approach also may be useful for explaining behavior changes and transitions during adulthood. From this perspective, both youthful and adult offenders may be coerced into becoming involved in prosocial behavior patterns that can increase their investments in conformity and their attachments to other people, employment, school, or the community. That is, the direct control of behavior through legal coercion is predicted to increase compliance with conventional norms, rules, and prosocial activities. These activities, in turn, may enhance the socialization process leading to increased social controls.

In this paper we hypothesize that the use of coercive interactions beyond childhood will be useful for decreasing the probability of future criminal behavior. Specifically, coercion of offenders to engage in prosocial behaviors should be associated with increased involvement in such behaviors. In addition, individuals who exhibit the greatest involvement in prosocial behaviors will exhibit reduced risk of subsequent involvement in criminal activity. Figure 26.1 presents a summary of the hypothesized relationships.

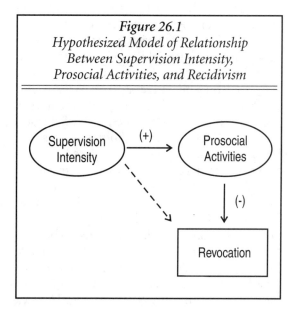

Figure 26.1
Hypothesized Model of Relationship Between Supervision Intensity, Prosocial Activities, and Recidivism

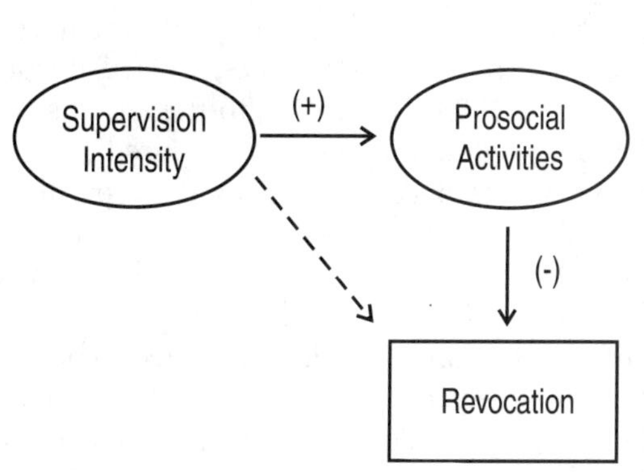

Socialization and the Internalization of Social Norms

The importance of coercion is perhaps most apparent in the literature on the implications of parenting practices for youths' future antisocial behavior. Rankin and Wells (1990:142), following Nye (1958), argue that coercion or "direct controls" on behavior take the form of "normative regulation" (i.e., the establishment of ground rules for children), "monitoring" (i.e., surveillance or direct supervision), and discipline or punishment for misbehavior. An important feature of such coercion is that it involves the "immediate application (or threat) of punishments and rewards to gain compliance with conventional norms" (Rankin and Wells 1990:142).

Coercive interactions in themselves have not traditionally been viewed as viable long-term solutions for controlling problem behavior (Gottfredson and Hirschi 1990:94–105; Nye 1958:7; Sampson and Laub 1993:65–71). The long-term value of coercive and controlling practices lies in their ability to induce socialization: for example, compliance with and (indeed) internalization of social norms (Gottfredson and Hirschi 1990:97; Sampson and Laub 1993:67). This individual internalization creates a web of disincentives for engaging in antisocial behaviors (Dishion and Patterson 1997; Nagin and Paternoster 1993, 1994).

Although some theorists assert that the tendency toward antisocial behavior is established early in life and does not change thereafter (Gottfredson and Hirschi 1990; Wilson and Herrnstein 1985), others take a different view (Nagin and Paternoster 1993, 1994; Sampson and Laub 1993). According to the latter, social bonds or "capital" that can be acquired in childhood, adolescence, or adulthood are predicted to be important barriers to offending in adulthood. From this viewpoint, individuals who have few social skills or who engage in frequent antisocial behavior are hypothesized to be relatively unlikely to acquire and maintain valuable relationships and ties to conventionality, but the possibility is not ruled out. For example, on the basis of their research on the Glueck and Glueck (1950) subjects, Sampson and Laub (1993) contend that factors such as conventional occupations and affective attachments to spouses constitute key barriers to adult offending, even among adults who offended as youths. Such attachments are associated with reduced criminal activity and are important in ending criminal careers. Yet, if social controls such as these are not strengthened, argue Sampson and Laub, offending is likely to continue.

In support of theories that identify temporally proximate causes of offending during the adult years, Horney, Osgood, and Marshall (1995) have shown how initiation and disruption of both informal and formal social controls, even if temporary or transient, can account respectively for short-term desistance from and resumption of criminal offending. Although these sources of social control may not produce meaningful increases in long-term socialization (i.e., "deep" change), Horney et al. (1995:670) speculate that these influences are likely to be important discriminators between those who exhibit meaningful change and those who do not.

Control theorists have not fully specified factors leading to the development of social controls beyond childhood. The etiology appears to be exogenous or even fortuitious (Laub and Sampson 1993:317–18; Nagin and Paternoster 1994:582–83; Sampson and Laub 1993:141–42,250). Thus social controls may develop through chance or highly circumstantial occurrences. In short, as Nagin and Paternoster observed, the development of social control may represent a critical pathway leading away from offending, but there is little available evidence or theoretical guidance indicating how these controls might develop initially.

In this paper we consider the idea that direct controls over the behavior of adult offenders may start a process of socialization, as in childhood. That is, the imposition of direct controls may coerce offenders to participate in prosocial activities; the activities, in turn, may initiate changes in offenders that increase their ties or commitments to conventional behavior patterns; these ties, in turn, create barriers to future offending. Thus intensive supervision is important not because of its direct impact on criminal activity, but because of its influence on the initiation of prosocial activities.

Intensive Community Supervision

Intensive supervision programs typically subject offenders to more frequent contact with supervising officers and compel them to engage in certain activities as conditions of supervision. Research on intensive community supervision has not yet found a consistent relationship between increased supervision and reduced recidivism (see Clear and Braga 1995; Erwin 1986; Land, McCall, and Williams 1990; Lurigio and Petersilia 1992; Pearson 1988; Petersilia and Turner 1993; Turner, Petersilia, and Deschenes 1992). Yet this research has demonstrated with some consistency that offenders in intensive supervision programs are more likely to enter counseling and treatment programs and to secure employment. This finding suggests that they are coerced, in some sense, into participating in these prosocial activities (Land et al. 1990; Latessa and Vito 1988; Pearson 1988; Petersilia and Turner 1993; Turner et al. 1992).

In line with the evaluations of intensive supervision, research on releasees from boot camps, conducted by MacKenzie and her colleagues (MacKenzie, Shaw, and Souryal 1992; MacKenzie and Souryal 1994), also yielded inconsistent results when these authors examined the direct association between supervision intensity (for probationers, parolees, and boot camp releasees) and recidivism. They found evidence, however, that the intensity of supervision was associated with increased involvement in prosocial activities such as accepting responsibility for actions, achieving financial and residential stability, making satisfactory progress in treatment and education programs, and job stability.

The drug treatment literature offers further evidence that prosocial activities can be coerced. Anglin and Hser (1990), for example, reviewed a large number of drug treatment evaluation studies. Some of these evaluations focused on the effects of legally coerced drug treatment on subsequent behavior. Traditionally the major objection to coerced treatment is that therapeutic interventions will not be effective unless the treated individual is motivated to respond. Yet Anglin and Hser concluded, from their review, that clients who participated in legally coerced treatment stayed in treatment for longer periods and that the length of participation was associated with better outcomes regardless of whether treatment was coerced (also see DeLeon 1988; Gendreau, Cullen, and Bonta 1994; Wexler, Lipton, and Johnson 1988; Wish and Johnson 1986).

Overall, previous research found no consistent relationship between intensity of community supervision and recidivism. Studies of drug treatment and intermediate sanctions, however, suggest that it may be possible to legally coerce involvement in prosocial activities. We hypothesize that involvement in such activities will be associated with a reduced probability of future offending. Unlike earlier analyses, this investigation is concerned with the relationship between involvement in prosocial activities and revocation for new criminal activity after taking into account all measured factors (including supervision intensity) thought to affect both outcomes. In previous analyses, these outcomes were examined separately; here we focus on their joint distribution. Although our analysis suffers several important limitations (which we discuss below), we believe that it provides a useful initial assessment of the problem and offers a framework for future analyses of this problem.

Methods

Research Design

The data for this study were collected as part of a larger eight-state evaluation of boot camp prisons (also called shock incarceration programs) (MacKenzie 1994; MacKenzie and Souryal 1994). In the analysis presented here we relied on data collected in four of these states (Florida, Georgia, Louisiana, and South Carolina), where data sufficient for examining the hypothesized links (see Figure 26.1) were available. Within each state, offenders from several comparison subsamples (boot camp completers, dropouts, prison parolees, and probationers) were followed during the first year of community supervision. Offenders were not assigned randomly to these samples, but they all met formal eligibility criteria for inclusion in the boot camp sample in their respective states. These subsamples' comparative performances have been examined elsewhere (MacKenzie 1994; MacKenzie and Souryal 1994). Here we emphasize the empirical validity of the hypothesized patterns of association between supervision intensity, involvement in prosocial activities, and recidivism (as measured by revocation for new criminal activity).

Study Variables

As shown in Table 26.1, the samples from the different states varied somewhat. Florida had the largest number of dropouts from the boot

Table 26.1
Descriptive Statistics

Variables	Florida (*N* = 274) Mean (SD) or %	Range	Georgia (*N* = 238) Mean (SD) or %	Range	Louisiana (*N* = 247) Mean (SD) or %	Range	South Carolina (*N* = 230) Mean (SD) or %	Range
Sample Categories								
Boot camp completers (%)	38.0		30.7		27.9		35.2	
Boot camp dropouts (%)	23.7				5.7			
Probationers (%)			32.4		37.7		37.8	
Prison releasees (%)	38.3		37.0		28.7		27.0	
Individual Characteristics								
Race (% nonwhite)	56.9		60.9		64.4		55.2	
Age (in years)	19.4 (1.8)	16 to 25	21.7 (2.8)	17 to 33	25.1 (5.4)	17 to 47	21.1 (2.3)	18 to 30
Current offense								
% Violent	32.8		14.3		9.3		13.9	
% Drug-related	14.6		27.7		29.6		22.6	
% Property & other	52.6		58.0		61.1		63.5	
Prior offending record (% Yes)	27.4		31.1		83.4		58.7	
Community Supervision Data								
Supervision intensity	1.4 (.9)	0 to 4.2	1.0 (.5)	0 to 3.4	.7 (.8)	0 to 4	.9 (.5)	0 to 2.6
Prosocial activities	.0 (1.0)	−1.4 to 2.3	.0 (1.0)	−1.7 to 2.5	.0 (1.0)	−2.6 to 2.7	.0 (1.0)	−1.7 to 2.0
% revoked by end of 12 months	11.3		16.4		6.5		9.6	

camp in the sample, and included only prison releasees in the comparison sample. For the other three states, the samples included both probationers and prison releasees. Also, compared with the other states, the Florida sample contained more violent offenders and fewer convicted of drug-related or property offenses, and the offenders were younger. Louisiana offenders were older, and more of them had a prior record of offending. Small percentages of cases were lost because of missing data in each state: Florida, 5.2 percent; Georgia, 9.2 percent; Louisiana, 11.1 percent; and South Carolina, 5.3 percent. All information was based on offenders' official records; all subjects were males.

Variables available for analysis included subsample membership (boot camp, prison, probation), age (in years) at the beginning of community supervision, race (1 = nonwhite, 0 = white), and presence of a prior offending record (1 = yes, 0 = no). We also included indicator variables for type of offense (1 = violent, 0 = otherwise; 1 = drug-related offense, 0 = otherwise; 1 = property/other, 0 = otherwise). Although we control for all of these variables in the analyses below, we are most interested in the empirical associations between intensity of supervision, involvement in prosocial activities, and revocation for new criminal activity.

Supervision intensity is the independent variable in which we are primarily interested. In three of the four states (excluding Louisiana), supervising officers maintained monthly records of their number of contacts with offenders. Because the distributions of these contact variables exhibited a strong positive skew, we used a natural log transformation of this variable in all of the analyses. In Louisiana, supervising officers maintained a monthly index measuring their surveillance of offenders. High scores on the composite represent high levels of supervision intensity (see Appendix 26.1). For individuals who were revoked for new criminal activities, we measured supervision by the average level of intensity until revocation. For individuals who were not revoked, we measured supervision by the average level of intensity throughout the one-year follow-up period.

Our key intervening variable, involvement in prosocial activities, was measured by an eight-item index (except in Louisiana, where we used a 13-item index) that tapped offenders' performances in an array of areas such as meeting family responsibilities, making satisfactory progress in education and treatment programs, and achieving residential and financial stability. The eight- and 13-item indexes included some (but not all) of the items used respectively by

Latessa and Vito (1988) and by MacKenzie and her colleagues (MacKenzie and Brame 1995; MacKenzie et al. 1992). All of the items were binary (yes/no) indicators of whether offenders were judged by their officers to be performing well in each area. In Florida, Georgia, and South Carolina these evaluations were compiled for three-month periods of the year following release as long as offenders remained in the community. In Louisiana the evaluations were conducted every month.

For individuals who were revoked for new criminal activities, we measured involvement in prosocial activities by the average level of involvement until the revocation. For individuals who were not revoked, we measured prosocial activities by the average level of involvement throughout the one-year follow-up period. Within each state, we standardized this variable to have zero mean and unit variance.[1]

The outcome of primary interest in this analysis is a binary variable that discriminates between those whose community supervision was revoked for new criminal activities and those whose supervision was not revoked within a one-year follow-up period. Revocation for new criminal activities differs from other possible outcomes such as being arrested or experiencing a revocation for technical violations of supervision conditions. Indeed, some of the items that we describe as prosocial activities also may be requirements for avoiding revocation for technical violations. Because arrests may initiate a process that leads to revocation proceedings for technical violations, arrests and technical violations may be related tautologically to our measure of involvement in prosocial activities. To avoid the ambiguity that such recidivism outcomes would introduce into our analysis, we measure recidivism by relying exclusively on involvement in new criminal activities. Table 26.1 presents descriptive statistics for each of the four states in our analysis.

Analysis

As Figure 26.1 indicates, the conceptual model that we have considered in this paper explicitly anticipates a two stage process: (1) a positive relationship between the amount of supervision an individual receives and that person's level of involvement in prosocial activities; and (2) an inverse relationship between prosocial activities and revocation. In short, we are interested in the joint distribution of prosocial activities and revocation.

This situation is fundamentally different and more complicated than the case in which each univariate outcome is studied separately. Moreover, our two dependent variables, prosocial activities and revocation, have been captured at different levels of measurement: prosocial activities is a continuous outcome, while revocation is a binary and therefore discrete outcome. Because of these issues, we implemented a statistical model that allows us to examine both outcomes simultaneously. Models like these are often estimated with structural equation software such as LISREL, but those packages require us to assume that both outcomes are continuous and are distributed normally. The problem we are addressing, however, cannot be adapted easily to this type of software. Because we must take some special steps to resolve this difficulty, we describe our methods in greater detail in the appendix. Methods such as those used here have proved useful for other problems with joint outcomes and mixed structures (see, e.g., Catalano and Ryan 1992:652; Cox and Snell 1989:163–65; Fitzmaurice and Laird 1995:846–47; Maddala 1983:120–22).

Do prosocial activities cause, or tend to cause, recidivism? For a number of technical reasons described in Appendix 26.2, we cannot resolve this issue in our analysis. Although some readers might view this inability as a limitation of the model, it actually reflects a limitation of theory and of the data at hand. The main limitation is that we need to identify a variable which exerts a causal effect on involvement in prosocial activities but has no direct effect on recidivism (i.e., an instrumental variable). The most obvious example of such a variable is random assignment to different levels of involvement in prosocial activities. If theory in this area were stronger, it also might be possible to find an instrumental variable that meets this requirement, other than randomized assignment. In the absence of such theory, however, our analysis must be limited to the study of correlations rather than causal effects. Even so, we believe that the model we have specified, which captures the association (which we call δ) between prosocial activities and revocation after the measured independent variables have explained as much variation as they can, makes the best use of all of the available data. Moreover, the estimates obtained from this model still should allow us to say something useful about the correspondence between observed associations and the pattern of relationships anticipated in Figure 26.1.

Results

Here we report results for each of the four states in our analysis. Although we control for a number of individual characteristics in each model, we are interested primarily in (1) whether supervision intensity is associated positively with involvement in prosocial activities; (2) whether supervision intensity exhibits any consistent pattern of association with recidivism across states; and (3) whether involvement in prosocial activities is associated inversely with recidivism after adjusting for individual characteristics.

Table 26.2 presents the results of this analysis across each of the four states. Our preliminary analysis suggested that the relationship between supervision intensity and prosocial activities could be modeled with a cubic polynomial regression function in Florida, Georgia, and South Carolina. Therefore, the effects of supervision intensity displayed in Table 26.2 include linear (supervision intensity), quadratic (supervision intensity squared), and cubic (supervision intensity cubed) coefficients. In addition, our preliminary analysis revealed that a linear coefficient adequately captured the relationship between supervision and prosocial activities in Louisiana. Even though a different functional form appears to capture the relationship between supervision intensity and involvement in prosocial activities, all of the analysis results imply a positive association between the two variables.[2]

The second interesting aspect of the results shown in Table 26.2 is the absence of a consistent relationship between supervision intensity and recidivism across the four states. The effect of supervision intensity on recidivism is negative and approaches statistical significance in Georgia; just the opposite is true in South Carolina. In neither Florida nor Louisiana do we find any evidence of a relationship between these two variables. Because the direct links between intensive supervision and recidivism are not clearly understood, we do not wish to read much into this result at this point. We merely note that weak and inconsistent correlations between supervision and recidivism seem to predominate in the literature; our analysis provides further support for this general finding.

The third and final noteworthy observation about the findings shown in Table 26.2 is the negative and statistically significant association between involvement in prosocial activities and recidivism after taking into account the effects of other covariates.[3] Net of the covariates in our models, then, individuals who exhibit high levels of prosocial activities are significantly less likely than others to be revoked for new criminal activities. This result is consistent with what we would expect to see if the model outlined in Figure 26.1 is faithful to the process that generated the data.

The four panels of Figure 26.2 present a summary of our results. These results do not vindicate the model depicted in Figure 26.1; they are merely consistent with that model. Any unmeasured variables (e.g., intelligence, early childhood differences in impulsivity, quality of childrearing) that affect both prosocial activities and recidivism would render the correlations shown in Table 26.2 at least partially spurious. Other possibilities also exist. For example, individuals who are supervised most intensively may be those who are most accessible to supervising officers. Indeed, they could be most accessible because they are involved in prosocial activities. In sum, Figure 26.1 depicts a plausible process by which the results in Table 26.2 could have been generated, but we must be aware that data involving more elaborate sets of covariates could produce different conclusions. Still, the results strike us as interesting, and the matter appears to deserve further study.

Figure 26.2
Summary of Estimated Relationships Between Supervision Intensity, Prosocial Activities, and Revocation

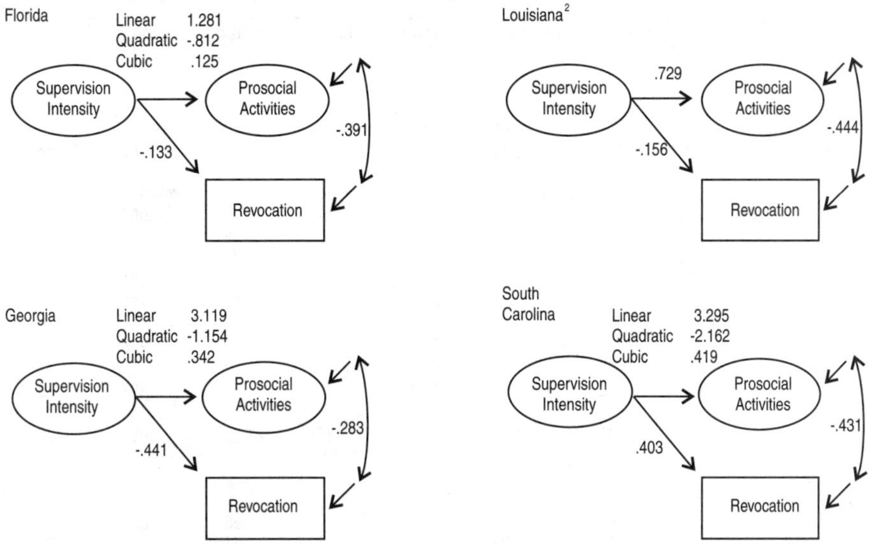

Note: None of the arrows from supervision intensity to revocation are statistically significant at a two-tailed 95% confidence level. All other arrows represent estimates that are statistically significant at that level.

[2] Supervising officers' numbers of contacts with offenders not available for this state.

Discussion and Conclusions

Theoretically we are proposing that intensive supervision acts as a direct control on these offenders' behavior. If it has the effect we anticipate, such control will coerce individuals to participate in prosocial activities that plausibly can be linked to socialization processes such as those described by Nye (1958) and by Rankin and Wells (1990). These, in turn, may decrease future involvement in crime. To make this possibility concrete, we considered a model of the relationship between supervision intensity, prosocial activities, and recidivism. We gathered three hypotheses from the extant literature relating to these variables.

First, we hypothesized that those who were supervised more intensively would exhibit greater involvement in prosocial activities. Second, we predicted that recidivism would be associated inversely with prosocial activities. Third, we anticipated that the main effects of supervision intensity on recidivism would be weak and/or erratic, and that the important effects would be indirect, through prosocial activities.

Our analysis suggests that these predictions are consistent with the data. Nonetheless, as we have suggested, a number of alternative models are also consistent with these results. Therefore, it would be premature to conclude that our findings demonstrate the validity of the model described in Figure 26.1.

As work in this area proceeds, we think that several issues deserve careful consideration. First, our analysis has emphasized the possibility of a link between supervision, involvement in prosocial activities, and recidivism. A key question left unanswered here and in other related work, such as that conducted by Horney and her colleagues (1995), is whether these short-term connections have more lasting implications for behavior. In other words, do individuals who experience increases in short-term prosocial behavior accumulate social capital or tools that will restrain them from future involvement in crime?

Table 26.2
Parameter Estimates for Statistical Model of Prosocial Activities and Recidivism

	Florida		Georgia		Louisiana		South Carolina	
Predictor Variables	**Estimate**	**|z|-ratio**	**Estimate**	**|z|-ratio**	**Estimate**	**|z|-ratio**	**Estimate**	**|z|-ratio**
Prosocial Activities								
Intercept	–3.803	5.48	–1.447	2.40	–1.132	4.56	–1.494	2.42
Boot camp completers	.335	2.48	–.096	.59	.212	1.29	–.082	.56
Boot camp dropouts	.001	.01			.219	1.04		
Probationers			Reference		Reference		Reference	
Prison releasees	Reference		–.181	.98	.124	1.04	–.067	.44
Nonwhite	–.416	3.28	–.392	2.99	–.426	4.32	–.576	4.76
Age	.140	4.28	.014	.55	.031	3.31	.030	1.09
Violent offense	.372	2.63	.275	1.51	–.209	1.25	.131	.72
Drug-related offense	.150	.88	.439	2.96	.174	1.57	.262	1.75
Property offense	Reference		Reference		Reference		Reference	
Prior record	–.287	2.10	–.372	2.53	–.054	.42	–.288	2.34
Supervision (linear)	1.781	3.32	3.119	4.68	.729	8.69	3.295	4.12
Supervision (quadratic)	–.812	2.45	–1.854	3.54			–2.162	2.69
Supervision (cubic)	.125	2.11	.342	2.91			.419	1.82
σ_1	.871	22.45	.886	20.78	.689	21.21	.855	20.37
Revocation								
Intercept	1.003	.69	.056	.05	–.518	.55	–.652	.50
Boot camp completers	–.707	2.53	.812	2.25	.377	.71	.085	.27
Boot camp dropouts	–.625	2.00			.225	.31		
Probationers			Reference		Reference		Reference	
Prison releasees	Reference		.767	1.94	.247	.59	–.254	.69
Nonwhite	.438	1.61	.372	1.39	1.174	2.46	.192	.71
Age	–.087	1.19	–.082	1.57	–.092	2.33	–.074	1.16
Violent offense	–.640	2.03	–.733	1.86	–.443	.71	.060	.14
Drug-related offense	–.392	1.06	–.379	1.29	.080	.22	–.149	.42
Property offense	Reference		Reference		Reference		Reference	
Prior record	–.259	.86	1.106	4.18	.140	.35	.534	1.78
Supervision	–.133	.99	–.441	1.49	–.156	.57	.403	1.46
δ (Residual Association)	–.391	2.76	–.283	2.04	–.444	2.11	–.431	2.84
Log-likelihood	–435.83		–390.66		–306.58		–353.18	

Note: |z|-ratios exceeding 1.96 are statistically significant at the 95% confidence level (two-tailed).

Second, the data for the current study were not collected with these hypotheses in mind. Ordinarily this would not be a major limitation, but in this study we cannot rule out the possibility that the relationship between prosocial activities and recidivism is spurious. As we have suggested, it would be difficult using data such as the information collected here to rule out this possibility. The development of more sophisticated statistical models does not strike us as productive for future research on this question. It would be more useful, we believe, to analyze other data sets containing more extensive sets of covariates. Through such work, we should be able to see whether the introduction of more control variables alters the conclusions obtained from the present analysis.

The possibility of reciprocal effects for supervision intensity and involvement in prosocial activities is an important rival hypothesis for our results. Like other researchers who have studied supervision effects by simply assuming their exogeneity, we assume that the effects of supervision intensity on prosocial activities can be captured with a recursive model. Nevertheless, we recognize that this is not a satisfactory long-term research strategy. In the future, researchers should analyze data in which individuals are assigned randomly to varying levels of supervision intensity. Such an approach will be a strong methodological platform for examining whether analysis results depend on the exogeneity of supervision intensity (see, e.g., Petersilia and Turner 1993).

Finally, more thought is needed for the kinds of supervision that would be most likely to lead to greater levels of prosocial activity. What mechanisms under the control of community supervision personnel hold the greatest promise for increasing involvement in prosocial activities? What is the optimal set of tactics for coercing individuals to engage in constructive behaviors? Researchers not only must continue studying the plausibility of the theoretical links discussed here, but also must give more attention to how these connections work in practice.

Notes

1. As an anonymous reviewer of this manuscript observed, the prosocial activities indexes used in this paper do not measure the actual acquisition of social skills; instead they measure the extent to which individuals are immersed in environments where they might reasonably be expected to acquire those skills.
2. We also estimated bivariate Spearman rank-order correlation coefficients between supervision intensity and involvement in prosocial activities in each state: Florida (+.312), Georgia (+.243), Louisiana (+.678), and South Carolina (+.234). All of these coefficients were statistically significant at .05.
3. We also calculated simple *t*-tests for the difference in prosocial activity means between those who recidivated within 12 months and those who did not: Florida ($t = -3.384$), Georgia ($t = -3.204$), Louisiana ($t = -2.141$), and South Carolina ($t = -3.595$). Each of these *t*-statistics was statistically significant at .05.

References

Anglin, M.D. and Y. Hser. 1990. "Treatment of Drug Abuse." Pp. 393–461, in *Crime and Justice: A Review of Research,* vol. 13, edited by M. Tonry and J.Q. Wilson. Chicago, IL: University of Chicago Press.

Catalano, P.J. and L.M. Ryan. 1992. "Bivariate Latent Variable Models for Clustered Discrete and Continuous Outcomes." *Journal of the American Statistical Association* 87:651–58.

Clear, T.R. and A.A. Braga. 1995. "Community Corrections." Pp. 421–44 in *Crime,* edited by J.Q. Wilson and J. Petersilia. San Francisco, CA: ICS.

Cox, D.R. and E.J. Snell. 1989. *Analysis of Binary Data.* 2nd ed. London: Chapman and Hall.

DeLeon, G. 1988. "Legal Pressure in Therapeutic Communities." Pp. 160–77 in *Compulsory Treatment of Drug Abuse: Research and Clinical Practice,* edited by C.G. Leukefeld and F.M. Tims. Washington, DC: National Institute on Drug Abuse.

Dishion, T.J. and G.R. Patterson. 1997. "The Timing and Severity of Antisocial Behavior: Three Hypotheses Within an Ecological Framework." Pp. 205–17 in *Handbook of Antisocial Behavior,* edited by D.M. Stoff, J. Breiling, and J.D. Maser. New York: Wiley.

Eliason, S.R. 1993. *Maximum Likelihood Estimation: Logic and Practice.* Newbury Park, CA: Sage.

Erwin, B.S. 1986. "Turning Up the Heat on Probationers in Georgia." *Federal Probation* 50:17–24.

Fitzmaurice, G.M. and N.M. Laird. 1995. "Regression Methods for a Bivariate Discrete and Continuous Outcome With Clustering." *Journal of the American Statistical Association* 90:845–52.

Gendreau, P., F.T. Cullen, and J. Bonta. 1994. "Intensive Rehabilitation Supervision: The Next Generation in Community Corrections?" *Federal Probation* 58:72–78.

Glueck, S. and E. Glueck. 1950. *Unraveling Juvenile Delinquency.* New York: Commonwealth Fund.

Gottfredson, M.R. and T. Hirschi. 1990. *A General Theory of Crime.* Stanford, CA: Stanford University Press.

Hirschi, T. 1969. *Causes of Delinquency.* Berkeley, CA: University of California Press.

Horney, J., D.W. Osgood, and I.H. Marshall. 1995. "Criminal Careers in the Short Term: Intra-Individual Variability in Crime and Its Relation to Local Life Circumstances." *American Sociological Review* 60:655–73.

Johnson, N.L. and S. Kotz. 1970. *Continuous Univariate Distributions—1.* New York: Wiley.

King, G. 1989. *Unifying Political Methodology: The Likelihood Theory of Statistical Inference.* New York: Cambridge University Press.

Land, K.C., P.L. McCall, and J.R. Williams. 1990. "Something That Works in Juvenile Justice: An Evaluation of the North Carolina Court Counselors' Intensive Protective Supervision Randomized Experimental Project, 1987–1989." *Evaluation Review* 14:574–606.

Latessa, E.J. and G.F. Vito. 1988. "The Effects of Intensive Supervision on Shock Probationers." *Journal of Criminal Justice* 16:319–30.

Laub, J.H. and R.J. Sampson. 1993. "Turning Points in the Life Course: Why Change Matters to the Study of Crime." *Criminology* 31:301–25.

Lurigio, A.J. and J. Petersilia. 1992. "The Emergence of Intensive Probation Supervision Programs in the United States." Pp. 3–17 in *Smart Sentencing: The Emergence of Intermediate Sanctions,* edited by J. Byrne, A. Lurigio, and J. Petersilia. Newbury Park, CA: Sage.

MacKenzie, D.L. 1994. "Results of a Multi-Site Study of Boot-Camp Prisons." *Federal Probation* 58:60–67.

MacKenzie, D.L. and R. Brame. 1995. "Shock Incarceration and Positive Adjustment During Community Supervision." *Journal of Quantitative Criminology* 11:111–42.

MacKenzie, D.L., J.W. Shaw, and C. Souryal. 1992. "Characteristics Associated With Successful Adjustment to Supervision: A Comparison of Parolees, Probationers, Shock Participants, and Shock Dropouts." *Criminal Justice and Behavior* 19:437–54.

MacKenzie, D.L. and C. Souryal. 1994. *Multisite Evaluation of Shock Incarceration.* Washington, DC: National Institute of Justice.

Maddala, G.S. 1983. *Limited-Dependent and Qualitative Variables in Econometrics.* New York: Cambridge University Press.

Nagin, D.S. and R. Paternoster. 1993. "Enduring Individual Differences and Rational Choice Theories of Crime." *Law and Society Review* 27:467–96.

——. 1994. "Personal Capital and Social Control: The Deterrence Implications of a Theory of Individual Differences in Criminal Offending." *Criminology* 32:581–606.

Nye, F.I. 1958. *Family Relationships and Delinquent Behavior.* New York: Wiley.

Pearson, F.S. 1988. "Evaluation of New Jersey's Intensive Supervision Program." *Crime and Delinquency* 34:437–48.

Petersilia, J. and S. Turner. 1993. "Intensive Probation and Parole." Pp. 281–335 in *Crime and Justice: A Review of Research,* edited by M. Tonry and N. Morris. Chicago, IL: University of Chicago Press.

Rankin, J.H. and L.E. Wells. 1990. "The Effect of Parental Attachments and Direct Controls on Delinquency." *Journal of Research in Crime and Delinquency* 27:140–65.

Sampson, R.J. and J.H. Laub. 1993. *Crime in the Making: Pathways and Turning Points Through Life.* Cambridge, MA: Harvard University Press.

Turner, S., J. Petersilia, and E.P. Deschenes. 1992. "Evaluating Intensive Supervision Probation/Parole (ISP) for Drug Offenders." *Crime and Delinquency* 38:539–56.

Wexler, H.K., D.S. Lipton, and B.D. Johnson. 1988. *A Criminal Justice System Strategy for Treating Cocaine-Heroin Abusing Offenders in Custody.* Washington, DC: National Institute of Justice.

Wilson, J.Q. and R. Herrnstein. 1985. *Crime and Human Nature.* New York: Simon and Schuster.

Wish, E.D. and B.D. Johnson. 1986. "The Impact of Substance Abuse on Criminal Careers." Pp. 52–88 in *Criminal Careers and "Career Criminals,"* edited by A. Blumstein, J. Cohen, J.A. Roth, and C.A. Visher. Washington, DC: National Academy Press.

Appendix 26.1

Prosocial Activities Measures Used in Florida, Georgia, Louisiana, and South Carolina and Surveillance Index Used in Louisiana

Eight-Item Prosocial Activities Index Used in Florida, Georgia, and South Carolina

1. Employed, enrolled in school, or participating in a training program for more than 50% of the follow-up period.
2. Held any one job (or continued in educational or vocational program) for more than a three-month period during the follow-up.
3. Attained vertical (upward) mobility in employment, educational, or vocational program.
4. For the last half of follow-up period, individual was self-supporting and supported any immediate family.
5. Individual shows stability in residency. Either lived in the same residence for three months or moved at suggestion or with the agreement of supervising officer.
6. Individual has avoided any critical incidents that show instability, immaturity, or inability to solve problems acceptably.
7. Attainment of financial stability. This is indicated by the individual living within his means, opening bank accounts, or meeting debt payments.
8. Participation in self-improvement programs. These could be vocational, educational, group counseling, alcohol, or drug maintenance programs.

Note: this index is based on measures described by Latessa and Vito (1988).

Thirteen-Item Prosocial Activity Index Used in Louisiana

1. Subject was employed.
2. Employer evaluates subject favorably.
3. Subject required to attend AA and is making satisfactory progress.
4. Subject required to attend drug treatment and is making satisfactory progress.
5. No positive alcohol-sensor tests.
6. No positive drug screen.
7. Subject actively pursuing job training or attending school and is making satisfactory progress.
8. Subject is experiencing no problems in relationships with family.
9. Subject is not spending time with other offenders.
10. Subject has satisfactory attitude or appearance.
11. Subject cooperates and complies with supervising officer decisions.
12. Subject completing community service requirements satisfactorily.

Appendix 26.2

Analytical Procedures

We begin by defining x_i as a set of predictor variables thought to be associated with outcome y_{i1}^*, and z_i as a set of predictor variables thought to be associated with a second outcome, y_2^*. These variables are indexed for $i = 1,2,\ldots,n$ observations. We assume, for the moment, that the y_i^* variables are fully observed continuous variables with $N(\mu,\sigma^2)$ distributions. Our interest then centers on the following two-equation model:

$$y_{i1}^* = \alpha_1 + \theta\chi_i + u_{i1}$$

$$y_{i2}^* = \alpha_2 + \gamma\chi_i + \beta y_{i1}^* + u_{i2}$$

Because $\text{cov}(u_1,u_2)$ generally is not equal to zero, it is not possible to obtain consistent estimates of the parameters in these two equations unless certain conditions are present.

To confront this problem we must study the joint distribution of the two outcomes rather than their respective marginal distributions (see, e.g., Eliason 1993:56). Steps for computing the joint density of the two y_i^* variables are

$$w_1 = \frac{1}{\sqrt{2\pi\sigma_1\sigma_2(1-\rho^2)}}$$

$$w_2 = -\frac{1}{2(1-\rho^2)}$$

$$w_{i3} = \left(\frac{y_{i1}^*-\mu_1}{\sigma_1}\right)^2 + \left(\frac{y_{i2}^*-\mu_2}{\sigma_2}\right)^2 - \rho\left(\frac{y_{i1}^*-\mu_1}{\sigma_1}\right) \times \left(\frac{y_{i2}^*-\mu_2}{\sigma_2}\right),$$

and the joint density itself is $f(y_{i1}^*,y_{i2}^*;\mu_1,\mu_2,\sigma_1,\sigma_2,\rho) = w_1\exp(w_2w_{i3})$, where ρ is the correlation between y_1^* and y_2^*.

If we allow the μs to depend on covariates, we face the problem of obtaining consistent estimates of all parameters in those equations. As King (1989:198) shows, it is possible to obtain such consistent estimates when $x_i \neq z_i$. This is the case where one can be confident not only on empirical grounds, but also on substantive grounds, that there are measured variables which generate variation in one outcome but not in the other. In practice, such "identification restrictions" are often quite difficult to justify.

The additional complication confronting us is the mixed observability of the outcomes. Specifically, we treat involvement in prosocial activities as a continuous variable (y_1), while revocation is a binary or dichotomous variable (y_2). The relationships between these variables and their latent random normal counterparts are

$$y_{i1} = y_{i1}^*$$

and

$$y_{i2} = \begin{cases} 0 \text{ if } y_{i2}^* < 0, \\ 1 \text{ if } y_{i2}^* > 0 \end{cases}$$

(see, e.g., Cox and Snell 1989:14-16). Although it is simple to estimate probabilities for the marginal distributions of y_1 and y_2, it is more complicated to derive the bivariate distribution of these two outcomes (see, e.g., Catalano and Ryan 1992:652; Cox and Snell 1989:163-65; Fitzmaurice and Laird 1995:846-47; Maddala 1983:120-22).

To address this problem, we rely on a method described by Catalano and Ryan (1992:652). Following their exposition, one can evaluate the joint density of a normally distributed continuous variable and a binary variable with a normally distributed latent counterpart by taking the product of the marginal distribution of y_1 and the distribution of y_2 conditional on y_1:

$$f(y_{i1},y_{i2}) = f(y_{i1})f(y_{i2}\,|\,y_{i1})$$

To estimate this joint density, we must break it down into its component parts. First, we define the expected value of y_{i1} by

$$E(y_{i1}) = \mu_1 = \alpha + \theta_{Xi}.$$

The residual term, μ_{i1}, is then given by

$$u_{i1} = y_{i1} - \mu_{i1}.$$

Following Johnson and Kotz (1970:40), we then form the density of y_{i1} by

$$f(y_{i1}\,|\,x_i) = \left(\frac{1}{\sqrt{2\pi}\sigma_1}\right) \times \exp\left[-\tfrac{1}{2}\left(\frac{u_{i1}}{\sigma_1}\right)^2\right].$$

Next, as Catalano and Ryan (1992:652) suggest, one must obtain the distribution of y_{i2} conditional on y_{i1} by dividing the $i = 1,2,\ldots,n$ observations into two groups. For the group of individuals with $y_{i2} = 0$ we estimate

$$\Pr(y_{i2} = 0\,|\,y_{i1},z_i) = \Phi[-(\alpha_2 + \gamma z_i + 0y_{i1} + \delta u_{i1})];$$

for the other group of observations, with $y_{i2} = 1$, we estimate

$$\Pr(y_{i2} = 1\,|\,y_{i1},z_i) = \Phi[(\alpha_2 + \gamma z_i + 0y_{i1} + \delta u_{i1}),$$

where $\Phi(\cdot)$ is the standard normal cumulative distribution function (Johnson and Kotz 1970:40-41). Under this formulation, the *effect* of y_{i1} on y_{i2} is assumed to be zero, and δ estimates the strength of association between the residuals of the two equations. Thus δ provides an estimate of the amount of change in the latent variable

Appendix 26.B
Analytical Procedures (continued)

associated with y_{i2}, given a unit change in the residual associated with y_{i1}. The log-likelihood is[a]

$$\log(L \mid \alpha, \beta = 0, \gamma, \theta, \delta) = \sum_{i=1}^{N} \log[f(y_{i1} \mid x_i)] + \log\,[\Pr(y_{i2} \mid y_{i1}, z_i)].$$

It would be desirable to estimate β along with the other parameters of the models described above. In the special cases where $\text{cov}(u_1,u_2) = 0$ or when $x_i \neq z_i$, we can relax the constraint that $\beta = 0$ and can obtain consistent estimates of $\alpha_1, \alpha_2, \theta, \gamma$, and β. In the current analysis, however, it is quite conceivable that the processes generating recidivism avoidance and involvement in prosocial activities are very similar. This essentially rules out, at least for now, any argument for imposing the constraint that $\text{cov}(u_1,u_2) = 0$ or $x_i \neq z_i$. Because of these limitations, the next best strategy seems to be to estimate the strength of association between y_1 and y_2 after the measured covariates have explained as much as they can.

[a] We wrote a computer program to maximize this log-likelihood function using the SAS/IML matrix programming language.

Chapter 27

Race, Religion, and Support for the Death Penalty

A Research Note

Chester L. Britt

Although prior research has shown race and affiliation with a fundamentalist Protestant church to be important predictors of support for using the death penalty, this research has given little attention to the combined effect that race and religious affiliation may have on views about capital punishment. In short, do blacks and whites with similar religious affiliations view the use of capital punishment in the same way? The author tests three explanations of the relationship between race and religious affiliation with views about the use of capital punishment: (1) political views, (2) salience of religion, and (3) religious ideology. Britt tests these explanations with data from the 1991 General Social Survey. Although he finds black and white fundamentalists to be very similar on measures of religious behavior and beliefs, black fundamentalists have the lowest levels of support for using the death penalty, while white fundamentalists have the highest levels of support. This pattern persists, even after controlling for the respondent's political views, salience of religion, and religious ideology. These results call into question the assumption of homogeneity among fundamentalist Protestants and indicate that future research on sensitive moral, social, and political issues should consider dual racial and religious contexts in understanding the public's views on these issues.

In the last four decades, public opinion in the United States has shifted dramatically in regard to criminal punishments, especially the use of capital punishment. Gallup Polls reveal that public support for the death penalty declined gradually through the 1960s, reaching a low of 44% in 1966, but has gradually increased over the past 30 years; thus 75 to 80% of the individuals now polled support capital punishment for convicted murderers (Moore, 1995; Zeisel and Gallup, 1989). Public support for capital punishment remains high even when researchers include life imprisonment without the option of parole as an alternative (Sandys and McGarrell, 1994, 1995; Zeisel and Gallup, 1989) or raise the possibility that an innocent person may be sentenced to death (Moore, 1995).

Throughout this period, support for using capital punishment among whites often has been 20 to 25 percentage points higher than among blacks (Cullen et al., 1985; Durham et al., 1996; Grasmick et al., 1992, 1993a, 1993b; Harris, 1986; Moore, 1995; Skovron et al., 1989; Young, 1991, 1992; Zeisel and Gallup, 1989). Similarly, individuals who claim membership in fundamentalist Protestant churches are more likely than the rest of the population to support harsh criminal sanctions in general, and the death penalty in particular (Grasmick et al., 1992, 1993a, 1993b; Grasmick and McGill, 1994; Young, 1992).

Although race and religion may be important predictors of support for capital punishment, relatively little research has examined how race and religion jointly affect these views and explanations. Explanations for support for capital punishment appear to fall into three broad categories: political views, salience of religion in everyday life, and religious ideology. According to the first explanation, blacks will be more likely than others to affiliate with religious organizations that tend to be less socially and politically conservative and more focused on issues of social justice. This view implies a selection process in which individuals affiliate with churches based on compatibility of religious, political, and social attitudes. According to the second explanation, blacks will be more active in their religious organizations and will find religion more salient in everyday life; this attitude appears to decrease punitive attitudes toward criminal offenders. According to the third explanation, blacks will be involved in religious organizations that hold to a less theologically conservative doctrine oriented around biblical literalism and the sinfulness of human nature; this outlook would lead individuals to be more supportive of harsh sanctions for criminal offenders.

The *political views* explanation suggests that support for capital punishment is one of a constellation of issues that distinguish individuals on a continuum of sociopolitical views ranging from liberal to conservative. Thus individuals who self-identify as conservatives are expected to be more supportive of the death penalty. Research on the links between political views and support for the death penalty is ambiguous, however. Langworthy and Whitehead (1986) found self-identified liberals to be less punitive; Longmire (1996), Sandys and McGarrell (1995), and Young (1991, 1992) found self-identified conservatives to be more supportive of the death penalty; other researchers found no effect of self-identified political views on punitiveness (Durham et al., 1996; Stinchcombe et al., 1980; Taylor et al., 1979; Tyler and Weber, 1982). In lieu of asking for self-identified political views, other researchers have used political party affiliation as a proxy for measuring an individual's liberalism or conservatism, assuming that Republicans will be more conservative, on average, than Democrats. These researchers have found weak to moderate support for Democrats' being less punitive than Republicans (Grasmick et al., 1992, 1993a, 1993b; Grasmick and McGill, 1994; Harris, 1986; Longmire, 1996).

Individuals often affiliate with religious organizations whose political and social views are compatible with their own outlook on the world. Roof and McKinney (1987) show that fundamentalist Protestants are more likely to self-identify as social and political conservatives; such identification should affect levels of support for the death penalty. Thus an apparent association between membership in a fundamentalist Protestant church and views about capital punishment may be spurious, and simply may reflect sociopolitical views that led to a particular religious affiliation. In recent research on the link between religious affiliation and support for the death penalty, members of fundamentalist Protestant churches continue to have greater levels of support for capital punishment, even when self-identified political views (Young, 1992) and political party membership are controlled statistically (Grasmick et al., 1992, 1993a, 1993b; Grasmick and McGill, 1994).

Racial differences in political views may explain some of the race variation in support for capital punishment. Blacks tend to hold more liberal sociopolitical views than whites in the United States (see, e.g., Niemi et al., 1989); these should be reflected in varying levels of support, by race, for the death penalty. The only meaningful test of this hypothesis appears in Young's (1991) analysis of data from the Detroit Area Study, which found that the effect of conservative political views on support for the death penalty was conditioned on race: White conservatives were most likely to support the death penalty, black liberals were least likely, and there were no apparent differences in level of support between white liberals and black conservatives.

Race may also be important to understanding how religious affiliation and political views affect support for capital punishment. Insofar as church membership is a function of sociopolitical views (Roof and McKinney, 1987), we would expect whites to be affiliated disproportionately with fundamentalist Protestant organizations and blacks to affiliate at higher rates with religious organizations that hold similar socially and politically liberal views.

The *religious salience* explanation suggests that the prevalence of religion in everyday life—the level of daily participation in religious activities—has a negative association with attitudes toward the death penalty. Grasmick et al. (1993a, 1993b; Grasmick and McGill, 1994) and Young (1992) found that individuals who participate more frequently in religious activities—attending Sunday church services, praying, or attending other church-sponsored events—tend to be less supportive of harsh criminal sanctions.

Research has not clarified whether the effect of salience of religion is independent of the effect of religious affiliation (Grasmick et al., 1993a, 1993b; Young, 1992). If participation in religious activities is independent of religious affiliation, then relatively lower support for capital punishment should be observed among both fundamentalist Protestants and nonfundamentalists who are more active in their churches. On the other hand, if the effects of religious salience and church affiliation are not independent, the effect is more complicated. For example, insofar as socialization is expected to occur in religious organizations, individuals with higher levels of participation in fundamentalist churches should have greater exposure to a church doctrine that emphasizes sin and the depravity of human nature and therefore should be more punitive than less active members of fundamentalist churches. Similarly, among nonfundamentalists, we should find that increased participation in religious activities may further decrease support for capital punishment, again on the basis of differential exposure to religious ideologies that either emphasize the goodness or humanity of individuals or deemphasize human sinfulness; as a result, more active nonfundamentalists should hold less punitive attitudes.

The impact of religious salience on the relationship of race with capital punishment is more ambiguous. Young's (1992) analysis of data from the 1988 General Social Survey represents the only test of this hypothesis. For whites but not for blacks, Young found a significant negative relationship between level of participation in religious activities and support for capital punishment.

The *religious ideology* explanation suggests that religious beliefs will directly influence the individual's support for capital punishment. Fundamentalist Protestant churches are characterized by an emphasis on a literal interpretation of the Bible, on the depravity of human nature, on the sinfulness of the individual, and on the need for punishment for immoral or wrongful behavior (Ellison and Sherkat, 1993; Ellison et al., 1996; Grasmick et al., 1992, 1993a, 1993b; Grasmick and McGill, 1994; Roof and McKinney, 1987; Smith, 1990; Young, 1992). The stronger the individual's belief in conservative theological beliefs, such as a literal interpretation of the Bible, the greater the individual's punitiveness (Ellison and Sherkat, 1993; Grasmick et al., 1992, 1993a, 1993b; Grasmick and McGill, 1994; Young, 1992).

Grasmick et al. (Grasmick et al., 1992, 1993a, 1993b; Grasmick and McGill, 1994) and Young (1992) argue that religious affiliation affects an individual's attribution style (i.e., views about the causes of behavior), which ostensibly affects support for the death penalty. Their arguments suggest that members of fundamentalist Protestant churches will be more likely to attribute the causes of criminal behavior to characteristics of the individual offender, while others will be more prone to attribute causes to environmental (e.g., social) characteristics. Although these researchers claim support for this position, they include few direct measures of attribution style, and appear to measure aspects of religious ideology (e.g., views about human nature) more directly. Furthermore, the link between religious affiliation and attribution style is tenuous; weak evidence shows that fundamentalist Protestants are more likely to view the causes of behavior in reference to individual characteristics (Lupfer and Wald, 1985; Spilka et al., 1985), while another study has found no evidence of such a link (Lupfer et al., 1988).

Researchers are ambiguous about the joint effect of race and religious ideology. There are significant differences between the religious ideology found in white fundamentalist churches and in predominately black Protestant churches (see, e.g., Frazier, 1974 [1963]; Lincoln and Mamiya, 1990; Sernett, 1975). Fundamentalist churches with predominantly white members tend to emphasize a doctrine of individual responsibility and blame; as religious organizations such as the Christian Coalition have developed in recent years, an increasing level of political and social activism has been aimed at a conservative sociopolitical agenda. In contrast, churches with predominantly black members have been politically and socially active in the United States for decades, but their efforts often have been aimed at issues related to civil rights and social justice (Lincoln and Mamiya, 1990). Thus, blacks' and whites' religious ideology should differ, especially those of white fundamentalists and all other race-religion groups. These differences in religious ideology will help to explain variations in support for using capital punishment (Young, 1992).

Data and Methods

Sample

The data used in the following analysis come from the 1991 General Social Survey (GSS), which is described in more detail by Davis and Smith (1993). To maximize the contrast between black and white respondents, I excluded individuals classified as a race other than black or white from the analysis. Of the 1,468 respondents identified as black or white (out of 1,517 total respondents), 1,257 provided a valid response to the question on their level of support for using the death penalty (described below). Complete information was available on 850 of the respondents to the death penalty item identified as black ($n = 90$) or white ($n = 760$).[1] As in most GSS samples, about 10% of the respondents did not report a valid response for income. Further analysis of missing values for all measures included in this study showed no systematic bias to the cases that were dropped.[2]

A Measure of Support for Using the Death Penalty

To assess the respondent's level of support for the use of the death penalty, the question "Do you agree or disagree that people convicted of murder should be subject to the death penalty?" provides the basis for the following analysis. The question includes five response categories ranging from strongly disagree (coded as 1) to strongly agree (coded as 5). Among respondents to this question, 48.9% strongly agree, 26.4% agree, 8.2% express no preference, 9.6% disagree, and 6.8% strongly disagree with using the death penalty for convicted murderers.

The 1991 GSS is the only year to include this question. This question, called DEATHPEN in the GSS Codebook (Davis and Smith, 1993), is considerably different from the question annually included in other editions of the GSS (the item CAPPUN), in which respondents are simply asked whether they favor or oppose the use of capital punishment. The single-item measure included in this study should provide a better indicator of the level, or degree, of support for the use of capital punishment, because it allows for moderate variation in the level at which respondents can claim support or opposition to the death penalty. For example, the five-category item used in this study allows for distinctions such as those between respondents who claim to strongly agree and who claim to agree, who claim no preference and who claim to disagree, or who claim to disagree and who claim to strongly disagree with the use of the death penalty. Such comparisons are not possible with the dichotomous choice question.

Durham et al.'s (1996) recent paper points to a potential limitation in this measure of support for the death penalty. Durham et al. (1996) show that when respondents are presented with a range of circumstances in which the death penalty might be used, support for using the death penalty tends to be more variable than suggested by a dichotomous response choice (also see Cullen et al., 1985; Harris, 1986; Sandys and McGarrell, 1994, 1995). Thus a five-category response choice will miss some of the more subtle aspects of death penalty support highlighted by Durham et al., but the range of response choices in this measure compensates for the lack of multiple support measures in the GSS, and should provide a reasonable proxy measurement for the degree to which the respondent approves of capital punishment.

Control and Independent Variables

Religious affiliation is coded 1 for membership in a denomination classified as *fundamentalist Protestant* (see Smith, 1990); 0 otherwise. Smith's (1990) classification of religious denominations as either "fundamentalist," "moderate," or "liberal" parallels Roof and McKinney's (1987) classification scheme for conservative Protestant denominations.[3] Approximately 33% of the GSS sample was classified as fundamentalist Protestant under this scheme.[4]

Race is coded 1 for blacks; 0 for whites. In view of the qualitative differences I hypothesize between predominantly black and predominantly white churches, an *interaction between race and membership in a fundamentalist church* is coded 1 for black and member of a fundamentalist Protestant church; 0 otherwise. *Sex* is coded 1 for females; 0 for males. *Education* is coded as years of education completed. *Family income* is coded on a 21-point scale. *Size of place of residence* is coded in millions of persons. Regional influences are measured through a contrast of *southerners* with all others: 1 if the respondent lives in the southern United States; 0 otherwise.

Political views are measured with two items. *Republican party membership* measures whether the respondent identifies as a Republican (coded 1) or as a Democrat or an Independent (coded 0). Self-identified *political conservatism* is measured by asking the respondent to locate his or her political views on a seven-point scale, ranging from "extremely liberal" (coded 1) through "moderate—middle of the road" (coded 4), to "extremely conservative" (coded 7).

The *salience of religion* is measured with three questions: "How often do you attend religious services?"; "How often do you take part in the activities and organizations of a church or place of worship other than attending services?" (responses for each item range from never, coded 1, to several times a week, coded 9); and, "About how often do you pray?" (responses range from never, coded 1, to several times a day, coded 11). The three questions are standardized and the mean taken so that the index for salience of religion is scored from 0 to 1. These three items measure how active and relevant religious activity is for the respondent at both an organizational (church) and personal level (alpha reliability = .793); high scores indicate greater levels of religious salience.

Religious ideology is measured with three items. *Biblical literalism* is measured with a question asking respondents for their interpretation of the Bible. A score of 1 was given to respondents who replied that the statement "The Bible is the actual word of God and it is to be taken literally, word for word" was closest to describing their interpretation of the Bible; all other respondents received 0. To measure respondents' *perceptions of human nature,* I use a Likert-type item with seven responses ranging from "Human nature is basically good" (coded 1) to "Human nature is perverse and fundamentally corrupt" (coded 7). *Conservative theology* is measured with responses to four questions: "Do you believe in life after death?"; "Do you believe in the Devil?"; "Do you believe in Hell?"; "Do you believe in Heaven?" (coded 1 = no, definitely not; 2 = no, probably not; 3 = yes, probably; 4 = yes, definitely). The conservative theology index is scored as the mean response to the four items (alpha reliability = .863); high scores indicate a belief system consistent with that found in fundamentalist Protestant denominations (Roof and McKinney, 1987; Smith, 1990).

Analysis

The analysis proceeds in two main stages. In the first stage I test for mean differences in the dependent and the independent variables among respondents based on race, religious affiliation, and combinations of race and religious affiliation (black fundamentalists, black nonfundamentalists, white fundamentalists, and white nonfundamentalists). In the second stage I use four equations that test for effects of race and religious affiliation on support for use of the death penalty. These equations sequentially add sociodemographic characteristics (equation 1), political views (equation 2), salience of religion (equation 3), and religious ideology (equation 4).[5]

Findings

Table 27.1 shows significant differences in the dependent and the independent variables by race and religious affiliation. In agreement with past research, blacks indicate lower levels of support for the death penalty than do whites. Blacks are also less likely to identify themselves as members of the Republican Party, but score higher on the salience of religion index and are more likely to claim a literal interpretation of the Bible.

In contrast to recent research on fundamentalist Protestants and support for the death penalty (Grasmick et al., 1992, 1993a, 1993b; Grasmick and McGill, 1994; Young, 1992), I

Table 27.1
Means and Standard Deviations for the Independent Variables by Race and Religious Affiliation

	Race		Religious Affiliation	
Variable	Blacks	Whites	Fundamentalist Protestants	Nonfundamentalist Protestants
Support for Using the Death Penalty for Persons Convicted of Murder	3.500* (1.392)	4.070 (1.224)	4.068 (1.286)	3.978 (1.238)
Republican Party Membership	0.033* (0.181)	0.361 (0.480)	0.314 (0.465)	0.332 (0.471)
Political Conservatism	4.000 (1.446)	4.158 (1.297)	4.379* (1.323)	4.016 (1.293)
Salience of Religion	0.640* (0.227)	0.530 (0.240)	0.610* (0.238)	0.505 (0.235)
Biblical Literalism	0.511* (0.503)	0.299 (0.458)	0.512* (0.501)	0.221 (0.415)
Views of Human Nature	3.489 (1.756)	3.214 (1.620)	3.519* (1.807)	3.099 (1.521)
Conservative Theology Index	3.328 (0.728)	3.200 (0.856)	3.543* (0.644)	3.040 (0.884)
Number of Cases	90	760	293	557

Notes: $N = 850$; standard deviation in parentheses.
* Mean differences across race or religious affiliation categories are significantly different at $p < .05$ (*t*-test).

found no direct effect of affiliation with a fundamentalist Protestant church on the level of support for the death penalty. At least three factors may contribute to the difference between the results presented here and those in past research. One possibility is due to the differences in measuring support for the death penalty. Grasmick and colleagues and Young use dichotomous indicators of support; I use a five-category response choice. Two other possibilities are explored below in greater detail.

Although fundamentalists and nonfundamentalists do not differ significantly as to membership in the Republican Party, fundamentalists do indicate higher levels of political conservatism. As expected, fundamentalists and nonfundamentalists differ significantly on all measures of religious behavior and beliefs. These findings validate Roof and McKinney's (1987) and Smith's (1990) classifications of fundamentalist denominations because respondents classified as fundamentalist score higher than nonfundamentalists on the salience of religion index, are more likely to hold to a literal interpretation of the Bible, are more likely to view human nature as evil, and are more likely to believe in Heaven, Hell, the Devil, and an afterlife.

The findings in Table 27.2 also clarify why these results differ from those obtained by Grasmick et al. If most of the respondents identified as fundamentalists in the Oklahoma City survey data used by Grasmick et al. are white, then the results in Table 27.2 are consistent with their research because the greater level of support for capital punishment that Grasmick at al. found among fundamentalist Protestants was essentially the effect for white fundamentalists that I show in Table 27.2.

Another possibility for differences between my results and those found by Grasmick et al. may be related to differences in measures of religious affiliation. I compare fundamentalist Protestants with all other respondents, whereas Grasmick et al. include three measures of religious affiliation—fundamentalist Protestants, Protestants, and Catholics—and use respondents with no religious affiliation as the reference category.

As I noted in regard to Table 27.1, whites are more likely than blacks to claim membership in

Table 27.2
Means and Standard Deviations for the Independent Variables by Race-Religion Category

Variable	Black Fundamentalist Protestants	Black Non-fundamentalists	White Fundamentalist Protestants	White Non-fundamentalists
Support for Using the Death Penalty for Persons Convicted of Murder*	3.208 (1.498)	3.919 (1.115)	4.258 (1.153)	3.983 (1.247)
Republican Party Membership*	0.000 (0.000)	0.081 (0.277)	0.383 (0.487)	0.350 (0.477)
Political Conservatism	4.019 (1.525)	3.973 (1.343)	4.458 (1.264)	4.019 (1.290)
Salience of Religion*	0.652 (0.213)	0.622 (0.246)	0.601 (0.242)	0.497 (0.232)
Biblical Literalism*	0.566 (0.500)	0.432 (0.502)	0.500 (0.501)	0.206 (0.405)
Views of Human Nature*	3.509 (1.793)	3.459 (1.726)	3.521 (1.813)	3.073 (1.504)
Conservative Theology Index*	3.405 (0.623)	3.216 (0.854)	3.573 (0.646)	3.028 (0.886)
Number of Cases	53	37	240	520

Notes: $N = 850$; standard deviations in parentheses.
* Race-Religion categories are significantly different at $p < .05$ (F-test).

the Republican Party, independent of religious affiliation. Across races, patterns of Republican Party membership differ by religious affiliation. Among whites, fundamentalists are more likely to identify as Republican; among blacks, nonfundamentalists are more likely to claim membership in the Republican Party. I found no significant differences in level of conservatism across race and religious affiliation.

Black fundamentalists score highest on the religious salience index, followed by black nonfundamentalists and white fundamentalists. In keeping with expectations, blacks (both fundamentalist and nonfundamentalist) have a greater level of religious salience than whites. Black fundamentalists are also more likely to hold to a literal interpretation of the Bible. White fundamentalists score higher on the conservative theology index, followed closely by black fundamentalists. Black and white fundamentalists are virtually indistinguishable on views of human nature. For all four measures of religious views and behavior, white nonfundamentalists' scores were well below those of the other three race-religion groups.

The OLS regression results appear in Table 27.3. The R^2 values are relatively low, a common result in research on public opinion and attitudes.[6] Equation 1 in Table 27.3 shows that race and affiliation with a fundamentalist Protestant church jointly affect support for the death penalty.[7] The significant coefficients for affiliation with a fundamentalist church and the interaction effect between race and fundamentalist church affiliation mean that the effects of race and religious affiliation on support for capital punishment cannot be easily disentangled. Black fundamentalists report the lowest levels of support for the death penalty, controlling for age, sex, education, family income, missing income, native southerner, and size of place of residence. White fundamentalists report the highest level of support. The lack of significance of the coefficient for race means that black and white nonfundamentalists hold similar views regarding the death penalty. Results for equation 1 also show, in agreement with much prior research on attitudes toward capital punishment, that women and people with higher levels of education are less supportive of the death penalty, while people with larger family incomes and who live in more populated areas support capital punishment more strongly.

Table 27.3
Regressions of Support for Using the Death Penalty for Convicted Murderers on Sociodemographic Characteristics (Equation 1), Political Views (Equation 2), Religious Salience (Equation 3), and Religious Ideology (Equation 4)

	Equation 1		Equation 2		Equation 3		Equation 4	
Variable	**b**	**Beta**	**b**	**Beta**	**b**	**Beta**	**b**	**Beta**
Fundamentalist Protestant	.269** (.100)	.102	.190* (.099)	.072	.234* (.101)	.089	.209* (.104)	.079
Black	–.143 (.213)	–.035	–.072 (.210)	–.018	–.007 (.212)	–.002	–.007 (.212)	–.002
Black x Fundamentalist Protestant	–.944*** (.280)	–.182	–.859** (.275)	–.166	–.889*** (.275)	–.171	–.868** (.275)	–.167
Sociodemographic Characteristics								
Age	–.002 (.003)	–.033	–.003 (.003)	–.047	–.002 (.003)	–.030	–.002 (.003)	–.024
Female	–.158† (.087)	–.062	–.144† (.086)	–.057	–.107 (.087)	–.042	–.104 (.087)	–.041
Education	–.048** (.017)	–.106	–.057*** (.017)	–.124	–.053** (.017)	–.116	–.050** (.017)	–.111
Income	.015† (.009)	.063	.011 (.009)	.045	.012 (.009)	.051	.013 (.009)	.053
Southerner	.018 (.096)	.007	.026 (.094)	.010	.033 (.094)	.012	.027 (.094)	.010
Size of Place	.081† (.044)	.065	.092* (.043)	.073	.095* (.043)	.076	.098* (.043)	.079
Political Views								
Republican Party Member			.359*** (.093)	.134	.372*** (.093)	.139	.365*** (.093)	.136
Political Conservatism			.119*** (.033)	.124	.127*** (.033)	.133	.122*** (.033)	.128
Religious Salience								
Salience of Religion Index					–.419* (.187)	–.080	–.545** (.209)	–.105
Religious Ideology								
Biblical Literalism							–.036 (.100)	–.013
Views of Human Nature							.021 (.026)	.027
Conservative Theology Index							.089 (.058)	.060
Intercept	4.577*** (.283)		4.187*** (.297)		4.206*** (.297)		3.907*** (.346)	
R^2		.056		.093		.099		.102

Notes: $N = 850$; standard errors in parentheses; b is the metric regression coefficient; Beta is the standardized regression coefficient.
† $p < .10$; * $p < .05$; ** $p < .01$; *** $p < .001$ (all two-tailed tests)

Political views are added in equation 2 of Table 27.3. Identifying as a member of the Republican Party and holding conservative political and social views both have significant positive effects on support for the death penalty. The addition of political views, however, does not substantially alter the combined effect of race and religious affiliation with a fundamentalist Protestant church on support for the death penalty. Black fundamentalists still report the lowest levels of support, while white fundamentalists continue to report the highest levels. Contrary to the expectations of the first hypothesis, I found unique effects of affiliation with a fundamentalist church that are not mediated by measures of sociopolitical views. When political views are added, family income no longer has a significant effect; this finding indicates that political views, as measured by Republican Party membership and self-identified conservative views, are correlated positively with family income and thus mediate the effect of family income.

The salience of religion index is added in equation 3 of Table 27.3. People who report greater participation in religious activities (public and private) report lower levels of support for the death penalty. The combined effect of race and religious affiliation is not altered by the inclusion of religious salience, and shows the same pattern found in equations 1 and 2. The only substantive changes in coefficient values and statistical significance found in equation 3 is that gender is no longer significant; this finding suggests that the lower level of support for the death penalty often expressed by women is mediated in part by the salience of religious acitivites in daily life.

Religious ideology measures are added in equation 4 of Table 27.3. None of the three measures of religious ideology—biblical literalism, views of human nature, and conservative theology—has a significant effect on support for the death penalty. Thus, despite significant differences in measures of religious ideology across the four race-religious affiliation groups (see Table 27.2), these measures have no effect on support for the death penalty, once sociodemographic characteristics, political views, and salience of religion are controlled. Moreover, the effect of race and fundamentalist church affiliation on support for the death penalty is altered only slightly by including religious ideology measures.

Taken together, political views, salience of religion, and religious ideology help to explain the level of support for the death penalty but hardly alter or explain the effect of race and religious affiliation on support. In all equations, black fundamentalists show significantly lower levels of support for the death penalty; white fundamentalists show much higher levels of support, regardless of whether measures of political and religious views are included in the analysis; [and] black and white nonfundamentalists show virtually identical levels of support for the death penalty, which falls between the levels expressed by black and white fundamentalists.

Conclusion

My results, using data from the 1991 General Social Survey, indicate that the effect of religious affiliation on support for the death penalty is contingent on the respondent's race. Regardless of whether the analysis included measures of the respondent's political views, salience of religion, or religious ideology, black fundamentalists reported the lowest levels of support for the death penalty, white fundamentalists reported the highest levels, and black and white nonfundamentalists were indistinguishable, once other respondent characteristics had been controlled.

Although these findings are broadly consistent with prior research on death penalty support, the results highlight the importance of a combined effect of race and affiliation with a fundamentalist Protestant church . . . on support for capital punishment. These findings also indicate an important gap in research on public views about capital punishment. Past research on attitudes toward criminal sanctions treated race and religious affiliation as factors that affect people's views independently. My results suggest that failure to consider the intersection of race and religion will leave a gap in our explanations and understanding of public attitudes on capital punishment. The importance of jointly considering race and religious affiliation is highlighted by the theological similarity between black and white fundamentalists, who reported similar views about biblical literalism, human nature, and beliefs in the Devil, Hell, Heaven, and an afterlife but held widely different views on using the death penalty, even after these characteristics were controlled statistically.

Past research on the effect of religious affiliation on moral, social, and political views assumed that socialization occurs in the church community, and that individuals who affiliate with religions possessing similar belief structures will hold similar views about other issues (see, e.g., Ellison and Sherkat, 1993; Grasmick et al., 1993a, 1993b). The findings reported here indicate that the link between religious beliefs and views on sociopolitical issues may be more complex. Two different groups of fundamentalist Protestants—black and white—hold similar religious beliefs but seem to apply these beliefs in very different ways. Possible explanations for this pattern—all of which require further study—may include the effects of racial identity in church congregations, the effects of alternative theological emphases (e.g., hope, forgiveness, "second chances") in fundamentalist churches, and the effects of a theology that focuses on issues of social justice. For example, Frazier's (1974 [1963]) study of predominately black churches in the United States illustrates how religion has played a more important role historically, culturally, and politically among blacks than among whites. Lincoln and Mamiya's (1990) recent study of black churches provides consistent evidence that blacks' religious experience is qualitatively different from that of whites in the United States.

Unfortunately, most of the survey data that could be used to study views about religious beliefs and about capital punishment are inadequate to test these additional explanations. Surveys that have focused on public views on crime and punishment may include more fully detailed measures of views about capital punishment, but often include only crude measures of religious affiliation (e.g., Durham et al., 1996). Similarly, more highly detailed studies of religious beliefs and attitudes tend to ignore sociopolitical issues altogether or include only crude measures of views on such issues as the death penalty (e.g., Young, 1991, 1992). Given our current lack of knowledge about how race and religious affiliation simultaneously affect views on capital punishment, these kinds of omissions will be corrected in future surveys of these topics.

Beyond the issue of capital punishment, this research suggests that future studies on other sensitive moral and sociopolitical issues, such as abortion, corporal punishment, and operation of the criminal justice system, should consider the joint influence of race and religious affiliation to gain a better understanding of the public views on these issues. Future researchers must abandon the popular conception that all fundamentalist Protestants are the same. The findings presented above suggest that this view is mistaken; additional study is required to understand how race and church membership affect attitudes about social and political issues.

Notes

1. In most national probability samples, a relatively small proportion of respondents is identified as black. The GSS is no exception: 10.6% of the sample used in this paper is identified as black, which reflects the population of the United States at the time of this survey.
2. In an attempt to test the robustness of our findings, I performed a complementary set of analyses with the 1,257 respondents to the death penalty item, using variable means or modes to replace missing values for continuous or dichotomous variables respectively. The findings I report below, using the 850 cases with complete information, are nearly identical to the findings based on imputed values for missing data. These results are available on request.
3. Denominations classified as fundamentalist in these schemes include Assembly of God, Church of Christ, Church of God, Four Square Gospel, Free Methodist, Mennonite, Nazarene, Pentecostal, Seventh Day Adventist, Jehovah's Witness, Southern Baptist, Lutheran Missouri Synod, Evangelical Reform, and various other sects.
4. In preliminary analysis I also explored the possibility that American Catholics would have significantly different views on the use of capital punishment than fundamentalist and nonfundamentalist Protestants. I found no effect of affiliation with the Catholic Church on views about the death penalty, and dropped the distinction in subsequent analyses.
5. In agreement with other research that has analyzed ordered dependent variables with at least five other categories (see, e.g., Ellison and Sherkat 1993; Sandys and McGarrell 1995), I use OLS to estimate these four equations. It is not clear that the added complexity of an ordered logit (or probit) model for a five-category response variable is necessary. I estimated ordered logit and probit models for all four equations, however, and reached the same substantive conclusions.
6. Although the relatively low R^2 values may be disappointing to some readers, I have not attempted to develop a comprehensive explanation of support for the death penalty. In recognition of the difficulty involved in developing an explanation for *any* attitude, I have focused on assisting future research in this area by demonstrating the combined importance of race and religion for views on the use of capital punishment.
7. I estimated common measures of multicollinearity (e.g., variance inflation factor and condition index) for all four equations reported in Table 27.3. In no instance did the results suggest that there was a collinearity problem with the analyses (see Belsley, Kuh, and Welsch 1980).

References

Belsley, D.A., E. Kuh, and R.E. Welsch. 1980. *Regression Diagnostics: Identifying Influential Data and Sources of Collinearity.* New York: John Wiley & Sons.

Cullen, F.T., G.A. Clark, J.B. Cullen and R.A. Mathers. 1985. "Attribution, Salience, and Attitudes Toward Criminal Sanctioning." *Criminal Justice and Behavior* 12:305–331.

Davis, J.A. and T.W. Smith. 1993. *General Social Surveys, 1972–1993: Cumulative Codebook.* Chicago: National Opinion Research Center.

Durham, A., H.P. Elrod, and P.T. Kinkead. 1996. "Public Support for the Death Penalty: Beyond Gallup." *Justice Quarterly* 13:705–736.

Ellison, C.G. and D.E. Sherkat. 1993. "Conservative Protestantism and Support for Corporal Punishment." *American Sociological Review* 58:131–144.

Ellison, C.G., J.P. Bartkowski, and M.L. Segal. 1996. "Conservative Protestantism and the Parental Use of Corporal Punishment." *Social Forces* 74:1003–1028.

Frazier, E.F. 1974 [1963]. *The Negro Church in America.* New York: Schocken Books.

Grasmick, H.G., R.J. Bursik, Jr., and B.S. Blackwell. 1993a. "Religious Beliefs and Public Support for the Death Penalty for Juveniles and Adults." *Journal of Crime and Justice* 16:59–86.

Grasmick, H.G., J.K. Cochran, R.J. Bursik, Jr., and M. Kimpel. 1993b. "Religion, Punitive Justice, and Support for the Death Penalty." *Justice Quarterly* 10:289–314.

Grasmick, H.G., E. Davenport, M.B. Chamlin, and R.J. Bursik, Jr. 1992. "Protestant Fundamentalism and the Retributive Doctrine of Punishment." *Criminology* 30:21–45.

Grasmick, H.G. and A.L. McGill. 1994. "Religion, Attribution Style, and Punitiveness Toward Juvenile Offenders." *Criminology* 32:23–46.

Harris, P.W. 1986. "Over-Simplification and Error in Public Opinion Surveys on Capital Punishment." *Justice Quarterly* 3:429–455.

Langworthy, R.H. and J.T. Whitehead. 1986. "Liberalism and Fear as Explanations of Punitiveness." *Criminology* 24:575–591.

Lincoln, C.E. and L.H. Mamiya. 1990. *The Black Church in the African American Experience.* Durham, NC: Duke University Press.

Longmire, D.R. 1996. "Americans' Attitudes About the Ultimate Weapon: Capital Punishment." Pp. 93–108 in *Americans View Crime and Justice: A National Public Opinion Survey* edited by T.J. Flanagan and D.R. Longmire. Thousand Oaks, CA: Sage.

Lupfer, M.B., P.L. Hopkinson, and P. Kelley. 1988. "An Exploration of Attribution Styles of Christian Fundamentalists and of Authoritarians." *Journal for the Scientific Study of Religion* 27:389–398.

Lupfer, M.B. and K. Wald. 1985. "An Exploration of Adults' Religious Orientations and Their Philosophies of Human Nature." *Journal for the Scientific Study of Religion* 24:293–304.

Moore, D.W. 1995. "Americans Firmly Support Death Penalty." *The Gallup Poll Newsletter* Volume 60, Number 5.

Niemi, R.C., J. Mueller, and T.W. Smith. 1989. *Trends in Public Opinion.* New York: Greenwood Press.

Roof, W.C. and W. McKinney. 1987. *American Mainline Religion: Its Changing Shape and Future.* New Brunswick, NJ: Rutgers University Press.

Sandys, M. and E.F. McGarrell. 1994. "Attitudes Toward Capital Punishment Among Indiana Legislators: Diminished Support in Light of Alternative Sentencing Options." *Justice Quarterly* 11:651–677.

——. 1995. "Attitudes Toward Capital Punishment: Preference for the Penalty or Mere Acceptance?" *Journal of Research in Crime and Delinquency* 32:191–213.

Sernett, M.C. 1975. *Black Religion and American Evangelicalism.* Metuchen, NJ: Scarecrow Press and the American Theological Library Association.

Skovron, S.E., J.E. Scott, and F.T. Cullen. 1989. "The Death Penalty for Juveniles: An Assessment of Public Support." *Crime and Delinquency* 35:546–561.

Smith, T.W. 1990. "Classifying Protestant Denominations." *Review of Religious Research* 31:225–245.

Spilka, B., P. Shaver, and L.A. Kirkpatrick. 1985. "A General Theory of Attribution for the Psychology of Religion." *Journal for the Scientific Study of Religion* 24:1–20.

Stinchcombe, A.L., R. Adams, C.A. Heimer, K.L. Schepple, T.W. Smith, and D.G. Taylor. 1980. *Crime and Punishment: Changing Attitudes in America.* San Francisco: Jossey-Bass.

Taylor, D.C., K.L. Schepple, and A.L. Stinchcombe. 1979. "Salience of Crime and Support for Harsher Criminal Sanctions." *Social Problems* 26:413–424.

Tyler, T.R. and R. Weber. 1982. "Support for the Death Penalty: Instrumental Response to Crime or Symbolic Attitude?" *Law and Society Review* 17:21–44.

Young, R.L. 1991. "Race, Conceptions of Crime and Justice, and Support for the Death Penalty." *Social Psychology Quarterly* 54:67–75.

——. 1992. "Religious Orientation, Race, and Support for the Death Penalty." *Journal for the Scientific Study of Religion* 31:76–81.

Zeisel, H. and A.M. Gallup. 1989. "Death Penalty Sentiment in the United States." *Journal of Quantitative Criminology* 5:285–296.

Chapter 28

Beyond Correctional Quackery

Professionalism and the Possibility of Effective Treatment

Edward J. Latessa
Francis T. Cullen
Paul Gendreau

Much that passes for professional correctional treatment is little more than custom, convenience, tradition, and baseless ideology; correctional treatment is often little more than correctional quackery. The result is not merely ineffective treatment, but a broader loss of faith and trust in the "profession" of corrections by the public at large. Correctional quackery has four main sources: failure to use research in designing programs; failure to follow appropriate assessment and classification practices; failure to use effective treatment models; and failure to evaluate what we do. Professionalism and effective treatment must overcome these procedural failures and establish an evidence-based culture.

Long-time viewers of Saturday Night Live will vividly recall Steve Martin's hilarious portrayal of a medieval medical practitioner—the English barber, Theodoric of York. When ill patients are brought before him, he prescribes ludicrous "cures," such as repeated bloodletting, the application of leeches and boar's vomit, gory amputations, and burying people up to their necks in a marsh. At a point in the skit when a patient dies and Theodoric is accused of "not knowing what he is doing," Martin stops, apparently struck by the transforming insight that medicine might abandon harmful interventions rooted in ignorant customs and follow a more enlightened path. "Perhaps," he says, "I've been wrong to blindly follow the medical traditions and superstitions of past centuries." He then proceeds to wonder whether he should "test these assumptions analytically through experimentation and the scientific method." And perhaps, he says, the scientific method might be applied to other fields of learning. He might even be able to "lead the way to a new age—an age of rebirth, a renaissance." He then pauses and gives the much-awaited and amusing punchline, "Nawwwwwww!"

The humor, of course, lies in the juxtaposition and the embrace of blatant quackery with the possibility and rejection of a more modern, scientific, and ultimately effective approach to medicine. For those of us who make a living commenting on or doing corrections, however, we must consider whether, in a sense, the joke is on us. We can readily see the humor in Steve Martin's skit and wonder how those in medieval societies "could have been so stupid." But even a cursory survey of *current* correctional practices yields the disquieting conclusion that we are a field in which quackery is tolerated, if not implicitly celebrated. It is not clear whether most of us have ever had that reflective moment in which we question whether, "just maybe," there might be a more enlightened path to pursue. If we have paused to envision a different way of doing things, it is apparent that our reaction, after a moment's contemplation, too often has been, "Nawwwwwww!"

This appraisal might seem overly harsh, but we are persuaded that it is truthful. When intervening in the lives of offenders—that is, intervening with the expressed intention of reducing recidivism—corrections has resisted becoming a true "profession." Too often, being a "professional" has been debased to mean dressing in a presentable way, having experience in the field, and showing up every day for work. But a profession is defined not by its surface appearance but by its intellectual core. An occupation may lay claim to being a "profession" only to the extent that its practices are based on research knowledge, training, and expertise—a triumvirate that promotes the possibility that what it does can be effective (Cullen, 1978; Starr, 1982). Thus, medicine's professionalization cannot be separated from its embrace of scientific knowledge as the ideal arbiter of how patients should be treated (Starr, 1982). The very concept of "malpractice" connotes that standards of service delivery have been established, are universally transmitted, and are capable of distinguishing acceptable from unacceptable interventions. The concept of liability for "correctional malpractice" would bring snickers from the crowd—a case where humor unintentionally offers a damning indictment of the field's standards of care.

In contrast to professionalism, *quackery* is dismissive of scientific knowledge, training, and expertise. Its posture is strikingly overconfident, if not arrogant. It embraces the notion that interventions are best rooted in "common sense," in personal experiences (or clinical knowledge), in tradition, and in superstition (Gendreau, Goggin, Cullen, and Paparozzi, forthcoming). "What works" is thus held to be "obvious," derived only from years of an individual's experience, and legitimized by an appeal to custom ("the way we have always done things around here has worked just fine"). It celebrates being anti-intellectual. There is never a need to visit a library or consult a study.

Correctional quackery, therefore, is the use of treatment interventions that are based on neither 1) existing knowledge of the causes of crime nor 2) existing knowledge of what programs have been shown to change offender behavior (Cullen and Gendreau, 2000; Gendreau, 2000). The hallmark of correctional quackery is thus ignorance. Such ignorance about crime and its cures at times is "understandable"—that is, linked not to the willful rejection of research but to being in a field in which professionalism is not expected or supported. At other times, however, quackery is proudly displayed, as its advocates boldly proclaim that they have nothing to learn from research conducted by academics "who have never worked with a criminal" (a claim that is partially true but ultimately beside the point and a rationalization for continued ignorance).

Need we now point out the numerous programs that have been implemented with much fanfare and with amazing promises of success, only later to turn out to have "no effect" on reoffending? "Boot camps," of course, are just one recent and salient example. Based on a vague, if not unstated, theory of crime and an absurd theory of behavioral change ("offenders need to be broken down"—through a good deal of humiliation and threats—and then "built back up"), boot camps could not possibly have "worked." In fact, we know of no major psychological theory that would logically suggest that such humiliation or threats are components of effective therapeutic interventions (Gendreau et al., forthcoming). Even so, boot camps were put into place across the nation without a shred of empirical evidence as to their effectiveness, and only now has their appeal been tarnished after years of negative evaluation studies (Cullen, Pratt, Miceli, and Moon, 2002; Cullen, Wright, and Applegate, 1996; Gendreau, Goggin, Cullen, and Andrews, 2000; MacKenzie, Wilson, and Kider, 2001). How many millions of dollars have been squandered? How many opportunities to rehabilitate offenders have been forfeited? How many citizens have been needlessly victimized by boot camp graduates? What has been the cost to society of this quackery?

We are not alone in suggesting that advances in our field will be contingent on the conscious rejection of quackery in favor of an *evidence-based corrections* (Cullen and Gendreau, 2000; MacKenzie, 2000; Welsh and Farrington, 2001). Moving beyond correctional quackery when intervening with offenders, however, will be a daunting challenge. It will involve overcoming four central failures now commonplace in correctional treatment. We review these four sources of correctional quackery not simply to show what is lacking in the field but also in hopes of illuminating what a truly professional approach to corrections must strive to entail.

Four Sources of Correctional Quackery

Failure to Use Research in Designing Programs

Every correctional agency must decide "what to do" with the offenders under its supervision, including selecting which "programs" or "interventions" their charges will be subjected to. But how is this choice made (a choice that is consequential to the offender, the agency, and the community)? Often, no real choice is made, because agencies simply continue with the practices that have been inherited from previous administrations. Other times, programs are added incrementally, such as when concern rises about drug use or drunk driving. And still other times—such as when punishment-oriented intermediate sanctions were the fad from the mid-1980s to the mid-1990s—jurisdictions copy the much-publicized interventions being implemented elsewhere in the state and in the nation.

Notice, however, what is missing in this account: The failure to consider the existing research on program effectiveness. The risk of quackery rises to the level of virtual certainty when nobody in the agency asks, "Is there any evidence supporting what we are intending to do?" The irrationality of not consulting the existing research is seen when we consider again, medicine. Imagine if local physicians and hospitals made no effort to consult "what works" and simply prescribed pharmaceuticals and conducted surgeries based on custom or the latest fad. Such malpractice would be greeted with public condemnation, lawsuits, and a loss of legitimacy by the field of medicine.

It is fair to ask whether research can, in fact, direct us to more effective correctional interventions. Two decades ago, our knowledge was much less developed. But the science of crime and treatment has made important strides in the intervening years. In particular, research has illuminated three bodies of knowledge that are integral to designing effective interventions.

First, we have made increasing strides in determining the *empirically established or known predictors* of offender recidivism (Andrews and Bonta, 1998; Gendreau, Little, and Goggin, 1996; Henggeler, Mihalic, Rone, Thomas, and Timmons-Mitchell, 1998). These include, most importantly: 1) antisocial values, 2) antisocial peers, 3) poor self-control, self-management, and prosocial problem-solving skills, 4) family dysfunction, and 5) past criminality. This information is critical, because interventions that ignore these factors are doomed to fail. Phrased alternatively, successful programs start by recognizing what causes crime and then *specifically design the intervention to target these factors for change* (Alexander, Pugh, and Parsons, 1998; Andrews and Bonta, 1998: Cullen and Gendreau, 2000; Henggeler et al., 1998).

Consider, however, the kinds of "theories" about the causes of crime that underlie many correctional interventions. In many cases, simple ignorance prevails; those working in correctional agencies cannot explain what crime-producing factors the program is allegedly targeting for change. Still worse, many programs have literally invented seemingly ludicrous theories of crime that are put forward with a straight face. From our collective experiences, we have listed in Table 28.1 crime theories that either 1) were implicit in programs we ob-

Table 28.1
Questionable Theories of Crime We Have Encountered in Agency Programs

- ✓ "Been there, done that" theory.
- ✓ "Offenders lack creativity" theory.
- ✓ "Offenders need to get back to nature" theory.
- ✓ "It worked for me" theory.
- ✓ "Offenders lack discipline" theory.
- ✓ "Offenders lack organizational skills" theory.
- ✓ "Offenders have low self-esteem" theory.
- ✓ "We just want them to be happy" theory.
- ✓ The "treat offenders as babies and dress them in diapers" theory.
- ✓ "Offenders need to have a pet in prison" theory.
- ✓ "Offenders need acupuncture" theory.
- ✓ "Offenders need to have healing lodges" theory.
- ✓ "Offenders need drama therapy" theory.
- ✓ "Offenders need a better diet and haircut" theory.
- ✓ "Offenders (females) need to learn how to put on makeup and dress better" theory.
- ✓ "Offenders (males) need to get in touch with their feminine side" theory.

served or 2) were voiced by agency personnel when asked what crime-causing factors their programs were targeting. These "theories" would be amusing except that they are commonplace and, again, potentially lead to correctional quackery. For example, the theory of "offenders (males) need to get in touch with their feminine side" prompted one agency to have offenders dress in female clothes. We cannot resist the temptation to note that you will now know whom to blame if you are mugged by a cross-dresser! But, in the end, this is no laughing matter. This intervention has no chance to be effective, and thus an important chance was forfeited to improve offenders' lives and to protect public safety.

Second, there is now a growing literature that outlines what does not work in offender treatment (see, e.g., Cullen, 2002; Cullen and Gendreau, 2000; Cullen et al., 2002; Cullen et al., 1996; Gendreau, 1996; Gendreau et al., 2000; Lipsey and Wilson, 1998; MacKenzie, 2000). These include boot camps, punishment-oriented programs (e.g., "scared straight" programs), control-oriented programs (e.g., intensive supervision programs), wilderness programs, psychological interventions that are non-directive or insight oriented (e.g., psychoanalytic), and non-intervention (as suggested by labeling theory). Ineffective programs also target for treatment low-risk offenders and target for change weak predictors of criminal behavior (e.g., self-esteem). Given this knowledge, it would be a form of quackery to continue to use or to freshly implement these types of interventions.

Third, conversely, there is now a growing literature that outlines what *does* work in offender treatment (Cullen, 2002; Cullen and Gendrau, 2000). Most importantly, efforts are being made to develop principles of effective intervention (Andrews, 1995; Andrews and Bonta, 1998; Gendreau, 1996). These principles are listed in Table 28.2. Programs that adhere to these principles have been found to achieve meaningful reductions in recidivism (Andrews, Dowden, and Gendreau, 1999; Andrews, Zinger, Hoge, Bonta, Gendreau, and Cullen, 1990; Cullen, 2002). However, programs that are designed without consulting these principles are almost certain to have little or no impact on offender recidivism and may even risk increasing reoffending. That is, if these principles are ignored, quackery is likely to result. We will return to this issue below.

Failure to Follow Appropriate Assessment and Classification Practices

The steady flow of offenders into correctional agencies not only strains resources but also creates a continuing need to allocate treatment resources efficaciously. This problem is not dissimilar to a hospital that must process a steady flow of patients. In a hospital (or doctor's office), however, it is immediately recognized that the crucial first step to delivering effective treatment is diagnosing or *assessing* the patient's condition and its severity. In the absence of such a diagnosis—which might involve the careful study of symptoms or a battery of tests—the treatment prescribed would have no clear foundation. Medicine would be a lottery in which the ill would hope the doctor assigned the right treatment. In a similar way, effective treatment intervention requires the appropriate assessment of both the risks posed by, and the needs underlying the criminality of, offenders. When such diagnosis is absent and no classification of offenders is possible, offenders in effect enter a treatment lottery in which their access to effective intervention is a chancy proposition.

Strides have been made to develop more effective classification instruments—such as the Level of Supervision Inventory (LSI) (Bonta, 1996), which, among its competitors, has achieved the highest predictive validity with recidivism (Gendreau et al., 1996). The LSI and similar instruments classify offenders by using a combination of "static" factors (such as criminal history) and "dynamic factors" (such as antisocial values, peer associations) shown by previous research to predict recidivism. In this way, it is possible to classify offenders by their level of risk and to discern the types and amount of "criminogenic needs" they possess that should be targeted for change in their correctional treatment.

At present, however, there are three problems with offender assessment and classification by

Table 28.2
Eight Principles of Effective Correctional Intervention

1. Organizational Culture
Effective organizations have well-defined goals, ethical principles, and a history of efficiently responding to issues that have an impact on the treatment facilities. Staff cohesion, support for service training, self-evaluation, and use of outside resources also characterize the organization.

2. Program Implementation/Maintenance
Programs are based on empirically-defined needs and are consistent with the organization's values. The program is fiscally responsible and congruent with stakeholders' values. Effective programs also are based on thorough reviews of the literature (i.e., meta-analyses), undergo pilot trials, and maintain the staff's professional credentials.

3. Management/Staff Characteristics
The program director and treatment staff are professionally trained and have previous experience working in offender treatment programs. Staff selection is based on their holding beliefs supportive of rehabilitation and relationship styles and therapeutic skill factors typical of effective therapies.

4. Client Risk/Need Practices
Offender risk is assessed by psychometric instruments of proven predictive validity. The risk instrument consists of a wide range of dynamic risk factors or criminogenic needs (e.g., anti-social attitudes and values). The assessment also takes into account the responsivity of offenders to different styles and modes of service. Changes in risk level over time (e.g., 3 to 6 months) are routinely assessed in order to measure intermediate changes in risk/need levels that may occur as a result of planned interventions.

5. Program Characteristics
The program targets for change a wide variety of criminogenic needs (factors that predict recidivism), using empirically valid behavioral/social learning/cognitive behavioral therapies that are directed to higher-risk offenders. The ratio of rewards to punishers is at least 4:1. Relapse prevention strategies are available once offenders complete the formal treatment phase.

6. Core Correctional Practice
Program therapists engage in the following therapeutic practices: anti-criminal modeling, effective reinforcement and disapproval, problem-solving techniques, structured learning procedures for skill-building, effective use of authority, cognitive self-change, relationship practices, and motivational interviewing.

7. Inter-Agency Communication
The agency aggressively makes referrals and advocates for its offenders in order that they receive high quality services in the community.

8. Evaluation
The agency routinely conducts program audits, consumer satisfaction surveys, process evaluations of changes in criminogenic need, and follow-ups of recidivism rates. The effectiveness of the program is evaluated by comparing the respective recidivism rates of risk-control comparison groups of other treatments or those of a minimal treatment group.

Note: Items adapted from the *Correctional Program Assessment Inventory—2000*, a 131-item questionnaire that is widely used in assessing the quality of correctional treatment programs (Gendreau and Andrews, 2001).

correctional agencies (Gendreau and Goggin, 1997). First, many agencies simply do not assess offenders, with many claiming they do not have the time. Second, when agencies do assess, they assess poorly. Thus, they often use outdated, poorly designed, and/or empirically unvalidated classification instruments. In particular, they tend to rely on instruments that measure exclusively static predictors of recidivism (which cannot, by definition, be changed) and that provide no information on the criminogenic needs that offenders have. If these "needs" are not identified and addressed—such as possessing antisocial values—the prospects for recidivism will be high. For example, a study of 240 (161 adult and 79 juvenile) programs assessed across 30 states found that 64 percent of the programs did not utilize a standardized and objective assessment tool that could distinguish risk/needs levels for offenders (Matthews, Hubbard, and Latessa, 2001; Latessa, 2002).

Third, even when offenders are assessed using appropriate classification instruments, agencies frequently ignore the information. It is not uncommon, for example, for offenders to be assessed and then for everyone to be given the same treatment. In this instance, assessment becomes an organizational routine in which paperwork is compiled but the information is ignored.

Again, these practices increase the likelihood that offenders will experience correctional quackery. In a way, treatment is delivered blindly, with agency personnel equipped with little knowledge about the risks and needs of the offenders under their supervision. In these circumstances, it is impossible to know which offenders should receive which interventions. Any hopes of individualizing interventions effectively also are forfeited, because the appropriate diagnosis either is unavailable or hidden in the agency's unused files.

Failure to Use Effective Treatment Models

Once offenders are assessed, the next step is to select an appropriate treatment model. As we have suggested, the challenge is to consult the empirical literature on "what works," and to do so with an eye toward programs that conform to the principles of effective intervention. At this stage, it is inexcusable either to ignore this research or to implement programs that have been shown to be ineffective. Yet, as we have argued, the neglect of the existing research on effective treatment models is widespread. In the study of 240 programs noted above, it was reported that two-thirds of adult programs and over half of juvenile programs did not use a treatment model that research had shown to be effective (Matthews et al., 2001; Latessa, 2002). Another study—a meta-analysis of 230 program evaluations (which yielded 374 tests or effect sizes)—categorized the extent to which interventions conformed to the principles of effective intervention. In only 13 percent of the tests were the interventions judged to fall into the "most appropriate" category (Andrews et al., 1999). But this failure to employ an appropriate treatment approach does not have to be the case. Why would an agency—in this information age—risk quackery when the possibility of using an evidence-based program exists? Why not select effective treatment models?

Moving in this direction is perhaps mostly a matter of a change of consciousness—that is, an awareness by agency personnel that quackery must be rejected and programs with a track record of demonstrated success embraced. Fortunately, depending on the offender population, there is a growing number of treatment models that might be learned and implemented (Cullen and Applegate, 1997). Some of the more prominent models in this regard are the "Functional Family Therapy" model that promotes family cohesion and affection (Alexander et al., 1998; Gordon, Graves, and Arbuthnot, 1995), the teaching youths to think and react responsibly peer-helping ("Equip") program (Gibbs, Potter, and Goldstein, 1995), the "Prepare Curriculum" program (Goldstein, 1999), "Multisystemic Therapy" (Henggeler et al., 1998), and the prison-based "Rideau Integrated Service Delivery Model" that targets criminal thinking, anger, and substance abuse (see Gendreau, Smith, and Goggin, 2001).

Failure to Evaluate What We Do

Quackery has long prevailed in corrections because agencies have traditionally, required no systematic evaluation of the effectiveness of their programs (Gendreau, Goggin, and Smith, 2001). Let us admit that many agencies may not have the human or financial capital to conduct ongoing evaluations. Nonetheless, it is not clear that the failure to evaluate has been due to a lack of capacity, as much as to a lack of desire. The risk inherent in evaluation, of course, is that practices that are now unquestioned and convenient may be revealed as ineffective. Evaluation, that is, creates accountability and the commitment threat of having to change what is now being done. The cost of change is not to be discounted, but so too is the "high cost of ignoring success" (Van Voorhis, 1987). In the end, a professional must be committed to doing not simply what is in one's self-interest but what is ethical and effective. To scuttle attempts at program evaluation and to persist in using failed interventions is wrong and a key ingredient to continued correctional quackery (more broadly, see Van Voorhis, Cullen, and Applegate, 1995).

Evaluation, moreover, is not an all-or-nothing procedure. Ideally, agencies would conduct experimental studies in which offenders were randomly assigned to a treatment or control group and outcomes, such as recidivism, were measured over a lengthy period of time. But let us assume that, in many settings, conducting this kind of sophisticated evaluation is not feasible. It is possible, however, for virtually all agencies to monitor, to a greater or lesser extent, the *quality* of the programs that they or outside vendors are supplying. Such evaluative monitoring would involve, for example, assessing whether treatment services are being delivered as designed, supervising and giving constructive feedback to treatment staff, and studying whether offenders in the program are making progress on targeted criminogenic factors (e.g., changing antisocial attitudes, manifesting more prosocial behavior). In too many cases, offenders are "dropped off" in intervention programs and then, eight or twelve weeks later, are deemed—without any basis for this conclusion—to have "received treatment." Imagine if medical patients entered and exited hospitals with no one monitoring their treatment or physical recovery. Again, we know what we could call such practices.

Conclusion—Becoming an Evidence-Based Profession

In assigning the label "quackery" to much of what is now being done in corrections, we run the risk of seeming, if not being, preachy and pretentious. This is not our intent. If anything, we mean to be provocative—not for the sake of causing a stir, but for the purpose of prompting correctional leaders and professionals to stop using treatments that cannot possibly be effective. If we make readers think seriously about how to avoid selecting, designing, and using failed correctional interventions, our efforts will have been worthwhile.

We would be remiss, however, if we did not confess that academic criminologists share the blame for the continued use of ineffective programs. For much of the past quarter century, most academic criminologists have abandoned correctional practitioners. Although some notable exceptions exist, we have spent much of our time claiming that "nothing works" in offender rehabilitation and have not created partnerships with those in corrections so as to build knowledge on "what works" to change offenders (Cullen and Gendreau, 2001). Frequently, what guidance criminologists have offered correctional agencies has constituted *bad* advice—ideologically inspired, not rooted in the research, and likely to foster quackery. Fortunately, there is a growing movement among criminologists to do our part both in discerning the principles of effective intervention and in deciphering what interventions have empirical support (Cullen and Gendreau, 2001; MacKenzie, 2000; Welsh and Farrington, 2001). Accordingly, the field of corrections has more information available to find out what our "best bets" are when intervening with offenders (Rhine, 1998).

We must also admit that our use of medicine as a comparison to corrections has been overly simplistic. We stand firmly behind the central message conveyed—that what is done in corrections would be grounds for malpractice in medicine—but we have glossed over the challenges that the field of medicine faces in its attempt to provide scientifically-based interventions. First, scientific knowledge is not static but evolving. Medical treatments that appear to work now may, after years of study, prove ineffective or less effective than alternative interventions. Second, even when information is available, it is not clear that it is effectively transmitted or that doctors, who may believe in their personal "clinical experience," will be open to revising their treatment strategies (Hunt, 1997). "The gap between research and knowledge," notes Millenson (1997, p. 4), "has real consequences. . . . When family practitioners in Washington State were queried about treating a simple urinary tract infection in women, eighty-two physicians came up with an extraordinary 137 different strategies." In response to situations like these, there is a renewed evidence-based movement in medicine to improve the quality of medical treatments (Millenson, 1997; Timmermans and Angell, 2001).

Were corrections to reject quackery in favor of an evidence-based approach, it is likely that agencies would face the same difficulties that medicine encounters in trying base treatments on the best scientific knowledge available. Designing and implementing an effective program is more complicated, we realize, than simply visiting a library in search of research on program effectiveness (although this is often an important first step). Information must be available in a form that can be used by agencies. As in medicine, there must be opportunities for training and the provision of manuals that can be consulted in how *specifically* to carry out an intervention. Much attention has to be paid to implementing programs as they are designed. And, in the long run, an effort must be made to support widespread program evaluation and to use the resulting data both to improve individual programs and to expand our knowledge base on effective programs generally.

To move beyond quackery and accomplish these goals, the field of corrections will have to take seriously what it means to be a *profession*. In this context, individual agencies and individuals within agencies would do well to strive to achieve what Gendreau et al. (forthcoming) refer to as the "3 C's" of effective correctional policies: First, employ *credentialed people;* second, ensure that the *agency is credentialed* in that it is founded on the principles of fairness and the improvement of lives through ethically defensive means; and third, base treatment decisions on *credentialed knowledge* (e.g., research from meta-analyses).

By themselves, however, given individuals and agencies can do only so much to implement effective interventions—although each small step away from quackery and toward an evidence-based practice potentially makes a meaningful difference. The broader issue is whether the *field* of corrections will embrace the principles that all interventions should be based on the best research evidence, that all practitioners must be sufficiently trained so as to develop expertise in how to achieve offender change, and that an ethical corrections cannot tolerate treatments known to be foolish, if not harmful. In the end, correctional quackery is not an inevitable state of affairs—something we are saddled with for the foreseeable future. Rather, although a formidable foe, it is ultimately rooted in our collective decision to tolerate ignorance and failure. Choosing a different future for corrections—making the field a true profession—will be a daunting challenge, but it is a future that lies within our power to achieve.

References

Alexander, James, Christie Pugh, and Bruce Parsons. 1998. *Functional Family Therapy: Book Three in the Blueprints and Violence Prevention Series.* Boulder, CO: Center for the Study and Prevention of Violence, University of Colorado.

Andrews, D. A. 1995. "The Psychology of Criminal Conduct and Effective Treatment." Pp. 35–62 in James McGuire (ed.), What Works: Reducing Reoffending. West Sussex, UK: John Wiley.

Andrews, D. A., and James Bonta. 1998. *Psychology of Criminal Conduct,* 2nd ed. Cincinnati: Anderson.

Andrews, D. A., Craig Dowden, and Paul Gendreau. 1999. "Clinically Relevant and Psychologically Informed Approaches to Reduced Re-Offending: A Meta-Analytic Study of Human Service, Risk, Need, Responsivity, and Other Concerns in Justice Contexts." Unpublished manuscript, Carleton University.

Andrews, D. A., Ivan Zinger, R. D. Hoge, James Bonta, Paul Gendreau, and Francis T. Cullen. 1990. "Does Correctional Treatment Work? A Clinically Relevant and Psychologically Informed Meta-Analysis." *Criminology* 28: 369–404.

Bonta, James. 1996. "Risk-Needs Assessment and Treatment." Pp. 18–32 in Alan T. Harland (ed.), *Choosing Correctional Options That Work: Defining the Demand and Evaluating the Supply.* Thousand Oaks, CA: Sage.

Cullen, Francis T. 2002. "Rehabilitation and Treatment Programs." Pp. 253–289 in James Q. Wilson and Joan Petersilia (eds.), *Crime: Public Policies for Crime Control.* Oakland, CA: ICS Press.

Cullen, Francis T. and Brandon K. Applegate, eds. 1997. *Offender Rehabilitation: Effective Correctional Intervention.* Aldershot, UK: Ashgate/Dartmouth.

Cullen, Francis T. and Paul Gendreau. 2000. "Assessing Correctional Rehabilitation: Policy, Practice, and Prospects." Pp. 109–175 in Julie Horney (ed.), *Criminal Justice 2000: Volume 3—Policies, Processes, and Decisions of the Criminal Justice System.* Washington, DC: U.S. Department of Justice, National Institute of Justice.

Cullen, Francis T. and Paul Gendreau. 2001. "From Nothing Works to What Works: Changing Professional Ideology in the 21st Century." *The Prison Journal* 81:313–338.

Cullen, Francis T., Travis C. Pratt, Sharon Levrant Miceli, and Melissa M. Moon. 2002. "Dangerous Liaison? Rational Choice Theory as the Basis for Correctional Intervention." Pp. 279–296 in Alex R. Piquero and Stephen G. Tibbetts (eds.), *Rational Choice and Criminal Behavior: Recent Research and Future Challenges.* New York: Routledge.

Cullen, Francis T., John Paul Wright, and Brandon K. Applegate. 1996. "Control in the Community: The Limits of Reform?" Pp. 69–116 in Alan T. Harland (ed.), *Choosing Correctional Interventions That Work: Defining the Demand and Evaluating the Supply.* Thousand Oaks, CA: Sage.

Cullen, John B. 1978. *The Structure of Professionalism.* Princeton, NJ: Petrocelli Books.

Gendreau, Paul. 1996. "The Principles of Effective Intervention with Offenders." Pp. 117–130 in Alan T. Harland (ed.), *Choosing Correctional Options That Work: Defining the Demand and Evaluating the Supply.* Newbury Park, CA: Sage.

Gendreau, Paul. 2000. "1998 Margaret Mead Award Address: Rational Policies for Reforming Offenders." Pp. 329–338 in Maeve McMahon (ed.), *Assessment to Assistance: Programs for Women in Community Corrections.* Lanham, MD: American Correctional Association.

Gendreau, Paul and D. A. Andrews. 2001. *Correctional Program Assessment Inventory—2000.* Saint John, Canada: Authors.

Gendreau, Paul and Claire Goggin. 1997. "Correctional Treatment: Accomplishments and Realities." Pp. 271–279 in Patricia Van Voorhis, Michael Braswell, and David Lester (eds.), *Correctional Counseling and Rehabilitation,* 3rd edition. Cincinnati: Anderson.

Gendreau, Paul, Claire Goggin, Francis T. Cullen, and D.A. Andrews. 2000. "The Effects of Community Sanctions and Incarceration on Recidivism." *Forum on Corrections Research* 12 (May): 10–13.

Gendreau, Paul, Claire Goggin, Francis T. Cullen, and Mario Paparozzi. Forthcoming. "The Common Sense Revolution in Correctional Policy." In James McGuire (ed.), *Offender Rehabilitation and Treatment: Effective Programs and Policies to Reduce Re-Offending.* Chichester, UK: John Wiley and Sons.

Gendreau, Paul, Claire Goggin, and Paula Smith. 2001. "Implementing Correctional Interventions in the 'Real' World." Pp. 247–268 in Gary A. Bernfeld, David P. Farrington, and Alan W. Leschied (eds.), *Inside the "Black Box" in Corrections.* Chichester, UK: John Wiley and Sons.

Gendreau, Paul, Tracy Little, and Claire Goggin. 1996. "A Meta-Analysis of the Predictors of Adult Offender Recidivism: What Works?" *Criminology* 34:575–607.

Gendreau, Paul, Paula Smith, and Claire Goggin. 2001. "Treatment Programs in Corrections." Pp. 238–263 in John Winterdyk (ed.), Corrections in Canada: Social Reaction to Crime. Toronto, Canada: Prentice-Hall.

Gibbs, John C., Granville Bud Potter, and Arnold P. Goldstein. 1995. *The EQUIP Program: Teaching Youths to Think and Act Responsibly Through a Peer-Helping Approach.* Champaign, IL: Research Press.

Goldstein, Arnold P. 1999. *The Prepare Curriculum: Teaching Prosocial Competencies.* Rev. ed. Champaign, IL: Research Press.

Gordon, Donald A., Karen Graves, and Jack Arbuthnot. 1995. "The Effect of Functional Family Therapy for Delinquents on Adult Criminal Behavior." *Criminal Justice and Behavior* 22: 60–73.

Henggeler, Scott W., with the assistance of Sharon R. Mihalic, Lee Rone, Christopher Thomas, and Jane Timmons-Mitchell. 1998. *Multsystemic Therapy: Book Six in the Blueprints in Violence Prevention Series.* Boulder, CO: Center for the Study and Prevention of Violence, University of Colorado.

Hunt, Morton. 1997. *How Science Takes Stock: The Story of Meta-Analysis.* New York: Russell Sage Foundation.

Latessa, Edward J. 2002. "Using Assessment to Improve Correctional Programming: An Update." Unpublished paper, University of Cincinnati.

Lipsey, Mark W. and David B. Wilson. 1998. "Effective Intervention for Serious Juvenile Offenders." Pp. 313–345 in Rolf Loeber and David P. Farrington (eds.), *Serious and Violent Juvenile Offenders: Risk Factors and Successful Intervention.* Thousand Oaks, CA: Sage.

MacKenzie, Doris Layton. 2000. "Evidence-Based Corrections: Identifying What Works." *Crime and Delinquency* 46:457–471.

MacKenzie, Doris Layton, David B. Wilson, and Suzanne B. Kider. 2001. "The Effects of Correctional Boot Camps on Offending." *Annals of the American Academy of Political and Social Science* 578 (November): 126–143.

Matthews, Betsy, Dana Jones Hubbard, and Edward J. Latessa. 2001. "Making the Next Step: Using Assessment to Improve Correctional Programming." *Prison Journal* 81:454–472.

Millenson, Michael L. 1997. *Demanding Medical Excellence: Doctors and Accountability in the Information Age.* Chicago: University of Chicago Press.

Rhine, Edward E. (ed.). 1998. *Best Practices: Excellence in Corrections.* Lanham, MD: American Correctional Association.

Starr, Paul. 1982. *The Social Transformation of American Medicine: The Rise of a Sovereign Profession and the Making of a Vast Industry.* New York: Basic Books.

Timmermans, Stefan and Alison Angell. 2001. "Evidence-Based Medicine, Clinical Uncertainty, and Learning to Doctor." *Journal of Health and Social Behavior* 42:342–359.

Van Voorhis, Patricia. 1987. "Correctional Effectiveness: The High Cost of Ignoring Success." *Federal Probation* 51 (March): 59–62.

Van Voorhis, Patricia, Francis T. Cullen, and Brandon K. Applegate. 1995. "Evaluating Interventions with Violent Offenders: A Guide for Practitioners and Policymakers." *Federal Probation* 59 (June): 17–28.

Welsh, Brandon C. and David P. Farrington. 2001. "Toward an Evidence-Based Approach to Preventing Crime." *Annals of the American Academy of Political and Social Science* 578 (November): 158–173.

Edward J. Latessa, Francis T. Cullen, and Paul Gendreau, "Beyond Correctional Quackery: Professionalism and the Possibility of Effective Treatment." Reprinted from *Federal Probation* September 2002, 66 (2): 43–49. Published by The Administrative Offices of the United States Courts. ✦

Unit IV

Discussion Questions

1. What is the purpose of punishment?
2. Does probation "work"? How do you define "work"?
3. Review the strengths and weaknesses of the various probation delivery models outlined by Whitehead and Braswell. Why do the authors conclude that the restorative justice and spiritual modes are the most promising for the future?
4. What probation model(s) would you endorse and why?
5. What can be done to improve probation services?
6. What are some examples of intermediate punishments? Should we utilize them more frequently?
7. Why have intermediate sentencing options been added to the sentencing guidelines grid? Are intermediate sanctions proving to be effective?
8. What is prison-based programming, what can it do, and why is it needed?
9. What are the principles of effective prison-based programming? Do you support prison-based programming? Why or why not?
10. Parole hearings are exempt from constitutionally protected due-process procedural rights. How does this constitutional reality impact the day-to-day operations of parole boards? What has the state of Colorado done with respect to this issue and how are they able to do this? Do you agree with the "Colorado model"? Why or why not?
11. Discuss the problems experienced by inmates in the context of the parole decision-making process.
12. What can be done to get inmates and parole board members on the "same page" when it comes to identifying parole release decision factors?
13. What is the relationship between community supervision, prosocial activities, and recidivism? In what way does community supervision seem to impact positively upon recidivism rates?
14. Why does the public support capital punishment? How are those perspectives formed? What are the impacts of race and religion upon public perspectives of capital punishment?
15. Do you support capital punishment? Why or why not? What are the arguments advanced by those who disagree with you on this topic?
16. The Supreme Court has ruled that the death penalty is not unconstitutional in part because a majority of the public does not con-

sider it to be so. If a majority of the people felt it was cruel and unusual punishment, would the Supreme Court then view it as unconstitutional?

17. Should the Supreme Court consider public opinion in determining the constitutionality of cases brought before it?

18. What needs to be done to move corrections in the direction of a legitimate profession? What measures need to be undertaken to increase the overall efficacy of correctional treatment?

19. What new correctional programs do you think should be implemented in this country?

20. Design a research evaluation effort to determine whether the new correctional programs you propose would positively impact the actual crime perpetration rate. ✦

Unit V

American Juvenile Justice

The juvenile justice system is a unique American creation that evolved from the child-saver movement of the 1800s (Platt, 1969). It was thought that separate proceedings were needed to address the special needs of young people. The first official juvenile court was formed in Illinois in 1899, with almost every state following suit in the next few years.

Consider the following material taken from a report prepared by the Bureau of Justice Statistics (1988, 78–79):

> Cases involving juveniles are handled much differently than adult cases. The juvenile court and a separate process for handling juveniles resulted from reform movements of the late 19th century. Until that time juveniles who committed crimes were processed through the criminal courts. In 1899 Illinois established the first juvenile court based on the concepts that a juvenile was a salvageable human being who needed treatment rather than punishment and that the juvenile court was to protect the child from the stigma of criminal proceedings. Delinquency and other situations such as neglect and adoption were deemed to warrant the court's intervention on the child's behalf. The juvenile court also handled "status offenses" (such as truancy, running away, and incorrigibility), which are not applicable to adults.
>
> While the juvenile courts and the handling of juveniles remain separated from criminal processing, the concepts on which they are based have changed. Today, juvenile courts usually consider an element of personal responsibility when making decisions about juvenile offenders.
>
> Juvenile courts may retain jurisdiction until a juvenile legally becomes an adult (generally at age 18 in most states). This limit sets a cap on the length of time juveniles may be institutionalized that is often much less than that for adults who commit similar offenses. Some jurisdictions transfer the cases of juveniles accused of serious offenses or with long criminal histories to criminal court so that the length of the sanction cannot be abridged.
>
> Juvenile courts are very different from criminal courts. The language used in juvenile courts is less harsh. For example, juvenile courts
>
> - accept "petitions of delinquency" rather than criminal complaints.
> - conduct "hearings," not trials.
> - "adjudicate" juveniles to be "delinquent" rather than find them guilty of a crime.
> - order one of a number of available "dispositions" rather than sentences.

Despite the wide discretion and informality associated with juvenile court proceedings, juveniles are protected by most of the due process safeguards associated with adult criminal trials.

Most referrals to juvenile court are for property crimes, but roughly 20 percent are for status offenses. . . .

Arrest is not the only means of referring juveniles to the courts. While adults may begin criminal justice processing only through arrest, summons, or citations, juveniles may be referred to court by law enforcement agencies, parents, schools, victims, probation officers, or other sources.

Law enforcement agencies refer three-quarters of the juvenile cases, and they are most likely to be the referral source in cases involving curfew violations, drug offenses, and property crimes. Other referral sources are most likely in cases involving status offenses (truancy, ungovernability, and running away).

"Intake" is the first step in the processing of juveniles. At intake, decisions are made about whether to begin formal proceedings. Intake is most frequently performed by the juvenile court or an executive branch intake unit, but increasingly prosecutors are becoming involved. In addition to beginning formal court proceedings, officials at intake may refer the juvenile for psychiatric evaluation, informal probation, or counseling, or, if appropriate, they may close the case altogether.

For a case involving a juvenile to proceed to a court adjudication, the intake unit must file a petition with the court. Intake units handle most cases informally without a petition. The National Center for Juvenile Justice estimates that more than half of all juvenile cases disposed of at intake are handled informally without a petition and are dismissed and/or referred to a social service agency.

Initial juvenile detention decisions are usually made by the intake staff. Prior to holding an adjudicatory hearing, juveniles may be released in the custody of their parents, put in protective custody (usually in foster homes or runaway shelters), or admitted to detention facilities. Relatively few juveniles are detained prior to court appearance.

Under certain circumstances, juveniles may be tried in criminal courts. Age at which criminal courts gain jurisdiction of young offenders ranges from 16 to 18.

Age of offender when under criminal court jurisdiction	States
16 years	Connecticut, New York, North Carolina
17	Georgia, Illinois, Louisiana, Massachusetts, Michigan, Missouri, New Hampshire, South Carolina, Texas, Wisconsin
18	Alabama, Alaska, Arizona, Arkansas, California, Colorado, Delaware, District of Columbia, Florida, Hawaii, Idaho, Indiana, Iowa, Kansas, Kentucky, Maine, Maryland, Minnesota, Mississippi, Montana, Nebraska, Nevada, New Jersey, New Mexico, North Dakota, Ohio, Oklahoma, Oregon, Pennsylvania, Rhode Island, South Dakota, Tennessee, Utah, Vermont, Virginia, Washington, West Virginia, Federal districts
19	Wyoming

Source: John T. Whitehead and Steven P. Lab, *Juvenile Justice*. Cincinnati, OH: Anderson, 1999, p. 6.

All states allow juveniles to be tried as adults in criminal courts. Juveniles are referred to criminal courts in one of three ways:

- ***Concurrent jurisdiction.*** The prosecutor has the discretion of filing charges for certain offenses in either juvenile or criminal courts.
- ***Excluded offenses.*** The legislature excludes from juvenile court jurisdiction certain offenses usually either very minor, such as traffic or fishing violations, or very serious, such as murder or rape.
- ***Judicial waiver.*** The juvenile court waives its jurisdiction and transfers the case to criminal court (the procedure is also known as "binding over" or "certifying" juvenile cases to criminal courts).

Less than 1 percent of all juvenile cases are referred to criminal court. Recent studies found that most juveniles referred to criminal court were age 17 and were charged with property offenses. However, juveniles charged with violent offenses or with serious prior offense histories were more likely to be adjudicated in criminal court. Waiver of juveniles to criminal court is less likely where court jurisdiction extends for several years beyond the juvenile's 18th birthday.

Juveniles tried as adults have a very high conviction rate, but most receive sentences of probation or fines. More than 90 % of the judicial waiver or concurrent jurisdiction cases in Hamparian's study resulted in guilty verdicts, and more than half the convictions led to fines or probation. Sentences to probation often occur because the criminal courts view juveniles as first offenders regardless of their prior juvenile record. However, serious violent juvenile offenders are more likely to be institutionalized. In a study of 12 jurisdictions with Habitual or Serious or Violent Juvenile Offender Programs, 63 percent of those convicted were sentenced to prison and 14 percent to jail. The average prison sentence was 6.8 years.

Correctional activities for juveniles tried as adults in most states occur within the criminal justice system. In . . . more than half the states, youths convicted as adults and given an incarcerative sentence could only be placed in adult corrections facilities. In [a number of states,] youths convicted as adults could be placed in either adult or juvenile corrections facilities, but sometimes this discretion was limited by special circumstances. [A small number of states] restrict placement of juveniles convicted as adults to state juvenile corrections institutions. Generally, youths sentenced in this manner will be transferred to adult facilities to serve the remainder of their sentence on reaching majority.

Parens Patriae

The original philosophy behind the creation of a separate juvenile system was based on the *parens patriae* concept: The state was to serve not as an adversary, but as a parent; it was to function on behalf of the child. Consequently, the adversarial nature that typified the adult court was rejected in favor of a more informal procedure. This procedure, however, often seemed to work against the child. There were often pressures to confess, rights to counsel were denied, decisions were made "off the record," and appellate rights were limited. Concerns over these procedurally lawless arrangements finally came to a head in the 1960s, when the Supreme Court began to take a more active interest in juvenile court operations. In a number of landmark cases, both the Warren and Burger Courts outlined a series of fundamental due-process elements that were to be included in juvenile court proceedings. Nevertheless, juvenile courts still function less formally than adult courts.

Serious Crimes

The founding philosophy of *parens patriae* has long since been abandoned as juvenile courts have struggled to deal with an increasingly violent and chronically delinquent juvenile clientele. Nearly all school violence studies find that the large majority of those surveyed report that the amount of violence has either stayed the same or has increased. The Center for Disease Control estimates that more than 100,000 guns are carried to school each day. A presidential executive order was signed in 1994 requiring schools to expel students caught with guns on campus. In addition, many schools have installed metal detectors and have hired security guards. From all available evidence, this has not seemed to deter young people from continuing to bring weapons to school. Tragic episodes of school shootings continue, from metropolitan areas like New York City and Los Angeles to suburban Denver, to rural communities like Jonesboro, Arkansas, and Springfield, Oregon.

Youth in Crisis

Across the board, young people appear to be in crisis—nearly half of 15- to 17-year-olds are sexually active, the annual birth rate for 15- to 19-year-olds is 55 per 1,000, nearly 40 percent of 12- to 17-year-olds use alcohol weekly, and nearly 10 percent of 12- to 17-year-olds are drug abusers. The suicide rate for 15- to 19-year-olds is 10 per 100,000, and nearly 2 million youth are arrested each year. The good news is that all these figures appear to be falling. The number of "kids having kids" is on the decline, and youth suicide rates are dropping as well.[1] Juvenile crime rates are also falling, including violent crime rates. By the same token, in a historical context, the numbers are still quite high. Though the juvenile violent crime index arrests have turned downward in the last few years, they still remain 50 percent above mid-1980s levels. Likewise, teenage birth rates and suicide rates, both in the midst of a several-year decline, are still higher than they were in 1980. Although some progress seems to have been made, the drug and alcohol abuse levels are still unacceptably high. Interestingly, nearly 30 perecent of all juvenile arrests are females. This figure represents a small but steady increase in the past few years in the proportion of female to male juvenile arrests, and is something that is currently being carefully monitored by the juvenile justice community.

Explaining why youth engage in delinquent and criminal behaviors has proven to be quite difficult, and numerous theories abound. Many youth appear not to have a stake in conventional society, and instead join gangs where they perpetuate the oppositional culture of the streets (Anderson 1990). Gang activity certainly had much to do with the rise in violent crime in the latter portion of the 20th century. There are no firm figures available as to how many gangs exist in the United States nor how many juveniles are actively involved. But there is no doubt as to the existence of juvenile gangs and gang activity, and it appears that recruiting efforts are now reaching into the elementary schools, enticing children as young as 8 years old into street gangs. Gang activity seems to be accelerating.

Responding to the Problem

At present, it can be argued that the justice system lacks the ability to respond effectively to the size, scope, and complexity of contemporary delinquency problems. Incarceration is emerging as a default option and is being used much more frequently than ever before. There are approximately 110,000 juveniles in custody (roughly 65 percent in public facilities and 35 percent in private institutions), up from 80,000 in the mid-1980s. Yet numerous studies have clearly documented that confinement is a short-term response at best, and that incarcerating a young person can actually increase the likelihood of further offenses upon release. Consequently, the deinstitutionalization of status offenders remains on the agenda of many writers, researchers, and government leaders.

Due in part to the concerns over institutionalizing young people, a number of social and psychological approaches are currently being used to respond to the delinquency problem, such as positive peer culture, diversion programs, guided group interaction, individual counseling, reality therapy, Project Head Start, tutoring-mentoring volunteer programs, drug and alcohol programming, halfway houses, boot camps, job corps, Outward Bound, transactional analysis, curfews, after-school programs, and teen courts, among many, many others. There is a good deal of controversy in the field, however, as to the effectiveness of these approaches, and to the proper course of action to be undertaken in the future. Critics argue that the present juvenile justice system lacks the ability to effectively deal with the delinquency problem because it is "embedded in a larger social context" (Bernard 1992, 187). Numerous researchers point out that the solutions to the present situation lie outside the justice system in the form of better family relations, improved educational and employment opportunities, enhanced social opportunities, and greater spiritual bonds. The delinquency problem clearly has its roots in areas that the government cannot do much about.

* * *

Some critics have proposed the abolition of the separate juvenile justice structure. However, its abandonment is highly unlikely, and there is little chance of realizing the fundamental social changes advocated by many juvenile justice researchers. Instead, system officials will likely continue to make marginal adjustments in the juvenile justice process. As a result, it is likely the crisis will only deepen as we move into the next century.

Note

1. The United States Bureau of the Census reported that suicide rates for youth aged 10 to 14 more than doubled from 1970 to 1985, and that 15- to 19-year-olds experienced a 70 percent increase in the same period. These figures do warrant some brief discussion. The upward surge for 15- to 19-year-olds seems to have peaked in 1988 and dropped slightly in the late 1990s. It is currently just below the national average of 12 per 100,000. The suicide rate for 10- to 14-year-olds has continued to rise, but the rates (less than 2 per 100,000) and the actual numbers (roughly 320 a year) are rather small and account for only 1 percent of the suicides in America each year.

References and Further Reading Materials

Anderson, Elijah. 1990. *Streetwise: Race, Class and Change in an Urban Community.* Chicago: University of Chicago Press.

Bernard, Thomas J. 1992. *The Cycle of Juvenile Justice.* Upper Saddle River, NJ: Prentice-Hall.

Bureau of Justice Statistics. 1988. *Report to the Nation on Crime and Justice.* Washington, DC: United States Department of Justice.

Chesney-Lind, Meda and Randall G. Shelden. 1998. *Girls: Delinquency and Juvenile Justice.* Belmont, CA: West/Wadsworth.

Curry, David and Scott Decker. 1998. *Confronting Gangs.* Los Angeles: Roxbury.

Miller, Jody, Cheryl L. Maxson, and Malcolm Klein. 2001. *The Modern Gang Reader.* Los Angeles: Roxbury.

Platt, Anthony M. 1969. *The Child Savers.* Chicago: University of Chicago Press.

Siegel, Larry J. and Joseph Senna. 2000. *Juvenile Delinquency.* Belmont, CA: Wadsworth.

Trojanowicz, Robert C., Merry Morash, and Pamela J. Schram. 2001. *Juvenile Delinquency.* Upper Saddle River, NJ: Prentice Hall. ✦

Chapter 29

Serious, Violent, and Chronic Juvenile Offenders

The Relationship of Delinquency Career Types to Adult Criminality

Kimberly Kempf-Leonard
Paul E. Tracy
James C. Howell

While significant research has been devoted to the most extreme juvenile offenders, few have studied the differences between serious, violent, and chronic delinquents. The authors examine the distinctions between different delinquent careers to study their impact on adult criminality. Finally, they look for demographic characteristics shared by each subgroup in hopes of identifying and rehabilitating those juvenile offenders who are most likely to go on to serious criminal behavior as adults.

Few topics currently receive as much policy and research attention as serious, violent, and chronic juvenile offenders. Although the current "feeding frenzy" of policy initiatives (Howell 1997; also see Doi 1998; Zimring 1996, 1998) has no obvious starting point, one can argue that it stems from media accounts stating that serious juvenile crime is approaching epidemic proportions (Blumstein 1995; DiIullio 1996; Fox 1996). These accounts gave rise to distorted notions of the "superpredator" (DiIullio 1996) and the liberated "female gangsta" (Chesney-Lind 1997:34–77; Maher and Curtis 1995) as relatively common phenomena. Fear of juvenile offenders committed to crime subsequently fueled public anxiety about teenagers in general (Bernard 1992; Feld 1999; Males 1996). As a result, recent policy action in nearly every state has created harsher, more restrictive juvenile codes and procedures for processing juvenile offenders defined according to broad categories as heinous (Torbet et al. 1996; Walker 1995).

Major research is now under way to identify those youths who are at risk of becoming the most extreme delinquents, to develop effective intervention strategies to stop their criminality, and to initiate prevention programs which will assure that youths in the future do not follow similar career paths in delinquency. Surprisingly little attention, however, has been devoted to the career distinctions between serious, violent, and chronic offenders. In this [chapter] we examine differences in prevalence and incidence of adult offending among serious, violent, and chronic delinquents in the 1958 Philadelphia birth cohort, by gender, race, and socioeconomic status. With a large number of subjects and extensive criminal history information through age 26, these data enable us to make comparisons across delinquent and criminal careers that are not available in many other investigations. On the basis of our findings, we suggest how knowledge about these career distinctions and demographic differences might affect future research and policy.

Developmental Theory and Research

"Chronic" offenders were introduced to the field when the results of the first Philadelphia birth cohort study were published (Wolfgang, Figlio, and Sellin 1972). This study, along with cohort studies conducted in Racine, Wisconsin by Shannon (1978, 1980) and in Columbus, Ohio by Hamparian et al. (1978), stimulated interest in serious and violent offender careers. These studies also helped to renew criminologists' interest in criminal careers and career criminals; consequently, in 1983 the National Academy of Sciences convened the Panel on Research on Criminal Careers to assess the evidence and recommend directions for future research (Blumstein et al. 1986). Because of the scarcity of longitudinal studies, the Panel could shed little light on the link between offending during adolescence and during adulthood.

Taken together, two seminal essays by Loeber and Le Blanc (1990) and Le Blanc and Loeber (1998) trace the growth of developmental criminology as a perspective guiding the study of delinquent and criminal careers. This theoretical perspective focuses research on crime and delinquency in two important areas: the causes and correlates of criminal offending, and the life course trajectories of criminal offending (Le Blanc and Loeber 1998:117).

"Trajectories," sometimes called "pathways" (Loeber et al. 1993; Sampson and Laub 1993), represent individuals' movements along developmental sequences. Usually these trajectories span more than one developmental period, such as childhood, adolescence, and adulthood (Le Blanc and Loeber 1998). Descriptors of offending patterns covering two or more of these periods are what Le Blanc and Loeber (1998) call "metatrajectories." Patterson, Capaldi, and Bank (1991) identified two distinct groups of offenders: those who start early, and those who start in adolescence and offend for only a short period. Moffitt (1993; also see Moffitt et al. 1996) separated early-onset offenders from others in her two metatrajectories: "life-course-persistent offenders" and "adolescence-limited offenders." The first group includes those who begin with oppositional behaviors and aggressive acts in childhood and persist into more violent behaviors through adolescence and into adulthood. The second group engages in violent acts only during adolescence. Neither research team attempted to identify differences between offenders within each of the two subgroups.

Wilson and Howell (1993) proposed three juvenile delinquent metatrajectories, consisting of subtypes that might be linked to adult criminal careers: serious, violent, and chronic. Snyder (1998) showed empirically the existence of these delinquent career subgroups in 16 birth cohorts of referrals to the Maricopa County (AZ) juvenile court. Using arrest data, Loeber, Van Kammen, and Fletcher (1996; cited in Loeber, Farrington, and Waschbusch 1998:18–19) replicated Snyder's (1998) analysis in the representative urban sample of boys in the Pittsburgh Youth Study. Their results also showed these three distinct subgroups.

The first aim of this study is to see whether these three main delinquent subgroups can be distinguished in the adolescent period in the 1958 Philadelphia birth cohort. Next we examine whether these subgroups are useful for examining the continuity of offender careers from childhood and adolescence to adulthood, and, if so, whether certain demographic factors characterize them. If this proves to be the case, we will have confirmed the need to examine subgroups of offenders beyond Moffitt's (1993; Moffitt et al. 1996) adolescence-limited and life-course persistent offenders.

Recent Research in Developmental Criminology

Not all studies agree about particular characteristics of the two groups identified by Patterson and Moffitt, nor about the strength of explanatory models (see Dean, Brame, and Piquero 1996; Krohn et al. 2001; Nagin, Farrington, and Moffit 1995; Nagin and Land 1993; Paternoster and Brame 1997).

Other subgroups of offenders have been identified: one, for whom onset occurs in adolescence (rather than in childhood), with continued offending into adulthood (Kempf 1988; Nagin et al. 1995); another, for whom onset occurs in adulthood (Tracy and Kempf-Leonard 1996); and yet another, who apparently cease offending in adolescence but resume in adulthood (Kempf 1989). Few studies, however, have followed the same participants into adulthood to see whether the adolescence-limited offenders indeed desist (see Nagin et al. 1995). Unfortunately, most of the research identifying the two groups is based on studies only of males.

After an initial concentration on chronic offenders, developmental criminologists focused on the early-onset hypothesis, positing that early-onset offenders would have more serious and more extensive careers than late-onset offenders. This hypothesis receives support in the literature. Of 22 studies reviewed by Krohn et al. (2001), 21 reported a significant relationship between early onset and later crime and delinquency. For example, Tracy and Kempf-Leonard's (1996) analysis of data on the 1958 Philadelphia birth cohort affirmed the importance of delinquency status on offending in adulthood. The study also revealed that early onset, frequency of offending, offense concentration or specialization (particularly weapons possession and having co-offenders), offense seriousness, and offense escalation as juveniles increased the likelihood of adult offending. These researchers did not distinguish subgroups defined by the interactions between sex, race, and socioeconomic status (e.g. lower-class black males). Most important, they did not identify the intersections between delinquency careers that were serious, violent, or chronic, nor did they examine the number of adult crimes for which these subgroups were responsible.

Other developmental criminologists have pursued offense specialization in offender careers (Farrington, Snyder, and Finnigan 1988; Hindelang 1971; Kempf 1987; Piquero et al. 1999; Rojek and Erickson 1982; Tracy, Wolfgang, and Figlio 1990). Generally these studies have found little offense specialization except for weapons possession and having co-offenders (as noted above; see Tracy and Kempf-Leonard 1996) and status offenses (especially running away) among female offenders. In a recent analysis of Philadelphia birth cohort data, Mazerolle et al. (2000) examined offense specialization within life-course-persistent (early-onset) and adolescence-limited (late-onset) offenders, using three offense categories: violent, property, and all other offenses. Following Moffitt (1993), they hypothesized that life-course-persistent offenders would demonstrate more diversity in types of offending than adolescence-limited offenders. Indeed, this was the case. Interestingly, males were not more versatile than females.

Krohn and his colleagues (2001) extended the developmental criminologists' early-onset hypothesis with respect to the ages of early-onset offenders. They proposed that offenders who begin very early (age 10 and under) have more serious and more violent offender careers in the adolescent and young adult years: "their criminal careers are of greater duration, extending further into their life course; . . . they will commit more offenses and have higher individual offending rates; and . . . their offenses will tend to be more serious and more violent than those of late onset offenders" (p. 68). These hypotheses were supported for the very youngest offenders in their analyses of data from two ongoing longitudinal studies, conducted in Rochester, NY and Montreal (Le Blanc and Frechette 1989); the data from the Montreal study were less consistent, however.

The federal Office of Juvenile Justice and Delinquency Prevention (OJJDP) established a Study Group on serious and violent juvenile offenders to review knowledge about serious, violent, and chronic juvenile offenders, and about the types of interventions that apparently can reduce their level of offending (Loeber and Farrington 1998a; for a summary, see Loeber and Farrington 1998b). The Study Group's overall conclusions were limited largely to serious and violent offenders because the group quickly discovered the problems of defining "chronic" offenders for comparison of results from existing studies (Loeber and Farrington 1998a:2). The term *chronic* usually incorporates two dimensions: frequency of offending and the length of time over which offending persists (see Laub and Lauritsen 1993). Studies using self-report measures, however, typically use operational definitions of chronicity based on a much larger number of offenses than do court studies; the latter are based on referral and adjudication measures, thus rendering comparisons difficult.

On the basis of their review of chronic offender studies for the OJJDP Study Group, Loeber et al. (1998) offer several conclusions. First, the proportions of chronic offenders vary considerably from study to study (from 7% to 25%). Second, the amount of crime accounted for by chronic offenders varies by ethnicity: nonwhite male chronic offenders account for a greater proportion of official serious delinquency. Third, there are large gender differences: chronic offending is lower in females than in males. Fourth, the amount of crime accounted for by chronic offenders varies by cohort in the same location (see Shannon 1988). Fifth, the amount of crime accounted for by chronic offenders varies by offense type: it is relatively low when all offenses are taken into account, and somewhat higher for violent offenses, especially robbery (see Tracy et al. 1990; Wolfgang et al. 1972).

Snyder's (1998) Study Group contribution offers the first empirical description of the parameters that distinguish serious, violent, and chronic juvenile offenders. Using a Maricopa County (AZ) sample of 151,209 court-referred youths (from 16 annual birth cohorts), Snyder examined their juvenile court careers. He found that almost two-thirds (64%) of these careers pertained to nonchronic (fewer than four referrals), nonserious, and nonviolent delinquents. About one-third (34%) of all careers contained a serious-nonviolent referral, 15 percent pertained to chronic offenders (four or more court referrals), 8 percent contained a violent referral, and slightly over 3 percent were chronic and included serious and violent offenses. (It is inappropriate to total these percentages because an individual offender can be represented in more than one career type.) Snyder also examined the overlap, or intersections, among juvenile offender subgroups.

For the OJJDP Study Group, Loeber and his colleagues (1996; cited in Loeber et al. 1998:18–19) replicated Snyder's (1998) analysis in the representative urban sample of boys in the Pittsburgh Youth Study. Using Pittsburgh police records, they found the Pittsburgh subgroups to be similar in size to Snyder's Arizona cohorts. About one-third (36%) of the chronic offenders were also violent offenders (versus 29% in Snyder's Arizona cohorts), nearly one-half (45%) of the violent offenders were also chronic offenders (versus 53% in the Arizona cohorts), and about one-third (35%) of the serious offenders also were chronic offenders (versus 35% in the Arizona cohorts). Thus, in both studies, most chronic offenders did not commit violent acts, although most violent delinquents were also chronic offenders. Further, the majority of chronic and violent offenders also were involved in serious but nonviolent offending. Regrettably, neither of these studies could determine the propensity for adult offending linked to each delinquency subgroup, nor did they examine differences associated with sociodemographic characteristics.

Previously the National Academy of Sciences' Panel on Research on Criminal Careers had argued that "demographic variables have received considerable attention, primarily because they are widely available in data on the general population, are easily observed by crime victims and police, and are routinely recorded for identification purposes in data from administrative and operational agencies" (Blumstein et al. 1986:24). Although this argument may be true for estimates of delinquency prevalence, it does not hold for career pathways that require more rigorous measurement and large numbers of subjects for observation. In particular, this void exists because of the difficulty of observing the low base rate for serious, violent, and chronic juvenile offenders in general, and especially for females. For example, Huizinga and Jakob-Chien contend, "[B]ecause statistical significance is dependent on sample sizes, some differences that appear to be substantively significant are not statistically different, especially for girls" (1998:53). Along this line, Tolan and Gorman-Smith (1998) report that "estimates for females are less stable." Even so, they find some evidence of (1) a lower proportion of high aggression among females but (2) a higher proportion of serious offending among the more aggressive females (p. 74). These authors concluded that because most studies have focused on males, researchers face serious limitations in applying knowledge developed only on males, and much of what can be concluded about serious, violent, and chronic juvenile offenders may apply only to males (p. 70).

In the OJJDP Study Group review of racial differences among serious juvenile offenders, Hawkins, Laub, and Lauritsen (1998) use national arrest data for 1995 to show that the disproportionate representation of black youths varies considerably by crime type (p. 34). Arguing for observations of within-group racial differences, these authors also note that "many of the social and ecological correlates of serious and chronic offending have not been fully incorporated into extant theory and explanation" (pp. 30–31). Unfortunately, the authors comment that gender differences are beyond the scope of their paper and refer to a single study based only on young black women (p. 46).

Even though demographic correlates of offenders' careers have received little attention in studies to date, this lack of information has not precluded some assertions about the applicability of findings across demographic subgroups. For example, Loeber and Hay (1994) argued that their conceptual model of three pathways based on 1,500 males in the Pittsburgh Youth Study can account for most delinquency career patterns. This model, however, has not been validated separately for females, nor have gender-specific analyses been conducted (Tolan and Gorman-Smith 1998). In addition, in their meta-analysis of the predictors of serious or violent offending in longitudinal studies, Lipsey and Derzon (1998:89), reported that the samples studied have been primarily male; yet they still identified gender as the most significant personal characteristic associated with violent and/or serious delinquency (pp. 96–98). These authors also observe that although gender and race are not "malleable," prediction models suggest that male gender is "not a feasible target" for preventive intervention in age groups 6 to 11 and 12 to 14 (p. 100).

In sum, the developmental perspective departs from traditional criminology or sociology, which usually compares groups of deviants with nondeviants or criminals with noncriminals, in an effort to understand the origins of deviancy and criminality. Developmental criminology concentrates mainly on changes within offender groups over the life course. In the words of Le Blanc and Loeber (1998), "[W]e know very little about changes in individuals' rates of offending and how rates of offending wax and wane over the life cycle . . . it remains to be seen to what extent individuals' mixture of offenses and degree of seriousness of delinquency develop over time and in an orderly and predictable manner" (p. 116). Farrington (1998) argues that comparisons across subgroups of serious offenders are precisely the focus now needed in criminological research. In addition, very little is known about the sociodemographic characteristics of subgroups that are represented in life-course offender careers.

With respect to life-course-persistent offenders, we propose that serious, violent, and chronic juvenile offender subgroups can be distinguished among adult criminal offenders and that they make a disproportionate contribution to adult crime. In addition, we hypothesize a cascading effect in these subgroups' contribution to adult crime. That is, following Wilson and Howell (1993), we propose that the serious, violent, and chronic juvenile offender subgroup is most likely to continue offending in adulthood and to account for the most disproportionate amount of adult crime. We cannot specify in advance the order in which other subgroups (serious delinquents, violent delinquents, chronic delinquents, serious and chronic delinquents, chronic and violent delinquents, and serious and violent delinquents) will continue offending in adulthood and contribute disproportionately to adult crime. This is the first study to conduct such an analysis. Neither Snyder (1998) nor Loeber and his colleagues (1996) analyzed the number of offenses committed by these subgroups. Therefore this analysis is exploratory. As a final aim of this study, we examine demographic differences across these offender trajectories. Given previous research, we anticipate a higher prevalence of "worse" offending among black males from lower-class neighborhoods.

The Present Study

The 1958 Philadelphia birth cohort constitutes a population. As such, it is not vulnerable to the usual threats to external validity posed by sampling procedures because every available subject is included regardless of delinquency or adult crime status. This cohort of 13,160 males and 14,000 females is the largest of its kind; it includes detailed information drawn from several sources able to identify its members' characteristics. The eligibility requirement for defining the cohort is Philadelphia residence from ages 10 and 18; this provides a uniform time frame and setting within which cohort members were at risk of offending. Sample mortality is not problematic in this longitudinal investigation because the retrospective data collection involved unobtrusive archival examination of records that are maintained routinely by the Philadelphia Police Department and area schools.

Measuring Delinquency and Crime

Police rap sheets and investigation reports were provided by the Juvenile Aid Division of the Philadelphia Police Department to characterize police encounters that members of the cohort experienced before age 18. In addition to official arrests, the rap sheet data contain "police contact" information. The police maintain records of these contacts that result in "remedial," informal, or diversionary handling of the youths by an officer, whereby youths generally are remanded to their parents' custody. Thus the juvenile delinquency data contain both official arrests and informal contacts that did not result in an arrest. In this way they represent a total record of official delinquency; further, they constitute a much fuller record of delinquency than data based solely on arrest information. We used the police investigation reports to supplement information provided in the rap sheets with detailed descriptions of the criminal event in which the subject was involved.

Arrest records for the subjects after age 18 were extracted from files maintained by the Municipal Court and the Court of Common Pleas of Philadelphia. Although obtained from a different source, these data are comparable to the police data for juveniles except that informal action by police was not recorded. Adult criminal history data are available through December 31, 1984, or through age 26 for all cohort members. These data do not capture adult women who changed their surname and whose arrest as adults was their first police encounter. Tracy and Kempf-Leonard (1996) and Tracy et al. (1985, 1990) provide further descriptions of the data collection procedures for the 1958 Philadelphia Birth Cohort Study and the results of a comparison study of the juvenile delinquency careers for males in the 1958 and 1945 Philadelphia cohorts.

Within-individual changes in offender patterns, as represented in official records, are compiled from the adolescent period through young adulthood (age 26) in the 1958 Philadelphia birth cohort data set. These careers are categorized into nondelinquent, serious, violent, and chronic offender subgroups. In the final step, we examine the transition of these respective subgroups from nondelinquent and delinquent careers to criminality during adulthood. In the present analysis we focus on serious, violent, and chronic offenders, rather than on other subgroups that might well be empirically valid, because this nomenclature is most directly relevant to policy and programs.

The data include records from all public and private schools in Philadelphia, and were used to identify the population of 27,160 males and females born in 1958 who lived in Philadelphia at least from ages 10 through 18. Together with the criminal history data that were collected for the cohort through age 26, these data are superior to those on which many previous investigations were based. The present data permit the systematic structuring of the longitudinal sequence of police contacts and thereby facilitate the identification of youths, both delinquents and nondelinquents, who are most likely to proceed to adult crime.

We use the definition of chronic offenders as those with a record of five or more police encounters (Hamparian et al. 1978; Shannon 1978; Wolfgang et al. 1972; Wolfgang, Thornberry, and Figlio 1987). We define violent offenders as those with a delinquency record including homicide, rape, robbery, aggravated assault, or aggravated sexual intercourse. We define serious offenders to include all violent offenders, plus those with records of burglary, theft, automobile theft, arson, and vandalism greater than $500.

Measuring Sociodemographic Factors

We used three sociodemographic correlates in the analyses: gender, race (i.e., white, African American, Hispanic, Asian, and American Indian), and socioeconomic status of the neighborhood. Only the latter requires any elaboration. We have adopted the position taken by Thornberry and Farnworth (1982): that measuring only a single indicator of social status is inadequate and should be abandoned in favor of multiple indicators (p. 507). Specifically, we used a complex measure of neighborhood social status that encompasses a number of separate indicators applied to residential address in 1970.[1] We developed this measure as follows.

From the 1970 Bureau of Census files for Philadelphia we selected a total of 15 census tract variables. We inspected the univariate distributions and performed logarithmic transformations because the data were skewed or otherwise unevenly distributed. From the pool of 30 variables (the original 15 variables and the 15 transformations) we selected a final set of 10 indicators of social status: median family income, percentage of families below median income, families below the poverty line, percent ages 18–24 with less than high school education, population on welfare, percent age 25 and older with less than high school education, percent age 16 and older out of school and unemployed, percent ages 16–21 out of school and unemployed, percent employed in unskilled labor, and percentage of female-headed households. These items were noted most often in previous studies of SES and crime, and they were distributed most normally across census tracts.

Although summary scales and additive indices are often used, we preferred to employ a multivariate technique for deriving the social status indicator. Thus we used principal-components factor analysis. From the first principal component extracted in the factor analysis, we computed the factor score, which we then assigned to each census tract. In turn, we noted the factor score for a cohort subject's census tract of residence as of 1970, or age 12. The factor scores ranged from –3.04 to +1.89; as in all standard scores, the mean was 0 and the standard deviation was 1. Because the great majority of our analyses consider SES as a qualitative variable, we dichotomized the factor scores (below and above the mean) to produce a discrete SES construct with two levels: low SES and high SES. We used very reliable census data and sophisticated statistical procedures; thus we have employed the best available measure of neighborhood social status. Even so, we are aware of the limitations of aggregate measures.

Results

In Figure 29.1, a Venn diagram with intersecting circles represents the proportion of delinquents in each of the career types, overlapping areas represent careers with attributes from two or more subgroups, and shading represents the percentage that also committed crime in adulthood. All 6,287 delinquents are included in the outer circle. Those delinquents who had no record of any serious offense and fewer than five encounters with the police are included in the proportion of the large circle outside the other circles. Adult offending was reported for 48.0 percent of the serious delinquents, 52.8 percent of the violent delinquents, 58.5 percent of the chronic delinquents, 62.5 percent of the delinquents with both serious and chronic offending, and 63.1 percent of the violent and chronic delinquents. These increasing percentages represent a strong trend toward adult criminality as the severity and/or chronicity of the delinquency career is examined.

Next we examine the distributions of adult offending (including the total number of offenses) among the delinquency subgroups, based separately on gender, race, and socioeconomic status. Within the cohort, the delinquents were distributed as 31.4 percent female, 64.5 percent black, 2.9 percent Hispanic, and 63.8 percent living in lower-class areas. The distributions of delinquency career types and adult offending by demographic traits are shown in Tables 29.1 through Table 29.4.

Among the 4,315 male delinquents, according to Table 29.1, 50.6 percent had a record of a serious offense, in contrast to only 16.5 percent of the 1,972 females. Given the smaller number of females, however, a gender comparison based merely on frequencies would be inappropriate because the males would obviously predominate. It is far more accurate to make gender comparisons based on percentage of delinquents, which adjust for the population size at risk. If we use the percentages to calculate the ratio of males to females among the serious delinquents, the ratio identifies three males for every one female who is a serious delinquent. Violent delinquents included 1,128 males, or 26.1

Figure 29.1
Venn Diagram Showing Intersection Between Delinquency Career Types

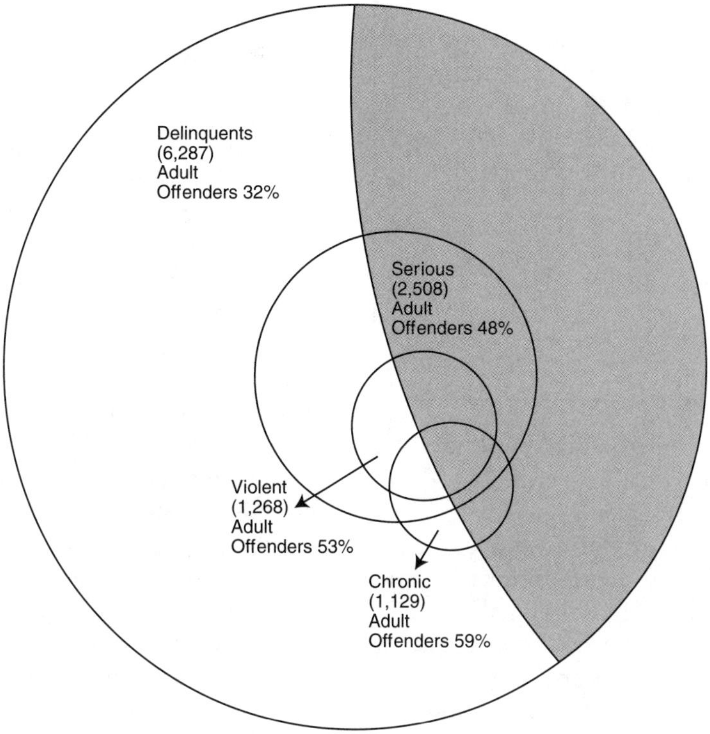

percent of the 4,315 male delinquents, and 140 females, or 7.1 percent of the 1,972 female delinquents. Thus we found nearly four violent delinquent males for every violent female. Chronic delinquents included 982 males (22.8%) and 147 females (7.4%), for a male-to-female ratio of 3 to 1.

Table 29.1 also shows the intersection among serious, violent, and chronic juvenile offenders, and the proportion of each that subsequently became adult offenders. There were 895 males who were classified as both serious and chronic offenders. Although they account for only one-fifth of all male delinquents, this group represents 91.1 percent of the total chronic subset and 41.0 percent of the serious male delinquents. In contrast, the 69 serious and chronic female delinquents made up less than 4 percent of the total delinquents, 46.9 percent of the chronic group, and 21.2 percent of the serious female delinquents. For each serious and chronic female delinquent, there were approximately six male delinquents.

Delinquents who were both violent and chronic offenders included 612 males, or 14.2 percent of males, and 39 females, or 2 percent of the female delinquents. This career type represented 62.3 percent of the male chronic offenders, 26.5 percent of the female chronic offenders, 54.2 percent of the violent males, and 27.9 percent of the violent females. Each violent and chronic female delinquent had seven male counterparts.

The data indicate parallel patterns for adult prevalence and share of adult criminality among the delinquency career types for males and females, although males were substantially more likely to exhibit every career type. The greatest differential in adult offending concerns "virgin" adult offenders, or those with no juve-

Table 29.1
Prevalance of Delinquency Career Types and Adult Offending, by Gender

Career Types	Category Total	% of Total Delinquents	% That Were Adult Offenders	# of Adult Crimes	% of Adult Crimes	Ratio, Career Types
Male						
Total subjects	13,160	—	23.4 (3,077)	8,149	100.0	—[a]
Not delinquents	8,845	—	14.4 (1,272)	2,573	31.6	—
Total delinquents	4,315	100.0	41.8 (1,805)	5,576	68.4	
Serious delinquents	2,182	50.6	51.5 (1,123)	3,965	48.7	3.1:1
Violent delinquents	1,128	26.1	56.2 (634)	2,404	29.5	3.7:1
Chronic delinquents	982	22.8	63.0 (619)	2,649	32.5	3.1:1
Serious and chronic del.	895	20.7	63.8 (571)	2,478	30.4	5.9:1
Violent and chronic del.	612	14.2	64.4 (394)	1,698	20.8	7.1:1
Female						
Total subjects	14,000	—	3.9 (540)	908	100.0	—[b]
Not delinquents	12,028	—	2.5 (304)	426	46.9	—
Total delinquents	1,972	100.0	12.0 (236)	482	53.1	—
Serious delinquents	326	16.5	24.8 (81)	240	26.4	.32:1
Violent delinquents	140	7.1	25.7 (36)	136	15.0	.27:1
Chronic delinquents	147	7.4	28.6 (42)	169	18.6	.32.1
Serious and chronic del.	69	3.5	43.5 (30)	141	15.5	.17:1
Violent and chronic del.	39	2.0	43.6 (17)	100	11.0	.14:1

NOTE: Numbers in parentheses indicate the number of adult offenders.
[a] Ratios, male to female
[b] Ratios, female to male

nile record: we observed adult crime for 14.4 percent of the males and 2.5 percent of the females, or a ratio of 5.8 males to one female. Yet when we examine the relationship of delinquency career type to adult criminality and crimes accumulated, we find that males and females follow the same patterns despite the lower prevalence (as expected) among females. Thus, for example, we see that among males, the proportion who go on to adult crime is 51.5 percent for serious delinquents, 56.2 percent for violent delinquents, 63 percent for chronic delinquents, 63.8 percent for the serious and chronic, and 64.4 percent for the violent and chronic. In comparison, the data for females show lower percentages but display the same trend of increasing risk as the career types escalate: 24.8 percent for serious delinquents, 25.7 percent for violent delinquents, 28.6 percent for chronic delinquents, 43.5 percent for the serious and chronic, and 43.6 percent for the violent and chronic.

We also find a remarkable similarity by gender in the results concerning the number of adult crimes for which the various delinquent career types were responsible. These data, however, indicate that the effect of career type is stronger among females than males—an important point. As we examine the more serious, more violent, and more chronic career types or their intersections, we find that females commit an even more disproportionate share of adult crime than their male counterparts. For example, the serious female delinquents (16.5%) committed 26.4 percent of all the adult crime by women; among males, the serious delinquents (50.6%) committed only 48.7 percent of the adult crime by men. Among the violent females (7.1%) and the chronic females (7.4%), these career types were responsible for more than twice their proportionate shares of adult crime: 15 percent and 18.6 percent respectively. The comparable data for males indicate that the violent and chronic delinquents represented slightly more than 20 percent of the males. These male delinquent types, however, did not commit more than twice their shares of adult crime, but only 29.5 percent and 32.5 percent respectively.

The intersections of the career types produce the most disparate results. For females, the intersection of serious and chronic consists of 69 delinquents. These offenders make up only 3.5 percent of female delinquents; yet 43.5 percent became adult criminals who committed 141 offenses, or 15.5 percent of all adult crime by women. Therefore, this small group of serious and chronic female delinquents was responsible for a share of adult crime 4.4 times greater than their size would suggest. Even more startling, for the violent and chronic female delinquents, the 39 offenders are only 2 percent of all the female delinquents, but 43.6 percent went on to adult careers in crime and amassed 100 criminal offenses as adults, or 11 percent of the total. Here the share is 5.5 times greater than parity would suggest.

The males do not show the same share of adult crimes. The serious and chronic male delinquents make up 20.7 percent of the male offenders but committed only 30.4 percent of the adult male crimes. Similarly, male delinquents who were both violent and chronic accounted for 14.2 percent of the male delinquents but committed only 20.8 percent of the adult male crimes. Clearly, males show a greater propensity toward serious components in their delinquency careers, but these components carry a greater risk of adult crime for females.

In Table 29.2 we examine the career types across the various racial categories. We wish to learn whether the relationships between delinquency career types and adult offending found for gender also hold true when the subjects' race is considered. Delinquency career distinctions show that serious offenders included 28.8 percent of the white delinquents, 45.4 percent of the black delinquents, and 39.6 percent of the Hispanic delinquents. These distributions of serious delinquency indicate that the ratio of black to white is 1.6 to 1, white to Hispanic is .7 to 1, and black to Hispanic is 1 to 1. Violence involved 8.9 percent of the white delinquents, 26.1 percent of the black delinquents, and 14.4 percent of the Hispanic delinquents; thus, for violent delinquency, the ratio of black to white is 2.9 to 1, white to Hispanic is .7 to 1, and black to Hispanic is 1.8 to 1. We observed chronic delinquency for 12 percent of the white delinquents, 21.1 percent of the black delinquents, and 15.0 percent of the Hispanic delinquents. Thus, we found nearly two black chronic delinquents for every one white chronic delinquent. Regardless of race, adult offending was least prevalent among the nondelinquents. Also, the association between delinquency career type and adult criminality is strong: prevalence was highest among chronic offenders who also had records of either violent or serious crimes.

Table 29.2
Prevalance of Delinquency Career Types and Adult Offending, by Race

Career Types	Category Total	% of Total Delinquents	% That Were Adult Offenders		# of Adult Crimes	% of Adult Crimes	Ratio, Career Types
White							
Total subjects	12,853	—	9.1	(1,172)	2,570	100.0	—[a]
Not delinquents	10,831	—	5.5	(597)	1,050	40.9	—
Total delinquents	2,022	100.0	28.4	(575)	1,520	59.1	—
Serious delinquents	583	28.8	44.4	(259)	864	33.6	.63:1
Violent delinquents	179	8.9	49.2	(88)	290	11.3	.34:1
Chronic delinquents	243	12.0	59.3	(144)	597	23.2	.57:1
Serious and chronic del.	193	9.5	63.7	(123)	544	21.2	.52:1
Violent and chronic del.	83	4.1	57.8	(48)	186	7.2	.30:1
Black							
Total subjects	13,529	—	17.4	(2,349)	6,245	100.0	—[b]
Not delinquents	9,465	—	9.8	(932)	1,854	29.7	—
Total delinquents	4,064	100.0	34.9	(1,417)	4,391	70.3	—
Serious delinquents	1,847	45.4	49.4	(913)	3,229	51.7	1.6:1
Violent delinquents	1,061	26.1	53.5	(568)	2,173	34.8	2.9:1
Chronic delinquents	857	21.1	58.3	(500)	2,148	34.4	1.8:1
Serious and chronic del.	747	18.4	61.7	(461)	2,002	32.1	1.9:1
Violent and chronic del.	556	13.7	63.7	(354)	1,559	25.0	3.3:1
Hispanic							
Total subjects	725	—	13.1	(95)	240	100.0	—[c]
Not delinquents	538	—	8.7	(47)	95	39.6	—
Total delinquents	187	100.0	25.7	(48)	145	60.4	—
Serious delinquents	74	39.6	43.2	(32)	112	46.6	.87:1
Violent delinquents	27	14.4	51.9	(14)	77	32.1	.55:1
Chronic delinquents	28	15.0	60.7	(17)	73	30.4	.81:1
Serious and chronic del.	24	12.8	70.8	(17)	73	30.4	.61:1
Violent and chronic del.	12	6.4	75.0	(9)	53	22.1	.47:1
Other Minorities							
Total subjects	53	—	1.9	(1)	2	100.0	—[d]
Not delinquents	39	—	na	(0)	na	na	—
Total delinquents	14	100.0	7.1	(1)	2	100.0	—
Serious delinquents	4	28.6	na	(0)	na	na	na
Violent delinquents	1	7.1	na	(0)	na	na	na
Chronic delinquents	1	7.1	na	(0)	na	na	na
Serious and chronic del.	0	na	na	na	na	na	na
Violent and chronic del.	0	na	na	na	na	na	na

NOTE: Numbers in parentheses indicate the number of adult offenders.
[a] Ratios, white to black
[b] Ratios, black to white
[c] Ratios, Hispanic to black
[d] Ratios, career types

Among white subjects, the proportion of adult offenders rises as one moves from serious (44.4%) to violent (49.2%) to chronic (59.3%). In regard to the intersections, however, the proportion with adult offenses was slightly higher among chronic delinquents (59.3%) than among chronic and violent delinquents (57.8%), while white youths with a record of serious and chronic offending subsequently produced the highest prevalence of adult crime (63.7%). Similarly, a substantial proportion of adult crimes may be attributed to the following delinquency career types: serious (33.6%), violent (11.3%), chronic (23.2%), serious and chronic (21.2%), and violent and chronic (7.2%).

The results for black subjects produce a more consistent and much stronger relationship than for white youths. That is, at each successive career type, black delinquents show an increasing proportion of adult criminals: serious (49.4%), violent (53.5%), chronic (58.3%), serious and chronic (61.7%), and violent and chronic (63.7%). The corresponding proportions of all adult crime by black subjects in the cohort are as follows: serious (51.7%), violent (34.8%), chronic (34.4%), serious and chronic (32.1%), and violent and chronic (25.0%).

The results for Hispanics in the cohort are even stronger than for blacks. At each successive career type, Hispanic subjects show an increasing proportion of adult criminals, which reaches a highly disproportionate figure: serious (43.2%), violent (51.9%), chronic (60.7%), serious and chronic (70.8%), and violent and chronic (75.0%). As with whites and blacks, the small groups of Hispanic offenders across the at-risk career types produce a greater share of adult offenses than their size would suggest: serious (46.6%), violent (32.1%), chronic (30.4%), serious and chronic (30.4%), and violent and chronic (22.1%).

In regard to socioeconomic status, one would expect that youths from low status areas would be at greater risk for delinquency, would be more likely to reflect higher percentages of the various career types, and consequently would be at greater risk for adult crime. Those from neighborhoods of higher social status, on the other hand, should be insulated . . . against delinquency and career type progression, and one would expect less association with adult crime. The results shown in Table 29.3, however, indicate that the career progression was strong regardless of SES.

Serious offenders included 1,768 (44.1%) of the delinquents from low-SES areas and 740 (32.5%) of those from high-SES areas; these figures represent a ratio of low SES to high SES of 1.4 to 1. In the low-SES subgroup, 49.9 percent of the serious delinquents became adult criminals and committed a total of 3,120 adult offenses, or 51.2 percent of all the adult crimes by cohort members from low-SES areas. Similarly, among serious delinquents from the high-SES subgroup, 43.5 percent became adult criminals with a total of 1,085 offenses, or 36.6 percent of the subgroup's crimes.

Violent delinquency also shows an increase. In the low-SES subgroup, 53.4 percent of the violent delinquents became adult criminals who contributed 32.1 percent of their total adult crimes; in the high-SES subgroup, 51.2 percent of the violent delinquents went on to adult crime and were responsible for 19.7 percent of their adult crimes.

Chronic delinquency continues the pattern. Of the delinquents from low-SES areas who were chronic, 60.2 percent were adult criminals and amassed a total of 2,152 crimes (35.3% of the total). Of the chronic delinquents from high-SES areas, 54.1 percent had records of adult crime showing a total of 666 crimes (22.4% of the total).

For the 718 delinquents (17.8% of the total) from the low-SES subgroup with both serious and chronic delinquency, 63.8 percent became adult criminals and had 2,000 adult arrests (32.8% of the total). We found 246 delinquents (10.8% of the total) from high-SES neighborhoods with this pattern; 58.1 percent of these went on to adult careers and committed a total of 619 adult offenses, or 20.9 percent of the total.

In the low-SES subgroup, 12.7 percent had a violent and chronic delinquency career, in contrast to only 6.2 percent of the high-SES subgroup. This career type produced the highest prevalence of adult crime: 64.4 percent for subjects from the low-SES areas and 58.5 percent for subjects from high-SES areas. The totals of adult crime were about twice as high as would be expected from this comparatively small concentration. That is, the violent chronic delinquents from low-SES areas accounted for only 12.7 percent of all offenders in the subgroup, but were responsible for 23.4 percent of all the adult crime. Even among delinquents from high-SES areas—whose neighborhood might have been expected to act as an insulator against further criminality—142 delinquents (6.2%) showed both violent and chronic delinquency. From this subgroup emerged 83 adult criminals who were responsible for 371 adult crimes, or 12.5 percent of all the adult crimes by cohort members from high-SES neighborhoods.

To distinguish the career offense patterns further and to ensure that the results held true regardless of demographic factors, we examined the intersections between gender, race, and socioeconomic status groups. These results are displayed in Table 29.4, with all factors cross-classified. We omitted Hispanics and subjects in the "other race" category because the cells contained insufficient cases to justify tabular analysis.

Table 29.3
Prevalence of Delinquency Career Types and Adult Offending by Socioeconomic Status

Career Types	Category Total	% of Total Delinquents	% That Were Adult Offenders	# of Adult Crimes	% of Adult Crimes	Ratio, L:H Career Types
Low SES						
Total subjects	13,362	—	17.1 (2,279)	6,090	100.0	—[a]
Not delinquents	9,354	—	9.6 (898)	1,831	30.1	—
Total delinquents	4,008	100.0	34.5 (1,381)	4,259	69.9	—
Serious delinquents	1,768	44.1	49.9 (882)	3,120	51.2	1.4:1
Violent delinquents	965	24.1	53.4 (515)	1,956	32.1	1.8:1
Chronic delinquents	826	20.6	60.2 (497)	2,152	35.3	1.5:1
Serious and chronic del.	718	17.9	63.8 (458)	2,000	32.8	1.7:1
Violent and chronic del.	509	12.7	64.4 (328)	1,427	23.4	2.0:1
High SES						
Total subjects	13,798	—	9.7 (1,338)	2,967	100.0	—[b]
Not delinquents	11,519	—	5.9 (678)	1,168	39.4	—
Total delinquents	2,279	100.0	29.0 (660)	1,799	60.6	—
Serious delinquents	740	32.5	43.5 (322)	1,085	36.6	.74:1
Violent delinquents	303	13.3	51.2 (155)	584	19.7	.55:1
Chronic delinquents	303	13.3	54.1 (164)	666	22.4	.84:1
Serious and chronic del.	246	10.8	58.1 (143)	619	20.9	.60:1
Violent and chronic del.	142	6.2	58.5 (83)	371	12.5	.49:1

NOTE: Numbers in parentheses indicate the number of adult offenders.
[a] Ratios, low to high
[b] Ratios, high to low

Table 29.4
Prevalence of Delinquency Career Types and Adult Offending by Gender, Race, and Socioeconomic Status

Career Types	Category Total	% of Total Delinquents	% That Were Adult Offenders	# of Adult Crimes	% of Adult Crimes	Ratio, M:F Career Types
Low SES White						
Male						
Total subjects	1,318	—	25.1 (331)	953	100.0	
Not delinquents	881	—	16.2 (143)	318	33.4	
Total delinquents	437	100.0	43.0 (188)	635	66.6	
Serious delinquents	198	45.3	57.1 (113)	447	46.9	
Violent delinquents	67	15.3	56.7 (38)	150	15.7	
Chronic delinquents	90	20.6	72.2 (65)	328	34.4	
Serious and chronic del.	80	18.3	73.8 (59)	307	32.2	
Violent and chronic del.	35	8.0	68.6 (24)	107	11.2	
Female						
Total subjects	1,478	—	3.0 (44)	73	100.0	—
Not delinquents	1,258	—	1.7 (22)	29	39.7	—
Total delinquents	220	100.0	10.0 (22)	44	60.3	—
Serious delinquent	24	10.9	25.0 (6)	22	30.1	4.2:1
Violent delinquents	9	4.1	44.4 (4)	7	9.6	3.7:1
Chronic delinquents	14	6.4	28.6 (4)	17	23.3	3.2:1
Serious and chronic del.	5	2.3	60.0 (3)	16	21.9	8.0:1
Violent and chronic del.	3	1.4	66.7 (2)	4	5.4	5.7:1
Low SES Black						
Male						
Total subjects	4,779	—	31.3 (1,496)	4,288	100.0	
Not delinquents	2,629	—	20.0 (526)	1,167	27.2	
Total delinquents	2,150	100.0	45.1 (970)	3,121	72.8	
Serious delinquents	1,275	59.3	52.8 (673)	2,371	55.3	
Violent delinquents	767	35.7	56.6 (434)	1,631	38.0	
Chronic delinquents	608	28.3	63.2 (384)	1,626	37.9	
Serious and chronic del.	568	26.4	63.4 (360)	1,519	35.4	
Violent and chronic del.	434	20.2	65.0 (282)	1,202	28.0	
Female						
Total subjects	5,153	—	6.2 (318)	543	100.0	—
Not delinquent	4,120	—	4.0 (165)	229	42.2	—
Total delinquents	1,033	100.0	14.8 (153)	314	57.8	—
Serious delinquents	206	19.9	28.2 (58)	168	30.9	3.0:1
Violent delinquents	97	9.4	25.8 (25)	91	16.8	3.8:1
Chronic delinquents	90	8.7	30.0 (27)	108	19.9	3.3:1
Serious and chronic del.	43	4.2	44.2 (19)	85	15.7	6.3:1
Violent and chronic del.	26	2.5	42.3 (11)	61	11.2	8.1:1
High SES White						
Male						
Total subjects	4,898	—	14.6 (715)	1,423	100.0	
Not delinquents	3,923	—	9.7 (381)	634	44.6	
Total delinquents	975	100.0	34.3 (334)	789	55.4	
Serious delinquents	318	32.6	42.1 (134)	388	27.3	
Violent delinquents	92	9.4	48.9 (45)	131	9.2	
Chronic delinquents	119	12.2	58.8 (70)	245	17.2	
Serious and chronic del.	99	10.2	58.6 (58)	217	15.2	
Violent and chronic del.	42	4.3	50.0 (21)	73	5.1	
Female						
Total subjects	5,159	—	1.6 (82)	121	100.0	—
Not delinquents	4,769	—	1.1 (51)	69	57.0	—
Total delinquents	390	100.0	7.9 (31)	52	43.0	—
Serious delinquents	43	11.0	14.0 (6)	7	5.8	3.0:1
Violent delinquents	11	2.8	9.1 (1)	2	1.7	3.4:1
Chronic delinquents	20	5.1	25.0 (5)	7	5.8	2.4:1
Serious and chronic del.	9	2.3	33.3 (3)	4	3.3	4.4:1
Violent and chronic del.	3	.8	33.3 (1)	2	1.7	5.4:1
High SES Black						
Male						
Total subjects	1,782	—	25.2 (449)	1,256	100.0	
Not delinquents	1,164	—	15.6 (182)	369	29.4	
Total delinquents	618	100.0	43.2 (267)	887	70.6	
Serious delinquents	322	52.1	53.4 (172)	648	51.6	
Violent delinquents	174	28.2	59.2 (103)	415	33.0	
Chronic delinquents	139	22.5	60.4 (84)	378	30.1	
Serious and chronic del.	125	20.2	62.4 (78)	363	28.9	
Violent and chronic del.	89	14.4	65.2 (58)	263	20.9	
Female						
Total subjects	1,815	—	4.7 (86)	158	100.0	—
Not delinquents	1,552	—	3.8 (59)	89	56.3	—
Total delinquents	263	100.0	10.3 (27)	69	43.7	—
Serious delinquents	44	16.7	22.7 (10)	42	26.6	3.1:1
Violent delinquents	23	8.7	26.1 (6)	36	22.8	3.2:1
Chronic delinquents	20	7.6	25.0 (5)	36	22.8	3.0:1
Serious and chronic del.	11	4.2	36.4 (4)	35	22.2	4.8:1
Violent and chronic del.	7	2.7	42.9 (3)	33	20.9	5.3:1

NOTE: Numbers in parentheses indicate the number of adult offenders.

The rank order of prevalence for each delinquency career type was the same, from highest percentage to lowest: (1) low-SES black males; (2) high-SES black males; (3) low-SES white males; (4) high-SES white males; (5) low-SES black females; (6) high-SES black females; (7) high-SES white females; and (8) low-SES white females. Serious delinquency was the most common career, and ranged from 10.9 percent of the low-SES white females to 59.3 percent of the low-SES black males. The least common career pattern was both violent and chronic delinquency: 1.4 percent of the low-SES white females to 20.2 percent of the low-SES black males.

In nearly all cases, adult crime was more prevalent among chronic delinquents who also had committed either serious or violent offenses. The results clearly indicate that regardless of gender, race, or socioeconomic status, delinquency career types carry an increasing risk of adult crime. In all cases, the serious and chronic type and the violent and chronic type, although only a small proportion of the subjects in their demographic subgroups, commit a far greater share of adult crimes than such a small proportion would produce under conditions of equal criminal propensity.

Last, to provide a multivariate test of the relationship between adult crime status and the various delinquent career subgroups, we conducted a series of logistic regression analyses. We partitioned serious delinquency into its two components: major violence and major property offenses. Using adult crime status as the dependent variable, we estimated various main-effects models to examine the predictive ability and statistical significance of the two demographic factors (race and residential social status) and the three delinquency career factors (chronic delinquency, major violence, and major property). We sequenced the various models to test the effects of the delinquency factors individually and in various combinations: (three paired comparisons and all three delinquency factors together simultaneously). We estimated the models separately for males and for females because the occurrence of the delinquency career factors and the criterion measure differed so substantially by sex. The data for males would affect the coefficients disproportionately in a joint model and might provide misleading information about career pathways in general. The logistic regression results are presented in Tables 29.5 and 29.6.

The logistic regression results provide useful information about the relationship between the delinquency career types and the status of adult offending. Table 29.6 indicates in all models that, for females, residential social status has a

Table 29.5
Logistic Regression Models: Delinquency Career Types on Adult Offending: Males

	Black	Hispanic	Other Race	Residence Status	Chronic Delinquent	Major Violence	Major Property
Model 1							
B	.094	−.235	−1.654	−.097*	1.085***		
SE	.081	.206	1.061	.040	.076		
Wald	1.362	1.297	2.428	5.967	202.790		
Exp (*B*)	1.099	.791	.191	.907	2.959		
Model 2							
B	.037	−.272	−1.689	−.111**		.739***	
SE	.081	.204	1.058	.039		.073	
Wald	.207	1.779	2.550	7.923		103.374	
Exp (*B*)	1.037	.762	.185	.895		2.093	
Model 3							
B	.148	−.245	−1.693	−.109**			.598***
SE	.079	.203	1.057	.039			.064
Wald	3.469	1.452	2.562	7.761			86.163
Exp (*B*)	1.159	.783	.184	.896			1.818
Model 4							
B	.036	−.257	−1.646	−.090*	.929***	.370***	
SE	.082	.206	1.059	.040	.083	.081	
Wald	.193	1.546	2.417	5.082	124.403	20.859	
Exp (*B*)	1.037	.774	.193	.914	2.532	1.447	
Model 5							
B	.091	−.243	−1.642	−.090*	.962***		.255***
SE	.081	.206	1.058	.040	.083		.072
Wald	1.260	1.381	2.408	5.091	132.917		12.594
Exp (*B*)	1.095	.785	.194	.914	2.617		1.291
Model 6							
B	.024	−.284	−1.680	−.090*		.666***	.525***
SE	.081	.205	1.057	.040		.074	.065
Wald	.090	1.928	2.525	5.089		81.619	64.220
Exp (*B*)	1.025	.752	.186	.914		1.946	1.690
Model 7							
B	.030	−.266	−1.635	−.082*	.790***	.386***	.274***
SE	.082	.207	1.056	.040	.091	.081	.072
Wald	.131	1.654	2.397	4.196	75.759	22.625	14.362
Exp (*B*)	1.030	.767	.195	.921	2.204	1.471	1.315

*$p < .05$; **$p < .01$; *** $p < .001$

Table 29.6
Logistic Regression Models: Delinquency Career Types on Adult Offending: Females

	Black	Hispanic	Other Race	Residence Status	Chronic Delinquent	Major Violence	Major Property
Model 1							
B	.258	−.866	−2.793	−.247**	1.174***		
SE	.185	.618	6.738	.880	.200		
Wald	1.944	1.966	.172	7.906	34.599		
Exp (*B*)	1.294	.420	.061	.781	3.234		
Model 2							
B	.243	−.820	−2.850	−.227**		.909***	
SE	.185	.616	6.740	.870		.210	
Wald	1.715	1.771	.179	6.789		18.658	
Exp (*B*)	1.275	.440	.058	.797		2.481	
Model 3							
B	.268	−.955	−2.744	−.229**			1.140***
SE	.186	.620	6.740	.089			.174
Wald	2.066	2.375	.166	6.690			42.768
Exp (*B*)	1.307	.385	.064	.795			3.128
Model 4							
B	.223	−.820	−2.773	−.234**	1.029***	.666**	
SE	.186	.618	6.739	.088	.208	.221	
Wald	1.443	1.765	.169	7.097	24.574	9.082	
Exp (*B*)	1.250	.440	.062	.791	2.797	1.946	
Model 5							
B	.245	−.928	−2.688	−.233**	.913***		.957***
SE	.187	.622	6.740	.890	.210		.182
Wald	1.717	2.222	.159	6.857	18.964		27.559
Exp (*B*)	.792	1.278	.680	.792	2.493		2.604
Model 6							
B	.228	−.891	−2.710	−.214*		.789***	1.081***
SE	.188	.619	6.741	.089		.215	.176
Wald	1.471	2.069	.162	5.836		13.422	37.544
Exp (*B*)	1.256	.410	.067	.807		2.201	2.947
Model 7							
B	.217	−.882	−2.673	−.221*	.779***	.605**	.932***
SE	.188	.621	6.741	.089	.219	.226	.184
Wald	1.335	2.013	.157	6.202	12.669	7.139	25.665
Exp (*B*)	1.243	.414	.069	.801	2.180	1.831	2.540

*$p < .05$; **$p < .01$; ***$p < .001$

significant inverse effect on the odds of becoming an adult criminal; none of the race effects are significant, however. Thus, disadvantaged conditions during a delinquent's youth, rather than race/ethnicity, bring a significant risk of adult criminality.

Across the various models in both Tables 29.5 and 29.6, we see a significant positive main effect of the delinquency career types: chronic delinquency (Model 1), major violence (Model 2), and major property (Model 3), when considered individually. In Models 4 to 6 we include pairs of these three factors to estimate the effect of each while controlling for a second delinquency factor. In all of these models, both of the delinquency career measures tested have significant main effects.

Finally, in Model 7, we estimated the effects when all three factors were included at the same time. Model 7 shows that all three delinquency career subgroups are significant predictors of adult crime when the effects of the other factors are controlled. Yet when major property is included with any other delinquency factor (Models 5, 6, and 7), it has the strongest effect and produces the highest odds ratio. Therefore it would appear that being a major property offender, rather than a chronic delinquent, places a female delinquent at the greatest risk of continuing her criminal career.

Table 29.5 indicates that the results for males are similar in form and nearly the same in substance as for females. First, in all seven models, residential social status again is significant and is related inversely to adult crime, while race has no significant effect.

Second, the models employing a single delinquency factor (Models 1 to 3) show that each of the delinquency career factors, in isolation from the other two, is related significantly to adult crime status: chronic delinquency is the strongest, followed by major violence and then major property. Third, when the delinquency career factors are paired (Models 4 to 6), each of the effects remains significant when any other delinquency factor is controlled. Again, however, chronic delinquency remains the strongest predictor.

Finally, when all three delinquency career types are included at the same time (Model 7), each of the factors is significant. Being a chronic delinquent, however, carries by far the strongest effect. Thus, among males, the quality of a delinquent's residential environment is related significantly to the probability of adult crime. Each career type carries significant odds of adult criminality, but a career as a chronic delinquent carries the significantly greatest risk.

Summary and Implications

This study shows the value of focusing on various types of delinquency careers in exploring the link between juvenile delinquency and differential involvement in adult crime. The examination of juvenile delinquent career subgroups reveals a cascading pattern of adult criminal behavior. Among both male and female juvenile offenders, the proportion who go on to adult crime increases incrementally among delinquent subgroups: from serious delinquents to violent delinquents, chronic delinquents, serious and chronic delinquents, and delinquents with histories of serious, violent and chronic offenses. Two types of delinquent careers are most common among life-course-persistent offenders: one includes both serious and chronic delinquency and the other, both violent and chronic delinquency. Persons of these types commit a disproportionate share of adult crimes.

Our general finding that certain delinquency career types carry an increased risk of adult crimes was replicated for all subgroups regardless of gender, race, or the socioeconomic status of their residential locations. Although the general patterns were consistent across the demographic subgroups we examined, the prevalence of offending differed by group. Moreover, the rank order of prevalence for each type of delinquency career was the same across subgroups: black males showed the highest prevalence, followed by white males, black females, and white females. Because of insufficient numbers of Hispanic, Asian, and Native American subjects, and our reliance on an ecological measure of socioeconomic status, we do not make broad interpretations related to these measures. Nonetheless, our findings certainly indicate that developmental criminology can benefit from greater attention both to demographic factors and to offense career transitions that extend into adulthood.

These findings support the distinction of life-course-persistent offenders from others whose criminality appears to be limited to adolescence (Moffitt 1993; Moffitt et al. 1996; Patterson et al. 1991). Moreover, the findings support suggestions that finer distinctions should be added to this classification scheme, particularly including typologies that not only capture the continuity of offending, but also distinguish serious and violent offending, and especially indicate how each of these delinquency traits interacts with high-rate offenders (Farrington 1998; Wilson and Howell 1993). Our findings also suggest that use of the serious, violent, and chronic offender subgroups to examine continuity of offending is a productive distinction for policy and practical purposes. A logical next step, for such purposes, would be to develop risk assessment instruments that can distinguish these subgroups from others in terms of potential for recidivism. It would be particularly valuable to make such a predictive distinction between serious-chronic and violent-chronic subgroups and others, given the disproportionate share of adult crimes committed by these two groups in our data.

Even though similar patterns are evident across gender, racial, and socioeconomic status groups, the differences in the magnitude of the patterns should indicate that developmental criminology must expand its scope. For example, the similarity in the patterns shown for females and for males is quite noteworthy: criminologists tend to ignore females, especially in regard to chronic and serious offending.

Even more important to future research, however, is the finding that the effect of career type is as strong for females as for males. That is, we found the most disparate gender results for the joint effects of the serious, violent, and chronic career subtypes. Our results reinforce previous findings that males are far more heavily involved in offending than females, and that males show a greater propensity for serious delinquency, but we also provide new information revealing that these components carry a substantial risk of adult crime for females as well. Thus our results show that among the more serious, violent, and chronic career types, or their intersections, females commit an even more disproportionate share of adult crime than their male counterparts. Still unknown is the extent to which our findings may be limited by official data sources that mask effects of differential treatment.

If gender differences are to be understood, researchers must work to understand gender-specific issues that relate to offending over the criminal career, or the life course, and to focus on crime-specific modeling. Important contextual differences across age, race, social class, geographic location, and justice system also merit much more attention (Chesney-Lind 1997; Simpson 1991). We must recognize that "[g]irls' pathways into crime, even into violence, are affected by the gendered nature of their environments and particularly their experiences as marginalized girls in communities racked by poverty" (Chesney-Lind 1997:176). In addition, we need a fuller understanding of the links between crime and responses to victimization, including how juvenile justice processing labels female victims' responses as offenses. Such knowledge should help illuminate the criminal career pathways that flow from such victimization (Maxfield and Widom 1996; Widom and Ames 1994). We also must examine gender similarities in order to understand the differences more clearly. For females and males alike, the system needs the capacity to combine knowledge of behavioral antecedents in pathways to serious, violent, and chronic offending with concomitant risk factors. Also, gender is only one of many factors that remain to be examined thoroughly in the context of developmental criminology.

Obvious public safety benefits could accrue from a more precise paradigm. Our results show the greater likelihood that adult criminality will correspond to chronic offending, severity, violence, and combinations of delinquency careers; these findings underscore the need to develop effective delinquency interventions and to apply them early, so as to reduce the propensities of these particular career types to proceed to adult crime.

In regard to policy, our findings also may provide some information with which to defeat current legislative and administrative actions, in which too many youths have been identified as serious juvenile offenders at risk of a life of crime. Almost without exception, the aim of policy reform is to hold juvenile offenders responsible for their actions (Albert 1998). The objective of accountability is sometimes linked to treatment (Bazemore and Day 1996; Bazemore and Umbreit 1995; Wilson and Howell 1993), but more often the focus is on punishment and retribution (Feld 1997). For example, in part on the basis of his interpretation that desistance from crime is a natural result of aging, Feld argues the following:

> In allocating scarce resources, [an explicitly punitive process] would use seriousness of the offense to rationalize charging decisions and "divert" or "decriminalize" most of the "kids' stuff" that provides the grist of the juvenile court mill until it became chronic or escalated in severity. (1997:128–29)

This position, which favors ignoring offending until it reaches an intolerable level that merits punishment, disregards research findings that show success for early interventions. Policy reforms predicated on notions of individual accountability should require us to know more about the high incidence of delinquency involving adolescents' miscalculation of risk (Bernard 1992; Feld 1997; Matza 1964).

Similarly, policy actions intended to curtail future criminality should be based on information about which delinquents can benefit most from the interventions. In their review of evaluations of programs, Lipsey and Wilson (1998) identify reductions in recidivism as high as 44 percent among the most effective programs for serious juvenile offenders; this effect is larger than for delinquents in general. They conclude, "If anything, then, it would appear that the typical intervention in these studies is *more* effective with serious offenders than with less serious offenders" (p. 23). In addition, Feld acknowledges that "youthful development is highly variable," and uses age to explain his view that "the ability to make responsible choices is learned behavior, and the dependent status of youth systematically deprives them of chances to learn to be responsible" (Feld 1997:121, 114). Given our findings that girls' prevalence of offending is lower but their continuity of offending is greater, and in the face of arguments that girls are more sheltered and are supervised more closely than boys, gender differences in response to independence and in learning responsibility also could prove very valuable for policy.

Our data do not allow us to explain when, or in what form, juvenile interventions should be imposed for the maximum effects on preventing adult criminality among serious, violent, and chronic offender careers. Our research, however, highlights the importance of continued efforts to isolate the elements leading from delinquent to criminal careers, and to identify the risk factors that seem to facilitate various pathways to offending. This information can be used to considerable advantage in the juvenile justice system in achieving a good fit between delinquents' position on pathways toward serious, violent, and chronic careers, sanctions that are graduated in concert with progression along delinquent pathways, and appropriate, effective treatment programs.

Note

1. We recorded addresses annually from school records through 1976, and observed little mobility.

References

Albert, R.L. 1998. "Juvenile Accountability Incentive Block Grants Program." *Fact Sheet* 76. Washington, DC: U.S. Department of Justice.

Bazemore, G. and S.E. Day. 1996. "Restoring the Balance: Juvenile and Community Justice." *Juvenile Justice* 1:3–14.

Bazemore, G. and M. Umbreit. 1995. "Rethinking the Sanctioning Function in Juvenile Court: Retributive or Restorative Responses to Youth Crime." *Crime and Delinquency* 49:296–316.

Bernard, T.J. 1992. *The Cycle of Juvenile Justice.* New York: Oxford University Press.

Blumstein, A. 1995. "Violence by Young People: Why the Deadly Nexus?" *NIJ Journal,* August, pp. 1–9.

Blumstein, A., J. Cohen, J.A. Roth, and C.A. Visher. 1986. *Criminal Careers and "Career Criminals."* Washington, DC: National Academy Press.

Chesney-Lind, M. 1997. *The Female Offender: Girls, Women, and Crime.* Thousand Oaks, CA: Sage.

Dean, C.W., R. Brame, and A.R. Piquero. 1996. "Criminal Propensities, Discrete Groups of Offenders, and Persistence in Crime." *Criminology* 34:547–74.

DiIullio, J.J. 1996. "They're Coming: Florida's Youth Crime Bomb." *Impact,* Spring, pp. 25–27.

Doi, D.J. 1998. "The Myth of Teen Violence." *State Government News,* April, pp. 17–19.

Farrington, D.P. 1998. "Understanding Risk Factors in Youth Violence." Pp. 421–76 in *Youth Violence: Crime and Justice,* vol. 24, edited by M. Tonry and M.H. Moore. Chicago, IL: University of Chicago Press.

Farrington, D.P., H.N. Snyder, and T.A. Finnegan. 1988. "Specialization in Juvenile Court Careers." *Criminology* 26:461–87.

Feld, B.C. 1997. "Abolish the Juvenile Court: Youthfulness, Criminal Responsibility, and Sentencing Policy." *Journal of Criminal Law and Criminology* 88:68–136.

——. 1999. *Bad Kids: Race and the Transformation of the Juvenile Court.* New York: Oxford University Press.

Fox, J.A. 1996. *Trends in Juvenile Violence: A Report to the U.S. Attorney General on Current and Future Rates of Juvenile Offending.* Boston, MA: Northeastern University Press.

Hamparian, D.M., R. Schuster, S. Dinitz, and J. Conrad. 1978. *The Violent Few.* Lexington, MA: Lexington Books.

Hawkins, D.F., J.H. Laub, and J.L. Lauritsen. 1998. "Race, Ethnicity, and Serious Juvenile Offending." Pp. 30–46 in *Serious and Violent Juvenile Offenders,* edited by R. Loeber and D.P. Farrington. Thousand Oaks, CA: Sage.

Hindelang, M.J. 1971. "Age, Sex, and the Versatility of Delinquent Involvements." *Social Problems* 18:522–35.

Howell, J.C. 1997. *Juvenile Justice and Youth Violence.* Thousand Oaks, CA: Sage.

Huizinga, D. and C. Jakob-Chien. 1998. "The Contemporaneous Co-Occurrence of Serious and Violent Juvenile Offending and Other Problem Behaviors." Pp. 47–67 in *Serious and Violent Juvenile Offenders,* edited by R. Loeber and D.P. Farrington. Thousand Oaks, CA: Sage.

Kempf, K.L. 1987. "Specialization and the Criminal Career." *Criminology* 25:399–420.

——. 1988. "Crime Severity and Criminal Career Progression." *Journal of Criminal Law and Criminology* 79:201–16.

——. 1989. "Delinquency: Do the Dropouts Drop Back In?" *Youth and Society* 20:269–89.

Krohn, M.D., T.P. Thornberry, C. Rivera, and M. Le Blanc. 2001. "Later Delinquency Careers." Pp. 67–94 in *Child Delinquents: Development, Intervention, and Service Needs,* edited by R. Loeber and D.P. Farrington. Thousand Oaks, CA: Sage.

Laub, J.H. and J.L. Lauritsen. 1993. "Violent Criminal Behavior Over the Life Course: A Review of the Longitudinal and Comparative Research." *Violence and Victims* 8:235–52.

Le Blanc, M. and M. Frechette. 1989. *Male Criminal Activity From Childhood Through Youth.* New York: Springer-Verlag.

Le Blanc, M. and R. Loeber. 1998. "Developmental Criminology Updated." Pp. 115–98 in *Crime and Justice: A Review of Research,* vol. 23, edited by M. Tonry. Chicago, IL: University of Chicago Press.

Lipsey, M. and J.H. Derzon. 1998. "Predictors of Violent or Serious Delinquency in Adolescence and Early Adulthood: A Synthesis of Longitudinal Research." Pp. 86–105 in *Serious and Violent Juvenile Offenders,* edited by R. Loeber and D.P. Farrington. Thousand Oaks, CA: Sage.

Lipsey, M. and D.B. Wilson. 1998. "Effective Interventions With Serious Juvenile Offenders: A Synthesis of Research." Pp. 313–45 in *Serious and Violent Juvenile Offenders,* edited by R. Loeber and D.P. Farrington. Thousand Oaks, CA: Sage.

Loeber, R. and D.P. Farrington, eds. 1998a. *Serious and Violent Juvenile Offenders.* Thousand Oaks, CA: Sage.

——. 1998b. "Never Too Early, Never Too Late: Risk Factors and Successful Interventions for Serious and Violent Juvenile Offenders." *Studies on Crime and Crime Prevention* 7:7–30.

Loeber, R., D.P. Farrington, and D.A. Waschbusch. 1998. "Serious and Violent Juvenile Offenders." Pp. 13–29 in *Serious and Violent Juvenile Offenders,* edited by R. Loeber and D.P. Farrington. Thousand Oaks, CA: Sage.

Loeber, R. and D.F. Hay. 1994. "Developmental Approaches to Aggression and Conduct Problems." Pp. 488–516 in *Development Through Life: A Handbook for Clinicians,* edited by M. Rutter and D.F. Hay. Oxford: Blackwell.

Loeber, R. and M. Le Blanc. 1990. "Toward a Developmental Criminology." Pp. 375– 473 in *Crime and Justice: An Annual Review of Research,* vol. 12 , edited by M. Tonry and N. Morris. Chicago, IL: University of Chicago Press.

Loeber, R., W.B. Van Kammen, and M. Fletcher. 1996. "Serious, Violent, and Chronic Offenders in the Pittsburgh Youth Study: Unpublished Data." Pittsburgh, PA: Western Psychiatric Institute and Clinic.

Loeber, R., P. Wung, K. Keenan, B. Girous, M. Stouthamer-Loeber, W.B. Van Kammen, and B. Maughan. 1993. "Developmental Pathways in

Disruptive Child Behavior." *Development and Psychopathology* 5:103–33.

Maher, L. and R. Curtis. 1995. "In Search of the Female Urban 'Gangsta': Change, Culture, and Crack Cocaine." Pp. 148–66 in *The Criminal Justice System and Women,* 2nd ed., edited by B.R. Price and N.J. Sokoloff. New York: McGraw-Hill.

Males, M.A. 1996. *The Scapegoat Generation: America's War on Adolescents.* Monroe, ME: Common Courage Press.

Matza, D. 1964. *Delinquency and Drift.* New York: Wiley.

Maxfield, M.G. and C.S. Widom. 1996. "The Cycle of Violence Revisited 6 Years Later." *Archives of Pediatric and Adolescent Medicine* 150:390–95.

Mazorelle, P., R. Brame, R. Paternoster, A. Piquero, and C. Dean. 2000. "Onset Age, Persistence, and Offending Versatility: Comparisons Across Gender." *Criminology* 38:1143–72.

Moffitt, T.E. 1993. "Adolescence-Limited and Life-Course-Persistent Antisocial Behaviour: A Developmental Taxonomy." *Psychological Review* 100:674–701.

Moffitt, T.E., A. Caspi, N. Dickson, P. Silva, and W. Stanton. 1996. "Childhood-Onset Versus Adolescent-Onset Antisocial Conduct Problems in Males: Natural History From Ages 3 to 18 Years." *Development and Psychopathology* 8:399–424.

Nagin, D.S., D.P. Farrington, and T.E. Moffitt. 1995. "Life-Course Trajectories of Different Types of Offenders." *Criminology* 33:111–39.

Nagin, D.S. and K.C. Land. 1993. "Age, Criminal Careers, and Population Heterogeneity: Specification and Estimation of a Nonparametric, Mixed Poisson Model." *Criminology* 31:327–62.

Paternoster, R. and R. Brame. 1997. "Multiple Routes to Delinquency? A Test of Developmental and General Theories of Crime." *Criminology* 35:49–84.

Patterson, G.R., D. Capaldi, and L. Bank. 1991. "An Early Starter Model for Predicting Delinquency." Pp. 139–68 in *The Development and Treatment of Childhood Aggression,* edited by D.J. Pepler and K.H. Rubin. Hillsdale, NJ: Erlbaum.

Piquero, A.R., R. Paternoster, R. Brame, P. Mazerolle, and C.W. Dean. 1999. "Onset Age and Specialization in Offending Behavior." *Journal of Research in Crime and Delinquency* 36:235–74.

Rojek, D.G. and M.L. Erickson. 1982. "Delinquent Careers: A Test of the Career Escalation Model." *Criminology* 20:5–28.

Sampson, R.J. and J.H. Laub. 1993. *Crime in the Making: Pathways and Turning Points Through Life.* Cambridge, MA: Harvard University Press.

Shannon, L.W. 1978. "A Longitudinal Study of Delinquency and Crime." Pp. 121–46 in *Quantitative Studies in Criminology,* edited by C. Wellford. Beverly Hills, CA: Sage.

——. 1980. *Assessing the Relationship of Adult Criminal Careers to Juvenile Careers.* Washington, DC: U.S. Government Printing Office.

——. 1988. *Criminal Career Continuity.* New York: Human Sciences Press.

Simpson, S. 1991. "Caste, Class, and Violent Crime: Explaining Difference in Female Offending." *Criminology* 29:115–35.

Snyder, H.N. 1998. "Serious, Violent, and Chronic Juvenile Offenders: An Assessment of the Extent of and Trends in Officially Recognized Serious Criminal Behavior in a Delinquent Population." Pp. 428–44 in *Serious and Violent Juvenile Offenders,* edited by R. Loeber and D.P. Farrington. Thousand Oaks, CA: Sage.

Thornberry, T.P and M. Farnworth. 1982. "Social Correlates of Criminal Involvement: Further Evidence on the Relationship Between Social Status and Criminal Behavior." *American Sociological Review* 47:505–18.

Tolan, P.H. and D. Gorman-Smith. 1998. "Development of Serious and Violent Offending Careers." Pp. 68–85 in *Serious and Violent Juvenile Offenders,* edited by R. Loeber and D.P. Farrington. Thousand Oaks, CA: Sage.

Torbet, P., R. Gable, H. Hurst, I. Montgomery, L. Szymanski, and D. Thomas. 1996. *State Reponses to Serious and Violent Juvenile Crime.* Washington, DC: Office of Juvenile Justice and Delinquency Prevention.

Tracy, P.E. and K. Kempf-Leonard. 1996. *Continuity and Discontinuity in Criminal Careers.* New York: Plenum.

Tracy, P.E., M.E. Wolfgang, and R.M. Figlio. 1985. *Delinquency in Two Birth Cohorts: Executive Summary.* Washington, DC: U.S. Government Printing Office.

——. 1990. *Delinquency Careers in Two Birth Cohorts.* New York: Plenum.

Walker, S. 1995. *Sense and Nonsense About Crime: A Policy Guide.* 3rd ed. Monterey, CA: Brooks/Cole.

Widom, C.S. 1989. "The Cycle of Violence." *Science* 244:160–66.

Widom, C.S. and M.A. Ames. 1994. "Criminal Consequences of Childhood Sexual Victimization." *Child Abuse and Neglect* 18:303–18.

Wilson, J.J. and J.C. Howell. 1993. *A Comprehensive Strategy for Serious, Violent, and Chronic Juvenile Offenders.* Washington, DC: Office of Juvenile Justice and Delinquency Prevention.

Wolfgang, M.E., R.M. Figlio, and T. Sellin. 1972. *Delinquency in a Birth Cohort.* Chicago, IL: University of Chicago Press.

Wolfgang, M.E., T.P. Thornberry, and R.M. Figlio. 1987. *From Boy to Man, From Delinquency to Crime.* Chicago, IL: University of Chicago Press.

Zimring, F.E. 1996. "Crying Wolf Over Teen Demons." *Los Angeles Times,* August 19, p. B5.

——. 1998. *American Youth Violence.* New York: Oxford University Press.

Kimberly Kempf-Leonard, Paul E. Tracy, and James C. Howell, "Serious, Violent, and Chronic Juvenile Offenders: The Relationship of Delinquency Career Types to Adult Criminality." Reprinted from *Justice Quarterly* 18 (3): 449–478. Copyright © 2001 Academy of Criminal Justice Sciences. Reprinted by permission ✦

Youth violence

gangs

Chapter 30

Preventing Adolescent Gang Involvement

Finn-Aage Esbensen

While gangs are hardly responsible for all youth violence and gang members are far from media portrayals of "superpredators," they are more likely to be drawn into delinquent behavior. Esbensen examines the key characteristics of gangs and gang members, cautioning that racial and socioeconomic profiles ignore increasing gang problems in rural and middle-income areas. He studies past gang prevention programs and analyzes which approaches have proved most successful, suggesting that a combination of programs aimed at adolescents as a whole, at targeted groups more likely to become involved with gangs, and at those who are already gang members is necessary to address the problem at large.

The expansion of the American youth gang problem during the past decade has been widely documented. National survey findings that have noted the spread of gangs throughout the United States indicate that law enforcement agencies across the country are acknowledging the presence of youth gangs in their communities.[1] In particular, recent survey results have documented the presence of youth gangs in rural areas. Most of these rural gangs appear to be primarily homegrown problems and not the result of the social migration of urban gang youth.

The emergence of youth gangs in rural areas and in cities previously without gangs coincided with the juvenile violent crime wave of the 1980's and early 1990's. The issue of whether youth gangs were responsible for the juvenile violent crime wave in the United States is beyond the scope of this [chapter]. However, given the relationship between gang membership and violent offending,[2] it makes sense to examine the youth gang problem within the larger context of youth violence.

American society demonstrated a heightened concern about juvenile violence during the past 30 years. Demographic consequences of the baby boom were, in large part, responsible for this concern. During the 1960's, the number of individuals ages 13–17 rose to 10 percent of the total population, leading to a corresponding increase in the number of crimes occurring within this cohort. By the mid-1980's, youth in this age range had fallen to 7 percent of the total population. However, the number of juvenile crimes did not see a similar decrease, resulting in an increase in the juvenile crime rate (Zimring, 1998). Public concern continued to focus on juvenile violence, drug use, and delinquent behavior. Following an apparent hiatus of youth gangs during the 1970's (Bookin-Weiner and Horowitz, 1983), American society witnessed a reemergence of youth gang activity and media interest in this phenomenon in the 1980's and 1990's. "Colors," "Boyz N the Hood," other Hollywood productions, and MTV brought Los Angeles gang life to suburban and rural America. Recent research also suggests that youth gangs now exist in Europe and other foreign localities (Covey, Menard, and Franzese, 1997; Klein, 1995).

Concurrent with the reemergence of gangs, the juvenile homicide rate doubled (Covey, Menard, and Franzese, 1997) and crack cocaine became an affordable drug of choice for urban youth. In spite of the decline in juvenile violence during the 1990's, concern about this issue continued as a dominant topic in public discourse. Fox (1996) and DiIulio (1995) were among the more widely cited authors who warned of an impending blood bath as a new cohort of superpredators (young, ruthless, violent offenders with casual attitudes about violence) would cause an increase in homicides in the 21st century. The media quickly spread this gloomy scenario. Zimring (1998), however, disputed these doomsday predictions by highlighting the erroneous assumptions underlying them. For example, the predictions were based on the belief that 6 percent of the population would become serious delinquents. DiIulio (1995) argued that by 2010, the population of boys under age 18 in the United States would grow from 32 million to 36.5 million, and that this increase would result in an additional 270,000 serious delinquents. However, this estimate suggested that 1.9 million superpredators already existed in the United States (6 percent of 32 million). Zimring (1998:62) noted, "That happens to be more young people than were accused of *any* form of delinquency last year in the United States" (emphasis added).

How is this discussion relevant to a [chapter] on gang prevention programs? Just as the superpredator notion took on a life of its own in the media, so too has the image of the drug-crazed, drug-dealing, gang-banging gang member. In fact, the tendency is to consider gang members and superpredators as one and the same. This depiction of youth gang members as marauding, drug-dealing murderers has underlying errors similar to those inherent in the superpredator concept. For the majority of the time, gang youth engage in the same activities as other youth—sleeping, attending school, hanging out, working odd jobs. Only a fraction of their time is dedicated to gang activity. Klein (1995:11) summarized gang life as being "a very dull life. For the most part, gang members do very little—sleep, get up late, hang around, brag a lot, eat again, drink, hang around some more. It's a boring life." In his book about Kansas City, MO, gang members, Fleisher (1998) provided numerous descriptive accounts of this lifestyle. Although gang life may not be as exciting or as violent as media portrayals might suggest, one consistent finding across all research methodologies is that gang youth are in fact more criminally involved than other youth. Illegal behavior attributed to youth gangs is a serious problem for which hype and sensationalism are neither required nor warranted. Regardless of study design or research methodology, considerable consensus exists regarding the high rate of criminal offending among gang members. With the increase in gang membership and in the violent juvenile crime rate during the past decade (Cook and Laub, 1998) and with the availability of increasingly lethal weapons, criminal activity by gang members has taken on new importance for law enforcement and prevention efforts.

What Is Known About American Youth Gangs?

Although this [chapter] focuses on gang prevention programs, it is essential to first review what is known about American youth gangs. Aside from the high rate of criminal activity among gang members, what is known about this adolescent phenomenon? What risk factors are associated with the emergence of gangs, and who joins these gangs once they have formed? Are gang members stable or transient? Are they delinquent prior to their gang associations? Are there identifiably different social processes (reasons for joining the gang or expected benefits from gang life) involved for girls and boys who join gangs? These are some of the questions that should help to shape gang prevention efforts.

In spite of years of research and years of suppression, intervention, and prevention efforts, considerable disagreement exists regarding the nature and extent of youth gangs. Debate still centers on how to define gangs. For instance, how many youth constitute a gang? Must the gang members commit crimes as a gang to be considered a gang? Must gangs have an organizational structure? Should skinhead groups, white supremacist groups, and motorcycle gangs be considered part of the youth gang problem? These definitional questions reveal both a lack of consensus about the magnitude of the gang problem and confusion about what policies might best address it (Covey, Menard, and Franzese, 1997; Klein, 1995; Spergel, 1995).

Generally, for a group to be classified a youth gang, the following elements should exist:

- The group must have more than two members. Given what is known about youth offending patterns (most offenses are committed in groups of two or more) and what has been learned from studying gangs, a gang seldom consists of only two members.

- Group members must fall within a limited age range, generally acknowledged as ages 12 to 24.
- Members must share some sense of identity. This is generally accomplished by naming the gang (often referring to a specific geographic location in the name) and/or using symbols or colors to claim gang affiliation. Hand signs, graffiti, specific clothing styles, bandannas, and hats are among the common symbols of gang loyalty.
- Youth gangs require some permanence. Gangs are different from transient youth groups in that they show stability over time, generally lasting a year or more. Historically, youth gangs have also been associated with a particular geographical area or turf.
- Involvement in criminal activity is a central element of youth gangs. While some disagreement surrounds this criterion, it is important to differentiate gangs from noncriminal youth groups such as school and church clubs, which also meet all of the preceding criteria.

For further discussion of the issues associated with defining youth gangs, consult Covey, Menard, and Franzese (1997); Curry and Decker (1998); or Klein (1995).

What Are the Risk Factors?

To prevent gangs from forming and to keep juveniles from joining existing gangs, it is necessary to understand the causes of gang formation and the underlying attraction of gangs. A considerable number of theoretical statements address these issues. Hagedorn (1988), Jackson (1991), and Klein (1995) are among the authors who argue that gang formation is a product of postindustrial development. Klein (1995:234) states, "Street gangs are an amalgam of racism, of urban underclass poverty, of minority and youth culture, of fatalism in the face of rampant deprivation, of political insensitivity, and the gross ignorance of inner-city (and inner-town) America on the part of most of us who don't have to survive there." The early work of Thrasher (1927) and other Chicago-based gang researchers emphasized the importance of structural and community factors. They believed that delinquency in general and youth gangs in particular were products of the social environment and that these societal factors may also contribute to juveniles' joining gangs. However, because most youth who reside in areas where gangs exist choose not to join these gangs, additional factors are required to explain why youth join gangs. The following sections provide an overview of the research examining risk factors associated with gang membership. They focus on the following five domains: individual and family demographics, personal attributes, peer group, school, and community.

Individual and Family Demographics

Traditionally, the typical gang member is male, lives in the inner city, and is a member of a racial or ethnic minority. Although these characteristics may be prevalent among gang members, it should not be assumed that all, or even the overwhelming majority of, gang members share these demographic qualities. In addition to changes in the geographical distribution of gangs (that is, the proliferation into nonurban areas) documented by Klein (1995); Curry, Ball, and Fox (1994); Curry, Ball, and Decker (1996); and the National Youth Gang Center (NYGC) surveys, research in the past 20 years has highlighted the presence of girls in gangs (Bjerregard and Smith, 1993; Chesney-Lind, 1997; Curry, 1998; and Esbensen and Winfree, 1998). Evidence also shows that gang membership is not restricted to youth from racial and ethnic minorities.

Gang behavior has been described almost exclusively as a male phenomenon. Law enforcement estimates generally indicate that more than 90 percent of gang members are male (Curry, Ball, and Fox, 1994). Early references to female gang members were usually restricted to their involvement in sexual activities or as tomboys; they were rarely included in any serious discussions about gangs. The little that was said about gang girls suggested that they were socially inept, maladjusted, and sexually promiscuous and that they suffered from low self-esteem.

Recent survey research, however, suggests that females may account for more than one-third of youth gang members (Esbensen and Winfree, 1998). In addition, a number of contemporary researchers have moved beyond the stereotypical notion that female gang members are merely auxiliary members of male gangs and have proposed gender-specific explanations of gang affiliation (Campbell, 1991; Chesney-Lind and Shelden, 1992; Fishman, 1995; Miller, 1998). Some researchers have explored the possibility that girls join gangs in search of a sense of belonging to a peer "familial" group (Giordano, 1978; Harris, 1988; Joe and Chesney-Lind, 1995). For example, in an ethnographic study of Latina gang members in male-dominated Hispanic gangs in the San Fernando Valley of Califomia, Harris (1988) concluded that Latina gang members were lost between two worlds—Anglo and Mexican American society and culture. The complex social and cultural roles of Latinas, according to Harris, are displayed in Latina gang membership and behavior in which females found peers with whom they could relate. The females would "fight instead of flee, assault instead of articulate, and kill rather than control their aggression" (Harris, 1988:174).

Another myth about the demographics of gang youth is that they are almost exclusively members of ethnic or racial minorities. Some law enforcement estimates and studies based on law enforcement samples indicate that 85 to 90 percent of gang members are African American or Hispanic (Covey, Menard, and Franzese, 1997). However, more recent law enforcement estimates from the 1998 National Youth Gang Survey (National Youth Gang Center, in press) indicate that earlier estimates may overstate the minority representation of gang members. The survey revealed that the race or ethnicity of gang members is closely tied to the size of the community. While Caucasians constituted only 11 percent of gang members in large cities (where most gang research has taken place), they accounted for approximately 30 percent of gang members in small cities and rural counties. Lending credence to law enforcement estimates are ethnographers' depictions of gang youth, usually based on research conducted in socially disorganized communities (that is, characterized by high rates of poverty, mobility, welfare dependency, and single-parent households) in Los Angeles, New York, or other urban areas with high concentrations of minority residents. More general surveys that examine youth gangs also tend to be restricted to specific locations that do not include diverse population samples. For example, longitudinal studies in Denver and Rochester (Bjerregard and Smith, 1993; Esbensen and Huizinga, 1993; Thornberry et al., 1993), part of the OJJDP-funded Program of Research on the Causes and Correlates of Delinquency, were concentrated in high-risk neighborhoods that (by definition) included disproportionate representation of racial and ethnic minorities.

It is worthwhile to note that the early gang studies provided a rich source of information about white urban gangs. These early gangs were usually described according to nationality and/or ethnicity, not race. Researchers began to identify gang members by race in the 1950's (Spergel, 1995). This change in gang composition is closely tied to the social disorganization of urban areas and the research focus on urban youth. Covey, Menard, and Franzese (1997:240) suggested that the scarcity of non-Hispanic, white, ethnic gangs may be attributable to the smaller proportion of non-Hispanic European Americans residing in neighborhoods characterized by social disorganization.

As research expands to more representative samples of the general population, a redefinition of the racial and ethnic composition of gang members is likely. Esbensen and Lynskey (in press) report that community-level demographics are reflected in the composition of youth gangs; that is, gang members are white in primarily white communities and are African American in predominantly African American communities.

Family characteristics of gang members, such as family structure and parental education and income, also have been revised, because the traditional stereotype of gang members as urban, minority males from single-parent families is too restrictive. In fact, gang youth are found in intact two-parent, single-parent, and recombined families. In addition, gang youth are not limited to homes in which parents have low educational achievement or low incomes. Klein (1995:75–76) summarizes gang characteristics as follows (emphasis added):

> [I]t is not sufficient to say that gang members come from lower-income areas, from minority populations, or from homes more often characterized by absent parents or reconstituted families. It is not sufficient because most youths from such areas, such groups, and such families do *not* join gangs.

Although it would be erroneous to conclude that demographic characteristics alone can explain gang affiliation, individual factors are nevertheless clearly associated with gang membership; that is, minority youth residing in single-parent households are at greater risk for joining gangs than are white youth from two-parent households.

Personal Attributes

Some researchers (for example, Yablonsky, 1962) have found that, compared with nongang youth, gang members are more socially inept, have lower self-esteem, and, in general, have sociopathic characteristics. Moffitt (1993) stated that youth gang members are likely to be "life-course persistent offenders." To what extent are such depictions accurate? Are gang youth substantially different from nongang youth? Recent surveys in which gang and nongang youth's attitudes were compared found few consistent differences.[3] This lack of consistent findings, however, may reflect differences in survey methods and question content. Comparisons between gang and nongang youth have been reported from Rochester (Bjerregard and Smith, 1993), Seattle (Hill et al., 1999), and San Diego (Maxson, Whitlock, and Klein, 1998). These authors used different questions and different sampling methods and reported slightly different findings. In the Seattle study, Hill and colleagues (1999) found that gang youth held more antisocial beliefs, while Maxson, Whitlock, and Klein (1998), among others, found that gang members had more delinquent self-concepts (based on statements such as the following: "I'm the kind of person who gets into fights a lot, is a bad kid, gets into trouble, and does things against the law."), had greater tendencies to resolve conflicts by threats, and had experienced more critical stressful events. On a more generic level, both the Seattle and San Diego studies found significant differences between gang and nongang youth within multiple contexts; that is, individual, school, peer, family, and community characteristics.

Extending this comparative approach, Esbensen, Huizinga, and Weiher (1993) examined gang youth, serious youthful offenders who were not gang members, and nondelinquent youth. Their findings indicated that the nondelinquent youth were different from the delinquent and gang youth—nondelinquent youth reported lower levels of commitment to delinquent peers, lower levels of social isolation, lower tolerance for deviance, and higher levels of commitment to positive peers. In a partial replication of the study by Esbensen, Huizinga, and Weiher (1993), Deschenes and Esbensen (1997) found a continuum extending from nondelinquent to minor delinquent to serious delinquent to gang member. Based on delinquency scores, they categorized eighth grade students into one of these four classifications. On every measure tested, gang members were significantly different from each of the other groups but were clearly the most distinct from nondelinquents (generally, at least one standard deviation above the mean). Gang members were more impulsive, engaged in more risk-seeking behavior, were less committed to school, and reported less communication with, and lower levels of attachment to, their parents. Nongang youth were more committed to prosocial peers and less committed to delinquent peers.

Using a somewhat different approach, Esbensen et al. (in press) examined differences among gang members. They classified gang members on a continuum, beginning with a broad definition of gang members and gradually restricting the definition to include only those youth who claimed to be core members of a delinquent gang that had a certain level of organizational structure. They found significant attitudinal and behavioral differences between core gang members and those more broadly classified as gang members. They did not find any differences in regard to demographic factors.

In another report from the Seattle study, Battin-Pearson and colleagues (1997) compared nongang youth, transient gang youth (members for 1 year or less), and stable gang youth (members for 2 or more years). Both the transient and stable gang members differed significantly from the nongang youth on a variety of attitudinal and behavioral measures. However, few distinctions between the transient and stable gang members were found. The measures on which differences occurred tended to represent individual- and peer-level measures (for example, personal attitudes and delinquency of friends).

Research shows that the notion of youth joining gangs for life is a myth. While some members make the gang a lifelong endeavor, findings from three longitudinal studies indicate that one-half to two-thirds are members for 1 year or less (Battin-Pearson et al., 1997; Esbensen and Huizinga, 1993; Thornberry, 1998).

Peer Group, School, and Community Factors

One consistent finding from research on gangs, as is the case for research on delinquency in general, is the overarching influence of peers on adolescent behavior (Battin-Pearson et al., 1997; Menard and Elliott, 1994; Warr and Stafford, 1991). In their comparison of stable and transient gang youth, Battin-Pearson and colleagues reported that the strongest predictors of sustained gang affiliation were a high level of interaction with antisocial peers and a low level of interaction with prosocial peers. Researchers have examined the influence of peers through a variety of measures, including exposure to delinquent peers, attachment to delinquent peers, and commitment to delinquent peers. Regardless of how this peer affiliation is measured, the results are the same: Association with delinquent peers is one of the strongest predictors (that is, risk factors) of gang membership.

Gang researchers examine school factors less frequently than other factors. However, they have found that these issues are consistently associated with the risk of joining gangs. Research indicates that gang youth are less committed to school than nongang youth (Bjerregard and Smith, 1993; Esbensen and Deschenes, 1998; Hill et al., 1999; Maxson, Whitlock, and Klein, 1998). Some gender differences have been reported in regard to this issue. In OJJDP's Rochester study, expectations for educational attainment were predictive of gang membership for girls but not for boys. In a similar vein, Esbensen and Deschenes (1998) found that commitment to school was lower among gang girls than nongang girls. No such differences were found for boys. Studies that examine juveniles' cultures and ethnic backgrounds also attest to the role of school factors in explaining gang membership (Campbell, 1991; Fleisher, 1998).

The community is the domain examined most frequently in regard to both the emergence of gangs and the factors associated with joining gangs. Numerous studies indicate that poverty, unemployment, the absence of meaningful jobs, and social disorganization contribute to the presence of gangs (Curry and Thomas, 1992; Fagan, 1990; Hagedorn, 1988, 1991; Huff, 1990; Vigil, 1988). There is little debate that gangs are more prominent in urban areas and that they are more likely to emerge in economically distressed neighborhoods. However, as previously stated, surveys conducted by NYGC during the 1990's identified the proliferation of youth gangs in rural and suburban communities. Except for law enforcement identification of this phenomenon, few systematic studies have explored these rural and suburban youth gangs. Winfree, Vigil-Backstrom, and Mays (1994) studied youth gang members in Las Cruces, NM, and Esbensen and Lynskey (in press) looked at gang youth in rural areas and small cities that were included in an 11-site study. Although neither of these reports addressed environmental characteristics, they did indicate a substantial level of violence by these gang members.

The traditional image of American youth gangs is characterized by urban social disorganization and economic marginalization; the housing projects or barrios of Chicago, Los Angeles, and New York are viewed as the stereotypical homes of youth gang members. The publication of Wilson's (1987) account of the underclass—those members of society who are truly disadvantaged and affected by changes in social and economic conditions—has renewed interest in the social disorganization perspective advanced by Thrasher (1927) and Shaw and McKay (1942). Los Angeles barrio gangs, according to Vigil (1988) and Moore (1991), are a product of economic restructuring and street socialization. Vigil (1988:9) refers to the multiple marginality (that is, the combined disadvantages of low socioeconomic status, street socialization, and segregation) of both male and female gang members who live in these socially disorganized areas. In addition to the pressures of marginal economics, these gang members experience the added burden of having marginal ethnic and personal identities. They look for identity and stability in the gang and adopt the cholo subculture—customs that are associated with an attachment to and identification with gangs—that includes alcohol and drug use, conflict, and violence. According to Moore (1991:137–138):

> Gangs as youth groups develop among the socially marginal adolescents for whom school and family do not work. Agencies of street socialization take on increased importance under changing economic circumstances, and have an increased impact on younger kids.

Social structural conditions, which have resulted in a lack of education and employment and in lives of poverty without opportunities (Short, 1996), are compounded for females, who experience the additional burden of sexual discrimination and traditional role expectations (Fishman, 1995; Swart, 1995). Social structural conditions alone, however, cannot account for the presence of gangs. Fagan (1990:207) comments that "inner-city youths in this study live in areas where social controls have weakened and opportunities for success in legitimate activities are limited. Nevertheless, participation in gangs is selective, and most youths avoid gang life." Therefore, addressing structural factors is not the only plausible strategy for gang prevention or intervention.

Prevention Strategies

Given the risk factors associated with violent offending and gang affiliation, are specialized prevention and intervention programs necessary for gang members? This is a critical question that has been asked all too infrequently in research on gang behavior. The trend has been to study gangs as a phenomenon distinct from delinquency in general. Despite the recent emphasis on gangs as a separate topic in research literature, there is reason to believe that gangs and gang programs should also be studied within the overall context of juvenile delinquency. For example, the works of Esbensen and Huizinga (1993), Thornberry et al. (1993), and Battin et al. (1998) suggest that, while the gang environment facilitates delinquency, gang members are already delinquent prior to joining the gang. However, rates of delinquent activity increase dramatically during the period of gang membership. From a prevention and intervention perspective, three thoughts emerge. First, the finding that delinquency generally precedes gang membership suggests that gang programs should not be limited to gang intervention or suppression. General prevention efforts that target the entire adolescent population may also prove beneficial in reducing youth gang involvement. Second, certain risk factors associated with gang membership have been identified. As such, prevention and intervention strategies that specifically target at-risk youth are warranted. Third, given the level of delinquent activity that occurs within the gang environment, specific programs that seek to intervene in the lives of gang-affiliated youth should also be encouraged.

This section addresses the following types of prevention efforts (Johnson, 1987):

- Primary prevention focuses on the entire population at risk and the identification of those conditions (personal, social, environmental) that promote criminal behavior.

- Secondary prevention targets those individuals who have been identified as being at greater risk of becoming delinquent.
- Tertiary prevention targets those individuals who are already involved in criminal activity or who are gang members.

The preceding discussion of risk factors emphasizes the necessity for all three strategies. In addition, law enforcement has tried a variety of suppression strategies designed to disrupt gang activity.

The past 60 years have seen a variety of gang prevention and intervention strategies. These strategies include efforts that focus on environmental factors and the provision of improved opportunities—for example, the Chicago Area Project developed by Shaw and McKay (1942), the Boston Midcity Project evaluated by Miller (1962), and the Mobilization for Youth program in New York (Bibb, 1967); programs with a distinct social work orientation [most notably the detached worker approach reported by Klein (1971) and Spergel (1966)]; and the strategy of gang suppression by law enforcement [for example, Chicago's Flying Squad (Dart, 1992)]. Most of these programs experienced short lifespans because changes did not take place immediately or because of a change in administrative priorities. For a review of past programmatic approaches to the gang problem, consult Howell (1995, 1998, and 2000), Klein (1995), or Spergel (1995). It is important to note that, in the overall history of America's response to youth gangs:

> Gang prevention programs have been rare. They require accurate knowledge of the predictors of gang membership, that is, identifying likely gang members, and they require knowledge of the causes of gangs and gang membership. Finally, they require knowledge of the likely impact of prevention efforts. (Klein, 1995: 137)

As indicated previously, there is a general lack of consensus about why gangs emerge and why juveniles join gangs. Therefore, it is more difficult to develop gang prevention programs and assess their impact.

Prevention Programs

Primary, Secondary, and Tertiary Prevention: The Chicago Area Project

> The history of gang intervention in the United States shows that early programs emphasized prevention. . . . The Chicago Area Project (CAP) (Sorrentino, 1959; Sorrentino and Whittaker, 1994), created in 1934, was designed to implement social disorganization theories, which suggested that community organization could be a major tool for reducing crime and gang problems. CAP was designed to involve local community groups, that is, indigenous community organizations, in improving neighborhood conditions that were believed to foster the formation of youth groups. (Howell, 1998:3)

CAP is representative of a community change approach and is perhaps the most widely known delinquency prevention program in American history. CAP was based on the theoretical perspective of Shaw and McKay and is summarized in their 1942 publication. Its intent was to prevent delinquency, including gang activity, through neighborhood and community development. CAP organized community residents through self-help committees based in preexisting community structures such as church groups and labor unions. Consistent with the research findings of Shaw and McKay, it was believed that the cause of maladaptive behavior was the social environment, not the individual. CAP and other similar programs are, at least in part, primary prevention efforts that target all adolescents in the neighborhood.

During the latter part of the 1940's, CAP introduced its detached worker program, which focused on either at-risk youth (secondary prevention) or, in some instances, current gang members (tertiary intervention). It recruited community members to help develop recreational activities and community improvement campaigns (e.g., health care, sanitation, education). These individuals worked with specific neighborhood gangs and served as advocates for gang members. This included advocating for gang members when they were confronted by the justice system and helping them find employment, health care, and educational assistance, among other services. The intent of the detached worker program was to transform the gang from an antisocial youth group to a prosocial group.

CAP's detached worker component was adopted by numerous other programs, including the Boston Midcity Project (Miller, 1962), Los Angeles' Group Guidance Program and Ladino Hills Project (Klein, 1968), and Chicago's Youth Development Project (Caplan et al., 1967). Although based on sound principles, Klein's Ladino Hills Project (which was a carefully designed implementation and evaluation of the detached worker program) led to the conclusion that the detached workers created an unintended outcome: increased gang cohesiveness, which resulted in increased gang crime. According to Klein (1995:143), "Increased group programming leads to increased cohesiveness (both gang growth and gang 'tightness'), and increased cohesiveness leads to increased gang crime." Klein (1995:147) concluded, "We had affected them but not their community. The lesson is obvious and important. Gangs are by-products of their communities: They cannot long be controlled by attacks on symptoms alone; the community structure and capacity must also be targeted."

Klein's research focused on detached workers targeting gang members (tertiary prevention), but the overall effectiveness of the CAP model remains in question. In regard to the community change approach described previously, subjective assessments by individuals involved with the project proclaimed its success. To date, however, the evaluations of this strategy have not reported a reduction in gangs or in gang activity. One review of delinquency programs stated that the measures collected by the program staff "have never been reported in ways that permit outsiders to assess the extent to which the Chicago Area Project accomplished its announced goal of preventing delinquency" (Lundman, 1993:74). In fact, evaluations of the Boston Midcity Project and other projects based on community organization and detached workers have documented that the programs failed to reduce delinquency and gang activity.

OJJDP promotes Spergel's Comprehensive Gang Model as a comprehensive communitywide response to gangs. This model consists of the following five strategies, which are representative of secondary and tertiary prevention:

> (1) Mobilizing community leaders and residents to plan, strengthen, or create new opportunities or linkages to existing organizations for gang-involved or at-risk youth; (2) using outreach workers to engage gang-involved youth; (3) providing or facilitating access to academic, economic, and social opportunities; (4) conducting gang suppression activities and holding gang-involved youth accountable; and (5) facilitating organizational change and development to help community agencies better address gang problems through a team 'problem-solving' approach that is consistent with the philosophy of community oriented policing. (Burch and Kane, 1999)

Evaluations of this program have been initiated, but to date no results have been published. An evaluation of the Little Village Project, a precursor to the Comprehensive Gang Model, has shown promising preliminary results (Spergel and Grossman, 1997; Spergel et al., 1999).

Primary Prevention: School-Based Prevention Programs

Schools provide one of the common grounds for American youth. Although growing numbers of children are being home schooled, the majority participate in the public education system. In recent years, schools have become a focal point for general delinquency prevention programs. The average middle school provides 14 different violence, drug, and other social problem prevention programs (Gottfredson and Gottfredson, 1999). One gang-specific prevention program that has received considerable attention is the Gang Resistance Education and Training (G.R.E.A.T.) program. The Phoenix Police Department introduced this school-based program in 1991 to provide "students with real tools to resist the lure and trap of gangs" (Humphrey and Baker, 1994:2). Modeled after the Drug Abuse Resistance Education (D.A.R.E.) program, the 9-week G.R.E.A.T. program introduces students to conflict resolution skills, cultural sensitivity, and the negative aspects of gang life. G.R.E.A.T. has spread throughout the country; to date, it has been incorporated in school curriculums in all 50 States and several other countries.

The objectives of the G.R.E.A.T. program are "to reduce gang activity and to educate a population of young people as to the consequences of gang involvement" (Esbensen and Osgood, 1999: 198). The curriculum consists of nine lessons offered once a week to middle school students (primarily seventh graders). Law enforcement officers (who always teach the program) are given detailed lesson plans that clearly state the purposes and objectives of the curriculum. The program consists of the following nine lessons: introduction; crime, victims, and your rights; cultural sensitivity and prejudice; conflict resolution (two lessons: discussion and practical exercises); meeting basic needs; drugs and neighborhoods; responsibility; and goal setting. The curriculum includes a discussion about gangs and their effects on the quality of people's lives and addresses the topic of resisting peer pressure.

To date, two evaluations have reported small but positive effects on students' attitudes and their ability to resist peer pressure (Palumbo and Ferguson, 1995; Esbensen and Osgood, 1999). Using a multisite, pre- and posttest research design, Palumbo and Ferguson reported that students in the G.R.E.A.T. program had a "slightly increased ability" to resist the pressures to join gangs. The authors acknowledged, however, that "the lack of a control group prevents assessments of the internal validity. Therefore, it cannot be concluded that the results . . . were due to G.R.E.A.T. as opposed to other factors" (Palumbo and Ferguson, 1995:600). A second multisite evaluation of G.R.E.A.T. examined the program's effectiveness. This evaluation compared eighth grade students who had completed the program with a comparable group of students who had not participated in G.R.E.A.T. The G.R.E.A.T. students self-reported less delinquency and had lower levels of gang affiliation, higher levels of school commitment, and greater commitment to prosocial peers, among other positive outcomes. However, the statistically significant effects were modest in terms of effect size, with an average between-group difference of about one-tenth of a standard deviation (Esbensen and Osgood, 1999).

As evidenced by the curriculum, the intent of the G.R.E.A.T. program is to provide life skills that empower adolescents with the ability to resist peer pressure to join gangs. The strategy is a cognitive approach that seeks to produce a change in attitude and behavior through instruction, discussion, and role-playing. Another notable feature of the program is its target population. In contrast to suppression and intervention programs, which are directed at youth who already are gang members, G.R.E.A.T. is intended for all youth. This is the classic, broad-based primary prevention strategy found in medical immunization programs: They intervene broadly, with a simple and relatively unintrusive program, well before any problem is detectable and without any attempt to predict who is most likely to be affected by the problem.

Secondary Prevention: Boys & Girls Clubs of America Program and the Montreal Program

The Boys & Girls Clubs of America (BGCA) has developed a program "to aggressively reach youth at risk of gang involvement and mainstream them into the quality programs the Club already offers" (Boys & Girls Clubs of America, 1993). This program, Gang Prevention Through Targeted Outreach, is an example of secondary prevention and consists of structured recreational, educational, and life skills programs (in conjunction with training) that are geared to enhance communication skills, problem-solving techniques, and decision-making abilities. This strategy targets youth who are at risk of becoming involved in gangs and seeks to alter their attitudes and perceptions and to improve their conflict resolution skills.

The BGCA outreach program also involves at-risk youth in conventional activities. Through its case management system, BGCA maintains detailed records on each youth, including participation in program activities, school attendance, contact with the justice system, and general achievements or problems. This information allows caseworkers to reward prosocial behavior or to take proactive measures in the event the youth engages in behaviors likely to lead to gang involvement (for example, skipping school, breaking curfew, and associating with delinquent friends).

Feyerherm, Pope, and Lovell (1992) conducted a process evaluation of 33 different BGCA gang intervention programs. Their examination focused on the degree to which the clubs implemented the gang intervention model and the extent to which clients received the various treatment components. The researchers concluded that "the youth gang prevention and early intervention initiative by Boys & Girls Clubs of America is both sound and viable in its approach" (Feyerherm, Pope, and Lovell, 1992:5). The researchers also collected descriptive information on risk factors and found that 48 percent of participants showed improvement in school (more than one-third of the youth improved their grades, and one-third improved their school attendance). However, to date, no evaluation results have been published that address the effectiveness of this strategy in reducing gang involvement. BGCA has also expanded this program in recent years to reach out to youth who have become involved with gangs.

The Montreal Preventive Treatment Program (Tremblay et al., 1996) is another secondary prevention program. It addresses early childhood risk factors for gang involvement by targeting boys from low socioeconomic backgrounds who display disruptive behavior while in kindergarten. It offers parents training sessions on effective discipline techniques, crisis management, and other parenting skills while the boys participate in training sessions that emphasize development of prosocial skills and self-control. An evaluation of the program showed that, compared with the control group, significantly fewer boys in the treatment group were gang members at age 15.

Tertiary Prevention

Tertiary prevention programs target individuals who are already involved with gangs. Although this approach includes detached worker programs such as those described above, a more common strategy implemented during the past decade has relied on law enforcement suppression tactics. Two such programs serve as examples. During the early 1990's, the Chicago Police Department experimented with the "Flying Squad," a special unit comprising young officers selected from the department's three gang units. According to Dart (1992), Chicago's chronic gang problem had left residents feeling intimidated and harassed. In response, the Chicago Police Department decided to give the impression of an omnipresent police force by assigning an additional 100 officers (the Flying Squad) to the Gang Crime Section and saturating an area of approximately 5 square blocks every night. It is interesting that while the intent of this tactic was to hold gangs accountable to the fullest measure of the law, the author acknowledges that "to win the war . . . there must be a marriage of intervention, prevention, and suppression strategies aimed at deterring and containing gang activity" (Dart, 1992:104). As with most gang prevention programs, this program was short lived and was disbanded by 1998.

The Los Angeles Police Department (LAPD), with its long history of dealing with gangs, organized a suppression unit in 1977. It was known as the Community Resources Against Street Hoodlums (CRASH) unit, and its mission was to combat gang crime. This unit was a "high profile gang control operation, carried out by uniformed patrol officers, stressing high visibility, street surveillance, proactive suppression activities, and investigative follow-through arrests" (Klein, 1995). At approximately the same time, LAPD began Operation Hammer, in which hundreds of officers saturated a predesignated area and arrested citizens for every possible legal violation and suspicious activity. Evaluations of these types of suppression efforts are lacking, but the consensus is that they are not likely to be an effective means of combating gang crime[4] (Klein, 1995; Spergel and Curry, 1995).

Law enforcement also has responded to juvenile violence and gangs with new ordinances, including curfew laws, anti-loitering laws, and civil injunctions. These suppression tactics limit the ability of certain groups of people (based on age or group affiliation) to congregate in public places based on the belief that such restrictions will reduce gang activity. However, constitutional concerns (that is, violations of the 1st, 4th, 5th, 9th, and 14th amendments) have been raised, and a 1999 U.S. Supreme Court decision declared that a Chicago antiloitering law was unconstitutional. This law targeted gang members (that is, persons the police believed to be gang members) by prohibiting the gathering of two or more people in any public place. Other jurisdictions have implemented civil injunctions and statutes that restrict or prohibit gang members from gathering in particular places (for example, parks, specific street corners, playgrounds) or from engaging in specific acts or wearing certain paraphernalia (wearing pagers or bandannas, riding bicycles, flashing gang signs). Evaluations of these city ordinances are mixed, as is legal opinion assessing their constitutionality (American Civil Liberties Union, 1997).

Conclusion

In light of the risk factors discussed at the outset of this [chapter], what conclusions can be made about gang prevention strategies? In regard to primary prevention, three facts are particularly salient. First, gang formation is not restricted to urban, underclass areas. Second, gang members come from a variety of backgrounds; they are not exclusively male, urban, poor, minority, or from single-parent households. Third, once juveniles join a gang, they engage in high levels of criminal activity. Therefore, it is appropriate to formulate primary gang prevention efforts that target the entire adolescent population.

In terms of secondary prevention approaches, some youth are at higher risk of joining gangs. Although social structural conditions associated with gang formation and demographic characteristics attributed to gang members are diverse (and despite the facts stated above), youth gangs are still more likely to be found in socially disorganized or marginalized communities. Secondary prevention strategies should, therefore, focus on communities and youth exposed to these greater risk factors. Community-level gang problem assessments may help guide prevention strategies by identifying areas and groups of youth that are most at risk for gang activity.

Tertiary prevention programs, such as CAP and a variety of gang suppression techniques, have shown little promise. Some detached worker programs produced the unintended consequence of increasing gang cohesion (Klein, 1995). Operation Hammer, CRASH, and similar law enforcement crackdowns have proven to be inefficient suppression approaches to gang activity and are not cost effective.

In conclusion, there is no clear solution to preventing or reducing gang activity, although some promising programs have been identified. As Short (1996:xvii) indicated (italics in original):

> *Systematic and sustained research is necessary if we are to understand gangs or any aspect of human behavior.* A corollary is equally important. If they are to be successful, *efforts to prevent, intervene with, or suppress gangs also must be systematic, sustained, and based on local knowledge and on research that is systematic and up to date.*

Recent findings from the Seattle study (Battin-Pearson et al., 1997), in which early predictors of gang affiliation were identified, highlight the importance of early primary prevention strategies. Additionally, given results from relatively recent studies of girls in gangs and girls who associate with gang members but are not part of the gang (Deschenes and Esbensen, 1999; Esbensen and Deschenes, 1998; Fleisher, 1998; Miller, 1998), prevention programs may need to consider gender as part of their efforts.

Much of this [chapter] has focused on individual factors. However, prevention efforts that concentrate only on individual characteristics will fail to address the underlying problems. As Short (1997:181–194) states:

> Effective interventions at the individual level that seek to control violence thus require that macro-level factors . . . be taken into consideration. . . . Absent change in the macro-level forces associated with these conditions, vulnerable individuals will continue to be pro-

duced. It follows that . . . to be effective in reducing overall levels of violent crime, interventions directed primarily at the individual level must address the macro-level as well. . . . A substantial body of research demonstrates . . . that single approaches, whether based on prevention, suppression, coordination of agency programs, community change, or law enforcement, are unlikely to prevent gang formation or to be successful in stopping their criminal behavior.

This overview of gang prevention strategies has sought to highlight the complexity of the youth gang issue, dispel some common stereotypes about youth gangs, and provide a framework within which to develop prevention programs. Clearly, there is no one "magic bullet" program or "best practice" for preventing gang affiliation and gang-associated violence. The youth gang problem is one that will be best addressed through a comprehensive strategy that incorporates primary, secondary, and tertiary prevention approaches. The Comprehensive Gang Model is one example of a multifaceted approach that targets individual youth, peer groups, families, and the community.

Notes

1. These include recent surveys by the National Youth Gang Center (1997, 1999a, 1999b, and in press; Moore and Terrett, 1999; Moore and Cook, 1999) and several earlier surveys (Miller, 1982; Spergel, 1990; Klein, 1995; Curry, Ball, and Fox, 1994; Curry, Ball, and Decker, 1996). For a review of these earlier surveys, see Howell, 1995.
2. Decker and van Winkle, 1996; Esbensen and Huizinga, 1993; Esbensen and Winfree, 1998; Thornberry et al., 1993.
3. Bjerregard and Smith, 1993; Esbensen, Huizinga, and Weiher, 1993; Esbensen and Deschenes, 1998; Hill et al., 1999; Maxson, Whitlock, and Klein, 1998.
4. During a weekend of Operation Hammer, for example, 1,453 arrests were made (half of those arrested were nongang members). Of these, 1,350 were released without charges being filed. Only 60 felony arrests were made; 32 of them resulted in charges being filed. This was the end product of 1,000 police officers saturating a small section of south central Los Angeles. In addition, this suppression and saturation approach assumes that gang members commit crimes based on a rational decisionmaking process. In reality, these crimes are more spontaneous and include fights, random assaults, and driveby shootings.

References

American Civil Liberties Union. 1997. *False Premises, False Promises: The Blythe Street Injunction and Its Aftermath.* Los Angeles, CA: ACLU Foundation of Southern California.

Battin, S., Hill, K.G., Abbott, R., Catalano, R.F., and Hawkins, J.D. 1998. The contribution of gang membership to delinquency beyond delinquent friends. *Criminology* 36(1):93–115.

Battin-Pearson, S., Guo, J., Hill, K.G., Abbott, R., Catalano, R.F., and Hawkins, J.D. 1997. Early predictors of sustained adolescent gang membership. Paper presented at the American Society of Criminology Annual Meeting, San Diego, CA.

Bibb, M. 1967. Gang related services of mobilization for youth. In *Juvenile Gangs in Context: Theory, Research, and Action,* edited by M.W. Klein. Englewood Cliffs, NJ: Prentice-Hall.

Bjerregard, B., and Smith, C. 1993. Gender differences in gang participation, delinquency, and substance use. *Journal of Quantitative Criminology* 9(4):329–355.

Bookin-Weiner, H., and Horowitz, R. 1983. The end of the youth gang: Fad or fact? *Criminology* 21(4):585–602.

Boys & Girls Clubs of America. 1993. *Youth Gang Prevention Through Targeted Outreach.* Atlanta, GA: Boys & Girls Clubs of America.

Burch, J., and Kane, C. 1999. *Implementing the OJJDP Comprehensive Gang Model.* Fact Sheet. Washington, DC: U.S. Department of Justice, Office of Justice Programs, Office of Juvenile Justice and Delinquency Prevention.

Campbell, A. 1991. *The Girls in the Gang,* 2d ed. Cambridge, MA: Basil Blackwell.

Caplan, N.S., Deshaies, D., Suttles, G.D., and Mattick, H. 1967. The nature, variety, and patterning of street club work in an urban setting. In *Youth Gangs in Context,* edited by M.W. Klein. Englewood Cliffs, NJ: Prentice-Hall.

Chesney-Lind, M. 1997. *The Female Offender: Girls, Women, and Crime.* Thousand Oaks, CA: Sage Publications, Inc.

Chesney-Lind, M., and Shelden, R.G. 1992. *Girls: Delinquency and Juvenile Justice.* Pacific Grove, CA: Brooks/Cole Publishing.

Cook, P.J., and Laub, J.H. 1998. The unprecedented epidemic in youth violence. In *Youth Violence,* edited by M. Tonry and M.H. Moore. Chicago, IL: University of Chicago Press, pp. 27–64.

Covey, H.C., Menard, S., and Franzese, R.J. 1997. *Juvenile Gangs,* 2d ed. Springfield, IL: Charles C. Thomas.

Curry, G.D. 1998. Female gang involvement. *Journal of Research in Crime and Delinquency* 35(1):100–118.

Curry, G.D., Ball, R.A., and Decker, S.H. 1996. *Estimating the National Scope of Gang Crime From Law Enforcement Data.* Research in Brief. Washington, DC: U.S. Department of Justice, Office of Justice Programs, National Institute of Justice.

Curry, G.D., Ball, R.A., and Fox, R.J. 1994. *Gang Crime and Law Enforcement Recordkeeping.* Research in Brief. Washington, DC: U.S. Department of Justice, Office of Justice Programs, National Institute of Justice.

Curry, G.D., and Decker, S.H. 1998. *Confronting Gangs: Crime and Community.* Los Angeles, CA: Roxbury.

Curry, G.D., and Thomas, R.W. 1992. Community organization and gang policy response. *Journal of Quantitative Criminology* 8(4):357–374.

Dart, R.W. 1992. Chicago's "Flying Squad" tackles street gangs. *Police Chief* (October):96–104.

Decker, S.H., and van Winkle, B. 1996. *Life in the Gang: Family, Friends, and Violence.* New York, NY: Cambridge University Press.

Deschenes, E.P., and Esbensen, F. 1997. Saints, delinquents, and gang members: Differences in attitudes and behavior. Paper presented at the American Society of Criminology Annual Meeting, San Diego, CA.

Deschenes, E.P., and Esbensen, F. 1999. Violence and gangs: Gender differences in perceptions and behavior. *Journal of Quantitative Criminology* 15(1):53–96.

DiIulio, J. 1995. The coming of the superpredators. *Weekly Standard* (November 27):23.

Esbensen, F., and Deschenes, E.P. 1998. A multisite examination of youth gang membership: Does gender matter? *Criminology* 36(4):799–828.

Esbensen, F., and Huizinga, D. 1993. Gangs, drugs, and delinquency in a survey of urban youth. *Criminology* 31(4):565–589.

Esbensen, F., Huizinga, D., and Weiher, A.W. 1993. Gang and non-gang youth: Differences in explanatory factors. *Journal of Contemporary Criminal Justice* 9(2):94–116.

Esbensen, F., and Lynskey, D.P. In press. Youth gang members in a school survey. In *The Eurogang Paradox: Street Gangs and Youth Groups in the U.S. and Europe,* edited by M.W. Klein, H. Kerner, C.L. Maxson, and E. Weitekamp. Amsterdam: Kluwer Press.

Esbensen, F., and Osgood, D.W. 1999. Gang Resistance Education and Training (G.R.E.A.T.): Results from the national evaluation. *Journal of Research in Crime and Delinquency* 36(2): 194–225.

Esbensen, F., and Winfree, L.T., Jr. 1998. Race and gender differences between gang and non-gang youth: Results from a multisite survey. *Justice Quarterly* 15(3):505–526.

Esbensen, F., Winfree, L.T., Jr., He, N., and Taylor, T.J. In press. Youth gangs and definitional issues: When is a gang a gang and why does it matter? *Crime and Delinquency.*

Fagan, J. 1990. Social processes of delinquency and drug use among urban gangs. In *Gangs in America,* edited by C.R. Huff. Newbury Park, CA: Sage Publications, pp. 183–219.

Feyerherm, W., Pope, C., and Lovell, R. 1992. Youth gang prevention and early intervention programs. Unpublished final research report. Portland, OR: Portland State University.

Fishman, L.T. 1995. The vice queens: An ethnographic study of black female gang behavior. In *The Modern Gang Reader,* edited by M.W. Klein, C.L. Maxson, and J. Miller. Los Angeles, CA: Roxbury Publishing Company.

Fleisher, M. 1998. *Dead End Kids.* Madison, WI: University of Wisconsin Press.

Fox, J.A. 1996. Trends in Juvenile Violence: A Report to the United States Attorney General on Current and Future Rates of Juvenile Offending. Boston, MA: Northeastern University Press.

Giordano, P. 1978. Girls, guys, and gangs: The changing social context of female delinquency. *Journal of Criminal Law and Criminology* 69(1):126–132.

Gottfredson, D., and Gottfredson, G. 1999. What do schools do to prevent problem behavior and promote school safety and how well do they do it? Paper presented at the Annual Conference on Criminal Justice Research and Evaluation, Washington, DC.

Hagedorn, J.M. 1988. *People and Folks: Gangs, Crime and the Underclass in a Rustbelt City.* Chicago, IL: Lakeview Press.

Hagedorn, J.M. 1991. Gangs, neighbor hoods, and public policy. *Social Problems* 38(4):529–542.

Harris, M.C. 1988. *Cholas: Latino Girls and Gangs.* AMS Press: New York, NY.

Hill, K.G., Howell, J.C., Hawkins, J.D., and Battin-Pearson, S.R. 1999. Childhood risk factors for adolescent gang membership: Results from the Seattle Social Development Project. *Journal of Research in Crime and Delinquency* 36(3):300–322.

Howell, J.C. 1995. Gangs and youth violence: Recent research. In *A Sourcebook: Serious, Violent, and Chronic Juvenile Offenders,* edited by J.C. Howell, B. Krisberg, J.D. Hawkins, and J.J. Wilson. Thousand Oaks, CA: Sage Publications.

Howell, J.C. 1998. Promising programs for youth gang violence prevention and intervention. In *Serious and Violent Juvenile Offenders: Risk Factors and Successful Interventions,* edited by R. Loeber and D.P. Farrington. Thousand Oaks, CA: Sage Publications.

Howell, J.C. 2000. *Youth Gang Programs and Strategies.* Summary. Washington, DC: U.S. Department of Justice, Office of Justice Programs, Office of Juvenile Justice and Delinquency Prevention.

Huff, C.R. 1990. Denial, overreaction, and misidentification: A postscript on public policy. In *Gangs in America,* edited by C.R. Huff. Newbury Park, CA: Sage Publications.

Humphrey, K.R., and Baker, P.R. 1994. The GREAT Program: Gang Resistance Education and Training. *FBI Law Enforcement Bulletin* (September):1–4.

Jackson, P.I. 1991. Crime, youth gangs, and urban transition: The social dislocations of postindustrial economic development. *Justice Quarterly* 8(3):379–397.

Joe, K.A., and Chesney-Lind, M. 1995. Just every mother's angel: An analysis of gender and ethnic variations in youth gang membership. *Gender and Society* 9(4):408–430.

Johnson, E.H. 1987. *Handbook on Crime and Delinquency Prevention.* New York, NY: Greenwood Press.

Klein, M.W. 1968. *The Ladino Hills Project: Final Report.* Los Angeles, CA: University of Southern California.

Klein, M.W. 1971. *Street Gangs and Street Workers.* Englewood Cliffs, NJ: Prentice-Hall.

Klein, M.W 1995. *The American Street Gang.* New York, NY: Oxford University Press.

Lundman, R. 1993. *Prevention and Control of Juvenile Delinquency.* New York, NY: Oxford University Press.

Maxson, C.L., Whitlock, M.L., and Klein, M.W. 1998. Vulnerability to street gang membership: Implications for practice. *Social Service Review* 72:70–91.

Menard, S., and Elliott, D.S. 1994. Delinquent bonding, moral beliefs, and illegal behavior: A three-wave panel model. *Justice Quarterly* 11(2):173–188.

Miller, J. 1998. Gender and victimization risk among young women in gangs. *Journal of Research in Crime and Delinquency* 35(4):429–453.

Miller, W.B. 1962. The impact of a 'total community' delinquency control project. *Social Problems* 10(Fall):168–191.

Miller, W.B. 1982. *Crime by Youth Gangs and Groups in the United States.* Washington, DC: U.S. Department of Justice, Office of Justice Programs, Office of Juvenile Justice and Delinquency Prevention.

Moffitt, T. 1993. Adolescence-limited and life-course-persistent antisocial behavior: A developmental taxonomy. *Psychological Review* 100(4):674–701.

Moore, J.P., and Cook, I.L. 1999. *Highlights of the 1998 National Youth Gang Survey.* Fact Sheet. Washington, DC: U.S. Department of Justice, Office of Justice Programs, Office of Juvenile Justice and Delinquency Prevention.

Moore, J.P., and Terrett, C.P. 1999. *Highlights of the 1997 National Youth Gang Survey.* Fact Sheet. Washington, DC: U.S. Department of Justice, Office of Justice Programs, Office of Juvenile Justice and Delinquency Prevention.

Moore, J.W. 1991. *Going Down to the Barrio.* Philadelphia, PA: Temple University Press.

National Youth Gang Center. 1997. *1995 National Youth Gang Survey.* Summary. Washington, DC: U.S. Department of Justice, Office of Justice Programs, Office of Juvenile Justice and Delinquency Prevention.

National Youth Gang Center. 1999a. *1996 National Youth Gang Survey.* Summary. Washington, DC: U.S. Department of Justice, Office of Justice Programs, Office of Juvenile Justice and Delinquency Prevention.

National Youth Gang Center. 1999b. *1997 National Youth Gang Survey.* Summary. Washington, DC: U.S. Department of Justice, Office of Justice Programs, Office of Juvenile Justice and Delinquency Prevention.

National Youth Gang Center. In press. *1998 National Youth Gang Survey.* Summary. Washington, DC: U.S. Department of Justice, Office of Justice Programs, Office of Juvenile Justice and Delinquency Prevention.

Palumbo, D.J., and Ferguson, J.L. 1995. Evaluating Gang Resistance Education and Training (GREAT): Is the impact the same as that of Drug Abuse Resistance Education (DARE)? *Evaluation Review* 19(6):591–619.

Shaw, C.R., and McKay, H.D. 1942. *Juvenile Delinquency and Urban Areas.* Chicago, IL: University of Chicago Press.

Short, J.F., Jr. 1996. Foreword: Diversity and change in U.S. gangs. In *Gangs in America,* 2d ed., edited by C.R. Huff. Thousand Oaks, CA: Sage Publications.

Short, J.F., Jr. 1997. *Poverty, Ethnicity, and Violent Crime.* Boulder, CO: Westview Press.

Sorrentino, A. 1959. The Chicago Area Project after twenty-five years. *Federal Probation* 23:40–45.

Sorrentino, A., and Whittaker, D.W. 1994. The Chicago Area Project: Addressing the gang problem. *FBI Law Enforcement Bulletin* 63(5):8–12.

Spergel, I.A. 1966. *Street Gang Work: Theory and Practice.* Reading, MA: Addison-Wesley.

Spergel, I.A. 1990. Youth gangs: Continuity and change. In *Crime and Justice: A Review of Research,* edited by M. Tonry and N. Morris. Chicago, IL: University of Chicago Press.

Spergel, I.A. 1995. *The Youth Gang Problem: A Community Approach.* New York, NY: Oxford University Press.

Spergel, I.A., and Curry, G.D. 1995. The National Youth Gang Survey: A research and development process. In *The Modern Gang Reader,* edited by M.W. Klein, C.L. Maxson, and J. Miller. Los Angeles, CA: Roxbury Publishing Company.

Spergel, I.A., and Grossman, S.F. 1997. The Little Village Project: A community approach to the gang problem. *Social Work* 42(5):456–470.

Spergel, I.A., Grossman, S.F., Wa, K.M., Choi, S., and Jacob, A. 1999. *Evaluation of the Little Village Gang Violence Reduction Project: The First Three Years.* Executive Summary. Chicago, IL: Illinois Criminal Justice Information Authority.

Swart, W.J. 1995. Female gang delinquency: A search for 'acceptable deviant behavior.' In *The Modern Gang Reader,* edited by M.W. Klein, C.L.

Maxson, and J. Miller. Los Angeles, CA: Roxbury Publishing Company.

Thornberry, T.P. 1998. Membership in youth gangs and involvement in serious violent offending. In *Serious and Violent Juvenile Offenders: Risk Factors and Successful Interventions,* edited by R. Loeber and D.P. Farrington. Thousand Oaks, CA: Sage Publications.

Thornberry, T.P., Krohn, M.D., Lizotte, A.J., and Chard-Wierschem, D. 1993. The role of juvenile gangs in facilitating delinquent behavior. *Journal of Research in Crime and Delinquency* 30(1):55–87.

Thrasher, F.M. 1927. *The Gang: A Study of One Thousand Three Hundred Thirteen Gangs in Chicago.* Chicago, IL: University of Chicago Press.

Tremblay, R.E., Masse, L., Pagani, L., and Vitaro, F. 1996. From childhood physical aggression to adolescent maladjustment: The Montreal Prevention Experiment. In *Preventing Childhood Disorders, Substance Abuse, and Delinquency,* edited by R.D. Peters and R.J. McMahon. Thousand Oaks, CA: Sage Publications, pp. 268–298.

Vigil, J.D. 1988. *Barrio Gangs: Street Life and Identity in Southern California.* Austin, TX: University of Texas Press.

Warr, M., and Stafford, M. 1991. The influence of delinquent peers: What they think or what they do? *Criminology* 29(4):851–865.

Finn-Aage Esbensen, "Preventing Adolescent Gang Involvement." Reprinted from *Juvenile Justice Bulletin,* September 2000, pp. 1–11. Published by the U.S. Department of Justice Office of Juvenile Justice and Delinquency Prevention. ✦

Chapter 31

A National Study Comparing the Environments of Boot Camps with Traditional Facilities for Juvenile Offenders

Doris Layton MacKenzie
Angela R. Gover
Gaylene Styve Armstrong
Ojmarrh Mitchell

One of the juvenile justice system's more recent innovations is the use of "boot camps" that combine strenuous physical activity and military discipline as an alternative to traditional incarceration. Although boot camps have not always been shown to affect recidivism rates, they may have other benefits. The authors surveyed staff and youth at boot camps and traditional facilities to determine how the different environments affected offenders' social bonds, attitudes, and stress levels, which are expected to affect future criminality.

During the 1990s, correctional boot camps became an increasingly popular sentencing option for juvenile delinquents. In 1996, 48 residential boot camps for adjudicated juveniles were operating in 27 States. Only one of those boot camps opened prior to 1990.

Boot camp programs are modeled after military basic training. Offenders often enter the programs in groups that are referred to as platoons or squads. They are required to wear military-style uniforms, march to and from activities, and respond rapidly to the commands of the "drill instructors." The rigorous daily schedule requires youths to wake up early and stay active throughout the day. Although programs differ somewhat, the schedule usually includes drill and ceremony practice, strenuous physical fitness activities, and challenge programs (e.g., ropes courses) as well as required academic education. Frequently, youths in the camps receive summary punishments, such as having to do pushups, for misbehavior.

Pros and Cons of Boot Camps

Despite their growing popularity, correctional boot camps are controversial. The controversy primarily is over whether the camps are an appropriate way to manage and treat juvenile delinquents and what impact the camps have on the adjustment and behavior of juveniles while they are confined and after they are released. Many people who visit or work in boot camps, as well as many youths in the camps, say the camp atmosphere is conducive to positive growth and change. Proponents of the camps believe that the structure of the programs and the control staff have over the participants create a safe environment in which the youths are less likely to fight with or be victimized by other youths than they would be in traditional correctional facilities. Furthermore, advocates argue that the incorporation of the military model builds camaraderie among youths and fosters respect for staff.

In contrast, boot camp critics say that the camps' confrontational environment is in direct opposition to the type of positive interpersonal relationships and supportive atmosphere that are needed for youths' positive development. From their perspective, the boot camp environment is antithetical to quality therapeutic programming. The boot camp atmosphere itself—strict control over juveniles' activities and confrontational interactions between drill instructors and youths—may cause juveniles to fear the correctional staff, which would create a negative environment for therapy and educational achievement.

Furthermore, critics argue, the camps' emphasis on group activities does not allow programs to address individual youths' problems. According to critics, juveniles' needs vary greatly, and effective programs should assess each individual's needs and provide appropriate individual programming. Many boot camps, however, manage juveniles in units or platoons. Youths enter the facility in a unit and remain with that unit for educational classes and treatment programs. Moreover, the military philosophy and highly structured daily schedule may not permit the flexibility needed to address individual problems.

Certain components of boot camps are also suspected of making it more difficult for juveniles to make the transition back to the community. Most delinquents will return to the community after being institutionalized for a relatively short time. For juveniles to succeed in the community, they need to receive help while they are institutionalized. Critics are concerned that boot camps, with their focus on group activities, regimentation, and military drill and ceremony, will not address what juveniles need to successfully make the transition back to the community. When returning to an environment that lacks such regimentation and positive group activities, the juveniles may revert to their old ways of surviving in and relating to the community in which they live.

Another problem critics find with group orientation is that it may cause youths to view the system as unjust. For example, juveniles may think the program is unfair or abusive if their entire platoon is punished because one member of the group misbehaved or because of the controversial nature of the interactions between themselves and drill instructors.

What Research Shows

Although the boot camp environment appears to be radically different from that of traditional residential facilities and some fear its potentially negative impact, studies have not shown that either type of facility is more effective in reducing recidivism. In general no significant differences have been found for either adults or juveniles when recidivism rates of boot camp participants have been compared with others receiving more traditional correctional options.[1]

In recent years, the importance of understanding the institutional environment or conditions of confinement has become a focus of attention in corrections. One reason for this interest is that research has shown that the prison environment has an impact on inmate adjustment and behavior. Facilities "possess unique and enduring characteristics that impinge on and shape individual behavior."[2] Because increasing numbers of juveniles are being confined in institutions, it is important to understand the effect this confinement is having on juveniles' behavior while they are confined and after they are released.

Furthermore, considerable research shows that correctional treatment programs can successfully change behavior. Results from meta-analyses, literature reviews, and assessments of the quality of the research on the effects of treatment show that treatment programs with particular characteristics are successful in reducing future delinquent and criminal activities.[3] Effective programs target offenders who are at risk of recidivism, are modeled after cognitive-behavior theoretical models and are sensitive to juveniles' learning styles and characteristics, and address the characteristics of youths directly associated with criminal activity. Youths should receive sufficient dosage of treatment (e.g., amount of contact, length of program), and the treatment should have therapeutic integrity (e.g., appropriately trained staff). From this perspective, measuring the conditions of confinement becomes important to understanding which program components are necessary for effective treatment.

Focus on Outcomes

Another justification for the interest in the conditions of confinement in juvenile institutions is the recent attention given to quality management and performance-based standards. Quality management has played an important role in the restructuring of private organizations and corporations, and these concepts are currently being applied to public agencies.[4] Quality management focuses on outcome-based decisionmaking. Traditionally, standards

Methodology

In 1996, the researchers surveyed juvenile correctional agencies and identified 48 boot camps in operation; another 2 jurisdictions were developing boot camp programs. Two programs were eliminated because they were nonresidential facilities. Of the remaining 46 programs, 27 in 20 States participated in the study. Although it was not possible to compare program aspects of those that were not in the study with those that were, the participating programs were geographically representative of the United States.

A matched comparison facility in the same State was identified for each participating boot camp. Each comparison facility was selected in consultation with the agency responsible for and/or the administrator of the boot camp. The comparison facility was selected as the most likely facility to which juveniles would have been sent had they not gone to boot camp. Comparison facilities were traditional institutions such as training schools and detention centers. For the study, 22 traditional institutions were compared with 27 boot camps.*

The 49 participating correctional facilities were visited between April 1997 and August 1998. During the site visits, 4,121 juveniles and 1,362 staff were surveyed. Structured interviews also were conducted with facility administrators to obtain data from institutional records and information on policies and procedures.

The juvenile survey contained 266 questions about demographic information, previous criminal history, attitudes, and experiences in the facility. The survey was administered in group settings of 15 to 20 juveniles. The informed consent and all items on the survey were videotaped and played on a VCR to reduce the amount of reading required of the youths.

The 216-item staff survey asked respondents to describe their demographic, background, and occupational characteristics. Both the juvenile and staff surveys included a series of items about perceptions of the facility's environmental conditions. Staff were asked additional questions about working conditions. Both surveys included items presented as statements (e. g., staff treat residents fairly; punishments given are fair), to which respondents answered according to a five-point scale ranging from "never" to "always."

The structured interviews with facility administrators consisted of 244 questions. Information was obtained about the facilities' policies and procedures, population characteristics, screening and admission criteria, the emphasis placed on programming components, staff and education issues, and visitation. The survey also requested statistical information from institutional records.

Fourteen scales were formed using factor analyses: control, resident danger, staff danger, environmental danger, activity, care, risks to residents, quality of life, structure, justice, freedom, therapeutic programming, preparation for release, and individual planning (see "Perceptual Environmental Conditions Scales" for scale descriptions). These scales were used to measure how staff and juveniles viewed the environment of the facility in which they lived or worked.

Across all facilities, juvenile and staff perceptions of the environments in boot camps were compared with perceptions of those in the comparison facilities using analysis-of-variance models. Overall differences between juveniles in the boot camps and those in the comparison facilities were compared on the 14 environmental scales. Similarly, boot camp staff perceptions were compared with traditional facility staff perceptions. Demographics (e.g., age, race/ethnicity, sex) were used as controls.

Note

* The number of boot camps exceeded the number of traditional facilities because two boot camps participated in one State, but there were no comparison sites for these facilities. One comparison site and two boot camps were selected in three other States.

for correctional institutions have been based on expert opinions about "best practices" in the field of corrections. Total quality management and performance-based standards change the focus from views on best practices to desired outcomes. From this perspective, the focus shifts from what is thought to be the best way to manage a facility to the actual outcomes desired. Broadly defined, outcomes include client and staff experiences, short-term changes, and long-term impacts.

In trying to understand the impact of correctional institutions and programs, many researchers have argued that outcomes must be broadened for various measures of effectiveness. The focus of the study described here was

Perceptual Environmental Conditions Scales

Control: Do staff have control over the residents? Do residents do what staff tell them? Do residents escape? Do residents have drugs or weapons?

Resident danger: Do residents worry about being hit or punched by other residents? Are they afraid of other residents? Are residents mean to one another? Do they fight? Do residents get sexually attacked?

Staff danger (juvenile perspective): Are residents afraid of staff? Do staff grab, push, or shove residents? Are staff mean to residents?

Staff danger (staff perspective): Are residents mean to staff? Are staff in danger of being hit or punched by residents? Do residents grab, push, or shove staff?

Environmental danger: Do staff protect residents? Is residents' property safe? Are gangs in the institution? Do staff catch and punish troublemakers? Are there enough staff to keep residents safe? Do staff prevent violence and forced sex among residents?

Activity: Do residents have activities to keep them busy? Do they spend time on school work? Are they busy at night? Do they plan what they will do when they leave? Do they exercise? Do they have activities when they are not in school?

Care: Do staff encourage residents to try new activities? Do staff help residents with school work after class? Do staff tease residents? Do they help residents with personal problems? Is the health care good? Are residents friendly? Will someone help if a resident has a problem? Do staff care about residents?

Risk to residents: Are insects, rodents, or dirt a problem? Is there a bad odor or poor air circulation? Do residents know what to do in case of fire? Do many accidents happen? Are the jobs safe?

Quality of life: Do residents exercise? Is it noisy? Is there a lot of space in the living area? Do residents have privacy in the shower and toilet? Is the food good? Do residents get enough to eat? Is the visiting area crowded?

Structure: Do residents follow a set schedule? Do they study at certain times? Do they know what will happen if they break a rule? Are they messy? Do staff change their minds about rules?

Justice: Are residents punished even when they do not do anything wrong? Do staff use force? Can residents file a grievance against staff? Are residents aware of the grievance process? Can staff and residents work out problems? Will something bad happen if a resident files a grievance? Do residents deserve the punishments they receive? Are punishments fair?

Freedom: Do residents have to work when they do not want to? Can they choose the type of work? Can they read or listen to music whenever they want? Are they encouraged to make decisions?

Therapeutic programming: Will the programs help residents find a job, understand themselves, keep focused on their goals, learn new skills, and/or return to school? Does the substance abuse treatment help residents? Are religious services offered? Do residents receive individual attention? Are they healthier since coming to the facility?

Preparation for release: Are residents encouraged to plan for release? Have they made plans to find a job, return to school, get drug treatment, and find a place to work? Do they set goals for the future?

Individual planning (staff only): Do residents have individual meetings with staff? Do they get help with their problems? Do they receive individual counseling?

to compare boot camps with more traditional facilities by measuring conditions of the institutional environment (see "Methodology"). The environments of the institutions were measured from several perspectives: the perceptions of staff and juveniles, data in institutional records and the policies and procedures (as reported by administrators). To examine the impact of the environment on juvenile offenders, changes experienced by juveniles while confined were studied. Changes in juveniles' attitudes, stress levels, and social bonds (ties to family, school, and work) were expected to reflect their responses to the institutional environment and to be associated with future criminal behavior.

Juvenile Perceptions of the Institutional Environment[5]

Demographics

The majority of the juveniles participating in the study in both facility types were black or white males who were approximately 16 years old. On average, these youths were 13 years old when they were arrested for the first time and had previously been committed to institutions 2.5 to 3 times. On average, juveniles in the boot camps had shorter sentence lengths than juveniles in comparison facilities (10 months compared with 16 months). They also had spent less time in the facility (3 months compared with 7 months). Juveniles in boot camps were significantly less likely than youths in traditional facilities to have experienced family violence and to have used illegal substances. Juveniles in boot camps, however, were significantly more likely than juveniles in traditional facilities to have problems with alcohol abuse.

Perceptions of the Institutional Environment

Juveniles in boot camps responded favorably to their institutional environments more frequently than juveniles in comparison facilities (see exhibit 31.1). Across all sites, juveniles in boot camps more frequently responded positively to their institutional environment, with the exception of safety from staff. Specifically, boot camp juveniles were more likely to report that they were in danger from staff. Juveniles in the boot camps reported more frequently that their environments prepared them for release, provided therapeutic programming, had structure and control, and kept them active. On average, juveniles in boot camps reported less environmental danger, less danger from other residents, and fewer environmental risks than juveniles in comparison facilities. Juveniles in boot camps reported less freedom.

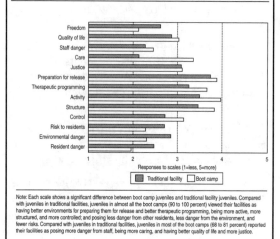

Exhibit 31.1
Boot Camp and Traditional Facility Youths' Perceptions of Their Envirnonment

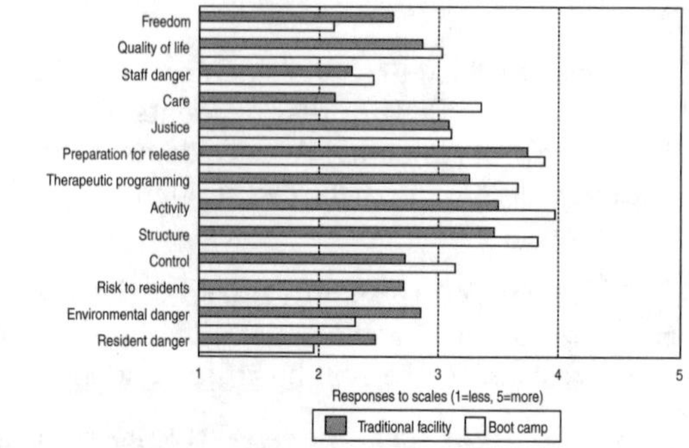

Note: Each scale shows a significant difference between boot camp juveniles and traditional facility juveniles. Compared with juveniles in traditional facilities, juveniles in almost all the boot camps (90 to 100 percent) viewed their facilities as having better environments for preparing them for release and better therapeutic programming, being more active, more structured, and more controlled; and posing less danger from other residents, less danger from the environment, and fewer risks. Compared with juveniles in traditional facilities, juveniles in most of the boot camps (68 to 81 percent) reported their facilities as posing more danger from staff, being more caring, and having better quality of life and more justice.

Staff Perceptions of the Institutional Environment[6]

Demographics

The majority of the staff in both facility types were male and white. Boot camp staff were an average age of 36; comparison facility staff were slightly older, on average, at 39 years old. Most boot camp (85 percent) and comparison (85 percent) staff had attended or graduated from college. More boot camp staff had military experience (49 percent compared with 29 percent of the comparison facility staff).

Perceptions of the Institutional Environment

As in the juvenile survey, staff in boot camps more frequently reported favorable perceptions of their institutional environment than traditional facility staff (see exhibit 31.2). Boot camp staff more frequently reported that juveniles were given more therapeutic programming and experienced a caring and just environment compared with reports of traditional facility staff. Boot camp staff also were more likely than staff in traditional facilities to say the juveniles were more active, and the camps had more structure and control and less freedom. Conversely, boot camp staff reported less frequently

Exhibit 31.2
Boot Camp and Traditional Facility Staff Perceptions of Their Envirnonment

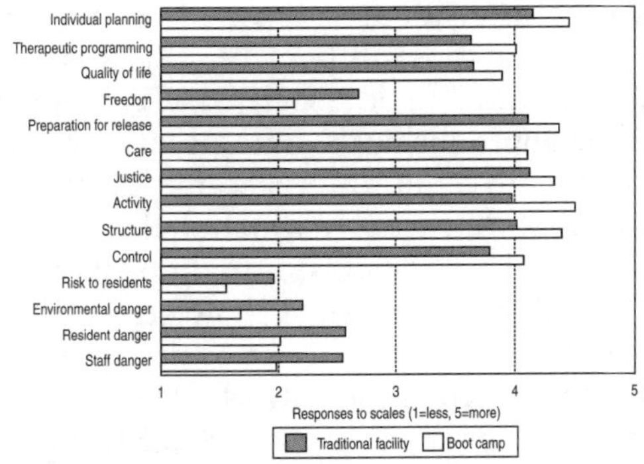

Note: Each scale shows a significant difference between boot camp staff and staff in traditional facilities. Compared with staff in traditional facilities, staff in almost all the boot camps (85 to 100 percent) viewed their facilities as being more caring, more active, more structured, and more controlled; having more justice, less freedom, and better therapeutic programming; and posing less danger from residents, less danger to staff, fewer environmental dangers, and fewer risks. Compared with staff in traditional facilities, staff in most of the boot camps (75 to 85 percent) reported their facilities as having better preparation for release and better quality of life and providing more individualized attention to residents.

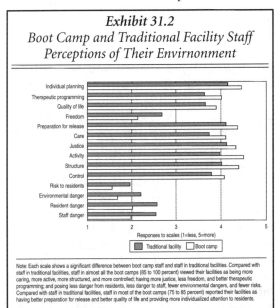

than traditional facility staff that there was danger to juveniles from the environment and other risks, from other juveniles, and from staff. Less consistent differences were found for the remaining three scales (quality of life, preparation for release, and individual planning).

Work Experiences

In comparison to staff in traditional facilities, boot camp staff also more frequently reported favorable working conditions (see exhibit 31.3). They reported less personal stress, better communication among staff, more support from the administration, and, in general, more satisfaction with their working conditions.

Exhibit 31.3
Boot Camp and Traditional Facility Staff Perceptions of Working Conditions

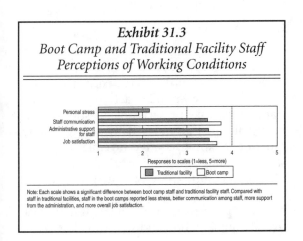

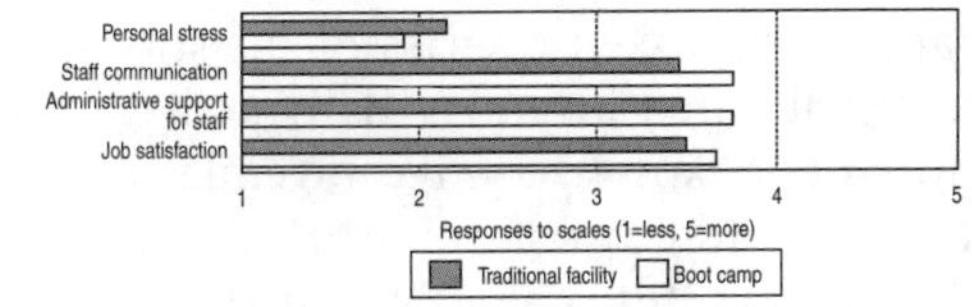

Note: Each scale shows a significant difference between boot camp staff and traditional facility staff. Compared with staff in traditional facilities, staff in the boot camps reported less stress, better communication among staff, more support from the administration, and more overall job satisfaction.

Comparison of Staff and Juvenile Perceptions

One interest of this research project was to find out whether juveniles and staff had the same perceptions of the particular facility in which they were confined or worked. Overall, there was strong agreement between juvenile and staff perceptions of the institutions' environments. The five juvenile and staff scales with the highest correlations were environmental danger, resident danger, care, quality of life, and control. For 10 of the scales, the correlations between staff and juveniles' environmental ratings were more than 0.85; the correlations for the remaining two scales were 0.38 (individual planning) and 0.60 (justice).

Individual Adjustment and Change

The survey was given to 550 youths in the facilities twice to examine changes in adjustment over time. This permitted an examination of the changes youths underwent while they were confined. Anxiety, depression, social bonds, dysfunctional impulsivity, and social adjustment were measured (see exhibit 31.4). The adjustment and change variables were selected for practical and theoretical reasons.

Critics of boot camps have been particularly concerned about the level of stress created by the strict, military-based, confrontational model. They fear such an atmosphere will create excessive stress and will mitigate any positive effects from academic and therapeutic treatment

Exhibit 31.4
Changes over Time for Juveniles in Boot Camps and Traditional Facilities

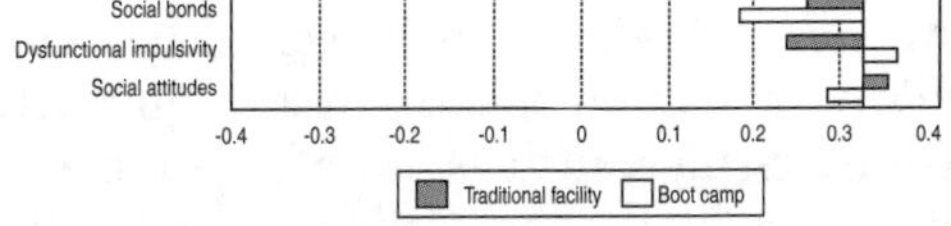

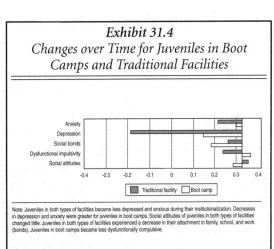

Note: Juveniles in both types of facilities became less depressed and anxious during their institutionalization. Decreases in depression and anxiety were greater for juveniles in boot camps. Social attitudes of juveniles in both types of facilities changed little. Juveniles in both types of facilities experienced a decrease in their attachment to family, school, and work (bonds). Juveniles in boot camps became less dysfunctionally compulsive.

programs that the camps may offer. Initial levels of anxiety were slightly higher for the boot camp juveniles, but initial levels of depression were higher for the comparison youths. The levels of anxiety and depression decreased over time for juveniles in both facilities; however, these reductions were greater for the boot camp youths.

Social bonds have been found to be associated with reductions in criminal activity.[7] If juvenile facilities improved such bonds, future criminal activities might be reduced. Disappointingly, juveniles in both types of facilities reported a weakening in their social bonds to family, school, and work while they were institutionalized. These changes, however, were small, and the differences were not statistically significant.

Theoretically, an inability to control one's impulses[8] and antisocial attitudes[9] is associated with delinquent and criminal activities. For this reason, changes in dysfunctional impulsivity (i.e., the inability to control one's impulses) and social attitudes (or, conversely, antisocial attitudes) during the time the youths were in the facility were examined. Juveniles in boot camps reported decreased dysfunctional impulsivity and increased prosocial attitudes (conversely, decreased antisocial attitudes). In contrast, juveniles in the comparison facilities reported more dysfunctional impulsivity and decreases in prosocial attitudes (conversely, increased antisocial attitudes).

Summary of Perceptions and Change

Overall, these results provided strong evidence that those who lived and worked in boot camps perceived their environment more positively than those who lived and worked in more traditional facilities. On average, both staff and juveniles in boot camps perceived less danger and more components that were conducive to positive change, such as more help in planning for release, more programming in the facility, a more just system, more activity, a more caring environment, and more individual attention. However, juveniles in boot camps more frequently reported perceptions of danger from staff.

Juveniles in both types of facilities became less depressed and anxious over time, but the decreases in depression and anxiety were greater for those in boot camps. Boot camps also appeared to be associated with more positive changes during the time juveniles were confined. Boot camp youths became less antisocial and reported less dysfunctional impulsivity compared with youths in traditional facilities. These changes were small, however, and youths in both facility types reported decreases in ties to family, school, and work. Thus, although youths in boot camps on average had a more positive view of their environments, there was little evidence that these perceptions translated into psychosocial changes that would reduce the likelihood of future delinquent or criminal activities.

Institutional Policies and Procedures[10]

The structured interview with facility administrators was designed to elicit information about the type of juveniles who enter the facility, the daily schedule, selection and admission procedures, facility characteristics, educational and staff issues, health and medical assistance policies, safety and security issues, and institutional impacts. While perceptions provide important information about the facilities, equally important is information about policies and procedures that might have an impact on those who live and work in the facilities.

Control and Structure

One explanation for juvenile and staff perceptions of a safe environment in boot camps could be a result of the increased structure and control over the juveniles' activities. Administrators were asked a series of questions about how structured juveniles' daily activities were. More boot camps required juveniles to get up, shower, and study according to a set daily schedule (see exhibit 31.5). Not surprising, boot camps also had more military-style components. Most of these components were indicative of regimentation and structure. For exam-

Exhibit 31.5
Structure and Military Components in Juvenile Boot Camps and Traditional Facilities

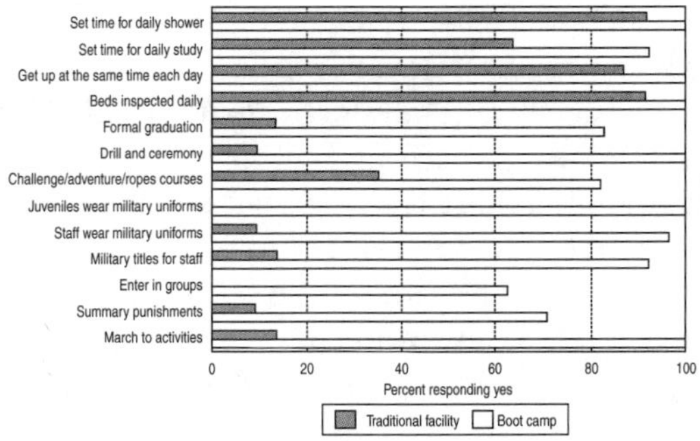

ple, in the majority of the boot camp facilities, staff and juveniles wore uniforms, and the youths practiced drill and ceremony, entered the facility in groups, and marched to activities. Thus, the information from the administrators was similar to the perceptions of staff and juveniles in suggesting that boot camps provide much more structure for juveniles than the traditional institutions. These differences may explain why juveniles in boot camps had more favorable perceptions of their institutional environments.

Characteristics of Juveniles in the Facilities

Another possible explanation for the differences in perceptions is that the juveniles in boot camps differed from those in traditional facilities. Although individual differences were controlled for statistically in the perceptual analyses, there is an inherent selection bias at the administrative level if those who entered boot camps differed from those who went to traditional facilities. This issue was examined by asking how selective facilities were about their populations. In general, boot camps were found to be much more selective (see exhibit 31.6). Fewer boot camps admitted juveniles who had psychological problems or were suicide risks. More boot camps required psychological, medical, and physical evaluations before juveniles were admitted into the facility. Additionally, more facility personnel in boot camps were able to se-

Exhibit 31.6
Selection Criteria Used by Boot Camps and Traditional Facilities

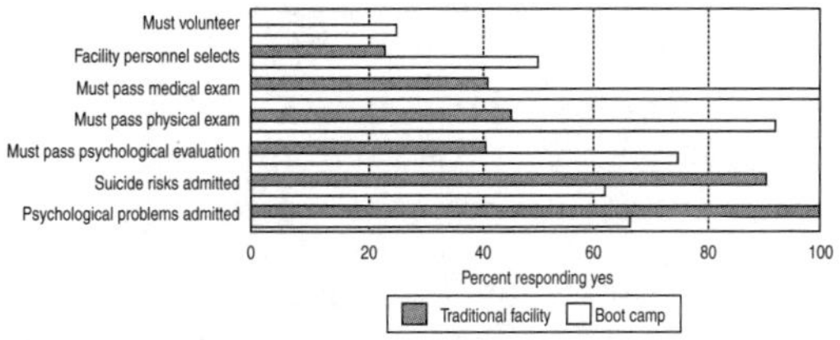

lect juveniles for their program, and in 25 percent of the boot camps, juveniles had to volunteer for the program. None of the traditional facilities required juveniles to volunteer.

The question of whether juveniles with certain past histories or offenses were admitted to the facilities was also examined (see exhibit 31.7). For example, administrators were asked whether juveniles who committed arson are permitted to enter the facility and, if so, whether the number of such individuals is limited. In general, comparison facilities admitted delinquents who committed more serious offenses.

The examination of the structure and admission components of the facilities suggested that the environments of the two types of facilities differed substantially. One possibility is that these different environments lead to different experiences and, hence, different perceptions of the environment. This investigation of the characteristics of the juveniles in the facilities and the selection process, however, suggests that the

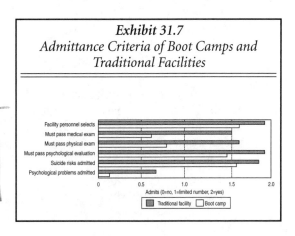

Exhibit 31.7
Admittance Criteria of Boot Camps and Traditional Facilities

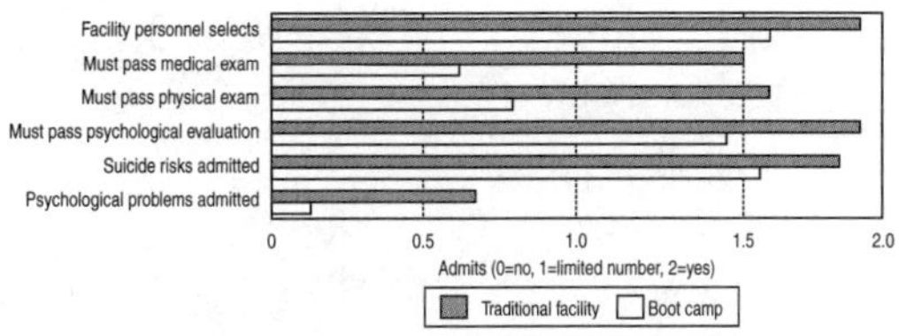

differences in perceptions may result from characteristics of the juveniles admitted. From this perspective, juveniles who enter boot camps are different from those who go to the traditional facilities (e.g., less aggressive, fewer psychological problems); therefore, because of this selection process, boot camp juveniles judged their environment more positively.

Therapeutic Components

It was somewhat surprising that juveniles and staff perceived the boot camp environment as having more components conducive to rehabilitation. In general, those who lived and worked in boot camps viewed their environment as being more just and caring, better preparing juveniles for release, and having more therapeutic programming. Staff in most of the boot camps also believed that their facilities provided more individual planning and therapeutic programming. This research attempted to verify the perceptions by obtaining information about programming, treatment, and the efforts facilities made to help youths maintain outside contacts (see "Differences in Therapeutic Programming and Individual Attention"). However, few differences were found in the average number of hours devoted to education per week.

Fewer boot camp youths took a General Educational Development (GED) test, but overall passing rates for those who did were about the same in both facility types. In 54.2 percent of the boot camps, juveniles attended classes with others in their grade levels, compared with 59.1 percent of comparison facilities. Comparison facilities had more teaching staff and more custody and treatment staff per juvenile, making it possible that juveniles in the traditional facilities would receive more individual attention. Boot camp facilities scheduled more physical fitness activities than traditional facilities, but this was not considered as treatment, education, or therapy.

Another project interest was visitation policies, because such activities would permit juveniles to stay in contact with their families. Community contact is important because many juveniles are confined for only a short period of time and will be released to live most likely with their families. Therefore, attempts at successful community reintegration should start while juveniles are confined.[11] Overall, the boot camps permitted less visitation (see "Contact with the

Differences in Therapeutic Programming and Individual Attention

- On average, boot camps scheduled 25.3 hours of educational classes per week compared with 25.7 hours scheduled in the comparison facilities.
- In boot camps, an average of 25.3 percent of juveniles took a General Educational Development (GED) test in the past year; 42.9 percent of the juveniles in the traditional facilities took a GED test.
- Of those who took a GED test, an average of 78.3 percent passed in the boot camp and 75.2 percent passed in the traditional facilities.
- Juveniles attended classes grouped according to their appropriate grade levels (not with groups, housing units, or platoons) in 54.2 percent of the boot camps and 59.1 percent of the comparisons.
- Boot camps had 10.1 juveniles for every 1 teaching staff; comparison facilities had 6.6 juveniles for each teaching staff member.
- Boot camps had 3.5 juveniles to every 1 custody or treatment staff; comparison facilities had 1.6 juveniles to every custody or treatment staff.
- On average, boot camps scheduled physical fitness activities (including drill and ceremony practice) for 18.8 hours per week compared with 12.3 hours in the comparison facilities.

Outside"). More than half the camps did not allow visits during the juveniles' first month of confinement, and almost one-fifth did not permit visits at any time. Comparison facilities had fewer restrictions on visitation. Boot camps also were more likely than traditional facilities to require visitors to schedule their visits in advance.

Conclusion

The perceptions of staff and youths provide important insight into the adequacy of these programs as correctional options for juvenile delinquents. This research found that juveniles and staff in the boot camps perceived their environment as more caring than did those living and working in the comparison facilities. These results show that youths in the boot camps were more likely to agree that staff members encourage residents to try new activities and help residents with schoolwork or other problems. Youths and staff also believed that the treatment of residents was more just in the boot camps.

Advantages

Not only did the boot camp youths perceive their facilities as more caring and just, they also believed the programs were more therapeutic and provided them with more preparation for their release. In comparison to those in traditional facilities, youths and staff in boot camps were more likely to agree that juveniles' experiences in the facility would help them get a job, understand themselves, keep them focused on their goals, learn new skills, return to school, and address substance abuse problems. Boot camp staff on average believed that youths got more individual attention, were healthier since entering the facility, and were planning for their release through activities such as finding a place to work, planning to return to school, and setting goals for the future. Another positive aspect of the boot camps was staff perceptions of their working environment. In comparison to staff in traditional facilities, the boot camp staff reported feeling less personal stress, better communication among staff, a more supportive atmosphere for staff, and more satisfaction with their work.

Concerns

The one finding that supports the criticism of boot camps as institutions that offer little to improve interpersonal relationships was the data indicating that youths in the boot camps more frequently reported feelings of being in danger from staff. In contrast, traditional facility youths more frequently reported feelings of danger from other residents.

An additional concern raised by critics of boot camps is that the military basic training and confrontational interactions may create undue stress on a vulnerable youth population. The findings from this research suggest that there initially is an increased level of anxiety for youths in boot camps compared with those in traditional institutions. This increased level of anxiety, however, did not appear to be greatly

Contact with the Outside

- Boot camps schedule 4.0 hours per week for visitation; comparison facilities schedule 7.1 hours.
- Fifty-four percent of the boot camps had a "no outside visits " rule during the first month juveniles were in the facility; 14 percent of the comparison facilities had such a policy.
- Seventeen percent of the boot camps had a "no outside visits" rule during the entire time juveniles were in the facility; none of the comparison facilities had such a policy.
- Sixty-seven percent of the boot camp programs required visitors to schedule their visits in advance; only 36 percent of the traditional facilities required this of visitors.
- Juveniles in the boot camps were permitted to make 1.2 phone calls per week on average; juveniles in the comparison facilities could make 1.6 phone calls.

dysfunctional. The juveniles were asked whether they agreed with statements indicating that they feel anxious, worried, upset, nervous, or not relaxed or calm; these questions reflect temporary emotions and not permanent anxiety or other dysfunctional traits. Therefore, the increased anxiety for the youths in the boot camps may reflect the difficult early period of adjustment to boot camp.[12] Although the data are not completely comparable to what some boot camp staff refer to as the "break down" and "build the youths up" phases, they suggest some similarities in that the early period in the boot camp may temporarily create more anxiety. Youths, however, do not become more depressed or exhibit permanent psychological dysfunction.

Findings from this study also indicated that in boot camps and traditional facilities, attachments or bonds to family, school, and work decreased for juveniles. This might be expected because youths are removed from their communities, schools, and work opportunities and have limited contact with their families. Boot camp youths, however, reported less dysfunctional impulsivity over time. Youths in the traditional facilities became slightly more impulsive, but the change was small. Similarly, traditional facility youths became less prosocial in attitudes over time, while boot camp youths became more prosocial. Prosocial changes for both boot camp and traditional facility youths, however, were small and statistically insignificant. Given the small changes in attitudes among both boot camp and traditional facility youths, it is not surprising that research to date has found little difference between the recidivism rates for these two groups.

The findings of administrator surveys of facility policies, procedures, and daily schedules were largely consistent with those from the perceptual surveys. Across all survey methods, boot camps were rated higher in institutional environments' structure, control, and "militaryness." Thus, some of the differences in perceptions of safety could be due to the structured nature of the environment. An environment that is structured and controlled by staff may be perceived by juveniles as safer.

Reasons for the Differences

However, differences between boot camps and traditional facilities in the juvenile selection process may also help explain why boot camps were perceived as having positive institutional environments. Boot camps, on average, were much more selective about who entered the facility. Therefore, one possible reason for the differences in perceptions may be that boot camp youths have characteristics that make them easier to work with, which can have an impact on all aspects of the institutional environment.

Another possibility is that differences in the facilities' policies, procedures, and daily schedules led to differences in staff and juvenile perceptions. For example, if juveniles in boot camps received more individual attention or spent more time in treatment or educational programs, this may explain the perceptions of boot camps' more therapeutic nature. Yet little measurable differences were found in the facilities' therapeutic atmospheres. The few differences that were found favored the traditional facilities. For example, the traditional facilities had higher teaching-staff-per-juvenile and custody-or-treatment-staff-to-juvenile ratios than the boot camps. The strict rules and regimented environment of the boot camps may mean that fewer staff are needed to control juveniles, but it also may mean that youths have less opportunity to receive individual attention.

Designing Better Programs

Together, the results from this study suggest that boot camps are successful in the first step—creating a positive environment. However, boot camps appear to lack the necessary focus on incorporating components of effective therapy.[13] As a result, it is not surprising that boot camps have not been effective in reducing recidivism. An additional concern was the finding that boot camp youths more frequently perceived that they were in danger from staff. This is disappointing because so many of the other aspects of boot camps were viewed positively.

Additionally, this study found that few of the boot camps or traditional facilities had information about what happens to youths after they are released. Because the majority of these youths will return to their home communities, it is hard to understand how a facility can design a successful program that does not include gathering information about what happens to youths after they are released. If juvenile correctional programs are expected to have a positive impact on the future lives of these youths, it is important that they have information on what happens to the juveniles after they return to their communities. Otherwise, how else can a program effectively evaluate its performance?

Notes

1. MacKenzie, D.L., "Criminal Justice and Crime Prevention," in *Preventing Crime: What Works, What Doesn't, What's Promising,* ed. L.W. Sherman, D.C. Gottfredson, D. MacKenzie, J. Eck, P. Reuter, and S. Bushway. Washington, DC: U.S. Department of Justice, National Institute of Justice, 1997, NCJ 165366.
2. Wright, K., and L. Goodstein, "Correctional Environments," in *The American Prison,* ed. L. Goodstein and D.L. MacKenzie, New York: Plenum Press, 1989: 266.
3. Andrews, D.A., I. Zinger, R.D. Hoge, J. Bonta, P. Gendreau, and F.T. Cullen, "Does Correctional Treatment Work? A Clinically Relevant and Psychologically Informed Meta-Analysis," *Criminology* 28 (3) (1990): 369–404; Lipsey, M., "Juvenile Delinquency Treatment: A Meta-Analytic Inquiry Into the Variability of Effects," in *Meta-Analysis for Explanation: A Casebook,* ed. T. Cook et al., New York: Russell Sage Foundation, 1992; and MacKenzie, D.L., "Criminal Justice and Crime Prevention."
4. MacKenzie, D.L., C.J. Styve, and A.R. Gover, "Performance-Based Standards for Juvenile Corrections," *Corrections Management Quarterly* 2 (1998): 28–35.
5. For a more detailed discussion, see Styve, G.J., D.L. MacKenzie, A.R. Gover, and O. Mitchell, "Perceived Conditions of Confinement: A National Evaluation of Juvenile Boot Camps and Traditional Facilities," *Law and Human Behavior* 24 (3) (2000): 297–308.
6. For a more detailed discussion, see Mitchell, O., D.L. MacKenzie, A.R. Cover, and G.J. Styve, "The Environment and Working Conditions in Juvenile Boot Camps and Traditional Facilities," *Justice Research and Policy* 1 (2) (1999): 1–22.
7. Sampson, R.J., and J.H. Laub, *Crime in the Making,* Cambridge, MA: Harvard University Press, 1993.
8. Gottfredson, M.R., and T. Hirschi, *A General Theory of Crime,* Stanford, CA: Stanford University Press, 1990.
9. Andrews, D.A., and J. Bonta, *The Psychology of Criminal Conduct,* Cincinnati: Anderson Publishing Co., 1998.
10. Gover, A.R., D.L. MacKenzie, and C.J. Styve, "Boot Camps and Traditional Correctional Facilities for Juveniles: A Comparison of the Participants, Daily Activities, and Environments," *Journal of Criminal Justice* 28 (1) (2000): 53–68.
11. Altschuler, D.M., T.L. Armstrong, and D.L. MacKenzie, *Reintegration, Supervised Release, and Intensive Aftercare,* Bulletin, Washington, DC: U.S. Department of Justice, Office of Juvenile Justice and Delinquency Prevention, 1999, NCJ 175715.
12. See Zamble, E., and F.J. Porporino, *Coping, Behavior, and Adaptation in Prison Inmates,* New York: Springer-Verlag, 1988, for a similar comparison to adult prison inmates.
13. See, for example, Lipsey, "Juvenile Delinquency Treatment"; and Andrews et al., "Does Correctional Treatment Work?"

Doris Layton MacKenzie, Angela R. Gover, Gaylene Styve Armstrong, and Ojmarrh Mitchell, "A National Study Comparing the Environments of Boot Camps with Traditional Facilities for Juvenile Offenders." Reprinted from *National Institute of Justice Research in Brief,* August 2001, pp. 1–11. Published by the U.S. Department of Justice Office of Justice Programs, National Institute of Justice. ✦

Chapter 32

Parental Efficacy and Delinquent Behavior

Do Control and Support Matter?

John Paul Wright
Francis T. Cullen

While control theory emphasize the role of parental control in preventing juvenile delinquency, Wright and Cullen suggest that parental social support may be equally important, and combine control and support into the idea of "parental efficacy." Their study measures control and support to determine whether support is indeed a distinct factor, and whether it lowers delinquency independent of parental controls.

In their innovative work on neighborhoods and crime, Sampson et al. (1997) draw on the concept of "self- or individual efficacy" to develop the notion of "collective efficacy" (see also Sampson et al., 1999). Sampson et al. (1997:919) propose that the two ideas are conceptually parallel in several ways. Thus, they observe that both neighborhoods and "individuals vary in their capacity for efficacious action." They proceed to note that both forms of efficacy are "situated rather than global (one has self-efficacy relative to a task or type of task)." They then note that the "reason we see an analogy between individual efficacy and neighborhood efficacy [is that] both are activated processes that seek to achieve an intended effect." In their work, the intended effect of collective efficacy was "supervising children and maintaining public order."

In Sampson et al.'s analysis, collective efficacy was, in a sense, an emergent concept. Originally, they had envisioned that neighborhood crime rates would be influenced by two separate factors or processes: informal social control by, and cohesion or mutual trust among, neighborhood residents. In reality, however, these two factors proved to be empirically intertwined. On reflection, Sampson et al. recognized that this close relationship made intuitive, if not criminological, sense, for "at the neighborhood level . . . the willingness of local residents to intervene for the common good"—that is, to exercise informal social control—"depends in large part on conditions of mutual trust and solidarity among neighbors" (p. 919).

These considerations form the conceptual context for the current study. Drawing on Sampson et al.'s revitalization of the concept of "efficacy," we argue that parents differ in the extent to which they effectively undertake the task of limiting their children's delinquency. Within criminology, control theory has provided the dominant understanding of how adults perform this parenting task—that is, through indirect and direct controls. We challenge this view of parenting as unnecessarily narrow. Borrowing research from other disciplines, we investigate how parental social support—a concept often neglected in criminological studies—diminishes delinquent involvement. Our analysis ultimately leads us, however, to a point parallel to that reached by Sampson et al. in their macrolevel work on collective efficacy: at the micro- or individual level, parental support and control are intertwined and form an important basis for "parental efficacy" in the task of keeping children out of trouble.

Parenting and Delinquent Involvement

Judith Rich Harris (1995) has set forth the provocative claim that parental behavior has few, if any, enduring effects on child development. Harris contends that beyond genetic effects, youths' conduct—including delinquency—is predominantly influenced by "group socialization"—that is, by the play groups in which children and adolescents participate. Her article, published in the *Psychological Bulletin,* recently earned an award from the American Psychological Association. The presentation of this award at the association's 1998 national meeting brought enormous attention outside academia to her contention that a child's "development is not derailed by the wide variations in parental behavior found within and between societies" (p. 458). Indeed, her central thesis—that parenting does not affect children's behavior—struck a chord with the media. For example, *Newsweek* (1998), *The New Yorker* (1998), and *The Chronicle of Higher Education* (1998) each printed lead stories about this "truly revolutionary idea" that has been heralded as a "paradigm shifter" (Harris, 1998). Perhaps not surprisingly, Harris (1998) has since conveyed her thesis in a book intended for popular consumption, which she titled, *The Nurture Assumption: Why Children Turn Out the Way They Do—"Parents Matter Less Than You Think and Peers Matter More."*

Ironically, criminology is proceeding in the opposite direction, with calls to "bring children back in" to criminological analysis (Sampson, 1993, 1994). With the emergence of developmental or life-course criminology, there is an increasing empirical and theoretical interest in the role played by family relations, especially between parent and child, in fostering and protecting against criminal involvement. Empirically, studies are documenting the family-related risk factors that increase criminogenic propensities (Lipsey and Derzon, 1998; Loeber and Stouthamer-Loeber, 1986). Theoretically, criminologists have most often explored the impact on delinquency of the informal social control exercised by parents and within families (see, e.g., Gottfredson and Hirschi, 1990; Hagan, 1989; Sampson and Laub, 1994).

The central role played by control theory in studying the influence of parents is not surprising. Even in the 1960s when criminology focused predominantly on class and adolescent peer group relationships (Cole, 1975), sociological control theories argued that parenting and attachments to parents insulated against wayward behavior (see Hirschi, 1969; Nye, 1958). In general, control theories maintain that parents induce their offspring to conform through indirect and/or direct controls. Indirect or "relational" (Hagan, 1989) controls operate through the attachment that children have to their parents. As Hirschi (1969:88) notes, "even when not physically present, parents can indirectly control their children if they are *psychologically* present when the temptation to commit a crime appears. If, in the situation of temptation, no thought is given to parental reaction, the child is to this extent free to commit the act." Parents matter to children—are "psychologically present"—to the extent that children are bonded or attached to their parents. In contrast, direct or "instrumental" (Hagan, 1989) control involves explicit efforts by parents to monitor their offspring's conduct and to punish misbehavior. Gottfredson and Hirschi's (1990) "general theory" is a variant of direct control theory: They argue that the propensity to commit crime, which they label "self-control," is inculcated in children by parents who exercise effective direct control—that is, who monitor, recognize, and punish wayward conduct.

Although control theories have illuminated important causal processes, as Cullen (1994; see also, Cullen et al., 1999) contends, criminologists have paid comparatively little attention to an alternative perspective on parenting within the field of child development: the effects on development of *social support*—that is, of the extent to which parents provide emotional and instrumental resources to their children (see, e.g., Pierce et al., 1996; for an exception, see Currie, 1985). The social support paradigm is a well-developed social-psychological perspective, which most often has been applied to the study of "internalized" reactions to stress, such as depression and other psychiatric symptoms (Linn et al., 1986; Thoits, 1995; Vaux, 1988). However, research has also investigated the impact of parental social support on "externalized" behavior, including delinquency and substance use/abuse (see, e.g., Alexander, 1973; Barrera and Li, 1996; Rothbaum and Weisz, 1994; Stice and Gonzales, 1998; Timko and Moos, 1996; Wills et al., 1996). Within criminology, although infrequent, empirical studies have been conducted linking social support to juvenile misconduct (Hepburn, 1977; Johnson et al., 1995).

Several conclusions can be drawn from the existing literature: Although the magnitude of effects varies across analyses, parental social support generally is negatively related to involvement in delinquency. It also appears that social support functions as a protective factor that fosters resiliency in children who are at risk for crime (Anisfeld et al., 1990; Barnes and Farrell, 1992; Cohen and Wills, 1985; Farrell et al., 1995; Jessor, 1993; Werner and Smith, 1982), and the data show that parental support has general effects on youths' lives. For example, parental support has been found to promote prosocial and altruistic behavior (Radke-Yarrow and Zahn-Waxler, 1986); to foster the assimilation of moral values, motives, and social skills (Hartup, 1986); and to produce and maintain affective attachments between youths and their parents (Cernkovich and Giordano, 1987; Hawkins et al., 1986; Sroufe and Fleeson, 1986).

Further, the thesis that social support lessens criminal involvement gains credence from Loeber and Stouthamer-Loeber's (1986) comprehensive meta-analysis of the family correlates of delinquency: Factors indicating a lack of parental support clearly increase delinquent involvement (see also, Rothbaum and Weisz, 1994). They conclude that delinquency is related inversely to "child-parent involvement, such as the amount of intimate communication, confiding, sharing of activities, and seeking help" (p. 42). Similarly, Rothbaum and Weisz (1994) found that children of accepting, responsive parents experienced fewer externalizing problems. These findings were particularly strong for studies employing experimental designs.

Thus far, we have juxtaposed control and social support as alternative explanations of why parents may affect delinquent involvement. To some degree, this characterization is misleading: Control theorists have not ignored the importance of parents caring about and being close to their offspring. Hirschi (1969), for example, focuses on the importance of intimate communications and attachment between parents and children. Still, in these theories, the concept of social support has not been systematically applied or has been relegated to a secondary influence. This is why virtually no summary of control theory mentions social support as a part of the theoretical tradition (see, e.g., Akers, 1994; Lilly et al., 1995).

More specifically, criminological control theories—either implicitly or explicitly—incorporate supportive aspects of parenting through the concept of attachment. Most often, however, the focus is on whether the child's attachment to parents reduces wayward conduct. In contrast to psychological research on attachment (Sroufe and Fleeson, 1986), there is not always a clear differentiation between (1) the support parents furnish and (2) the level of attachment this produces. This confusion is seen in empirical studies testing control theory that use measures of "attachment" that include either how parents treat their children or how their children feel about their parents (Rankin and Kern, 1994; Rankin and Wells, 1990; Wells and Rankin, 1988).

Relatedly, criminological research on control theory typically does not seek to distinguish the effects of parental social support as opposed to the effects of control. Instead, support is "folded into" control in the sense that its effects are seen to operate by making control possible. For example, in Hirschi's (1969) social bond theory, parental intimacy or "support" presumably reduces delinquency by increasing attachment and thus indirect parental control. What is not considered, however, is the possibility that social support has direct effects on delinquent behavior—a position that social support theory takes (see, e.g., Cullen, 1994; Cullen et al., 1998; Drennon-Gala, 1995).

Finally, because control theory sees support as a subsidiary concept, there is typically no attempt to explore systematically the interrelationship between parental support and features of control. For example, psychological research shows that parental support is related to attachment and to the internalization of self-control (Berscheid, 1986; Rankin and Kern, 1994; Sroufe and Fleeson, 1986; Wills et al., 1996), but empirical tests of control theories do not assess these possibilities. Further, Gottfredson and Hirschi (1990) suggest that parents' attachment to a child motivates them to monitor and sanction the child's behavior. It is noteworthy that no empirical study has tested this feature of their general theory (see, e.g., Gibbs et al., 1998).

Most important, with some exceptions (see McCord, 1979; Wilson and Herrnstein, 1985), criminologists have not explored whether control and support are features of parenting that occur coterminously and, if so, whether this is the most efficacious form of parenting. Existing research suggests that this is, in fact, the case. There is evidence, for example, that parents who are affectionate are also likely to have higher levels of supervision (McCord, 1979; see also Patterson and Stouthamer-Loeber, 1984). Further, Wilson and Herrnstein (1985) argue that the most effective parents are those who are "warm and restrictive." That is, parents who maintain an affectively close relationship and provide clear rules regarding the child's behavior promote prosocial behavior in the child. Echoing this view of the benefits of support and control, Baumrind (1991) contends that an "authoritative" parenting style facilitates children's development and prevents misconduct. According to Baumrind (p. 62), the hallmark of authoritative parents is that they are "both demanding and responsive. They monitor and impart clear standards for their children's conduct. . . . Their disciplinary methods are supportive rather than punitive."

These considerations set the context for the current study, which explores the effects of parental control and support on delinquent involvement.

Three issues are examined. First, we test the central contention of social support theory that parental support will reduce delinquency independent of parental controls. Again, previous research—mainly drawn from the social-psychological literature—has found that support has a direct and inverse relationship to misconduct among youngsters.

Second, we investigate whether support and control are empirically distinct or, in a factor analysis, load on the same factor. After exploring the extent to which parental support and control are interrelated, we assess whether this single construct is a strong predictor of delinquent involvement. Again, Sampson et al. (1997) have used the term "collective efficacy" to refer to the macrolevel feature of neighborhoods that involves the presence of both informal social control and trusting/cohesive relationships among residents. Arguing that control and support were integral to functioning communities, they showed that crime was inversely related to collective efficacy. In an analogous way, we use the term "parental efficacy" to refer to parents who control and support their children. Based on both support and control theory, we suggest that delinquent involvement will be inversely related to parental efficacy.

Third, our research provides an opportunity to assess Harris's (1995, 1998) contention that parents "don't matter" in delinquency causation. Although a strict test of Harris's theory is beyond the scope of the current study, we are able to address certain of the issues emphasized by Harris. First, Harris and other genetic researchers maintain that most research on the effects of parenting behaviors on delinquency is misspecified because only one youth within a household is typically assessed, along with the youth's parent(s). As Harris points out, however, youths reared within the same family environment are likely to experience, subjectively or objectively, different parenting styles due to their unique personality and physical traits. To combat this potentially important source of bias, we use a data set that includes measures of all youths living within a home.

Second, Harris argues that findings relating parenting to delinquency are also likely biased by "child effects." In this view, parenting behavior is not a cause of, but rather a reaction to, the personality and behavior of children. Well-mannered children, for example, are likely to solicit higher levels of parental support than are youths who misbehave consistently, thus "accounting" for the finding that supportive parenting leads to lower levels of misconduct among children. To address this issue, we use longitudinal data to statistically control for the effects of past behavior, and when appropriate, we control for the effects of adolescent delinquency on contemporaneous parental behavior.

Finally, Harris maintains that child behavior is accounted for by two sources of variation: inherited genes from the parents (parental heterogeneity) and peers. Without the use of genetic design studies, it is difficult to partition the variance in child outcomes to shared and nonshared sources—that is, between inherited traits and the environment. However, we include statistical controls for potential sources of parental heterogeneity and note that past research has found that as much as 40% of the variance in delinquency is associated with inherited traits from parents (Plomin, 1990). We also include the effects of delinquent peers in our models. Peers, argues Harris, are the most important source of socialization, outstripping the influence of parenting behaviors.

Methods

Sample

Data from the 1992 wave of the Children of the National Longitudinal Survey of Youth (NLSY) are used in this analysis. Respondents in the NLSY have been interviewed annually since 1979 about various economic, social, and personal experiences. Assessment of the development of children born to mothers in the NLSY began in 1986 and has continued at two-year intervals since then. The NLSY contains dual informant reports of adolescent and maternal behaviors and attitudes. Moreover, extensive measures exist detailing the mothers' delinquent and criminal involvement in 1980, allowing us to control for transmitted parental effects.

Because base rates for delinquent behaviors are low within samples of the general population, the use of high-risk samples has been encouraged. The NLSY sample of children can be considered a sample of high-risk adolescents and their mothers due to the overrepresentation of children born to teenage mothers. Young women in the NLSY sample were originally interviewed in 1979 when they were between the ages of 14 and 21. In the 1992 wave, these mothers were between the ages of 27 and 34. Thus, most of children over the age of 12 in 1992 were born to teenage mothers. Comparably, teenage mothers in this sample are less well educated, disadvantaged, and members of minority groups (Center for Human Resource Research, 1992). As of 1992, however, the degree of sample censoring has been reduced by the continued addition of older mothers whose inclusion into the sample fosters more generalizable results. Children included in the 1992 wave represent over two-thirds of the childbearing to a cohort of American women (Center for Human Resource Research, 1992).

The initial respondent selection procedure used multistage, stratified cluster sampling designed to include an overrepresentation of minorities. Given the sampling procedure involved, selection probabilities differ across various groups. We employ sampling weights to correct for differential selection probabilities to obtain unbiased descriptive statistics. However, the use of sampling weights in multiple linear regression is unadvisable, and thus, we employ unweighted data in the main analysis (Center for Human Resources Research, 1992).

We chose to limit our analysis to children age ten and over for two reasons: First, child self-report instruments were administered only to children over the age of ten. Second, the design of the survey includes the measurement of current and subsequent youths born to mothers. The size of the sample of youths then increases over time (new births) and ages. Subsequently, the number of youths age ten and over by 1992 includes a sufficient number for analysis ($N =$ 1526).

Measures

Parental Controls. The 1992 wave of the NLSY contains measures of both indirect parental controls and direct parental controls. The former, which we label attachment, focuses on the strength of the emotional bond between the child and parent (Bowlby, 1969; Hirschi, 1969; Rankin and Kern, 1994). Hagan (1989) refers to this dimension of control as "relational" control, whereas Nagin and Paternoster (1994) include attachment as a component of personal capital. Similarly, Sampson and Laub (1993) incorporate attachment under their theory of informal social control. We measure attachment through a two-item scale that assesses the degree of closeness children feel to their parents. These two items ask the children about how close they feel to their mothers and their fathers.

Current social control theories, however, have placed less emphasis on indirect controls, such as attachment, and more emphasis on direct mechanisms of child restraint. Direct parental controls, according to Patterson (1980), involve close monitoring, parental supervision, clearly articulated family rules, and rational punishment for transgressions. Similarly, Gottfredson and Hirschi (1990) argue that direct parental control is the mechanism through which self-control is established and offending prevented. We include three dimensions of direct parental controls in the analysis: parental supervision, parental expectations of the child, and parental household rules. These constructs are derived from contemporary control theory perspectives and have been found predictive of delinquency in past studies (Burton et al., 1995; Hagan, 1989; Loeber and Stouthamer-Loeber, 1986).

Parental supervision is measured by two items. First, mothers were asked how many of their child's close friends they know well. Second, mothers were asked how often they know where their child is (alpha = .52). Combined, these items tap into the extent to which mothers are aware of their children's activities and associates. The second measured dimension of direct controls is parental expectations. We employ a ten-item scale that includes both child and mother reports. Children, for example, were asked how often they were expected to straighten their room, clean the house, do dishes, and cook. Similarly, mothers reported how often they expected their children to make their bed, clean their room, help in household maintenance, do routine chores, and manage their time wisely (alpha = .80). Higher scores on the scale reflect greater parental expectations of the child.

In accordance with current control theories, we also include a measure of the presence of rules parents employ within the household. Children were asked about the existence of parental rules concerning the watching of television, keeping their parents informed of their whereabouts, doing their homework, and their dating (alpha = .45). We note that this measure is an index—that is, a simple count of the number of rules within the household. There is no reason to believe that the presence of one household rule would necessitate the presence of another, largely unrelated, household rule. Therefore, a low reliability for this measure is not unexpected.

Parental Support. We measured two dimensions of parental social support: parental reliability and support. The first construct, parental reliability, is measured through a two-item scale. Adolescents were asked how often both their mothers and fathers miss important events or activities. Responses were scored 1 = often, 2 = sometimes, and 3 = hardly ever. Higher scores on the scale reflect greater parental reliability.

We constructed a parental support scale that taps into the extent to which parents provide their children with various types of support, such as emotional support or instrumental support. We employ a 15-item scale that includes both mother and child reports of support given or received. For example, mothers were asked whether they encourage hobbies, whether the child receives special lessons or activities, and how often the child is praised, shown affection, and complimented. Similarly, children were asked if they have gone to the movies, to dinner, gone shopping specifically for them, gone on an outing, to church, done things together, worked on school work, or played a game or sport with their parent(s) in either the last week or month (alpha = .75).

Control Variables. Harris (1998) argues that parents essentially "pass on" behaviors and attitudes to their children through genetic inheritance. Although it is impossible to completely account for the influence of shared genetic influences—what we term "parental heterogeneity"—we include controls that ostensibly capture variation in parental heterogeneity. The strongest of these measures taps into individual differences between parents in their prior level of criminal offending. In 1980, then 14 to 21 years old, mothers were administered self-report questionnaires detailing their involvement in a number of delinquent and criminal events. Moreover, questions were also asked concerning their penetration into the criminal justice system. We used an 11-item scale to measure mothers' past involvement in drug use, selling drugs, conning someone to obtain property, automobile theft, breaking and entering, possessing or selling stolen property, gambling, and ever being stopped, charged, booked, or convicted of a criminal offense (alpha = .88).

Similarly, given the overrepresentation of teenage mothers in the sample, we include a dichotomous measure of whether the mother gave birth to a child while an adolescent.

Although often implicated in the etiology of delinquency, the effects of family structure on delinquency are subject to substantial empirical debate (Matsueda and Heimer, 1987; Van Voorhis et al., 1988; Wells and Rankin, 1991). However, current variants of control theory relate single-parent households to reduced direct parental controls (Gottfredson and Hirschi, 1990; Sampson and Laub, 1994; Wilson and Herrnstein, 1985). Thus, we include a single dichotomous measure of whether the child lives with only the mother.

The stress associated with sustained family poverty has also been shown to influence parenting, namely, by reducing parental control efforts (Amato and Booth, 1997) and thereby increasing the misbehavior of youths. Therefore, we include in the analysis a measure of chronic family poverty. NLSY staff ascertained from parents their income from all available sources for the years 1991 and 1992, as well as the number of dependents within the household. The family's poverty status was then determined by using federal guidelines.

According to Harris (1998), peers serve as the master socializing agent of a youth. Thus, we account for the influence that peers have on youths. Although we do not have direct measures of the number of delinquent friends, the NLSY does contain questions on delinquent peer pressure. This scale is composed of five items that tap into the extent to which adolescents have felt pressure from their friends to try cigarettes, marijuana, drink alcohol, skip school, or commit crime (alpha = .78).

Finally, we include a dichotomous measure of the adolescent's sex (1 = female), race (1 = minority), and age (in years).

Delinquency. Lastly, a 13-item delinquency scale was constructed through the use of child and mother reports. Children age ten and over were asked about the number of times they committed various delinquent acts, such as stealing from a store or hurting someone so badly they needed to see a doctor, and their experience with cigarettes, alcohol, marijuana, and cocaine. Mother reports ascertained whether their child(ren) had ever repeated a grade, been suspended or expelled, or if their child's behavior had ever required them to visit school officials (alpha = .88). A similar delinquency scale is used in our longitudinal analyses (alpha = .85). The delinquency scale used in this analysis has been subject to substantial pretesting and empirical validation, and it has been shown to have a high degree of predictive validity (Mott and Quinlan, 1993).

Statistical Models

The NLSY employs a total-population design and includes age-appropriate measures of all children. Therefore, these data can be considered clustered with children residing within families. The clustered nature of these data make standard regression analyses problematic. Clustered data substantially reduce the amount of independence between measures, biasing estimates of slope standard errors, and also potentially biasing slope estimates (Bryk and Raudenbush, 1992; Hedeker et al., 1994; Hox and Kreft, 1994).

To account for the clustering of observations within families, we employ a random-effects regression model (RRM). RRM's, also known as multilevel models or hierarchical linear models, account for the clustering of data within varying contexts. The general equation follows the form:

$$y_i = X_i\beta + 1_i\alpha_i + \varepsilon_i,$$

where y_i = an n_i X 1 response vector for family i, i = 1,2,. . . . ,N, X_i = an n_i X $(p + 1)$ covariate matrix with p covariates, β = a $(p + 1)$ X 1 vector of unknown population parameters, 1_i = an n_i X 1 vector of ones, α_i = the unknown cluster effect, and ε_i = an n_i X 1 vector of residuals. The two error components are correspondingly distributed $N(0, \phi^2{}_\alpha)$ and $N(0, \phi^2 I_{ni})$. Such a model allows for the simultaneous estimation of both random and fixed effects and produces estimates of the variance at each level. We use a program called MIXREG to estimate all model equations (Hedecker et al., 1994). MIXREG utilizes empirical Bayes methods to estimate cluster effects and maximum marginal likelihood methods to estimate both variance parameters and covariate effects.

Hierarchical linear models (HLM) assess the impact of parenting practices on individual levels of delinquent involvement, independent of individual family characteristics. We estimate a random intercept model with grand mean-centered Level 1 covariates (Bryk and Raudenbush, 1992). Level 2 measures, the between-family parenting practices, measure the adjusted true mean of delinquent involvement for family j controlling for variation in Level 1 control variables. The parameter estimates for the Level 2 variables represent the effects of parenting practices on the adjusted mean—that is, with the effects of within-family variables partialed out. Consistent with the analytical strategy of Elliott et al. (1996), we estimate only "fixed effects" models because of the relatively small within-cluster sample sizes. "Fixed effects" models assume that variables exert similar effects across individuals within families.

Results

Table 32.1 provides parameter estimates for model equations. Model equation (1) represents the baseline model in which only the intercept was entered into the equation and allowed to vary across families. The model is similar to the traditional analysis of variance (ANOVA) procedure and is used as a baseline to evaluate follow-on analyses. The baseline model follows the form:

$$Y_{ij} = \beta_{0j} + r_{ij},$$

where β_{0j} = a randomly varying intercept and r_{ij} a normally distributed error term with a zero mean and constant variance. β_{0j}, therefore, equals the mean level of delinquency across all families (5.42). The results indicate that there is substantial variation within families in child delinquency and, to a lesser but still substantive extent, across families. Moreover, the intraclass correlation coefficient shows substantial cross-family variation in child delinquency. This finding is congruent with past research that shows that delinquency is confined to a relatively small number of households (Farrington, 1986). Moreover, the substantial intraclass correlation coefficient, a measure of family homogeneity, is also consistent with past research that shows that the highest levels of group homogeneity are likely to be found within families (Kreft and De Leeuw, 1998).

The analysis of covariance (ANCOVA) model includes the household background factors and serves as a benchmark to evaluate the full models. This procedure allows us to estimate the unique contribution of parenting practices on juvenile delinquency. Accordingly, all of the background factors are statistically significant ($p < .05$), except for the effects of teenage motherhood and race. The strongest background predictor of delinquency is delinquent peer pressure.

An examination of the random components shows that the addition of the Level 1 covariates

Table 32.1

Hierarchical Linear Models of Family and Individual Effects on Delinquency

	Model Equation			
Variable	ANOVA	ANCOVA	Full Model	Parental Efficacy
Between Family Grand Mean	5.42*	.51	11.51*	1.29
Within Families				
Gender		−1.93*	−1.52*	−1.83*
Teenage Mother		.32	.38	.36
Mother's Delinquency		.18*	.16*	.15*
Mother's Marital Status (1 = single)		−.18*	−.02	.38*
Delinquent Peer Pressure		1.60*	1.50*	1.50*
Age (in years)		.56*	.43*	.44*
Race (1 = minority)		1.29	1.23	.90
Between Family Parental Controls				
Child–Parent Attachment			−.21*	
Parental Expectations			.03	
Household Rules			−.27*	
Parental Supervision			−.80*	
Between Family Parental Supports				
Parental Reliability			−.51*	
Parental Support			−.05*	
Between Family Parental Efficacy				−1.28*
Random Part				
Φ^2,	18.98*	16.73*	16.02*	15.94*
T_{00} (intercept)	9.74*	5.94*	5.61*	5.44*
Intra-cluster Correlation	.340	.262	.260	.250
Proportional Decrease of Variance				
Of Φ^2,		12%	16%	16%
Of T_{00}		39%	42%	44%
Percent Reduction in Total Conditional Error Variance			4.6%	6.6%
Model R^2		.21	.25	.26

* Parameter estimate at least twice its standard error.
Maximum Marginal Likelihood estimates (MML).

reduced the intraclass correlation from .34 to .26, and reduced the residual (individual level) variance (ϕ^2_ε) by 12% and the between-family variance by 39%. Overall, the model reduced the total error variance (in contrast with the ANOVA analysis) by 21%.

The third column in Table 32.1 shows the parameter estimates for the full model—that is, with the effects of parenting characteristics introduced. We first note that the introduction of the parenting variables reduced the effects of family structure to statistical insignificance and generally reduced the magnitude of the other coefficients, although not to insignificance. Thus, even with parenting practices included in the model, most of the within-family variables maintain significant effects in the predicted direction. Especially salient are the effects of delinquent peer pressure and mother's criminal involvement.

All of the parental control and parental support variables, however, exerted independent and significant effects in the predicted direction, except for the effects of parental expectations. Notably, the effects of parental supports withstood the effects of parental controls; both parental reliability and parental support were significantly and inversely related to delinquency. Thus, parental support does not appear to be able to be subsumed under other control theory constructs.

HLM computes variance statistics to allow for the partialling of the variance between levels of explanatory variables. In this way, we can assess the overall predictive power of Level 2 predictors on the individual outcome and in relation to Level 1 predictors. In essence, this part of the analysis allows us to answer "do parents matter" and, if so, "how much do they matter?"

An examination of the random components of the full model again show substantial within- and between-family variation in delinquency ($\rho = .260$). Compared with the ANOVA model, the addition of the parenting variables reduced the individual level variance by 16% and the between-family variance by 42%. However, the overall direct effect, as calculated by the percent reduction in the total conditional error variance, was only 4.6%. Accordingly, the net effect of parenting characteristics on adolescent delinquent involvement was modest. It would be unwise, however, to argue that "parents do not matter" for three reasons: First, the between-family variation is only a small part of the total variance. Given the design and sampling of the NLSY, only a modest amount of variance in delinquency can be associated with parenting. Second, including the parenting measures did provide a significant increase to the predictive power of the equation. The overall level of explained variance associated with the full model, $R^2 = .25$, is only modest, but the parenting variables account for almost 20% of this variation. Finally, if the proportional decrease of variance estimates are interpreted as explained variance, then the parenting variables are accounting for a substantial level of variance at the household level. Thus, even in our sample of high-risk youths with a substantial age range, parents who support and control their offspring appear capable of reducing wrongful behavior.

Parental Efficacy: Overlap in Support and Control

Having established the independent influence of the various dimensions of parenting, we next examine the joint influence of parental support and control. As we discussed earlier, Sampson et al. (1999) examined whether communities able to provide support and exercise control were associated with lower crime rates. What is instructive about their analysis, and pertinent to ours, is that they were largely unable to disentangle the effects of neighborhood support from levels of neighborhood informal control. To resolve the apparent overlap, they combined their measures of support with their measures of informal social control to form a measure that they termed "collective efficacy." Collective efficacy refers, at the macrolevel, to the ability of a community to provide support and exercise control.

The work of Sampson et al. thus prompted us to examine the interrelationship between support and control. We began by investigating the relationship among the different components of control and support, regressing each parenting variable on the other parenting dimensions. In this analysis, we also included a control for child delinquency to correctly specify our equations, thus limiting the possibility that our results are due to "child effects" or to individual differences between children in their behavior. The results are shown in Table 32.2. First, and most important, parental controls appear to be related inconsistently to other parental controls. For example, parental attachment is significantly and positively associated with supervision, inversely related to parental expectations, and unrelated to parental rules. On the other hand, the effects of parental support on dimensions of parental control are consistent across the equations and in the predicted direction—that is, parental support is significantly associated with each of the parenting dimensions, even with controls in place for child misbehavior. These data suggest, therefore, that parents who provide support to their children are also more likely to exercise a greater number of direct controls, such as supervision, and indirect controls, such as attachment. We address this issue specifically in the discussion section.

Second, it is instructive that the effects of parental support and control appear to operate at different levels. Most of the variation in parental controls occurs at the individual level. Youths residing within the same home vary in their levels of attachment, supervision, the number of rules they are subject to, and, to a much lesser extent, how much support they receive from their parents. However, parental support appears to be a defining characteristic among households. Indeed, the baseline model for parental support generated the highest intraclass correlation (.81) of all baseline models, indicating that youths within families share perceptions about how much their parents support them.

Table 32.2
Examining the Interrelationship Between Parenting Factors

Variable	Attachment	Supervision	Expectations	Parental Rules	Reliability	Support
	Model Equation					
Between Family Grand Mean	4.75*	5.10*	16.22*	.94*	1.100*	10.51*
Within Families						
Gender	–.28*	.43*	1.57*	.14*	.02	–3.02*
Teenage Mother	–.15*	–.14*	.72*	–.02	.03	–.53*
Mother's Delinquency	–.04*	.01	–.02	–.00	.00	.04
Marital Status (1 = single)	–.19*	–.06	–2.5*	–.08	.05	–6.37*
Delinquent Peer Pressure	–.07	–.02	–.04	.00	–.01	–.02
Age	–.05*	–.10*	.40*	–.01	.00	.01
Race	.02	.28	1.15	–.27	.05	.02
Child's Delinquency	–.02*	–.05	.02	–.00	–.01*	–.06*
Parental Controls						
Child–Parent Attachment	n/a	.07*	–.61*	–.00	.02	1.15*
Parental Supervision	.11*	n/a	–.10	.04	.06*	.30*
Parental Expectations	–.07*	–.01	n/a	.00	.00	.52*
Household Rules	–.00	.07*	.03	n/a	–.00	.57*
Parental Social Supports						
Parental Reliability	.13*	.16*	.14	–.00	n/a	.45*
Parental Support	.11*	.02*	.40*	.02*	.01*	n/a
Random Part						
Φ^2,	1.46*	.89*	7.84*	.45*	.38*	9.08*
T_{00} (intercept)	.45*	.30*	12.10*	.22*	.07*	18.76*
Intra-cluster Correlation	.235	.251	.607	.330	.160	.674
Proportional Decrease of Variance						
Of Φ^2,	18%	10%	33%	10%	1%	16%
Of T_{00}	46%	46%	20%	4%	75%	60%
Model R^2	.27	.23	.26	.06	.32	.52

* Parameter estimate at least twice its standard error.
Maximum Marginal Likelihood estimates (MML).

The preceding analysis suggests that parental support and parental controls are intertwined. To examine this issue further, we again followed Sampson et al.'s (1999) lead and factor analyzed the parental control and parental support variables. The analysis indicated that, indeed, the measures loaded on a single factor. We then entered the factor variable, which we term "parental efficacy," into the equation predicting delinquent involvement. Returning to Table 32.1, the results reveal that our measure of parental efficacy is inversely and moderately related to adolescent misbehavior. The effect of parental efficacy reduced the intercept variance, increased the overall explanatory power of the model, and generated a slightly stronger direct effect (6.6%) than did the individual components. Moreover, parental efficacy reduced the variation between families to statistical insignificance. From these data, it appears that parents who are nurturing, reliable, and closely attached to their youths and who provide guidance in the form of rules and supervision reduce the delinquency of their adolescents, even when the effects of delinquent peers and sources of parental heterogeneity are controlled.

Age-Graded Effects of Parental Efficacy

Because the effects of parenting variables have been found to decline as youths age (see, e.g., LaGrange and White, 1985), it is conceivable that the influence of parental efficacy is age-graded. To assess this possibility, we divided the overall sample into three age-graded categories: 10 to 12 years old, 13 to 14 years old, and 15 years old and above.[1] In these analyses, we used longitudinal data and, in addition to background characteristics, controlled for two strong predictors of delinquency: prior delinquent involvement and delinquent peer pressure.

The results are shown in Table 32.3. For the entire sample, age, delinquent peer pressure, and prior delinquency are positively and significantly associated with misbehavior, whereas gender is inversely associated with misbehavior. Even so, the effects of parental efficacy are significant and in the expected direction of reducing delinquent participation. Across the three age groups, we again find that parental efficacy is significantly and negatively related to delinquency. In each case, its relationship to delinquency is stronger than all variables in the analysis except for prior delinquency and delinquent peer pressure. It is noteworthy, moreover, that the influence of parental efficacy on delinquency is consistent across the age categories (with the Betas in the three models ranging from –.178 to –.192). In short, the pattern of results clearly suggests that parental efficacy has general effects across the age groups—that is, its influence is not limited to early age groups but extends into late adolescence.

Discussion

For more than three decades, control theory has had a continuing influence on criminological thinking. Theories that place family processes at their core have been particularly likely to emphasize the role of various forms of control in crime and delinquency causation (see, e.g., Gottfredson and Hirschi, 1990; Hagan, 1989; Hirschi, 1969; Sampson and Laub, 1994; Wilson and Herrnstein, 1985). Our research both reinforces and specifies the contention that control is central to the etiology of delinquent involvement.

Our empirical analysis found that delinquency was reduced by child-parent attachment, household rules, and parental supervision. These results are consistent with Hirschi's (1969) social bond theory, which stresses the importance of indirect or relational control, and with perspectives that emphasize the role of direct or instrumental control in fostering conformity by inducing self-control (Gottfredson and Hirschi, 1990), by reducing risk preferences (Hagan, 1989), or by increasing prosocial learning (Patterson, 1980; Wilson and Herrnstein, 1985). At the same time, our analysis also revealed that even with a range of social control and risk factors in the model, social support was inversely related to delinquency. In short, social support appears to have direct effects on juvenile waywardness that are not explained by or contingent on parental control (cf., Gottfredson and Hirschi, 1990). As a result, our findings join with those of other studies (Baumrind, 1991; Rollins and Thomas, 1979) in suggesting that theories of delinquency that focus exclusively on control and not on support are likely to be misspecified.

It is especially instructive, we believe, that parents who support their children are also parents who control and are attached to their children. Although support and control are conceptually distinct, it appears that in real-life parenting, they are often inextricably intertwined. In fact, empirically, the items measuring control and support loaded on the same factor. Theoretically, this finding makes sense. Both support and control require the investment of parental time and energies—that is, the expenditure of parental "capital."

Recall as well that the combined support-control measure—"parental efficacy"—had strong effects on delinquency. This result is consistent with the growing body of psychological research suggesting that effective parenting involves both expressing warmth and setting limits (Maccoby, 1980, 1992; Wilson and Hernnstein, 1985). As noted, within developmental psychology, this form of parenting is often termed "authoritative." Research indicates that the healthy development of both boys and girls across developmental stages is facilitated by parents who exercise firm but supportive control—that is, who are restrictive but responsive (Baumrind, 1991). Again, we suggest that control theory misses an important dimension of

Table 32.3
Examining the Age-Graded Effects of Parental Efficacy on Delinquency (b/Beta)

Independent Variables	Entire Sample		10–12		13–14		15 and Above	
	b	*Beta*	*b*	*Beta*	*b*	*Beta*	*b*	*Beta*
Gender	–.95	–.082*	–.780	–.080	–.815	–.073	–1.845	–.146*
Teenage Mother	–.57	–.044	.275	.028	–1.192	–.099	–2.203	–.091
Mother's Delinquency	.07	.032	.005	.003	–.001	–.006	.121	.049
Delinquent Peer Pressure	1.35	.238*	.855	.189*	1.993	.352*	1.490	.249*
Marital Status	.60	.051	–.009	–.001	–.340	–.030	.328	.026
Age	.38	.113*	1.914	.123*	.371	.041	.572	.106*
Race	.86	.015	4.852	.071	–1.556	–.032	.925	.018
Parental Efficacy	–1.32	–.225*	–.950	–.189*	–1.167	–.192*	–1.210	–.178*
Prior Delinquency (1990)	.55	.339*	.593	.343*	.394	.240	.563	.344*
R^2		.370		.277		.342		.363
N		582		195		223		259

* Indicates parameter estimate significant at the .05 level, two-tailed test.

effective parenting to the extent that social support is not integrated into the model (see also Braithwaite, 1989; Cullen, 1994; Currie, 1985).

This reality lends credence to the possibility that support may be intricately related to various types of parental control efforts. Recall that our measure of parental support was associated with each measure of parental control, but that parental controls were inconsistently related to other parental controls. Although microlevel longitudinal data are needed, this finding suggests that parental support makes it more likely that parents will control their children and exercise different types of controls.

This process, which will have to be confirmed in future studies, is theoretically important because it can potentially shed light on the multiple mechanisms parents employ to socialize their offspring. For example, in our data, we find that parental support is positively related to child-parent attachment, which is seen as an indirect control. Although we cannot establish causal ordering, there is a substantial psychological literature showing that parental nurturance or support is the foundation for attachment (Coble et al., 1996; Sroufe and Fleeson, 1986). Similarly, Gottfredson and Hirschi (1990) argue that direct control—monitoring, recognizing, and punishing deviant acts—is the cause of self-control. Research by Wills et al. (1996:539) also shows, however, that "parental support is a protective factor because it is conducive to the development of self-control skills." Our analysis lends empirical support to this possibility in another way—that is, by specifying the level at which parental support and control variables operate. We found that the support variables, which appear to operate at the household level, consistently predicted variation in parental controls, which mostly operated at the individual level. Taken together, the pattern of results suggests that parental controls are embedded in parental efforts to provide emotional and instrumental types of support. Future analyses of parental controls and supports that do not account [for] the level of parenting variables are likely to be misspecified by failing to estimate the effect of parental support at the household level.

Future research may also profit by being informed by the concept of "efficacy." As Sampson et al. (1999) note—albeit with regard to collective processes—efficacy involves "agency" or action taken to achieve intended goals or outcomes. It is noteworthy, then, that parental agency is implicit in the concepts of control and support. Parents must take steps to exercise control and to deliver social support. Although not designed directly for this purpose, many of the items in the scales we used in this study capture this parental agency, for they assess the concrete choices made by parents to structure, guide, know about, and be involved meaningfully in their children's lives (e.g., setting expectations and rules, monitoring their choice of friends and their whereabouts, attending games, supplying praise and affection).

Still, we suspect that research specially designed to measure parental efficacy may be able to move our understanding of parenting effects to a more advanced level. For example, we may profit from knowing the role of parental efficacy in preventing the onset of delinquency as opposed to its role when parents must respond to a crisis situation in which their children have "gotten into trouble." Further, existing criminological data sets rarely contain measures in which parents and children evaluate whether parental actions—in this case, the delivery of controls and supports—are experienced as positive, just, or useful. This issue is potentially important, given the emerging theorizing in criminology emphasizing how attempts at control can be counterproductive (Colvin, 2000; Sherman, 1993; Tittle, 1995) and the research in social psychology on the salience of "perceptions" of social support (Vaux, 1988). Of course, studies such as ours that depend on data sets like the NLSY make the plausible assumption that parents build attachments, set rules, monitor behavior, and spend time with their offspring precisely because they believe that this form of parenting will enhance their children's prosocial development and, conversely, insulate against wayward influences. Again, however, deepening our understanding, parental efficacy will require efforts to probe this matter more directly and to create measures that assess how parents and children experience and evaluate steps taken to deliver control and support.

Finally, the findings reported here address the current debate about the relevance of parenting to adolescent misbehavior. Our goal, aside from evaluating the impact of parental supports and controls, was to assess the relative impact of parenting variables on delinquency. According to Harris, parenting exerts little direct influence on youths above and beyond the effects of genes and peer groups. The reason parenting has so little effect is that youths who reside within the same home have very different experiences and perceptions—what she terms "microenvironments"—with their parents. And outside of the home, peer groups serve as the master socializing agent. Our analyses, which controlled for potential sources of parental heterogeneity and delinquent peer pressure, provide some support for Harris's contention. Within families, individual youths appear to be subject to varying levels of attachment, supervision, and rules. These variables, in turn, account for variation in delinquency. Similarly, we found that the direct effect of parenting variables on misbehavior ranged from 4.6% to 6.6%. That is, the overall direct effect of parenting on delinquency once sources of parental heterogeneity and delinquent peers were removed was relatively modest in the hierarchical models.

At the same time, our analyses call into question the position that "parents don't matter" in delinquency causation. The parental support and control measures produced independent and inverse effects on delinquency in our cross-sectional models, even with the effects from within-family variables controlled. Although the direct effect of the individual control and support measures was modest, the effect of "parental efficacy" rivaled that of delinquent peers in the cross-sectional model and in the longitudinal models that controlled for unobserved heterogeneity in offending. Contrary to Harris, parental efficacy appears to be capable of limiting delinquent involvement initially and capable of reducing delinquent involvement over a two-year period—for younger as well as for older youths.

Similarly, our analysis of parenting behaviors revealed that parental socializing efforts are not substantially reduced by the misbehavior of their offspring. Although it is likely that delinquency can influence parenting styles, can create conflict within the home, and can restrict the amount of support parents provide to their deviant adolescent, parents also appear able to adjust to instances of misbehavior. Delinquent youths may be more difficult to parent, but it does not appear that a youth's delinquency is the sole determinate of parenting behavior, as inferred by Harris.

It is undoubtedly tempting for researchers of family process to ignore Harris's critical assessment of the findings generated from a wide body of family socialization research. After all, her claim that parenting styles are of limited value to understanding differences between youths strikes many as nonsensical, if not blasphemous. Although the data presented here appear to show that Harris has overstated certain of her claims, we believe that it would be unwise to discount Harris or many of her criticisms of the family process literature. Future research would benefit from incorporating Harris's alternative position by including measures of each child and parent within the household, by examining the factors that differentiate the experiences of youths within each household, and by employing longitudinal designs that include multiple measurement waves so that individuals can serve as their own controls. In the end, Harris's challenge to family socialization researchers may sponsor a deeper understanding of the relationship between parental management styles and juvenile delinquency.

Note

1. Because of the sampling design employed in the NLSY, the inclusion of the measure of past delinquency restricts our sample to $N = 582$ youths who were assessed in 1990 and 1992. The subsample thus becomes comparably older and more likely to be born to teenage mothers. Moreover, the inclusion of our measure of past delinquency controls for unobserved heterogeneity in offending and thereby correctly specifies variable relationships (Thornberry, 1996). If Harris (1998) is correct, the parenting measure should be reduced to statistical insignificance once the measure of prior delinquency is introduced. On the other hand, if our hypothesis concerning the effects of parental efficacy is correct, the effect of parenting should not only be statistically significant, but also substantively important. We calculate OLS regression equations to assess the magnitude of effects within

models because the maximum likelihood estimates generated from the hierarchical models do not allow for standardized comparisons between parameter estimates.

Appendix 32.1
Zero-Order Pearson Correlation Matrix, Means, and Standard Deviations for NLSY Sample Variables

		X1	X2	X3	X4	X5	X6	X7	X8	X9	X10	X11	X12
Delinquency	x1	1.00											
Teenmom	x2	.16*	1.00										
Sex	x3	–.19*	.01	1.00									
MomDel	x4	.07*	.06*	.01	1.00								
Peer Pressure	x5	.37*	.08*	–.06*	–.01	1.00							
Reliability	x6	–.16*	–.02	.06*	–.01	–.07*	1.00						
Rules	x7	–.12*	–.05	.08*	–.03	–.01	.05	1.00					
Expectations	x8	–.04	.06	.18*	–.03	–.01	.08*	.09*	1.00				
Supervision	x9	–.33*	–.12*	.18*	–.01	–.13*	.17*	.13*	.09*	1.00			
Support	x10	–.20*	–.14*	.01	–.01	–.07*	.21*	.15*	.37*	.23*	1.00		
Attachment	x11	–.20*	–.16*	–.11*	–.07*	–.11*	.15*	.07*	–.03	.19*	.43*	1.00	
Marital Status	x12	–.10*	–.14*	–.01	–.08*	–.04	.14*	.04	.02	.11*	.56*	.24*	1.00
Mean		5.56	.583	1.48	1.31	0.49	2.37	1.97	29.10	6.80	39.66	7.00	.519
S.D.		5.33	.493	.50	2.87	1.08	0.70	.84	5.06	1.23	7.43	1.61	.500

* Indicates significant correlation at the .05 level, two–tailed.

References

Akers, Ronald L. 1994. Criminological Theories: Introduction and Evaluation. Los Angeles, Calif.: Roxbury.

Alexander, James R. 1973. Defensive and supportive communications in normal and deviant families. Journal of Consulting and Clinical Psychology 40:223–231.

Amato, Paul R. and Allen Booth. 1997. A Generation at Risk: Growing Up in an Era of Family Upheaval. Cambridge, Mass.: Harvard University Press.

Anisfeld, Elizabeth, Virginia Casper, Molly Nozyce, and Nicholas Cunningham. 1990. Does infant carrying promote attachment? An experimental study of the effects of increased physical contact on the development of attachment. Child Development 61:1617–1627.

Barnes, Grace M. and Michael P. Farrell. 1992. Parental support and control as predictors of adolescent drinking, delinquency, and related problem behaviors. Journal of Marriage and the Family 54:763–776.

Barrera, Manuel Jr. and Susan A. Li. 1996. The relation of family support to adolescents' psychological distress and behavior problems. In Gregory R. Pierce, Barbara R. Sarason, and Irvin G. Sarason (eds.), Handbook of Social Support and the Family. New York: Plenum Press.

Baumrind, Diana. 1991. The influence of parenting style on adolescent competence and substance abuse. Journal of Early Adolescence 11:56–95.

Berscheid, Ellen. 1986. Emotional experience in close relationships: Some implications for child development. In William W. Hartup and Zick Rubin (eds.), Relationships and Development. New Jersey: Lawrence Erlbaum Associates.

Braithwaite, John. 1989. Crime, Shame and Reintegration. Cambridge, U.K.: Cambridge University Press.

Bryk, Anthony S. and Stephen W. Raudenbush. 1992. Hierarchical Linear Models: Applications and Data Analysis Methods. Newbury Park, Calif.: Sage.

Bowlby, John. 1969. Attachment and Loss. Vol. 1, Attachment. New York: Basic.

Burton, Velmer S. Jr., Francis T. Cullen, T. Dave Evans, R. Gregory Dunaway, Sesha R. Kethineni, and Gary L. Payne. 1995. The impact of parental controls on delinquency. Journal of Criminal Justice 23:111–126.

Center for Human Resource Research. 1992. NLS Handbook: 1992. Center for Human Resource Research. The Ohio State University.

Cernkovich, Stephen A. and Peggy C. Giordano. 1987. Family relationships and delinquency. Criminology 25:295–321.

Coble, Hellen M., Diana L. Gantt, and Brent Mallinckrodt. 1996. Attachment, social competency, and the capacity to use social support. In Gregory R. Pierce, Barbara R. Sarason, and Irwin G. Sarason (eds.), Handbook of Social Support and the Family. New York: Plenum Press.

Cohen, Sheldon and Thomas A. Wills. 1985. Stress, social support, and the buffering hypothesis. Psychological Bulletin 98:321–357.

Cole, Stephen. 1975. The growth of scientific knowledge: Theories of deviance as a case study. In Lewis A. Costner (ed.), The Idea of Social Structure: Essays in Honor of Robert K. Merton. New York: Harcourt-Brace Jovanovich.

Colvin, Mark. 2000. Crime and Coercion: An Integrated Theory of Chronic Criminality. New York: St. Martin's Press.

Cullen, Francis T. 1994. Social support as an organizing concept for criminology: Presidential address to the Academy of Criminal Justice Sciences. Justice Quarterly 11:527–559.

Cullen, Francis T., John Paul Wright, and Mitchell B. Chamlin. 1999. Social support and social reform: A progressive crime control agenda. Crime and Delinquency 45:188–207.

Currie, Elliott. 1985. Confronting Crime: An American Challenge. New York: Pantheon Books.

Drennon-Gala, Don. 1995. Delinquency and High School Drop-Outs: Reconsidering Social Correlates. Lanham, Md.: University Press of America.

Elliott, Delbert, William Julius Wilson, David Huizinga, Robert J. Sampson, Amanda Elliott, and Bruce Rankin. 1996. The effects of neighborhood disadvantage on adolescent development. Journal of Research in Crime and Delinquency 33:389–426.

Farrell, Michael P., Grace M. Barnes, and Sarbani Banerjee. 1995. Family cohesion as a buffer against the effects of problem-drinking fathers on psychological distress, deviant behavior, and heavy drinking in adolescents. Journal of Health and Social Behavior 36:377–385.

Farrington, David P. 1986. Stepping stones to adult criminal careers. In Dan Olweus, Jack Block, and Marilyn Radke-Yarrow (eds.), Development of Antisocial and Prosocial Behavior. New York: Academic Press.

Gibbs, John J., Dennis Giever, and Jamie S. Martin. 1998. Parental management and self-control: An empirical test of Gottfredson and Hirschi's General Theory. Journal of Research in Crime and Delinquency 35:40–70.

Gottfredson, Michael R. and Travis Hirschi. 1990. A General Theory of Crime. Stanford, Calif.: Stanford University Press.

Hagan, John. 1989. Structural Criminology. New Brunswick, N.J.: Rutgers University Press.

Harris, Judith R. 1995. Where is the child's environment? A group socialization theory of development. Psychological Review 102:458–489.

——. 1998. The Nurture Assumption: Why Children Turn Out the Way They Do. Parents Matter Less Than You Think. New York: The Free Press.

Hartup, William W. 1986. On relationships and development. In William W. Hartup and Zick Rubin (eds.), Relationships and Development. New Jersey: Lawrence Erlbaum Associates.

Hawkins, J. David, Denise M. Lishner, Richard F. Catalano, and M. O. Howard. 1986. Childhood predictors of adolescent substance abuse: Toward an empirically grounded theory. Journal of Children in Contemporary Society 8:11–40.

Hedeker, Donald, Robert D. Gibbons, and Brian R. Flay. 1994. Random-effects regression models for clustered data with an example from smoking prevention research. Journal of Consulting and Clinical Psychology 62:57–65.

Hepburn, John R. 1977. Testing alternative models of delinquency causation. Journal of Criminal Law and Criminology 67:450–460.

Hirschi, Travis. 1969. Causes of Delinquency. Berkeley: University of California Press.

Hox, J. Joop and Ita Kreft. 1994. Multilevel analysis methods. Sociological Methods and Research 22:283–299.

Jessor, Richard. 1993. Successful adolescent development among youth in high-risk settings. American Psychologist 48:117–126.

Johnson, Robert A., Susan S. Su, Dean R. Gerstein, Hee-Choon Shin, and John P. Hoffmann. 1995. Parental influences on deviant behavior in early adolescence: A logistic response analysis of age and gender differentiated effects. Journal of Quantitative Criminology 11:167–194.

Kreft, Ita, and Jan De Leeuw. 1998. Introducing Multilevel Modeling. Thousand Oaks, Calif.: Sage.

LaGrange, Randy L. and Helene Raskin White. 1985. Age differences in delinquency: A test of theory. Criminology 23:19–45.

Laub, John H. and Robert J. Sampson. 1988. Unraveling families and delinquency: A reanalysis of the Gluecks' data. Criminology 26:355–380.

Lilly, J. Robert, Francis T. Cullen, and Richard A. Ball. 1995. Criminological Theory: Context and Consequences. 2d ed. Thousand Oaks, Calif.: Sage.

Linn, Nan, Alfred Dean, and Walter Ensel. 1986. Social Support, Life Events, and Depression. Coral Gables, Fl.: Academic Press.

Lipsey, Mark W. and James H. Derzon. 1998. Predictors of violent or serious delinquency in adolescence and early adulthood: A synthesis of longitudinal research. In Rolf Loeber and David P. Farrington (eds.), Serious and Violent Juvenile Offenders: Risk Factors and Successful Interventions. Thousand Oaks, Calif.: Sage.

Loeber, Rolf and Magda Stouthamer-Loeber. 1986. Family factors as correlates and predictors of juvenile conduct problems and delinquency. In Michael Tonry and Norval Morris (eds.), Crime and Justice: An Annual Review of Research. Chicago, Ill.: University of Chicago Press.

Maccoby, Eleanor E. 1980. Social Development: Psychological Growth and the Parent-Child Relationship. New York: Harcourt Brace Jovanovich.

——. 1992. The role of parents in the socialization of children: An historical overview. Developmental Psychology 28:1006–1017.

Matsueda, Ross L. and Karen Heimer. 1987. Race, family structure, and delinquency: A test of differential association and social control theories. American Sociological Review 52:826–840.

McCord, Joan. 1979. Some child-rearing antecedents of criminal behavior in adult men. Journal of Personality and Social Psychology 37:1477–1486.

Mott, Frank L. and S. V. Quinlan. 1993. The Ten-and-Over Years: Self-Reports from the Children of the NLSY. 1990 Tabulations and Summary Discussion. Columbus, Ohio: Center for Human Resource Research, The Ohio State University, 1991.

Nagin, Daniel S. and Raymond Paternoster. 1994 Personal capital and social control: The deterrence implications of a theory of individual differences in criminal offending. Criminology 32:581–606.

Nye, F. Ivan. 1958. Family Relationships and Delinquent Behavior. New York: John Wiley and Sons.

Patterson, Gerald R. 1980. Children who steal. In Travis Hirschi and Michael Gottfredson (eds.), Understanding Crime: Current History and Research. Beverly Hills, Calif.: Sage.

Patterson, Gerald R. and Magda Stouthamer-Loeber. 1984. The correlation of family management practices and delinquency. Child Development 55:1299–1307.

Pierce, Gregory R., Barbara R. Sarason, and Irwin G. Sarason (eds.). 1996. Handbook of Social Support and the Family. New York: Plenum.

Plomin, Robert. 1990. Nature and Nurture: An Introduction to Human Behavioral Genetics. Pacific Grove, Calif.: Brooks/Cole Publishing.

Radke-Yarrow, Marylin, and Carolyn Zahn-Waxler. 1986. The role of familial factors in the development of prosocial behavior: Research findings and questions. In Dan Olweus, Jack Block, and Marilyn Radke-Yarrow (eds.), Development of Antisocial and Prosocial Behavior. New York: Academic Press.

Rankin, Joseph H. and Roger Kern. 1994. Parental attachments and delinquency. Criminology 32:495–515.

Rankin, Joseph H. and L. Edward Wells. 1990. The effects of parental attachments and direct controls on delinquency. Journal of Research in Crime and Delinquency 27:140–165.

Rollins, Boyd C. and Darwin L. Thomas. 1979. Parental support, power and control techniques in the socialization of children. In W. R. Burr, R. Hill, F. I. Nye, and I. L. Reiss (eds.), Contemporary Theories About the Family. Vol. 1. New York: The Free Press.

Rothbaum, F. and J. R. Weisz. 1994. Parental caregiving and child externalized behavior in nonclinical samples: A meta-analysis. Psychological Bulletin 116:55–74.

Sampson, Robert J. and John H. Laub. 1993. Crime in the Making: Pathways and Turning Points Through Life. Cambridge, Mass.: Harvard University Press.

——. 1994. Urban poverty and the family context of delinquency: A new look at structure and process in a classic study. Child Development 94:523–540.

Sampson, Robert J., Stephen W. Raudenbush, and Felton Earls. 1997. Neighborhoods and violent crime: A multilevel study of collective efficacy. Science 277:918–924.

Sampson, Robert J., Jeffrey D. Morenoff, and Felton Earls. 1997. Beyond social capital: Spatial dynamics of collective efficacy for children. American Sociological Review 64:633–660.

Sherman, Lawrence W. 1993. Defiance, deterrence, and irrelevance: A theory of the criminal sanction. Journal of Research in Crime and Delinquency 30:445–473.

Sroufe, L. Allen and J. Fleeson. 1987. Attachment and the construction of relationships. In William W. Hartup and Zick Rubin (eds.), Relationships and Development. New Jersey: Lawrence Erlbaum Associates.

Stice, Eric and Nancy Gonzales. 1997. Adolescent temperament moderates the relation of parenting to antisocial behavior and substance abuse. Journal of Adolescent Research 13:5–31.

Thoits, Peggy A. 1995. Stress, coping, and social support processes: Where are we? What next? Journal of Health and Social Behavior (Extra Issue):53–79.

Thornberry, Terence P. 1996. Empirical support for interactional theory: A review of the literature. In J. David Hawkins (ed.), Delinquency and Crime: Current Theories. Cambridge, U.K.: Cambridge University Press.

Timko, Christine and Rudolf H. Moos. 1996. The mutual influence of family support and youth adaptation. In Gregory R. Pierce, Barbara R. Sarason, and Irwin G. Sarason (eds.), Handbook of Social Support and the Family. New York: Plenum Press.

Tittle, Charles R. 1995. Control Balance: Toward a General Theory of Deviance. Boulder, Colo.: Westview Press.

Van Voorhis, Patricia, Francis T. Cullen, Richard A. Mathers, and Connie Chenowith Garner. 1988. The impact of family structure and quality on delinquency: A comparative assessment of structural and functional factors. Criminology 26:235–261.

Vaux, Allen. 1988. Social Support: Theory, Research, and Intervention. New York: Praeger.

Wells, L. Edward and Joseph H. Rankin. 1988. Direct parental controls and delinquency. Criminology 26:263–285.

——. 1991. Families and delinquency: A meta-analysis of the impact of broken homes. Social Problems 38:71–93.

Werner, Emmy E. and Ruth S. Smith. 1982. Overcoming the Odds: High Risk Children from Birth to Adulthood. Ithaca, N.Y.: Cornell University Press.

Wills, Thomas A., John Mariani, and Marnie Filer. 1996. The role of family and peer relationships in adolescent substance abuse. In Gregory R. Pierce, Barbara R. Sarason, and Irwin G. Sarason (eds.), Handbook of Social Support and the Family. New York: Plenum Press.

Wilson, James Q. and Richard J. Herrnstein. 1985. Crime and Human Nature: The Definitive Study of the Causes of Crime. New York: Simon and Schuster.

Chapter 33

Sentencing Guidelines and the Transformation of Juvenile Justice in the 21st Century

Daniel P. Mears

At the end of its first century, the juvenile justice system has made significant departures from its original mission of protecting and rehabilitating youthful offenders. But while research on the transfer of juveniles to adult courts has led some to question the need for a separate system, Mears argues that juvenile justice still tempers punishment with rehabilitation. By focusing on sentencing guidelines that outline set punishments for specific crimes, Mears acknowledges that the juvenile justice system has moved away from its historical model of substantive *fairness—individually tailored punishment that considers offenders' circumstances and characteristics—toward* procedural *fairness—consistent punishment for similar crimes. But while the juvenile justice system has changed to emphasize punishment as a goal, Mears maintains that sentencing guidelines show that it also balances a host of other aims, like prevention, diversion, rehabilitation, and treatment, that make it a valuable and necessary tool.*

The past decade witnessed dramatic changes to juvenile justice in America, changes that have altered the focus and administration of juvenile justice as it enters the 21st century (Butts & Mitchell, 2000; Feld, 1991; Harris, Welsh, & Butler, 2000). In contrast to the philosophical foundation and practice of the first juvenile courts, punishment and due process today constitute central features of processing. These emphases, which run counter to the rehabilitative *parens patriae* ("state as parent") foundation of the first juvenile courts, emerged in the 1960s with a series of U.S. Supreme Court decisions. In cases such as *In re Gault,* the Supreme Court recognized that juvenile courts served not only a rehabilitative function but also a punishment function, and that consequently due process rights and procedures should figure more prominently in juvenile proceedings (Feld, 1999). In recent years, the transition has become more pronounced, with states enacting sweeping legislative changes affecting all aspects of the juvenile justice system (National Criminal Justice Association, 1997; Torbet et al., 1996; Torbet & Szymanski, 1998).

It is important to recognize, however, that the changes have not been entirely or even primarily focused on punishment. One would not know this from a review of research, the bulk of which has examined patterns, correlates, and effects of transfer (for a review, see Butts & Mitchell, 2000). The focus is understandable—transfer provides an easily identifiable symbol for debates about the merits of maintaining two separate juvenile and adult systems (Feld, 1999; Hirschi & Gottfredson, 1993). Indeed, why have a juvenile justice system if youth are being sent into adult courts? But the fact is that only about 1% of all formally processed delinquency cases ultimately are transferred (Snyder & Sickmund, 1999, p. 171).

Focusing solely on transfer ignores the fact that other equally, if not more significant, transformations have occurred in juvenile justice. These include enactment of sentencing guidelines; creation of blended sentencing options for linking the juvenile and criminal justice systems; enhanced correctional programming, with an increasing emphasis on treatment; greater interagency and cross-jurisdiction cooperation and information sharing; reduced confidentiality of court records and proceedings; and increased participation of victims in juvenile justice processing (Fagan & Zimring, 2000; Guarino-Ghezzi & Loughran, 1996; National Criminal Justice Association, 1997; Torbet et al., 1996). In addition, states increasingly are turning their attention to prevention, early intervention, rehabilitation, and the use of specialized courts to address juvenile crime (Butts & Harrell, 1998; Butts & Mears, 2001; Cocozza & Skowyra, 2000; Coordinating Council on Juvenile Justice and Delinquency Prevention, 1996; Cullen & Gendreau, 2000; Howell, 1995; Lipsey, Wilson, & Cothern, 2000; Rivers & Anwyl, 2000).

It is apparent that juvenile justice has been evolving along many dimensions. With all of these changes, the question arises: What, if any, are the common trends and issues underlying these different changes? To answer this question, I examine sentencing guidelines, showing that they reflect many of the major trends and issues in juvenile justice. I focus on guidelines because typically they apply to all juvenile offenders and embody a range of goals, thus reflecting many of the conflicts and tensions inherent in attempts to modify the focus and administration of juvenile justice. By contrast, transfer laws, which have received much more attention in the research literature, focus only on select age groups and offenders and have the delimited purpose of punishing and deterring offenders.

The primary goal of this [chapter], in short, is to use an analysis of sentencing guidelines to highlight a range of critical underlying trends and issues in juvenile justice. A secondary goal is to show that research on transfer laws provides little insight into juvenile justice as it is practiced today and, in the absence of research on or attention to other reforms, can provide a distorted picture of current practice. To achieve these goals, I begin by briefly describing the history of the juvenile court and the emergence of juvenile sentencing guidelines. I then use this discussion to identify key trends and issues in juvenile justice.

Foundation of the Juvenile Justice System

Juveniles have not always been viewed the same way throughout U.S. history. For example, in the 18th century, juvenile offenders were treated as adults and received the same types of punishments. During the 19th century, a movement began that focused on the unique, less-than-adult capacities and needs of youth. This movement highlighted the need for a specialized sanctioning process, one that emphasized rehabilitation and deemphasized punishment.

The result of this movement was the development of the first U.S. juvenile court in Cook County, Illinois, in 1899. By 1925, juvenile courts were established in all but two states, with most courts defining juveniles as individuals who were aged 17 years or younger. (For histories of the juvenile court, see Platt [1977], Bernard [1992], Feld [1999], and Butts and Mitchell [2000].)

These new youth-centered courts were grounded in the doctrine of *parens patriae.* The guiding rationale was that states had an obligation to intervene in the lives of children whose parents provided inadequate care or supervision. Juvenile court interventions were to be benevolent and in the "best interests" of the child.

For this reason, court processing entailed fundamentally different notions of procedural and substantive justice. Unlike adult court proceedings, juvenile court proceedings were to be informal and conducted on a case-by-case basis, with the aim of improving the lives of children through individualized treatment and varying dispositional options, ranging from warnings to probation to confinement.

The basis for intervening in the lives of juvenile offenders derived not from criminal law but civil law, further highlighting the focus on helping youth rather than sanctioning them for their crimes. Similarly, the philosophy of *parens patriae* clearly suggested that the courts had an obligation to help youth who committed crimes or who clearly needed help. As a result, juvenile courts could use coercive means to help youth, even when relatively minor crimes had been committed or when there was insufficient basis for determining that a crime in fact was committed.

The potential for abuse of this discretionary authority is evident in critiques of the juvenile court (see Feld, 1999). Indeed, as many scholars have shown, the transition to establishing a juvenile justice system was not motivated entirely by benevolent concerns. Under the guise of providing social services and crime control, juvenile courts could, for example, be used instead to provide a form of social control over "undesirable classes," including minorities, immigrants, and indigents (Butts & Mitchell, 2000).

By the 1960s, deep-rooted concerns arose about the procedural and substantive unfairness of juvenile court proceedings, leading the U.S. Supreme Court, through a series of decisions, to emphasize greater procedural parity with criminal court proceedings. The result was an increasingly criminal-like juvenile court. This trend, coupled with tougher transfer provisions in the 1990s, led to considerable debate about the merits of having two separate court systems, one for juveniles and one for adults (Feld, 1999).

Juvenile Sentencing Guidelines: An Overview

The early juvenile court emphasized individualized, offender-based treatment and sanctioning. Indeed, almost every justification of the juvenile court rests on the notion that the most appropriate and effective intervention for youth is one that takes into account their particular needs and resources. Ironically, despite the establishment of this view more than 100 years ago, recent research provides considerable empirical support for it—the most effective interventions are those premised on addressing the specific risk, needs, and capacities of youth (Cullen & Gendreau, 2000; Lipsey, 1999).

Under the Office of Juvenile Justice and Delinquency Prevention's (OJJDP's) Comprehensive Strategy for Serious, Violent, and Chronic Juvenile Offenders (Howell, 1995; Wilson & Howell, 1993), states have been encouraged to adopt individualized sanctioning and to emphasize risk and needs assessment. Many have responded by enacting guideline systems that are modeled to a considerable extent on the Comprehensive Strategy.

In some states, these guideline systems are voluntary, in others there are incentives to use them, and in still others they are required. In each instance, the guidelines typically are offense-based and outline a sequence of increasingly tougher sanctions, while at the same time emphasizing rehabilitative interventions when appropriate.

In 1995, far example, Texas enacted what it termed the Progressive Sanctions Guidelines. The Guidelines outline seven tiers of sanctioning, with each linked to the instant offense and the offender's prior record. Once the appropriate level of sanctioning is established, courts are encouraged to include additional, nonpunitive interventions. Although the Guidelines are voluntary, Texas documents the extent to which county-level sanctioning deviates from the recommendations of the Guidelines (Texas Criminal Justice Policy Council, 2001). Similar approaches have been implemented in other states, including Illinois, Kansas, Nebraska, New York, Utah, Virginia, and Washington (Corriero, 1999; Demleitner, 1999; Fagan & Zimring, 2000; Lieb & Brown, 1999; National Criminal Justice Association, 1997; Torbet et al., 1996).

State guideline systems often identify their goals explicitly. In Texas, for example, the Progressive Sanction Guidelines are used to "guide" dispositional decision making in providing "appropriate" sanctions and to promote "uniformity" and "consistency" in sentencing (Dawson, 1996). At the same time, the Guidelines are seen as furthering the newly established and explicitly stated goal of the Texas Juvenile Justice Code—namely, punishment of juveniles. But they also promote rehabilitative sanctioning by encouraging appropriate treatment and interventions for each recommended sanction level. In addition, the Guidelines implicitly promote certain goals, including public safety through incapacitation of the most serious or chronic offenders and reduced crime through get-tough, deterrence-oriented sanctioning.

Other states have followed similar paths. For example, Washington established sentencing guidelines aimed directly at reducing the perceived failings of a system founded on practitioner discretion (Lieb & Brown, 1999). The guidelines focus not only on offense-based considerations but also on the juvenile's age, with younger offenders receiving fewer "points" and thus more lenient sanctions. Similarly, Utah has enacted sentencing guidelines focusing on proportionate sentencing, early intervention, and progressively intensive supervision and sanctioning for more serious and chronic offenders (Utah Sentencing Commission, 1997).

Because many states increasingly are adopting sentencing guidelines and because the guidelines focus on all youth rather than simply those who may be transferred, an examination of them can help to identify underlying trends and issues emergent in juvenile justice. By contrast, a focus on transfer, typical of most research on recent reforms, provides relatively little leverage to do so. Transfer laws typically focus on "easy cases," those in which the seriousness of the offense largely vitiates, rightly or wrongly, concerns many would have about individualized or rehabilitative sanctioning. Any resulting debate therefore centers on extremes: Should we retain or eliminate the juvenile court?

But a broader issue in juvenile justice is how to balance individualized, offender-based sanctioning with proportional and consistent punishment. These issues, among several others, are a consideration in almost every case coming before the juvenile court. It is appropriate, therefore, to focus on a recent reform, such as sentencing guidelines, that typically target, in one manner or another, all youth and that reflects attempts to shape the entire juvenile justice system. For this reason, the remainder of this [chapter] uses a focus on sentencing guidelines to identify key trends and issues in the transformation of juvenile justice.

Juvenile Sentencing Guidelines: Trends and Issues in the Transformation of Juvenile Justice in the New Millennium

Balancing Multiple and Conflicting Goals

The motivation for transforming juvenile justice has come from many sources. Scholars cite a range of factors, including the desire to address violent crime, inconsistency and racial/ethnic disproportionality in sentencing, financial burdens faced by counties versus states, and public support for get-tough and rehabilitative measures (Bazemore & Umbreit, 1995; Bishop, Lanza-Kaduce, & Frazier, 1998; Butts & Mitchell, 2000).

As suggested by the different motivations for reform, a key trend in juvenile justice is the move toward balancing multiple and frequently competing goals, only one of which includes the punitive focus associated with transfer (Bazemore & Umbreit, 1995; Guarino-Ghezzi & Loughran, 1996; Mears, 2000). Today, many juvenile justice codes and policies focus on retributive/punitive sanctioning (through get-tough sanctions generally), incapacitation, deterrence, rehabilitation, individualized as well as consistent and proportional sentencing, and restorative sanctioning.

Reduced crime is a broad goal underlying many but not all of these more specific goals. For example, get-tough sanctions are viewed as a primary mechanism to instill fear and achieve specific or general deterrence (i.e., reduced offending among sanctioned or would-be offenders) or to reduce crime through temporary incapacitation of offenders. In many instances, retribution serves as the primary focus of sanctioning, irrespective of any potential crime control impact.

Some goals, like rehabilitation, serve as steps toward enhancing the lives of juveniles, not simply reducing their offending. Others, such as restorative sanctioning, focus on reintegrating offenders into their communities while at the same time providing victims with a voice in the sanctioning and justice process. Still others, including proportional and consistent sentencing, focus primarily on fairness rather than crime control. That is, the motivation is to provide sanctions that are proportional to the crime and that are consistent within and across jurisdictions so that juveniles sanctioned by Judge *X* or in County *X* receive sanctions similar to those administered by Judge *Y* or in County *Y*.

Historically these different goals, including what might be termed intermediate goals leading to reduced crime, have overlapped considerably with those of the criminal justice system (Snyder & Sickmund, 1999, pp. 94–96). In general, though, criminal justice systems have given greater weight to punishment than rehabilitation, whereas juvenile justice systems generally have favored rehabilitation more than punishment.

In reality, the goals in each system are diverse, as are the weightings given to each goal. Indeed, the diversity of goals and their weightings can make it difficult to determine how exactly the two systems differ, especially if we focus only on new transfer laws (see, however, Bishop & Frazier, 2000). But one major difference between the two is that juvenile justice systems—as is evident in their sentencing guideline systems—are actively struggling to balance as wide a range of goals as possible. By contrast, most criminal justice systems have veered strongly toward retribution and incapacitation (Clark, Austin, & Henry, 1997).

Giving Priority to Punishment Through Offense-Based Guidelines and Changes in Discretion

Most state guideline systems use offense-based criteria for determining which types of sanctions to apply (Coolbaugh & Hansel, 2000). Once the punishment level has been established, the court is supposed to consider the needs of the offender and how these may best be addressed. However, these needs frequently are only vaguely specified and rarely assessed. One result is that priority implicitly and in practice may be given to punishment. This priority can be reinforced through various mechanisms that place greater discretion in the hands of prosecutors rather than judges. For example, laws that stipulate automatic sanctions for certain offenses do not eliminate discretion; instead, they shift it to prosecutors, who can determine whether and how to charge an offense (Feld, 1999; Mears, 2000; Sanborn, 1994; Singer, 1996). Consequently, in practice, many guideline systems make punishment a priority not just for youth who may be transferred but for all youth referred to juvenile court.

Sentencing guidelines have not gone unopposed. For example, research on the Texas Progressive Sanction Guidelines indicates that many judges resisted enactment of the Guidelines and then, once they became law, resisted using them (Mears, 2000). One reason is their belief that offense-based criteria provide too limited a basis for structuring decision making. Thus, even though compliance with the Guidelines is voluntary, some judges feel that the Guidelines symbolize too narrow a focus, one that draws attention from factors they believe are more important, such as the age and maturity of the youth and their family and community contexts. Such concerns have been expressed about adult sentencing guidelines (e.g., see Forer, 1994). One difference with juvenile sentencing guidelines is that, despite the views of opponents, they generally state explicitly that there are multiple goals associated with sanctioning and that practitioners should consider a range of mitigating factors (Howell, 1995).

Balancing Discretion Versus Disparity and Consistency, and Procedural Versus Substantive Justice

In stark contrast to the early foundation of the juvenile court, many states today are intent on eliminating disparity and inconsistency in sentencing (Feld, 1999; Torbet et al., 1996). The widespread belief, evident in many sentencing guidelines, is that (a) judicial discretion causes disparity and inconsistency and (b) that offense-based systems can eliminate or reduce these problems. Both beliefs prevail despite the fact that little empirical evidence exists to support them (Mears & Field, 2000; Sanborn, 1994; Yellen, 1999).

But the fact that such strategies may not work does not belie the underlying trend toward discovering ways to promote fairness and consistency in sentencing. Nor does it belie the fact that, as with adult sanctioning, there likely will continue to be an ongoing tension between the use of discretion and the need to have sanctions that are relatively similar for different populations and within and across jurisdictions.

This tension is captured in part by the distinction in the sociology of law between procedural and substantive justice. From the perspective of procedural justice, fairness emerges from decisions that are guided by established rules and procedures for sanctioning cases that exhibit specific characteristics. By contrast, from the perspective of substantive justice, fairness emerges from decisions that are guided by consideration of the unique situational context and characteristics of the defendant (Gould, 1993; Ulmer & Kramer, 1996).

In recent years, and as exemplified by the creation of offense-based sentencing guidelines, juvenile justice systems increasingly are focusing on procedural justice. In the case of transfer particularly, the Supreme Court and state legislatures have attempted to ensure that there is procedural parity with adult proceedings. Yet despite the increased proceduralization, for most cases facing the juvenile courts, substantive justice also remains a priority, especially when sanctioning first-time and less serious offenders. In these instances, states have devised strategies, outlined in their guidelines, that promote diversion, rehabilitation, and treatment.

Maintaining the View That Most Youth Are 'Youth,' Not Adults

Public opinion polls show that whereas most people consistently support rehabilitative sanctioning of youth, they also support punitive, get-tough measures for serious and violent offenders (Roberts & Stalans, 1998). Moreover, even when the public supports transferring youth to the adult system, they generally prefer youth to be housed in separate facilities and to receive individualized, rehabilitative treatment (Schwartz, Guo, & Kerbs, 1993).

The apparent contradiction likely constitutes the primary reason that wholesale elimination of the juvenile justice system has not prevailed. In the debate about abolishing the juvenile court, this fact frequently is omitted, perhaps because so much attention has centered on changes in transfer laws. Indeed, were one to focus solely on recent trends in transfer, one might conclude that an eventual merging of juvenile and adult systems is inevitable (Feld, 1999).

Yet the focus and structure of juvenile sentencing guidelines, which explicitly call for rehabilitation and early intervention, suggest otherwise. In contrast to get-tough developments in the criminal justice system (Clark et al., 1997), most states—even those without guideline systems—have struggled to maintain a focus not only on the most violent offenders but also on efficient and effective intervention with less serious offenders.

This trend is reflected in the proliferation of alternative, or specialized, courts, including community, teen, drug, and mental health courts (Butts & Harrell, 1998; Office of Justice Programs, 1998; Santa Clara County Superior Court, 2001). These courts focus on timely and rehabilitative sanctioning that draws on the strengths of families and communities and the cooperation and assistance of local and state agencies.

Some authors suggest that these courts threaten the foundation of the juvenile court (Butts & Harrell, 1998). But specialized courts can be viewed as symbolic of the reemergence of the juvenile justice system as historically conceived—namely, as a system designed to intervene on an individualized, case-by-case basis, addressing the particular risks and needs of offenders (Butts & Mears, 2001). Indeed, to this end, many guidelines promote diversion of first- and second-time, less serious offenders from formal processing to informal alternatives available through specialized courts.

Limited Conceptualization and Assessment of the Implementation and Effects of Changes in the Juvenile Justice System

One last and prominent trend in juvenile justice bears emphasizing—the lack of systematic attention to conceptualizing and assessing the implementation and effects of recently enacted laws. A focus on sentencing guidelines illustrates the point: Few states have systematically articulated precisely what the goals of the guidelines are, how specifically the guidelines are expected to achieve these goals, or what in fact the effects of the guidelines have been (Coolbaugh & Hansel, 2000; Fagan & Zimring, 2000; Mears, 2000).

One example common to many guidelines is the focus on consistency. Several questions illustrate the point. What exactly does *consistency* mean? Is it identical sentencing of like offenders within jurisdictions? Across jurisdictions? Does it involve similar weighting of the same factors by all judges or judges within each jurisdiction in a state? Across states? Apart from definitional issues, does consistency lead to reduced crime or increased perceptions of fairness? If so, how? What precisely are the mechanisms by which increased consistency would lead to changes in crime or perceptions of fairness? The failure to address these questions means that it is impossible to assess whether there has been more or less consistency resulting from guideline systems.

Similar questions about many other aspects of recent juvenile justice reforms remain largely unaddressed, with two unfortunate consequences. First, as noted above, it is impossible to assess the effects of the reforms without greater clarity concerning their goals and the means by which these goals are to be reached. As a result, it is difficult if not impossible to make informed policy decisions, including those focusing on maintaining or eliminating the juvenile justice system (Schneider, 1984; Singer, 1996). Second, without conceptualization and assessment of the effects of recent reforms, there is an increased likelihood that research on delimited aspects of juvenile justice systems will be generalized into statements about entire systems, even though there may be little to no correspondence between the two.

Conclusion

Recent changes to juvenile justice systems throughout the United States indicate a trend toward developing more efficient and effective strategies for balancing different and frequently competing goals. This trend is evident in recent juvenile sentencing guidelines. As the above discussion demonstrates, guidelines focus on more than transferring the most serious offenders to the criminal justice system. They also focus on balancing competing goals, reducing discretion and promoting fair and consistent sanctioning, and tempering procedural with substantive justice. More generally, guidelines aim to preserve the notion that youth are not adults.

One result of such trends is increasing interest in alternative administrative mechanisms for processing youthful offenders. Specialized "community," "teen," "drug," "mental health," and other such courts have been developed to do what the original juvenile court was supposed to do—provide individualized and rehabilitative sanctioning. But the "modern" approach involves doing so in a more timely and sophisticated fashion, and in a way that draws on the cooperation and assistance of local and state agencies as well as families and communities.

In the new millennium, juvenile justice thus involves more than an emphasis on due process and punishment. It also involves substantive concerns, including a range of competing goals, a belief in the special status of childhood, and the desire to develop more effective strategies for preventing and reducing juvenile crime.

By focusing on sentencing guidelines, these types of issues become more apparent, highlighting the need for researchers to look beyond transfer laws in assessing recent juvenile justice reforms. Indeed, there is a need for research on many new and different laws, policies, and programs in juvenile justice, most of which remain unassessed. As we enter the new millennium, it will be critical to redress this situation, especially if we are to move juvenile justice beyond "juvenile" versus "adult" debates and to develop more efficient and effective interventions.

References

Bazemore, G., & Umbreit, M. (1995). Rethinking the sanctioning function in juvenile court: Retributive or restorative responses to youth crime. *Crime & Delinquency, 41,* 296–316.

Bernard, T. J. (1992). *The cycle of juvenile justice.* New York: Oxford University Press.

Bishop, D. M., & Frazier, C. E. (2000). Consequences of transfer. In J. Fagan & F. E. Zimring (Eds.), *The changing boundaries of juvenile justice: Transfer of adolescents to the criminal court* (pp. 227–276). Chicago: University of Chicago Press.

Bishop, D. M., Lanza-Kaduce, L., & Frazier, C. E. (1998). Juvenile justice under attack: An analysis of the causes and impact of recent reforms. *Journal of Law and Public Policy, 10,* 129–155.

Butts, J. A., & Harrell, A. V. (1998). *Delinquents or criminals? Policy options for juvenile offenders.* Washington, DC: The Urban Institute.

Butts, J. A., & Mears, D. P. (2001). Reviving juvenile justice in a get-tough era. *Youth & Society, 33,* 169–198.

Butts, J. A., & Mitchell, O. (2000). Brick by brick: Dismantling the border between juvenile and adult justice. In C. M. Friel (Ed.), *Criminal Justice 2000: Boundary changes in criminal justice organizations* (Vol. 2, pp. 167–213). Washington, DC: National Institute of Justice.

Clark, J., Austin, J., & Henry, D. A. (1997). *"Three strikes and you're out": A review of state legislation.* Washington, DC: National Institute of Justice.

Cocozza, J. J., & Skowyra, K. (2000). Youth with mental health disorders: Issues and emerging responses. *Juvenile Justice, 7,* 3–13.

Coolbaugh, K., & Hansel, C. J. (2000). *The comprehensive strategy: Lessons learned from the pilot sites.* Washington, DC: Office of Juvenile Justice and Delinquency Prevention.

Coordinating Council on Juvenile Justice and Delinquency Prevention. (1996). *Combating violence and delinquency: The national juvenile justice action plan.* Washington, DC: Office of Juvenile Justice and Delinquency Prevention.

Corriero, M. A. (1999). Juvenile sentencing: The New York youth part as a model. *Federal Sentencing Reporter, 11,* 278–281.

Cullen, F. T., & Gendreau, P. (2000). Assessing correctional rehabilitation: Policy, practice, and prospects. In J. Horney (Ed.), *Criminal justice 2000: Policies, processes, and decisions of the criminal justice system* (Vol. 3, pp. 109–175). Washington, DC: National Institute of Justice.

Dawson, R. O. (1996). *Texas juvenile law* (4th ed.). Austin: Texas Juvenile Probation Commission.

Demleitner, N. V. (1999). Reforming juvenile sentencing. *Federal Sentencing Reporter, 11,* 243–247.

Fagan, J., & Zimring, F. E. (Eds.). (2000). *The changing borders of juvenile justice.* Chicago: University of Chicago Press.

Feld, B. C. (1991). The transformation of the juvenile court. *Minnesota Law Review, 75,* 691–725.

Feld, B. C. (1999). *Bad kids: Race and the transformation of the juvenile court.* New York: Oxford University Press.

Forer, L. (1994). *A rage to punish: The unintended consequences of mandatory sentencing.* New York: Norton.

Gould, M. (1993). Legitimation and justification: The logic of moral and contractual solidarity in Weber and Durkheim. *Social Theory, 13,* 205–225.

Guarino-Ghezzi, S., & Loughran, E. J. (1996). *Balancing juvenile justice.* New Brunswick, NJ: Transaction.

Harris, P. W., Welsh, W. N., & Butler, F. (2000). A century of juvenile justice. In G. LaFree (Ed.), *Criminal justice 2000: The nature of crime: Continuity and change* (Vol. 1, pp. 359–425). Washington, DC: National Institute of Justice.

Hirschi, T., & Gottfredson, M. R. (1993). Rethinking the juvenile justice system. *Crime & Delinquency, 39,* 262–271.

Howell, J. C. (1995). *Guide for implementing the comprehensive strategy for serious, violent, and chronic juvenile offenders.* Washington, DC: Office of Juvenile Justice and Delinquency Prevention.

Lieb, R., & Brown, M. E. (1999). Washington state's solo path: Juvenile sentencing guidelines. *Federal Sentencing Reporter, 11,* 273–277.

Lipsey, M. W. (1999). Can rehabilitative programs reduce the recidivism of juvenile offenders? An inquiry into the effectiveness of practical programs. *Virginia Journal of Social Policy and Law, 6,* 611–641.

Lipsey, M. W., Wilson, D. B., & Cothern, L. (2000). *Effective intervention for serious juvenile offenders.* Washington, DC: Office of Juvenile Justice and Delinquency Prevention.

Mears, D. P. (2000). Assessing the effectiveness of juvenile justice reforms: A closer look at the criteria and impacts on diverse stakeholders. *Law and Policy, 22,* 175–202.

Mears, D. P., & Field, S. H. (2000). Theorizing sanctioning in a criminalized juvenile court. *Criminology, 38,* 101–137.

National Criminal Justice Association. (1997). *Juvenile justice reform initiatives in the states: 1994–1996.* Washington, DC: Office of Juvenile Justice and Delinquency Prevention.

Office of Justice Programs. (1998). *Juvenile and family drug courts: An overview.* Washington, DC: Author.

Platt, A. M. (1977). *The child savers: The invention of delinquency.* Chicago: University of Chicago Press.

Rivers, J. E., & Anwyl, R. S. (2000). Juvenile assessment centers: Strengths, weaknesses, and potential. *The Prison Journal, 80,* 96–113.

Roberts, J. V., & Stalans, L. J. (1998). Crime, criminal justice, and public opinion. In M. Tonry (Ed.), *The handbook of crime and punishment* (pp. 31–57). New York: Oxford University Press.

Sanbom, J. A. (1994). Certification to criminal court: The important policy questions of how, when, and why. *Crime & Delinquency, 40,* 262–281.

Santa Clara County Superior Court. (2001). *Santa Clara County Superior Court commences juvenile mental health court.* San Jose, CA: Author.

Schneider, A. L. (1984). Sentencing guidelines and recidivism rates of juvenile offenders. *Justice Quarterly, 1,* 107–124.

Schwartz, I. M., Guo, S., & Kerbs, J. J. (1993). The impact of demographic variables on public opinion regarding juvenile justice: Implications for public policy. *Crime & Delinquency, 39,* 5–28.

Singer, S. I. (1996). Merging and emerging systems of juvenile and criminal justice. *Law and Policy, 18,* 1–15.

Snyder, H. N., & Sickmund, M. (1999). *Juvenile offenders and victims: 1999 national report.* Washington, DC: Office of Juvenile Justice and Delinquency Prevention.

Texas Criminal Justice Policy Council. (2001). *The impact of progressive sanction guidelines: Trends since 1995.* Austin, TX: Author.

Torbet, P., Gable, R., Hurst, H. IV, Montgomery, I., Szymanski, L., & Thomas, D. (1996). *State responses to serious and violent juvenile crime.* Washington, DC: Office of Juvenile Justice and Delinquency Prevention.

Torbet, P., & Szymanski, L. (1998). *State legislative responses to violent juvenile crime: 1996–97 update.* Washington, DC: Office of Juvenile Justice and Delinquency Prevention.

Ulmer, J. T., & Kramer, J. H. (1996). Court communities under sentencing guidelines: Dilemmas of formal rationality and sentencing disparity. *Criminology, 34,* 383–407.

Utah Sentencing Commission. (1997). *Juvenile sentencing guidelines manual.* Salt Lake City, UT: Author.

Wilson, J. J., & Howell, J. C. (1993). *Comprehensive strategy for serious, violent, and chronic juvenile offenders: Program summary.* Washington, DC: Office of Juvenile Justice and Delinquency Prevention.

Yellen, D. (1999). Sentence discounts and sentencing guidelines. *Federal Sentencing Reporter, 11,* 285–288.

Chapter 34

Moving Toward Justice for Female Juvenile Offenders in the New Millennium

Modeling Gender-Specific Policies and Programs

Barbara Bloom
Barbara Owen
Elizabeth Piper Deschenes
Jill Rosenbaum

***H**istorically delinquency has been considered a male problem, with little attention and few resources devoted to female offenders. But with female delinquency on the rise, the authors argue that their specific needs must be addressed. In a survey of criminal justice professionals in fifty-eight California counties, they identify the risks and problems juvenile female offenders face, what programs and services are available, and what is still needed. Their study of how the current justice system accommodates female offenders highlights where it has to improve and outlines the paths it must take in order to effectively address a dangerously overlooked population.*

Until recently, girls and young women have been largely overlooked in the development of juvenile justice policy and programs and few resources have been directed at them (Chesney-Lind & Shelden, 1998). With the increase in the number of female offenders committing violent and property index crimes between 1992 and 1996, the Office of Juvenile Justice and Delinquency Prevention (OJJDP) increased federal support to state and local efforts to address the issue of gender-specific services for girls (Budnick & Shields-Fletcher, 1998). The experiences of several states are described in the OJJDP publication *Female Juvenile Offenders: A Status of the States Report* (Community Research Associates, 1998). Training and technical assistance on the best practices are being offered by Greene, Peters & Associates (1998). In at least one state, gender-specific programs are being developed and implemented with funding from the Bureau of Justice Assistance. OJJDP has sponsored the Safe Futures demonstration program for at-risk girls and female offenders. Despite the importance of these federal efforts, they remain limited in scope and it is up to the states to take action.

Moving toward justice for female juvenile offenders in the new millennium means that states must invest additional resources, conduct an assessment of the problem, and implement new policies. The common challenges facing states include: a growing number of female juvenile offenders committing more serious crimes and resulting in a greater number of juveniles in custody, a limited understanding of what works for girls, a demand for comprehensive needs assessments that identify gaps in the provision of services for girls, the need to develop and implement gender-specific services and programs designed to meet the unique needs of girls, and the competition for scarce resources in implementing these programs and policies (Budnick & Shields-Fletcher, 1998).

Even though advances have been made toward the goal of improving the status of juvenile justice for young women, there remains a paucity of programs and there is a need to seek solutions through federal, state, and local legislation (Acoca, 1999). This article presents a brief overview of national and state efforts to address gender-specific programming for young women in the juvenile justice system and summarizes findings from an assessment in the state of California that was conducted in 1997 and 1998 (Owen, Bloom, Deschenes, & Rosenbaum, 1998). This assessment included a review of the literature, a snapshot of trends in female juvenile offending and a profile of the offender, a review of federal and state policy initiatives, a series of interviews and focus groups with female youth and professionals serving this population, and a statewide survey of representatives of various agencies and programs.

National Efforts

In 1992, as part of the reauthorization of the Juvenile Justice and Delinquency Prevention (JJDP) Act of 1974, the following language was added:

> to develop and adopt policies to prohibit gender bias in placement and treatment and establishing programs to ensure female youth have access to the full range of health and mental health services, treatment for physical or sexual assault and abuse, self-defense instruction, education in parenting, education in general, and other training and vocational services. (Community Research Associates, 1998, p. 6)

The amendment, known as the Challenge Activity E component, required all states applying for federal formula grant dollars to examine their juvenile justice systems, identify gaps in services to juvenile female offenders, and plan for providing needed gender-specific services for the prevention and treatment of juvenile delinquency.

According to a review of the literature by the Evaluation and Training Institute (1996), additional work needs to be done if the JJDP Act is to be responsive to the realities of young women involved in the juvenile justice system. For example, the language of some of the legislation is not gender-neutral. Some of the recommended programs or services continue to be oriented toward young men. There are no specific directives on how the increased services for young women will be developed and/or funded. Many of the policies that are written specifically for young women focus on pregnancy-related issues with no recognition of other gender-specific needs. There remains a strong emphasis on placement of girls in a facility close to home, which ignores the fact that many young women have been physically or sexually abused at home and consequently family reunification services may not be beneficial. There is a failure to address the need for culturally competent services. There are requirements for juveniles to attend treatment programs or other mental health services without consideration as to whether the services are gender-specific. In sum, there are many areas for improvement.

Since the passage of the Challenge Activity E component in 1992, most of the progress on a national level has focused on program planning and training for practitioners as well as policy development, with little attention to research and evaluation. The first national training workshop on girls in the juvenile justice system was hosted by the American Correctional Association in 1994. The workshop included training on developmental differences between boys and girls and their implications for services, as well as models of gender-sensitive programming.

A second training workshop for practitioners working with girls in institutional settings was held by the National Institute of Corrections in 1995. At the same time OJJDP awarded funds to Girls, Inc. for a national symposium on girls' issues. The National Girls' Caucus, which is an advocacy group initiated by the Practical and Cultural Educational (PACE) Center for Girls, Inc., held a national roundtable in 1994 to address issues of policy, programming, and service delivery for at-risk girls. A report on the roundtable by Raviora (1999) contends that gender-specific programming should focus on some of the societal problems that challenge at-risk girls. These include: the death or loss of a family member due to violence, sexual and physical abuse, domestic violence, high-risk sexual behavior, the incarceration of close family members, gang involvement, the use of alcohol or tobacco and other drugs, and adolescent health issues.

In 1997, OJJDP awarded a 3-year grant to Greene, Peters & Associates to identify "promising programs" for juvenile girls throughout the United States and to develop curricula and implement training for practitioners working with girls involved in the juvenile justice system. One product is the report entitled *Guiding Principles for Promising Female Programming* (1998), which focuses on structural issues and programmatic elements. In developing a program, Greene, Peters & Associates suggested that attention should be paid to organization and management, which includes cooperation, respect, and good communication skills; diversity of staff and training in female development as well as risk factors and cultural sensitivity; and individualizing the intake and reentry process. Specific programmatic elements include education, skills training, and elements that promote positive development such as problem solving, relationship building, culturally relevant activities, career opportunities, health services, mentoring, community involvement, positive peer relationships, and family involvement. Specific treatment concerns such as prenatal or postpartum care, parenting and health care for babies, and substance abuse are also mentioned.

For several years, the OJJDP's Special Emphasis Division has offered grants to local jurisdictions for the development of gender-specific programs for female offenders. The Comprehensive Community-Based Services for At-Risk Girls and Adjudicated Juvenile Female Offenders is part of OJJDP's SafeFutures program. Community Research Associates (1998) provides support to national organizations working to address the needs of girls, disseminate information to states, and develop resource materials for individuals interested in the issue.

State Efforts

The OJJDP reports a high level of interest among states in the Challenge Activity E component, but it is clear that there is much to be done to meet this challenge. During 1997, 24 states embarked on such efforts (Chesney-Lind, 1997). The examination by Community Research Associates (1998) of girls' service needs within the juvenile justice system provided examples of some states that have developed unique approaches to addressing the needs of female juvenile offenders within their jurisdictions by using funding from the OJJDP.

Colorado and Delaware have established statewide committees to address the issues of girls and young women in the juvenile justice system, develop gender-specific services, and distribute federal formula grant dollars. Technical assistance to develop staff-secure cottages for girls or train staff in secure facilities has been requested in Colorado, Delaware, and Iowa. The Florida Female Initiative of 1994 coordinated the Florida Department of Juvenile Justice, state and private programs, and one staff member from each juvenile justice district to advocate for high-risk girls in their areas. In addition, Florida is home to PACE, which provides nonresidential, community-based education programs designed to prevent juvenile delinquency.

In Maryland, the Female Population Task Force has identified program components for gender-specific services for girls, including community-based residential treatment facilities as a means for diverting young women out of the justice system, and has requested technical assistance to work with a committee to redesign the programming at the Cheltenham Young Women's Facility. Baltimore has a specially trained unit of nine probation officers that serve all the female cases.

In Milwaukee, Wisconsin, the Continuum of Care for Girls project is a multiphase, court-ordered program teaching vocational and educational skills, providing drug and alcohol treatment, and providing the opportunities for gradual reintegration of participants into mainstream society. The program includes community-based residential treatment facilities as a means for diverting young women out of the justice system.

Minnesota and Oregon have been at the forefront of the movement for several years, working to address the needs of girls and women in the juvenile and criminal justice system. State legislation in Minnesota mandates equity in services. The Office of Planning for Female Offenders works with the Adolescent Female Subcommittee Advisory Task Force to expand parity of program funding, develop a continuum for care throughout the state, and create a Center for Adolescent Female Development and Studies. Oregon's House Bill 3576 mandates all state agencies to develop plans ensuring equal access for all services and calls for the strict monitoring of implementation of improved services for young women in the areas of teen pregnancy, physical and sexual abuse, alcohol and drug abuse, and services for runaway and homeless girls.

Current Study

In California, the Office of Criminal Justice Planning (OCJP) has addressed the needs of girls and young women at risk or currently involved in the juvenile justice system through the governor's State Advisory Group (SAG). In 1993, SAG convened a task force of researchers, policy makers, program providers, and youth advocates to determine the nature of this problem and develop research strategies to obtain the data necessary to make informed policy decisions. To identify gender-specific responses for at-risk girls and young women, OCJP contracted with researchers from the California State University system to develop a series of reports to address these issues, which are summarized in the final report (Owen et al., 1998). The researchers conducted an overview of the literature, reviewed federal and state policy initiatives, conducted a survey of officials from various state agencies, and conducted a series of interviews and focus groups with female youth and professionals serving this population.

Legislative Review

In 1998, California passed Senate Bill 1657 creating the Juvenile Female Offender Intervention Program, which would award competitive grants to counties to develop intervention programs designed to reduce juvenile crime committed by female offenders as specified. The bill would authorize the Board of Corrections to award up to $500,000 to counties that (a) develop and implement a comprehensive, multiagency plan that provides for a continuum of responses to juvenile crime and delinquency committed by female offenders; and (b) demonstrate a collaborative and integrated approach for implementing a system of swift, certain, and graduated responses targeted to meet the unique needs of at-risk female youth and female juvenile offenders. Unfortunately, Senate Bill 1657 was not signed by the governor.

Collaborations between agencies and jurisdictions (e.g., mental health, education, and family and children's services) present additional possibilities for a more holistic approach to juvenile justice issues. The Juvenile Crime Enforcement and Accountability Challenge Grant Program (S. 1760, 1997) provided $50 million to eligible counties for the purpose of reducing juvenile crime and delinquency. Grants were awarded by the Board of Corrections to (a) develop and implement a comprehensive multiagency plan that provides for a continuum of responses to juvenile crime and delinquency and (b) demonstrate a collaborative and integrated approach for implementing graduated responses for at-risk youth and juvenile offenders. Subsequent to this legislation, the Board of Corrections awarded grants totaling $45.7 million to 16 counties to implement their local action plans. Three county local action plans (Alameda, San Diego, and San Francisco) included provisions for services to at-risk girls and female juvenile offenders.

Other state legislation, compiled by the California Task Force to Review Juvenile Crime and the Juvenile Justice Response (1996), provided for policy and program opportunities that can be used to develop and expand gender-specific services. Assembly Bill 3220 (1995) established the Repeat Offender Prevention Project to provide comprehensive social services for wards 15 years or younger who are at risk of becoming chronic juvenile offenders. Senate Bill 1763 (1995) requires the California Youth Authority (CYA) to develop a 5-year plan with strategies for treatment and housing of CYA wards. Other legislation (Assembly Bill 2189, 1997) encourages the use of innovation and experimentation in the operation of juvenile detention facilities. Senate Bill 604 (1996) authorizes funding for educational, vocational, and special education services for young offenders. The use of collaboratives to develop peer teen courts (Assembly Bill 3324, 1995) and the establishment of a pilot project for intensive wraparound services to children in foster care (Assembly Bill 2297, 1997) provide opportunities for an interdisciplinary approach to the needs of at-risk youth, especially if implemented with a gender-specific focus.

Survey and Focus Group Methodology

Quantitative and qualitative data collection techniques were used in this study. A cross-sectional survey was designed to obtain data on the types of services available to girls and young women at risk of involvement or already involved in California's juvenile justice system and to learn more about problems that are faced by various providers. Focus groups and interviews were conducted with probation officers, program staff, and program participants in 11 counties.

The survey was distributed via mail to probation chiefs, detention supervisors, juvenile court judges, commissioners, and referees in each of the 58 counties and to 387 program providers in November 1997. Probation officers for each county were identified based on the Juvenile Challenge Grant Contact List. Names of detention supervisors were obtained through a directory of criminal justice agencies. The list of judges, commissioners, and referees was obtained from the Judicial Council of California. Several sources were used to create a list of agencies that provide services to girls and young women. One source was information provided by the Juvenile Justice Coordinating Councils in each county and another was the mailing list maintained by the Office of Criminal Justice Planning. One follow-up contact was made via telephone or fax approximately 1 month following the initial mail out. The response rate varied by type of respondent, with the highest rate among chief probation officers (71%), a moderate rate for detention supervisors (38%), and a low rate (17%) for the judges and programs. Overall, there was at least 1 survey returned from 53 out of the 58 counties in the state.

The survey included questions related to risk and protective factors for young women and men and program needs in terms of barriers to treatment and suggestions for system change.[1] Program providers were asked additional questions about their program, such as target population, program characteristics, demographic characteristics of staff and clients, and program information. Data were analyzed using SPSS with various techniques, including frequency distributions, cross-tabulations, *t* tests of means, and analysis of variance. Most of the results included in this article represent the overall descriptive statistics.[2]

Project staff conducted interviews and focus groups with a wide range of individuals, including probation officers, program staff, and girls and young women in 11 counties between August and December 1997. The counties were purposively selected to be representative of geographical location, urban or rural characteristics, or program reputation or interest. The focus group interview lasted between 60 and 90 minutes, and questions addressed the following areas: factors contributing to delinquency and other risk behavior, types of problems experienced by girls and young women, types of help and services needed, obstacles in seeking help, program gaps and barriers, and effective program elements.

Study Findings

The research results are divided into two sections. The first section summarizes the findings from the two data collection efforts and literature review and provides information for a basic understanding of at-risk girls and young women that is necessary to program development. Many of these findings parallel the conclusions made by Acoca (1999) and support the need for gender-specific programs. The second section provides recommendations for policy and program change within the state of California, which can be generalized to other states.

Research Results

Family problems, victimization, violence, and drugs are critical factors that contribute significantly to female involvement in juvenile of-

Table 34.1
Rank Order of Risk and Protective Factors by Survey Respondents

	Mean Score	
	Risk Factor	Protective Factor
Family issues	1.82	1.71
Individual problems	2.07	2.13
Peer group	3.09	3.31
School-related problems	3.25	3.22
Community	4.34	4.19

fending. Survey and focus group respondents alike indicated that the family is the primary risk and protective factor (see Table 34.1). As shown in Table 34.2 and as reported in the focus groups, family issues include conflicts and lack of communication within the family, parents who are ill-equipped or unprepared, and a range of problems presented by the parents themselves. Survey respondents indicated that positive family communication, along with rules and structure within the family, are primary protective factors (see Table 34.3). Individual experiences and problems are second in importance in determining the risks and needs of females (see Table 34.1). The lack of self-esteem is a primary problem displayed by many delinquent girls (see Table 34.2). Second, substance abuse is often a sign of other problems that lead to risky behavior. Sexual, physical, and emotional abuse are significant factors in producing risky and delinquent behavior among girls and young women. As mentioned in the focus groups, the effect of abuse is long lasting and creates problems with running away, emotional adjustments, trust and secrecy, future sexuality, and other risky behaviors. Gang involvement and fighting with peers contribute to delinquency for a significant number of girls and young women. According to survey respondents, creating a positive self-image and helping youth with skills related to problem solving, conflict resolution, and relationship building are among the primary protective factors for young women (see Table 34.3).

School difficulties and negative attitudes toward school contribute to truancy, dropping out, and other early warning signs of delinquency (see Table 34.2). Girls and young

Table 34.2
Risk Factors and Common Problems Identified by Survey Respondents (N = *167)*

	%
Family	
Family conflict	95.8
Family management problems	89.8
Parent or sibling history of criminal or violent behavior	88.7
Parental attitudes favorable to involvement in problem behavior	69.9
Individual	
Lack of self-esteem	95.8
Substance abuse	92.2
Sexual abuse	88.6
Emotional abuse	88.0
Sexual activity or awareness	88.0
Delinquency	86.7
Homeless or runaway youth	84.9
Pregnancy	81.9
Suicidal tendencies	80.1
Physical abuse	78.3
Gang involvement	77.1
Developmental or learning disabilities	74.1
Severe trauma or emotional disturbance	73.5
Eating disorders	64.5
School	
Discipline problems	91.0
Truancy	88.0
Academic failure	84.9
Dropout	72.5
Peer group	
Friends who engage in alcohol or drug use	90.4
Friends who engage in delinquency	89.2
Friends with favorable attitudes toward problem behavior	74.7
Community and other	
Availability of drugs	90.4
Values favorable toward problem behavior	71.1
Low neighborhood attachment, lack of community organization	69.9
Extreme economic deprivation	64.5
Lack of safe or adequate housing	59.6
Availability of firearms	52.4
Immigration problems	48.8

women at risk of future delinquency and those currently in programs reported that they lack a range of academic and social skills. Girls may also lack basic information about the world of work and planning for the future. Focus group respondents identified schools as a prime opportunity for early intervention in the lives of girls and young women but noted that they are often ill-equipped to deal with the high-risk student. Survey respondents indicated parental involvement in schooling is an important protective factor (see Table 34.3). According to focus group participants, there are few after-school and other recreational programs and activities designed for girls and young women. Girls and young women desire programs that promote active involvement in addressing their problems and needs.

Peer groups and the community are important settings for delinquency prevention. Survey respondents noted the availability of drugs and peer use of substances as important risk factors (see Table 34.2). Positive peer influences and community service were identified as important protective factors (see Table 34.3). Overall, it appears that girls and young women have multiple service needs.

The types of services provided by the 67 programs that responded to the survey are displayed in Table 34.4.[3] Some services are provided within the agency, whereas other services are referrals, depending on the type of program (residential or community-based outpatient).[4] The majority of programs include individual, family, and group counseling, as well as specific skills training such as education, life skills, and anger management. About half of the agencies provide individual counseling for substance abuse and more than half refer clients to 12-step groups. Programs are as likely to provide services as to make referrals for various types of general services. Focus group interviews suggested that few programs address the serious problem of victimization or provide needed

Table 34.3
Protective Factors Identified by Survey Respondents (N = 167)

	%
Family	
Positive family communication	97.6
Rules and structure within family	89.8
Parent involvement in schooling	89.2
High level of love and support within the family	88.6
Ongoing relationship with caring adult other than parent	75.3
Lack of family stress	72.9
Individual	
Positive self-image or self-worth	97.6
Problem solving skills	91.6
Positive values (integrity, honesty, responsibility)	89.8
Conflict resolution skills	88.6
Social skills or competence	84.3
Relationship building skills	83.7
Ability to express opinions, values, perspectives	78.9
Resistance skills	75.9
Ability to express range of feelings	75.9
Sense of personal safety	74.1
Ability to empathize with others	72.9
Spiritual values	61.4
School	
School engagement or bonding to school	81.2
Youth involvement in creative activities	79.5
Youth involvement in sports, athletic activities	77.7
Caring school climate	77.1
Rules and structure in school environment	74.1
Peer group	
Positive peer influences	89.2
Community and other	
Youth performing community service	73.5
Nonviolent and caring neighborhood	70.5
Community valuing youth	70.5
High expectations for youth by adults	62.7

Table 34.4
Type of Services Provided for Female Clients by Programs (N = *167)*

	% Provide	% Refer	% Provide or Refer
Counseling			
Individual	65.6	11.5	14.8
Family	57.4	19.7	13.1
Peer support group (coed)	54.1	18.0	3.3
Peer support group (single gender)	67.2	14.8	1.6
Skills training			
Education/tutoring	50.8	31.1	8.2
General Equivalency Diploma (GED)	23.0	55.7	0.0
Vocational	21.3	52.5	1.6
Victim awareness	37.7	34.4	1.6
Life skills	60.7	18.0	4.9
Anger management	63.9	21.3	1.6
Grief management	44.3	34.4	0.0
Parenting skills (clients)	49.2	23.0	1.6
Family planning (sex education)	44.3	34.4	4.9
Substance abuse treatment			
Individual counseling	50.8	21.3	6.6
Group counseling (coed)	41.0	26.2	1.6
Group counseling (single gender)	42.6	26.2	1.6
12-step groups	19.7	55.7	1.6
Residential or inpatient	13.1	54.1	0.0
Sober living home	11.5	42.6	1.6
Detoxification	3.3	60.7	0.0
General services			
Recreational activities	57.4	32.8	4.9
Mentoring	49.2	24.6	4.9
Food/clothing	42.6	36.1	4.9
Transportation	42.6	34.4	4.9
Housing	29.5	47.5	1.6
Foster care	18.0	47.5	1.6
Independent living	18.0	47.5	1.6
Temporary shelter	14.8	49.2	1.6
Medical and/or dental care	19.7	60.7	0.0
Child care	13.1	50.8	3.3

Note: Row percentages do not sum to 100%, as the responses that were left blank were not included in the table.

services for prevention or treatment of substance abuse. Health services are inadequate across the board. In particular, pregnant and parenting teens are neglected in terms of comprehensive health programs and services. Focus group participants suggested that special attention should be given to prevention and education programs concerning pregnancy and sexually transmitted diseases.

There is a multitude of barriers to program services for girls and young women. Even though funding was identified as the most serious barrier confronted by programs, girls and young women confront many individual barriers in seeking help and treatment for their problems (see Table 34.5). Focus group interviews documented that these barriers include: distrust and fear, lack of knowledge about services, teen attitudes and resistance, lack of personal contact with staff, transportation and lack of service accessibility, domestic responsibility, difficulty in making and accessing referrals, and cultural and immigration issues. In addition, racial, ethnic, gender, and economic discrimination may contribute to decreased opportunity, disparities in treatment, gender bias, and lack of program parity, although these were not identified as serious problems by survey respondents.

Survey respondents made many suggestions for program change (see Table 34.6) and indicated ways in which OCJP can help facilitate change (see Table 34.7). For example, the majority of respondents indicated that they want more information about what works for girls. Half of the respondents indicated a need to identify the best practices and provide program models. Additional resources and funding were

Table 34.5
Barriers to Program Services by Survey Respondents (N = 167)

	% Not a Problem	% Somewhat a Problem	% Serious Problem
Administrative barriers			
Funding/resources	14.5	27.7	57.9
Transportation	33.3	42.8	23.9
Staffing	33.3	44.9	21.8
Access/waiting list	36.7	43.0	20.3
Geographic location	36.7	46.8	16.5
Appointment hours	50.6	44.8	4.5
Individual barriers			
Support system	7.0	49.0	43.9
Lure of the streets	13.0	48.7	38.3
Motivation	10.3	56.4	33.3
Peer resistance	15.7	53.6	30.7
Family resistance	10.6	66.6	23.1
Acceptance of program rules	21.0	56.1	22.9
Lack of information	26.1	52.9	20.9
Cultural	30.6	58.0	11.5
Gender bias	52.3	37.4	10.3
Language	36.3	56.1	7.6
Sexual orientation	49.7	45.2	5.2
Economic barriers			
Employment	16.9	42.9	40.3
Education	24.0	37.0	39.0
Program cost	24.8	41.8	33.3
Social environmental barriers			
Childcare	30.9	44.3	24.8
Housing	29.4	51.0	19.6
Shelter	33.6	48.0	18.4
Treatment barriers			
Mental health issues	23.2	44.5	32.3
Medical issues	34.4	53.6	11.9
Disability	48.6	45.3	6.1

also high on the list. Improvements in communication and collaboration along with workshops, training, and staff development were among the primary areas targeted for change. In focus group interviews, respondents indicated that the juvenile justice system does not identify and address the needs of girls and young women in policy and program development. Most female delinquents continue to commit relatively minor offenses, which suggests a need for prevention and intervention programs rather than increased secure institutions. Female youth rarely participate in program development or case management planning. Program managers

Table 34.6
Suggestions for Program Change by Survey Respondents (N = 167)

	%
Improved or more information about what works for girls	72.3
Additional resources	54.8
Reallocation of existing resources	30.1
Better fit between funding criteria and characteristics of girls	34.9
Improved intra-agency communication/collaboration	40.4
Improved interagency communication/collaboration	38.6
Modified or new service delivery models	36.7
Improved client information systems	35.5
Enhanced public information efforts	35.5
Improved or more clarification of measurable outcomes	26.5
Improved/different opportunities for staff or management training	29.5
Less bureaucratic and/or administrative red tape	30.1
Changes in state laws or administrative rules	22.9
Organizational or managerial restructuring	12.7
Written policies or procedures	10.8
Lowered resistance to working with girls	18.1

Table 34.7
Ways to Facilitate Change Suggested by Survey Respondents (N = 167)

	%
Provide program funding	81.3
Conduct training	63.3
Provide program models	56.6
Identify best practices	54.2
Conduct workshops	54.2
Increase curriculum or program development	50.6
Promote staff development	48.8
Provide funding for program evaluation	47.0
Enhance public information efforts	41.0
Provide funding for program monitoring	39.2

lack information about available models and program effectiveness and see that funding for gender-appropriate programs is critically inadequate. Graduated sanctions and a continuum of care are not available to girls and young women in most counties. This includes front-end prevention and back-end aftercare programs. There are few linkages across and within programs. Meeting the needs of girls and young women requires specialized staffing and training, particularly in terms of relationship and communication skills, gender differences in delinquency, substance abuse education, the role of abuse, developmental stages of female adolescence, and available programs and appropriate placements and limitations.

Recommendations

The findings from this statewide assessment and review of current policy support the need for gender-appropriate policies and programs. The following recommendations are drawn from statements made by the focus group and survey respondents, as well as analysis of the scientific and applied literature. To date, California lacks any organized state office, task force, or policy division devoted solely to the needs of female adolescents or delinquents. Analyzing the standards for services and program development utilized by several other states in the public and private sector can provide California with the necessary references to move forward. A comprehensive effort should be undertaken to ensure an eventual parity between services for young men and women. Policy development must involve decision makers from all aspects of the community, the juvenile justice system, and girls and young women.

Even though the following recommendations were developed specifically for the state of California, they may be useful to policy makers in other states.

- County and state decision makers should develop specific policies aimed at addressing the needs of girls and young women.
- Funding should be targeted to address the needs of girls and young women at the state and county level.
- To meet the multifaceted needs of girls and young women, collaborative efforts in policy, grant development, and program planning should be encouraged.
- Girls and young women require a continuum of care that incorporates graduated sanctions and addresses prevention, intervention, intermediate sanctions, appropriate custodial settings, transitional housing, and aftercare.
- Community-based program opportunities must be developed to address these gender-specific needs and problems, such as abuse, teen pregnancy, running away, substance abuse, and family conflicts.
- Schools and school-based prevention programs should develop a more focused and collaborative approach in addressing the needs of girls and young women.
- Programs at all levels should provide family-focused services that include the fam-

ily, when appropriate, in addressing the problems that lead to delinquency.

- Family-focused services involve the family in assessment, case management, service delivery, and aftercare.
- Counties need to develop substance abuse programming for female adolescents including day treatment, clinical treatment, and residential programming.
- Local jurisdictions should increase services to female detention populations. These services include education, mental and physical health care, recreation, substance abuse treatment, and release planning.
- Health care services at all levels need to be provided in the community and detention settings. Programs that provide health education, clinical health services, and services addressing teen pregnancy and parenting should be developed and expanded.
- Staff at all levels of the juvenile justice and school systems should be provided with training and education concerning gender-specific issues such as adolescent development, sexual exploitation, awareness of family backgrounds, trust and emotional issues, relationship needs, and strategies and techniques for working with girls and young women.
- Programs and services to teen runaways should be implemented in every community.
- Academic and applied research on at-risk and delinquent female youth should be conducted. Inquiry into the causes of female delinquency, population descriptions and needs assessments, offense patterns and trends, and effectiveness-of-program models could provide useful data toward the development of effective policies and programs.

In sum, effective programming for girls and women should be shaped by and tailored to their unique situations and problems. To do this, a theoretical approach to treatment that is gender-sensitive and addresses the realities of girls' lives must be developed (Bloom, 1997). Appropriate services for girls and young women must have multiple components that address the complex issues that adolescent girls face. These services consist of educational opportunities, employment and vocational training, placement options, and mental and physical health services, all of which must be delivered in a culturally appropriate manner. Bloom (1997) discusses the need to incorporate the concept of the female sense of self, which manifests and develops differently in female-specific groups as opposed to coed groups. She describes how the unique needs and issues of women and girls can be addressed in a safe, trusting, and supportive girl-focused environment.

Conclusion

Even though girls and young women represent a minority within the juvenile justice system, there is little justification for the overall lack of policy, program, and research attention given to this neglected population, and there is a general consensus that federal, state, and local strategies should invest in programs and policies for girls. The review of the literature and data collected in this study point to three conclusions. First, the research shows that the needs of girls and young women facing involvement in the juvenile justice system are tied to specific, identifiable risk factors. These risk factors include such personal factors as family issues; sexual, physical, and emotional abuse; and inadequate academic and social skills. Although this study did not focus on the effect of social risk factors such as racism, sexism, and economic discrimination, these too must be understood in any discussion of female delinquency. Running away, truancy, early sexual behavior, substance abuse, and other predelinquent behaviors are related to these initial risk factors.

Second, girls and young women have been largely ignored in the development of policy and programs. The juvenile justice system is ill-equipped to deal with the risks and needs of girls and young women. The critical lack or early identification and assessment opportunities is aggravated by the scarcity of appropriate and effective community-based prevention and early intervention strategies. Inadequate planning and funding, the absence of a continuum of care, and the general lack of gender-appropriate programs, placement, detention, and aftercare services is further evidence of this inattention. Even though more rigorous evaluation and monitoring efforts are required, the basic elements and gender-appropriate interventions have been articulated through research and best practices. These elements are based on the developmental, psychological, social, educational, and cultural characteristics of girls and young women and the need to provide collaborative and comprehensive services to female youth and their families in a continuum of care.

Finally, it is clear that some states, like Minnesota and Oregon, have invested in gender-specific programming and policies and are leading the way. In comparison, other states have only begun to address the issue in conducting an assessment of the problem. Even though the Challenge Activity E amendment to the JJDP Act of 1974 has provided the initial momentum toward shaping the policies and programs for the new millennium, there is still a long way to go to achieve justice for female juvenile offenders.

Notes

1. Risk factors are those factors that increase the risk of delinquency or place youth at greater risk for system intervention. Protective factors act to prevent delinquency or problem behaviors.
2. The full report (Owen, Bloom, Deschenes, & Rosenbaum, 1998), which includes more detailed analyses, is available from the Office of Criminal Justice Planning. Some of the results have been reported in journal articles.
3. The most common type of program responding to the survey was a delinquency prevention program; some were group treatment homes and others were counseling centers.
4. In response to the type of services provided, in those cases where survey respondents checked both "provide" and "refer," the response is indicated as "provide or refer." If no box was checked, the percentage is unknown but is not reported in the table.

References

Acoca, L. (1999). Investing in girls: A 21st century strategy. *Juvenile Justice, 6* (1), 3–13.

Assembly Bill 2189, Poochigian, Chap. 100 (1997).

Assembly Bill 2297, Cunneen, Chap. 274 (1997).

Assembly Bill 3220, Connolly, Chap. 730 (1995).

Assembly Bill 3324, Connolly, Chap. 607 (1995).

Bloom, B. (1997, September). *Defining "gender-specific": What does it mean and why is it important?* Paper presented at the National Institute of Corrections' Intermediate Sanctions for Women Offenders National Project Meeting, Longmont, CO.

Budnick, K. J., & Shields-Fletcher, E. (1998). *What about girls ?* (OJJDP Fact Sheet No. 84). Washington, DC: U.S. Department of Justice, Office of Justice Programs, Office of Juvenile Justice and Delinquency Prevention.

California Task Force to Review Juvenile Crime and the Juvenile Justice Response. (1996). *Final report.* Sacramento: State of California.

Chesney-Lind, M. (1997). *What about girls? Hidden victims of congressional juvenile crime control.* Hawaii: University of Hawaii at Manoa, Women's Studies Program.

Chesney-Lind, M., & Shelden, R. G. (1998). *Girls, delinquency and juvenile justice.* Belmont, CA: West/Wadsworth.

Community Research Associates. (1998). *Female juvenile offenders: A status of the states report.* Washington, DC: U.S. Department of Justice, Office of Justice Programs, Office of Juvenile Justice and Delinquency Prevention.

Evaluation and Training Institute. (1996). *Study of gender-specific services: Initial review of the literature.* Sacramento, CA: Office of Criminal Justice Planning.

Greene, Peters & Associates. (1998). *Guiding principles for promising female programming: An inventory of best practices.* Washington, DC: U.S. Department of Justice, Office of Justice Programs, Office of Juvenile Justice and Delinquency Prevention.

Owen, B., Bloom, B., Deschenes, E. P., & Rosenbaum, J. (1998). *Modeling gender-specific services in juvenile justice: Policy and program recommendations.* Final report submitted to the Office of Criminal Justice Planning, Sacramento, CA.

Raviora, L. (1999). National girls' caucus. *Juvenile Justice, 6* (1), 21–28.

S. 604, Rosenthal, Chap. 72 (1996).

S. 1760, Lockyer, Chap. 133 (1997).

S. 1763, Wright, Chap. 905 (1995).

Unit V

Discussion Questions

1. What juvenile trajectories or pathways increase the likelihood of adult criminality?
2. In your experience, what portion of youth successfully avoid involvement in violence throughout adolescence, and why?
3. What risk factors and what protective factors do you think are the most powerful forces in the delinquency milieu, and why?
4. Are delinquents failures in school, or is school failure a cause of delinquency?
5. What type of youth tends to join gangs and why? What are the race and gender differences?
6. Do you know anyone who actually is a gang member? Why do you think that person joined a gang?
7. What type of intervention programs should be put in place to dissuade youth from joining gangs?
8. What are juvenile "boot camps" and how do they differ from traditional juvenile sentencing options? Discuss the pros and cons of "boot camps." How do they compare with traditional youth facilities in terms of impact/outcome assessment?
9. What impact does exposure to violence, through both direct victimization and witnessing victimization, have on adolescents? Explore the gender differences that surface relative to this topic.
10. What impact do parents have on controlling delinquency? How much impact did your parents have on your youthful behavior? What can and will you do differently if you become a parent?
11. What can be done to create nonviolent means for young people (particularly young males) to gain the self-esteem and opportunities they need to function as responsible members of society?
12. Many argue that the deterrence approach should be the main focus of the juvenile justice system. What is your opinion?
13. What are some of the current trends being implemented in the juvenile justice system? Which of these juvenile justice practices do you support and why?
14. Are the causes of delinquency similar for males and females?
15. Why do young males receive more programs and services than females? What kinds of programs do you think juvenile correctional facilities should offer?

16. What can be done to enhance the level of justice realized for female juvenile offenders?
17. It is generally agreed that our communities cannot be kept safe simply by locking up offenders, that while incarceration clearly needs to be a part of an overall strategy, it is overused. What other approaches need to be used more frequently when it comes to juveniles?
18. Should juveniles under the age of 16 be tried in capital cases? Why or why not?
19. How should society respond to the needs of delinquent youth?
20. Design a research evaluation effort to determine whether the delinquency prevention programs you propose would really prevent or reduce delinquency. ✦

Unit VI

The Future of Justice in America

It is difficult to speak to the future of justice in America without making reference to the events of September 11, 2001, and more importantly to the state of justice worldwide. Political borders have become increasingly irrelevant, and interdependence and interaction have become the realities of the day. While there is much to be said regarding the realization of justice on the domestic front, the nature of the current international socio-political-economic landscape suggests that there is a need to consider the state of justice throughout the world.

While marginal ebbs and flows are inevitable, the Western world is in the midst of an astounding and unparalleled era of economic growth. But this is also an era of startling contrast elsewhere in the world, for growth has been decidedly asymmetric. The least developed countries have clearly missed the "new wave," are still wallowing in the old economies, and are becoming increasingly marginalized. Survival, not social justice and commonweal responsibility, remains a primary motivating factor for tens of millions of people. While off the typical American's radar screen, there are areas of the world where poverty prevails, prosperity is inconceivable, hatred endures, fanatical nationalism survives, and hopelessness reigns. That world continues to be plagued with all manner of ongoing crises—extreme ethnic and religious conflict, pollution, disease, corruption. Such nations are contending with a multi-headed hydra. Corruption in particular is deeply embedded in the corporate traditions and legal cultures throughout nearly all of these nations. Successful anticorruption campaigns will require multisectional efforts over many generations.

Due to the increased level of international interdependence, I believe that the problems of the Third World will in time become the problems of the West. Sustained growth in the West, and in the end a greater sense of social justice for all, will necessitate a stable and more prosperous Third World, and particularly a more stable and prosperous Islamic community.

In partial response to this dynamic, the United States has quite deliberately attempted to utilize economic convergence theory to imprint a sense of justice upon our international neighbors—open up markets, allow cross-cultural consumption, build highways and byways, enhance infrastructure and agricultural output, and allow a middle class to develop, and their interests will converge with ours, democracy will get a foothold, and war will be averted. The theory has worked reasonably well on the Indian subcontinent and in South America, China, and Russia. But the message of peace through social and economic convergence has not infiltrated the Arabic peninsula, for many reasons, and as a result we now face a most difficult future.

In this latter context, it must be stressed that September 11 and its aftermath have littered the landscape with new obstacles that must be identified and surmounted. As of this writing, events in the Middle East are cause for the very devil to dance. The realization of justice in that region of the world remains a great challenge, and the potential negative spillover effect of failure has ominous negative implications.

The twentieth century was ushered in on June 28, 1914, when Gavrilo Princip assassinated the arrogant and audacious Archduke Francis Ferdinand. That act set in motion a series of events that not only led to World War I, but resulted in the total upheaval of the Western world; aristocracies were dismantled, the erosion of provincial territorialism accelerated, and many began to break out of the economic lockstep that had engulfed Europeans for centuries. The impacts of that assassination are still reverberating, as evidenced in part by the growth and development of the European Union.

In this same context, the twenty-first century was ushered in on September 11, 2001, when 19 individuals sacrificed their lives to "assassinate" what they saw as arrogant and audacious Americans. The acts of September 11 have set in motion a series of events that may not end the world as we know it, but will certainly change it. The nature of our global community is such that justice in America will be increasingly dependent upon the realization of a greater sense of universal socioeconomic justice.

On the domestic front, crime rates have been dropping in recent years, yet representatives from both political parties continue to engage in an ongoing game of one-upmanship, each trying to appear tougher on crime. One result of the politicizing of crime issues has been the passage of numerous federal crime bills in the last 30 years that tend to include increasingly stiffer penalties, a reduction in social programming, and more money for the wars on drugs and crime, more law enforcement personnel, and funding for more prison construction.

Careful and calm research has clearly demonstrated such measures to be "shortsighted, ineffective, and, in the case of drug policy, counterproductive" (Skolnick 1995, 11). Reason is being sacrificed on the altar of public policy. In part due to outcry from the criminological community, Congress did authorize a massive evaluation of criminal justice policy in the mid-1990s (Sherman et al. 1997). With the change of administration in the year 2001, however, the report's recommendations were largely relegated to the proverbial scrap heap. At present, it appears that the nation as a whole has become so converted to the crime-control orientation that today's popular hard-line crime policies will likely retain their mass appeal well into the new century.

Many on both sides of the debate are dissatisfied with the operation of the current justice system and are calling for a complete overhaul in order to reduce crime. In so doing, however, many miss a major point. Gurr (1979) has noted that justice systems can only be effective if they reinforce the dominant social view; they are viable only if they function as a supplement to social and cultural forces moving in the same direction. In much the same vein, McFarland (1986) observed:

> We cannot devise a perfect political system to make all people good, honest, fair, and considerate. Unless reform legislation is supported by the moral and ethical conscience of the citizenry, our laws will be ineffective in producing the desired social justice.

This crucial concept is often overlooked. Laws and justice systems are ineffective unless they are supported by society at large. "The high level of lawlessness in American society," wrote Walter Lippmann, "is maintained by the fact that Americans desire to do so many things which they also desire to prohibit." The problem, then, may not be the large supply of criminals, but the colossal demand for deviant goods and services from the public at large. The drug trade, for example, could not profit if there were no demand for the product.

Of course, societal change of this nature and magnitude is not likely to occur in the near future. In the meantime, justice system officials will continue striving to develop and promote new techniques, programs, and procedures that will allow the system to function more effectively and equitably.

A number of potential justice system reforms have been suggested in recent years. Below, a list of many such ideas has been compiled. It should be stressed that this list comes from a variety of sources and philosophical vantage points. Each of the reforms has its supporters, but no one individual or institution would be likely to concur with all of the recommendations.

Potential Justice System Reforms

Police

Increase use of neighborhood crime-watch programs

Adopt a social-service/problem-solving community policing model

Implement the 311 emergency phone system to augment the 911 system

Increase the use of foot patrols

Increase the use of bicycle patrols

Decrease the use of random automobile patrols

Open precinct homes throughout communities as per the Japanese *koban* model

Expand concealed camera projects:

- along highways to ticket speeders
- in high-density neighborhoods
- on squad cars to record police interactions with the public

Expand forensic capabilities in all scientific fields

Increase the use of creative sting operations

Adopt differentiated response dispatching

Adopt repeat offender programs

Increase the use of referral programs, such as:

- drug and alcohol treatment
- mental health counseling
- family crisis intervention
- dispute resolution centers

Increase the use of computers:

- as management information systems
- to develop probability models
- to develop solvability models
- to develop work schedules and personnel deployment systems
- to develop crime-incident mapping systems

Consolidate area law enforcement and emergency dispatching services

Encourage officers to join community committees/clubs (use work time to participate in such organizations)

Develop a two-track promotional system (patrol vs. management)

Encourage continuing education for officers (release time, educational sabbaticals, financial incentives, no promotions without degrees)

Encourage physical fitness among officers (add one dollar to all fines to advance physical fitness goals; pay officers for staying in shape)

Develop a statewide officer ranking system and encourage interdepartmental lateral transfers

Place a liaison officer full-time in the prosecutor's office

Develop outreach programs with immigrant and refugee neighborhoods:

- encourage officers to learn foreign languages
- translate departmental brochures into foreign languages
- hire representatives from these neighborhoods as Public Service Officer (PSO) liaisons
- develop bilingual newsletters
- provide translators for members of these neighborhoods

Increase interaction and cooperation with others who are "out and about":

- taxi drivers (use taxis to transport prisoners)
- gas meter readers
- real estate agents
- insurance agents

- social welfare agents
- probation and parole officers

Courts

Start neighborhood justice centers/community courts

Extend court hours; 24-hour court in urban communities

Expand the number of waiverable offenses

Expand the use of pretrial diversion:

- drug and alcohol treatment
- mental health counseling
- family crisis counseling
- dispute resolution centers
- support for the vocationally disadvantaged
- traditional deferred prosecution diversion

Abolish traditional bail bonds and adopt the 10 percent system, the ROR (Release on Recognizance) system, and the ROS (Release on Supervision) system

Allow fewer continuances, and no continuances within 24 hours of trial

Hire associate judges/magistrates/hearing officers to screen cases (dental hygienist analogy)

Establish a one-day/one-trial rule

Maximum one-day jury duty with limited juror exclusion rights

Establish substantive appellate review of sentences

Create sentencing councils of judges that handle only sentences

Set trial dates and specify trial judges at arraignments

Abolish the central docket and adopt an individual calendar

Allow no plea bargaining within 24 hours of trial

Organize periodic trial festivals

Hire judges pro tem (temporarily)

Shift judges from jurisdiction to jurisdiction to meet caseload needs

Obtain services of local attorneys to serve as judges and prosecutors on a voluntary basis

Expand the use of fines, restitution, and community service sentences

Expand victim-offender mediation programs, particularly with juveniles

Require pretrial mediation before a judge pro tem and/or magistrate in all civil cases and in all appeals

Simplify jury instructions

Establish a one-day/one-trial jury duty rule

During trials, judges need to:

- limit the number of expert witnesses
- narrow the issues before trial
- break into the proceeding and give simple explanations to confusing points of law and testimony
- allow fewer objections
- solve more legal disputes over evidence and procedures before trial (judges themselves or utilize judges pro tem and/or magistrates)
- allow judges pro tem/magistrates to empanel juries
- allow juries to take notes and to ask questions

Limit the number of cases that one attorney or one firm can bring to court

Organize periodic judicial mock sentencing conferences

Circulate a list of average sentences among state judges

Centralize state court systems

Make appellate court adjustments to:

- allow for fewer oral arguments
- allow for less opinion writing by judges and attorneys
- mandate pretrial mediation and settlement conferences

Corrections

Expand prison industry programs

Increase the use of citizen volunteers in:

- probation
- parole
- prison

Allow greater citizen interaction with prison inmates

Abolish indeterminate sentencing and adopt shorter, flat-time sentencing

Expand the use of counseling and treatment programs for:

- alcohol
- drug abuse
- mental health problems

Expand the use of fines and day fines

Expand the use of boot-camp prisons

Expand the use of home confinement programs

Expand the use of electronic monitoring supervision programs

Expand the use of prison furloughs:

- work release
- study release
- general family release

Identify a presumed prison release date within 60 days of admission to the correctional system

Expand the use of shock probation and shock parole programs

Increase the use of restitution and community service sentences

Expand the use of halfway houses

Expand the use of intensive supervision probation programs

Expand the use of Outward Bound–type programs for juveniles

Expand the use of job corps programs for both juveniles and adults

Expand the use of intermittent incarceration/weekend confinement

Abolish mandatory parole supervision

Reassess incarceration classification coding with a goal of placing fewer in maximum security and more in minimum security

Expand the use of pretrial release programs

Expand the use of pretrial diversion programs

General

Increase citizen participation in all phases of the judicial process

Organize community justice councils

Develop agency citizen advisory boards

Adopt strict handgun control laws; require handgun liability insurance similar to automobile insurance

Marginalize or decriminalize certain drugs, particularly marijuana

Increase the use of interactive cable television systems to facilitate a more informed and faster police response and enhance police-community relations

Start crime-stopper programs

Continue use of 911 emergency phone systems

Adopt a more aggressive media campaign regarding the problems of drug and alcohol abuse

Make possession of large amounts of cash illegal

Start community justice system ombudsman programs

Create powerful white-collar crime units located in state offices of the attorney general

Engage in statewide, regional, and national comprehensive justice system planning

Enhance public relations campaigns, such as:

- Bite out of Crime programs/McGruff the Crime Dog
- Just Say No campaign

Critical need for general socioeconomic reform to:

- promote economic growth
- enhance opportunity across social classes
- increase funding for project Head Start and Job Corps
- create tax incentives for hiring ex-cons
- hire more schoolteachers
- encourage community tutors/mentors in the classroom
- increase scholarship and grant funds for higher education (i.e., pay tuition at state university for all in-state high school graduates)

Adopt a global/transnational perspective on crime:

- rewrite extradition treaties
- rewrite international communication laws
- exchange law enforcement officers between countries
- promote aggressive international law enforcement cooperative efforts and information exchanges
- expand the role of INTERPOL and its central data bank
- enhance cooperative international money laundering investigative activities

* * *

Few would publicly argue against the premise that there is a need to reform the justice process. The system, in fact, is often openly castigated and reviled even by those who work within it. Yet due to the variety of forces involved both in and out of the system, change will always be slow in coming. Significant reform awaits an increased willingness on the part of citizens as a whole to become more involved in their communities in general and in the administration of justice process in particular with government officials, community leaders, and justice professionals working together toward the common goal of social justice for all. Justice in America will also increasingly depend upon an enhanced realization of socioeconomic justice on the global level.

References and Further Reading Materials

Barak, Gregg, Jeanne M. Flavin, and Paul S. Leighton. 2001. *Class, Race, Gender and Crime.* Los Angeles: Roxbury.

Braithwaite, John. 2002. *Restorative Justice and Responsive Regulation.* New York, NY: Oxford.

Gurr, Ted R. 1979. *Violence in America.* Beverly Hills, CA: Sage.

McFarland, James. 1986. Personal correspondence with the then Nebraska State Senator.

Messner, Steven F. and Richard Rosenfeld. 2001. *Crime and the American Dream.* Belmont, CA: Wadsworth.

Neubauer, David W. 2001. *Debating Crime: Rhetoric and Reality.* Belmont, CA: Wadsworth.

Sherman, Lawrence, Denise Gottfredson, Doris MacKenzie, John Eck, Peter Reuter, and Shawn Bushway. 1997. *Preventing Crime: What Works, What Doesn't, What's Promising.* Washington, DC: National Institute of Justice.

Skolnick, Jerome. 1995. "What Not to Do About Crime," *Criminology,* February, pp. 1–15.

Walker, Samuel. 2001. *Sense and Nonsense About Crime and Drugs.* Belmont, CA: Wadsworth.

Westervelt, Saundra D. and John A. Humphrey (Eds.). 2001. *Wrongly Convicted.* New Brunswick, NJ: Rutgers University Press.

Wilson, James Q. and Joan Petersilia (Eds.). 2002. *Crime: Public Policies for Crime Control.* Oakland, CA: Institute for Contemporary Studies. ✦

Chapter 35

Understanding and Preventing Violence

Jeffrey Roth

This chapter reviews the findings of the National Academy of Sciences Panel on the Understanding and Control of Violent Behavior. The panel concluded that the level of violent crime in this country has reached high, though not unprecedented levels. Because evaluations are not yet conclusive enough to warrant a commitment to any single strategy, violence control policy should proceed through a problem-solving strategy in which many tactics are tested, evaluated, and refined. According to Roth, this approach will require sustained, integrated efforts by criminal justice, social service, and community-based organizations.

The National Academy of Sciences Panel on the Understanding and Control of Violent Behavior was established to review existing knowledge about violence, with a view toward controlling it in the United States. The panel, set up at the request of three Federal agencies—the National Institute of Justice, the National Science Foundation, and the Centers for Disease Control and Prevention—reached the following fundamental conclusions:

- While present murder and other violent crime rates per capita are not unprecedented for the United States in this century, they are among the highest in the industrialized world.
- While sentencing for violent crimes grew substantially harsher between 1975 and 1989, the number of violent crimes failed to decrease. This happened apparently because the violence prevented by longer and more common prison sentences was offset by increases due to other factors and suggests a need for greater emphasis on preventing violent events before they occur.
- Although findings of research and program evaluations suggest promising directions for violence prevention strategies, developing effective prevention tactics will require long-term collaborations between criminal justice and juvenile justice practitioners, other social service agencies, and evaluation researchers.
- More research and better measurement are needed to identify the causes of violence and opportunities for preventing it—in situations where violence occurs, in communities, and in psychosocial and biological facets of individual human behavior.

This [chapter] more fully explains these conclusions and their implications.

Patterns and Trends in Violence

Violence is a serious social problem. In 1990, 23,438 Americans were murdered—a rate of 9.4 for every 100,000 people. In the latest years for which comparative data are available, this rate was nearly double that of Spain, which had the second highest rate in the industrialized world. The murder rate in the United States in 1988 was four times that of Canada.

Violent crime short of murder is also a frequent occurrence in this country. An estimated 2.9 million serious nonfatal violent victimizations—rapes, personal robberies, and aggravated assaults—occurred in 1990, according to the National Crime Victimization Survey (NCVS). The rates per 100,000 population for these crimes were also among the world's highest. In addition, the NCVS reported more than 3.1 million simple assaults—less serious crimes that neither involved a weapon nor injured the victim. National reporting systems do not include many other violent acts, especially those committed in families, between friends and intimates, by caregivers, by law enforcement officers, in prisons, and in schools. And no statistics fully capture the devastating effects of violence on local communities—their economies, neighborhoods, and quality of life.

Violence falls most heavily on ethnic minority males and occurs most often in urban areas. The lifetime risk of being murdered is about 42 per 1,000 for black males and 18 per 1,000 for Native American males. By contrast, it is only 6 per 1,000 for white males and 3 per 1,000 for white females. Except for forcible rape, serious violent crime reported through the FBI's Uniform Crime Reporting Program is highest in our largest cities. The violent crime rate is 2,243 per 100,000 population in cities with populations greater than 1 million. This is three times the rate for the country as a whole. Since 1980, however, serious violent crime rates in the third population tier (cities between 250,000 and 499,999) have exceeded those in the second tier (cities between 500,000 and 999,999).

Violence in America today is not unprecedented. Nor, despite the statistics above and some news media portrayals, is it limited predominantly to young men, or common in all areas of large cities, or primarily a matter of attacks by strangers, as the following panel findings attest:

- Murder rates have been as high as they are now twice before in this century—around 1931–34 and again in 1979–81. Because the U.S. population today is higher than ever, however, these per capita *rates* are producing unprecedented *numbers* of deaths.
- The 1990 count of serious violent crimes (2.9 million) is at about its 1975 level, following a peak around 1980, a decrease during the early 1980s, and an increase that began in 1986.
- Blacks' murder victimization rates have generally exceeded those of whites throughout this century. However, the trends for the two races do not always move together over time. Between 1970 and 1980, for example, the rate at which white males became murder victims rose from 7.3 to 10.9 per 100,000 population, while the rate for black males fell from 82.1 to 71.9.
- The black/white difference in murder victimization rates appears primarily to reflect conditions in low-income neighborhoods and tends to disappear altogether in high-income neighborhoods (according to the four available studies of this topic).
- Although teenagers and young adults are more likely than older adults to be murdered in any given year, three-fourths of all murder victims are killed after age 24, regardless of ethnicity. Minority murder rates are higher than white rates at all ages.
- Not all types of violent victimization rates move together over time. After 1973, aggravated assault and rape increased fairly steadily in cities of all sizes, but murder increases were greatest in large cities, and robbery rose during some periods and fell during others.
- Variations in violent crime rates by neighborhood in large cities are comparable to the variations in rates between large and small cities, and only a small percentage of all street addresses may account for a substantial share of a city's violent crimes.
- In nearly 40 percent of all murders, the relationship between victims and their killers is unknown to police at the time the statistics are reported. Among the remaining murders, strangers account for only 2 of every 10, while intimate partners or family members account for 3 of every 10, and other acquaintances for 5 of every 10.
- Women face only about one-third the murder risk faced by men. However, among murder victims, women are more than four times as likely as men to have been killed by spouses or other intimate partners. Male victims are nearly twice as likely as female victims to be killed by friends, acquaintances, or strangers.

The Need for Prevention

Usually the criminal justice system responds *after* a violent event occurs. The event must be reported to, or observed by, the police. Then an arrest may be made, the arrestee convicted, and the offender punished. Between 1975 and 1989, the probability of clearing a violent crime by arrest remained roughly constant. However, sentencing policy became much harsher. Increases in both a convicted violent offender's chance of being imprisoned and the average prison time served if imprisoned at all combined to cause a near tripling of the expected prison time served per violent crime.

The criminal justice system's increased use of prison reduced violent crime levels in two ways. First, it prevented 10 to 15 percent of potential violent crimes through incapacitation—the isolation that prevents prisoners from committing crimes in the community. Second, it prevented additional violent crimes through deterrence, by discouraging people in the community from committing them.

There is no reliable means of estimating the size of the deterrence effect and the total number of violent crimes the harsher sentencing policy averted. Whatever the number, however, those potential crimes must have been "replaced" by others, because the actual number of serious violent crimes was about the same in 1989 as in 1975—2.9 million. This suggests that by itself the criminal justice response to violence could accomplish no more than running in place. An effective control strategy must also include preventing violent events before they happen.

Risk Factors and Violence Prevention

Every violent event is a chance occurrence, in the sense that no human characteristic, set of circumstances, or chain of events makes violence inevitable. It seems reasonable to assume that some intervention might have prevented each violent event, but the correct intervention cannot be known in advance for every individual case. As starting points for exploring prevention, there are well-documented risk factors, which increase the odds that violence will occur. Some risk factors can be modified to reduce those odds. There is always a chance, however, that violence will occur in a low-risk setting or fail to occur in a very high-risk setting.

As shown in exhibit 35.1, risk factors for violence can be classified in a framework that has two dimensions. The first is temporal proximity—how close in time the factor is to the violent event. Furthest removed in time are predisposing risk factors, which increase the probability of violent events months or even years ahead. Situational risk factors are circumstances that surround an encounter between people and that increase either the chance that violence will occur or the harm that will take place if it does. Activating events are those that immediately lead to a violent act. The second dimension of the framework is the level at which the risk factor is most directly observed. The panel thought in terms of four levels:

- Macrosocial: Characteristics of large social units such as countries and communities. Examples are social values that promote or discourage violence against women, the structures of economic rewards and penalties for violent and nonviolent behavior, and catalytic events such as the 1992 announcement of the Rodney King beating trial verdicts.

- Microsocial: Characteristics of encounters among people. Examples are whether insults are exchanged, whether weapons are easily accessible, and how bystanders respond to an escalating confrontation.

- Psychosocial: Individuals' characteristics or temporary states that influence patterns of interaction with others. Examples are individuals' customary ways of expressing anger, or of behaving under the temporary influence of alcohol or stress.

- Biological: Chemical, electrical, and hormonal interactions, primarily in the brain, which underlie all human behavior.

Exhibit 35.2 illustrates the framework with two descriptions of murders, which were adapted from actual murder cases adjudicated during 1988 and recorded for other purposes. Just these two cases are sufficient to illustrate three principles about understanding and preventing violence:

- The diversity of these two events demonstrates the inadequacy of broad legal and

Exhibit 35.1
Matrix for Organizing Risk Factors for Violent Behavior

Units of Observation and Explanation	Proximity to Violent Events and Their Consequences		
	Predisposing	**Situational**	**Activating**
SOCIAL **Macrosocial**	–Concentration of poverty –Opportunity structures –Decline of social capital –Oppositional cultures –Sex role socialization	–Physical structure –Routine activities –Access: weapons, emergency medical services	–Catalytic social event
Microsocial	–Community organizations –Illegal markets –Gangs –Family disorganization –Pre-existing structures	–Proximity of responsible monitors –Participants' social relationships –Bystanders' activities –Temporary communication impairments –Weapons: carrying, displaying	–Participants' communication exchange
INDIVIDUAL **Psychosocial**	–Temperament –Learned social responses –Perceptions of rewards/ penalties for violence –Violent deviant sexual preferences –Social, communication skills –Self-identification in social hierarchy	–Accumulated emotion –Alcohol/drug consumption –Sexual arousal –Premeditation	–Impulse –Opportunity recognition
Biological	–Neurobehavioral* traits –Genetically mediated traits –Chronic use of psychoactive substances or exposure to neurotoxins	–Transient neurobehavioral* states –Acute effects of psycho-active substances	–Sensory signal processing errors

*Includes neuroanatomical, neurophysiological, neurochemical, and neuroendocrine. "Traits" describe capacity as determined by status at birth, trauma, and aging processes such as puberty. "States" describe temporary conditions associated with emotions, external stressors, etc.

Source: Adapted from Reiss, Albert J., Jr., and Jeffrey A. Roth, eds., *Understanding and Preventing Violence,* Washington D.C.: National Academy Press, 1993, p. 297.

statistical categories such as "murder" for understanding and preventing violent events. The risk factors and associated prevention strategies in just these two murders are quite different, and they represent only a small slice of the diversity in murder.

- It is important for prevention purposes to view a violent event as the outcome of a long chain of preceding events, which might have been broken at any of several links, rather than as the product of a set of factors that can be ranked in order of importance. To devise a strategy that might have prevented Jason's death (see box), one need not designate either Dave's accumulated humiliations or Jason's crying as the more "important" cause; rather, one must search for interventions that might have broken some link in a chain of events.

- Encouragingly, the two murders described here suggest a broad set of intervention points for preventing violent deaths before they occur.

It is useful to speculate about strategies that might have prevented Jason's and Andy's deaths. Conceivably, Jason's death might have been prevented if Dave had been raised to have higher self-esteem, if Evelyn had sought help when

Jason's and His Father's Story

Dave, Evelyn, and their 10-month-old son Jason were struggling. Jason was born just a few weeks after Evelyn's 20th birthday and 4 months before Dave was laid off from his job as a day laborer.

Things had clearly gone wrong since the layoff. Dave had become moody. They argued more frequently, mostly about money. During several of the arguments, Dave had slapped Evelyn, but begged forgiveness each time and promised never to hit her again. Worst of all, Dave seemed to have begun resenting Jason. He had never quite mastered feeding and changing and had stopped trying to learn. He had almost stopped playing with the baby, and what playing he did struck Evelyn as too rough.

Evelyn finally figured out a solution: she'd get back her old job as a waitress. Even though she would miss being [with] Jason, they needed the money. Less financial pressure might relieve the psychological pressures that, she believed, were making Dave more abusive. Dave didn't fight her idea, but Evelyn had mixed feeling about leaving Jason in his care. He was no model babysitter, but perhaps time alone together would build his bonds with Jason and take his attention off his joblessness. Anyway, there was no choice. She knew none of their neighbors, especially none whom she would trust with Jason, and the local day-care center had a 3-month waiting list.

As Evelyn left for her first day of work, Dave "hit bottom." All the humiliation—over the layoff, the rejections, loans from Evelyn's parents, and his new status as babysitter—descended at once. He heard Jason's bawling as yet another insult, not a cry for mother. Whatever Jason's problem was, Dave couldn't fix it. The more he tried, the louder the bawling, and the deeper his own despair and frustration.

Dave's self-control finally broke when Jason wet him. He turned on the "hot" tap, filled the bathtub with scalding water, and held Jason in the tub by his arm and leg. Jason's crying eventually stopped, but not until third-degree burns covered 35 percent of his body, according to the medical examiner's report.

Dave first slapped her, if a nurse or social worker making regular home visits had noticed the inadequate family functioning or Dave's poor parenting skills and shown Dave how to deal with problems more constructively, or if the neighborhood were characterized by more active social networks or more accessible child care services. Andy's death might have been avoided if Bob's early adolescent patterns of drinking and fighting had led to a referral for successful alcohol abuse treatment, if someone had thought of a recreational alternative to the usual Sunday beer party, if Andy's older brother had used his influence to stop the escalating fight instead of moving it outside, or if emergency medical services had been more accessible. The point is not that any single strategy will eliminate all violence, but that violence levels can be reduced by a variety of individual decisions and nonintrusive public policies.

Comprehensive Violence Prevention

Murder was only one of many types of violence explored by the panel. Research and evaluation findings concerning all forms of interpersonal violence suggest a variety of strategies that merit consideration and testing in any comprehensive violence prevention effort.

During Child Development

Promising violence prevention strategies include:

- Programs and materials to encourage and teach parents to be nonviolent role models, provide consistent discipline, and limit children's exposure to violent entertainment.
- Regular postpartum home visits by public nurses to provide health information, teach parenting skills, and give well-baby care, while taking the opportunity to detect signs of possible child abuse.
- Programs such as Head Start preschool enrichment and early-grade tutoring to reduce the risk of early-grade school failure, a well-known precursor of violent behavior.
- Social learning programs for parents, teachers, and children to teach children social skills for avoiding violence, ways to view television critically, and nonviolent

Exhibit 35.2
Examples of Possible Risk Factors in Two Murders

Units of Observation and Explanation	**Proximity to Violent Events and Their Consequences**		
	Predisposing	**Situational**	**Activating**
SOCIAL Macrosocial	1. Low neighborhood social interaction. 2. Neighborhood culture values fighting, drinking, sexual prowess.	1. No child care providers in neighborhood. 2. No local emergency medical services.	
Microsocial	1. Dave began hitting Evelyn months ago. 2. Widespread expectations of wild drinking parties at Andy's house.	1. Baby cries. Dave unable to cope. 2. Charlene humiliates Bob by resisting his advances.	1. Baby wets Dave. 2. Older brother says "take it outside," crowd goes outside to watch and cheer.
INDIVIDUAL Psychosocial	1. Dave has low self-esteem. 2. Bob develops adolescent pattern of drinking and violent behavior.	1. Dave humiliated by Evelyn's new job, his own lack of parenting skills. 2. Threats to Andy's family status, Bob's personal status.	
Biological	2. Possible familial traits of alcoholism and antisocial behavior in Bob's family.	2. Andy, Bob, and bystanders under alcohol influence.	

Murder 1: 10-month-old baby, scalded to death by father; no witnesses.

Murder 2: 20-year-old male beaten and intentionally run over by automobile; many witnesses.

Note: This is an illustration of the Exhibit 35.1 framework.

means to express anger and meet other needs.

- School-based anti-bullying programs.

Neurological and Genetic Processes

All human behavior, including aggression and violence, is the outcome of complex processes in the brain. Because of ethical constraints on research involving human subjects, the most firmly established knowledge about these processes concerns aggressive behavior by animals. Its applicability to violent human behavior is still speculative.

Available research suggests that violent behavior may be associated with certain relatively permanent conditions and temporary states of the nervous system. These possibilities relate to the following processes: the functioning in the brain of certain hormones and other body chemicals called neurotransmitters; certain physical abnormalities in the brain, which could be present at birth or develop as a result of brain injuries or maturation; certain abnormal brain wave responses to outside stress; brain dysfunctions that, by interfering with communication and thought processes, lead to school failure and other childhood problems that are

Andy's and Bob's Story

Wrightstown had long been known as a tough blue-collar suburb. Residents rarely ventured downtown, with its open-air drug markets and drive-by shootings. Still, "men were men," and their reputations depended on toughness, sexual and beer-drinking prowess, and family honor. Big Sunday-afternoon beer parties were a local ritual, and everyone knew that some of the biggest and wildest happened at Andy's house.

In a tough town, Andy's friend Bob was one of the toughest. Like his father before him, Bob had begun drinking heavily as a teenager and had accumulated records of school fights and simple assaults. He nearly always won the fights, but had recently lost his job for missing work—he had been in jail after a bar brawl that got out of hand.

Late one Sunday afternoon, on a run to replenish the beer supply, Andy ran into his out-of-luck friend and invited him back to join the party. Once there, Bob quickly drank up a six-pack and began making passes at Andy's sister Charlene. Charlene had never liked Bob. The more she resisted his advances, the more aggressive he became, until she slapped him hard across the mouth. Bob stepped back and tripped over a coffee table. As he picked himself up, half the crowd was laughing at him. The other half was yelling at Charlene to "Make it up to him like a good girl," and Andy saw his sister's honor at stake.

Andy came at Bob. The two fought in the living room until Andy's older brother told them to "take it outside" after they broke the coffee table. As the crowd moved out to the porch to watch and cheer, Bob yanked a tire iron out of his trunk and used it to knock Andy to the ground, unconscious. The crowd fell silent only after Bob jumped into his car, ran over Andy twice, and roared away. After what seemed like forever, an ambulance responded and took Andy to the hospital emergency room, where he died 4 hours later of massive internal injuries.

well-known precursors of violent behavior; and temporary effects of drinking alcohol, perhaps heightened by hypoglycemia or other health problems.

The roles of these processes in human behavior are far too uncertain to specify any neurological "markers" for violence or to warrant any wholesale biomedical interventions solely to prevent violent behavior. However, they do suggest that violence prevention may be a positive side-effect of certain interventions intended to achieve other goals.

Based on its review of available evidence, the panel concluded that potentially useful biomedical violence prevention strategies include:

- Programs to reduce maternal substance abuse during pregnancy, children's exposure to lead in the environment, and head injuries.
- Intensive alcohol abuse treatment and counseling programs for those in their early adolescent years whose behavior patterns include both conduct disorder and alcohol abuse, especially if alcohol dependence runs in their families.
- Developing pharmacological therapies to reduce craving for nonopiate illegal drugs, much as methadone reduces demand for heroin.
- Completing the development of medicines that reduce potentials for violent behavior during withdrawal from opiate addiction.

In statistical studies of twins, adoptees, and their families, researchers have found correlations suggesting that genetic and social processes interact as influences on the probabilities of many human behaviors, including alcoholism, antisocial behavior, and juvenile delinquency. However, the few available studies of human violent behavior have produced mixed results, suggesting at most a weak genetic influence on the chance of violent behavior. The statistical patterns make clear that, even if eventually discovered, any such influence would involve many genes rather than any single "violence gene" and would involve interactions with social conditions and life events.

Social and Community-Level Interventions

Research on social and community-level influences on violence is difficult to carry out, and evaluations of interventions at these levels are scarce. As a result, the knowledge base for formulating violence prevention strategies at these levels is not as strong as it should be. Research conducted thus far highlights the need for further development in the following areas:

- Housing policies to reverse the geographic concentration of low-income families.
- Programs to strengthen community organizations, social networks, and families that promote strong prosocial values.
- Economic revitalization in urban neighborhoods to restore opportunities for economic self-advancement through prosocial, nonviolent activities.
- Stronger community policing programs as a means of improving police responsiveness to community needs, stronger community-based violence prevention initiatives, reinforcement of prosocial values, and increased certainty of arrest and punishment for violent crimes.
- Strategies to reduce the violence-promoting effects of community transitions that occur in the course of new construction, gentrification, and other disruptions.
- Programs to reduce violence associated with prejudice and with the activities of some gangs.

Situational Approaches

The strategies outlined above are long-range approaches rather than immediate means to prevent violence. Time is needed to change the pathways through which a few aggressive children develop into violent adults and to change the communities in which they live.

Shorter-term strategies for violence prevention require altering or eliminating situations that present immediate opportunities for violent events. One approach involves cooperation between police and business proprietors to diagnose and remove the risk factors in "hot spots"—addresses or telephone locations that generate unexpectedly high volumes of "911" calls for emergency police assistance to deal with violence.

The diversity of violence means that different "hot spots" will require different remedies. However, a large body of research points directly to three commodities that should often be considered in situational violence prevention:

- Alcohol: Use of prevention educations, laws and law enforcement, taxes, and social pressure, among other measures to deal with underage drinking. Such measures appear to reduce teenagers' involvement in automobile crashes and may therefore reduce their excessive involvement in violence.
- Illegal drugs: Reducing the demand that fuels violence-ridden illegal drug markets; and using drug abuse prevention, drug treatment, coordination of in-prison drug treatment with post-release treatment, and (in the near future) methadone equivalents for drugs other than heroin.
- Firearms: Better enforcement of laws that regulate the allocation and uses of guns, and especially reducing juveniles' access to guns by enforcing laws prohibiting gun sales to minors and by disrupting illegal gun markets.

Diversified Problem-Solving in Violence Prevention

The strategies discussed above constitute a portfolio of promising violence prevention opportunities. The findings of program evaluations are not yet conclusive enough to warrant a national commitment to any single strategy. Therefore, violence control policy should be diversified through small investments in testing many strategies rather than a major commitment to nationwide implementation of one or two. Interventions that succeed in one setting sometimes fail in another because of the unintended consequences of interactions that are poorly understood. Even when the potential effectiveness of a specific strategy is fairly clear, the choice of implementation tactics may not be. Strategies aimed at predisposing risk factors, even when they are effective, require time to demonstrate that they will work. And while some strategies will doubtless prove more effective than others, the diversity of violent events guarantees that no single strategy will prevent more than a small fraction of them. For these reasons, "diversified investments" in many small-scale but sustained problem-solving initiatives are needed. Like initiatives to develop vaccines for preventing a single disease, each problem-solving initiative should focus on a specific source of violence. Each initiative involves five steps:

1. Diagnose the problem, using criminological and epidemiological techniques to document its importance and identify risk factors that suggest a preventive strategy.
2. Develop prototypes of several tactics for strategy implementation that show promise based on theory, research findings, or experience.
3. Compare the effectiveness of the alternative tactics through rigorous evaluations that use randomized assignment wherever feasible.
4. Refine the tactic for implementation, using the evaluation findings as the basis.
5. Replicate the evaluation and refinement steps to sharpen the effectiveness of the interventions and adapt them to local community characteristics.

The panel called for problem-solving initiatives aimed at sources of violence in several areas: childhood development; "hot spot" locations, routine activities, and situations; illegal markets, especially for drugs, guns, and prostitution; firearms, alcohol, and drugs; bias crimes, gang activities, and community transitions; and relationships between intimate partners.

Over time, this problem-solving approach may reduce the levels of different types of violence in large enough numbers to make a significant "dent" in the overall problem. Such progress in prevention is especially likely when the chances of early success can be maximized by focusing on certain categories of problems and interventions: those for which the risk factors are most firmly established, those for which evaluation findings are most positive, and those for which tactics are most easily marshaled. Progress in prevention also requires treating initial evaluation failures (which are inevitable) as indicators of the need for tactical refinements rather than as signals to abandon a strategy entirely. Simultaneously, progress in understanding violence will be made to the extent social scientists make greater use of findings from well-controlled outcome evaluations as evidence of the causes of violent events.

The preventive, problem-solving approach to violence is not intended to replace arrest and other traditional criminal justice responses. But it would involve integrating criminal justice responses with a broad range of preventive interventions, which are often administered by other public and private agencies. For example, arrest at the crime scene has been found to break the cycle of spouse assault/intervention under some conditions. However, arrest has never been systematically compared to, or integrated with, such interventions as referring battered women to shelters, teaching batterers nonviolent ways to deal with anger, or requiring batterers to participate in alcohol abuse treatment. Coordinating and evaluating all these elements of a spouse assault prevention initiative would require cooperation between police departments and the agencies that provide the other services.

More generally, violence problem-solving will require long-term collaboration and new organizational arrangements among local law enforcement, criminal justice, schools, and public health, emergency medicine, and social service agencies, all working with program evaluators and other researchers. Developing these arrangements will also require new leadership approaches by administrators of all agencies involved.

Building Knowledge for Future Use

To strengthen the knowledge base for developing the next generation of violence prevention strategies, three research initiatives are needed: better systems to measure violence, research in neglected topics, and a long-term study of the factors operating in communities and in individual development that cause a small percentage of children to have high potential for violent behavior as adults, while most do not.

Measurement Systems

Because of certain basic limitations in systems for gathering information on violence, many important questions in policy and science cannot be answered today, and emerging violence problems are sometimes slow to be discovered. For these reasons relevant information systems should be modified and expanded to provide:

- Better counts of intra-family violence, robberies committed in commercial establishments, violent bias crimes, and violence in schools and correctional facilities.
- More comprehensive recording of sexual violence, especially events involving intimates, and acts (for example, serial killings) in which the sexual component may not be immediately apparent.
- Baseline measures of the prevalence and incidence of risk factors for violence (for example, arguments between intoxicated spouses or intimates, drug transactions, and situations in which employees handle cash alone, especially at night).
- Links between the systems that measure all aspects of a violent event—the consequences, the treatment of victims, and the circumstances precipitating the event.
- Better systems for measuring violence levels in small geographic areas, to facilitate evaluating the effects of intervention.
- More detail about the attributes of violent events and their participants, to facilitate better studies of risk factors.

Neglected Research Areas

Certain research areas are of special concern because, having been largely devoid of resources, they could make rapid progress with relatively small-scale infusion of funds. These areas include:

- The effects of weapon type on death rates in assaults and robberies.
- Interactions among demographic, situational, and spatial risk factors for violent events and violent deaths.
- Comparisons of how individuals' potentials for violent behavior develop in ethnically and socioeconomically different communities.
- The nature of neurological responses that indicate elevated potentials for violent behavior.
- Development of medications that prevent violent behavior without the debilitating side effects of "chemical restraint."
- Interactions among cultural, developmental, and neuropsychological causes of sexual violence against strangers, intimate partners, and other family members.
- Violent behavior of custodians (for example, caretakers, correctional officers) against wards (for example, children in day care and prison inmates).

Multicommunity Longitudinal Studies

To lay the scientific groundwork for the next generation of preventive interventions, a multicommunity program of developmental studies of aggressive, violent, and antisocial behaviors is needed. By tracing the influences of the community, the family, and other individuals on children as they grow up, this program should improve the understanding of causes and lead to improved medical, developmental, and social interventions. The program should include randomized experiments that will identify developmental and social interventions for preventing high potentials for violent behavior in children. With support from the National Institute of Justice and the John D. and Catherine T. MacArthur Foundation, implementation of this recommendation has begun through a Program on Human Development and Criminal Behavior. Additional support is being solicited from a consortium of private and public sources.

Conclusion and Implications

Violence is a pervasive national problem, more serious in the United States than in the rest of the industrialized world, and especially serious for males who belong to demographic and ethnic minorities. However, the problem is neither unprecedented nor intractable. Existing knowledge reveals a number of promising prevention strategies involving factors at work in communities, in individuals, and in hazardous situations that present special risks of violence.

Implementing effective prevention strategies requires recognizing that the criminal justice response is not enough to reduce violence levels. Rather, prevention requires comprehensive problem-solving strategies that involve criminal justice agencies, schools, and public health, emergency medicine, and social service agencies. Cooperation among these agencies and community-based organizations is needed in specific problem-solving initiatives to systematically test and refine promising violence prevention tactics. At the same time, to lay the groundwork for the next generation of approaches to violence prevention, research should be carried out to improve the measurement of violence, to study certain topics neglected in recent years, and to learn more about what causes a small proportion of all children to commit violent acts as adults.

Jeffrey Roth, "Understanding and Preventing Violence." Reprinted from *NIJ Research in Brief*, Washington, D.C.: U.S. Department of Justice, February 1994, 11 pp. ✦

Chapter 36

Criminal Justice and the Future of Civil Liberties

Marvin Zalman

A *quarter of a century ago, Marvin Zalman predicted that technological advances and greater bureaucratization would lead to a twenty-first century justice system that would simultaneously increase crime control and ensure civil liberties. In light of the last decades' developments, here he revisits his prognosis; while crime rates have indeed declined, he argues that an ambiguous criminal justice system that simultaneously promotes both democratic and autocratic policies impinges on civil liberties, and may even make the United States a "quasi-authoritarian" state.*

Introduction: Past as Prologue

In 1980 I published an article forecasting that trends of legality and bureaucratization in criminal justice would in the "short run" (i.e., from the years 2000 to 2020) increase public safety and civil liberties. This would occur as the criminal justice system became more effective by wedding new technology to better crime control strategies and by gathering information from community members (Zalman, 1980, pp. 276, 278–280). Greater legality and bureaucratization would "steer criminal justice agencies toward the enhancement of liberal and democratic values" (p. 290). A conservative turn in the Supreme Court's criminal rulings would not divert the general democratic direction of criminal justice policies and practices (p. 281). As to the long-range future, the article noted that if pessimistic economic thinkers of the 1970s (e.g., Heilbroner, 1976) were correct in forecasting the end of capitalism and the material collapse of the broad middle classes, then criminal justice would adopt authoritarian means and ends, spelling the collapse of liberty and the rule of law.

That article correctly forecast greater success in crime control. "The current despair over the inability to control crime, then, masks the growing reality that government has been steadily increasing its net of control over citizens, and this trend is likely to continue" (Zalman, 1980, p. 277). The substantial drop in crime since the mid-1990s, possibly due to a variety of causes, seems to bear this out (Silverman, 1999; Symposium, 1998). Also, the historic link between the rule of law and classic liberalism and capitalism, emphasized in the 1980 article, has been demonstrated by the collapse of the Soviet empire. In short, the article projected a criminal justice system in 2000 that would effectively control crime and be a guarantor of civil liberties.

In light of criminal justice practices, the optimistic thesis that the system will invariably move toward enhancing civil liberties must be revised. The picture of criminal justice policies and practices since 1980 has been mixed, and any assessment of the future of civil liberties in America must take the current criminal justice situation into account. The thesis of the present essay, revising the 1980 article, is that some criminal justice developments are consistent with liberal democracy (e.g., community policing) while others are not (e.g., the "war on drugs"). Thus, along the civil liberties axis, I posit an ambiguous criminal justice system that operates simultaneously in democratic and autocratic modes. This, in turn, reflects on American society, which, although priding itself on being in the forefront of liberal democracies, may instead be seen to share, in an attenuated manner, the attributes of what I will describe as a "quasi-autocratic state." This indicates that in the next 20 to 40 years the criminal justice system will continue in its dualistic, quasi-authoritarian mode, marking the United States as a flawed liberal democracy.

A criminal justice system reflects its social and political environment; a liberal democracy's criminal justice system should operate in a "democratic mode" (Klockars, 1985, pp. 23–

24). Policing a democratic society, therefore, should stress service and crime reduction, unlike policing an autocratic society, which stresses control and repression (Turk, 1982, pp. 115–166). Nevertheless, evidence for democratic and autocratic criminal justice practices abound. Community policing, effective and narrowly focused crime reduction programs, independent courts, the guarantee of defense counsel, the concern with reducing domestic violence—all point to a democratically responsive criminal justice system (Buzawa & Buzawa, 1992; Silverman, 1999; Skogan & Hartnett, 1997). On the other hand, "zero-tolerance policing," widespread police brutality, the "war on drugs," get tough/three strike policies, racial profiling, asset forfeiture, the quintupling of prison populations in 30 years, the failure to provide adequate defense counsel, the weakening of constitutional protections for suspects and prisoners, and the failures of the juvenile justice system all point to a system bent on repression and control of the "usual suspects"—poor people, people of color, immigrants. A system operating in this autocratic mode threatens the liberties of all citizens even if it primarily targets more vulnerable populations (Anderson, 1995; Gordon, 1990; Human Rights Watch, 1998; Massing, 1998; Schichor & Sechrest, 1996; Tonry, 1995).

This essay, like the one before it, seeks to "make statements (guesses) as to the likely impact that the altered nature of criminal justice will have on civil liberties as we conceive of them today. The stability of these forecasts depends on a sound assessment of the current state of criminal justice as well as on a set of assumptions about the nature of society in the future, and even of human nature" (Zalman, 1980, p. 275). Accurately describing a component of society (e.g., "the economy") is difficult not only because social reality is complex but also because the observer's predisposition makes every description selective and partial. An essay unmoored from scientific methodology is hostage to the author's leanings and choice of evidence. The long-range projection that civil liberties would decline by 2080 (pp. 282–283), for example, rested on Robert Heilbroner's pessimism (1976), reflecting the social and economic pessimism of that period. In return for a narrower "objectivity," this essay seeks to impart some insight into deeper currents of reality.

The essay proceeds as follows. First, it draws on social evidence to support the self-congratulatory view of America as a liberal, constitutional democracy. Second, it examines policies and procedures in criminal justice that point to ambiguity and inconsistency: a criminal justice system that operates in democratic and autocratic modes. Third, it canvasses several analyses of criminal justice that help to explain this state of affairs. Fourth, it defines a "quasi-autocratic state" and asks whether the undemocratic features of contemporary criminal justice are so pervasive as to modify the view of the United States as a liberal democracy. The last section forecasts the likelihood of American criminal justice becoming unambiguously democratic in the next generation, concluding that the best that can be expected is some progress in the movement toward democratic criminal justice. I suggest that deeply entrenched conditions will sustain autocratic policies and practices.

A Land of Rights

There is no crisis of civil liberties in American society today. A half century ago—during the McCarthy era at the onset of the Cold War—a crisis existed. Consider that in 1954 an author of Henry Steele Commager's standing required courage to advocate the "free enterprise in ideas" and the dangers of "guilt by association" in a free society, on pain of being marked a traitor. Or that a white person advocating the civil rights of African-Americans stood a good chance of being investigated by the FBI for being a "subversive." Samuel Walker's *The Rights Revolution* (1998b) reminds us how far America has traveled in opening society to minorities, in protecting free speech, and in restraining the coercive power of the state. Nevertheless, the existence of a civil liberties crisis did not mean that the United States was something other than a constitutional democracy in that era. It does suggest that a constitutional democracy can deviate from its core values in times of great strain and that socially accepted and demanded levels of personal liberty have been "defined up" following the 1960s. Today, a return to legal segregation is unthinkable and free speech is generally protected by a conservative Supreme Court. Any assessment of civil liberties today and for the future has to take similar developments into account.

Contemporary meanings of liberty and civil rights, catalogued by Stephen Holmes, include four core norms of liberalism:

> *personal security* (the monopolization of legitimate violence by agents of the state who are themselves monitored and regulated by law), *impartiality* (a single system of law applied equally to all), *individual liberty* (a broad sphere of freedom from collective or governmental supervision, including freedom of conscience, the right to be different, the right to pursue ideals one's neighbors thinks wrong [sic], the freedom to travel and emigrate, and so forth), and *democracy* or the right to participate in lawmaking by means of elections and public discussion through a free press. (S. Holmes, 1993, p. 4)

These norms encompass, at a minimum, such practices as "religious toleration, freedom of discussion, personal security, free elections, constitutional government, and the freedom to buy and sell in a market of goods and services" (S. Holmes, 1995, pp. 13–14). David Fromkin's synoptic history of humankind (1999) places these political and ideological principles, which "prove[d] to be so especially congenial to the modernizing revolution" (p. 149), among the core ideas not only of Western but of world culture. "More of the world's peoples than ever before enjoy political freedom" (p. 238). Fromkin suggests that these ideals, originally developed in Anglo-American politics, are best suited to sustain the open society and the rule of law needed "to deal with the opportunities afforded by the civilization of science" (pp. 238–239). Does evidence exist to support the belief that these civil liberties are firmly entrenched? Several empirical studies of America's middle-class majority support the view that most Americans enjoy a strong sense of civil liberties (Bellah, Madsen, Sullivan, Swidler, & Tipton, 1985, 1991; Wattenberg, 1985; Wolfe, 1998).

Wattenberg challenged pundits of the right and left in the mid-1980s—who described an America beset with moral decay or middle-class decline—with telling statistics indicating improvements in health, ethnic toleration, political participation, patriotism, pollution, and the economy. Statistics identified increasing crime as a real problem. Although incarceration rates were rising dramatically, public opinion nevertheless saw criminal justice as too lenient, exacerbated by media broadcasts of "bad" crime news. Noting that earlier crime waves led to government action and decreased crime rates, Wattenberg believed that this would soon recur (1985, p. 313). His surveys gave no indication of concerns that heavy-handed government crime control would destroy American civil liberties. Robert Bellah and colleagues (1985) in the 1980s, and Alan Wolfe (1998) in the 1990s, conducted in-depth interviews with middle-class individuals to assess deep personal concerns about what gave meaning to life. Neither survey detected a sense of threat to civil liberties. Wolfe found that ordinary people included "the Constitution's basic principles" as a constituent element of their moral sense and concluded that "the words they use to express their support for individual freedom and the moral equality and dignity of all people are not just random noise" (p. 301).

In contrast to these sociological studies, two ideological perspectives arrived at opposite conclusions about rights held by citizens. A libertarian journalist, drawing on news stories, deduced that government tyranny has stripped Americans of civil liberties via historic preservation laws, the EPA, the war on drugs, labor unions, and many other commonly accepted institutions and laws (Bovard, 1995). Missing from this parade of horribles is any indication that individual rights are compromised by the private sector, as for example in widespread drug testing by employers (Ehrenreich, 2000) or in companies monitoring the on-line activities of employees and consumers (Conlin, 2000; Munro, 2000). In sharp contrast, communitarians worry that Americans have too much liberty, which they seek to curb by legislation favoring more communal programs (Etzioni,

1993). The "rapidly expanding catalogue of rights—extending to trees, animals, smokers, nonsmokers, consumers, and so on . . . risks trivializing core democratic values" (Glendon, 1991, pp. x–xi). "Rights talk," in this view, has become absolute in its tenor and a sense of individual rights "trumps every other consideration," destroying community and undermining a sense of responsibility (p. 18). Although libertarians and communitarians both perceive a crisis of civil liberties, their diametrically opposed assessments seem to cancel each other out.

Legal historian–sociologist Lawrence Friedman's comments on legal culture today are in sync with Bellah's and Wolfe's picture of middle-class life. American belief in "total justice"—an expectation that there is a recompense for every injury—helps to explain high rates of litigation (Friedman, 1985, pp. 91, 99). Furthermore, the growth of due process rights, by definition, implies a decline of traditional authority as those subjected to authority challenge it in court (p. 89). The legal culture of ordinary people, and not just lawyers, is a natural result of modernity, rationality, mobility, and a growing sense of individualism and personal autonomy—social changes that reflect the triumph of liberal democracy (Friedman, 1990, pp. 18–50). Twentieth-century expressive individualism "stresses self-expression, that is, cultivating the inner human being, expanding the self, developing the special qualities and uniqueness of each person. The idea seeps into legal culture as well" (p. 35). Widespread comfort with rights that protect Bellah's "expressive individualism" and that exalt autonomy and freedom of choice in personal matters displays no apprehension about the erosion of civil rights (Friedman, 1990, p. 96). A deft example is the Americans With Disabilities Act, signed into law by a conservative president, who sensed the temper of the times as giving those who were formerly marginalized a legally enforceable right to participate in society. People are given second chances today, both socially and legally (pp. 99–106). As a result, a rights-oriented "lifestyle society" has transformed authority, making it far less hierarchical and more "horizontal" (Friedman, 1999). In this society the authority structures of criminal justice and the penal law remain the most "vertical," adhering most to older forms of authority. Yet even criminal law has been affected by the legal culture of expressive individualism, for example by decriminalizing sexual acts between consenting adults (adultery, fornication, same-sex activity, cohabitation, etc.) (Friedman, 1990, pp. 141–145).

Two caveats must be added. It may be said that the existence of injustices or the centrality of force undermines the thesis that America is a liberal democracy with a non-autocratic criminal justice system. As to the first point, injustices exist in every country. The point at which injustice or corruption becomes so great as to delegitimize an entire government depends as much on an observer's ideological perspective as on the facts. I assume that Bellah's and Wolfe's middle-class respondents have it more or less right: By contemporary standards America is a constitutional democracy. Of course, there is much room for dispute and improvement. "That public disagreement is a creative force may have been the most novel and radical principle of liberal politics" (S. Holmes, 1993, p. 4).

As for the second objection, the classic recognition of the state's monopoly of force should need little elaboration (Dahl, 1989, pp. 44–47). Still, some citizens of the modern polity reflect a therapeutic temperament hostile to coercion (Bellah et al., 1985, pp. 121–138). For them essential elements of criminal justice—the use of force, legitimation of retribution, hierarchical exposition of state authority, and the law's rigidity and clarity—are distasteful or abhorrent (Menninger, 1969). What might be called "therapeutic liberalism," as opposed to "constitutional liberalism," seeks to replace force, law, and retributive notions of right with treatment, health standards, and utilitarian goals (Menninger, 1969; Wootton, 1963). Constitutional liberalism, inherently legalistic, accepts retribution as long as it is tempered by limits on cruel and unusual punishment. It subordinates treatment to standards of just punishment. At least one case has revealed the danger of repression under the guise of therapy (*McNeil v. Director, Patuxent Institution*, 1972). Thus, another assumption underlying this article is that constitutional liberalism, necessitating the state's monopoly of force and retributive justice, is a proper basis of governance.

The Ambiguous Criminal Justice System: Democratic and Autocratic Policing

The Two Faces of Criminal Justice

What is striking—and it is the point of departure for the concept of an ambiguous criminal justice system—is that stories about the same agencies and processes are written in a fully condemnatory voice by some while others are optimistic paeans. Two reading lists could present radically different views of criminal justice. Thus, at the time that the Los Angeles Police Department was in the throes of the Rampart Division scandal involving the gross abuse of citizens' rights, other divisions and other officers of the same agency were promoting community policing (Neely, 1998; "Police Division to Train," 1999; Sterngold, 2000).

Police brutality is rare in a liberal democracy and is not supported by the courts, who see themselves as guardians of liberty and maximize constitutional protections. In a democratic polity legislation supports courts' efforts to "patrol" prisoners' rights, juvenile offenders receive full due process of law but are subject to rules of criminal law and sentencing that take their age into account, citizens of all races and classes are treated with dignity and on an equal basis in the courts and on the streets, criminal penalties are rationally apportioned according to the heinousness of the crime, substance abuse is seen primarily as a public health issue, and the cost of absolute drug prohibition in the loss of civil rights is taken into account before waging an unwinnable "war" (Duke & Gross, 1993). This catalogue of a liberal-democratic criminal justice system is not a pipe dream. Some aspects of this exist in other Western nations and, to some extent, American criminal justice follows this outline (Walker, 1998a).

Nevertheless, American criminal justice, which has improved greatly in professionalism and legality since the 1960s, relentlessly pursues policies that befit an autocratic state more comfortably than a liberal democracy. The irrationality and excess of these policies have been detailed over and over again in careful studies by the best criminologists and policy analysts. There is general agreement, for example, that drug policy since 1970 has failed to actually reduce the availability of illicit substances and produces harmful side effects (Krauss & Lazear, 1991; MacKenzie & Uchida, 1994; Massing, 1998; McCoy & Block, 1992; Zimring & Hawkins, 1992). The sudden growth of the use of DNA testing has revealed to the general public the stunning extent to which adversarial justice is flawed (Sheck, Neufeld, & Dwyer, 2000). As a result of many innocent persons being released from death row, Governor George Ryan of Illinois imposed a moratorium on the death penalty and the death penalty emerged as an issue in the 2000 presidential campaign ("The New Death Penalty Politics," 2000). Court and criminal justice specialists, however, are not surprised that defense attorney incompetence, prosecutorial misconduct, or judicial obtuseness occurs with discomfiting frequency. Miscarriages of justice occur too often (Cooper & Sheppard, 1995; Eberle & Eberle, 1993; Hirsch, 2000) while many crimes go unsolved.

At this point, a small slice of this body of work is examined to contrast the autocratic and democratic faces of criminal justice. The focus on policing does not exempt other facets of criminal justice from critical scrutiny, e.g., the correctional gulag (Tonry, 1995), conditions of prison life and the withdrawal of judicial protection (Herman, 1998; Sullivan, 2000), or deep problems with the juvenile justice system (Feld, 1997).

Autocratic Policing

Most Americans probably believe that police brutality is rare and is perpetrated only by aberrational police like Justin Volpe, the New York City officer convicted of sodomizing Haitian immigrant Abner Louima with a stick (Bandes, 1999, pp. 1283–1284; Cooper, 1997). There is strong evidence, however, that police brutality occurs with regularity, in unacceptably high numbers, and disproportionately aimed at racial minorities. A report by Human Rights

Watch detailed numerous recent cases of excessive use of force in 14 large cities, including New York, Chicago, and Los Angeles. The report, based on interviews conducted over 2 and a half years, detailed many cases of unambiguous abuse. The incidents were drawn largely from news accounts of both notorious and obscure incidents of criminal abuse by police. The report is especially useful in demonstrating the grossly inadequate way in which the police are policed. Officers with many abuse reports account disproportionately for brutality, but they are routinely protected by the blue code of silence "and by flawed systems of reporting, oversight and accountability" (Human Rights Watch, 1998, pp. 20, 66–71). Police typically criticize the findings of special commissions on brutality rather than utilize them as bases for reform (p. 46). Unnecessary roadblocks are placed in the way of citizens seeking to file complaints (pp. 49–52). Civilian review boards are weak (pp. 53–61). As for self-policing, Human Rights Watch considers it "alarming . . . that no outside review, including our own, has found the operations of internal affairs divisions in any of the major U.S. cities satisfactory" (p. 63). Local and federal prosecutors almost never press criminal charges and do so only in the most egregious cases (pp. 85–105). Disciplinary action against abusive officers tends to be lenient (pp. 71–74). Police officers involved in shootings in some cities are protected by rules against being questioned for up to 48 hours (excluding weekends), allowing some time to "get their stories straight" (p. 75). From this outrageous situation of planned ineffectiveness it is fair to conclude that many more cases of police brutality occur than are determined officially to exist.

The Human Rights Watch report fails to document the prevalence of police brutality, leaving it open to the charge that the reported cases amount only to anecdotal evidence of some "rotten apples" and not proof of systemic abuse. The report did refer to a Department of Justice study on official misconduct complaints made in urban police departments between 1985 and 1990, undertaken "in response to the uproar over the [Rodney] King beating in Los Angeles" (p. 106). The DOJ concluded that "no pattern emerges from these figures" (p. 107). It appears that the DOJ was in error. A careful multivariate reanalysis of the DOJ data, along with variables added from the Uniform Crime Reports and the 1990 U.S. Census, concludes, "The findings for the additive equation . . . show that city population, percent black, percent Hispanic, and majority/minority income inequality were related positively and strongly to the average number of civil rights criminal complaints in cities of 150,000+ population, net of the effects of other variables in the equation" (M. Holmes, 2000, p. 358). This strongly supports the hypothesis that police brutality increases with minority population, because police officers, whether themselves white or racial minority, perceive minorities as a threat. "This study validates and extends findings of earlier ones by demonstrating a broad pattern of civil rights complaints alleging police brutality, particularly in large cities with relatively large and relatively poor minority populations" (M. Holmes, 2000, p. 361). This careful study confirms the now classic conclusion of Jerome Skolnick (1966) that police view minority citizens as "symbolic assailants." Because the police have frequent contact with people from marginal and powerless segments of society, who disproportionately are members of racial minorities, they tend to stereotype by viewing all people of color—lower, middle, and upper class—as threats based on their pigmentation.

M. Holmes (2000, p. 347) referred to two earlier studies of police–citizen encounters in which incidents of excessive force were observed. The number of excessive force incidents was deemed a "limited number"—42 incidents out of 5,012 police transactions (Reiss, 1971, p. 142) and 23 incidents of excessive force in 5,688 police–citizen encounters (Worden, 1996, p. 36). Holmes judged these numbers to be "limited" because they did not allow multivariate analysis. Although the numbers of observed cases of abuse are small they are not negligible. Abusive encounters occurred in 0.84% of Reiss's data and in 0.4% of Worden's data. These rates may underestimate the extent of police abuse, given that "a nationwide survey of residents of U.S. cities in 1982 found that 13.6% of respondents believed they personally had been the victims of police misconduct in the preceding year" (M. Miller, 1998, p. 149, n. 5, citing Pate & Fridell, 1993). Whether a police brutality rate of about 0.6% of all citizen encounters is unacceptably large is a moral and policy conclusion. A commercial airline crash rate of 0.6% is clearly unacceptable. Is an error rate of 6 out of 1,000 routine surgical operations acceptable? In my view, an error rate of 0.6% mistaken probable cause arrests is acceptable, for this measures honest mistakes made when quick judgment is exercised. Excessive force is another thing. Given the risks of police work, there are undoubtedly cases where the "actual" use of excessive force can be exonerated. But a "brutality rate" of 0.6% in two observational studies, combined with careful analysis of a large data set of citizen complaints over a five-year period that demonstrates statistically significant and strong relationships between complaints and minority populations, points to a conclusion that the number of cases of police brutality is unacceptably high.

This is supported by Bandes' study (1999), which applies a restrictive definition of police brutality—not excessive force but, in effect, torture: "conduct that is not merely mistaken, but taken in bad faith with the intent to dehumanize and degrade its target" (p. 1276). Bandes applies this standard to accounts of torture by Chicago's Area Two Violent Crimes Unit officers running unchecked from about 1971 to 1991 when, after years of rumors and ineffective efforts to uncover the situation, it became known that "more than sixty men, all of them black, had been systematically tortured by members of a group of approximately fifteen Area Two officers, all of them white" (Bandes, 1999, pp. 1288–1289; Human Rights Watch, 1998, pp. 152–157). All of the roadblocks to complaint and investigation reviewed by the Human Rights Watch report were detailed by Bandes (1999, pp. 1289–1294). Her account follows up the effects of police brutality: The victimized suspects all confessed and later sought to suppress the confessions or, if convicted, to overturn their convictions. What is especially unnerving is the extent to which some judges ruled in order to protect police torture. For example, one trial judge refused to allow testimony by a suspect who had been tortured by electroshock in the same investigation in which the defendant was tortured by electroshock because "Jones claimed he was shocked using tweezers rather than alligator clips" (Bandes, 1999, p. 1300). After the scandal broke, the city of Chicago disposed of it by the firing of Commander John Burge, the ringleader. "No criminal charges were brought against Burge or any of the other Area Two officers. No federal investigation was undertaken. The other Area Two officers . . . continue to be decorated and promoted" (p. 1302). Bandes goes on to enumerate the reasons why most citizens and most judges, and apparently the administration of the City of Chicago in the early 1990s, cling to the "rotten barrel" thesis: an ingrained belief in a "just world," selective empathy, fear of chaos, the need to find individual motive and blame (a scapegoat), the valorization of public officers, the belief that the state and the defendant are equally matched in the courtroom, and a judicial retreat to formalism (pp. 1317–1340). These mechanisms, then, help to explain why police brutality, prevalent though it is, remains invisible to the public and to officials.

Police brutality is hardly the only aspect of policing that has been subject to sharp criticism for autocratic policing. The "offense of driving while black" ("police using traffic offenses as an excuse to stop and conduct roadside investigations of innocent black drivers and their cars, usually to look for drugs") is pervasive (Harris, 1999, p. 266). It has led to major lawsuits in New Jersey and Maryland and a shake-up of the New Jersey State Police and has recently been carefully documented by David Harris (1999). Police perjury routinely comes into play in cases involving the application of the Fourth Amendment exclusionary rule so as to allow the police to virtually nullify the rule and to cover virtually all kinds of misconduct (Cloud, 1994; Dorfman, 1999, pp. 461–462). Police enthusiasm for drug asset forfeiture makes them lawfully complicit in maintaining the illicit drug trade (Blumenson & Nilsen, 1998; Zalman, 1996).

Any evaluation of autocratic policing is incomplete without a discussion of at least three contextual elements: the "war on drugs," the Supreme Court's role in shrinking the constitutional protections of suspects, and race (Kennedy, 1997). Space does not permit a disquisition on these critical aspects of contemporary criminal justice. To state the obvious, each subject is quite complicated, each contributes to problematic policing, and ameliorations in each may reduce the pressures that appear to make abusive policing more prevalent than it has to be.

Democratic Policing

A century ago most police departments were corrupt appendages of political machines, complicit with vice purveyors, routinely brutal, inveterately racist, marginally effective in preventing crime and capturing criminals, and often used to break labor unions with force. In the south, they enforced segregation and often allowed lynchings to occur. The professional policing model, which began in the 1930s and in many ways holds sway today, combined with deep structural changes in American life, has substantially improved or eliminated these problems (Fogelson, 1977; Walker, 1998a). Although many problems remain, the trend of more educated and more managerial- and result-oriented police officials, informed by policy prescriptions from the Justice Department's National Institute of Justice and organizations such as PERF (the Police Executive Research Forum) and the Police Foundation, augurs well for democratic policing.

Community policing has been perhaps the leading topic of police discourse and study in the last 15 years. It is currently enjoying the flush of success as plummeting crime rates have led to the revival of urban slum areas that were a few short years ago unsafe for investment and development, although the causes of the crime rate bust are not known with certainty and rates of crime have dropped even in cities that have not emulated community policing (Belluck, 2000; Butterfield, 2000). Although the success of community policing is important, it is not critical to my thesis of democratic policing, for what has been more important is that the highly fragmented police world has moved, haltingly perhaps, toward democratic solutions to its basic functions for the last four decades. The community policing movement has been built on a growing realization of the limits of the professional policing model (Walker, 1999, p. 39) and on the failure of similar initiatives from the 1960s to the 1990s. These include team policing, community relations units, community crime prevention programs, and the immediate precursor to community policing, the foot patrol experiments, as well as the very slow adoption of the intimately linked approach of problem-solving policing (Moore, 1992, pp. 128–138). Despite their failures, each of these initiatives was based on a desire and on an attempt to implement models of policing that were essentially democratic.

Community policing cannot be understood as a specific set of procedures. "To a great extent, problem-solving and community policing are overlapping concepts. . . . A commitment to problem solving leads quite naturally to the invention of solutions that involve the broader community" (Moore, 1992, p. 126; also see Goldstein, 1979). Skogan and Hartnett (1997, p. 5) posit that community policing programs share three general features: (a) "organizational decentralization and a reorientation of patrol in order to facilitate two-way communication between police and the public," (b) "a commitment to broadly focused, problem-oriented policing [that] requires that police be responsive to citizens' demands," and (c) a commitment to helping neighborhoods solve crime problems on their own, through community organizations and crime-prevention programs." As Patrick Murphy (1995, p. 746) has noted, "the proper role of the police in a free society, as distinguished from a police state, is to assist the people to prevent and reduce crime."

Few political concepts are as elusive as democracy, and talk of democratic policing runs the risk of succumbing to bombast. Jones, Newburn, and Smith (1996) tackle the issue and in doing so downplay the participation element of democratic policing, the one that ordinarily comes first to mind. Thus, despite the fact that in many successful community policing programs community participation is secondary to police initiative, it is nevertheless democratic policing. This is so because community policing actuates other ideals of democracy: responsiveness to community needs, the absolute reliance on information (i.e., crime intelligence), and the effective delivery of system outputs (i.e., lower crime and disorder). Community policing involves community participation to a greater degree than the professional policing model allowed, and to the extent that it does it also enhances the democratic value of the distribution of power to prevent excessive concentration and repression. Also, given the centrality of organizational decentralization to community policing, it incorporates the democratic ideal of redress or "competition between elites, in which the ultimate sanction of the electorate is to remove an incompetent or malevolent administration from office" (p. 192). As the most recent application of the new policing in New York City shows, tenure in command positions depends on performance (Silverman, 1999). The most fundamental democratic ideal is a concern for fairness or equity (p. 186). If community policing has been responsible for municipalities to cause, or to help to cause, the return of normal, peaceful, civil public intercourse on city streets in areas that were previously devastated because of economic disadvantage, then equity has been achieved by extending a basic attribute of social life to those who were most deprived of it.

A detailed examination of community policing at the present moment is beyond the scope of this essay. As recently as 1992 there was some question as to whether this promising idea would in fact meet its promise (Moore, 1992). Yet the idea was the centerpiece of President Clinton's 1992 campaign proposal to fund 100,000 municipal police (Marion, 1994, pp. 221–222; Treaster, 1992). This program was passed into legislation in 1994 and has been institutionalized in the Justice Department's Office of Community Oriented Policing Services (Bureau of Justice Assistance, 1994; COPS, 2000 [On-line]; Johnston, 1994). Patrick Murphy (1995, p. 748), commenting on the severe fragmentation of American policing, lists services and functions that are essential to modern, democratic policing: "Fifteen thousand local departments cannot work successfully without a comprehensive national support structure of planning, coordination, intelligence, statistics, research, experimentation, demonstrations, technical assistance, training, education, personnel exchanges and standards." The federal COPS program indeed provides these functions for those departments who wish to participate.

Alongside this effort has been the explosive interest on the other side of community policing—the problem-solving approach. Labeled "CompStat," after the widely publicized approach taken in New York City, its dramatic crime reduction results have caused the program to spread to so many municipal police departments so rapidly that it may indeed be the paradigm shift away from professional policing that reformers have called for (Walsh, 2000). Powerful new computer crime mapping technology, disseminated by the National Institute of Technology, has been instrumental in acceptance of the new model (Rich, 1999). As Larry Hoover points out, what is significant is not the adoption of new technology in itself but the fact that, unlike earlier adoptions of tactical apparatus (e.g., improved body armor), more recent inventions including geographic information systems, global positioning systems, DNA databases, broadband communication, and in-car laptop computers are "emergent technologies that have profound *strategy* implication [italics added]" (Hoover, 2000). Hoover warns that traditional role conceptions and organizational structures can subvert the move toward the new paradigm of policing and that what is occurring at the present time must be seen as only the first steps of institutional change. Nevertheless, the extent of change in the last five years is stunning. Detailed accounts of the application of the new model show an intense focus on reducing crime by gathering comprehensive information (intelligence) that allows commanders and officers to innovate specific solutions to particular crime problems. Responsibility has been devolved down to the precinct level where the officers, supervisors, and commanders can best assess local problems and solutions while the higher administration uses the CompStat data and organizational structure to ensure compliance. Despite intramural debates as to whether CompStat is community policing, whether "zero tolerance" policing subverts the community policing model, and whether the new model works as well as it could, the examples found in the relevant literature, taken as a whole, point to profound changes in the way in which police departments operate internally (organizationally) and externally in their relations to the community. Both trends are clearly in the democratic direction (Bratton & Knobler, 1998; Kelling & Coles, 1996; Skogan & Hartnett, 1997; Walker, 1999).

Explaining Contemporary Criminal Justice

Numerous authors have sought to explain the negative features of the criminal justice system in broad social and political terms. Some of the more promising approaches include American exceptionalism (Lipset, 1996), moral panics (Cohen, 1985; Goode & Ben-Yehuda, 1994; Jenkins, 1999), governing through crime (Caplow & Simon, 1999), and the "great disruption" concept (Fukuyama, 1999). The valuable insights of these analyses provide a foundation for the thesis of this article—that the ambiguous nature of criminal justice casts a shadow on the characterization of the American polity as a liberal democracy, which is discussed in the next section.

American exceptionalism, a familiar theme in political discourse first made popular by de Tocqueville, is, according to Seymour Martin Lipset (1996, p. 18), a double-edged concept that helps explain "the worst as well as the best" in American society. "The American Creed can be described in five terms: liberty, egalitarianism, individualism, populism, and laissez-faire" (p. 19). It includes a disdain for authority. This mix helps to explain such disparate facts as American rejection and Canadian adoption of the metric system in the 1970s or the fact that America leads the world in the proportion of people receiving college degrees. On the other hand, "European countries have devoted a much larger share of their GNP, of their public funds, to bettering the living conditions of their working classes and the less privileged generally" (p. 22). America is characterized by its "emphasis on adversarial relations among groups, and by intense, morally based conflicts about public policy, precisely because its people quarrel sharply about how to apply the basic principles of Americanism they purport to agree about" (p. 26). Lipset's inquiry into high drug use and crime rates and the nation's astronomical prison rate (p. 17) leads him to note the paradoxical feature of a crime-ridden society that is also rooted in law. The cause of this paradox lies in distinctive American patterns such as competition, achievement, expressive individualism, weak traditional-communal norms, and, in the case of alcohol and opiates, a long history of use and abuse that has not changed much (pp. 46–49, 269–271). This points us on the right track. Understanding America's wildly excessive response to crime, like crime itself, should be sought in our cultural belief system and in political values that are deeply rooted in social and economic reality. Also, analysis should not be forced into an ideological or Manichean mold, for American values are complex, paradoxical, double-edged, and moralistic (p. 268).

Given the centrality of the excessive "war on drugs" to any explanation of American criminal justice, the notion of moral panics offers a necessary but not a sufficient explanation of the autocratic features and ambiguous nature of American criminal justice (Cohen, 1985; Goode & Ben-Yehuda, 1994). The moral panic, then, is characterized by the feeling, held by a substantial number of the members of a given society, that evildoers pose a threat to the society and to the moral order as a consequence of their behavior and, therefore, "something should be done" about them and their behavior. A major focus of that "something" typically entails strengthening the social control apparatus of the society—tougher or renewed rules, more intense public hostility and condemnation, more laws, longer sentences, more police, more arrests, and more prison cells. If society has become morally lax, a revival of traditional values may be necessary; if innocent people are victimized by crime, a crackdown on offenders will do the trick; if the young and the morally weak, wavering, and questionable are dabbling (or might dabble) in evil, harmful deeds, they should be made aware of what they are doing and its consequences (Goode & Ben-Yehuda, 1994, pp. 31–32).

Moral panics can arise over unlikely or even nonexistent problems (e.g., satanic ritual abuse) or can be generated by a real cause of concern such as drug use. Moral panics tend to arise in troubled times. Characterized by a "heightened level of concern over the behavior of a certain group or category," "an increased level of hostility toward the group or category," "widespread agreement or consensus . . . that the threat is real," a disproportionate view of the threat so that people gripped by the panic substantially overestimate the threat, and the volatility of moral panics, they may lie fallow for a time and suddenly arise or they may become routinized or institutionalized (pp. 33–41). This perspective sees moral rules not only as deeply embedded customs but also as constructs subject to manipulation and creation by moral entrepreneurs and reflections of a society's power arrangements (pp. 76–86). Goode and Ben-Yehuda (pp. 205–223) convincingly propose that American drug policies of the 1980s reflected a moral panic and suggest a framework and methodology for better understanding the excessive response to drugs and crime. The depth of their explanation is limited by a tendency to dismiss moral panics as calculated disinformation campaigns designed to divert public attention from real problems (p. 32). In any event, moral panics continue to occur, most recently concerning "designer drugs" (Jenkins, 1999). The moral panic framework is a useful aid to understanding the paradox of autocratic criminal justice practices in a liberal democracy. It suggests that the police will not rise above the grip of the mass overreaction—that they will enforce the law against the object of the panic with sufficient conviction in its manifest "evils" so as to create a blind spot regarding the tangible benefits arising from their enforcement posture. Prominent examples in history include the enforcement of Prohibition laws in the 1920s and the role of the FBI and many police department "red squads" during the McCarthy era (Donner, 1990; Powers, 1987; Stolberg 1995, pp. 73–75).

A powerful concept developed by Simon (1997) and expanded and applied by Caplow and Simon (1999) is "governing through crime." The thesis is that increased prison rates and populations, and other criminal justice practices that set the United States off from other advanced democratic nations, especially the continued use of the death penalty, cannot entirely be explained by increases in crime. It is better explained by a crisis of governance. There has been a collapse in confidence in the problem-solving ability of government, a growing reliance on market solutions, and a post-industrial/postmodern shift away from traditional politics of bargaining over material goals toward value and identity politics that are not amenable to compromise. Into this consensus vacuum, the one set of ideas that most people can agree on (perhaps especially the middle-class respondents to Bellah's and Wolfe's surveys) are the minimal moral requirements of the criminal law. Being "tough on crime" has been a sure avenue to electoral success, but, more fundamentally, crime control has become a "source of legitimacy" for government. Governing through crime transcends the older conservative–liberal divide as social movements, including liberal ones, seek to utilize arrest, prosecution, and imprisonment as modes of effective action and as ways to legitimate their own goals. Thus, a criminal justice approach becomes important to Mothers Against Drunk Driving, mandatory arrest laws are sought by activists against domestic violence, the pro-choice movement lobbies to make it a federal crime to block abortion clinics, gay rights become legitimated through hate crime legislation, and so forth (Eilperin & Nakashima, 2000; Merida, 1994; Sherman, 1992; Weed, 1995). The tendency to legitimate government through crime control—when combined with fear of the "dangerous classes," racism, a war on drugs run amok, and a "reflexive" penal system that maintains a large pool of parolees who can be more swiftly and easily sent to prison than criminal defendants—makes the phenomenal increase in the prison population less perplexing. The "governing through crime" hypothesis, although it focuses only on the pathological side of criminal justice policy and practice, implicitly supports the thesis of this essay. It unfavorably contrasts America's criminal justice system to that of other democratic nations by examining criminal justice in its sociopolitical context, incorporating elements of American exceptionalism and moral panics, and concludes that a partial breakdown of "normal" politics has elevated criminal justice to a position of unwarranted prominence.

Francis Fukuyama (1999), a moderate-conservative social thinker, advances the "great disruption" thesis to explain trends in Western society from 1960 to 1990. This was a period marked by overall decline in social capital, as seen by increasing crime rates, declining family cohesion, increased individuality, decreased association and community, and decreased trust in others. This great disruption was also, and not coincidentally, linked to the transformation from an industrial to an information economy (pp. 3–60). Fukuyama discounts but does not entirely dismiss conventional explanations for the negative social indicators, including American exceptionalism, poverty and inequality, greater wealth, mistaken government policies (e.g., welfare), or a broad cultural shift (pp. 61–76). Instead, he sees more plausible causes in demography, the dramatic increase in the numbers of youths in the crime-prone age cohort from 1963 to 1980, modernization and urbanization, and social diversity. Each of these factors is associated with higher rates of crime. Fukuyama thinks that the crack epidemic from 1985 to the early 1990s merely prolonged the higher than normal crime rates. He further assumes that disruptions in family cohesion weakened the mode by which self-control is instilled in people. Rather than see linear cause and effect, he has suggested common causes for both crime and family breakdown (pp. 77–91): women's control over fertility ("the pill") and women entering a transformed workforce where "an information age economy substitutes mental for physical labor" (p. 106). This in turn weakened the biological and social bonds that tied men to families, exacerbated by the collapse of blue-collar manufacturing jobs that "hit men more sharply than it did women [and caused] their real incomes [to] fall at what was often an astonishing rate" (p. 108). Men untethered to the traditional family were more prone to commit crimes.

This analysis, coming after a decade of sustained economic growth that has drawn formerly unemployable young, poor, black men into the workforce (Nasar & Mitchell, 1999), suggests a socioeconomic approach to understanding the ambiguous criminal justice system that takes into account the deep anxieties that affect individuals. The era of imposed external suffering (the Depression, World War II) that called for individual sacrifice on behalf of the community (family, country) ended. It was replaced by an America whose political and economic hegemony was challenged (e.g., 1970's oil crisis). People were not threatened with death or injury but with assaults on that which gave life meaning: the value of one's work, one's status in relation to family members, fears about the future status of one's children, and so forth. In this framework, the rise of a conservative political movement is understandable. The New Deal liberal coalition cohered as long as its social and economic foundations were in place, but it collapsed in the face of a fundamental economic realignment (from an industrial to an information economy) and through a decline in social capital (Putnam, 2000). "The rightward shift reflected a new reality" (Berman, 1998).

This framework can be applied to the work of the Supreme Court. Moralistic legal observers like Cole (1999) see perversity in the Supreme Court's conservative criminal procedure agenda. But the views of conservative justices were shaped by ideas similar to those that influenced many voting Americans in 1968 who thought that "the Supreme Court's 'rights revolution' seemed more concerned with protecting, in the words of journalist Harold Myerson, 'the one against the many—not the many against the powerful' " (Berman, 1998, p. 1). Conservative rulings and the excesses of autocratic criminal justice policies like the "war on drugs" reflect this age of anxiety. The demonization of black criminals (the Willie Horton syndrome), for example, pandered to racism not at a time of Jim Crow reaction but at a period of genuine advances by African-Americans and a period of transitional thinking among many whites (Anderson, 1995; Jaynes & Williams, 1989; Kennedy, 1997). Anxieties about family and work are not subject to easy solution. Laid off white-collar workers who have found new careers are not likely to join trade unions and rail against those corporations that survived mergers. Middle- and working-class blacks who have a stake in society want police protection as much as they want an end to racial profiling (Tierney, 1999). Parents' normal concerns and fears for their children's future are not easily allayed in a world where most have no idea what the world of meaningful work will look like in 30 years.

Fukuyama's "great disruption" (1999) thus describes a social and economic milieu that complements Berman's political analysis (1998). It provides a plausible contextual account of the causes of a turn to the right in criminal justice policies. This conservative shift was generated by fears that caused "typical" middle-class citizens (i.e., Bellah's and Wolfe's respondents), and the people they elected to office, to be less concerned with autocratic elements of the criminal justice system. That system, after all, operates mostly to police "others." If the great disruption is coming to an end, does this presage a return to more moderate (even liberal) policies? The implications of this for the future of criminal justice and civil liberties are delineated in the final section.

The Quasi-Autocratic State

If a nation's criminal justice system reflects its sociopolitical character, America's ambiguous criminal justice system suggests, at best, a flawed liberal democracy. Can a constitutional democracy tolerate police practices that mark Third World dictatorships? To answer this, it may be instructive to consider the notion of the "quasi-autocratic state." A fully autocratic state is characterized by centralized despotic rule with no real political opposition, pervasive and ruthless police power, a judiciary powerless to rule against the state, central control over communications, and governmental arbitrariness and unaccountability. Some people are materially advantaged in every autocracy, although at a moral cost and with an understanding that personal security is precarious (Willhoite, 1988, pp. 155–244). In Nazi Germany, for example, even a full "Aryan" citizen could be treated in the most arbitrary and unjust manner by the courts with no recourse (Müller, 1991, pp. 138–139). Liberal democracies, in contrast, are characterized by citizen participation, the rule of law, an independent judiciary, and other factors specified above (S. Holmes, 1993, 1995). The existence of problems and discontents is not a basis for claiming that a liberal democracy is an autocratic state (as did 1960s antiwar protesters), as long as the polity adheres to basic liberal norms and retains the capacity to expose and correct problems.

A "quasi-totalitarian" or "quasi-tyrannous" or "quasi-autocratic" state is not meant to describe a flawed or emerging democracy but more specifically to characterize a regime that is genuinely democratic and liberal for one part of its population (even if its democracy is not perfect), while a distinct group of people live under a dictatorial or autocratic regime. Examples that fit this description are the United States under slavery, the American south under legalized Jim Crow segregation (c. 1890 to c. 1966), and South Africa's apartheid nationalist government (1948–1994). The level of tyranny for the subjected populations differs from one regime to another but these regimes share the odd characteristic that a part of the population genuinely enjoys civil rights that are denied to another part.

From 1776 to 1865 white citizens of the United States lived in the most advanced liberal republic and democracy of its day, however imperfect by modern standards. It was a genuine constitutional republic based on Enlightenment notions of liberty. It progressively eliminated religious qualifications for voting and office holding at the local level, reduced economic fetters such as indentured servitude and imprisonment for debt, extended the franchise to propertyless white males, and began to eliminate the limits on married women's property rights (Morison, 1965). Due process in the courts "was no hollow ideal. Trial judges took seriously their responsibility to do justice without fear or favor. . . . With certain exceptions, notably blacks, there is little evidence to suggest that state and local governments made blatant or systematic use of criminal law to suppress unpopular groups or individuals" (Bodenhamer, 1992, p. 64). Not perfect, but heading in the right direction.

When we turn to Americans of African descent at that time, free as well as slaves, the picture is radically different. The free black person in the most enviable position lived in fear of enslavement and was subjected to severe legal and political restrictions. The slave, even one whose physical condition of life might have been one of greater ease than particular whites, nevertheless knew that he lived under a regime that could at any moment exert totally arbitrary force against him backed up, ironically, by the same legal regime that extended so many rights to whites. This was so despite the fitful existence of some legal protections (Genovese, 1972, pp. 25–49). This dictatorial regime was, of course, confirmed by the Supreme Court in the *Dred Scott* case (Schwartz, 1993, pp. 105–125). The juxtaposition of free and slave societies in the same nation was exposed by the inability of abolitionists to freely circulate mail in southern states and by the monumental battle against the southern gag rule that for some time prevented even Congress from discussing the question of slavery (W. L. Miller, 1996). White Americans lived in a democracy; black Americans lived in a dictatorship (de Tocqueville, 1850/1969).

If America during slavery could be called "quasi-dictatorial," Jim Crow America might be given a softer label such as "quasi-autocratic." African-Americans were free, after all, and some social and economic progress did occur, especially for blacks not living in the south. Nevertheless, the Jim Crow regime was designed to replicate as many conditions of slavery as was possible. Blacks were forced into conditions of economic peonage, often by the penal contract labor system (Oshinsky, 1996). Political participation through voting, jury service, and office holding was virtually denied. Lynching and arbitrary criminal justice enforced this political, economic, and social repression (Finkelman, 1992; Woodward, 1966). In the same period, democratic political participation was the norm for working-class whites, labor organizations and left-wing political parties were active and able to struggle, and the foundation was laid for the New Deal social welfare state (Morison, 1965).

A similar picture can be drawn of the apartheid South Africa regime, in which "a person's political, civil, economic, and social rights are determined by the race or ethnic group to which he belongs," fixed by law (Dugard, 1978, p. 59). Although aimed at black Africans, it appears that the regime's ability to suppress white dissenters was quite severe and effective. The rule of law was more limited, and the risk of a slide into a totally autocratic state seemed more possible than in Jim Crow America (Dugard, 1978; Ellmann, 1992). Nevertheless, even in the face of a very repressive regime, political opposition was carried on and courts operated with a substantial level of impartiality (Fine & Hansson, 1990). The apartheid regime succumbed in part to external international pressures, but the fact that it ended in a political settlement and parliamentary vote rather than in a violent revolution is an indication that the regime was quasi-autocratic rather than fully dictatorial (Noble, 1993).

No label can adequately capture the complexity and ambiguity of contemporary criminal justice in America. In a quasi-autocratic state, the criminal justice system is mobilized to suppress a particular minority politically, economically, and even culturally. It is not difficult to find powerful examples in the Jim Crow era: lynching (Finkelman, 1992), convict lease systems that were "worse than slavery" (Oshinsky, 1996), lynch mob justice (Carter, 1979), torture in the administration of justice (*Brown v. Mississippi,* 1936). The abuses seen in criminal justice today do not rise to the level of brutality, or the deliberateness, or the clear motive of political suppression of that era. Yet it would be an intellectual and moral mistake to hold today's criminal justice system to past standards of civility. Does the existence of an ambiguous criminal justice system mark the United States as a quasi-autocratic state?

The Future: Toward a Less Ambiguous Criminal Justice System

This essay raises two hypotheses: first, that the criminal justice system is ambiguous—part autocratic, part democratic—and, second, that autocratic elements in the criminal justice system mark the American polity as a quasi-autocratic or quasi-authoritarian state. I am confident that the first proposition has been demonstrated. Those whose ideological lenses differ from mine may see criminal justice in a far more negative or far more positive light, but they do not discuss the other side of the equation (Cole, 1999; Constantine, 2000). The second hypothesis is more speculative.

As for the first hypothesis, it seems to me that the short-run optimism and long-run pessimism of 1980 (Zalman, 1980) need to be reversed. The powerful social, economic, and political dynamics that shape today's ambiguous criminal justice system are not likely to abate in the next 20 to 40 years. The brightest prospect for the near-term future is that the criminal justice system will move closer to democratic than to autocratic modes, but for several reasons it seems that the emergence of a fully democratic criminal justice system is unlikely.

There are several reasons for this pessimism. Fukuyama's tempered optimism (1999) at the passing of the "great disruption" applies primarily to the middle class. Caplow and Simon (1999, p. 88) gloomily concluded that, even if crime rates drop, the pressures that have generated governing through crime "will probably sustain a continued demand for strict crime control policies." A prime reason is that the deep fears that have generated the quasi-military response to drugs are likely to continue. In a captivating analysis, Michael Massing (1998) showed how middle-class suburban parents, ignorant and disdainful of urban ghetto life, captured the national drug policy office, turned off the spigot that provided effective treatment modes for inner-city hard drug users (which for a short time in the early 1970s helped to reduce crime rates), and instead channeled their anxieties about their children's life prospects into a fear of marijuana. The strong economy of the late 1990s has not lessened income inequality and thus is not likely to lessen the fears of middle-class parents for the prospects of their offspring, ensuring more drug panics and making a rational approach to drugs less likely (Jenkins, 1999). Fears of terrorism and narco-terrorism are also likely to fan the fears that maintain the autocratic side of criminal justice. This in turn will sustain the conditions that motivate police corruption, perjury, and brutality (Duke & Gross, 1993). However costly the stocking of the penal system with a large and easily arrested supply of minor drug offenders has been, internal criminal justice system dynamics are at work to keep on waging the war on drugs and expanding prisons. These dynamics include the political power of prison guard unions (Butterfield, 1995) and the allure of asset forfeiture. The latter gives police a powerful and licit rationale to keep illegal drug markets alive and to "tax" them, rather than take a problem-oriented approach to eliminating the trade (Blumenson & Nilsen, 1998; Zalman, 1996).

The nation's homicide and violence rates, even after their recent declines, are still far above the levels of Europe and Japan. Given the huge stock of weapons in this country, it is unlikely that positive effects of more strenuous gun control policies will reduce the level of lethal violence to that of other advanced nations. Fears of violence, then, abetted by a hyperactive press that reports every lurid crime, will continue to exert independent pressure to govern through crime. American exceptionalism, supported by strong lobbies and a deep pro-gun strain in public opinion, will operate to make it unlikely that gun control will advance very far beyond what has been accomplished by 2000. As of this writing there is a remarkable sudden concern that death penalty states may be executing innocent persons (Johnson, 2000). This appeal to the generous and humane side of the American character is likely to be short-lived and not translated into a deep questioning of governing through crime, as a self-absorbed populace soon returns to its more traditional concerns with material satiation or religious triumphalism or both.

The Supreme Court is not likely to reverse the general tenor of its counterrevolution in criminal procedure of the last three decades, even if a Democratic president were to nominate the next two or three justices. The racial divide, and the symbolic fears that it stirs up, add to the dynamic of governing through crime. Progress in the conditions of African-Americans, combined with continuous lags in equality, marks contemporary race relations (Jaynes & Williams, 1989). Close observations indicate that much racial hostility exists and may be intensified by immigration and by a globalized economy that will continue to put severe economic pressure on those at the bottom (LeDuff, 2000). In a cynical vein, perhaps the best that can be expected is that racial profiling will abate as police become sufficiently sophisticated to distinguish "safe" middle-class blacks and Latinos from "unsafe" poor people—white and colored alike.

This stream of negativism may be overdone, but, if enough of these guesses of the future are accurate, it means that the criminal justice system will not move rapidly toward a fully democratic mode. Although positive court and prison programs (e.g., drug courts) can likely be found among the negatives, a precise forecast of the direction of the entire criminal justice system would be foolish. Nevertheless, I believe it is more likely than not that the criminal justice system will have improved only marginally in 20 to 40 years in democratic directions; it will continue to operate in quasi-autocratic modes. It is worth recalling that the termination of team policing and a national drug policy that stressed treatment in the early 1970s coincided with a troubled economy and American malaise. For a decade from the mid-1970s to the mid-1980s the buzzword in police administration was "cutback management." Even if the current run of prosperity continues, it seems to generate a level of income inequality that is socially corrosive and that coincides with a measured decline in social capital that, in turn, undermines crime control efforts like community policing (Putnam, 2000).

A longer-term forecast (to the year 2100) is necessarily unstable because it is not based on existing and reasonably foreseeable realities. Extremely long-range forecasts tend to rely on utopian or apocalyptic visions of the future or to veer into science fiction. We are living through astonishing scientific and technological revolutions that are harnessing information (if a horse-and-buggy metaphor may be permitted). Perhaps the genetic and computer revolutions will ameliorate the human condition to such an extent that civil liberties and the civil society will continue to spread. On the other hand, with a world population likely to reach 9 billion by the year 2050, the chance of an ecological collapse is not pure fantasy (Leslie, 2000). Doomsday conditions would necessarily generate harsh and authoritarian modes of control.

The second hypothesis is concerned with the question of whether the ambiguous criminal justice system implies that the American polity can be described as quasi-autocratic, or, to put it more gently, quasi-authoritarian. This question cannot be definitively answered; its value lies in the asking. The democratic nature of American government depends on many values and processes that lie outside the criminal justice system. Nevertheless, persistent autocratic criminal justice practices, with their corrosive impact on minority communities (Tonry, 1995), cast a shadow on democratic pretensions. They undercut the principle of equity and pose threats to the civil liberties of all. It is fanciful to imagine America becoming a police state. But a quasi-autonomous criminal justice system, bent on its own vision of law and order, can be contained only with difficulty by a constitutional regime and can be poised to exercise its power autocratically if released from restraint. Indeed, something like this happened in the FBI during J. Edgar Hoover's long reign (Powers, 1987; Wise, 1976).

To answer the question, one must ask whether the abuses of American criminal justice outweigh its positive practices, whether the impact of criminal justice on African-Americans and Hispanics is malign or, on balance, beneficial, whether the current governmental approach to illicit drug use is balanced or whether the "war on drugs" is unwinnable and corrosive of American values (Duke & Gross, 1993), whether prison, probation, and parole populations that swallow up the 1 in 20 males under penal supervision enhance public safety or destroy political community. These are difficult questions that deserve sustained attention. Their answers are important in their own right as critical problems of the justice system today. More importantly, the answers to these questions tell us what kind of country we live in.

Author's Note

The author wishes to thank members of the Wayne State Justice Studies Working Group (Phil Abbott, Shel Alexander, Eric Cades, Jim Chalmers, Steve Patterson, Fred Pearson, Brad Roth, Ed Wise) and Leo Carroll, Diana Gordon, Jonathan Simon, William Walsh, Chris Zimmerman, and, of course, Greta Zalman, for their helpful comments and encouragement. I take full responsibility for any errors, for all interpretations, and for all incorrect predictions.

References

Anderson, D. C. (1995). *Crime and the politics of hysteria: How the Willie Horton story changed American justice.* New York, NY: Times Books.

Bandes, S. (1999). Patterns of injustice: Police brutality in the courts. *Buffalo Law Review, 47,* 1275–1341.

Bellah, R. N., Madsen, R., Sullivan, W. M., Swidler, A., & Tipton, S. M. (1985). *Habits of the heart: Individualism and commitment in American life.* New York, NY: Harper & Row.

Bellah, R., Madsen, R., Sullivan, W., Swidler, A., & Tipton, S. (1991). *The good society.* New York, NY: Alfred A. Knopf.

Belluck, P. (2000, May 29). Blighted areas are revived as crime rate falls in cities. *New York Times,* p. A1.

Berman, W. C. (1998). *America's right turn: From Nixon to Clinton* (2nd ed.). Baltimore, MD: Johns Hopkins University Press.

Blumenson, E., & Nilsen, E. (1998). Policing for profit: The drug war's hidden economic agenda. *University of Chicago Law Review, 65,* 35–114.

Bodenhamer, D. J. (1992). *Fair trial: Rights of the accused in American history.* New York, NY: Oxford University Press.

Bovard, J. (1995). *Lost rights: The destruction of American liberty.* New York, NY: St. Martin's Press.

Bratton, W., & Knobler, P. (1998). *Turnaround.* New York, NY: Random House.

Brown v. Mississippi. 297 U.S. 278 (1936).

Bureau of Justice Assistance. (1994, August). *Understanding community policing: A framework for action* (Bureau of Justice Assistance Monograph, NCJ 148457). Washington, DC: Author.

Butterfield, F. (1995, November 7). Political gains by prison guards. *New York Times,* p. A1.

Butterfield, F. (2000, March 4). Cities reduce crime and conflict without New York-style hardball. *New York Times,* p. A1.

Buzawa, E., & Buzawa, C. (Eds.). (1992). *Domestic violence: The changing criminal justice response.* Westport, CT: Auburn House.

Caplow, T., & Simon, J. (1999). Understanding prison policy and population trends. In M. Tonry & J. Petersilia (Eds.), *Crime and justice: A review of research: Vol. 26. Prisons* (pp. 63–120). Chicago, IL: University of Chicago Press.

Carter, D. T. (1979). *Scottsboro: A tragedy of the American south* (Rev. ed.). Baton Rouge, LA: Louisiana State University Press.

Cloud, M. (1994). The dirty little secret. *Emory Law Journal, 43,* 1311.

Cohen, S. (1985). *Visions of social control: Crime, punishment and classification.* Cambridge, England: Polity Press.

Cole, D. (1999). *No equal justice: Race and class in the American criminal justice system today.* New York, NY: The Free Press.

Conlin, M. (2000, June 12). Workers, surf at your own risk: More and more companies are monitoring their employees' abuse of the Internet [On-line]. *Business Week Online.* Available: http://www.businessweek.com/2000/00_24/b3685257.htm

Constantine, T. A. (2000). Victims: The forgotten ingredient. *Albany Law Review, 63*(3), 687–701.

Cooper, C. L., & Sheppard, S. R. (1995). *Mockery of justice: The true story of the Sheppard murder case.* Boston, MA: Northeastern University Press.

Cooper, M. (1997, August 14). Charges of brutality: The officer. Differing views of policeman accused of assaulting man in custody. *New York Times,* p. B3.

COPS. (2000, June 19). *Community policing resources* [On-line]. Available: www.usdoj.gov/cops/cp_resources/default.htm

Dahl, R. (1989). *Democracy and its critics.* New Haven, CT: Yale University Press.

de Tocqueville, A. (1969). *Democracy in America* (J. P. Mayer, Ed., G. Lawrence, Trans.). Garden City, NY: Anchor Books. (Original work published 1850)

Donner, F. (1990). *Protectors of privilege: Red squads and police repression in urban America.* Berkeley, CA: University of California Press.

Dorfman, D. N. (1999). Proving the lie: Litigating police credibility. *American Journal of Criminal Law, 26,* 455–503.

Dugard, J. (1978). *Human rights and the South African legal order.* Princeton, NJ: Princeton University Press.

Duke, S., & Gross, A. C. (1993). *America's longest war: Rethinking our tragic crusade against drugs.* New York, NY: Putnam.

Eberle, P., & Eberle, S. (1993). *The abuse of innocence: The McMartin preschool case.* Buffalo, NY: Prometheus Books.

Ehrenreich, B. (2000, March 5). Warning: This is a rights-free workplace. *New York Times Magazine,* p. 88.

Eilperin, J., & Nakashima, E. (2000, September 7). Clinton makes hate-crime bill a top priority. *Washington Post,* p. A5.

Ellmann, S. (1992). *In a time of trouble: Law and liberty in South Africa's state of emergency.* Oxford, England: Clarendon Press.

Etzioni, A. (1993). *The spirit of community: Rights, responsibilities and the communitarian agenda.* New York, NY: Crown Publishers.

Feld, B. (1997). Abolish the juvenile court: Youthfulness, criminal responsibility, and sentencing policy. *Journal of Criminal Law and Criminology, 88,* 68–136.

Fine, D., & Hansson, D. (1990). Community responses to police abuse of power: Coping with the kitskonstabels. In D. Hansson & D. Van Zyl Smit (Eds.), *Towards justice? Crime and state control in South Africa* (pp. 209–231). Cambridge, MA: Oxford University Press.

Finkelman, P. (Ed.). (1992). *Lynching, racial violence, and law.* New York, NY: Garland Publishing.

Fogelson, R. M. (1977). *Big-city police.* Cambridge, MA: Harvard University Press.

Friedman, L. M. (1985). *Total justice.* New York, NY: Russell Sage Foundation.

Friedman, L. M. (1990). *The republic of choice: Law, authority, and culture.* Cambridge, MA: Harvard University Press.

Friedman, L. M. (1999). *The horizontal society.* New Haven, CT: Yale University Press.

Fromkin, D. (1999). *The way of the world: From the dawn of civilizations to the eve of the twenty-first century.* New York, NY: Knopf.

Fukuyama, F. (1999). *The great disruption: Human nature and the reconstitution of social order.* New York, NY: The Free Press.

Genovese, E. D. (1972). *Roll, Jordan, roll: The world the slaves made.* New York, NY: Vintage Books.

Glendon, M. A. (1991). *Rights talk: The impoverishment of political discourse.* New York, NY: The Free Press.

Goldstein, H. (1979). Improving policing: A problem-oriented approach. *Crime & Delinquency, 25*(2), 236–258.

Goode, E., & Ben-Yehuda, N. (1994). *Moral panics: The social construction of deviance.* Oxford, England: Blackwell.

Gordon, D. (1990). *The justice juggernaut: Fighting street crime, controlling citizens.* New Brunswick, NJ: Rutgers University Press.

Harris, D. A. (1999). The stories, the statistics, and the law: Why "driving while black" matters. *Minnesota Law Review, 84,* 265–326.

Heilbroner, R. (1976). *Business civilization in decline.* New York, NY: Norton.

Herman, S. (1998). Slashing and burning prisoners' rights: Congress and the Supreme Court in dialogue. *Oregon Law Review, 77,* 1229–1303.

Hirsch, J. S. (2000). *Hurricane: The miraculous journey of Rubin Carter.* Boston, MA: Houghton Mifflin.

Holmes, M. (2000). Minority threat and police brutality: Determinants of civil rights criminal complaints in U.S. municipalities. *Criminology, 38*(2), 343–367.

Holmes, S. (1993). *The anatomy of antiliberalism.* Cambridge, MA: Harvard University Press.

Holmes, S. (1995). *Passions and constraints: On the theory of liberal democracy.* Chicago, IL: University of Chicago Press.

Hoover, L. (2000, May). *Technology and police strategy.* Paper presented at the annual meeting of the Academy of Criminal Justice Sciences, New Orleans, LA.

Human Rights Watch. (1998). *Shielded from justice: Police brutality and accountability in the United States.* New York, NY: Human Rights Watch.

Jaynes, G. D., & Williams, R. M., Jr. (1989). *A common destiny: Blacks and American society.* Washington, DC: National Academy Press.

Jenkins, P. (1999). *Synthetic panics: The symbolic politics of designer drugs.* New York, NY: New York University Press.

Johnson, D. (2000, February 1). Illinois, citing faulty verdicts, bars executions. *New York Times,* p. A1.

Johnston, D. (1994, September 14). Experts doubt effectiveness of crime bill. *New York Times,* p. A16.

Jones, T., Newburn, T., & Smith, D. J. (1996). Policing and the idea of democracy. *British Journal of Criminology, 36*(2), 182–198.

Kelling, G. L., & Coles, C. M. (1996). *Fixing broken windows: Restoring order and reducing crime in our communities.* New York, NY: Touchstone.

Kennedy, R. (1997). *Race, crime, and the law.* New York, NY: Pantheon Books.

Klockars, C. (1985). *The idea of police.* Newbury Park, CA: Sage.

Krauss, M. B., & Lazear, E. P. (1991). *Searching for alternatives: Drug control policy in the United States.* Stanford, CA: Hoover Institution Press.

LeDuff, C. (2000, June 16). At a slaughterhouse, some things never die: Who kills, who cuts, who bosses can depend on race. *New York Times,* p. A1.

Leslie, J. (2000, July). Running dry. *Harper's Magazine,* pp. 37–52.

Lipset, S. M. (1996). *American exceptionalism: A double-edged sword.* New York, NY: Norton.

MacKenzie, D. L., & Uchida, C. (Eds.). (1994). *Drugs and crime: Evaluating policy initiatives.* Thousand Oaks, CA: Sage.

Marion, N. (1994). *A history of federal crime control initiatives, 1960–1993.* Westport, CT: Praeger.

Massing, M. (1998). *The fix.* New York, NY: Simon & Schuster.

McCoy, A. W., & Block, A. A. (Eds.). (1992). *War on drugs: Studies in the failure of U.S. narcotics policy.* Boulder, CO: Westview Press.

McNeil v. Director, Patuxent Institution. 407 U.S. 245 (1972).

Menninger, K. (1969). *The crime of punishment.* New York, NY: Viking Press.

Merida, K. (1994, May 13). Abortion clinic bill approved: Legislation seeking to end harassment sent to White House. *Washington Post,* p. A1.

Miller, M. (1998). Note: Police brutality. *Yale Law & Policy Review, 17,* 149.

Miller, W. L. (1996). *Arguing about slavery: The great battle in the United States Congress.* New York, NY: Knopf.

Moore, M. (1992). Problem-solving and community policing. In M. Tonry & N. Morris (Eds.), *Modern policing* (pp. 99–158). Chicago, IL: University of Chicago Press.

Morison, S. E. (1965). *The Oxford history of the American people.* New York, NY: Oxford University Press.

Müller, I. (1991). *Hitler's justice: The courts in the Third Reich* (D. L. Schneider, Trans.). Cambridge, MA: Harvard University Press.

Munro, N. (2000, September 2). Privacy's price. *The National Journal, 32*(35), Technology Section.

Murphy, P. V. (1995). Violent crime control and law enforcement act of 1994: The impact of additional police. *University of Dayton Law Review, 20,* 745.

Nasar, S., & Mitchell, K. B. (1999, May 23). Booming job market draws young black men into fold. *New York Times,* sec. 1, p. 1.

Neely, L. (1998, November 3). Stability predicted with two new chiefs: Change. Police and fire department heads bring extensive experience. *Ventura County Star,* p. A1.

The new death penalty politics. (2000, June 7). *New York Times,* p. A30.

Noble, K. B. (1993, December 23). South African parliament adopts new constitution. *New York Times,* p. A3.

Oshinsky, D. M. (1996). *"Worse than slavery": Parchman Farm and the ordeal of Jim Crow justice.* New York, NY: The Free Press.

Pate, A., & Fridell, L. (1993). *Police use of force: Official reports, citizen complaints, and legal consequences, Volumes I and II.* Washington, DC: The Police Foundation.

Police division to train in conflict resolution. (1999, June 26). *Los Angeles Times,* p. B4.

Powers, R. G. (1987). *Secrecy and power: The life of J. Edgar Hoover.* New York, NY: The Free Press.

Putnam, R. (2000). *Bowling alone: The collapse and revival of American community.* New York, NY: Simon and Schuster.

Reiss, A. J., Jr. (1971). *The police and the public.* New Haven, CT: Yale University Press.

Rich, T. (1999, October). Mapping the path to problem solving. *National Institute of Justice Journal,* pp. 3–9.

Schichor, D., & Sechrest, D. (Eds.). (1996). *Three strikes and you're out: Vengeance as public policy.* Thousand Oaks, CA: Sage.

Schwartz, B. (1993). *A history of the Supreme Court.* New York, NY: Oxford University Press.

Sheck, B., Neufeld, P., & Dwyer, J. (2000). *Actual innocence.* New York, NY: Doubleday.

Sherman, L. (1992). *Policing domestic violence: Experiments and dilemmas.* New York, NY: The Free Press.

Silverman, E. (1999). *NYPD battles crime: Innovative strategies in policing.* Boston, MA: Northeastern University Press.

Simon, J. (1997). Governing through crime. In L. M. Friedman & G. Fisher (Eds.), *The crime conundrum: Essays on criminal justice* (pp. 171–189). Boulder, CO: Westview Press.

Skogan, W., & Hartnett, S. (1997). *Community policing, Chicago style.* New York, NY: Oxford University Press.

Skolnick, J. (1966). *Justice without trial.* New York, NY: John Wiley and Sons.

Sterngold, J. (2000, February 24). Investigation into police is broadened in Los Angeles. *New York Times,* p. A12.

Stolberg, M. M. (1995). *Fighting organized crime: Politics, justice and the legacy of Thomas E. Dewey.* Boston, MA: Northeastern University Press.

Sullivan, J. (2000, January 30). States and cities removing prisons from courts' grip. *New York Times,* sec. 1, p. 1.

Symposium. (1998). Why is crime declining. *Journal of Criminal Law and Criminology, 88*(4).

Tierney, J. (1999, February 18). The big city: Once, racism meant leaving Harlem alone. *New York Times,* p. B1.

Tonry, M. (1995). *Malign neglect: Race, crime and punishment in America.* New York, NY: Oxford University Press.

Treaster, J. (1992, October 22). The 1992 campaign: Issues—the drug problem. Candidates seek little change in antidrug efforts. *New York Times,* p. A22.

Turk, A. (1982). *Political criminality.* Beverly Hills, CA: Sage.

Walker, S. (1998a). *Popular justice: A history of American criminal justice* (2nd ed.). New York, NY: Oxford University Press.

Walker, S. (1998b). *The rights revolution: Rights and community in modern America.* New York, NY: Oxford University Press.

Walker, S. (1999). *The police in America* (3rd ed.). Boston, MA: McGraw-Hill.

Walsh, W. (2000, March). *Analysis of an emerging paradigm: The strategic management of police organization.* Paper presented at the annual meeting of the Academy of Criminal Justice Sciences, New Orleans, LA.

Wattenberg, B. J. (1985). *The good news is the bad news is wrong.* New York, NY: Touchstone.

Weed, F. (1995). *Certainty of justice: Reform in the crime victim movement.* Hawthorne, NY: Aldine de Gruyter.

Willhoite, F. H. (1988). *Power and governments: An introduction to politics.* Pacific Grove, CA: Brooks/Cole.

Wise, D. (1976). *The American police state.* New York, NY: Random House.

Wolfe, A. (1998). *One nation, after all.* New York, NY: Viking.

Woodward, C. V. (1966). *The strange career of Jim Crow* (2nd ed.). New York, NY: Oxford University Press.

Wootton, B. (1963). *Crime and the criminal law: Reflections of a magistrate and social scientist.* London, England: Stevens.

Worden, R. E. (1996). The causes of police brutality: Theory and evidence on police use of force. In W. A. Geller & H. Toch (Eds.), *Police violence: Understanding and controlling police abuse of force* (pp. 23–51). New Haven, CT: Yale University Press.

Zalman, M. (1980). The future of criminal justice administration and its impact upon civil liberties. *Journal of Criminal Justice, 8,* 275–286.

Zalman, M. (1996). Judges in their own case: A Lockean analysis of drug asset forfeiture. *Criminal Justice Review, 21*(2), 197–230.

Zimring, F. E., & Hawkins, G. (1992). *The search for rational drug control.* New York, NY: Cambridge University Press.

Chapter 37

Restoring Justice to the Community

A Realistic Goal?

Susan Sarnoff

The American criminal justice system has historically focused on offenders—punishing them, incapacitating them, rehabilitating them. The victims' rights movement raised issues that forced some consideration of the needs of the victimized, but even restitution programs fail to truly embrace restorative justice. But although a restorative system that considered the needs of victims, offenders, and the community as a whole might go deeper than current efforts to address the root causes of crime, Sarnoff argues that only a complete systemic overhaul could result in such a change.

The last half of the 20th century was the setting for extensive changes in the criminal justice system, many of which were precipitated by the victims' rights movement. Early victims' groups complained, quite accurately, that the criminal justice system had lost sight of victims, redefining and relating to them only as witnesses to "crimes against the state" (Schafer, 1977).

Since the 1960s, much has been done to improve the status of victims in the system, as well as to meet victims' financial and other tangible needs caused by crime (Karmen, 1996; Galaway and Hudson, 1981). Some observers even claim that such efforts are steps toward the development of a restorative justice system (Carey, 1995). Restorative justice is quite different from our present criminal justice system, however, despite isolated efforts to implement programs which reflect restorative justice elements (Zuni, 1992). Superimposing restorative justice components onto a system as adversarial and compartmentalized as our criminal justice system does not result in a restorative justice system. True implementation of restorative justice might require no less than a complete overhaul and reorientation of the justice system. In fact, the concept of a *criminal* justice system suggests the very issue to which victims originally objected: a focus on criminals to the exclusion of other parties affected by crime.

The adversarial nature of the criminal justice system (Dooley, 1995) and the separation of punishment and recompense into respective criminal and civil tort proceedings (Schafer, 1970) exemplify two of the major, longstanding impediments to transforming our *criminal* justice system to reflect a *restorative* justice orientation. A more recent third is the unwillingness of representatives of the victims' rights movement to have victims perceived as anything but completely innocent. This paper will explore the inherent difficulties in implementing a restorative justice model. It will review instances in which restorative justice has been reflected in the criminal justice system, opposition to the restorative justice model and the requisite attitudinal as well as programmatic changes that would have to occur if restorative justice were to become more than a term applied, often inappropriately, to a range of criminal justice innovations. Finally, it will address the fact that the community is the most-ignored potential participant in restorative justice.

Elements of the Restorative Model

While there is no single definition of restorative justice, and ideas about it differ depending upon whether religious, ethnic, or proscriptive models are used, the concept encompasses several principles. Kurki (1999) observes that these include that:

- crime consists of more than violation of criminal law and defiance of government authority;
- crime disrupts victims, communities, and offenders;
- the primary goals of restitution are the repair of harm and healing of victim and community;

- the victim, community, and offender should all participate in determining the outcome of crime—government should surrender its monopoly over the process;
- case dispositions are based on victim and community needs, not solely on offender needs, culpability, danger or criminal history;
- components reflect a holistic philosophy.

The model used by the Balanced and Restorative Justice Project at the University of Minnesota is "founded on the belief that justice is best served when the community, victim and youth[ful offender] receive balanced attention, and all gain tangible benefits" (Center for Restorative Justice and Peacemaking, 1999). This is an ideal balance, but also limits use of the program to offenders involved in the juvenile justice system.

Restorative justice prioritizes reimbursement to the victim and the community over other forms of punishment, and is generally reserved for nonviolent offenders (Carey, 1995). In some cases, offenders are sentenced to work on projects in local neighborhoods; while in others, court staff link offenders with drug treatment, health care, education and other social services, with community members rather than criminal justice professionals charged with developing sanctions (Kurki, 1999).

The most extensive examples of restorative justice within the borders of the United States are those of indigenous tribes. These systems of justice exist apart from the Anglo-American system, which long disdained and undermined them. They have recently regained attention and respect from outsiders, however.

Indigenous methods of conflict resolution include dispute resolution, peace making, talking circles, family or community gatherings, and meditation. These methods are immersed in tradition and religion, and incorporate use of ritual, cleansing, ceremonial sweats, fasting, and purification. It is no surprise that they have as their goal no less than the restoration of mental, spiritual, and emotional well-being and communal harmony. Verbal accountability by the offender and the offender's family, remorse, and face-to-face apology and forgiveness are important aspects of the process, which seeks to renew damaged personal and communal relationships so vital in small, tribal cultures. These processes are used even when there are no identified victims, as in problems between parents and children, individual misconduct, and excessive alcohol consumption. In such cases, anyone concerned with the offender's welfare may participate (Melton, undated).

It is interesting to note that these "primitive" forms of justice recognized centuries before more familiar criminal justice systems that crime, delinquency, and deviance are symptoms of larger problems which can be attributed to families and communities as well as individuals (Melton, undated). Similarly, these forms of justice require a deep understanding of how behavior affects others, a willingness to acknowledge that behavior results from choices that could have been made differently, and action to repair that harm and make changes necessary to avoid such behavior in the future (United States Department of Justice, undated).

Zuni (1992) notes that restorative justice requires an understanding of the difference between vertical and fluid modes of communication. It also requires the promotion of resolution and healing through trust, rather than the use of adversarial and conflict-oriented methods; incorporates representation by family members rather than by strangers; and focuses on victim and communal rather than individual rights (Zuni, 1992). In reality, however, programs operate on a continuum—some strongly reflect restorative justice priorities while others are closer to traditional criminal justice models (Umbreit and Greenwood, 2000a.)

Many religious groups have developed ministries based upon what they refer to as restorative justice principles. These differ markedly from the tribal model, particularly because they do not replace the criminal justice system, but are superimposed upon it, generally after sentencing has occurred. In fact, the Mennonite version of restorative justice, which is undoubtedly the most fully developed, "addresses injustices in the criminal justice system . . . with a conviction that healing . . . comes only with truth-telling . . . emphasiz[ing] accountability by offenders, safety and healing for victims, and hope, the possibility of change, for all people," reflecting more of a reiteration of the criminal justice system, and an emphasis on rehabilitating offenders by encouraging them to confess and repent than on balancing responsibility and restoring relationships among participants. Typical programs provide services to those affected by the criminal justice system, opportunities for community participation in healing, and encouragement to reduce abuses and enhance the effectiveness of the criminal justice system (Mennonite Central Committee, undated). But it is the very nature of the criminal justice system that runs counter to restorative justice principles; so enhancing it, rather than replacing or at least reforming it, is antithetical to restorative justice regardless of the worthy intentions of the program implementers. Even proponents of restorative justice acknowledge that many disparate programs exist that are referred to as restorative justice programs, with some doing so inaccurately (Evers, 1998), and others misapplying restorative justice principles to inappropriate victims, offenders, and crimes.

Restoring Victims or Restoring Justice?

In response to organized efforts by victim groups, many of the previously unmet needs of victims were satisfied by government during the last third of the 20th century (Karmen, 1996; Galaway and Hudson, 1981). Victims are now better informed about the criminal justice process, and have the right to be heard in regard to sentencing and parole. But these rights can be exercised in only the small proportion of cases in which crimes are reported and criminals are caught and convicted.

Victims have a greater chance of being financially "restored" after crime (or more accurately, being given access to resources that make such restoration possible). But, contrary to restorative justice principles, offenders are often circumvented in that process. Offenders have been assessed fines and fees to support victim compensation (United States Department of Justice, 1990), and restitution orders and collection have increased in some jurisdictions (Dooley, 1995)—but only a few, primarily corporate, criminals pay for the bulk of victim compensation (United States Department of Justice, 1990). Restitution also continues to go uncollected, when ordered, more often than not (Victims Assistance Legal Organization, 1996); due primarily to the reality that most criminals are poor (Geis, 1967), and imprisonment makes it nearly impossible for offenders to meet restitution obligations (Elias, 1993).

Historically, restitution was designed to benefit the offender rather than the victim (Edelhertz et al., 1975). Restitution was viewed as less severe, more humane, and rehabilitative toward the offender. It also had benefits for the criminal justice system and society, because it reduced the "need" for vengeance, and resulted in the offender's remaining integrated in society (Galaway, 1977). While restitution is still used for minor crimes or young first offenders in lieu of other punishment, the current victim focus uses restitution less for leniency than for efficiency or added punishment.

Restitution has many potential merits that dovetail with the goals of restorative justice: Garafalo (1975) observed that it can relieve prison overcrowding (when it is used traditionally, that is, in lieu of prison rather than in addition to it); it can place the burden of compensating the victim on the offender (Barnett and Hagel, 1977); and it can arguably offer treatment benefits to both the victim and the offender (Goldstein, 1974). These are theoretical advantages, however. The reality of restitution is far less perfect, because the majority of offenders are never caught or convicted; many offenders who are convicted are indigent, unable to work, or simply unwilling to make restitution payments; and poor collection methods fail to obtain most of the restitution that is ordered by the courts (Galaway and Hudson, 1981). For example, in 1994, restitution was ordered from only 32 percent of the offenders convicted of violent crimes (Maguire and Pastore, 1994), despite increasing restitution mandates. Sometimes, too, restitution is a condition of parole, but parole violation or subsequent crimes lead to reincarceration. And even when it is both ordered and received, restitution rarely arrives in time to actually help with the costs for which it was intended (Elias, 1983). In fact, victim compensation was created to respond to victims' immediate need for assistance whether or not they would eventually receive restitution. Finally, particularly as a result of mandates, restitution does not always involve negotiation between parties.

A study conducted jointly by the New York State Division of Criminal Justice Services and the New York State Crime Victims Board (1988) found that many victims elect not to request restitution because they have received or are eligible for victim compensation, which tends to be more timely, more certain, and better keyed to victims' needs. As the bulk of crimes are committed by criminals while they are young (Wilson, 1975), it is no surprise that so many are indigent, and only a handful of states make parents responsible for restitution ordered from minors. However, no studies have attempted to track criminals to determine how many would be able to pay restitution later if these costs followed them throughout their lives as child support, debts to the IRS, and student loans increasingly do.

This suggests that restitution may be appropriate in more cases than are currently realized, and that practice, rather than policy, is the cause of its underuse. Additional evidence that restitution can be used more frequently is that Vermont, which mandated reparations in all criminal offenses in its state constitution in 1791 (Dooley, 1995), was the last state to develop a victim compensation agency.

For restitution to reflect a restorative justice orientation, however, it must also involve discussion between the victim and offender and some level of agreement on the necessity for the payment, the appropriateness of the amount and payment schedule, and acceptance of satisfaction of the claim once it has been met. In fact, perhaps the greatest examples of restitution as a component of restorative justice are the vast but undocumented number of cases in which offenders privately and voluntarily make peace with their victims to dissuade the victims not to report their crimes. While the criminal justice system generally frowns on such arrangements unless the crimes are very minor and the criminals are juveniles, there has been no systematic study to determine the effectiveness of such private arrangements, or whether they ever produce better results than those formalized by the criminal justice system.

Victim-oriented legislation has also increased victims' rights to sue their offenders civilly. Yet again, offenders are often unknown, [or] victims often cannot afford the time and expense to bring tort actions against them (Wolfgang, 1965); and because perpetrators of crimes are typically poor (Geis, 1967), judgments against them are often uncollectible. Lawsuits against offenders are also antithetical to the restorative justice model because the process is so adversarial.

Opposition to Restorative Justice

For restitution to reflect restorative justice principles, it must enable victims and offenders to come together in a "meeting of the minds" (a face-to-face meeting, while usually encouraged, is not absolutely necessary to effect this). It requires more than restitution: It demands that negotiation of amounts and payment mechanisms address the suffering inflicted and the payer's assumption of responsibility for at least some of that suffering. As noted, this does not always occur, and even when it does, restitution rarely takes into consideration the effects of the crime on people other than the primary victim.

Presser and Lowenkamp (1999) observe that offenders are generally selected for participation in restorative justice programs according to the types of crimes they have committed and their willingness to participate, but that these "screening" mechanisms may be inadequate. They recommend developing mechanisms to determine whether the offender has the cognitive and expressive skills necessary to make the interaction a positive experience for the victim and the community. In this sense, willingness must be defined as willingness to express remorse and accept responsibility, rather than mere willingness to participate in a procedure that may result in a more lenient sentence.

Presser and Lowenkamp (1999) also note that victims should be screened to ensure that they truly wish to participate, rather than being pressured to do so or to express forgiveness to the offender that they do not really feel. It might be added that victims should be screened not only for these factors, but to ensure that their expectations are not unrealistic, which could lead to disappointment if those expectations are not met.

Community attitudes affect many aspects of restorative justice programs, including the types of offenders and victims referred to them, how they are funded, and the backgrounds and qualifications of their volunteers (Umbreit and Greenwood, 2000b). Bazemore (1998) observes that judges commonly act as gatekeepers to restorative justice projects, but that their methods vary and, in the absence of clear selection guidelines, judges may use restorative justice mechanisms inappropriately. In many cases, too, criminal justice personnel are so threatened by alternative methods that they resist them in all cases (Umbreit and Carey, undated). There is also an underlying dilemma regarding whether the purpose of the justice system is punishment or correction (Umbreit, 1998).

Victim-offender reconciliation and mediation programs, because they seek to "reconcile" not only financial accounts, but also emotional ones, are especially effective when the victim knows and still has some positive feelings for the offender, and is therefore reluctant to engage in an adversarial process, as well as when fault is shared. This is common in bar fights between friends, in adolescent-parent disputes and even in some marital altercations.

But victims are often discouraged by attorneys and victim advocates from taking any responsibility for the circumstances that placed them in harm's way. While such cautions may be necessary to win a case in our adversarial system, it does disservice to the healing of victims: It not only thwarts the restoration process, but limits victims' ability to learn from mistakes and change behaviors that place them in danger. This also impedes victims' healing, because it is harder to feel safe when attempts to assess danger are countered with assertions about the randomness of crime.

Karmen (1991) analyzed the "blameworthy" actions of victims and noted that they can be categorized in three distinct ways:

- *victim facilitation:* making the criminal's task easier by neglecting security precautions;
- *victim precipitation:* risk-taking behavior on the part of the victim;
- *victim provocation:* inciting acts that instigate violent responses.

Karmen's analysis is a modern distillation of the more extreme one of von Hentig (1948), who believed that all crime was "caused" by the interaction between offender and victim. Many victims clearly bear no blame for the crimes committed against them, and are ill-served by a system that abandons the constructs of guilt and innocence. But recognizing the victim's culpability, if any, is an important aspect of balancing justice. Some victims do bear some blame for crimes committed against them, such as those who provoke violence by making threats or using racial epithets. Other victims, while not provoking violence, take excessive risks or are careless about security measures. Still other victims are forced into unsafe positions unwittingly (as when expected security devices are absent or malfunction) or due to poverty. In such instances blame might be diffused, even if the victim is blameless. Restorative justice can address these distinctions and mete out responsibility accordingly, although it is rarely used in this manner.

When they are used at all, restorative justice methods are often used to handle cases defined by the criminal justice system as too "minor" to warrant more traditional treatment—although what is minor to the system may not seem minor to a victim (Karmen, 1996). And this points up another potential pitfall in implementing restorative justice: that it can be misused for inappropriate cases or political purposes.

Perhaps the most useful, but also most controversial, application of restorative justice is with people in ongoing relationships. (This suggests why it is common to tribal, intentional, and other small communities, in which virtually all relationships are ongoing.) Restorative justice is in many ways well-suited to these cases, because it assumes that many past behaviors led up to the incident in question as well as participants' feelings about the incident, that this totality of behaviors affected others in the community as well as the victim and offender, and that settlement must look to future prevention as well as to the incident in question. Victim groups have been reticent to acknowledge that mutual patterns of behavior are ever a factor in violence, particularly domestic violence. And there are clearly cases in which this approach would be wrong. In addition, modern societies are less concerned than are traditional ones with repairing troubled relationships and enabling participants to interact peacefully if not lovingly.

Mediation can also reflect power differentials among parties. People with more negotiating skill—or with less to lose—may always have the advantage in mediation. While some experts claim that mediation is "dialogue driven," rather than "settlement driven" (Umbreit, 1998), this distinction is more dependent on the program and the orientation and skill of the mediator (Umbreit and Greenwood, 2000b).

Substantive and procedural due process issues, such as avoiding coercion and achieving fundamental fairness, so that efforts and results are acceptable to all parties, participation is voluntary, and all parties understand the implications of their participation, are vital if restorative justice is to be effective (National Institute of Justice, 1998). As noted, restorative justice may be inappropriate for many, and perhaps most such cases, especially if serious violence is likely to recur. However, in cases of minor or mutual violence, and in cases in which an ongoing relationship is desired by both parties and would not pose significant danger, it might offer the best hope. This seeming paradox reiterates the need for further research and screening to determine the factors which make mediation and reconciliation successful. Research does demonstrate that restorative justice programs tend to be isolated from other facets of the criminal justice system, which has a negative impact on program operations (Umbreit and Greenwood, 2000b), and that program staff are not always trained to understand and mediate cultural differences that can contribute to crime or hamper the mediation process, such as misread body language perceived as disrespect (Umbreit and Coates, 2000).

These issues raise two concerns about the types of cases appropriate to restorative justice modalities. On the one hand, it is clear that restorative justice is not appropriate for all offenders, victims, or types of crimes. Power differentials among intimates can challenge the bases for mediation (Presser and Lowenkamp, 1999). On the other hand, the type of crime maybe less significant than the willingness of participants to negotiate and the motivation of participants to reconcile their differences interpersonally.

Potential Applications of Restorative Justice

What might benefit victims most, while essentially being what most victims (although not necessarily the most vocal victims) want, is a less adversarial criminal justice process. This would be especially helpful in cases where both participants bear some blame for the altercation or when the participants have an ongoing relationship. However, in all criminal cases the adversarial system discourages offenders from admitting guilt or showing remorse.

Witnessing the offender's guilt and remorse is healing to victims, and helps them forgive the offender and put closure on the crime. Restitution has the best chance of being awarded, and paid, when offenders admit guilt and show remorse. Making the criminal justice system less adversarial, and linking it to restitution, could lead to a re-melding of civil and criminal procedures, so victims would not have to go to court a second time to obtain civil damages. However, for this to occur, hard choices would have to be made: Should the strict procedural protections of criminal litigation, the looser requirements of civil procedures, or some combination of the two be used to determine criminal guilt on the one hand and civil fault on the other? Or should a universal benefit, such as victim compensation or even national health care, replace the right and need for victims to sue civilly?

Victims should not be denied the right to obtain damages, but there may be other ways to satisfy victims' need for justice. Our system translates damages into dollars, but a different system might translate "pain and suffering" into healing or forgiveness. (Note that this does not incorporate third-party negligence, which would have to be addressed in a separate forum in any case.)

The criminal justice system has defined crime in terms of offenders' acts, but to victims, other characteristics or circumstances of crimes, such as the relationship of the victim to the offender or the violence of the act, are often more significant. The criminal justice system defines crimes as assaults, sex crimes, and homicides, for example, but these distinctions say little about the victimizations they represent. Was the assault an unprovoked shooting that left the victim paralyzed, for instance, or a punch in the nose that may have been provoked by ethnic slurs or drunken advances?

Forgiveness may be difficult for victims, but it results in better resolution and healing than does revenge (Henderson, 1985). Furthermore, harsh punishments give more power to the government, which is not generally the "friend of victims" it purports to be (Brants and Koh, 1986). One way to encourage forgiveness, or at least reconciliation, is to recognize how both victims and offenders are victims of circumstances that promote injustice, and that both share an interest in preserving human rights (Elias, 1993).

Reimbursement itself can serve as a means of reconciling victims, particularly if the crime was property-based or resulted in only minor injury. Reimbursement demonstrates offenders' willingness to make their victims whole again, which can improve offenders' self-image as well as victims' image of offenders. Of course, failure to comply with a restitution order can result in the opposite reactions.

Changes Necessary to Implement Restorative Justice

Restitution could be improved if methods of apprehending and convicting criminals, performing and paying for prison labor, determining indigence, and collecting restitution from the non-indigent were improved. One factor that may facilitate this is the increased use of telecommunications in work situations. In theory, some offenders should be able to bring their work to prison via telecommunication, lessening the need for corrections departments to find jobs for all inmates and enabling some workers to earn more than prison wages. This has yet to be tested, although some prisons currently provide telecommunication work for their prisoners. These include the South Ventura California Youth Facility, which operates TWA's reservation operation. But this very system exemplifies the problems as well as the advantages of prison labor—the program was set up to counter a TWA strike (Parenti, 1995).

Requiring restitution to be paid while the offender is in prison is fraught with further problems. A substantial raise in prison wages would be necessary in any system requiring restitution to be paid by incarcerated offenders. In the United States, businesses have opposed this as unfair competition, and labor unions view it as potentially reducing jobs (Jacob, 1977). Therefore, prison labor has been seriously curtailed since the Great Depression.

Alternative sentencing, sometimes called community service or service restitution, is one alternative to traditional criminal justice practices that incorporates elements of restorative justice (Eglash, 1977). One of the benefits of alternative sentencing is that it costs approximately one-tenth of the cost of incarceration (Nassau County Community Services Agency, 1989). Restitution availability might be improved if more criminals were permitted to serve alternative sentences. DiMascio (1995) identified escalating punishments, including probation, intensive probation, community service, day reporting, house arrest, and electronic monitoring and halfway houses, as methods used to punish criminals without incarceration. While these may not be appropriate for violent criminals or nonviolent recidivist criminals, they increase the possibility that some offenders can remain employed at their regular jobs, making it easier for them to pay restitution.

Vermont streamlined its restitution system in 1994 by ordering that restitution that compensates victims already reimbursed by that state's victim compensation program be automatically forwarded to the state program. And California regularly publishes a "Restitution Review" newsletter that provides information on restitution and commends those judges who have ordered the most substantial fines (Crime Victims Compensation Quarterly, 1994).

During the debate on how to improve the collection of cash restitution, some innovators have tried more unusual methods. A judge in Memphis allows victims of property crimes to go to the home of the offender, under guard, to select their choice of the offender's possessions. In one such case, a victim found satisfaction in destroying a photograph of the offender's girlfriend.

A great deal of attention has been paid to restitution and other forms of victim reimbursement, not because they are the only forms of restorative justice, but because they are the most extensive, long-standing, and well-developed. As noted, mediation and reconciliation programs are more controversial because they apply to so few cases and because some individuals find them ideologically repugnant.

Restoring the Community

So far this discussion has focused on the elements of restorative justice that have currently been implemented, even if some are used in only certain locations or for discrete types of crimes or criminals. When the community component of restorative justice is addressed at all, it is most often in using community *members* in roles as mediators, or in community *service* as offender punishment. Few programs reflect recognition of the community as *victim* in any meaningful way. Perhaps this is inevitable, given that victims and offenders have constituencies and advocates, but few if any communities have advocates that enable them to be perceived as victims. This is unlike Eastern European countries, which have traditionally measured the magnitude of crimes by the number of people they affect, and have used this as the primary determinant of harm and punishment (Separaovic, 1985), reflecting a unique recognition of community rights.

Restitution, again, has been found to significantly reduce recidivism among juvenile offenders (United States Department of Justice, 1992), suggesting that its early and consistent use could contribute to crime reduction. Crime prevention is one of the ways that restorative justice can restore communities as a whole. Another form of crime prevention is retraining of criminals who have used crime as their primary means of income. While this is conceptually sound, it is not clear that it is effective in practice. Typical retraining programs train criminals for hard or minimum wage labor, which may not have the desired effect of inducing offenders to turn away from crime, since many criminals commit crimes not because there is no legitimate employment available to them but because the employment that is available to them is harder or less lucrative than criminal activity.

Sentencing circles are a form of restorative justice that rely on community members to establish sentences and see that they are carried out. Yet "community" in this sense is a source of service providers, and limited to those members willing to donate their free time to the process. This may leave out a large number of community members, and more significant, may result in a group that is far from a cross section of the community. (Paying community members as jurors are paid might mitigate the latter concern.)

Sentencing circles often bear responsibility for mentoring offenders to help them carry out their sentences, which may include restitution, community service, letters of apology, drug treatment, or job training (Simon, 1999). Peacemaking circles go to the heart of restorative justice, as they help victims make sense of the offense, help offenders understand the harm done, and help all involved to understand what led to the event, how it might be made right, and how offenders can regain the trust of the community after successful completion of their "sentence" (Pranis, 1997).

A very practical and effective use of community restorative justice is the creation of work crews made up of petty criminals who vandalize property or cover it with graffiti. While this is one of the more common forms of community restorative justice, it also reflects the unusual case in which the community is the actual, primary victim.

It is more unusual for the community to recover damages in cases where there are traditional victims. An interesting example of this is an Iowa case in which the judge granted 25 percent of a $4.2 million civil suit settlement to the victims, and the remainder to the Iowa State Reparations Fund (*Newsday,* 1992). The couple sued for less than $1 million, but the jury was so outraged by the crime (the couple was one of many videotaped through the hotel's mirror) that it more than quadrupled the requested award.

None of these approaches go far enough, however. Consider drunken brawls after professional sports events. While the responsibility of offenders should not be minimized, society's obsession with sports and tolerance of public drunkenness clearly affect such activities. If the community is to assume the role of victim at times, it must also accept the role of offender at others. Similarly, many crimes affect perceptions about genders, age cohorts, racial and ethnic groups, and so forth. Offenders, and in some cases even victims, need to be held accountable for ways that their behavior affects perceptions of groups to which they belong, and atone to that community.

Communities suffer in many ways from crime—not only from vandalism, but from notoriety, drops in property values, citizen fear, and loss of trust and community. Restorative justice could help in many such cases if, during reconciliation, mediation, or other meetings of victims, offenders, and other affected parties, damages to the community (including damages to infrastructure, values, and perceptions) were assessed and means of restoring the community, or undoing the damage to the degree possible, were determined. In fairness, community responsibility for crime should also be considered.

Conclusions

Full restorative justice is incompatible with our present criminal justice system. Although some elements of restorative justice are in use in isolated areas and cases, this use is not only extremely limited in scope, but is focused on victims, and to a lesser degree on offenders. The community as a whole has not received attention from those implementing restorative justice components. While there could be many benefits to extending such implementation, it would require a major overhaul of our criminal justice system and diversion of attention from victims and offenders alone to the broader causes and effects of crime. Yet this is the only way that true restorative justice can be achieved.

References

Barnett, R., and J. Hagel. (1977). "Assessing the Criminal." In Barnett, R., and J. Hagel, eds., *Assessing the Criminal: Restitution, Retribution and the Criminal Process.* Cambridge, MA: Ballinger, 1–31.

Bazemore, G. (1998). "Crime Victims and Restorative Justice in Juvenile Courts: Judges as Obstacle or Leader?" *Western Criminology Review 1* (1), http://wcr.sonoma.edu/v1n1/bazemore.html.

Brants, C., and E. Koh. (1986). "Penal Sanctions as a Feminist Strategy: Contradiction in Terms." *International Journal of the Sociology of Law,* 14, 269–86.

Carey, M. (1995). "It's Time to Amend Our Community Correction Acts to Restorative Justice Acts." Unpublished.

Center for Restorative Justice and Peacemaking. (October 27, 1999). *The Balanced and Restorative Justice Project.* St. Paul, MN: University of Minnesota, Center for Restorative Justice and Peacemaking, http://ssw.che.umn.edu/rjp/BARJ.htm.

Crime Victims Compensation Quarterly. (1994). "Vermont Authorizes Restitution to Compensation," *Crime Victims Compensation Quarterly,* 5.

DiMascio, W. (1995). *Seeking Justice.* New York: The Edna McConnell Clark Foundation.

Dooley, M. (1995). "Restorative Justice in Vermont: A Work in Progress." In *Topics in Community Corrections 1995.* Washington, DC: U.S. Department of Justice.

Edelherz, H. et al. (1975). *Restitutive Justice: A General Survey and Analysis.* Seattle: Battelle Human Affairs Research Centers.

Eglash, A. (1977). "Beyond Restitution—Creative Restitution." In Hudson, J., and B. Galaway, eds., *Restitution in Criminal Justice.* Lexington, MA: Lexington Books, 91–99.

Elias, R. (1993). *Victims Still.* Newbury Park, CA: Sage Publications.

—— (1983). *Victims of the System: Crime Victims and Compensation in American Politics and Criminal Justice.* New Brunswick, NJ: Transaction Books.

Evers, T. (September 1998). "A Healing Approach to Crime," *The Progressive,* 30–33.

Galaway, B. (1977). "Toward the Rational Development of Restitution." In Hudson, J., and B. Galaway, eds., *Restitution in Criminal Justice.* Lexington, MA: D. C. Heath.

—— and J. Hudson, eds. (1981). *Perspectives on Crime Victims.* St. Louis, MO: C. V. Mosby Co.

Galper, J. (1975). *The Politics of Social Services.* Englewood Cliffs, NJ: Prentice-Hall.

Garofalo, R. (1975). "Enforced Reparation as a Substitute for Imprisonment." In Hudson, J., and B. Galaway, eds., *Considering the Victim: Readings in Restitution and Victim Compensation.* Springfield, IL: Charles C. Thomas, Publisher, 43–53.

Geis, G. (1967). "State Compensation to Victims of Violent Crime." President's Commission on Law Enforcement and Administration of Justice. *Task Force Report: Crime and Its Impact—An Assessment.* Washington, DC: U.S. Department of Justice.

Goldstein, N. (1974). "Reparation by the Offender to the Victim as a Method of Rehabilitation for Both." In Drapkin, I. and E. Viano, eds., *Victimology—A New Focus.* Lexington, MA: Lexington Books, 193–206.

Henderson, L. (1985). "The Wrongs of Victims' Rights." *Stanford Law Review* 37, 937–1021.

Jacob, B. (1977). "The Concept of Restitution: An Historical Overview." In Hudson, J., and B. Galaway, eds., *Restitution in Criminal Justice.* Lexington, MA: Lexington Books, 45–62.

Karmen, A. (1991). "The Controversy over Shared Responsibility." In Sank, D., and D. Kaplan, eds., *To Be a Victim.* New York: Plenum Press, 395–408.

——. (1996). *Crime Victims,* Third Edition. Belmont, CA: Wadsworth.

Kurki, L. (September 1999). *Incorporating Restorative and Community Justice Into American Sentencing and Corrections.* Washington, DC: U.S. Dept. of Justice.

Maguire, K., and A. Pastore. (1994). *Sourcebook of Criminal Justice Statistics 1994.* Albany, NY: Hindelang Criminal Justice Research Center.

Melton, A. P. (Undated). *Indigenous Justice Systems and Tribal Society.* Washington, DC: U.S. Department of Justice.

Mennonite Central Committee. (Undated). *Restorative Justice.* Akron, PA: Mennonite Central Committee.

Nassau County Community Services Agency. (1989). *Community Services: Who, What, When, Where, Why & How.* Mineola, NY: NCCSA.

National Institute of Justice. (March 1998). "An Interview with Former Visiting Fellow of NIJ, Thomas Quinn," *National Institute of Justice Journal.*

Newsday. (June 27, 1992). "Jury Awards $1 Million to Couple Exposed by Hotel's Mirror," *Newsday,* 9.

New York State Division of Criminal Justice Services and New York State Crime Victims Board. (June 1988). *Restitution in New York State: Recommendations for Improvement.* New York: New York State Division of Criminal Justice Services and New York State Crime Victims Board.

Parenti, C. (November 3, 1995). "Inside Jobs." *New Statesman and Society,* 20.

Pranis, K. (December 1997). "Restorative Justice: Peacemaking Circles," *Corrections Today,* 72.

Presser, L. and C. T. Lowenkamp. (1999). "Restorative Justice and Offender Screening," *Journal of Criminal Justice,* 27, 4, 333–343.

Schafer, S. (1977). *Victimology: The Victim and His Criminal.* Reston, VA: Prentice-Hall.

—— (1970). *Compensation and Restitution to Victims of Crime.* Montclair, NJ: Patterson Smith.

Separovic, Z. (1985). *Victimology.* Zagreb, Yugoslavia: Pravni Fakultet.

Simon, S. (May 13, 1999). "Throwing Offenders a Curve," *Los Angeles Times,* A1.

Stephens, G. (November 1999). "Preventing Crime: The Promising Road Ahead," *Futurist,* 29–34.

Umbreit, M. (1998). "Restorative Justice Through Victim-Offender Mediation: A Multi-Site Assessment," *Western Criminology Review* 1 (1), http://wcr.sonoma.edu/v1nl/umbreit.html.

—— (Undated). *Restorative Justice: Implications for Organizational Change,* http://www.ojp.usdoj.gov/nij/rest-just/ch3/implications.html.

—— and R. B. Coates. (April 2000). *Multicultural Implications of Restorative Justice: Potential Pitfalls and Dangers.* St. Paul, MN: University of Minnesota, Center for Restorative Justice and Peacemaking.

Umbreit, M. and Jean Greenwood. (April 2000a). *Guidelines for Victim-Sensitive Victim-Offender Mediation: Restorative Justice through Dialogue.* St. Paul, MN: University of Minnesota, Center for Restorative Justice and Peacemaking.

—— (April 2000b). *National Survey of Victim-Offender Mediation Programs in the United States.* St. Paul, MN: University of Minnesota, Center for Restorative Justice and Peacemaking.

United States Department of Justice. (Undated). *Implementing the Balanced and Restorative Justice Model.* Washington, DC: United States Department of Justice.

—— (April 1990). *Office for Victims of Crime Report to Congress.* Washington, DC: United States Department of Justice.

—— (September 1992). *Restitution and Juvenile Recidivists.* Washington, DC: United States Department of Justice.

Victims' Assistance Legal Organization, Inc. (March 1996). *Restitution: Policies and Procedures for a Coordinated Team Model* (Draft). McLean, VA: VALOR.

Von Hentig, H. (1948). *The Criminal and His Victim.* New Haven, CT: Yale University Press.

Wilson, J. (1975). *Thinking About Crime.* New York: Basic Books.

Wolfgang, M. (1965). "Victim Compensation in Crimes of Personal Violence." *Minnesota Law Review* 50.

Zuni, C. (1992). "Justice Based on Indigenous Concepts," paper presented at the Indigenous Justice Conference.

Susan Sarnoff, "Restoring Justice to the Community: A Realistic Goal?" Reprinted from *Federal Probation* 65 (1): 33–39. Published by The Administrative Offices of the United States Courts. ✦

Chapter 38

Wrongful Conviction and Public Policy

The American Society of Criminology 2001 Presidential Address

C. Ronald Huff

Convicting the innocent is among the most serious miscarriages of justice, and one that any society that purports to be just cannot tolerate. The advent of DNA technology brought wrongful conviction into the public eye, and Huff argues that the American system doesn't do enough to protect the innocent. In his survey of law enforcement and criminal justice officials, he found that while perceptions of the incidence of wrongful conviction are low, the huge number of convictions in the United States means that even at the lowest levels, thousands may be affected each year. Huff looks at the causes and effects of wrongful convictions, and offers an array of policy recommendations aimed at enhancing the rights of innocent defendants and establishing a truly just system—including ending the death penalty.

The topic of wrongful conviction has recently attracted much more attention due to two major factors: (1) the highly-publicized post-conviction DNA exonerations of individuals who served long prison sentences and (2) the moratorium imposed by the governor of Illinois on the use of the death penalty, sparking debates in a number of other state legislatures and executive offices. In Illinois, the governor was reacting to a period of time in which more death row inmates had been exonerated than had been executed. He was concerned about the clear-cut evidence that the criminal justice system had made a number of errors and, therefore, the possibility that innocent persons might be executed. Indeed, Radelet, Bedau, and Putnam (1992) have argued that at least 23 innocent persons have already been executed.

What Is Wrongful Conviction?

There are a number of ways in which "wrongful conviction" might be defined. In an earlier publication, we said the following: "Convicted innocents . . . are people who have been arrested on criminal charges . . . who have either pleaded guilty to the charge or have been tried and found guilty; and who, notwithstanding plea or verdict, are in fact innocent" (Huff, Rattner, and Sagarin, 1996:10). Others have used broader definitions, including cases in which the charges were dropped without retrial or convictions were overturned in court and the defendant found not guilty.

Instead, we have focused on cases in which innocence was established beyond a reasonable doubt. We have excluded many cases in which the conviction was overturned and either the charges were dropped or the defendant was found not guilty, because neither of those outcomes by itself establishes innocence beyond a reasonable doubt. A "not guilty" finding does not necessarily mean that the person was actually innocent.

How Often Does Wrongful Conviction Occur?

It is certainly not necessary to artificially inflate the magnitude of the problem by including in our analysis cases that are not clear-cut. When we began this research in the 1980s, we were unaware of any attempt to estimate the magnitude of this problem. Therefore, we conducted a survey, utilizing an intentionally conservative sample so as not to be accused of inflating the magnitude of this problem. The sample had two components: an Ohio sample dominated by prosecutors, judges, and law enforcement officials, and a national sample of attorneys general. The total sample size was 353 and we received 229 responses, a 65% response rate (Huff et al., 1996:55).

That survey measured respondents' perceptions of the accuracy of the system. It is not possible to know with certainty what proportion of convictions are erroneous, since no systematic data are collected and since we know it is likely that many errors go undiscovered. In that sense, the challenge of estimating the actual rate of wrongful conviction makes the estimation of actual crime look easy, since systematic victimization surveys have facilitated that task.

We asked our conservative sample to estimate what proportion of all felony convictions resulted in wrongful convictions. The responses ranged from 0% to 5%. Ten of our respondents actually said that wrongful conviction never happens. Of those who provided an estimate, 72% said that wrongful conviction occurs in less than 1% of all felony cases. To be conservative, we took the midpoint of the category of response they selected ("less than 1%") and decided to see what it would really mean in terms of the magnitude of this problem if the criminal justice system is, indeed, 99.5% accurate and errs in only one-half of 1% of all felony cases. Updating our previous analysis, based on Uniform Crime Reports data for 2000 (U.S. Department of Justice, Federal Bureau of Investigation, 2001), there were in that year about 2.2 million arrests *for index crimes alone.* We know that about 70% of those arrested for felonies are ultimately convicted of either a felony or a misdemeanor (U.S. Department of Justice, Bureau of Justice Statistics, 2001)—about 1.5 million in the year 2000. Therefore, if we assume that the system is 99.5% accurate, that would mean that about 7,500 persons arrested for index crimes were wrongfully convicted in the year 2000. Thus, it is clear that our nation has such a large base rate of arrests for serious crimes that only a small error rate will produce thousands of wrongful convictions each year.

Also, Scheck, Neufeld, and Dwyer (2000) recently reported that in DNA testing conducted in 18,000 criminal cases, more than 25% of *prime suspects* were excluded *prior to trial.* Because the great majority of criminal cases do not produce biological material to be tested, one can only speculate as to the error rate in those cases. They also noted that in the past 25 years of the U.S. experience with the death penalty, 553 individuals were executed while 80 were released and had their sentences vacated, suggesting a possible one in seven error rate in the *most* carefully scrutinized criminal cases (Scheck et al., 2000). Finally, Liebman et al.'s (2000) massive study of capital cases from 1973–1995 suggested the possibility of an even higher error rate in capital cases. These findings raise serious questions about the accuracy of the system and, in light of that concern, the justification for retaining the death penalty.

Why Is Wrongful Conviction an Important Problem?

There are a number of reasons that this is an important problem, but the two most compelling are the implications for justice and the implications for public safety. In 1747, Voltaire wrote, "It is better to risk saving a guilty person than to condemn an innocent one." Just two decades later, Sir William Blackstone increased that ratio with his famous admonition, "It is better that ten guilty persons escape than one innocent suffer" (Blackstone, 1765–1769). Most people can readily understand that convicting an innocent person is unjust, even though they might express more concern with the guilty who go free. A society that views itself as just and fair simply cannot afford to ignore this problem.

If the cause of justice itself is not a sufficient motivation for some people, they might be more responsive to the threat posed to public safety. There is an inverse relationship between Type I and Type II errors, so every time we convict an innocent person, the real offender is likely to remain free to victimize others. How many murders, rapes, robberies, and other crimes are committed each year by criminals while innocent persons are serving unjust prison sentences? Placing equal emphasis on public safety is, in my judgment, one of the best ways to build a broad-based coalition of interests in addressing this problem, since wrongful convictions jeopardize public safety.

What Are the Causes of Wrongful Conviction?

Scholars, jurists, journalists, and activists have documented and analyzed cases of wrongful conviction since Borchard's (1932) seminal work. Causes include eyewitness error; overzealous law enforcement officers and prosecutors who engage in misconduct, including withholding evidence; false/coerced confessions and suggestive interrogations; perjury; misleading lineups; inappropriate use of informants, or "snitches"; ineffective assistance of counsel; community pressure for a conviction; forensic science errors, incompetence, and fraud; and the "ratification of error" (the tendency to "rubber stamp" decisions made at lower levels as cases move up through the system). Usually, more than one factor contributes to the error and there are interaction effects among these factors. For example, police or prosecutorial overzealousness might be combined with perjury, withholding of evidence, and the inappropriate use of jailhouse "snitches"—all occurring in a case in which the defendant has inadequate assistance of counsel and is therefore unable to discover these errors. Let us consider some of these factors.

Eyewitness Error

The general public and jurors tend to believe that if people actually witness a crime, they must be the best possible source of evidence because, after all, "they were there and they saw what happened." Eyewitness identification error, usually unintentional, is the factor that is most often associated with wrongful convictions. In our survey, 79% of our respondents ranked witness error as the most frequent type of error resulting in wrongful conviction (Huff et al., 1996:67). Scheck et al. (2000) report that 84% of the DNA exonerations that they examined rested, at least in part, on mistaken eyewitness identification. Loftus (1979), Wells and his colleagues (Wells et al., 1998), and other scholars have written extensively about eyewitness perception, how it can be significantly affected by psychological, societal, cultural, and systemic factors, and how police lineups should and should not be conducted in fairness to suspects.

The U.S. Supreme Court recognized the problem of eyewitness identification error in 1967 in several cases that were addressed in a single decision, known informally as the "Wade trilogy." The Court said, in part:

> The vagaries of eyewitness identification are well known; the annals of criminal law are rife with instances of mistaken identification. . . . [I]mproper suggestion upon identifying witnesses probably accounts for more miscarriages of justice than any other single factor. . . . (*United States v. Wade,* 1967)

Overzealous and Unethical Cops and Prosecutors

We delegate to law enforcement officers and prosecutors a great deal of discretionary authority in dealing with crime in our society, and their use of that discretion and authority is largely invisible to us. In the 17th century, Pascal observed that, "Justice without strength is helpless, strength without justice is tyrannical. . . . Unable to make what is just strong, we have made what is strong just" (Pascal, 1670). Misuse of official authority is an exercise in strength and power, not justice.

Some law enforcement officers and prosecutors, caught up in ultra suppression-oriented organizational subcultures, engage in unprofessional, unethical, and sometimes even criminal behavior in the name of getting the "scum bags" off the streets and protecting the public. Instead, their behavior sometimes *jeopardizes* public safety by arresting and convicting the wrong person, leaving the real criminal free to continue victimizing citizens. Sometimes cops believe that they have the right suspect or defendant, especially if he has a previous record, and to ensure that they get a conviction, all they need to do is induce the suspect to confess, embellish or alter the evidence, offer perjured testimony, "help" witnesses remember "what really happened," and/or pick out the "right" person in a lineup. Some prosecutors aid and abet this process by uncritically reviewing the evidence, by looking the other way when perjured testimony is offered, and by withholding from the defense potentially exculpatory evidence.

Of the post-conviction DNA exonerations reported by Scheck et al. (2000), 63% involved police and/or prosecutorial misconduct. Prosecutors who behave in this unethical manner ignore both federal and state court decisions and the ethical standards of professional conduct. The seminal opinion on prosecutorial misconduct in the United States involved a 1935 federal case and still stands as the clearest and most eloquent statement, in my judgment:

> The United States Attorney is the representative not of an ordinary party to a controversy, but of a sovereignty whose obligation to govern impartially is as compelling as its obligation to govern at all; and whose interest, therefore, in a criminal prosecution is not that it shall win a case, but that justice shall be done. . . . It is as much his duty to refrain from improper methods calculated to produce a wrongful conviction as it is to use every legitimate means to bring about a just one. (*Berger v. United States,* 1935)

Scheck et al. (2000) reported that in examining 381 murder convictions that had been reversed due to police or prosecutorial misconduct, not once was a prosecutor disbarred, even when knowingly allowing perjured testimony or deliberately concealing exculpatory evidence. Most of the time, they were not even disciplined.

False and Coerced Confessions and Suggestive Interrogations

Another important factor in wrongful convictions is false and coerced confessions, often related to suggestive interrogations. Scheck et al. (2000) reported that 15 of the first 62 post-conviction DNA exonerations in their database, or about 1 in 4, involved false confessions. Leo (2001) has created a typology that includes five kinds of false confession. Extracting such confessions, he argues, involves a two-step process in which interrogators first shift suspects' perceptions from one of confidence to one of hopelessness and then offer inducements to confess as a way of dealing with the "hopeless" situation confronting them. One can see this at work almost any week on television "cop shows" such as *NYPD Blue,* as Andy Sipowicz and his partner play "good cop/bad cop" and say things like, "We want to help you, but you have to help us and then we can help you with the D.A. Right now, you're looking at dying in prison on a gurney with a needle in your arm."

Some law enforcement units seem especially prone to unethical behavior. These include "elitist" units that tend to operate with more independence from the rest of the organization, such as elite narcotics enforcement and street gang units. Consider, for example, the recent, highly-publicized scandal in the Los Angeles Police Department's Rampart Division, where its anti-gang unit has been at the center of multiple investigations that have led to indictments and convictions of police officers for engaging in lawless tactics. Referring to the subculture that can exist in such elite special units, a Los Angeles Times writer recently observed:

> Cops in these units are, by definition, set apart—even from other police. For most of his career, [Rafael] Perez, the man at the center of the LAPD Rampart scandal, worked in two of these units: gang suppression and undercover narcotics. It is common, particularly among the hardest charging cops in these units, to come to believe they reign over secret domains, that they are governed by codes of behavior of their own devising, liberated from normal life and its bothersome rules. In this shadow world, they can come to feel like royalty, true princes of the city and masters of all they survey. (McDermott, 2000: A1)

Even more compelling is this excerpt from Officer Perez's own testimony:

> Well, sir, make no bones about it, what we did was wrong—planting evidence . . . fabricating evidence, perjuring ourselves—but our mentality was us against them. . . . We knew that Rampart's crime rate, murder rate, was the highest in the city. . . . [L]ieutenants, captains, and everybody else would come to our roll calls and say this has to end and you guys are in charge of things. Do something about it. That's your responsibility. . . . And the mentality was, it was like a war, us against them. . . . (McDermott, 2000:A22)

Inappropriate Use of Informants, or 'Snitches'

Another important contributing factor is the widespread and often unprincipled use of informants, or "snitches," by police, prosecutors, and jail officers. For example, the perjury and other unethical and illegal conduct in the highly-publicized "snitch crisis" in the Los Angeles County Jail in the 1980s was ultimately linked to 225 felony convictions (Reinhold, 1989). Also, 5 of the first 13 Illinois death row inmates found to have been wrongfully convicted were prosecuted using jailhouse informants (Armstrong and Mills, 2000), and 21% of the DNA exoneration cases reported by Scheck et al. (2000) involved the use of "jailhouse snitches." Such informants, many of whom have been used repeatedly, are often willing to shape their stories to fit whatever is needed—in return, of course, for favorable considerations of various kinds. And although prosecutors are understandably cynical about the stories told to them by defendants, some of them seem to be able to routinely suspend that cynicism and accept as truthful the stories told by jailhouse informants and other "snitches."

Ineffective Assistance of Counsel

Ineffective assistance of counsel has been a basis for appeal since the famous Scottsboro Boys case (*Powell v. Alabama,* 1932), but such appeals are rarely successful, despite the widespread acknowledgment by judges at the state and federal levels that many attorneys are inadequately prepared for trial work. Unfortunately, being inadequately represented by defense counsel is a widespread problem that is likely to worsen due to the inadequate budgets allocated for defense work.

Given the assumptions of the adversarial system of justice, ineffective assistance of counsel poses a special problem that challenges those assumptions. An authoritative opinion was offered by Judge David Bazelon:

> The adversary system assumes that each side has adequate counsel. This assumption probably holds true for giant corporations or well to do individuals, but what I have seen in 23 years on the bench leads me to believe that a great many—if not most—indigent defendants do not receive the effective assistance of counsel guaranteed them by the Sixth Amendment.... [T]he criminal justice system goes to considerable lengths to bury the problem. But no one could seriously dispute that ineffective assistance is a common phenomenon. A very able trial judge described some of the counsel coming before the courts as "walking violations of the sixth amendment." (Bazelon, 1973)

Bazelon cited a few examples: a lawyer who told the judge that he'd sum up in 10 minutes to avoid a parking ticket; one who spent only 15 minutes with his client and then pleaded him guilty to a capital offense despite his client's statement that he could produce exculpatory witnesses; another who met his client for the first time on his way to court and had no knowledge of the facts of the case; and yet another who slept through the prosecutor's questioning of his witnesses (Bazelon, 1973). Even more threatening to our adversarial system's assumptions are the "guilty plea wholesalers" (Huff et al., 1996:55), who make comfortable livings by pleading defendants guilty without investigating cases or even interviewing the defendants.

Forensic Errors, Incompetence, and Fraud

Forensic science, like nuclear energy, can be used constructively or destructively. Recent advances in forensic science offer tremendous opportunities to improve the accuracy of our criminal justice system. However, the technology is ahead of the quality control, training, and, in some cases, ethics, of those working in crime labs. Scheck and Neufeld's Innocence Project has relied on DNA analyses to exonerate many wrongfully convicted persons. They, along with others such as Thompson (1997) and Castelle and Loftus (2001) have also discussed the factors affecting subjective human judgment as well as the incompetent, unethical, and unprofessional behavior of "junk scientists" and masters of fraud and deception supervising or working in crime labs that have assisted in scores of wrongful convictions. These include the well-known case of Fred Zain, who directed the West Virginia State Police Crime Lab. Zain's fraudulent lab reports and perjured testimony over a 16-year career contributed to many wrongful convictions (Castelle and Loftus, 2001:30–34).

What Theoretical Perspectives Help Explain Wrongful Conviction?

In developing my own theoretical framework for analyzing and understanding wrongful conviction, I have been influenced most heavily by Herbert Packer's (1968) classic work, *The Limits of the Criminal Sanction,* and by more recent contributions made by Daniel Givelber (1997, 2001) and by William Lofquist (2001). While many cases of wrongful conviction clearly involve the overzealous, unethical, and even illegal behavior of individual actors, I believe that it is essential, from a theoretical perspective, to place those actions in a broader structural and organizational framework. In doing so, I have incorporated the contributions of these three scholars and our own conceptualization of the "ratification of error" in cases of wrongful conviction (Huff et al., 1996).

Packer's (1968) "crime control" and "due process" models, though they are theoretical constructs, are useful in assessing the relative emphases of particular aspects of the criminal justice process. Not surprisingly, those aspects that emphasize crime control objectives, such as plea bargaining, may not only help control crime but also contribute to system error and wrongful conviction. Givelber's (1997, 2001) focus on the adequacy of the adversarial system is also useful in understanding wrongful conviction at the macrolevel of analysis. He argues that our system relies on parties to frame the legal dispute, which is then to be resolved by a fact finder (either a judge or a jury). Along the way, we provide a number of protections and advantages for the defendant, but Givelber points out that these actually benefit the guilty more than the innocent defendant. Furthermore, the adversarial system assumes that cases are filtered from the initial arrest through the trial and that this filtering will "weed out" the cases involving innocent defendants. Givelber argues, however, that in practice, the filtering process actually stops when prosecutors decide to go to trial, at which point they tend to become advocates for conviction, rather than for justice.

Finally, Lofquist (2001) helps place all of this in a structural, organizational perspective that I find consistent with my own research and analysis. Lofquist draws upon earlier theoretical explanations of corporate wrongdoing, David Sudnow's (1965) classic conceptualization of "normal crimes," and, especially, Vaughan's (1996) well-developed organizational and structural analysis of the *Challenger* disaster. From this perspective, the actions of individuals and the injustices that I've been describing are more often attributable to the routine operations of our criminal justice system—one that operates within an overall social, cultural, and organizational context. In this sense, the errors made in our system that result in these miscarriages of justice are more comparable to what Vaughan concluded about the *Challenger* tragedy—that is, that it represented ". . . an incremental descent into poor judgment" (Vaughan, 1996:xiii). From my perspective, the organizational subcultures that are developed and sustained in many police departments, crime labs, and prosecutors' offices shape the ways in which human actors view their jobs and view the suspects and defendants with whom they deal.

Theoretically, then, wrongful conviction might be seen as a generally unintended consequence in an adversarial system of justice whose basic premise (that the prosecution and the defense will adequately represent the state and the accused, respectively) is not empirically valid and that the system, beginning with the arrest of a suspect, tends to ratify errors made at lower levels while serving both the "crime control" and the "due process" models, neither of which adequately addresses the needs of the innocent defendant.

What Are the Consequences for the Wrongfully Convicted?

The experience of wrongful conviction can exact a heavy toll on its victims and their families. Many of the wrongfully convicted spend years incarcerated in prison. While there, they experience anger, fear, and trauma—sometimes including victimization—in varying degrees. Inmates have their own status hierarchy and varying degrees of tolerance for different types of crimes and criminals. Those who are wrongfully convicted and sentenced to prison for child molestation or for raping a child or a woman, for example, are especially vulnerable and have sometimes been attacked by other prisoners, scalded with hot water, and subjected to severe ridicule that may have long-lasting effects.

Imagine what it would be like to be an innocent person serving time in prison with some of the state's most dangerous offenders. One of the most powerful statements on that experience came from Randall Dale Adams. Wrongfully convicted of murdering a Dallas police officer in a case that led to the prize-winning documentary, *The Thin Blue Line* (Morris, 1988), Adams served 12½ years in prison and was just 72 hours from execution when Supreme Court Justice Powell ordered a stay. When asked to describe what life in prison was like for him, he said:

> . . . To live inside a penitentiary . . . everybody that I respect—law enforcement, correctional officers—they're looking at me: "You're a cop killer!" That's not a nice look! All the people that I disrespect— the rapists, the killers—[are saying]: "You've been on death row, convicted of killing a cop, doing life!" . . . The people that I respect, hate me; the people that I don't respect, respect me. It was a strange situation. . . . (Huff et al., 1996:40)

For those wrongfully convicted of a crime, the stigma of having been convicted is hard to overcome, and many people remain suspicious and distrustful. Getting a job can be very difficult. Much has been written by criminologists concerning the argument that unemployment causes crime, but less has been said about crime causing unemployment. Even the *belief* that one committed a crime, although he has been exonerated, can be the unspoken reason that employment is hard to find, even in a good economy.

Those who spend years in prison for crimes they didn't commit must then readjust to society when they are released, and while prison sentences are based on a linear calculation of time, with each year being weighted equally, societal change in the late twentieth and early twenty-first century is decidedly nonlinear. The innocent ex-inmate, upon release, has fallen even further behind—socially, psychologically, and economically—than might be implied even by a lengthy sentence.

There is a paucity of good research on the impact of wrongful conviction on human lives. Some of the best in-depth research on this subject has been done by Adrian Grounds, a forensic psychiatrist at the Institute of Criminology at Cambridge. Grounds cautions that his work is still at the preliminary stage and has not yet been published because he wants to expand his sample further. He has completed clinical assessments of 11 wrongfully convicted men, 5 of whom were victims of injustice in the notorious British cases known as "the Birmingham Six" and "the Guildford Four."

Grounds followed up on 11 wrongfully convicted men who were, on average, 30 years old when incarcerated and about 42 when released. As he put it, "Those who had been in . . . longest had lost a generation of family life. Parents had died and children had grown up. Young men who entered prison as fathers of young children were released as middle aged men with grandchildren" (Grounds, 2001:2).

Grounds acknowledges that he "didn't expect to find much," based on the absence of prior histories of mental illness and the general findings in the research literature, which implied that there was little solid evidence of psychological deterioration in long-term imprisonment. What he discovered was "wholly unexpected." His assessments revealed a pattern of severe disabling symptoms and psychological problems that were comparable in all 11 cases. He returned to the research literature and found striking similarities in symptomatology in documented cases involving hostages and the victims of natural disasters. In 10 of the 11 cases, the personality change was "enduring" and included estrangement, loss of capacity for intimacy, moodiness, inability to settle, and loss of a sense of purpose and direction (Grounds, 2001:1–3).

Eight of the men were diagnosed as having post-traumatic stress symptoms, generally related to specific threats or violence they experienced following arrest or while in prison. Three had made false and coerced confessions. Ten reported being terrified of being assaulted or killed. Three suffered serious violence (two were sexually assaulted and one was stabbed). Several said that they had learned to be "highly aggressive and intimidating as a form of self-protection." They also suffered in their social adjustment following their sudden release from prison. They could not cope with ordinary tasks such as shopping, operating mechanical controls, and using credit cards or automatic teller machines. One of the men told Grounds that he felt humiliated by his lack of ability and the need to ask his wife to teach him basic skills. "It's like when someone has a stroke," he said, "you have to be taught how to do things again" (Grounds, 2001:3–4).

Some children of the wrongfully convicted, having suddenly lost their fathers, developed significant psychological problems. Some had to cope with sudden poverty and hunger, as well. Families were shunned because they were related to the men who had been arrested and because they were Irish. A mother was physically attacked several times. One woman told Dr. Grounds that she and her children were sworn at, spat at, had their house vandalized, a noose hung on their gate, and graffiti painted on the house that said "Hang Irish Bastards" and "Scum." The women became seriously depressed, and one considered using her gas oven to kill herself. They used alcohol to cope with their depression and stress, leading one of the children to say, "She turned to drink. I hated her for it. . . . As young children, we blamed her. She didn't have any more to give us" (Grounds, 2001:7–8).

Based on my familiarity with some of the victims of wrongful conviction in the United States and information reported in the literature, I believe that there are striking similarities in symptomatology, although wrongful conviction cases rarely involve the highly political contexts associated with the Birmingham Six and the Guildford Four. The common sense of estrangement and the difficulties experienced in reintegrating into society pose significant challenges.

Public Policy Recommendations

There is an urgent need for public policy responses to this problem. In a free, democratic society, depriving innocent citizens of their freedom—and perhaps even their lives—is a challenge deserving of serious reforms in both policies and practices. Reinhold Niebuhr (1944) once said, "Man's capacity for justice makes democracy possible, but man's inclination to injustice makes democracy necessary." In our democracy, the people can pursue reforms in the law and in public policy. I'd like to offer eight major recommendations concerning law and public policy.

POLICY RECOMMENDATION #1: States should enact measures to fairly compensate those who are wrongfully convicted, at least those who serve time in jail or prison following their convictions. States should also assign a "case manager" for each of these individuals and make available to them and their families a full range of counseling, social services, and employment assistance to help reintegrate them into society.

POLICY RECOMMENDATION #2: The death penalty should be abolished and replaced with sentences of 20 years, 30 years, or life imprisonment without parole, depending on the facts of each case. Because all convictions are based on a probabilistic assessment of guilt and are subject to error, they ought to be reversible, allowing the innocent person to be freed and compensated. All criminal sentences *except* the death penalty allow this opportunity, but execution of the innocent forecloses this option. Samuel Gross (1998) recently found that a majority of Americans surveyed, both supporters and opponents of the death penalty, indicated that the issue of actual innocence caused them concern about the propriety of the death penalty. Finally, this would bring the United States in line with other nations that have abolished the death penalty. Such abolition is, for example, a requirement of membership in the Council of Europe and in the European Union. Also, Russia has had a moratorium on the use of capital punishment since 1996, with President Putin recently stating his opposition to reviving the death penalty (Reynolds, 2001). In fact, the United States increasingly finds itself so isolated on this issue that our government is unable to secure the extradition of those wanted for violent crimes, including mass murder, unless our government provides assurances that the defendant will not face the death penalty.

POLICY RECOMMENDATION #3: Those convicted of crimes in which biological evidence is available for testing should be allowed to request such tests and prosecutors should agree to such testing, as recommended by the National Commission on the Future of DNA Evidence (1999). Also, biological evidence in criminal cases should be preserved for testing throughout the duration of an offender's sentence. The rate of DNA exonerations tripled between 1996 and 2000 (Scheck and Neufeld, 2001:241), and further advances in forensic science will continue to produce scientific evidence of innocence in many cases.

POLICY RECOMMENDATION #4: In cases in which eyewitness identification is involved, the court should always permit the use of qualified expert witnesses and should issue precise cautionary instructions to juries, informing them of the possibility of eyewitness misidentification.

POLICY RECOMMENDATION #5: No identification procedure (pre- or post-indictment) should be conducted in the absence of legal counsel for the suspect/accused.

POLICY RECOMMENDATION #6: Police interrogations of suspects in the United States should be recorded in full. Electronic recording of interrogations is now either common or mandatory in England, Australia, and Canada (Westling and Waye, 1998). Leo (1996) has noted that electronically recording custodial interrogations promotes the goals of truth finding, fair treatment, and accountability in the legal process and creates an objective and retrievable record of police questioning.

POLICY RECOMMENDATION #7: Law enforcement officers, criminalists, and prosecutors who engage in unethical, unprofessional, or illegal conduct contributing to wrongful conviction should be removed from their positions of public trust and subjected to the most severe civil, professional, and (when appropriate) criminal penalties. For prosecutors, this should include disbarment proceedings, because such misconduct, if proved, is a clear violation of public trust.

Although some may view tolerance for such behaviors as promoting Packer's (1968) crime control model, it is also arguable that it undermines that model by eroding public confidence in the criminal justice system. In the case of law enforcement and the police, such behavior can exacerbate public cynicism and increase jurors' reluctance to convict. Conversely, reducing the number of wrongful convictions may increase confidence in the criminal justice system and may actually increase the conviction rate.

POLICY RECOMMENDATION #8: Criminal cases review commissions (or "innocence commissions") should be established at the national and state levels in the United States. As Griffin (2001) has noted, the commissions could review appeals, then refer appropriate cases to trial-level courts that could then entertain collateral attacks on the conviction. They could hold hearings and decide to dismiss the appeal/referral, order a new trial, or vacate the conviction.

Although state and local bar associations and the courts must become more active in punishing and deterring such behavior, that is not likely to be sufficient, nor will the efforts of Scheck's and Neufeld's Innocence Project, Jim McCloskey and Centurion Ministries, and a number of journalists and activists. I believe that the time has come to do what the United Kingdom has done. We should establish commissions similar to their Criminal Cases Review Commission (CCRC) to review post-appellate claims of wrongful conviction and, when appropriate, refer those cases to the appropriate courts.

According to Griffin (2001), by October 2000 the Commission had received 3,680 appeals, had reviewed 2,381 and had referred 203 cases (4.3%) to courts of appeal. Of those 203 cases, 49 had been heard by the courts, resulting in 38 convictions having been overturned. These 38 overturned convictions represent 77.5% of the cases referred to the courts by the Commission but only 1.6% of all appeals. Thus, the argument that such a review commission would overburden the courts does not find empirical support thus far, at least with respect to the British experience.

Questions for Future Research

Finally, the subject of wrongful conviction presents rich opportunities for future research—within jurisdictions, across jurisdictions, and cross-nationally. In fact, I believe that a cross-national, comparative study by a team of social scientists and legal scholars could make an important contribution to our knowledge, and I hope to begin organizing such a group. One model for such an undertaking is Malcolm Klein's initiative, which has led to the Eurogang network of European and American scholars researching gangs and similar groups with other preferred names in a number of European nations (Klein et al., 2001). One of the best ways to improve our understanding of social problems and the law is to view them in the context of other nations and cultures.

Some potentially fruitful questions for future research might include the following:

(1) Are some criminal justice systems more likely to produce wrongful convictions than others? If so, why?

(2) What is the level of public tolerance for errors leading to the conviction of those who are factually innocent, as opposed to errors that free those who are factually guilty? This question should be addressed within a single jurisdiction over time, as well as across multiple jurisdictions.

(3) Are some individuals more at risk for wrongful conviction than others? Does this vary across jurisdictions? Does it vary within the same jurisdiction over multiple points in time?

(4) In wrongful conviction cases, what is the nature and magnitude of the crimes committed by the actual offender while the wrong person was the prime suspect and, later, while he was incarcerated?

(5) In societies that are relatively homogeneous with respect to race and ethnicity, is eyewitness identification any more accurate than is the case elsewhere, such as in the United States?

(6) In assessing the role of unethical police behavior, what differences are there in nations where police investigations are carried out under the supervision of a state's attorney or are conducted by an independent magistrate?

(7) In nations that utilize inquisitorial systems, wherein the presiding judge examines the evidence while the attorneys for the state and for the accused play only supplementary roles, is it less likely that evidence favorable to the defense will be suppressed?

(8) How do wrongfully convicted prisoners adapt to and cope with life in prison, as compared with other prisoners?

(9) In follow-up studies of those released following long-term imprisonment, how do the psychological, social, and economic adjustments made by the wrongfully convicted compare to those made by other prisoners?

References

Armstrong, Ken and Steve Mills. 2000. Ryan: 'Until I can be sure' Illinois is first state to suspend death penalty. Chicago Tribune. February 1:1.

Bazelon, David. 1973. The defective assistance of counsel. University of Cincinnati Law Review 42:1–2.

Blackstone, Sir William. 1809 [1765–1769]. Commentaries on the Laws of England. Book IV:27. London: Strahan (15th edition).

Borchard, Edwin M. 1932. Convicting the Innocent: Sixty-Five Actual Errors of Criminal Justice. Garden City, N.Y.: Doubleday.

Castelle, George and Elizabeth F. Loftus. 2001. Misinformation and wrongful convictions. In Saundra D. Westervelt and John A. Humphrey (eds.), Wrongly Convicted: Perspectives on Failed Justice. New Brunswick, N.J.: Rutgers University Press.

Givelber, Daniel. 1997. Meaningless acquittals, meaningful convictions: Do we reliably acquit the innocent? Rutgers Law Review 49:1317–1396.

——. 2001. The adversary system and historical accuracy: Can we do better? In Saundra D. Westervelt and John A. Humphrey (eds.), Wrongly Convicted: Perspectives on Failed Justice. New Brunswick, N.J.: Rutgers University Press.

Griffin, Lissa. 2001. The correction of wrongful convictions: A comparative perspective. American University International Law Review 16:1241–1308.

Gross, Samuel R. 1998. Update: American public opinion on the death penalty—it's getting personal. Cornell Law Review 83:1448–1475.

Grounds, Adrian. 2001. Psychological consequences of wrongful imprisonment. Unpublished paper presented at Institute of Criminology, Cambridge, England. April 26.

Huff, C. Ronald, Arye Rattner, and Edward Sagarin. 1996. Convicted but Innocent: Wrongful Conviction and Public Policy. Thousand Oaks, Calif.: Sage.

Klein, Malcolm W., Hans-Juergen Kerner, Cheryl Maxson, and Elmar Weitekamp (eds.). 2001. The Eurogang Paradox: Street Gangs and Youth Groups in the U.S. and Europe. Dordrecht, The Netherlands: Kluwer.

Leo, Richard A. 1996. The impact of Miranda revisited. Journal of Criminal Law and Criminology 86:621–692.

——. 2001. False confessions: Causes, consequences, and solutions. In Saundra D. Westervelt and John A. Humphrey (eds.), Wrongly Convicted: Perspectives on Failed Justice. New Brunswick, N.J.: Rutgers University Press.

Liebman, James S., Jeffrey Fagan, Valerie West, and Jonathan Lloyd. 2000. Capital attrition: Error rates in capital cases, 1973–1995. Texas Law Review 78:1839–1865.

Lofquist, William S. 2001. Whodunit? An examination of the production of wrongful convictions. In Saundra D. Westervelt and John A. Humphrey (eds.), Wrongly Convicted: Perspectives on Failed Justice. New Brunswick, N.J.: Rutgers University Press.

Loftus, Elizabeth F. 1979. Eyewitness Testimony. Cambridge, Mass.: Harvard University Press.

McDermott, Terry. 2000. Perez's bitter saga of lies, regrets, and harm. Los Angeles Times. 31 December, A1, A22–24.

Morris, Errol (director). 1988. The Thin Blue Line (film). New York: Miramax Films.

National Institute of Justice. 1999. National Commission on the Future of DNA Evidence Postconviction DNA Testing. Washington: National Institute of Justice, Office of Justice Programs.

Niebuhr, Reinhold. 1944. The Children of Light and the Children of Darkness. New York: Scribner's.

Packer, Herbert. 1968. The Limits of the Criminal Sanction. Stanford, Calif.: Stanford University Press.

Pascal, Blaise. 1995 [1670]. Pensées. New York: Penguin (reissue).

Radelet, Michael L., Hugo Adam Bedau, and Constance Putnam. 1992. In Spite of Innocence. Boston, Mass.: Northeastern University Press.

Reinhold, Robert. 1989. California shaken over an informer. New York Times. 17 February, A1.

Reynolds, Maura. 2001. Russian president takes stand against reviving death penalty. Los Angeles Times, 11 July:A7.

Scheck, Barry and Peter Neufeld. 2001. DNA and innocence scholarship. In Saundra D. Westervelt and John A. Humphrey (eds.), Wrongly Convicted: Perspectives on Failed Justice. New Brunswick, N.J.: Rutgers University Press.

Scheck, Barry, Peter Neufeld, and Jim Dwyer. 2000. Actual Innocence. New York: Doubleday.

Sudnow, David. 1965. Normal crimes: Sociological features of the penal code in a public defender office. Social Problems (Winter):255–276.

Thompson, William C. 1997. A sociological perspective on the science of forensic testing. University of California Davis Law Review 30:1113–1136.

U.S. Department of Justice, Bureau of Justice Statistics. 2001. Criminal Case Processing. Washington: U.S. Department of Justice.

U.S. Department of Justice, Federal Bureau of Investigation. 2001. Crime in the United States—2000. Washington: U.S. Department of Justice.

Vaughan, Diane. 1996 The *Challenger* Launch Decision. Chicago, Ill.: University of Chicago Press.

Voltaire, Francois Marie Arouet. 1961 [1747]. Zadig. Chapter 6. New York: Signet (reissue).

Wells, Gary L., Mark Small, Steven Penrod, Roy S. Malpass, Solomon Fulero, and C. Elizabeth Brimacombe. 1998. Eyewitness identification procedures: Recommendations for lineups and photospreads. Law and Human Behavior 22:603–647.

Westling, Wayne T. and Vicki Waye. 1998. Videotaping police interrogations: Lessons from Australia. American Journal of Criminal Law 25 (Summer):493–543.

Cases

Berger v. United States 295 U.S. 78 (1935)

Powell v. Alabama 287 U.S. 45 (1932)

United States v. Wade 388 U.S. 218 (1967)

Unit VI

Discussion Questions

1. What can be done to help invigorate the nation's inner cities? What role should justice system officials have in such an effort? What types of welfare reforms would you propose to achieve this end? Some argue that welfare can't be reformed without a dramatic reduction in single parenthood. How do you respond to that observation?

2. What were the key findings of the National Academy of Sciences Panel on the Understanding and Control of Violent Crime?

3. According to the National Academy of Sciences Panel, what violence control strategies should be adopted in this country?

4. Zalman argues that in the context of civil liberties, the criminal justice system is "ambiguous," promoting both autocratic and democratic policies. Provide examples of each type of policy. Which perspective would you tend to embrace and why?

5. Maintenance of the bifurcated system as outlined by Zalman suggests the possible application of a dual standard of justice—a more autocratic mode toward lower-class persons of color, and a more liberal, democratic response toward the middle and upper classes. What can be done to negate this dual standard?

6. What is restorative justice and how does it differ from the traditional justice model?

7. What programmatic changes must be made to realize a viable restorative justice model?

8. Would you support the creation of a restorative justice model in your community? Why or why not?

9. What role should research play in developing public policy?

10. Huff outlines a number of policy recommendations that he believes would reduce the number of wrongful convictions. Which of his recommendations do you support and why?

11. If you could personally bring about one major change in the justice system today, what would it be?

12. Design a research evaluation effort to determine whether the change you propose would really prevent or reduce crime or favorably impact justice system operations. ✦

Appendices

Appendix A

Criminal Justice–Related Professional Organizations

There are many professional organizations in the field. Students should consider joining one or more of these organizations and/or subscribing to the journals and newsletters that they publish. Some of the more prominent national organizations in the field are noted below. For a more complete listing, go to http://www.asc41.com/AGENCIES.html.

Academy of Criminal Justice Sciences
7319 Hanover Parkway, Suite C
Greenbelt, MD 20770
800-757-2257
http://www.acjs.org

American Correctional Association
4380 Forbes Blvd.
Lanham, MD 20706
800-222-5646
http://www.aca.org

American Criminal Justice Association
P.O. Box 601047
Sacramento, CA 95860
916-484-6553
http://www.acjalae.org

American Jail Association
1135 Professional Court
Hagerstown, MD 21740
301-790-3930
http://www.corrections.com/aja

American Judicature Society
2700 University Ave.
Des Moines, IA 50311
515-271-2281
http://www.ajs.org

American Probation and Parole Association
2760 Research Park Dr.
Lexington, KY 40511-8410
859-244-8203
http://www.appa-net.org

American Society of Criminology
1314 Kinnear Road
Columbus, OH 43212
614-292-2907
http://www.asc41.com

Canadian Criminal Justice Association
383 Parkdale Avenue, # 207
Ottawa, Ontario
CANADA K1Y 4R4
613-725-3715
http://www.ccja-acjp.ca/en/

International Association for the Study of Organized Crime
Criminal Justice Department
Virginia Commonwealth University
Richmond, VA 23284-2017
804-828-1050
http://www.iasoc.net

International Association of Chiefs of Police
515 North Washington Street
Alexandria, VA 22314
800-843-4227
http://www.theiacp.org

Justice Research and Statistics Association
777 N. Capital St., NE, Suite 801
Washington, DC 20002
202-842-9330
http://www.jrsainfo.org

Law and Society Association
205 Hampshire House
University of Massachusetts
Amherst, MA 01003-9257
413-545-4617
http://www.lawandsociety.org

National Association of Blacks in Criminal Justice
North Carolina Central University
P.O. Box 19788
Durham, NC 27707
919-683-1801
http://www.nabcj.org

National Association of Police Organizations
750 First Street NE, Suite 920
Washington, DC 20002-4241
202-842-4420
http://www.napo.org

National Council on Crime and Delinquency
1970 Broadway, Suite 500
Oakland, CA 94612
510-218-0500
http://www.nccd-crc.org

National Crime Prevention Council
1000 Connecticut Ave., NW
Washington, DC 20036
202-466-6272
http://www.ncpc.org

National District Attorneys Association
99 Canal Center Plaza, Suite 510
Alexandria, VA 22314
703-549-9222
http://www.ndaa-apri.org

National Juvenile Detention Association
301 Perkins Building
Eastern Kentucky University
Richmond, KY 40475-3102
859-622-6259
http://www.njda.com

Southern Criminal Justice Association
Department of Correctional Services
Eastern Kentucky University
Richmond, KY 40475
606-622-1155
http://www.scja.net

Western Society of Criminology
Criminal Justice Program
San Diego, CA 92181
691-594-4089
http://www.sonoma.edu/cja/wsc/wscmain.html ✦

Appendix B

100 Leading Justice System–Related Supreme Court Cases*

Abel v. United States, 362 U.S. 217, 80 S.Ct. 683 (1960) Abel was a foreign spy living in a New York hotel who was suspected of espionage. Reliable informants gave FBI and INS agents sufficient information to incriminate him. INS agents obtained an administrative deportation warrant seeking to deport him as an undocumented or unregistered alien. They went to Abel's hotel with their warrant, seeking first to obtain his cooperation regarding his espionage activities. FBI agents accompanied INS agents but without a search or arrest warrant. When INS agents entered Abel's apartment, they placed him under arrest and proceeded to search the premises. The search, with FBI agents acting only as "observers," yielded a false birth certificate and other forged identities used by Abel in his espionage activities. This evidence was subsequently turned over to the United States Attorney for investigation and prosecution. Abel was subsequently convicted. He appealed, alleging that the items seized should have been suppressed because the FBI had not obtained a valid search warrant. The SC (Supreme Court) upheld Abel's conviction, contending that the INS had every right to search his premises following reliable evidence of his culpability as an unregistered alien and spy. The INS justified the search based upon the administrative deportation warrant. As the evidence was obtained by INS agents during the lawful discharge of their responsibilities, it was not subject to suppression.

Aguilar v. Texas, 378 U.S. 108, 84 S.Ct. 1509 (1964) On the basis of an informant's information, police in Texas obtained a search warrant to search the home of Aguilar for possible heroin, marijuana, and other narcotics. The police searched Aguilar's home, finding large quantities of narcotics. After Aguilar was convicted, he appealed, contending that there was no probable cause upon which a valid search warrant could be issued. The SC overturned Aguilar's conviction, saying that whenever information supplied by informants is used as the basis for search warrants, some information must be provided to the issuing magistrate that supports the credibility and reliability of the informant. That is, in what capacity do officers know the informant, and has the informant provided reliable information in the past? This, in short, is the two-pronged test of informant reliability. Thus the SC established that the standard for obtaining a search warrant by state officers is the same as applies under the Fourth and Fourteenth Amendments; a search warrant may be defective when it does not specify any factual basis for the magistrate to form a decision regarding issuance; officers need to outline the factual basis for the search. This test of informant reliability as the basis for a valid search warrant was effectively rejected in the case of *Illinois v. Gates* (1983), which opened the door to a totality-of-circumstances test where the identity of the informant was unknown to police.

Apodaca v. Oregon, 406 U.S. 404, 92 S.Ct. 1628 (1972) Apodaca and others were found guilty of various serious crimes by less-than-unanimous jury verdicts. Oregon has a statute mandating a conviction or acquittal on the basis of a 10 to 2 vote, or what is referred to by the Oregon Legislature as a 10 of 12 vote. In Apodaca's case, the vote favoring conviction was 11 to 1. Apodaca challenged this vote as not being unanimous, and the SC heard the case contemporaneously with the case of *Johnson v. Louisiana* (1972) on an identical issue. In Apodaca's case, the SC

* With the exception of *Whren v. United States* and *Wilson v. Arkansas,* all case summaries are reprinted from Dean J. Champion, *The Roxbury Dictionary of Criminal Justice,* copyright © 1997 by Roxbury Publishing Company.

upheld the constitutionality of the Oregon jury voting provision, declaring that votes of these kinds do not violate one's right to due process under either the Sixth or the Fourteenth Amendments. The significance of this case is that less-than-unanimous jury votes among the states are constitutional and do not violate one's right to due process.

Argersinger v. Hamlin, 407 U.S. 25, 92 S.Ct. 2006 (1972) Argersinger was an indigent charged with carrying a concealed weapon. In Florida, this crime is a misdemeanor punishable by imprisonment of up to six months and a $1,000 fine. Argersinger was not allowed to have court-appointed counsel, as required for a *felony,* because his crime was not a felony (*see Gideon v. Wainwright* [1963]). He was convicted of the misdemeanor and sentenced to 90 days in jail. He appealed, and the SC overturned his misdemeanor conviction. The SC said that any indigent defendant is entitled to counsel for *any* offense involving imprisonment, regardless of the shortness of the length of incarceration. Thus it extended the *Gideon* decision to include misdemeanor offenses, holding that no sentence involving the loss of liberty (incarceration) can be imposed where there has been a denial of counsel; defendants have a right to counsel when imprisonment might result.

Arizona v. Fulminante, 499 U.S. 279, 111 S.Ct. 1246 (1991) Fulminante was suspected of killing his daughter. Insufficient evidence existed to charge him, and he left the state of Arizona and traveled to New Jersey, where he was arrested and convicted for another crime. In prison, his cellmate, Sarivola, advised Fulminante that other inmates had heard that Fulminante was a "child murderer," and thus, his life was in jeopardy. Sarivola offered him protection in exchange for his confession to the murder of Fulminante's daughter. Fulminante confessed to Sarivola and later to Sarivola's wife. Later, he was charged in Arizona with the murder of his daughter, and the Sarivolas, who were also government informants, testified against him. Fulminante was convicted. He appealed on the ground that his confession had been coerced because Sarivola had implied a threat. The SC overturned his conviction on the basis of this argument. It ordered a new trial without the use of the confessions he had given to the Sarivolas. The SC stressed that the "harmless error" doctrine exists to govern involuntary confessions. However, the government had failed to show harmless error beyond a reasonable doubt. The trial judge had erred by permitting a coerced confession to be used against Fulminante. The judge's error would not have resulted in a reversal of a conviction, but it must be judged as harmless by using the "beyond a reasonable doubt" standard.

Baldwin v. New York, 399 U.S. 66, 90 S.Ct. 1886 (1970) Baldwin was arrested and prosecuted for "jostling" (picking pockets), a Class A misdemeanor punishable by a maximum term of imprisonment of one year in New York. According to New York law at the time, this was a petty offense not entitling a defendant to a jury trial. Baldwin asked for and was denied a jury trial. He then appealed. The SC declared that petty offenses carrying a one-year prison term are serious in that jury trials are required if requested. Specifically, the months of imprisonment constituted serious time. The SC said that a potential sentence in excess of six-month imprisonment is sufficiently severe by itself to take an offense out of the category of "petty" as respects right to jury trial (at 1886, 1891). The SC overturned Baldwin's conviction and sent the case back to the lower court for a jury trial.

Barker v. Wingo, 407 U.S. 514, 92 S.Ct. 2182 (1972) Barker and Manning were alleged to have shot an elderly couple in Kentucky in July 1958. They were arrested later and a grand jury indicted them in September 1958. Kentucky prosecutors sought 16 continuances to prolong Barker's trial. Manning was subjected to five different trials, each with a hung jury until the fifth trial, in which Manning was convicted. Then, Barker's trial was scheduled. During these five trials, Barker made no attempt to protest or to encourage a trial on his own behalf. After postponement for various reasons, his trial was finally held in October 1963, when he was convicted. He appealed, alleging a violation of his right to a speedy trial. The SC heard the case and declared that since from every apparent circumstance, Barker did not want a speedy trial, he was not entitled to one. The principle is that defendants must assert their desire to have a speedy trial in order to invoke the speedy-trial provision and to have Amendment rights be enforceable.

Batson v. Kentucky, 476 U.S. 79, 106 S.Ct. 1712 (1986) In Kentucky, a black man, Batson, was convicted by an all-white jury of second-degree burglary. The prosecutor had used all of his peremptory challenges to exclude the few black prospective jurors from the jury pool. Ordinarily, peremptory challenges may be used to strike particular jurors, without the prosecutor's having to provide a reason for doing so. In this case, the use of peremptory challenges was rather transparent, and Batson appealed. In a landmark case, the SC decided that peremptory challenges may not be used for a racially discriminatory purpose. Thus, creating an all-white jury by deliberately eliminating all prospective black candidates was discriminatory. The SC ruled in favor of Batson.

Bell v. Wolfish, 441 U.S. 520, 99 S.Ct. 1861 (1979) This case involved the minimum-security Metropolitan Correctional Center in New York City, a facility operated by the United States Bureau of Prisons and designed to accommodate 449 federal prisoners, including many pretrial detainees. It had been constructed in 1975 and was considered architecturally progressive and modern, generally a comfortable facility. Originally, the facility was designed to house inmates in individual cells. But soon, the capacity of the facility was exceeded by inmate overpopulation. Inmates were obliged to share their cells with other inmates. This double-bunking and other issues related to overcrowding eventually led to a class-action suit against the facility by several of the pretrial detainees and prisoners, including Bell. A lower court ruled in favor of the prisoners, holding that "compelling necessity" had not been demonstrated by prison officials in their handling of the overcrowding situation. But the SC overturned the lower court and said that the "intent" of prison officials should decide whether double-bunking was intended as "punishment" or a simple deprivation because of necessity. Since no "intent" to punish pretrial detainees could be demonstrated, there was no punishment. Hence, the Eighth Amendment was not violated.

Brady v. United States, 397 U.S. 742, 90 S.Ct. 1463 (1970) Brady and a codefendant were charged with kidnapping. The offense carried a maximum penalty of death. Brady initially entered a not-guilty plea, but his codefendant pleaded guilty under a plea-bargain arrangement. When Brady learned that his companion had confessed and agreed to testify against him, Brady changed his plea to guilty, in exchange for a lengthy prison sentence. He knew that if the case proceeded through trial, the jury could impose the death penalty. After he received a 50-year sentence, it was commuted to 30 years. Brady appealed, claiming that his plea of guilty had been involuntarily given, that he had done so only to avoid the possible imposition of the death penalty. The SC upheld Brady's conviction and sentence, saying that the guilty plea had not been coerced. The SC stated that a plea of guilty is not invalid merely because it is entered to avoid the possibility of a death penalty. Thus, although Brady's plea of guilty may well have been motivated in part by a desire to avoid a possible death penalty, the court was convinced that his plea was voluntary and intelligently made and it had no reason to doubt that his solemn admission of guilt was truthful.

Brown v. Mississippi, 287 U.S. 278, 56 S.Ct. 461 (1936) Brown was a suspect in a murder. He was visited at his home by a deputy sheriff and brought to the murder scene. He denied committing the murder. The deputy and others hanged him from a tree, let him down, and then hanged him again. Later they tied him to a tree and beat him. A few days later the deputy came to his home again and arrested him. Brown was taken to jail, where he was beaten repeatedly and told that the beatings would continue until he confessed. He confessed to the murder and was subsequently convicted and sentenced to death. He filed an appeal on the grounds that he had been denied due process. The SC agreed. It argued further that the brutality of police officers had rendered his confession and other statements inadmissible in court against him. Coerced confessions to crimes are unconstitutional. His conviction was overturned.

Burch v. Louisiana, 441 U.S. 357, 99 S.Ct. 1623 (1979) Burch was convicted 5–1 by a six-person jury on charges of exhibiting obscene motion pictures. He appealed to the SC, which overturned his conviction. The SC used precedent to justify its action where a less-than-unanimous six-person jury is unconstitutional (*see Duncan v. Louisiana* and *Ballew v. Georgia*). After an overly lengthy opinion (in view of the fact that the matter had already been settled in two landmark cases earlier), the SC said, again, that six-person juries must be unanimous; if they are not, then the defendant has been deprived of the right to a fair jury trial under the Sixth and Fourteenth Amendments.

California v. Acevedo, 500 U.S. 565, 111 S.Ct. 1982 (1991) DEA agents discovered a Federal Express package shipped from Hawaii to California that contained a large quantity of marijuana. They allowed Federal Express personnel to deliver the package to a house and placed the house under surveillance. Subsequently, a man entered the house and left later carrying a tote bag. They intercepted him and found about a pound of marijuana in the bag. Later they observed Acevedo arrive at the house and leave later carrying a brown paper bag about the size of the tote bag. Police officers stopped Acevedo's car thereafter, searched the brown paper bag without a warrant, and discovered marijuana. The police lacked probable cause to search the vehicle itself, although they did have probable cause to believe that the paper bag held marijuana. Acevedo was convicted and he appealed. The SC upheld Acevedo's conviction, saying that probable cause to believe that a container has contraband may enable officers to search that container, even if it is in a vehicle that they lack probable cause to search. This case modified greatly two other cases, *United States v. Chadwick* (1977) and *Arkansas v. Sanders* (1979), because it permitted officers to open containers, even large ones, if there was probable cause to do so, even if those containers were in vehicles that police lacked probable cause to search in their entirety.

California v. Ciraolo, 476 U.S. 207, 106 S.Ct. 1809 (1986) Ciraolo was growing marijuana in his backyard, according to an anonymous tip received by police. The yard could not be seen from the street, so police flew over Ciraolo's home in an airplane and photographed the backyard. After viewing photographs and detecting marijuana plants, officers obtained a search warrant for Ciraolo's premises, where they found growing marijuana plants. Ciraolo was convicted of cultivating marijuana. He appealed, contending that he had a reasonable expectation of privacy, which included his backyard, and that planes flying over his yard viewing it constituted a Fourth Amendment unreasonable search. The SC upheld the aerial use of photography in identifying illegal contraband, such as growing marijuana. It declared that one's property, such as a backyard, cannot be barred from public view from the air; thus, anything, such as marijuana or other illegal contraband, is subject to being viewed and seized.

California v. Greenwood, 486 U.S. 35, 108 S.Ct. 1625 (1988) Greenwood, a suspected drug dealer, was under surveillance by the police. They observed that from time to time, he would place trash out for trash collectors. They inspected some of his trash and discovered sufficient incriminating evidence to obtain a search warrant of the premises based upon probable cause. A search yielded large quantities of cocaine and hashish and resulted in Greenwood's arrest and conviction for various drug violations. He appealed, contending that his trash should have been subject to a search warrant before police inspected it, and thus, the evidence later discovered and used against him in court should have been excluded. The SC disagreed and said that warrantless searches of trash or garbage are permissible, because persons give up their right to privacy of refuse whenever they place it in public places in trash containers, readily accessible to others.

California v. Hodari D., 499 U.S. 621, 111 S.Ct. 1547 (1991) Hodari was a juvenile who was observed by police late at night with others huddled around a vehicle in a high-crime neighborhood of Oakland. Everyone fled in different directions when seeing the approaching police vehicle. One officer, Pertoso, drove around the block to intercept one of the fleeing persons, Hodari. Hodari ran into Pertoso and a brief scuffle ensued. Hodari broke free, began to run away again, and threw away what appeared to be a small rock. The officer tackled Hodari and arrested him. The recovered rock turned out to be crack cocaine. After Hodari was convicted, he appealed, contending that he had been seized unreasonably and that Petroso had lacked probable cause to arrest him and use the thrown-away cocaine against him. The SC disagreed with Hodari and upheld his conviction, saying that the thrown-away cocaine constituted *abandonment*, that Petroso had not *seized* Hodari before this abandonment, and thus, that the cocaine was admissible against Hodari. If Petroso had tackled Hodari and arrested him before Hodari threw away the crack cocaine, then the eventual discovery of cocaine would have been excluded as evidence against Hodari because Petroso would not have been able to establish probable cause for his arrest.

Carroll v. United States, 267 U.S. 132, 45 S.Ct. 280 (1925) Carroll was a suspected bootlegger of illegal liquor. Police had tried several times to stop his car but had failed to do so. One evening officers saw Carroll's car returning to Grand Rapids from Detroit. They stopped the car and proceeded, without warrant, to search it extensively. Eventually, after tearing apart seats and other automobile components, they discovered illegal whiskey. Carroll was convicted of transporting intoxicating liquor. He appealed, arguing that the whiskey evidence was the result of an illegal search of his vehicle without probable cause and also without a valid search warrant. The SC upheld his conviction, saying that officers did, indeed, have probable cause to stop him and did not need a search warrant. It stressed that automobiles, unlike houses, are highly mobile entities, and therefore the police were authorized to search it before its occupants could destroy any illegal contraband.

Chapman v. California, 386 U.S. 18, 87 S.Ct. 824 (1967) Chapman and a confederate, Teale, were charged with robbing, kidnapping, and murdering a bartender. During the trial, Chapman did not testify. At that time, California had a statute permitting the judge and prosecutor to comment on the fact that the defendant did not testify in his or her own defense and that inferences about guilt could be drawn from the defendant's failure to testify. The trial judge told the jury that they could draw adverse inferences from the defendant's failure to testify. Chapman was convicted. Before she appealed, the SC decided another case, *Griffin v. California* (1965), which held that commentary by a judge or prosecutor about a defendant's refusal to testify in a criminal case must not infringe on his right not to be compelled to be a witness against himself, guaranteed by the Fifth Amendment. The California Supreme Court, therefore, admitted that Chapman had been denied a federal constitutional right because of the judge's instructions to the jury about that silence, but it held that the error was *harmless*. Chapman appealed. The SC reversed Chapman's conviction, holding that the error was *not harmless* when the state prosecutor's argument and the trial judge's jury instructions continuously and repeatedly impressed the jury that the refusal of the defendant to testify required inferences to be drawn in the state's favor. Chapman was granted a new trial, where judicial and prosecutorial commentary on her refusal to testify in her own case were prohibited.

Chapman v. United States, 365 U.S. 610, 81 S.Ct. 776 (1961) Chapman rented a dwelling in a wooded area near Macon, Georgia. The landlord went to the house to invite him to church. Chapman wasn't home and the landlord smelled "sour mash," a whiskey odor. He advised police, who went to the house and entered it through a window, without a warrant, although the landlord had given his permission for police to enter. The police found a distillery and 1,300 gallons of whiskey. Subsequently, federal officers were summoned to the house. Their investigation led to Chapman's arrest and conviction of making illegal whiskey. He appealed, alleging that the police should have obtained a valid warrant before entering his premises, and that the landlord had no right to admit officers to the dwelling he was renting. The SC reversed Chapman's conviction, holding that the warrantless search was unjustified. The federal officers had had time to obtain a warrant but had failed to do so. Even the search by Georgia police was in violation of the Fourth Amendment provision against unreasonable searches and seizures, because they had not known at the time that the premises were being used for illegal whiskey manufacture. A Georgia ordinance provides that an information must be filed by the solicitor-general before a "public nuisance" can be abated, such as the dwelling where the whiskey was being manufactured illegally. (*See Weeks v. United States* [1914] for a comparative case.)

Chimel v. California, 395 U.S. 752, 89 S.Ct. 2034 (1969) Chimel was suspected of being involved in the burglary of a coin company in California. Police officers obtained a valid arrest warrant and went to his home to arrest him. When Chimel returned from work, police were waiting for him. They placed him under arrest and then proceeded to search his entire house, as a "search incident to an arrest." In Chimel's attic, they found some of the stolen coins, which were used against him in court. He was convicted of burglary. Chimel appealed. The SC overturned his conviction, arguing that the police search of Chimel's residence was well beyond the scope of the *arrest* warrant. The police should have obtained a *search* warrant, but they had not. The SC said that in a search incident to an arrest under the circumstances in *Chimel*, police are permitted to search only the defendant's person and the area within the immediate vicinity. Thus, they may search the room where the suspect is arrested but cannot extend their search to other areas of his residence without a valid search warrant. (*See Cupp v. Murphy* [1973] and *Schmerber v. California* [1966] for related issues.)

Colorado v. Bertine, 479 U.S. 367, 107 S.Ct. 738 (1987) Bertine was arrested for DWI. Police officers conducted a "routine" inventory of his van's contents, which yielded illegal drugs. The van was towed to the police impound lot, and Bertine was subsequently convicted of cocaine possession. He appealed. The police argued that the departmental policy and routine investigation without warrant was to protect a car owner's property and to insure against any claims of loss following a car's impoundment. The SC upheld Bertine's conviction, thus condoning police policy of conducting warrantless inventories of impounded vehicles.

Coolidge v. New Hampshire, 403 U.S. 443, 91 S.Ct. 2022 (1971) Coolidge was a suspect in the murder of a 14-year-old girl. She had been called by a man who wanted her to work as a babysitter. She soon was missing but her body was not discovered until 13 days later. Coolidge was questioned by police and took a lie-detector test. Simultaneously, as the result of a search warrant issued by the state attorney general, police seized his vehicle, which they searched several times over a period of days. They also went to Coolidge's home and asked his wife for any guns in the home and for the clothes Coolidge was wearing the night the girl disappeared. Coolidge's wife turned several guns over to police as well as the clothes. This evidence, together with trace evidence from Coolidge's vehicle, was sufficient to convict him of the girl's murder. Coolidge appealed, contending that *all* evidence seized should have been excluded. The SC agreed in part and disagreed in part. It suppressed the evidence seized on the basis of the search warrant because it had not been issued by a neutral and detached magistrate. The SC stressed the fact that the attorney general was not a "neutral and detached" party and thus was not in the position of issuing a valid search warrant in this particular case. However, it allowed the evidence provided by Coolidge's wife, because it was the result of consent and did not require a warrant. Coolidge's conviction was upheld.

County of Riverside v. McLaughlin, 500 U.S. 44, 111 S.Ct. 1661 (1991) McLaughlin was arrested without a warrant and detained for several days over a weekend in the Riverside County Jail in California. The policy of arrest and detention in Riverside County provided for arraignments, without unnecessary or undue delay, within 48 hours after persons are arrested, excluding weekends and holidays. The SC heard the case and determined that a 48-hour period is presumptively reasonable, provided that an arraignment immediately follows. If not, then the government bears the burden of showing why a period beyond 48 hours is reasonable detention of an accused person. If the period is less than 48 hours, the burden shifts to the accused to show unreasonable delay.

Delaware v. Prouse, 440 U.S. 648, 99 S.Ct. 1391 (1979) Prouse was randomly stopped by a police officer, who observed nothing illegal about Prouse's vehicle or the way Prouse was driving it. The officer asked Prouse for his driver's license and vehicle registration. While doing so, the officer smelled marijuana and saw it in plain view on the floor of the vehicle. Prouse was subsequently convicted of marijuana possession. He appealed, contending that the officer had had no probable cause to stop him in the first place, so all evidence found should have been suppressed. The SC agreed with Prouse, saying that officers must have probable cause in order to stop vehicles; they may not stop vehicles randomly for spot checks. This case did not make spot checks of vehicles unconstitutional. The SC allowed for states to devise schemes whereby spot checks could be made less intrusively, such as DWI stops, which are currently permitted.

Duncan v. Louisiana, 391 U.S. 145, 88 S.Ct. 1444 (1968) Duncan was convicted in a bench trial of simple battery in a Louisiana court. The crime was punishable as a misdemeanor, with two years' imprisonment and a fine of $300. In Duncan's case, he was sentenced to only 60 days and a fine of $150. He appealed, saying that he had demanded a jury trial and none was provided. The SC agreed with Duncan, saying that a crime with a potential punishment of two years is a serious crime, despite the sentence of 60 days imposed. Thus, for serious crimes, under the Sixth Amendment, Duncan was entitled to a jury trial.

Elkins v. United States, 364 U.S. 206, 80 S.Ct. 1437 (1960) The SC overturned the so-called silver-platter doctrine, which had previously allowed state authorities who discovered evidence of a federal crime in an illegal search to turn the evidence over to federal agencies for prosecution, as long as federal agents did not participate in the search.

Escobedo v. Illinois, 378 U.S. 478, 84 S.Ct. 1758 (1963) An informant told police that Escobedo had murdered someone. Without an arrest warrant, the police arrested Escobedo and commenced to interrogate him, without benefit of counsel, on his way to the police station. Escobedo asked to speak with an attorney on several occasions during a subsequent long interrogation period. At certain points, he was escorted about the station to various rooms, and at these times, he would see his attorney at a distance down the hall. The attorney was denied access to his client, who was told that his attorney "did not wish to see him" or was "unavailable." After many hours of intensive interrogation, Escobedo eventually confessed to murder and was convicted. He appealed. The SC overturned the conviction on the grounds that Escobedo had been denied counsel and that interrogation had proceeded despite his plea to have counsel present. Thus, the denial of counsel to Escobedo when he requested it had violated his right to due process. The case is also significant because the SC stressed the fact that initially, police officers were merely investigating a murder. At some early point, their mode shifted to accusation, where they accused Escobedo of murder. Thus, whenever police officers shift their questioning from investigatory to accusatory, defendants are entitled to counsel and to refrain from conversing with officers unless counsel is present.

Faretta v. California, 422 U.S. 806, 95 S.Ct. 2525 (1975) Faretta, who was charged with grand theft, desired to represent himself. The judge ruled that he had no constitutional right to represent himself in the case and appointed a public defender to defend him. Faretta was convicted. He appealed, arguing that he had a right to represent himself. The SC overturned his conviction, holding that Faretta indeed had a right knowingly and intelligently to waive his right to counsel and represent himself in the criminal proceeding. Thus, he had been denied his constitutional right to act as his own counsel.

Florida v. Bostick, 501 U.S. 429, 111 S.Ct. 2382 (1991) Bostick was a passenger on a bus from Miami to Atlanta. Florida police boarded the bus without any suspicion but rather with a simple intent to catch drug smugglers. They approached Bostick, asked him a few questions, asked to see his ticket, and then asked if they could search his bag. They advised Bostick he had a right to refuse, but he gave his consent. They discovered cocaine in his bag and he was subsequently convicted of cocaine possession. He appealed and the SC upheld the conviction, because given the totality of circumstances, Bostick had not been under arrest and had given his consent at the time of the search. Further, the fact that Bostick was on a bus did not constitute a "seizure" in the Fourth Amendment context. The SC concluded that the governing test is whether a reasonable person would feel free to decline the police offer to search his or her luggage, given the totality of circumstances.

Florida v. Royer, 460 U.S. 491, 103 S.Ct. 1319 (1983) Royer was an airline passenger in the Miami airport. DEA agents thought he fit a "drug courier profile," inasmuch as he bought a one-way ticket for cash and under an assumed name; he also was young, nervous, casually dressed, with heavy luggage. He gave police his driver's license with his correct name when requested. He also followed them to a room, again at their request, where they asked him if they could look through his luggage. He consented. They found marijuana, and Royer was eventually found guilty. He appealed, alleging that his Fourth Amendment rights had been violated because of the unreasonableness of his original stop and detention and the subsequent search. The SC agreed and overturned his conviction, saying that it is insufficient for police merely to have consent, without probable cause, to make a warrantless search of personal effects, such as luggage. The SC stressed Royer's lengthy detention and noted it was a serious intrusion into his privacy, especially as police had no probable cause to engage him in further searches. Consent given after an illegal act by police is tainted by the illegal act.

Gagnon v. Scarpelli, 411 U.S. 778, 92 S.Ct. 1756 (1973) Scarpelli pled guilty to a charge of robbery in July 1965 in a Wisconsin court. He was sentenced to 15 years in prison. But the judge suspended this sentence on August 5, 1965, and placed Scarpelli on probation for 7 years. The next day, August 6, Scarpelli was arrested and charged with burglary. His probation was revoked without a hearing, and he was placed in the Wisconsin State Reformatory to serve his 15-year term. About 3 years later, Scarpelli was paroled. Shortly before his parole, he filed a habeas corpus petition, alleging that his probation revocation had been invoked without a hearing and without benefit of counsel; thus he had been denied due process. Following his parole, the SC acted on his petition and ruled in his favor. Specifically, it said that Scarpelli had been denied his right to due process, because no revocation hearing had been held and he had not been represented by court-appointed counsel as an indigent. In effect, the Court, referring to *Morrissey v. Brewer* (1972), said that "a probation revocation, like parole revocation, is not a stage of a criminal prosecution, but does result in loss of liberty. . . . We hold that a probationer, like a parolee, is entitled to a preliminary hearing and a final revocation hearing in the conditions specified in *Morrissey v. Brewer*." The significance of this case is that it equated probation with parole as well as equating the respective revocation proceedings. Although the Court did not say that all parolees and probationers have a right to representation by counsel in all probation and parole revocation proceedings, it did say that counsel should be provided in cases where the probationer or parolee makes a timely claim contesting the allegations. No constitutional basis exists for providing counsel in all probation or parole revocation proceedings, but subsequent probation and parole revocation hearings usually involve defense counsel if legitimately requested. The SC declaration has been liberally interpreted in subsequent cases.

Gideon v. Wainwright, 372 U.S. 335, 83 S.Ct. 792 (1963) Gideon broke into a poolroom allegedly with the intent to commit larceny. This act was regarded as a felony in Florida. Gideon was indigent and asked for a lawyer to represent him. He was advised by the judge that counsel could only be appointed to persons if the offense involved the death penalty. Therefore, Gideon represented himself and was convicted. He appealed. The SC overturned his conviction, saying that all indigent defendants are entitled to court-appointed counsel in felony cases. (*See Argersinger v. Hamlin* [1972] for a narrowing of this provision to minor crimes or misdemeanor cases.)

Greenholtz v. Inmates of Nebraska, 442 U.S. 1, 99 S.Ct. 2100 (1979) The Nebraska prison system annually reviews files of inmates who are parole-eligible, and the Nebraska Parole Board decides whether they should be released in a two-stage proceeding: one phase consists of an initial review, and the second phase is a final parole hearing. The Parole Board decides whether the inmate is a good or bad parole risk, partially on the basis of evidence presented at these hearings. Inmate rights given by the Parole Board include the right to present evidence, call witnesses, be represented by counsel, and receive a written statement of reasons in the event parole is denied. Inmates believed that they were entitled to more constitutional rights relating to their early release than those given by the Parole Board and appealed to the SC. The Court upheld the Nebraska Parole Board and declared that inmates have no inherent constitutional rights to be released conditionally before the expiration of their valid sentences. Parole is a *privilege,* not a *right.* Furthermore, parole is optional with each state. For instance, Maine and the federal prison system have abolished parole. These jurisdictions currently use a form of supervised release.

Gregg v. Georgia, 428 U.S. 153, 96 S.Ct. 2909 (1976) Gregg was convicted of robberies and murders in Atlanta and sentenced to death. According to newly enacted provisions by the Georgia legislature, death penalty cases required bifurcated trials (two-stage trials), where guilt or innocence could be determined in the first stage, and the penalty could be assessed in the second stage. The provisions further required that in the penalty phase the jury was to consider and weigh aggravating and mitigating circumstances, and if the former outweighed the latter, the death penalty was to be imposed. An automatic appeal of the death sentence was also prescribed by law. Gregg appealed his death sentence, but the SC upheld it, saying that the procedures Georgia had instituted for applying the death penalty were constitutional and were not in violation of either the Eighth or Fourteenth Amendments.

Harris v. United States, 390 U.S. 234, 88 S.Ct. 992 (1968) Harris' automobile had been observed leaving the scene of a bank robbery. Later, Harris was arrested by police and his car was impounded. The car was subjected to a routine search. Incriminating evidence was obtained from his car and later used against him in court, when he was convicted. He appealed, but the SC upheld his conviction, saying that anything in plain view in an automobile during an inventory search is subject to seizure and admissible in court later.

Herrera v. Collins, 506 U.S. 390, 113 S.Ct. 853 (1993) On the basis of a handwritten confession, two eyewitness accounts and identifications, and two additional and critical pieces of circumstantial evidence, Herrera was convicted of first-degree murder and sentenced to death in Texas in 1982. Ten years later, he initiated a habeas corpus petition alleging that he was innocent of these murders because of "newly discovered evidence." Texas statutes have provisions governing the time limits to bring new appeals on newly discovered evidence. Herrera had gone well beyond these limits, and considering his confession, eyewitnesses to the murders, and the incriminating circumstantial evidence, the threshold for questioning Herrera's original conviction had not been reached. The SC upheld Herrera's conviction and death sentence, although it did offer one other avenue of relief. The SC said that Herrera could appeal to the Texas governor for clemency on a post-trial demonstration of actual innocence. Thus, if Herrera could show that the newly discovered evidence was exonerating, then the governor could grant clemency.

Hewitt v. Helms, 459 U.S. 460, 103 S.Ct. 864 (1983) Following riots in a Pennsylvania prison, an inmate, Helms, was given several misconduct reports. He was placed in solitary confinement for a period of time. Subsequent misconduct reports resulted in his being placed in solitary confinement for six months. Helms filed suit under Title 42, U.S.C. Section 1983, alleging that his Fourteenth Amendment right to due process had been violated because he had been denied full hearings on the two punishments. The SC denied Helms relief, saying that administrative segregation (solitary confinement) requires no formal hearings and is often ordered to insure prisoner safety. Specifically, inmates are not entitled to hearings to determine whether administrative segregation should be imposed for *protection*. The SC stressed, however, that for purposes of *punishment*, inmates are entitled to hearings as set forth in *Wolff v. McDonnell* (1974). Thus, there is a difference between administrative segregation, where no hearing is required, and punitive segregation, where it is.

Hurtado v. California, 110 U.S. 516 (1884) In 1879, California dropped the grand jury system, replacing it with broad prosecutorial discretionary powers, such as filing information against minor offenders and felons. In 1884, absent an indictment, Hurtado was charged with murder through a piece of criminal information, convicted, and sentenced to death. He appealed. The SC upheld the death sentence, holding that the grand jury is merely a procedure that the states can abolish at will. The significance of this case is that grand juries are not required for death-penalty cases to be conducted in state courts.

Illinois v. Gates, 462 U.S. 213, 103 S.Ct. 2317 (1983) Based upon an anonymous letter received by police officers, a couple, Lance and Sue Gates, of Bloomingdale, was accused of selling drugs. A fairly detailed description of the Gateses' activities was contained in the letter. Police placed the Gateses under surveillance, and everything described in the letter was observed to occur. The Gateses were moving large quantities of drugs between Florida and Illinois by automobile and air. The police obtained a search warrant from a judge and searched the Gates home, discovering large quantities of drugs. They were convicted. They appealed to the SC, arguing that the reliability of the informant could not be determined; thus, no basis existed to support the search warrant leading to the drug discovery. The Gateses moved to suppress all drugs found as the result of this allegedly faulty search. The landmark decision in this case was that the totality of circumstances, not informant reliability (previously used in *Aguilar v. Texas* [1964]), justified the search warrant issued. Thus it is now easier for police to obtain search warrants where they allege that a totality of circumstances suggests a crime is or has been committed and specific suspects have been named.

Illinois v. Rodriguez, 497 U.S. 177, 110 S.Ct. 2793 (1990) A woman, Fischer, called police and reported that she had been beaten by her boyfriend, Rodriguez, who was living elsewhere. The police went with Fisher to Rodriguez's apartment. She allowed them entry, since she lived there with Rodriguez and had a key. Indeed, her clothes, furniture, and other personal effects were in the apartment as proof of her statements. When police entered, they saw in plain view containers of cocaine and drug paraphernalia and arrested Rodriguez. The seized evidence was used against him and he was convicted. He appealed, contending that Fischer had moved out weeks before she and the police came to his apartment, and that she did not have the right to permit police entry. In fact, Fischer had moved out. Nevertheless, the police were acting in good faith that she did, indeed, have the authority to admit them. Thus, the court upheld Rodriguez's conviction, saying that a warrantless entry and search based on the consent of someone they believed to possess common authority over the premises was valid, even if the person actually lacked that authority.

In re Gault, 387 U.S. 1, 87 S.Ct. 1428 (1967) Gault was a 15-year-old in Arizona who, with another boy, allegedly made an obscene telephone call to an adult neighbor, Mrs. Cook. Police arrested Gault and took him to jail for questioning. In several subsequent one-sided juvenile court proceedings, Gault was not permitted to cross-examine his accuser or to testify in his own behalf. He was not initially permitted counsel or advised of his rights. Later, the juvenile court judge adjudicated his case and confined him in the Arizona State Industrial School until he reached age 21. He appealed, and the SC reversed the decision. This landmark case established a juvenile's right to have counsel, to confront and cross-examine accusers, to have protection from self-incrimination, and to have adequate notice of charges when there is the possibility of confinement as a punishment.

In re Winship, 397 U.S. 358, 90 S.Ct. 1068 (1970) Winship, age 12, purportedly entered a locker and stole $112 from a woman's pocketbook in New York City. He was charged with larceny. Under Section 712 of the New York Family Court Act, a juvenile delinquent is defined as "a person over seven and less than sixteen years of age who does any act, which, if done by an adult, would constitute a crime." Interestingly, the juvenile judge in the case acknowledged that the proof to be presented by the prosecution might be insufficient to establish the guilt of Winship beyond a reasonable doubt, although he did indicate that the New York Family Court Act provided that "any determination at the conclusion of [an adjudicatory hearing] that a [juvenile] did an act or acts must be based on a preponderance of the evidence" standard (397 U.S. at 360). Winship was adjudicated as a delinquent and ordered to a training school for 18 months, subject to annual extensions of his commitment until his 18th birthday. Appeals to New York courts were unsuccessful. The SC subsequently heard Winship's appeal and reversed the New York Family Court ruling because the beyond-a-reasonable-doubt standard had not been used in a case where incarceration or loss of freedom was likely. The standard of proof of beyond a reasonable doubt applies to juvenile delinquency proceedings where incarceration or incapacitation is a judicial adjudicatory option.

Johnson v. Louisiana, 406 U.S. 356, 92 S.Ct. 1620 (1972) Johnson was arrested without a warrant at his home based upon a photograph identification by a robbery victim. He was later subjected to a lineup, where he was identified again. Johnson was represented by counsel. He was subjected to trial by jury for the robbery offense and convicted in a jury vote of 9 to 3. Johnson appealed, contending that the jury verdict should be unanimous. The SC affirmed his conviction, saying, in effect, that states have the right to determine whether conviction requires unanimity of jury votes or only a majority vote. The SC concluded by saying that the verdicts rendered by 9 out of 12 jurors are not automatically invalidated by the disagreement of the dissenting 3. Johnson was not deprived of due process or a fair trial because of the 9 to 3 vote. (*See also Apodaca v. Oregon* [1972] for a comparative case.) This SC decision applies to states only and does not affect federal jury voting, which must be unanimous in their verdicts. Federal criminal jury sizes of 12 may be reduced to 11 under special conditions with judicial approval; either size must be unanimous.

Kent v. United States, 383 U.S. 541, 86 S.Ct. 1045 (1966) In 1959, Kent, a 14-year-old in the District of Columbia, was apprehended and charged with several housebreakings and attempted purse snatchings. He was judged delinquent and placed on probation. Subsequently in 1961, an intruder entered the apartment of a woman, took her wallet, and raped her. Fingerprints at the crime scene were later identified as those of Kent, who had been fingerprinted in connection with his delinquency case in 1959. On September 5, 1961, Kent admitted the offense as well as other crimes, and the juvenile court judge advised him of his intent to waive Kent to criminal court. In the meantime, Kent's mother had obtained an attorney, who advised the court that he intended to oppose the waiver. The judge ignored the attorney's motion and transferred Kent to the United States district court for the District of Columbia, where Kent was tried and convicted of six counts of housebreaking by a federal jury, although the jury found him "not guilty by reason of insanity" on the rape charge. Kent appealed. His conviction was reversed by the SC. The SC held that a full hearing, with assistance of counsel, must be held concerning the question of transferring a juvenile case to an adult court; children or their attorneys must have full access to social records used to make determinations, and the judge must state in writing the reasons for the transfer. The majority held that his rights to due process and to the effective assistance of counsel had been violated when he was denied a formal hearing on the waiver and his attorney's motions were ignored. The SC said that the matter of a waiver to criminal court was a "critical stage," relating to the defendant's potential loss of freedoms, and thus attorney representation was fundamental to due process. Because of the *Kent* decision, waiver hearings are now considered critical stages.

Mallory v. United States, 354 U.S. 449, 77 S.Ct. 1356 (1957) In an apartment house in the early morning hours of April 7, 1954, a woman doing laundry in the basement encountered trouble with the washing machine. She called the janitor, Mallory, who lived in the building with his wife and two sons. The janitor fixed the washing machine, left the laundry room, and later reappeared masked with his two sons. These men raped the woman and left the apartment shortly thereafter. The victim gave an account of the rape to police and named Mallory as a key suspect. Later that afternoon, Mallory and his sons were arrested and taken to police headquarters and questioned. Mallory was subjected to intensive questioning and a lie detector test. At about 10 p.m. that evening, he confessed. Because a magistrate could not be found, Mallory was brought before a commissioner the following morning and arraigned. Because of various delays, Mallory's trial occurred a year later. He was convicted. He appealed, arguing that he had not been brought before a magistrate without undue delay and that his extensive interrogation by police had been without probable cause and of unreasonable duration. The SC heard Mallory's case and overturned his conviction, holding that police had had only reasonable suspicion when Mallory was originally arrested, and that the subsequent detention and interrogation yielded probable cause for which rape charges could be filed against Mallory. The SC also noted that during the afternoon when Mallory was first arrested, numerous magistrates had been available to police. Thus Mallory had not been brought before them without undue delay, a violation of his due-process rights. The SC said that it is not the function of police to arrest, as it were, at large and to use an interrogating process at police headquarters to determine whom they should charge before a committing magistrate on "probable cause."

Mapp v. Ohio, 367 U.S. 1081, 81 S.Ct. 1684 (1961) Police in Cleveland suspected someone of bomb making or possessing bomb materials. The suspect was believed to be at the home of Mapp, a woman friend. Officers went to Mapp's home and asked to come in. Mapp refused, suggesting that officers get a warrant. The officers left and Mapp called her attorney. The officers returned later, waving a piece of paper and saying that they had a warrant to conduct their search of her premises. Mapp's attorney arrived at the same time. Neither he nor Mapp was permitted to see the "warrant." Mapp grabbed the piece of paper and shoved it down her bosom. A police officer quickly retrieved it and handcuffed her. A thorough search of her home disclosed no bomb materials. However, a trunk in Mapp's basement yielded pencil sketches and drawings depicting what officers believed to be "pornography." Mapp was subsequently convicted of possessing pornographic material. She appealed to the SC, claiming that the officers had had no right to search her home. The SC agreed with Mapp and overturned her conviction. No warrant had ever been issued and it was unknown what the piece of paper was that police waved in front of Mapp and her attorney preceding their unlawful search of her premises. This is a landmark SC case, because it established the *exclusionary rule* to deter police misconduct in search-and-seizure cases. It made the rule applicable to *both* state and federal law enforcement officers. Thus, any evidence seized illegally is inadmissible later in court against criminal suspects. Overruled cases relating to the exclusionary rule were *Weeks v. United States* (1914), *Wolf v. Colorado* (1949), and *Wong Sun v. United States* (1963). The Fourth Amendment protects citizens from unreasonable searches and seizures by the states; this decision by the SC overturned the *Wolf* decision and made the Fourth Amendment applicable to states through the due-process clause of the Fourteenth Amendment.

Maryland v. Buie, 494 U.S. 325, 110 S.Ct. 1093 (1990) Police suspected Buie of involvement in an armed robbery and went to his home with a valid arrest warrant. The officers fanned out and commenced searching the home for Buie, who was in the basement. He surrendered. While the police investigated the basement to see if anyone else was there who might pose a danger to them, they observed a red running suit like the one used in the armed robbery. This evidence was seized and used in a subsequent trial where Buie was convicted of armed robbery. He appealed, arguing that the police had had no business entering parts of his home searching for evidence without a valid search warrant. The SC disagreed and said that in this case, officers were merely attempting to determine whether anyone else might be on the premises who would pose a danger to them. The SC stressed that this was a protective sweep for the safety of officers, and that contraband or evidence seen in plain view during such a sweep was not immune from a Fourth Amendment reasonable seizure.

Massachusetts v. Sheppard, 468 U.S. 981, 104 S.Ct. 3424 (1984) Sheppard, a murder suspect, was investigated by police. Officers attempted to obtain a search warrant articulating the places to be searched and things or items to be seized. For some reason, conventional search warrants were not available, so the officers decided to use alternative warrants used for searching for controlled substances. These warrants were in a different form from those of conventional search warrants. The officers crossed out certain phraseology and wrote in other pertinent phraseology so that the warrant would be worded correctly. After further modification by a judge, the contrived search warrant against Sheppard was signed. Incriminating evidence was obtained as the result of executing the search warrant. Sheppard's attorney made a pretrial motion alleging that the contrived search warrant was invalid; thus, according to the exclusionary rule, the evidence obtained by its execution ought to be suppressed. The trial judge allowed the evidence against Sheppard, who was convicted of first-degree murder. He appealed, but the SC upheld his conviction, despite the faulty nature of the search warrant. The SC declared that in a manner similar to *United States v. Leon* (1984), the police officers executing the search warrant had done so in good faith. The difference between *United States v. Leon* (1984) and *Sheppard* is that in *Sheppard*, it was alleged that the officers *knew* that the warrant was defective in advance, since it had been substantially revised and rewritten; whereas in *Leon*, officers *did not know* the defectiveness of the warrant. The SC concluded that the officers in *Sheppard* believed the warrant-issuing judge, who had advised them that the warrant was valid when, in fact, it wasn't.

Massiah v. United States, 377 U.S. 201, 84 S.Ct. 1199 (1964) Massiah was believed to be transporting illegal drugs into the United States from South America. He was indicted by a federal grand jury on drug charges. While he was under indictment and awaiting trial, a friend of Massiah's was directed by FBI agents to sit in Massiah's car and elicit incriminating statements about the drugs from Massiah. Massiah's friend was wearing a wire transmitter, and an FBI agent was sitting in a car behind Massiah's car in order to record these incriminating statements. Massiah did make incriminating statements that were recorded and he was subsequently convicted. He appealed. The SC overturned his conviction, saying that the conversation he had with his friend in Massiah's car constituted an *interrogation*, since the friend was *acting on behalf of and at the instruction of the government.* Thus, because Massiah was under indictment and represented by counsel, who was entitled to be present during the interrogation but was not present, Massiah's constitutional rights had been violated.

McCleskey v. Kemp, 481 U.S. 279, 107 S.Ct. 1756 (1987) McCleskey, a black man, was convicted of murdering a police officer during a grocery store robbery in 1978. He was sentenced to death. McCleskey appealed, introducing evidence to show that statistically more black criminals receive the death penalty than white criminals and claiming that such disproportion is unconstitutional. The SC rejected McCleskey's claim. Georgia's death penalty, the SC said, was not arbitrary and capricious, nor was it being applied in a discriminatory manner, regardless of statistical evidence to the contrary.

McCleskey v. Zant, 499 U.S. 467, 111 S.Ct. 1454 (1991) McCleskey was charged with murder and armed robbery. A cellmate of McCleskey's, Evans, was called to testify against him. Evans said that McCleskey had boasted about the killing and admitted it. McCleskey was convicted and sentenced to death. He appealed, claiming that the cellmate-induced conversations had been made without the assistance of his counsel. The SC rejected his claim, stating that they could have been made in an earlier appeal proceeding. The fact that McCleskey was making it in a subsequent proceeding nullified the claim. Thus, in order for such claims to be considered, they must be made at the right time, shortly after they occur, not after several appeals have been unsuccessfully lodged with state and federal courts.

McKeiver v. Pennsylvania, 403 U.S. 528, 91 S.Ct. 1976 (1971) In May 1968, McKeiver, age 16, was charged with robbery, larceny, and receiving stolen goods. He was represented by counsel, who asked the court for a jury trial "as a matter of right." This request was denied. McKeiver was subsequently adjudicated delinquent. On appeal to the SC later, McKeiver's adjudication was upheld. The case is important because the SC said that jury trials for juveniles are not a matter of constitutional right but rather at the discretion of the juvenile court judge. In about a fifth of the states today, jury trials for juveniles in juvenile courts are held under certain conditions.

McNabb v. United States, 318 U.S. 332, 63 S.Ct. 608 (1943) The McNabb family in Chattanooga, Tennessee, was a clan of mountaineers dealing in illegal whiskey by operating an illegal still. Agents from the Alcohol Tax Unit raided their settlement one evening when it was learned that they planned to sell a large quantity of illegal liquor. During their raid, one federal officer was shot and killed. Later, federal agents visited the home of the McNabbs and arrested the brothers Freeman and Raymond. They took the men to the federal building in Chattanooga, where they were not brought before any United States magistrate or other judicial official but kept in a small room for 14 hours and not permitted to see relatives or lawyers. There is no evidence that they requested counsel. Neither had passed the fourth grade in school. Following intensive questioning by agents, they eventually confessed to the killing and were tried, convicted of murder, and sentenced to 45 years in prison. They appealed. The SC reversed their convictions, holding that coerced confessions are not admissible. Further, the officers had erred by not providing suitable counsel for these defendants and the interrogation conditions were inherently illegal and contrary to due process. Thus, their confessions had been improperly received as evidence against them.

McNeil v. Wisconsin, 501 U.S. 171, 111 S.Ct. 2204 (1991) McNeil was charged with armed robbery in West Allis, Wisconsin. He requested and was represented by a public defender. While in police custody, McNeil signed a Miranda rights waiver and agreed to talk with police about the West Allis robbery; during that time, he made incriminating statements about his involvement in a murder in Caledonia, Wisconsin. He was then formally charged with the murder in Caledonia. In a pretrial motion, he moved to suppress his former incriminating statements. This motion was denied. He was convicted. He appealed on the grounds that his statements should have been barred from evidence, because he had requested counsel during his initial appearance and because police were initially telling him his Miranda rights concerning an unrelated crime. McNeil believed he must be told his rights for *each* of the crimes with which he had been charged. The SC heard McNeil's appeal and rejected it, holding that the assertion of the Sixth Amendment right to counsel does not imply invocation of the Miranda Fifth Amendment right; such a rule would seriously impede effective law enforcement by precluding uncounseled but uncoerced admissions of guilt pursuant to valid Miranda warnings.

Mempa v. Rhay, 389 U.S. 128, 88 S.Ct. 254 (1967) Mempa was convicted of joyriding in a stolen vehicle on June 17, 1959. He was placed on probation for two years by a Spokane, Washington, judge. Several months later, Mempa was involved in a burglary on September 15. Mempa admitted participating in the burglary. The county prosecutor in Spokane moved to have Mempa's probation revoked. At his probation revocation hearing, the sole testimony about his involvement in the burglary came from his probation officer. Mempa was not represented by counsel, was not asked if he wanted counsel, and was not given an opportunity to offer statements in his own behalf. Furthermore, there was no cross-examination of the probation officer about his statements. The court revoked Mempa's probation and sentenced him to 10 years in the Washington State Penitentiary. Six years later in 1965, Mempa filed a writ of habeas corpus, alleging that he had been denied a right to counsel at the revocation hearing. The Washington Supreme Court denied his petition, but he appealed, and the United States SC elected to hear it. The SC overturned the Washington decision and ruled in Mempa's favor. Specifically, the SC said Mempa had been entitled to an attorney but had been denied one. While the Court did not question Washington authority to defer sentencing in the probation matter, it said that any indigent (including Mempa) is entitled at every stage of a criminal proceeding to be represented by court-appointed counsel, where "substantial rights of a criminal accused may be affected." Thus, the SC considered a probation revocation hearing to be a "critical stage" that falls within the due-process provisions of the Fourteenth Amendment. In subsequent years, several courts also applied this decision to parole revocation hearings.

Michigan v. Harvey, 494 U.S. 344, 110 S.Ct. 1176 (1990) Harvey was arraigned on rape charges, and counsel was appointed for him. Initially, he wanted to make a statement to police but didn't know whether he ought to have his attorney present. The police advised Harvey that he could make a statement *without* his attorney present, since the attorney would eventually get a copy of his statement anyway. Subsequently, Harvey signed a rights waiver form and made incriminating statements to police without his attorney present. Later in court, Harvey gave conflicting statements, and police used his earlier statement, given without the attorney present, to impeach his court testimony. Harvey was convicted of first-degree criminal sexual conduct. He appealed. A Michigan court overturned his conviction, saying that it is unconstitutional for prosecutors to use statements otherwise inadmissible under the *Jackson* rule (see *Michigan v. Jackson* [1986]) to impeach a defendant's later testimony in court. The State of Michigan appealed, and the SC reinstated Harvey's conviction, holding that a statement to police taken in violation of *Jackson* may be used to impeach a defendant's testimony (in court later). The important point here is that Harvey's statements had been initiated by Harvey, not by police, even though Harvey had invoked his Sixth Amendment right to counsel. This information *could not* be used by prosecutors in their case-in-chief against the defendant, but *it could* be used for impeachment purposes.

Minnesota v. Dickerson, 508 U.S. 366, 113 S.Ct. 2130 (1993) Dickerson emerged from a known "crack house" and was observed by police officers walking down an alley. When he saw the officers approaching him, he reversed direction and walked away from them. They decided to stop him for an investigative pat-down. They discovered no weapons, but one of the officers thrust his hand into Dickerson's pockets and found a small quantity of crack cocaine in a glassine envelope. He claimed that he had "felt a small lump that felt like crack cocaine" through Dickerson's clothing after the initial pat-down and frisk. Dickerson was charged with cocaine possession and convicted. He appealed, and the SC overturned his conviction on the ground that the search of Dickerson went well beyond the scope specified in *Terry v. Ohio*, where police officer pat-downs and frisks of suspects were used exclusively for the purpose of determining whether they possessed a dangerous weapon that might be used to harm the police. This specific type of incident is directly on point and consistent with a SC ruling in another case involving excessive officer intrusion into a suspect's pocket in a search for contraband: *Sibron v. New York* (1968).

Minnick v. Mississippi, 498 U.S. 146, 111 S.Ct. 486 (1990) A day after escaping from a Mississippi county jail, Minnick and an accomplice killed two men during the burglary of a trailer. Minnick fled to California, where he was arrested on Friday, August 22, 1986, by Lemon Grove police. On August 23, FBI agents advised Minnick of his right to counsel and his right not to answer their questions. Minnick made a partial confession to FBI agents, although he advised them to "come back Monday" when he would have an attorney present. The same day, Minnick was appointed an attorney, who advised him to say nothing to police. On Monday, August 25, a deputy sheriff from Mississippi, Denham, flew to the San Diego jail where Minnick was being held. Minnick was reluctant to talk to Denham, but jailers told him he "had to talk." Minnick related all the incidents following his jail escape and admitted committing one of the murders. He was subsequently convicted on two counts of capital murder and sentenced to death. He appealed, moving to suppress his statements to FBI agents and to Denham. The SC reversed Minnick's conviction and sentence and remanded the case to a lower court, reasoning that once the Miranda warning had been given and an attorney appointed, further questioning by police might not resume without an attorney present, if the defendant had invoked the right to have counsel present.

Miranda v. Arizona, 384 U.S. 436, 86 S.Ct. 1602 (1966) Miranda was arrested on suspicion of rape and kidnapping. He was not permitted to talk to an attorney, nor was he advised of his right to one. He was interrogated by police for several hours, eventually confessing and signing a written confession. He was convicted. Miranda appealed, contending that his right to due process had been violated because he had not first been advised of his right to remain silent and to have an attorney present during a custodial interrogation. The SC agreed and set forth the *Miranda warning.* This monumental decision provided that confessions made by suspects who were not notified of their due-process rights cannot be admitted as evidence. Suspects must be advised of certain rights before they are questioned by police; these rights include the right to remain silent, the right to counsel, the right to free counsel if suspects cannot afford one, and the right to terminate questioning at any time.

Mistretta v. United States, 488 U.S. 361, 109 S.Ct. 647 (1989) Mistretta was convicted of selling cocaine. The United States Sentencing Guidelines were officially in effect after November 1, 1987. Mistretta's criminal acts and conviction occurred after this date, and thus he was subject to guidelines-based sentencing rather than indeterminate sentencing, which the federal district courts had previously followed. Under the former sentencing scheme, Mistretta might have been granted probation. However, the new guidelines greatly restricted the use of probation as a sentence in federal courts, and thus, Mistretta's sentence involved serving an amount of time in prison. Mistretta appealed his conviction, arguing that the new guidelines violated the separation-of-powers doctrine, as several federal judges were members of the United States Sentencing Commission and helped to formulate laws and punishments, an exclusive function of Congress.The SC upheld Mistretta's conviction and declared the new guidelines to be constitutional, not in violation of the separation of powers doctrine.

Moran v. Burbine, 475 U.S. 412, 106 S.Ct. 1135 (1986) Burbine, a murder suspect, was arrested by police and given the Miranda warning. The police, knowing that Burbine's sister had had counsel appointed for him and that the attorney was attempting to reach Burbine, elected to question Burbine for a few hours anyway, before he was allowed to see his counsel. Burbine did not know that his sister had appointed counsel for him or know that his counsel was attempting to reach him. Further, the police had advised Burbine's attorney that no interrogation was planned for the evening and that the attorney could see him "in the morning." Burbine made a confession to police about the murder and was subsequently convicted. He appealed, alleging that his Fifth Amendment right against self-incrimination had been violated when police forbade the attorney to talk to him. The SC upheld Burbine's conviction, saying that he had been properly told his Miranda rights and was in the position of knowingly giving or not giving incriminating statements to police, regardless of other events occurring around him and of which he was unaware. The SC said that events outside the defendant's knowledge could have no bearing on the defendant's invocation of his right to silence. Thus, when Burbine decided to talk with police about the murder and confess, he was knowingly waiving his right to silence.

Morrissey v. Brewer, 408 U.S. 471, 92 S.Ct. 2593 (1972) Morrissey was a parolee who allegedly violated several parole conditions. The violations included (1) failing to report his place of residence to his parole officer, (2) buying an automobile under an assumed name and operating it without parole officer permission, (3) obtaining credit under an assumed name, and (4) giving false statements to police after a minor traffic accident. The paroling authority summarily revoked his parole, and he was returned to prison. Morrissey appealed the summary revocation and the SC heard his case. Among other things, the Court in this landmark case established the minimum due process requirements for parole revocation: (1) Two hearings are required: the first is a preliminary hearing to determine whether probable cause exists that a parolee has violated any specific parole condition; the second is a general revocation proceeding. (2) Written notice must be given to the parolee prior to the general revocation proceeding. (3) Disclosure must be made to the parolee concerning the nature of parole violation(s) and evidence obtained. (4) Parolees must be given the right to confront and cross-examine their accusers unless adequate cause can be given for prohibiting such a cross-examination. (5) A written statement must be provided containing the reasons for revoking the parole and the evidence used in making that decision. (6) The parolees are entitled to have the facts judged by a detached and neutral hearing committee.

New Jersey v. T.L.O., 469 U.S. 325, 105 S.Ct. 733 (1985) A 14-year-old girl was caught smoking a cigarette in the school bathroom, violating school rules. When confronted by the principal, she denied that she had been smoking. The principal examined her purse and discovered a pack of cigarettes, some rolling papers, money, marijuana, and other drug materials. This information was turned over to police, who charged the girl with delinquency. She was convicted. The girl's attorney sought to exclude the seized evidence because it was believed to be in violation of her Fourth Amendment right against unreasonable searches and seizures. The SC heard the case and ruled in favor of school officials, declaring that they only need reasonable suspicion, not probable cause, in order to search students and their possessions while on school property. When students enter their schools, they are subject to a lower standard than that applied to adult suspects when suspected of wrongdoing or carrying illegal contraband in violation of school rules.

New York v. Quarles, 467 U.S. 649, 104 S.Ct. 2626 (1984) A woman reported that she had just been raped by an armed man, who ran into a supermarket. Police went to the market and saw Quarles. They approached him and had him place his hands on his head. A pat-down led to the discovery of an empty shoulder holster. Fearing that a firearm was near Quarles, making the issue of public safety of paramount concern, police asked Quarles where the gun was. He identified where he had thrown it among some empty cartons. The officers retrieved the gun and then read Quarles his Miranda rights. He was charged with rape and convicted. Quarles appealed, arguing that the initial statements he gave about the whereabouts of his gun should have been excluded as evidence against him, since officers had not told him his rights prior to questioning him about the gun's whereabouts. The SC upheld Quarles's conviction, saying that officer concern for public safety, where a firearm was near a potentially dangerous suspect, overrides the matter of advising suspects of their right to silence and other Miranda warnings. Thus the SC created a public-safety exception to allow investigating officers to bypass the Miranda warning when public safety is believed to be in jeopardy.

Nix v. Williams, 467 U.S. 431, 104 S.Ct. 2501 (1984) On Christmas Eve, a 10-year-old girl was missing from a YMCA building in Des Moines, Iowa. Eyewitnesses reported later observing Williams leaving the YMCA building carrying a large bundle wrapped in a blanket, with two skinny legs protruding. Officers found Williams's car the next day 160 miles east of Des Moines. At a rest stop between where the car was found and the YMCA building, they discovered items of clothing and other articles. They assumed that the girl's body was probably somewhere between Des Moines and where Williams's car was found. Williams was subsequently found in a nearby town and arrested. While he was being driven back to Des Moines in a police vehicle, police officers engaged him in conversation relating to the girl's whereabouts. Because it had recently snowed, finding her body would be difficult. Officers suggested to Williams that he ought to tell them where her body was so that they could give her a "Christian burial." (This became known as the *Christian Burial Case.*) Williams confessed and directed officers to the girl's body. Williams was charged with and convicted of first-degree murder. He appealed, and his conviction was overturned inasmuch as police officers had not advised him of his Miranda rights. He was subjected to a second trial, in which his original confession was excluded. He was convicted again, but this time because the prosecutor showed that the girl's body would have been discovered eventually, thus providing the conclusive evidence against Williams. The significance of this case is that it introduced the inevitable-discovery exception to the exclusionary rule, whereby prosecutors may argue that inculpatory evidence may be introduced against criminal suspects if it can be shown that police would have eventually discovered the incriminating evidence anyway.

Oliver v. United States, 466 U.S. 170, 104 S.Ct. 1735 (1984) Oliver grew marijuana on some land near his home. He had fenced in the property and posted a "No Trespassing" sign. Acting on reports from an informant that Oliver was growing marijuana in the field, officers went to the field and found a footpath. Without an arrest warrant or a search warrant, they followed it about a mile until they came to some marijuana plants growing in the middle of the field. Oliver was arrested and convicted of marijuana manufacturing. He appealed, contending that the "No Trespassing" sign required police to obtain a search warrant before they trespassed on his property. The SC disagreed with Oliver and upheld the conviction, saying that "No Trespassing" signs are not sufficient to create the reasonable expectation of privacy that requires police to have a warrant; further, the open field was such that the privacy expectation that an owner would have relating to it does not exist. Police may "trespass" and search any such open area without a warrant and without probable cause.

Oregon v. Elstad, 470 U.S. 298, 105 S.Ct. 1285 (1985) Elstad was suspected of burglary, and police officers went to his home with an arrest warrant. They entered the house at the mother's invitation and proceeded to Elstad's room, where they advised him that he was implicated in the burglary. Elstad told officers, "I was there," before being given his Miranda warning. He was placed under arrest and taken to the police station, where he requested to talk to officers. He gave a full and voluntary confession to the burglary and signed a typed statement. After he was convicted, he appealed, contending that his original statement was an inculpatory one, and because it had been given before he was told his Miranda rights, it should have been excluded as well as the confession he made later resulting from the incriminating statement. The SC disagreed with Elstad and upheld the burglary conviction. They noted that prior statements made by suspects before Miranda warnings are given are admissible so long as they are voluntary, especially if subsequent confessions are given following Miranda warnings, where earlier statements are substantiated.

Powell v. Alabama, 287 U.S. 45, 53 S.Ct. 55 (1932) During a train trip in Alabama, two white women were allegedly raped by several young black men. At an unscheduled stop, the train was searched by police, who arrested nine black young men and charged them with rape. Not until the trial date did the judge assign an attorney to represent each man. In one-day trials, each young man was convicted and sentenced to death. They appealed. The SC overturned their convictions, citing several violations of constitutional rights. Among other things, the men had not been permitted the assistance of counsel in their own defense until the trial date. Additionally, unreliable and incompetent evidence had been admitted against the men, evidence that would not have been admitted in other courts. The charges had not been properly formulated or delivered to the men, so that they did not understand fully what it was they were supposed to have done and when. Considering the time of the incident, the early 1930s, and race relations in the State of Alabama, their treatment by authorities was consistent with inequities against blacks in the South generally during that time period.

Powers v. Ohio, 499 U.S. 400, 111 S.Ct. 1364 (1991) Powers was charged with murder, aggravated murder, and attempted aggravated murder, all with firearm specifications (calling for mandatory minimum sentences). A white man, he objected to the government's use of peremptory challenges to strike seven black prospective jurors from the jury. Subsequently, Powers was convicted. He appealed, alleging that his Fourteenth Amendment right had been violated under the equal-protection clause because of the alleged discriminatory use of peremptory challenges. The matter of excluding prospective black jurors by the use of peremptory challenges had already been decided in *Batson v. Kentucky* (1986), where it was declared unconstitutional to use peremptory challenges to achieve a racially pure jury. In the *Batson* case, however, the defendant was black, and government prejudice was obvious in the use of these peremptory challenges. In the *Powers* case, the defendant was white and prospective black jurors had been excluded. The SC heard Powers' appeal and overturned his conviction on the same grounds as *Batson*, holding that criminal defendants may object to race-based exclusions of jurors effected through peremptory challenges whether or not defendants and excluded jurors share the same race.

Rhodes v. Chapman, 452 U.S. 337, 101 S.Ct. 2392 (1981) Kelly Chapman and Richard Jaworski, two inmates of the Southern Ohio Correctional Facility, were housed in the same cell. They objected, contending that double-celling violated their constitutional rights. Furthermore, in support of their claim, they cited the facts that their confinement was *long-term* and not *short-term* as it was in *Bell v. Wolfish* (1979), that physical and mental injury would be sustained through such close contact and limited space for movement, and that the Ohio facility was housing 38 percent more inmates than its design capacity specified. The SC ruled that double-celling in this long-term prison facility was neither cruel and unusual punishment nor unconstitutional per se. The court based its holding on the "totality of circumstances" associated with Chapman's and Jaworski's confinement. The "cruel and unusual" provisions of the Eighth Amendment must be construed in a "flexible and dynamic" manner. Thus, when all factors were considered, no evidence existed that Ohio authorities were wantonly inflicting pain on these or other inmates. These conditions, considered in their totality, did not constitute serious deprivation. Double-celling, made necessary by the unanticipated increase in prisoners in the facility, had not resulted in food deprivations, a decrease in the quality of medical care, or a decrease in sanitation standards.

Rochin v. California, 342 U.S. 165, 72 S.Ct. 205 (1952) Rochin, a suspect allegedly trafficking in narcotics, was visited by sheriff's deputies one evening. Officers found him sitting on his bed partially dressed. Several white capsules were on a nearby nightstand in plain view. When officers attempted to seize them, Rochin grabbed the capsules and swallowed them. Officers immediately brought Rochin to a nearby hospital and ordered physicians to give him an emetic solution to cause him to vomit. The capsules were obtained through a stomach pump and turned out to be morphine. These capsules were used against him later in court and he was convicted. He appealed. His conviction was overturned because of the unreasonableness of the manner of the officer's search and seizure of the capsules. In a written opinion, the SC labeled the police tactics offensive and "conduct that shocks the conscience."

Rummel v. Estelle, 445 U.S. 263, 100 S.Ct. 1133 (1980) Rummel had previously been convicted of two nonviolent felonies. Under a Texas recidivist statute, he was convicted and given a life sentence. He appealed to the SC, which upheld the sentence. The SC said that life sentences for violating habitual-offender statutes are *not* cruel and unusual in violation of the Eighth Amendment. (*See Solem v. Helm* [1983] for a comparative case.)

Santobello v. New York, 404 U.S. 257, 92 S.Ct. 495 (1971) Santobello was charged with two felony counts and pleaded guilty to a lesser included offense following a promise by the prosecutor not to make a sentence recommendation at the plea bargain hearing. Several months lapsed, and in the meantime, a new prosecutor was appointed and represented the government at Santobello's plea hearing. At this time, the prosecutor recommended the maximum sentence under the law, and Santobello moved to withdraw his guilty plea. The judge refused to allow the withdrawal of the guilty plea, and Santobello was sentenced to the maximum sentence. The SC heard Santobello's appeal. Santobello alleged that the prosecutor was honor bound to stand by his statement not to make a sentence recommendation, despite the fact that the judge said that he was "uninfluenced" by the prosecutor's recommendation. The SC overturned Santobello's conviction and allowed him to withdraw his guilty plea, saying that when a guilty plea rests to a significant degree on a promise or agreement by the prosecutor, then such a promise must be fulfilled. The significance of this case is that prosecutors cannot make promises to defendants to elicit guilty pleas unless they fulfill their promises.

Schall v. Martin, 467 U.S. 253, 104 S.Ct. 2403 (1984) Martin, age 14, was arrested at 11:30 p.m. on December 13, 1977, in New York City. He was charged with first-degree robbery, second-degree assault, and criminal possession of a weapon. Martin lied to police at the time, giving a false name and address. Between the time of his arrest and December 29, when a fact-finding hearing was held, Martin was detained (a total of 15 days). His detention was based largely on the false information he had supplied to police and the seriousness of the charges pending against him. Subsequently, he was adjudicated a delinquent and placed on two years' probation. Later, his attorney filed an appeal, contesting his preventive detention as violative of the due-process clause of the Fourteenth Amendment. The SC eventually heard the case and upheld the detention as constitutional.

Schmerber v. California, 384 U.S. 757, 86 S.Ct. 1826 (1966) Schmerber was arrested in California for driving under the influence of alcohol following an accident. He was brought to a hospital, where a nurse drew a sample of his blood against his will, while he was being treated for injuries. The blood specimen became inculpatory evidence against him later in court, and he was convicted of DWI. He appealed, contending that the seizure of his blood had been unreasonable and had violated his Fourth Amendment rights. Furthermore, he argued that his own blood used against him was tantamount to self-incrimination and thus violated his Fifth Amendment rights. The SC disagreed on both counts, declaring that drawing blood without one's consent, when done by medical personnel, does not violate one's constitutional rights against unreasonable search and seizure. The SC rejected the Fifth Amendment violation argument by noting that this right pertained only to testimony, not blood evidence. The court added that exigent circumstances existed in that situation, because a delay would have prevented officers from obtaining a valid sample of Schmerber's blood to show its true alcohol content at or near the time of the accident.

Schneckloth v. Bustamonte, 412 U.S. 218, 93 S.Ct. 2041 (1973) One evening, police observed an automobile with a broken tail light and stopped it. The driver had no driver's license and was asked to step out of the car together with several other occupants. One passenger, Alcala, had a driver's license and told police that the automobile belonged to his brother. The officers asked if they could search the vehicle and Alcala consented. While conducting their search, the officers discovered stolen checks from a car wash and arrested one of the passengers, Bustamonte. Bustamonte was later convicted of possessing checks with intent to defraud. He appealed, seeking to have the checks suppressed as evidence against him. The SC disagreed, saying that Alcala, who had constructive possession of the vehicle, was in a position to give police consent to conduct their search. Therefore, the evidence they later discovered as the result of that search was valid and had not violated Bustamonte's Fourth Amendment rights.

Sherman v. United States, 356 U.S. 369, 78 S.Ct. 819 (1958) A paid government informant was instructed to meet Sherman, a drug addict, in a doctor's office and inquire about possible sources of drugs. Sherman repeatedly declined to provide the informant with drug information or sources of drugs. At some point, however, he eventually provided small quantities of drugs to the informant at his own cost plus expenses. Eventually, after several transactions, government agents arrested Sherman and he was convicted of drug offenses. Sherman appealed, alleging entrapment. The SC agreed and overturned his conviction. The SC stressed the significance of the phrase "entrapment occurs whenever the government induces persons to commit crimes they otherwise would never have committed." The persistence of the government informant in requesting drugs and Sherman's repeated avoidance and denials of involvement in drug trafficking were clear evidence to the SC that Sherman had never intended to traffic in drugs, without the substantial inducement and entrapment by the government and their paid informant.

Singer v. United States, 380 U.S. 24, 85 S.Ct. 783 (1965) Singer, charged with a federal crime, requested to have a bench trial instead of a jury trial. His request was denied, and he was subsequently convicted of the crime by a federal jury. He appealed, arguing that he should have been entitled to a bench trial. The SC disagreed and said that although Singer had a right to a jury trial under the circumstances, the constitutional requirement did not entitle a citizen to the opposite of that right, namely, a bench trial. Thus, defendants cannot elect to have a bench trial as a matter of right if jury trials are prescribed in federal proceedings (*see Duncan v. Louisiana* [1968]).

Spinelli v. United States, 394 U.S. 410, 89 S.Ct. 584 (1972) An informant alerted the FBI to Spinelli's allegedly illegal bookmaking activities in St. Louis. Spinelli was placed under FBI surveillance. During this surveillance, FBI agents observed Spinelli enter an apartment where a telephone was located, one supposedly used in this bookmaking activity. The FBI filed an affidavit with a United States magistrate, detailing its observations of Spinelli and its belief that he was engaged in illegal interstate bookmaking. Little information was relayed to the magistrate about the informant and the basis for the informant's reliability. FBI agents entered Spinelli's apartment, searched, and found materials implicating Spinelli in illegal bookmaking. He was convicted. He appealed and the SC overturned the conviction primarily because the FBI agents had not met the two-pronged test established by *Aguilar v. Texas* (1964). The two-pronged test is (1) How well is the informant known by the law enforcement officer? and (2) How reliable has been previous information furnished by the informant? The SC also rejected a totality-of-circumstances test, concluding in part that it "paints too broad a brush," making an affidavit too vague to substantiate probable cause. Subsequently, in the case of *Illinois v. Gates* (1983), the SC modified the two-pronged test established in *Aguilar* and created an additional totality-of-circumstances test, making it currently unnecessary for law enforcement officers to detail the nature of their relations with informants and informant reliability.

Stack v. Boyle, 342 U.S. 1, 72 S.Ct. 1 (1951) Stack was charged with conspiracy to commit a crime, and bail was set at $50,000. He protested, saying that the bail was excessive and that no hearing was ever held to determine how much bail should be set. The SC agreed with Stack and remanded the case back to the district court, where a hearing could be held on the bail issue. The Court held that bail had not been fixed by proper methods in this case. It did not try to determine or define "proper methods," however.

Stone v. Powell, 428 U.S. 465, 96 S.Ct. 3037 (1976) An inmate filed a habeas corpus petition in a federal court seeking release from prison. The prisoner had already filed the same petition in a state court and the petition had been denied. The SC heard the appeal and rejected the argument of the inmate, concluding that a habeas corpus petition will not be heard in federal court after it has already been rejected in a state court. The SC stressed the fact that the inmate had a full and fair opportunity to argue the case in a state appellate court.

Tennessee v. Garner, 471 U.S. 1, 105 S.Ct. 1694 (1985) A 15-year-old boy, Garner, and a friend were in an empty home in Memphis late at night when neighbors reported the "breaking and entering" to police. Police officers approached the home and saw someone fleeing. They shouted warnings to the fleeing suspects and finally shot at them. One bullet struck Garner in the back of the head, killing him instantly. The standard governing the use of deadly force was that *any* force could be employed, even deadly force, to prevent the escape of fleeing felons. Because burglary is a felony, those fleeing from the empty home were felony suspects and police believed they were entitled to shoot at them. Many years later, in 1985, the SC declared that deadly force had not been warranted in this case, as burglary is punishable with a few years in prison, not the death penalty. This landmark case was significant because it effectively nullified the fleeing-felon standard for using deadly force. Since then, deadly force may be applied to fleeing suspects only (1) if they pose a threat to the lives of officers or (2) if they pose a threat to the lives of others.

Terry v. Ohio, 392 U.S. 1, 88 S.Ct. 1868 (1968) A 35-year veteran police officer observed Terry and two companions standing on a Cleveland street corner. They moved up and down the street, looking in store windows, returning frequently to the corner and conversing. The officer was suspicious of this behavior and confronted them about their identities and business. He patted down Terry and discovered a revolver. Terry was charged with carrying a concealed weapon and convicted. Terry appealed and the SC eventually heard the case. The argument was whether police officers may "pat down and frisk" suspicious persons if they have reasonable suspicion that a crime is being contemplated. The SC upheld Terry's conviction, determining that police officers may pat down suspects as a means of protecting themselves and determining whether suspicious persons may be armed and pose a danger to them. (*See Sibron v. New York* [1968] as a limitation to the pat-down-and-frisk ruling in *Terry*.)

Thompson v. Oklahoma, 487 U.S. 815, 108 S.Ct. 2687 (1988) Thompson was 15 years old when his brother-in-law was brutally murdered. Thompson was suspected. Under Oklahoma law, the district attorney filed a statutory petition to have him waived to criminal court, where he could be tried for murder as an adult. The waiver was granted and Thompson was tried, convicted, and sentenced to death. Thompson appealed, and his case was eventually reviewed by the SC. The SC concluded that "the Eighth and Fourteenth Amendments prohibit the execution of a person who was under 16 years of age at the time of his or her offense" (108 S.Ct. at 2700). Thompson's death sentence was overturned. Thompson's attorney had originally requested the Court to draw a line so that all those under age 18 would be exempt from the death penalty as a punishment, regardless of their crimes. The SC refused to do this. (*See also Stanford v. Kentucky* and *Wilkins v. Missouri*.)

United States v. Dunn, 480 U.S. 294, 107 S.Ct. 1134 (1987) Drug agents investigated Dunn, who was suspected of manufacturing drugs in large quantities in a private laboratory located on his property. With a properly executed warrant, police placed a beeper in a container used by Dunn to transport drugs. Eventually, the officers located Dunn's farm. Passing through several gates, fences, and other perimeter guards, they shined their flashlights into a large barn about 50 yards from Dunn's house. They could hear a motor running, and they saw drug equipment through the side boards. They secured a search warrant and entered the barn, where they seized a quantity of illegal drugs. Dunn was convicted of drug manufacturing. He appealed, seeking to suppress the barn evidence because he believed that police had had no legal authority to observe his barn in the middle of a heavily protected area. The SC upheld Dunn's conviction, saying that because the barn itself was not part of the curtilage of Dunn's home but rather was separately fenced, police were not required to obtain a search warrant to look at it or through its side boards. The SC stressed how close the barn was to Dunn's house; whether it was in a separate enclosure; the nature and uses of the area; and any evident concealment attempts. These guidelines gave greater parameters for police when conducting searches of open fields or yards (*see Oliver v. United States* [1984] for comparison).

United States v. Havens, 446 U.S. 620, 100 S.Ct. 1912 (1980) Havens was suspected of importing and conspiring to import cocaine. During his trial and under direct examination, he denied various facts pertaining to the cocaine allegations. While cross-examining him, the prosecutor used illegally obtained evidence to contradict Havens, who was subsequently convicted. He appealed to the SC, alleging that because the evidence used against him had been illegally seized and was otherwise inadmissible, it should have been excluded. The SC disagreed and upheld his conviction, holding that evidence that is otherwise inadmissible as the result of a Fourth Amendment violation may be used to impeach the credibility of the defendant when the defendant gives testimony that is contradicted by such illegally seized evidence. Thus, when defendants testify, they must testify truthfully "or suffer the consequences" (at 1912).

United States v. Hensley, 469 U.S. 221, 105 S.Ct. 675 (1985) A motorist, Hensley, was a convicted felon from St. Bernard, Ohio, traveling through Kentucky. A recent robbery in Kentucky led police officers to suspect Hensley, although there was no evidence linking him to the crime. A "wanted" poster of Hensley was circulated among contiguous states, and a Covington, Kentucky, police officer observed Hensley on a highway. He stopped and questioned Hensley and then arrested him, largely because of the "wanted" poster he had seen. In a search incident to the arrest, the officer found weapons in Hensley's automobile. Hensley was never charged with the robbery, but he was charged with, and convicted of, being a felon in possession of firearms, a prohibited act. He appealed, arguing that the police had lacked probable cause to stop him initially and therefore the weapons subsequently found in his car should have been excluded as evidence. The SC upheld the conviction of Hensley, contending that the "wanted" poster had provided police with sufficient grounds to stop and question Hensley. The SC stressed the increasing mobility of United States citizens and the greater importance of information exchanges about felons and crimes among the states.

United States v. Leon, 468 U.S. 897, 104 S.Ct. 3405 (1984) Leon, a suspected drug trafficker, was placed under surveillance by Burbank, California, police. Subsequently, police obtained search warrants for three residences and several automobiles under Leon's control. Acting on the search warrants, they seized large quantities of inculpatory drug evidence, which was used against Leon at a trial later, where he was convicted. He appealed to the SC, which upheld his conviction. Although the SC declared the search warrants invalid, they noted in a rambling and extensive opinion that the officers who abided by the directives outlined by the invalid warrants had been acting in good faith, presuming that the issued warrants were valid. The SC also noted that this decision was not to be interpreted as a blanket generalization authorizing officers to act in all instances where defective warrants are issued. The SC simply weighed the benefits of suppressing the evidence obtained in Leon's case against the costs of exclusion. The significance of this case is that it creates a good-faith exception to the exclusionary rule. The SC's message is that evidence may be admissible if the fault for defective warrants rests with judges, not police officers. The target of the exclusionary rule is police misconduct, not judicial misconduct.

United States v. Ross, 456 U.S. 798, 102 S.Ct. 2157 (1982) A reliable informant advised police that Ross was dealing drugs out of his car in a designated location. Police went to the location, observed Ross as described by the informant, and made a warrantless arrest. Then they searched his vehicle, where they found heroin and other illegal substances in containers in the trunk. He was convicted, but he appealed, arguing that police had violated his Fourth Amendment rights against unreasonable searches and seizures. The SC upheld Ross' conviction, saying that following a lawful arrest based upon probable cause, a person's car may be searched without warrant, as well as bags and other containers found within it. (*See United States v. Chadwick* [1977], which prohibits warrantless searches of large footlockers, even if found in vehicles being searched incident to an arrest and the police have time to get a warrant.)

United States v. Salerno, 481 U.S. 739, 107 S.Ct. 2095 (1987) Salerno and others were arrested for several serious crimes and held without bail under the Bail Reform Act of 1984 as dangerous. He was convicted and sentenced to 100 years in prison. He appealed, being among the first to challenge the constitutionality of the new Bail Reform Act and its provision that specifies that dangerous persons may be detained prior to trial until such time as their case may be decided. He objected that the new act violated the Eighth Amendment provision against "cruel and unusual" punishment. The SC upheld the constitutionality of pretrial detention and declared that it did not violate the defandant's rights under the Eighth Amendment if a specific defendant was found to be dangerous.

United States v. Sokolow, 490 U.S. 1, 109 S.Ct. 1581 (1989) The Drug Enforcement Administration has developed a drug courier profile for use at ports of entry, airports, and bus and train depots. On the basis of this profile, Sokolow and a companion were observed at an airport purchasing with cash two roundtrip tickets to Hawaii. Both men appeared nervous and possessed only carry-on luggage. They were stopped by DEA agents and taken to a private airport office, where their luggage was examined by narcotics-detecting dogs. The dogs reacted as though the luggage contained drugs. Officers obtained a search warrant, and the bags were searched. The search yielded more than 1,000 grams of cocaine. Sokolow was subsequently convicted. He appealed, arguing that DEA agents had lacked probable cause to stop initially and search his personal effects. Essentially, he was contesting use of the drug courier profile. The SC downplayed the significance of profiling, favoring the totality-of-circumstances justification for stopping, questioning, and subsequently searching persons who fit profiles as drug couriers.

United States v. Verdugo-Urquidez, 494 U.S. 259, 110 S.Ct. 1056 (1990) Verdugo-Urquidez was arrested by Mexican police, who delivered him to United States authorities. Subsequently, United States authorities conducted a warrantless search of Verdugo-Urquidez's residence in Mexico and obtained incriminating information against him, which was used to convict him in a United States court. He appealed. A lower appellate court ruled to suppress the evidence seized in Mexico, because the Fourth Amendment right against unreasonable search and seizure had been violated. The SC upheld Verdugo-Urquidez's conviction, saying that the Fourth Amendment does not apply in Mexico against persons who are Mexican residents, who are not United States citizens, and who have no voluntary attachment to the United States.

United States v. Wade, 388 U.S. 218, 87 S.Ct. 1926 (1967) Wade was a participant in a bank robbery. He drove away from the bank with an accomplice. Eyewitnesses saw them in the bank and gave descriptions to police. Subsequently, Wade was arrested and indicted for robbery. A lawyer was appointed for him. Later at the jail, police placed Wade in a lineup with other men for two bank workers to view. Both bank workers identified Wade as the robber. Wade's attorney was not notified of the lineup. Later, at Wade's trial, the same bank employees reidentified Wade as the robber and he was convicted, in some part, upon the testimony of these eyewitnesses. Wade appealed, moving to suppress the testimony of the eyewitnesses, because he had been subjected to a lineup without his attorney present. The SC agreed and overturned Wade's conviction, saying that lineups are critical stages, and whenever indicted offenders have counsel appointed for them, those attorneys should be present at these critical stages. In Wade's case, because he was represented by counsel and his counsel was not present at his lineup, his right to counsel had been violated.

Weeks v. United States, 232 U.S. 383, 34 S.Ct. 351 (1914) Weeks was suspected of using the mails to send lottery tickets, a form of prohibited gambling. United States marshals entered Weeks' home without a warrant, conducted a search, and discovered lottery tickets, which were used as evidence against Weeks in his later trial. Weeks was convicted of unlawful use of the mail. He appealed, arguing that law enforcement officers should have obtained a search warrant before entering his home and seizing materials later used in his conviction. The SC agreed with Weeks and overturned his conviction. Weeks had been gainfully employed at the time and was an unlikely flight risk, and the United States marshals had had plenty of time to obtain a valid search warrant. They simply failed to do so. This case set a precedent, at least for *federal* law enforcement officers. It established the *exclusionary rule*, which says that evidence seized illegally is inadmissible in court. Subsequently, some states chose to abide by the exclusionary rule, while other states chose not to abide by it, citing various exceptions or special circumstances. These became known as *exclusionary* and *nonexclusionary* states. An unusual situation developed following *Weeks*, whereby states would obtain evidence against criminal suspects illegally and turn over this information to federal authorities for their own prosecutions of these same suspects. The reasoning behind the practice became known as the *silver-platter doctrine*, since state officers were delivering illegally obtained evidence to federal prosecutors on a "silver platter," so to say. Ultimately, in *Elkins v. United States* (1960) and *Mapp v. Ohio* (1961), the silver-platter doctrine was eliminated, and both state and federal laws were harmonized relative to protocol to be followed in searches and seizures conducted against criminal suspects.

Whren v. United States, 517 U.S. 806, 116 S.Ct. 690 (1996) Whren and a number of associates were traveling in a truck in a high drug crime area. Officers driving in an unmarked car noticed that the vehicle had stopped at a stop sign, and remained at that stop sign for a long period of time. The officers turned their vehicle around and approached the truck. At that moment, the truck made a right turn without signaling and left the area at an "unreasonable" speed. The officers gave chase and overtook the truck when it stopped at a red light. As the officers approached the truck, they saw two bags of what seemed to be cocaine in the lap of Whren. It was in fact cocaine, and Whren and his associates were arrested. Whren sought to exclude the evidence, arguing that plainclothes officers would not, in the normal course of business, stop a vehicle for relatively minor traffic violations. The stop, he contested, was a pretextual stop on the part of the police—an excuse used to extend their ability to search for what they were really looking for: drugs. Minus the evidence uncovered in the pretextual stop, there was no probable cause present to support the stop and search for drugs. The lower courts upheld the stop and the search, and Whren and his associates were convicted on the drug charges. On appeal, the SC ruled, "the temporary detention of a motorist upon probable cause to believe that he has violated the traffic laws does not violate the Fourth Amendment's prohibition against unreasonable seizures, even if a reasonable officer would not have stopped the motorist absent some additional law enforcement objective."

Williams v. Florida, 399 U.S. 78, 90 S.Ct. 1893 (1970) Williams was arrested and charged with robbery. At his subsequent trial, a 6-member jury found him guilty. Williams appealed, alleging among other things that he should have had a jury of 12 members, rather than 6 members. Florida law proclaimed that 12-member juries would be convened in capital cases, but only 6-member juries would hear all other types of cases. The SC heard Williams' appeal and affirmed the Florida provision, saying that the "jury . . . composed of 12 is a historical accident, unnecessary to effect the purposes of the jury system and wholly without significance except to mystics."

Wilson v. Arkansas, 514 U.S. 927, 115 S.Ct. 1914 (1995) Wilson had made several drug purchases from an undercover agent. On the basis of these actions, both an arrest warrant for Wilson and a search warrant of Wilson's residence were obtained. The police identified themselves when executing the warrants, and directly entered the home through an unlocked door without adhering to the common law "knock and announce" procedure. Contraband was obtained from the Wilson residence. Wilson sought to exclude that evidence due to the fact that the police did not knock and announce when they served the warrants. The SC agreed with Wilson, and noted that police should generally "knock and announce" before entering a home, even if they are armed with a valid warrant. This case did not, however, "mandate a rigid rule of announcement." The SC indicated that given exigent circumstances the police would not be required to "knock and announce." The SC left to the lower courts the discretion to determine what constitutes unreasonable unannounced entries.

Wilson v. Seiter, 501 U.S. 294, 111 S.Ct. 2321 (1991) Wilson was a felon incarcerated in the Hocking, Ohio, Correctional Facility. Filing a Title 42, U.S.C. Section 1983 civil-rights claim against prison officials, he alleged that the conditions of his confinement violated his constitutional rights under the Eighth and Fourteenth Amendments. These conditions were improper ventilation, inadequate heating and cooling, excessive noise, unclean and inadequate restrooms, unsanitary dining facilities and food preparation, and housing with mentally and physically abusive inmates. The suit was rejected by the SC, which declared that prison officials must exhibit deliberate indifference to prisoner needs and living conditions before inmates will successfully prevail in their suits. Further, a culpable state of mind must be demonstrated on the part of prison officials. These difficult criteria mean that suits by prisoners alleging poor prison conditions will be difficult to sustain.

Wolff v. McDonnell, 418 U.S. 539, 94 S.Ct. 2963 (1974) Basic elements of a procedural due process must be present when decisions are made concerning the discipline of a prison inmate. In this Nebraska case, the SC ruled that in procedures resulting in loss of good-time or in solitary confinement, due process requires the following: advance written notice of the violation, written statement of fact findings, the prisoner's right to call witnesses and present evidence where it will not be hazardous to the operation of the institution, mail from attorneys to be opened and inspected in the presence of inmates, and prison records to be expunged if not in accord with required procedures. This case also dealt with the question of whether letters determined to be from attorneys may be opened by prison authorities in the presence of the inmate or whether such mail must be delivered unopened if normal detection techniques fail to indicate contraband. The SC did not add a great deal of clarity to this issue in their decision. It indicated that attorneys must clearly identify themselves by placing their names and addresses in plain view on envelopes and that the letters should show that they came from lawyers. In any event, prison authorities may inspect and read any document leaving and entering the institution in an effort to determine whether inmates are abusing their rights by communicating about "restricted matters." ✦

Brief Index of Covered Topics

Criminal Justice: Concepts and Issues will comfortably stand alone as a single assigned text. However, some instructors may choose to use this anthology to supplement another text. These instructors may find the following index helpful, which lists the selections in the book by topic and chapter number.